BKmos
(a)

2023

JUL

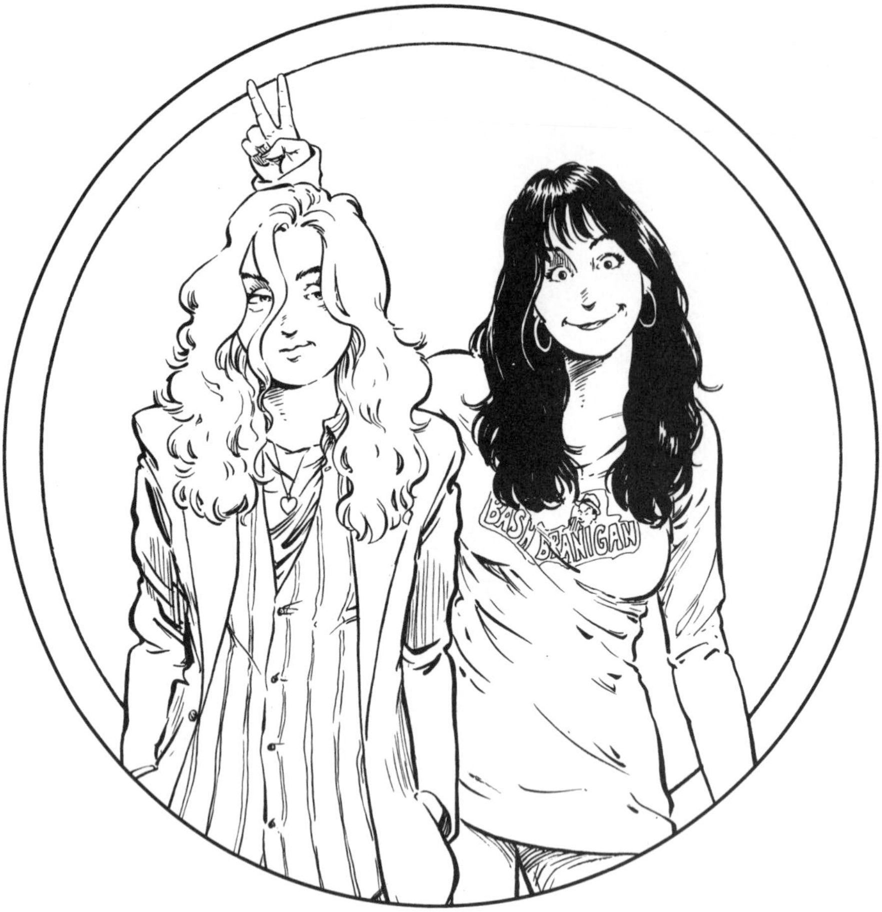
BASH BRANIGAN

Publisher
Robyn Moore

Color by:
Brian Miller

Pages 340-344 pencils and inks by
Jim Lee and Scott Williams

AbstractStudioComics.com

Softcover ISBN: 978-1-892597-91-5
Hardcover ISBN 978-1-892597-93-9
Library of Congress control number: 2023930686

Published by Abstract Studio, Inc., P. O. Box 271487, Houston, TX 77277-1487.

Printed in Canada.

STRANGERS IN PARADISE

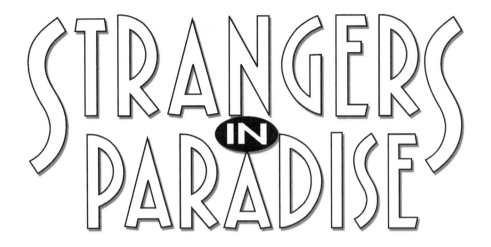

by

Terry Moore

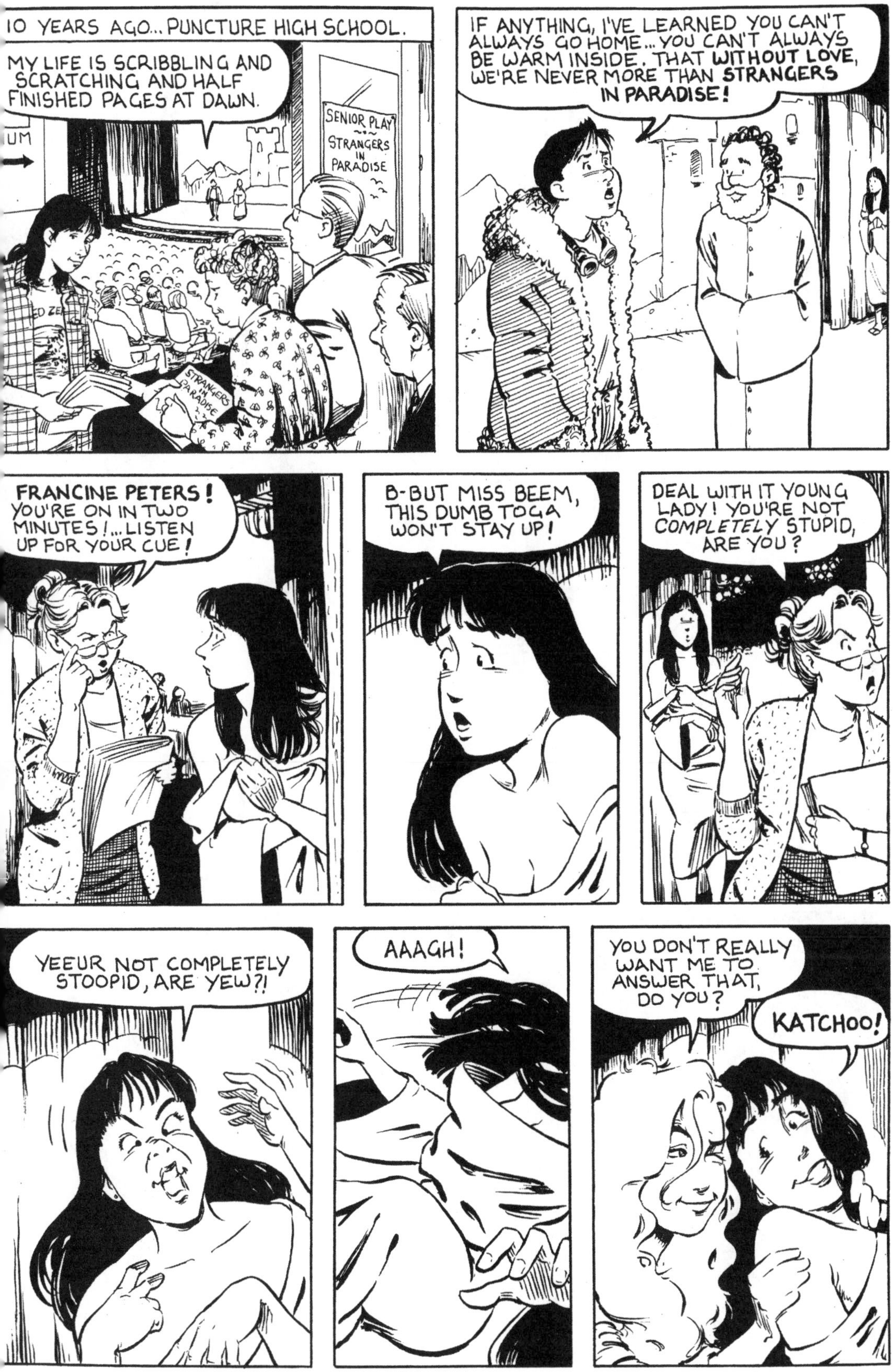
10 YEARS AGO... PUNCTURE HIGH SCHOOL.
MY LIFE IS SCRIBBLING AND SCRATCHING AND HALF FINISHED PAGES AT DAWN.
SENIOR PLAY STRANGERS IN PARADISE
STRANGERS IN PARADISE
IF ANYTHING, I'VE LEARNED YOU CAN'T ALWAYS GO HOME... YOU CAN'T ALWAYS BE WARM INSIDE. THAT WITHOUT LOVE, WE'RE NEVER MORE THAN STRANGERS IN PARADISE!
FRANCINE PETERS! YOU'RE ON IN TWO MINUTES!... LISTEN UP FOR YOUR CUE!
B-BUT MISS BEEM, THIS DUMB TOGA WON'T STAY UP!
DEAL WITH IT YOUNG LADY! YOU'RE NOT COMPLETELY STUPID, ARE YOU?
YEEUR NOT COMPLETELY STOOPID, ARE YEW?!
AAAGH!
YOU DON'T REALLY WANT ME TO ANSWER THAT, DO YOU?
KATCHOO!

KATCHOO! WHAT ARE YOU DOING HERE? I THOUGHT YOU WERE SUSPENDED YESTERDAY!

YEAH, WELL WHATEVER...

HEY! I COULDN'T MISS SEEING MY BEST FRIEND MAKE A FOOL OF HERSELF IN FRONT OF THE WHOLE SCHOOL, NOW COULD I?

OH GOD! HOW DO I LET MYSELF GET TALKED INTO THESE THINGS?

'CAUSE YOU'RE EASY GIRL! ...AND EVERYBODY KNOWS IT! YOU EVER HEARD OF THE WORD NO?

I AM NOT EASY! JUST BECAUSE I DON'T GO AROUND BLOWING UP GUYS' LOCKERS!

HEY! A GUY SCREWS ME AROUND HE'S GOING TO PAY FOR IT!

FRANCINE! WHERE IS THAT GIRL?

I BETTER GO.

OK... BREAK A BUTT!

LEG! I'M S'PPOSED TO BREAK A LEG!

GEE, SHOWBIZ IS HELL, HUH?

WHERE HAVE YOU BEEN? YOU'RE ON NEXT! GET OUT THERE!

...UH...I SAID, WHAT YOU NEED IS REFRESHMENT!......

BUT MY TOGA!

GO!

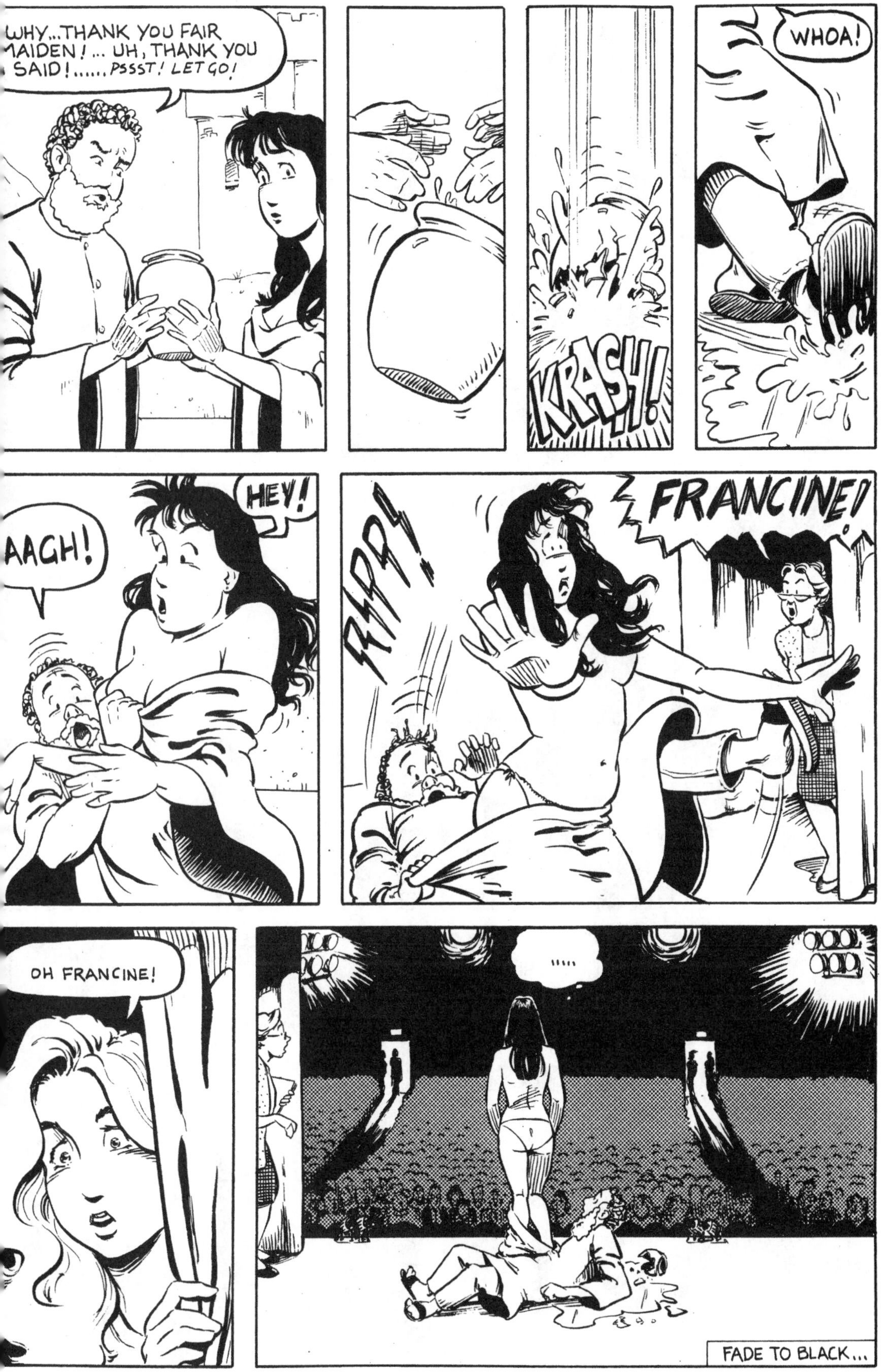
WHY...THANK YOU FAIR
MAIDEN! ... UH, THANK YOU
SAID!...... PSSST! LET GO!
KRASH!
WHOA!
AAGH!
HEY!
RIPP!
FRANCINE!
OH FRANCINE!
.....
FADE TO BLACK...

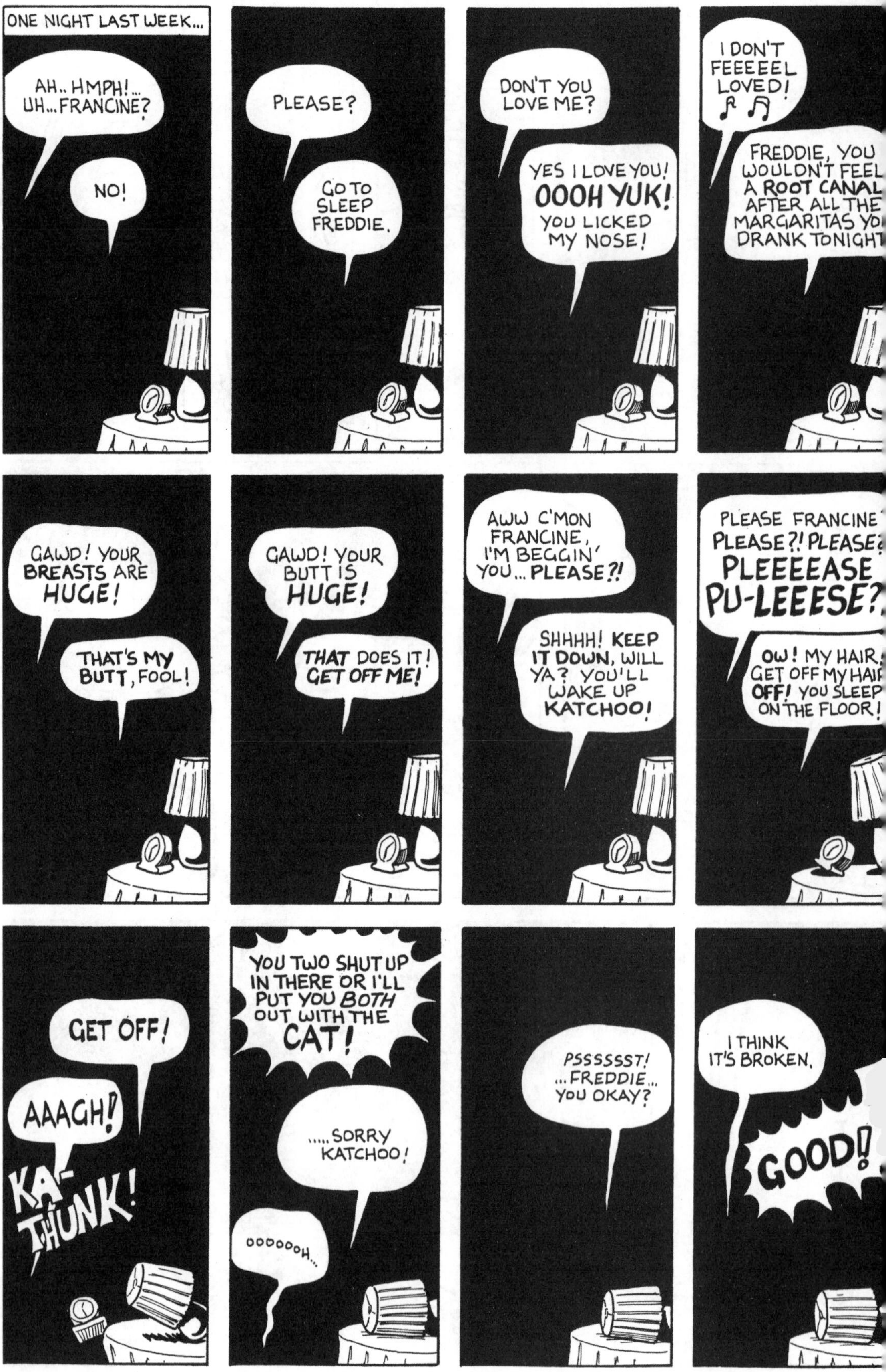
ONE NIGHT LAST WEEK...
AH.. HMPH!... UH... FRANCINE?
NO!
PLEASE?
GO TO SLEEP FREDDIE.
DON'T YOU LOVE ME?
YES I LOVE YOU! OOOH YUK! YOU LICKED MY NOSE!
I DON'T FEEEEEL LOVED!
FREDDIE, YOU WOULDN'T FEEL A ROOT CANAL AFTER ALL THE MARGARITAS YO DRANK TONIGHT
GAWD! YOUR BREASTS ARE HUGE!
THAT'S MY BUTT, FOOL!
GAWD! YOUR BUTT IS HUGE!
THAT DOES IT! GET OFF ME!
AWW C'MON FRANCINE, I'M BEGGIN' YOU... PLEASE?!
SHHHH! KEEP IT DOWN, WILL YA? YOU'LL WAKE UP KATCHOO!
PLEASE FRANCINE PLEASE?! PLEASE PLEEEEASE PU-LEEESE?
OW! MY HAIR GET OFF MY HAIR OFF! YOU SLEEP ON THE FLOOR!
GET OFF!
AAAGH!
KA-THUNK!
YOU TWO SHUT UP IN THERE OR I'LL PUT YOU BOTH OUT WITH THE CAT!
.....SORRY KATCHOO!
OOOOOOH...
PSSSSSST! ...FREDDIE... YOU OKAY?
I THINK IT'S BROKEN.
GOOD!

RINNG!

BAN BANG

GOOD MORNING DEAR, SLEEP WELL? HEH! HEH! HEH!

KATCHOO!

GESUNDHEIT.

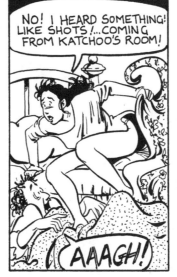

NO! I HEARD SOMETHING! LIKE SHOTS!...COMING FROM KATCHOO'S ROOM!

AAAGH!

PROBABLY JUST HER VIBRATOR BACKFIRING AGAIN!....I TELL YOU THAT GIRL NEEDS TO GET OUT MORE!

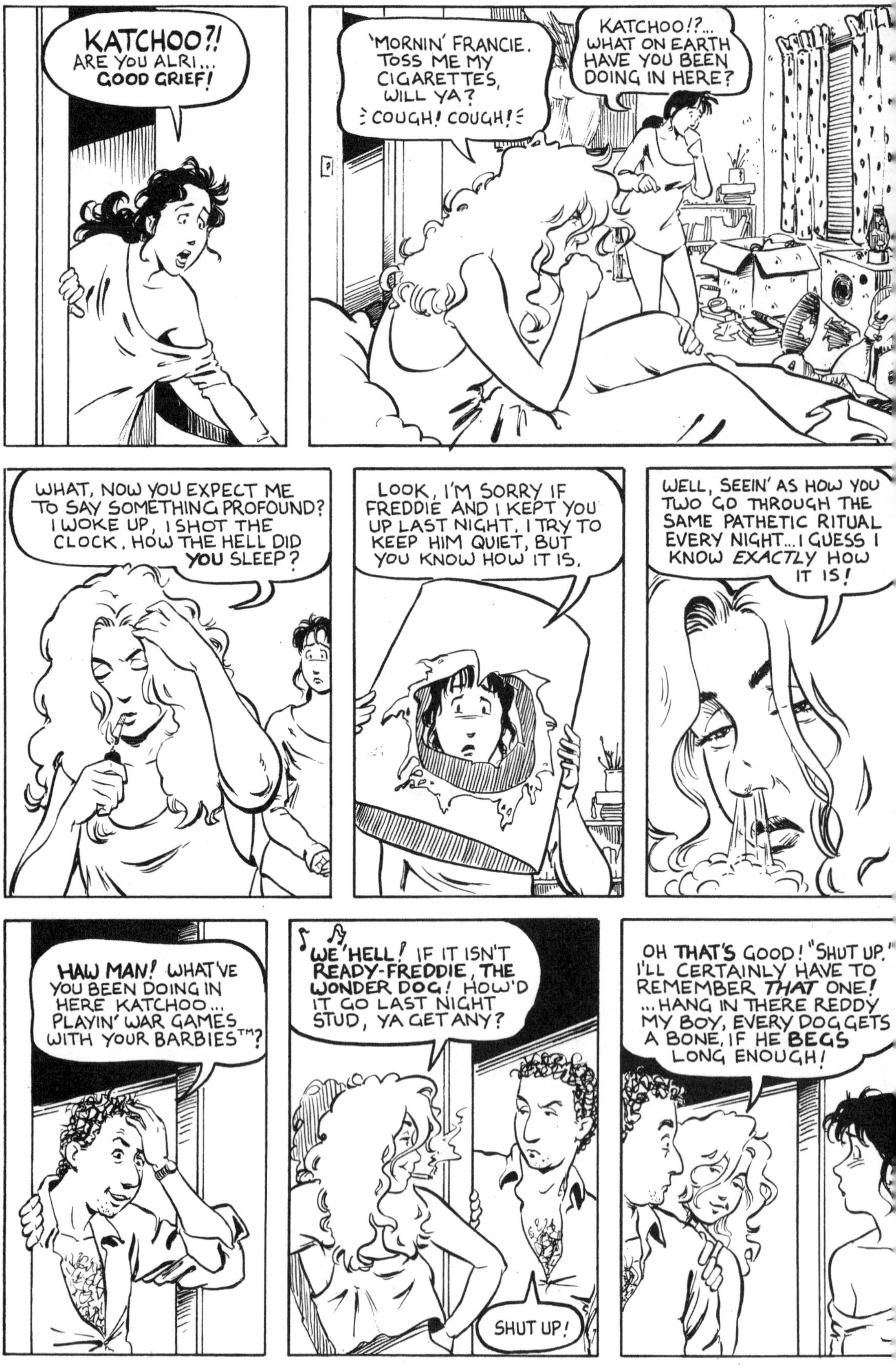
KATCHOO?! ARE YOU ALRI... GOOD GRIEF!
'MORNIN' FRANCIE. TOSS ME MY CIGARETTES, WILL YA? COUGH! COUGH!
KATCHOO!?... WHAT ON EARTH HAVE YOU BEEN DOING IN HERE?
WHAT, NOW YOU EXPECT ME TO SAY SOMETHING PROFOUND? I WOKE UP, I SHOT THE CLOCK. HOW THE HELL DID YOU SLEEP?
LOOK, I'M SORRY IF FREDDIE AND I KEPT YOU UP LAST NIGHT. I TRY TO KEEP HIM QUIET, BUT YOU KNOW HOW IT IS.
WELL, SEEIN' AS HOW YOU TWO GO THROUGH THE SAME PATHETIC RITUAL EVERY NIGHT... I GUESS I KNOW EXACTLY HOW IT IS!
HAW MAN! WHAT'VE YOU BEEN DOING IN HERE KATCHOO... PLAYIN' WAR GAMES WITH YOUR BARBIES™?
WE'HELL! IF IT ISN'T READY-FREDDIE, THE WONDER DOG! HOW'D IT GO LAST NIGHT STUD, YA GET ANY?
SHUT UP!
OH THAT'S GOOD! "SHUT UP." I'LL CERTAINLY HAVE TO REMEMBER THAT ONE! ...HANG IN THERE REDDY MY BOY, EVERY DOG GETS A BONE, IF HE BEGS LONG ENOUGH!

IT WAS A JOKE FREDDIE.

YEAH WELL I'M NOT LAUGHING! IT'S HUMILIATING TO STAND THERE AND TAKE HER CRAP!... ESPECIALLY WHEN SHE'S *RIGHT!*

FREDDIE...PLEASE! LET'S DON'T GO INTO THIS AGAIN, I THOUGHT WE AGREED TO WAIT.

WAIT FOR WHAT FRANCINE? YOU NEVER SAY *WHAT* WE'RE WAITING FOR! ...GODOT? CHRISTMAS? THE EASTER BUNNY? ...WHAT?!!

OOK, WE'VE EEN ALL THRU HIS BEFORE! THOUGHT E HAD AN NDERSTA...

I'M SORRY, TO ME THIS JUST DEFIES UNDERSTANDING.

I MEAN, HERE WE ARE IN A MATURE RELATIONSHIP, TWO CONSENTING ADULTS ...AND *YOU'RE NOT CONSENTING!*

HONEY, BELIEVE ME, IT'S NOT THAT I DON'T WANT TO ...IT'S JUST THAT... WELL...

WELL *WHAT?!*

...I...OH GOD, THIS IS SO HARD...

WHAT?!

I'M AFRAID IF I SLEEP WITH YOU...IT'LL RUIN EVERYTHING...AND YOU'LL LEAVE ME LIKE ALL THE OTHERS.

...YOU'RE JOKING RIGHT? I MEAN YOU CAN'T BE SERIOUS?!

NO! I MEAN IT! I KNOW HOW MEN ARE! YOU ALL HAVE THIS *CONQUEST* THING! THEN WHEN YOU GET WHAT YOU WANT IT'S 1-800 SEE-YA!

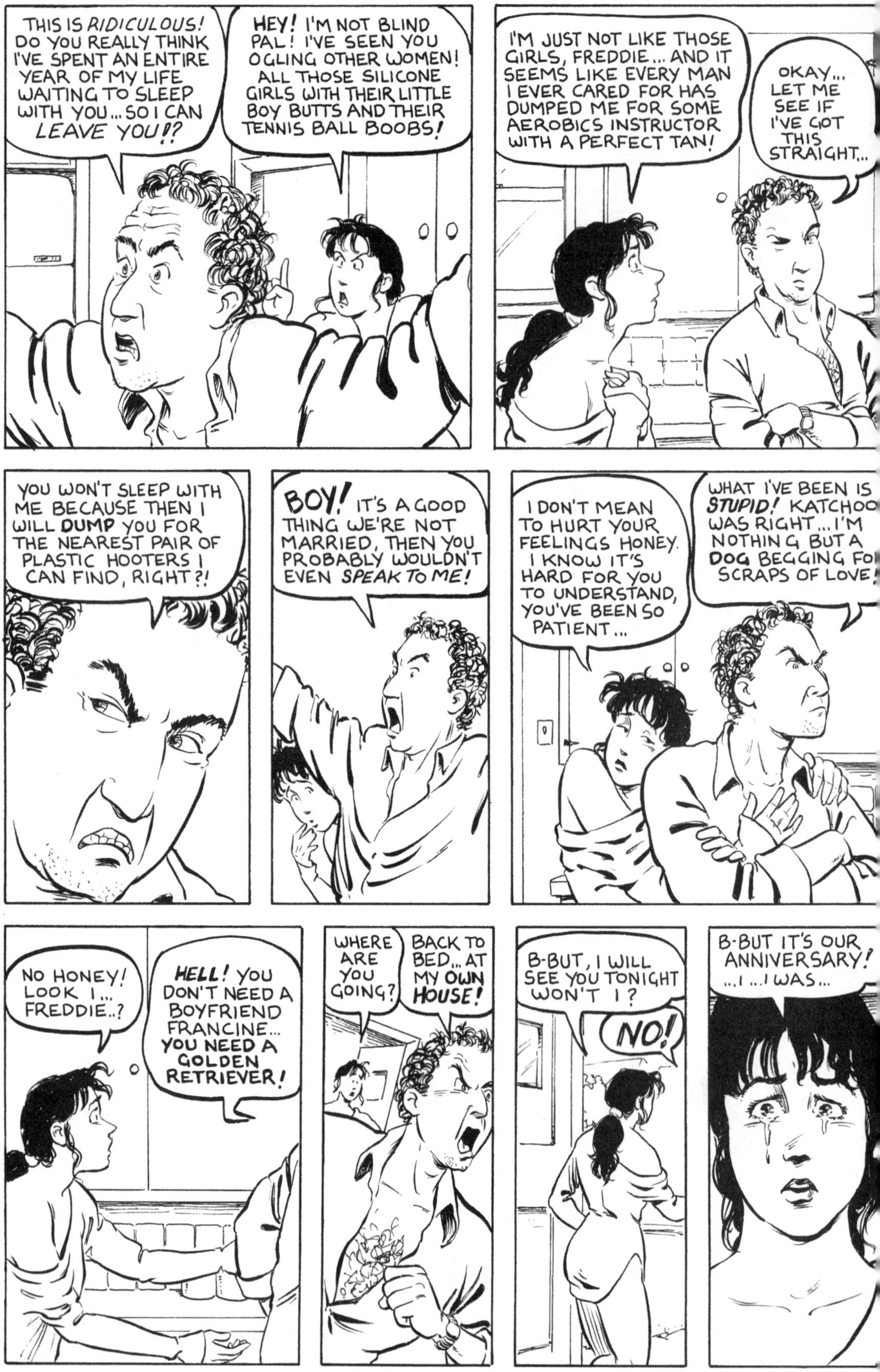
THIS IS RIDICULOUS! DO YOU REALLY THINK I'VE SPENT AN ENTIRE YEAR OF MY LIFE WAITING TO SLEEP WITH YOU... SO I CAN LEAVE YOU!?
HEY! I'M NOT BLIND PAL! I'VE SEEN YOU OGLING OTHER WOMEN! ALL THOSE SILICONE GIRLS WITH THEIR LITTLE BOY BUTTS AND THEIR TENNIS BALL BOOBS!
I'M JUST NOT LIKE THOSE GIRLS, FREDDIE... AND IT SEEMS LIKE EVERY MAN I EVER CARED FOR HAS DUMPED ME FOR SOME AEROBICS INSTRUCTOR WITH A PERFECT TAN!
OKAY... LET ME SEE IF I'VE GOT THIS STRAIGHT...
YOU WON'T SLEEP WITH ME BECAUSE THEN I WILL DUMP YOU FOR THE NEAREST PAIR OF PLASTIC HOOTERS I CAN FIND, RIGHT?!
BOY! IT'S A GOOD THING WE'RE NOT MARRIED, THEN YOU PROBABLY WOULDN'T EVEN SPEAK TO ME!
I DON'T MEAN TO HURT YOUR FEELINGS HONEY. I KNOW IT'S HARD FOR YOU TO UNDERSTAND, YOU'VE BEEN SO PATIENT...
WHAT I'VE BEEN IS STUPID! KATCHOO WAS RIGHT... I'M NOTHING BUT A DOG BEGGING FO SCRAPS OF LOVE!
NO HONEY! LOOK I... FREDDIE..?
HELL! YOU DON'T NEED A BOYFRIEND FRANCINE... YOU NEED A GOLDEN RETRIEVER!
WHERE ARE YOU GOING?
BACK TO BED... AT MY OWN HOUSE!
B-BUT, I WILL SEE YOU TONIGHT WON'T I?
NO!
B-BUT IT'S OUR ANNIVERSARY! ...I ...I WAS...

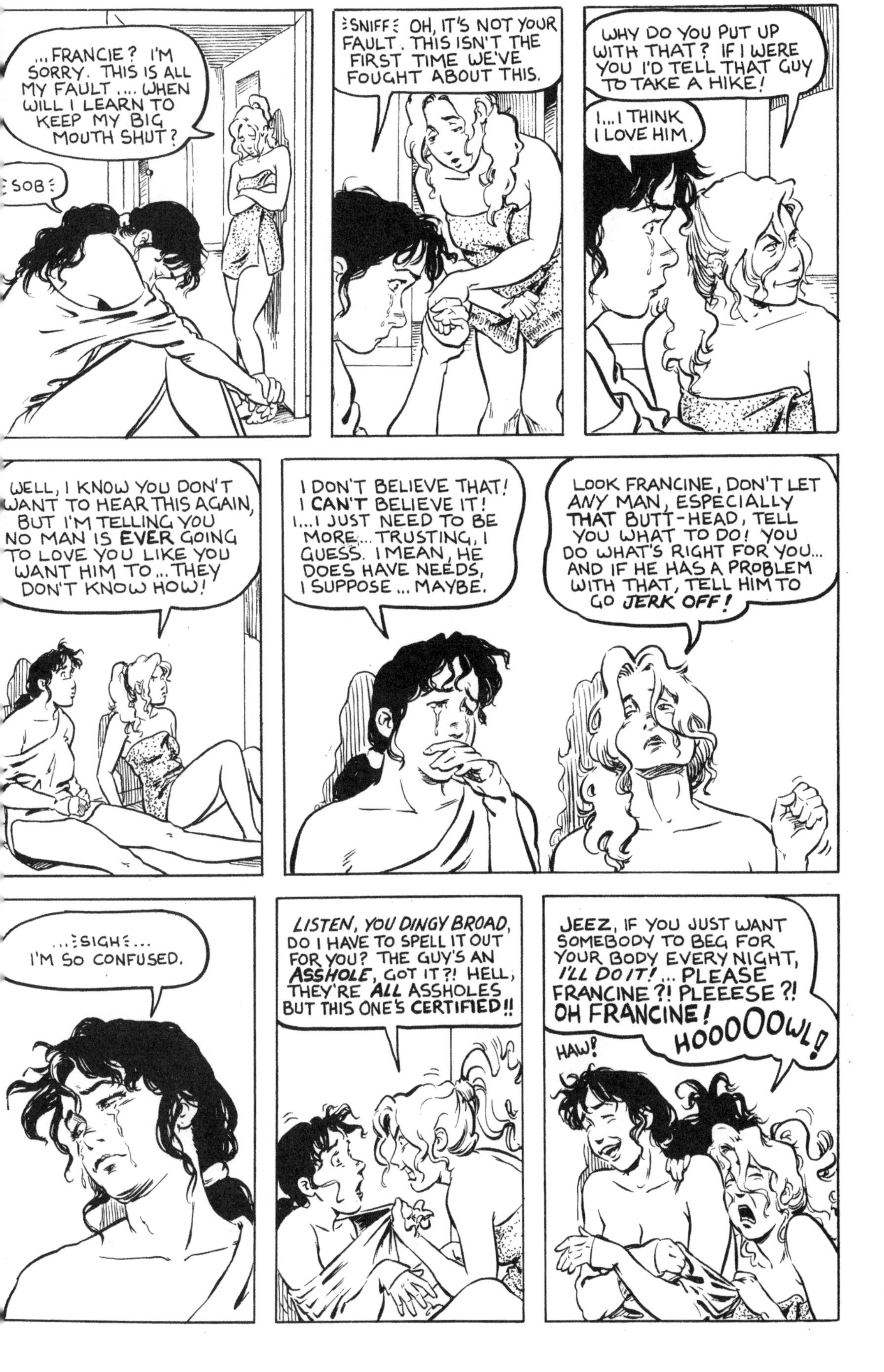
...FRANCIE? I'M SORRY. THIS IS ALL MY FAULT.... WHEN WILL I LEARN TO KEEP MY BIG MOUTH SHUT?
SOB
SNIFF OH, IT'S NOT YOUR FAULT. THIS ISN'T THE FIRST TIME WE'VE FOUGHT ABOUT THIS.
WHY DO YOU PUT UP WITH THAT? IF I WERE YOU I'D TELL THAT GUY TO TAKE A HIKE!
I...I THINK I LOVE HIM.
WELL, I KNOW YOU DON'T WANT TO HEAR THIS AGAIN, BUT I'M TELLING YOU NO MAN IS EVER GOING TO LOVE YOU LIKE YOU WANT HIM TO... THEY DON'T KNOW HOW!
I DON'T BELIEVE THAT! I CAN'T BELIEVE IT! I...I JUST NEED TO BE MORE... TRUSTING, I GUESS. I MEAN, HE DOES HAVE NEEDS, I SUPPOSE... MAYBE.
LOOK FRANCINE, DON'T LET ANY MAN, ESPECIALLY THAT BUTT-HEAD, TELL YOU WHAT TO DO! YOU DO WHAT'S RIGHT FOR YOU... AND IF HE HAS A PROBLEM WITH THAT, TELL HIM TO GO JERK OFF!
...SIGH... I'M SO CONFUSED.
LISTEN, YOU DINGY BROAD, DO I HAVE TO SPELL IT OUT FOR YOU? THE GUY'S AN ASSHOLE, GOT IT?! HELL, THEY'RE ALL ASSHOLES BUT THIS ONE'S CERTIFIED!!
JEEZ, IF YOU JUST WANT SOMEBODY TO BEG FOR YOUR BODY EVERY NIGHT, I'LL DO IT! ... PLEASE FRANCINE?! PLEEESE?! OH FRANCINE!
HAW!
HOOOOOWL!

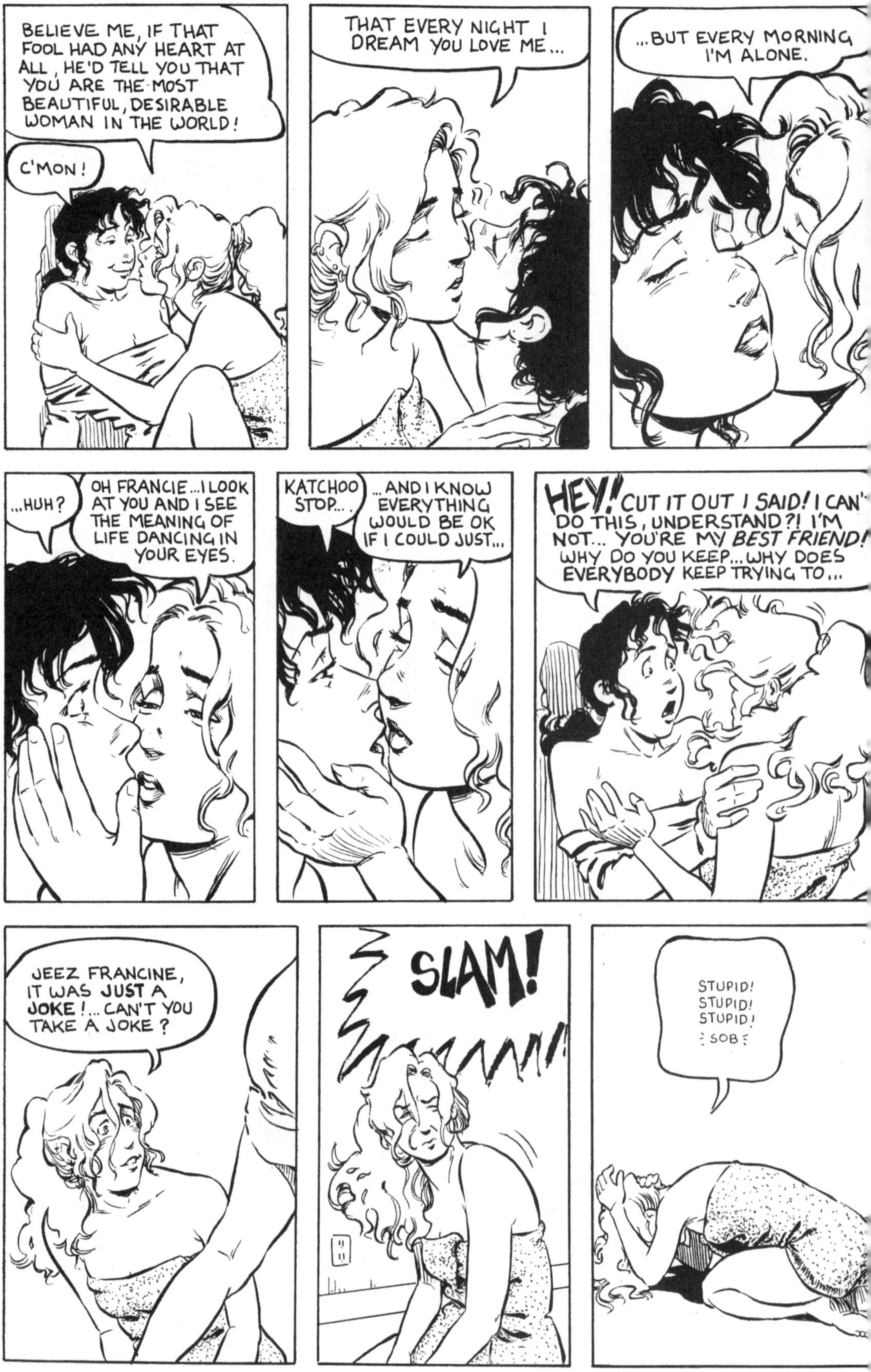
BELIEVE ME, IF THAT FOOL HAD ANY HEART AT ALL, HE'D TELL YOU THAT YOU ARE THE MOST BEAUTIFUL, DESIRABLE WOMAN IN THE WORLD!
C'MON!
THAT EVERY NIGHT I DREAM YOU LOVE ME...
...BUT EVERY MORNING I'M ALONE.
...HUH?
OH FRANCIE...I LOOK AT YOU AND I SEE THE MEANING OF LIFE DANCING IN YOUR EYES.
KATCHOO STOP...
...AND I KNOW EVERYTHING WOULD BE OK IF I COULD JUST...
HEY! CUT IT OUT I SAID! I CAN'T DO THIS, UNDERSTAND?! I'M NOT... YOU'RE MY *BEST FRIEND!* WHY DO YOU KEEP...WHY DOES EVERYBODY KEEP TRYING TO...
JEEZ FRANCINE, IT WAS **JUST A JOKE**!... CAN'T YOU TAKE A JOKE?
SLAM!
STUPID! STUPID! STUPID! SOB

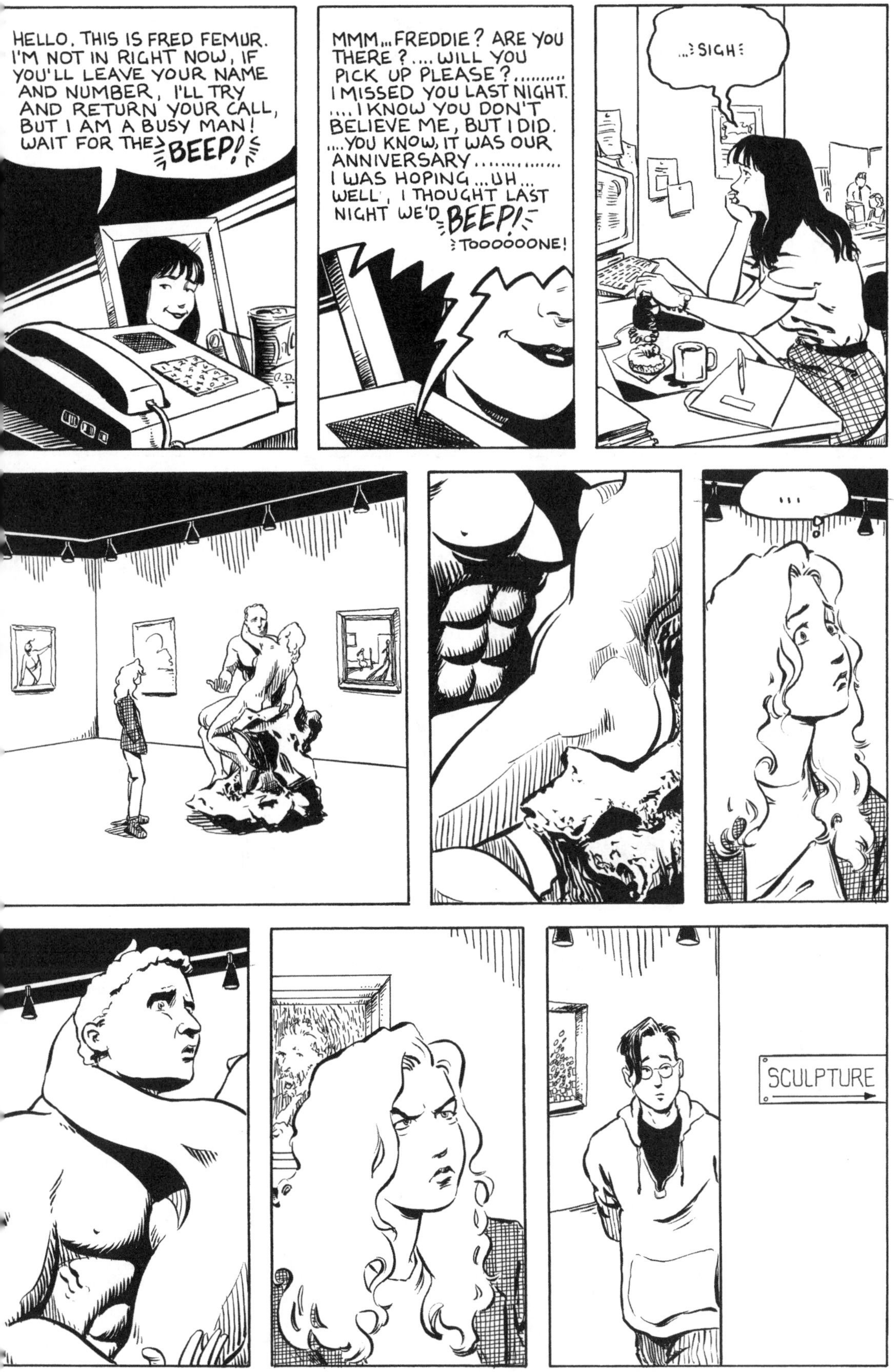
HELLO. THIS IS FRED FEMUR. I'M NOT IN RIGHT NOW, IF YOU'LL LEAVE YOUR NAME AND NUMBER, I'LL TRY AND RETURN YOUR CALL, BUT I AM A BUSY MAN! WAIT FOR THE BEEP!
MMM... FREDDIE? ARE YOU THERE?.... WILL YOU PICK UP PLEASE?......... I MISSED YOU LAST NIGHT. ....I KNOW YOU DON'T BELIEVE ME, BUT I DID. ....YOU KNOW, IT WAS OUR ANNIVERSARY.............. I WAS HOPING ... UH ... WELL, I THOUGHT LAST NIGHT WE'D BEEP!
TOOOOOONE!
...SIGH
...
SCULPTURE

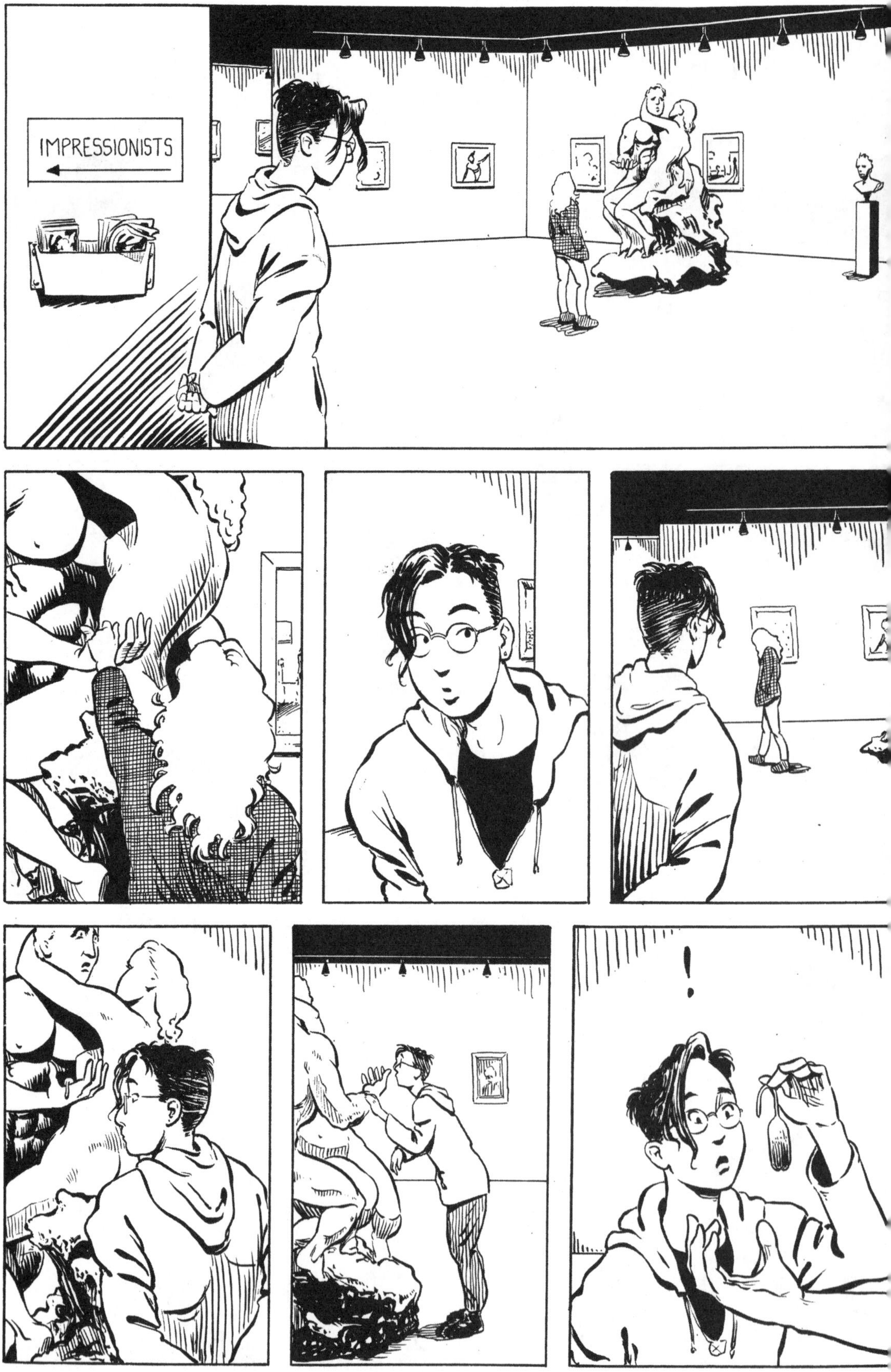
IMPRESSIONISTS
!

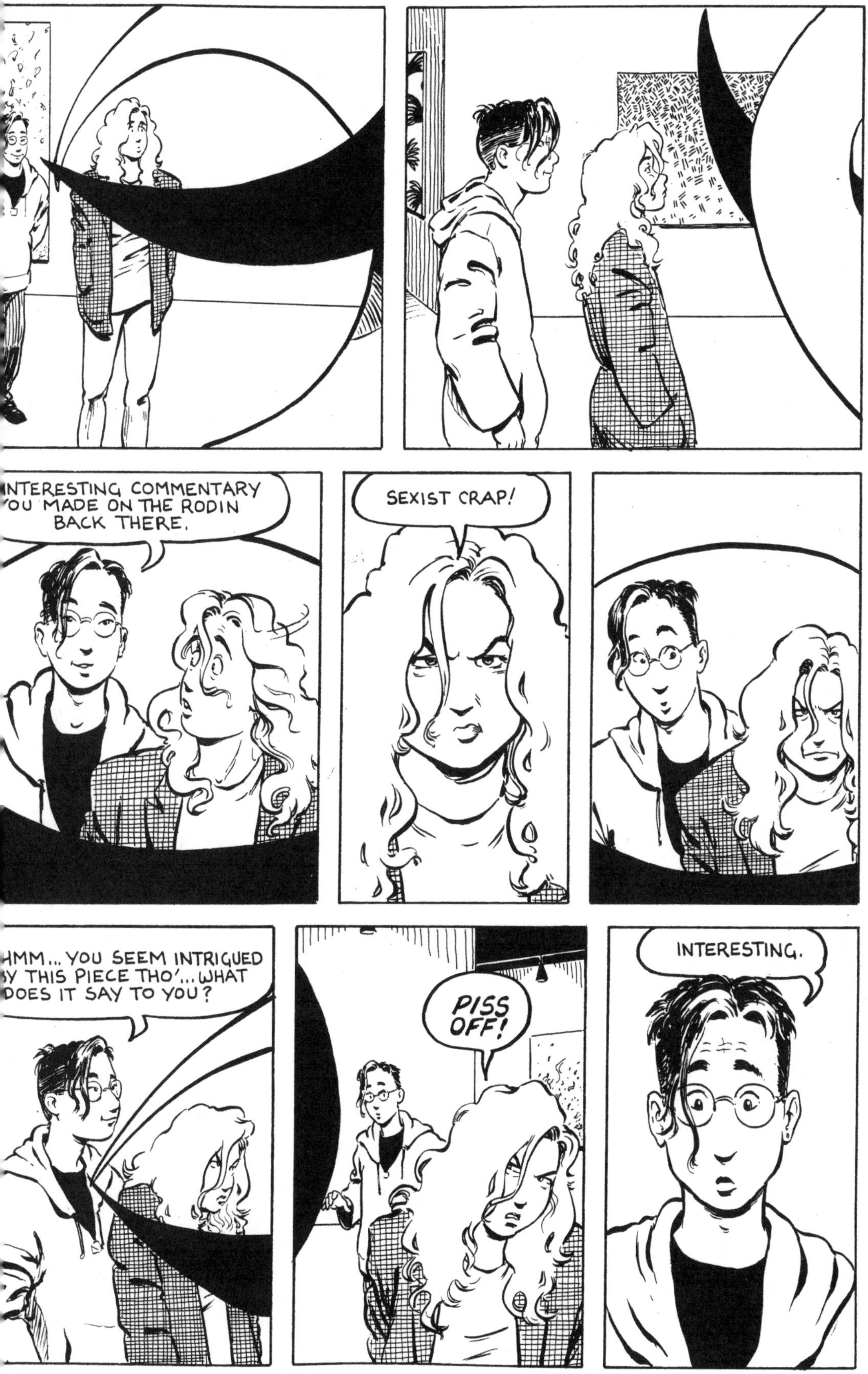
INTERESTING COMMENTARY YOU MADE ON THE RODIN BACK THERE.
SEXIST CRAP!
HMM... YOU SEEM INTRIGUED Y THIS PIECE THO'... WHAT DOES IT SAY TO YOU?
PISS OFF!
INTERESTING.

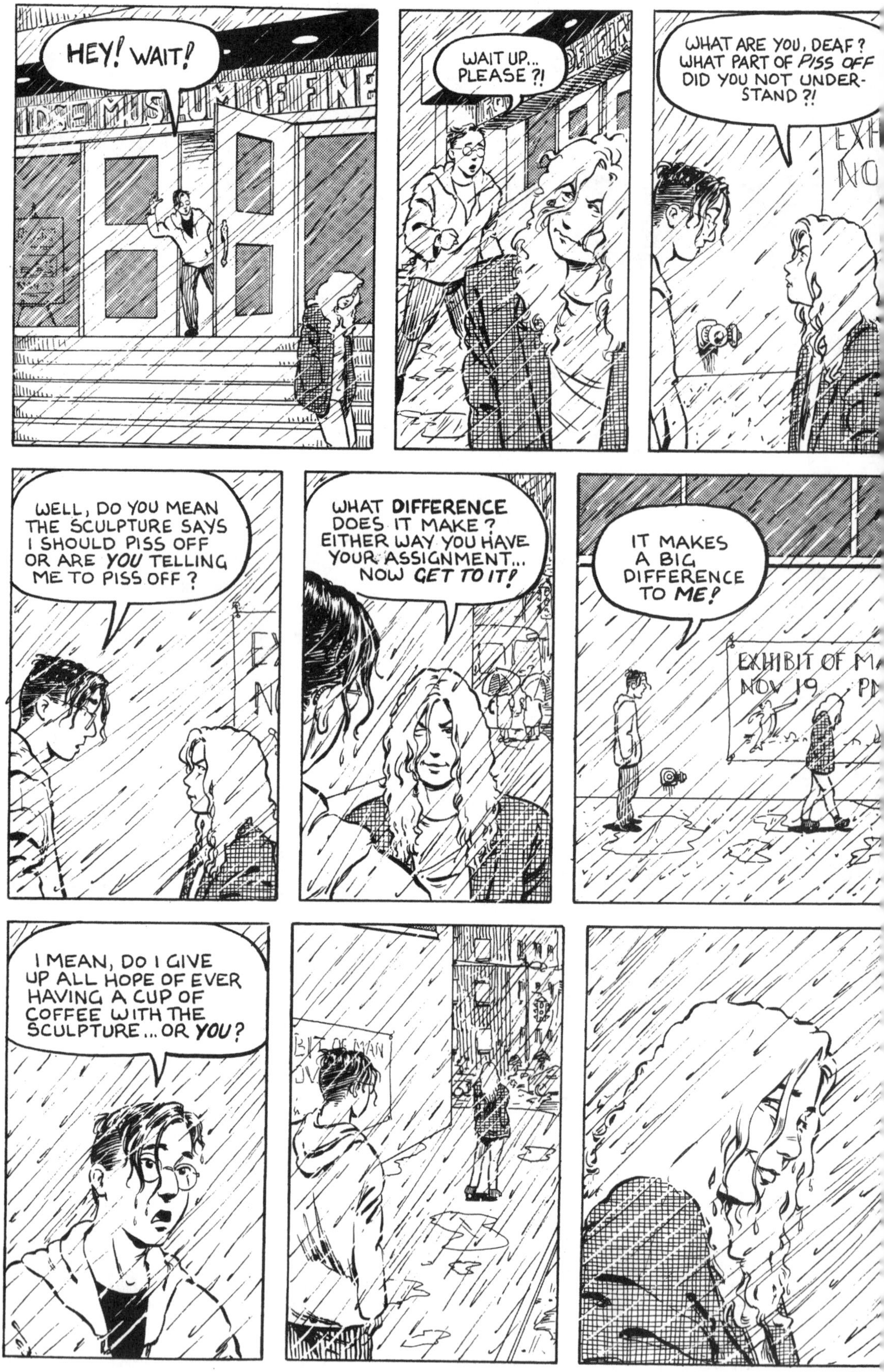
HEY! WAIT!
WAIT UP... PLEASE ?!
WHAT ARE YOU, DEAF? WHAT PART OF PISS OFF DID YOU NOT UNDERSTAND ?!
WELL, DO YOU MEAN THE SCULPTURE SAYS I SHOULD PISS OFF OR ARE YOU TELLING ME TO PISS OFF ?
WHAT DIFFERENCE DOES IT MAKE? EITHER WAY YOU HAVE YOUR ASSIGNMENT... NOW GET TO IT!
IT MAKES A BIG DIFFERENCE TO ME!
EXHIBIT OF M
NOV 19 PM
I MEAN, DO I GIVE UP ALL HOPE OF EVER HAVING A CUP OF COFFEE WITH THE SCULPTURE... OR YOU?

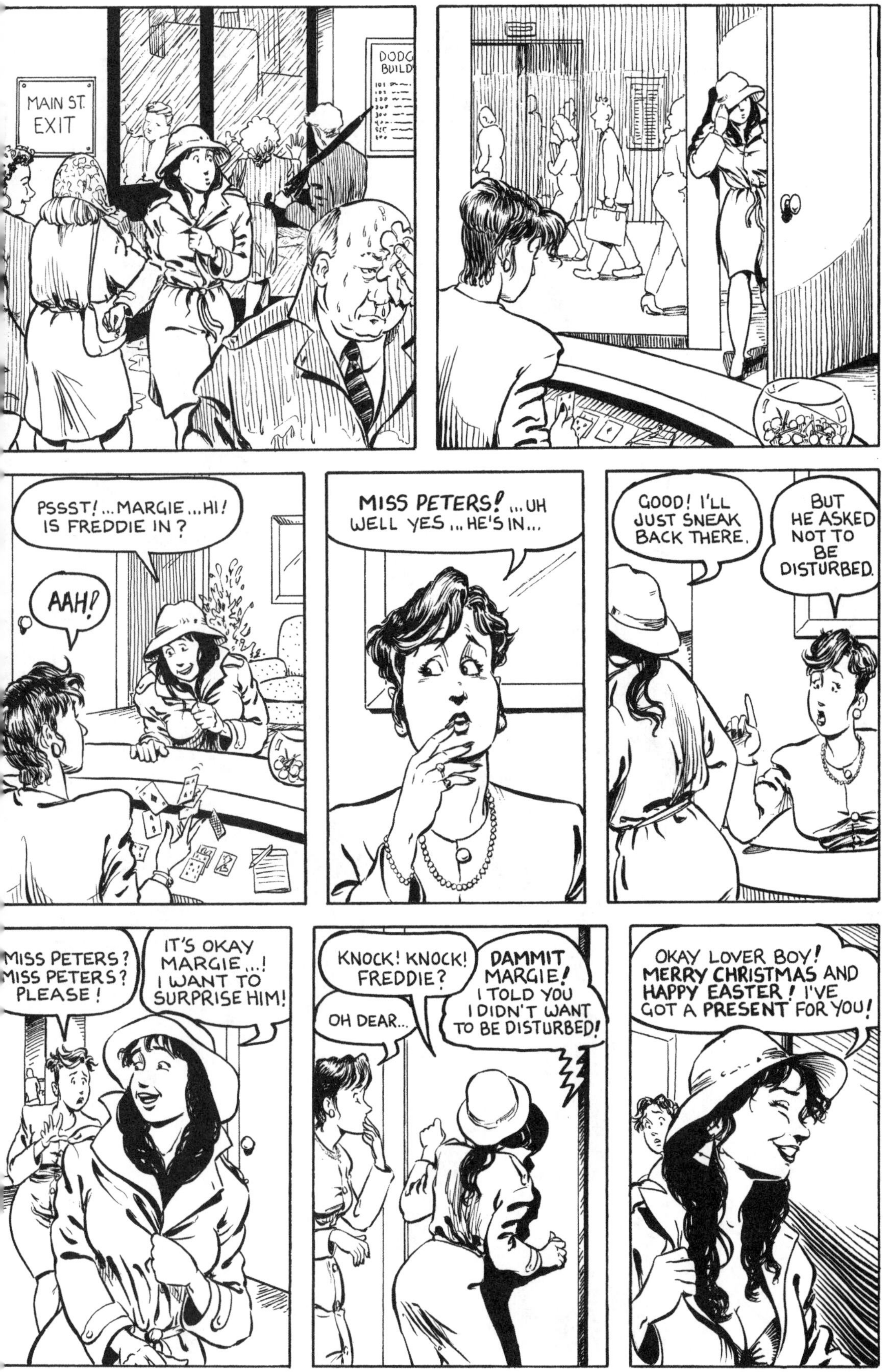
MAIN ST. EXIT
DODG BUILD
PSSST! ... MARGIE ... HI! IS FREDDIE IN?
AAH!
MISS PETERS! ... UH WELL YES ... HE'S IN...
GOOD! I'LL JUST SNEAK BACK THERE.
BUT HE ASKED NOT TO BE DISTURBED.
MISS PETERS? MISS PETERS? PLEASE!
IT'S OKAY MARGIE ...! I WANT TO SURPRISE HIM!
KNOCK! KNOCK! FREDDIE?
OH DEAR...
DAMMIT MARGIE! I TOLD YOU I DIDN'T WANT TO BE DISTURBED!
OKAY LOVER BOY! MERRY CHRISTMAS AND HAPPY EASTER! I'VE GOT A PRESENT FOR YOU!

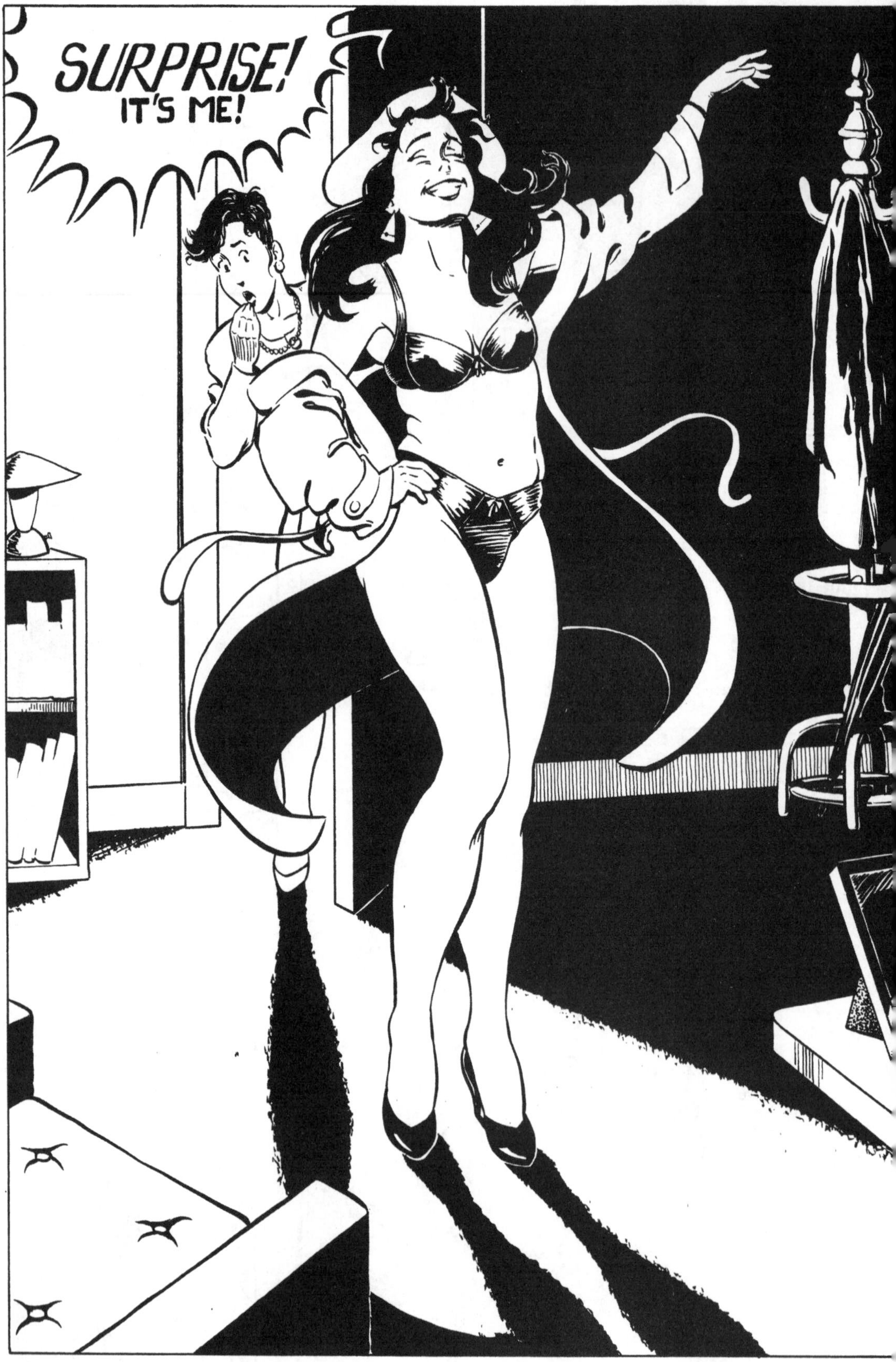
SURPRISE! IT'S ME!

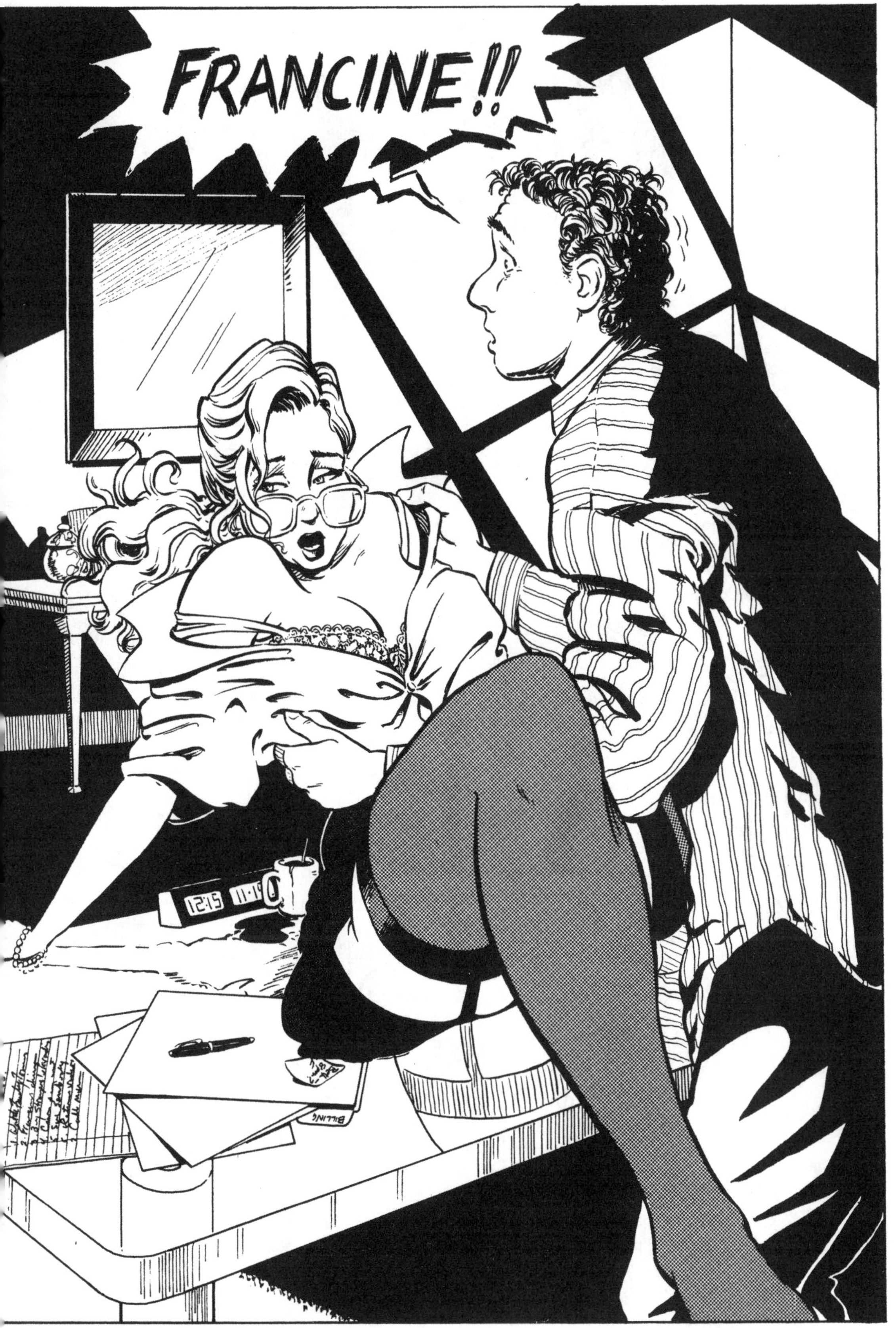
FRANCINE!!

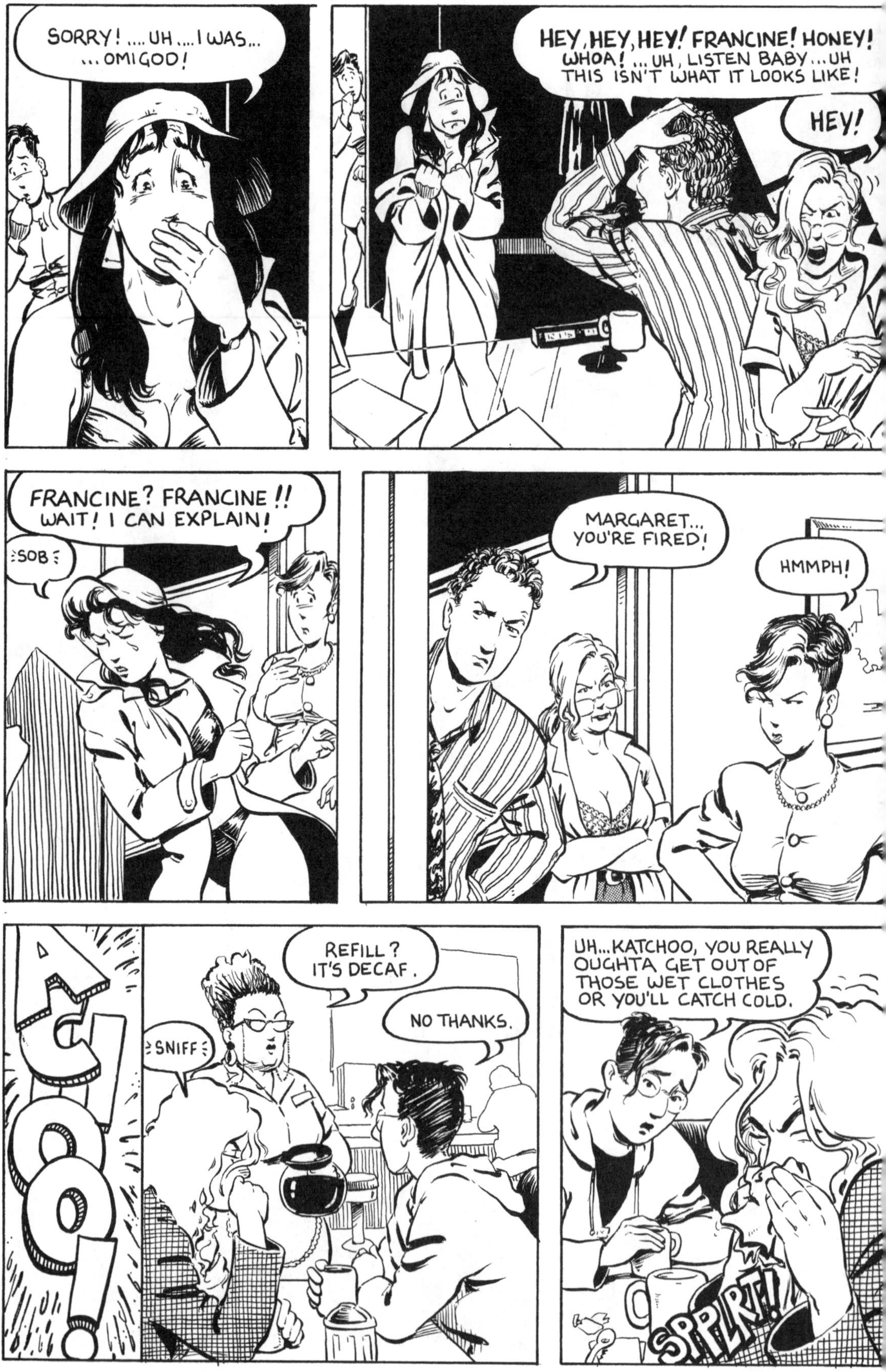
SORRY! ....UH....I WAS... ...OMIGOD!
HEY, HEY, HEY! FRANCINE! HONEY! WHOA! ...UH, LISTEN BABY...UH THIS ISN'T WHAT IT LOOKS LIKE!
HEY!
FRANCINE? FRANCINE!! WAIT! I CAN EXPLAIN!
SOB
MARGARET... YOU'RE FIRED!
HMMPH!
ACHOO!
SNIFF
REFILL? IT'S DECAF.
NO THANKS.
UH...KATCHOO, YOU REALLY OUGHTA GET OUT OF THOSE WET CLOTHES OR YOU'LL CATCH COLD.
SPPLRT!

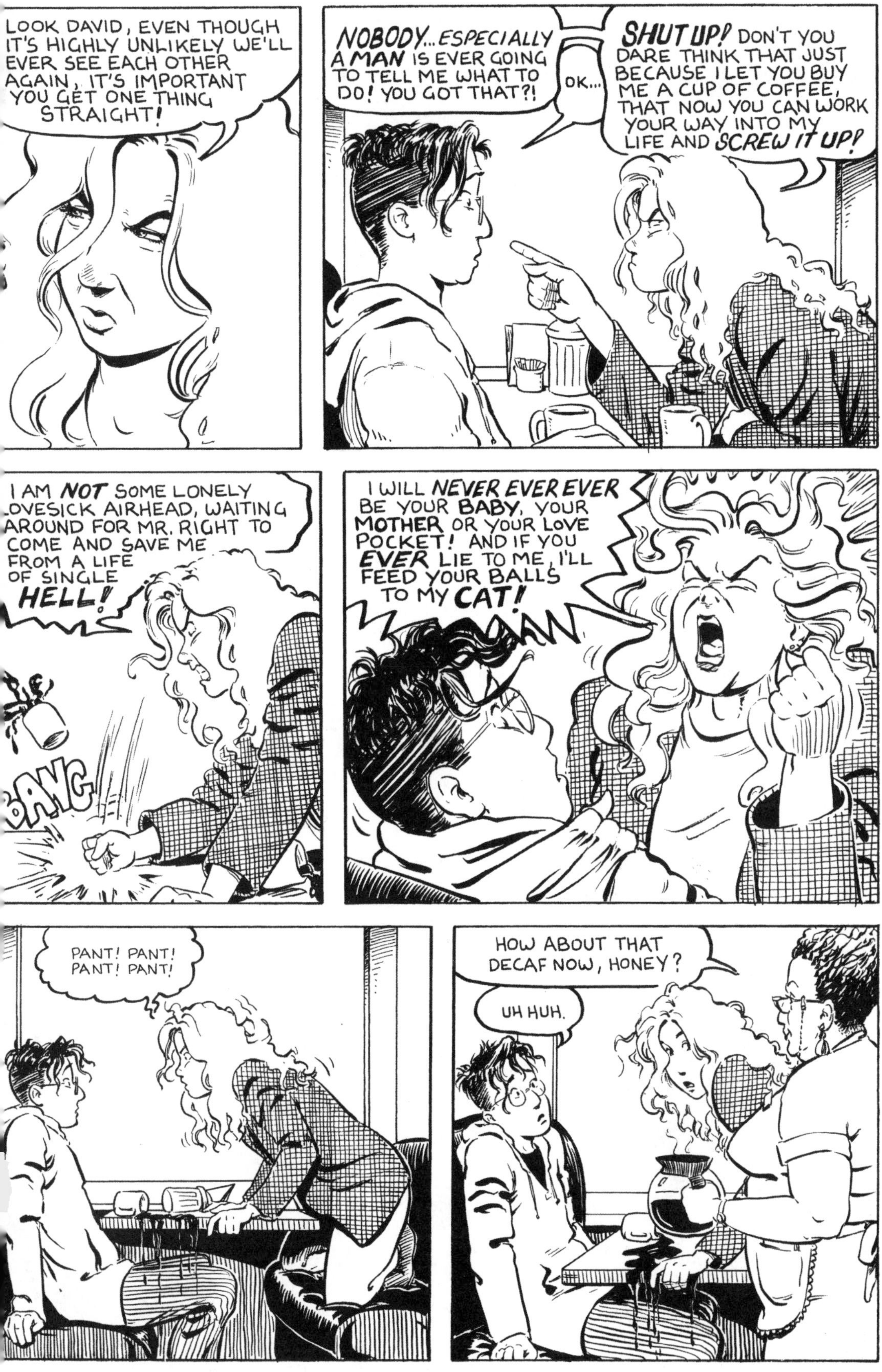
LOOK DAVID, EVEN THOUGH IT'S HIGHLY UNLIKELY WE'LL EVER SEE EACH OTHER AGAIN, IT'S IMPORTANT YOU GET ONE THING STRAIGHT!
NOBODY...ESPECIALLY A MAN IS EVER GOING TO TELL ME WHAT TO DO! YOU GOT THAT?!
OK...
SHUT UP! DON'T YOU DARE THINK THAT JUST BECAUSE I LET YOU BUY ME A CUP OF COFFEE, THAT NOW YOU CAN WORK YOUR WAY INTO MY LIFE AND SCREW IT UP!
I AM NOT SOME LONELY LOVESICK AIRHEAD, WAITING AROUND FOR MR. RIGHT TO COME AND SAVE ME FROM A LIFE OF SINGLE HELL!
BANG
I WILL NEVER EVER EVER BE YOUR BABY, YOUR MOTHER OR YOUR LOVE POCKET! AND IF YOU EVER LIE TO ME, I'LL FEED YOUR BALLS TO MY CAT!
PANT! PANT! PANT! PANT!
HOW ABOUT THAT DECAF NOW, HONEY?
UH HUH.

THE NEXT MORNING...

TICK TOK
TICK TOK
TICK TOK

RING!!

Call Freddie back 512-6002

FRANCIE?
...YOU AWAKE?

FREDDIE'S ON THE PHONE... DO YOU WANT TO TALK...

...TO HIM?

WHOOPS!

?

SUGAR
COFFEE

HELLO? FREDDIE? ARE YOU THERE?!

FRANCINE, LISTEN, WE NEED TO TALK...

WHY DON'T YOU MEET ME FOR LUNCH... SAY AT THE PARK, OK? ....
...WELL, LOOK, LET'S WAIT AND TALK ABOUT IT THEN, OK? SEE YA.

DON'T WORRY BABS, THIS WON'T TAKE LONG, THEN WE'LL GO EAT.

GOOD, I'M FAMISHED!

SNIFF

Nope. SNIFF

THIS SEAT TAKEN?

FRANCINE..... ABOUT WHAT HAPPENED IN MY OFFICE...

YOU DON'T HAVE TO APOLOGIZE FREDDIE, IT'S NOT YOUR FAULT!

...EH?

I ONLY HAVE MYSELF TO BLAME. I DROVE YOU TO HER... I SEE THAT NOW. I JUST WANT TO WIPE THE SLATE CLEAN AND TRY TO START OVER.

WHAT? AND GO BACK TO THE WAY THINGS WERE? NO THANKS! I'VE HAD IT!

C'MON, YOU DON'T REALLY MEAN THAT! LOOK, I KNOW YOU LOVE ME AND I LOVE YOU... I'M READY TO TRUST YOU NOW, REALLY! I CAN MAKE YOU HAPPY!.....FREDDIE?

...I'M SORRY FRANCINE, I REALLY AM. YOU'RE A SWEET GIRL, BUT TO BE BLUNT... YOU'RE NOT WORTH IT!

FREDDIE, STOP IT! LISTEN HONEY, THIS IS ME, FRANCINE! I KNOW WHAT MAKES YOU HAPPY! I KNOW WHAT YOU WANT, WHAT YOU NEED...AND I CAN DO IT! YOU KNOW I CAN!

NAH! I DON'T THINK SO. LOOK, I HAVE TO GET GOING, I HAVE SOMEBODY WAITING IN THE PORSCHE.

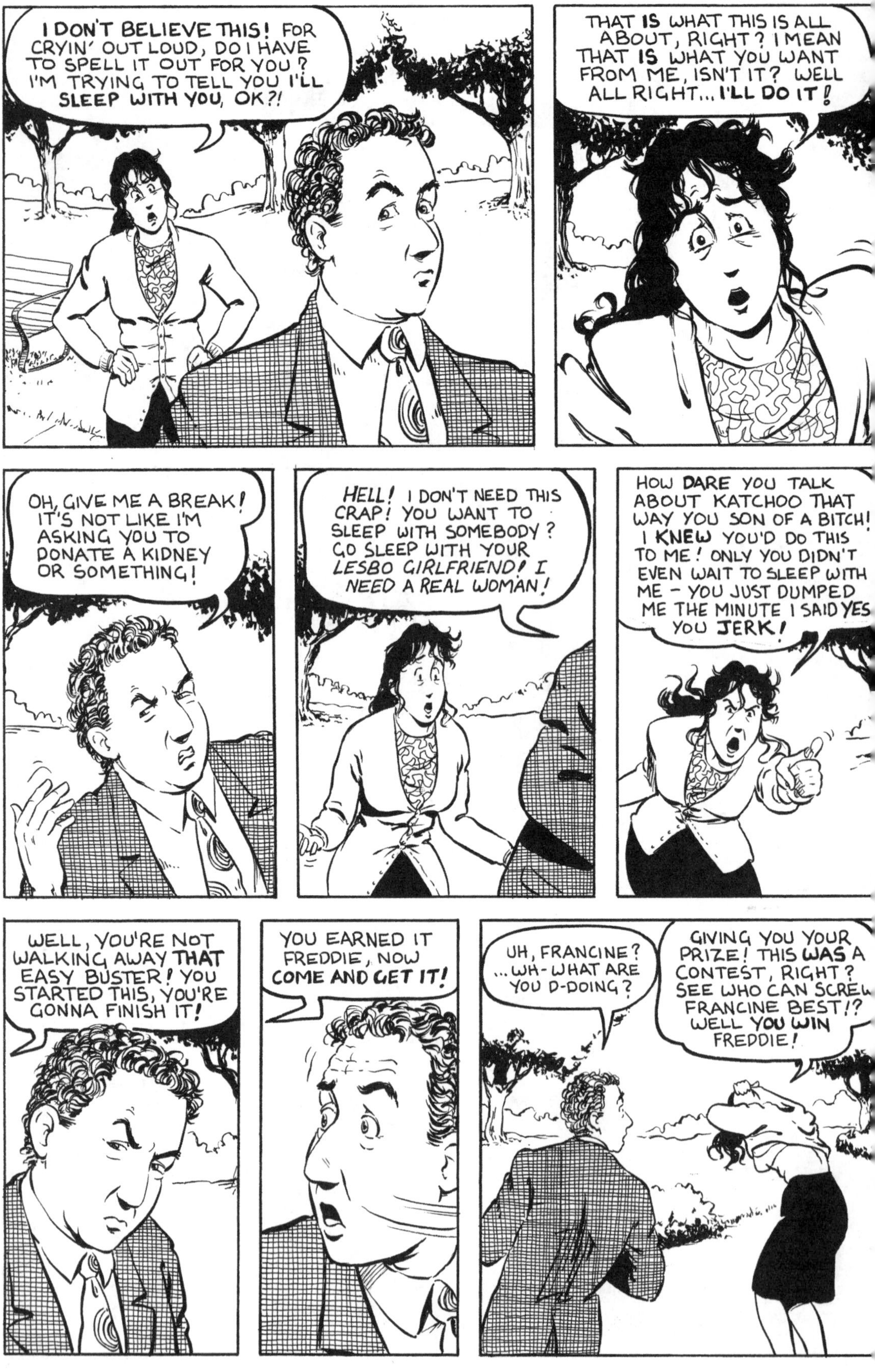
I DON'T BELIEVE THIS! FOR CRYIN' OUT LOUD, DO I HAVE TO SPELL IT OUT FOR YOU? I'M TRYING TO TELL YOU I'LL SLEEP WITH YOU, OK?!
THAT IS WHAT THIS IS ALL ABOUT, RIGHT? I MEAN THAT IS WHAT YOU WANT FROM ME, ISN'T IT? WELL ALL RIGHT... I'LL DO IT!
OH, GIVE ME A BREAK! IT'S NOT LIKE I'M ASKING YOU TO DONATE A KIDNEY OR SOMETHING!
HELL! I DON'T NEED THIS CRAP! YOU WANT TO SLEEP WITH SOMEBODY? GO SLEEP WITH YOUR LESBO GIRLFRIEND! I NEED A REAL WOMAN!
HOW DARE YOU TALK ABOUT KATCHOO THAT WAY YOU SON OF A BITCH! I KNEW YOU'D DO THIS TO ME! ONLY YOU DIDN'T EVEN WAIT TO SLEEP WITH ME - YOU JUST DUMPED ME THE MINUTE I SAID YES YOU JERK!
WELL, YOU'RE NOT WALKING AWAY THAT EASY BUSTER! YOU STARTED THIS, YOU'RE GONNA FINISH IT!
YOU EARNED IT FREDDIE, NOW COME AND GET IT!
UH, FRANCINE? ...WH-WHAT ARE YOU D-DOING?
GIVING YOU YOUR PRIZE! THIS WAS A CONTEST, RIGHT? SEE WHO CAN SCREW FRANCINE BEST!? WELL YOU WIN FREDDIE!

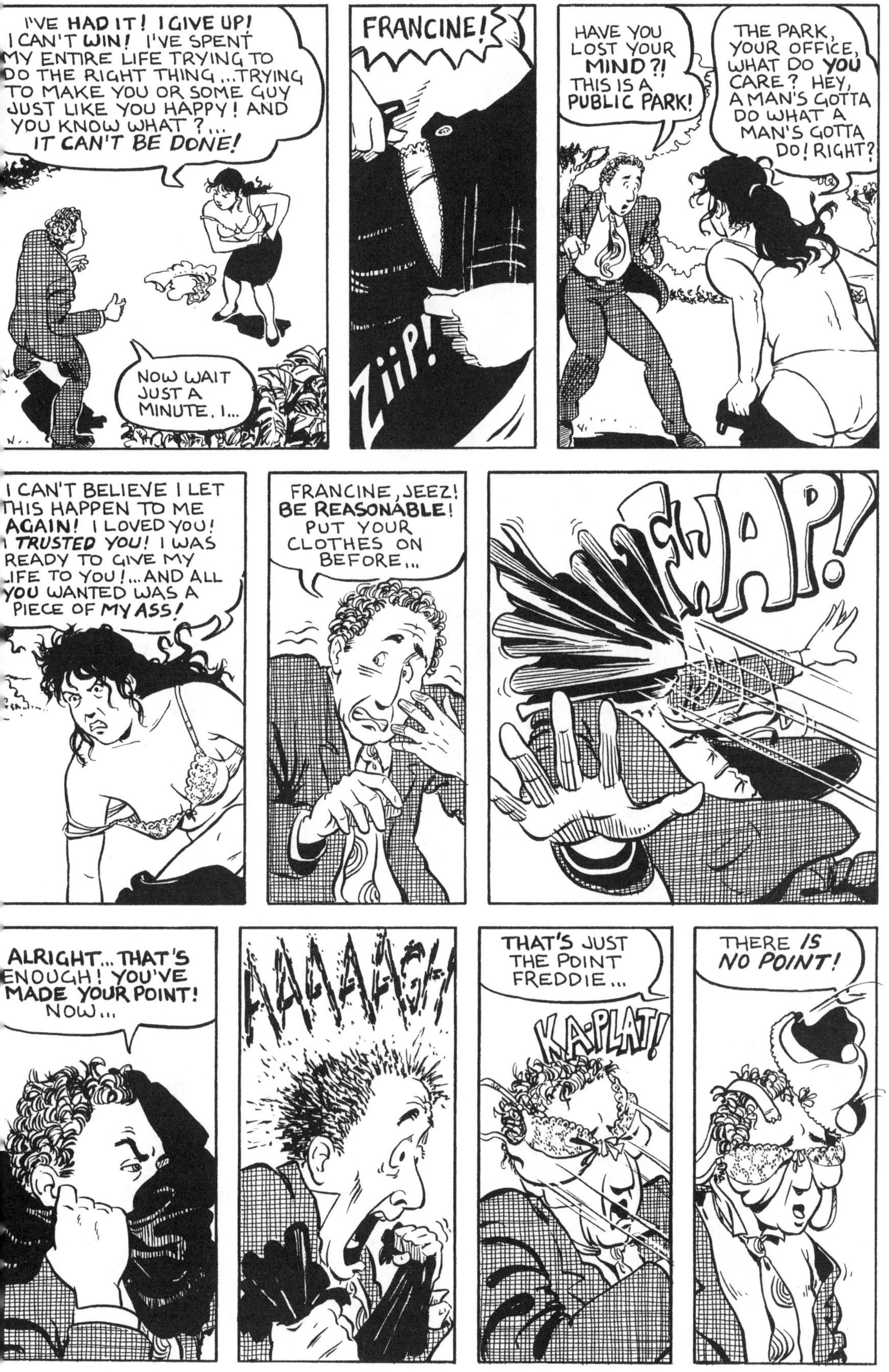
I'VE HAD IT! I GIVE UP! I CAN'T WIN! I'VE SPENT MY ENTIRE LIFE TRYING TO DO THE RIGHT THING...TRYING TO MAKE YOU OR SOME GUY JUST LIKE YOU HAPPY! AND YOU KNOW WHAT?... IT CAN'T BE DONE!
NOW WAIT JUST A MINUTE. I...
FRANCINE!
ZIIP!
HAVE YOU LOST YOUR MIND?! THIS IS A PUBLIC PARK!
THE PARK, YOUR OFFICE, WHAT DO YOU CARE? HEY, A MAN'S GOTTA DO WHAT A MAN'S GOTTA DO! RIGHT?
I CAN'T BELIEVE I LET THIS HAPPEN TO ME AGAIN! I LOVED YOU! I TRUSTED YOU! I WAS READY TO GIVE MY LIFE TO YOU!...AND ALL YOU WANTED WAS A PIECE OF MY ASS!
FRANCINE, JEEZ! BE REASONABLE! PUT YOUR CLOTHES ON BEFORE...
SWAP!
ALRIGHT...THAT'S ENOUGH! YOU'VE MADE YOUR POINT! NOW...
THAT'S JUST THE POINT FREDDIE...
KA-PLAT!
THERE IS NO POINT!

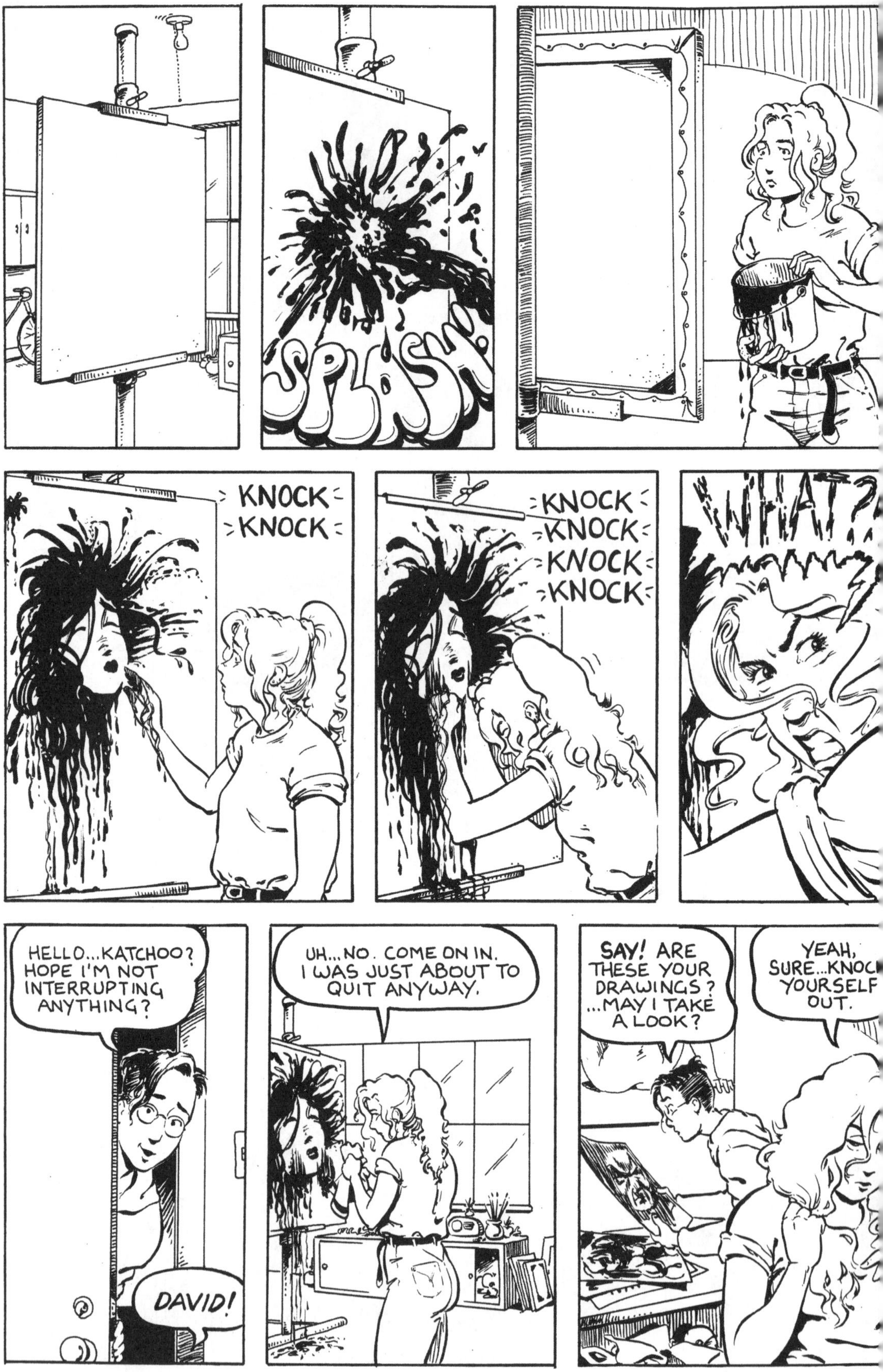
SPLASH!
KNOCK KNOCK
KNOCK KNOCK KNOCK KNOCK
WHAT?
HELLO...KATCHOO? HOPE I'M NOT INTERRUPTING ANYTHING?
DAVID!
UH...NO. COME ON IN. I WAS JUST ABOUT TO QUIT ANYWAY.
SAY! ARE THESE YOUR DRAWINGS? ...MAY I TAKE A LOOK?
YEAH, SURE...KNOC YOURSELF OUT.

LOOKS LIKE IT'S GOING TO RAIN AGAIN TONIGHT.

GOOD!

I LIKE THE RAIN NOW... IT REMINDS ME OF MEETING YOU.

OHMIGOSH, WHO'VE I LET IN MY HOUSE, PEPE LE PEW?

KATCHOO!...THIS IS AWESOME! I'VE NEVER SEEN ANYTHING LIKE IT!

SURE YOU HAVE! YOU TOOK GYM IN SCHOOL DIDN'T YOU?

NO, NO! I MEAN YOUR STYLE! IT'S SO STRONG! SO...SO BOLD!...SUCH A BIG VOICE FOR SUCH A DELICATE CREATURE.

YES?

DAVID?

...SHUT UP.

SKREEEEEECH!

WHAT WAS THAT?

HOOOOUUUUUUNK!

FRANCINE!

29

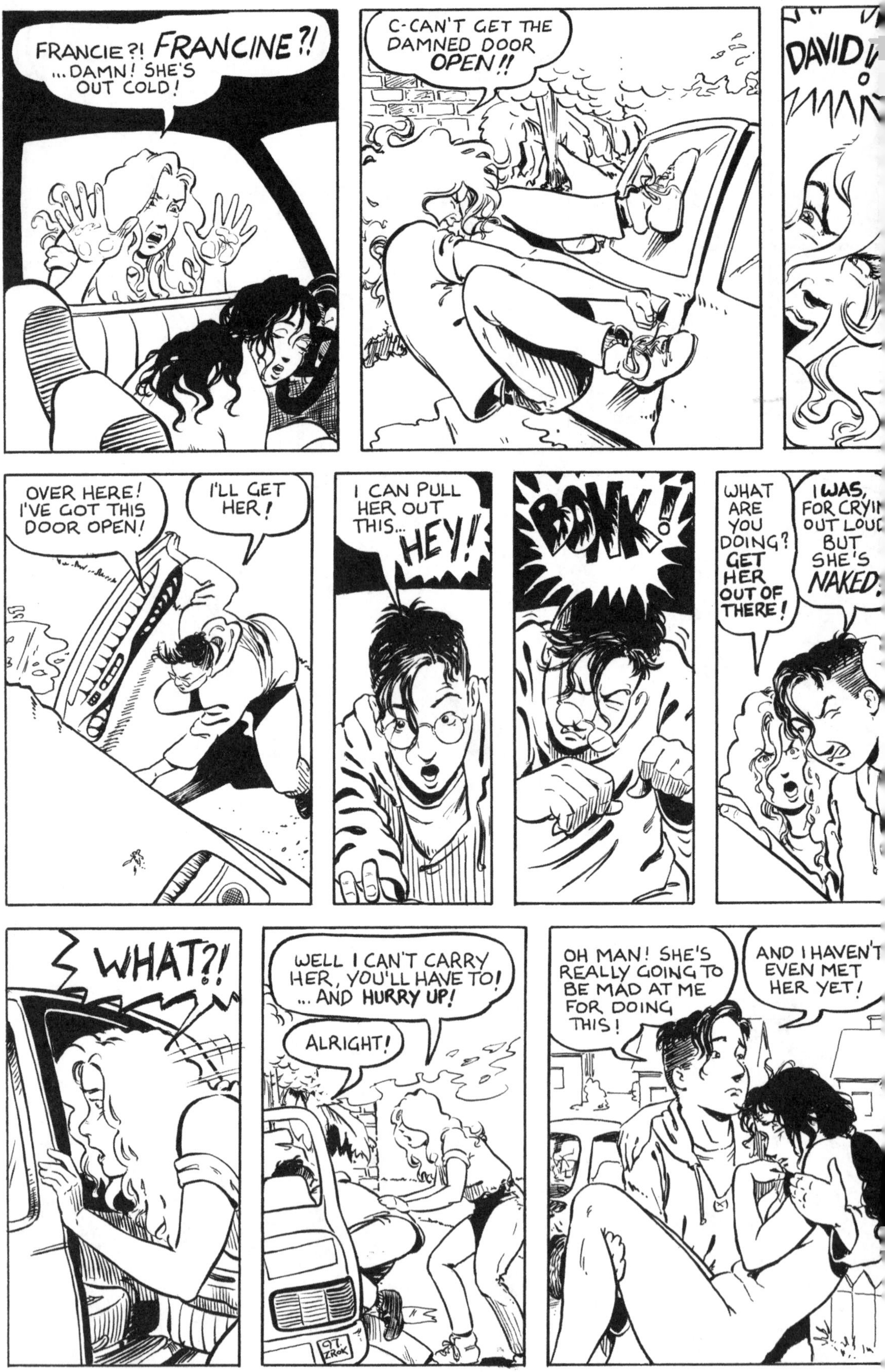
FRANCIE?! FRANCINE?! ...DAMN! SHE'S OUT COLD!
C-CAN'T GET THE DAMNED DOOR OPEN!!
DAVID!
OVER HERE! I'VE GOT THIS DOOR OPEN!
I'LL GET HER!
I CAN PULL HER OUT THIS... HEY!
BONK!
WHAT ARE YOU DOING? GET HER OUT OF THERE!
I WAS, FOR CRYIN OUT LOUD BUT SHE'S NAKED!
WHAT?!
WELL I CAN'T CARRY HER, YOU'LL HAVE TO! ...AND HURRY UP!
ALRIGHT!
OH MAN! SHE'S REALLY GOING TO BE MAD AT ME FOR DOING THIS!
AND I HAVEN'T EVEN MET HER YET!

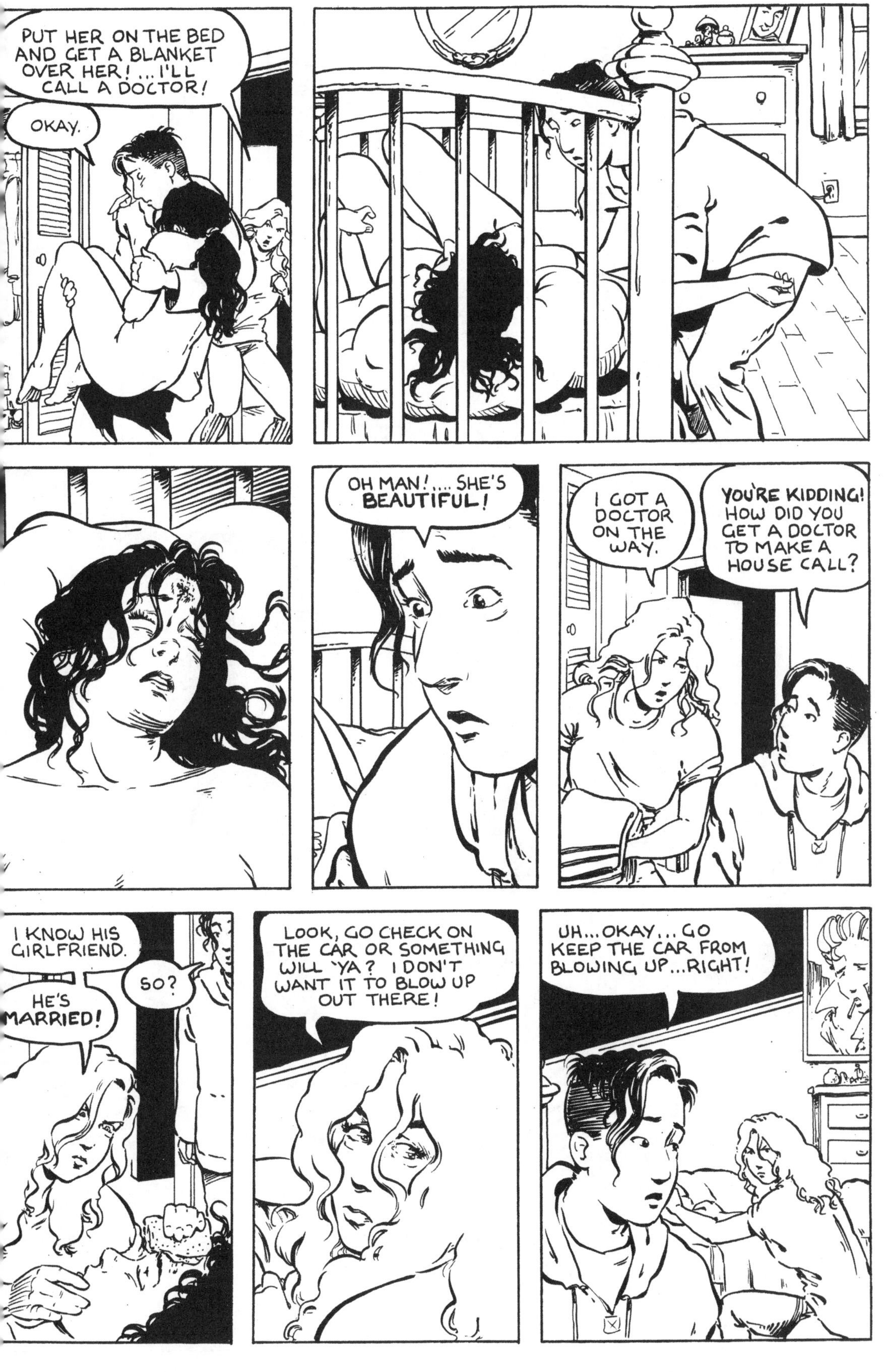
PUT HER ON THE BED AND GET A BLANKET OVER HER! ...I'LL CALL A DOCTOR!
OKAY.
OH MAN!.... SHE'S BEAUTIFUL!
I GOT A DOCTOR ON THE WAY.
YOU'RE KIDDING! HOW DID YOU GET A DOCTOR TO MAKE A HOUSE CALL?
I KNOW HIS GIRLFRIEND.
SO?
HE'S MARRIED!
LOOK, GO CHECK ON THE CAR OR SOMETHING WILL 'YA? I DON'T WANT IT TO BLOW UP OUT THERE!
UH...OKAY...GO KEEP THE CAR FROM BLOWING UP...RIGHT!

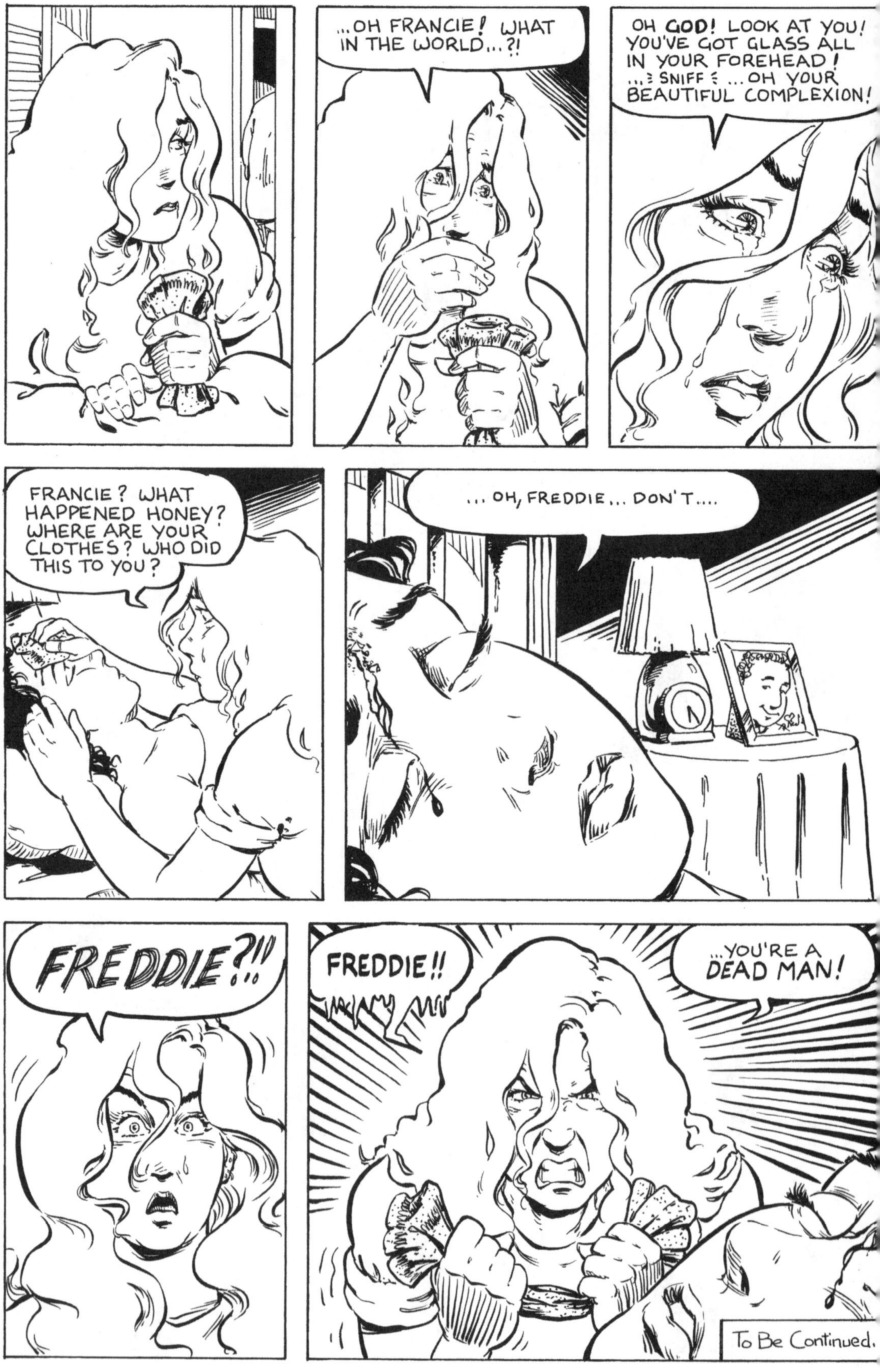
...OH FRANCIE! WHAT IN THE WORLD...?!
OH GOD! LOOK AT YOU! YOU'VE GOT GLASS ALL IN YOUR FOREHEAD! ...⁝ SNIFF ⁝ ...OH YOUR BEAUTIFUL COMPLEXION!
FRANCIE? WHAT HAPPENED HONEY? WHERE ARE YOUR CLOTHES? WHO DID THIS TO YOU?
...OH, FREDDIE... DON'T....
FREDDIE?!!
FREDDIE!!
...YOU'RE A DEAD MAN!
To Be Continued.

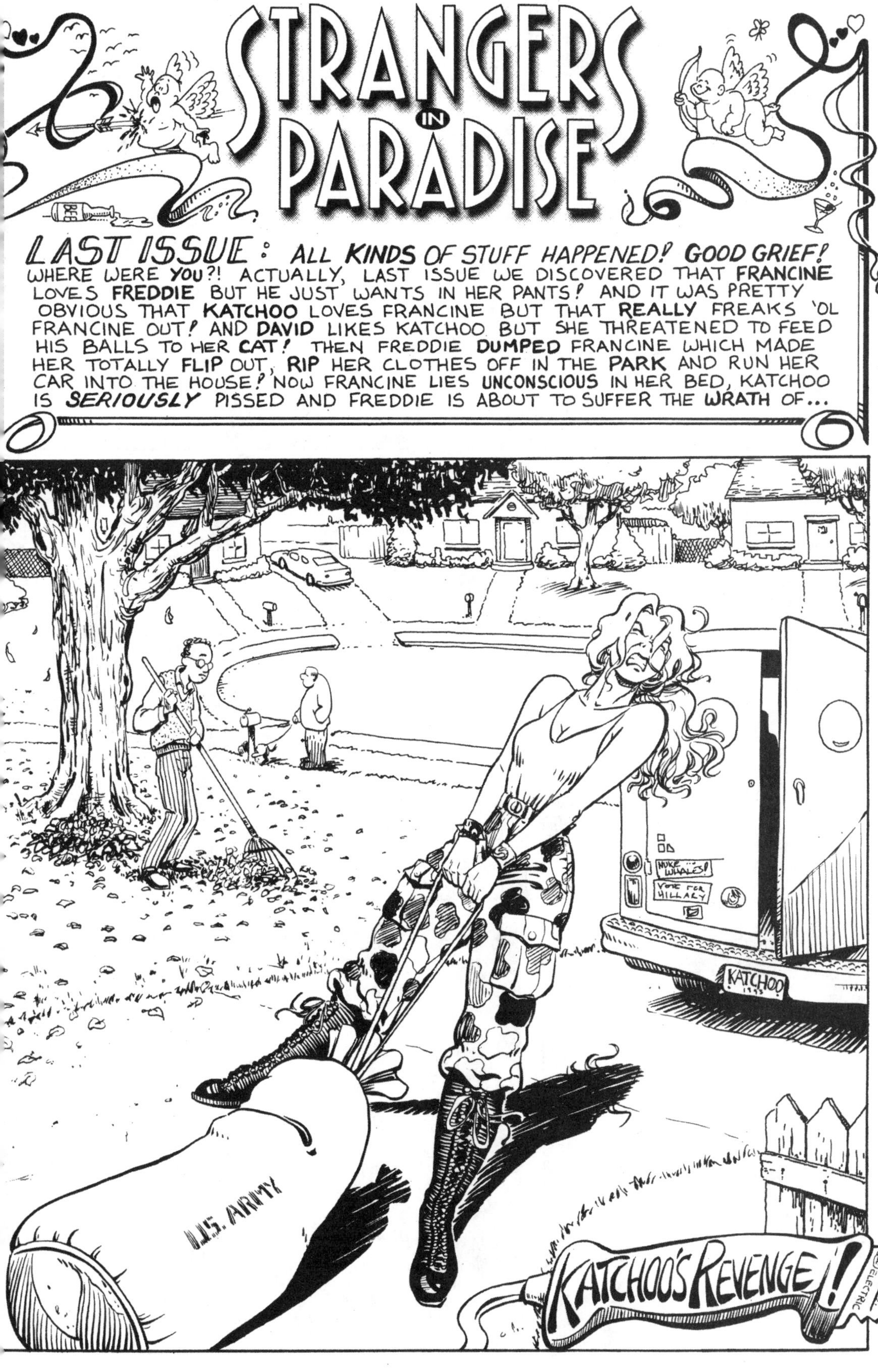

STRANGERS IN PARADISE
LAST ISSUE: ALL KINDS OF STUFF HAPPENED! GOOD GRIEF! WHERE WERE YOU?! ACTUALLY, LAST ISSUE WE DISCOVERED THAT FRANCINE LOVES FREDDIE BUT HE JUST WANTS IN HER PANTS! AND IT WAS PRETTY OBVIOUS THAT KATCHOO LOVES FRANCINE BUT THAT REALLY FREAKS 'OL FRANCINE OUT! AND DAVID LIKES KATCHOO BUT SHE THREATENED TO FEED HIS BALLS TO HER CAT! THEN FREDDIE DUMPED FRANCINE WHICH MADE HER TOTALLY FLIP OUT, RIP HER CLOTHES OFF IN THE PARK AND RUN HER CAR INTO THE HOUSE! NOW FRANCINE LIES UNCONSCIOUS IN HER BED, KATCHOO IS SERIOUSLY PISSED AND FREDDIE IS ABOUT TO SUFFER THE WRATH OF...
NUKE ... WHALES!
VOTE FOR HILLARY
KATCHOO
U.S. ARMY
KATCHOO'S REVENGE!

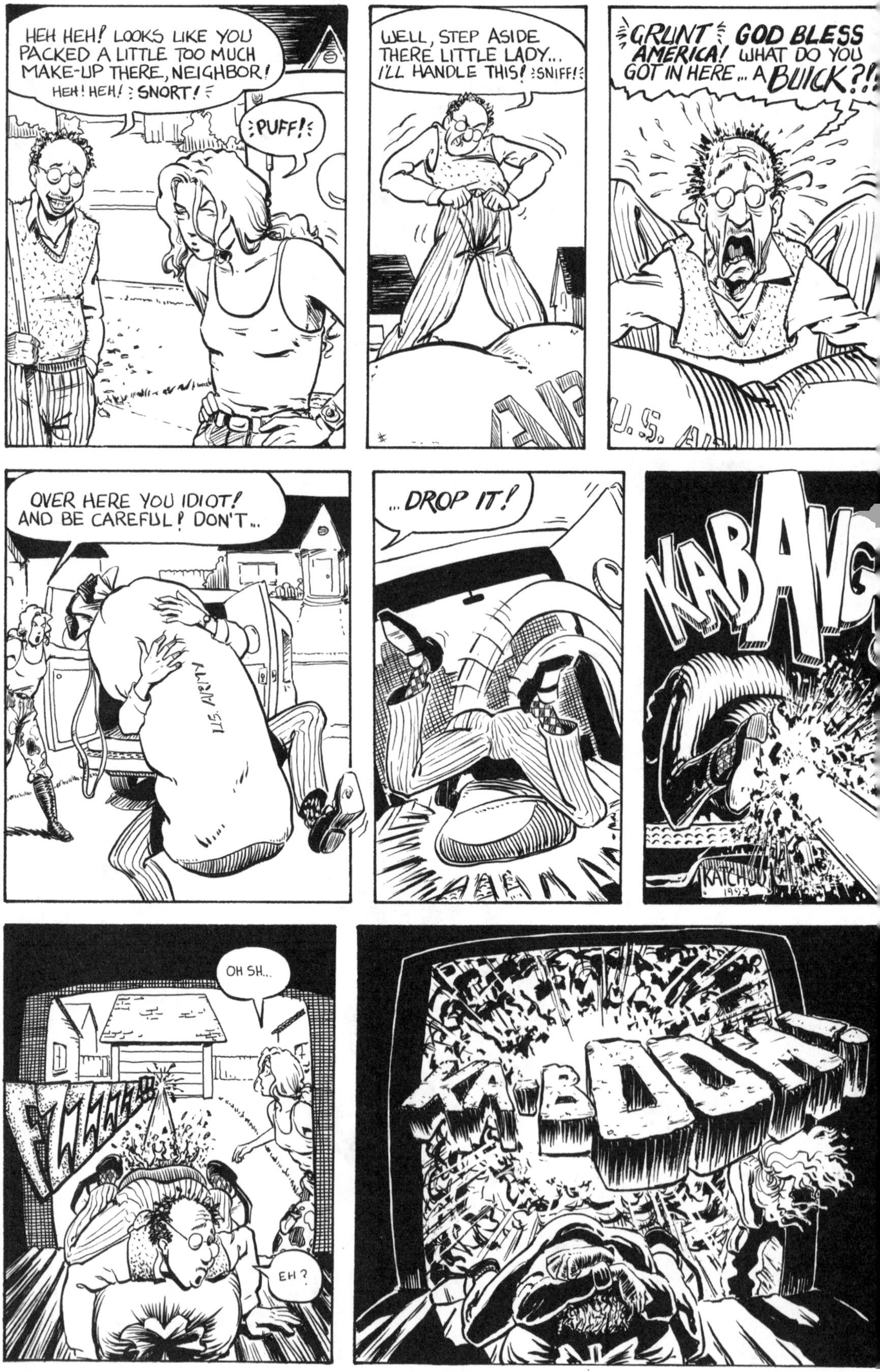
HEH HEH! LOOKS LIKE YOU PACKED A LITTLE TOO MUCH MAKE-UP THERE, NEIGHBOR! HEH! HEH! SNORT!
PUFF!
WELL, STEP ASIDE THERE LITTLE LADY... I'LL HANDLE THIS! SNIFF!
GRUNT GOD BLESS AMERICA! WHAT DO YOU GOT IN HERE... A BUICK?!
U.S.
OVER HERE YOU IDIOT! AND BE CAREFUL! DON'T...
U.S. ARMY
...DROP IT!
KABANG
KATCHOO
1993
OH SH...
EH?
KA-BOOM

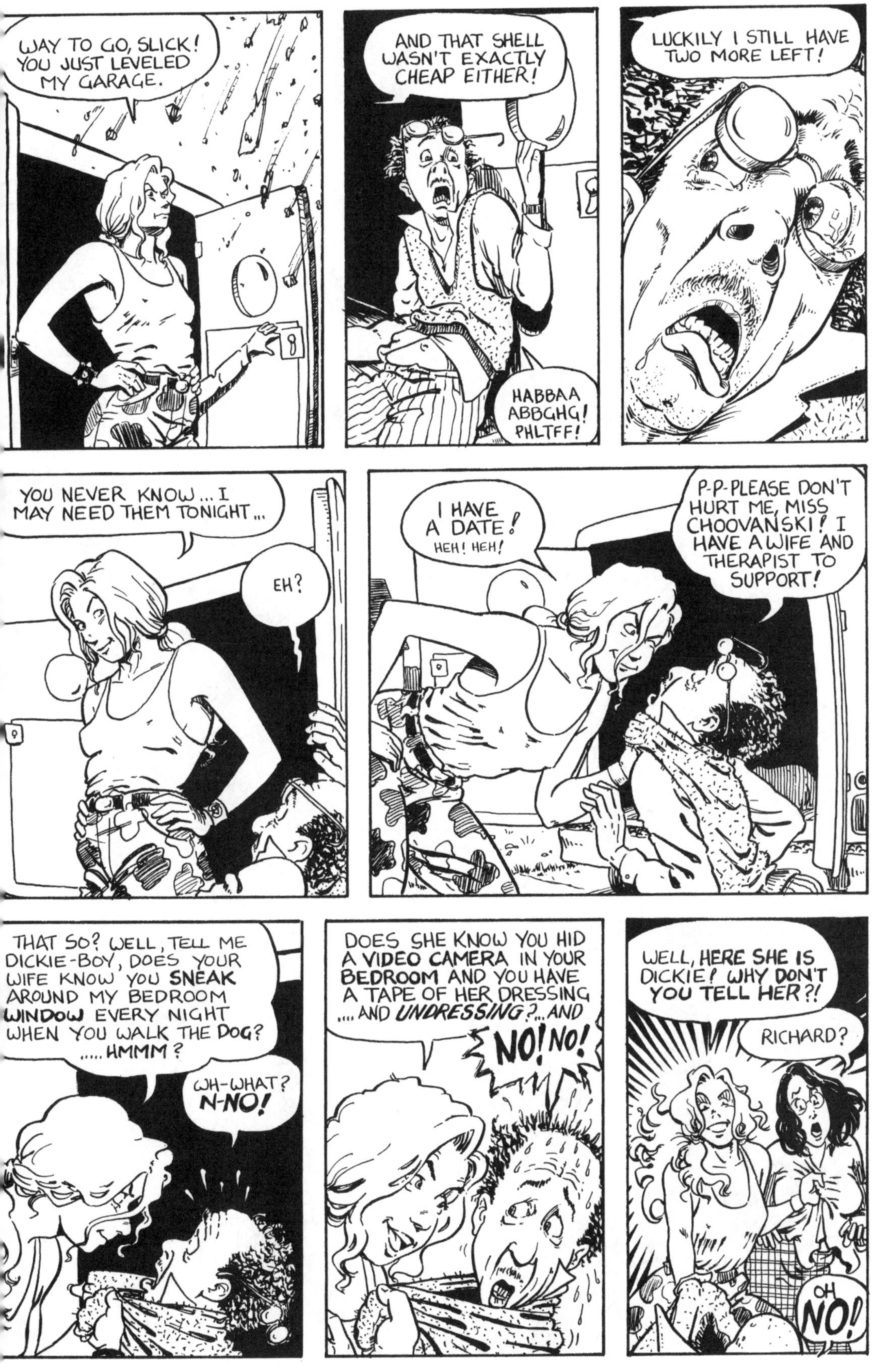

WAY TO GO, SLICK! YOU JUST LEVELED MY GARAGE.
AND THAT SHELL WASN'T EXACTLY CHEAP EITHER!
HABBAA ABBGHG! PHLTFF!
LUCKILY I STILL HAVE TWO MORE LEFT!
YOU NEVER KNOW... I MAY NEED THEM TONIGHT...
EH?
I HAVE A DATE! HEH! HEH!
P-P-PLEASE DON'T HURT ME, MISS CHOOVANSKI! I HAVE A WIFE AND THERAPIST TO SUPPORT!
THAT SO? WELL, TELL ME DICKIE-BOY, DOES YOUR WIFE KNOW YOU **SNEAK** AROUND MY BEDROOM **WINDOW** EVERY NIGHT WHEN YOU WALK THE DOG? .....HMMM?
WH-WHAT? N-NO!
DOES SHE KNOW YOU HID A **VIDEO CAMERA** IN YOUR **BEDROOM** AND YOU HAVE A TAPE OF HER DRESSING ....AND ***UNDRESSING***?...AND
NO! NO!
WELL, **HERE SHE IS** DICKIE! WHY **DON'T YOU TELL HER**?!
RICHARD?
OH NO!

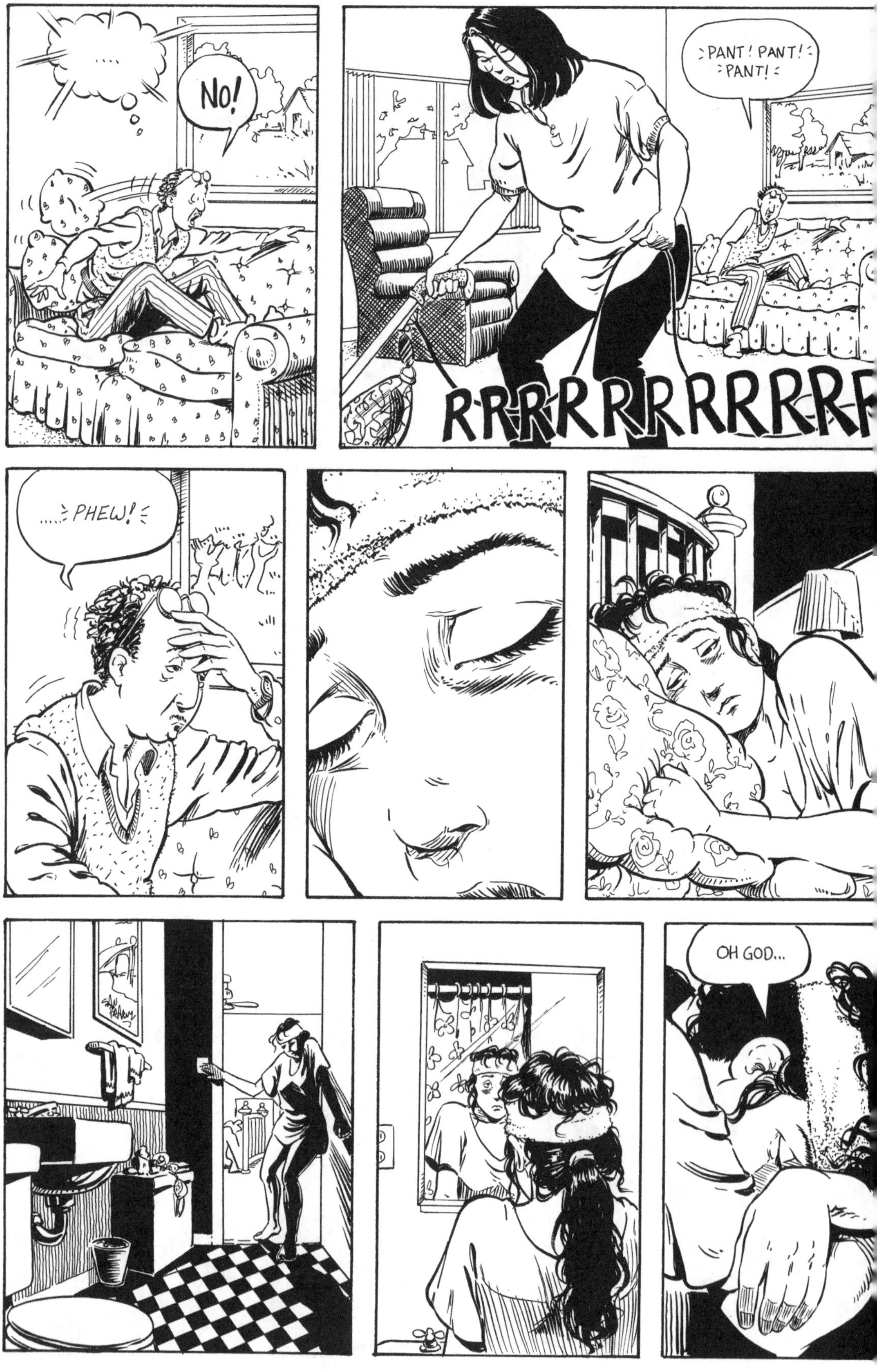
....
No!
PANT! PANT! PANT!
RRRRRRRRRRRR
....PHEW!
OH GOD...

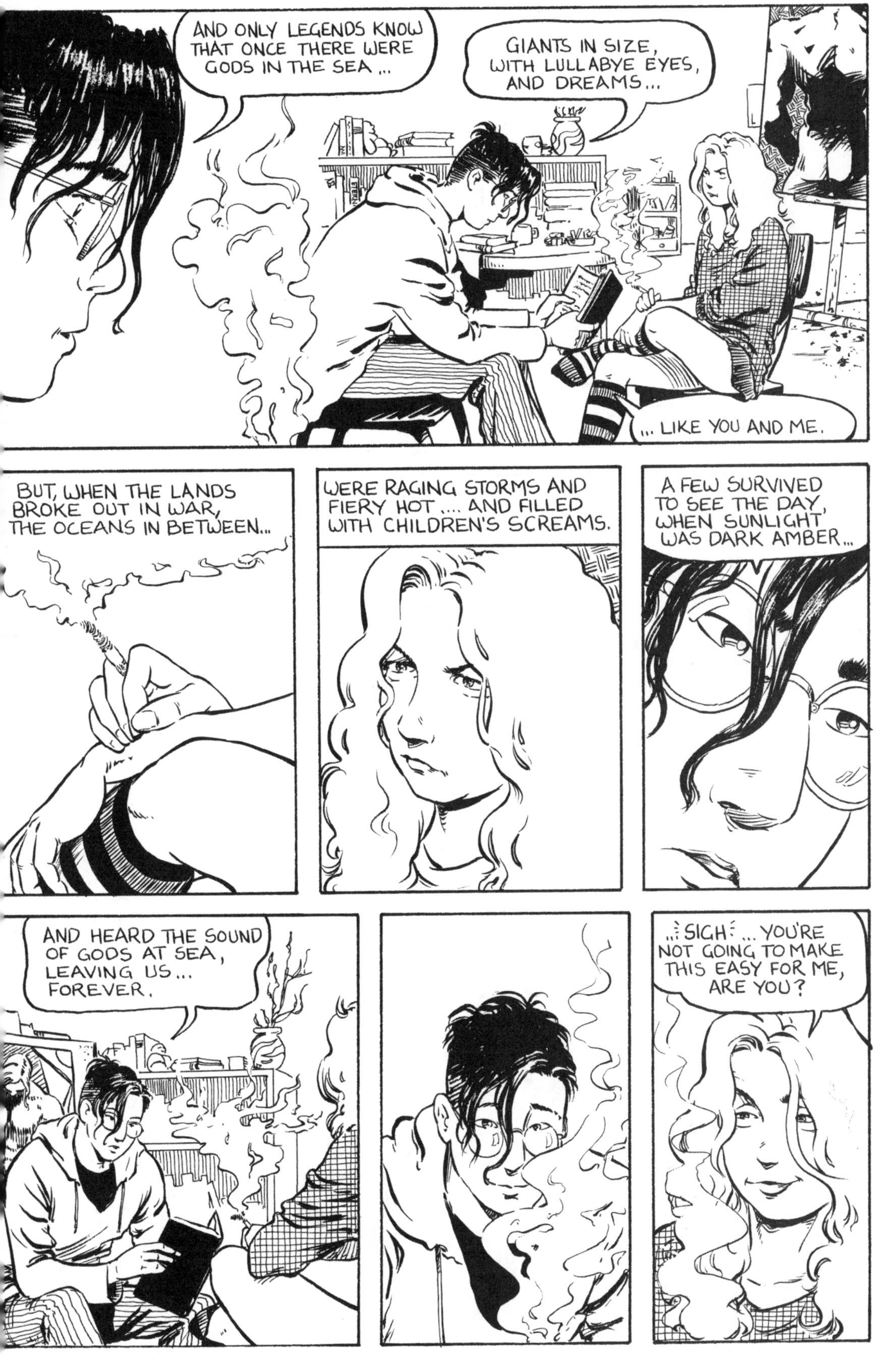
AND ONLY LEGENDS KNOW THAT ONCE THERE WERE GODS IN THE SEA ...
GIANTS IN SIZE, WITH LULLABYE EYES, AND DREAMS...
... LIKE YOU AND ME.
BUT, WHEN THE LANDS BROKE OUT IN WAR, THE OCEANS IN BETWEEN...
WERE RAGING STORMS AND FIERY HOT .... AND FILLED WITH CHILDREN'S SCREAMS.
A FEW SURVIVED TO SEE THE DAY, WHEN SUNLIGHT WAS DARK AMBER...
AND HEARD THE SOUND OF GODS AT SEA, LEAVING US... FOREVER.
... SIGH ... YOU'RE NOT GOING TO MAKE THIS EASY FOR ME, ARE YOU?

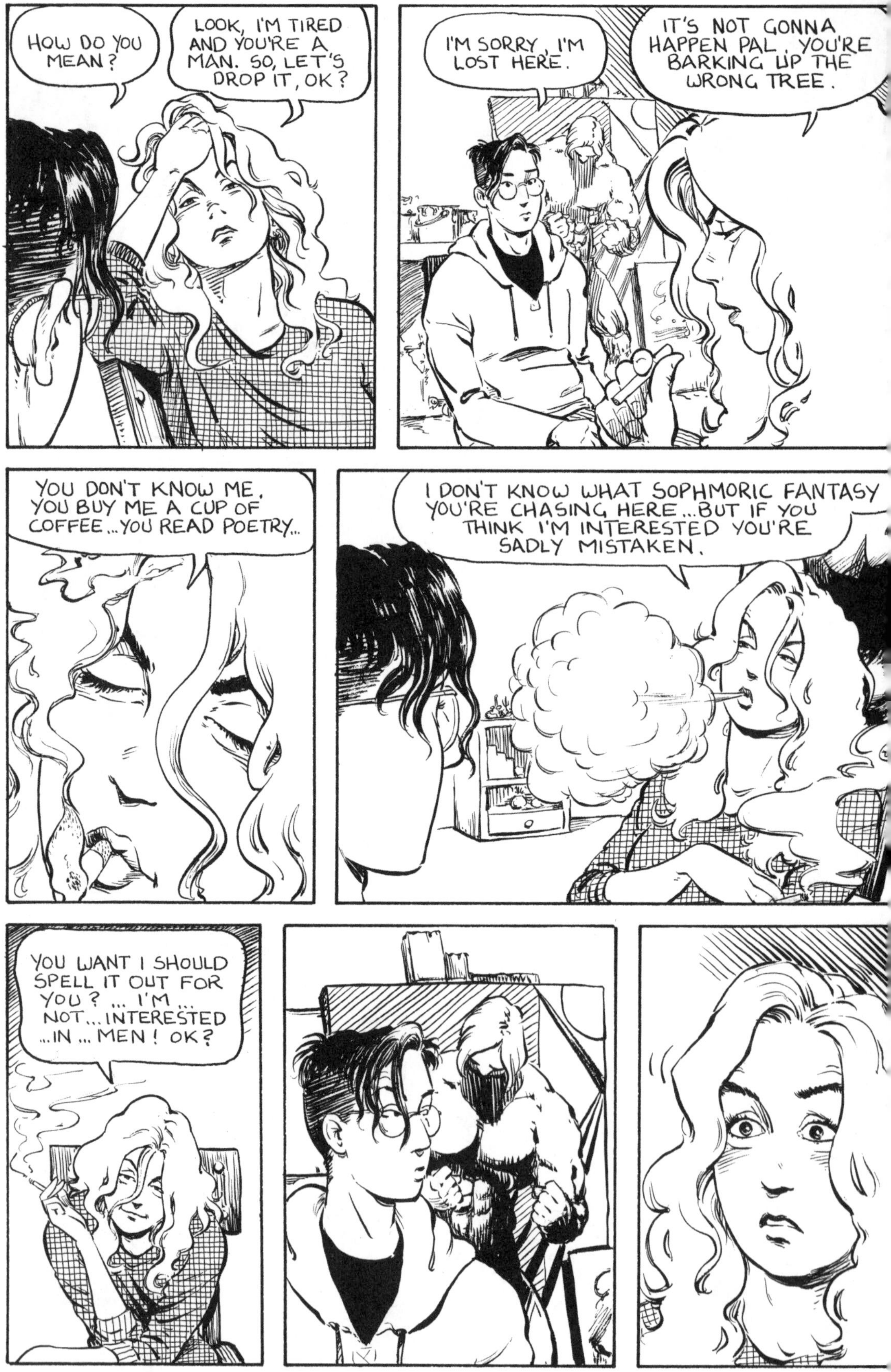
HOW DO YOU MEAN?
LOOK, I'M TIRED AND YOU'RE A MAN. SO, LET'S DROP IT, OK?
I'M SORRY, I'M LOST HERE.
IT'S NOT GONNA HAPPEN PAL. YOU'RE BARKING UP THE WRONG TREE.
YOU DON'T KNOW ME. YOU BUY ME A CUP OF COFFEE... YOU READ POETRY...
I DON'T KNOW WHAT SOPHMORIC FANTASY YOU'RE CHASING HERE... BUT IF YOU THINK I'M INTERESTED YOU'RE SADLY MISTAKEN.
YOU WANT I SHOULD SPELL IT OUT FOR YOU? ... I'M ... NOT... INTERESTED ...IN ... MEN! OK?

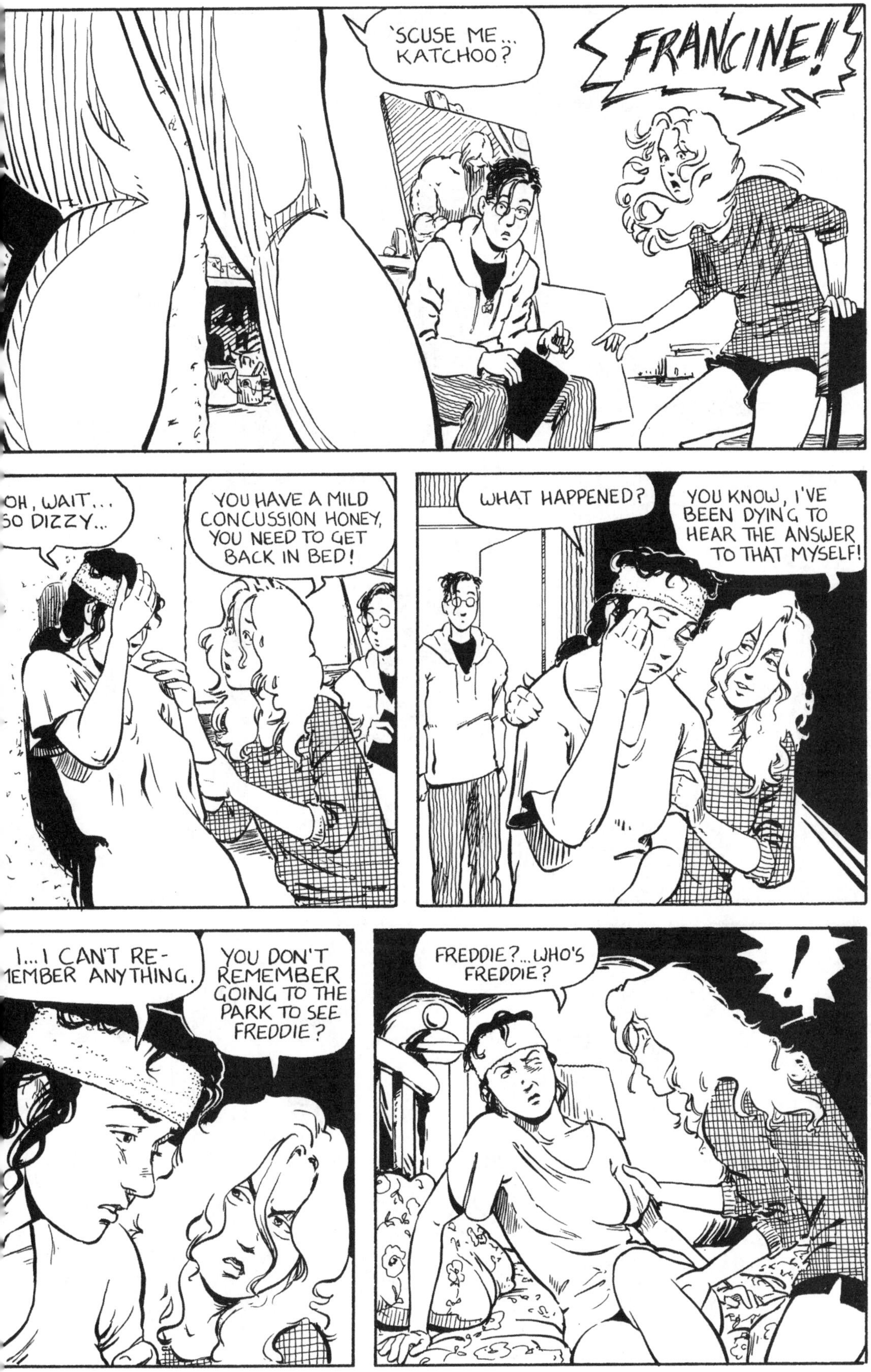
'SCUSE ME... KATCHOO?
FRANCINE!
OH, WAIT... SO DIZZY...
YOU HAVE A MILD CONCUSSION HONEY, YOU NEED TO GET BACK IN BED!
WHAT HAPPENED?
YOU KNOW, I'VE BEEN DYING TO HEAR THE ANSWER TO THAT MYSELF!
I... I CAN'T REMEMBER ANYTHING.
YOU DON'T REMEMBER GOING TO THE PARK TO SEE FREDDIE?
FREDDIE?... WHO'S FREDDIE?
!

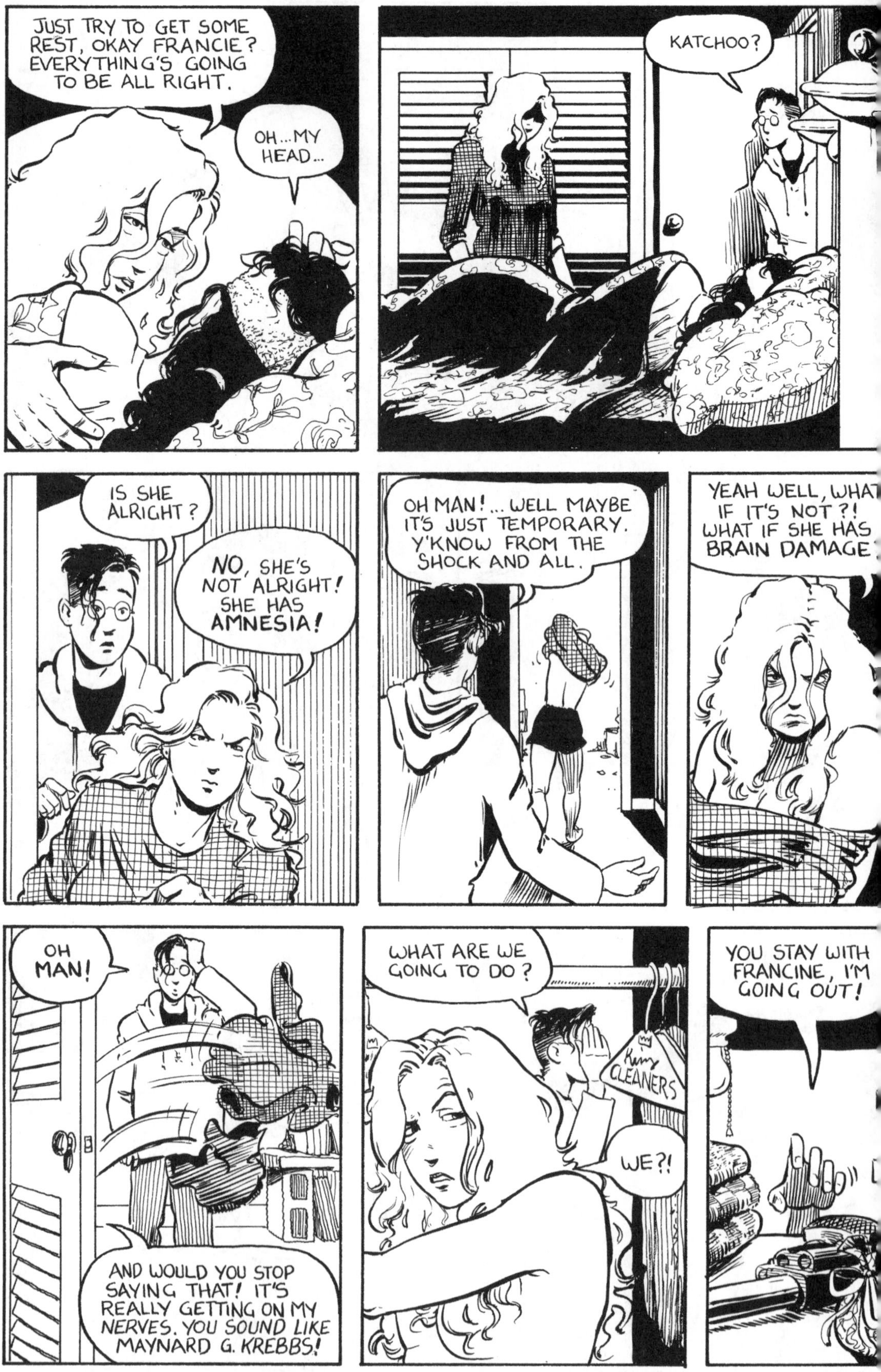

JUST TRY TO GET SOME REST, OKAY FRANCIE? EVERYTHING'S GOING TO BE ALL RIGHT.
OH... MY HEAD...
KATCHOO?
IS SHE ALRIGHT?
NO, SHE'S NOT ALRIGHT! SHE HAS AMNESIA!
OH MAN! ... WELL MAYBE IT'S JUST TEMPORARY. Y'KNOW FROM THE SHOCK AND ALL.
YEAH WELL, WHAT IF IT'S NOT?! WHAT IF SHE HAS BRAIN DAMAGE
OH MAN!
AND WOULD YOU STOP SAYING THAT! IT'S REALLY GETTING ON MY NERVES. YOU SOUND LIKE MAYNARD G. KREBBS!
WHAT ARE WE GOING TO DO?
CLEANERS
WE?!
YOU STAY WITH FRANCINE, I'M GOING OUT!

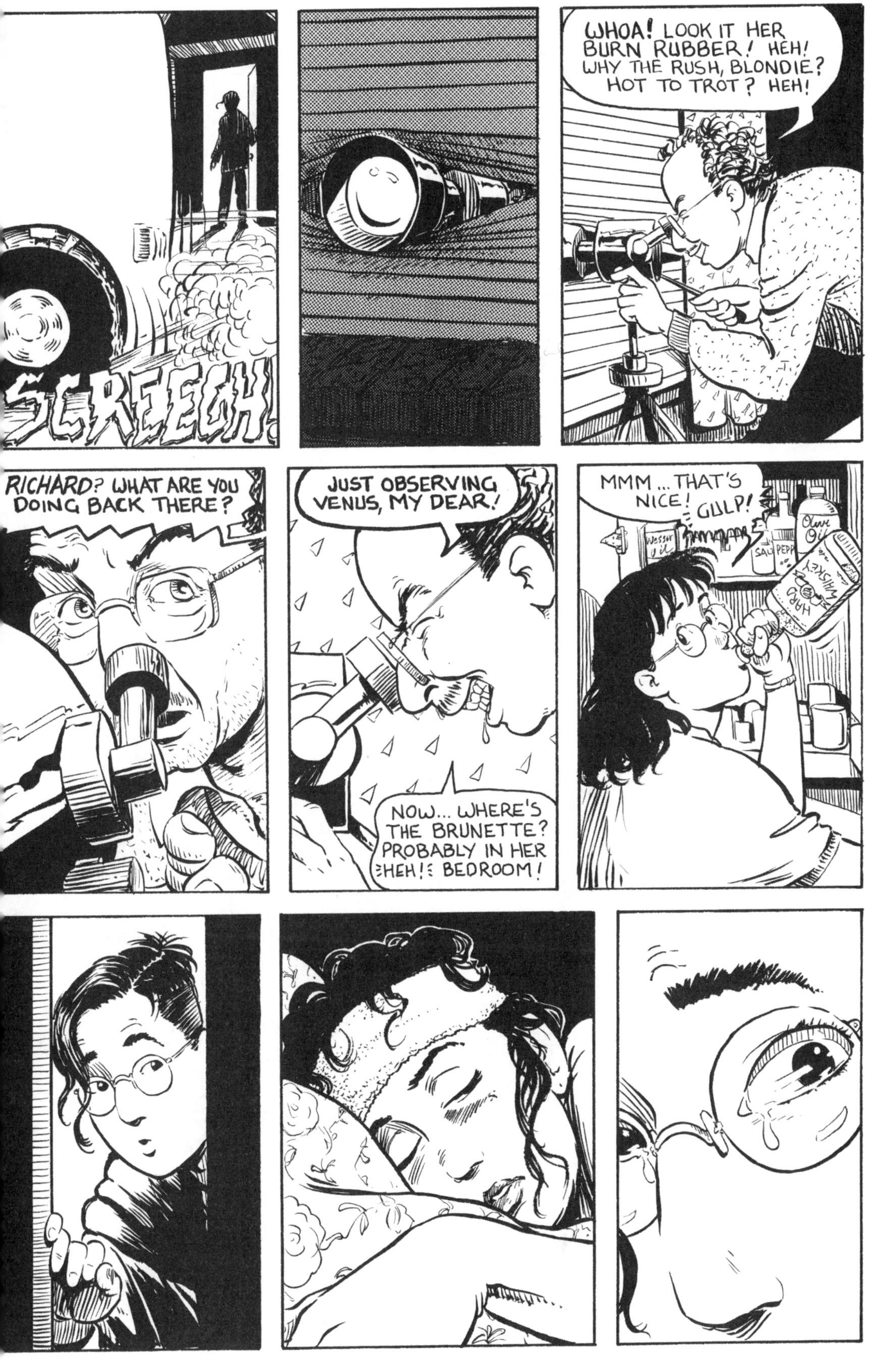
SCREECH!
WHOA! LOOK IT HER BURN RUBBER! HEH! WHY THE RUSH, BLONDIE? HOT TO TROT? HEH!
RICHARD? WHAT ARE YOU DOING BACK THERE?
JUST OBSERVING VENUS, MY DEAR!
NOW... WHERE'S THE BRUNETTE? PROBABLY IN HER HEH! BEDROOM!
MMM... THAT'S NICE!
GULP!
Wesson Oil
SALT
PEPP
Olive Oil
HARD WHISKEY

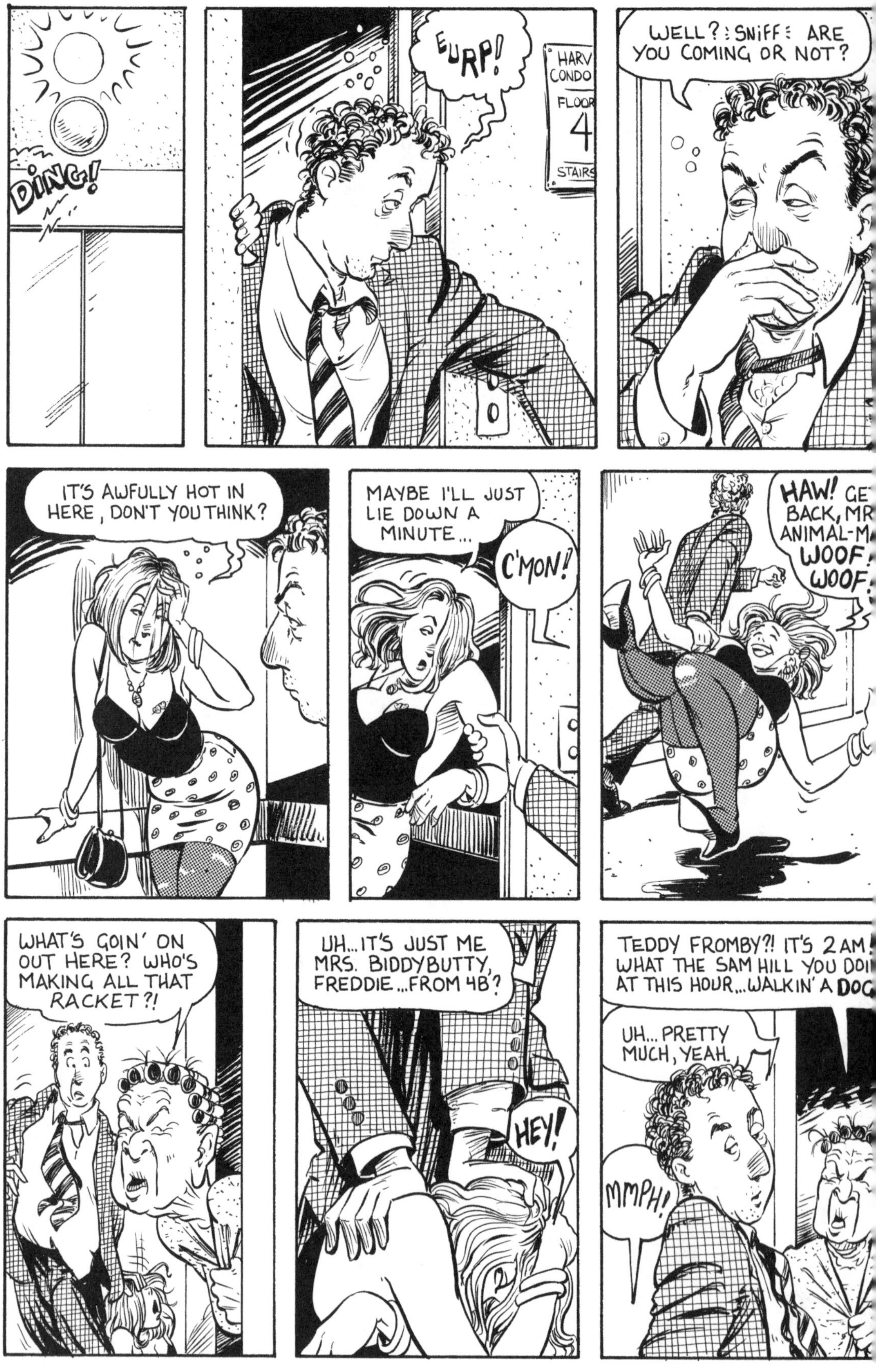
DING!
EURP!
HARV
CONDO
FLOOR
4
STAIRS
WELL? :SNIFF: ARE YOU COMING OR NOT?
IT'S AWFULLY HOT IN HERE, DON'T YOU THINK?
MAYBE I'LL JUST LIE DOWN A MINUTE...
C'MON!
HAW! GE
BACK, MR
ANIMAL-M
WOOF!
WOOF
WHAT'S GOIN' ON OUT HERE? WHO'S MAKING ALL THAT RACKET?!
UH...IT'S JUST ME MRS. BIDDYBUTTY, FREDDIE...FROM 4B?
HEY!
TEDDY FROMBY?! IT'S 2 AM
WHAT THE SAM HILL YOU DOI
AT THIS HOUR...WALKIN' A DOG
UH... PRETTY MUCH, YEAH.
MMPH!

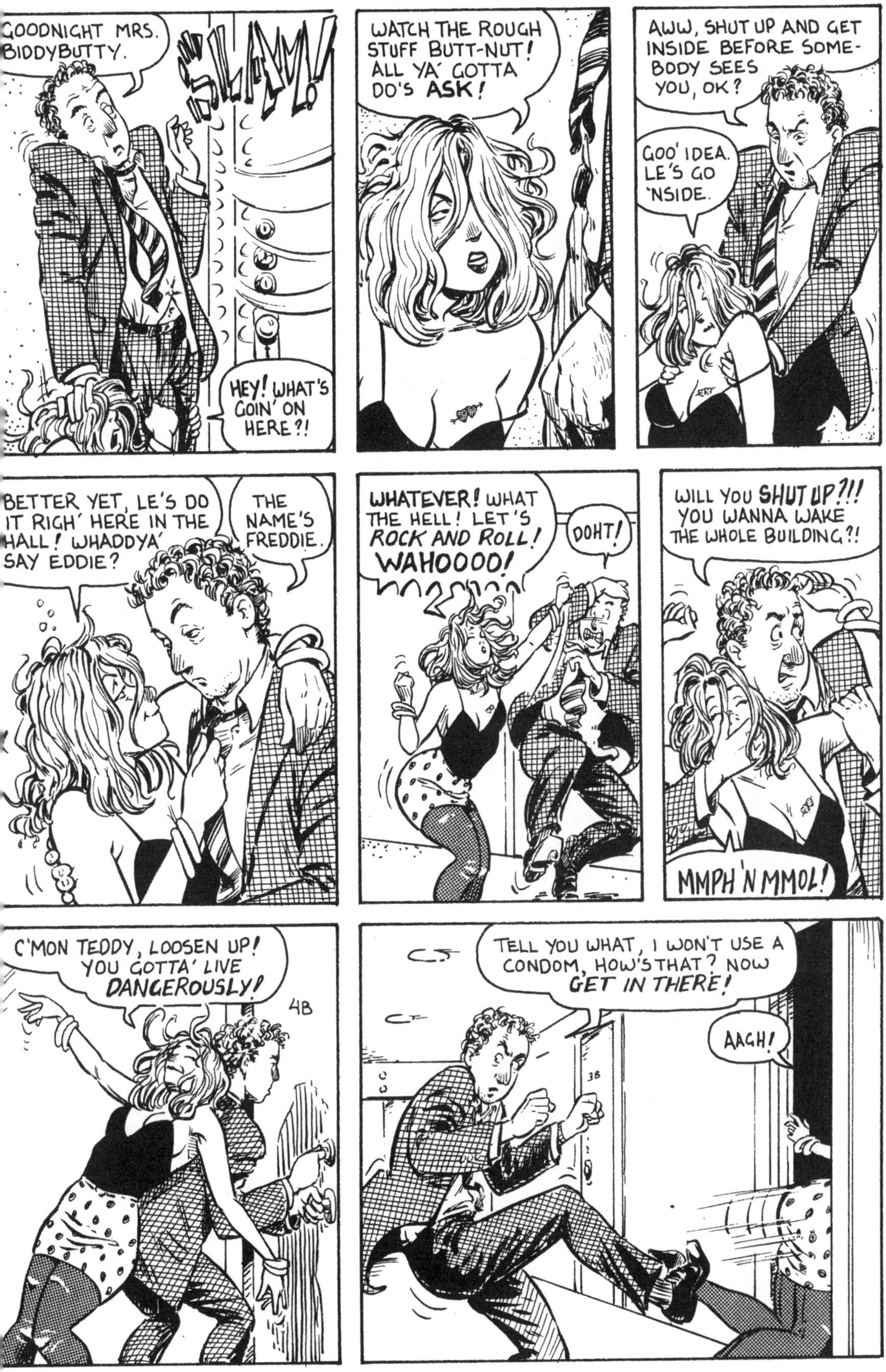
GOODNIGHT MRS. BIDDYBUTTY.
SLAM!
HEY! WHAT'S GOIN' ON HERE?!
WATCH THE ROUGH STUFF BUTT-NUT! ALL YA' GOTTA DO'S ASK!
AWW, SHUT UP AND GET INSIDE BEFORE SOME-BODY SEES YOU, OK?
GOO' IDEA. LE'S GO 'NSIDE.
BETTER YET, LE'S DO IT RIGH' HERE IN THE HALL! WHADDYA' SAY EDDIE?
THE NAME'S FREDDIE.
WHATEVER! WHAT THE HELL! LET'S ROCK AND ROLL! WAHOOOO!
DOHT!
WILL YOU SHUT UP?!! YOU WANNA WAKE THE WHOLE BUILDING?!
MMPH 'N MMOL!
C'MON TEDDY, LOOSEN UP! YOU GOTTA' LIVE DANGEROUSLY!
4B
TELL YOU WHAT, I WON'T USE A CONDOM, HOW'S THAT? NOW GET IN THERE!
AAGH!
3B

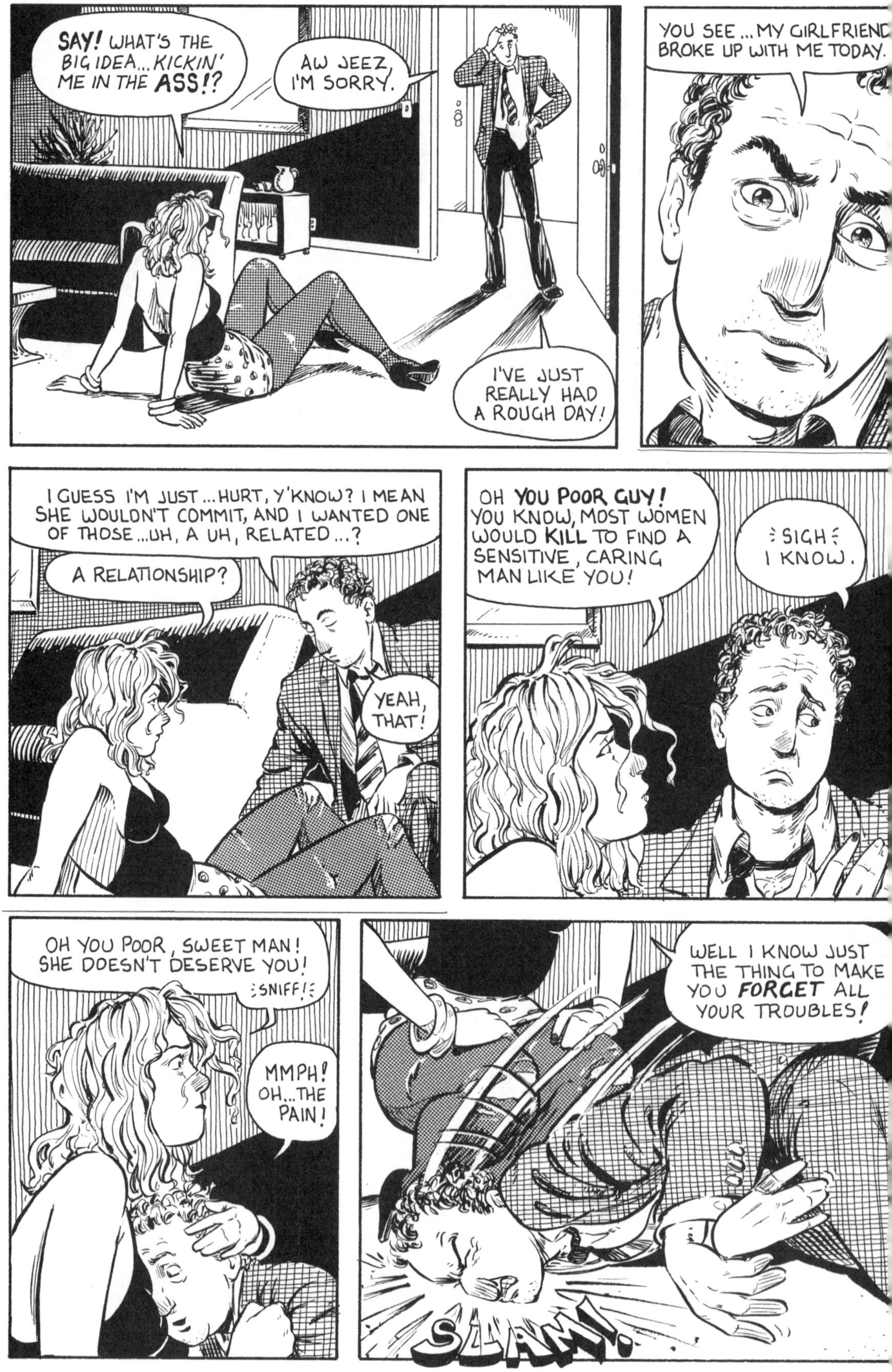
SAY! WHAT'S THE BIG IDEA... KICKIN' ME IN THE ASS!?
AW JEEZ, I'M SORRY.
I'VE JUST REALLY HAD A ROUGH DAY!
YOU SEE... MY GIRLFRIEND BROKE UP WITH ME TODAY.
I GUESS I'M JUST... HURT, Y'KNOW? I MEAN SHE WOULDN'T COMMIT, AND I WANTED ONE OF THOSE... UH, A UH, RELATED...?
A RELATIONSHIP?
YEAH, THAT!
OH YOU POOR GUY! YOU KNOW, MOST WOMEN WOULD KILL TO FIND A SENSITIVE, CARING MAN LIKE YOU!
SIGH I KNOW.
OH YOU POOR, SWEET MAN! SHE DOESN'T DESERVE YOU!
SNIFF!
MMPH! OH... THE PAIN!
WELL I KNOW JUST THE THING TO MAKE YOU FORGET ALL YOUR TROUBLES!
SLAM!

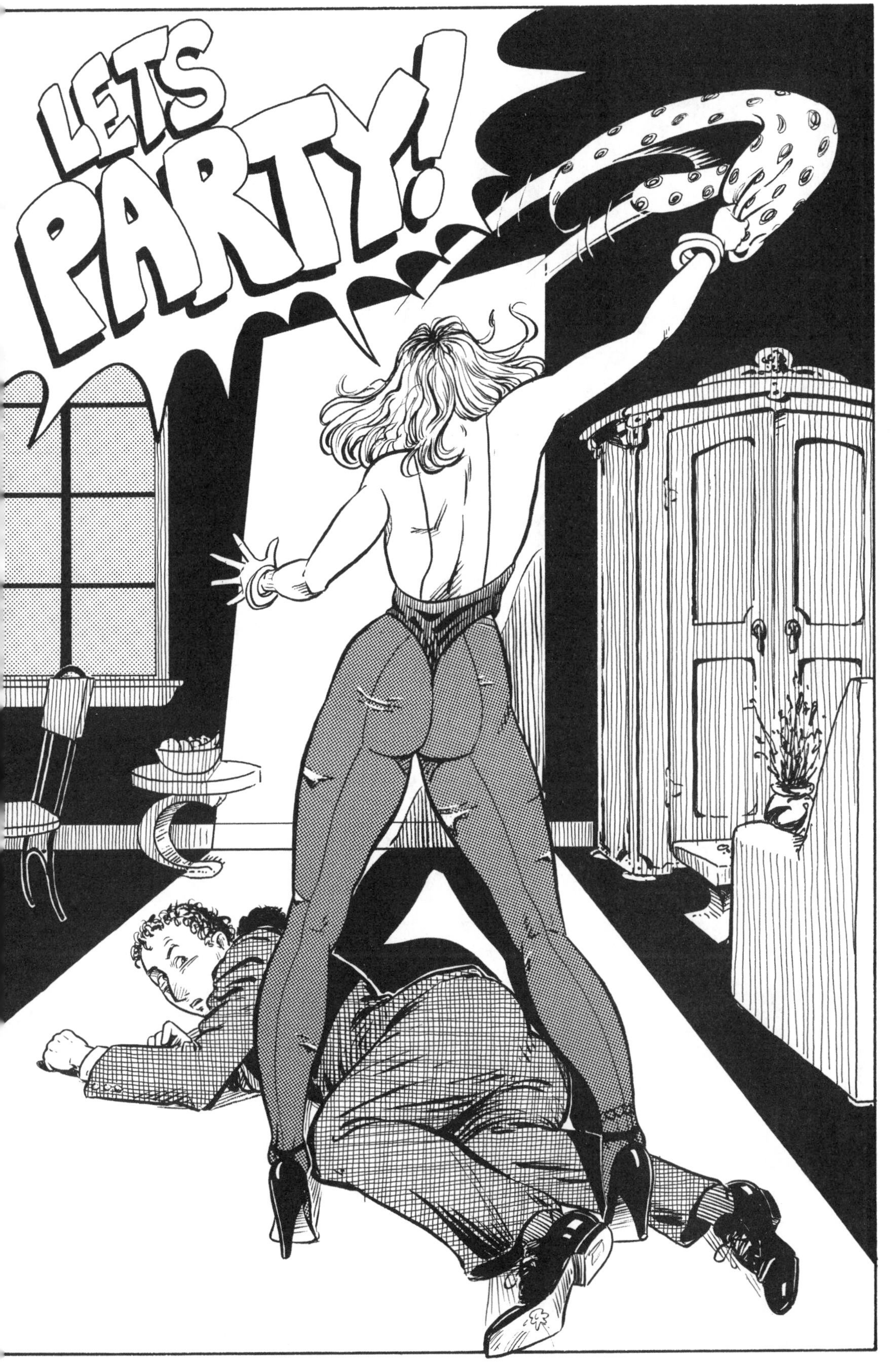
LETS PARTY!

ALL RIGHT! COUNT ME IN BABE! HEH! HEH!

HEY! HEY! HEY! CAREFUL WITH THE MERCHANDISE THERE! DON'T BE SO...

ROOOUGH!

COME ON EDDIE! I'M HOT TO TROT!

ALRIGHT ALRIGHT! KEEP YOUR PANTS ON!

NO WAIT... STRIKE THAT LAST COMMENT!

GIGGLE!

GINGER... WAIT... WAIT A SECOND... LET ME SHUT THE DOOR.

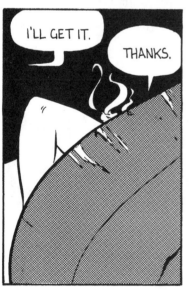

I'LL GET IT.

THANKS.

?

YOU JUST CAN'T KEEP IT IN YOUR PANTS, CAN YOU... READY-FREDDIE?

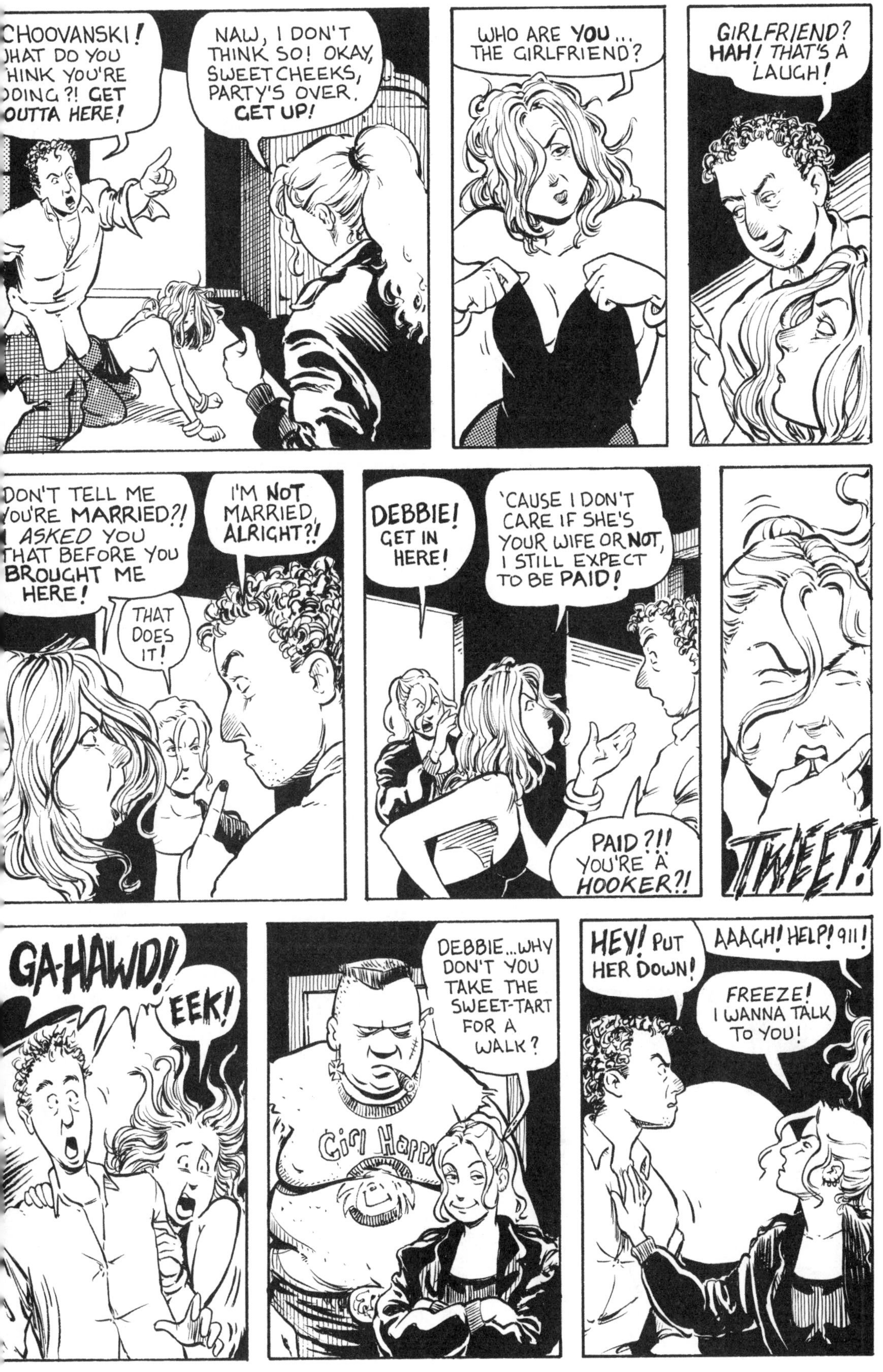
CHOOVANSKI! WHAT DO YOU THINK YOU'RE DOING?! GET OUTTA HERE!
NAW, I DON'T THINK SO! OKAY, SWEETCHEEKS, PARTY'S OVER. GET UP!
WHO ARE YOU... THE GIRLFRIEND?
GIRLFRIEND? HAH! THAT'S A LAUGH!
DON'T TELL ME YOU'RE MARRIED?! I ASKED YOU THAT BEFORE YOU BROUGHT ME HERE!
I'M NOT MARRIED, ALRIGHT?!
THAT DOES IT!
DEBBIE! GET IN HERE!
'CAUSE I DON'T CARE IF SHE'S YOUR WIFE OR NOT, I STILL EXPECT TO BE PAID!
PAID?!! YOU'RE A HOOKER?!
TWEET!
GA-HAWD!
EEK!
DEBBIE...WHY DON'T YOU TAKE THE SWEET-TART FOR A WALK?
Girl Happy
HEY! PUT HER DOWN!
AAAGH! HELP! 911!
FREEZE! I WANNA TALK TO YOU!

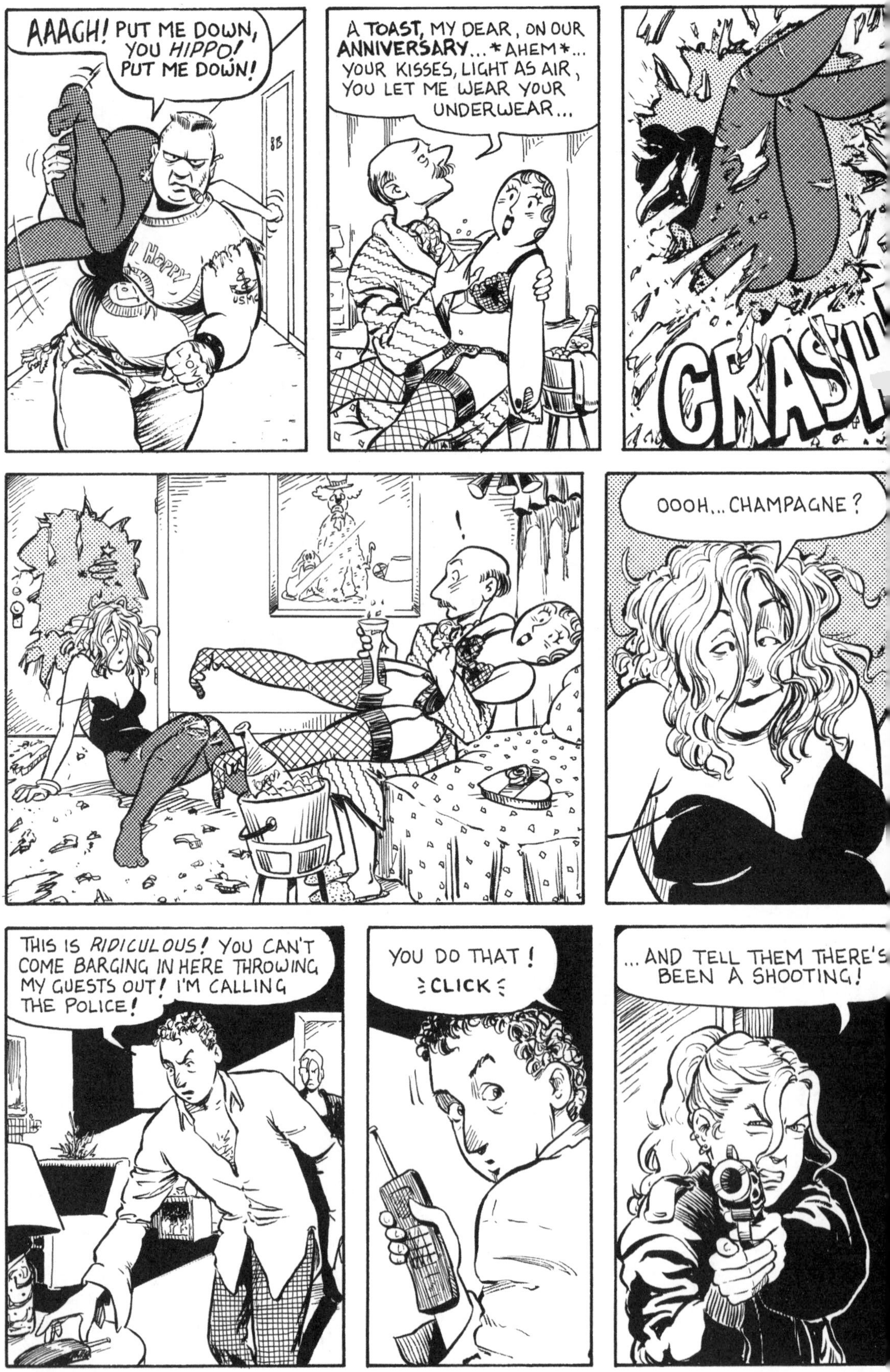
AAAGH! PUT ME DOWN, YOU HIPPO! PUT ME DOWN!
8B
I Happy
USMC
A TOAST, MY DEAR, ON OUR ANNIVERSARY... *AHEM*... YOUR KISSES, LIGHT AS AIR, YOU LET ME WEAR YOUR UNDERWEAR...
CRASH
!
OOOH... CHAMPAGNE?
THIS IS RIDICULOUS! YOU CAN'T COME BARGING IN HERE THROWING MY GUESTS OUT! I'M CALLING THE POLICE!
YOU DO THAT!
CLICK
...AND TELL THEM THERE'S BEEN A SHOOTING!

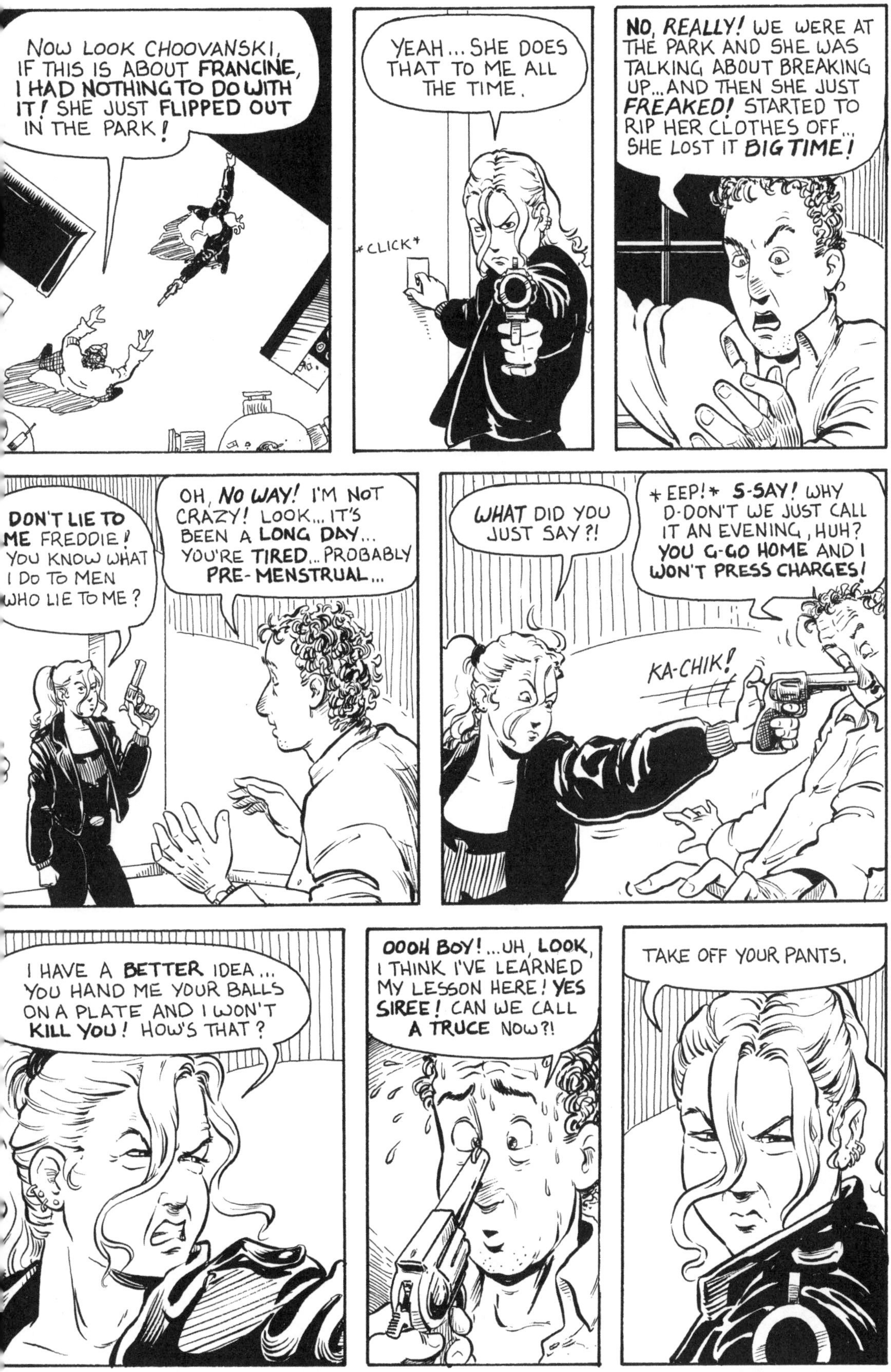
NOW LOOK CHOOVANSKI, IF THIS IS ABOUT FRANCINE, I HAD NOTHING TO DO WITH IT! SHE JUST FLIPPED OUT IN THE PARK!
YEAH... SHE DOES THAT TO ME ALL THE TIME.
CLICK
NO, REALLY! WE WERE AT THE PARK AND SHE WAS TALKING ABOUT BREAKING UP... AND THEN SHE JUST FREAKED! STARTED TO RIP HER CLOTHES OFF... SHE LOST IT BIG TIME!
DON'T LIE TO ME FREDDIE! YOU KNOW WHAT I DO TO MEN WHO LIE TO ME?
OH, NO WAY! I'M NOT CRAZY! LOOK... IT'S BEEN A LONG DAY... YOU'RE TIRED... PROBABLY PRE-MENSTRUAL...
WHAT DID YOU JUST SAY?!
EEP! S-SAY! WHY D-DON'T WE JUST CALL IT AN EVENING, HUH? YOU G-GO HOME AND I WON'T PRESS CHARGES!
KA-CHIK!
I HAVE A BETTER IDEA... YOU HAND ME YOUR BALLS ON A PLATE AND I WON'T KILL YOU! HOW'S THAT?
OOOH BOY! ...UH, LOOK, I THINK I'VE LEARNED MY LESSON HERE! YES SIREE! CAN WE CALL A TRUCE NOW?!
TAKE OFF YOUR PANTS.

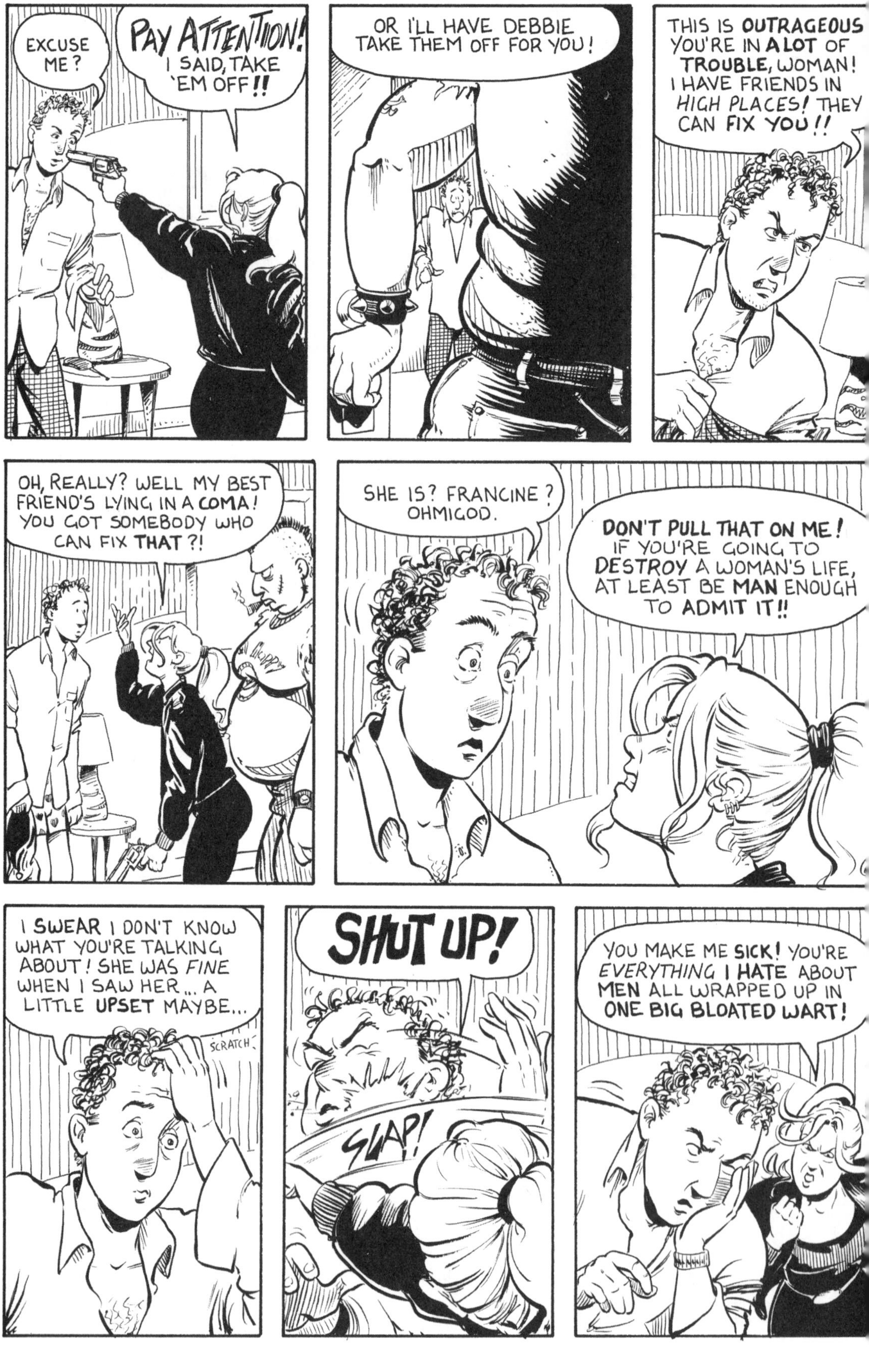
EXCUSE ME?
PAY ATTENTION! I SAID, TAKE 'EM OFF!!
OR I'LL HAVE DEBBIE TAKE THEM OFF FOR YOU!
THIS IS OUTRAGEOUS YOU'RE IN A LOT OF TROUBLE, WOMAN! I HAVE FRIENDS IN HIGH PLACES! THEY CAN FIX YOU!!
OH, REALLY? WELL MY BEST FRIEND'S LYING IN A COMA! YOU GOT SOMEBODY WHO CAN FIX THAT?!
SHE IS? FRANCINE? OHMIGOD.
DON'T PULL THAT ON ME! IF YOU'RE GOING TO DESTROY A WOMAN'S LIFE, AT LEAST BE MAN ENOUGH TO ADMIT IT!!
I SWEAR I DON'T KNOW WHAT YOU'RE TALKING ABOUT! SHE WAS FINE WHEN I SAW HER... A LITTLE UPSET MAYBE...
SCRATCH
SHUT UP!
SLAP!
YOU MAKE ME SICK! YOU'RE EVERYTHING I HATE ABOUT MEN ALL WRAPPED UP IN ONE BIG BLOATED WART!

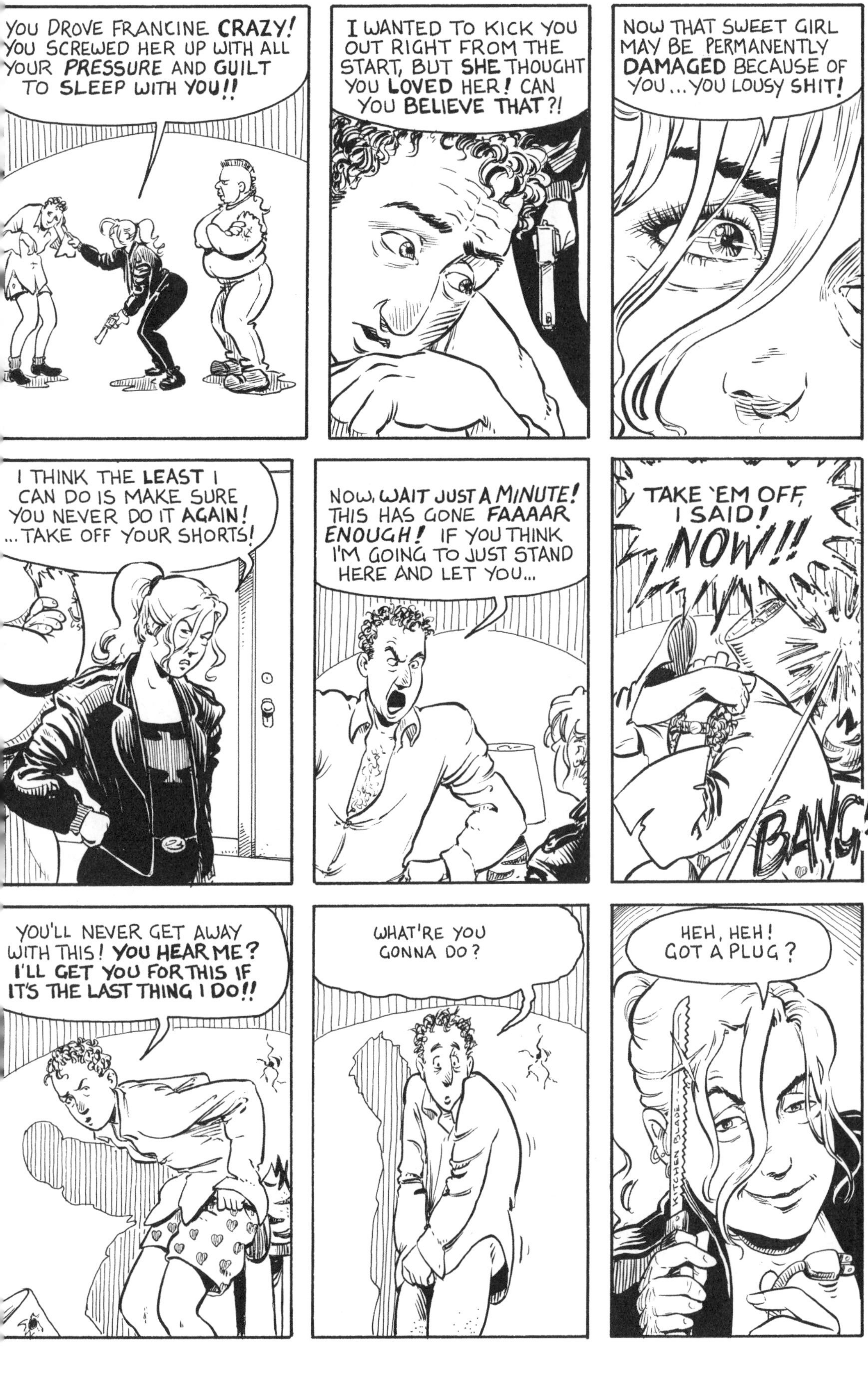
YOU DROVE FRANCINE CRAZY! YOU SCREWED HER UP WITH ALL YOUR PRESSURE AND GUILT TO SLEEP WITH YOU!!
I WANTED TO KICK YOU OUT RIGHT FROM THE START, BUT SHE THOUGHT YOU LOVED HER! CAN YOU BELIEVE THAT?!
NOW THAT SWEET GIRL MAY BE PERMANENTLY DAMAGED BECAUSE OF YOU... YOU LOUSY SHIT!
I THINK THE LEAST I CAN DO IS MAKE SURE YOU NEVER DO IT AGAIN! ...TAKE OFF YOUR SHORTS!
NOW, WAIT JUST A MINUTE! THIS HAS GONE FAAAAR ENOUGH! IF YOU THINK I'M GOING TO JUST STAND HERE AND LET YOU...
TAKE 'EM OFF, I SAID! NOW!!
BANG!
YOU'LL NEVER GET AWAY WITH THIS! YOU HEAR ME? I'LL GET YOU FOR THIS IF IT'S THE LAST THING I DO!!
WHAT'RE YOU GONNA DO?
HEH, HEH! GOT A PLUG?
KITCHEN BLADE

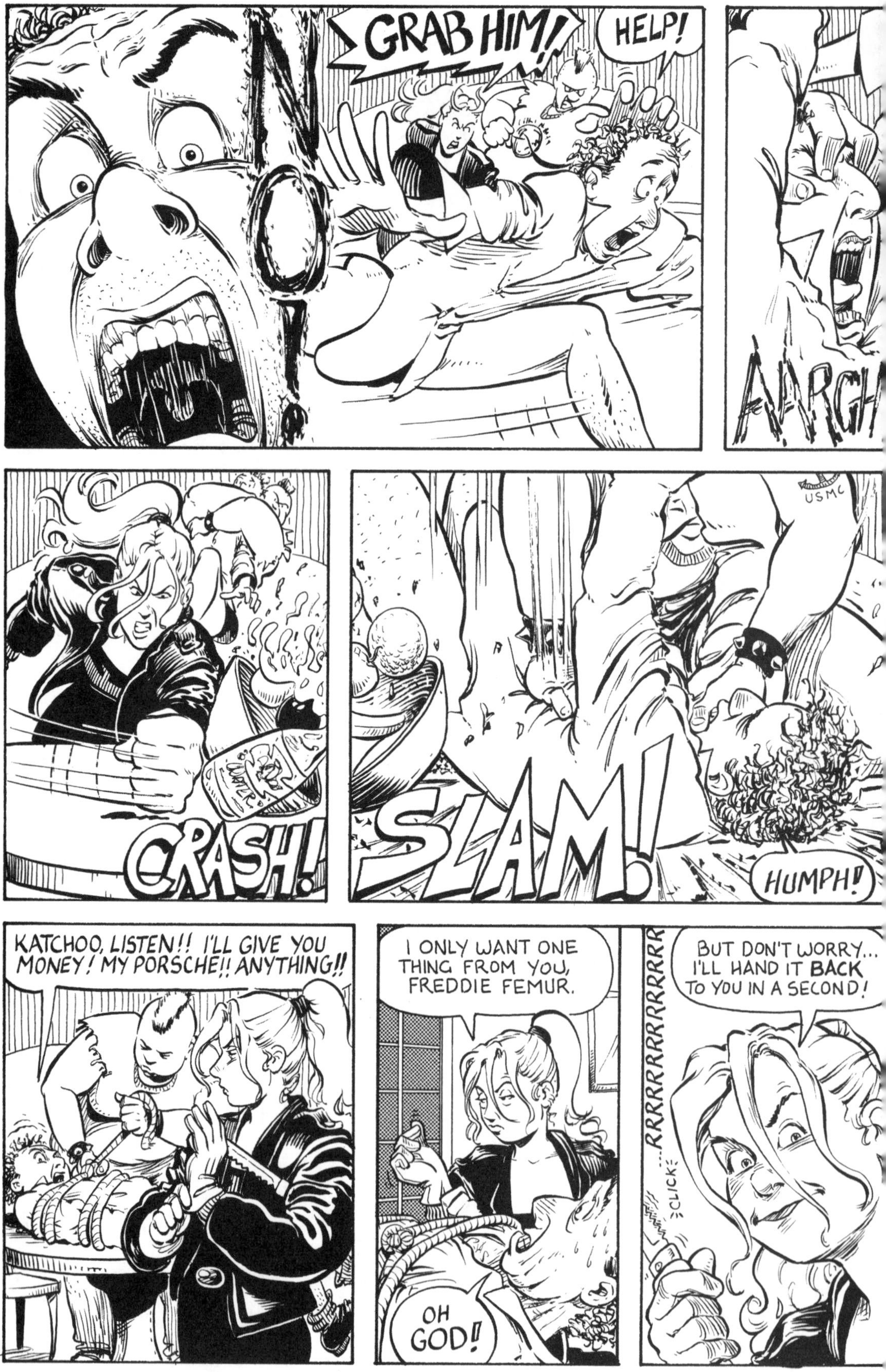
NO!
GRAB HIM!
HELP!
AARGH
CRASH!
USMC
SLAM!
HUMPH!
KATCHOO, LISTEN!! I'LL GIVE YOU MONEY! MY PORSCHE!! ANYTHING!!
I ONLY WANT ONE THING FROM YOU, FREDDIE FEMUR.
OH GOD!
...CLICK!
RRRRRRRRRRRRRRRR
BUT DON'T WORRY... I'LL HAND IT **BACK** TO YOU IN A SECOND!

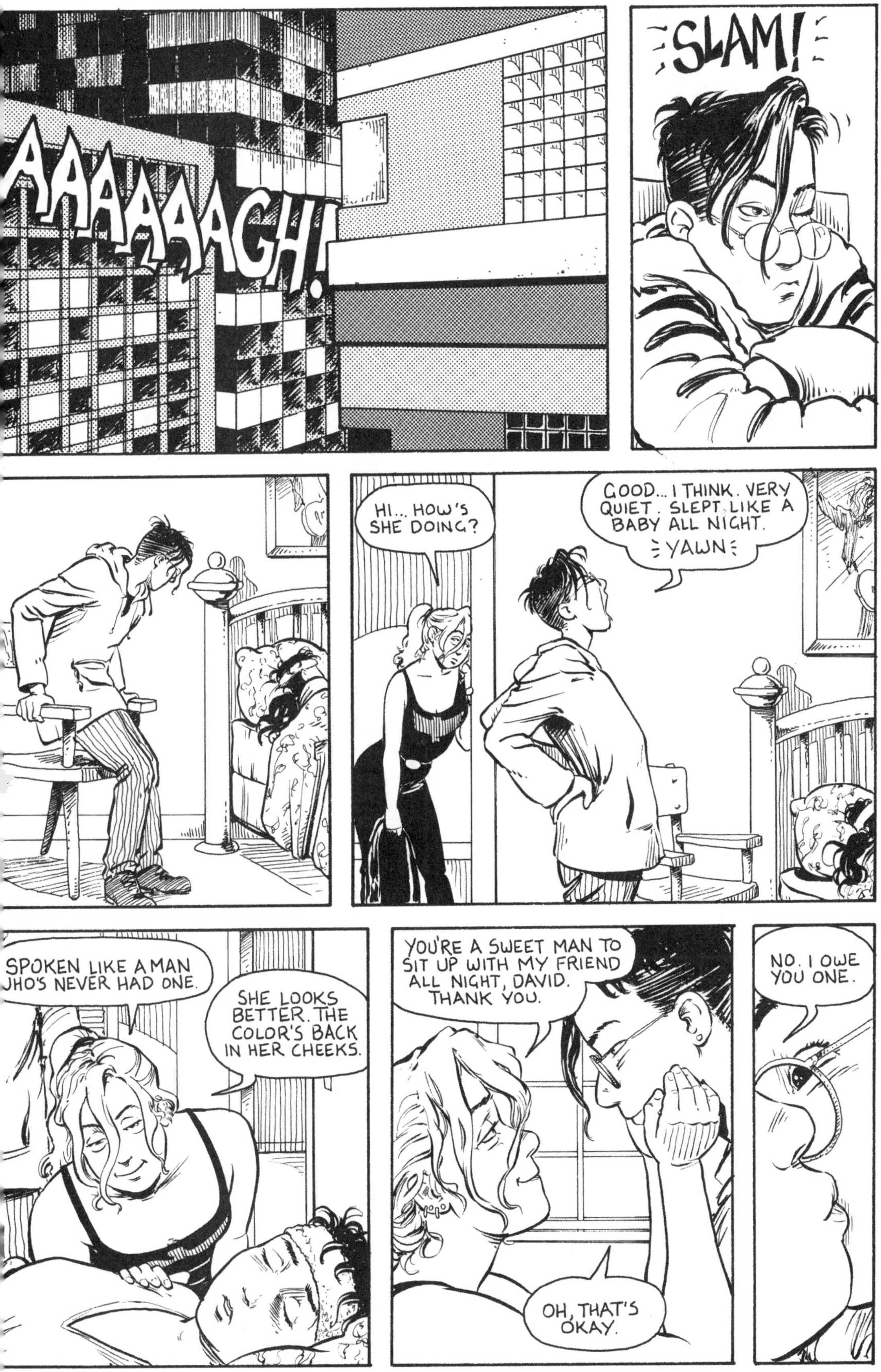
AAAAAACH!
SLAM!
HI... HOW'S SHE DOING?
GOOD... I THINK. VERY QUIET. SLEPT LIKE A BABY ALL NIGHT.
YAWN
SPOKEN LIKE A MAN WHO'S NEVER HAD ONE.
SHE LOOKS BETTER. THE COLOR'S BACK IN HER CHEEKS.
YOU'RE A SWEET MAN TO SIT UP WITH MY FRIEND ALL NIGHT, DAVID. THANK YOU.
OH, THAT'S OKAY.
NO. I OWE YOU ONE.

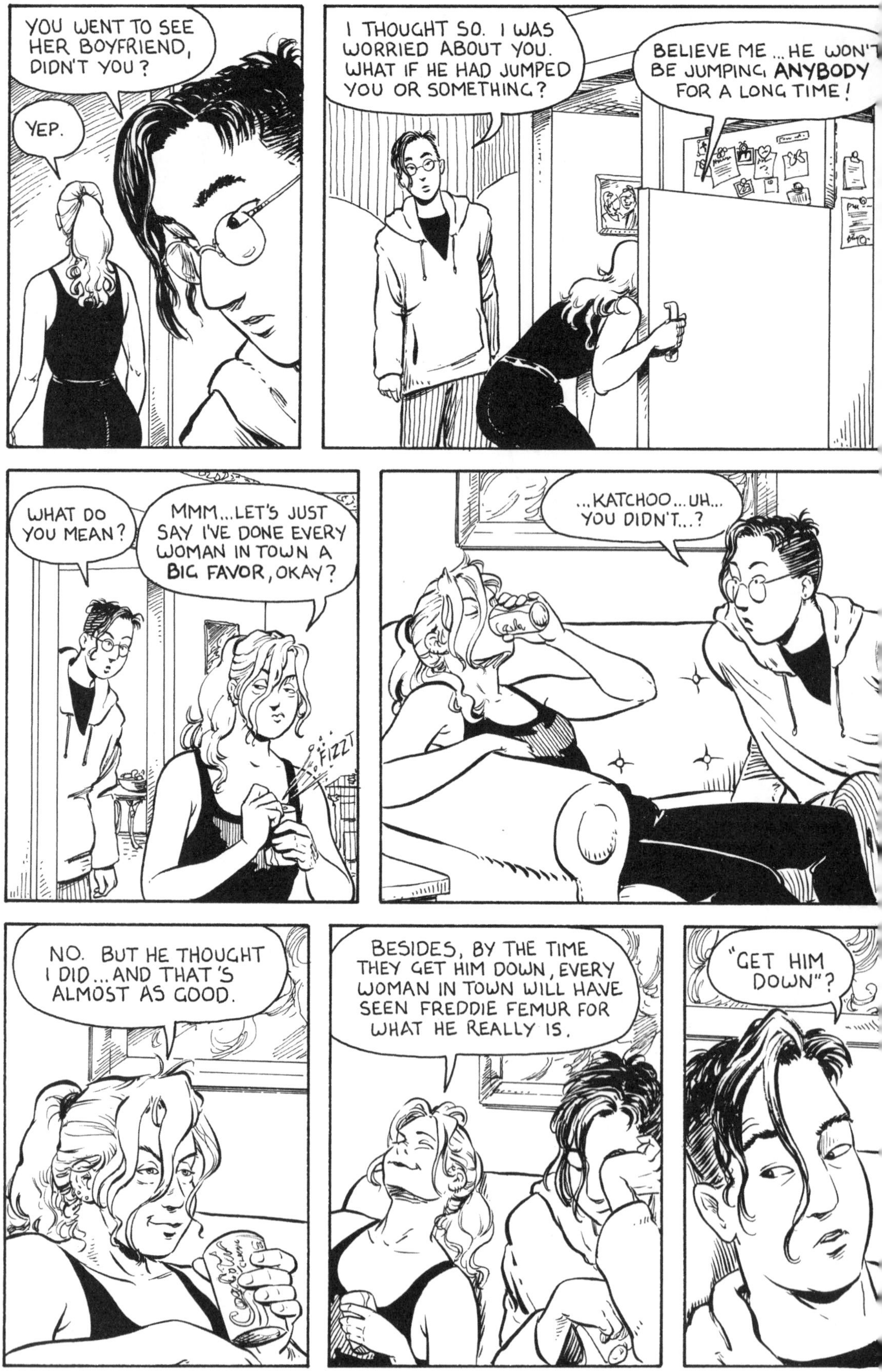
YOU WENT TO SEE HER BOYFRIEND, DIDN'T YOU?
YEP.
I THOUGHT SO. I WAS WORRIED ABOUT YOU. WHAT IF HE HAD JUMPED YOU OR SOMETHING?
BELIEVE ME ... HE WON'T BE JUMPING **ANYBODY** FOR A LONG TIME!
WHAT DO YOU MEAN?
MMM...LET'S JUST SAY I'VE DONE EVERY WOMAN IN TOWN A **BIG FAVOR**, OKAY?
FIZZT
...KATCHOO...UH... YOU DIDN'T...?
NO. BUT HE THOUGHT I DID...AND THAT'S ALMOST AS GOOD.
BESIDES, BY THE TIME THEY GET HIM DOWN, EVERY WOMAN IN TOWN WILL HAVE SEEN FREDDIE FEMUR FOR WHAT HE REALLY IS.
"GET HIM DOWN"?

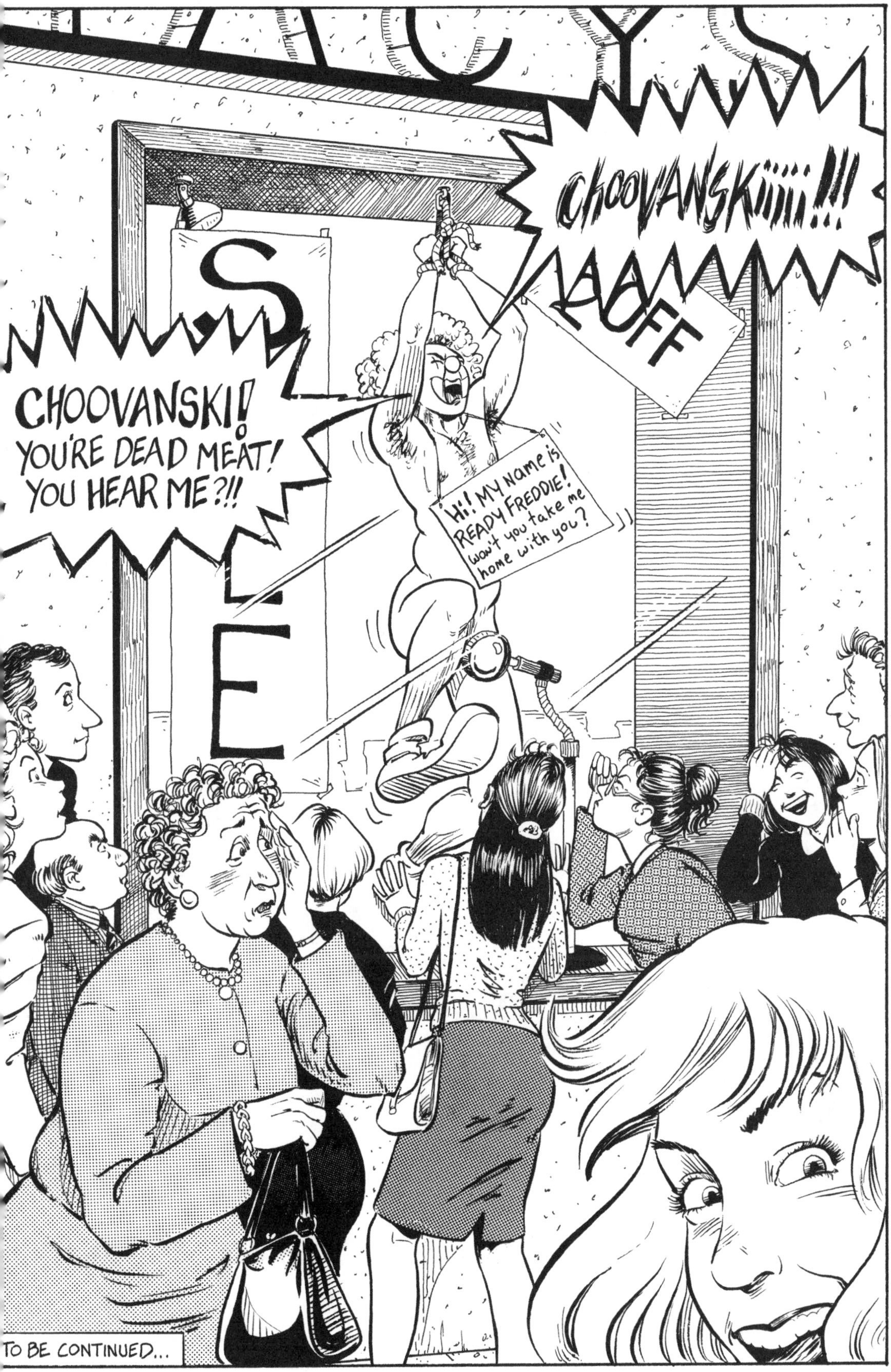
CHOOVANSKIiiiii!!!
CHOOVANSKI! YOU'RE DEAD MEAT! YOU HEAR ME?!!
% OFF
Hi! My name is READY FREDDIE! won't you take me home with you?
TO BE CONTINUED...

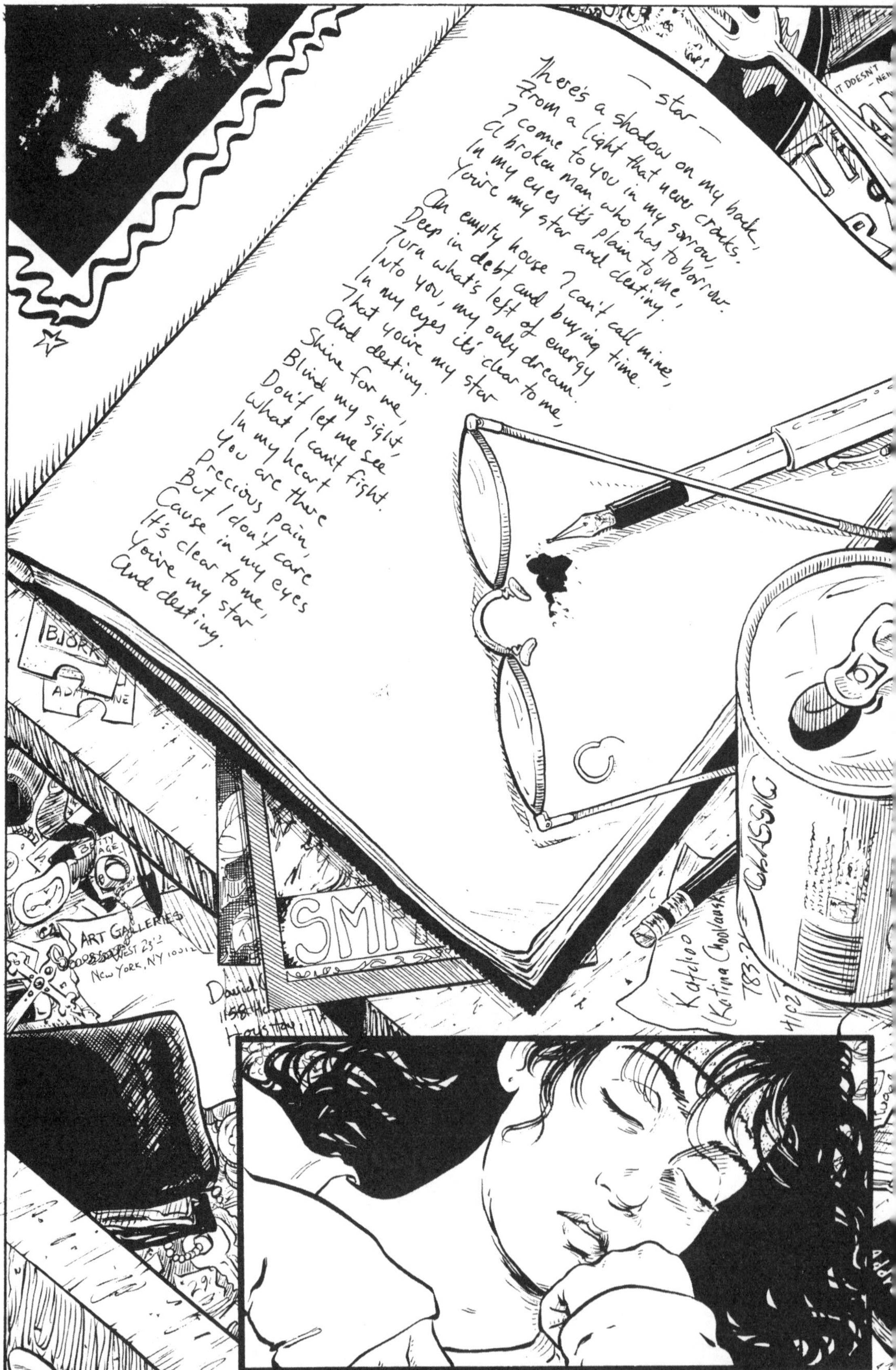
— star —
There's a shadow on my back,
From a light that never cracks.
I come to you in my sorrow,
A broken man who has to borrow.
In my eyes it's plain to me,
You're my star and destiny.
An empty house I can't call mine,
Deep in debt and buying time.
Turn what's left of energy
Into you, my only dream.
In my eyes it's clear to me,
That you're my star
And destiny.
Shine for me,
Blind my sight,
Don't let me see,
What I can't fight.
In my heart
You are there
Precious pain,
But I don't care
Cause in my eyes
It's clear to me,
You're my star
And destiny.
IT DOESN'T
BJORK
ART GALLERIES
NEW YORK, NY
CLASSIC

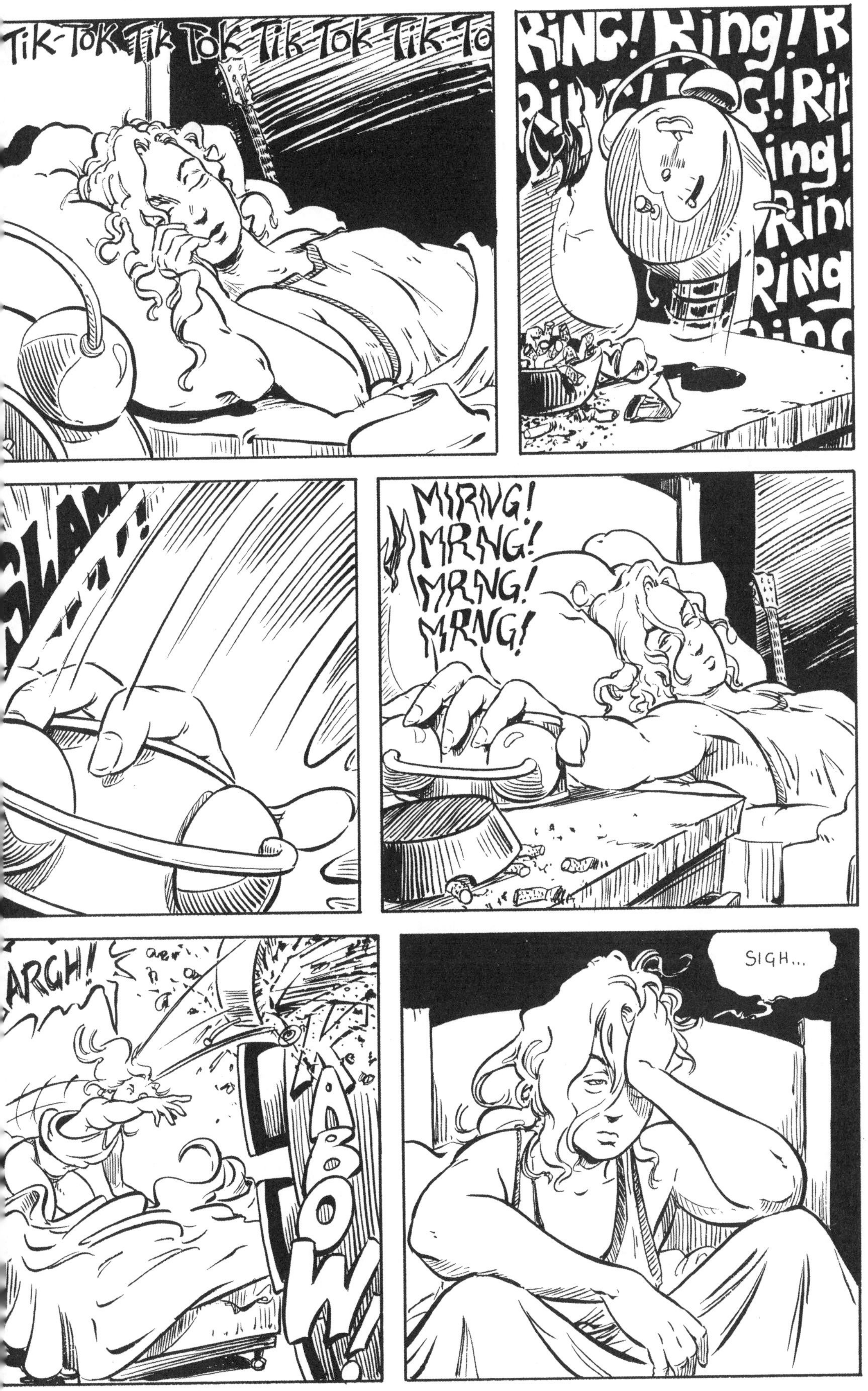
TIK-TOK TIK TOK TIK-TOK TIK-TO
RING! RING! R
RING! RING! RING!
SLAM!!
MRNG! MRNG! MRNG! MRNG!
ARGH!
KA BOOW!
SIGH...

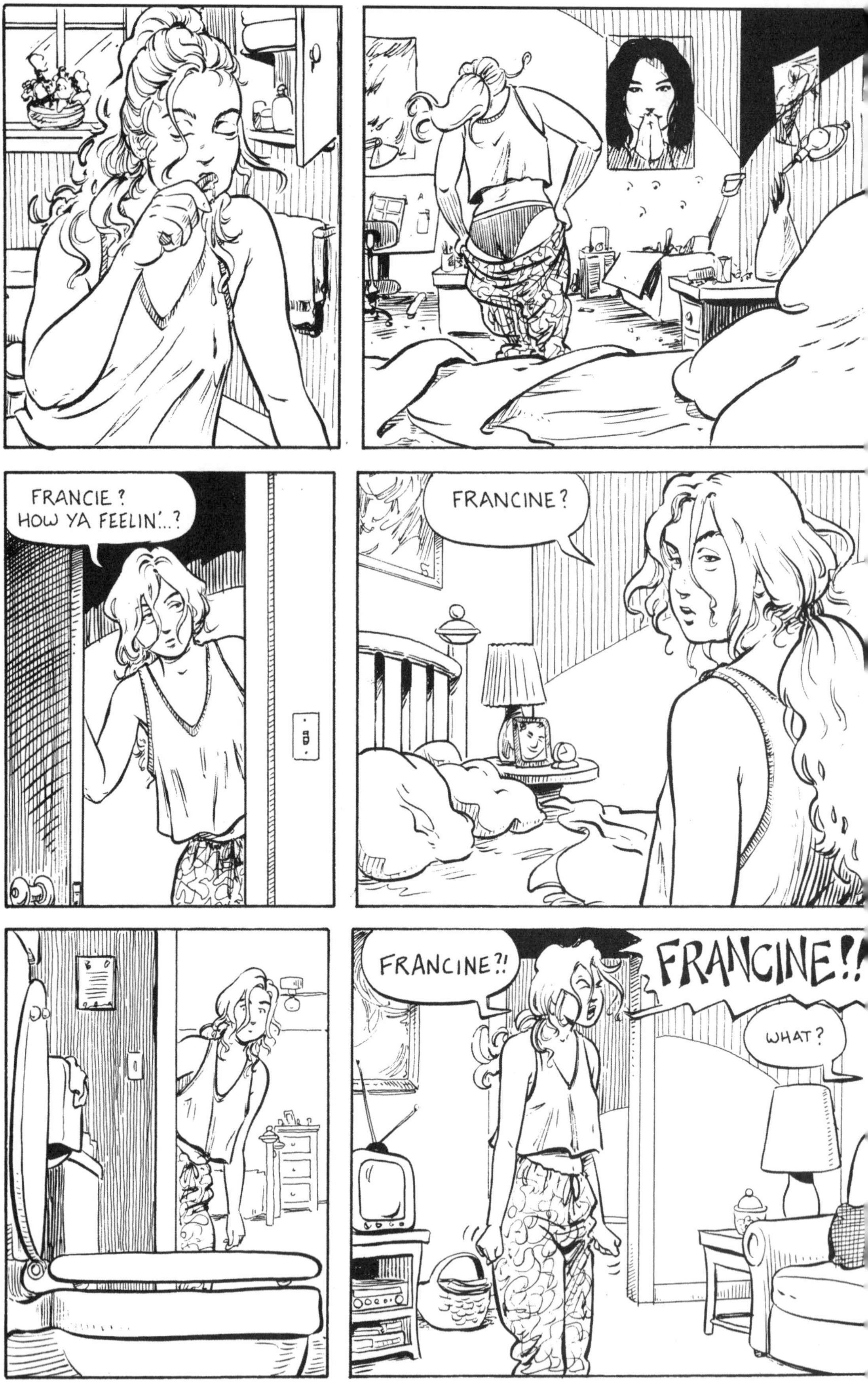
FRANCIE? HOW YA FEELIN'...?
FRANCINE?
FRANCINE?!
FRANCINE!!
WHAT?

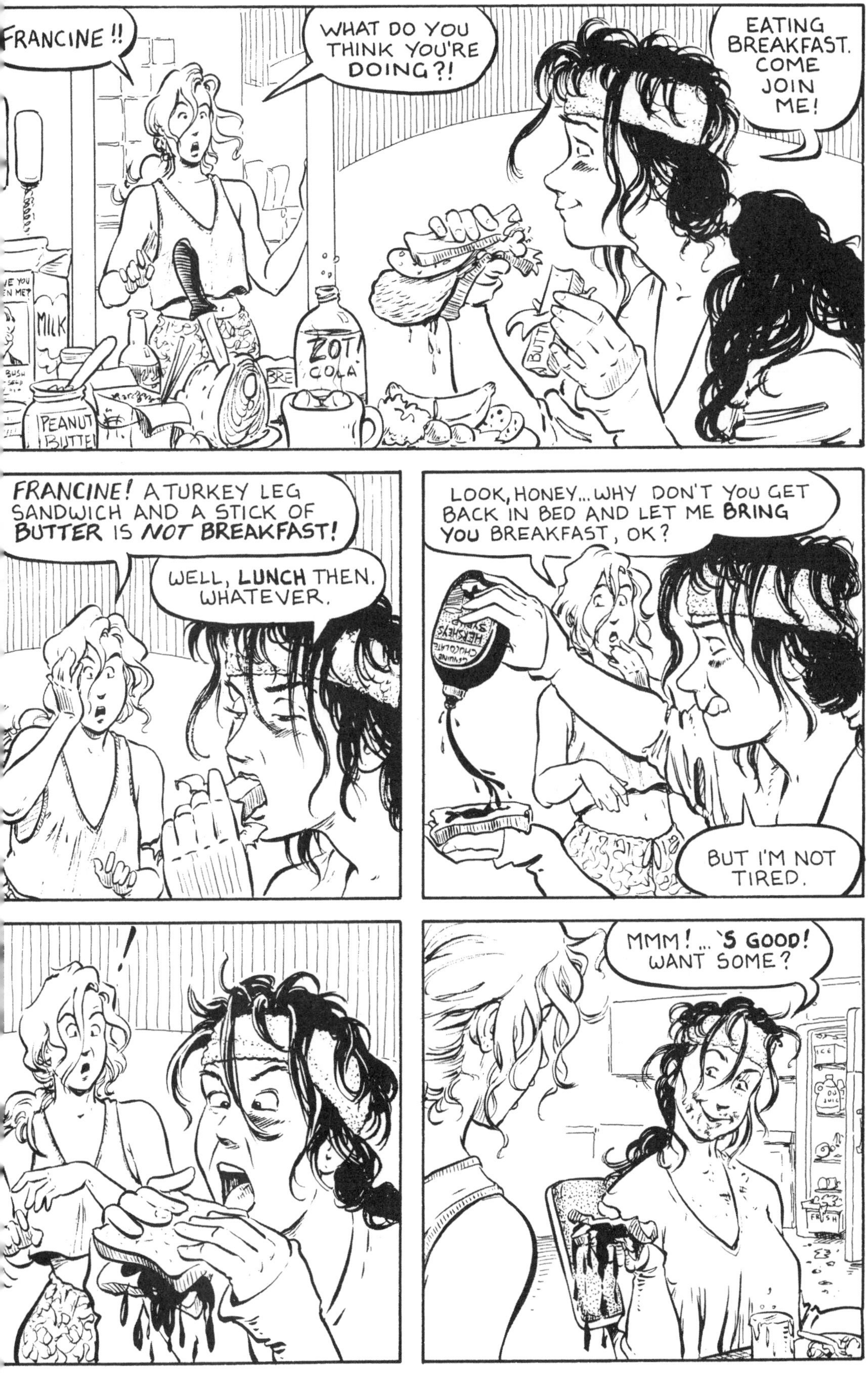
FRANCINE !!
WHAT DO YOU THINK YOU'RE DOING ?!
EATING BREAKFAST. COME JOIN ME!
MILK
PEANUT BUTTE
ZOT! COLA
FRANCINE! A TURKEY LEG SANDWICH AND A STICK OF BUTTER IS NOT BREAKFAST!
WELL, LUNCH THEN. WHATEVER.
LOOK, HONEY... WHY DON'T YOU GET BACK IN BED AND LET ME BRING YOU BREAKFAST, OK?
GENUINE CHOCOLATE HERSHEY'S SYRUP
BUT I'M NOT TIRED.
!
MMM! ... 'S GOOD! WANT SOME?

THAT DOES IT! COME ON, IT'S **BACK TO BED** WITH YOU!

OKEY DOKEY.

RING! RING!

HINEY CATSUP
OLIVES

DAMMIT FREDDIE YOU SORRY STINKIN' LOUSY...

CATSUP

RI... RI...

KATCHOO... YOU KNOW WHAT WE HAVEN'T HAD IN A LONG TIME...? **LIVER!** MMMMM! *SMACK! SMACK!* **DELISH**, HUH?

MMM, DELISH, YEAH. LOOK, JUST SIT HERE, OK? FRANCIE? JUST... **STAY!**

RING! RING!

RING! RI....

WHAT THE HELL DO YOU WANT?!!

UH... KATCHOO IT'S DAVID

LIVER AND MILKSHAKE

DID I CATCH YOU AT A BAD TIME?

A **LIVER** MILKSHAKE

OH... UH, HI, DAVID. YEAH, I'M KIND OF BUSY RIGHT NOW. FRANCINE'S UP, AND SHE'S ACTING REALLY **WEIRD**... UH, HOLD ON A SECOND...

FRANCINE!!! GET THAT OUT OF YOUR MOUTH! YOU DON'T KNOW WHERE IT'S BEEN!

IS THIS LIVER?

AT&T

DAVID? I'LL HAVE TO CALL YOU BACK LATER, OKAY?

LIVER!! I NEED LIVER!

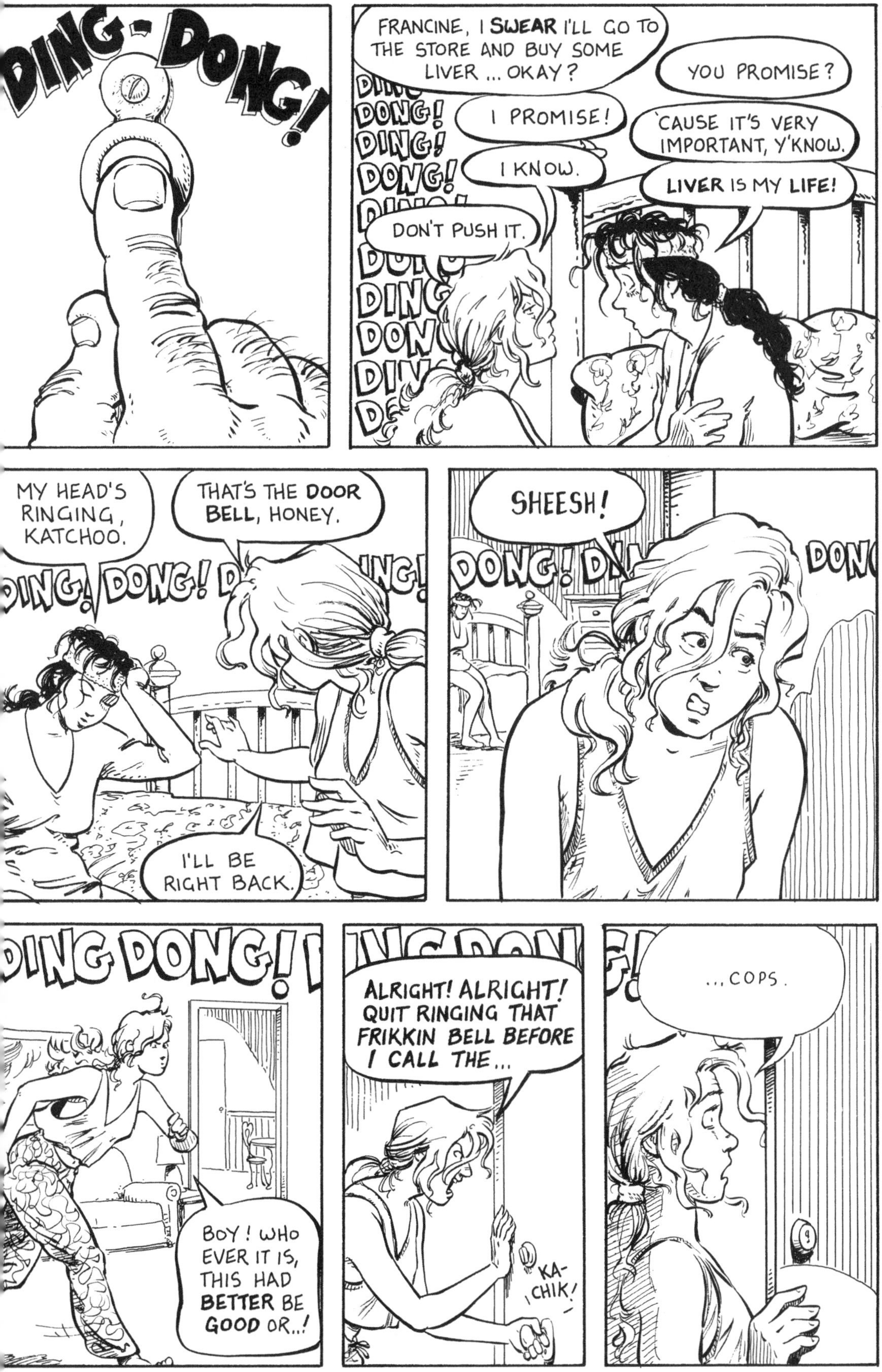

DING-DONG!
FRANCINE, I SWEAR I'LL GO TO THE STORE AND BUY SOME LIVER ... OKAY?
YOU PROMISE?
DING DONG! DING! DONG!
I PROMISE!
'CAUSE IT'S VERY IMPORTANT, Y'KNOW.
I KNOW.
LIVER IS MY LIFE!
DON'T PUSH IT.
DING DONG
MY HEAD'S RINGING, KATCHOO.
THAT'S THE DOOR BELL, HONEY.
DING! DONG!
I'LL BE RIGHT BACK.
SHEESH!
DONG!
DING DONG!
BOY! WHO EVER IT IS, THIS HAD BETTER BE GOOD OR..!
ALRIGHT! ALRIGHT! QUIT RINGING THAT FRIKKIN BELL BEFORE I CALL THE...
KA-CHIK!
...COPS.

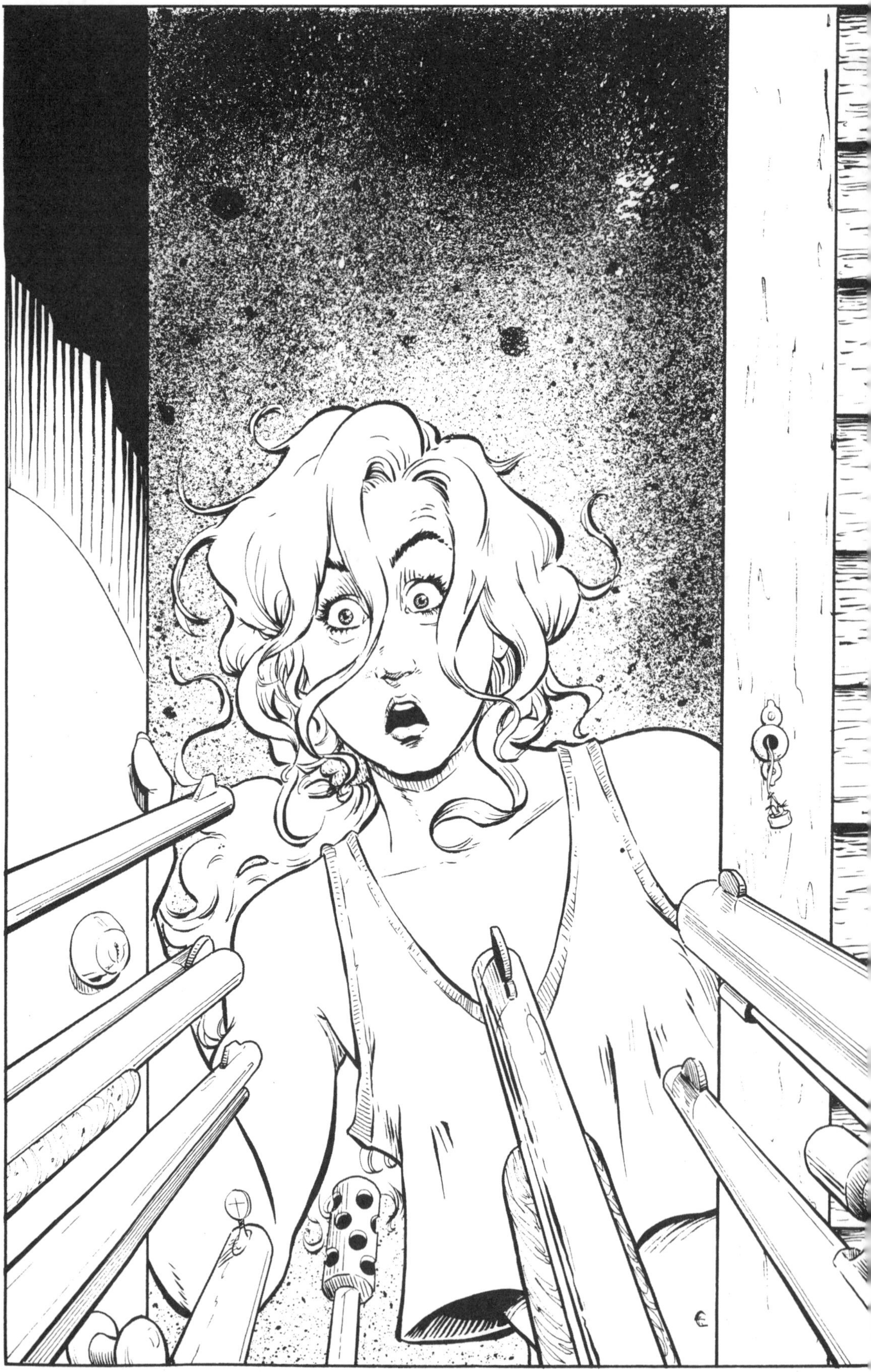

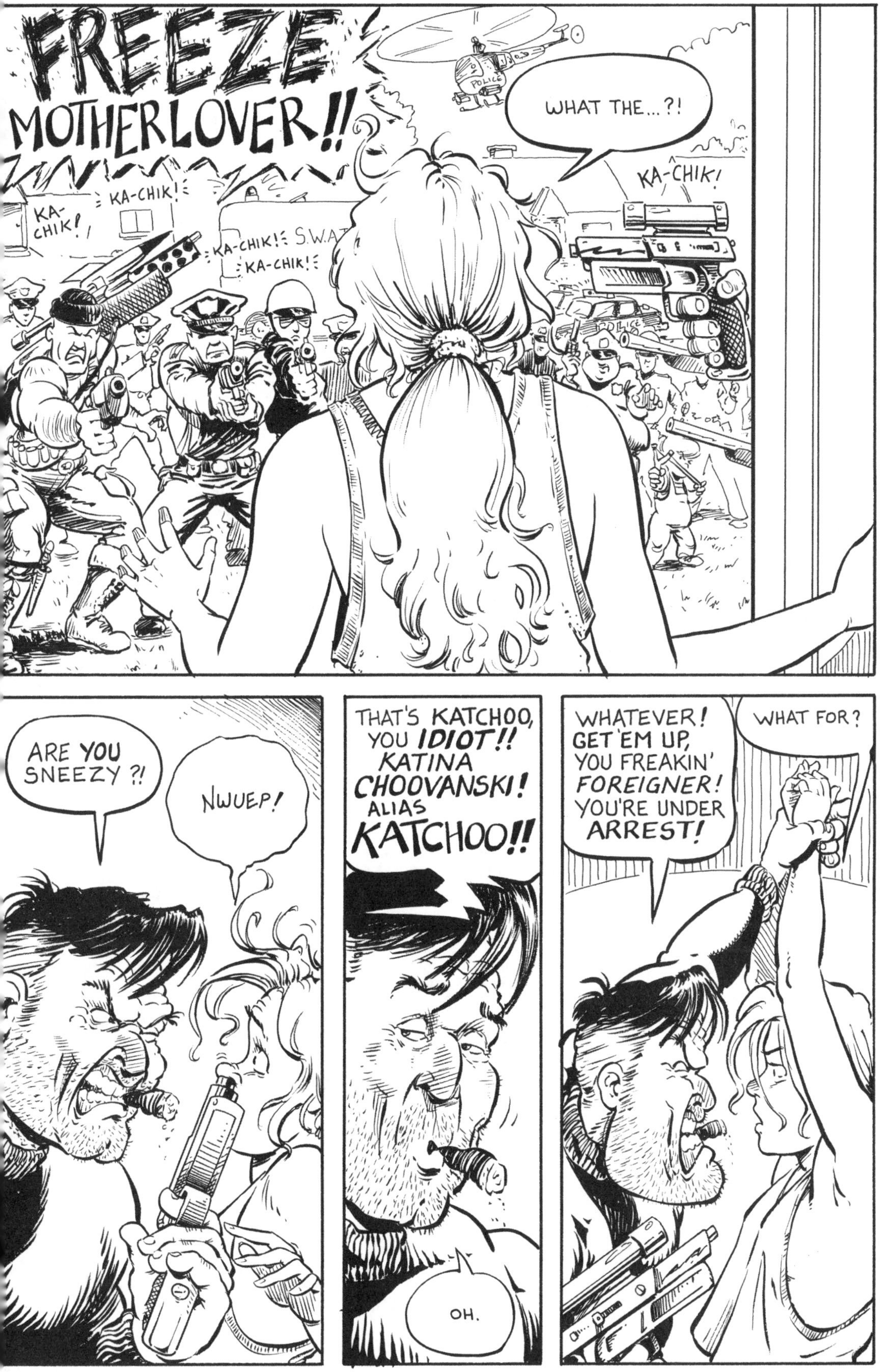
FREEZE MOTHERLOVER!!
POLICE
WHAT THE...?!
KA-CHIK!
KA-CHIK!
KA-CHIK!
KA-CHIK!
KA-CHIK!
S.W.A
POLICE
ARE YOU SNEEZY ?!
NWUEP!
THAT'S KATCHOO, YOU IDIOT!! KATINA CHOOVANSKI! ALIAS KATCHOO!!
OH.
WHATEVER! GET 'EM UP, YOU FREAKIN' FOREIGNER! YOU'RE UNDER ARREST!
WHAT FOR?

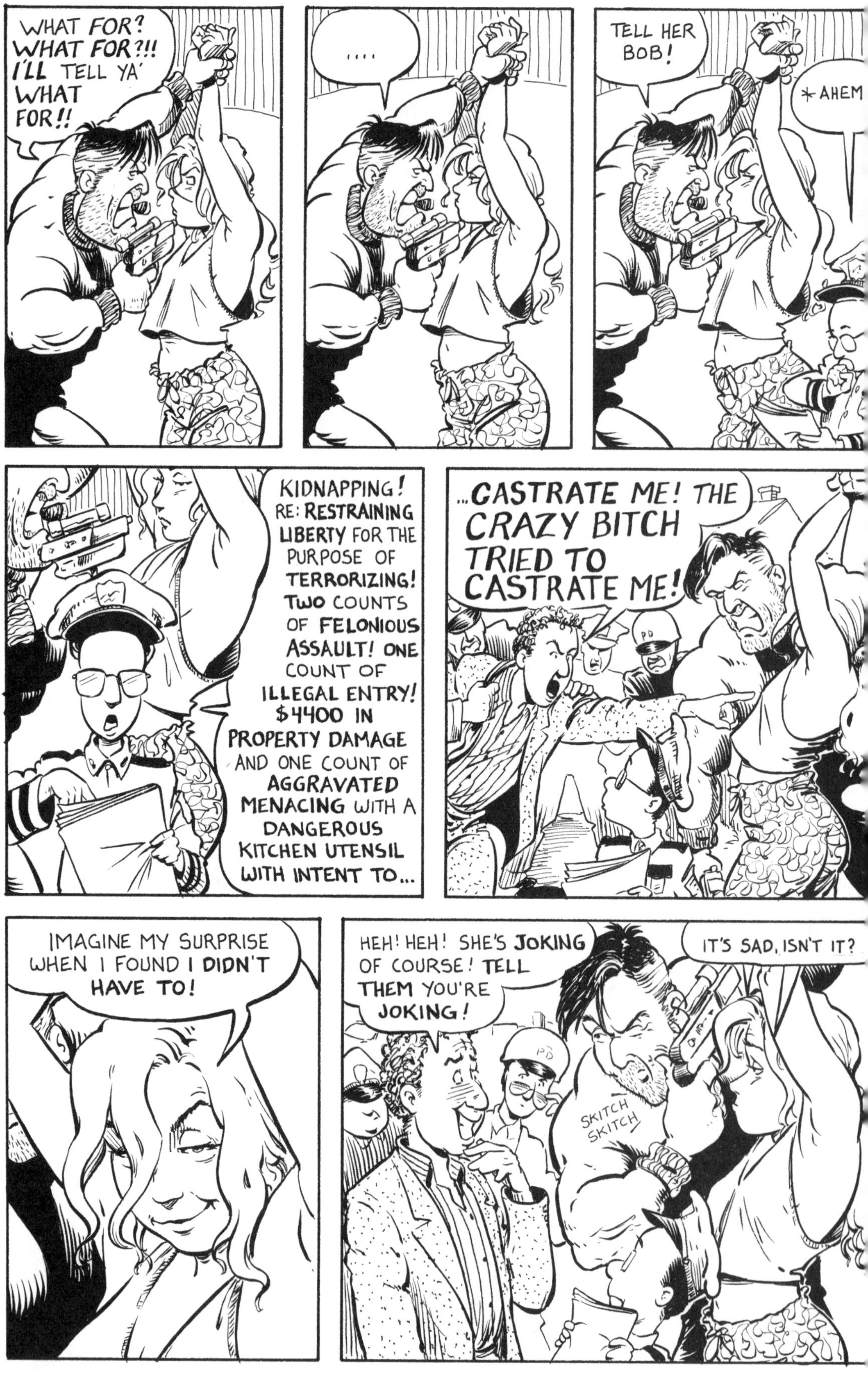
WHAT FOR? WHAT FOR?!! I'LL TELL YA' WHAT FOR!!
....
TELL HER BOB!
*AHEM
KIDNAPPING! RE: RESTRAINING LIBERTY FOR THE PURPOSE OF TERRORIZING! TWO COUNTS OF FELONIOUS ASSAULT! ONE COUNT OF ILLEGAL ENTRY! $4400 IN PROPERTY DAMAGE AND ONE COUNT OF AGGRAVATED MENACING WITH A DANGEROUS KITCHEN UTENSIL WITH INTENT TO...
...CASTRATE ME! THE CRAZY BITCH TRIED TO CASTRATE ME!
PD
IMAGINE MY SURPRISE WHEN I FOUND I DIDN'T HAVE TO!
HEH! HEH! SHE'S JOKING OF COURSE! TELL THEM YOU'RE JOKING!
IT'S SAD, ISN'T IT?
PD
SKITCH SKITCH

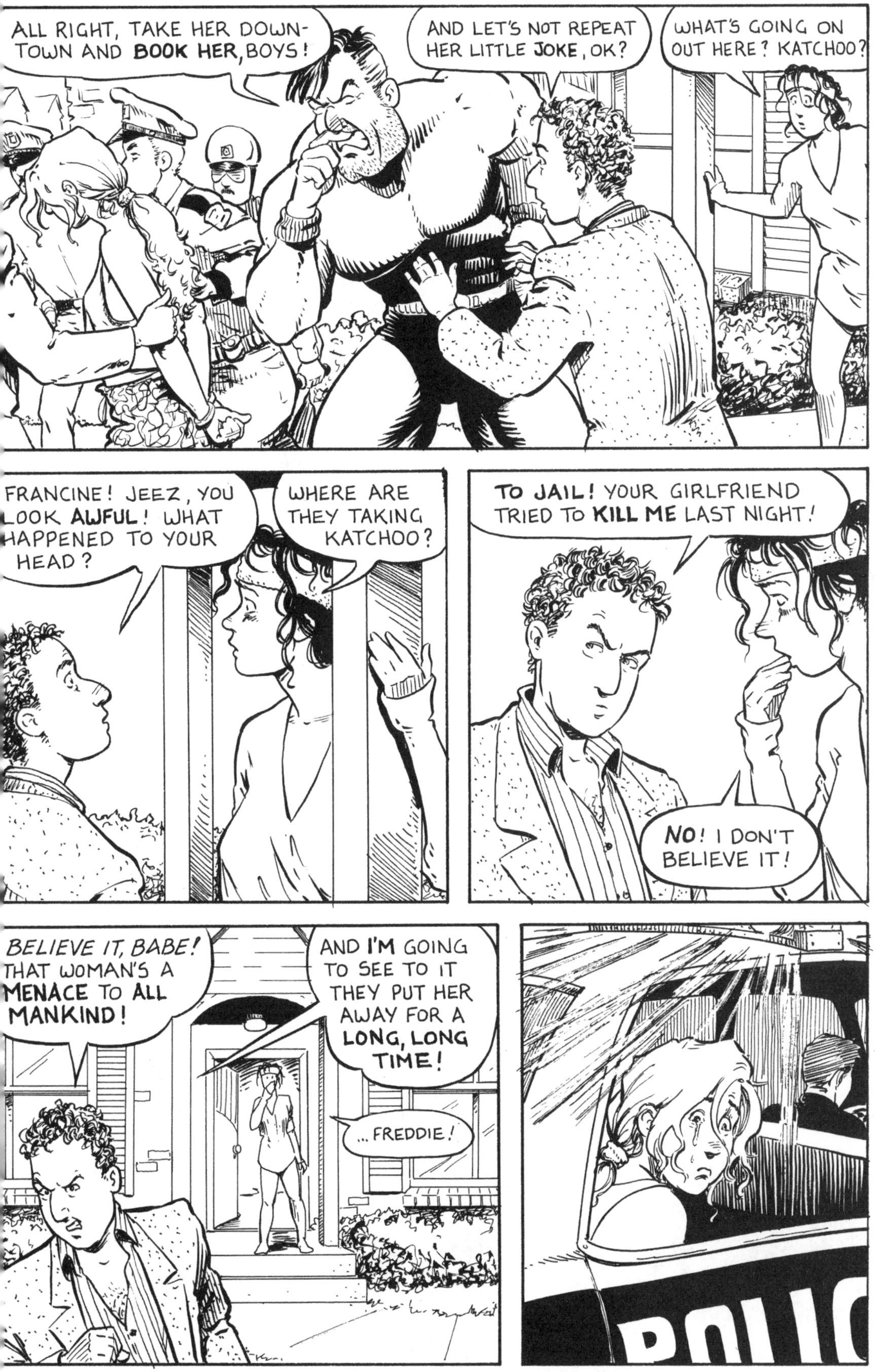
ALL RIGHT, TAKE HER DOWN-TOWN AND BOOK HER, BOYS!
AND LET'S NOT REPEAT HER LITTLE JOKE, OK?
WHAT'S GOING ON OUT HERE? KATCHOO?
FRANCINE! JEEZ, YOU LOOK AWFUL! WHAT HAPPENED TO YOUR HEAD?
WHERE ARE THEY TAKING KATCHOO?
TO JAIL! YOUR GIRLFRIEND TRIED TO KILL ME LAST NIGHT!
NO! I DON'T BELIEVE IT!
BELIEVE IT, BABE! THAT WOMAN'S A MENACE TO ALL MANKIND!
AND I'M GOING TO SEE TO IT THEY PUT HER AWAY FOR A LONG, LONG TIME!
... FREDDIE!

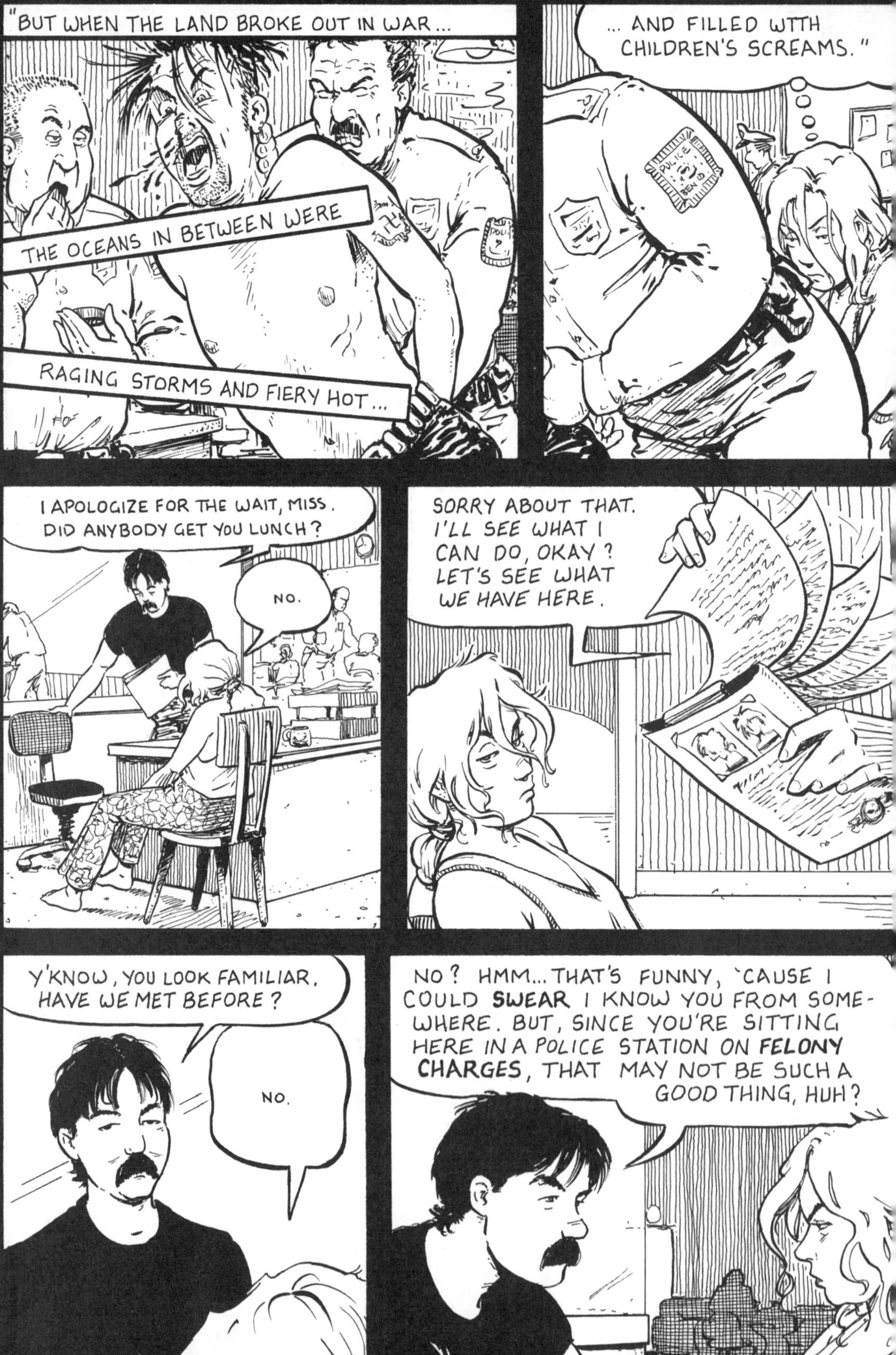
"BUT WHEN THE LAND BROKE OUT IN WAR...
THE OCEANS IN BETWEEN WERE
RAGING STORMS AND FIERY HOT...
... AND FILLED WITH CHILDREN'S SCREAMS."
I APOLOGIZE FOR THE WAIT, MISS. DID ANYBODY GET YOU LUNCH?
NO.
SORRY ABOUT THAT. I'LL SEE WHAT I CAN DO, OKAY? LET'S SEE WHAT WE HAVE HERE.
Y'KNOW, YOU LOOK FAMILIAR. HAVE WE MET BEFORE?
NO.
NO? HMM... THAT'S FUNNY, 'CAUSE I COULD **SWEAR** I KNOW YOU FROM SOMEWHERE. BUT, SINCE YOU'RE SITTING HERE IN A POLICE STATION ON **FELONY CHARGES**, THAT MAY NOT BE SUCH A GOOD THING, HUH?

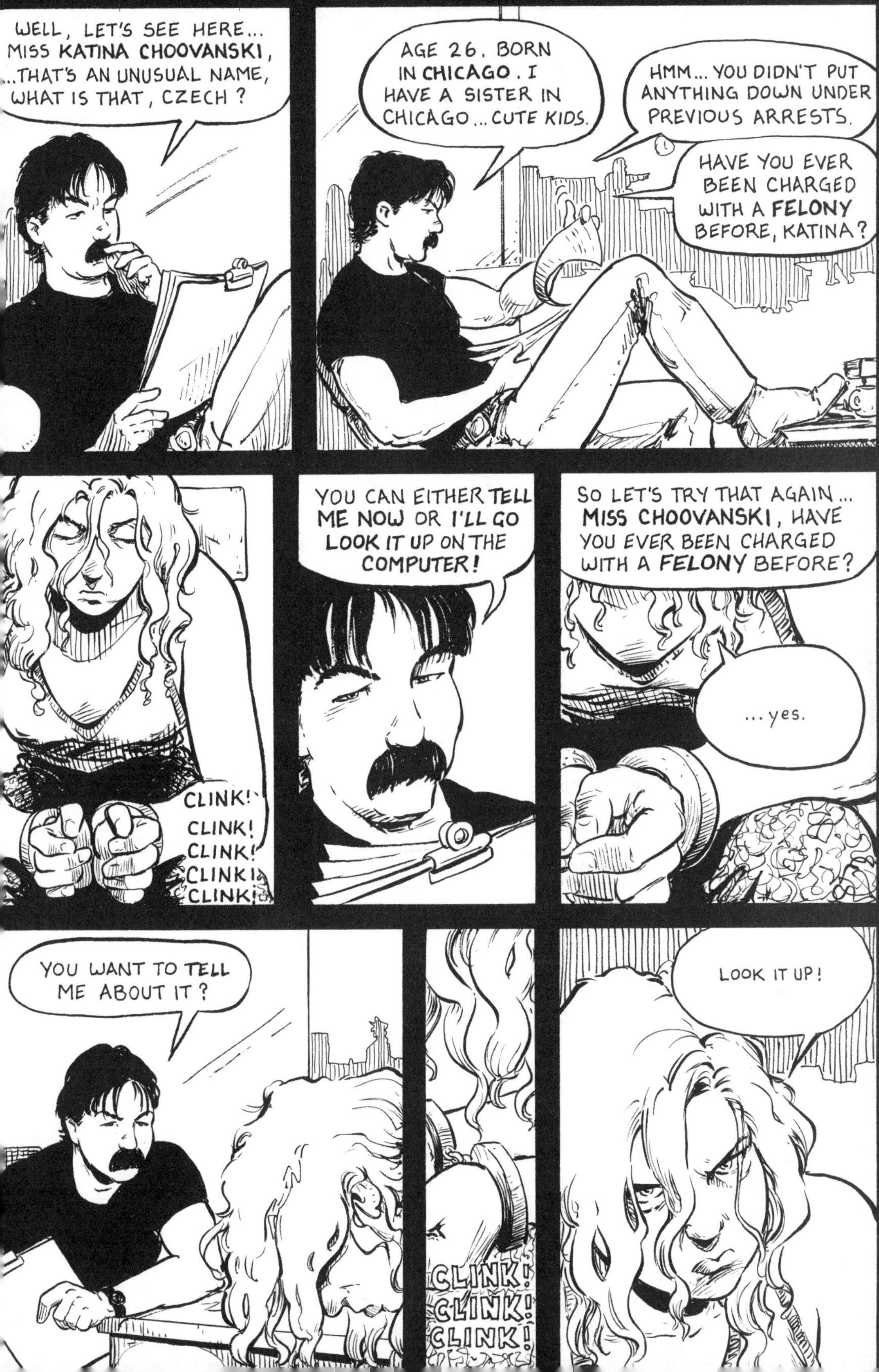
WELL, LET'S SEE HERE... MISS KATINA CHOOVANSKI, ...THAT'S AN UNUSUAL NAME, WHAT IS THAT, CZECH?
AGE 26. BORN IN CHICAGO. I HAVE A SISTER IN CHICAGO... CUTE KIDS.
HMM... YOU DIDN'T PUT ANYTHING DOWN UNDER PREVIOUS ARRESTS.
HAVE YOU EVER BEEN CHARGED WITH A FELONY BEFORE, KATINA?
CLINK! CLINK! CLINK! CLINK! CLINK!
YOU CAN EITHER TELL ME NOW OR I'LL GO LOOK IT UP ON THE COMPUTER!
SO LET'S TRY THAT AGAIN... MISS CHOOVANSKI, HAVE YOU EVER BEEN CHARGED WITH A FELONY BEFORE?
...yes.
YOU WANT TO TELL ME ABOUT IT?
CLINK! CLINK! CLINK!
LOOK IT UP!

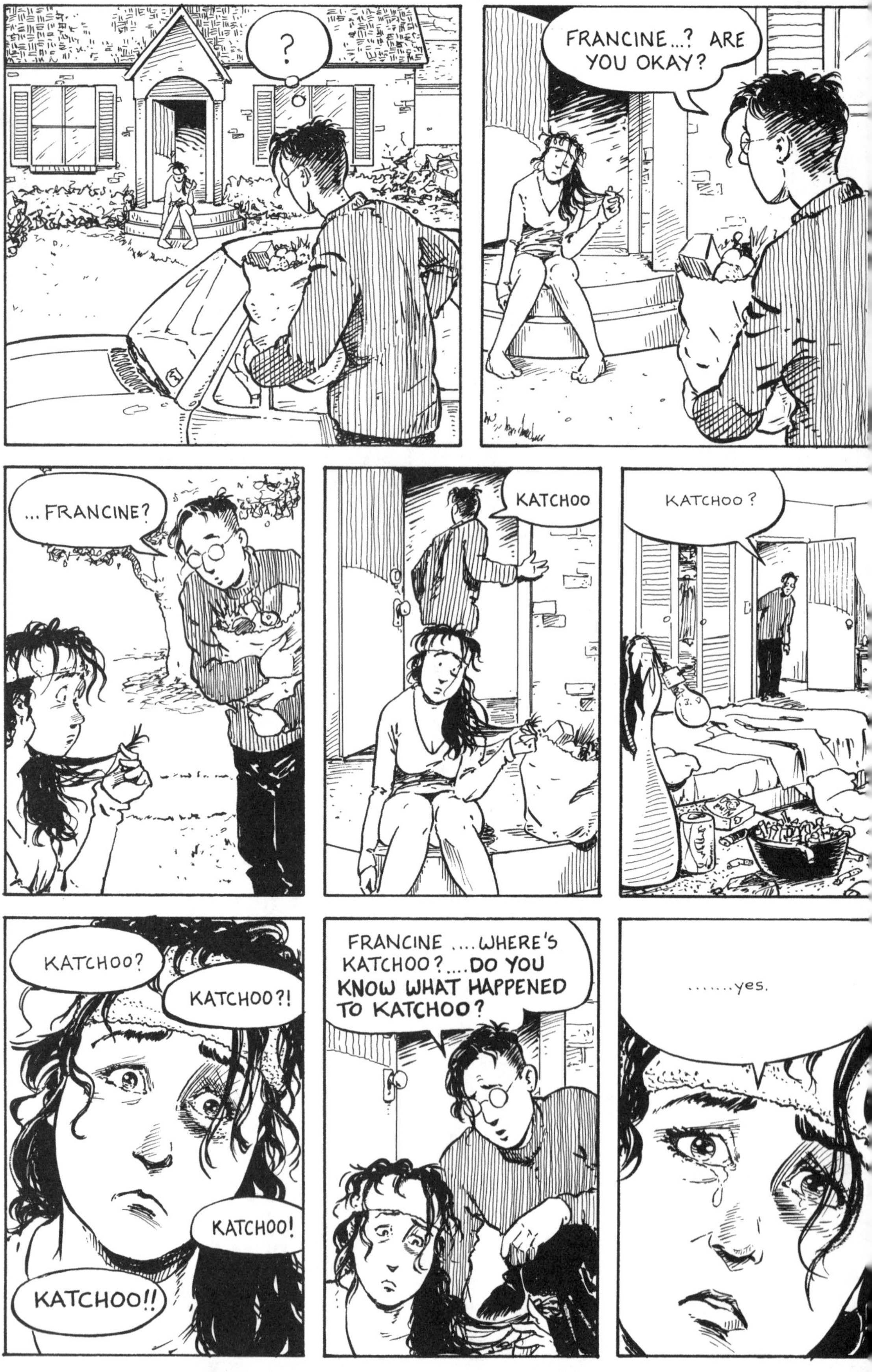
?
FRANCINE...? ARE YOU OKAY?
...FRANCINE?
KATCHOO
KATCHOO?
KATCHOO?
KATCHOO?!
KATCHOO!
KATCHOO!!
FRANCINE ....WHERE'S KATCHOO?....DO YOU KNOW WHAT HAPPENED TO KATCHOO?
.......yes.

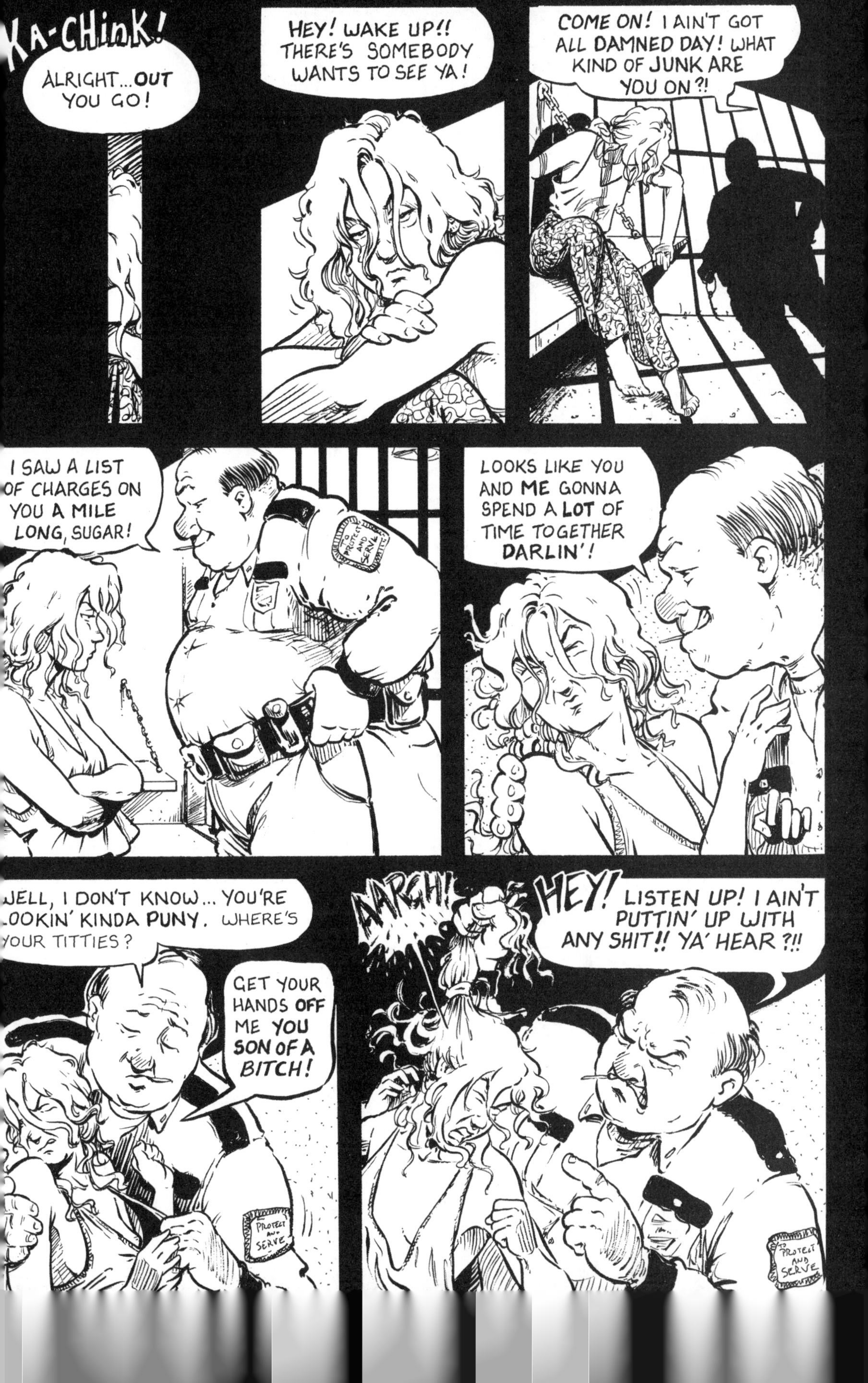
KA-CHINK!
ALRIGHT... OUT YOU GO!
HEY! WAKE UP!! THERE'S SOMEBODY WANTS TO SEE YA!
COME ON! I AIN'T GOT ALL DAMNED DAY! WHAT KIND OF JUNK ARE YOU ON?!
I SAW A LIST OF CHARGES ON YOU A MILE LONG, SUGAR!
TO PROTECT AND SERVE
LOOKS LIKE YOU AND ME GONNA SPEND A LOT OF TIME TOGETHER DARLIN'!
WELL, I DON'T KNOW... YOU'RE LOOKIN' KINDA PUNY. WHERE'S YOUR TITTIES?
GET YOUR HANDS OFF ME YOU SON OF A BITCH!
PROTECT AND SERVE
AARGH!
HEY! LISTEN UP! I AIN'T PUTTIN' UP WITH ANY SHIT!! YA' HEAR?!!
TO PROTECT AND SERVE

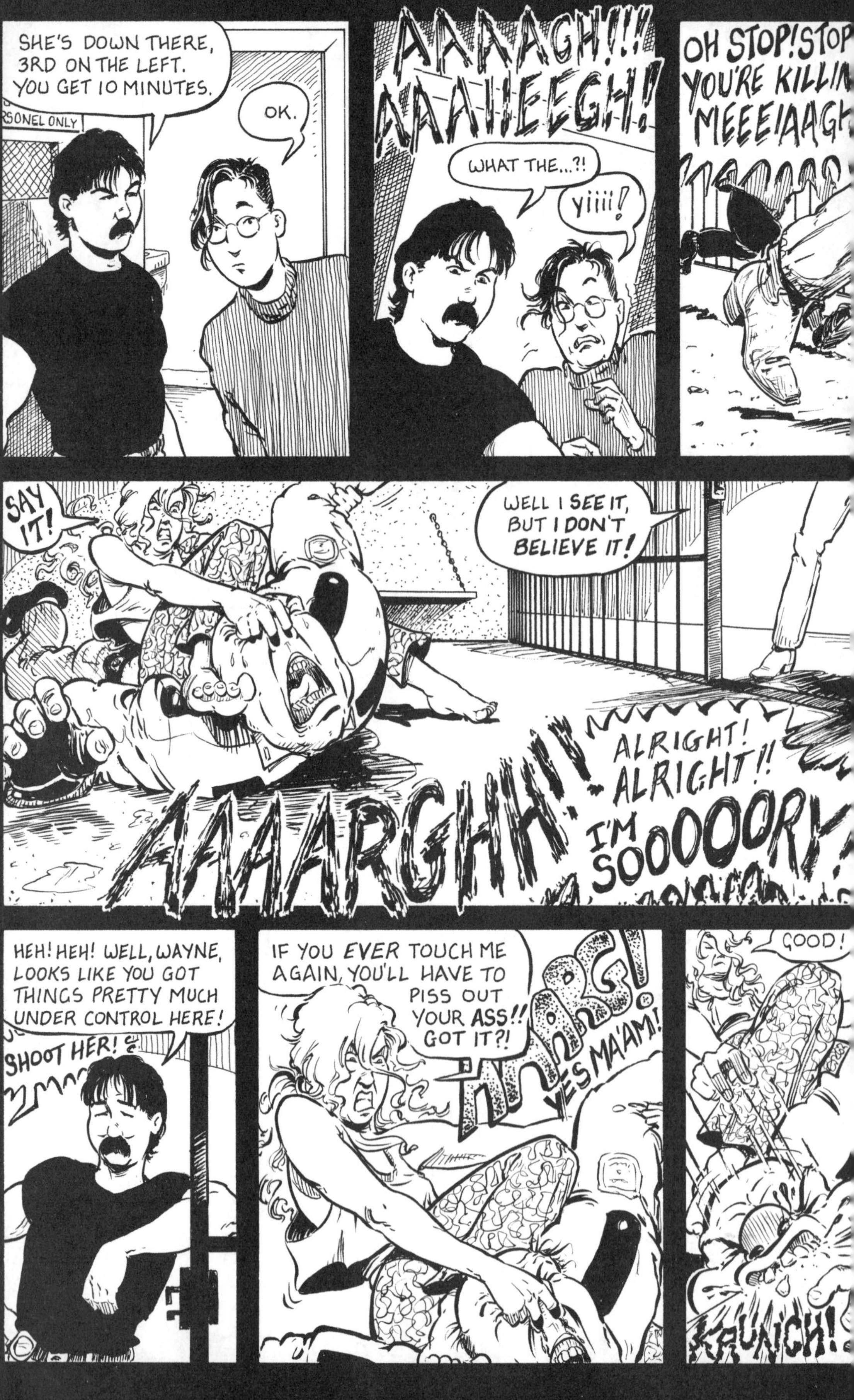
SHE'S DOWN THERE, 3RD ON THE LEFT. YOU GET 10 MINUTES.
OK.
AAAAGH!!! AAAIIEEGH!
WHAT THE...?!
yiiii!
OH STOP! STOP YOU'RE KILLIN MEEE!AAGH
SAY IT!
WELL I SEE IT, BUT I DON'T BELIEVE IT!
AAAARGHH!!
ALRIGHT! ALRIGHT!! I'M SOOOOORY!
HEH! HEH! WELL, WAYNE, LOOKS LIKE YOU GOT THINGS PRETTY MUCH UNDER CONTROL HERE!
SHOOT HER!
IF YOU EVER TOUCH ME AGAIN, YOU'LL HAVE TO PISS OUT YOUR ASS!! GOT IT?!
YES MA'AM!
GOOD!
KRUNCH!

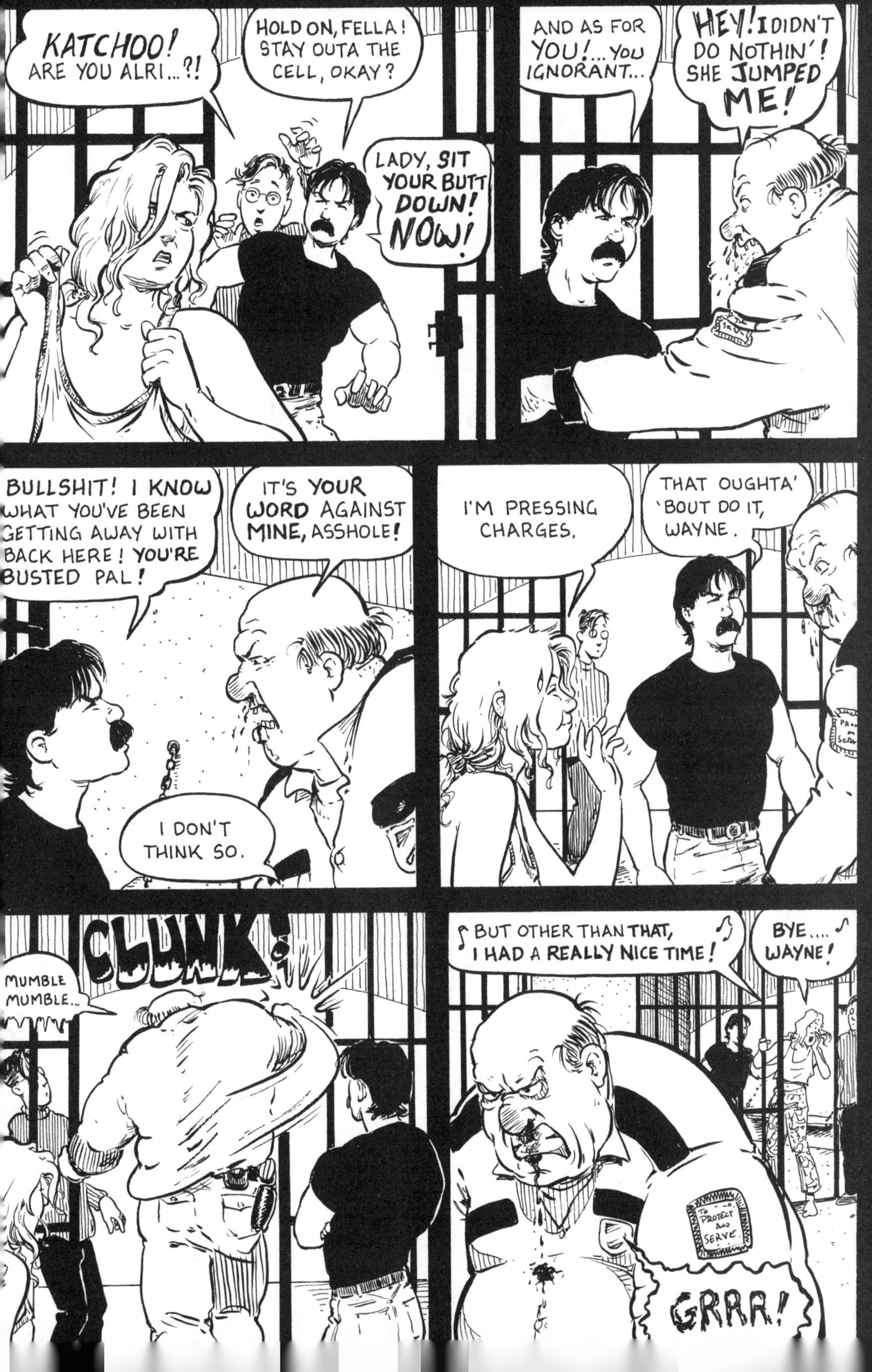
KATCHOO! ARE YOU ALRI...?!
HOLD ON, FELLA! STAY OUTA THE CELL, OKAY?
LADY, SIT YOUR BUTT DOWN! NOW!
AND AS FOR YOU!... YOU IGNORANT...
HEY! I DIDN'T DO NOTHIN'! SHE JUMPED ME!
BULLSHIT! I KNOW WHAT YOU'VE BEEN GETTING AWAY WITH BACK HERE! YOU'RE BUSTED PAL!
IT'S YOUR WORD AGAINST MINE, ASSHOLE!
I DON'T THINK SO.
I'M PRESSING CHARGES.
THAT OUGHTA' 'BOUT DO IT, WAYNE.
CLUNK!
MUMBLE MUMBLE...
BUT OTHER THAN THAT, I HAD A REALLY NICE TIME!
BYE.... WAYNE!
TO PROTECT AND SERVE
GRRR!

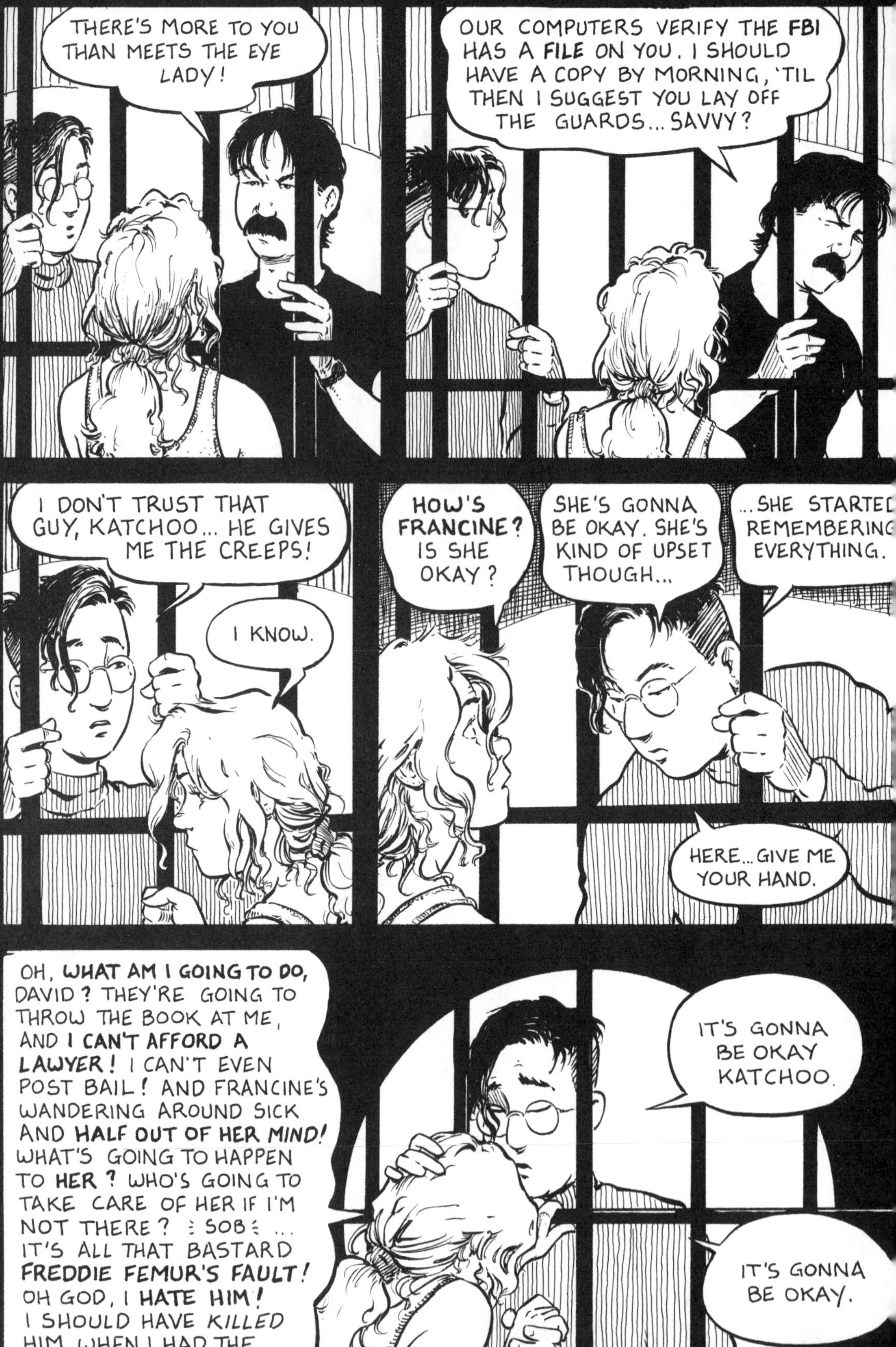
THERE'S MORE TO YOU THAN MEETS THE EYE LADY!
OUR COMPUTERS VERIFY THE FBI HAS A FILE ON YOU. I SHOULD HAVE A COPY BY MORNING, 'TIL THEN I SUGGEST YOU LAY OFF THE GUARDS... SAVVY?
I DON'T TRUST THAT GUY, KATCHOO... HE GIVES ME THE CREEPS!
I KNOW.
HOW'S FRANCINE? IS SHE OKAY?
SHE'S GONNA BE OKAY. SHE'S KIND OF UPSET THOUGH...
...SHE STARTED REMEMBERING EVERYTHING.
HERE... GIVE ME YOUR HAND.
OH, WHAT AM I GOING TO DO, DAVID? THEY'RE GOING TO THROW THE BOOK AT ME, AND I CAN'T AFFORD A LAWYER! I CAN'T EVEN POST BAIL! AND FRANCINE'S WANDERING AROUND SICK AND HALF OUT OF HER MIND! WHAT'S GOING TO HAPPEN TO HER? WHO'S GOING TO TAKE CARE OF HER IF I'M NOT THERE? SOB ... IT'S ALL THAT BASTARD FREDDIE FEMUR'S FAULT! OH GOD, I HATE HIM! I SHOULD HAVE KILLED HIM WHEN I HAD THE CHANCE! ... SOB
IT'S GONNA BE OKAY KATCHOO.
IT'S GONNA BE OKAY.

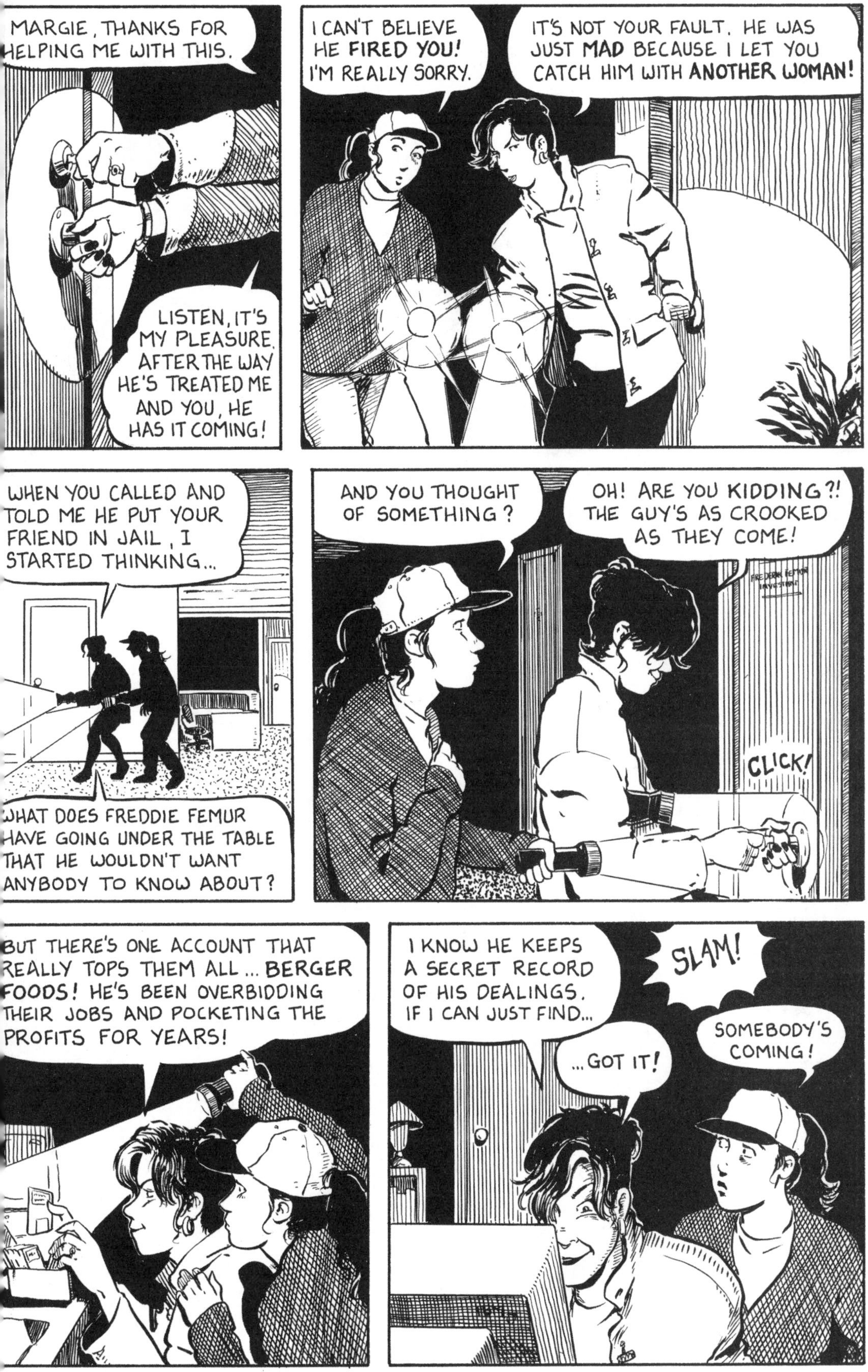
MARGIE, THANKS FOR HELPING ME WITH THIS.
LISTEN, IT'S MY PLEASURE. AFTER THE WAY HE'S TREATED ME AND YOU, HE HAS IT COMING!
I CAN'T BELIEVE HE FIRED YOU! I'M REALLY SORRY.
IT'S NOT YOUR FAULT. HE WAS JUST MAD BECAUSE I LET YOU CATCH HIM WITH ANOTHER WOMAN!
WHEN YOU CALLED AND TOLD ME HE PUT YOUR FRIEND IN JAIL, I STARTED THINKING...
WHAT DOES FREDDIE FEMUR HAVE GOING UNDER THE TABLE THAT HE WOULDN'T WANT ANYBODY TO KNOW ABOUT?
AND YOU THOUGHT OF SOMETHING?
OH! ARE YOU KIDDING?! THE GUY'S AS CROOKED AS THEY COME!
CLICK!
BUT THERE'S ONE ACCOUNT THAT REALLY TOPS THEM ALL ... BERGER FOODS! HE'S BEEN OVERBIDDING THEIR JOBS AND POCKETING THE PROFITS FOR YEARS!
I KNOW HE KEEPS A SECRET RECORD OF HIS DEALINGS. IF I CAN JUST FIND...
SLAM!
...GOT IT!
SOMEBODY'S COMING!

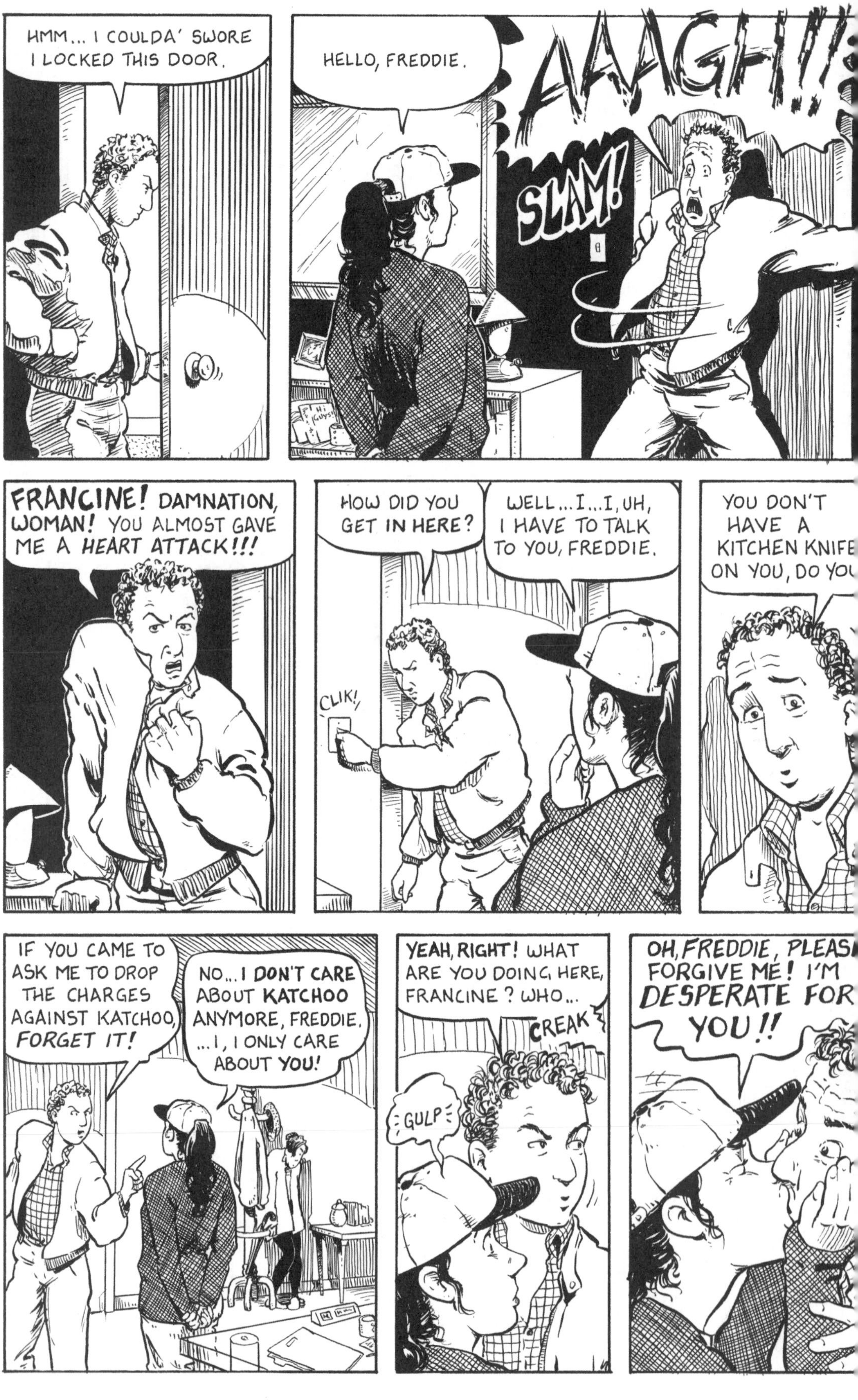
HMM... I COULDA' SWORE I LOCKED THIS DOOR.
HELLO, FREDDIE.
AAAGH!!
SLAM!
FRANCINE! DAMNATION, WOMAN! YOU ALMOST GAVE ME A HEART ATTACK!!!
HOW DID YOU GET IN HERE?
CLIK!
WELL... I... I, UH, I HAVE TO TALK TO YOU, FREDDIE.
YOU DON'T HAVE A KITCHEN KNIFE ON YOU, DO YOU
IF YOU CAME TO ASK ME TO DROP THE CHARGES AGAINST KATCHOO, FORGET IT!
NO... I DON'T CARE ABOUT KATCHOO ANYMORE, FREDDIE. ...I, I ONLY CARE ABOUT YOU!
YEAH, RIGHT! WHAT ARE YOU DOING HERE, FRANCINE? WHO...
CREAK
GULP
OH, FREDDIE, PLEASE FORGIVE ME! I'M DESPERATE FOR YOU!!

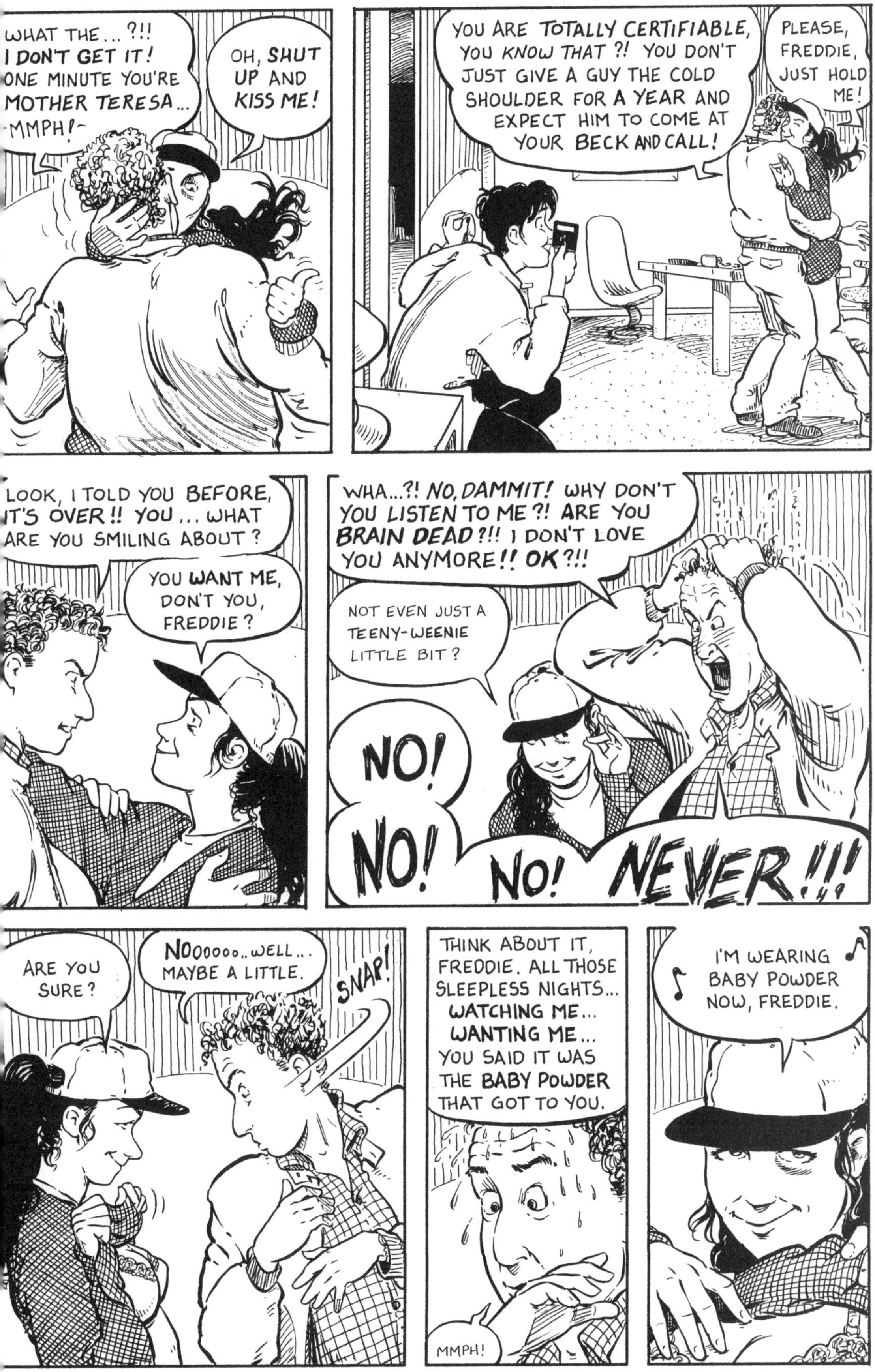
WHAT THE...?!! I DON'T GET IT! ONE MINUTE YOU'RE MOTHER TERESA... MMPH!
OH, SHUT UP AND KISS ME!
YOU ARE TOTALLY CERTIFIABLE, YOU KNOW THAT?! YOU DON'T JUST GIVE A GUY THE COLD SHOULDER FOR A YEAR AND EXPECT HIM TO COME AT YOUR BECK AND CALL!
PLEASE, FREDDIE, JUST HOLD ME!
LOOK, I TOLD YOU BEFORE, IT'S OVER!! YOU... WHAT ARE YOU SMILING ABOUT?
YOU WANT ME, DON'T YOU, FREDDIE?
WHA...?! NO, DAMMIT! WHY DON'T YOU LISTEN TO ME?! ARE YOU BRAIN DEAD?!! I DON'T LOVE YOU ANYMORE!! OK?!!
NOT EVEN JUST A TEENY-WEENIE LITTLE BIT?
NO! NO! NO! NEVER!!!
ARE YOU SURE?
NOoooo.. WELL... MAYBE A LITTLE.
SNAP!
THINK ABOUT IT, FREDDIE. ALL THOSE SLEEPLESS NIGHTS... WATCHING ME... WANTING ME... YOU SAID IT WAS THE BABY POWDER THAT GOT TO YOU.
MMPH!
I'M WEARING BABY POWDER NOW, FREDDIE.

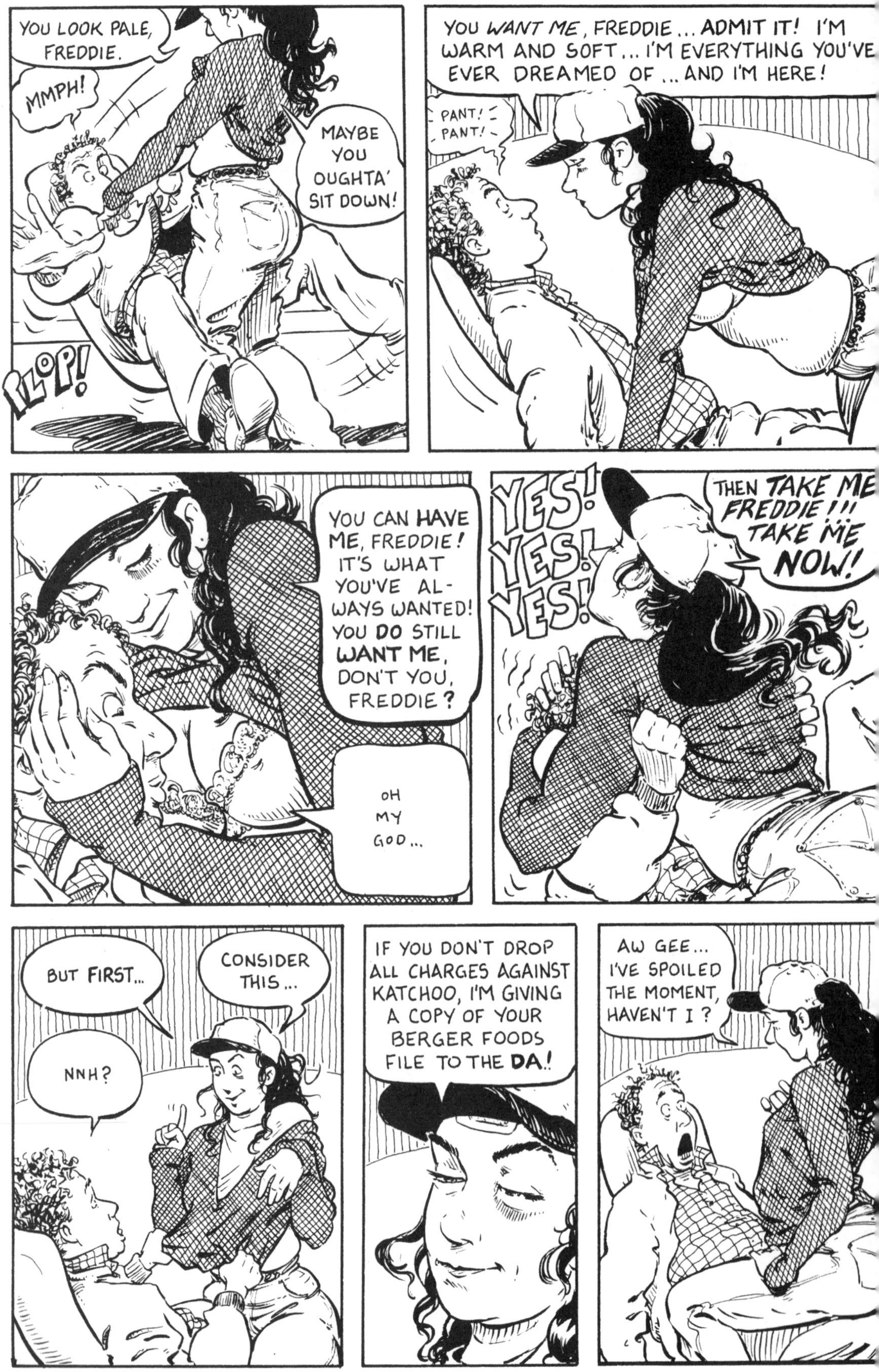
YOU LOOK PALE, FREDDIE.
MMPH!
MAYBE YOU OUGHTA' SIT DOWN!
FLOP!
YOU WANT ME, FREDDIE... ADMIT IT! I'M WARM AND SOFT... I'M EVERYTHING YOU'VE EVER DREAMED OF... AND I'M HERE!
PANT! PANT!
YOU CAN HAVE ME, FREDDIE! IT'S WHAT YOU'VE ALWAYS WANTED! YOU DO STILL WANT ME, DON'T YOU, FREDDIE?
OH MY GOD...
YES! YES! YES!
THEN TAKE ME FREDDIE!!! TAKE ME NOW!
BUT FIRST...
CONSIDER THIS...
NNH?
IF YOU DON'T DROP ALL CHARGES AGAINST KATCHOO, I'M GIVING A COPY OF YOUR BERGER FOODS FILE TO THE DA!
AW GEE... I'VE SPOILED THE MOMENT, HAVEN'T I?

WHAT DO YOU KNOW ABOUT BERGER FOODS?

ENOUGH TO SEND YOU TO PRISON.

YOU'RE BLUFFING!

NO...FREDDIE, I'M NOT.

I WANT KATCHOO RELEASED, IMMEDIATELY!

UNDERSTAND?

YES.

I'M GLAD WE HAD THIS LITTLE CHAT. I FEEL SO MUCH BETTER, DON'T YOU?

I'M SORRY IT DIDN'T WORK OUT FOR US, FREDDIE, 'CAUSE I'LL TELL YOU A LITTLE SECRET...

I'M INCREDIBLE. BETTER THAN YOUR WILDEST DREAMS. ALL I WAS WAITING FOR WAS OUR ONE YEAR ANNIVERSARY.

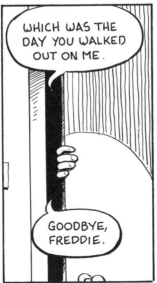

WHICH WAS THE DAY YOU WALKED OUT ON ME.

GOODBYE, FREDDIE.

SLAM!

FADE TO BLACK...

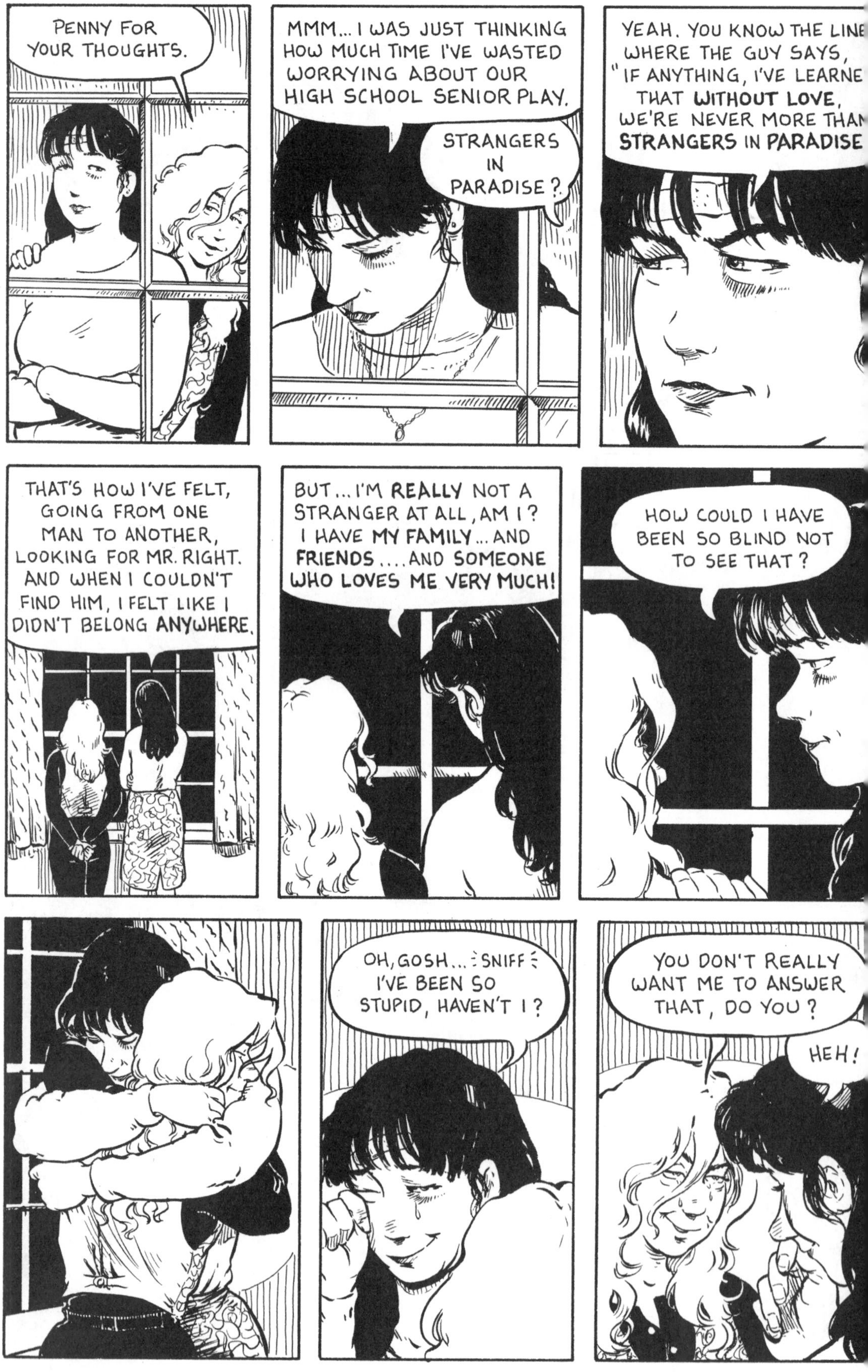
PENNY FOR YOUR THOUGHTS.
MMM... I WAS JUST THINKING HOW MUCH TIME I'VE WASTED WORRYING ABOUT OUR HIGH SCHOOL SENIOR PLAY.
STRANGERS IN PARADISE?
YEAH. YOU KNOW THE LINE WHERE THE GUY SAYS, "IF ANYTHING, I'VE LEARNED THAT WITHOUT LOVE, WE'RE NEVER MORE THAN STRANGERS IN PARADISE."
THAT'S HOW I'VE FELT, GOING FROM ONE MAN TO ANOTHER, LOOKING FOR MR. RIGHT. AND WHEN I COULDN'T FIND HIM, I FELT LIKE I DIDN'T BELONG ANYWHERE.
BUT... I'M REALLY NOT A STRANGER AT ALL, AM I? I HAVE MY FAMILY... AND FRIENDS.... AND SOMEONE WHO LOVES ME VERY MUCH!
HOW COULD I HAVE BEEN SO BLIND NOT TO SEE THAT?
OH, GOSH... SNIFF I'VE BEEN SO STUPID, HAVEN'T I?
YOU DON'T REALLY WANT ME TO ANSWER THAT, DO YOU?
HEH!

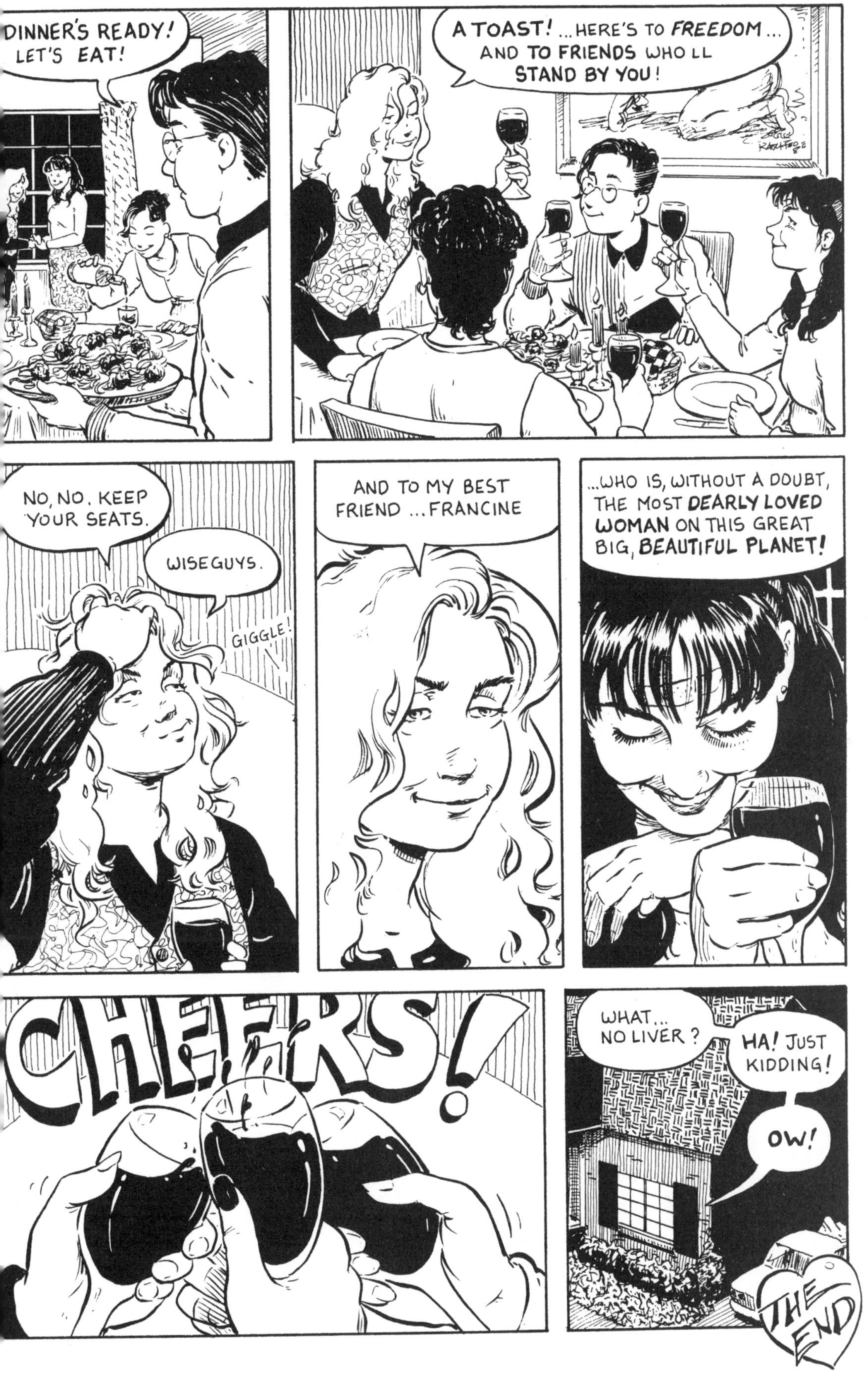
DINNER'S READY! LET'S EAT!
A TOAST! ...HERE'S TO FREEDOM... AND TO FRIENDS WHO'LL STAND BY YOU!
NO, NO. KEEP YOUR SEATS.
WISEGUYS.
GIGGLE!
AND TO MY BEST FRIEND ...FRANCINE
...WHO IS, WITHOUT A DOUBT, THE MOST DEARLY LOVED WOMAN ON THIS GREAT BIG, BEAUTIFUL PLANET!
CHEERS!
WHAT... NO LIVER?
HA! JUST KIDDING!
OW!
THE END

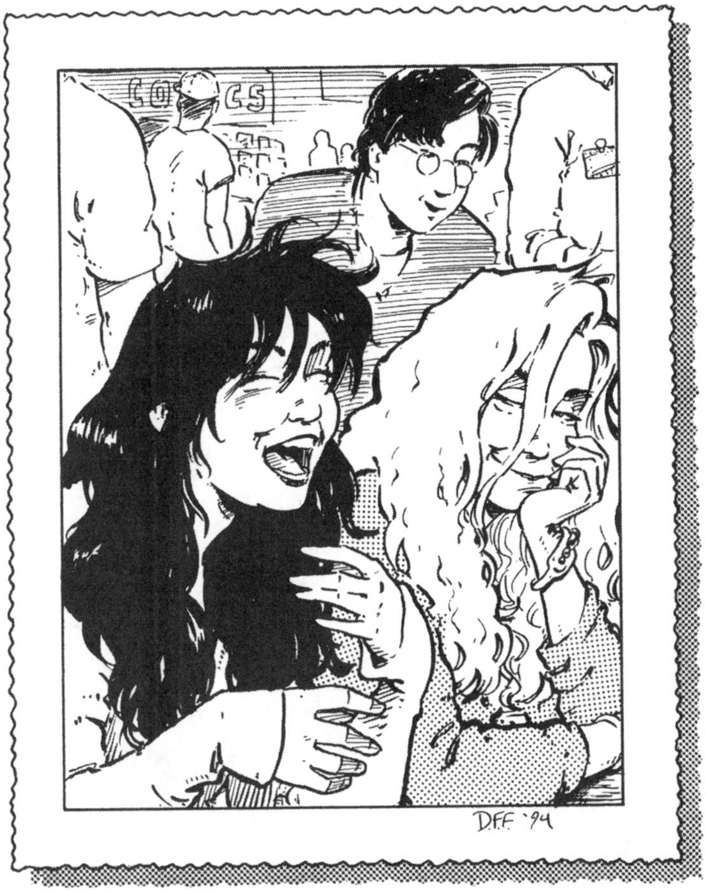
D.F.F. '94

The heart has it's reasons, that reason cannot know.

—Pascal

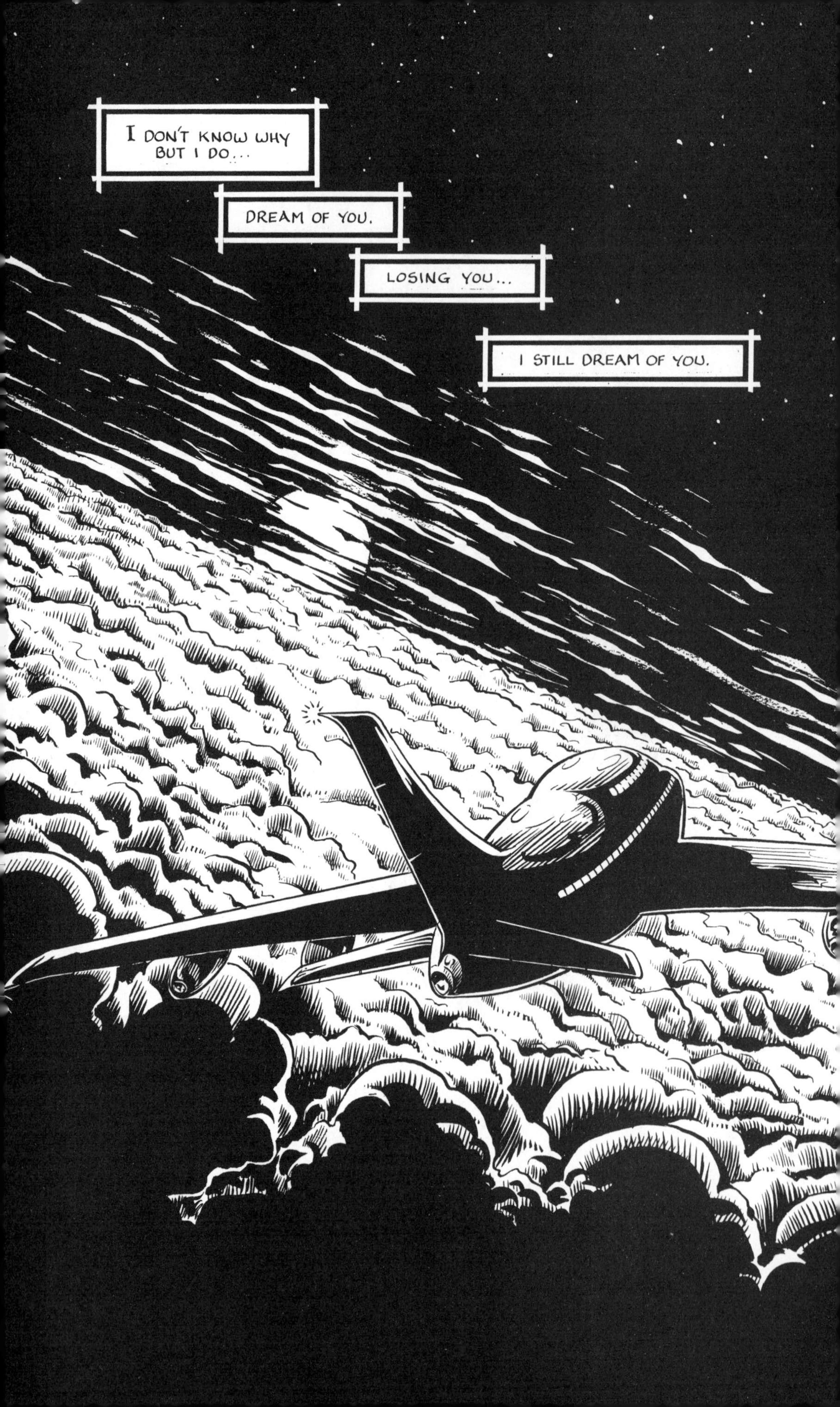
I DON'T KNOW WHY BUT I DO...
DREAM OF YOU.
LOSING YOU...
I STILL DREAM OF YOU.

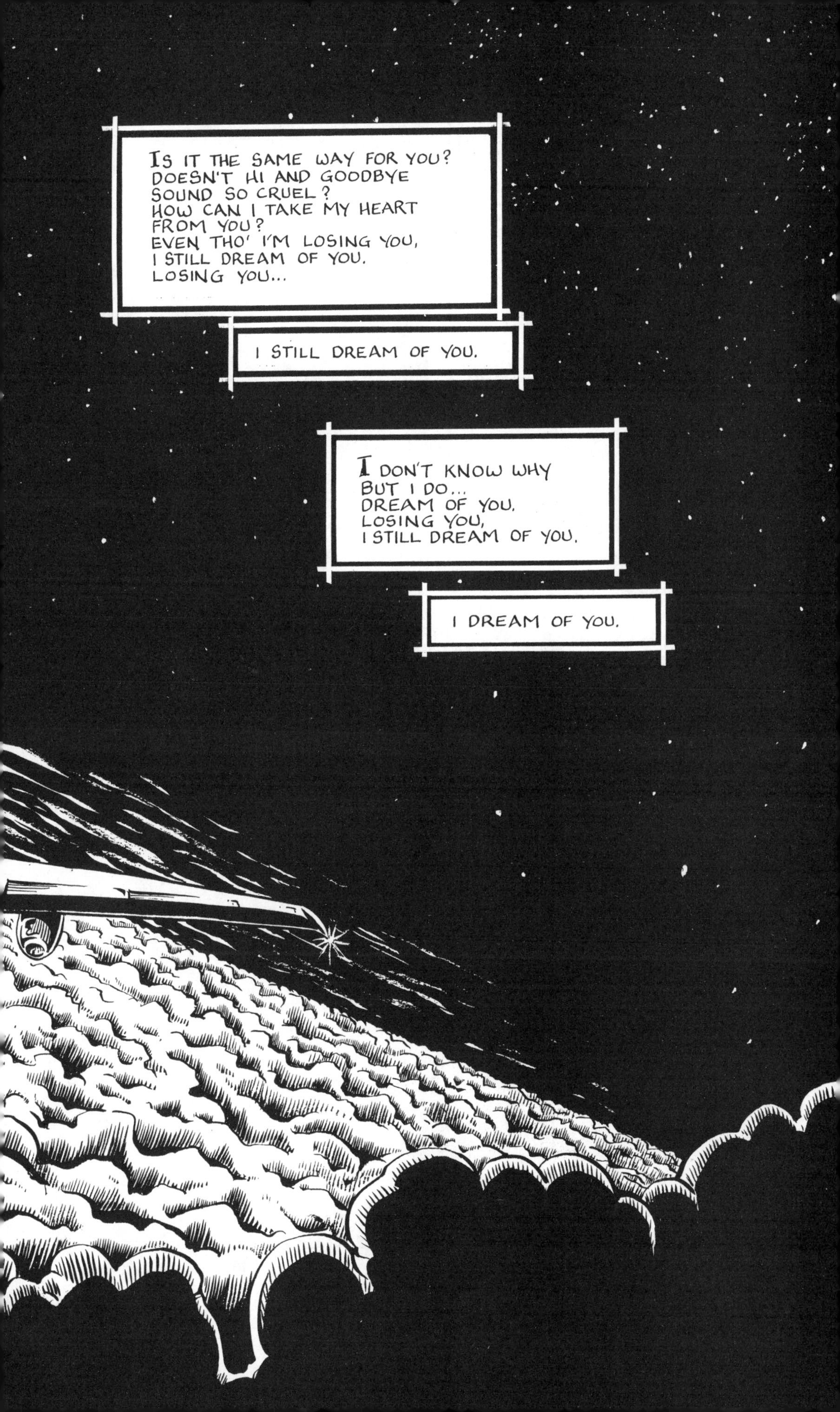
IS IT THE SAME WAY FOR YOU?
DOESN'T HI AND GOODBYE
SOUND SO CRUEL?
HOW CAN I TAKE MY HEART
FROM YOU?
EVEN THO' I'M LOSING YOU,
I STILL DREAM OF YOU.
LOSING YOU...
I STILL DREAM OF YOU.
I DON'T KNOW WHY
BUT I DO...
DREAM OF YOU.
LOSING YOU,
I STILL DREAM OF YOU.
I DREAM OF YOU.

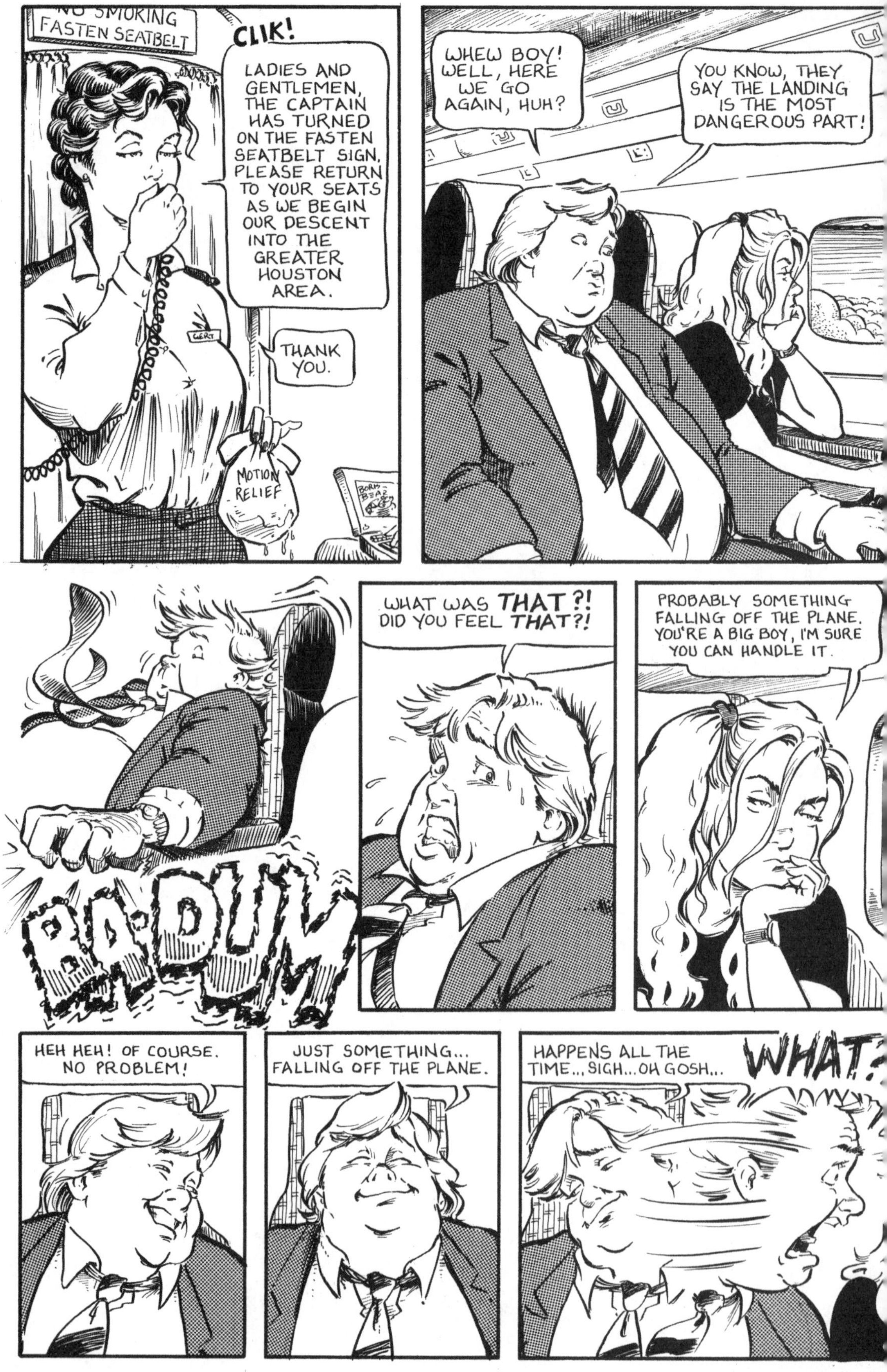
NO SMOKING
FASTEN SEATBELT
CLIK!
LADIES AND GENTLEMEN, THE CAPTAIN HAS TURNED ON THE FASTEN SEATBELT SIGN. PLEASE RETURN TO YOUR SEATS AS WE BEGIN OUR DESCENT INTO THE GREATER HOUSTON AREA.
THANK YOU.
GERT
MOTION RELIEF
WHEW BOY! WELL, HERE WE GO AGAIN, HUH?
YOU KNOW, THEY SAY THE LANDING IS THE MOST DANGEROUS PART!
BA-DUM
WHAT WAS THAT?! DID YOU FEEL THAT?!
PROBABLY SOMETHING FALLING OFF THE PLANE. YOU'RE A BIG BOY, I'M SURE YOU CAN HANDLE IT.
HEH HEH! OF COURSE. NO PROBLEM!
JUST SOMETHING... FALLING OFF THE PLANE.
HAPPENS ALL THE TIME... SIGH... OH GOSH...
WHAT?

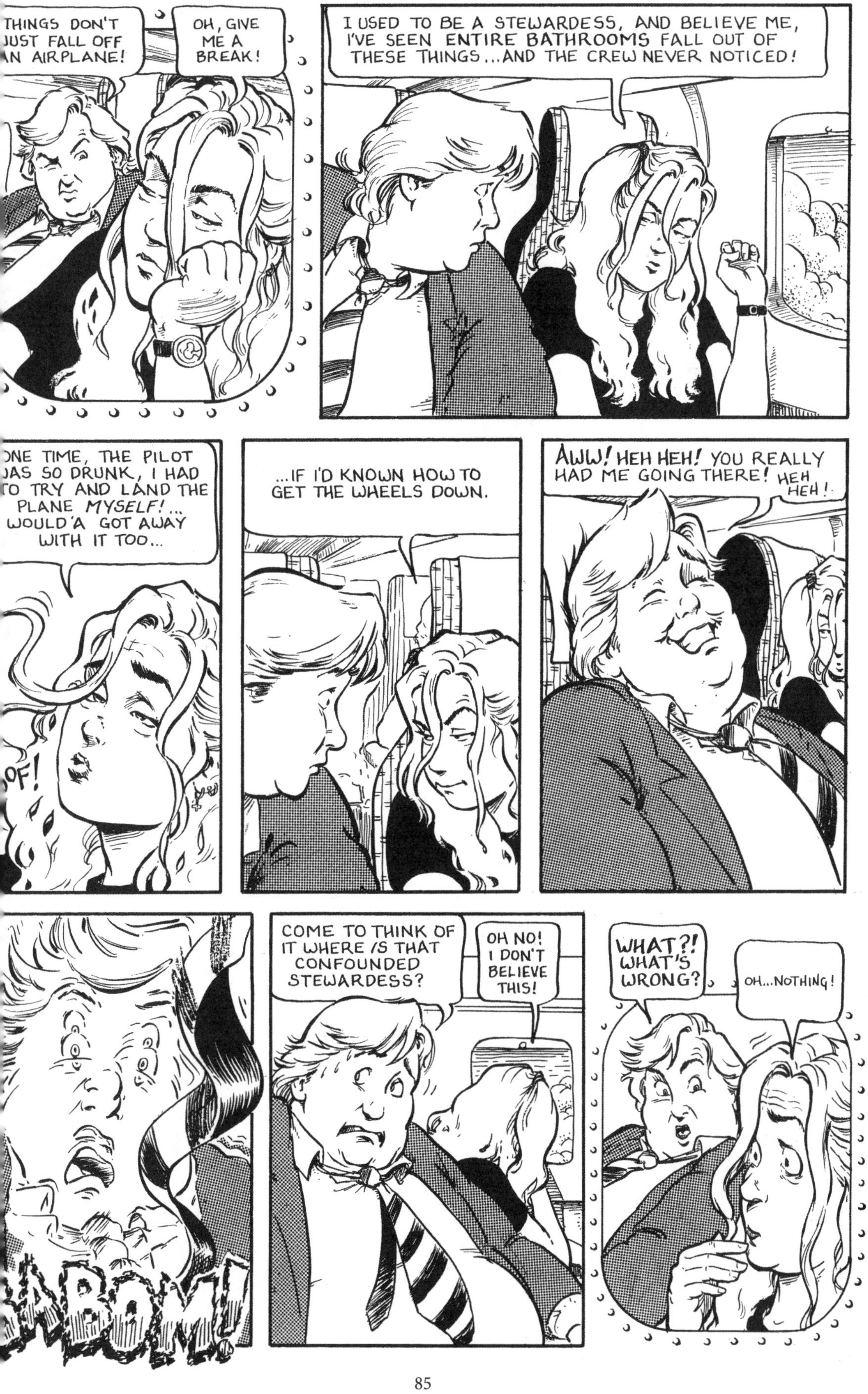

THINGS DON'T JUST FALL OFF AN AIRPLANE!
OH, GIVE ME A BREAK!
I USED TO BE A STEWARDESS, AND BELIEVE ME, I'VE SEEN ENTIRE BATHROOMS FALL OUT OF THESE THINGS... AND THE CREW NEVER NOTICED!
ONE TIME, THE PILOT WAS SO DRUNK, I HAD TO TRY AND LAND THE PLANE MYSELF!... WOULD'A GOT AWAY WITH IT TOO...
...IF I'D KNOWN HOW TO GET THE WHEELS DOWN.
AWW! HEH HEH! YOU REALLY HAD ME GOING THERE!
HEH HEH!
COME TO THINK OF IT WHERE IS THAT CONFOUNDED STEWARDESS?
OH NO! I DON'T BELIEVE THIS!
WHAT?! WHAT'S WRONG?
OH...NOTHING!

EXCUSE ME. EXCUSE ME, PLEASE.

WELCOME HOME!

FRANCINE!

BAGGAGE CLAIM

WELCOME HOME

DAVID! WHERE YOU BEEN?

LOOK WHAT I FOUND IN THE GIFT SHOP! WHADD'YA THINK?

ICE C

WELCOME HOME!

YOU DIDN'T BUY THAT FOR KATCHOO DID YOU?

OOF! HEY!

OH SORRY! THAT'LL WASH RIGHT OUT.

WELL YEAH. I THOUGHT IT'D BE KIND OF A...UH FUN LITTLE...ER...UH...

NO, NO I DIDN'T.

GOOD. I'D HATE TO SEE YOU GET HURT.

WELCOME HOME

...sigh

YOU MIGHT AS WELL HAVE A SEAT. ≡SMACK≡ SMACK≡ THESE LATE NIGHT FLIGHTS ARE NEVER ON TIME.

86

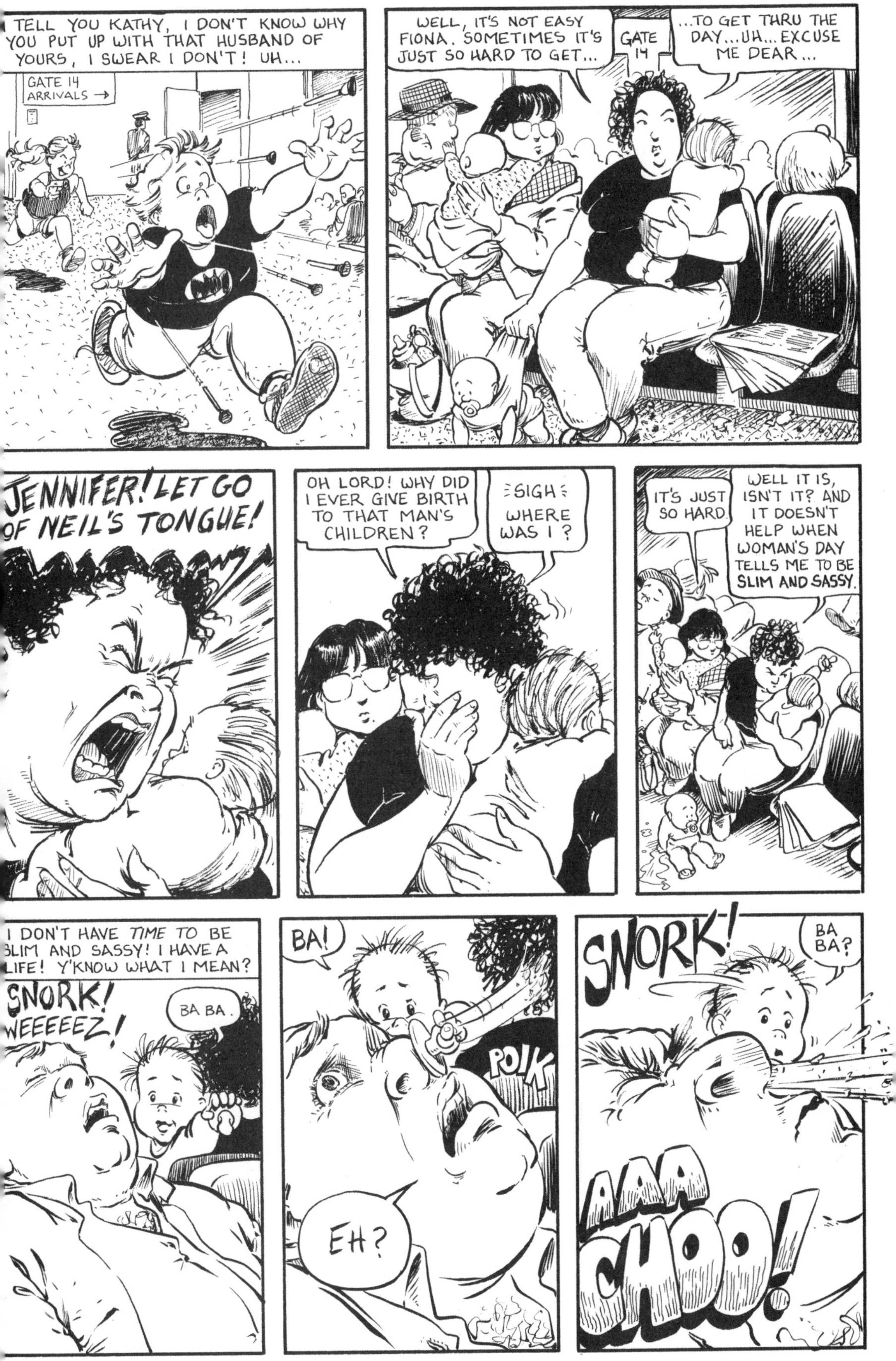
I TELL YOU KATHY, I DON'T KNOW WHY YOU PUT UP WITH THAT HUSBAND OF YOURS, I SWEAR I DON'T! UH...
GATE 14 ARRIVALS →
WELL, IT'S NOT EASY FIONA. SOMETIMES IT'S JUST SO HARD TO GET...
GATE 14
...TO GET THRU THE DAY...UH...EXCUSE ME DEAR...
JENNIFER! LET GO OF NEIL'S TONGUE!
OH LORD! WHY DID I EVER GIVE BIRTH TO THAT MAN'S CHILDREN?
SIGH WHERE WAS I?
IT'S JUST SO HARD.
WELL IT IS, ISN'T IT? AND IT DOESN'T HELP WHEN WOMAN'S DAY TELLS ME TO BE SLIM AND SASSY.
I DON'T HAVE TIME TO BE SLIM AND SASSY! I HAVE A LIFE! Y'KNOW WHAT I MEAN?
SNORK! WEEEEEZ!
BA BA.
BA!
POIK
EH?
SNORK!
BA BA?
AAA CHOO!

BONK!

OW!

FFFFFT!

WHAT?

SOMETHING JUST *HIT* ME!

FLY AMERICA AIRLINE

DEPAR DAILY PARA

WET FUR SALE! 1% OFF!

BOY, WHEN YOU GET AN IDEA, YOU GO NUTS, HUH?

NO, I MEAN *REALLY* HIT ME!

GATE 15

WET FUR SALE! 1% OFF!

THE HOUS PENTAGON ADVISE TO NEVER INVADE POLAND NOW "IT'S NEVER TOO LATE!" GEN HIT HERE WE GO AGAIN!

YOUR ATTENTION PLEASE... AMERICAN AIRLINES FLIGHT 232 FROM TORONTO IS NOW ARRIVING AT GATE 15!

THAT'S OUR GIRL!

WHOOPITA!

EXCUSE ME! COMIN' THRU!

HEY!

?!

OH, KATCHOO... PLEASE BE ON THIS PLANE... PLEASE BE ON THIS PLANE...

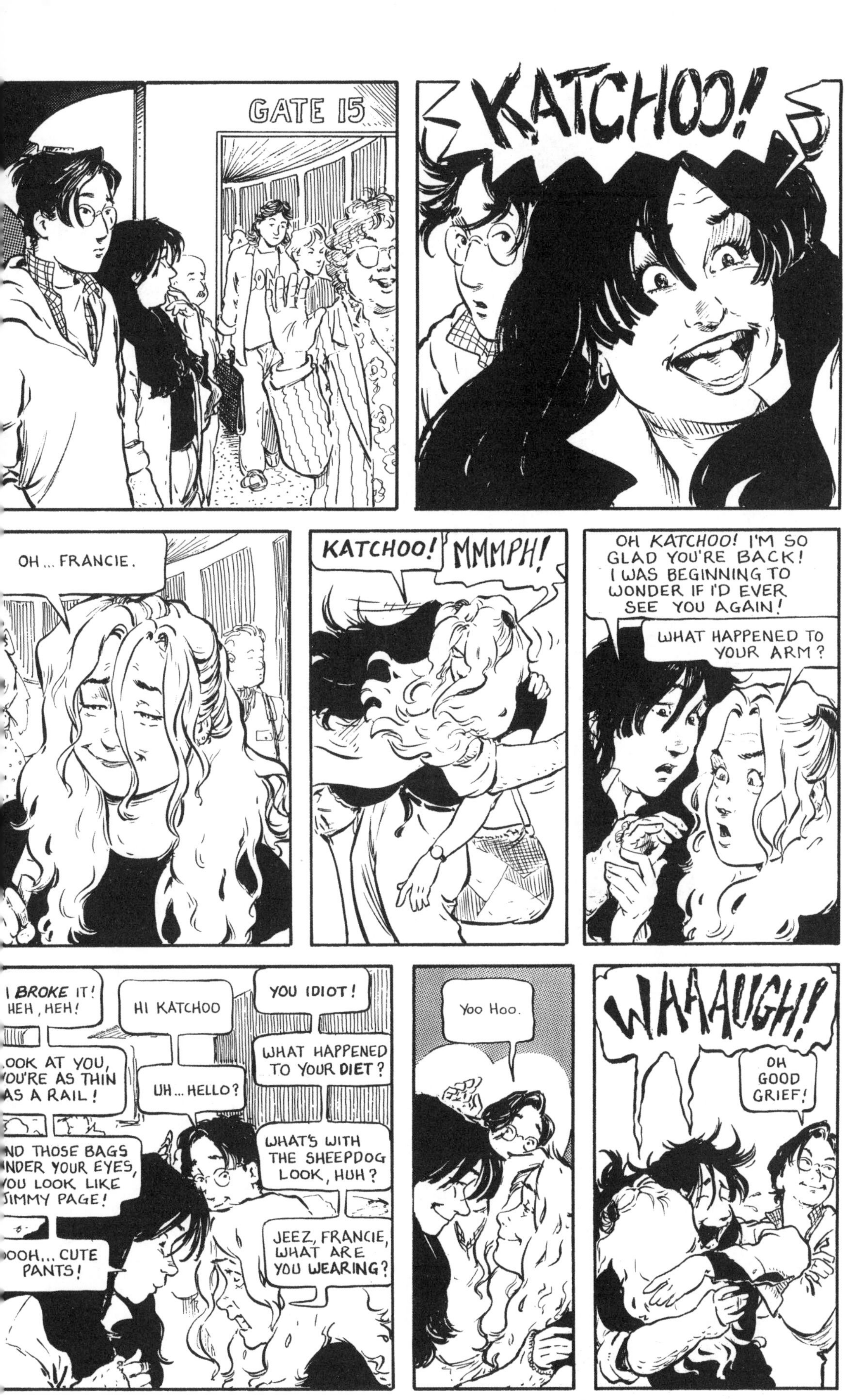
GATE 15
KATCHOO!
OH... FRANCIE.
KATCHOO!
MMMPH!
OH KATCHOO! I'M SO GLAD YOU'RE BACK! I WAS BEGINNING TO WONDER IF I'D EVER SEE YOU AGAIN!
WHAT HAPPENED TO YOUR ARM?
I BROKE IT! HEH, HEH!
HI KATCHOO
YOU IDIOT!
OOK AT YOU, OU'RE AS THIN AS A RAIL!
UH... HELLO?
WHAT HAPPENED TO YOUR DIET?
ND THOSE BAGS NDER YOUR EYES, OU LOOK LIKE IMMY PAGE!
WHAT'S WITH THE SHEEPDOG LOOK, HUH?
OOH... CUTE PANTS!
JEEZ, FRANCIE, WHAT ARE YOU WEARING?
Yoo Hoo.
WAAAUGH!
OH GOOD GRIEF!

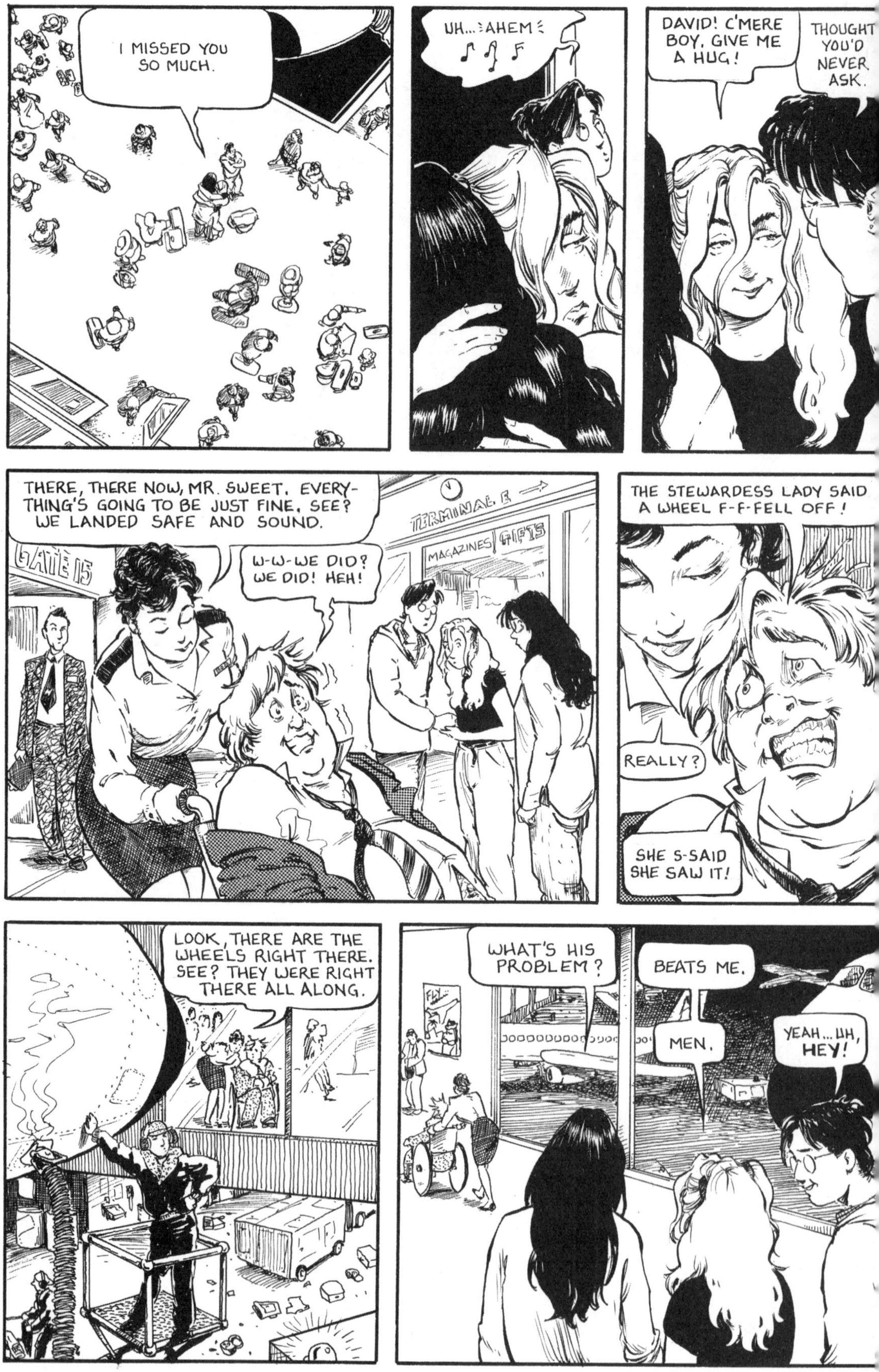

I MISSED YOU SO MUCH.
UH...AHEM
DAVID! C'MERE BOY, GIVE ME A HUG!
THOUGHT YOU'D NEVER ASK.
THERE, THERE NOW, MR. SWEET. EVERYTHING'S GOING TO BE JUST FINE, SEE? WE LANDED SAFE AND SOUND.
TERMINAL E
GATE 15
MAGAZINES
GIFTS
W-W-WE DID? WE DID! HEH!
THE STEWARDESS LADY SAID A WHEEL F-F-FELL OFF!
REALLY?
SHE S-SAID SHE SAW IT!
LOOK, THERE ARE THE WHEELS RIGHT THERE. SEE? THEY WERE RIGHT THERE ALL ALONG.
WHAT'S HIS PROBLEM?
FLY
BEATS ME.
MEN.
YEAH...UH, HEY!

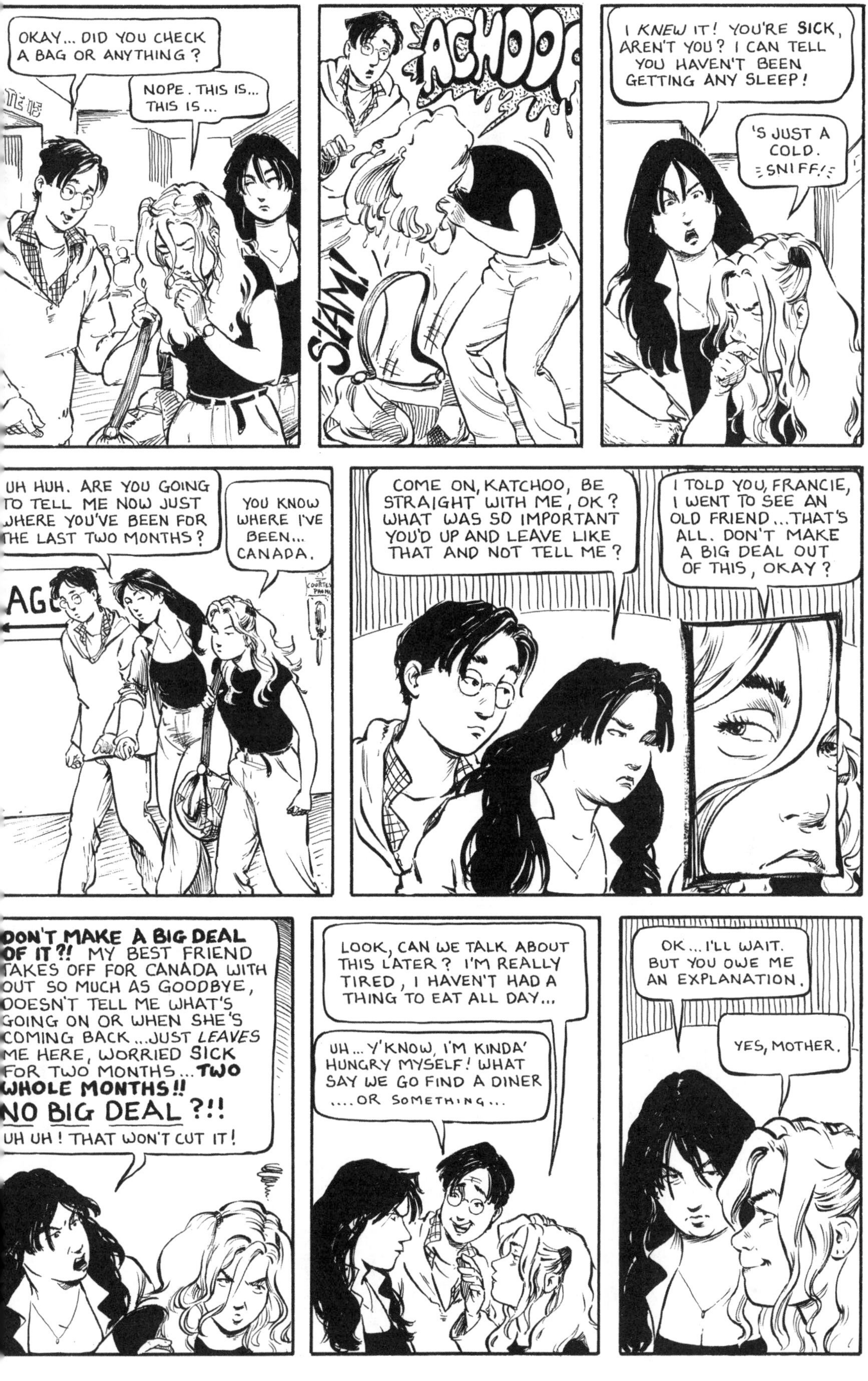
OKAY... DID YOU CHECK A BAG OR ANYTHING?
NOPE. THIS IS... THIS IS...
ACHOO!
SLAM!
I KNEW IT! YOU'RE SICK, AREN'T YOU? I CAN TELL YOU HAVEN'T BEEN GETTING ANY SLEEP!
'S JUST A COLD. SNIFF!
UH HUH. ARE YOU GOING TO TELL ME NOW JUST WHERE YOU'VE BEEN FOR THE LAST TWO MONTHS?
YOU KNOW WHERE I'VE BEEN... CANADA.
COME ON, KATCHOO, BE STRAIGHT WITH ME, OK? WHAT WAS SO IMPORTANT YOU'D UP AND LEAVE LIKE THAT AND NOT TELL ME?
I TOLD YOU, FRANCIE, I WENT TO SEE AN OLD FRIEND... THAT'S ALL. DON'T MAKE A BIG DEAL OUT OF THIS, OKAY?
DON'T MAKE A BIG DEAL OF IT?! MY BEST FRIEND TAKES OFF FOR CANADA WITH OUT SO MUCH AS GOODBYE, DOESN'T TELL ME WHAT'S GOING ON OR WHEN SHE'S COMING BACK... JUST LEAVES ME HERE, WORRIED SICK FOR TWO MONTHS... TWO WHOLE MONTHS!! NO BIG DEAL?!! UH UH! THAT WON'T CUT IT!
LOOK, CAN WE TALK ABOUT THIS LATER? I'M REALLY TIRED, I HAVEN'T HAD A THING TO EAT ALL DAY...
UH... Y'KNOW, I'M KINDA' HUNGRY MYSELF! WHAT SAY WE GO FIND A DINER .... OR SOMETHING...
OK... I'LL WAIT. BUT YOU OWE ME AN EXPLANATION.
YES, MOTHER.

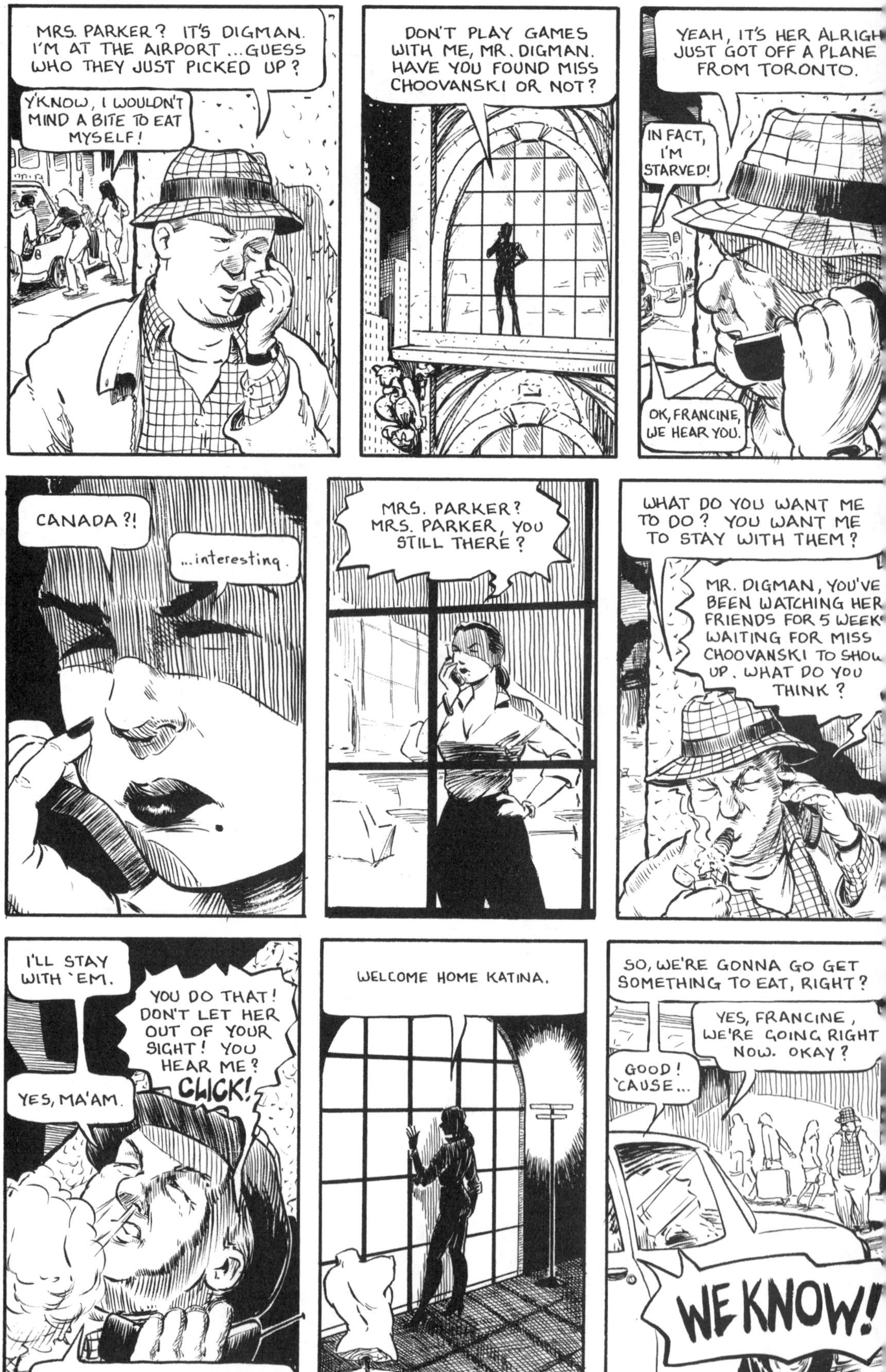
MRS. PARKER? IT'S DIGMAN. I'M AT THE AIRPORT ...GUESS WHO THEY JUST PICKED UP?
Y'KNOW, I WOULDN'T MIND A BITE TO EAT MYSELF!
DON'T PLAY GAMES WITH ME, MR. DIGMAN. HAVE YOU FOUND MISS CHOOVANSKI OR NOT?
YEAH, IT'S HER ALRIGH
JUST GOT OFF A PLANE FROM TORONTO.
IN FACT, I'M STARVED!
OK, FRANCINE, WE HEAR YOU.
CANADA?!
...interesting.
MRS. PARKER? MRS. PARKER, YOU STILL THERE?
WHAT DO YOU WANT ME TO DO? YOU WANT ME TO STAY WITH THEM?
MR. DIGMAN, YOU'VE BEEN WATCHING HER FRIENDS FOR 5 WEEK WAITING FOR MISS CHOOVANSKI TO SHOW UP. WHAT DO YOU THINK?
I'LL STAY WITH 'EM.
YOU DO THAT! DON'T LET HER OUT OF YOUR SIGHT! YOU HEAR ME?
CLICK!
YES, MA'AM.
LOVE YOU TOO... YA WITCH!
WELCOME HOME KATINA.
SO, WE'RE GONNA GO GET SOMETHING TO EAT, RIGHT?
YES, FRANCINE, WE'RE GOING RIGHT NOW. OKAY?
GOOD! 'CAUSE...
WE KNOW!

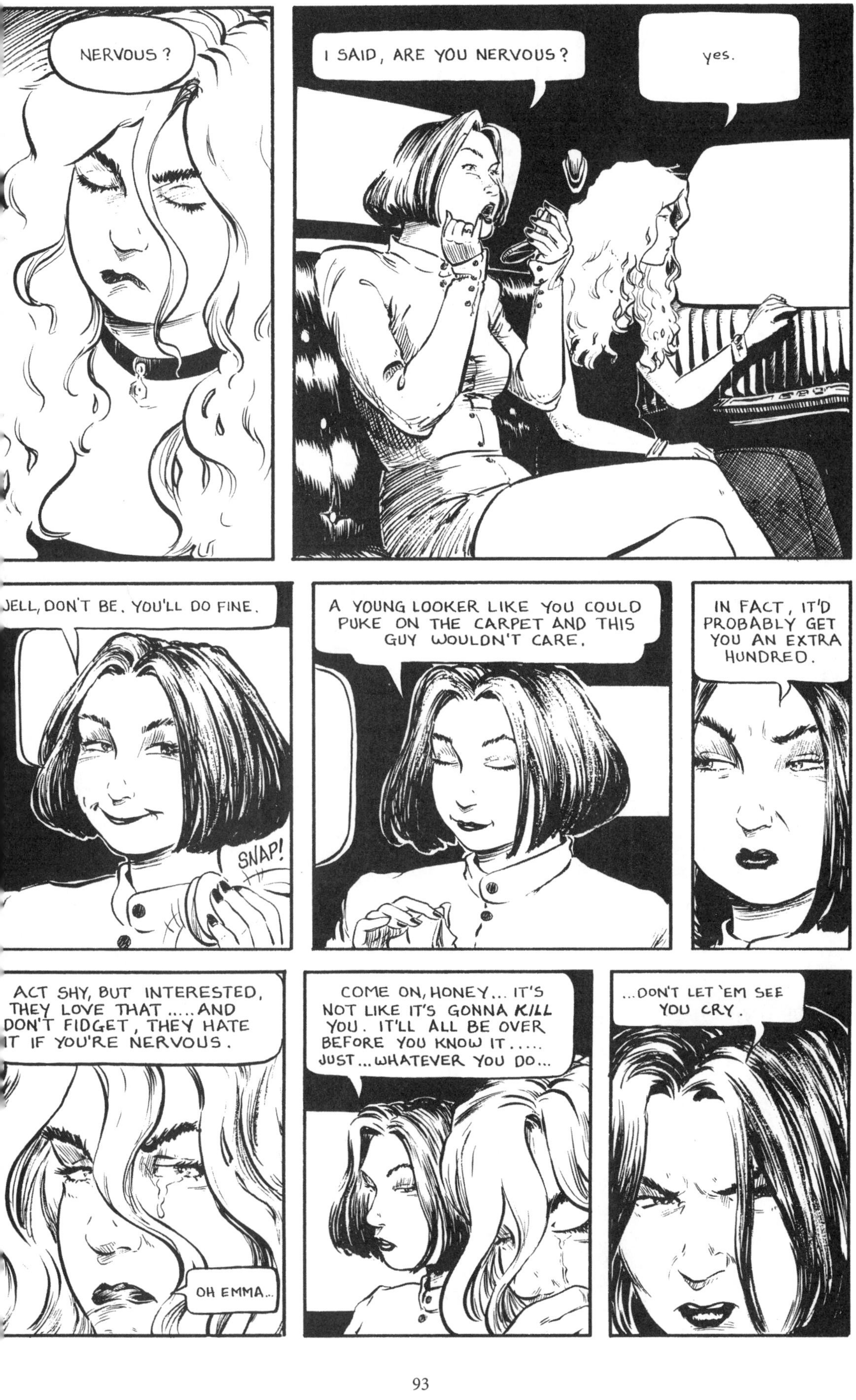
NERVOUS ?
I SAID, ARE YOU NERVOUS ?
yes.
WELL, DON'T BE. YOU'LL DO FINE.
SNAP!
A YOUNG LOOKER LIKE YOU COULD PUKE ON THE CARPET AND THIS GUY WOULDN'T CARE.
IN FACT, IT'D PROBABLY GET YOU AN EXTRA HUNDRED.
ACT SHY, BUT INTERESTED, THEY LOVE THAT .....AND DON'T FIDGET, THEY HATE IT IF YOU'RE NERVOUS.
OH EMMA...
COME ON, HONEY... IT'S NOT LIKE IT'S GONNA *KILL* YOU. IT'LL ALL BE OVER BEFORE YOU KNOW IT..... JUST... WHATEVER YOU DO...
...DON'T LET 'EM SEE YOU CRY.

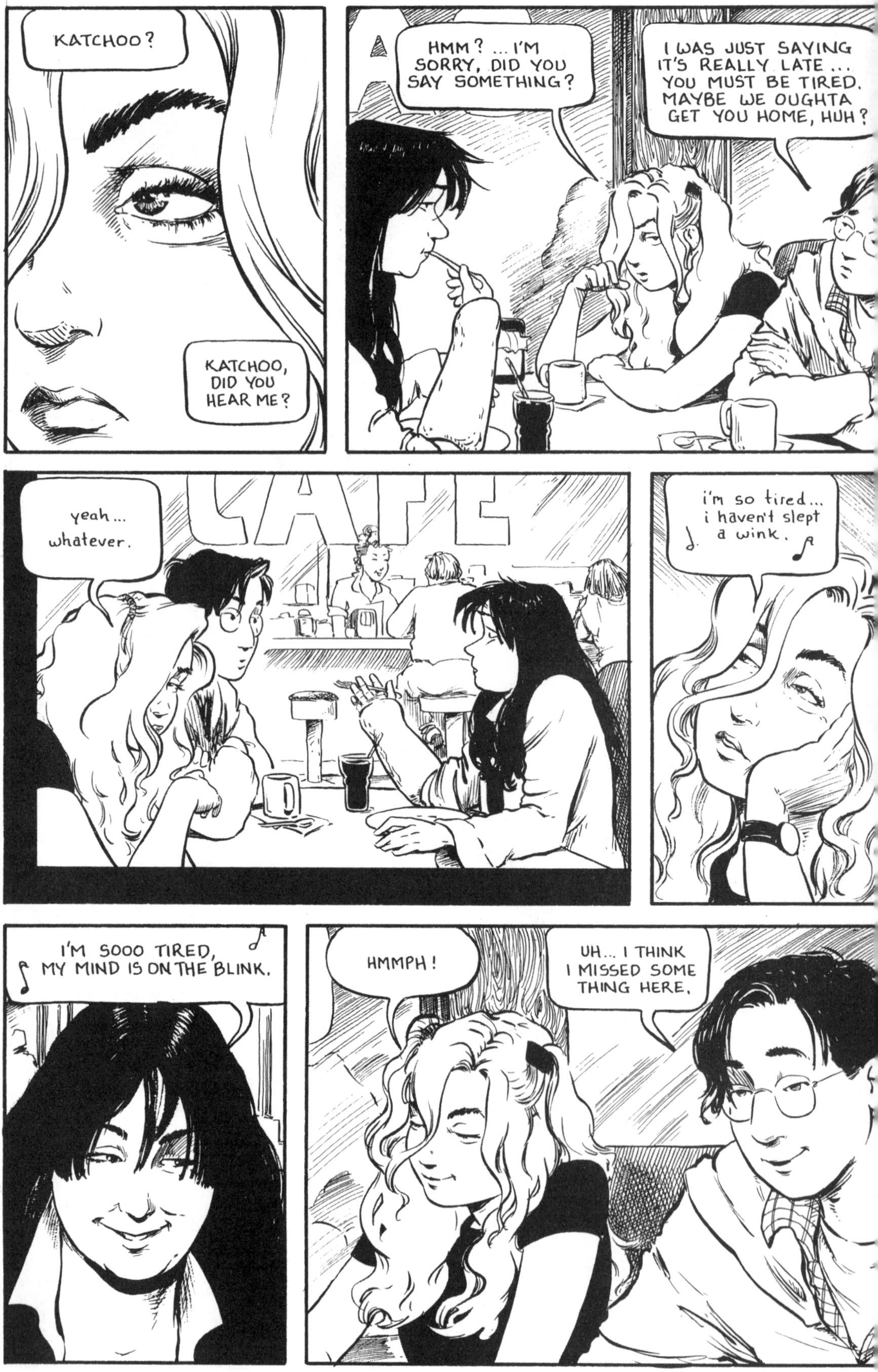

KATCHOO?
KATCHOO, DID YOU HEAR ME?
HMM? ... I'M SORRY, DID YOU SAY SOMETHING?
I WAS JUST SAYING IT'S REALLY LATE ... YOU MUST BE TIRED. MAYBE WE OUGHTA GET YOU HOME, HUH?
yeah ... whatever.
i'm so tired... i haven't slept a wink.
I'M SOOO TIRED, MY MIND IS ON THE BLINK.
HMMPH!
UH... I THINK I MISSED SOME THING HERE.

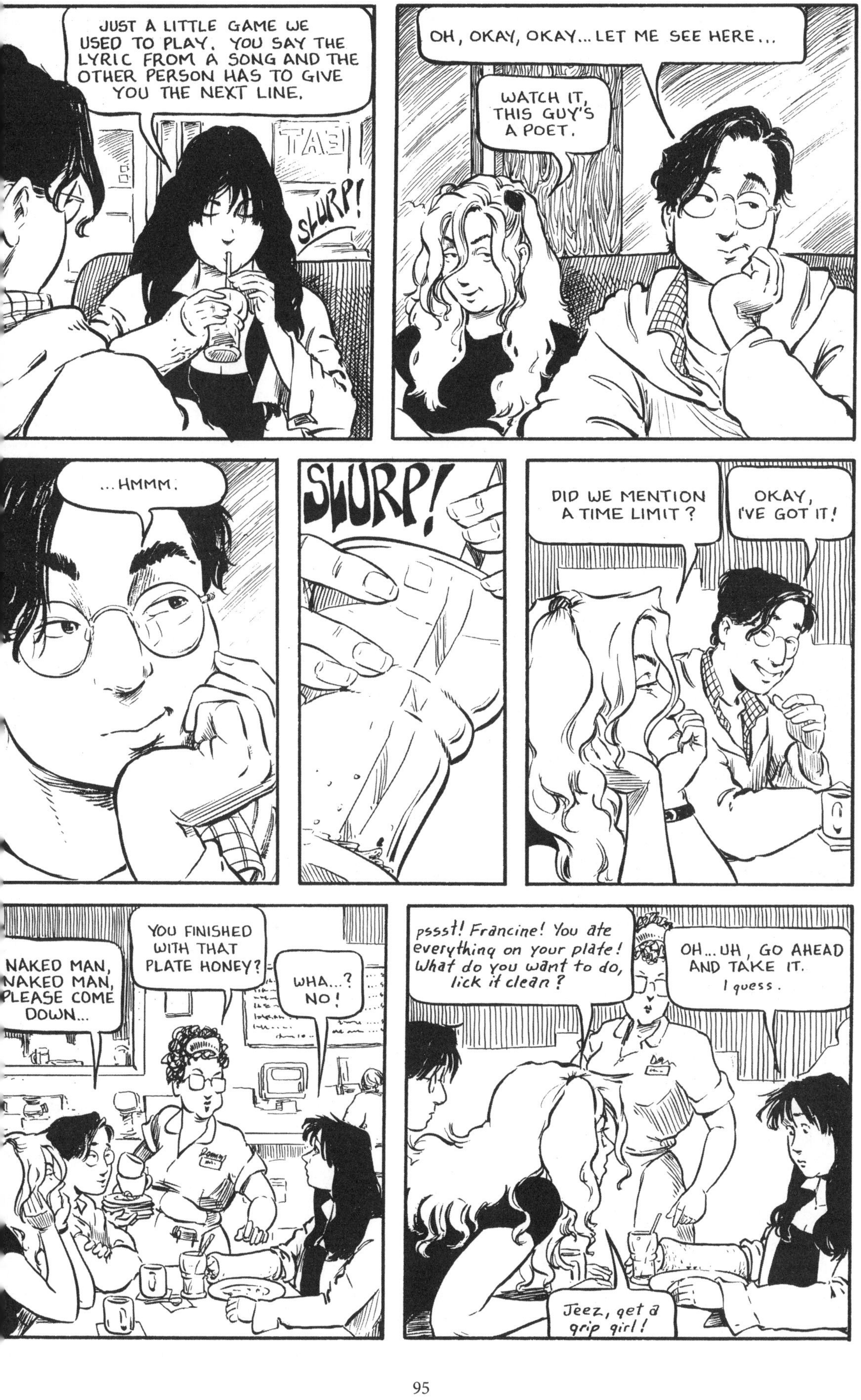
JUST A LITTLE GAME WE USED TO PLAY. YOU SAY THE LYRIC FROM A SONG AND THE OTHER PERSON HAS TO GIVE YOU THE NEXT LINE.
TAB
SLURP!
OH, OKAY, OKAY... LET ME SEE HERE...
WATCH IT, THIS GUY'S A POET.
... HMMM.
SLURP!
DID WE MENTION A TIME LIMIT?
OKAY, I'VE GOT IT!
NAKED MAN, NAKED MAN, PLEASE COME DOWN...
YOU FINISHED WITH THAT PLATE HONEY?
WHA...? NO!
pssst! Francine! You ate everything on your plate! What do you want to do, lick it clean?
OH... UH, GO AHEAD AND TAKE IT.
I guess.
Jeez, get a grip girl!

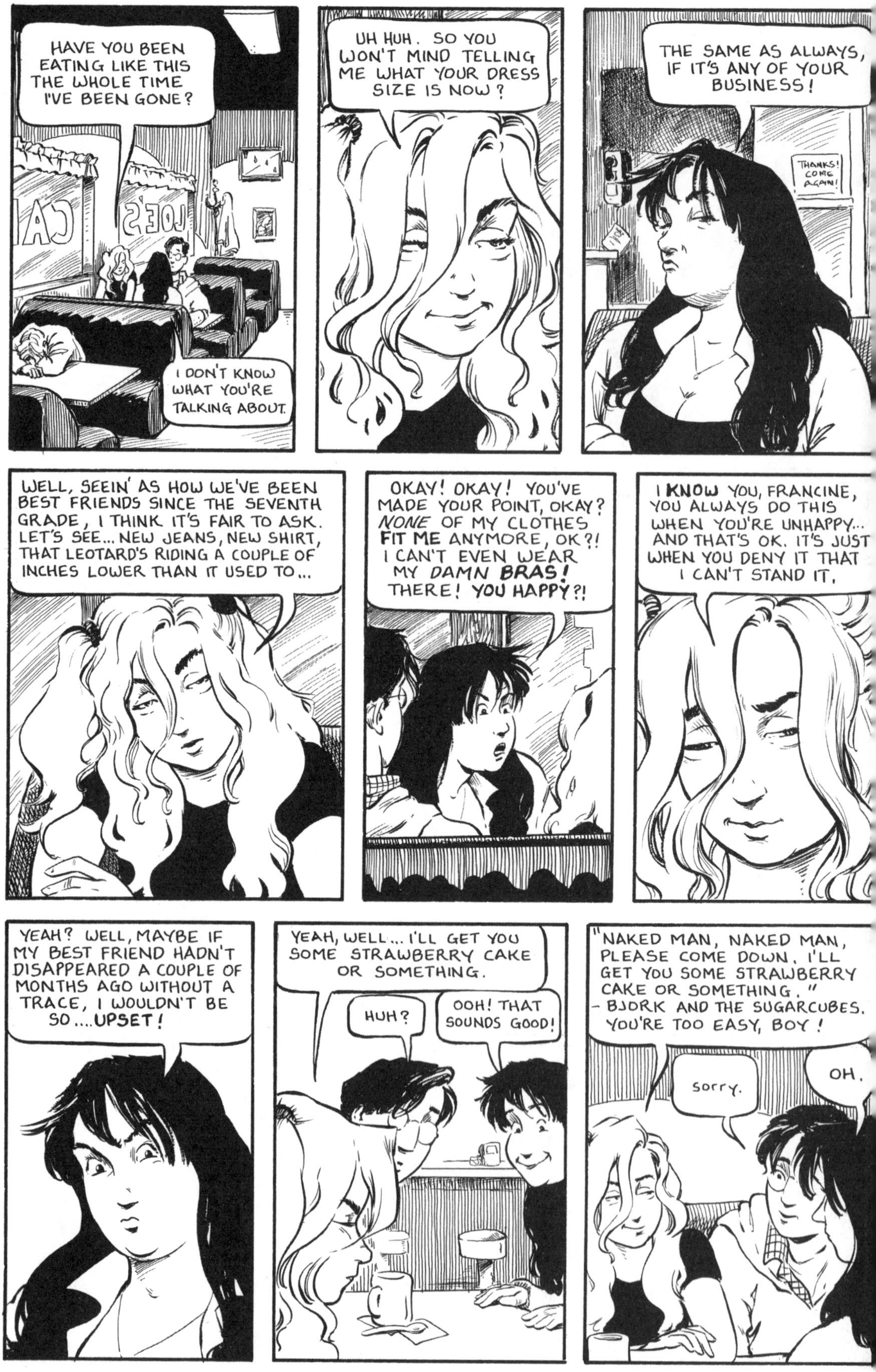
HAVE YOU BEEN EATING LIKE THIS THE WHOLE TIME I'VE BEEN GONE?
LOE'S CA
I DON'T KNOW WHAT YOU'RE TALKING ABOUT.
UH HUH. SO YOU WON'T MIND TELLING ME WHAT YOUR DRESS SIZE IS NOW?
THE SAME AS ALWAYS, IF IT'S ANY OF YOUR BUSINESS!
THANKS! COME AGAIN!
WELL, SEEIN' AS HOW WE'VE BEEN BEST FRIENDS SINCE THE SEVENTH GRADE, I THINK IT'S FAIR TO ASK. LET'S SEE... NEW JEANS, NEW SHIRT, THAT LEOTARD'S RIDING A COUPLE OF INCHES LOWER THAN IT USED TO...
OKAY! OKAY! YOU'VE MADE YOUR POINT, OKAY? NONE OF MY CLOTHES FIT ME ANYMORE, OK?! I CAN'T EVEN WEAR MY DAMN BRAS! THERE! YOU HAPPY?!
I KNOW YOU, FRANCINE, YOU ALWAYS DO THIS WHEN YOU'RE UNHAPPY... AND THAT'S OK. IT'S JUST WHEN YOU DENY IT THAT I CAN'T STAND IT.
YEAH? WELL, MAYBE IF MY BEST FRIEND HADN'T DISAPPEARED A COUPLE OF MONTHS AGO WITHOUT A TRACE, I WOULDN'T BE SO....UPSET!
YEAH, WELL... I'LL GET YOU SOME STRAWBERRY CAKE OR SOMETHING.
HUH?
OOH! THAT SOUNDS GOOD!
"NAKED MAN, NAKED MAN, PLEASE COME DOWN. I'LL GET YOU SOME STRAWBERRY CAKE OR SOMETHING." - BJORK AND THE SUGARCUBES. YOU'RE TOO EASY, BOY!
sorry.
OH.

I SHOULD'VE PICKED SOMETHING REALLY OLD.

...sigh

LIKE A TONY BENNETT SONG.

TRUST ME, SHE KNOWS 'EM ALL.

HAM AND EGGS .....
BACON AND EGGS.....
PORK BUTT AND EGGS....
PIG EARS AND EGGS ...
SNOUT OF PIG AND EGGS..
KNEE OF PORK AND EGGS..
PORK FAT AND EGG YOLK
PEPTO BISMOL & EGG.

...HEN THE WHITE QUEEN'S TALKING BACKWARDS...

AND THE RED QUEEN'S ON HER HEAD...

UH...

WELL?

THINK MAN, THINK!

OH JEEZ! I KNOW THIS! ...mumble mumble mumble...

OH! REMEMBER WHAT THE DOOR-MOUSE SAID?

FEED YOUR HEAD!

OH MAN! YOU'RE DIGGING WAY TOO DEEP IN THE PAST FOR ME!

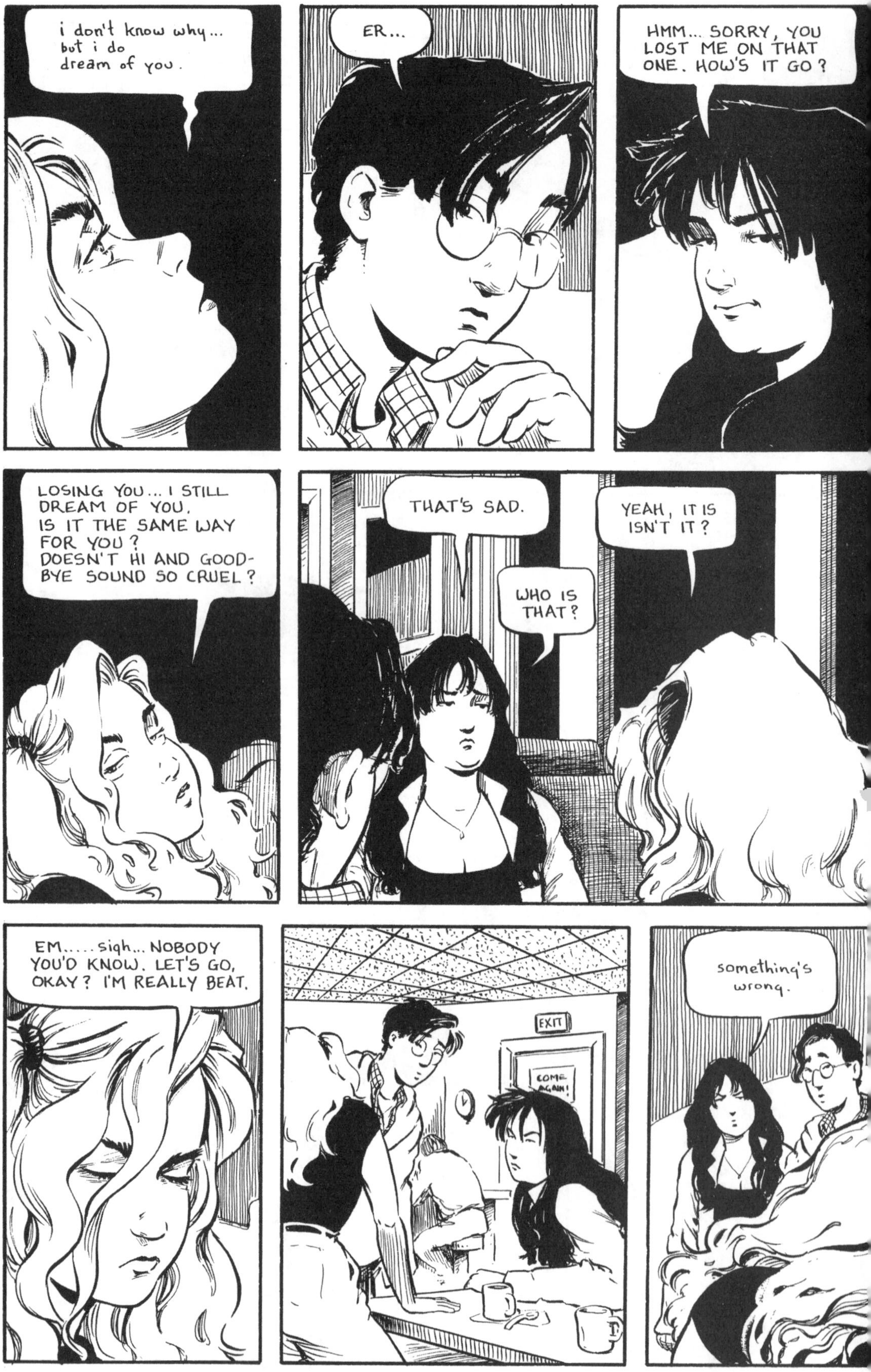
i don't know why...
but i do
dream of you.
ER...
HMM... SORRY, YOU LOST ME ON THAT ONE. HOW'S IT GO?
LOSING YOU... I STILL DREAM OF YOU. IS IT THE SAME WAY FOR YOU? DOESN'T HI AND GOOD-BYE SOUND SO CRUEL?
THAT'S SAD.
WHO IS THAT?
YEAH, IT IS ISN'T IT?
EM.....sigh... NOBODY YOU'D KNOW. LET'S GO, OKAY? I'M REALLY BEAT.
EXIT
COME AGAIN!
something's wrong.

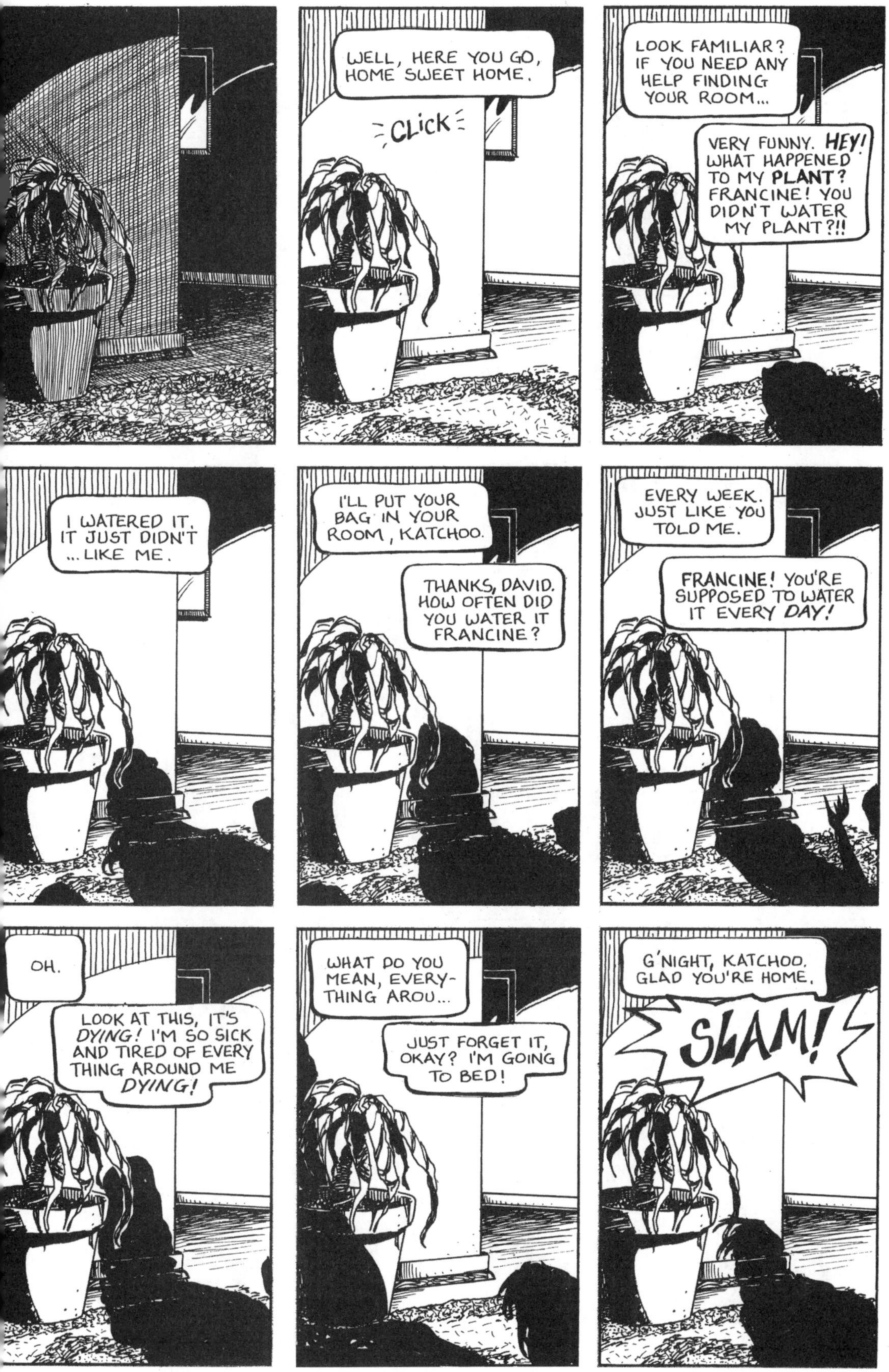
WELL, HERE YOU GO, HOME SWEET HOME.
CLICK
LOOK FAMILIAR? IF YOU NEED ANY HELP FINDING YOUR ROOM...
VERY FUNNY. HEY! WHAT HAPPENED TO MY PLANT? FRANCINE! YOU DIDN'T WATER MY PLANT?!!
I WATERED IT. IT JUST DIDN'T ...LIKE ME.
I'LL PUT YOUR BAG IN YOUR ROOM, KATCHOO.
THANKS, DAVID. HOW OFTEN DID YOU WATER IT FRANCINE?
EVERY WEEK. JUST LIKE YOU TOLD ME.
FRANCINE! YOU'RE SUPPOSED TO WATER IT EVERY DAY!
OH.
LOOK AT THIS, IT'S DYING! I'M SO SICK AND TIRED OF EVERY THING AROUND ME DYING!
WHAT DO YOU MEAN, EVERY-THING AROU...
JUST FORGET IT, OKAY? I'M GOING TO BED!
G'NIGHT, KATCHOO. GLAD YOU'RE HOME.
SLAM!

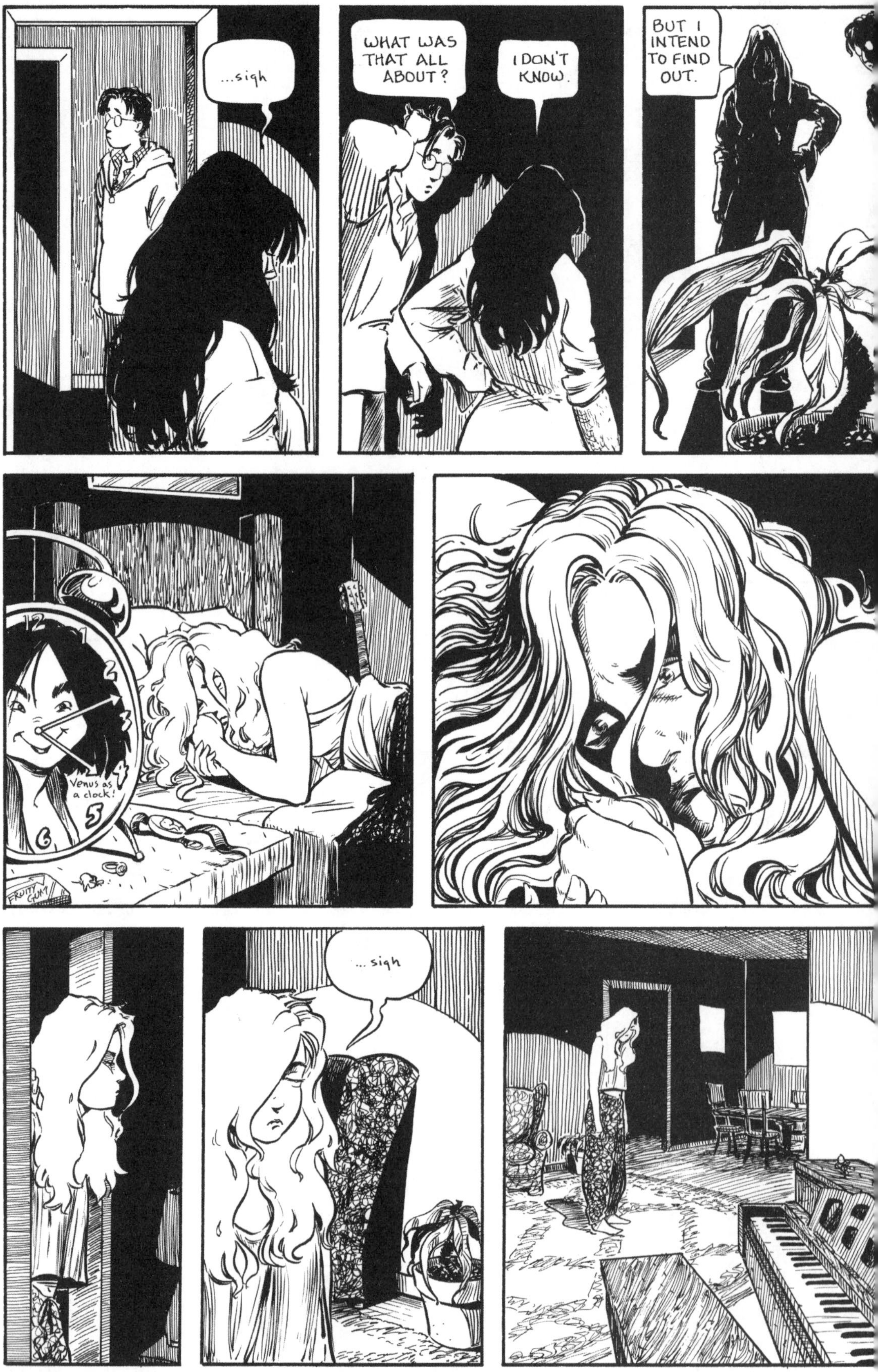
...sigh
WHAT WAS THAT ALL ABOUT?
I DON'T KNOW.
BUT I INTEND TO FIND OUT.
Venus as a clock!
FRUITY GUM
...sigh

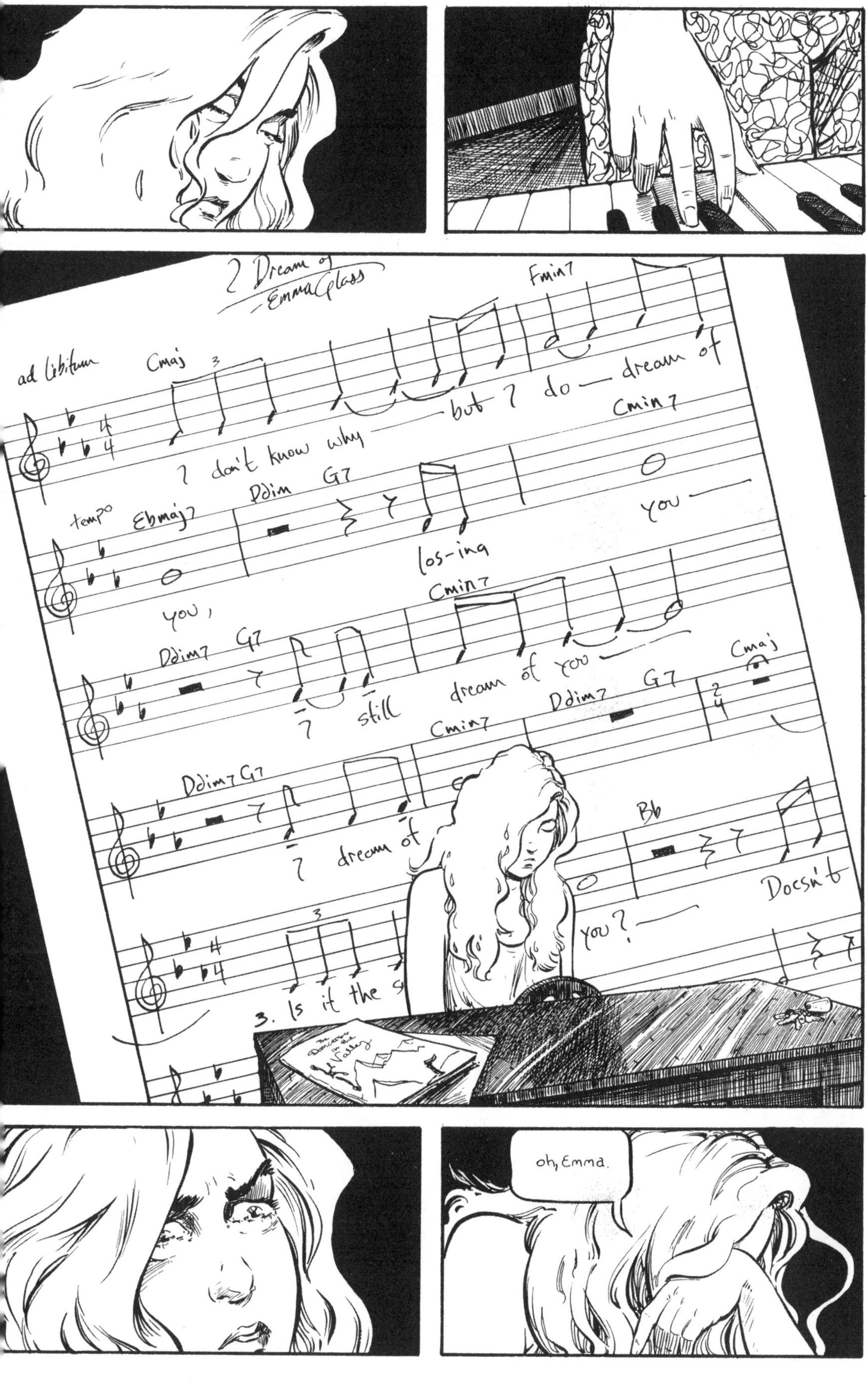
I Dream of
- Emma Glass
ad Libitum
Cmaj
Fmin7
I don't know why — but I do — dream of
Cmin7
tempo
Ebmaj7
Ddim G7
los-ing
you —
you,
Cmin7
Ddim7 G7
I still dream of you —
Cmaj
Cmin7
Ddim7 G7
Ddim7 G7
I dream of
Bb
Doesn't
you? —
3. Is it the
oh, Emma.

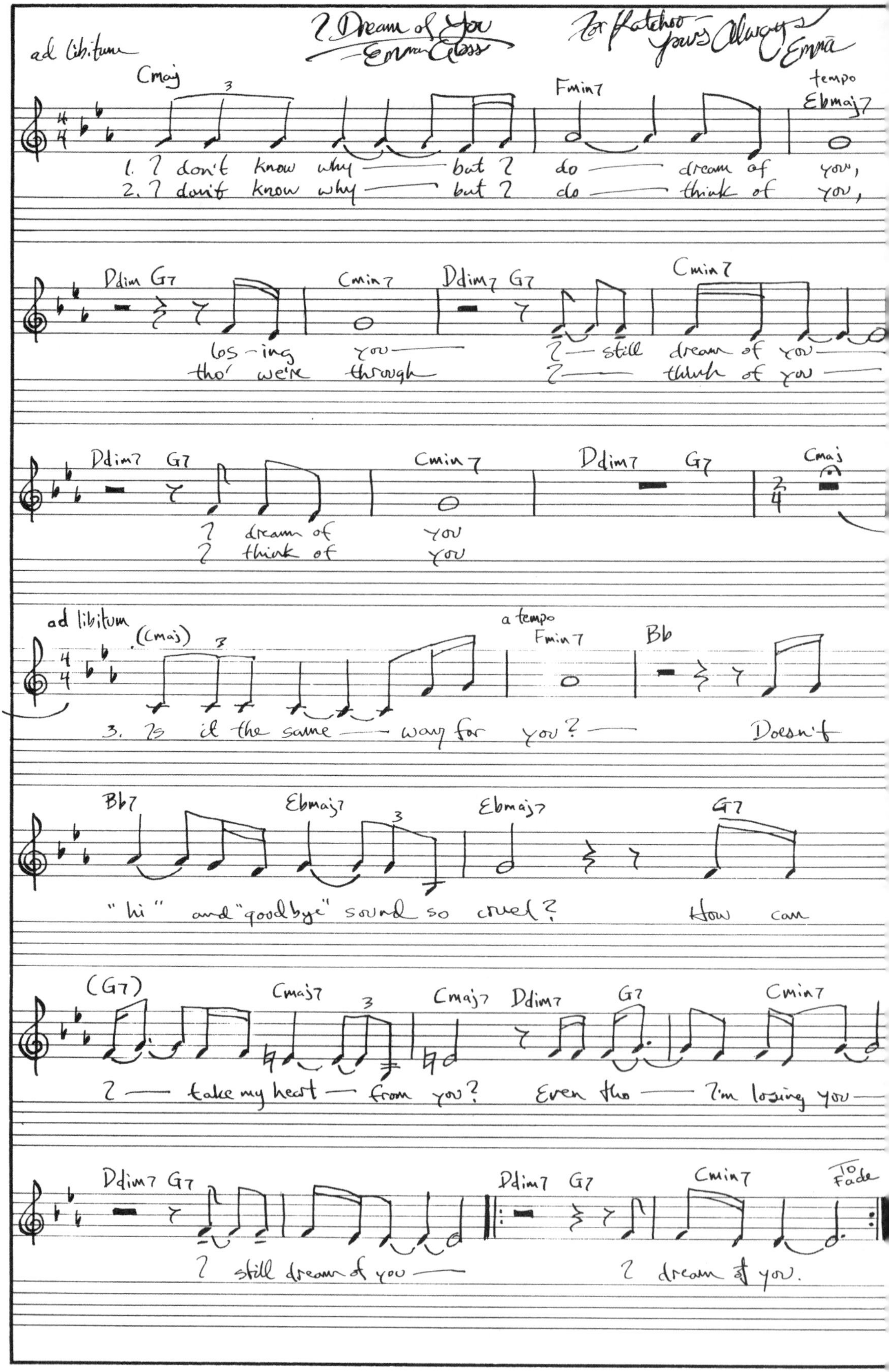
I Dream of You
Emma Gloss
For Klatchoo yours Always Emma
ad libitum
Cmaj
Fmin7
tempo
Ebmaj7
1. I don't know why but I do dream of you,
2. I don't know why but I do think of you,
Ddim G7
Cmin7
Ddim7 G7
Cmin7
los-ing you
tho' we're through
I still dream of you
I think of you
Ddim7 G7
Cmin7
Ddim7 G7
Cmaj
I dream of you
I think of you
ad libitum
(Cmaj)
a tempo
Fmin7
Bb
3. Is it the same way for you? Doesn't
Bb7
Ebmaj7
Ebmaj7
G7
"hi" and "goodbye" sound so cruel? How can
(G7)
Cmaj7
Cmaj7
Ddim7
G7
Cmin7
I take my heart from you? Even tho I'm losing you
Ddim7 G7
Ddim7 G7
Cmin7
To Fade
I still dream of you
I dream of you.

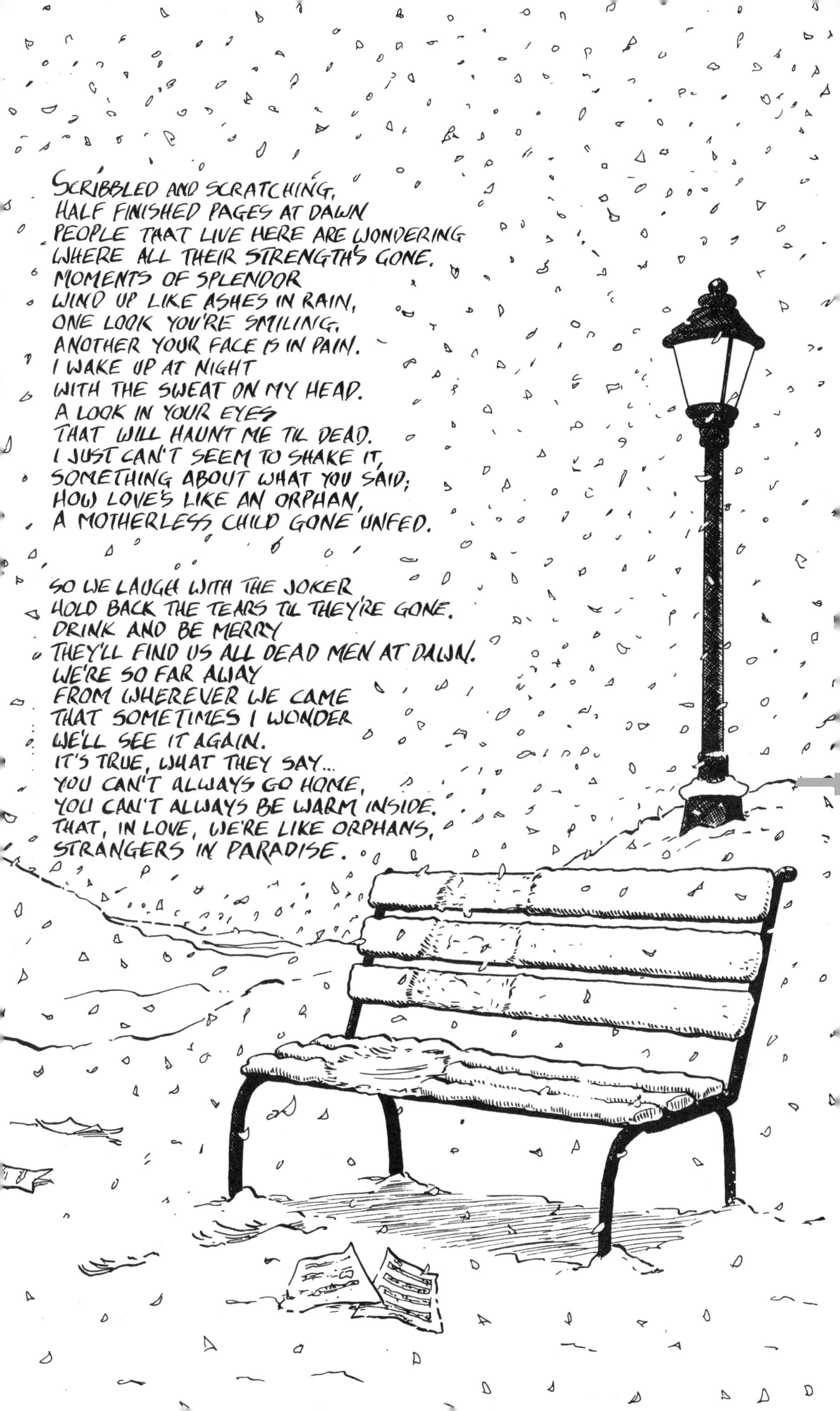
SCRIBBLED AND SCRATCHING,
HALF FINISHED PAGES AT DAWN
PEOPLE THAT LIVE HERE ARE WONDERING
WHERE ALL THEIR STRENGTH'S GONE.
MOMENTS OF SPLENDOR
WIND UP LIKE ASHES IN RAIN,
ONE LOOK YOU'RE SMILING,
ANOTHER YOUR FACE IS IN PAIN.
I WAKE UP AT NIGHT
WITH THE SWEAT ON MY HEAD.
A LOOK IN YOUR EYES
THAT WILL HAUNT ME TIL DEAD.
I JUST CAN'T SEEM TO SHAKE IT,
SOMETHING ABOUT WHAT YOU SAID;
HOW LOVE'S LIKE AN ORPHAN,
A MOTHERLESS CHILD GONE UNFED.
SO WE LAUGH WITH THE JOKER
HOLD BACK THE TEARS TIL THEY'RE GONE.
DRINK AND BE MERRY
THEY'LL FIND US ALL DEAD MEN AT DAWN.
WE'RE SO FAR AWAY
FROM WHEREVER WE CAME
THAT SOMETIMES I WONDER
WE'LL SEE IT AGAIN.
IT'S TRUE, WHAT THEY SAY...
YOU CAN'T ALWAYS GO HOME,
YOU CAN'T ALWAYS BE WARM INSIDE.
THAT, IN LOVE, WE'RE LIKE ORPHANS,
STRANGERS IN PARADISE.

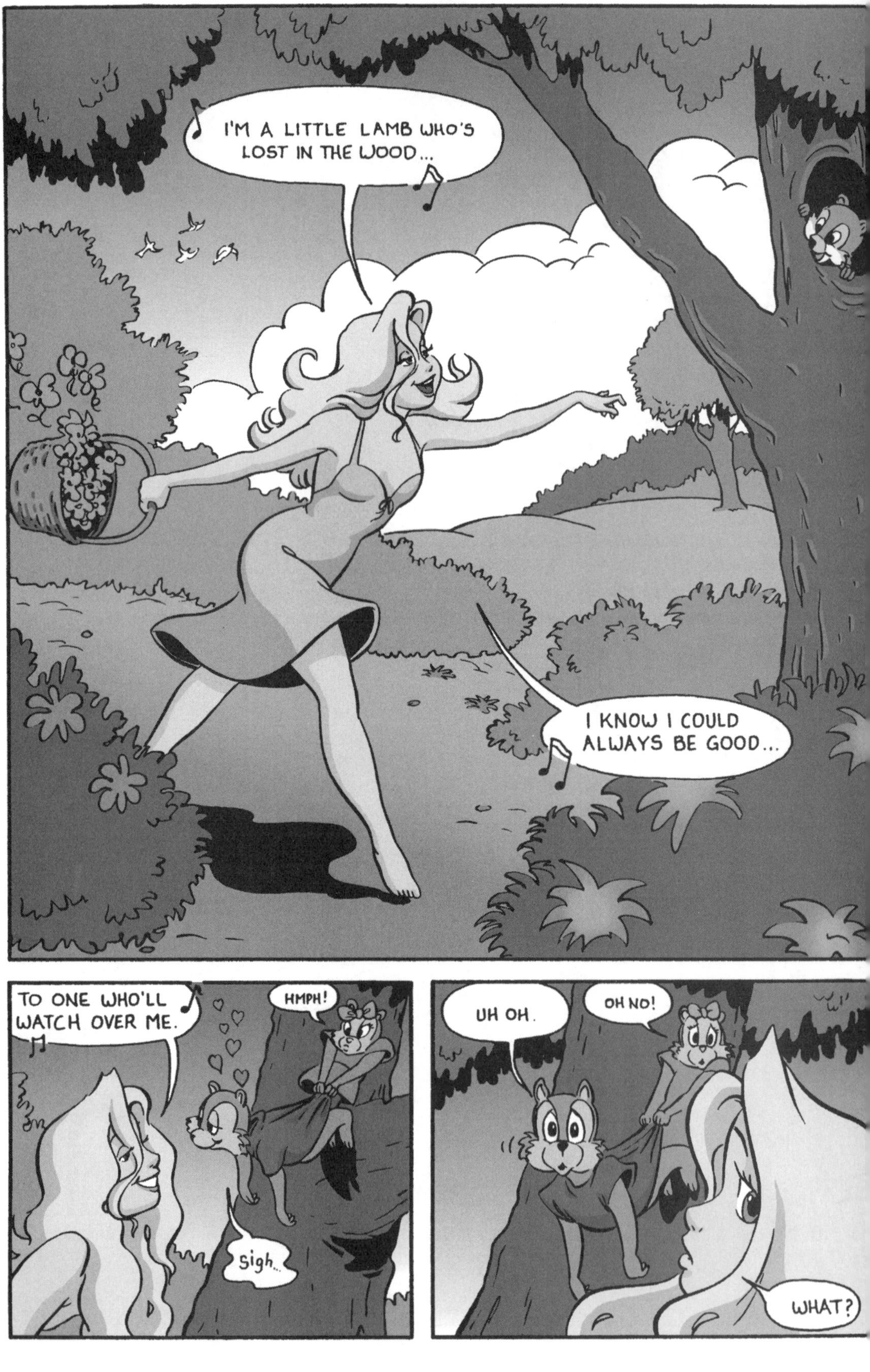
I'M A LITTLE LAMB WHO'S LOST IN THE WOOD...
I KNOW I COULD ALWAYS BE GOOD...
TO ONE WHO'LL WATCH OVER ME.
HMPH!
Sigh..
UH OH.
OH NO!
WHAT?

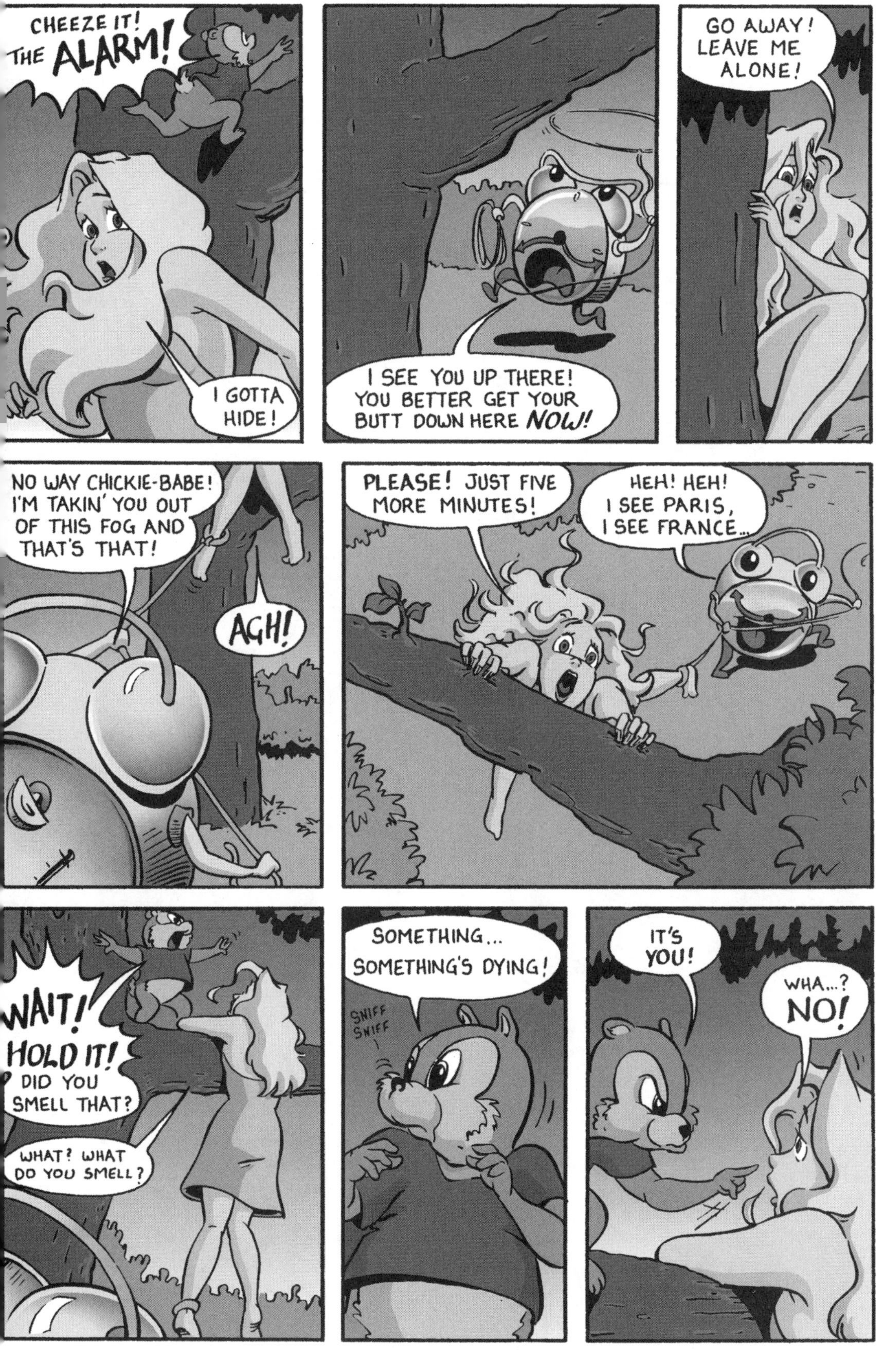
CHEEZE IT! THE ALARM!
I GOTTA HIDE!
I SEE YOU UP THERE! YOU BETTER GET YOUR BUTT DOWN HERE NOW!
GO AWAY! LEAVE ME ALONE!
NO WAY CHICKIE-BABE! I'M TAKIN' YOU OUT OF THIS FOG AND THAT'S THAT!
AGH!
PLEASE! JUST FIVE MORE MINUTES!
HEH! HEH! I SEE PARIS, I SEE FRANCE...
WAIT! HOLD IT! DID YOU SMELL THAT?
WHAT? WHAT DO YOU SMELL?
SOMETHING... SOMETHING'S DYING!
SNIFF SNIFF
IT'S YOU!
WHA...? NO!

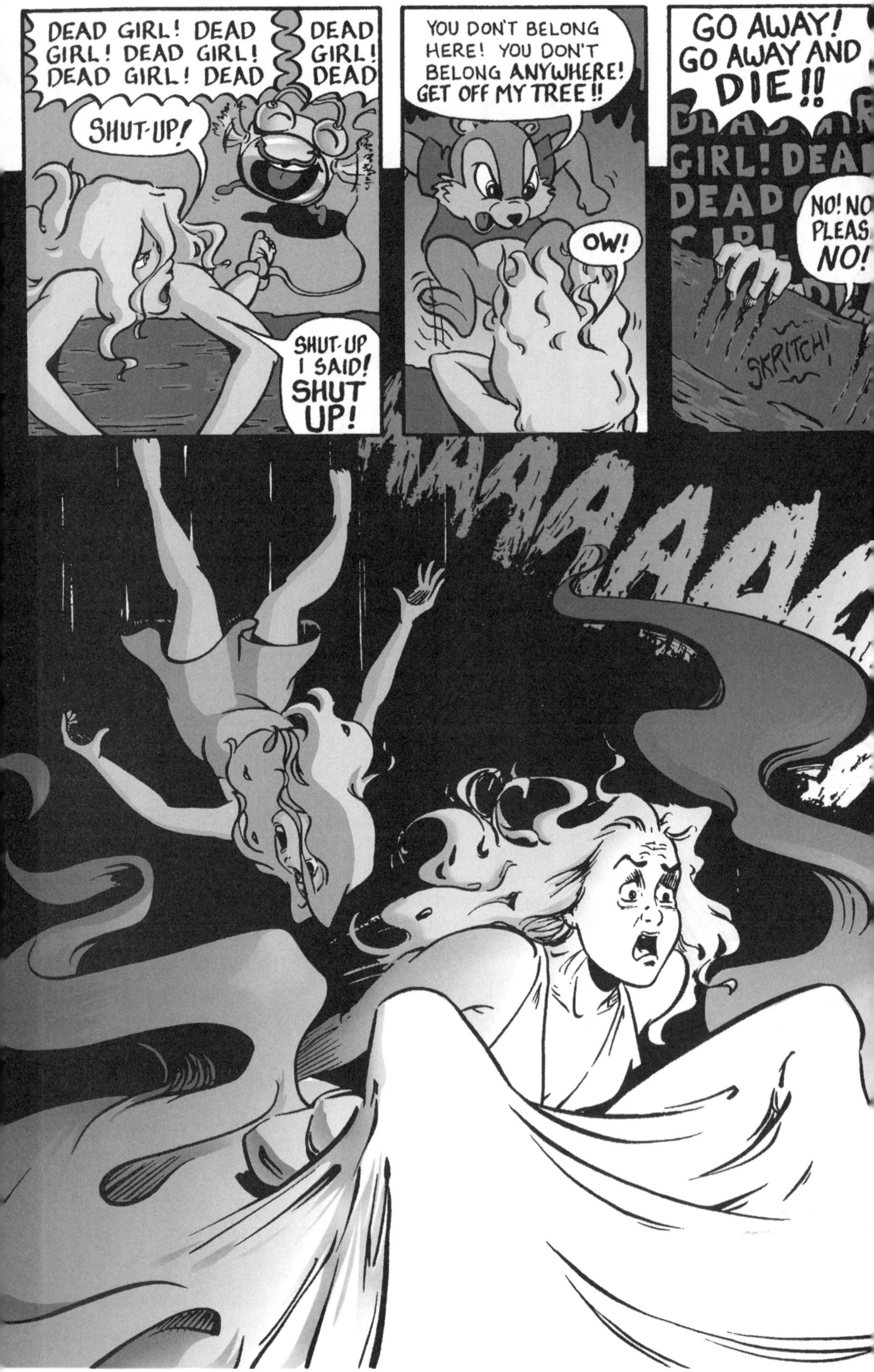
DEAD GIRL! DEAD GIRL! DEAD GIRL! DEAD GIRL! DEAD
DEAD GIRL! DEAD
SHUT-UP!
SHUT-UP I SAID! SHUT UP!
YOU DON'T BELONG HERE! YOU DON'T BELONG ANYWHERE! GET OFF MY TREE!!
OW!
GO AWAY! GO AWAY AND DIE!!
GIRL! DEA
DEAD
NO! NO PLEAS NO!
SKRITCH!

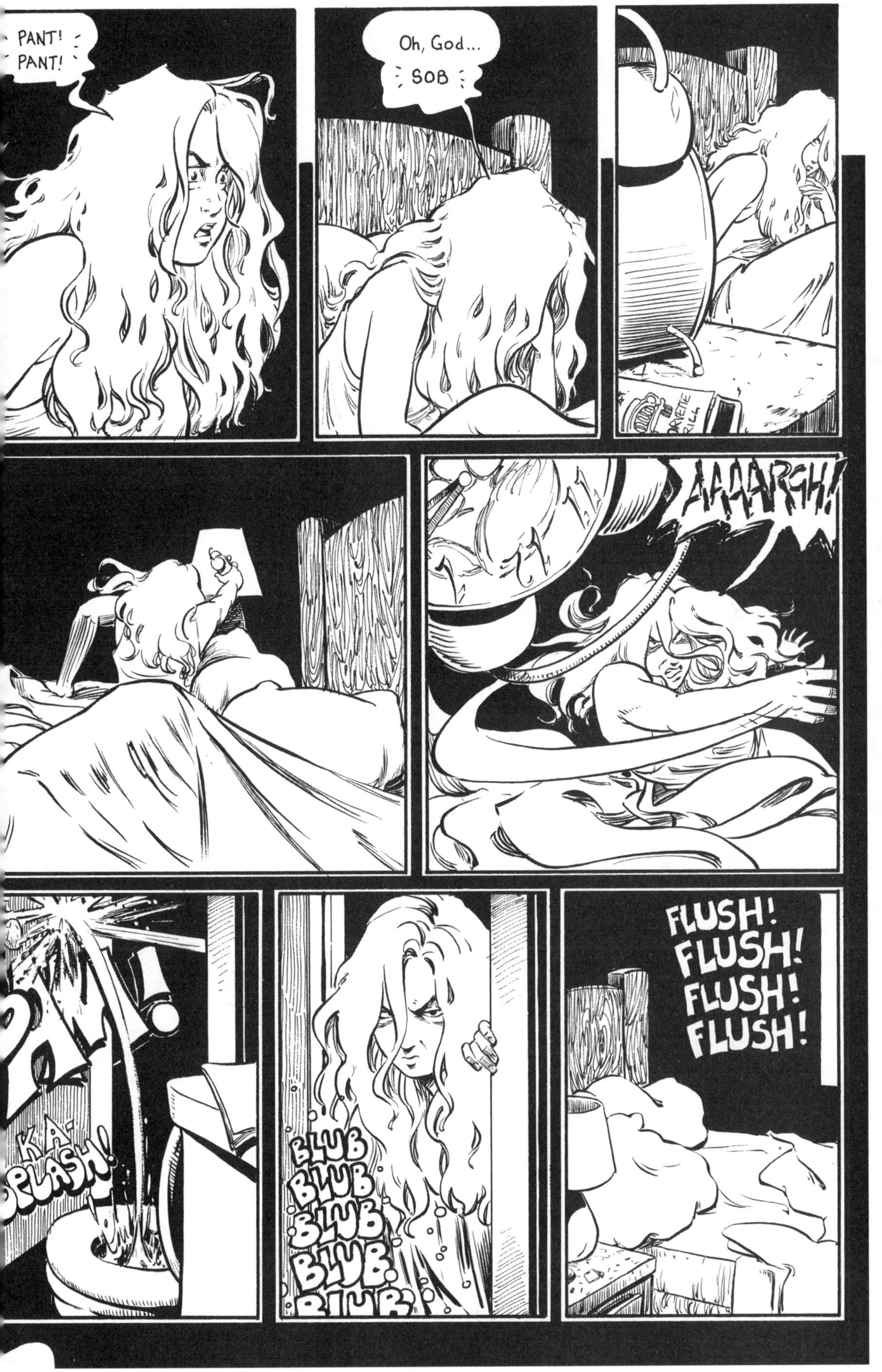
PANT! PANT!
Oh, God... SOB
AAAARGH!
KA-SPLASH!
BLUB BLUB BLUB BLUB
FLUSH! FLUSH! FLUSH! FLUSH!

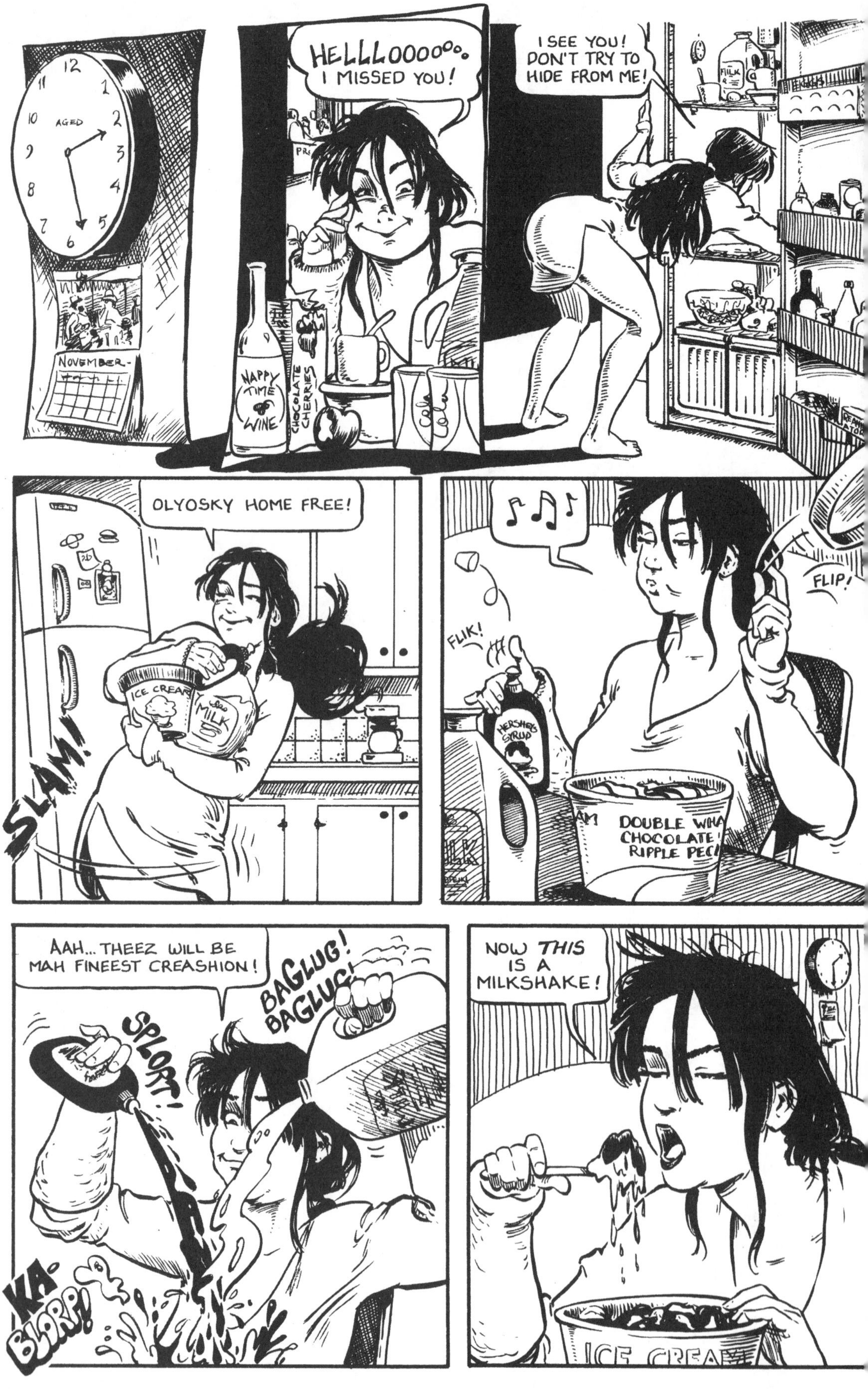

AGED
NOVEMBER
HELLLOOOOooo
I MISSED YOU!
NAPPY TIME WINE
CHOCOLATE CHERRIES
I SEE YOU! DON'T TRY TO HIDE FROM ME!
OLYOSKY HOME FREE!
ICE CREAM
MILK
SLAM!
FLIK!
FLIP!
HERSHEY'S SYRUP
DOUBLE WHA
CHOCOLATE
RIPPLE PEC
AAH... THEEZ WILL BE MAH FINEEST CREASHION!
BAGLUG! BAGLUG!
SPLORT!
KA-BLORP!
NOW THIS IS A MILKSHAKE!
ICE CREAM

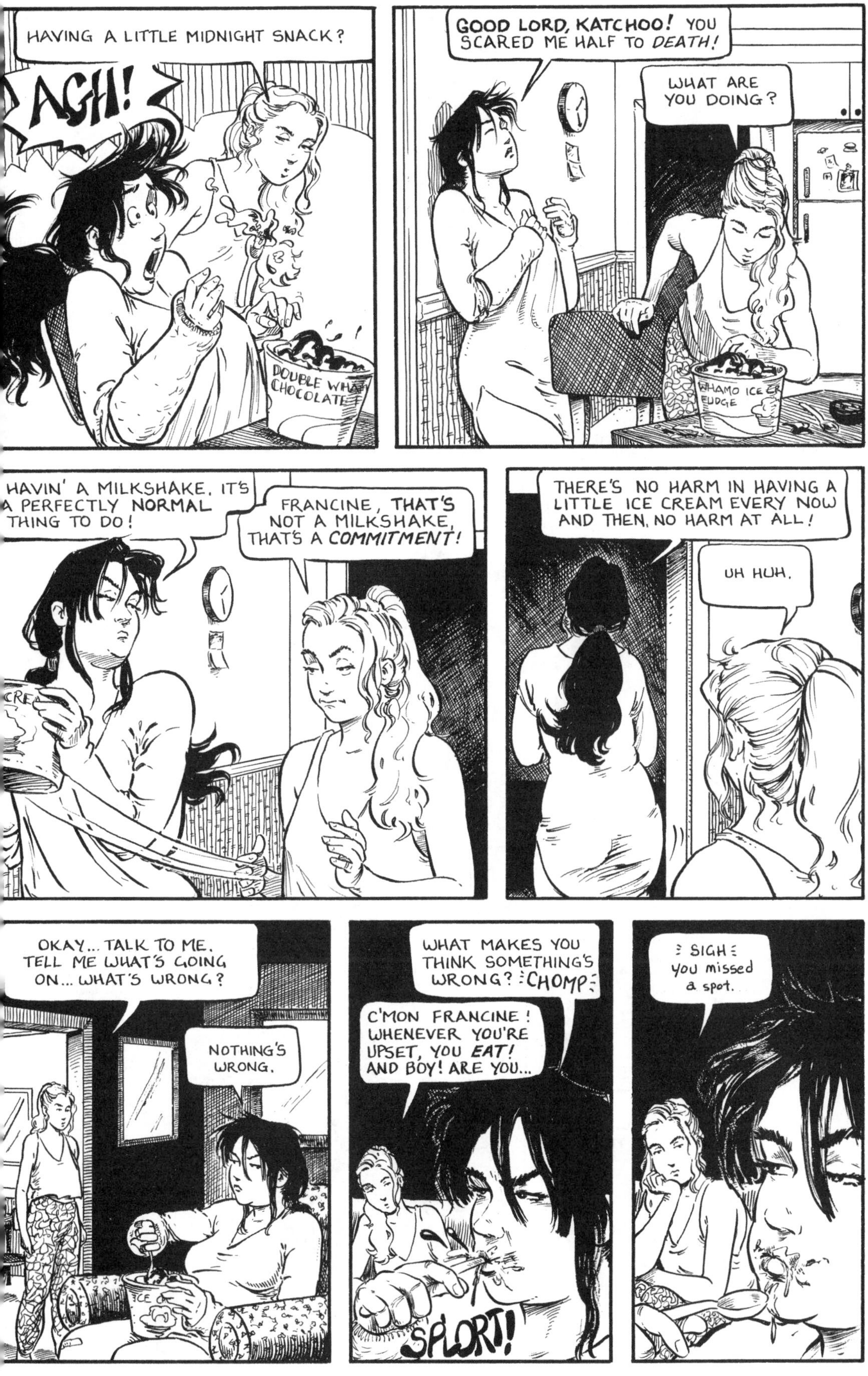
HAVING A LITTLE MIDNIGHT SNACK?
AGH!
DOUBLE WHA
CHOCOLATE
GOOD LORD, KATCHOO! YOU SCARED ME HALF TO DEATH!
WHAT ARE YOU DOING?
WHAMO ICE CR
FUDGE
HAVIN' A MILKSHAKE. IT'S A PERFECTLY NORMAL THING TO DO!
FRANCINE, THAT'S NOT A MILKSHAKE, THAT'S A COMMITMENT!
THERE'S NO HARM IN HAVING A LITTLE ICE CREAM EVERY NOW AND THEN, NO HARM AT ALL!
UH HUH.
OKAY... TALK TO ME. TELL ME WHAT'S GOING ON... WHAT'S WRONG?
NOTHING'S WRONG.
WHAT MAKES YOU THINK SOMETHING'S WRONG? CHOMP
C'MON FRANCINE! WHENEVER YOU'RE UPSET, YOU EAT! AND BOY! ARE YOU...
SPLORT!
SIGH
you missed a spot.

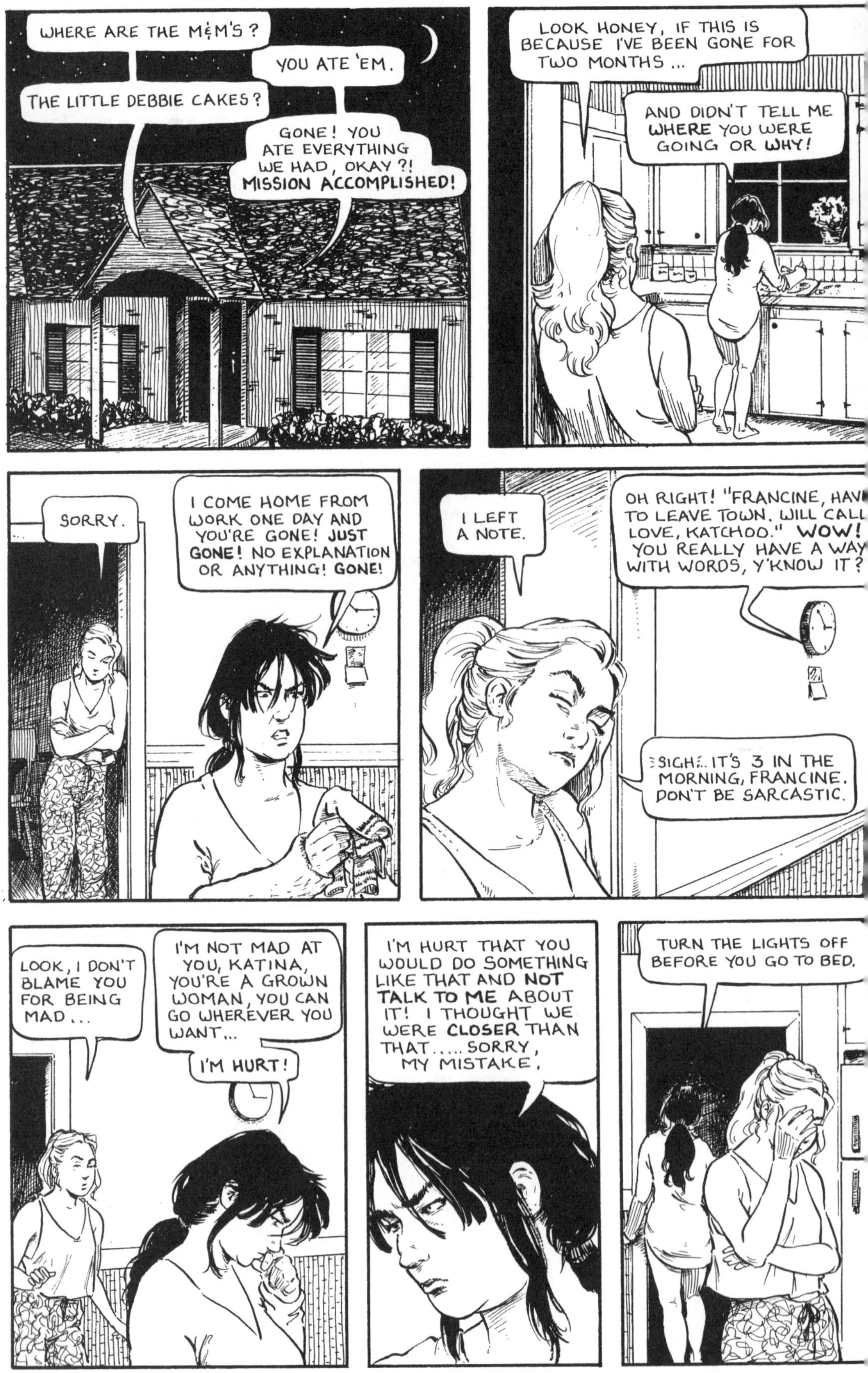
WHERE ARE THE M&M'S?
YOU ATE 'EM.
THE LITTLE DEBBIE CAKES?
GONE! YOU ATE EVERYTHING WE HAD, OKAY?! MISSION ACCOMPLISHED!
LOOK HONEY, IF THIS IS BECAUSE I'VE BEEN GONE FOR TWO MONTHS...
AND DIDN'T TELL ME WHERE YOU WERE GOING OR WHY!
SORRY.
I COME HOME FROM WORK ONE DAY AND YOU'RE GONE! JUST GONE! NO EXPLANATION OR ANYTHING! GONE!
I LEFT A NOTE.
OH RIGHT! "FRANCINE, HAV TO LEAVE TOWN. WILL CALL LOVE, KATCHOO." WOW! YOU REALLY HAVE A WAY WITH WORDS, Y'KNOW IT?
SIGH... IT'S 3 IN THE MORNING, FRANCINE. DON'T BE SARCASTIC.
LOOK, I DON'T BLAME YOU FOR BEING MAD...
I'M NOT MAD AT YOU, KATINA, YOU'RE A GROWN WOMAN, YOU CAN GO WHEREVER YOU WANT...
I'M HURT!
I'M HURT THAT YOU WOULD DO SOMETHING LIKE THAT AND NOT TALK TO ME ABOUT IT! I THOUGHT WE WERE CLOSER THAN THAT..... SORRY, MY MISTAKE.
TURN THE LIGHTS OFF BEFORE YOU GO TO BED.

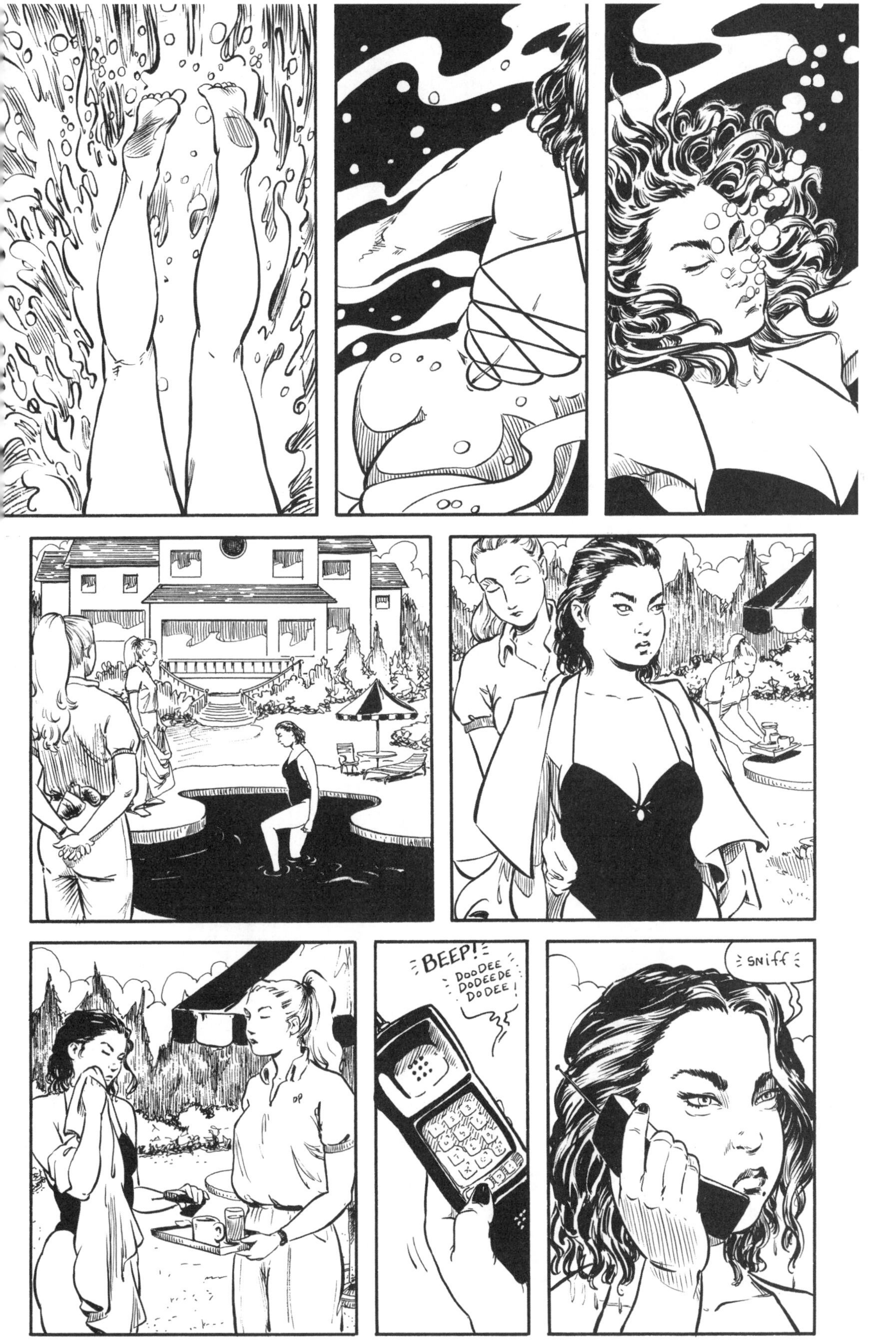
BEEP!
DOODEE DODEEDE DODEE!
SNIFF

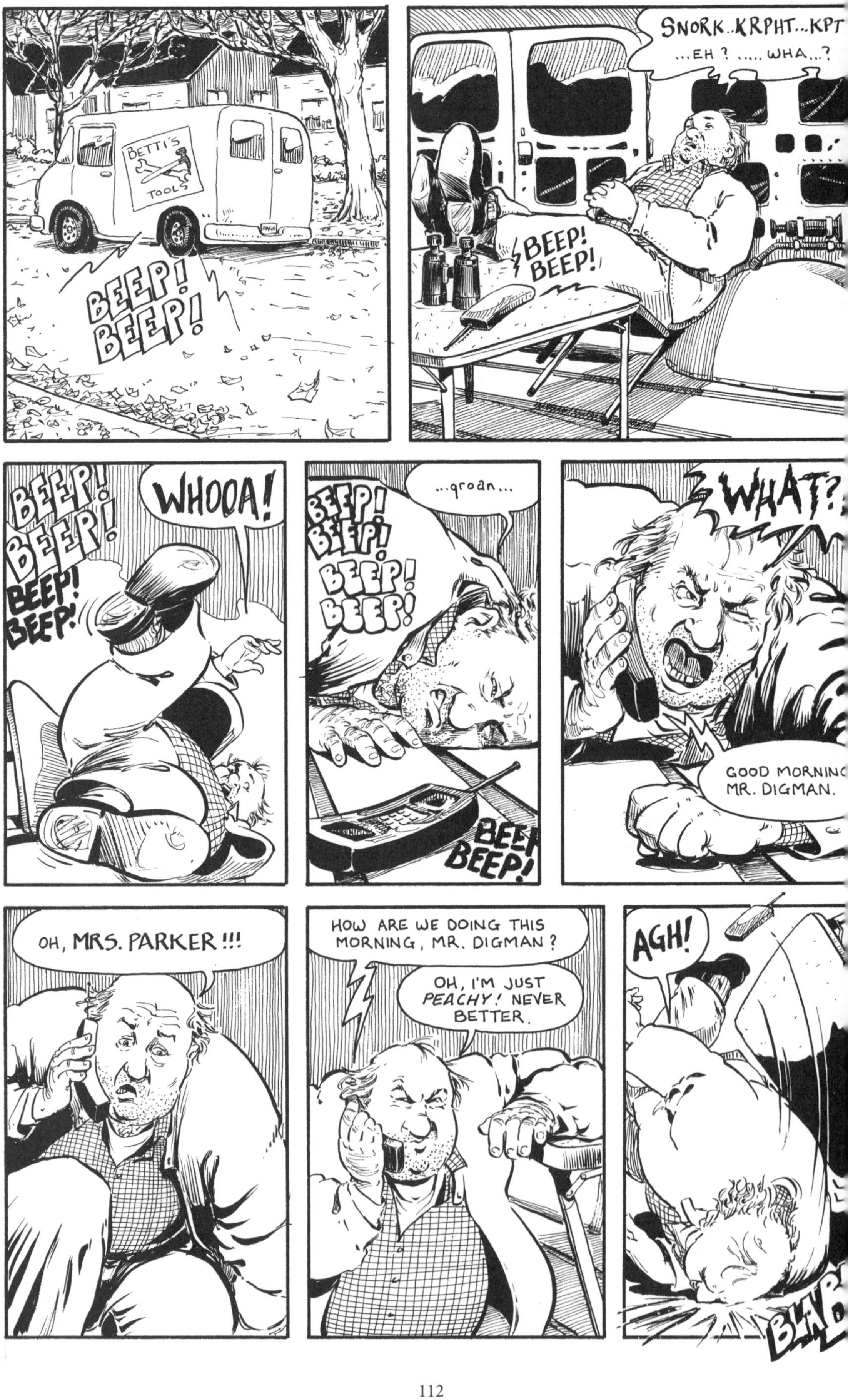
BETTI'S TOOLS
BEEP! BEEP!
SNORK..KRPHT...KPT
...EH ? ..... WHA...?
BEEP! BEEP!
BEEP! BEEP! BEEP! BEEP!
WHOOA!
BEEP! BEEP! BEEP! BEEP!
...groan...
BEEP! BEEP!
WHAT?
GOOD MORNING MR. DIGMAN.
OH, MRS. PARKER!!!
HOW ARE WE DOING THIS MORNING, MR. DIGMAN?
OH, I'M JUST PEACHY! NEVER BETTER.
AGH!

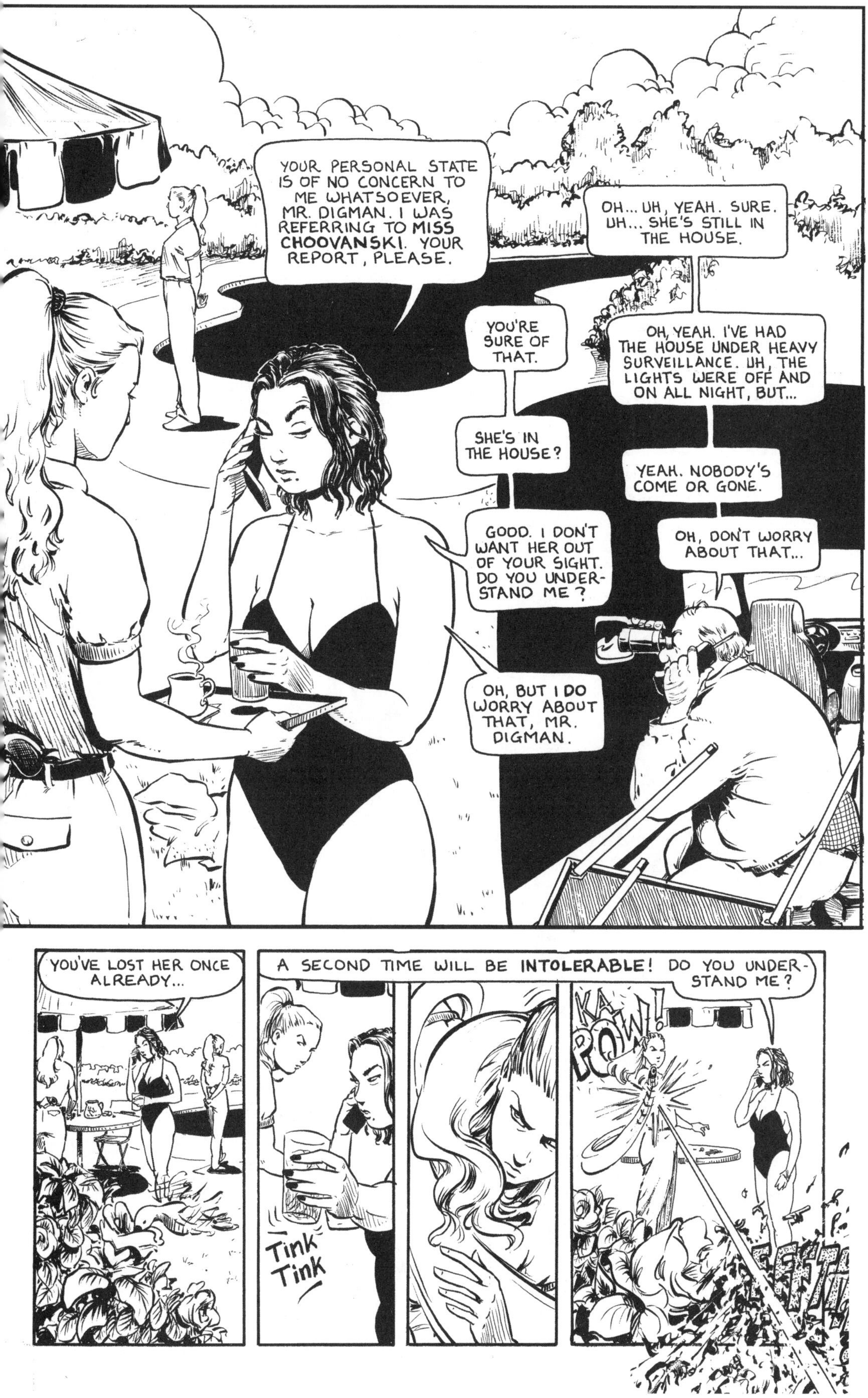
YOUR PERSONAL STATE IS OF NO CONCERN TO ME WHATSOEVER, MR. DIGMAN. I WAS REFERRING TO MISS CHOOVANSKI. YOUR REPORT, PLEASE.
OH... UH, YEAH. SURE. UH... SHE'S STILL IN THE HOUSE.
YOU'RE SURE OF THAT.
OH, YEAH. I'VE HAD THE HOUSE UNDER HEAVY SURVEILLANCE. UH, THE LIGHTS WERE OFF AND ON ALL NIGHT, BUT...
SHE'S IN THE HOUSE?
YEAH. NOBODY'S COME OR GONE.
GOOD. I DON'T WANT HER OUT OF YOUR SIGHT. DO YOU UNDERSTAND ME?
OH, DON'T WORRY ABOUT THAT...
OH, BUT I DO WORRY ABOUT THAT, MR. DIGMAN.
YOU'VE LOST HER ONCE ALREADY...
A SECOND TIME WILL BE INTOLERABLE! DO YOU UNDERSTAND ME?
Tink Tink
KA POW!

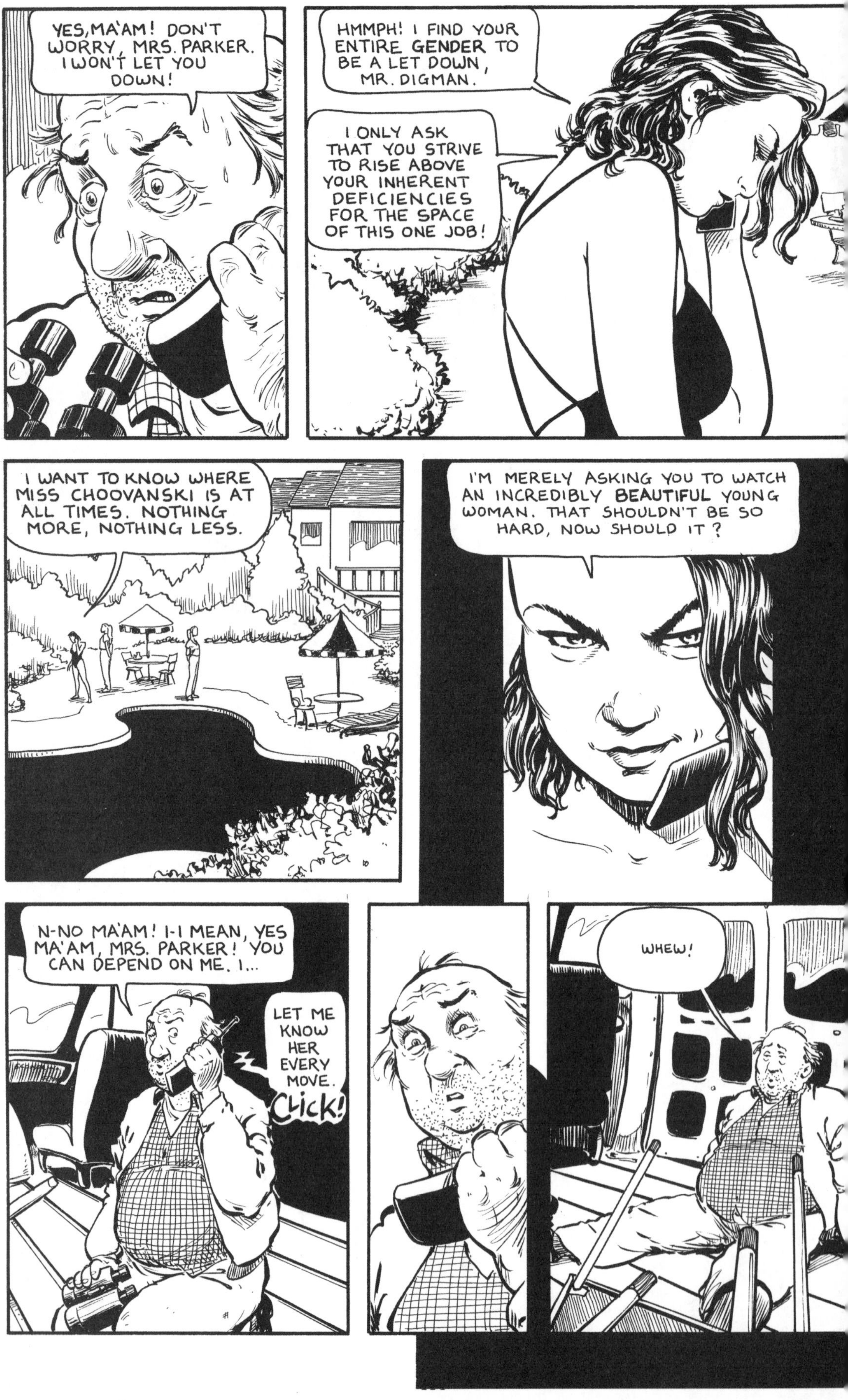
YES, MA'AM! DON'T WORRY, MRS. PARKER. I WON'T LET YOU DOWN!
HMMPH! I FIND YOUR ENTIRE GENDER TO BE A LET DOWN, MR. DIGMAN.
I ONLY ASK THAT YOU STRIVE TO RISE ABOVE YOUR INHERENT DEFICIENCIES FOR THE SPACE OF THIS ONE JOB!
I WANT TO KNOW WHERE MISS CHOOVANSKI IS AT ALL TIMES. NOTHING MORE, NOTHING LESS.
I'M MERELY ASKING YOU TO WATCH AN INCREDIBLY BEAUTIFUL YOUNG WOMAN. THAT SHOULDN'T BE SO HARD, NOW SHOULD IT?
N-NO MA'AM! I-I MEAN, YES MA'AM, MRS. PARKER! YOU CAN DEPEND ON ME. I...
LET ME KNOW HER EVERY MOVE.
CLICK!
WHEW!

RING! RING!

BLOOP! BLOOP

RING! RING

RING! RING! RING! RING! RING! R!

WHAT THE...?!

...OH.

Ring! Ring!

lo?

HELLO? KATCHOO? IT'S DAVID, I DIDN'T WAKE YOU, DID I?

..............KATCHOO?

..;lo?

HEH! KATCHOO, IT'S DAVID! LISTEN, I HAVE A SURPRISE FOR YOU! CAN YOU MEET ME AT THE O'NEAL GALLERY IN AN HOUR?

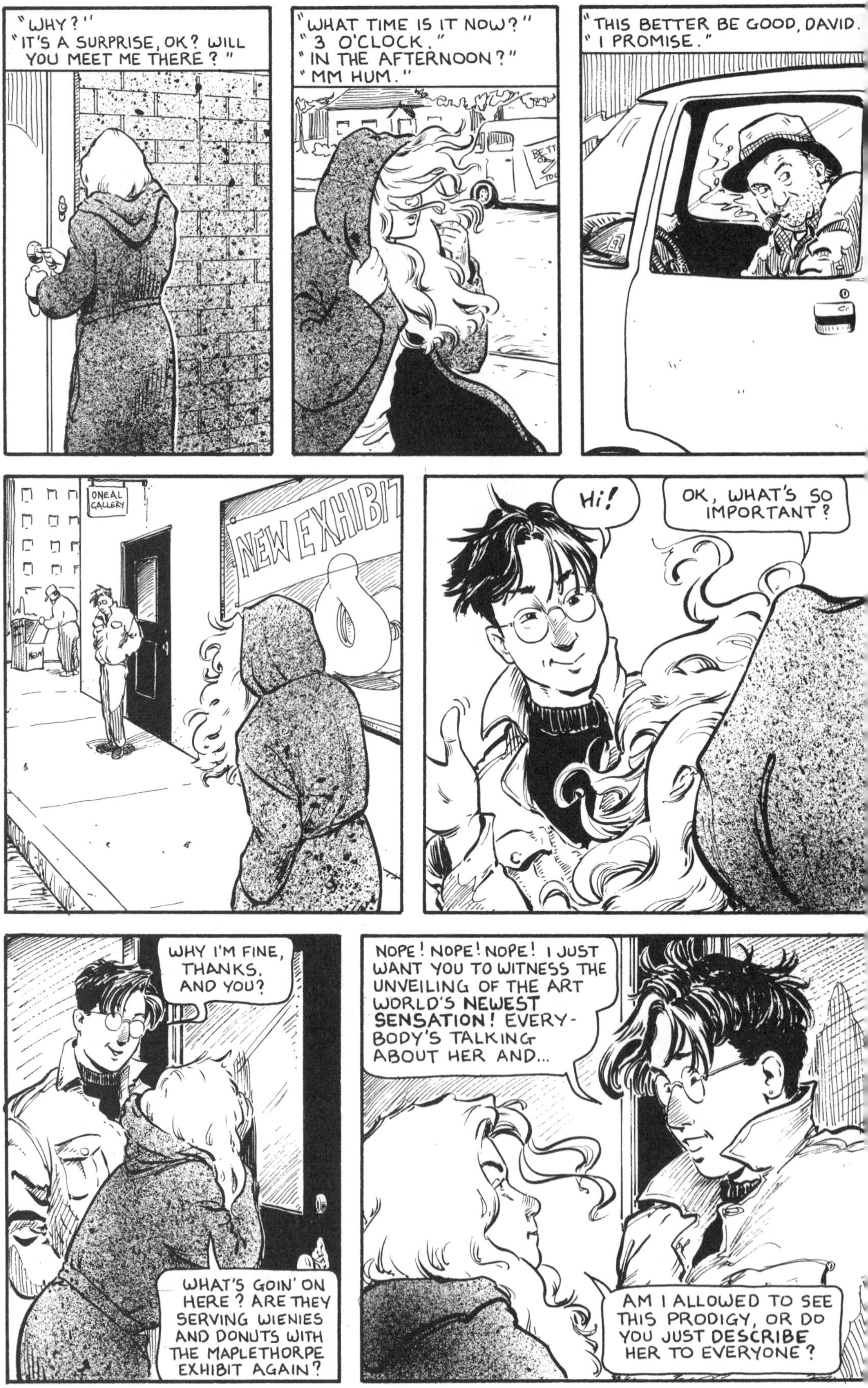
"WHY?"
"IT'S A SURPRISE, OK? WILL YOU MEET ME THERE?"
"WHAT TIME IS IT NOW?"
"3 O'CLOCK."
"IN THE AFTERNOON?"
"MM HUM."
"THIS BETTER BE GOOD, DAVID."
"I PROMISE."
ONEAL GALLERY
NEW EXHIBIT
Hi!
OK, WHAT'S SO IMPORTANT?
WHY I'M FINE, THANKS. AND YOU?
WHAT'S GOIN' ON HERE? ARE THEY SERVING WIENIES AND DONUTS WITH THE MAPLETHORPE EXHIBIT AGAIN?
NOPE! NOPE! NOPE! I JUST WANT YOU TO WITNESS THE UNVEILING OF THE ART WORLD'S **NEWEST SENSATION!** EVERY-BODY'S TALKING ABOUT HER AND...
AM I ALLOWED TO SEE THIS PRODIGY, OR DO YOU JUST **DESCRIBE** HER TO EVERYONE?

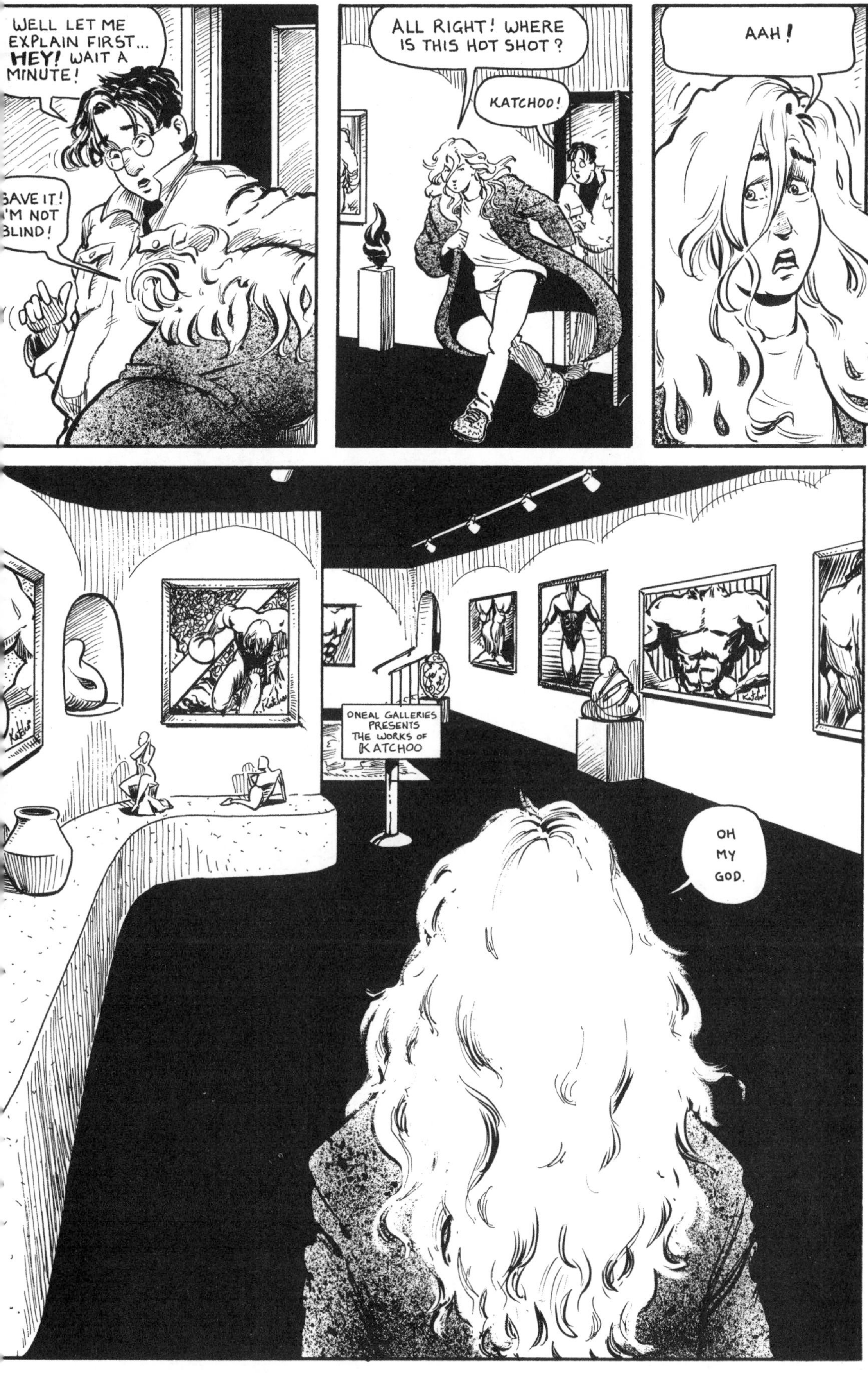
WELL LET ME EXPLAIN FIRST... HEY! WAIT A MINUTE!
SAVE IT! I'M NOT BLIND!
ALL RIGHT! WHERE IS THIS HOT SHOT?
KATCHOO!
AAH!
ONEAL GALLERIES PRESENTS THE WORKS OF KATCHOO
OH MY GOD.

WELL... AS YOU CAN SEE, THE NEWEST SENSATION IS......**YOU!**

THIS...THESE ARE **MY** PAINTINGS!

I KNOW! ISN'T IT FANTASTIC?! KATCHOO, THEY **LOVE YOU!!**

b-but, how...

I SHOWED SOME OF YOUR PAINTINGS TO AN ART DEALER WHILE YOU WERE IN CANADA, ...AND HE WENT **NUTS!**

OH MY GOD!

O'NEAL'S INSISTED ON A SHOWING RIGHT AW— THEY'VE BEEN GETTING CALLS FROM GA— OVER THE COUNTRY EVER SINCE! BELIEVE T— PRICES YOU' —NIUS! —DINC —EVEN THAT— —ER TO TOUR T— —AL —AND THEN— GOT RO— —TO GO EVERYB— U.K. YOU CA— OR MAGA— TH STUDI— ALL Y— USED DREA— TO IT— THE — BELIE— UNRE— AL! I AVE— NO ID— —T YO— REAL WELL LET SAY T— HAT PRICE— ARE T— =SOB=

AND —IES A— —WOULD —OFFERE —MANHAT —ALL NEX —HEY! WA —YOU'RE H —MONEY A —TOWNHO— —PAINTINC —ECAUSE T —OFFERS A —JBODY C —IT! I ME —ARE JU —BET YO —EA HOW —LY ARE— —ME JUST —ALREAD— —HRU THE **ROOF**

AND THAT'S JUST THE BEGINNING! ...UH, KATCHOO?

UH, I KNOW I SHOULD'VE ASKED PERMISSION FIRST, BUT WE DIDN'T KNOW WHERE YOU WERE, OR WHEN YOU'D BE BACK.

...AND I DIDN'T WANT YOU TO MISS A BIG BREAK LIKE THIS, BECAUSE YOU REALLY DESERVE IT, Y'KNOW?

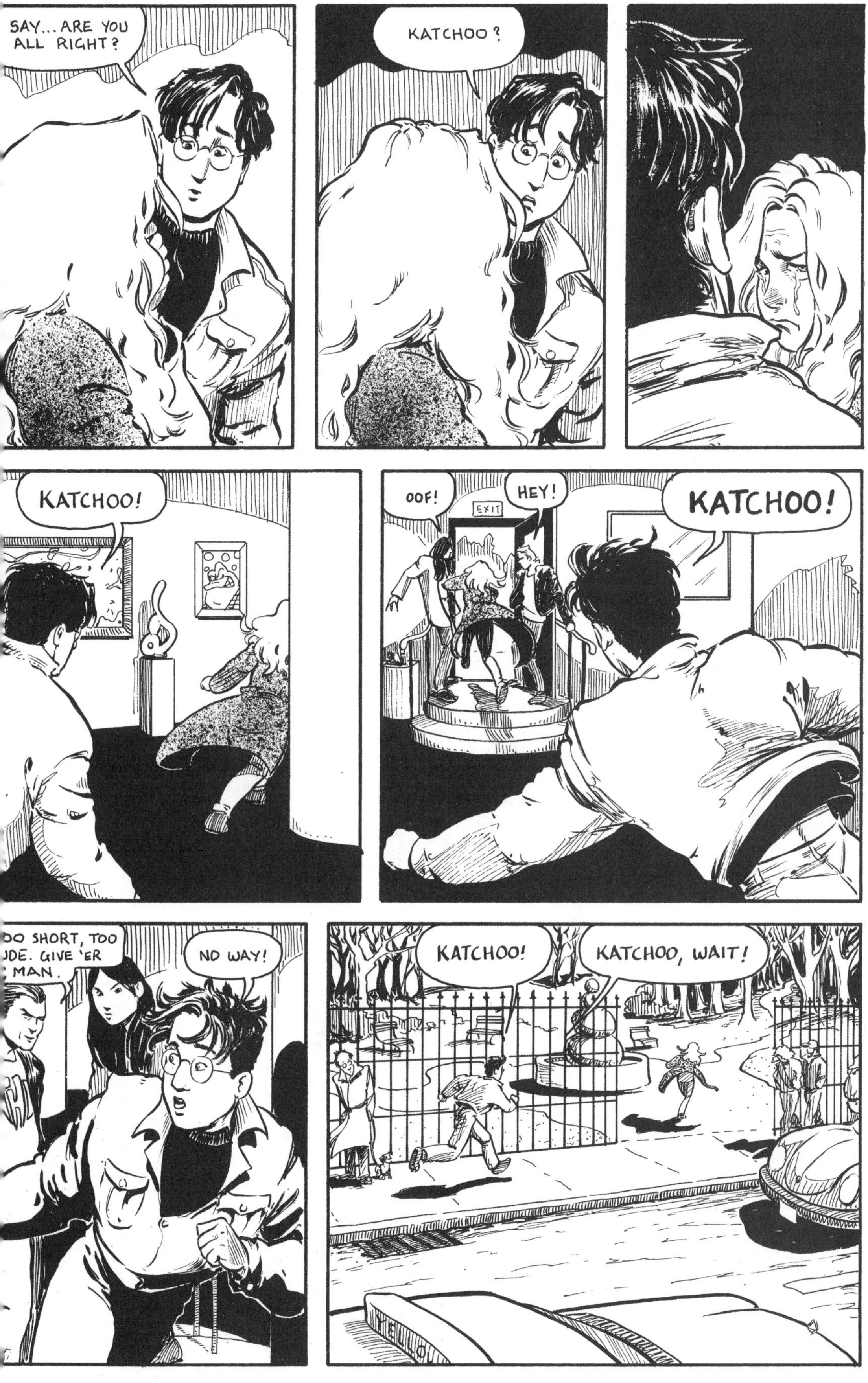
SAY... ARE YOU ALL RIGHT?
KATCHOO?
KATCHOO!
OOF!
HEY!
KATCHOO!
OO SHORT, TOO
UDE. GIVE 'ER
MAN.
NO WAY!
KATCHOO!
KATCHOO, WAIT!

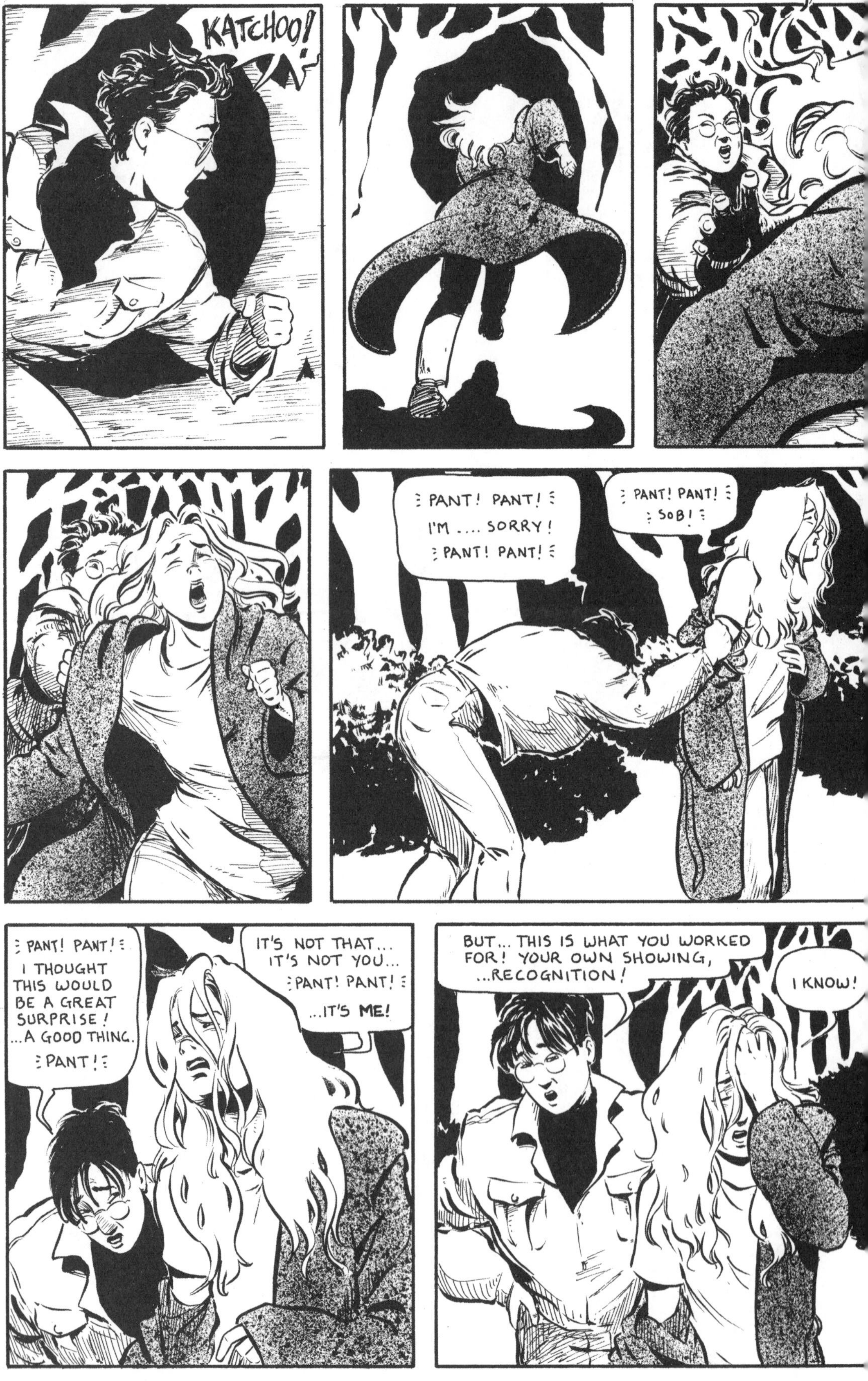
KATCHOO!
PANT! PANT! I'M.... SORRY! PANT! PANT!
PANT! PANT! SOB!
PANT! PANT! I THOUGHT THIS WOULD BE A GREAT SURPRISE! ...A GOOD THING. PANT!
IT'S NOT THAT... IT'S NOT YOU... PANT! PANT! ...IT'S ME!
BUT... THIS IS WHAT YOU WORKED FOR! YOUR OWN SHOWING, ...RECOGNITION!
I KNOW!

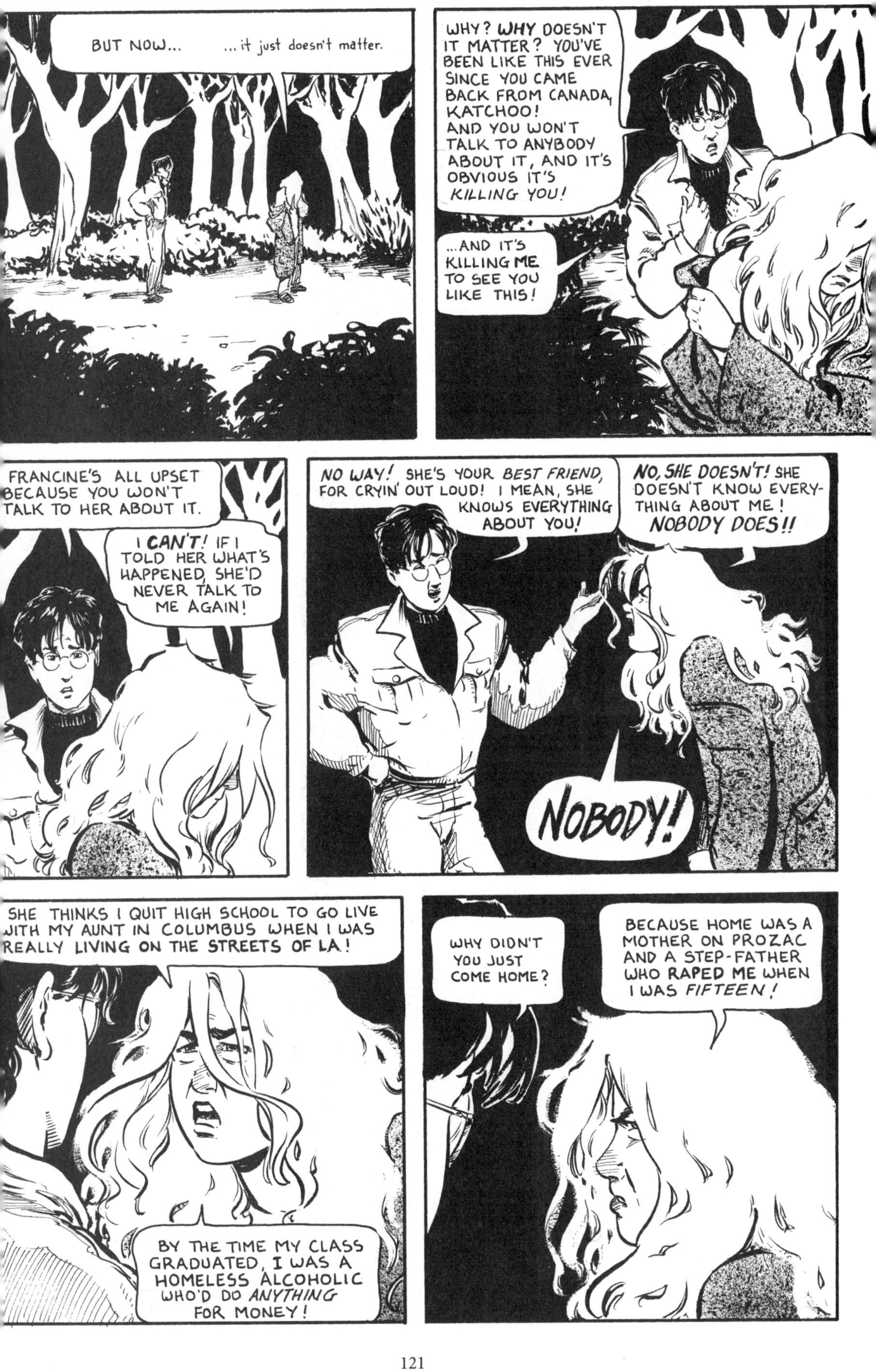
BUT NOW... ...it just doesn't matter.
WHY? WHY DOESN'T IT MATTER? YOU'VE BEEN LIKE THIS EVER SINCE YOU CAME BACK FROM CANADA, KATCHOO! AND YOU WON'T TALK TO ANYBODY ABOUT IT, AND IT'S OBVIOUS IT'S KILLING YOU!
...AND IT'S KILLING ME TO SEE YOU LIKE THIS!
FRANCINE'S ALL UPSET BECAUSE YOU WON'T TALK TO HER ABOUT IT.
I CAN'T! IF I TOLD HER WHAT'S HAPPENED, SHE'D NEVER TALK TO ME AGAIN!
NO WAY! SHE'S YOUR BEST FRIEND, FOR CRYIN' OUT LOUD! I MEAN, SHE KNOWS EVERYTHING ABOUT YOU!
NO, SHE DOESN'T! SHE DOESN'T KNOW EVERYTHING ABOUT ME! NOBODY DOES!!
NOBODY!
SHE THINKS I QUIT HIGH SCHOOL TO GO LIVE WITH MY AUNT IN COLUMBUS WHEN I WAS REALLY LIVING ON THE STREETS OF LA!
BY THE TIME MY CLASS GRADUATED, I WAS A HOMELESS ALCOHOLIC WHO'D DO ANYTHING FOR MONEY!
WHY DIDN'T YOU JUST COME HOME?
BECAUSE HOME WAS A MOTHER ON PROZAC AND A STEP-FATHER WHO RAPED ME WHEN I WAS FIFTEEN!

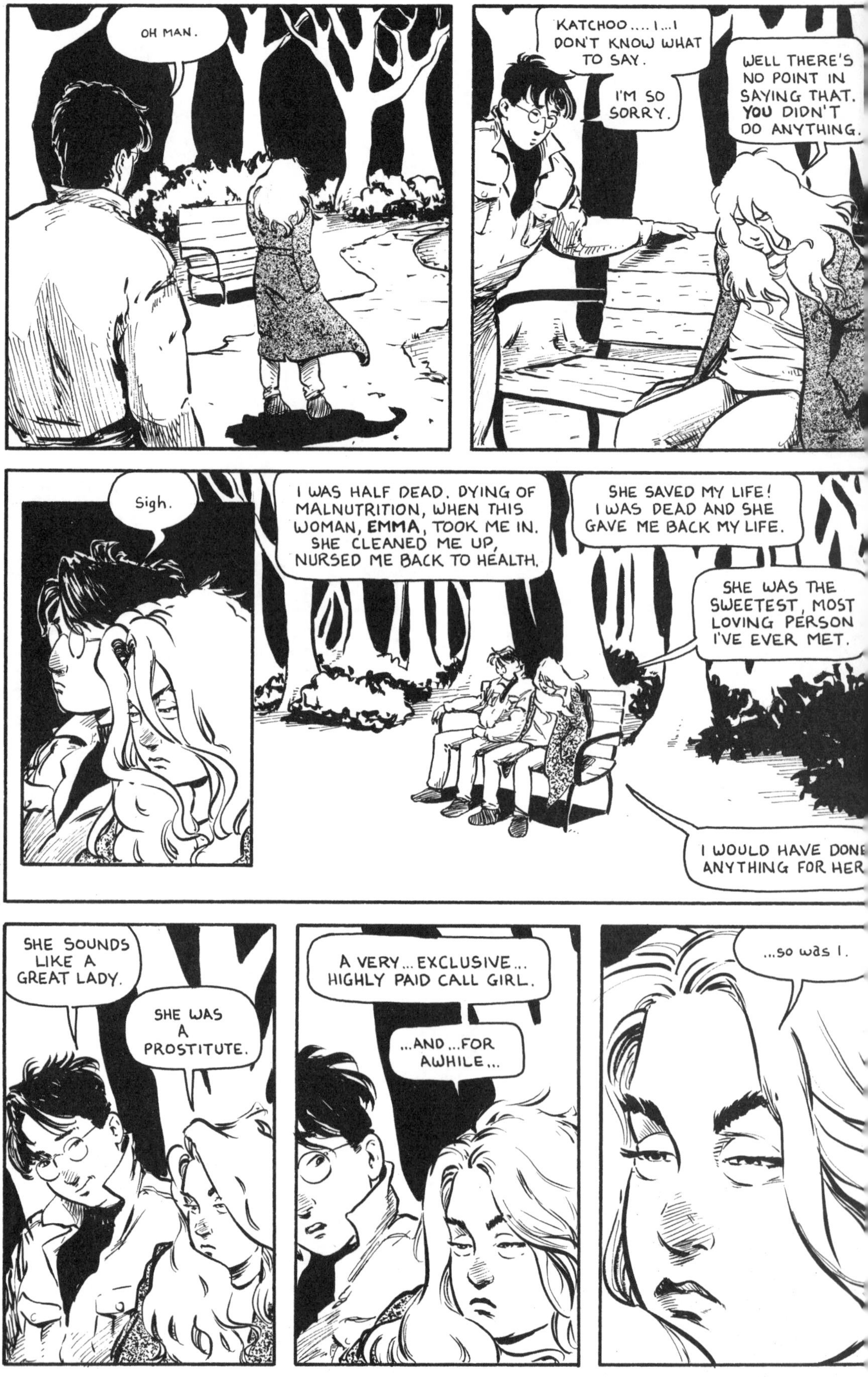
OH MAN.
KATCHOO.... I...I DON'T KNOW WHAT TO SAY.
I'M SO SORRY.
WELL THERE'S NO POINT IN SAYING THAT. YOU DIDN'T DO ANYTHING.
Sigh.
I WAS HALF DEAD. DYING OF MALNUTRITION, WHEN THIS WOMAN, EMMA, TOOK ME IN. SHE CLEANED ME UP, NURSED ME BACK TO HEALTH.
SHE SAVED MY LIFE! I WAS DEAD AND SHE GAVE ME BACK MY LIFE.
SHE WAS THE SWEETEST, MOST LOVING PERSON I'VE EVER MET.
I WOULD HAVE DONE ANYTHING FOR HER
SHE SOUNDS LIKE A GREAT LADY.
SHE WAS A PROSTITUTE.
A VERY... EXCLUSIVE... HIGHLY PAID CALL GIRL.
...AND...FOR AWHILE...
...so was I.

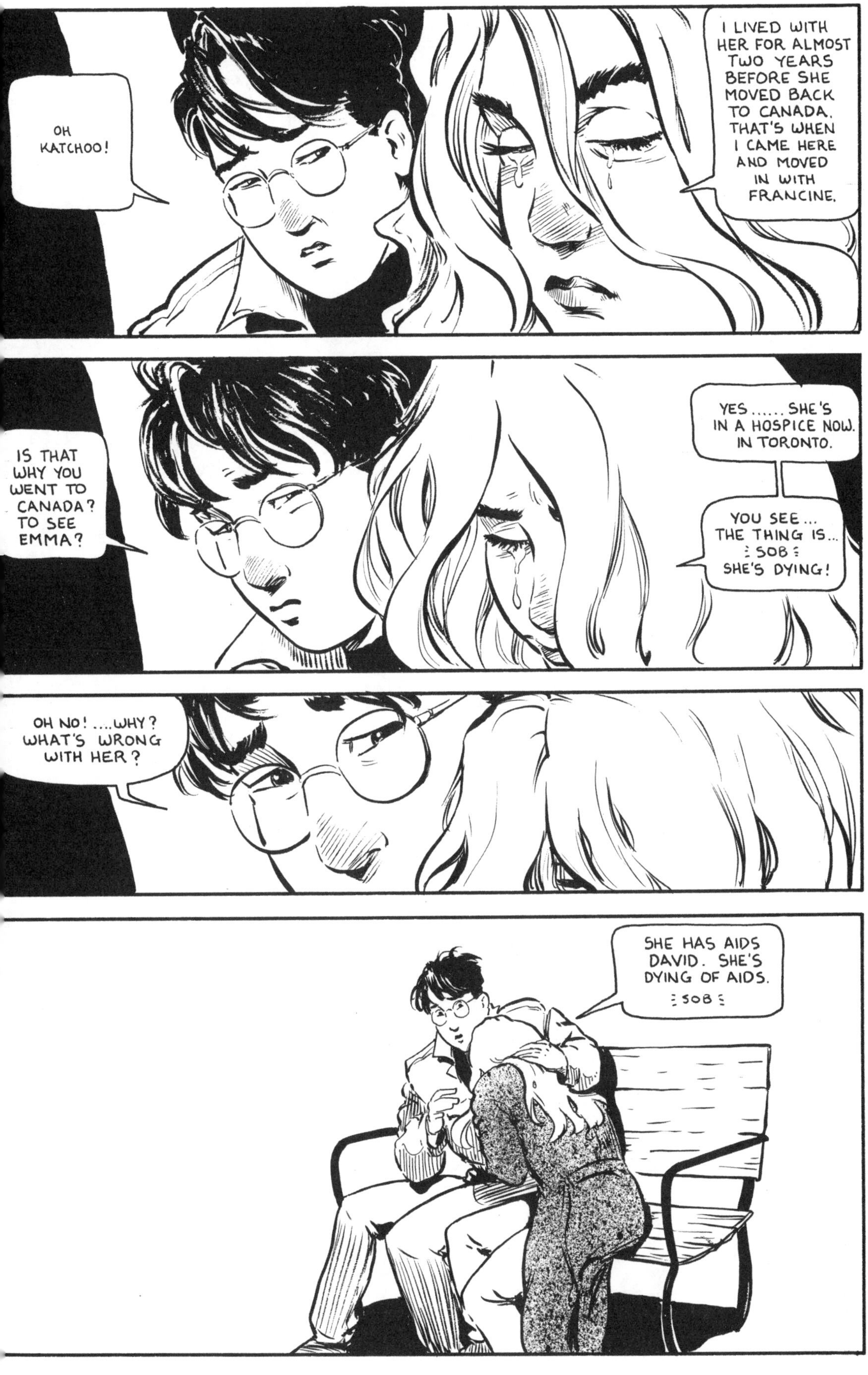
I LIVED WITH HER FOR ALMOST TWO YEARS BEFORE SHE MOVED BACK TO CANADA. THAT'S WHEN I CAME HERE AND MOVED IN WITH FRANCINE.
OH KATCHOO!
YES...... SHE'S IN A HOSPICE NOW. IN TORONTO.
YOU SEE... THE THING IS... SOB SHE'S DYING!
IS THAT WHY YOU WENT TO CANADA? TO SEE EMMA?
OH NO! ....WHY? WHAT'S WRONG WITH HER?
SHE HAS AIDS DAVID. SHE'S DYING OF AIDS. SOB

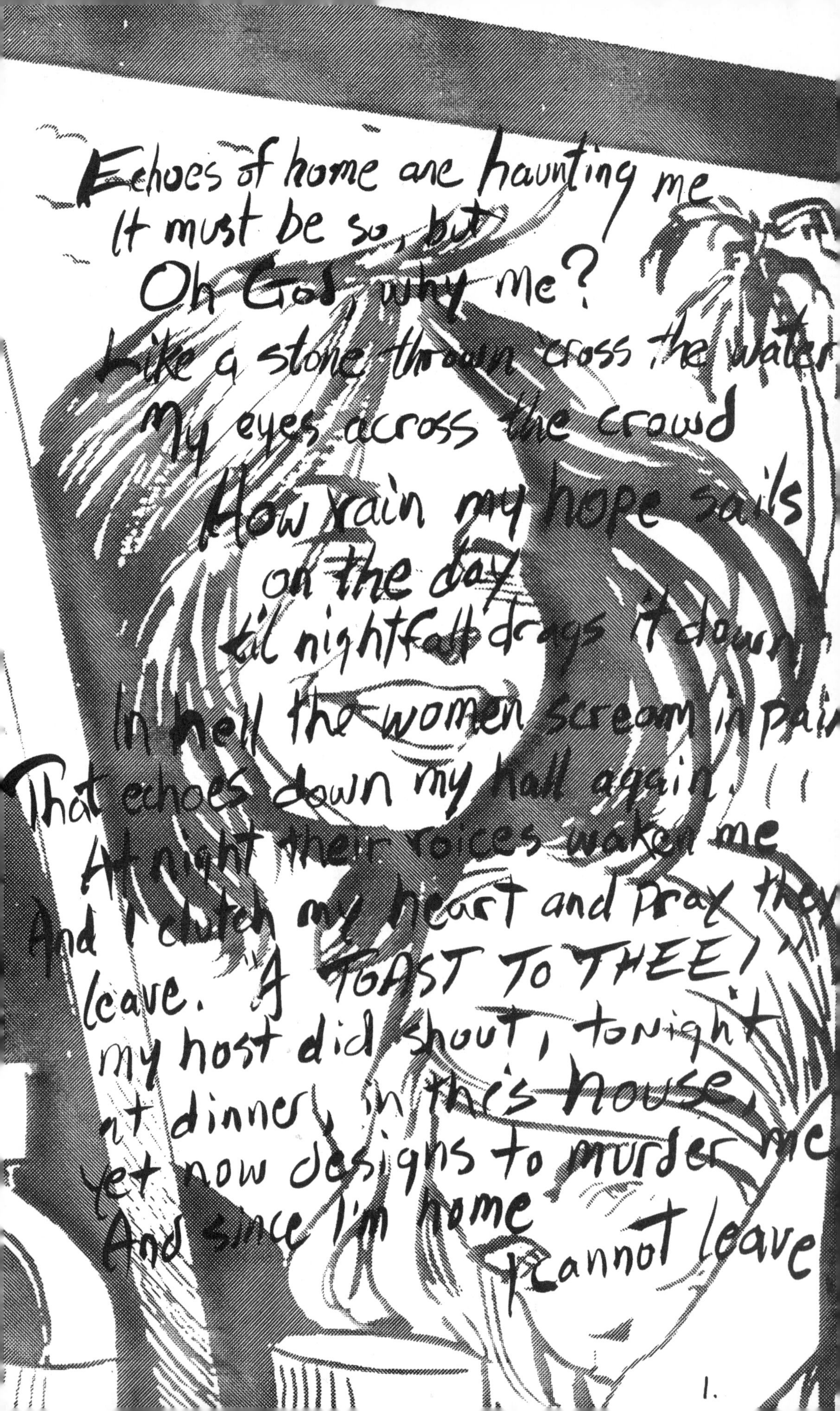
Echoes of home are haunting me
It must be so, but
Oh God, why me?
Like a stone thrown cross the water
My eyes across the crowd
How vain my hope sails
on the day
'til nightfall drags it down
In hell the women scream in pai
That echoes down my hall again.
At night their voices waken me
And I clutch my heart and pray they
leave. "A TOAST TO THEE!"
my host did shout, tonight
at dinner, in this house,
yet now designs to murder me
And since I'm home
I cannot leave
1.

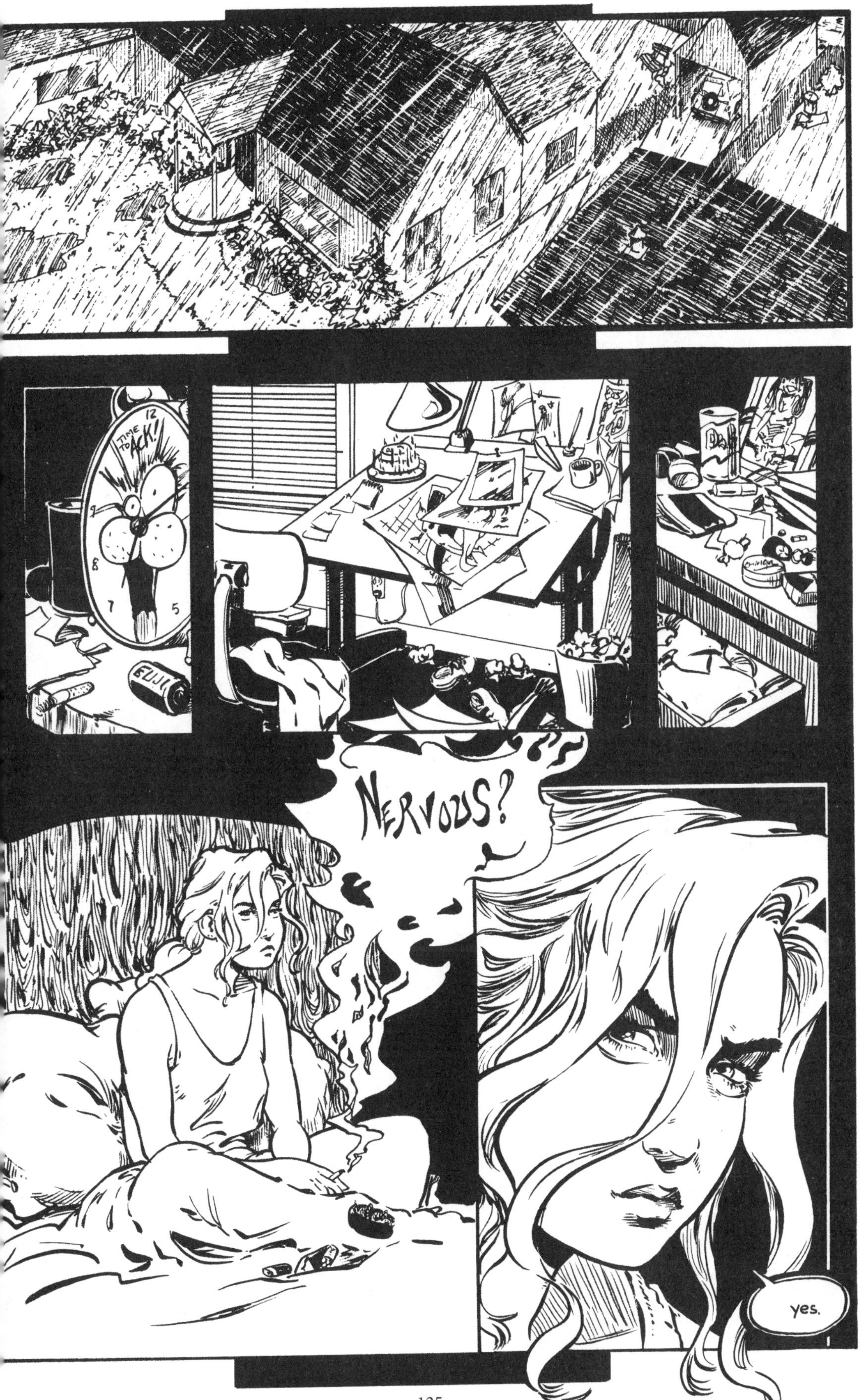
TIME TO ACK!
ELIJ
NERVOUS?
yes.

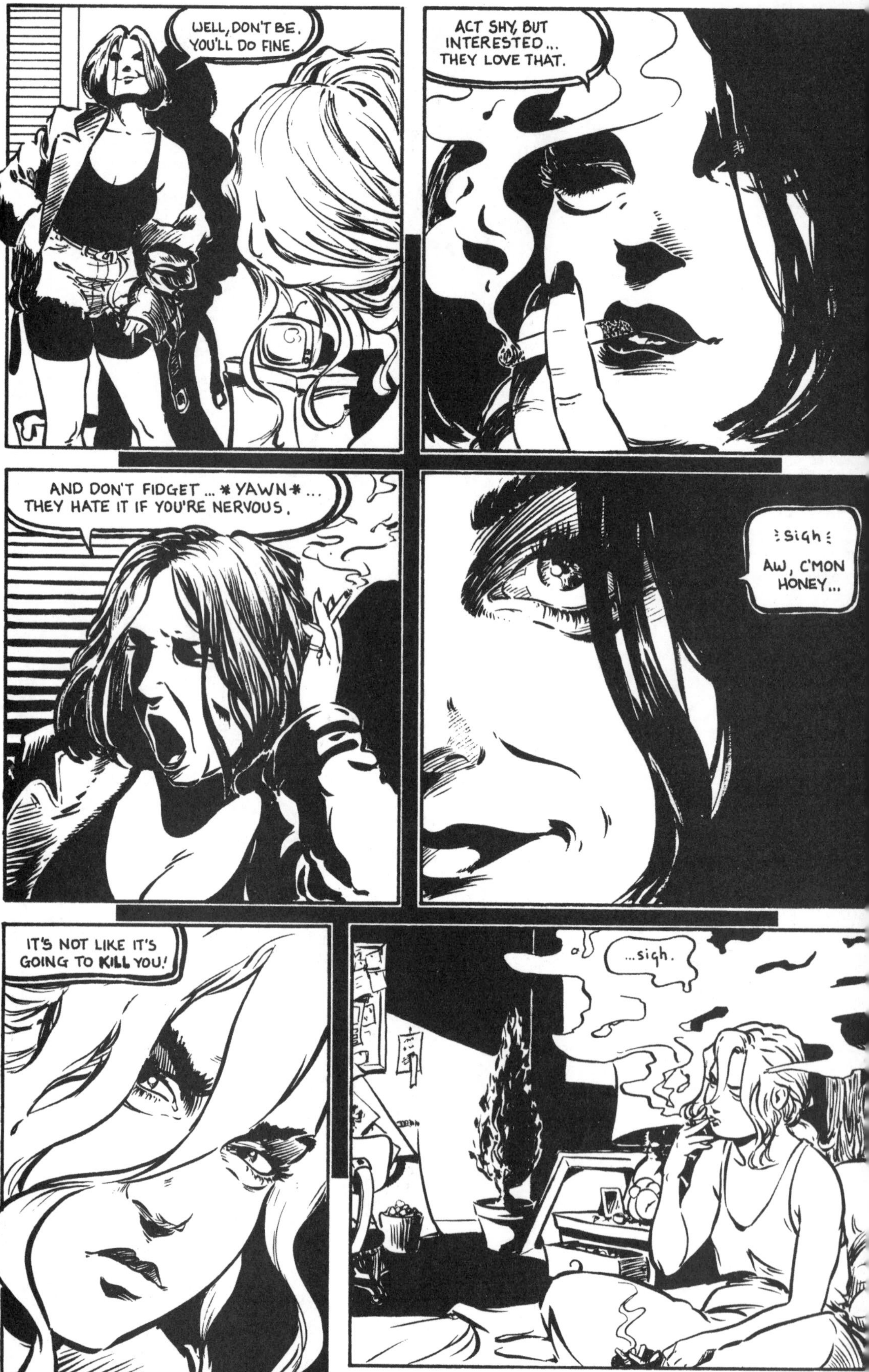
WELL, DON'T BE. YOU'LL DO FINE.
ACT SHY, BUT INTERESTED... THEY LOVE THAT.
AND DON'T FIDGET... *YAWN*... THEY HATE IT IF YOU'RE NERVOUS.
SIGH
AW, C'MON HONEY...
IT'S NOT LIKE IT'S GOING TO KILL YOU!
...sigh.

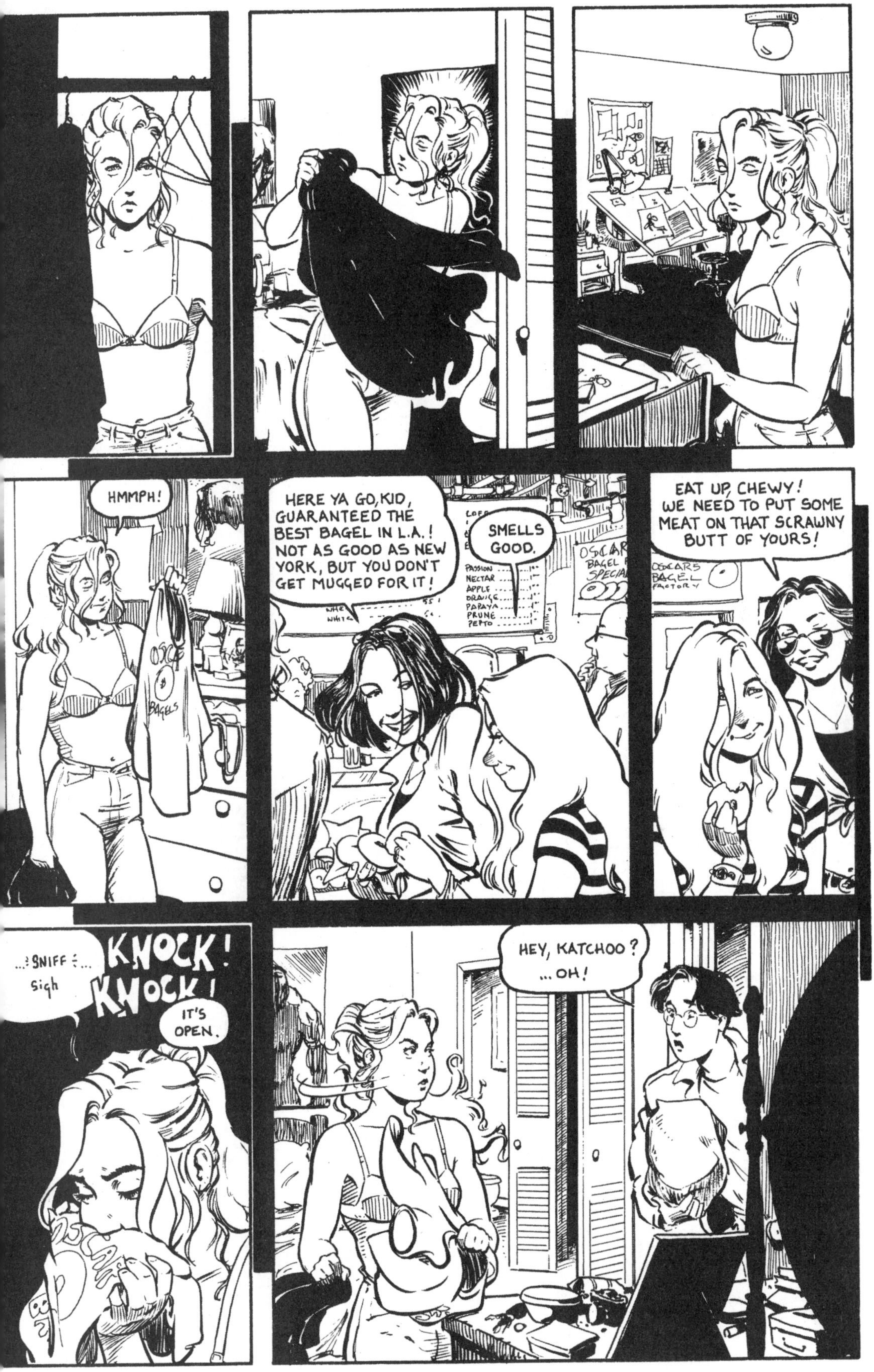
HMMPH!
HERE YA GO, KID, GUARANTEED THE BEST BAGEL IN L.A.! NOT AS GOOD AS NEW YORK, BUT YOU DON'T GET MUGGED FOR IT!
SMELLS GOOD.
EAT UP, CHEWY! WE NEED TO PUT SOME MEAT ON THAT SCRAWNY BUTT OF YOURS!
...SNIFF... sigh
KNOCK! KNOCK!
IT'S OPEN.
HEY, KATCHOO? ...OH!

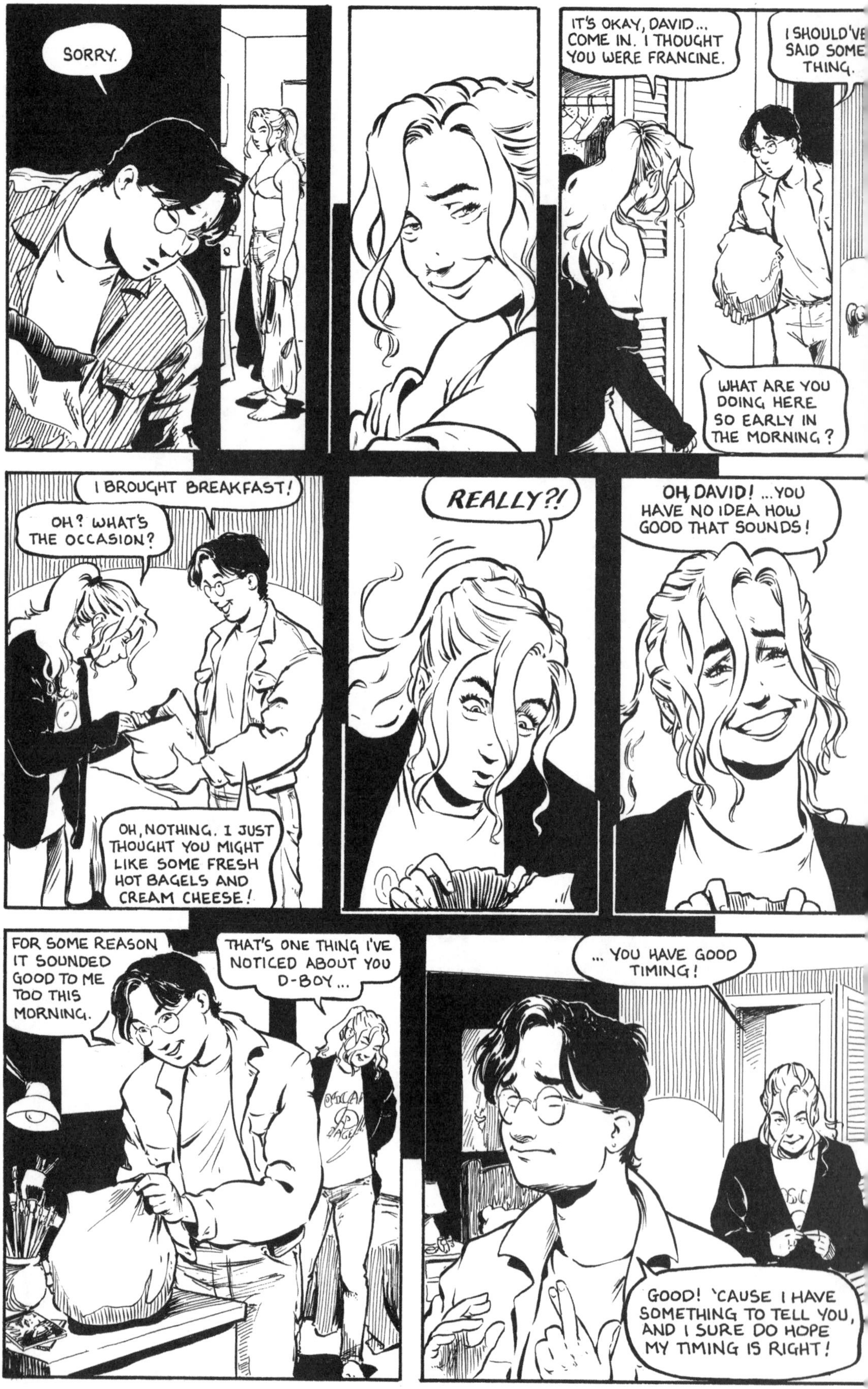
SORRY.
IT'S OKAY, DAVID... COME IN. I THOUGHT YOU WERE FRANCINE.
I SHOULD'VE SAID SOME THING.
WHAT ARE YOU DOING HERE SO EARLY IN THE MORNING?
I BROUGHT BREAKFAST!
OH? WHAT'S THE OCCASION?
OH, NOTHING. I JUST THOUGHT YOU MIGHT LIKE SOME FRESH HOT BAGELS AND CREAM CHEESE!
REALLY?!
OH, DAVID! ...YOU HAVE NO IDEA HOW GOOD THAT SOUNDS!
FOR SOME REASON IT SOUNDED GOOD TO ME TOO THIS MORNING.
THAT'S ONE THING I'VE NOTICED ABOUT YOU D-BOY...
... YOU HAVE GOOD TIMING!
GOOD! 'CAUSE I HAVE SOMETHING TO TELL YOU, AND I SURE DO HOPE MY TIMING IS RIGHT!

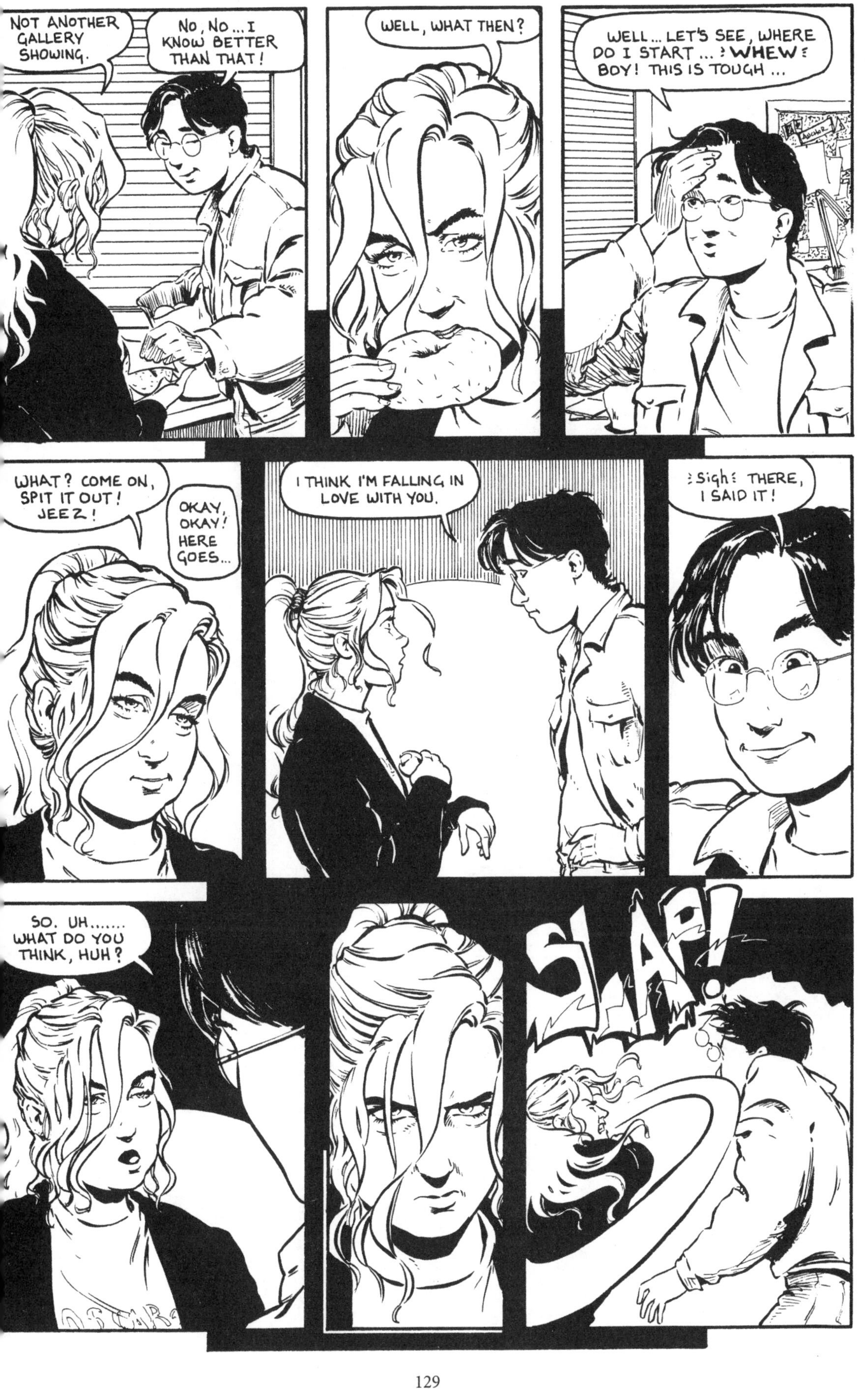
NOT ANOTHER GALLERY SHOWING.
NO, NO... I KNOW BETTER THAN THAT!
WELL, WHAT THEN?
WELL... LET'S SEE, WHERE DO I START... ꞉WHEW꞉ BOY! THIS IS TOUGH...
WHAT? COME ON, SPIT IT OUT! JEEZ!
OKAY, OKAY! HERE GOES...
I THINK I'M FALLING IN LOVE WITH YOU.
꞉Sigh꞉ THERE, I SAID IT!
SO. UH....... WHAT DO YOU THINK, HUH?
SLAP!

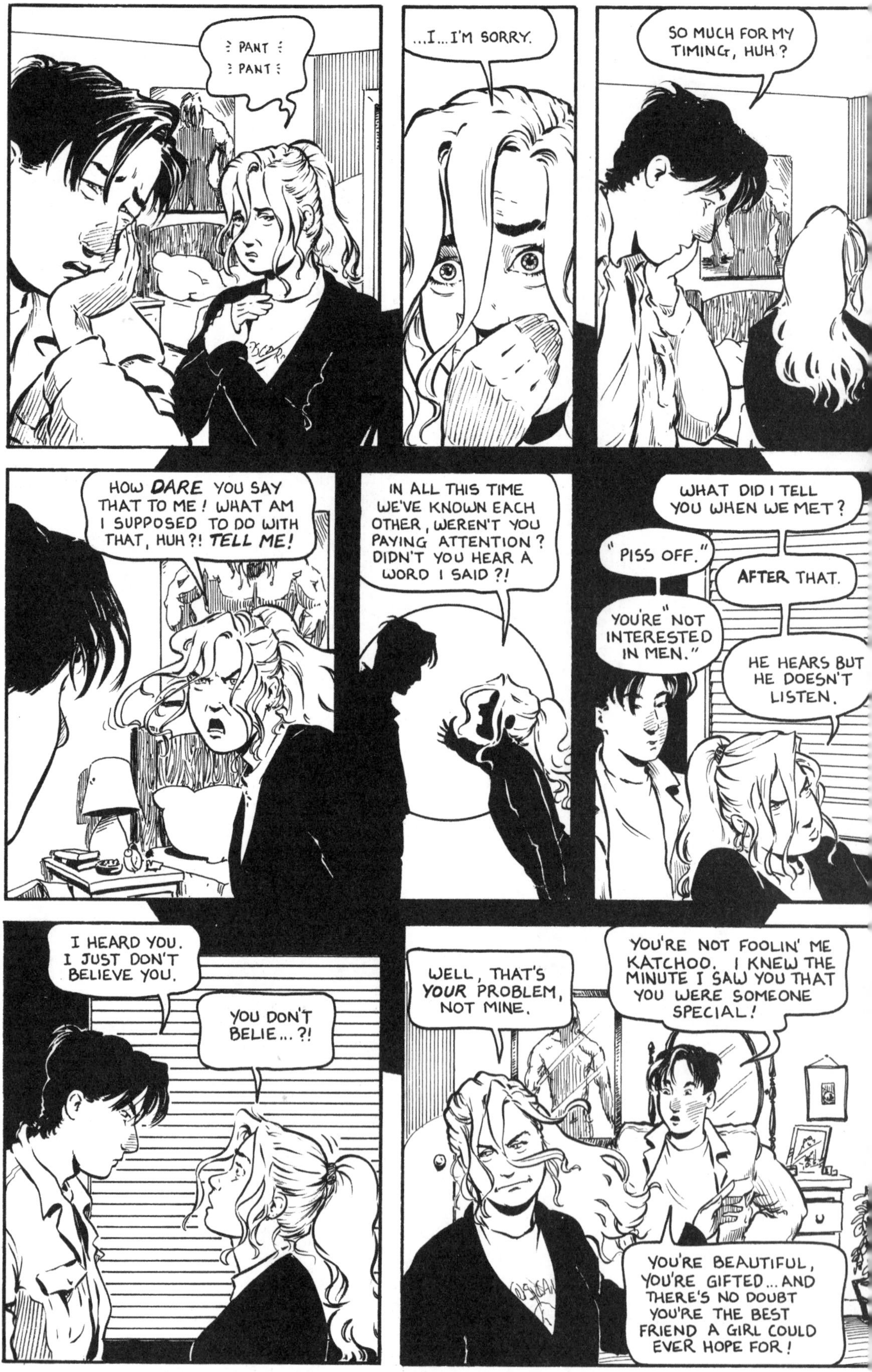

PANT
PANT
...I...I'M SORRY.
SO MUCH FOR MY TIMING, HUH?
HOW DARE YOU SAY THAT TO ME! WHAT AM I SUPPOSED TO DO WITH THAT, HUH?! TELL ME!
IN ALL THIS TIME WE'VE KNOWN EACH OTHER, WEREN'T YOU PAYING ATTENTION? DIDN'T YOU HEAR A WORD I SAID?!
WHAT DID I TELL YOU WHEN WE MET?
"PISS OFF."
AFTER THAT.
YOU'RE "NOT INTERESTED IN MEN."
HE HEARS BUT HE DOESN'T LISTEN.
I HEARD YOU. I JUST DON'T BELIEVE YOU.
YOU DON'T BELIE...?!
WELL, THAT'S YOUR PROBLEM, NOT MINE.
YOU'RE NOT FOOLIN' ME KATCHOO. I KNEW THE MINUTE I SAW YOU THAT YOU WERE SOMEONE SPECIAL!
YOU'RE BEAUTIFUL, YOU'RE GIFTED... AND THERE'S NO DOUBT YOU'RE THE BEST FRIEND A GIRL COULD EVER HOPE FOR!

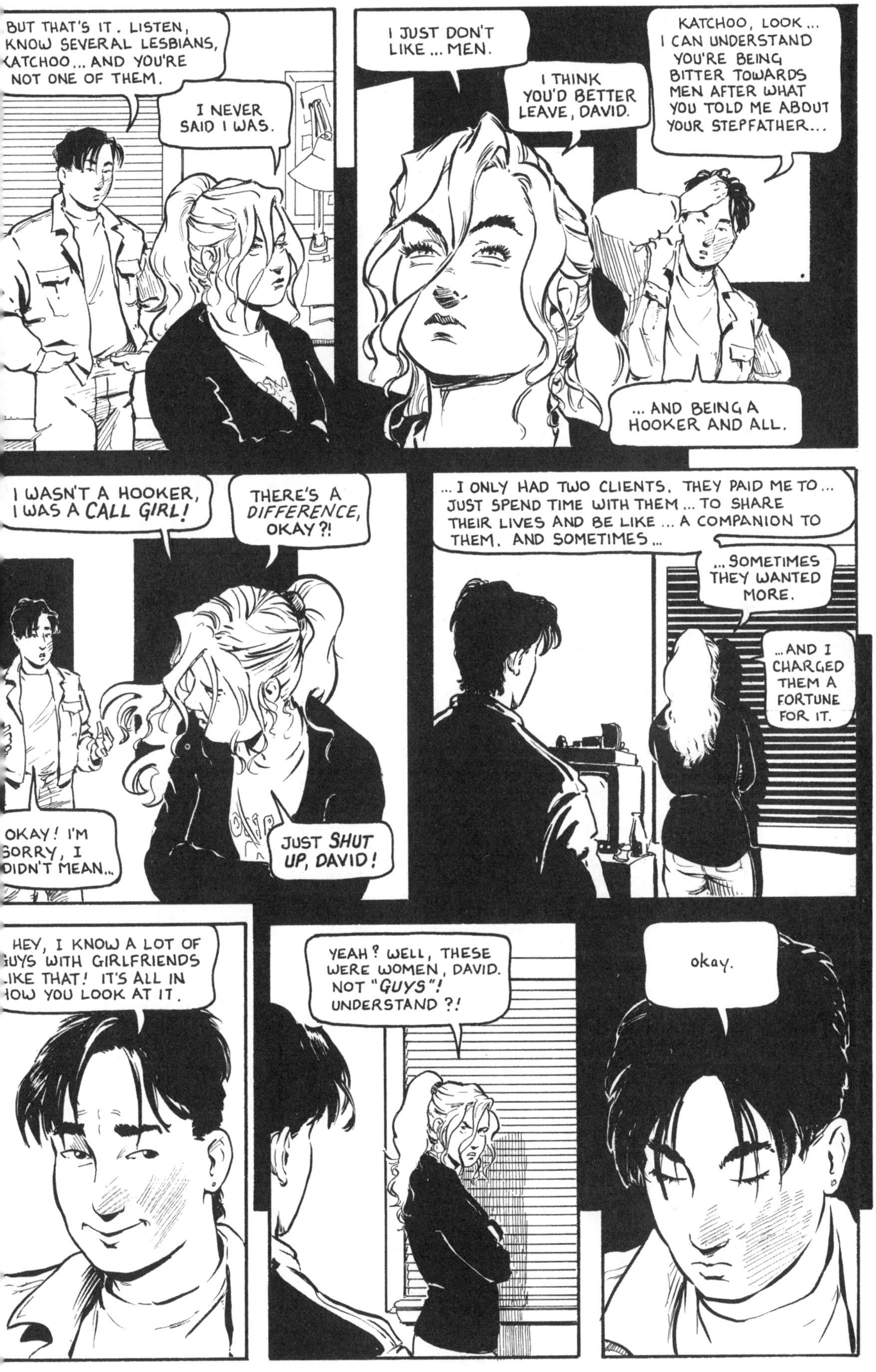
BUT THAT'S IT. LISTEN, KNOW SEVERAL LESBIANS, KATCHOO... AND YOU'RE NOT ONE OF THEM.
I NEVER SAID I WAS.
I JUST DON'T LIKE... MEN.
I THINK YOU'D BETTER LEAVE, DAVID.
KATCHOO, LOOK... I CAN UNDERSTAND YOU'RE BEING BITTER TOWARDS MEN AFTER WHAT YOU TOLD ME ABOUT YOUR STEPFATHER...
... AND BEING A HOOKER AND ALL.
I WASN'T A HOOKER, I WAS A CALL GIRL!
THERE'S A DIFFERENCE, OKAY?!
OKAY! I'M SORRY, I DIDN'T MEAN...
JUST SHUT UP, DAVID!
... I ONLY HAD TWO CLIENTS. THEY PAID ME TO... JUST SPEND TIME WITH THEM... TO SHARE THEIR LIVES AND BE LIKE... A COMPANION TO THEM. AND SOMETIMES...
... SOMETIMES THEY WANTED MORE.
... AND I CHARGED THEM A FORTUNE FOR IT.
HEY, I KNOW A LOT OF GUYS WITH GIRLFRIENDS LIKE THAT! IT'S ALL IN HOW YOU LOOK AT IT.
YEAH? WELL, THESE WERE WOMEN, DAVID. NOT "GUYS"! UNDERSTAND?!
okay.

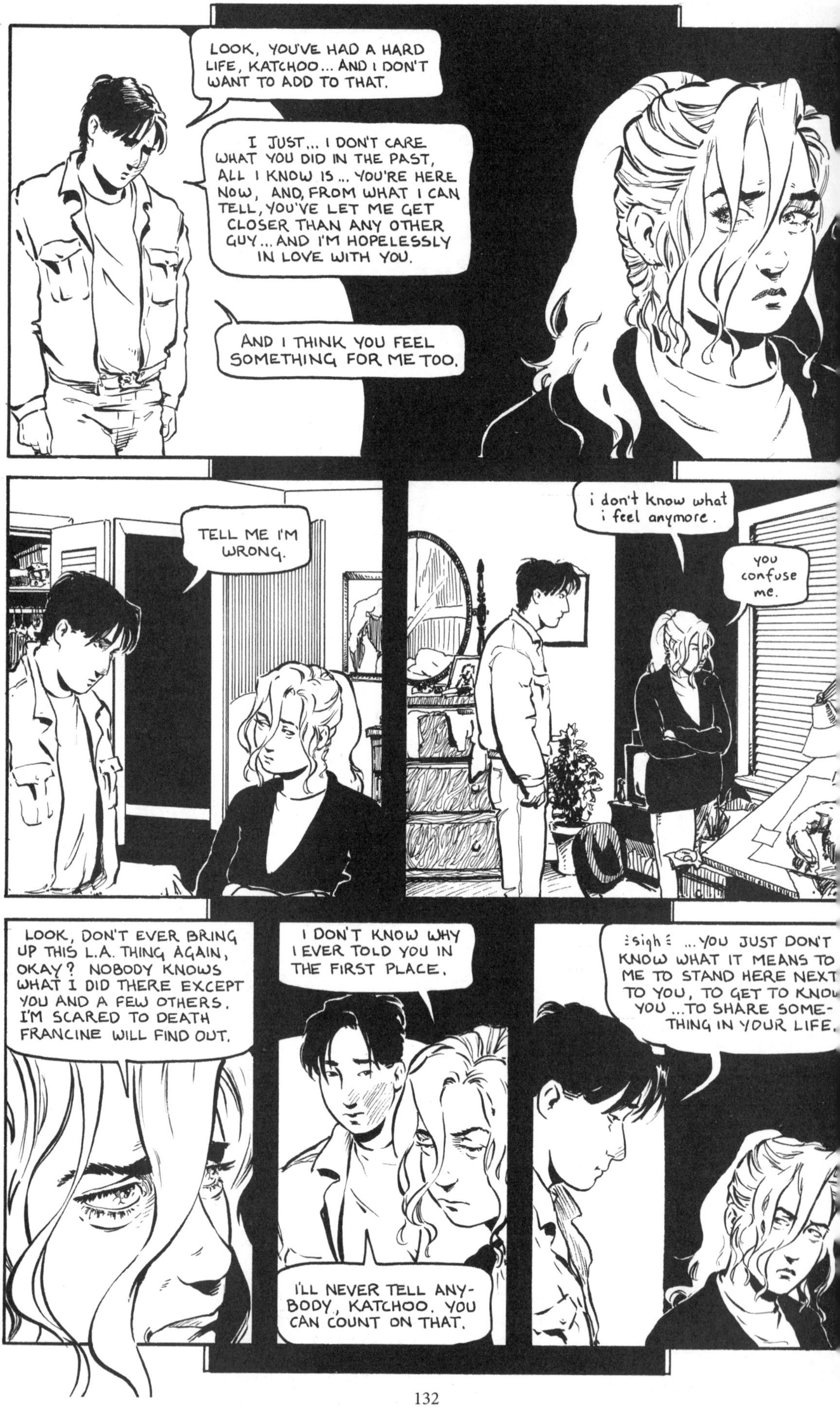
LOOK, YOU'VE HAD A HARD LIFE, KATCHOO... AND I DON'T WANT TO ADD TO THAT.
I JUST... I DON'T CARE WHAT YOU DID IN THE PAST, ALL I KNOW IS... YOU'RE HERE NOW, AND, FROM WHAT I CAN TELL, YOU'VE LET ME GET CLOSER THAN ANY OTHER GUY... AND I'M HOPELESSLY IN LOVE WITH YOU.
AND I THINK YOU FEEL SOMETHING FOR ME TOO.
TELL ME I'M WRONG.
i don't know what i feel anymore.
you confuse me.
LOOK, DON'T EVER BRING UP THIS L.A. THING AGAIN, OKAY? NOBODY KNOWS WHAT I DID THERE EXCEPT YOU AND A FEW OTHERS. I'M SCARED TO DEATH FRANCINE WILL FIND OUT.
I DON'T KNOW WHY I EVER TOLD YOU IN THE FIRST PLACE.
I'LL NEVER TELL ANYBODY, KATCHOO. YOU CAN COUNT ON THAT.
sigh ...YOU JUST DON'T KNOW WHAT IT MEANS TO ME TO STAND HERE NEXT TO YOU, TO GET TO KNOW YOU ...TO SHARE SOMETHING IN YOUR LIFE.

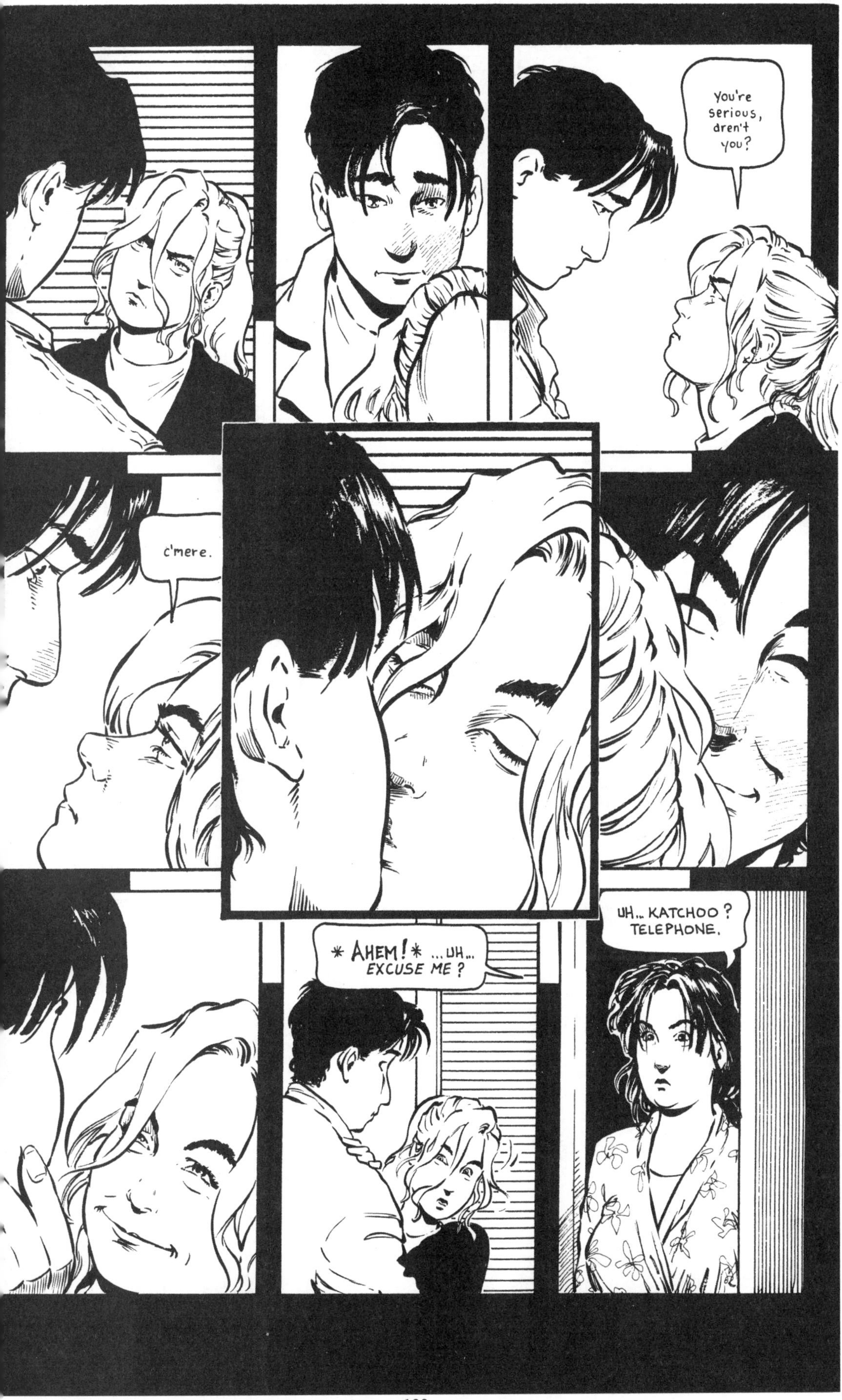
You're serious, aren't you?
c'mere.
AHEM! ...UH... EXCUSE ME?
UH.. KATCHOO? TELEPHONE.

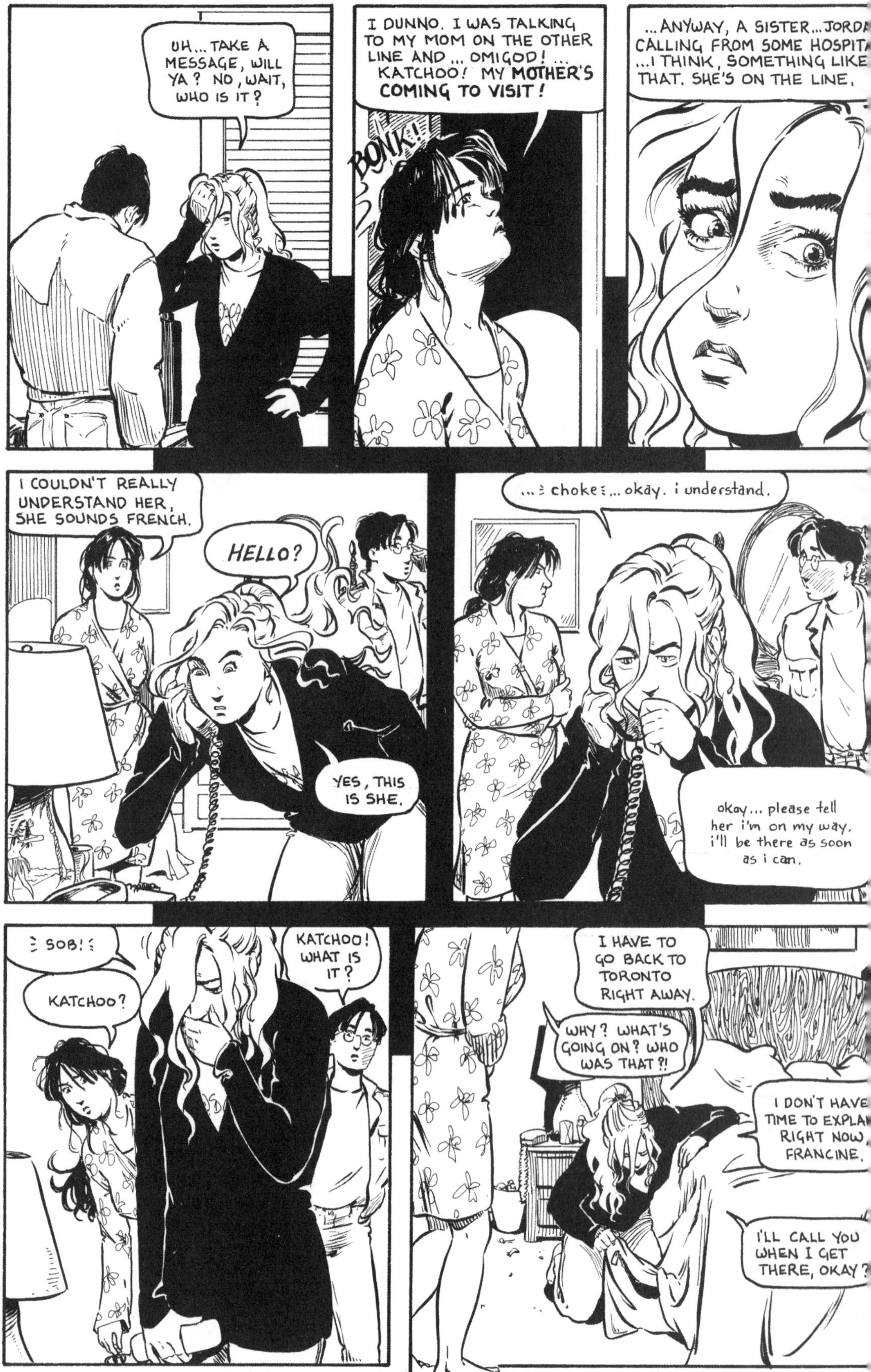
UH... TAKE A MESSAGE, WILL YA? NO, WAIT, WHO IS IT?
I DUNNO. I WAS TALKING TO MY MOM ON THE OTHER LINE AND... OMIGOD! ... KATCHOO! MY MOTHER'S COMING TO VISIT!
BONK!
...ANYWAY, A SISTER...JORDA CALLING FROM SOME HOSPITA ...I THINK, SOMETHING LIKE THAT. SHE'S ON THE LINE.
I COULDN'T REALLY UNDERSTAND HER, SHE SOUNDS FRENCH.
HELLO?
YES, THIS IS SHE.
...:choke:... okay. i understand.
okay... please tell her i'm on my way. i'll be there as soon as i can.
:SOB!:
KATCHOO?
KATCHOO! WHAT IS IT?
I HAVE TO GO BACK TO TORONTO RIGHT AWAY.
WHY? WHAT'S GOING ON? WHO WAS THAT?!
I DON'T HAVE TIME TO EXPLA RIGHT NOW, FRANCINE.
I'LL CALL YOU WHEN I GET THERE, OKAY?

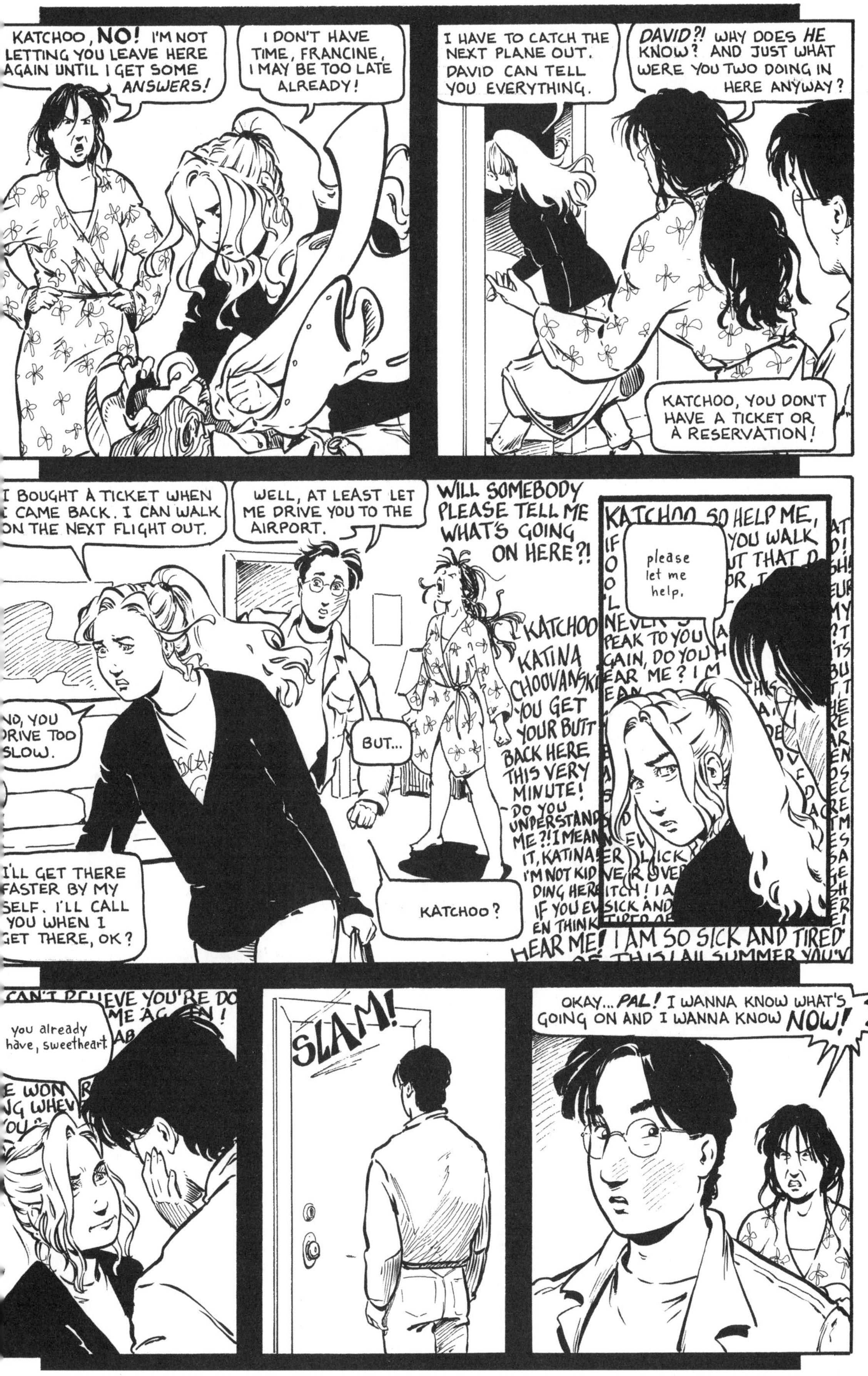
KATCHOO, NO! I'M NOT LETTING YOU LEAVE HERE AGAIN UNTIL I GET SOME ANSWERS!
I DON'T HAVE TIME, FRANCINE, I MAY BE TOO LATE ALREADY!
I HAVE TO CATCH THE NEXT PLANE OUT. DAVID CAN TELL YOU EVERYTHING.
DAVID?! WHY DOES HE KNOW? AND JUST WHAT WERE YOU TWO DOING IN HERE ANYWAY?
KATCHOO, YOU DON'T HAVE A TICKET OR A RESERVATION!
I BOUGHT A TICKET WHEN I CAME BACK. I CAN WALK ON THE NEXT FLIGHT OUT.
WELL, AT LEAST LET ME DRIVE YOU TO THE AIRPORT.
WILL SOMEBODY PLEASE TELL ME WHAT'S GOING ON HERE?!
NO, YOU DRIVE TOO SLOW.
BUT...
KATCHOO KATINA CHOOVANSKI YOU GET YOUR BUTT BACK HERE THIS VERY MINUTE! DO YOU UNDERSTAND ME?! I MEAN IT, KATINA! I'M NOT KIDDING HERE! IF YOU EVEN THINK
I'LL GET THERE FASTER BY MYSELF. I'LL CALL YOU WHEN I GET THERE, OK?
KATCHOO?
KATCHOO SO HELP ME, IF YOU WALK OUT THAT DOOR,
please let me help.
PEAK TO YOU AGAIN, DO YOU HEAR ME? I MEAN
HEAR ME! I AM SO SICK AND TIRED
you already have, sweetheart.
SLAM!
OKAY... PAL! I WANNA KNOW WHAT'S GOING ON AND I WANNA KNOW NOW!

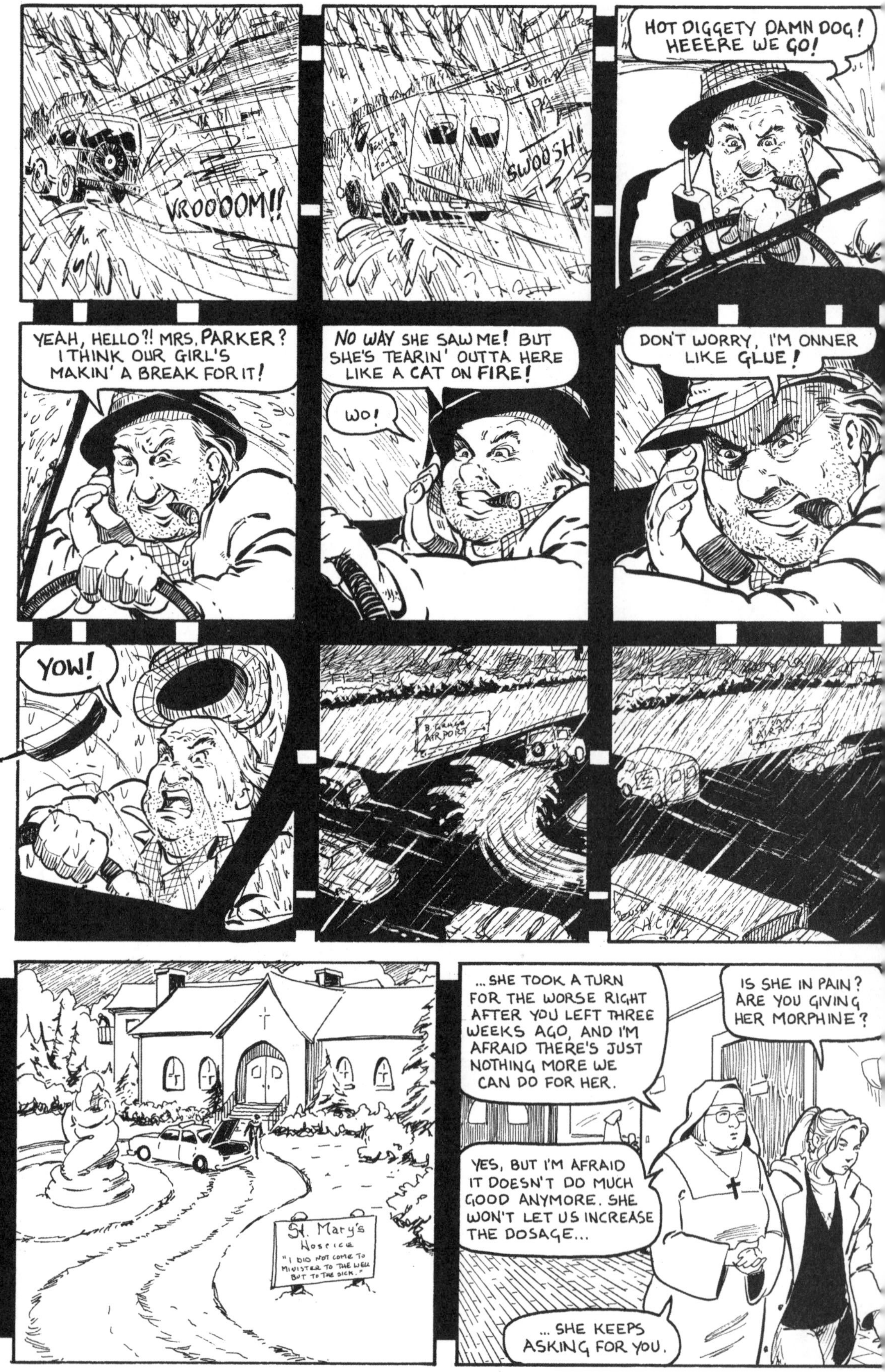
VROOOOM!!
SWOOSH!
HOT DIGGETY DAMN DOG! HEEERE WE GO!
YEAH, HELLO?! MRS. PARKER? I THINK OUR GIRL'S MAKIN' A BREAK FOR IT!
NO WAY SHE SAW ME! BUT SHE'S TEARIN' OUTTA HERE LIKE A CAT ON FIRE!
WO!
DON'T WORRY, I'M ONNER LIKE GLUE!
YOW!
AIRPORT
St. Mary's Hospice
"I DID NOT COME TO MINISTER TO THE WELL BUT TO THE SICK."
...SHE TOOK A TURN FOR THE WORSE RIGHT AFTER YOU LEFT THREE WEEKS AGO, AND I'M AFRAID THERE'S JUST NOTHING MORE WE CAN DO FOR HER.
IS SHE IN PAIN? ARE YOU GIVING HER MORPHINE?
YES, BUT I'M AFRAID IT DOESN'T DO MUCH GOOD ANYMORE. SHE WON'T LET US INCREASE THE DOSAGE...
...SHE KEEPS ASKING FOR YOU.

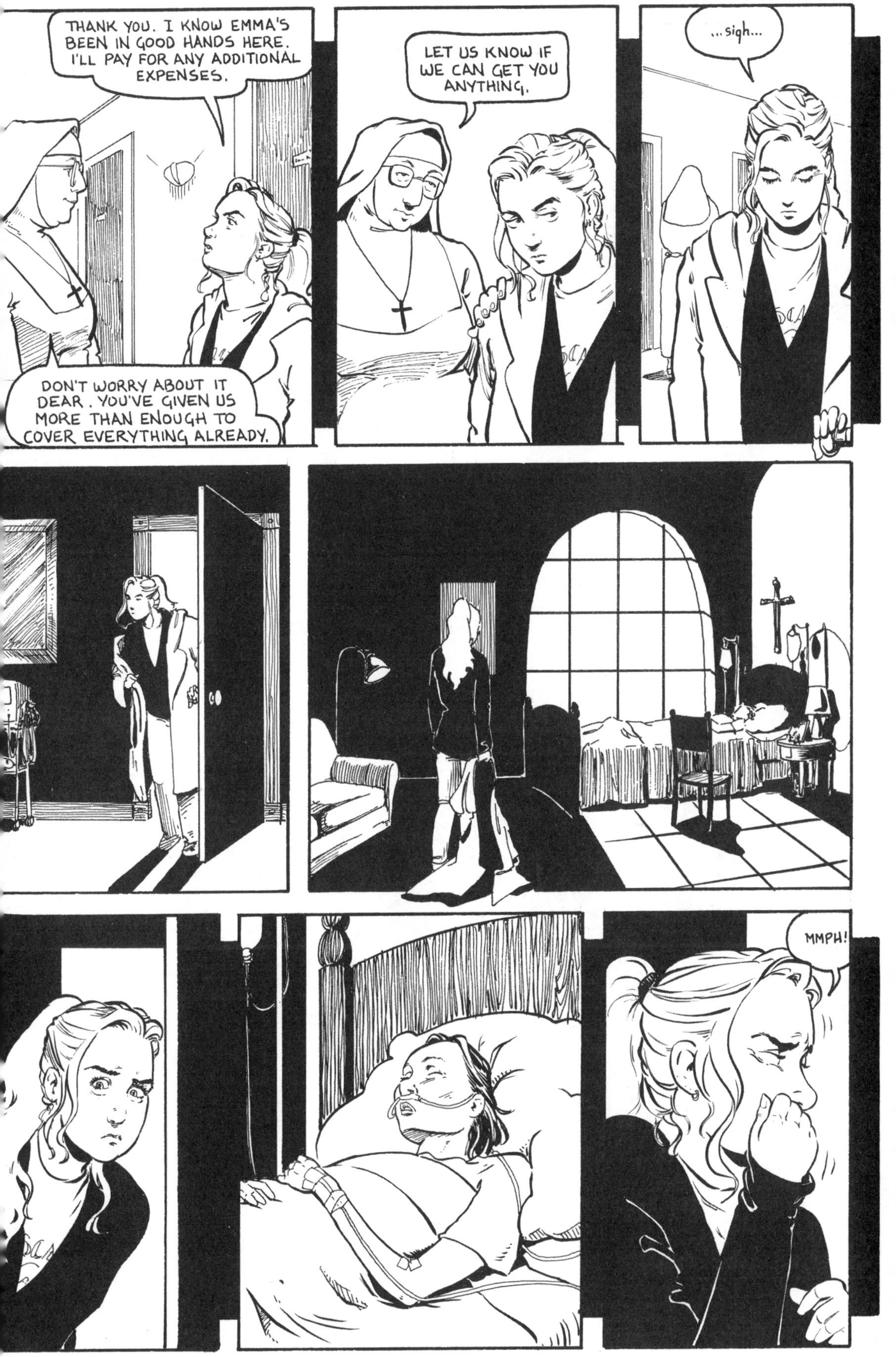

THANK YOU. I KNOW EMMA'S BEEN IN GOOD HANDS HERE. I'LL PAY FOR ANY ADDITIONAL EXPENSES.
DON'T WORRY ABOUT IT DEAR. YOU'VE GIVEN US MORE THAN ENOUGH TO COVER EVERYTHING ALREADY.
LET US KNOW IF WE CAN GET YOU ANYTHING.
...sigh...
MMPH!

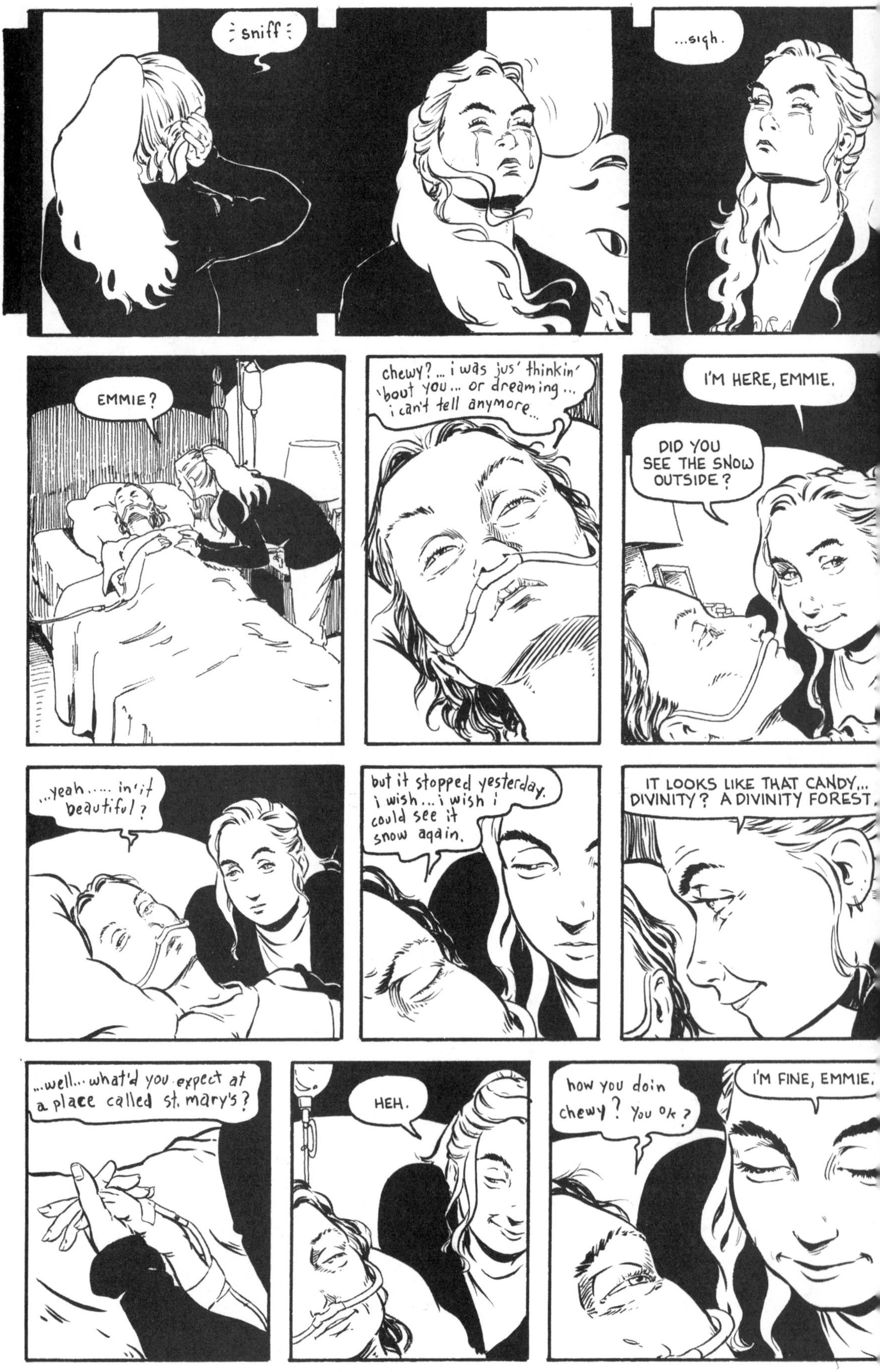

sniff
...sigh.
EMMIE?
chewy? ... i was jus' thinkin' 'bout you... or dreaming... i can't tell anymore...
I'M HERE, EMMIE.
DID YOU SEE THE SNOW OUTSIDE?
...yeah..... in'it beautiful?
but it stopped yesterday. i wish... i wish i could see it snow again.
IT LOOKS LIKE THAT CANDY... DIVINITY? A DIVINITY FOREST.
...well... what'd you expect at a place called st. mary's?
HEH.
how you doin chewy? you ok?
I'M FINE, EMMIE.

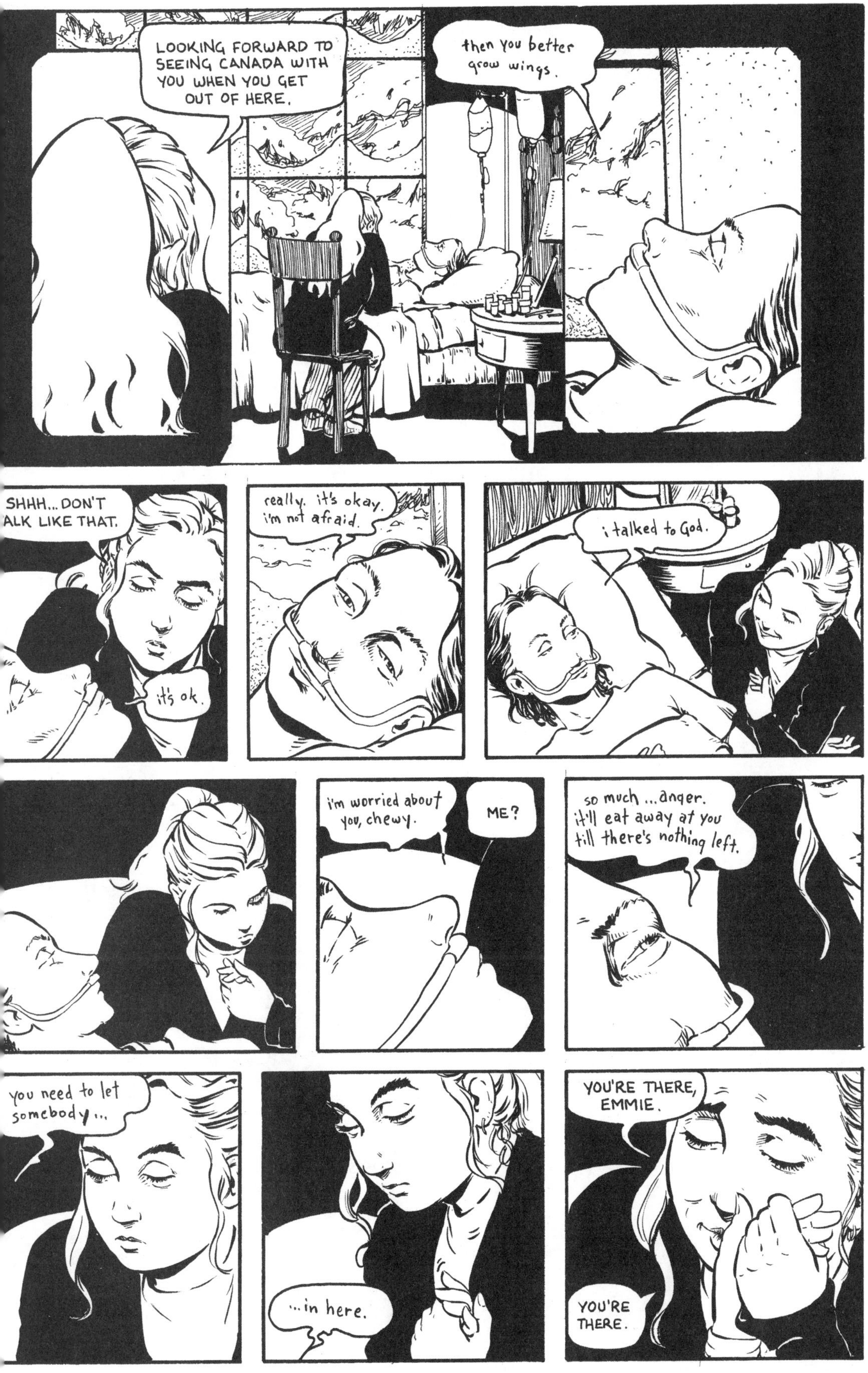
LOOKING FORWARD TO SEEING CANADA WITH YOU WHEN YOU GET OUT OF HERE.
then you better grow wings.
SHHH... DON'T ALK LIKE THAT.
it's ok.
really. it's okay. i'm not afraid.
i talked to God.
i'm worried about you, chewy.
ME?
so much ...anger. it'll eat away at you till there's nothing left.
you need to let somebody...
...in here.
YOU'RE THERE, EMMIE.
YOU'RE THERE.

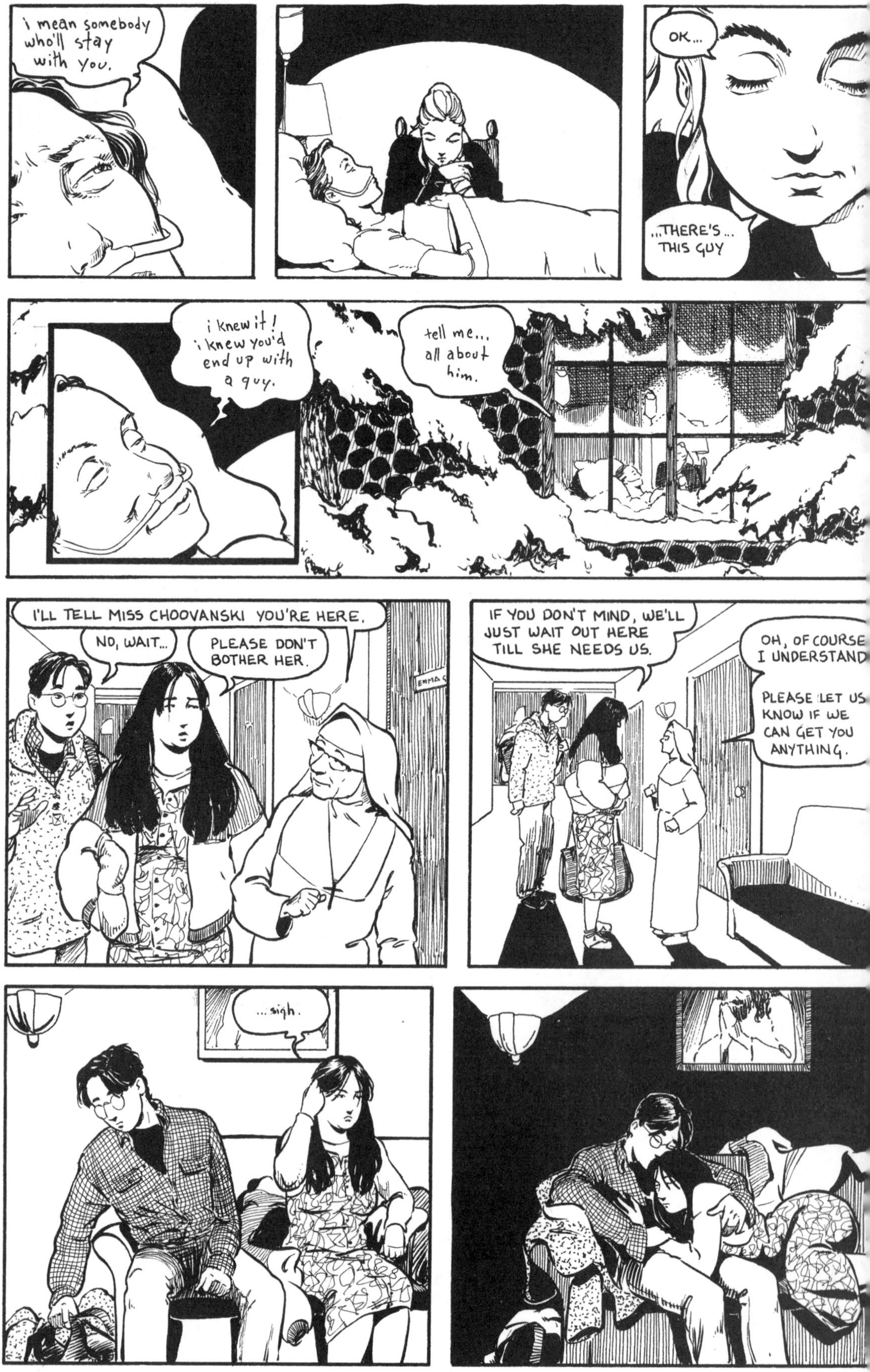
i mean somebody who'll stay with you.
OK...
...THERE'S... THIS GUY
i knew it! i knew you'd end up with a guy.
tell me... all about him.
I'LL TELL MISS CHOOVANSKI YOU'RE HERE.
NO, WAIT...
PLEASE DON'T BOTHER HER.
IF YOU DON'T MIND, WE'LL JUST WAIT OUT HERE TILL SHE NEEDS US.
OH, OF COURSE I UNDERSTAND
PLEASE LET US KNOW IF WE CAN GET YOU ANYTHING.
...sigh.

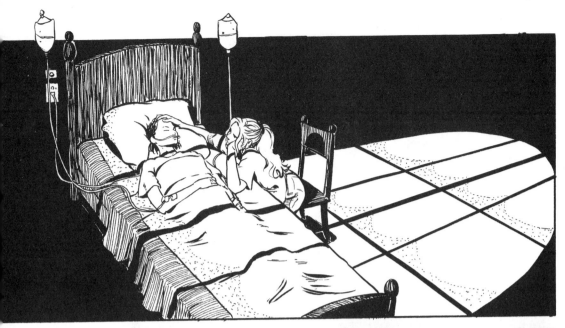

WHAT'CHA THINKING ABOUT?

WHAT, EMMIE? ...what?

BABY JUNE? ...THE SONG? WHAT MADE YOU THINK OF THAT?

I REMEMBER WHEN YOU WROTE THAT. WE WERE STAYING IN THAT LITTLE HOUSE IN HANA, REMEMBER?

WE WERE SO BROWN.

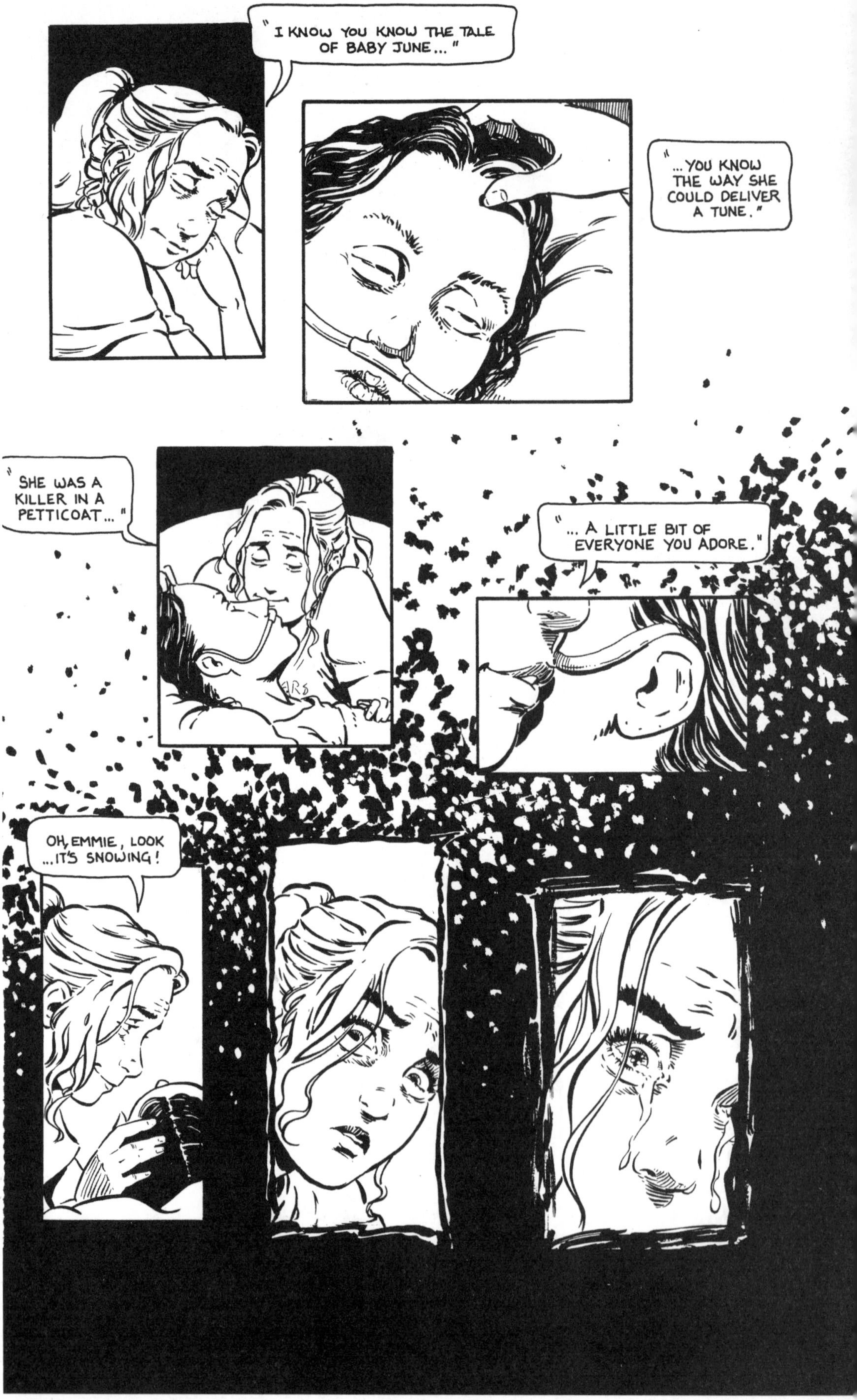
"I KNOW YOU KNOW THE TALE OF BABY JUNE..."
"...YOU KNOW THE WAY SHE COULD DELIVER A TUNE."
"SHE WAS A KILLER IN A PETTICOAT..."
"... A LITTLE BIT OF EVERYONE YOU ADORE."
OH, EMMIE, LOOK ...IT'S SNOWING!

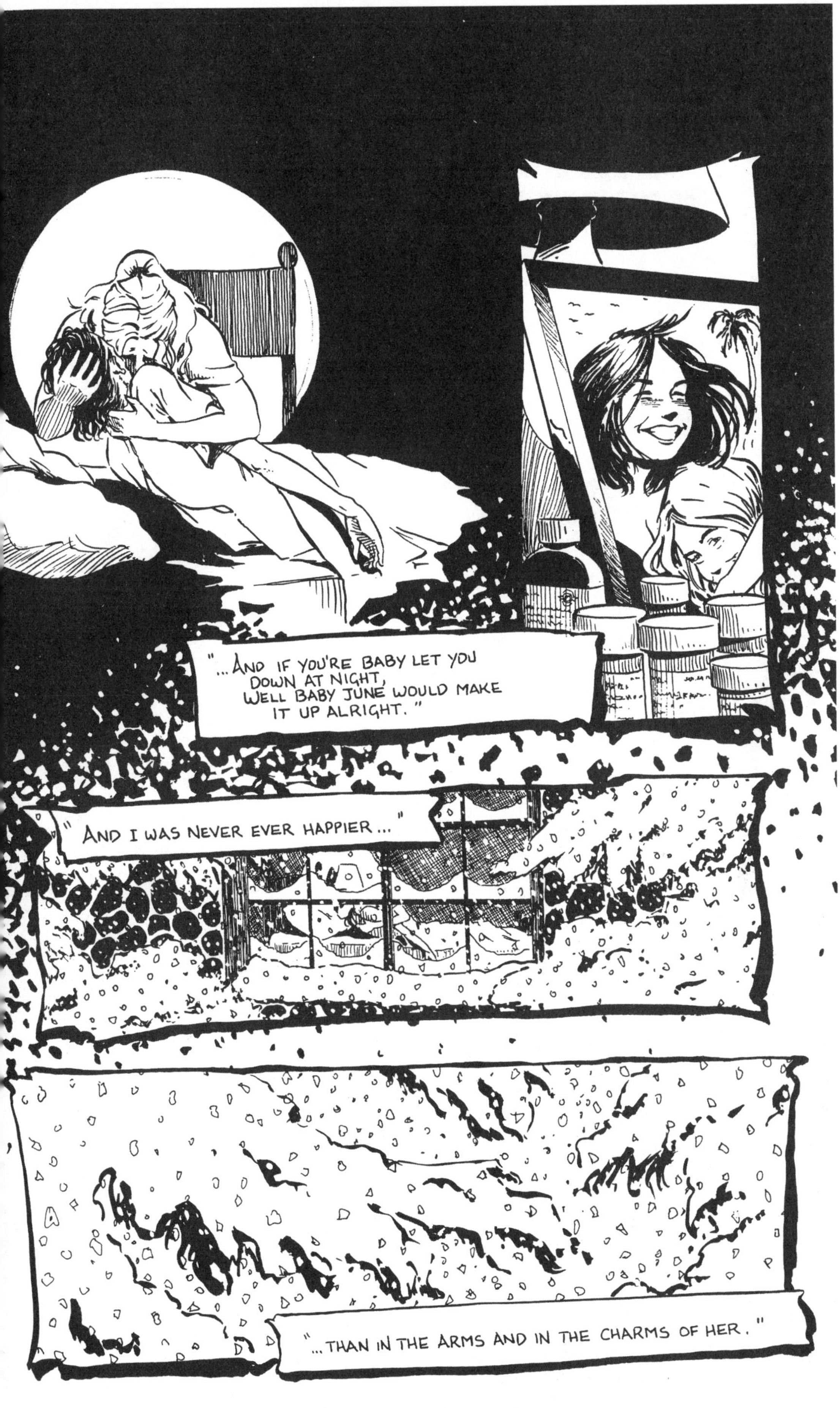
"...AND IF YOU'RE BABY LET YOU DOWN AT NIGHT, WELL BABY JUNE WOULD MAKE IT UP ALRIGHT."
"AND I WAS NEVER EVER HAPPIER..."
"...THAN IN THE ARMS AND IN THE CHARMS OF HER."

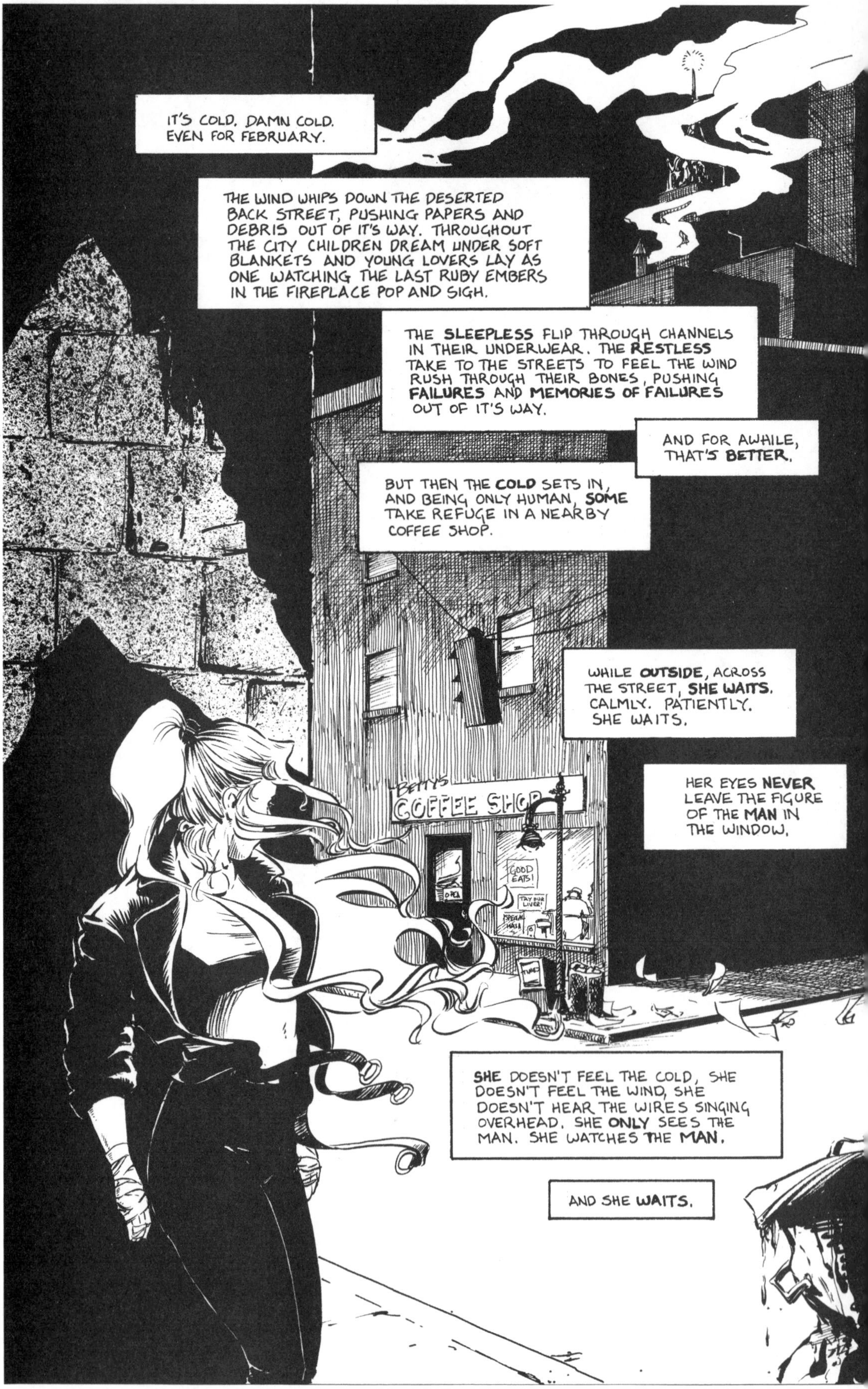
IT'S COLD. DAMN COLD. EVEN FOR FEBRUARY.
THE WIND WHIPS DOWN THE DESERTED BACK STREET, PUSHING PAPERS AND DEBRIS OUT OF IT'S WAY. THROUGHOUT THE CITY CHILDREN DREAM UNDER SOFT BLANKETS AND YOUNG LOVERS LAY AS ONE WATCHING THE LAST RUBY EMBERS IN THE FIREPLACE POP AND SIGH.
THE **SLEEPLESS** FLIP THROUGH CHANNELS IN THEIR UNDERWEAR. THE **RESTLESS** TAKE TO THE STREETS TO FEEL THE WIND RUSH THROUGH THEIR BONES, PUSHING **FAILURES** AND **MEMORIES OF FAILURES** OUT OF IT'S WAY.
AND FOR AWHILE, THAT'S **BETTER**.
BUT THEN THE **COLD** SETS IN, AND BEING ONLY HUMAN, **SOME** TAKE REFUGE IN A NEARBY COFFEE SHOP.
WHILE **OUTSIDE**, ACROSS THE STREET, **SHE WAITS**. CALMLY. PATIENTLY. SHE WAITS.
HER EYES **NEVER** LEAVE THE FIGURE OF THE **MAN** IN THE WINDOW.
BETTY'S
COFFEE SHOP
GOOD EATS!
TRY OUR LIVER!
TIMES
SHE DOESN'T FEEL THE COLD, SHE DOESN'T FEEL THE WIND, SHE DOESN'T HEAR THE WIRES SINGING OVERHEAD. SHE **ONLY** SEES THE MAN. SHE WATCHES THE **MAN**.
AND SHE **WAITS**.

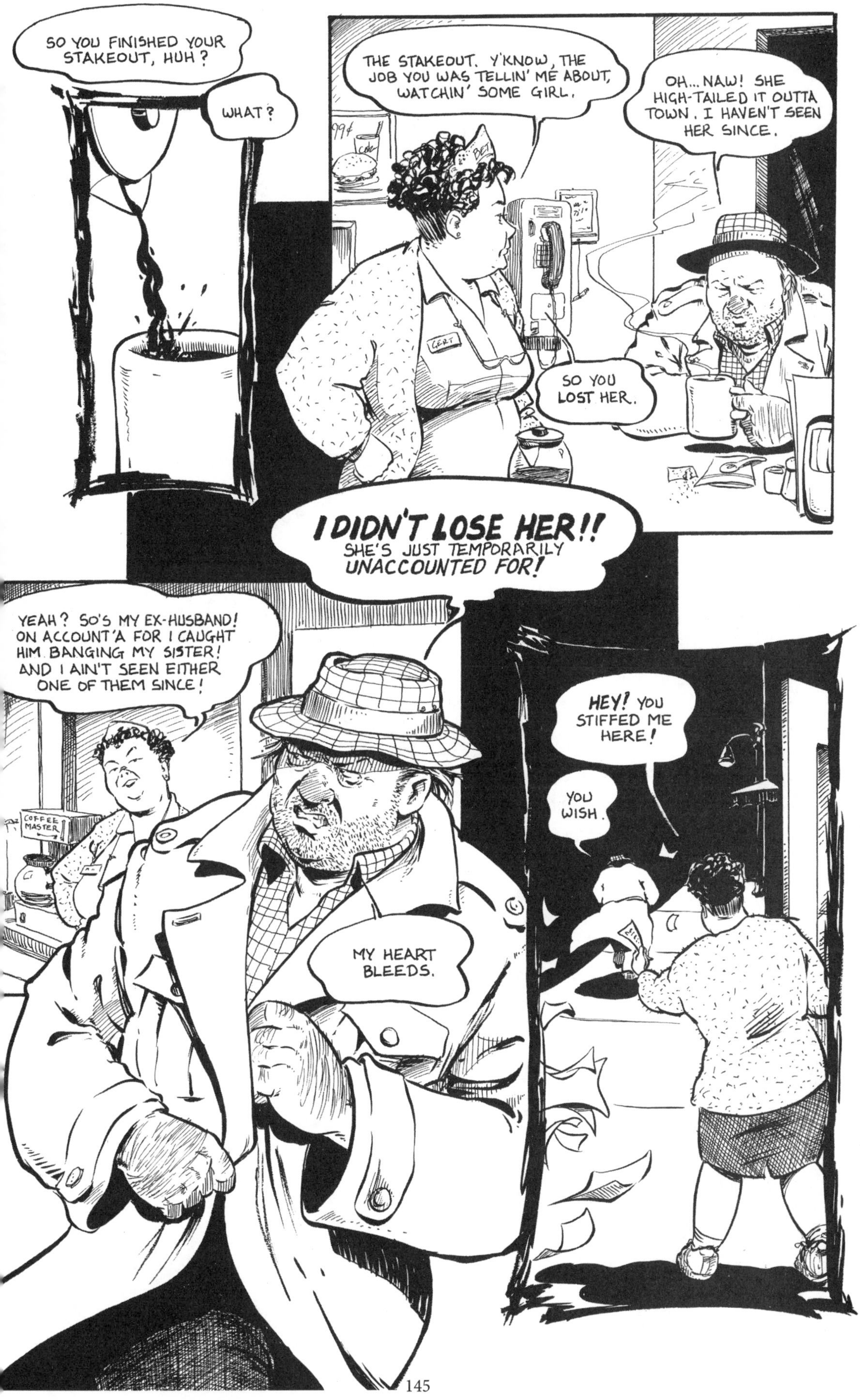
SO YOU FINISHED YOUR STAKEOUT, HUH?
WHAT?
THE STAKEOUT. Y'KNOW, THE JOB YOU WAS TELLIN' ME ABOUT, WATCHIN' SOME GIRL.
OH... NAW! SHE HIGH-TAILED IT OUTTA TOWN. I HAVEN'T SEEN HER SINCE.
SO YOU LOST HER.
I DIDN'T LOSE HER!! SHE'S JUST TEMPORARILY UNACCOUNTED FOR!
YEAH? SO'S MY EX-HUSBAND! ON ACCOUNT'A FOR I CAUGHT HIM BANGING MY SISTER! AND I AIN'T SEEN EITHER ONE OF THEM SINCE!
MY HEART BLEEDS.
HEY! YOU STIFFED ME HERE!
YOU WISH.

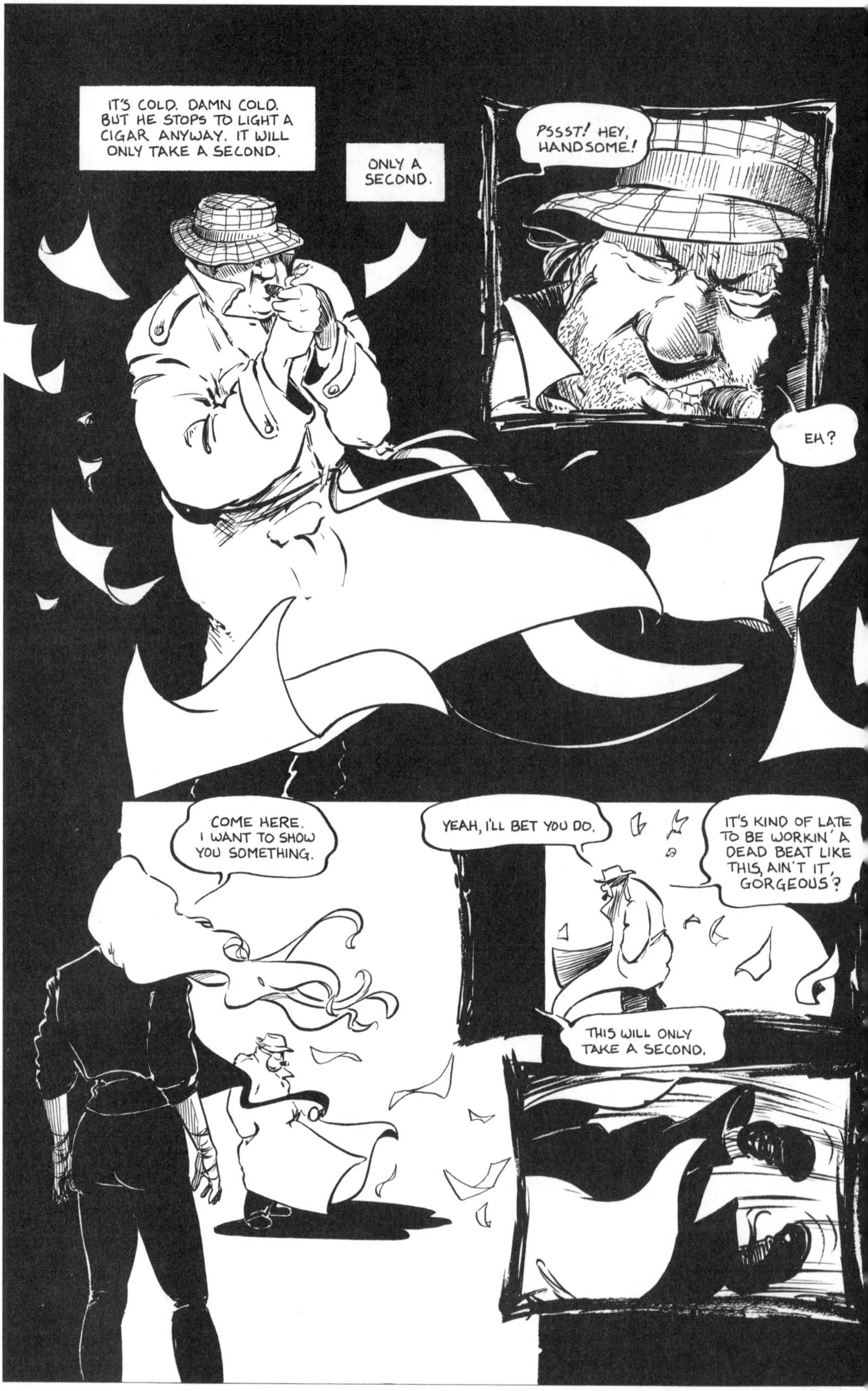

IT'S COLD. DAMN COLD. BUT HE STOPS TO LIGHT A CIGAR ANYWAY. IT WILL ONLY TAKE A SECOND.
ONLY A SECOND.
PSSST! HEY, HANDSOME!
EH?
COME HERE. I WANT TO SHOW YOU SOMETHING.
YEAH, I'LL BET YOU DO.
IT'S KIND OF LATE TO BE WORKIN' A DEAD BEAT LIKE THIS, AIN'T IT, GORGEOUS?
THIS WILL ONLY TAKE A SECOND.

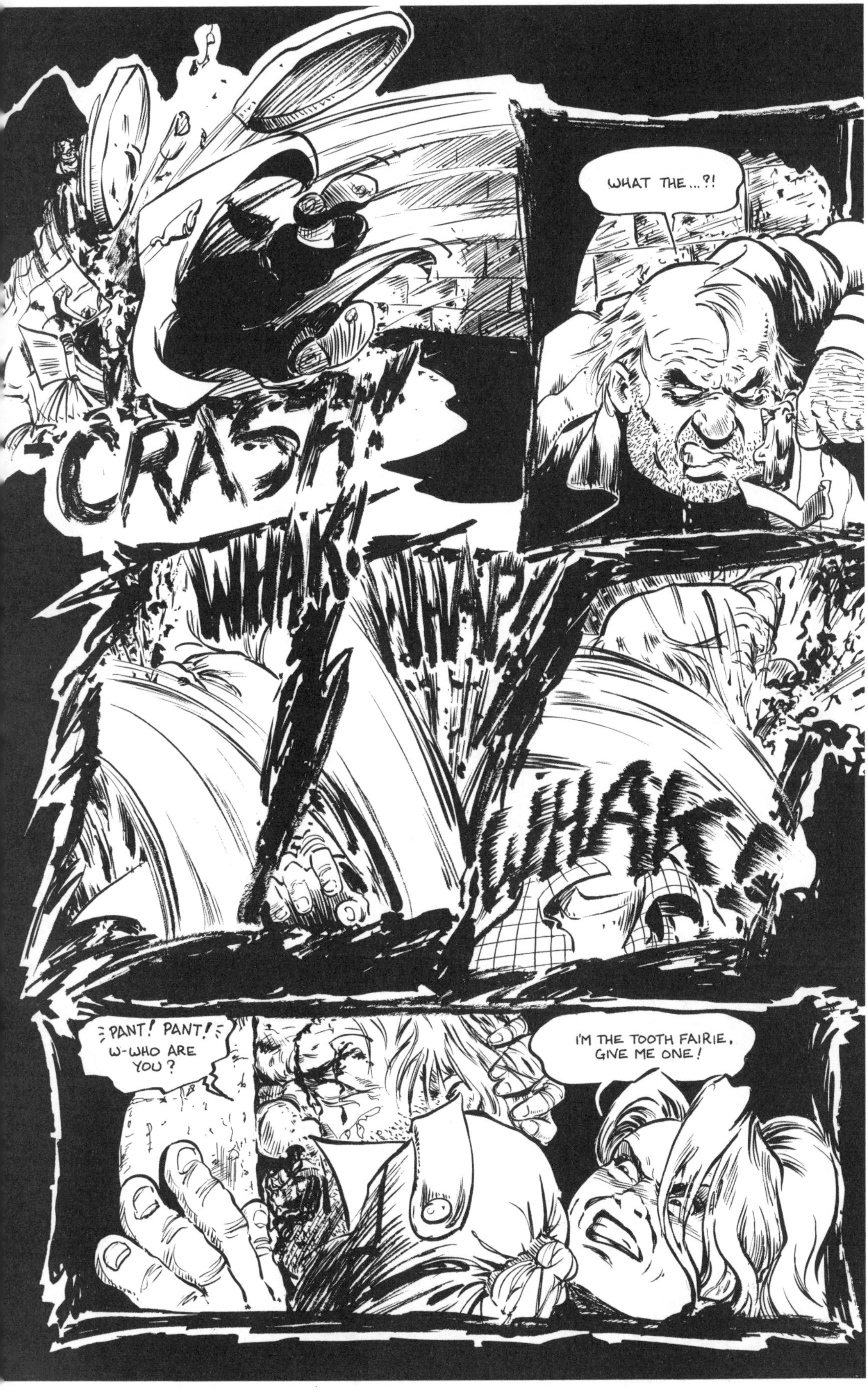
CRASH!
WHAT THE...?!
WHAK!
WHAP!
WHAK!
PANT! PANT!
W-WHO ARE YOU?
I'M THE TOOTH FAIRIE, GIVE ME ONE!

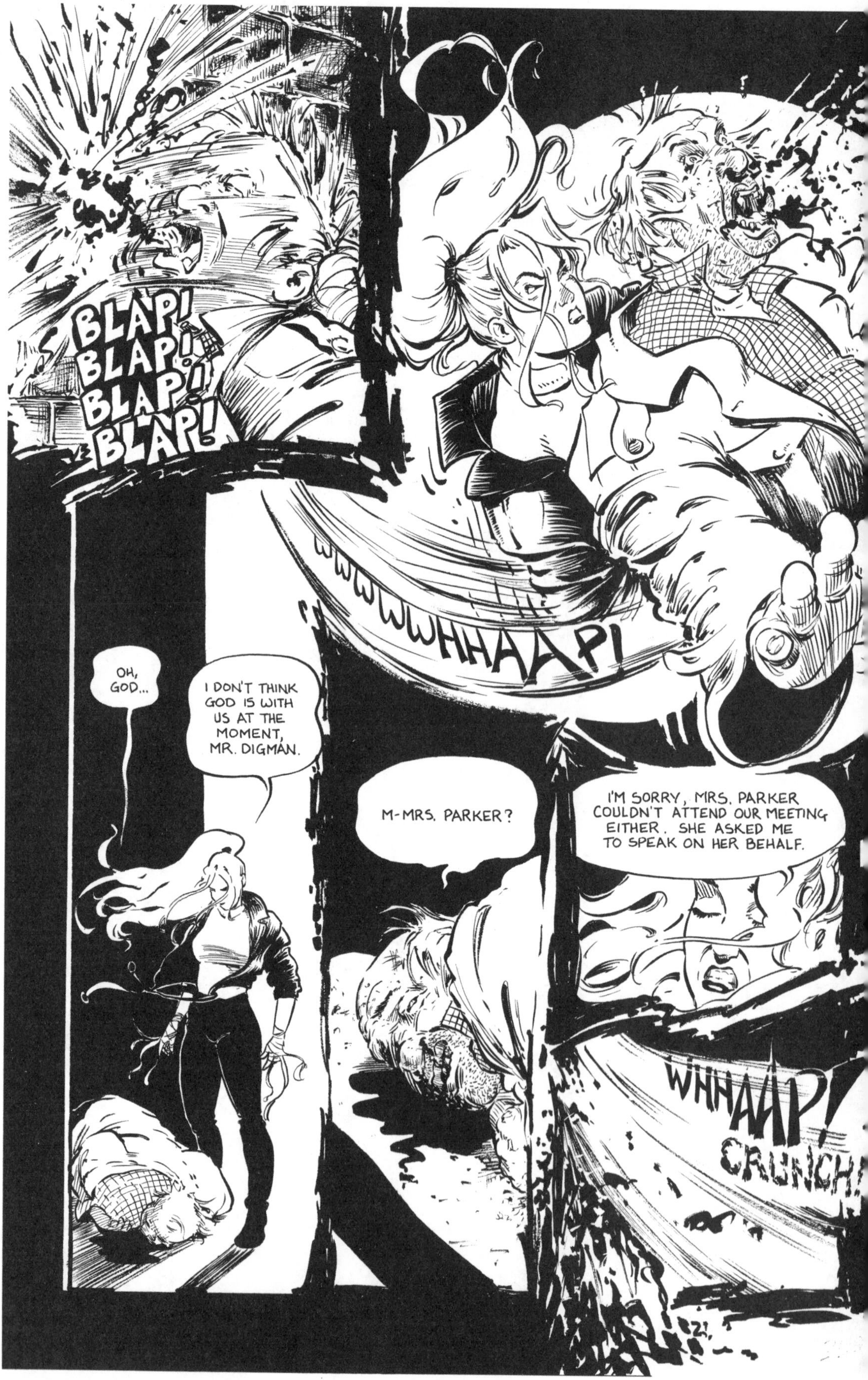
BLAP! BLAP! BLAP! BLAP!
WWWWWWHHAAP!
OH, GOD...
I DON'T THINK GOD IS WITH US AT THE MOMENT, MR. DIGMAN.
M-MRS. PARKER?
I'M SORRY, MRS. PARKER COULDN'T ATTEND OUR MEETING EITHER. SHE ASKED ME TO SPEAK ON HER BEHALF.
WHHAAP!
CRUNCH!

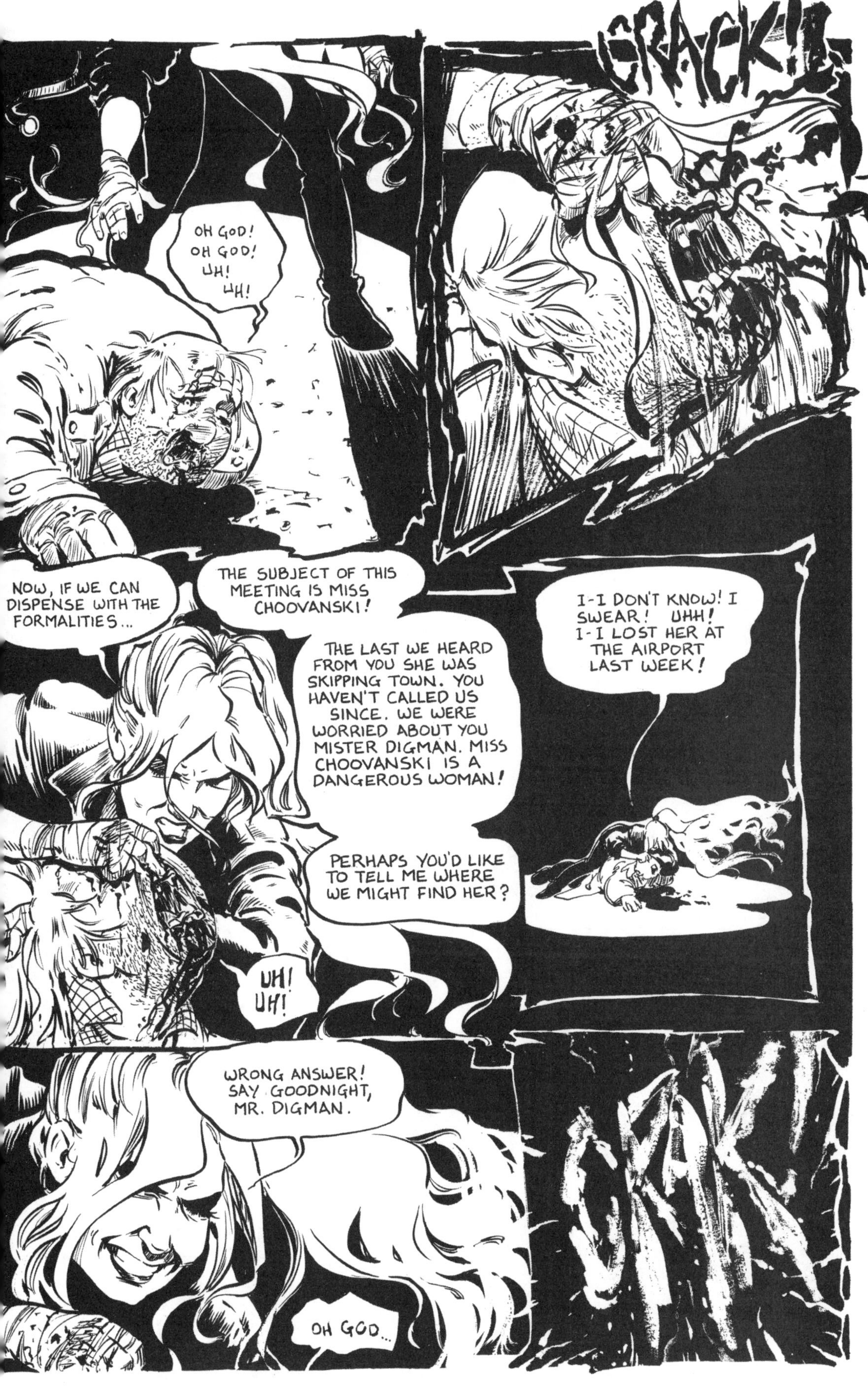

CRACK!!
OH GOD! OH GOD! UH! UH!
NOW, IF WE CAN DISPENSE WITH THE FORMALITIES...
THE SUBJECT OF THIS MEETING IS MISS CHOOVANSKI!
THE LAST WE HEARD FROM YOU SHE WAS SKIPPING TOWN. YOU HAVEN'T CALLED US SINCE. WE WERE WORRIED ABOUT YOU MISTER DIGMAN. MISS CHOOVANSKI IS A DANGEROUS WOMAN!
PERHAPS YOU'D LIKE TO TELL ME WHERE WE MIGHT FIND HER?
UH! UH!
I-I DON'T KNOW! I SWEAR! UHH! I-I LOST HER AT THE AIRPORT LAST WEEK!
WRONG ANSWER! SAY GOODNIGHT, MR. DIGMAN.
OH GOD...

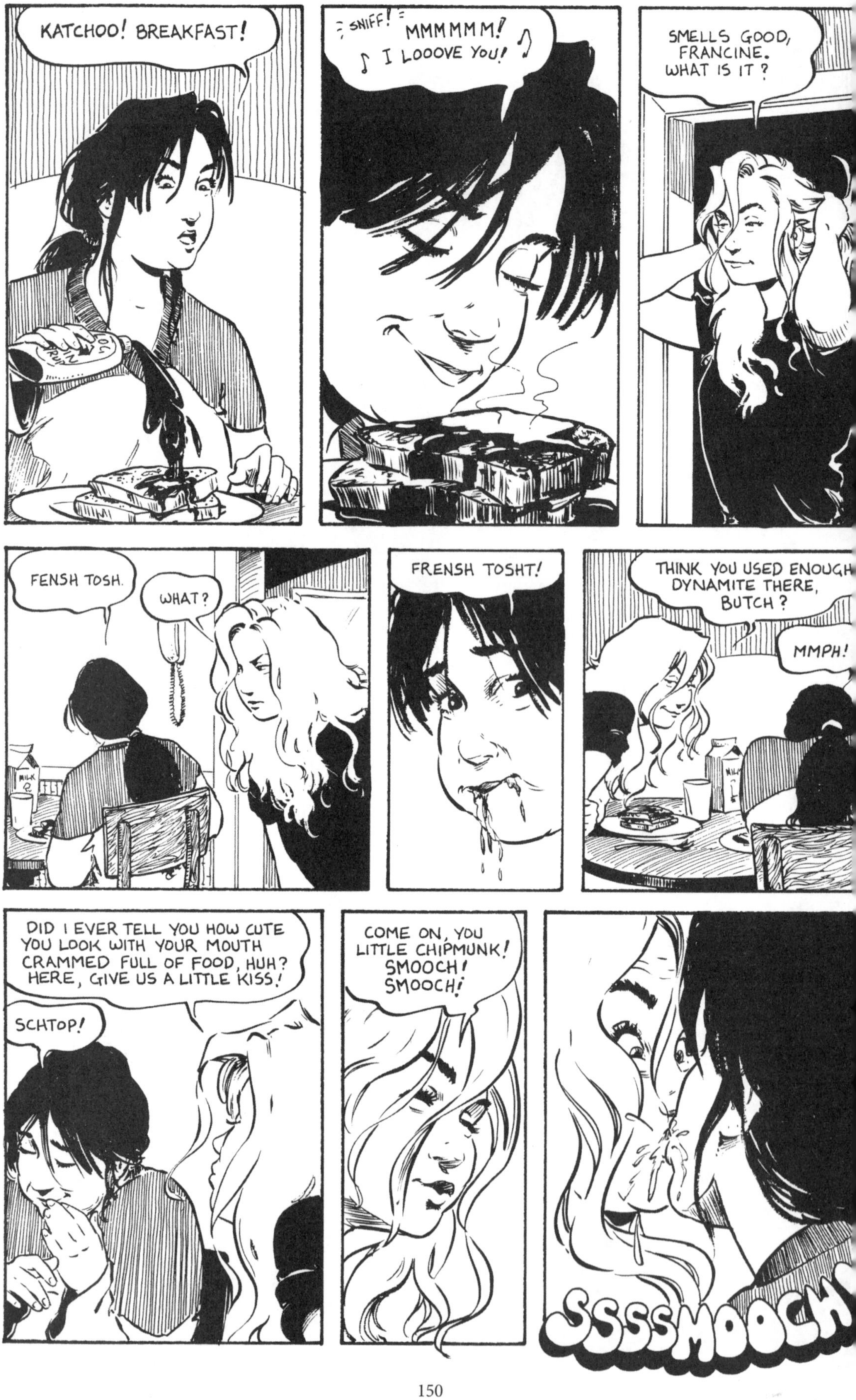

KATCHOO! BREAKFAST!
SNIFF!
MMMMMM! I LOOOVE YOU!
SMELLS GOOD, FRANCINE. WHAT IS IT?
FENSH TOSH.
WHAT?
FRENSH TOSHT!
THINK YOU USED ENOUGH DYNAMITE THERE, BUTCH?
MMPH!
DID I EVER TELL YOU HOW CUTE YOU LOOK WITH YOUR MOUTH CRAMMED FULL OF FOOD, HUH? HERE, GIVE US A LITTLE KISS!
SCHTOP!
COME ON, YOU LITTLE CHIPMUNK! SMOOCH! SMOOCH!
SSSSMOOCH

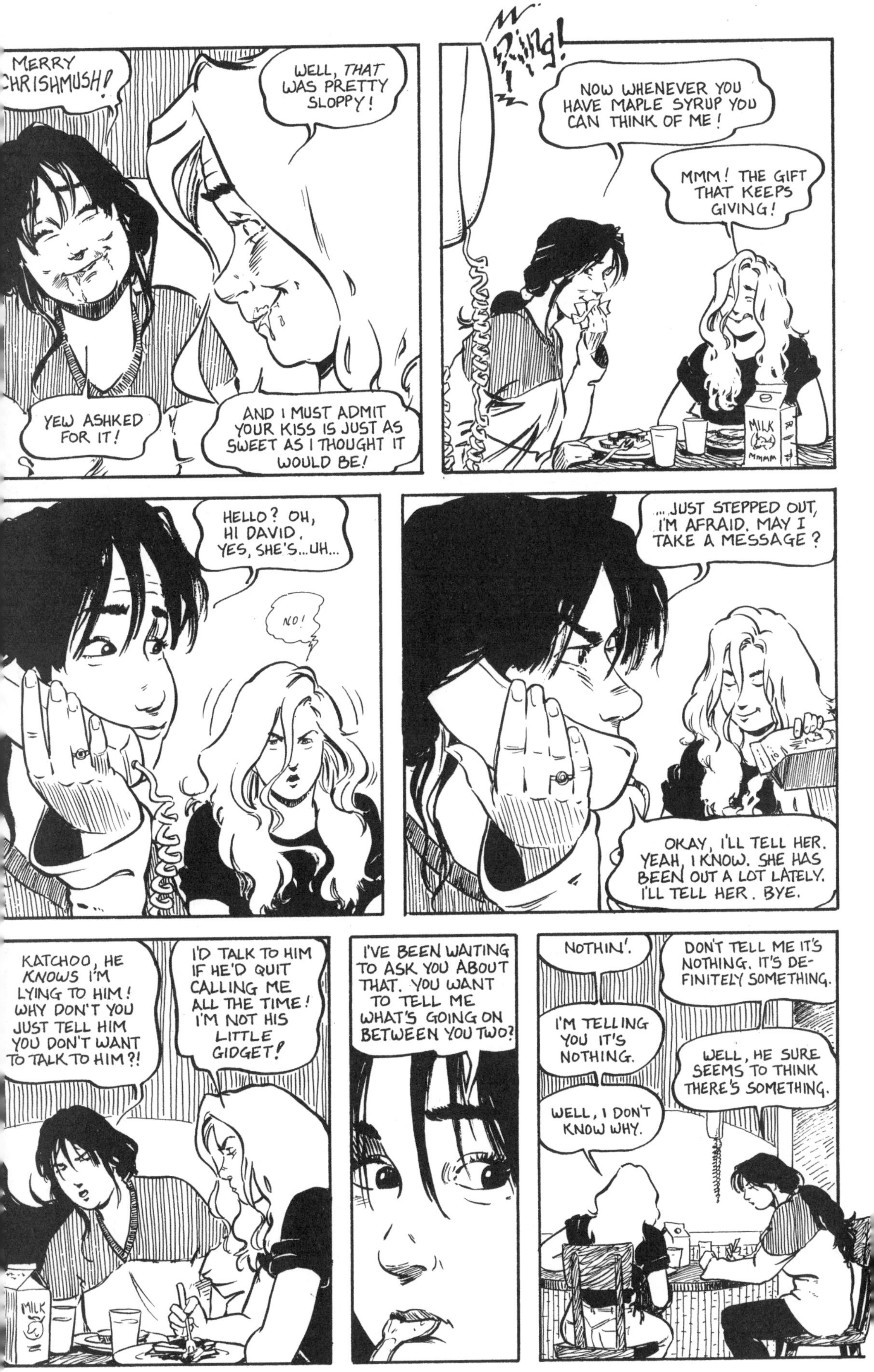
MERRY CHRISHMUSH!
WELL, THAT WAS PRETTY SLOPPY!
YEW ASHKED FOR IT!
AND I MUST ADMIT YOUR KISS IS JUST AS SWEET AS I THOUGHT IT WOULD BE!
Ring!
NOW WHENEVER YOU HAVE MAPLE SYRUP YOU CAN THINK OF ME!
MMM! THE GIFT THAT KEEPS GIVING!
MILK
HELLO? OH, HI DAVID. YES, SHE'S...UH...
NO!
...JUST STEPPED OUT, I'M AFRAID. MAY I TAKE A MESSAGE?
OKAY, I'LL TELL HER. YEAH, I KNOW. SHE HAS BEEN OUT A LOT LATELY. I'LL TELL HER. BYE.
KATCHOO, HE KNOWS I'M LYING TO HIM! WHY DON'T YOU JUST TELL HIM YOU DON'T WANT TO TALK TO HIM?!
I'D TALK TO HIM IF HE'D QUIT CALLING ME ALL THE TIME! I'M NOT HIS LITTLE GIDGET!
MILK
I'VE BEEN WAITING TO ASK YOU ABOUT THAT. YOU WANT TO TELL ME WHAT'S GOING ON BETWEEN YOU TWO?
NOTHIN'.
DON'T TELL ME IT'S NOTHING. IT'S DEFINITELY SOMETHING.
I'M TELLING YOU IT'S NOTHING.
WELL, HE SURE SEEMS TO THINK THERE'S SOMETHING.
WELL, I DON'T KNOW WHY.

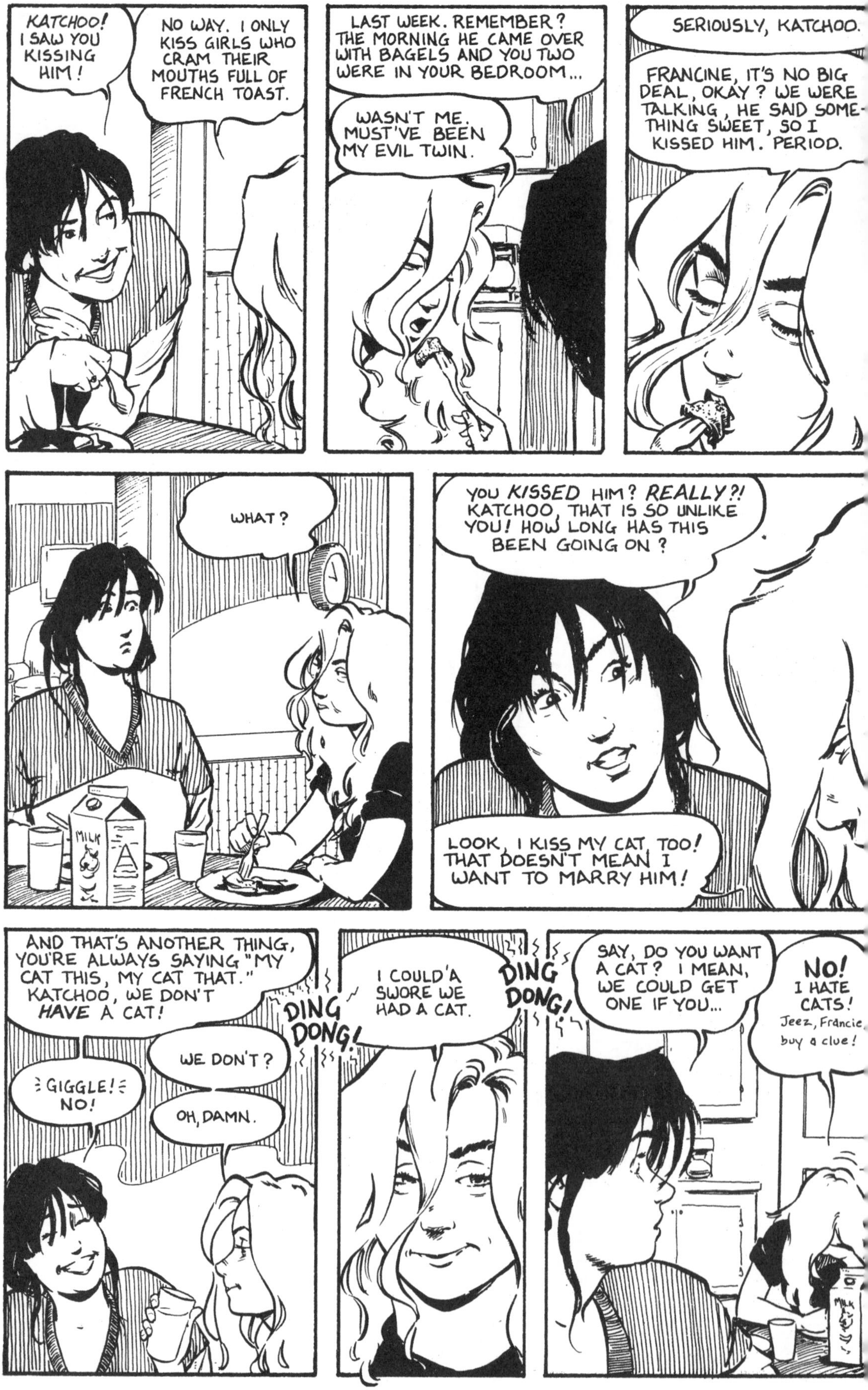

KATCHOO! I SAW YOU KISSING HIM!
NO WAY. I ONLY KISS GIRLS WHO CRAM THEIR MOUTHS FULL OF FRENCH TOAST.
LAST WEEK. REMEMBER? THE MORNING HE CAME OVER WITH BAGELS AND YOU TWO WERE IN YOUR BEDROOM...
WASN'T ME. MUST'VE BEEN MY EVIL TWIN.
SERIOUSLY, KATCHOO.
FRANCINE, IT'S NO BIG DEAL, OKAY? WE WERE TALKING, HE SAID SOMETHING SWEET, SO I KISSED HIM. PERIOD.
WHAT?
YOU KISSED HIM? REALLY?! KATCHOO, THAT IS SO UNLIKE YOU! HOW LONG HAS THIS BEEN GOING ON?
LOOK, I KISS MY CAT, TOO! THAT DOESN'T MEAN I WANT TO MARRY HIM!
AND THAT'S ANOTHER THING, YOU'RE ALWAYS SAYING "MY CAT THIS, MY CAT THAT." KATCHOO, WE DON'T HAVE A CAT!
WE DON'T?
GIGGLE! NO!
OH, DAMN.
DING DONG!
I COULD'A SWORE WE HAD A CAT.
DING DONG!
SAY, DO YOU WANT A CAT? I MEAN, WE COULD GET ONE IF YOU...
NO! I HATE CATS! Jeez, Francie, buy a clue!
MILK

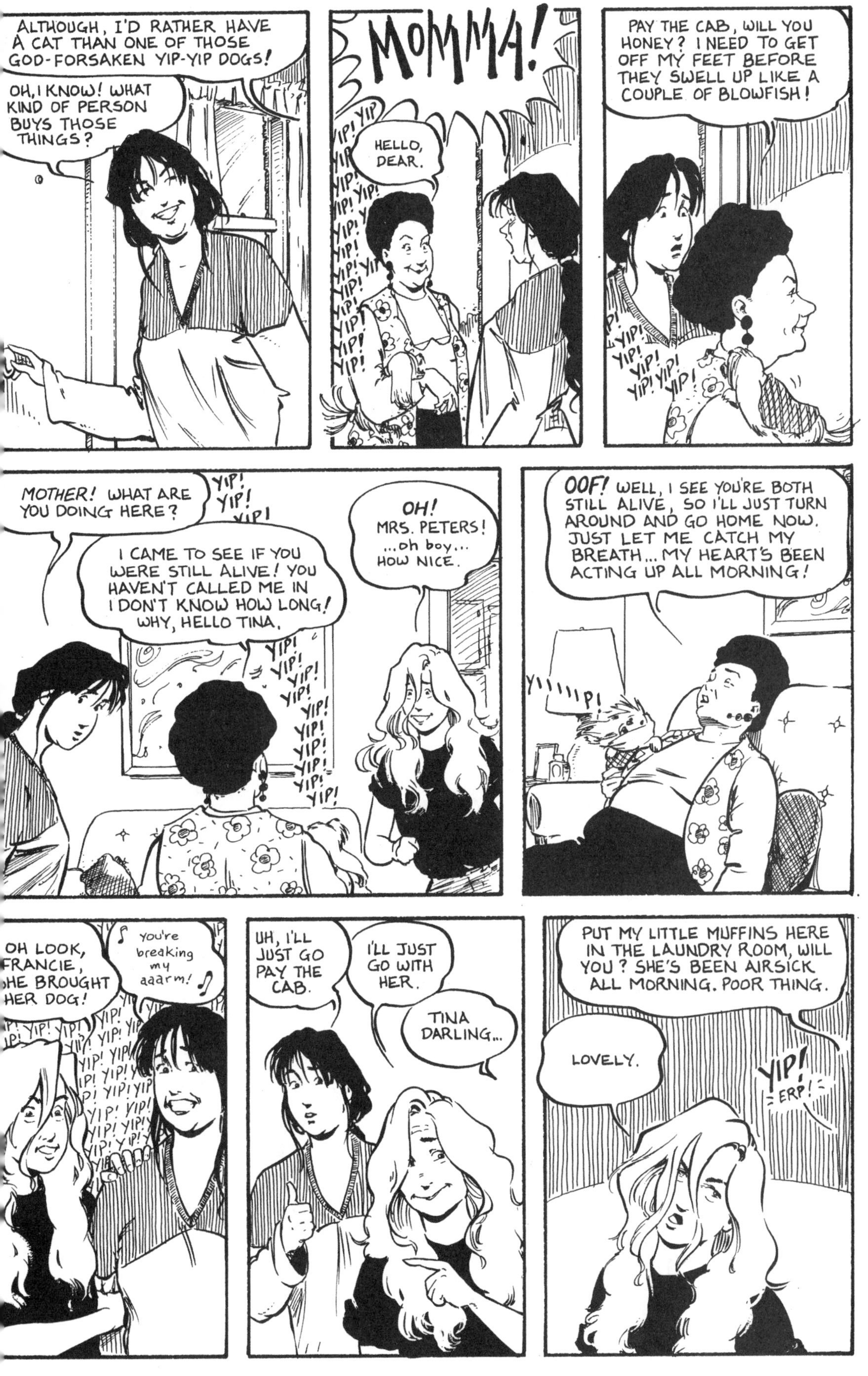
ALTHOUGH, I'D RATHER HAVE A CAT THAN ONE OF THOSE GOD-FORSAKEN YIP-YIP DOGS!
OH, I KNOW! WHAT KIND OF PERSON BUYS THOSE THINGS?
MOMMA!
YIP! YIP!
HELLO, DEAR.
PAY THE CAB, WILL YOU HONEY? I NEED TO GET OFF MY FEET BEFORE THEY SWELL UP LIKE A COUPLE OF BLOWFISH!
YIP! YIP! YIP! YIP!
MOTHER! WHAT ARE YOU DOING HERE?
YIP! YIP!
I CAME TO SEE IF YOU WERE STILL ALIVE! YOU HAVEN'T CALLED ME IN I DON'T KNOW HOW LONG! WHY, HELLO TINA.
OH! MRS. PETERS! ...oh boy... HOW NICE.
YIP! YIP! YIP! YIP!
OOF! WELL, I SEE YOU'RE BOTH STILL ALIVE, SO I'LL JUST TURN AROUND AND GO HOME NOW. JUST LET ME CATCH MY BREATH... MY HEART'S BEEN ACTING UP ALL MORNING!
YIIIIIP!
OH LOOK, FRANCIE, SHE BROUGHT HER DOG!
You're breaking my aaarm!
UH, I'LL JUST GO PAY THE CAB.
I'LL JUST GO WITH HER.
TINA DARLING...
PUT MY LITTLE MUFFINS HERE IN THE LAUNDRY ROOM, WILL YOU? SHE'S BEEN AIRSICK ALL MORNING. POOR THING.
LOVELY.
YIP!
ERP!

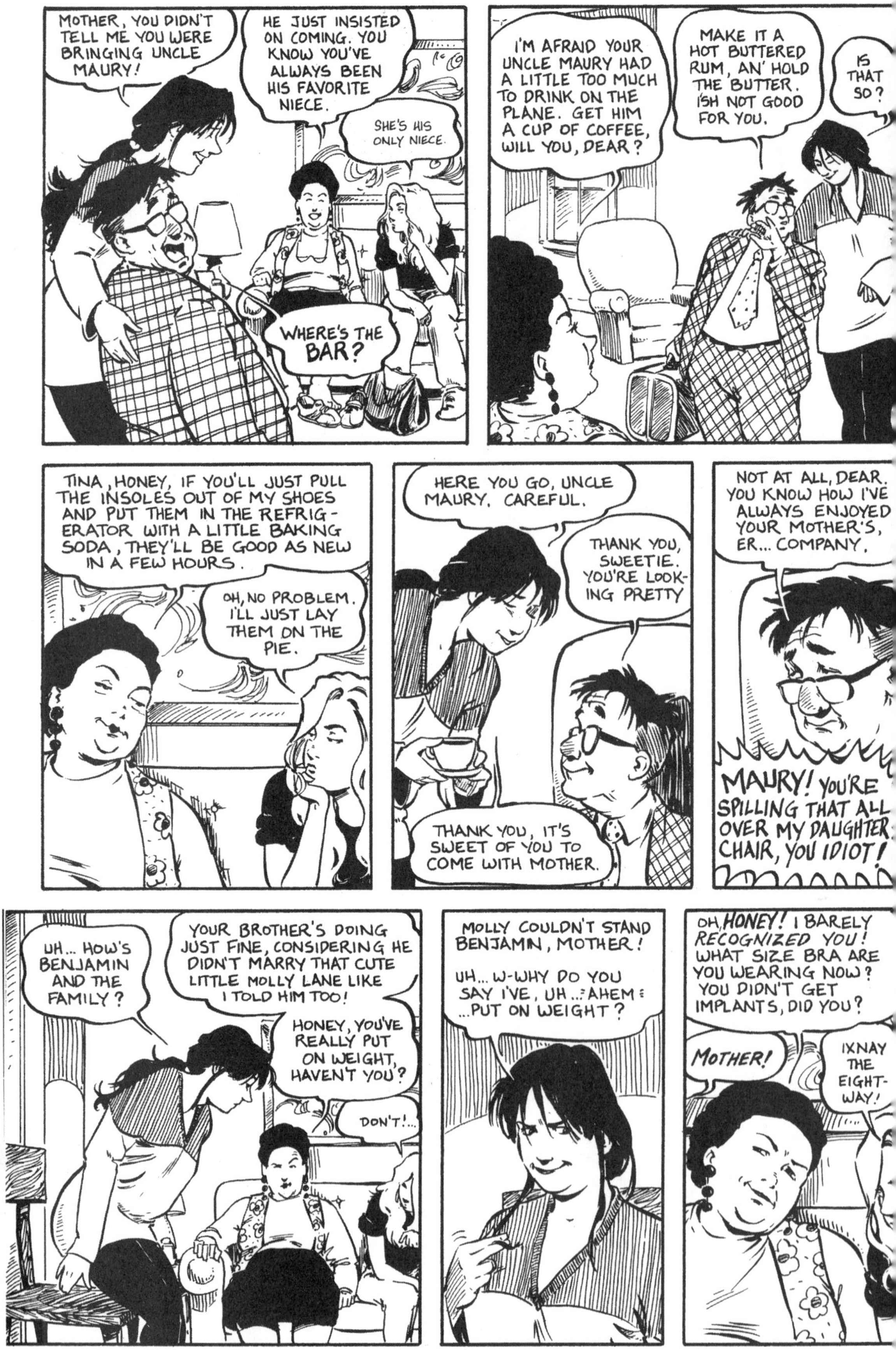
MOTHER, YOU DIDN'T TELL ME YOU WERE BRINGING UNCLE MAURY!
HE JUST INSISTED ON COMING. YOU KNOW YOU'VE ALWAYS BEEN HIS FAVORITE NIECE.
SHE'S HIS ONLY NIECE.
WHERE'S THE BAR?
I'M AFRAID YOUR UNCLE MAURY HAD A LITTLE TOO MUCH TO DRINK ON THE PLANE. GET HIM A CUP OF COFFEE, WILL YOU, DEAR?
MAKE IT A HOT BUTTERED RUM, AN' HOLD THE BUTTER. 'ISH NOT GOOD FOR YOU.
IS THAT SO?
TINA, HONEY, IF YOU'LL JUST PULL THE INSOLES OUT OF MY SHOES AND PUT THEM IN THE REFRIGERATOR WITH A LITTLE BAKING SODA, THEY'LL BE GOOD AS NEW IN A FEW HOURS.
OH, NO PROBLEM. I'LL JUST LAY THEM ON THE PIE.
HERE YOU GO, UNCLE MAURY. CAREFUL.
THANK YOU, SWEETIE. YOU'RE LOOKING PRETTY
THANK YOU, IT'S SWEET OF YOU TO COME WITH MOTHER.
NOT AT ALL, DEAR. YOU KNOW HOW I'VE ALWAYS ENJOYED YOUR MOTHER'S, ER... COMPANY.
MAURY! YOU'RE SPILLING THAT ALL OVER MY DAUGHTER CHAIR, YOU IDIOT!
UH... HOW'S BENJAMIN AND THE FAMILY?
YOUR BROTHER'S DOING JUST FINE, CONSIDERING HE DIDN'T MARRY THAT CUTE LITTLE MOLLY LANE LIKE I TOLD HIM TOO!
HONEY, YOU'VE REALLY PUT ON WEIGHT, HAVEN'T YOU?
DON'T!...
MOLLY COULDN'T STAND BENJAMIN, MOTHER!
UH... W-WHY DO YOU SAY I'VE, UH ... AHEM ... PUT ON WEIGHT?
OH, HONEY! I BARELY RECOGNIZED YOU! WHAT SIZE BRA ARE YOU WEARING NOW? YOU DIDN'T GET IMPLANTS, DID YOU?
MOTHER!
IXNAY THE EIGHT-WAY!

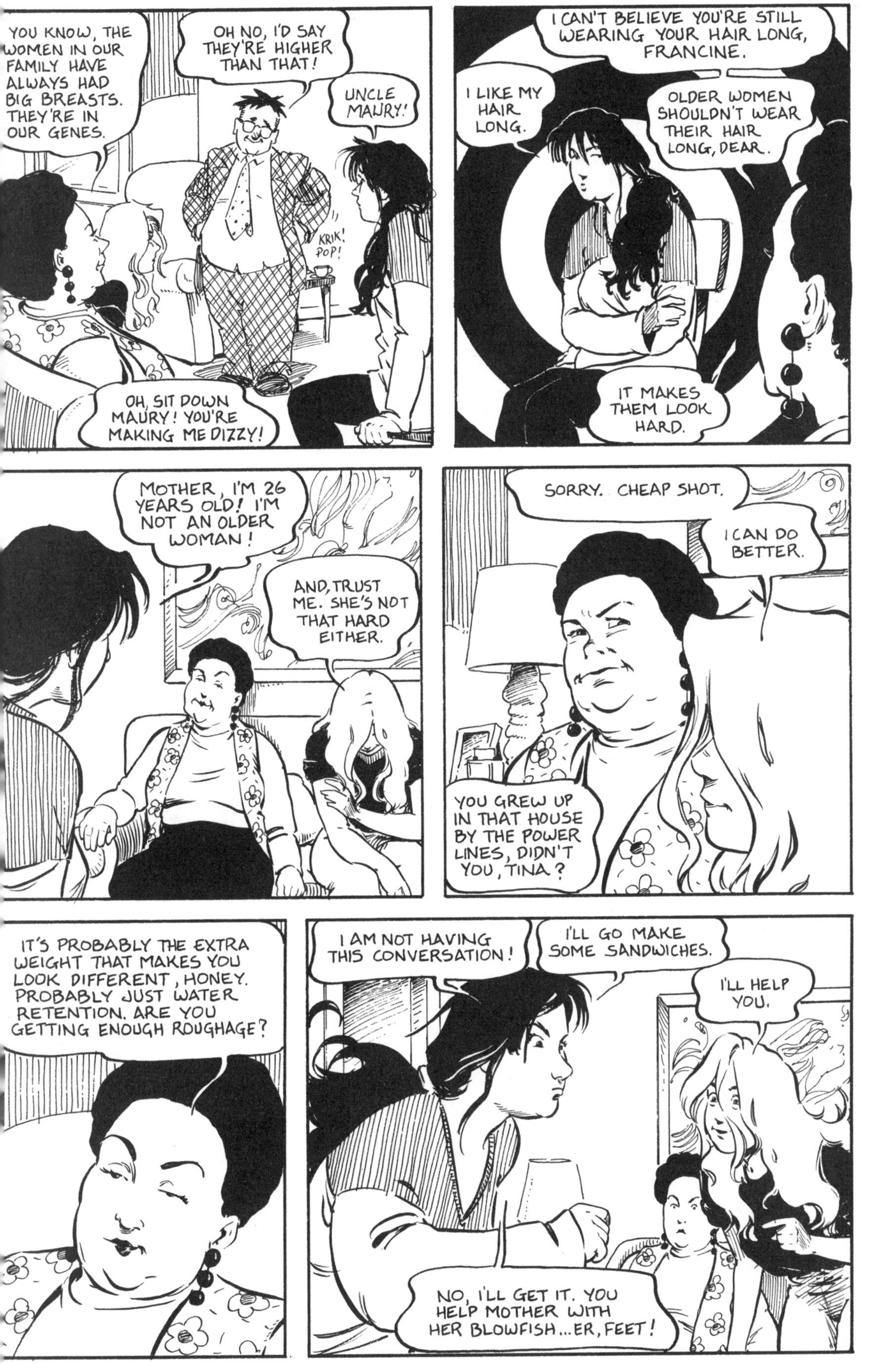

YOU KNOW, THE WOMEN IN OUR FAMILY HAVE ALWAYS HAD BIG BREASTS. THEY'RE IN OUR GENES.
OH NO, I'D SAY THEY'RE HIGHER THAN THAT!
UNCLE MAURY!
KRIK! POP!
OH, SIT DOWN MAURY! YOU'RE MAKING ME DIZZY!
I CAN'T BELIEVE YOU'RE STILL WEARING YOUR HAIR LONG, FRANCINE.
I LIKE MY HAIR LONG.
OLDER WOMEN SHOULDN'T WEAR THEIR HAIR LONG, DEAR.
IT MAKES THEM LOOK HARD.
MOTHER, I'M 26 YEARS OLD! I'M NOT AN OLDER WOMAN!
AND, TRUST ME. SHE'S NOT THAT HARD EITHER.
SORRY. CHEAP SHOT.
I CAN DO BETTER.
YOU GREW UP IN THAT HOUSE BY THE POWER LINES, DIDN'T YOU, TINA?
IT'S PROBABLY THE EXTRA WEIGHT THAT MAKES YOU LOOK DIFFERENT, HONEY. PROBABLY JUST WATER RETENTION. ARE YOU GETTING ENOUGH ROUGHAGE?
I AM NOT HAVING THIS CONVERSATION!
I'LL GO MAKE SOME SANDWICHES.
I'LL HELP YOU.
NO, I'LL GET IT. YOU HELP MOTHER WITH HER BLOWFISH... ER, FEET!

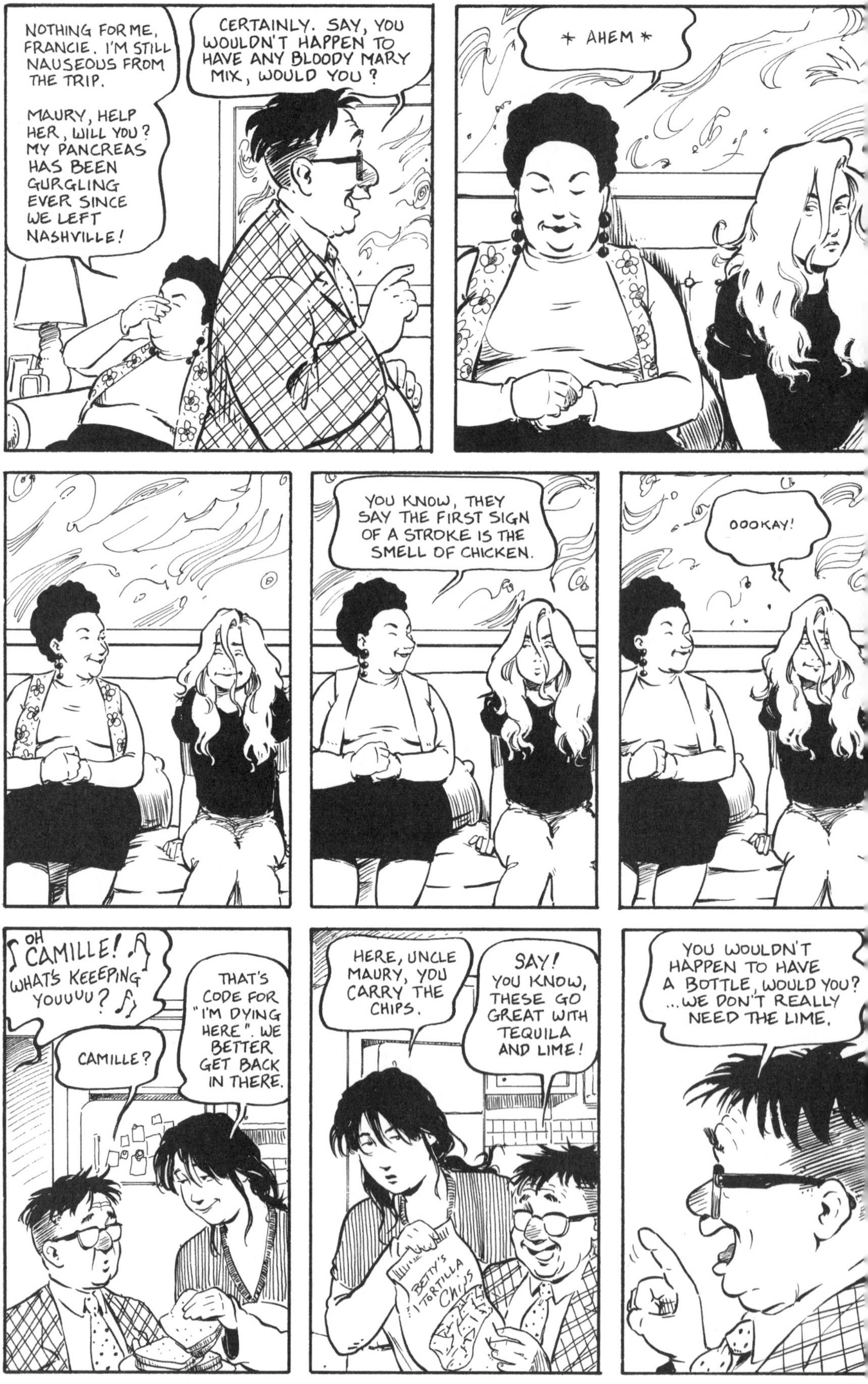
NOTHING FOR ME, FRANCIE. I'M STILL NAUSEOUS FROM THE TRIP.
MAURY, HELP HER, WILL YOU? MY PANCREAS HAS BEEN GURGLING EVER SINCE WE LEFT NASHVILLE!
CERTAINLY. SAY, YOU WOULDN'T HAPPEN TO HAVE ANY BLOODY MARY MIX, WOULD YOU?
* AHEM *
YOU KNOW, THEY SAY THE FIRST SIGN OF A STROKE IS THE SMELL OF CHICKEN.
OOOKAY!
OH CAMILLE! WHAT'S KEEEPING YOUUUU?
CAMILLE?
THAT'S CODE FOR "I'M DYING HERE". WE BETTER GET BACK IN THERE.
HERE, UNCLE MAURY, YOU CARRY THE CHIPS.
SAY! YOU KNOW, THESE GO GREAT WITH TEQUILA AND LIME!
BETTY'S TORTILLA CHIPS
YOU WOULDN'T HAPPEN TO HAVE A BOTTLE, WOULD YOU? ...WE DON'T REALLY NEED THE LIME.

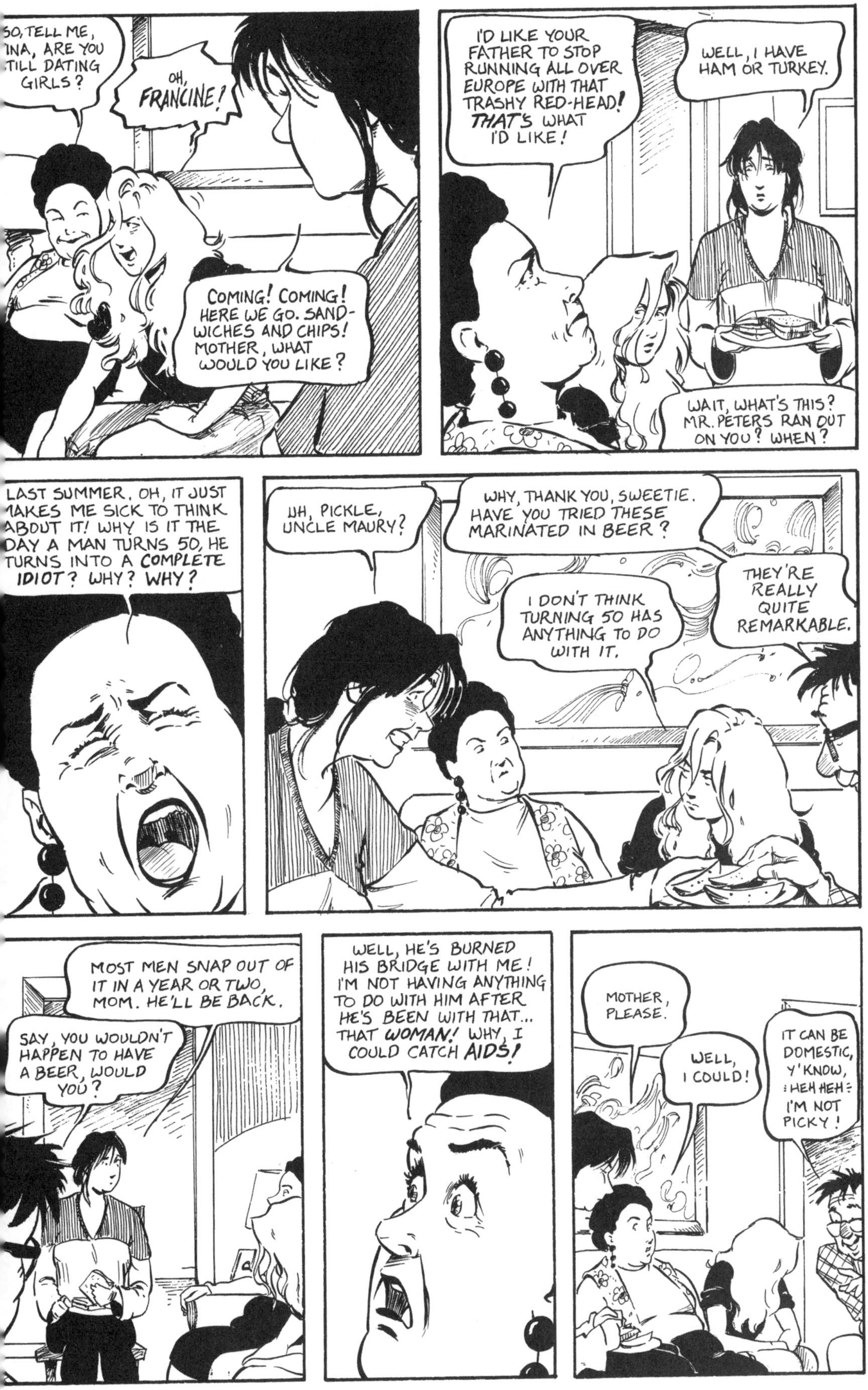
SO, TELL ME, INA, ARE YOU STILL DATING GIRLS?
OH, FRANCINE!
COMING! COMING! HERE WE GO. SANDWICHES AND CHIPS! MOTHER, WHAT WOULD YOU LIKE?
I'D LIKE YOUR FATHER TO STOP RUNNING ALL OVER EUROPE WITH THAT TRASHY RED-HEAD! THAT'S WHAT I'D LIKE!
WELL, I HAVE HAM OR TURKEY.
WAIT, WHAT'S THIS? MR. PETERS RAN OUT ON YOU? WHEN?
LAST SUMMER. OH, IT JUST MAKES ME SICK TO THINK ABOUT IT! WHY IS IT THE DAY A MAN TURNS 50, HE TURNS INTO A COMPLETE IDIOT? WHY? WHY?
UH, PICKLE, UNCLE MAURY?
WHY, THANK YOU, SWEETIE. HAVE YOU TRIED THESE MARINATED IN BEER?
I DON'T THINK TURNING 50 HAS ANYTHING TO DO WITH IT.
THEY'RE REALLY QUITE REMARKABLE.
MOST MEN SNAP OUT OF IT IN A YEAR OR TWO, MOM. HE'LL BE BACK.
SAY, YOU WOULDN'T HAPPEN TO HAVE A BEER, WOULD YOU?
WELL, HE'S BURNED HIS BRIDGE WITH ME! I'M NOT HAVING ANYTHING TO DO WITH HIM AFTER HE'S BEEN WITH THAT... THAT WOMAN! WHY, I COULD CATCH AIDS!
MOTHER, PLEASE.
WELL, I COULD!
IT CAN BE DOMESTIC, Y'KNOW, HEH HEH I'M NOT PICKY!

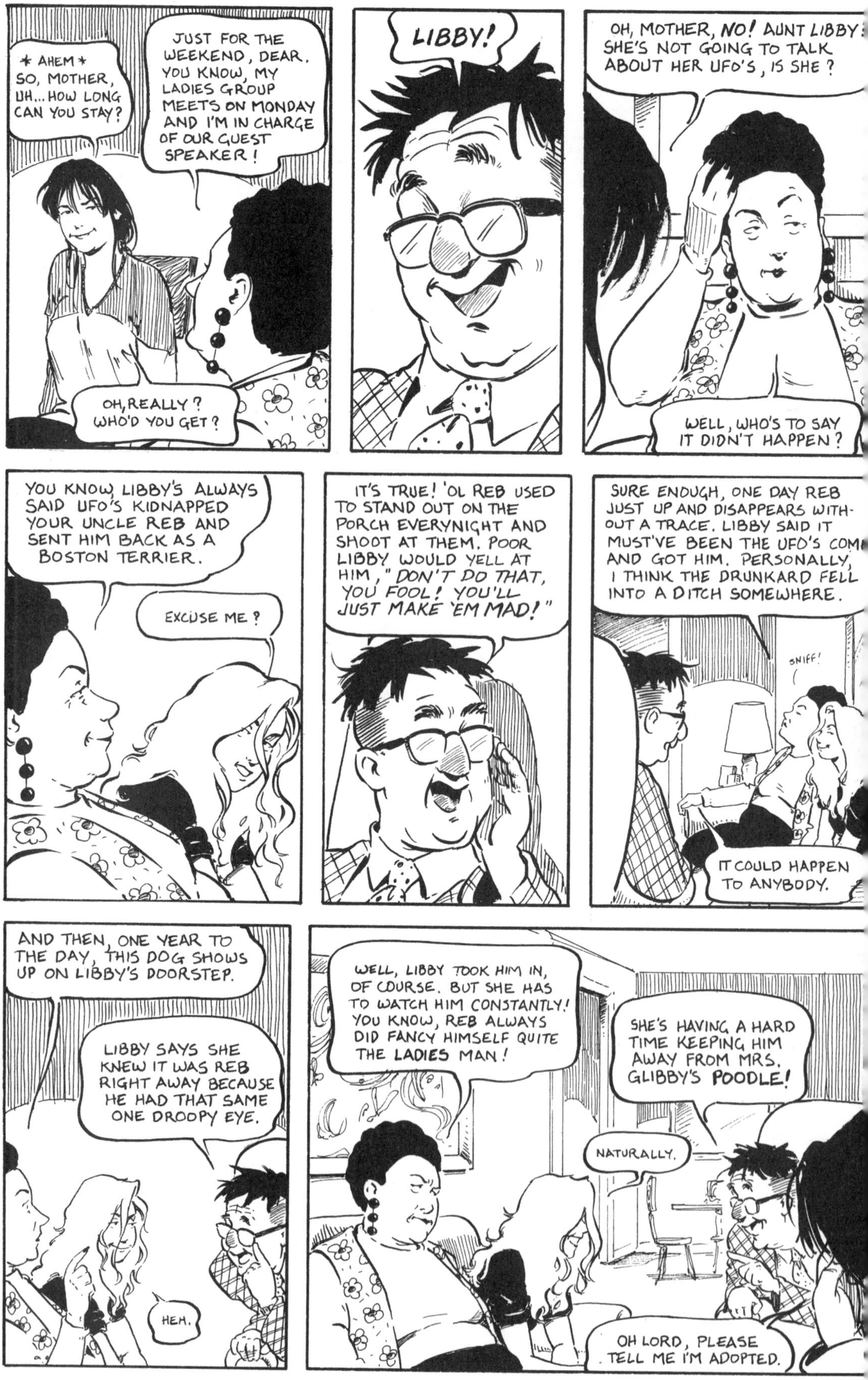
* AHEM * SO, MOTHER, UH... HOW LONG CAN YOU STAY?
JUST FOR THE WEEKEND, DEAR. YOU KNOW, MY LADIES GROUP MEETS ON MONDAY AND I'M IN CHARGE OF OUR GUEST SPEAKER!
OH, REALLY? WHO'D YOU GET?
LIBBY!
OH, MOTHER, NO! AUNT LIBBY! SHE'S NOT GOING TO TALK ABOUT HER UFO'S, IS SHE?
WELL, WHO'S TO SAY IT DIDN'T HAPPEN?
YOU KNOW, LIBBY'S ALWAYS SAID UFO'S KIDNAPPED YOUR UNCLE REB AND SENT HIM BACK AS A BOSTON TERRIER.
EXCUSE ME?
IT'S TRUE! 'OL REB USED TO STAND OUT ON THE PORCH EVERYNIGHT AND SHOOT AT THEM. POOR LIBBY WOULD YELL AT HIM, "DON'T DO THAT, YOU FOOL! YOU'LL JUST MAKE 'EM MAD!"
SURE ENOUGH, ONE DAY REB JUST UP AND DISAPPEARS WITHOUT A TRACE. LIBBY SAID IT MUST'VE BEEN THE UFO'S COM AND GOT HIM. PERSONALLY, I THINK THE DRUNKARD FELL INTO A DITCH SOMEWHERE.
SNIFF!
IT COULD HAPPEN TO ANYBODY.
AND THEN, ONE YEAR TO THE DAY, THIS DOG SHOWS UP ON LIBBY'S DOORSTEP.
LIBBY SAYS SHE KNEW IT WAS REB RIGHT AWAY BECAUSE HE HAD THAT SAME ONE DROOPY EYE.
HEH.
WELL, LIBBY TOOK HIM IN, OF COURSE. BUT SHE HAS TO WATCH HIM CONSTANTLY! YOU KNOW, REB ALWAYS DID FANCY HIMSELF QUITE THE LADIES MAN!
SHE'S HAVING A HARD TIME KEEPING HIM AWAY FROM MRS. GLIBBY'S POODLE!
NATURALLY.
OH LORD, PLEASE TELL ME I'M ADOPTED.

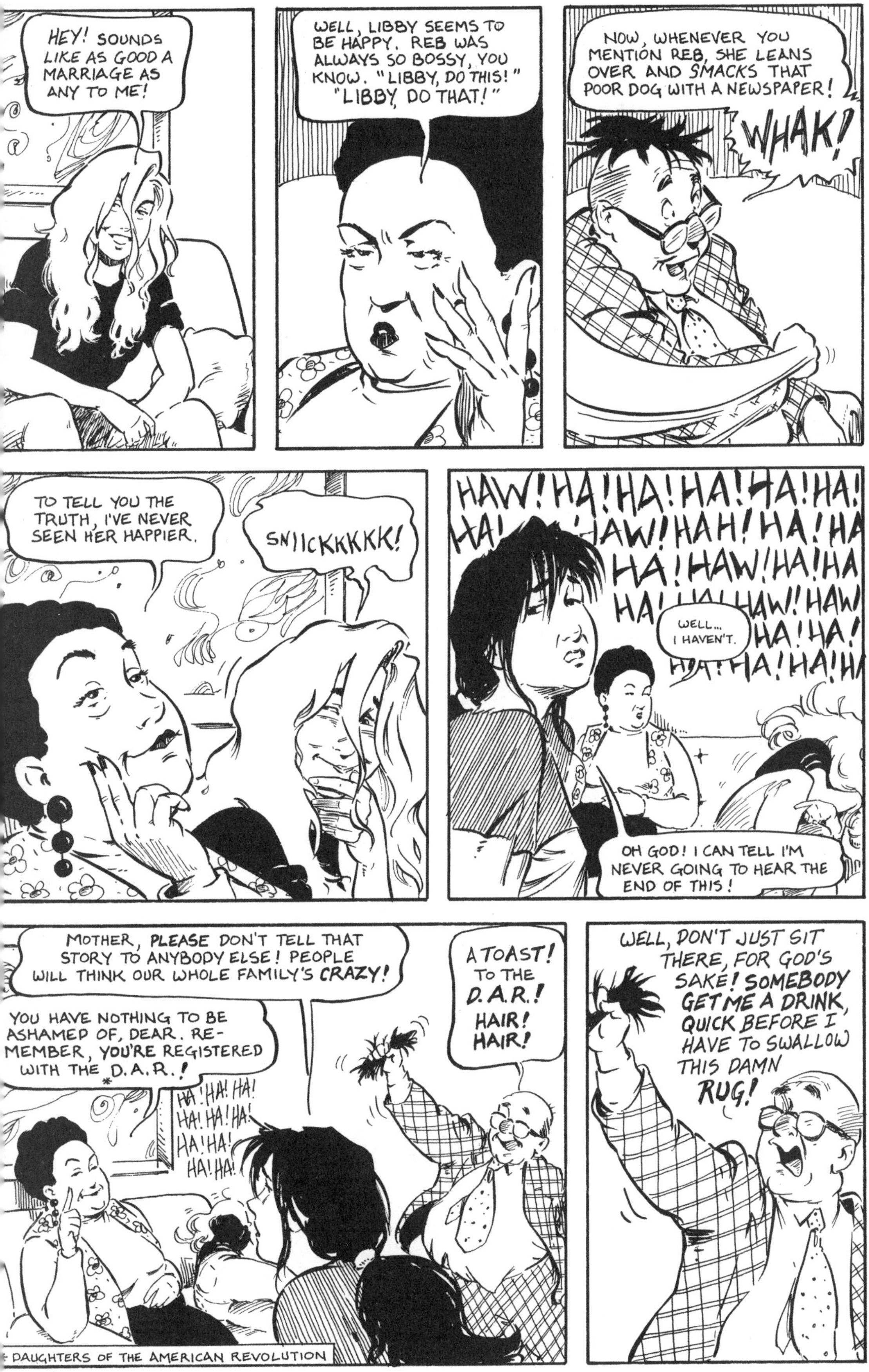
HEY! SOUNDS LIKE AS GOOD A MARRIAGE AS ANY TO ME!
WELL, LIBBY SEEMS TO BE HAPPY. REB WAS ALWAYS SO BOSSY, YOU KNOW. "LIBBY, DO THIS!" "LIBBY, DO THAT!"
NOW, WHENEVER YOU MENTION REB, SHE LEANS OVER AND SMACKS THAT POOR DOG WITH A NEWSPAPER!
WHAK!
TO TELL YOU THE TRUTH, I'VE NEVER SEEN HER HAPPIER.
SNIICKKKKK!
HAW! HA! HA! HA! HA! HA! HA! HAW! HAH! HA! HA HA! HAW! HA! HA HA! HAW! HAW HA! HA! HA! HA! HA!
WELL... I HAVEN'T.
OH GOD! I CAN TELL I'M NEVER GOING TO HEAR THE END OF THIS!
MOTHER, PLEASE DON'T TELL THAT STORY TO ANYBODY ELSE! PEOPLE WILL THINK OUR WHOLE FAMILY'S CRAZY!
YOU HAVE NOTHING TO BE ASHAMED OF, DEAR. REMEMBER, YOU'RE REGISTERED WITH THE D.A.R.*!
HA! HA! HA! HA! HA! HA! HA! HA! HA! HA!
A TOAST! TO THE D.A.R.! HAIR! HAIR!
* DAUGHTERS OF THE AMERICAN REVOLUTION
WELL, DON'T JUST SIT THERE, FOR GOD'S SAKE! SOMEBODY GET ME A DRINK, QUICK BEFORE I HAVE TO SWALLOW THIS DAMN RUG!

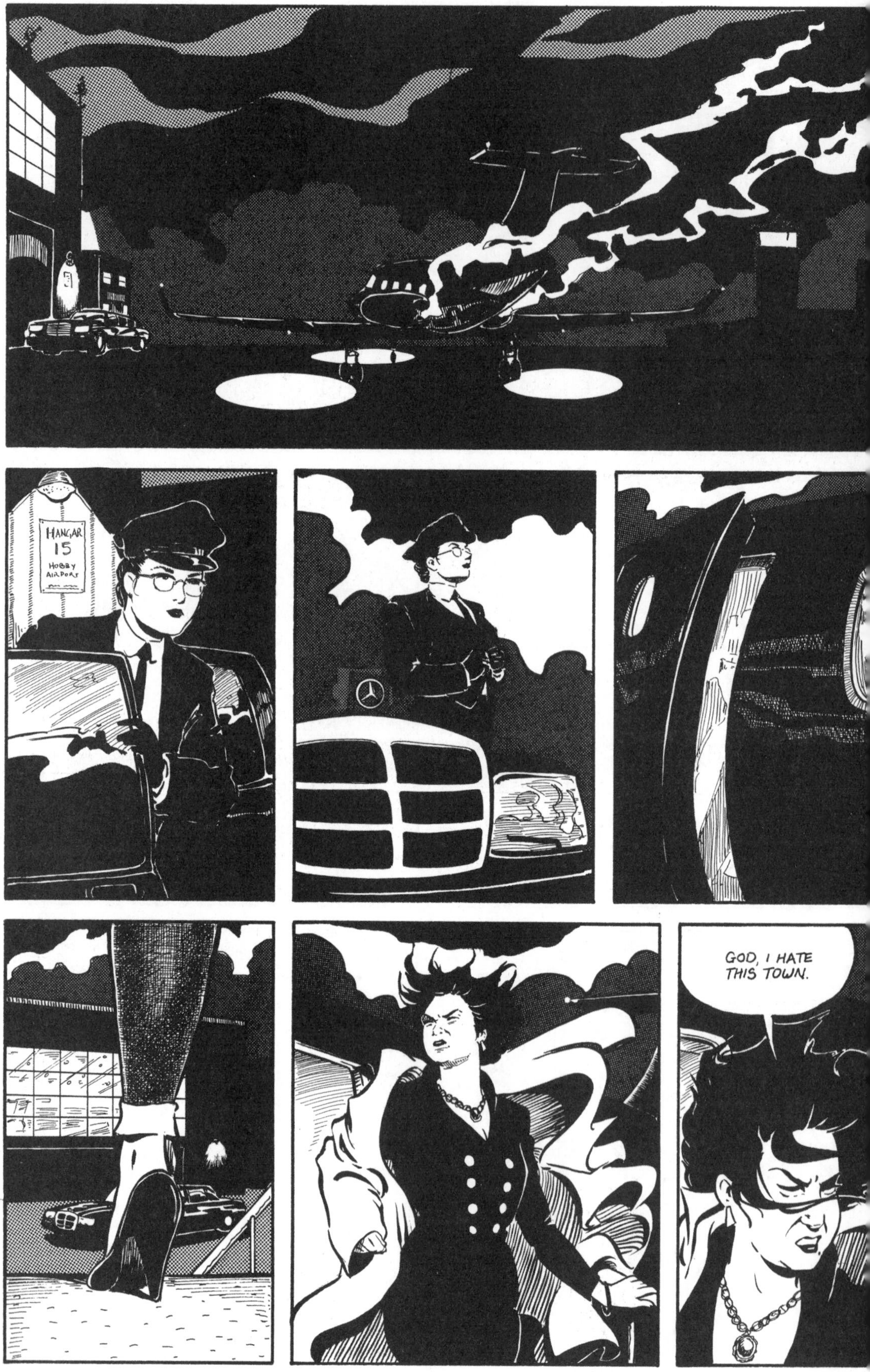
HANGAR
15
HOBBY
AIRPORT
GOD, I HATE
THIS TOWN.

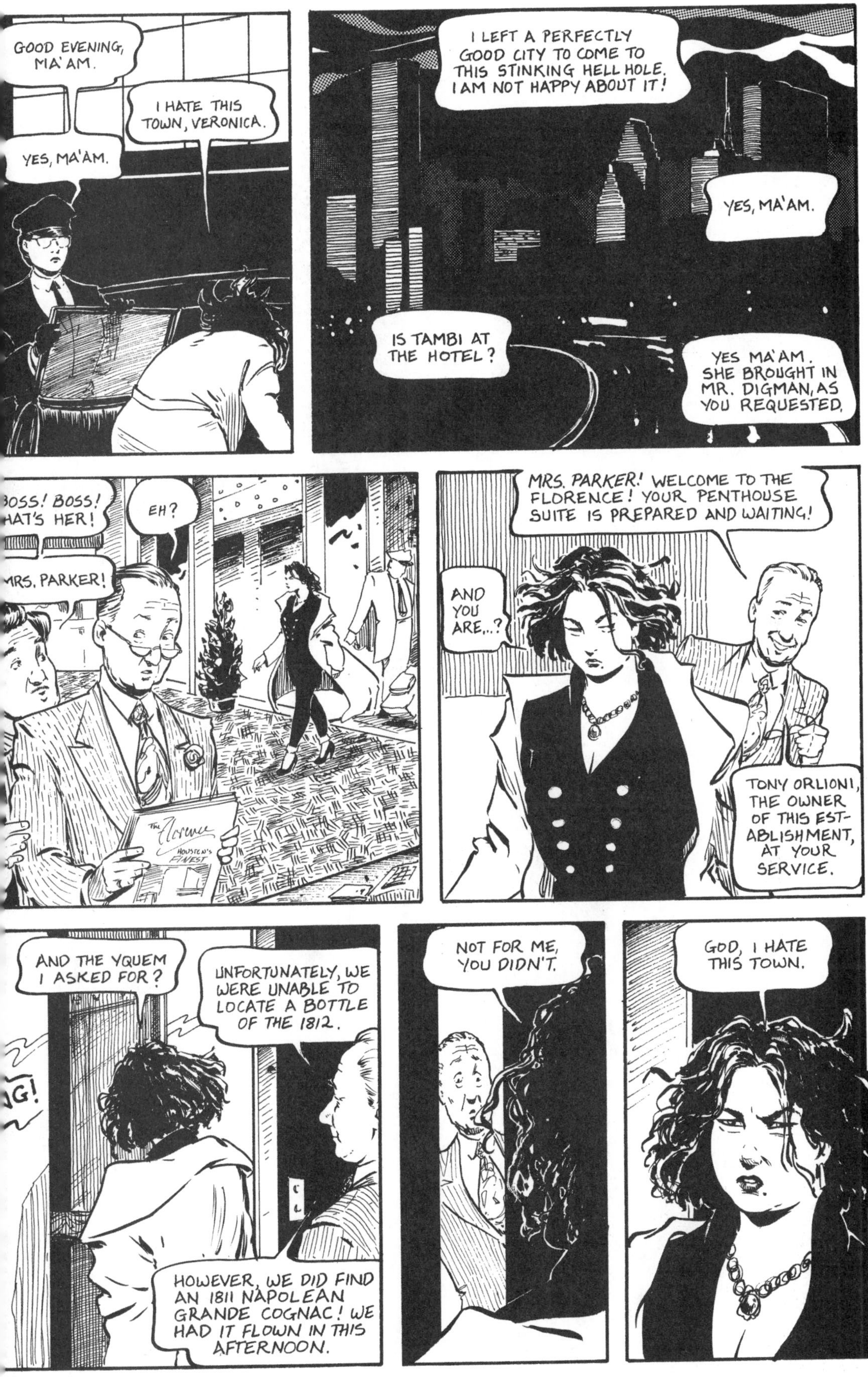
GOOD EVENING, MA'AM.
I HATE THIS TOWN, VERONICA.
YES, MA'AM.
I LEFT A PERFECTLY GOOD CITY TO COME TO THIS STINKING HELL HOLE. I AM NOT HAPPY ABOUT IT!
YES, MA'AM.
IS TAMBI AT THE HOTEL?
YES MA'AM. SHE BROUGHT IN MR. DIGMAN, AS YOU REQUESTED.
BOSS! BOSS! THAT'S HER!
EH?
MRS. PARKER!
The Florence HOUSTON'S FINEST
MRS. PARKER! WELCOME TO THE FLORENCE! YOUR PENTHOUSE SUITE IS PREPARED AND WAITING!
AND YOU ARE...?
TONY ORLIONI, THE OWNER OF THIS ESTABLISHMENT, AT YOUR SERVICE.
AND THE YQUEM I ASKED FOR?
UNFORTUNATELY, WE WERE UNABLE TO LOCATE A BOTTLE OF THE 1812.
HOWEVER, WE DID FIND AN 1811 NAPOLEAN GRANDE COGNAC! WE HAD IT FLOWN IN THIS AFTERNOON.
NOT FOR ME, YOU DIDN'T.
GOD, I HATE THIS TOWN.

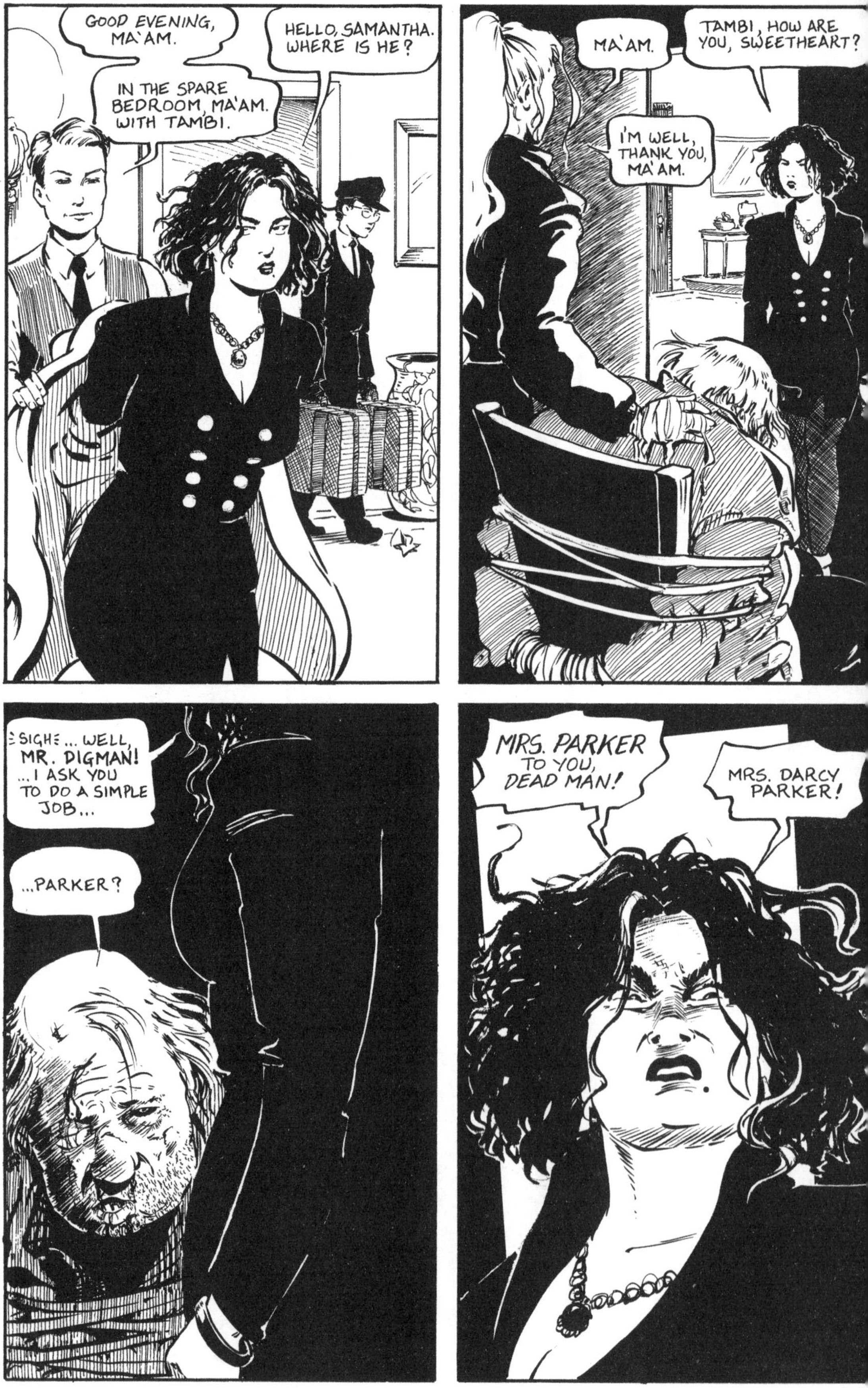
GOOD EVENING, MA'AM.
HELLO, SAMANTHA. WHERE IS HE?
IN THE SPARE BEDROOM, MA'AM. WITH TAMBI.
MA'AM.
TAMBI, HOW ARE YOU, SWEETHEART?
I'M WELL, THANK YOU, MA'AM.
SIGH ... WELL, MR. DIGMAN! ...I ASK YOU TO DO A SIMPLE JOB...
...PARKER?
MRS. PARKER TO YOU, DEAD MAN!
MRS. DARCY PARKER!

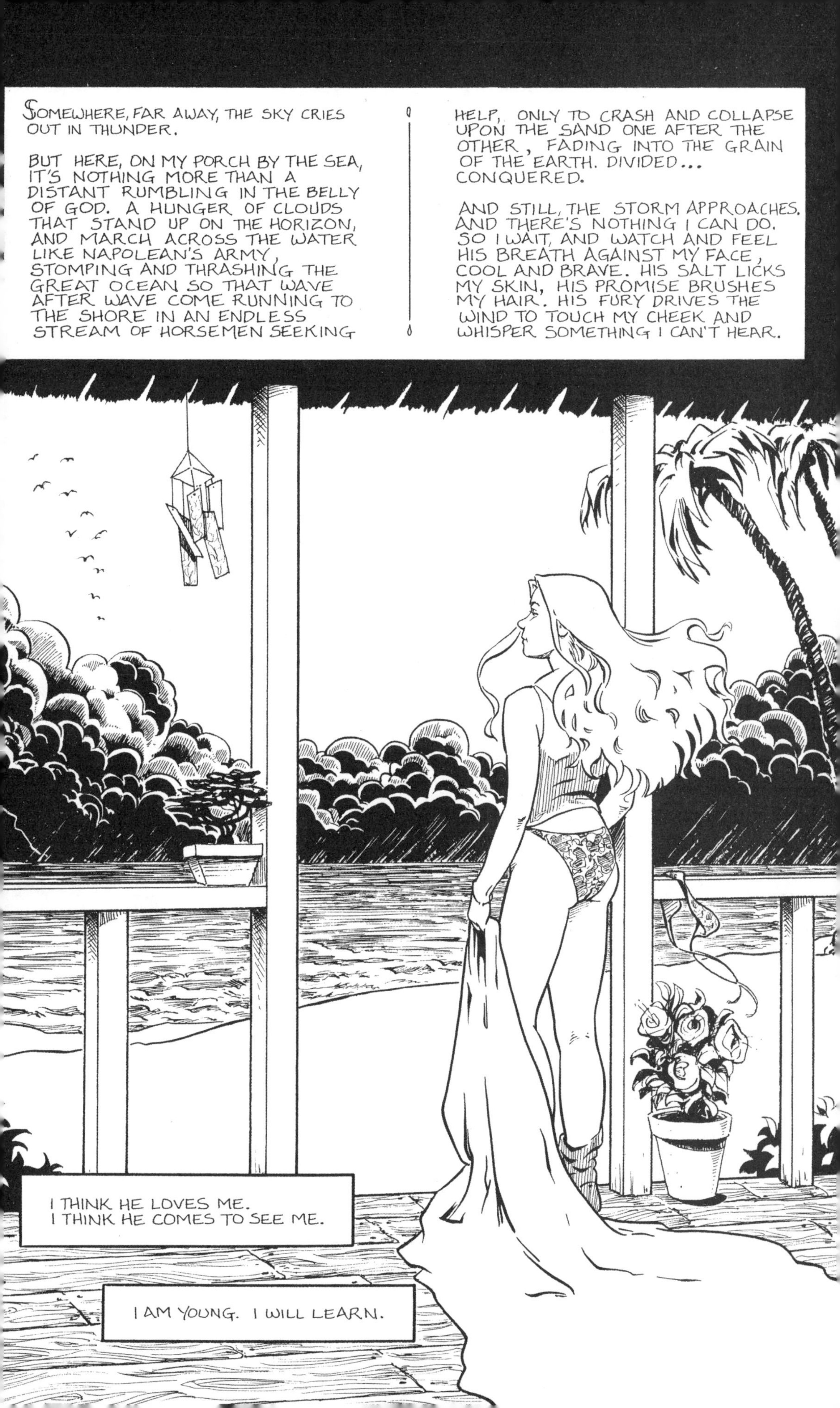
SOMEWHERE, FAR AWAY, THE SKY CRIES OUT IN THUNDER.
BUT HERE, ON MY PORCH BY THE SEA, IT'S NOTHING MORE THAN A DISTANT RUMBLING IN THE BELLY OF GOD. A HUNGER OF CLOUDS THAT STAND UP ON THE HORIZON, AND MARCH ACROSS THE WATER LIKE NAPOLEAN'S ARMY, STOMPING AND THRASHING THE GREAT OCEAN SO THAT WAVE AFTER WAVE COME RUNNING TO THE SHORE IN AN ENDLESS STREAM OF HORSEMEN SEEKING HELP, ONLY TO CRASH AND COLLAPSE UPON THE SAND ONE AFTER THE OTHER, FADING INTO THE GRAIN OF THE EARTH. DIVIDED... CONQUERED.
AND STILL, THE STORM APPROACHES. AND THERE'S NOTHING I CAN DO. SO I WAIT, AND WATCH AND FEEL HIS BREATH AGAINST MY FACE, COOL AND BRAVE. HIS SALT LICKS MY SKIN, HIS PROMISE BRUSHES MY HAIR. HIS FURY DRIVES THE WIND TO TOUCH MY CHEEK AND WHISPER SOMETHING I CAN'T HEAR.
I THINK HE LOVES ME.
I THINK HE COMES TO SEE ME.
I AM YOUNG. I WILL LEARN.

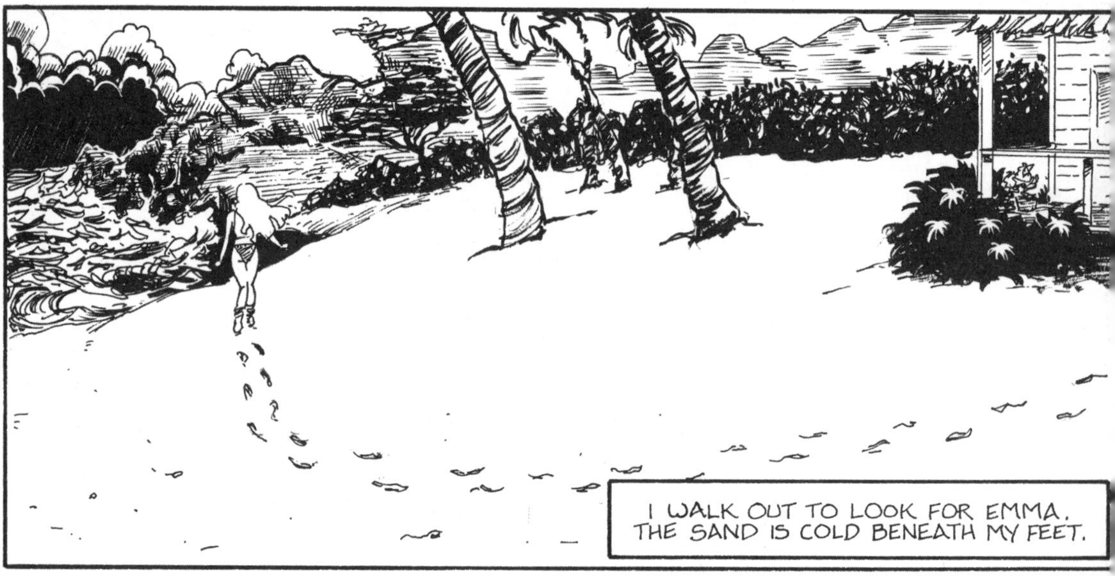
I WALK OUT TO LOOK FOR EMMA.
THE SAND IS COLD BENEATH MY FEET.

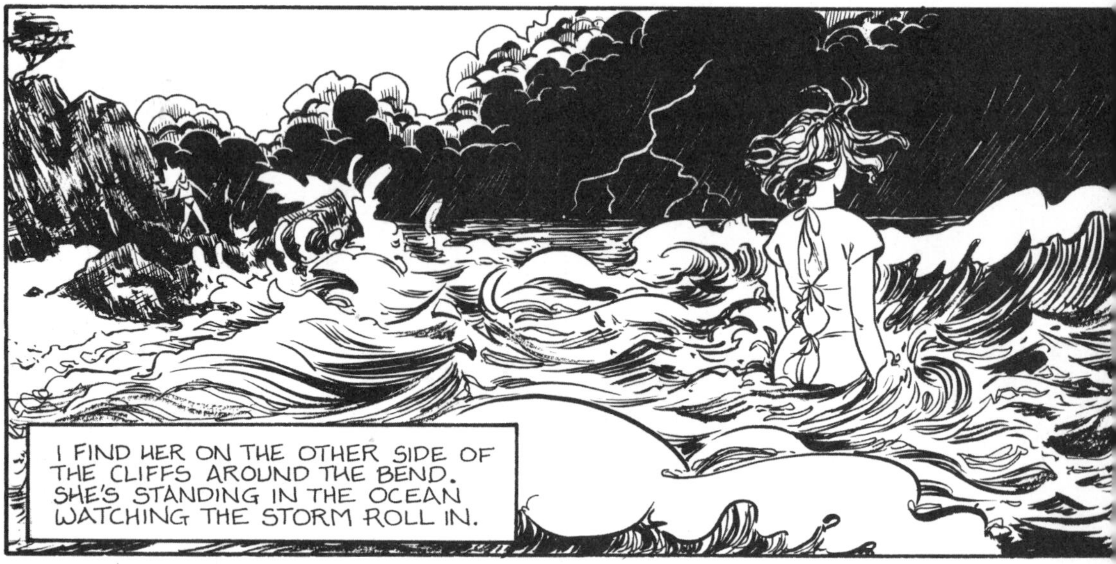
I FIND HER ON THE OTHER SIDE OF THE CLIFFS AROUND THE BEND. SHE'S STANDING IN THE OCEAN WATCHING THE STORM ROLL IN.

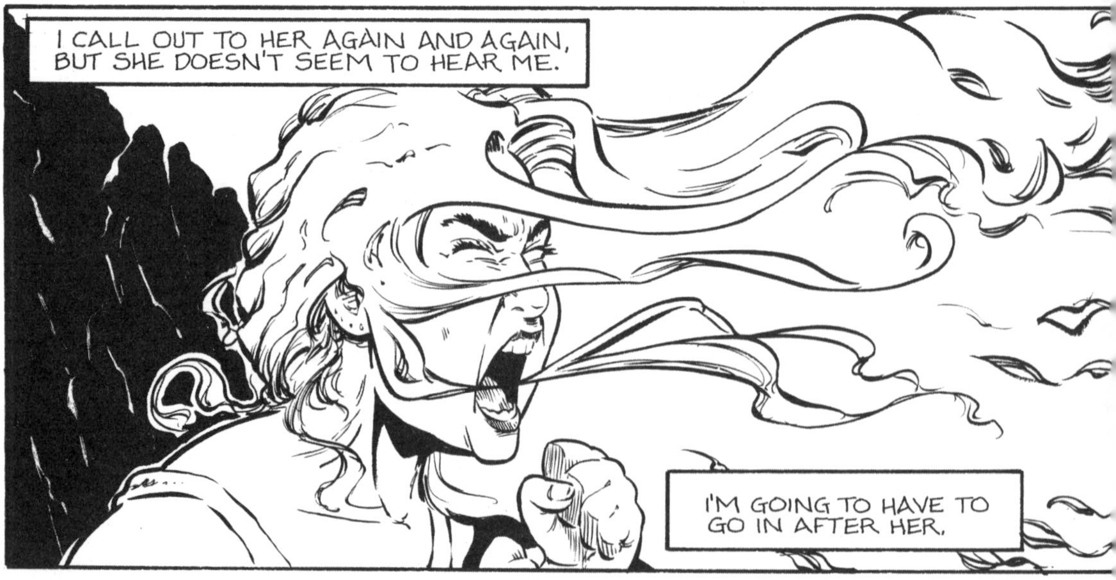
I CALL OUT TO HER AGAIN AND AGAIN, BUT SHE DOESN'T SEEM TO HEAR ME.
I'M GOING TO HAVE TO GO IN AFTER HER.

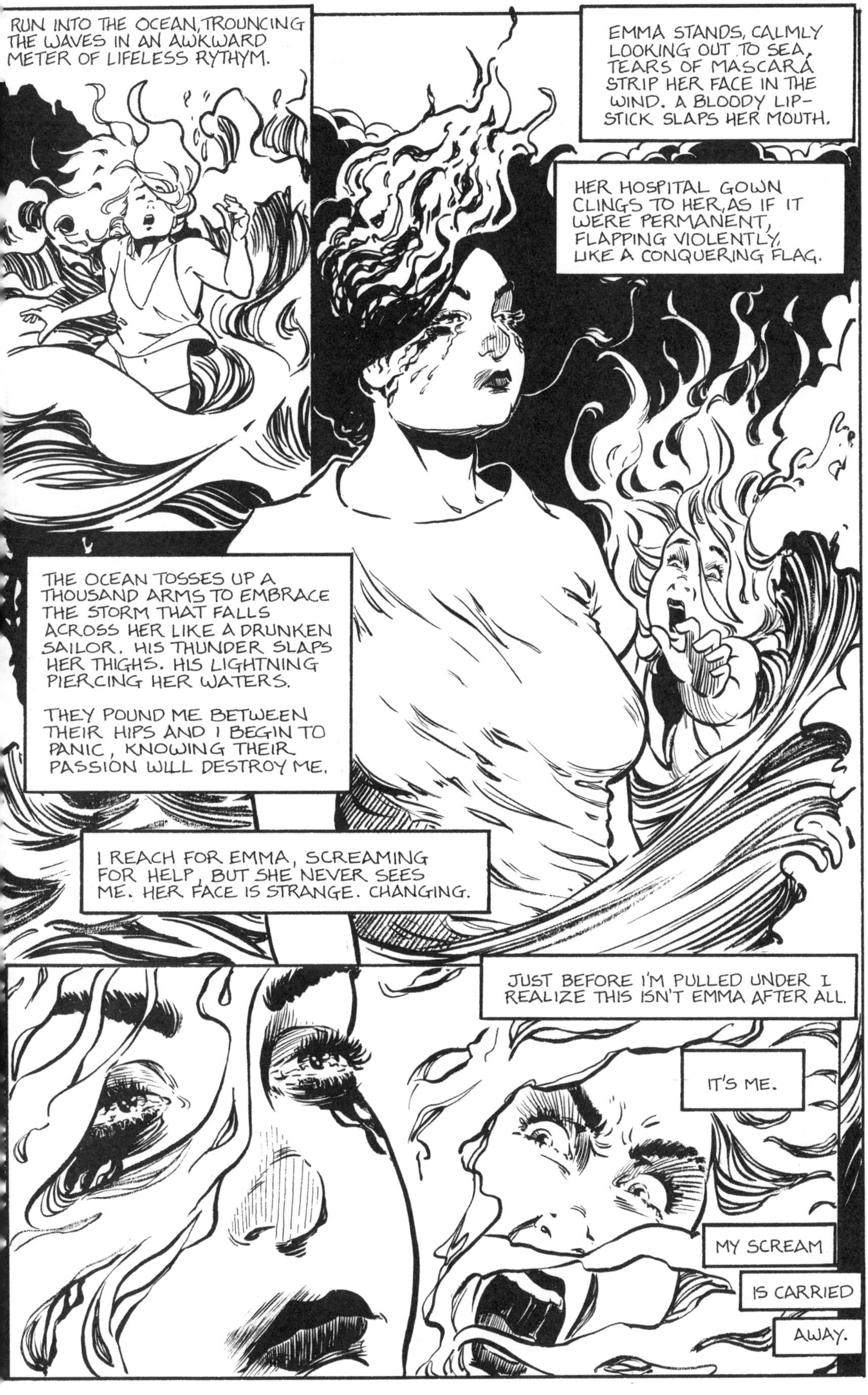
RUN INTO THE OCEAN, TROUNCING THE WAVES IN AN AWKWARD METER OF LIFELESS RYTHYM.
EMMA STANDS, CALMLY LOOKING OUT TO SEA. TEARS OF MASCARA STRIP HER FACE IN THE WIND. A BLOODY LIP-STICK SLAPS HER MOUTH.
HER HOSPITAL GOWN CLINGS TO HER, AS IF IT WERE PERMANENT, FLAPPING VIOLENTLY, LIKE A CONQUERING FLAG.
THE OCEAN TOSSES UP A THOUSAND ARMS TO EMBRACE THE STORM THAT FALLS ACROSS HER LIKE A DRUNKEN SAILOR. HIS THUNDER SLAPS HER THIGHS. HIS LIGHTNING PIERCING HER WATERS.
THEY POUND ME BETWEEN THEIR HIPS AND I BEGIN TO PANIC, KNOWING THEIR PASSION WILL DESTROY ME.
I REACH FOR EMMA, SCREAMING FOR HELP, BUT SHE NEVER SEES ME. HER FACE IS STRANGE. CHANGING.
JUST BEFORE I'M PULLED UNDER I REALIZE THIS ISN'T EMMA AFTER ALL.
IT'S ME.
MY SCREAM
IS CARRIED
AWAY.

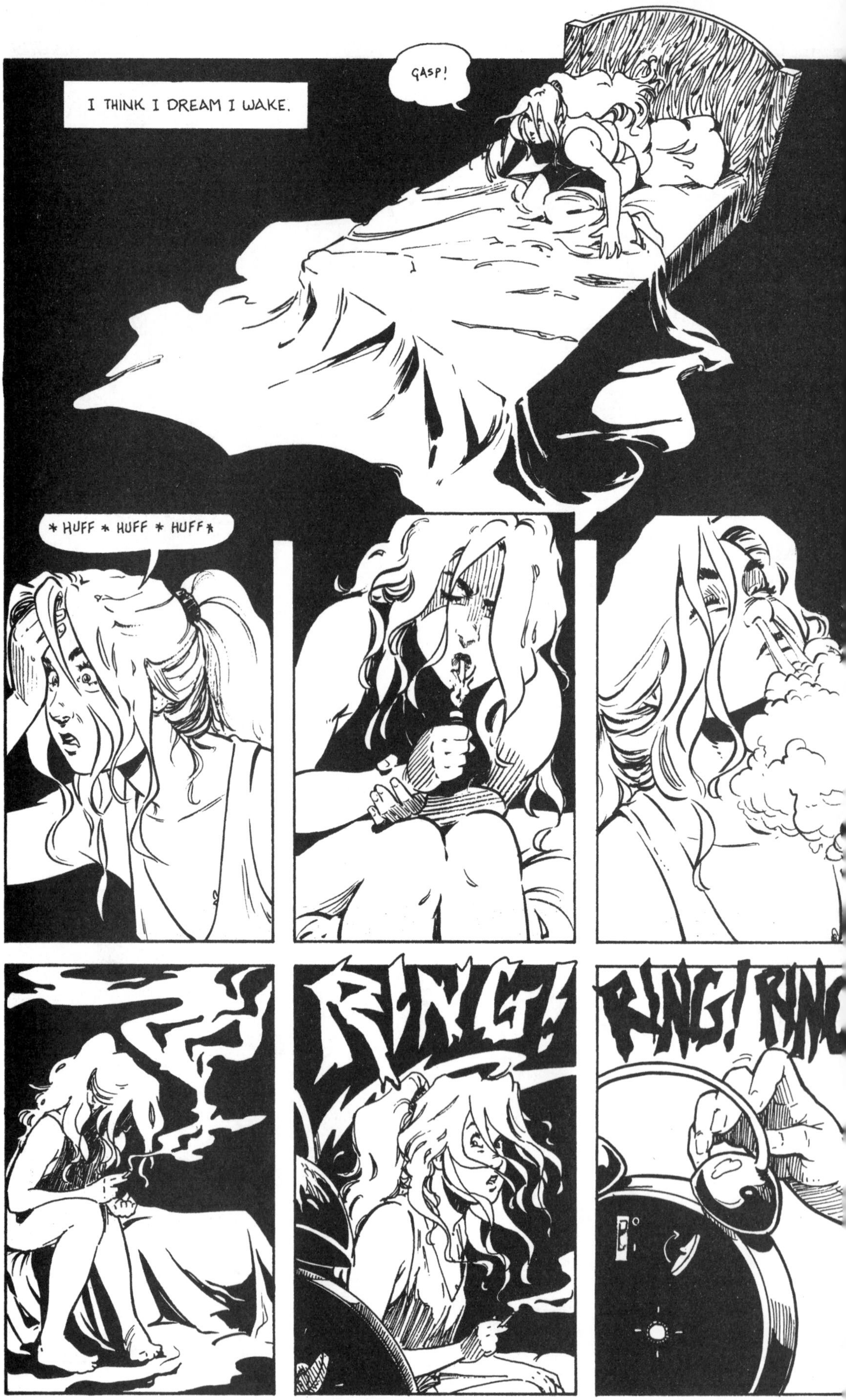
I THINK I DREAM I WAKE.
GASP!
* HUFF * HUFF * HUFF *
RING!
RING! RING

RING! RING! RING!

CLIK! CLIK! CLIK!

RING RING RING RIN RIN

CLIK! CLIK! CLIK! CLIK!

RING! RING! RING! RING! RING! RING! NG INC ING RING RING RIN

THAT'S THE TROUBLE WITH TURNING THINGS ON, BABY JUNE. SOMETIMES YOU CAN'T TURN THEM OFF.

EMMA?

SURE. IF THAT'S WHO YOU WANT ME TO BE.

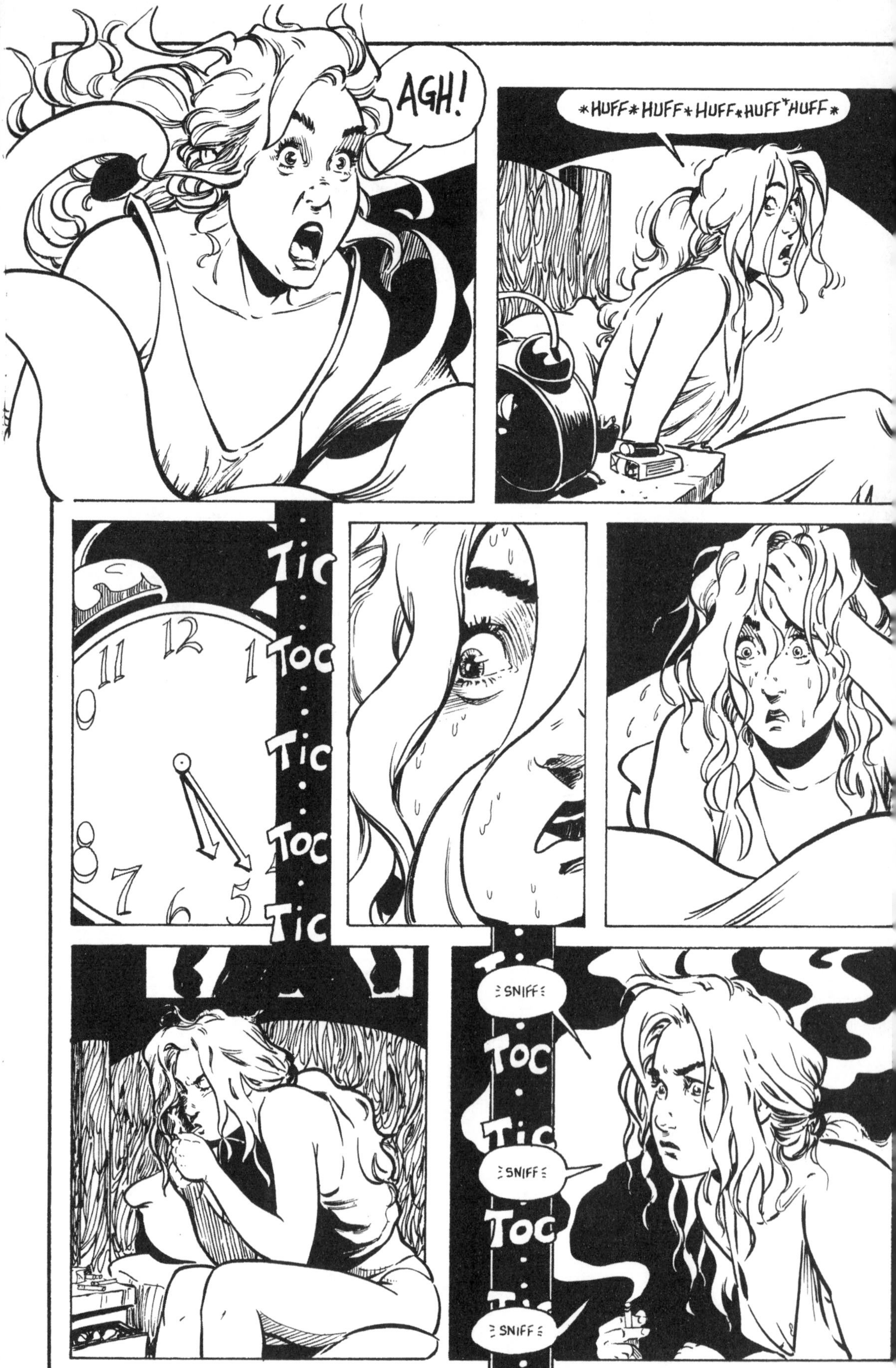
AGH!
*HUFF*HUFF*HUFF*HUFF*HUFF*
TIC
TOC
TIC
TOC
TIC
SNIFF
TOC
TIC
SNIFF
TOC
SNIFF

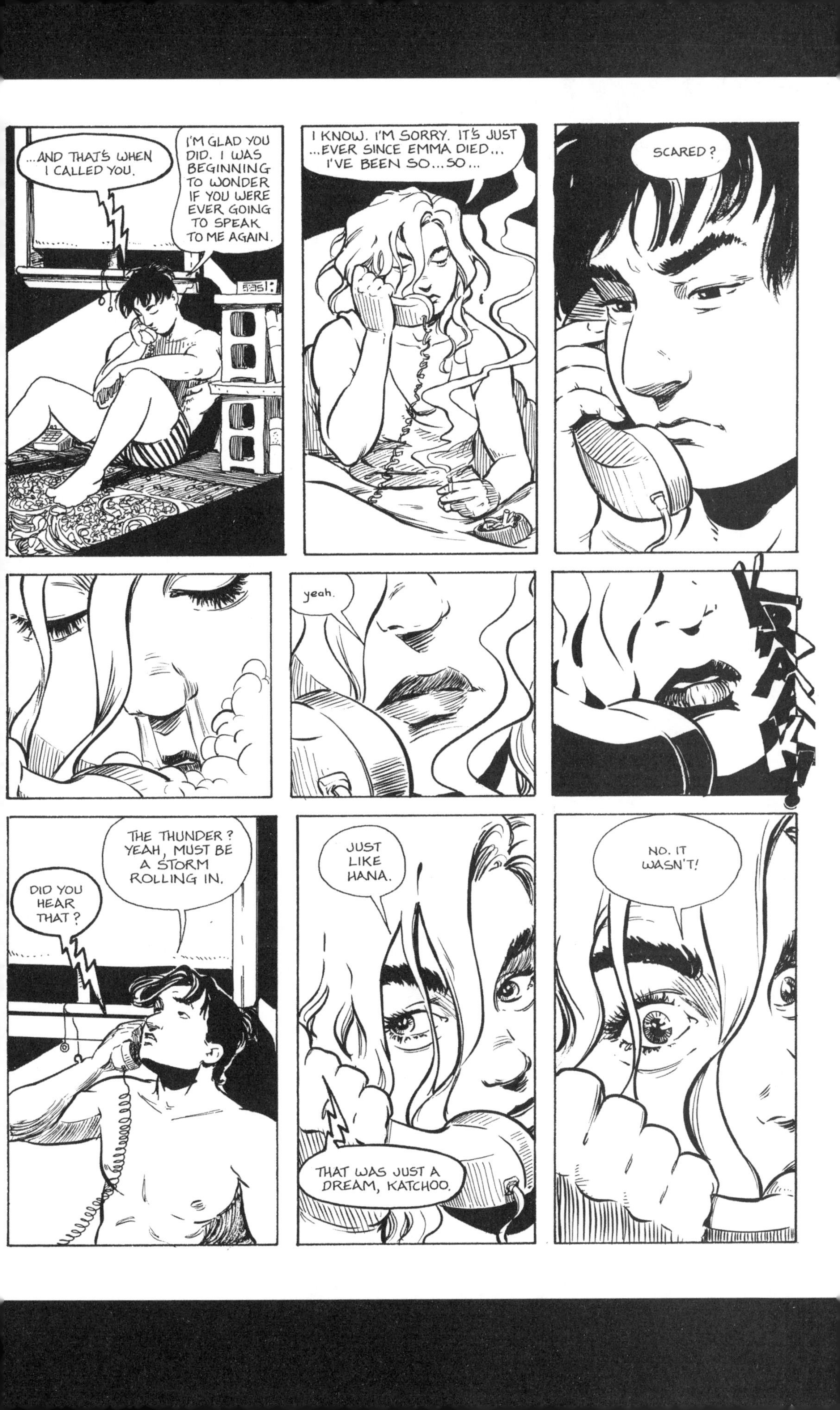
...AND THAT'S WHEN I CALLED YOU.
I'M GLAD YOU DID. I WAS BEGINNING TO WONDER IF YOU WERE EVER GOING TO SPEAK TO ME AGAIN.
I KNOW. I'M SORRY. IT'S JUST ...EVER SINCE EMMA DIED... I'VE BEEN SO...SO...
SCARED?
yeah.
DID YOU HEAR THAT?
THE THUNDER? YEAH, MUST BE A STORM ROLLING IN.
JUST LIKE HANA.
THAT WAS JUST A DREAM, KATCHOO.
NO. IT WASN'T!

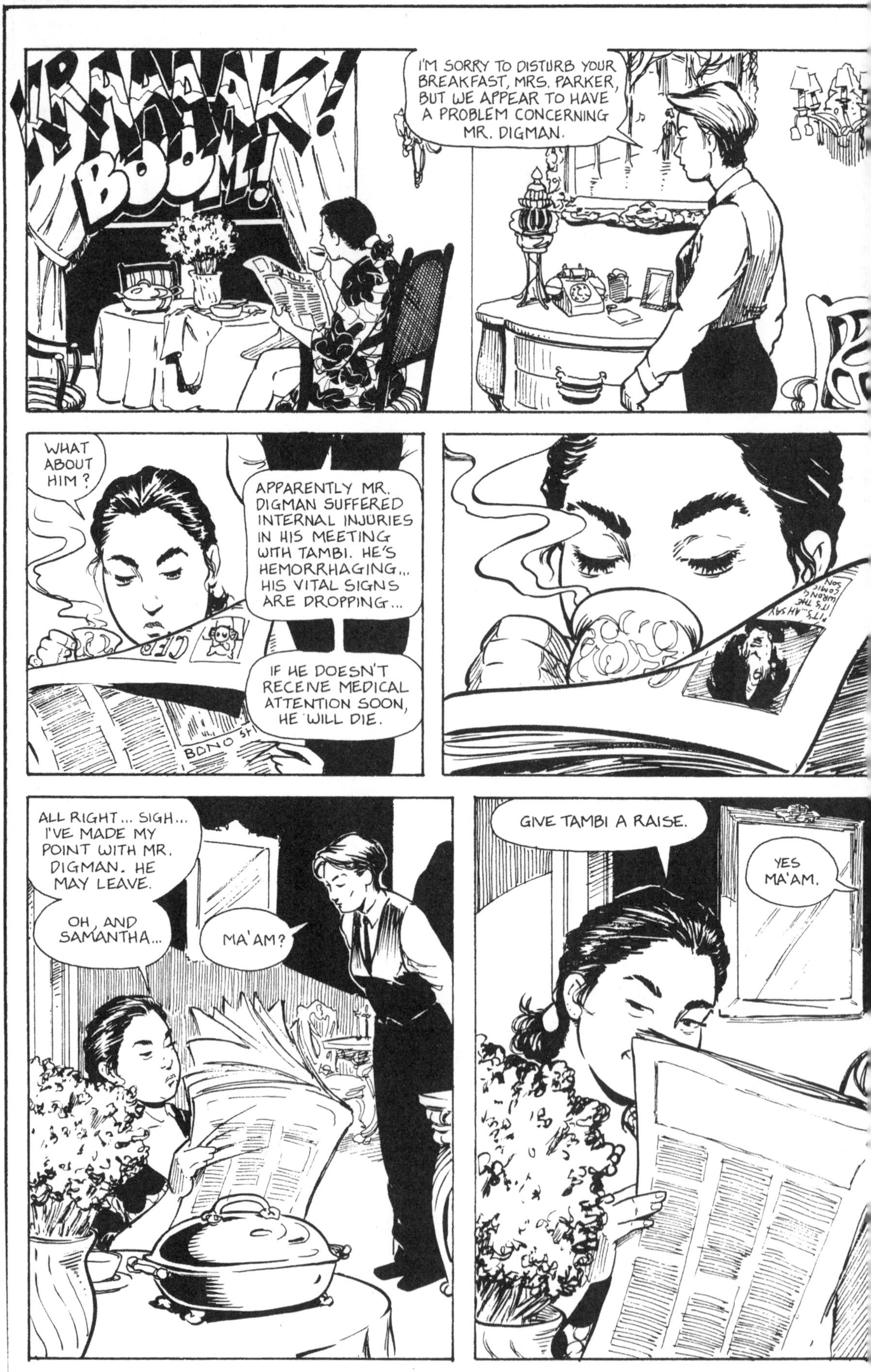
BOOM!
I'M SORRY TO DISTURB YOUR BREAKFAST, MRS. PARKER, BUT WE APPEAR TO HAVE A PROBLEM CONCERNING MR. DIGMAN.
WHAT ABOUT HIM?
APPARENTLY MR. DIGMAN SUFFERED INTERNAL INJURIES IN HIS MEETING WITH TAMBI. HE'S HEMORRHAGING... HIS VITAL SIGNS ARE DROPPING...
IF HE DOESN'T RECEIVE MEDICAL ATTENTION SOON, HE WILL DIE.
ALL RIGHT... SIGH... I'VE MADE MY POINT WITH MR. DIGMAN. HE MAY LEAVE.
OH, AND SAMANTHA...
MA'AM?
GIVE TAMBI A RAISE.
YES MA'AM.

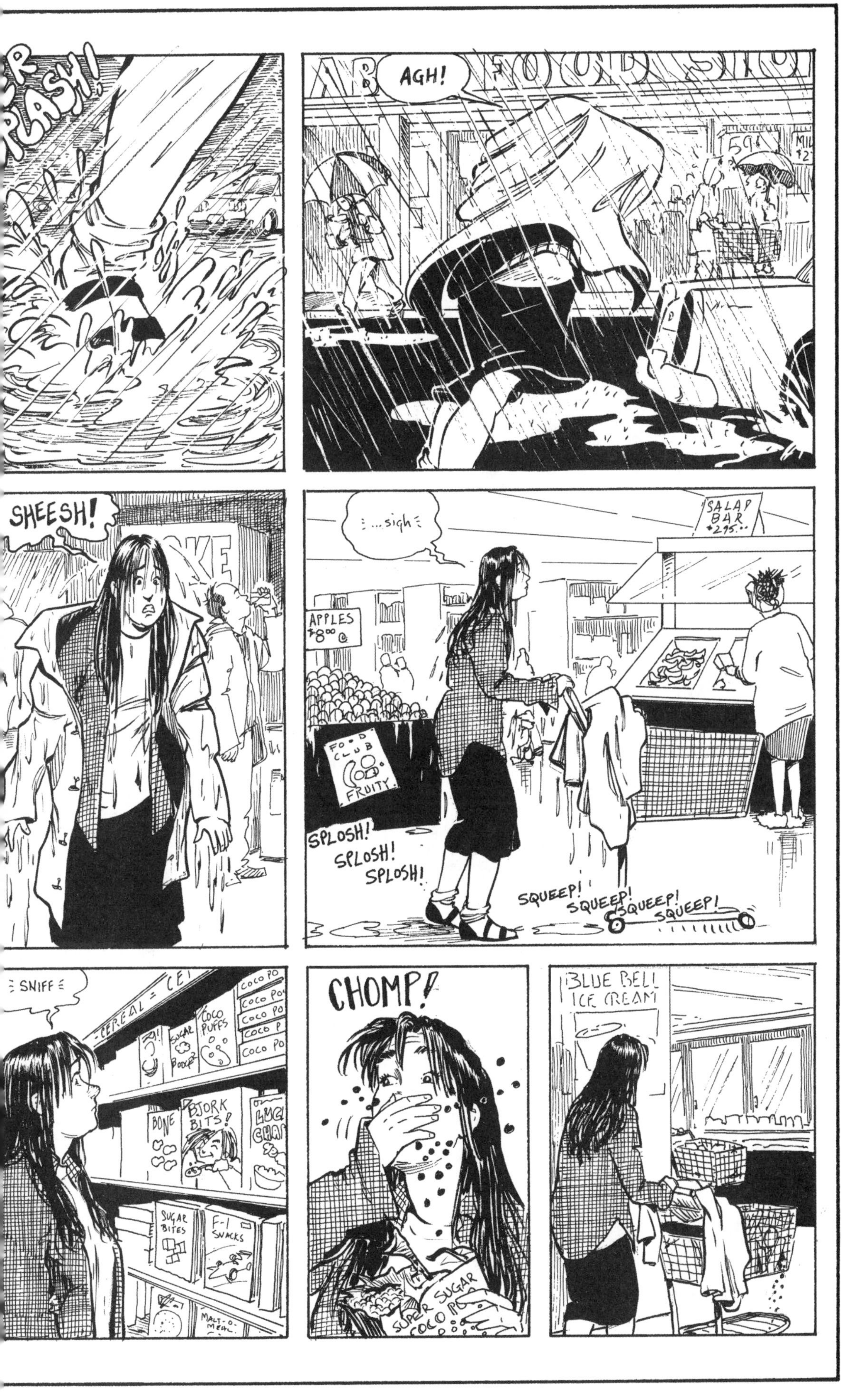
SPLASH!
AGH!
FOOD SHO
SHEESH!
...sigh
SALAD BAR
APPLES $8.00 @
FOOD CLUB FRUITY
SPLOSH! SPLOSH! SPLOSH!
SQUEEP! SQUEEP! SQUEEP! SQUEEP!
SNIFF
CEREAL
COCO PUFFS
SUGAR BOOGERS
BONE
BJORK BITS!
SUGAR BITES
F-1 SNACKS
MALT-O-MEAL
CHOMP!
SUPER SUGAR COCO PO
BLUE BELL ICE CREAM

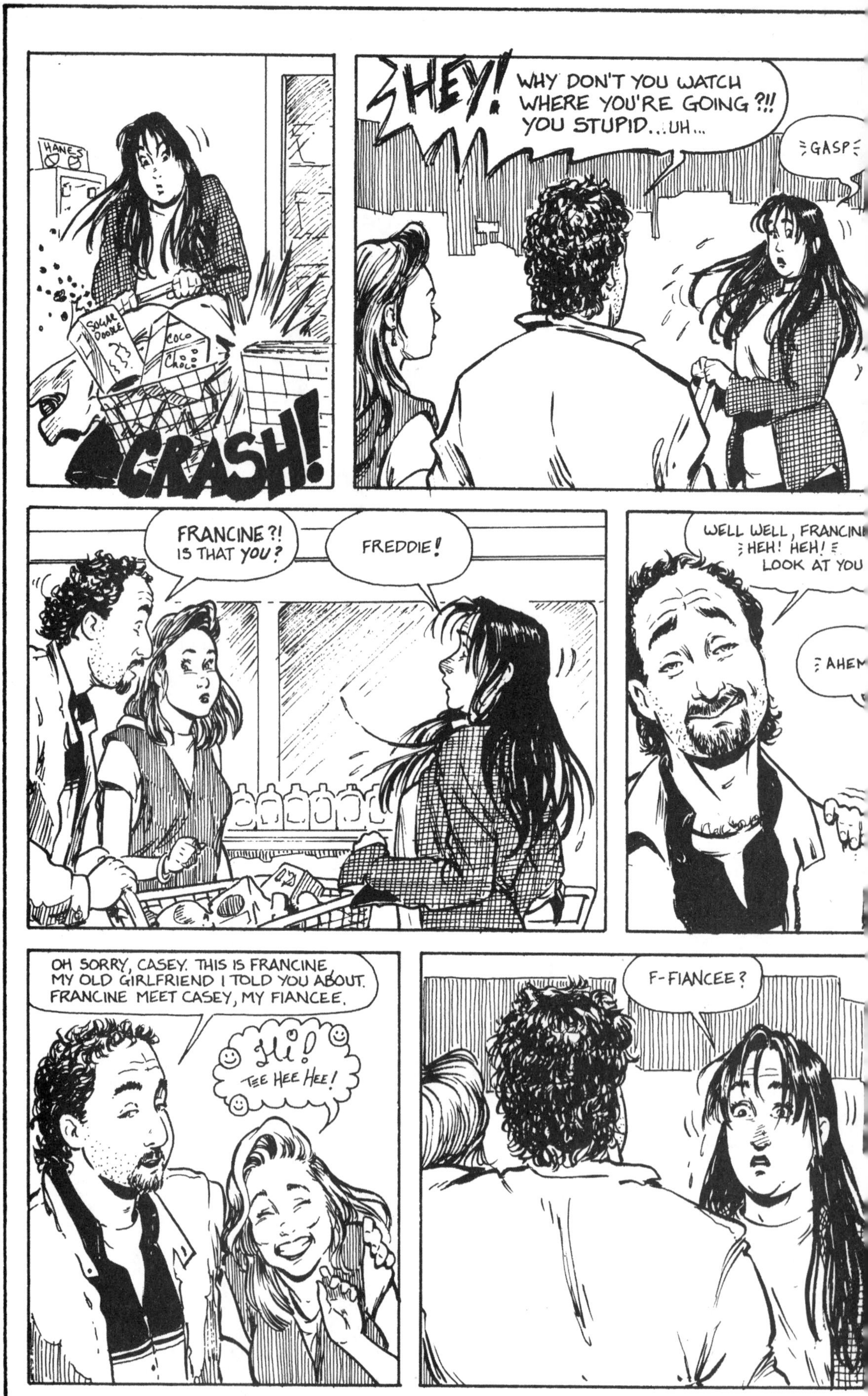
HANES
SUGAR DOODLE
COCO CHOCO
CRASH!
HEY!
WHY DON'T YOU WATCH WHERE YOU'RE GOING ?!! YOU STUPID...UH...
GASP
FRANCINE ?! IS THAT YOU?
FREDDIE!
WELL WELL, FRANCIN
HEH! HEH!
LOOK AT YOU
AHEM
OH SORRY, CASEY. THIS IS FRANCINE, MY OLD GIRLFRIEND I TOLD YOU ABOUT. FRANCINE MEET CASEY, MY FIANCEE.
Hi!
TEE HEE HEE!
F-FIANCEE?

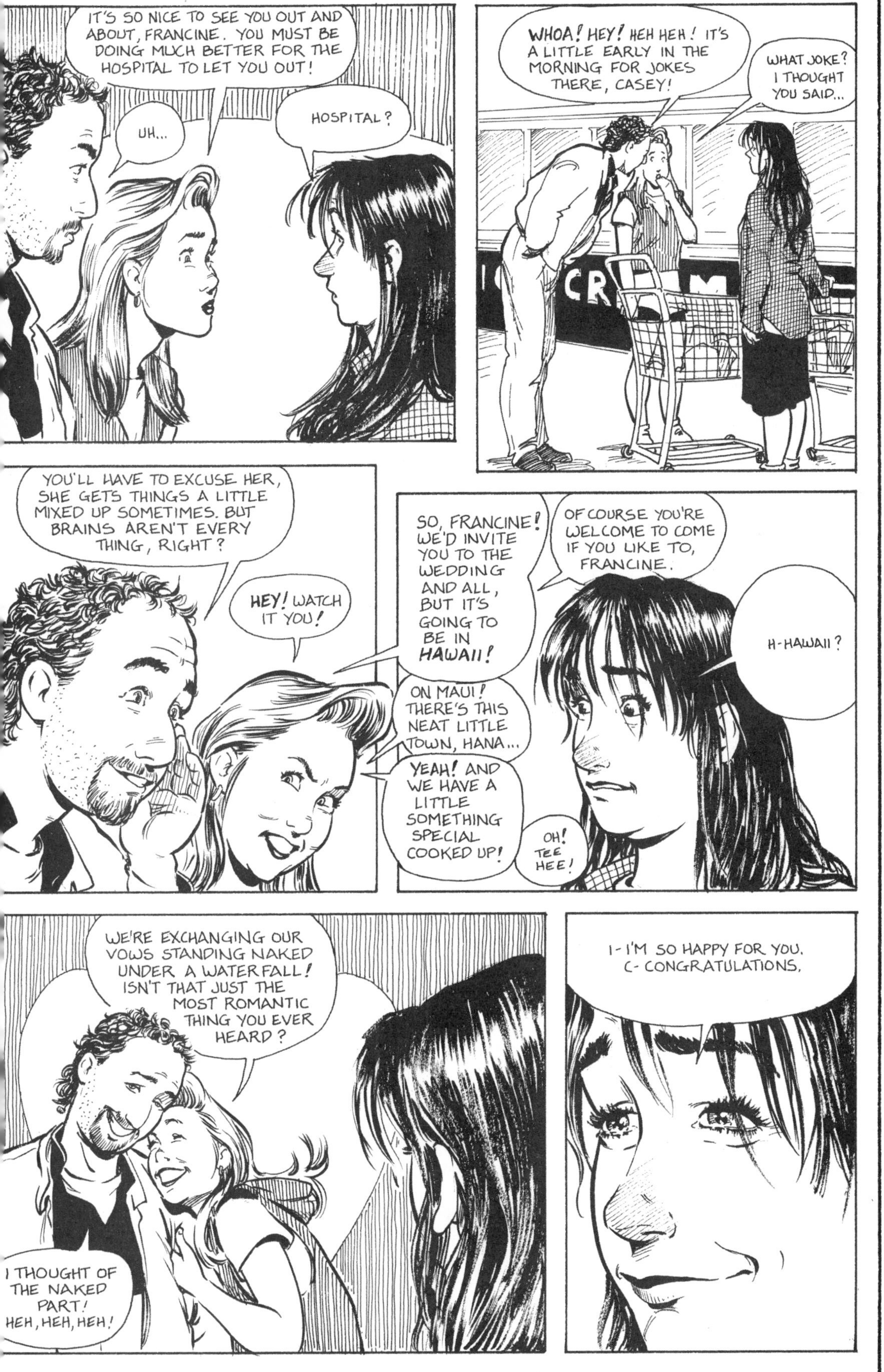
IT'S SO NICE TO SEE YOU OUT AND ABOUT, FRANCINE. YOU MUST BE DOING MUCH BETTER FOR THE HOSPITAL TO LET YOU OUT!
UH...
HOSPITAL?
WHOA! HEY! HEH HEH! IT'S A LITTLE EARLY IN THE MORNING FOR JOKES THERE, CASEY!
WHAT JOKE? I THOUGHT YOU SAID...
YOU'LL HAVE TO EXCUSE HER, SHE GETS THINGS A LITTLE MIXED UP SOMETIMES. BUT BRAINS AREN'T EVERY THING, RIGHT?
HEY! WATCH IT YOU!
SO, FRANCINE! WE'D INVITE YOU TO THE WEDDING AND ALL, BUT IT'S GOING TO BE IN HAWAII!
OF COURSE YOU'RE WELCOME TO COME IF YOU LIKE TO, FRANCINE.
H-HAWAII?
ON MAUI! THERE'S THIS NEAT LITTLE TOWN, HANA...
YEAH! AND WE HAVE A LITTLE SOMETHING SPECIAL COOKED UP!
OH! TEE HEE!
WE'RE EXCHANGING OUR VOWS STANDING NAKED UNDER A WATERFALL! ISN'T THAT JUST THE MOST ROMANTIC THING YOU EVER HEARD?
I THOUGHT OF THE NAKED PART! HEH, HEH, HEH!
I-I'M SO HAPPY FOR YOU. C-CONGRATULATIONS.

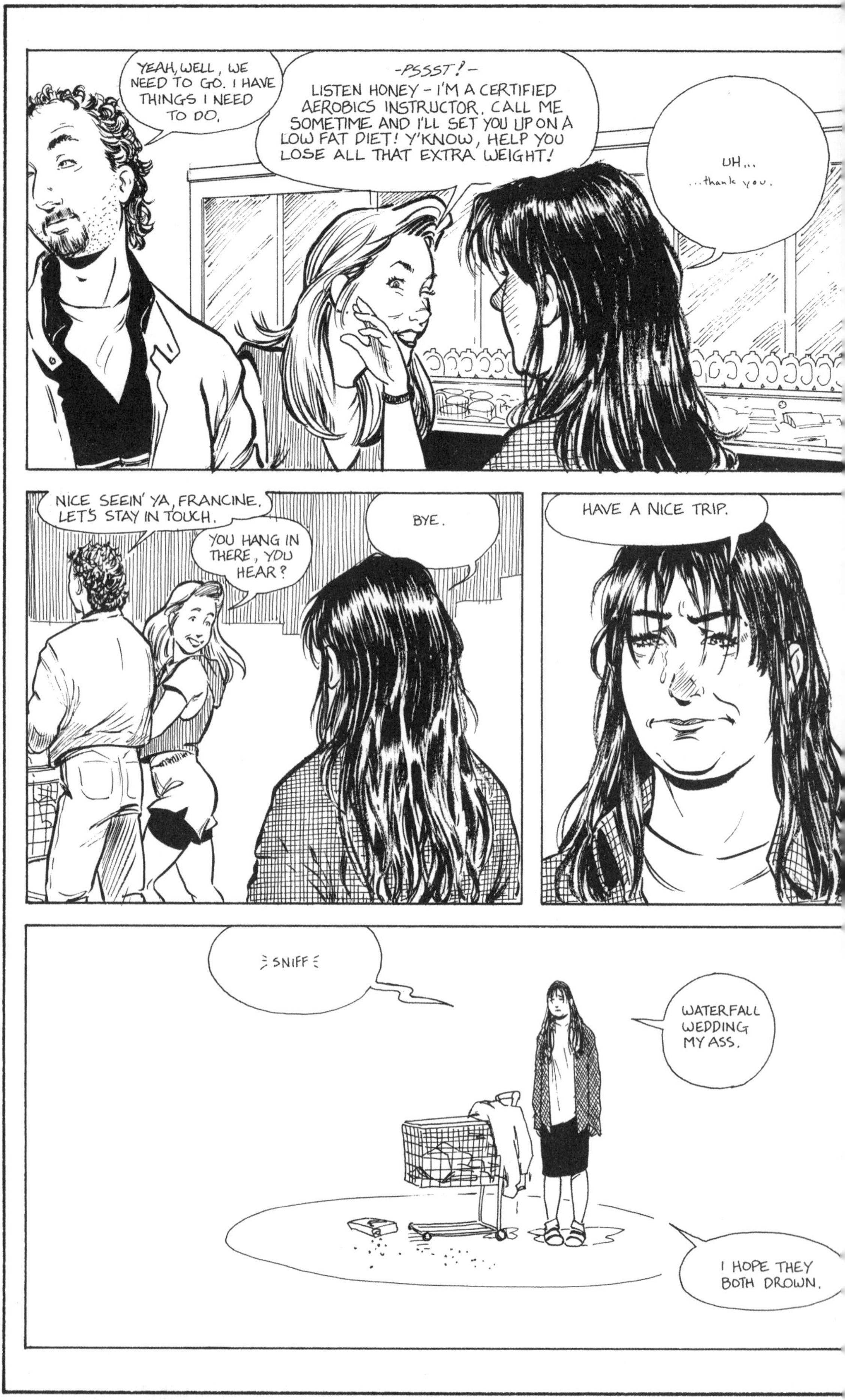
YEAH, WELL, WE NEED TO GO. I HAVE THINGS I NEED TO DO.
-PSSST!- LISTEN HONEY - I'M A CERTIFIED AEROBICS INSTRUCTOR. CALL ME SOMETIME AND I'LL SET YOU UP ON A LOW FAT DIET! Y'KNOW, HELP YOU LOSE ALL THAT EXTRA WEIGHT!
UH... ...thank you.
NICE SEEIN' YA, FRANCINE. LET'S STAY IN TOUCH.
YOU HANG IN THERE, YOU HEAR?
BYE.
HAVE A NICE TRIP.
SNIFF
WATERFALL WEDDING MY ASS.
I HOPE THEY BOTH DROWN.

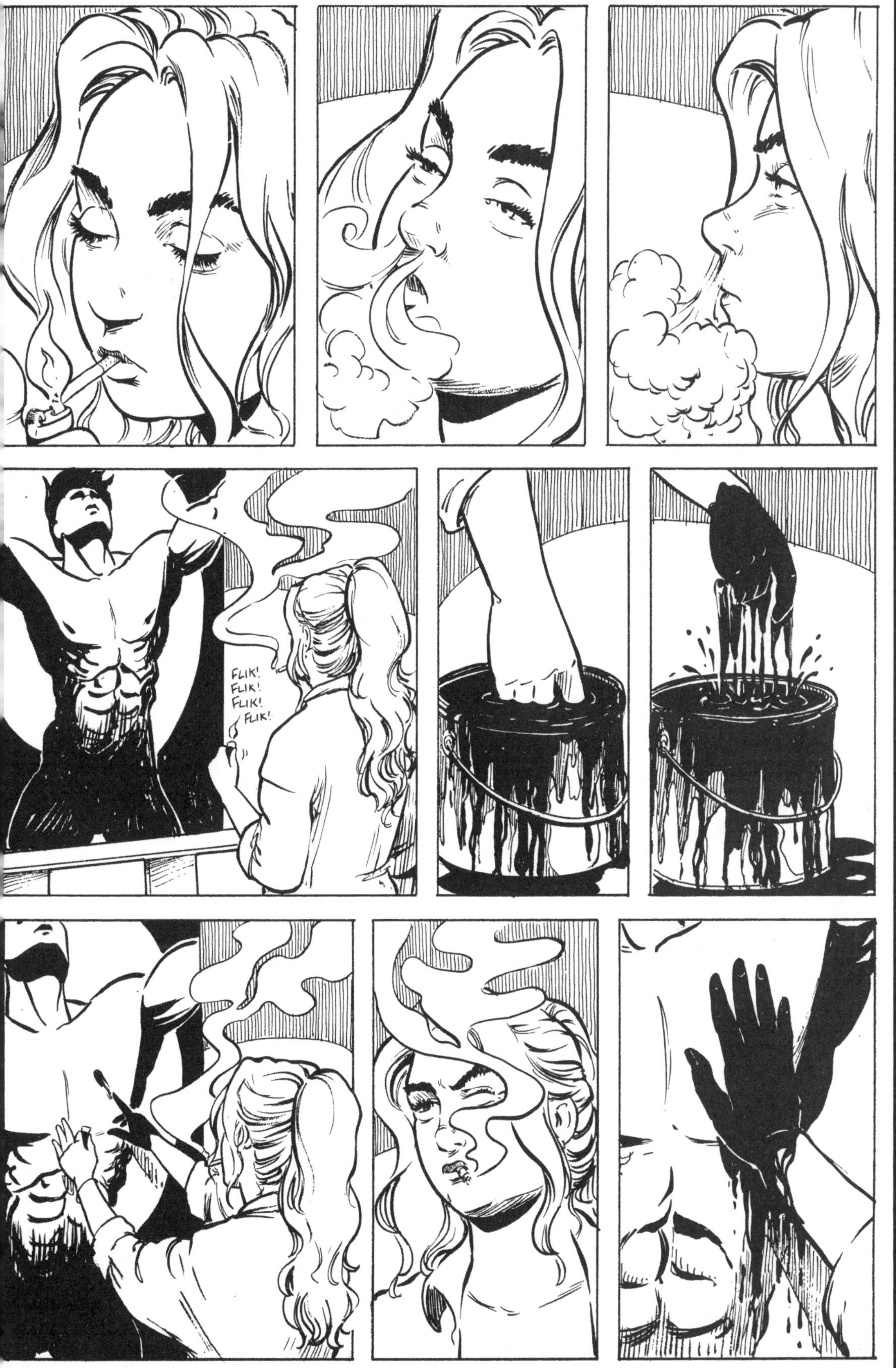
FLIK!
FLIK!
FLIK!
FLIK!

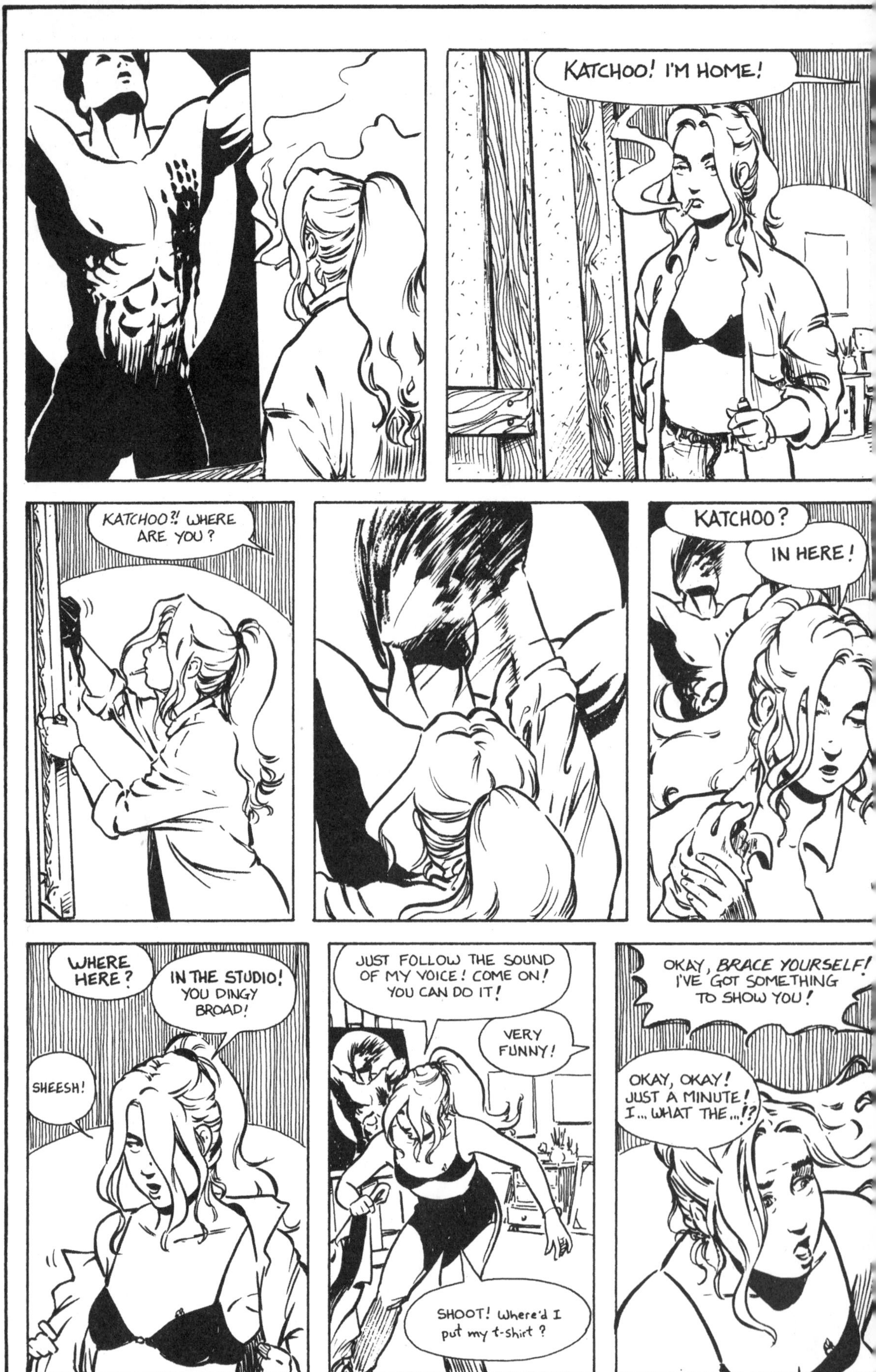
KATCHOO! I'M HOME!
KATCHOO?! WHERE ARE YOU?
KATCHOO?
IN HERE!
WHERE HERE?
IN THE STUDIO! YOU DINGY BROAD!
SHEESH!
JUST FOLLOW THE SOUND OF MY VOICE! COME ON! YOU CAN DO IT!
VERY FUNNY!
SHOOT! Where'd I put my t-shirt?
OKAY, *BRACE YOURSELF!* I'VE GOT SOMETHING TO SHOW YOU!
OKAY, OKAY! JUST A MINUTE! I... WHAT THE...!?

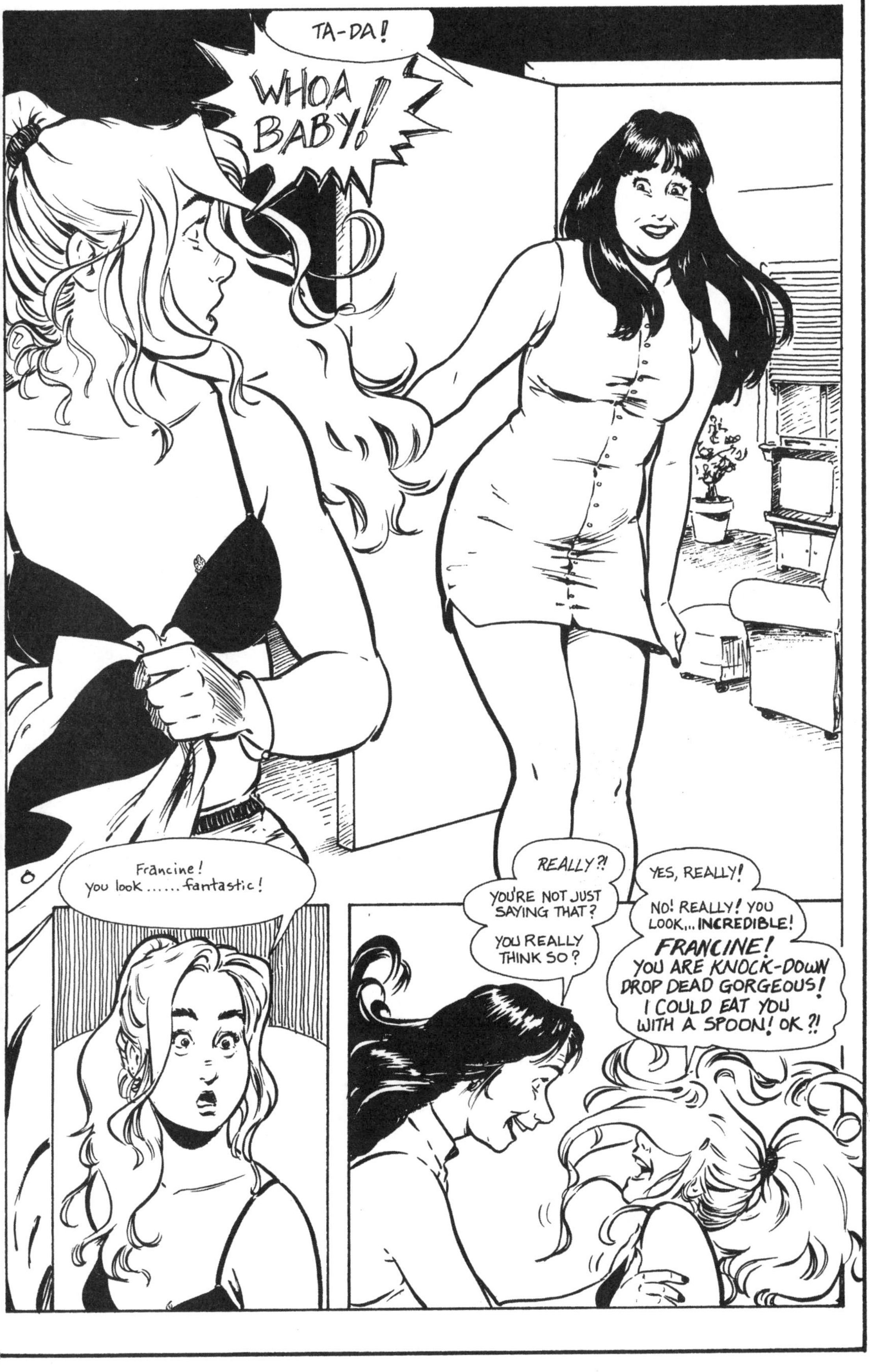

TA-DA!
WHOA BABY!
Francine! you look...... fantastic!
REALLY?!
YOU'RE NOT JUST SAYING THAT?
YOU REALLY THINK SO?
YES, REALLY!
NO! REALLY! YOU LOOK... INCREDIBLE!
FRANCINE! YOU ARE KNOCK-DOWN DROP DEAD GORGEOUS! I COULD EAT YOU WITH A SPOON! OK?!

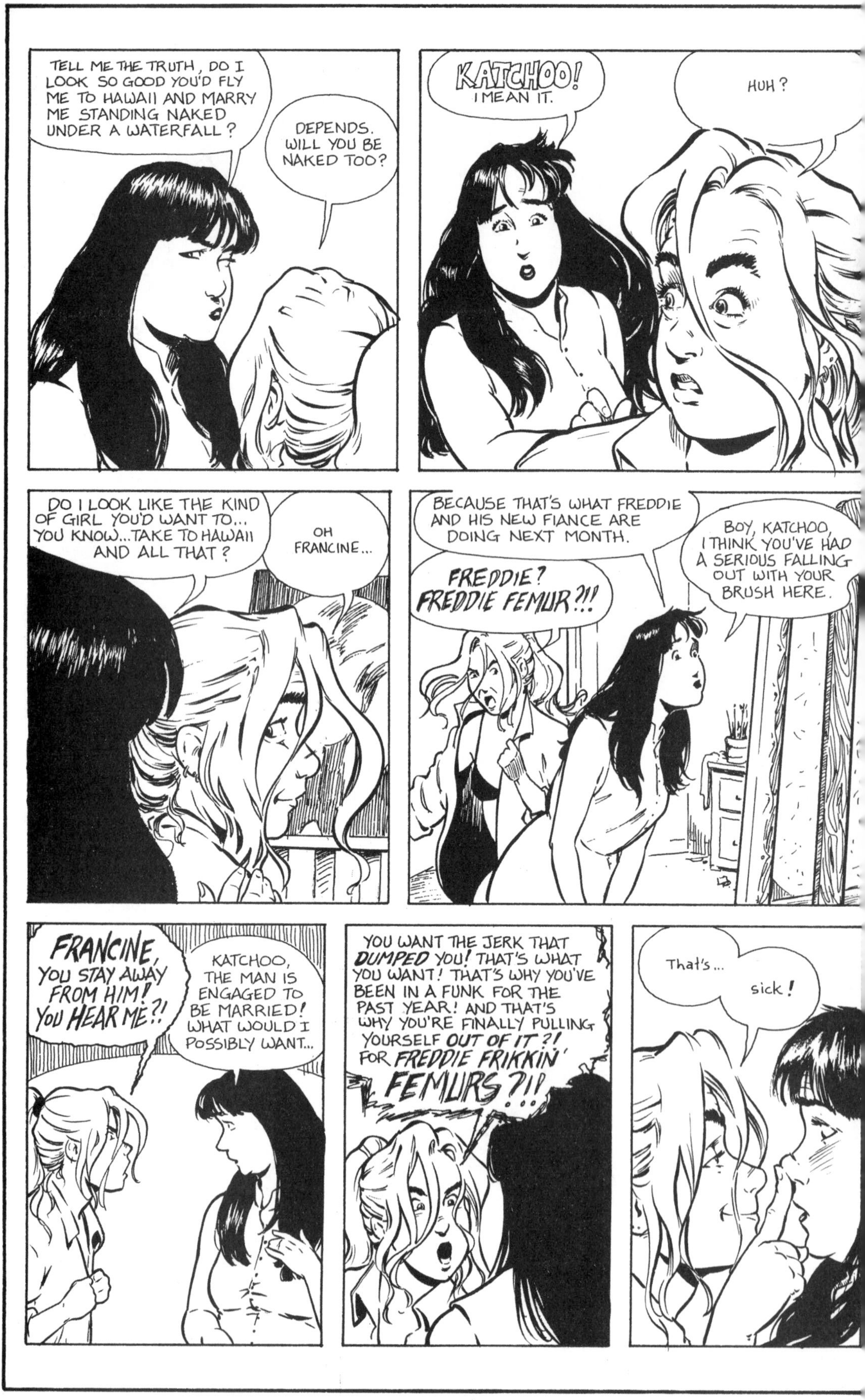
TELL ME THE TRUTH, DO I LOOK SO GOOD YOU'D FLY ME TO HAWAII AND MARRY ME STANDING NAKED UNDER A WATERFALL?
DEPENDS. WILL YOU BE NAKED TOO?
KATCHOO! I MEAN IT.
HUH?
DO I LOOK LIKE THE KIND OF GIRL YOU'D WANT TO... YOU KNOW...TAKE TO HAWAII AND ALL THAT?
OH FRANCINE...
BECAUSE THAT'S WHAT FREDDIE AND HIS NEW FIANCE ARE DOING NEXT MONTH.
FREDDIE? FREDDIE FEMUR?!!
BOY, KATCHOO, I THINK YOU'VE HAD A SERIOUS FALLING OUT WITH YOUR BRUSH HERE.
FRANCINE, YOU STAY AWAY FROM HIM! YOU HEAR ME?!
KATCHOO, THE MAN IS ENGAGED TO BE MARRIED! WHAT WOULD I POSSIBLY WANT...
YOU WANT THE JERK THAT DUMPED YOU! THAT'S WHAT YOU WANT! THAT'S WHY YOU'VE BEEN IN A FUNK FOR THE PAST YEAR! AND THAT'S WHY YOU'RE FINALLY PULLING YOURSELF OUT OF IT?! FOR FREDDIE FRIKKIN' FEMURS?!!
That's...
sick!

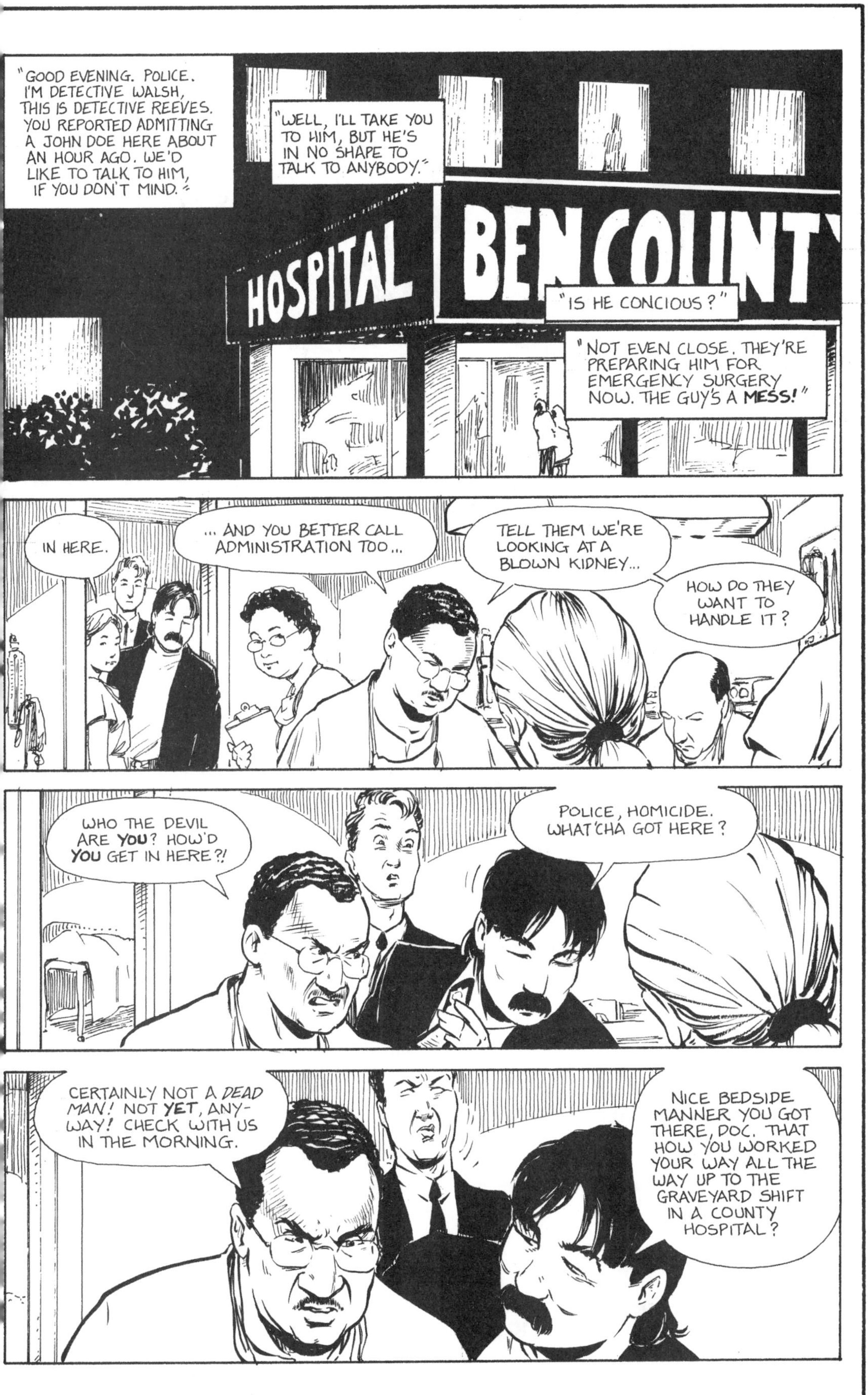
"GOOD EVENING. POLICE. I'M DETECTIVE WALSH, THIS IS DETECTIVE REEVES. YOU REPORTED ADMITTING A JOHN DOE HERE ABOUT AN HOUR AGO. WE'D LIKE TO TALK TO HIM, IF YOU DON'T MIND."
"WELL, I'LL TAKE YOU TO HIM, BUT HE'S IN NO SHAPE TO TALK TO ANYBODY."
HOSPITAL
BEN COUNT
"IS HE CONCIOUS?"
"NOT EVEN CLOSE. THEY'RE PREPARING HIM FOR EMERGENCY SURGERY NOW. THE GUY'S A MESS!"
IN HERE.
... AND YOU BETTER CALL ADMINISTRATION TOO...
TELL THEM WE'RE LOOKING AT A BLOWN KIDNEY...
HOW DO THEY WANT TO HANDLE IT?
WHO THE DEVIL ARE YOU? HOW'D YOU GET IN HERE?!
POLICE, HOMICIDE. WHAT'CHA GOT HERE?
CERTAINLY NOT A DEAD MAN! NOT YET, ANY-WAY! CHECK WITH US IN THE MORNING.
NICE BEDSIDE MANNER YOU GOT THERE, DOC. THAT HOW YOU WORKED YOUR WAY ALL THE WAY UP TO THE GRAVEYARD SHIFT IN A COUNTY HOSPITAL?

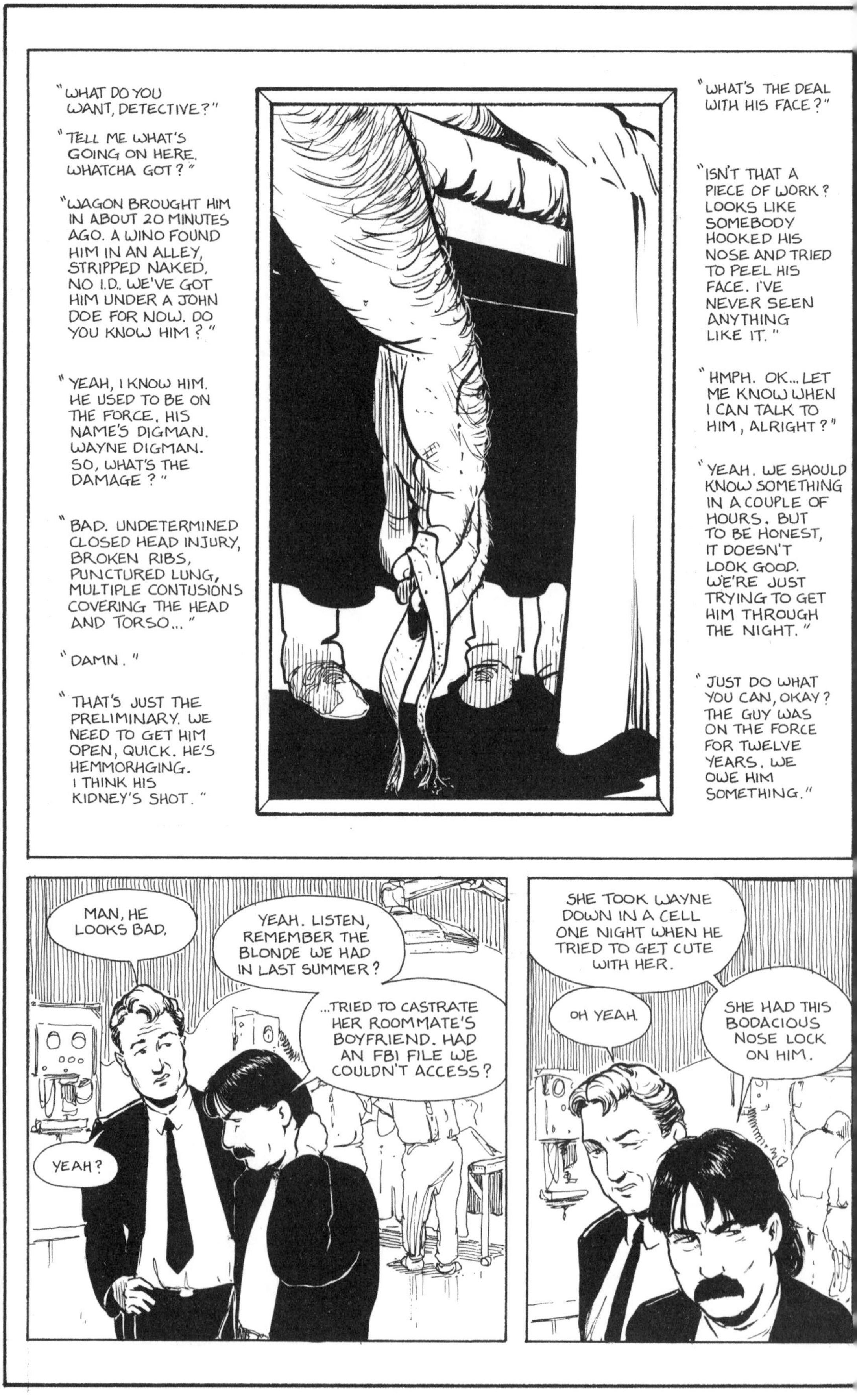
"WHAT DO YOU WANT, DETECTIVE?"
"TELL ME WHAT'S GOING ON HERE. WHATCHA GOT?"
"WAGON BROUGHT HIM IN ABOUT 20 MINUTES AGO. A WINO FOUND HIM IN AN ALLEY, STRIPPED NAKED, NO I.D., WE'VE GOT HIM UNDER A JOHN DOE FOR NOW. DO YOU KNOW HIM?"
"YEAH, I KNOW HIM. HE USED TO BE ON THE FORCE. HIS NAME'S DIGMAN. WAYNE DIGMAN. SO, WHAT'S THE DAMAGE?"
"BAD. UNDETERMINED CLOSED HEAD INJURY, BROKEN RIBS, PUNCTURED LUNG, MULTIPLE CONTUSIONS COVERING THE HEAD AND TORSO..."
"DAMN."
"THAT'S JUST THE PRELIMINARY. WE NEED TO GET HIM OPEN, QUICK. HE'S HEMMORHGING. I THINK HIS KIDNEY'S SHOT."
"WHAT'S THE DEAL WITH HIS FACE?"
"ISN'T THAT A PIECE OF WORK? LOOKS LIKE SOMEBODY HOOKED HIS NOSE AND TRIED TO PEEL HIS FACE. I'VE NEVER SEEN ANYTHING LIKE IT."
"HMPH. OK... LET ME KNOW WHEN I CAN TALK TO HIM, ALRIGHT?"
"YEAH. WE SHOULD KNOW SOMETHING IN A COUPLE OF HOURS. BUT TO BE HONEST, IT DOESN'T LOOK GOOD. WE'RE JUST TRYING TO GET HIM THROUGH THE NIGHT."
"JUST DO WHAT YOU CAN, OKAY? THE GUY WAS ON THE FORCE FOR TWELVE YEARS. WE OWE HIM SOMETHING."
MAN, HE LOOKS BAD.
YEAH. LISTEN, REMEMBER THE BLONDE WE HAD IN LAST SUMMER?
YEAH?
...TRIED TO CASTRATE HER ROOMMATE'S BOYFRIEND. HAD AN FBI FILE WE COULDN'T ACCESS?
SHE TOOK WAYNE DOWN IN A CELL ONE NIGHT WHEN HE TRIED TO GET CUTE WITH HER.
OH YEAH.
SHE HAD THIS BODACIOUS NOSE LOCK ON HIM.

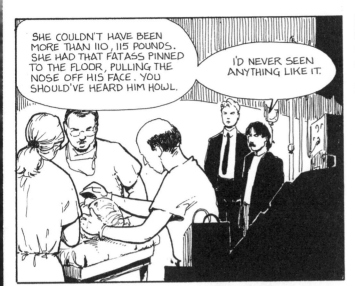

SHE COULDN'T HAVE BEEN MORE THAN 110, 115 POUNDS. SHE HAD THAT FATASS PINNED TO THE FLOOR, PULLING THE NOSE OFF HIS FACE. YOU SHOULD'VE HEARD HIM HOWL.

I'D NEVER SEEN ANYTHING LIKE IT.

NOW I'VE SEEN IT TWICE.

WHAT WAS HER NAME?

POLISH GIRL...FROM CHICAGO...**CHOOVANSKI**, SOMETHING CHOOVANSKI.

SEE IF YOU CAN FIND HER FILE. GET A WARRANT FOR HER ARREST. PICK HER UP, SUSPICION OF FELONIOUS ASSAULT.

TAKE A COUPLE OF MEN WITH YOU.

OH... AND PETE...

YEAH?

WHILE YOU'RE AT IT, GET A SECOND WARRANT ON HER, JUST IN CASE.

WHAT FOR?

MURDER ONE.

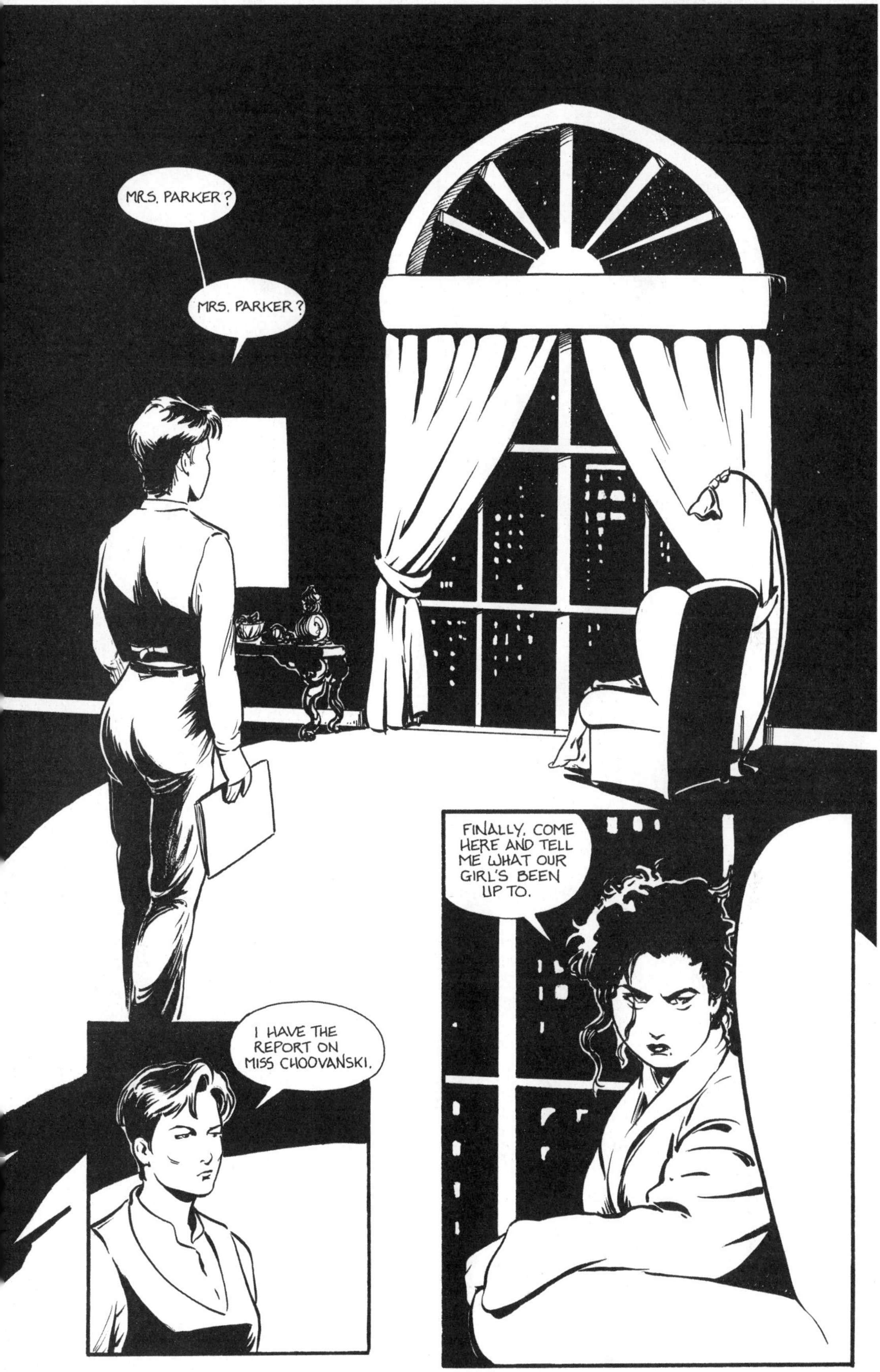
MRS. PARKER?
MRS. PARKER?
FINALLY. COME HERE AND TELL ME WHAT OUR GIRL'S BEEN UP TO.
I HAVE THE REPORT ON MISS CHOOVANSKI.

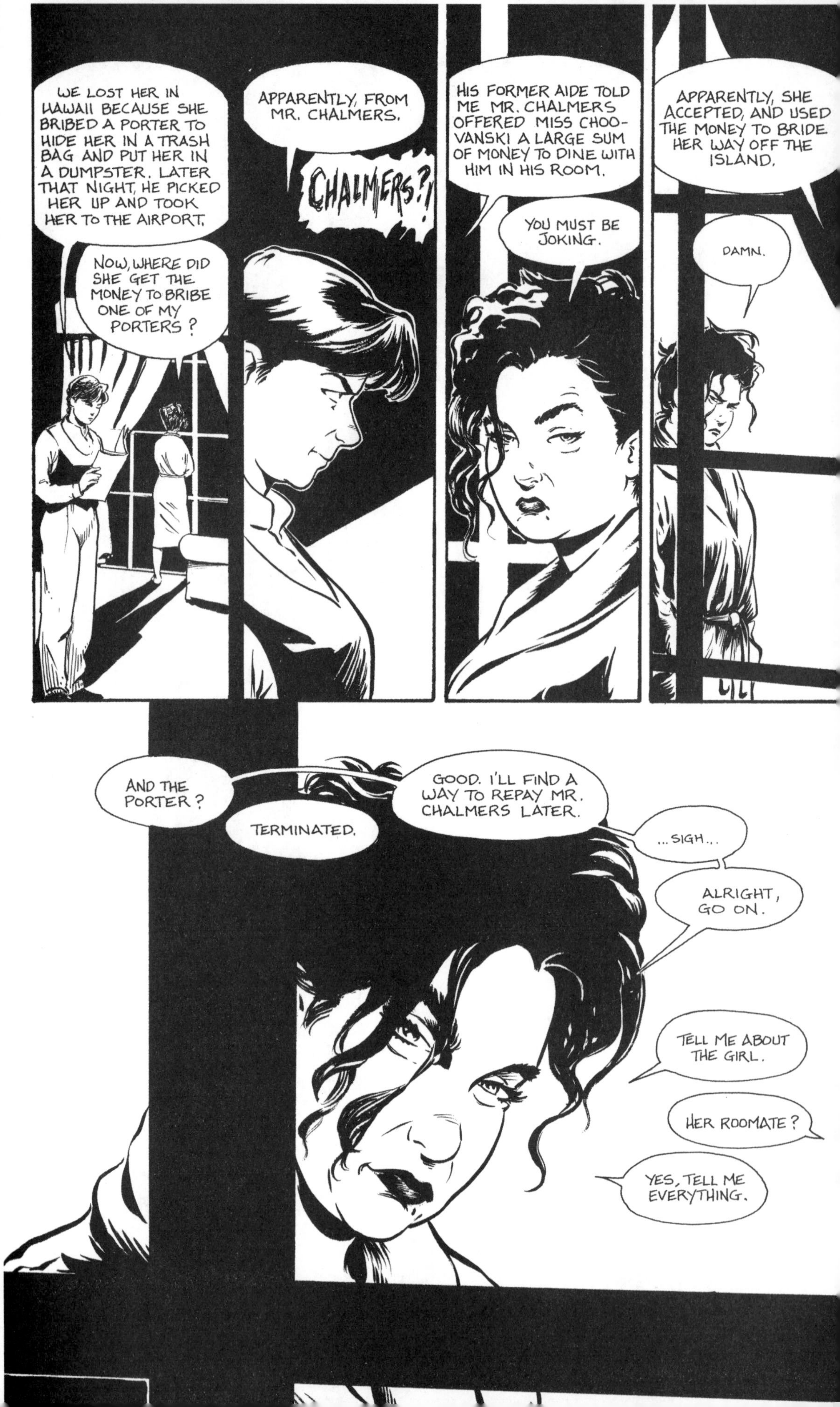

WE LOST HER IN HAWAII BECAUSE SHE BRIBED A PORTER TO HIDE HER IN A TRASH BAG AND PUT HER IN A DUMPSTER. LATER THAT NIGHT, HE PICKED HER UP AND TOOK HER TO THE AIRPORT,
NOW, WHERE DID SHE GET THE MONEY TO BRIBE ONE OF MY PORTERS ?
APPARENTLY, FROM MR. CHALMERS.
CHALMERS?!
HIS FORMER AIDE TOLD ME MR. CHALMERS OFFERED MISS CHOO-VANSKI A LARGE SUM OF MONEY TO DINE WITH HIM IN HIS ROOM.
YOU MUST BE JOKING.
APPARENTLY, SHE ACCEPTED, AND USED THE MONEY TO BRIDE HER WAY OFF THE ISLAND.
DAMN.
AND THE PORTER ?
TERMINATED.
GOOD. I'LL FIND A WAY TO REPAY MR. CHALMERS LATER.
...SIGH...
ALRIGHT, GO ON.
TELL ME ABOUT THE GIRL.
HER ROOMATE ?
YES, TELL ME EVERYTHING.

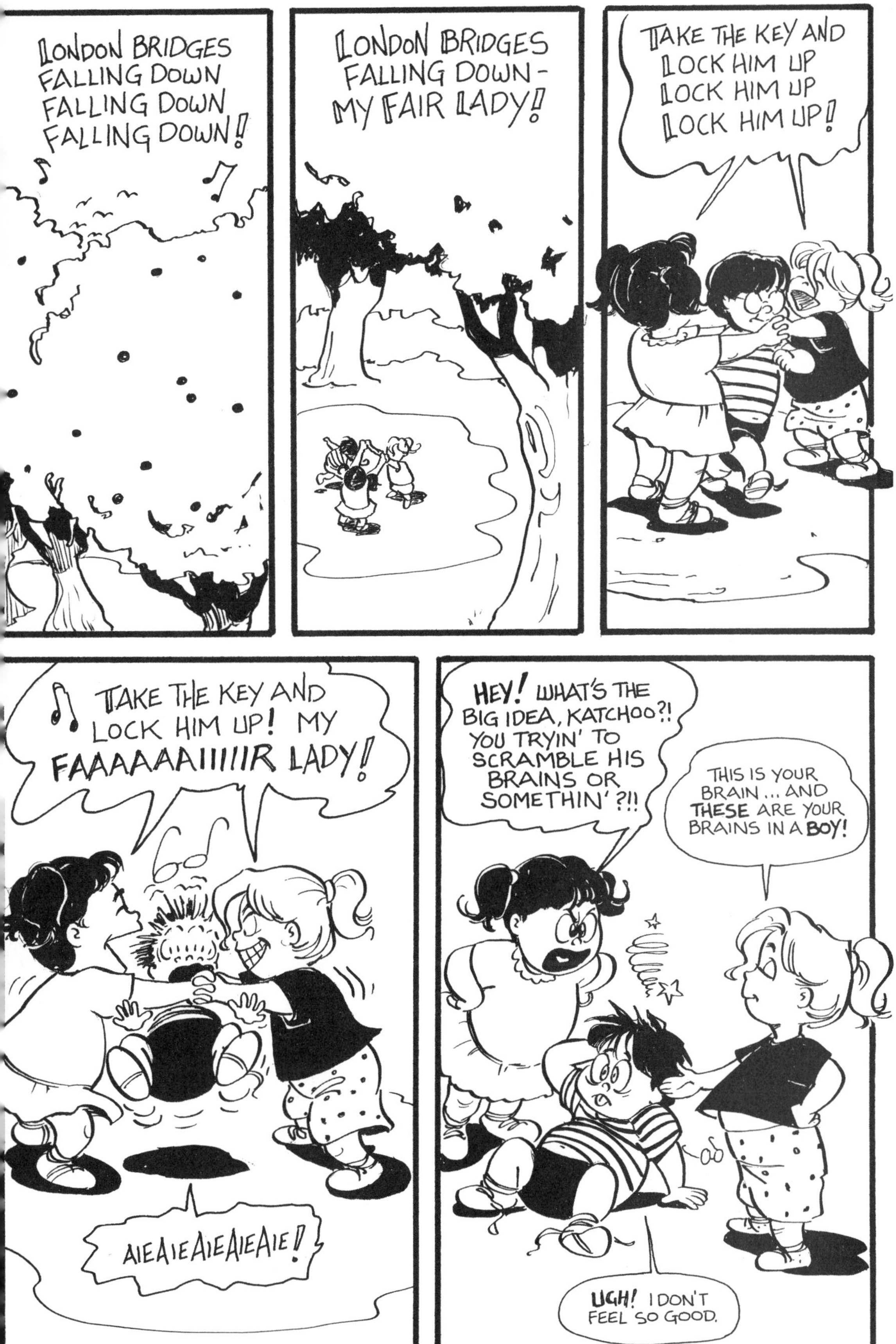
LONDON BRIDGES FALLING DOWN FALLING DOWN FALLING DOWN!
LONDON BRIDGES FALLING DOWN - MY FAIR LADY!
TAKE THE KEY AND LOCK HIM UP LOCK HIM UP LOCK HIM UP!
TAKE THE KEY AND LOCK HIM UP! MY FAAAAAAIIIIIR LADY!
AIEAIEAIEAIEAIE!
HEY! WHAT'S THE BIG IDEA, KATCHOO?! YOU TRYIN' TO SCRAMBLE HIS BRAINS OR SOMETHIN'?!!
THIS IS YOUR BRAIN ... AND THESE ARE YOUR BRAINS IN A BOY!
UGH! I DON'T FEEL SO GOOD.

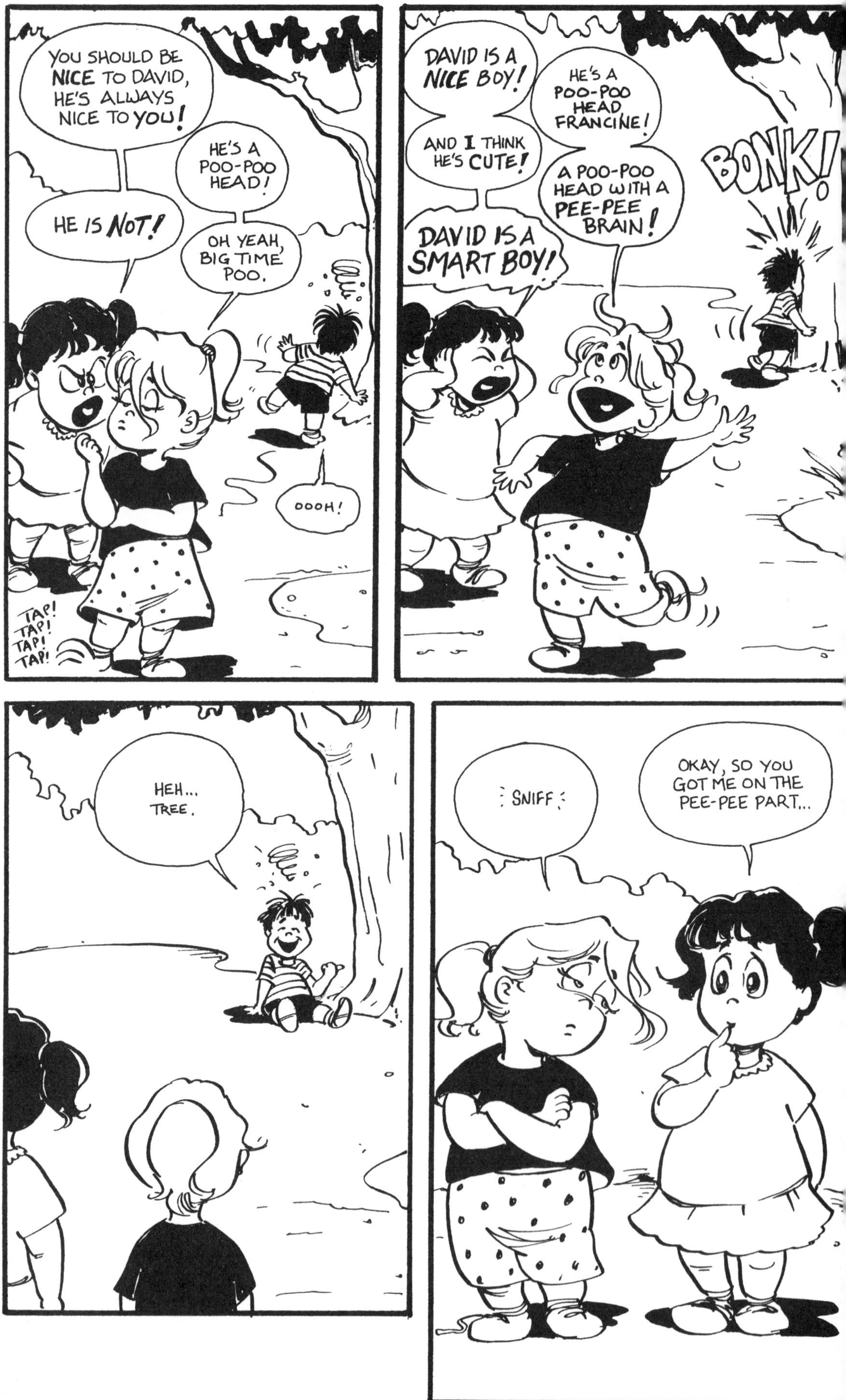

YOU SHOULD BE NICE TO DAVID, HE'S ALWAYS NICE TO YOU!
HE IS NOT!
HE'S A POO-POO HEAD!
OH YEAH, BIG TIME POO.
OOOH!
TAP! TAP! TAP! TAP!
DAVID IS A NICE BOY!
AND I THINK HE'S CUTE!
DAVID IS A SMART BOY!
HE'S A POO-POO HEAD FRANCINE!
A POO-POO HEAD WITH A PEE-PEE BRAIN!
BONK!
HEH... TREE.
SNIFF
OKAY, SO YOU GOT ME ON THE PEE-PEE PART...

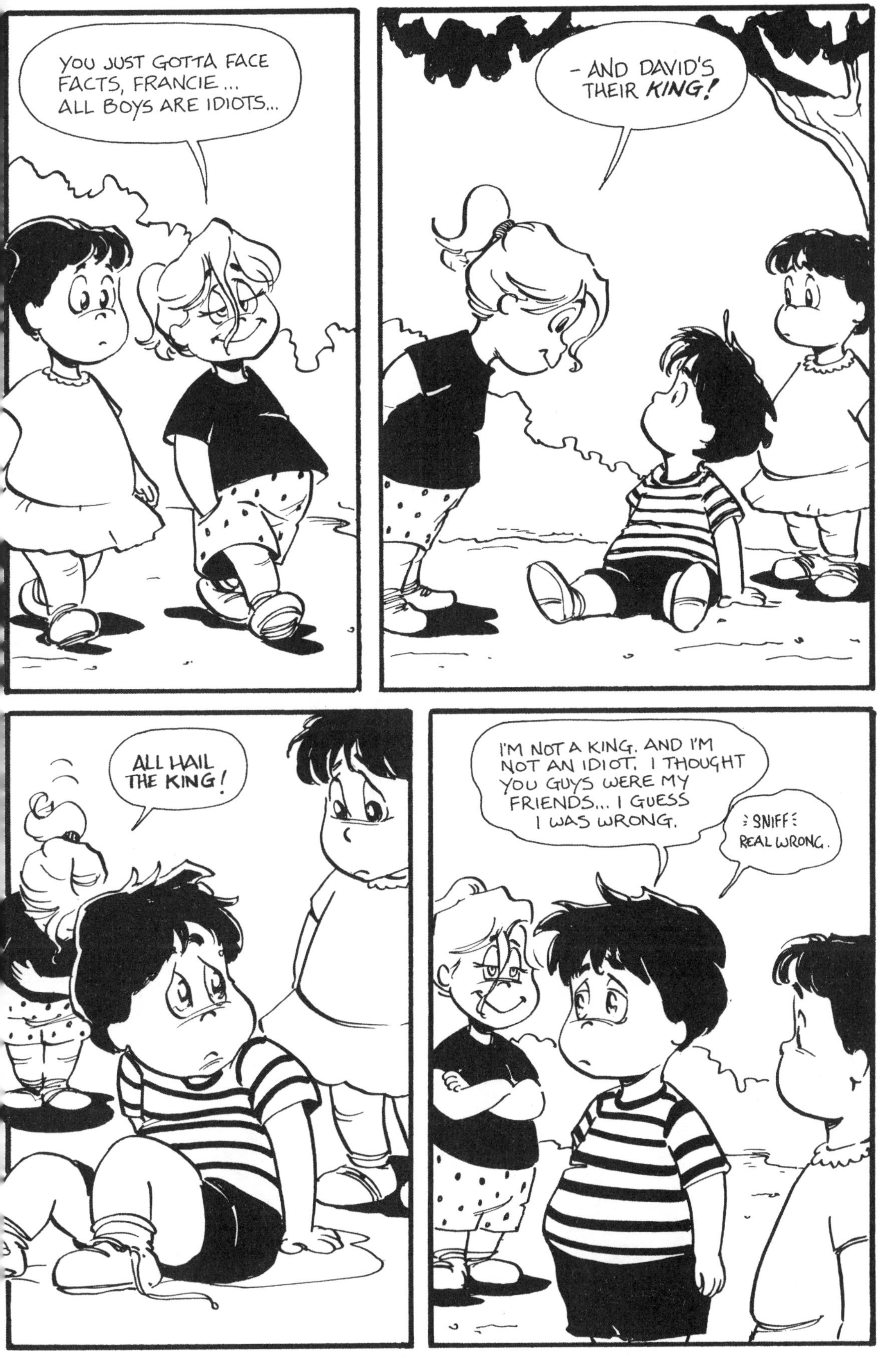
YOU JUST GOTTA FACE FACTS, FRANCIE... ALL BOYS ARE IDIOTS...
- AND DAVID'S THEIR KING!
ALL HAIL THE KING!
I'M NOT A KING. AND I'M NOT AN IDIOT. I THOUGHT YOU GUYS WERE MY FRIENDS... I GUESS I WAS WRONG.
SNIFF REAL WRONG.

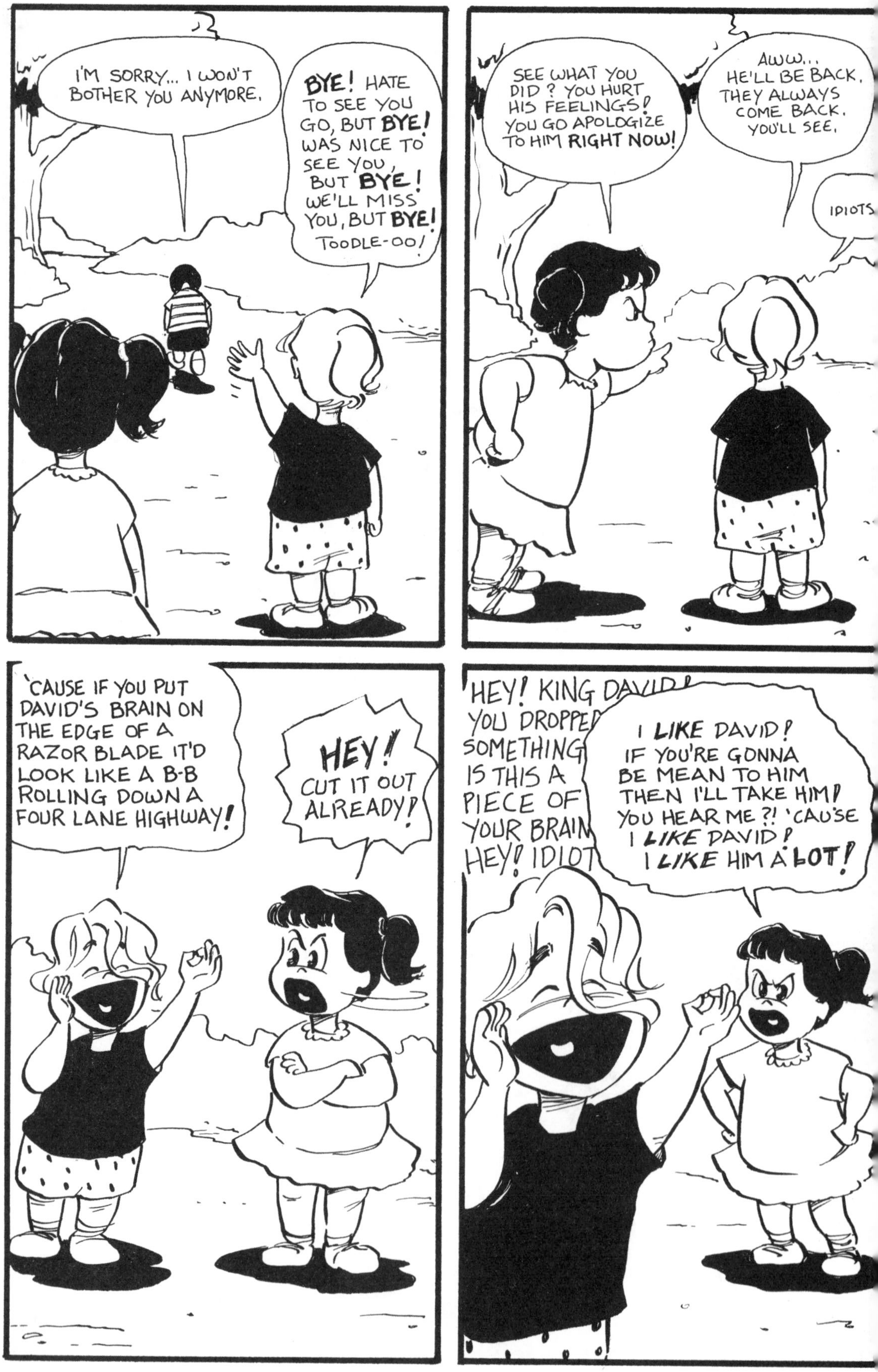
I'M SORRY... I WON'T BOTHER YOU ANYMORE.
BYE! HATE TO SEE YOU GO, BUT BYE! WAS NICE TO SEE YOU, BUT BYE! WE'LL MISS YOU, BUT BYE! TOODLE-OO!
SEE WHAT YOU DID? YOU HURT HIS FEELINGS! YOU GO APOLOGIZE TO HIM RIGHT NOW!
AWW... HE'LL BE BACK. THEY ALWAYS COME BACK. YOU'LL SEE.
IDIOTS
'CAUSE IF YOU PUT DAVID'S BRAIN ON THE EDGE OF A RAZOR BLADE IT'D LOOK LIKE A B-B ROLLING DOWN A FOUR LANE HIGHWAY!
HEY! CUT IT OUT ALREADY!
I LIKE DAVID! IF YOU'RE GONNA BE MEAN TO HIM THEN I'LL TAKE HIM! YOU HEAR ME?! 'CAUSE I LIKE DAVID! I LIKE HIM A LOT!

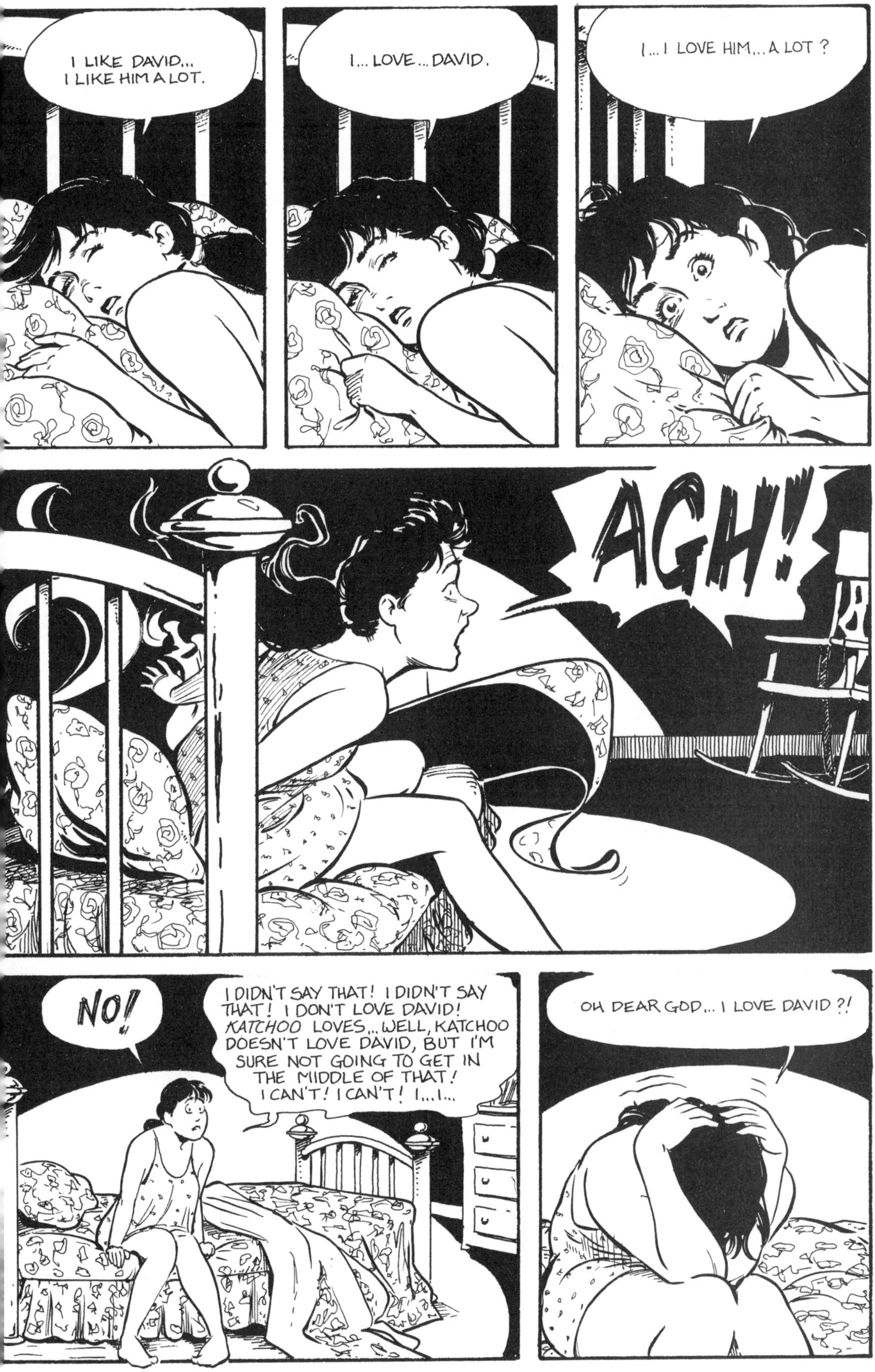
I LIKE DAVID...
I LIKE HIM A LOT.
I... LOVE... DAVID.
I... I LOVE HIM... A LOT ?
AGH!
NO!
I DIDN'T SAY THAT! I DIDN'T SAY THAT! I DON'T LOVE DAVID! KATCHOO LOVES... WELL, KATCHOO DOESN'T LOVE DAVID, BUT I'M SURE NOT GOING TO GET IN THE MIDDLE OF THAT! I CAN'T! I CAN'T! I...I...
OH DEAR GOD... I LOVE DAVID ?!

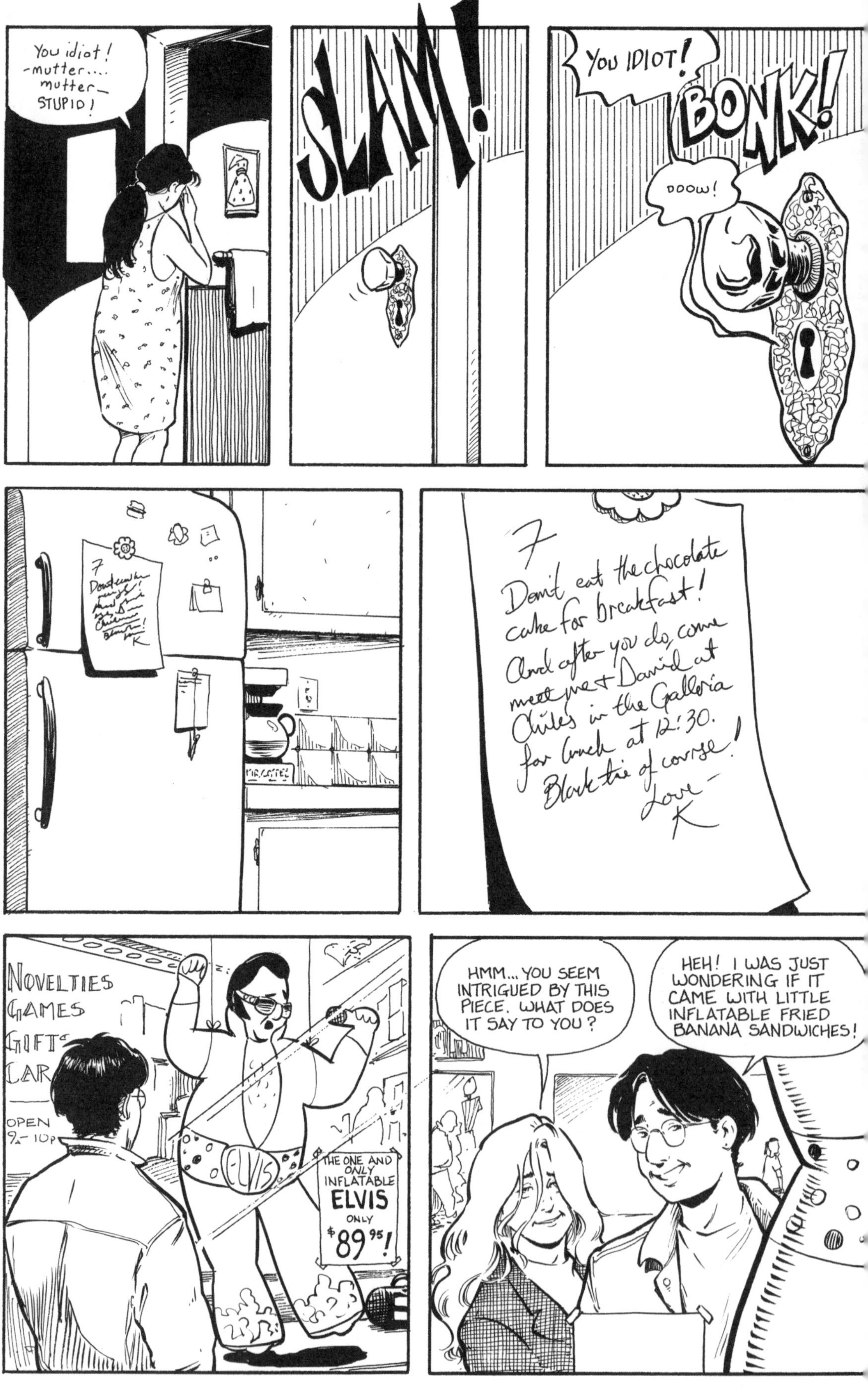

You idiot! -mutter.... mutter_ STUPID!
SLAM!
YOU IDIOT!
BONK!
OOOW!
7
Don't eat the chocolate cake for breakfast! And after you do, come meet me + David at Chile's in the Galleria for lunch at 12:30. Black tie of course! Love - K
NOVELTIES GAMES GIFTS CAR
OPEN 9A-10P
ELVIS
THE ONE AND ONLY INFLATABLE ELVIS ONLY $89.95!
HMM... YOU SEEM INTRIGUED BY THIS PIECE. WHAT DOES IT SAY TO YOU?
HEH! I WAS JUST WONDERING IF IT CAME WITH LITTLE INFLATABLE FRIED BANANA SANDWICHES!

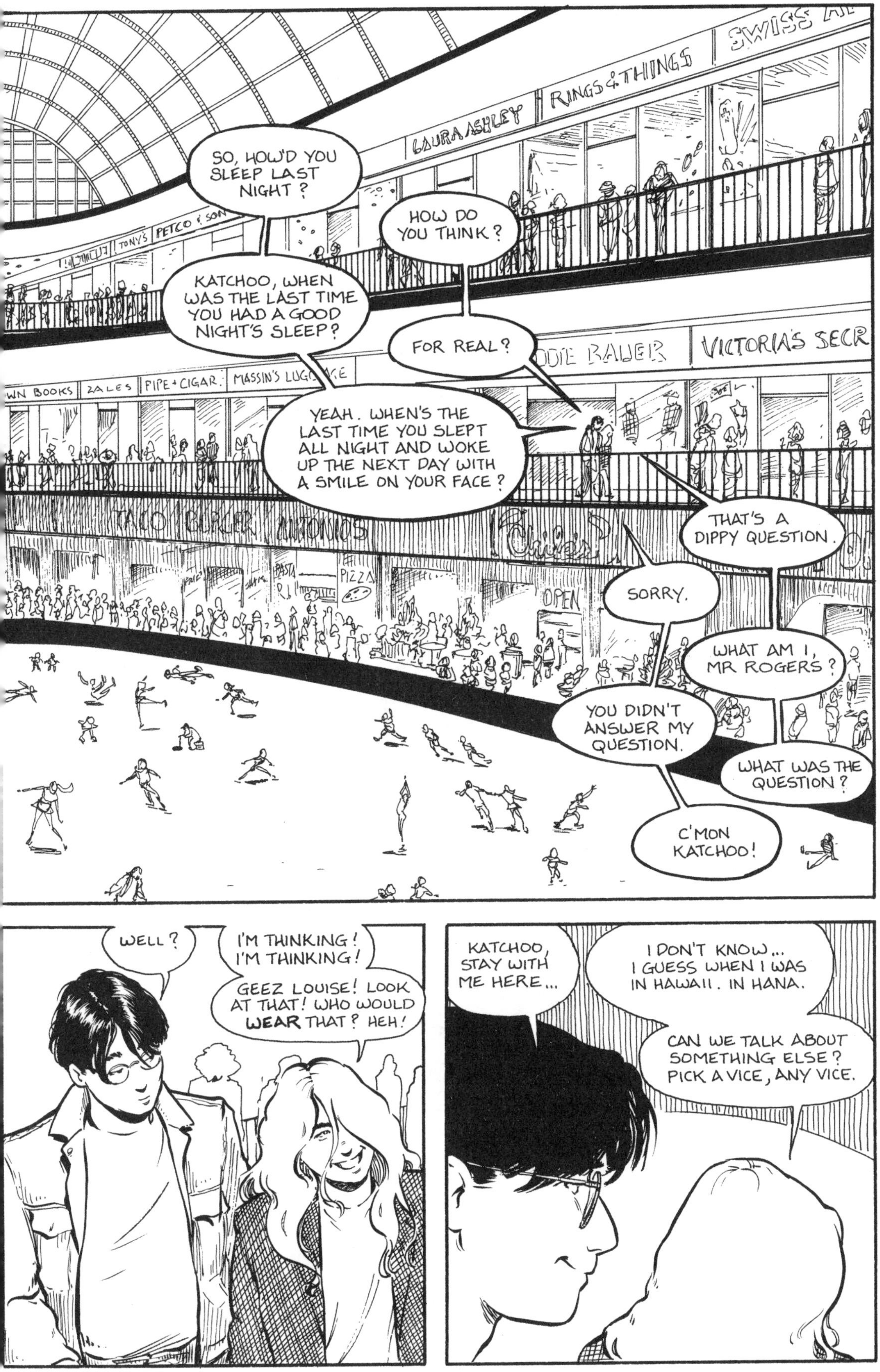

SO, HOW'D YOU SLEEP LAST NIGHT?
HOW DO YOU THINK?
KATCHOO, WHEN WAS THE LAST TIME YOU HAD A GOOD NIGHT'S SLEEP?
FOR REAL?
YEAH. WHEN'S THE LAST TIME YOU SLEPT ALL NIGHT AND WOKE UP THE NEXT DAY WITH A SMILE ON YOUR FACE?
THAT'S A DIPPY QUESTION.
SORRY.
WHAT AM I, MR ROGERS?
YOU DIDN'T ANSWER MY QUESTION.
WHAT WAS THE QUESTION?
C'MON KATCHOO!
WELL?
I'M THINKING! I'M THINKING!
GEEZ LOUISE! LOOK AT THAT! WHO WOULD WEAR THAT? HEH!
KATCHOO, STAY WITH ME HERE...
I DON'T KNOW... I GUESS WHEN I WAS IN HAWAII. IN HANA.
CAN WE TALK ABOUT SOMETHING ELSE? PICK A VICE, ANY VICE.

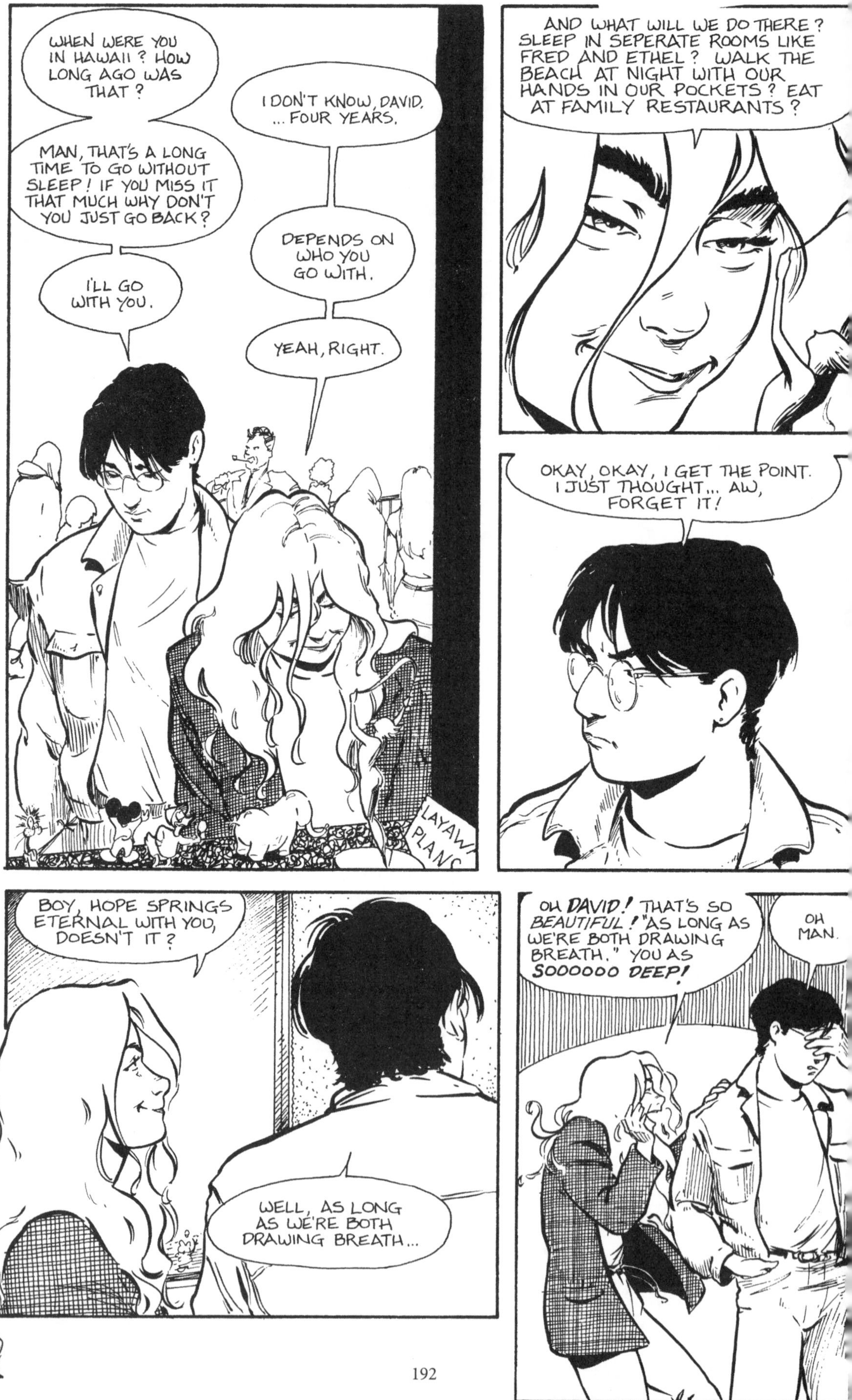
WHEN WERE YOU IN HAWAII? HOW LONG AGO WAS THAT?
I DON'T KNOW, DAVID. ... FOUR YEARS.
MAN, THAT'S A LONG TIME TO GO WITHOUT SLEEP! IF YOU MISS IT THAT MUCH WHY DON'T YOU JUST GO BACK?
DEPENDS ON WHO YOU GO WITH.
I'LL GO WITH YOU.
YEAH, RIGHT.
LAYAW PLANS
AND WHAT WILL WE DO THERE? SLEEP IN SEPERATE ROOMS LIKE FRED AND ETHEL? WALK THE BEACH AT NIGHT WITH OUR HANDS IN OUR POCKETS? EAT AT FAMILY RESTAURANTS?
OKAY, OKAY, I GET THE POINT. I JUST THOUGHT... AW, FORGET IT!
BOY, HOPE SPRINGS ETERNAL WITH YOU, DOESN'T IT?
WELL, AS LONG AS WE'RE BOTH DRAWING BREATH...
OH DAVID! THAT'S SO BEAUTIFUL! "AS LONG AS WE'RE BOTH DRAWING BREATH." YOU AS SOOOOOO DEEP!
OH MAN.

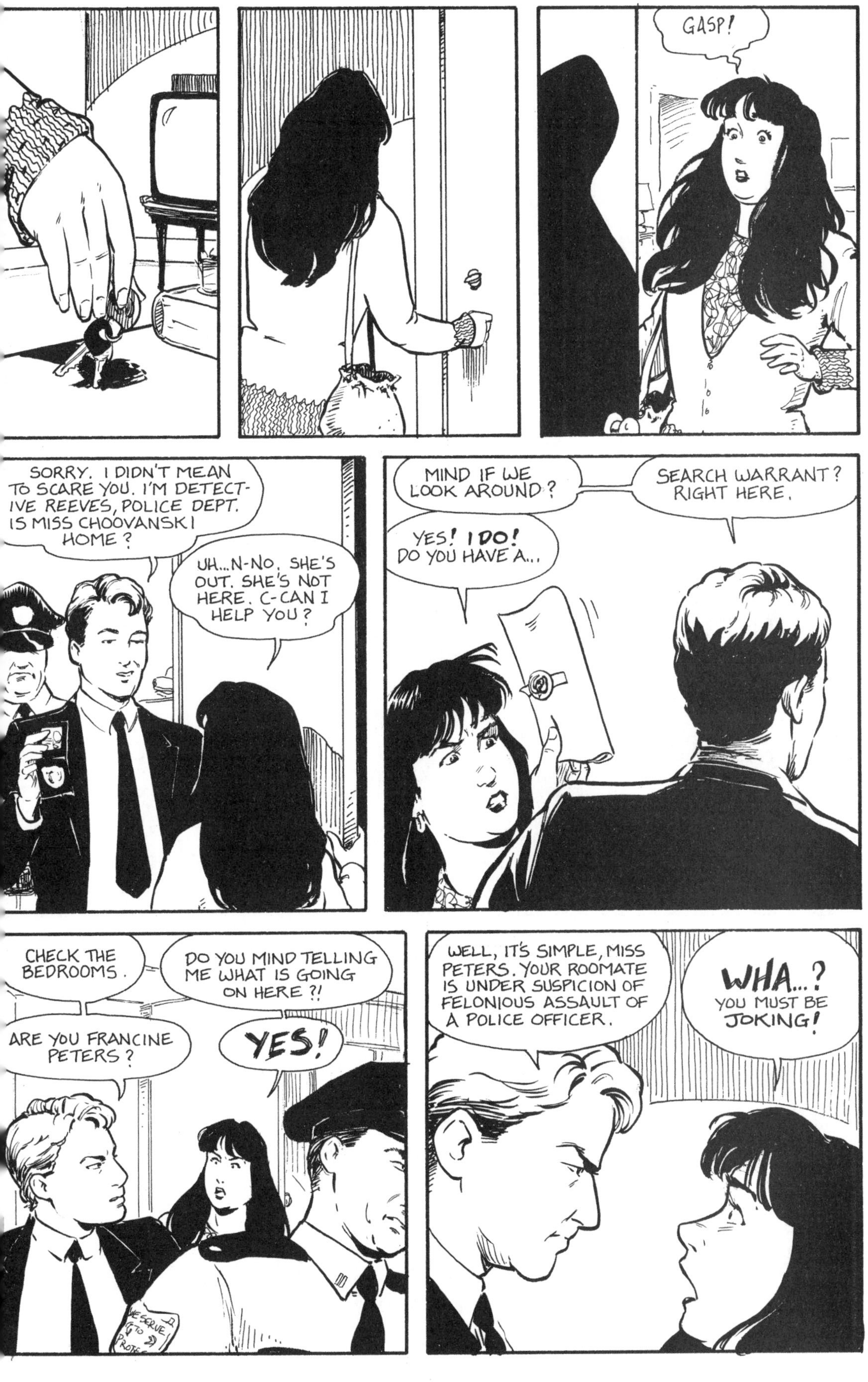
GASP!
SORRY. I DIDN'T MEAN TO SCARE YOU. I'M DETECTIVE REEVES, POLICE DEPT. IS MISS CHOOVANSKI HOME?
UH...N-NO. SHE'S OUT. SHE'S NOT HERE. C-CAN I HELP YOU?
MIND IF WE LOOK AROUND?
YES! I DO! DO YOU HAVE A...
SEARCH WARRANT? RIGHT HERE.
CHECK THE BEDROOMS.
ARE YOU FRANCINE PETERS?
DO YOU MIND TELLING ME WHAT IS GOING ON HERE?!
YES!
WELL, IT'S SIMPLE, MISS PETERS. YOUR ROOMATE IS UNDER SUSPICION OF FELONIOUS ASSAULT OF A POLICE OFFICER.
WHA...? YOU MUST BE JOKING!

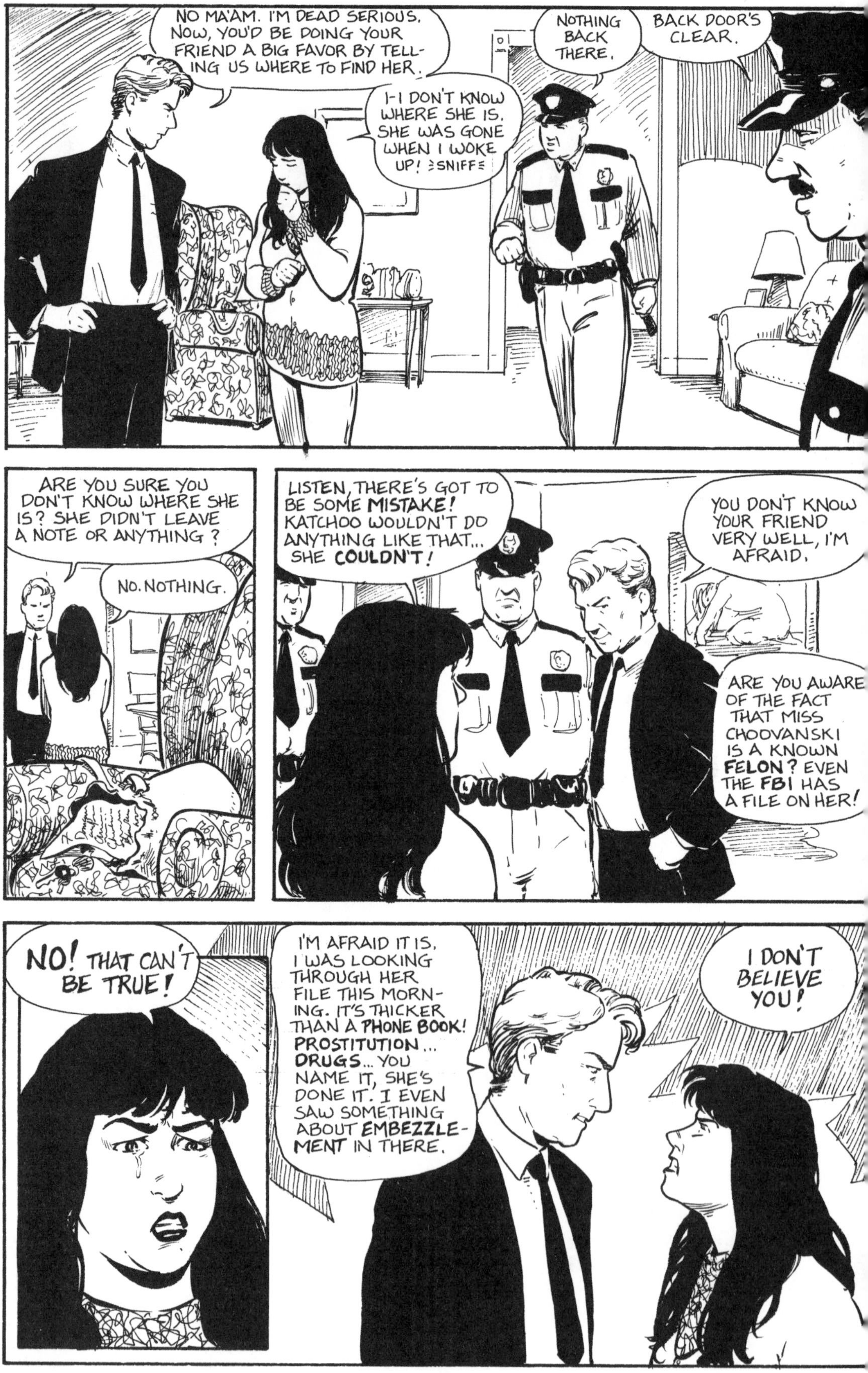
NO MA'AM. I'M DEAD SERIOUS. NOW, YOU'D BE DOING YOUR FRIEND A BIG FAVOR BY TELLING US WHERE TO FIND HER.
I-I DON'T KNOW WHERE SHE IS. SHE WAS GONE WHEN I WOKE UP! SNIFF
NOTHING BACK THERE.
BACK DOOR'S CLEAR.
ARE YOU SURE YOU DON'T KNOW WHERE SHE IS? SHE DIDN'T LEAVE A NOTE OR ANYTHING?
NO. NOTHING.
LISTEN, THERE'S GOT TO BE SOME MISTAKE! KATCHOO WOULDN'T DO ANYTHING LIKE THAT... SHE COULDN'T!
YOU DON'T KNOW YOUR FRIEND VERY WELL, I'M AFRAID.
ARE YOU AWARE OF THE FACT THAT MISS CHOOVANSKI IS A KNOWN FELON? EVEN THE FBI HAS A FILE ON HER!
NO! THAT CAN'T BE TRUE!
I'M AFRAID IT IS. I WAS LOOKING THROUGH HER FILE THIS MORNING. IT'S THICKER THAN A PHONE BOOK! PROSTITUTION... DRUGS... YOU NAME IT, SHE'S DONE IT. I EVEN SAW SOMETHING ABOUT EMBEZZLEMENT IN THERE.
I DON'T BELIEVE YOU!

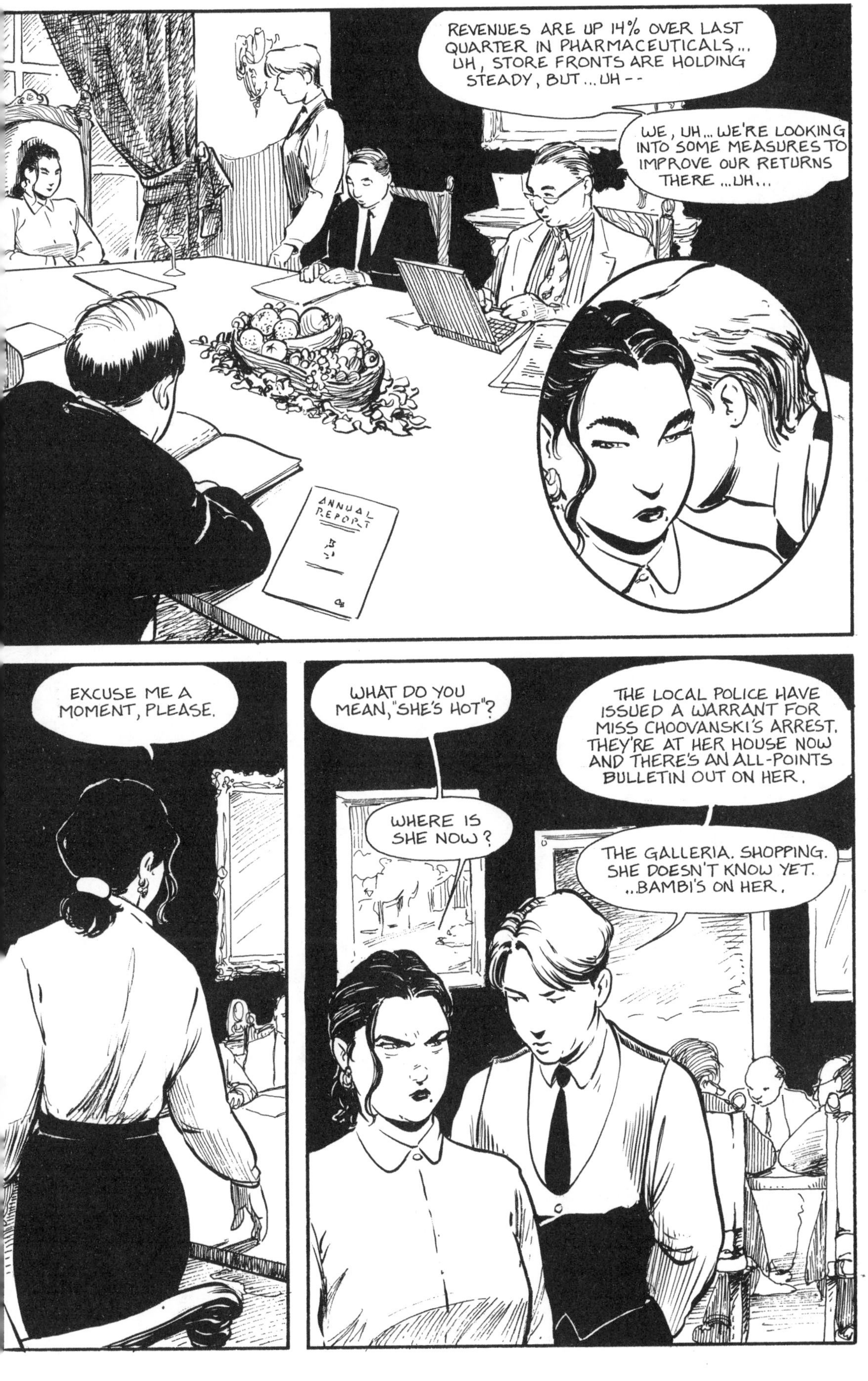
REVENUES ARE UP 14% OVER LAST QUARTER IN PHARMACEUTICALS... UH, STORE FRONTS ARE HOLDING STEADY, BUT... UH --
WE, UH... WE'RE LOOKING INTO SOME MEASURES TO IMPROVE OUR RETURNS THERE ...UH...
ANNUAL REPORT
EXCUSE ME A MOMENT, PLEASE.
WHAT DO YOU MEAN, "SHE'S HOT"?
THE LOCAL POLICE HAVE ISSUED A WARRANT FOR MISS CHOOVANSKI'S ARREST. THEY'RE AT HER HOUSE NOW AND THERE'S AN ALL-POINTS BULLETIN OUT ON HER.
WHERE IS SHE NOW?
THE GALLERIA. SHOPPING. SHE DOESN'T KNOW YET. ..BAMBI'S ON HER.

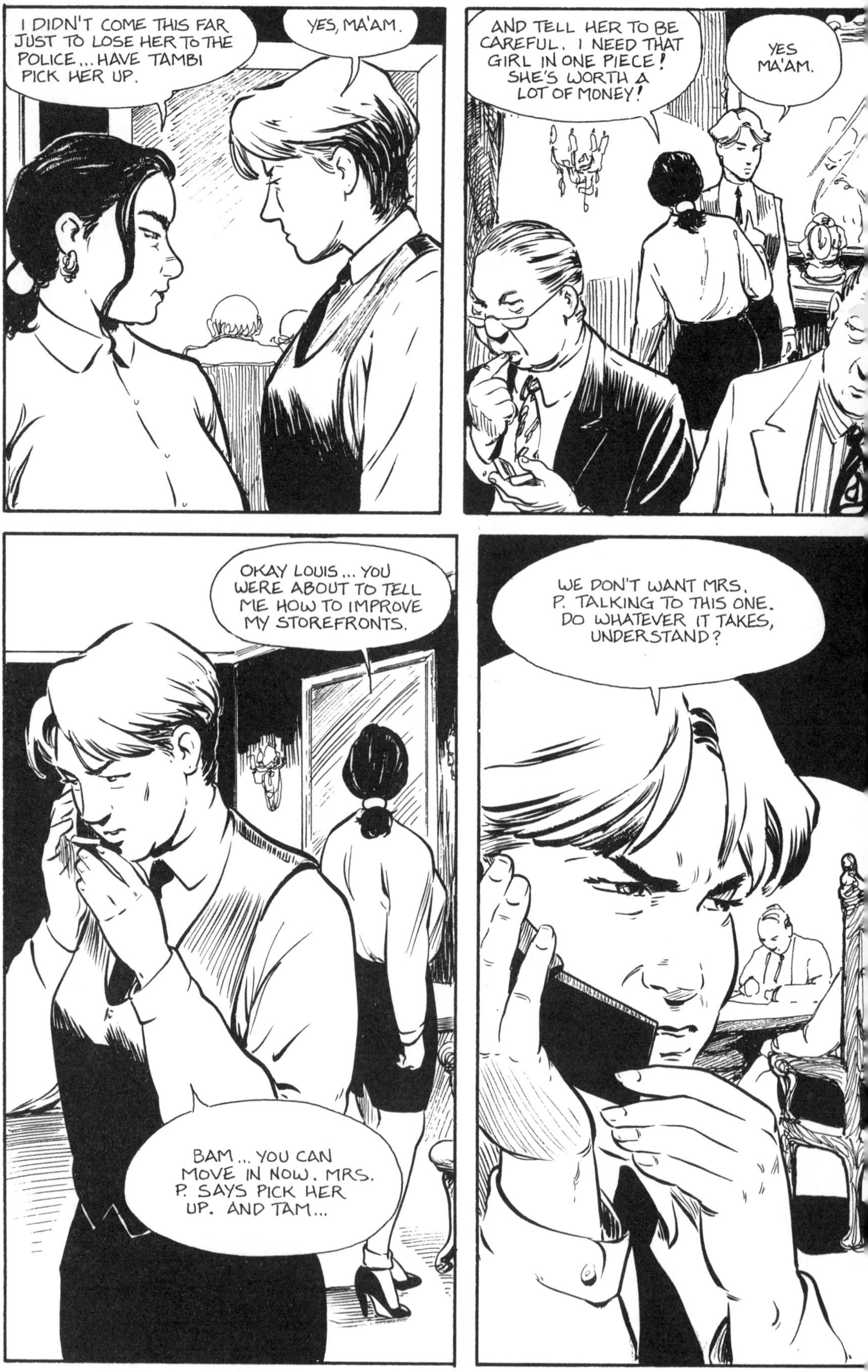
I DIDN'T COME THIS FAR JUST TO LOSE HER TO THE POLICE... HAVE TAMBI PICK HER UP.
YES, MA'AM.
AND TELL HER TO BE CAREFUL. I NEED THAT GIRL IN ONE PIECE! SHE'S WORTH A LOT OF MONEY!
YES MA'AM.
OKAY LOUIS... YOU WERE ABOUT TO TELL ME HOW TO IMPROVE MY STOREFRONTS.
BAM... YOU CAN MOVE IN NOW. MRS. P. SAYS PICK HER UP. AND TAM...
WE DON'T WANT MRS. P. TALKING TO THIS ONE. DO WHATEVER IT TAKES, UNDERSTAND?

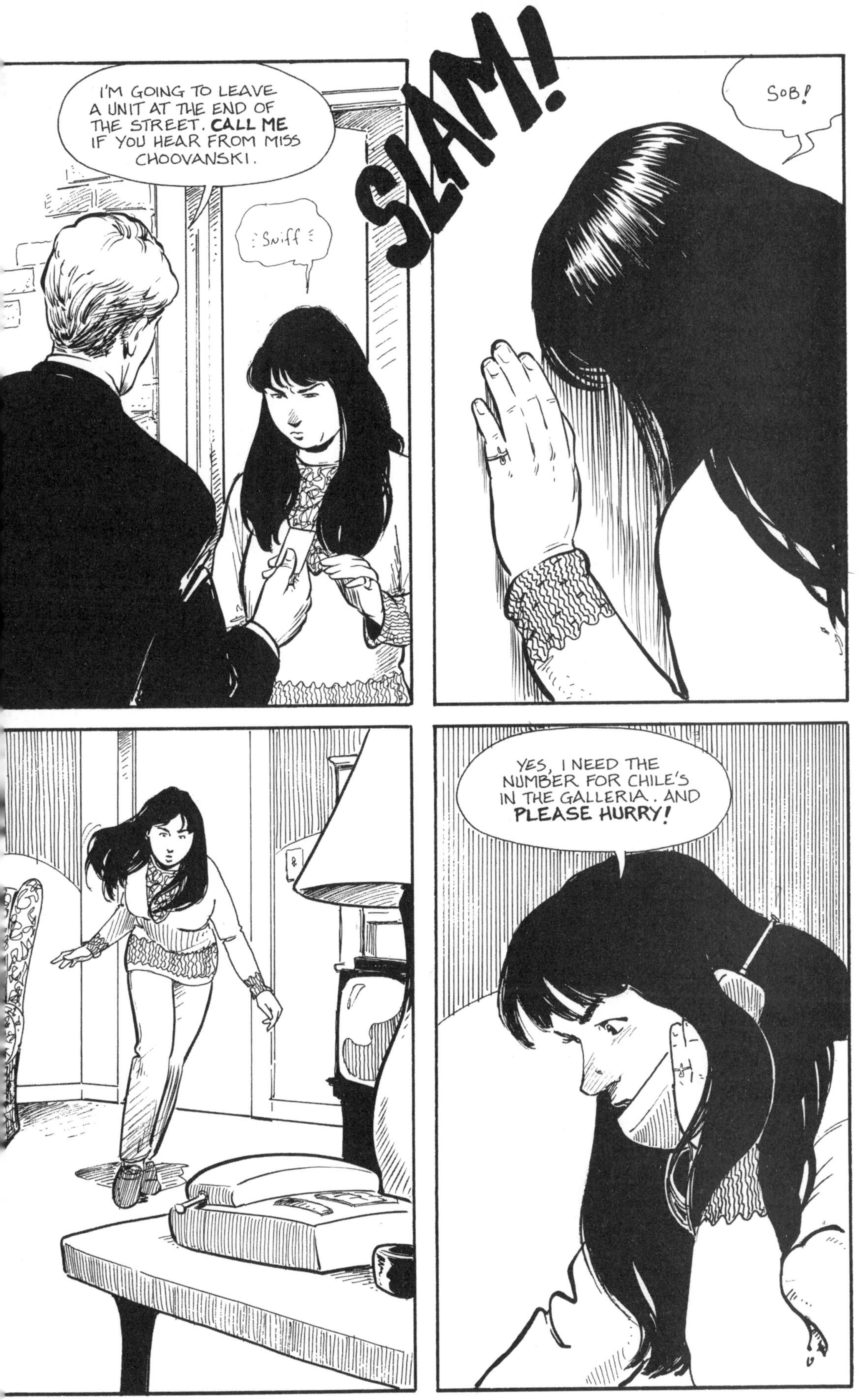
I'M GOING TO LEAVE A UNIT AT THE END OF THE STREET. **CALL ME** IF YOU HEAR FROM MISS CHOOVANSKI.
Sniff
SLAM!
SOB!
YES, I NEED THE NUMBER FOR CHILE'S IN THE GALLERIA. AND **PLEASE HURRY!**

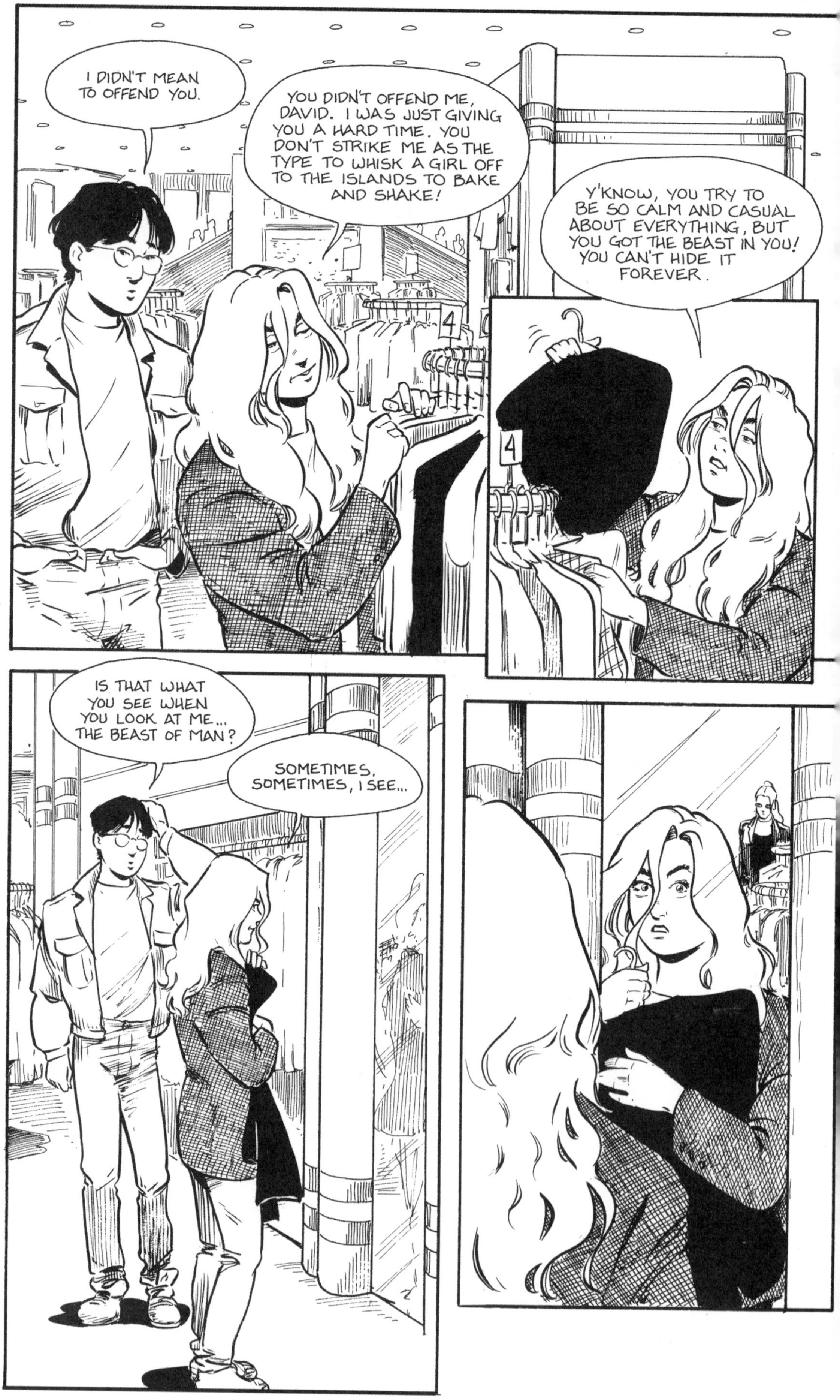
I DIDN'T MEAN TO OFFEND YOU.
YOU DIDN'T OFFEND ME, DAVID. I WAS JUST GIVING YOU A HARD TIME. YOU DON'T STRIKE ME AS THE TYPE TO WHISK A GIRL OFF TO THE ISLANDS TO BAKE AND SHAKE!
4
Y'KNOW, YOU TRY TO BE SO CALM AND CASUAL ABOUT EVERYTHING, BUT YOU GOT THE BEAST IN YOU! YOU CAN'T HIDE IT FOREVER.
4
IS THAT WHAT YOU SEE WHEN YOU LOOK AT ME... THE BEAST OF MAN?
SOMETIMES, SOMETIMES, I SEE...

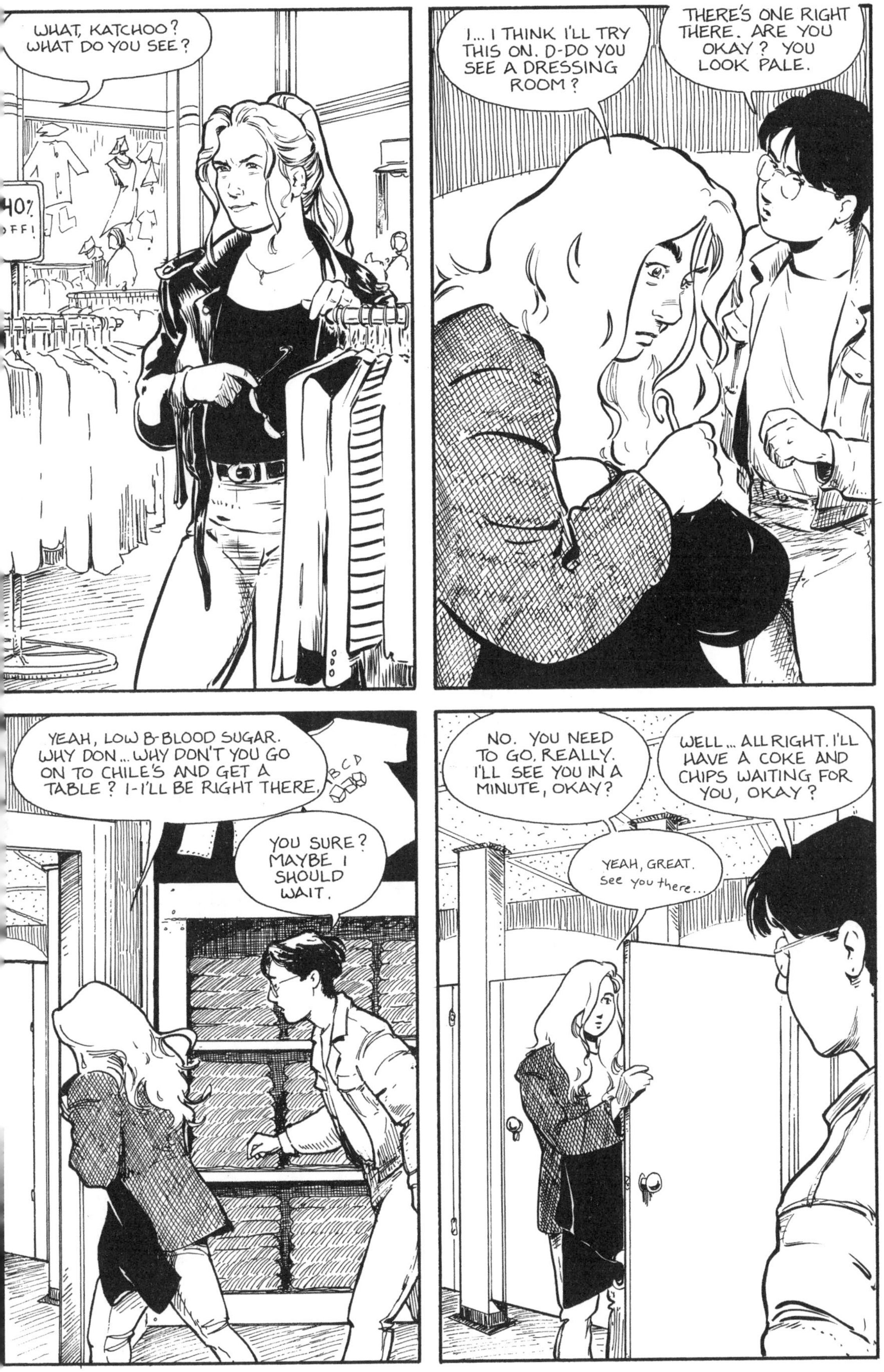
WHAT, KATCHOO? WHAT DO YOU SEE?
40% OFF!
I... I THINK I'LL TRY THIS ON. D-DO YOU SEE A DRESSING ROOM?
THERE'S ONE RIGHT THERE. ARE YOU OKAY? YOU LOOK PALE.
YEAH, LOW B-BLOOD SUGAR. WHY DON... WHY DON'T YOU GO ON TO CHILE'S AND GET A TABLE? I-I'LL BE RIGHT THERE.
YOU SURE? MAYBE I SHOULD WAIT.
NO. YOU NEED TO GO, REALLY. I'LL SEE YOU IN A MINUTE, OKAY?
WELL... ALL RIGHT. I'LL HAVE A COKE AND CHIPS WAITING FOR YOU, OKAY?
YEAH, GREAT. See you there...

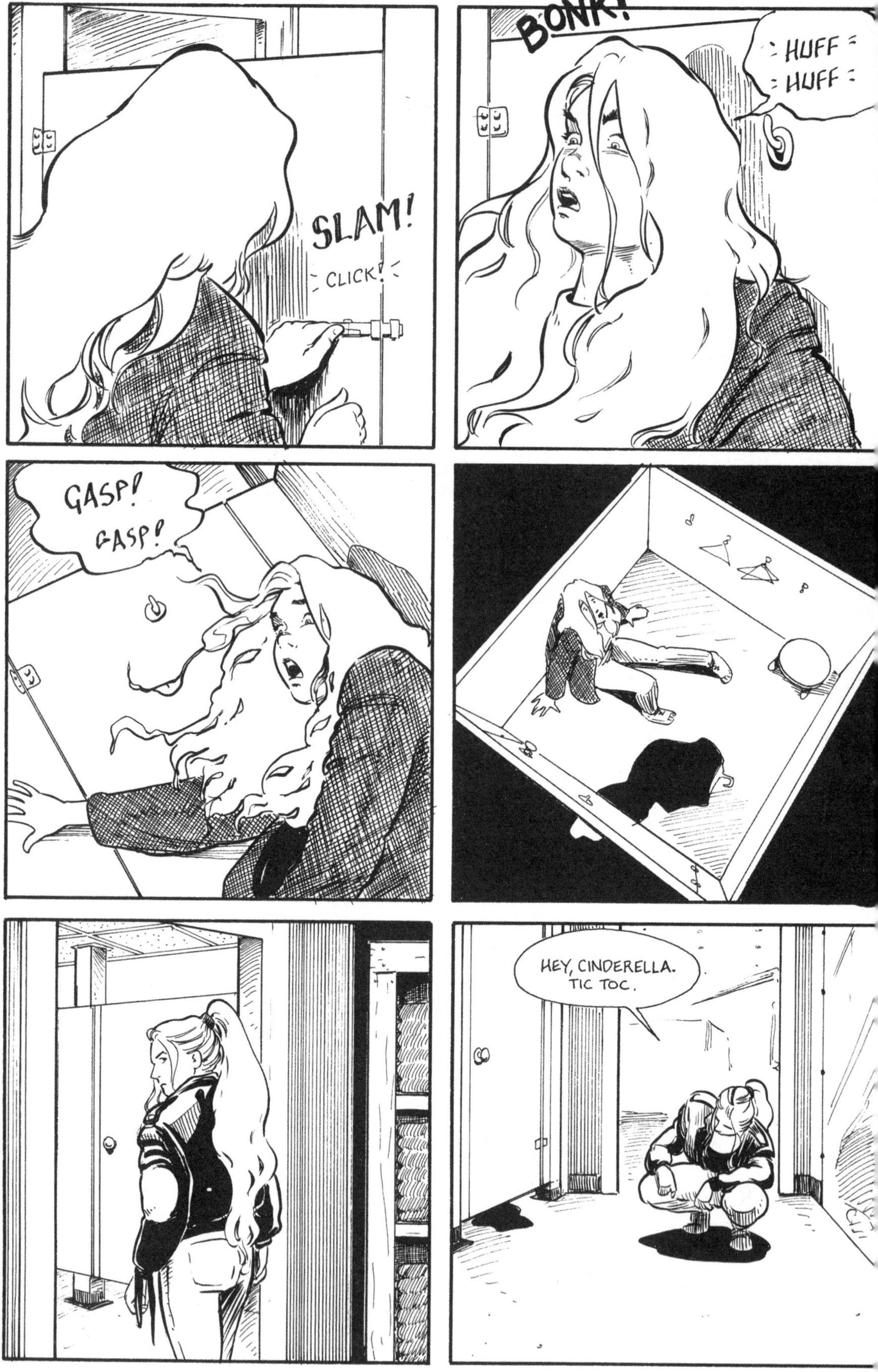
SLAM!
CLICK!
BONK!
HUFF
HUFF
GASP!
GASP!
HEY, CINDERELLA.
TIC TOC.

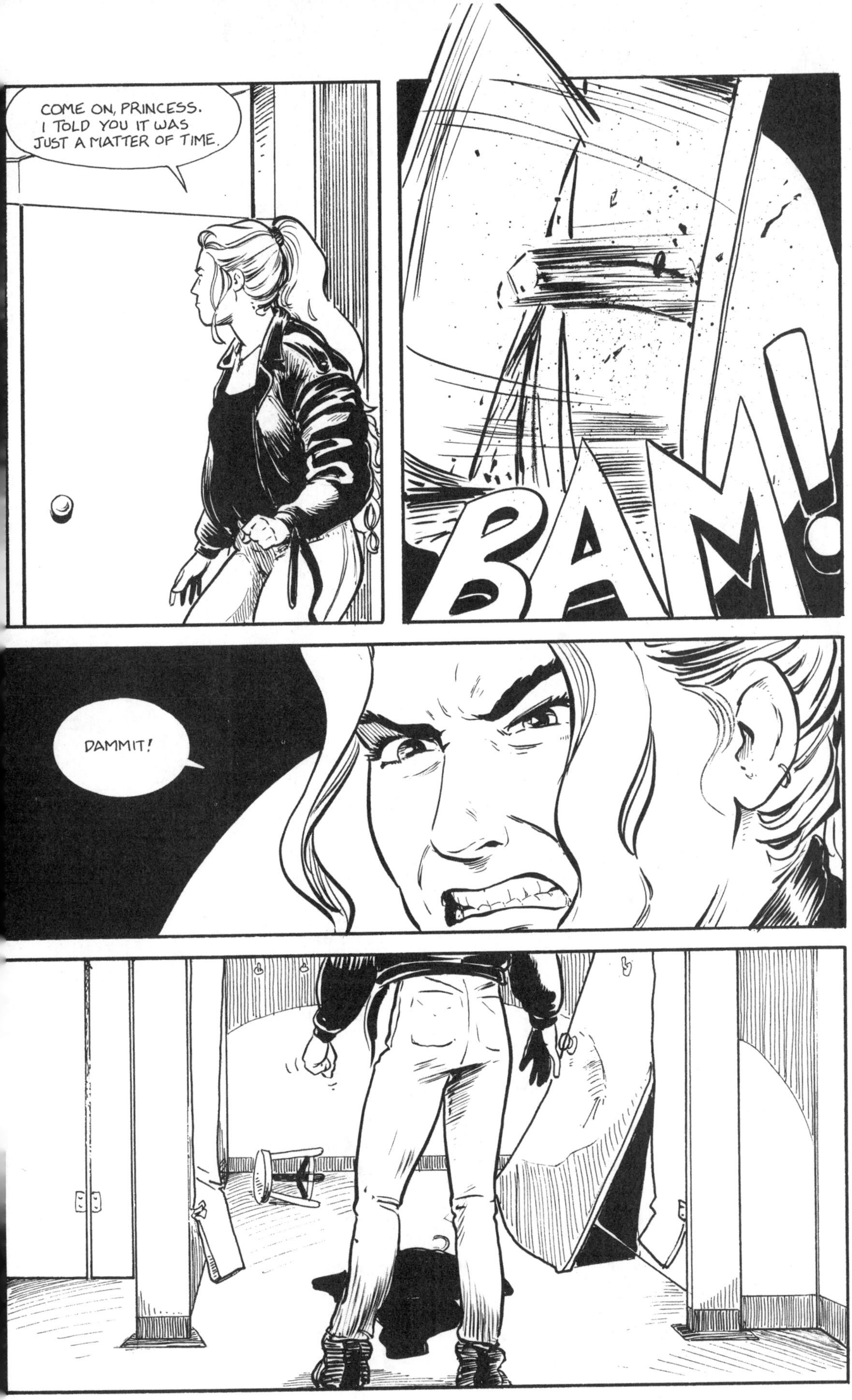
COME ON, PRINCESS. I TOLD YOU IT WAS JUST A MATTER OF TIME.
BAM!
DAMMIT!

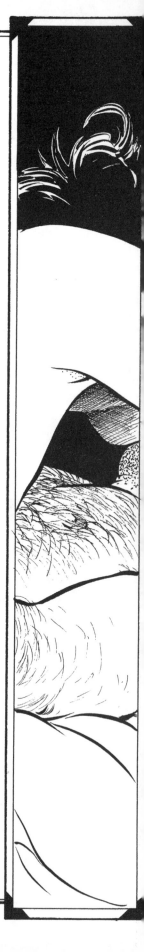

WHAT THE HELL ARE WE LISTENING TO ?

KING CRIMSON. THAT'S MY FAVORITE CD! YOU DON'T LIKE IT ?

WHAT IS IT? SOME KIND OF GAY SONG OR SOMETHING ? STRAIGHT MEN, LATE MEN... IF I SAW SOMEBODY TALKIN' TO THE WIND, I DON'T CARE IF HE'S GAY, STRAIGHT OR NOT, I'D LOCK HIM UP.

I THINK IT'S BEAUTIFUL. I LOVE SAD SONGS. ...≋SIGH≋... HOW'S THAT FEEL ?

FEELS NICE. I THINK. I LOST ALL FEELING A COUPLE OF HOURS AGO.

YOU'RE GETTING OLD ON ME, AREN'T YOU ?

DARLIN', I'VE AGED 10 YEARS TONIGHT ALONE!

GUESS I'LL JUST HAVE TO FIND ME A **YOUNG** STUD...

SLAP!

OW! HEY! ≋GIGGLE≋ NO SPANKING**!**

SORRY... HEH, HEH! IT JUST WENT OFF BY ACCIDENT. I HATE IT WHEN IT DOES THAT.

≋GIGGLE!≋ **C'MERE**, BUSTER... ≋MMPH≋ I'M NOT FINISHED WITH YOU YET!

OH, LORD, TAKE ME NOW, BEFORE THIS WILD WOMAN **KILLS** ME!

SHHH! .....SHUT UP! I'M WORTH IT. ...HOW'S THAT FEEL ?

SLOWER... SLOWER...WAIT, DON'T MOVE...WAIT A MINUTE ...**AGH!** AH!...AH! ....I SAID, DON'T MOVE.

HEH! SORRY, IT JUST WENT OFF. I HATE WHEN IT DOES THAT.

RING! RING!

TELL YOUR GIRLFRIENDS TO QUIT CALLING HERE.

IT'S PROBABLY YOUR SISTER.

DON'T ANSWER IT, HONEY. C'MERE.

RING! RING!

RING!
RING!
RING!
RING!

WALSH HERE.

CLICK!

HE IS?

ALL RIGHT. I'M ON MY WAY. NO, NO... YOU DID THE RIGHT THING. I'LL BE THERE IN TWENTY MINUTES.

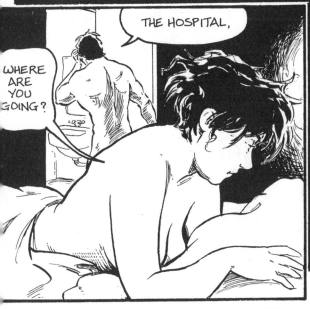

THE HOSPITAL.

WHERE ARE YOU GOING?

DAMN, I'M GOOD.

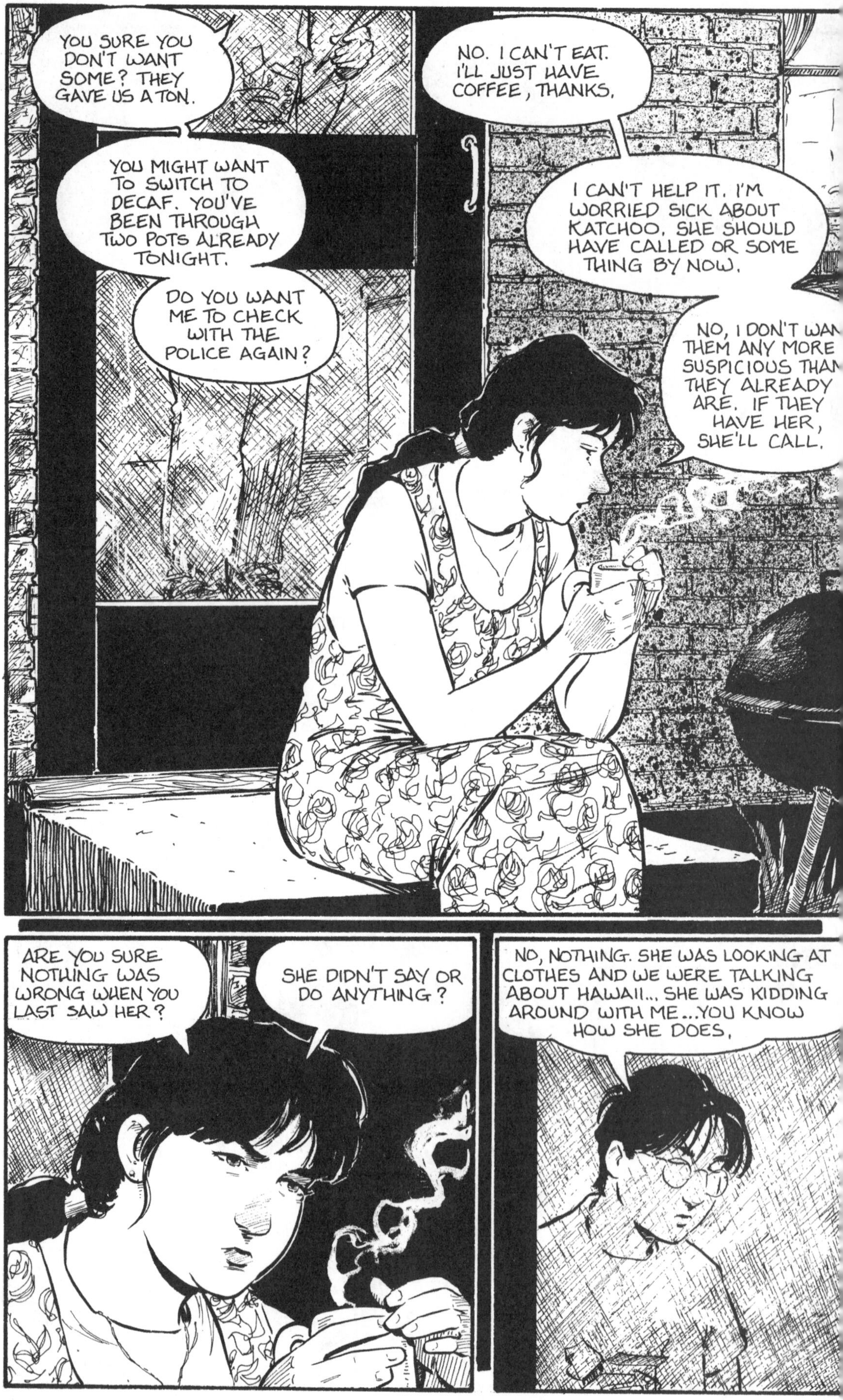
YOU SURE YOU DON'T WANT SOME? THEY GAVE US A TON.
NO. I CAN'T EAT. I'LL JUST HAVE COFFEE, THANKS.
YOU MIGHT WANT TO SWITCH TO DECAF. YOU'VE BEEN THROUGH TWO POTS ALREADY TONIGHT.
I CAN'T HELP IT. I'M WORRIED SICK ABOUT KATCHOO. SHE SHOULD HAVE CALLED OR SOME THING BY NOW.
DO YOU WANT ME TO CHECK WITH THE POLICE AGAIN?
NO, I DON'T WAN THEM ANY MORE SUSPICIOUS THAN THEY ALREADY ARE. IF THEY HAVE HER, SHE'LL CALL.
ARE YOU SURE NOTHING WAS WRONG WHEN YOU LAST SAW HER?
SHE DIDN'T SAY OR DO ANYTHING?
NO, NOTHING. SHE WAS LOOKING AT CLOTHES AND WE WERE TALKING ABOUT HAWAII... SHE WAS KIDDING AROUND WITH ME...YOU KNOW HOW SHE DOES.

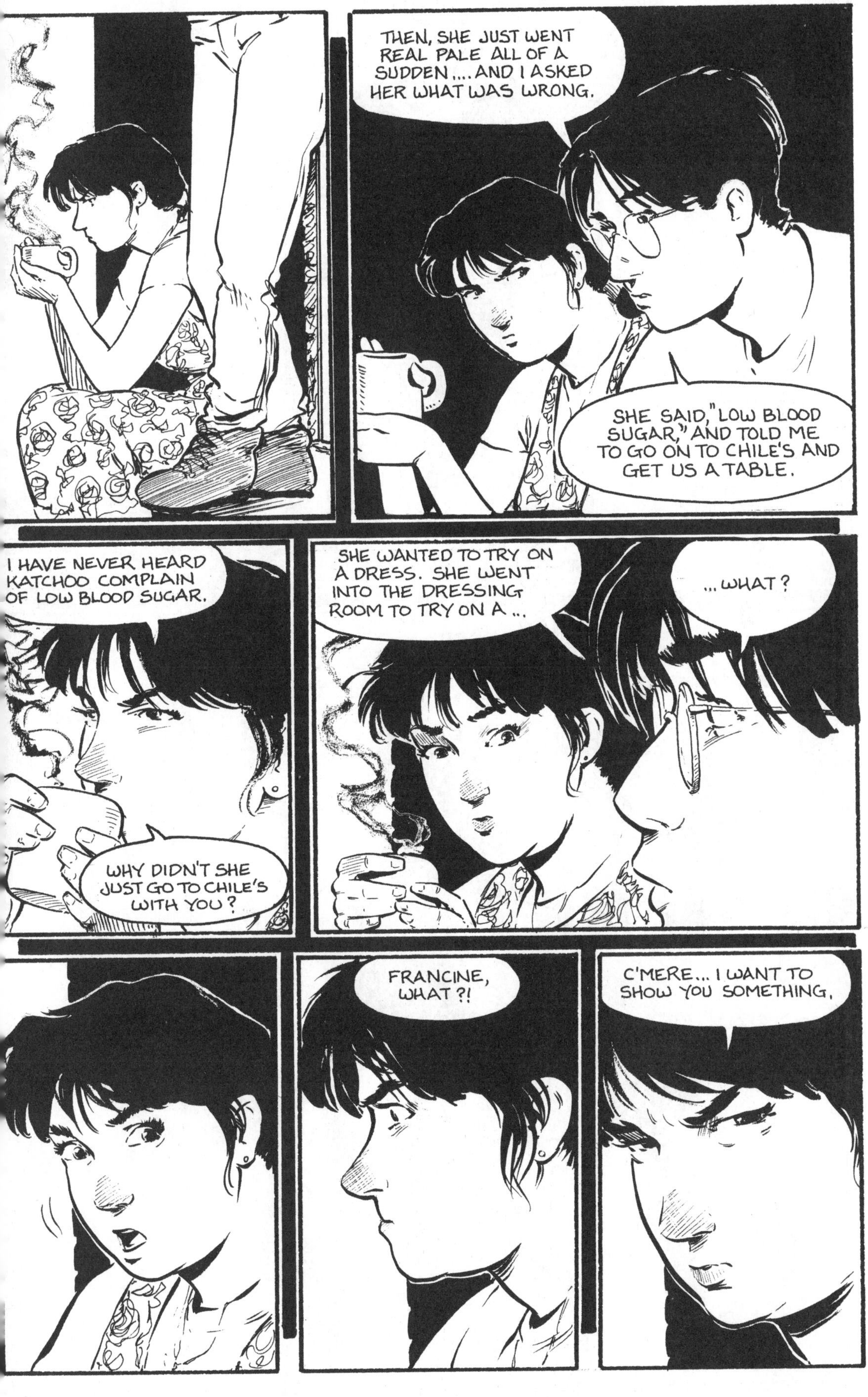
THEN, SHE JUST WENT REAL PALE ALL OF A SUDDEN.... AND I ASKED HER WHAT WAS WRONG.
SHE SAID, "LOW BLOOD SUGAR," AND TOLD ME TO GO ON TO CHILE'S AND GET US A TABLE.
I HAVE NEVER HEARD KATCHOO COMPLAIN OF LOW BLOOD SUGAR.
WHY DIDN'T SHE JUST GO TO CHILE'S WITH YOU?
SHE WANTED TO TRY ON A DRESS. SHE WENT INTO THE DRESSING ROOM TO TRY ON A ..
... WHAT?
FRANCINE, WHAT?!
C'MERE... I WANT TO SHOW YOU SOMETHING.

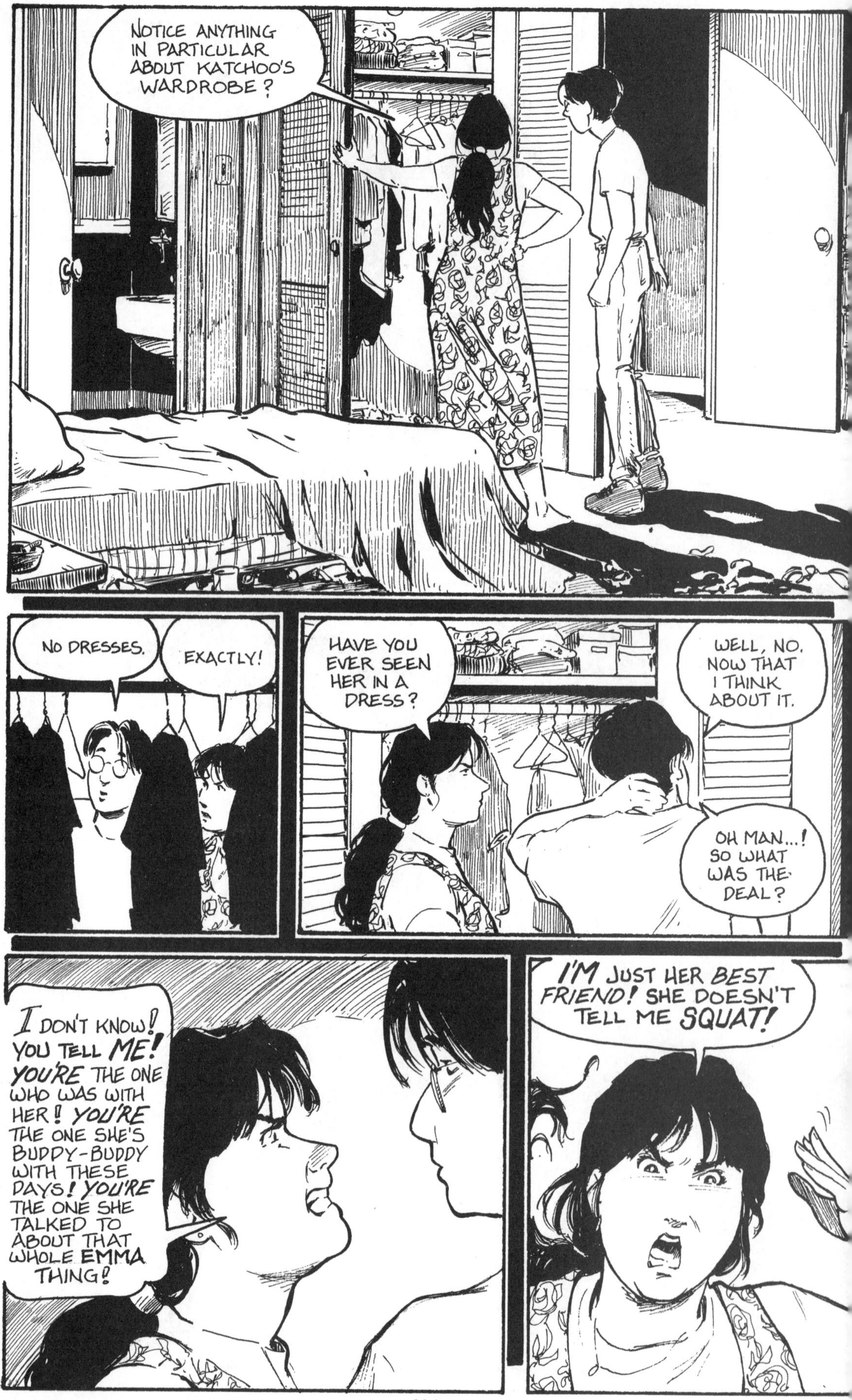
NOTICE ANYTHING IN PARTICULAR ABOUT KATCHOO'S WARDROBE?
NO DRESSES.
EXACTLY!
HAVE YOU EVER SEEN HER IN A DRESS?
WELL, NO. NOW THAT I THINK ABOUT IT.
OH MAN...! SO WHAT WAS THE DEAL?
I DON'T KNOW! YOU TELL ME! YOU'RE THE ONE WHO WAS WITH HER! YOU'RE THE ONE SHE'S BUDDY-BUDDY WITH THESE DAYS! YOU'RE THE ONE SHE TALKED TO ABOUT THAT WHOLE EMMA THING!
I'M JUST HER BEST FRIEND! SHE DOESN'T TELL ME SQUAT!

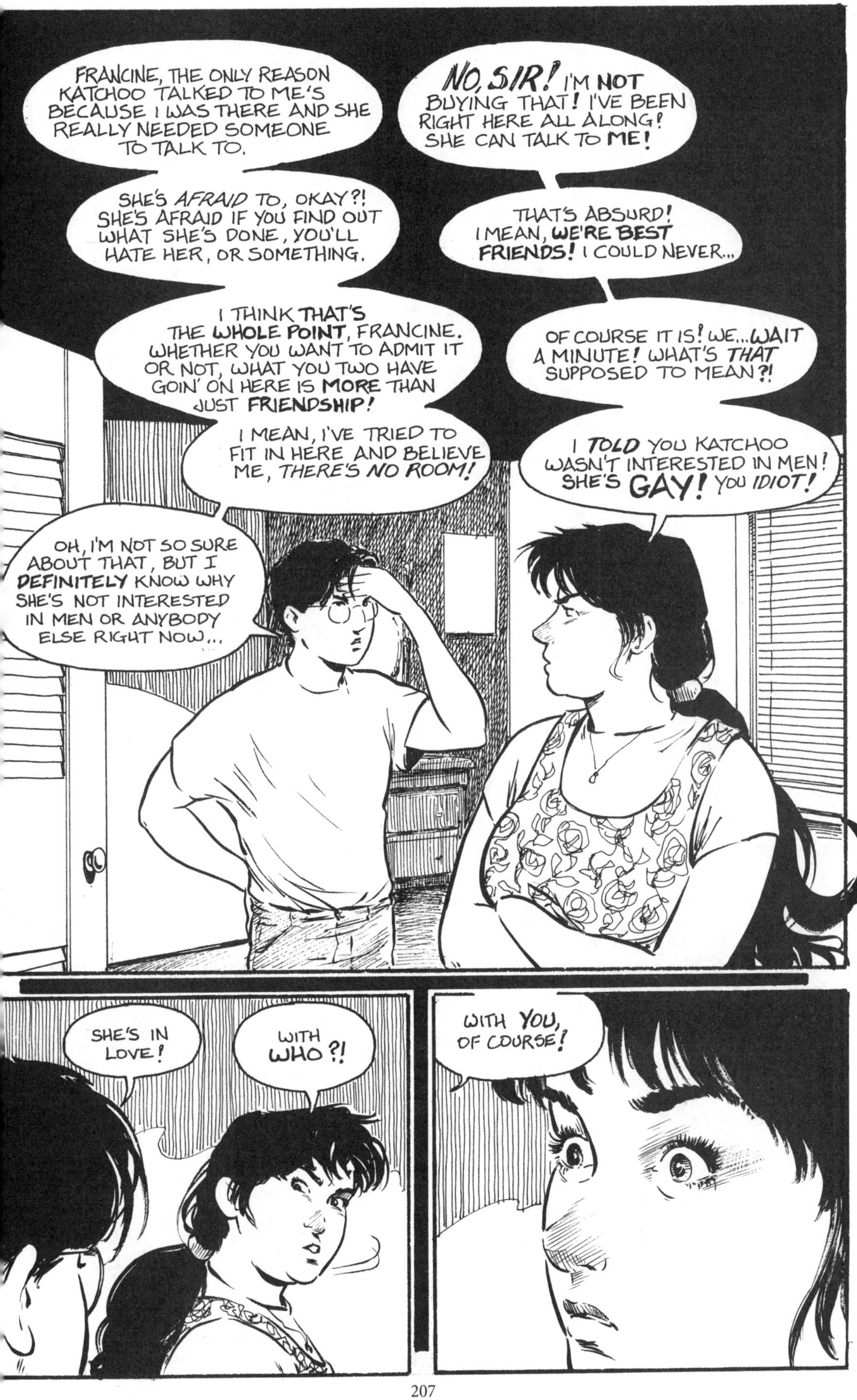
FRANCINE, THE ONLY REASON KATCHOO TALKED TO ME'S BECAUSE I WAS THERE AND SHE REALLY NEEDED SOMEONE TO TALK TO.
NO, SIR! I'M NOT BUYING THAT! I'VE BEEN RIGHT HERE ALL ALONG! SHE CAN TALK TO ME!
SHE'S AFRAID TO, OKAY?! SHE'S AFRAID IF YOU FIND OUT WHAT SHE'S DONE, YOU'LL HATE HER, OR SOMETHING.
THAT'S ABSURD! I MEAN, WE'RE BEST FRIENDS! I COULD NEVER...
I THINK THAT'S THE WHOLE POINT, FRANCINE. WHETHER YOU WANT TO ADMIT IT OR NOT, WHAT YOU TWO HAVE GOIN' ON HERE IS MORE THAN JUST FRIENDSHIP!
OF COURSE IT IS! WE...WAIT A MINUTE! WHAT'S THAT SUPPOSED TO MEAN?!
I MEAN, I'VE TRIED TO FIT IN HERE AND BELIEVE ME, THERE'S NO ROOM!
I TOLD YOU KATCHOO WASN'T INTERESTED IN MEN! SHE'S GAY! YOU IDIOT!
OH, I'M NOT SO SURE ABOUT THAT, BUT I DEFINITELY KNOW WHY SHE'S NOT INTERESTED IN MEN OR ANYBODY ELSE RIGHT NOW...
SHE'S IN LOVE!
WITH WHO?!
WITH YOU, OF COURSE!

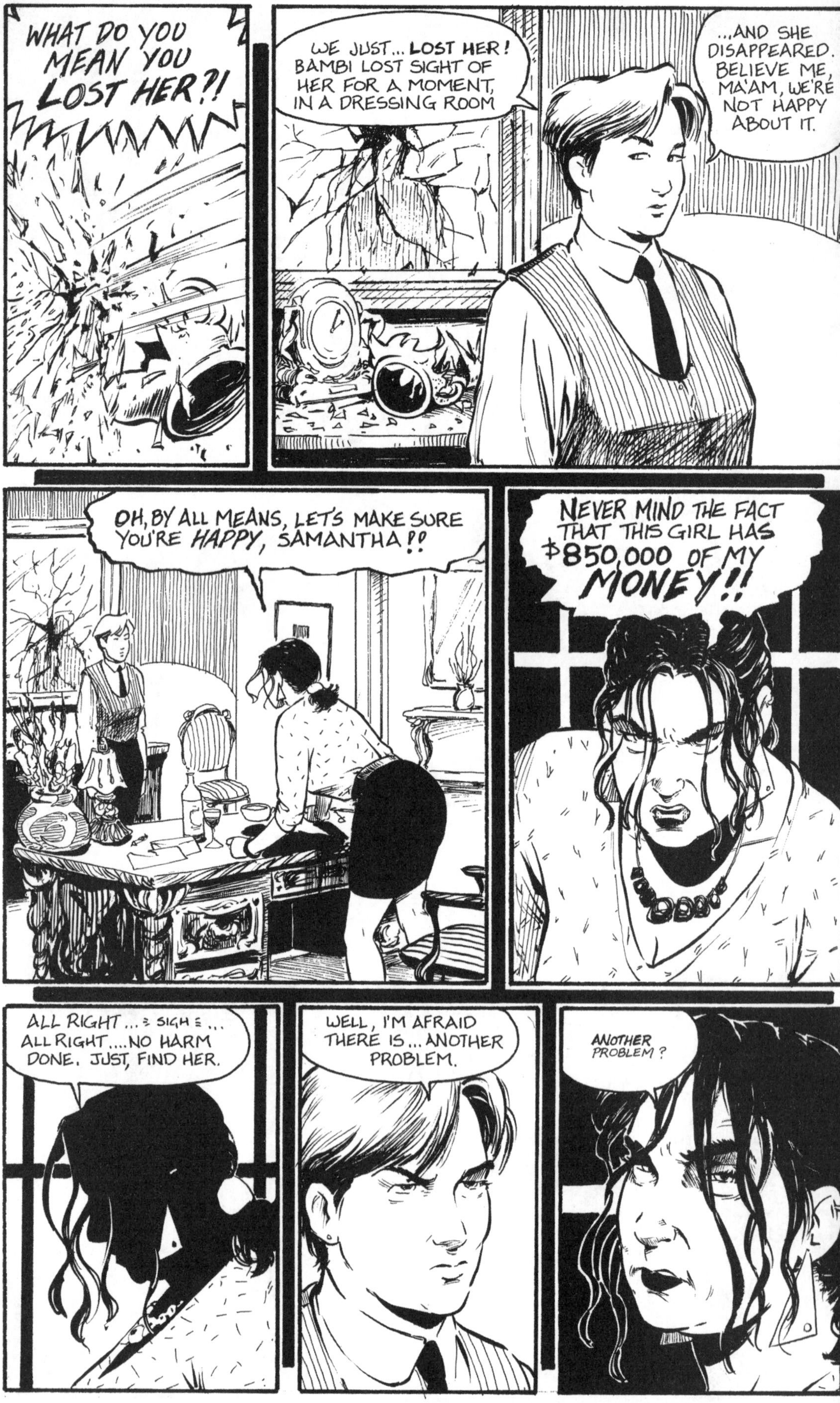
WHAT DO YOU MEAN YOU LOST HER?!
WE JUST... LOST HER! BAMBI LOST SIGHT OF HER FOR A MOMENT, IN A DRESSING ROOM
...AND SHE DISAPPEARED. BELIEVE ME, MA'AM, WE'RE NOT HAPPY ABOUT IT.
OH, BY ALL MEANS, LET'S MAKE SURE YOU'RE HAPPY, SAMANTHA!!
NEVER MIND THE FACT THAT THIS GIRL HAS $850,000 OF MY MONEY!!
ALL RIGHT... ⁝SIGH⁝... ALL RIGHT....NO HARM DONE. JUST, FIND HER.
WELL, I'M AFRAID THERE IS... ANOTHER PROBLEM.
ANOTHER PROBLEM?

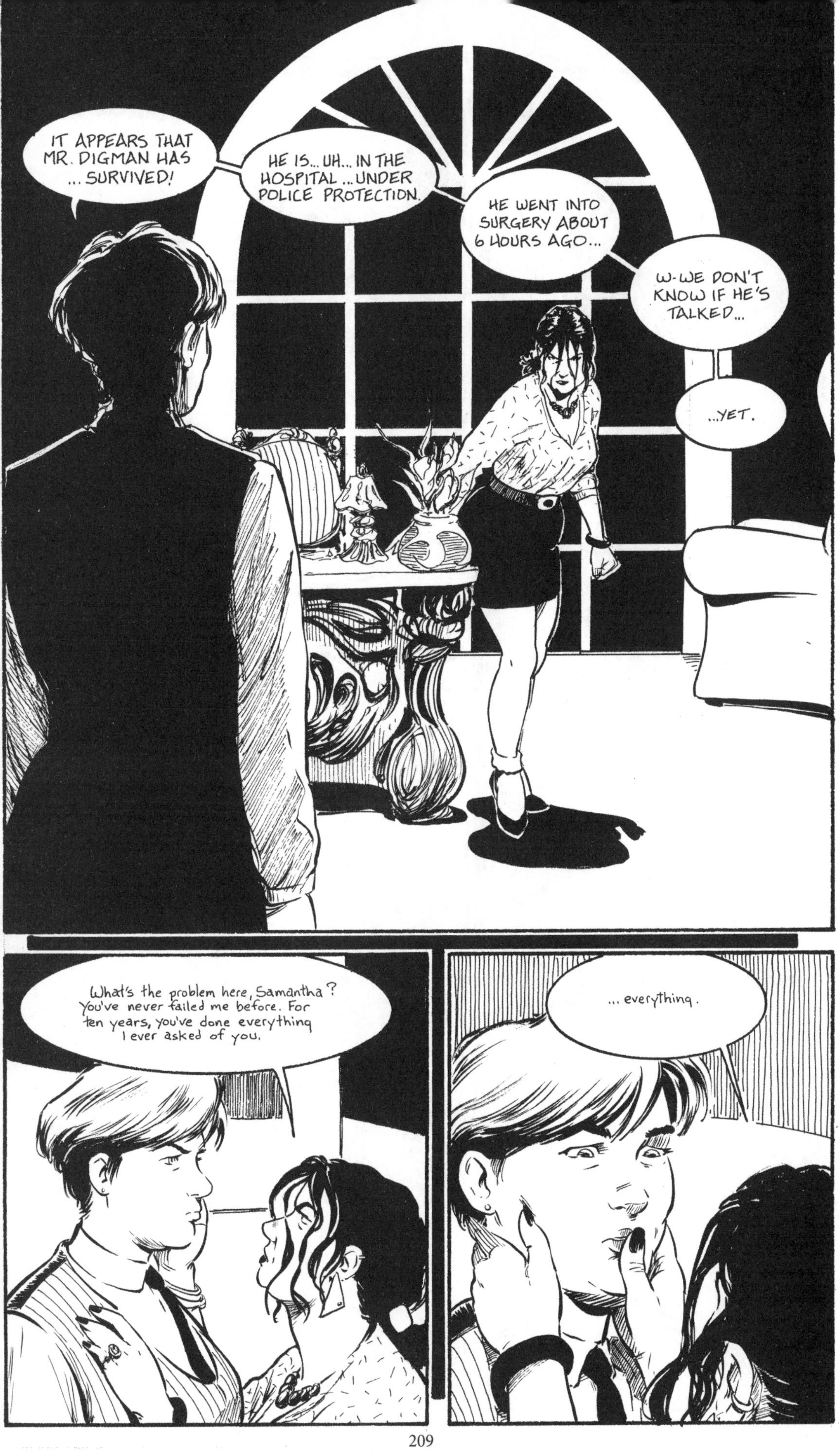
IT APPEARS THAT MR. DIGMAN HAS ... SURVIVED!
HE IS... UH... IN THE HOSPITAL ...UNDER POLICE PROTECTION.
HE WENT INTO SURGERY ABOUT 6 HOURS AGO...
W-WE DON'T KNOW IF HE'S TALKED...
...YET.
What's the problem here, Samantha? You've never failed me before. For ten years, you've done everything I ever asked of you.
... everything.

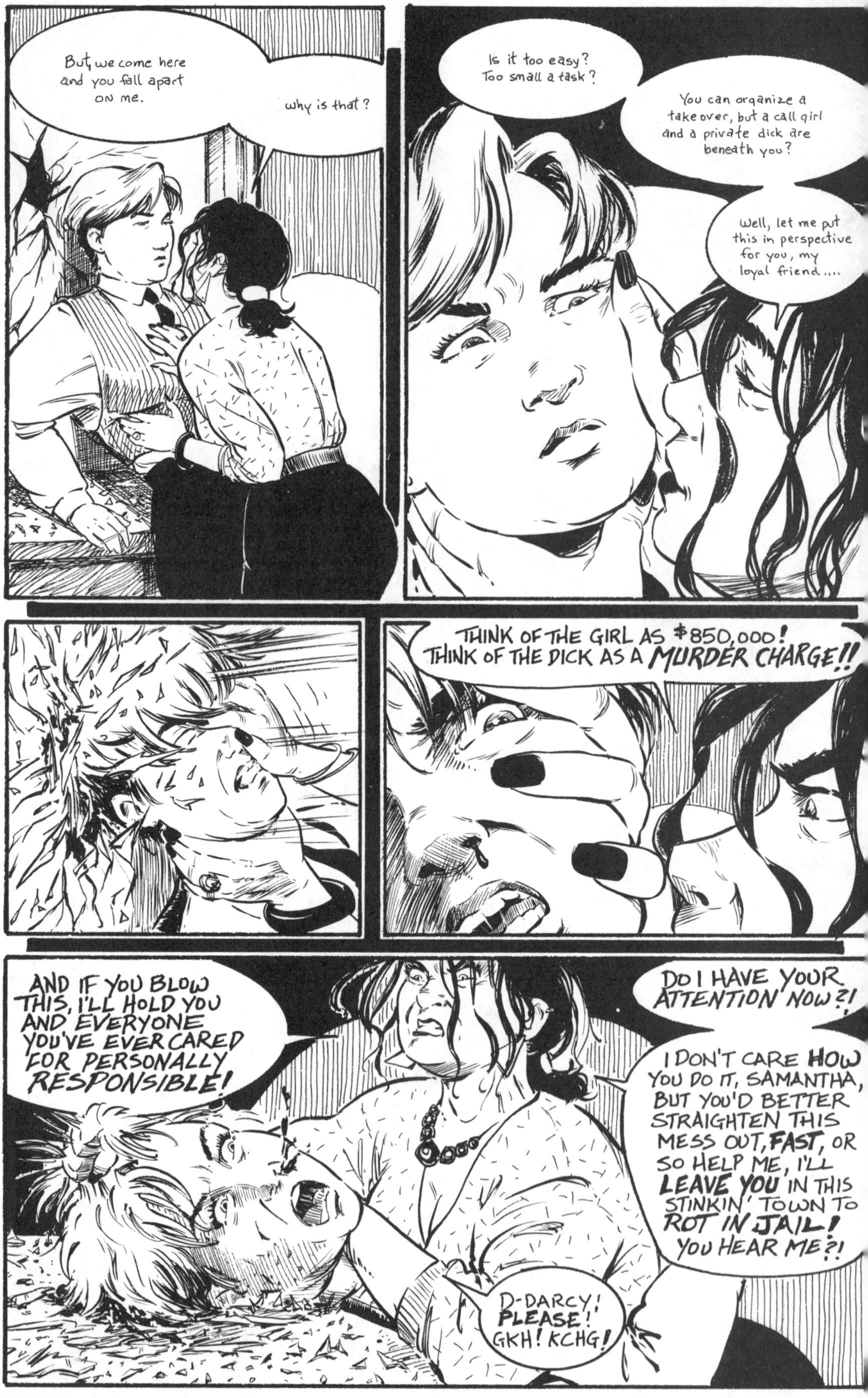
But, we come here and you fall apart on me.
why is that?
Is it too easy? Too small a task?
You can organize a take over, but a call girl and a private dick are beneath you?
Well, let me put this in perspective for you, my loyal friend....
THINK OF THE GIRL AS $850,000! THINK OF THE DICK AS A MURDER CHARGE!!
AND IF YOU BLOW THIS, I'LL HOLD YOU AND EVERYONE YOU'VE EVER CARED FOR PERSONALLY RESPONSIBLE!
DO I HAVE YOUR ATTENTION NOW?!
I DON'T CARE HOW YOU DO IT, SAMANTHA, BUT YOU'D BETTER STRAIGHTEN THIS MESS OUT, FAST, OR SO HELP ME, I'LL LEAVE YOU IN THIS STINKIN' TOWN TO ROT IN JAIL! YOU HEAR ME?!
D-DARCY! PLEASE! GKH! KCHG!

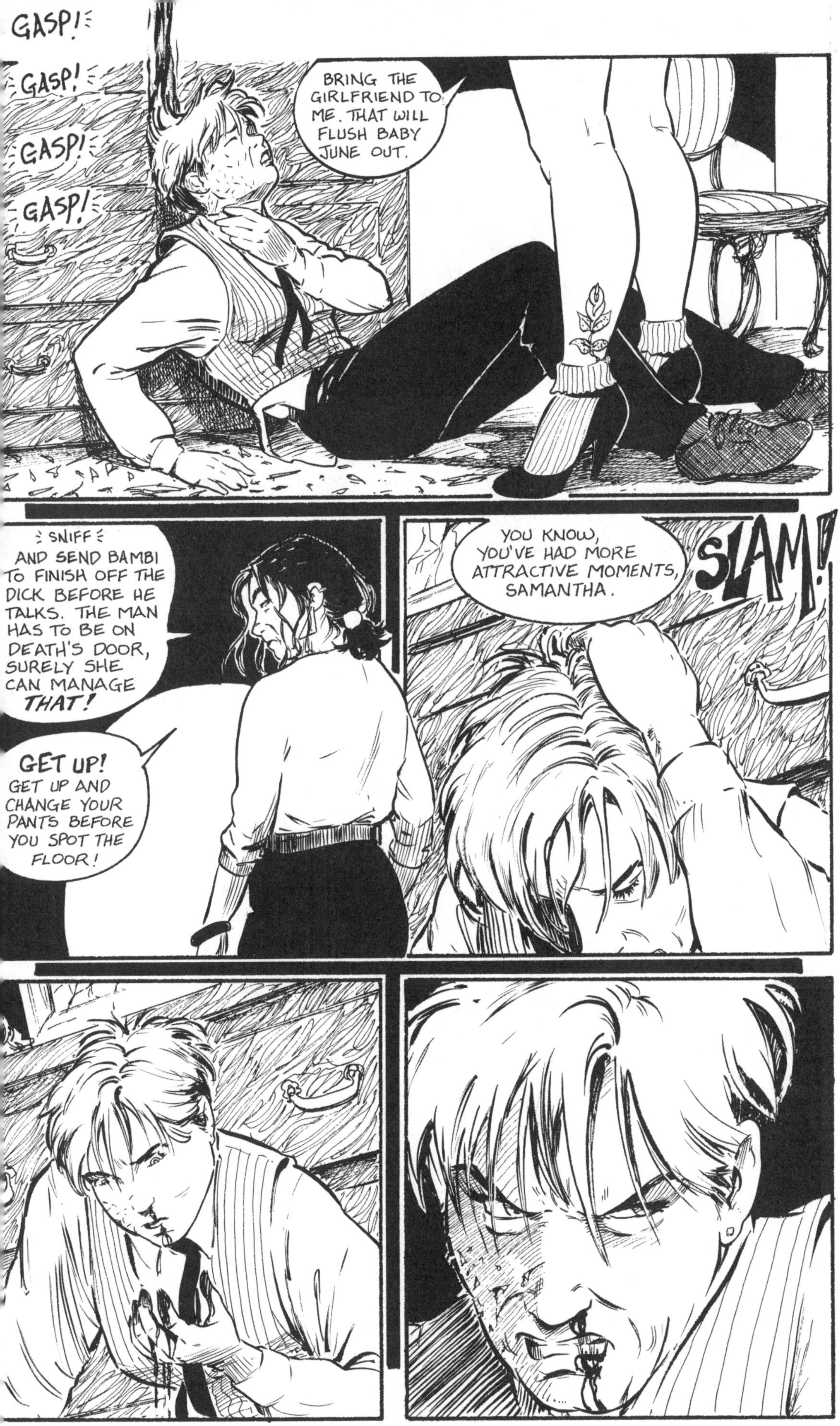
GASP!
GASP!
GASP!
GASP!
BRING THE GIRLFRIEND TO ME. THAT WILL FLUSH BABY JUNE OUT.
SNIFF
AND SEND BAMBI TO FINISH OFF THE DICK BEFORE HE TALKS. THE MAN HAS TO BE ON DEATH'S DOOR, SURELY SHE CAN MANAGE THAT!
GET UP! GET UP AND CHANGE YOUR PANTS BEFORE YOU SPOT THE FLOOR!
YOU KNOW, YOU'VE HAD MORE ATTRACTIVE MOMENTS, SAMANTHA.
SLAM!

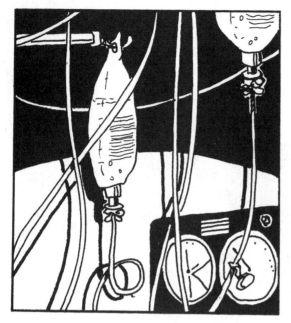

Detective Walsh stepped around the galvanized mop bucket that slid slowly across the floor in a soapy spill of dirty water.

"Excuse me," he said quietly.

The janitor never looked up, but waited, motionless, with his chin in his chest, for the detective to pass. Somewhere around the corner, Walsh could hear the muted whirring of someone waxing the floors of the sleeping hospital, removing the tracks of yesterday. Walsh made his way towards the critical care unit.

A handsome black man in police uniform sat in a chair positioned outside the large double doors that led into the CCU.

"Hey, Jesse. Who'd you piss off?" Walsh said as he approached the entrance.

"Man, I'm tellin' you!" the officer replied with a pained expression. "What ever happened to the ol' 9 to 5, you know? I mean, who's supposed to be watchin' my wife in the middle of the night while I'm watching this guy, know what I mean?"

"I hear ya, buddy. I hear ya," Walsh smiled as he opened one of the wide oak doors and stepped through. The door closed silently behind him and the officer resumed the careful cleaning of his fingernails with a pocket knife.

The critical care unit of Ben County Hospital was designed in hub and wheel fashion. A large nurses station filled the center of the circular lobby and served as a command center for monitoring the nine rooms that circled the crowded rotunda. All but one of the rooms were occupied, their guests in various stages of hope.

Walsh stood by the entrance for a moment until he saw a room to the right with an officer and several plain clothesmen huddled by the foot of the bed. He walked slowly towards the room, taking another look around the lobby. Habit.

The small room was dark except for a dim overhead bed light that lit the body beneath it in an eerie black-orange glow. Wayne Digman, former police officer and college all-star, lay under a scaffold of tubes and probes. Monitors and rolling carts jammed the area by the bed, pulsing, chirping and beeping in a medical symphony. Digman's face was half obscured by bandages and a respirator extended from his throat. A clean white sheet was folded down to his stomach revealing a massive, hairy torso wrapped tight in bandages and a number of tubes that either fed or drained dark fluids off to the side. Digman's bare arms lay motionless by his side, except for the continuous twitching of the index finger of his right hand. Nerve damage, Walsh decided. Three IV's ran up Digman's left arm that lay wrapped in a splint to keep him from bending his arm back on the needles.

Walsh pursed his lips and took a deep breath. The scene was made more unsettling by the lack of blood. Except for the swelling and the bruises, Digman was spotless with clean white bandages. Like most modern victims, Walsh noted, the real damage was internal.

Detective Reeves left the hushed conversation in the corner to come over and greet him, a grim smile on his face. "Sorry to get you out of bed," he said.

"That's alright," Walsh replied, rubbing the back of his neck. "You probably saved my life."

"I wouldn't know," Reeves smiled tightly. "You're the only couple I know still acts like they're on their honeymoon."

"Well, when you marry the right woman...." Walsh smiled into his hand as he wiped his face. He turned his attention to the detective and sighed heavily, "So, what's goin' on here? Where're we at?"

"He's in and out. Woke up about 45 minutes ago and answered a couple of questions for the nurses. I thought I'd better get you down here."

"How's he doing?" Walsh asked.

"Uh, not so good," Reeves replied, pointing to the bed. "They have him on this kidney dialysis thing, and whatever that wicked looking thing is plugged into his throat. He needs a kidney, but it's complicated. Since he came in under a John Doe and he's not with the force anymore the insurance is a big problem. But, I'll tell you, Mike, whoever did this is some piece of work."

"Yeah, well, everybody's tough with a baseball bat," Walsh replied. " Hell, for all we know he walked into some gang's territory... "

"No." Reeves said flatly, "This was done by hand. The bruises are focused and deep, the internal damage is pinpoint. Accurate. No, this was done by hand, by somebody who knew where to hit, like a surgeon with their fists. And they're strong."

"Any word yet from the lab on the strip of bandage we found in his hand?" Walsh muttered as he flipped through Digman's chart.

"The blood samples don't match his type, or your suspect's, Katina Choovanski."

"What about the strands of hair?"

"Well, they're female, bleached blonde. Our assailant, or one of the assailants anyway, is a brunette with bleached blonde hair. But I tell you, you're going to have a hard time convincing me a woman did this, " Reeves said.

"You'd be amazed at some of the things I've seen a woman do." Walsh said as he stepped carefully towards the head of the bed, pausing a moment to make sure he didn't interfere with one of the many tubes and wires running from the bed. He leaned over and spoke softly to Digman, "Wayne? Wayne, can you hear me?"

Digman eyes opened slightly and closed again.

"Wayne? It's me, Mike Walsh. Can you tell me who did this to you buddy?" Walsh whispered.

Digman's head flinched and his body shivered once before the big man's eyes fluttered briefly and closed again. He looked asleep except for the slight movement his head made every time the respirator pushed air into his lungs. Walsh looked back at Reeves who chewed on a piece of gum nervously, staring intently at the scene. Reeves gave the detective a puzzled look with a shrug of his shoulders. Walsh turned back to Digman. "Wayne? Can you tell me who did this to you?"

Digman turned his head toward Walsh, his movements slow and pained. Silently, he mouthed the word, "Parker."

"Parker?" Walsh frowned, "Parker who?"

Digman tried to lick his lips, but his mouth was dry. He continued slowly, his lips and tongue working without air, "Mrs. Parker... file on desk."

On hearing this, Walsh snapped his fingers behind his back at Reeves, who turned and spoke briefly with the uniformed officer that stood next to him. The officer left immediately for Digman's one room office on the south end of downtown.

Digman's head twitched in a small intense spasm and stopped. One of the monitors by the bed fluttered twice, then resumed its rhythmic sucking, fluttering sound. With great effort, Digman closed, then opened, his eyes and tried to look at the detective. The bandages across his nose and upper lip prevented him from closing his mouth all the way.

"Who's Mrs. Parker?" Walsh asked again.

"Mafia," Digman mouthed, then closed his eyes and seemed to drift away again.

"Excuse me, gentlemen," came a woman's voice from behind, "I need to ask you to leave now. I need to check Mr. Digman's status."

Walsh stood up straight and ran his hands through his hair with a heavy sigh. Reeves reached over and tapped him on the arm, "C'mon Mike, let's go grab a cup of coffee while they do their thing."

Walsh turned to follow Reeves and the other detective, smiling at the nurse who stood patiently by the foot of the bed, waiting for him to step by.

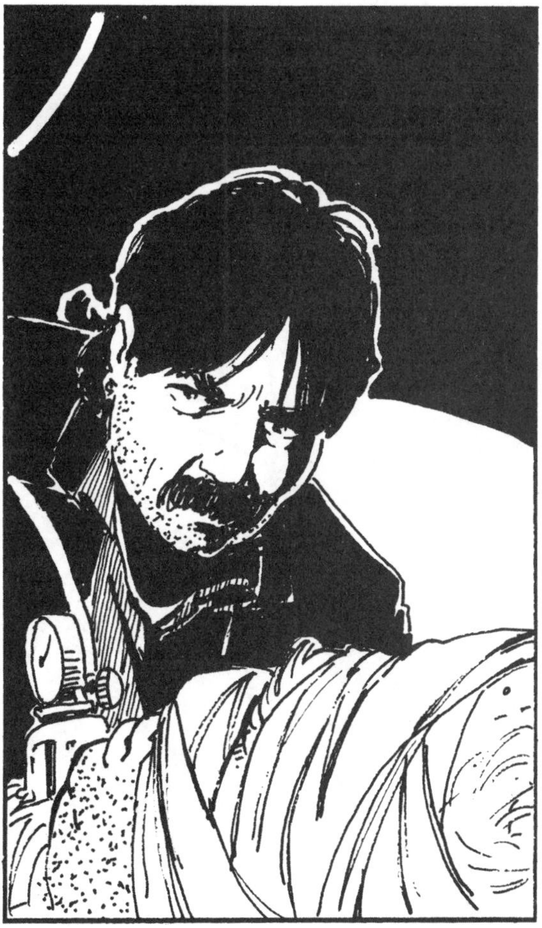

She was tall and statuesque, a little over six feet. Walsh noted her size and broad shoulders as he squeezed between her and the wall. She smiled a tight, polite smile that seemed to only accent her sharp features. She was pretty enough, even with no makeup and her blonde hair pulled tight in a bun behind her white nurse's cap, but there was something oddly cold and unattractive about her as well. Something... military.

Walsh paused at the door and turned to look at Digman, who lay sleeping, as the nurse bent over to check his pulse. Her hands were large and strong, like a man's, her long fingers easily wrapping around Digman's fat wrist. Walsh stared at the muscles in her arms as they filled out the short sleeves of the uniform. This woman has a serious workout, he noted with some admiration. She looked up at Walsh briefly, her gaze cool and unemotional. She lay Digman's hand back on the bed and began to attach a blood pressure strap to his arm in the quick, efficient manner that one acquires through years of routine. Walsh sighed, rubbing the back of his neck. She knows what she's doing, he thought to himself, and turned to leave.

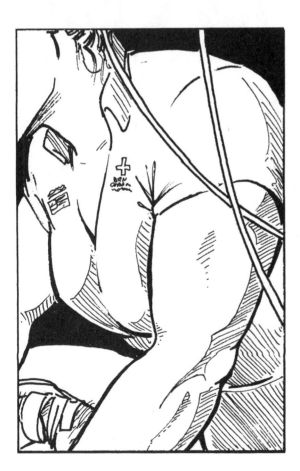

Reeves was waiting for Walsh by the elevators that would take them to the basement cafeteria. "Did you get a look at her?" Reeves chuckled as he pushed the down button, "Damnation! What a body! Can you imagine dating someone stronger than you? Talk about a woman that could kill you!

Walsh and Reeves stared at each other as the words hung between them.

"Did you see her hands?" Walsh said quietly.

"No, but I saw the back of her neck. Mike, she has dark roots. She's bleached blonde."

"Shit!" Walsh snapped, and immediately began running full speed back down the hall. "Seal off the exits!" he shouted back to Reeves, who was already giving the command over a 2 way radio.

Walsh burst loudly through the CCU doors with Jesse, the guard, close on his heels. "What's goin' on?" Jesse asked. Walsh didn't answer but ran across the small lobby directly to Digman's room and stopped in his tracks inside the doorway. Two nurses and a doctor were bent over Digman's body, the doctor barking instructions as he worked Digman's chest with his hands. One nurse was checking the tubing and IV bags around Digman's bed, giving the status of each one out loud as she moved around the bed.

Reeves ran into the room with two uniformed officers on his heels and pulled up beside Walsh at the foot of the bed. The medical symphony had lost it's rhythm. Only the steady monotone alarm of several monitors sounded as they stood and watched the doctor pump Digman's chest for three minutes before he stood up and wiped his brow.

Three men from cardiology came hurrying into the room with a cart and chest spreader, but the doctor waved them off.

Behind him, Walsh could hear Reeves outside the doorway checking the posts around the building. All the replies came back the same, "Nothing here."

Walsh bit his lip and suppressed a string of profanities as he watched one of the nurses turn off the monitors one by one. The doctor noted the time and cause of death, sudden cardiac arrest, to one of the nurses.

"Nothing," Reeves said quietly to Walsh as he walked out of the room into the lobby where several nurses stood off to one side watching and whispering.

"What do you want to do, Mike?" Reeves asked.

"I want Mrs. Parker's ass!" Walsh growled between his teeth. "This is now priority one, got it? I want the file Digman talked about brought to me right now. Do a complete, complete records search.

214

Give me everything you can find on her, state, federal, international, everything! If she's with the syndicate there should be something."

"What about the APB on Katina Choovanski?"

"Drop it. Pull the watch off her house. I want every man you got combing the city for this blonde body builder. If Miss Choovanski turns up I want to talk to her, but I think we know who we're looking for now."

"Right. Listen, Mike, I'm sorry I didn't clue onto the nurse sooner. I knew there was something different about her when I saw her. I just assumed..."

"I know. Me too. Sometimes you just can't tell who the bad guys are."

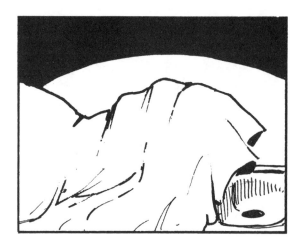

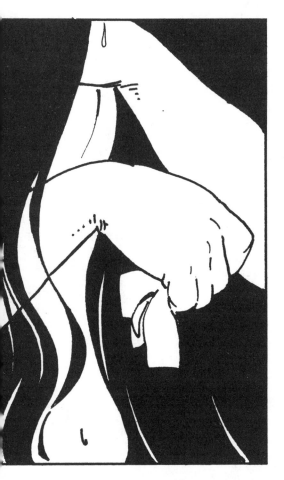

David put the last of the chinese food in a beat up, pink tupperware bowl and closed the lid. The refrigerator was packed, so he balanced the bowl on top of an opened can of fruit cocktail and rinsed his hands. Folding the dish towel neatly, he hung it back on the oven handle and turned off the lights. He checked the front door locks and peeked out the curtains, the street was empty. The sound of running water in the hall bath finally stopped. David turned and left the room, turning out the lights as he went. Francine came out of the bathroom wiping her nose with a tissue, her eyes red, her face pale and splotchy. She'd been crying for some time. She walked into her bedroom and slumped onto the bed. David followed her in and sat next to her gingerly.

"You okay?" he asked tenderly.

"Yeah," Francine sniffed. She folded her tissue nervously and wiped her eyes, the tears welling up and streaming down her face again.

"It's just... everytime I ever need help, she's there, you know? I mean, last year... she went to jail for me, you know?" Francine's voice broke.

"And now she needs me, I mean really needs me...and I can't do anything to help her. I don't know what's going on, I don't even know where she is!" Francine sobbed and fell into David's arms, crying hard for a long, long time.

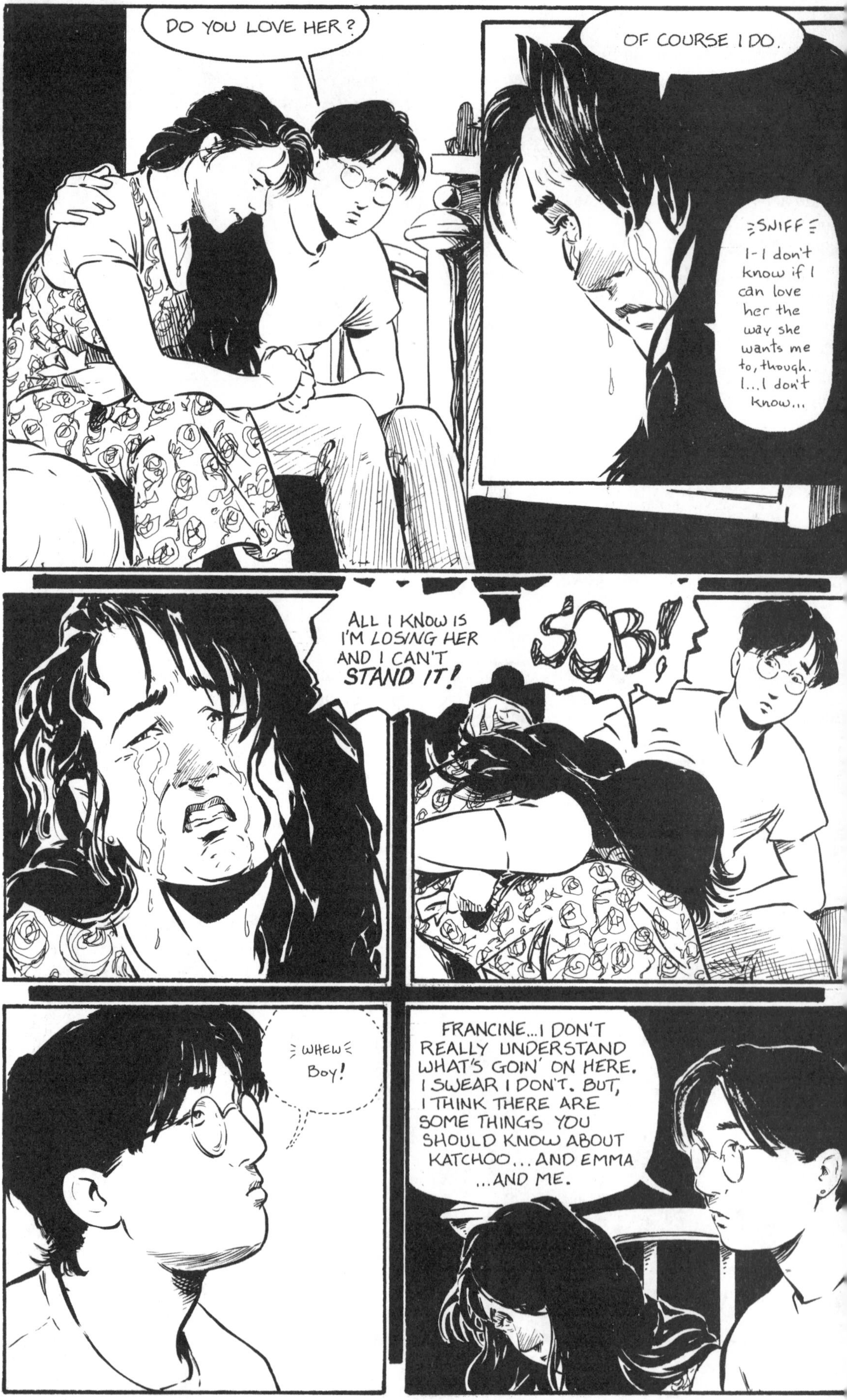
DO YOU LOVE HER?
OF COURSE I DO.
SNIFF
I-I don't know if I can love her the way she wants me to, though. I...I don't know...
ALL I KNOW IS I'M LOSING HER AND I CAN'T STAND IT!
SOB!
WHEW
Boy!
FRANCINE...I DON'T REALLY UNDERSTAND WHAT'S GOIN' ON HERE. I SWEAR I DON'T. BUT, I THINK THERE ARE SOME THINGS YOU SHOULD KNOW ABOUT KATCHOO... AND EMMA ...AND ME.

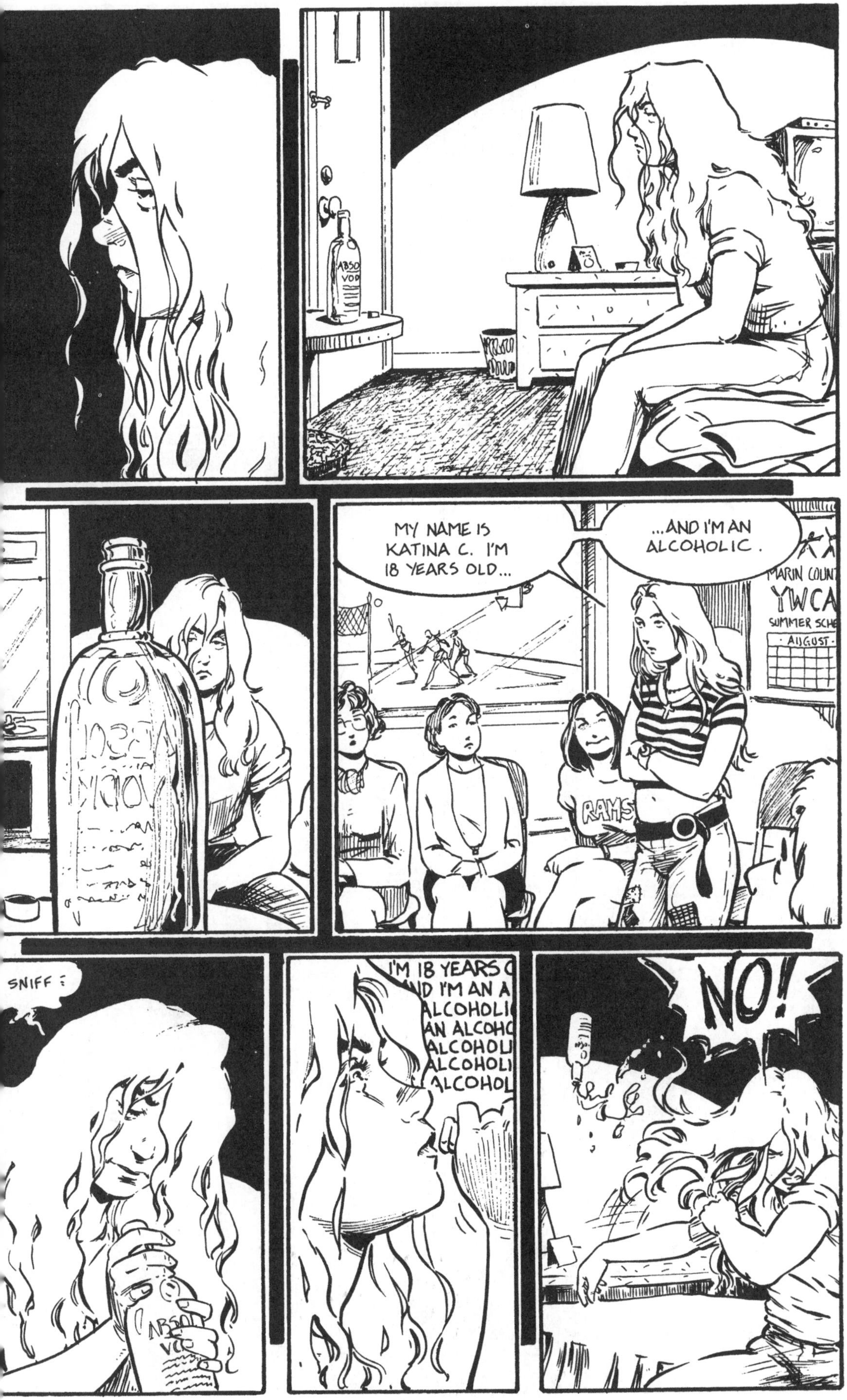
MY NAME IS KATINA C. I'M 18 YEARS OLD...
...AND I'M AN ALCOHOLIC.
MARIN COUNT
YWCA
SUMMER SCHE
AUGUST
RAMS
SNIFF
I'M 18 YEARS O
AND I'M AN A
ALCOHOLI
AN ALCOHO
ALCOHOLI
ALCOHOLI
ALCOHOL
NO!

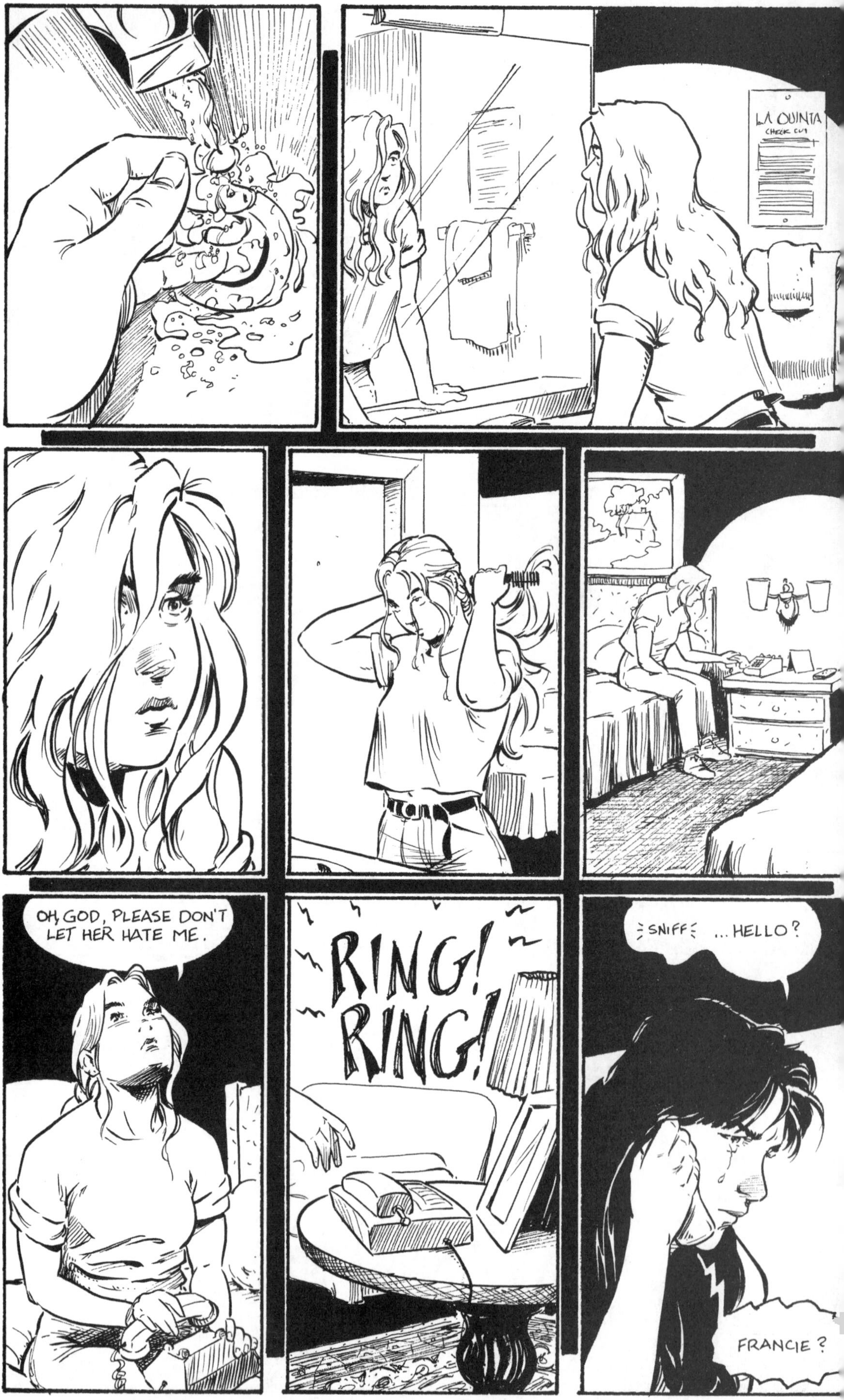
LA QUINTA
CHECK OUT
OH, GOD, PLEASE DON'T LET HER HATE ME.
RING! RING!
SNIFF ...HELLO?
FRANCIE?

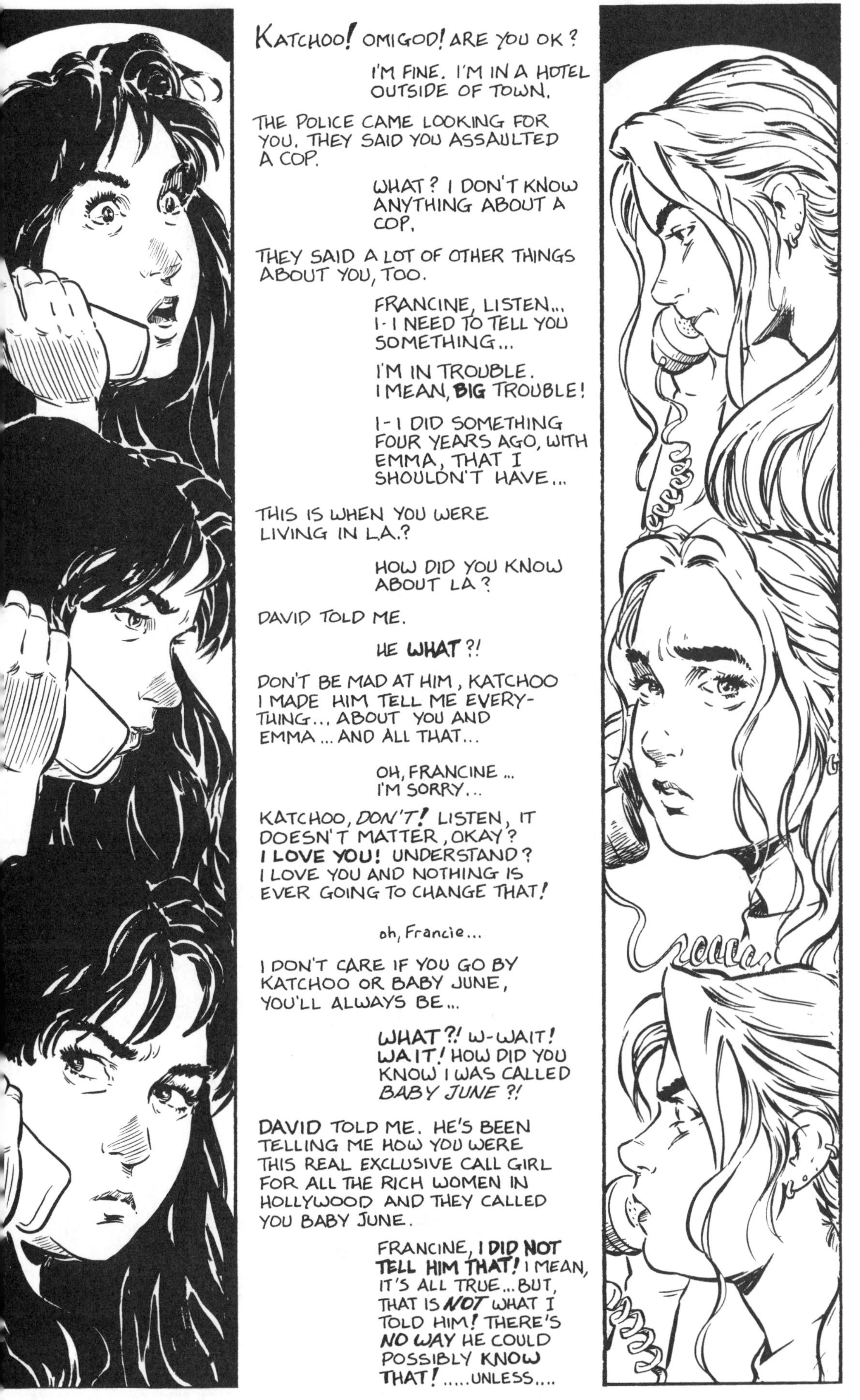
KATCHOO! OMIGOD! ARE YOU OK?
I'M FINE. I'M IN A HOTEL OUTSIDE OF TOWN.
THE POLICE CAME LOOKING FOR YOU. THEY SAID YOU ASSAULTED A COP.
WHAT? I DON'T KNOW ANYTHING ABOUT A COP.
THEY SAID A LOT OF OTHER THINGS ABOUT YOU, TOO.
FRANCINE, LISTEN... I-I NEED TO TELL YOU SOMETHING...
I'M IN TROUBLE. I MEAN, **BIG** TROUBLE!
I-I DID SOMETHING FOUR YEARS AGO, WITH EMMA, THAT I SHOULDN'T HAVE...
THIS IS WHEN YOU WERE LIVING IN L.A.?
HOW DID YOU KNOW ABOUT LA?
DAVID TOLD ME.
HE **WHAT**?!
DON'T BE MAD AT HIM, KATCHOO I MADE HIM TELL ME EVERY-THING... ABOUT YOU AND EMMA... AND ALL THAT...
OH, FRANCINE... I'M SORRY...
KATCHOO, *DON'T!* LISTEN, IT DOESN'T MATTER, OKAY? **I LOVE YOU!** UNDERSTAND? I LOVE YOU AND NOTHING IS EVER GOING TO CHANGE THAT!
oh, Francie...
I DON'T CARE IF YOU GO BY KATCHOO OR BABY JUNE, YOU'LL ALWAYS BE...
WHAT?! W-WAIT! **WAIT!** HOW DID YOU KNOW I WAS CALLED *BABY JUNE*?!
DAVID TOLD ME. HE'S BEEN TELLING ME HOW YOU WERE THIS REAL EXCLUSIVE CALL GIRL FOR ALL THE RICH WOMEN IN HOLLYWOOD AND THEY CALLED YOU BABY JUNE.
FRANCINE, **I DID NOT TELL HIM THAT!** I MEAN, IT'S ALL TRUE... BUT, THAT IS ***NOT*** WHAT I TOLD HIM! THERE'S ***NO WAY*** HE COULD POSSIBLY **KNOW THAT!** .....UNLESS....

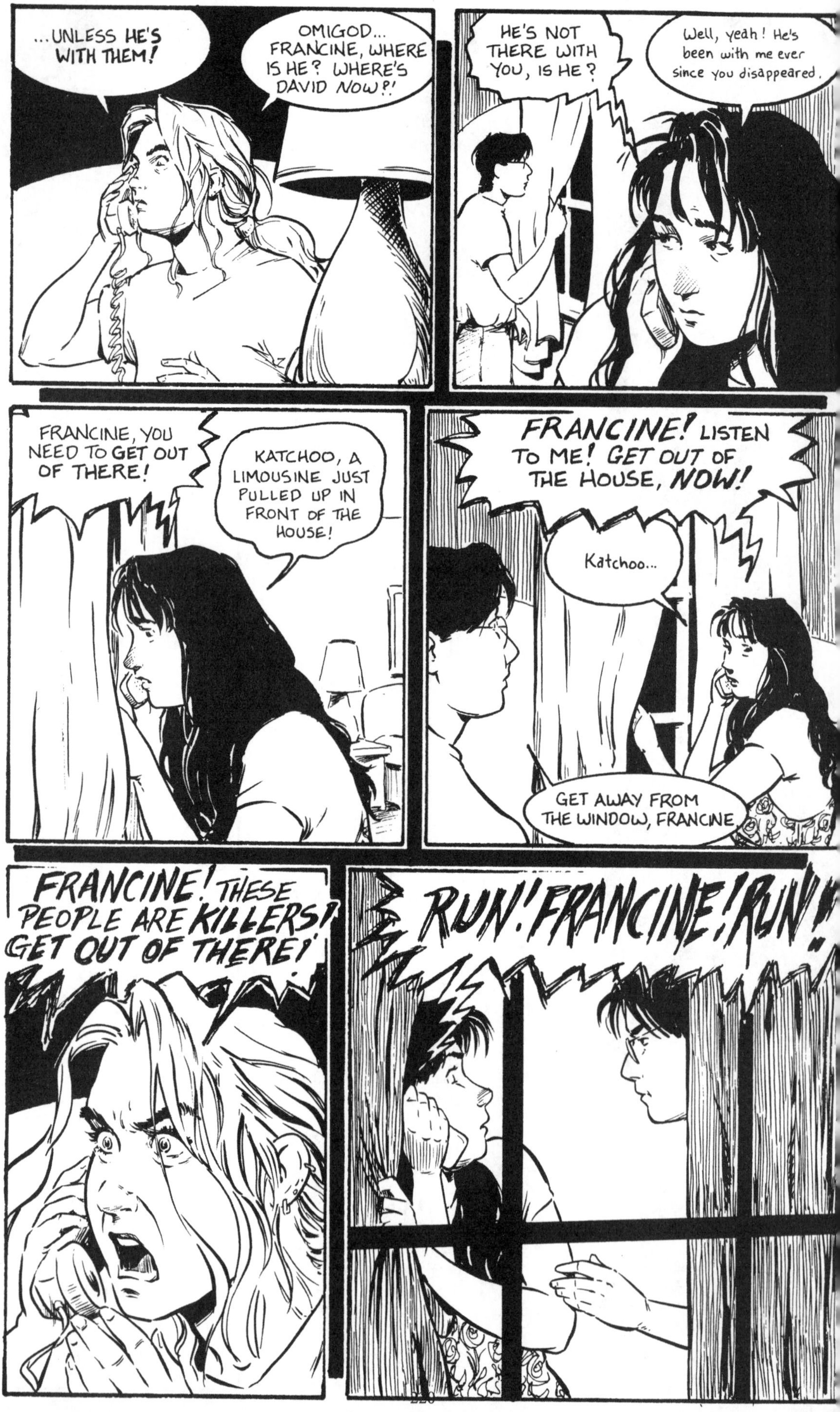
...UNLESS HE'S WITH THEM!
OMIGOD... FRANCINE, WHERE IS HE? WHERE'S DAVID NOW?!
HE'S NOT THERE WITH YOU, IS HE?
Well, yeah! He's been with me ever since you disappeared.
FRANCINE, YOU NEED TO GET OUT OF THERE!
KATCHOO, A LIMOUSINE JUST PULLED UP IN FRONT OF THE HOUSE!
FRANCINE! LISTEN TO ME! GET OUT OF THE HOUSE, NOW!
Katchoo...
GET AWAY FROM THE WINDOW, FRANCINE
FRANCINE! THESE PEOPLE ARE KILLERS! GET OUT OF THERE!
RUN! FRANCINE! RUN!!

Do you remember yesterdays?
Do you remember what I was like down?
I feel that madness come my way
I must drink to the vicious clowns.
I don't know if they found your ears
But I used to have a lot of names
Then one so tender pushed me here
And I watched as they fade away.
Again I wake up on the tiles
It's like I was never gone,
And just before the pain comes on,
Remember, this is where I started from.

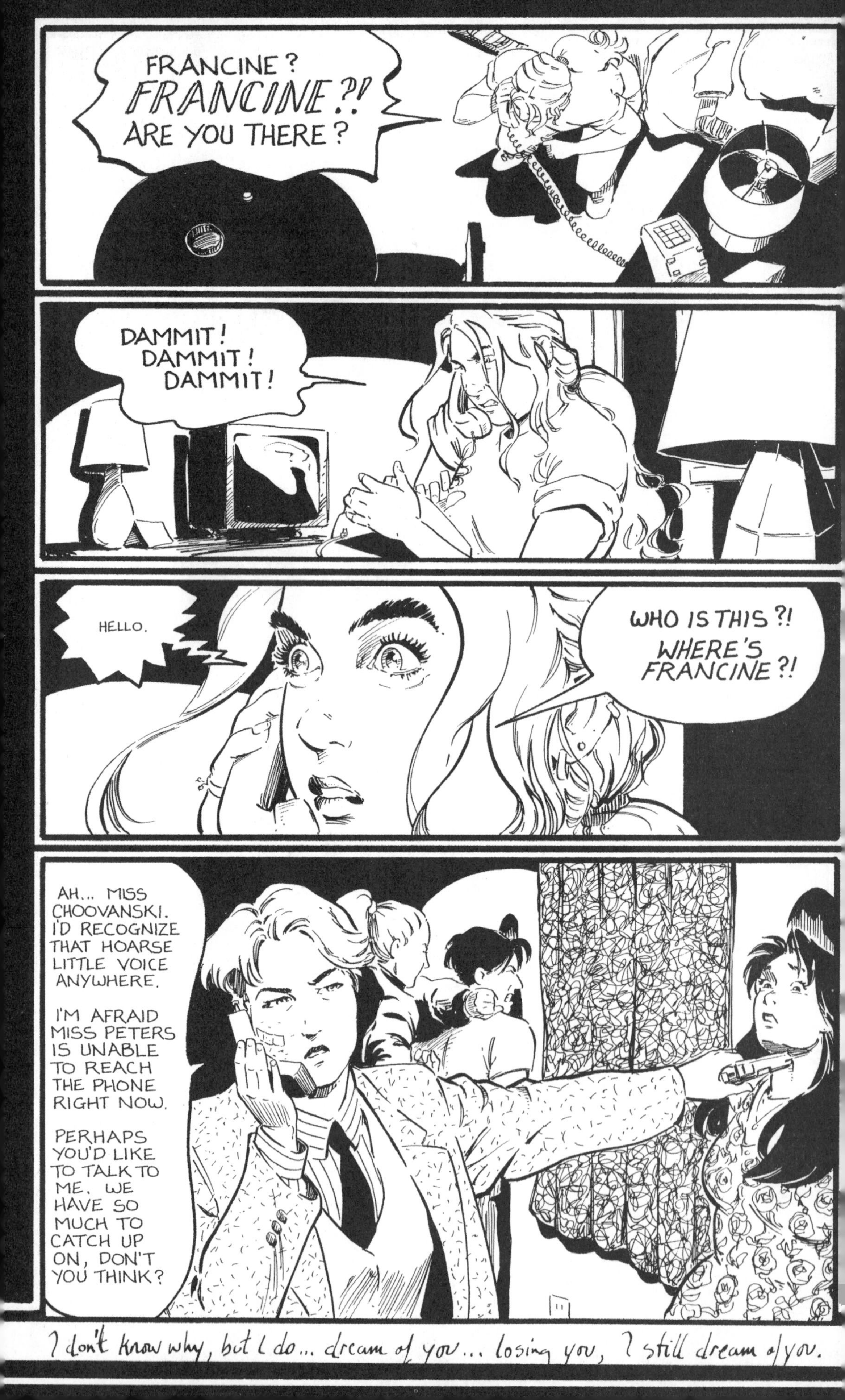
FRANCINE? FRANCINE?! ARE YOU THERE?
DAMMIT! DAMMIT! DAMMIT!
HELLO.
WHO IS THIS?! WHERE'S FRANCINE?!
AH... MISS CHOOVANSKI. I'D RECOGNIZE THAT HOARSE LITTLE VOICE ANYWHERE.
I'M AFRAID MISS PETERS IS UNABLE TO REACH THE PHONE RIGHT NOW.
PERHAPS YOU'D LIKE TO TALK TO ME. WE HAVE SO MUCH TO CATCH UP ON, DON'T YOU THINK?
I don't know why, but I do... dream of you... losing you, I still dream of you.

SA-SAMANTHA? WHAT THE **HELL** IS GOING ON HERE? WHAT HAVE YOU DONE WITH FRANCINE?!

I THOUGHT WE HAD A DEAL, MISS CHOOVANSKI.

LET ME TALK TO FRANCINE!

THE DEAL WAS, YOU DISAPPEAR FOREVER... WE DON'T KILL YOU.

I SWEAR TO GOD, SAMANTHA, IF YOU HURT HER... *I'LL KILL YOU!*

AND YET, HERE WE ARE, ONCE AGAIN...

DON'T PLAY GAMES WITH ME! LET ME TALK TO FRANCINE! I HAVE TO KNOW SHE'S ALL RIGHT!

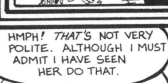

MRS. PARKER WOULD LIKE TO TALK TO YOU.

HMPH! *THAT'S* NOT VERY POLITE. ALTHOUGH I MUST ADMIT I HAVE SEEN HER DO THAT.

Is it the same way for you? ...Doesn't hi and goodbye sound so cruel?

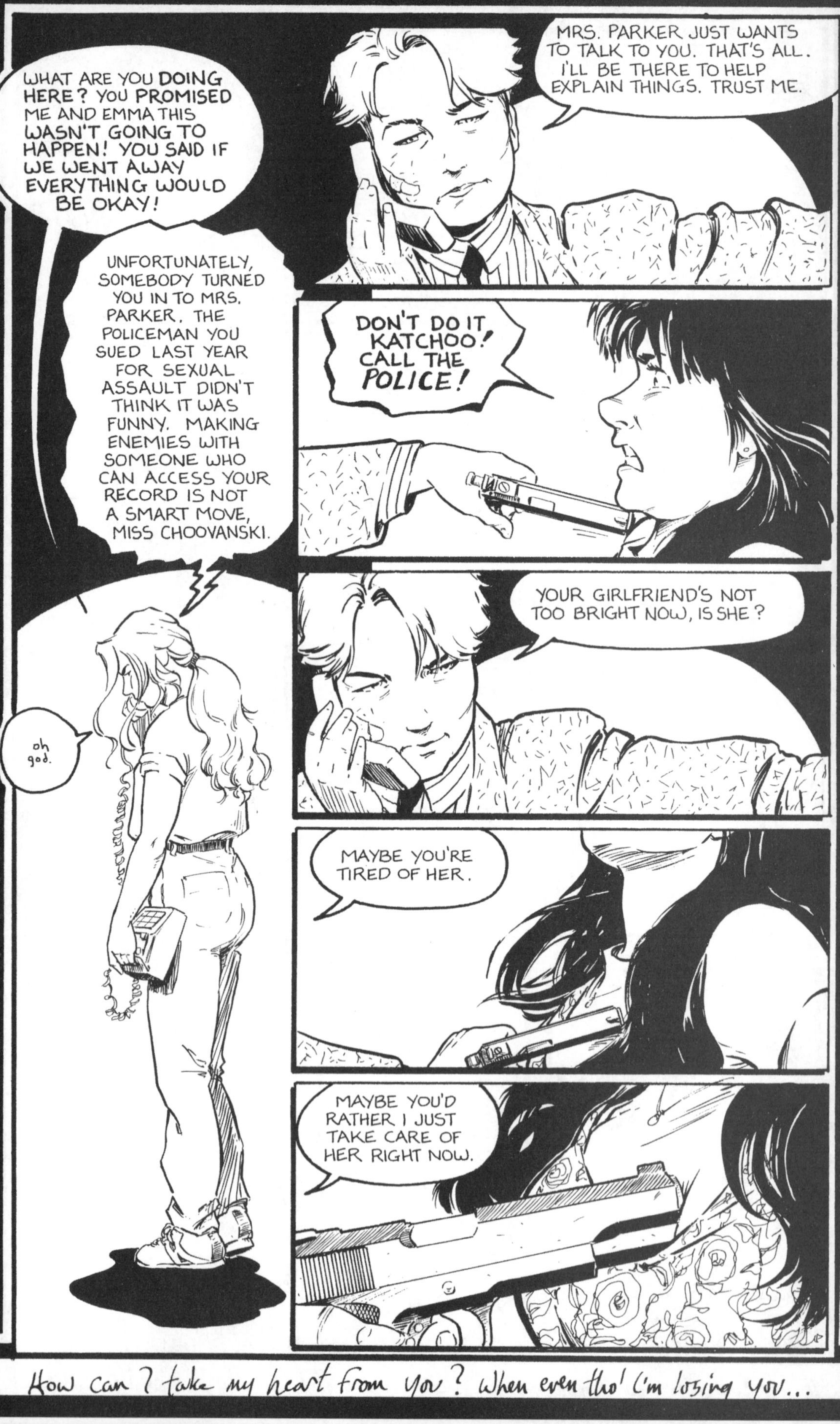
WHAT ARE YOU DOING HERE? YOU PROMISED ME AND EMMA THIS WASN'T GOING TO HAPPEN! YOU SAID IF WE WENT AWAY EVERYTHING WOULD BE OKAY!
MRS. PARKER JUST WANTS TO TALK TO YOU. THAT'S ALL. I'LL BE THERE TO HELP EXPLAIN THINGS. TRUST ME.
UNFORTUNATELY, SOMEBODY TURNED YOU IN TO MRS. PARKER. THE POLICEMAN YOU SUED LAST YEAR FOR SEXUAL ASSAULT DIDN'T THINK IT WAS FUNNY. MAKING ENEMIES WITH SOMEONE WHO CAN ACCESS YOUR RECORD IS NOT A SMART MOVE, MISS CHOOVANSKI.
DON'T DO IT KATCHOO! CALL THE POLICE!
YOUR GIRLFRIEND'S NOT TOO BRIGHT NOW, IS SHE?
oh god.
MAYBE YOU'RE TIRED OF HER.
MAYBE YOU'D RATHER I JUST TAKE CARE OF HER RIGHT NOW.

How can I take my heart from you? When even tho' I'm losing you...

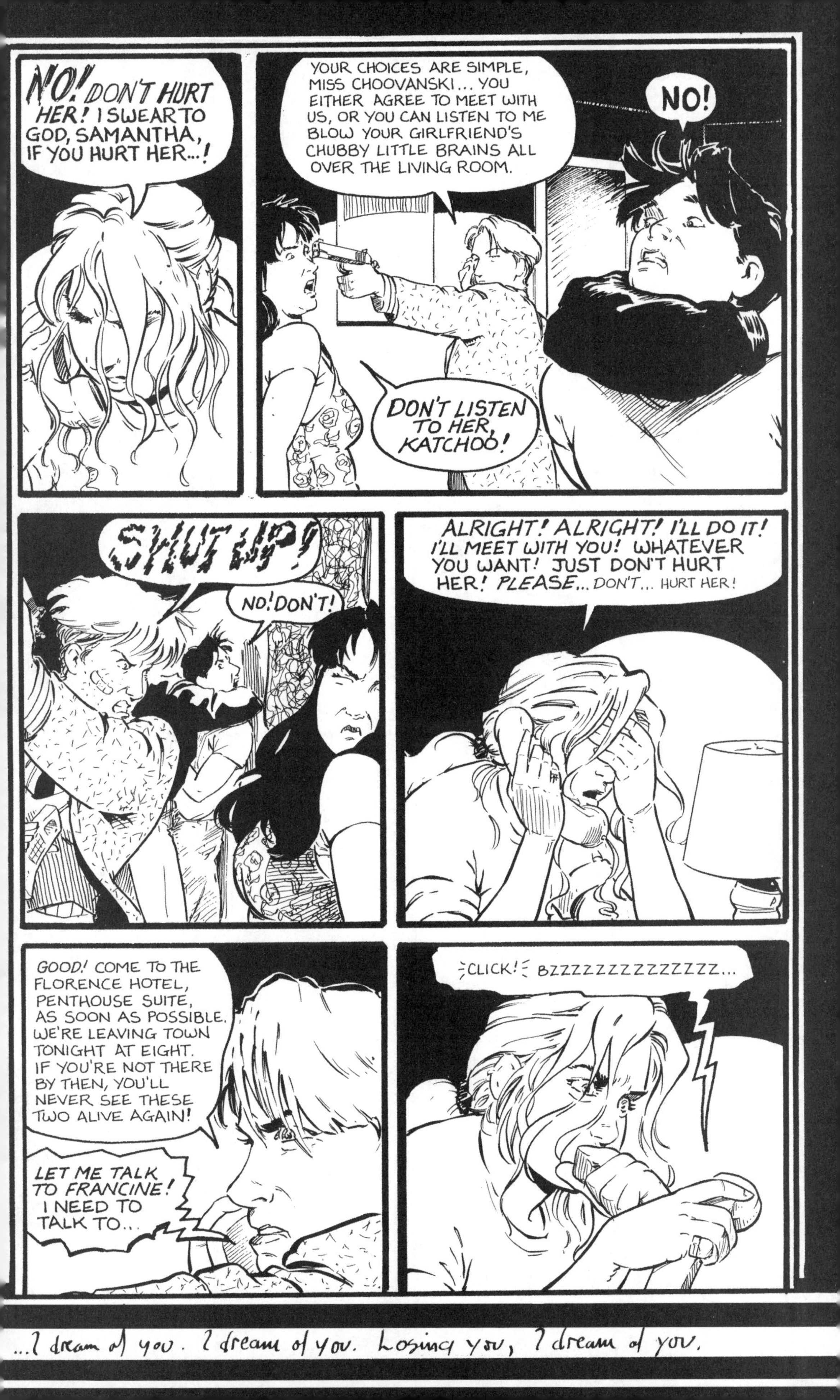

NO! DON'T HURT HER! I SWEAR TO GOD, SAMANTHA, IF YOU HURT HER...!
YOUR CHOICES ARE SIMPLE, MISS CHOOVANSKI... YOU EITHER AGREE TO MEET WITH US, OR YOU CAN LISTEN TO ME BLOW YOUR GIRLFRIEND'S CHUBBY LITTLE BRAINS ALL OVER THE LIVING ROOM.
NO!
DON'T LISTEN TO HER, KATCHOO!
SHUT UP!
NO! DON'T!
ALRIGHT! ALRIGHT! I'LL DO IT! I'LL MEET WITH YOU! WHATEVER YOU WANT! JUST DON'T HURT HER! PLEASE... DON'T... HURT HER!
GOOD! COME TO THE FLORENCE HOTEL, PENTHOUSE SUITE, AS SOON AS POSSIBLE. WE'RE LEAVING TOWN TONIGHT AT EIGHT. IF YOU'RE NOT THERE BY THEN, YOU'LL NEVER SEE THESE TWO ALIVE AGAIN!
LET ME TALK TO FRANCINE! I NEED TO TALK TO...
CLICK! BZZZZZZZZZZZZZZ...
...I dream of you. I dream of you. Losing you, I dream of you.

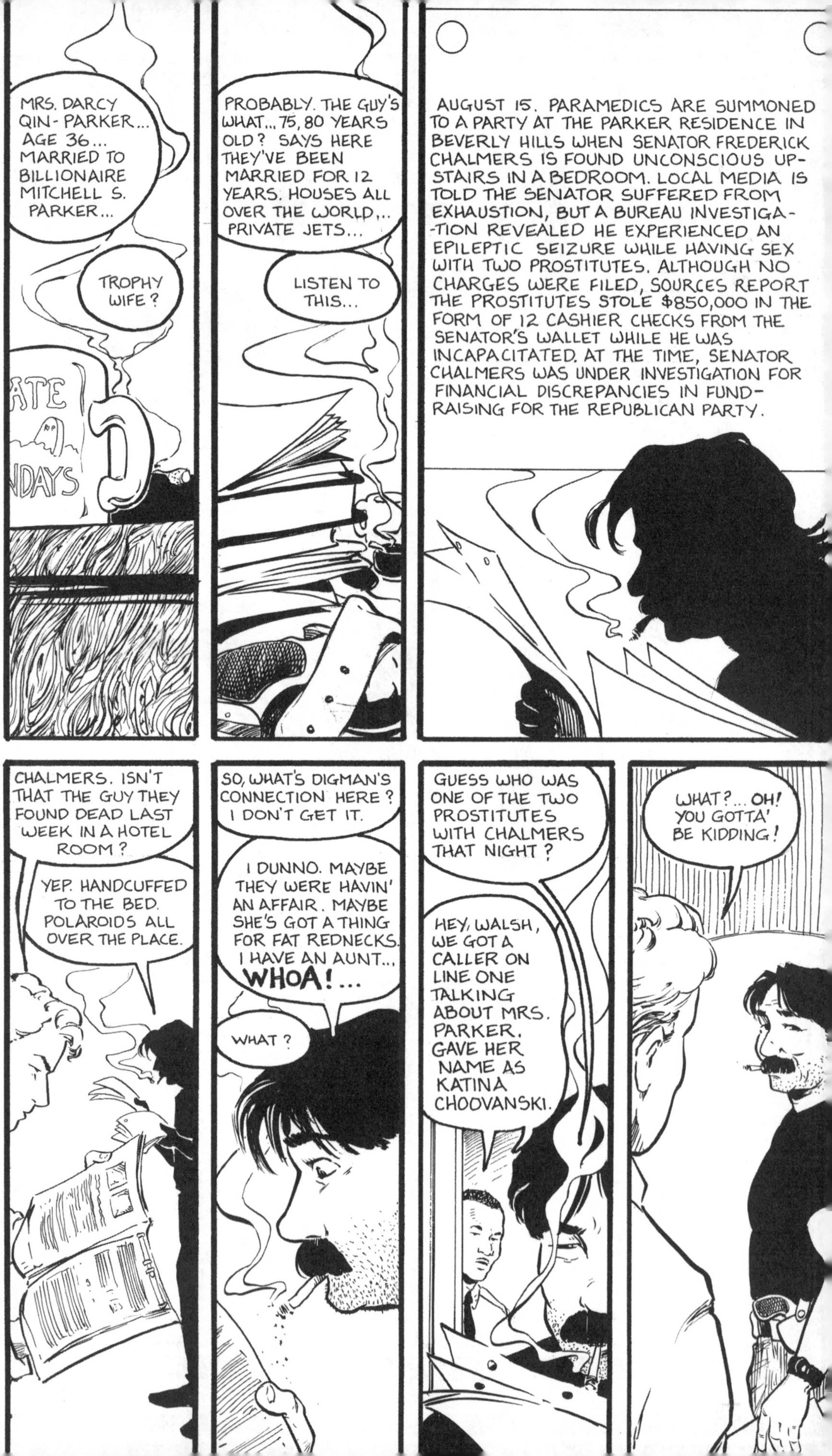

MRS. DARCY QIN-PARKER... AGE 36... MARRIED TO BILLIONAIRE MITCHELL S. PARKER...
TROPHY WIFE?
PROBABLY. THE GUY'S WHAT... 75, 80 YEARS OLD? SAYS HERE THEY'VE BEEN MARRIED FOR 12 YEARS. HOUSES ALL OVER THE WORLD,... PRIVATE JETS...
LISTEN TO THIS...
AUGUST 15. PARAMEDICS ARE SUMMONED TO A PARTY AT THE PARKER RESIDENCE IN BEVERLY HILLS WHEN SENATOR FREDERICK CHALMERS IS FOUND UNCONSCIOUS UPSTAIRS IN A BEDROOM. LOCAL MEDIA IS TOLD THE SENATOR SUFFERED FROM EXHAUSTION, BUT A BUREAU INVESTIGATION REVEALED HE EXPERIENCED AN EPILEPTIC SEIZURE WHILE HAVING SEX WITH TWO PROSTITUTES. ALTHOUGH NO CHARGES WERE FILED, SOURCES REPORT THE PROSTITUTES STOLE $850,000 IN THE FORM OF 12 CASHIER CHECKS FROM THE SENATOR'S WALLET WHILE HE WAS INCAPACITATED. AT THE TIME, SENATOR CHALMERS WAS UNDER INVESTIGATION FOR FINANCIAL DISCREPANCIES IN FUND-RAISING FOR THE REPUBLICAN PARTY.
CHALMERS. ISN'T THAT THE GUY THEY FOUND DEAD LAST WEEK IN A HOTEL ROOM?
YEP. HANDCUFFED TO THE BED. POLAROIDS ALL OVER THE PLACE.
SO, WHAT'S DIGMAN'S CONNECTION HERE? I DON'T GET IT.
I DUNNO. MAYBE THEY WERE HAVIN' AN AFFAIR. MAYBE SHE'S GOT A THING FOR FAT REDNECKS. I HAVE AN AUNT... WHOA!...
WHAT?
GUESS WHO WAS ONE OF THE TWO PROSTITUTES WITH CHALMERS THAT NIGHT?
HEY, WALSH, WE GOT A CALLER ON LINE ONE TALKING ABOUT MRS. PARKER. GAVE HER NAME AS KATINA CHOOVANSKI.
WHAT?... OH! YOU GOTTA' BE KIDDING!

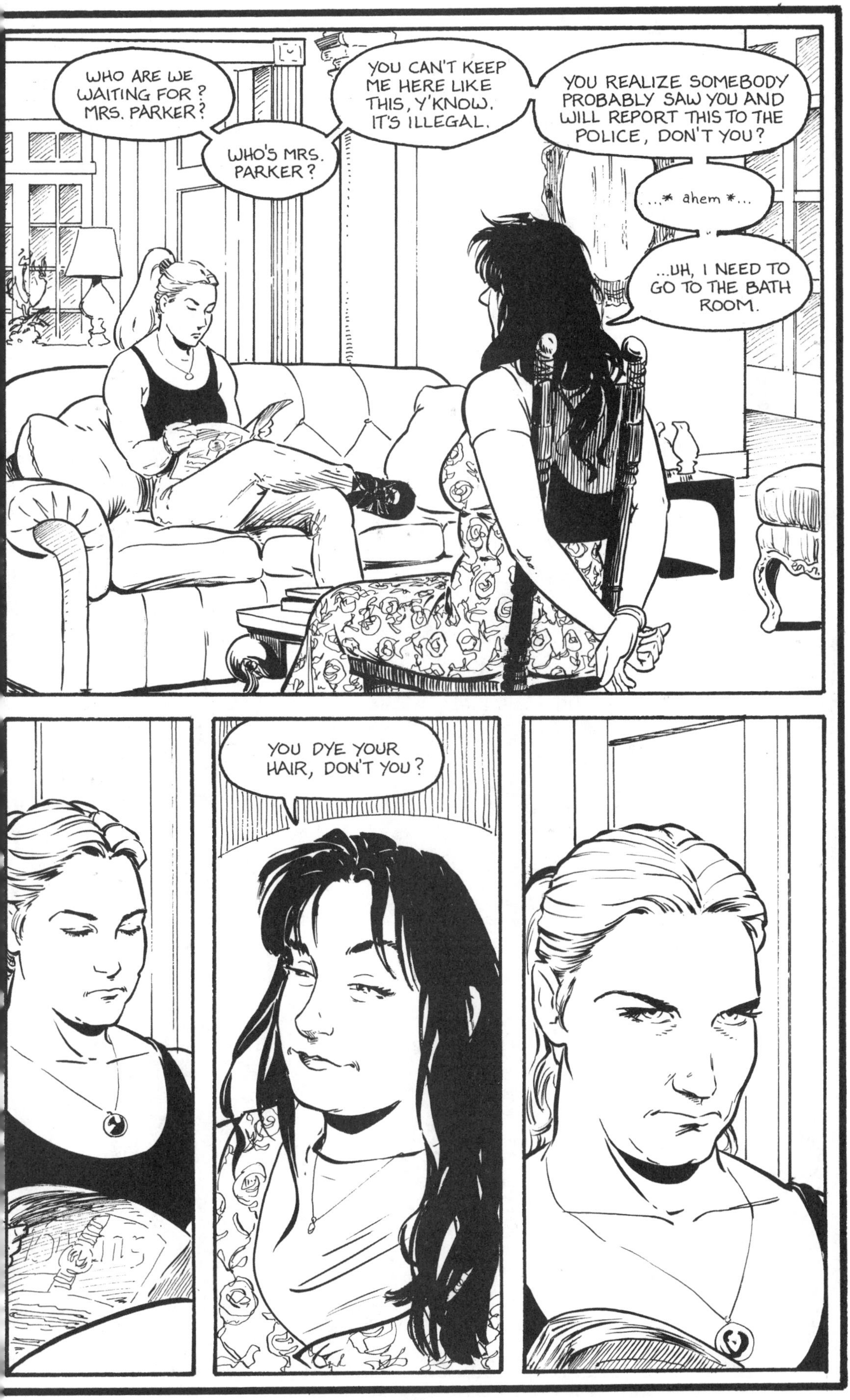
WHO ARE WE WAITING FOR? MRS. PARKER?
WHO'S MRS. PARKER?
YOU CAN'T KEEP ME HERE LIKE THIS, Y'KNOW. IT'S ILLEGAL.
YOU REALIZE SOMEBODY PROBABLY SAW YOU AND WILL REPORT THIS TO THE POLICE, DON'T YOU?
...* ahem *...
...UH, I NEED TO GO TO THE BATH ROOM.
YOU DYE YOUR HAIR, DON'T YOU?

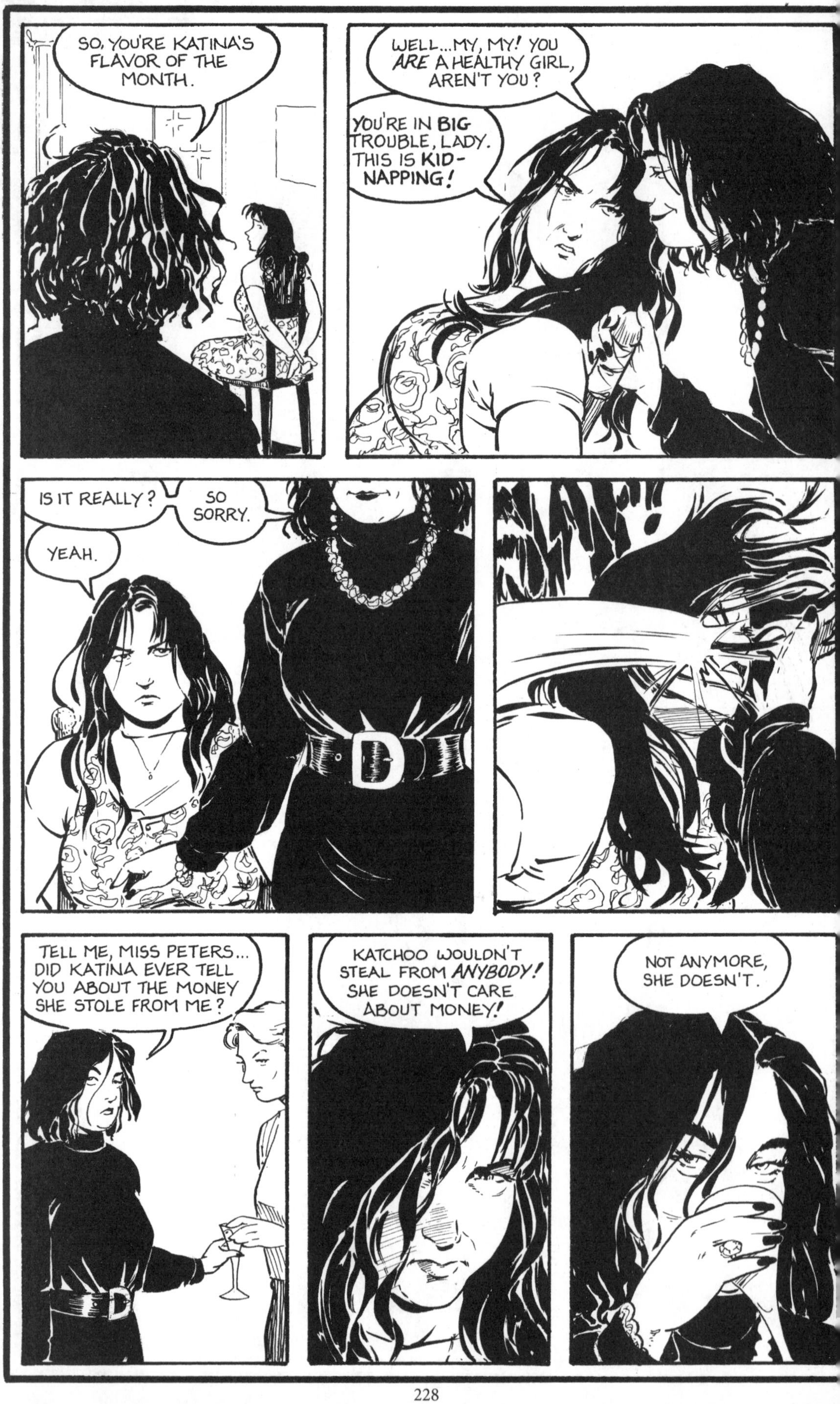

SO, YOU'RE KATINA'S FLAVOR OF THE MONTH.
WELL...MY, MY! YOU ARE A HEALTHY GIRL, AREN'T YOU?
YOU'RE IN BIG TROUBLE, LADY. THIS IS KID-NAPPING!
IS IT REALLY?
SO SORRY.
YEAH.
TELL ME, MISS PETERS... DID KATINA EVER TELL YOU ABOUT THE MONEY SHE STOLE FROM ME?
KATCHOO WOULDN'T STEAL FROM ANYBODY! SHE DOESN'T CARE ABOUT MONEY!
NOT ANYMORE, SHE DOESN'T.

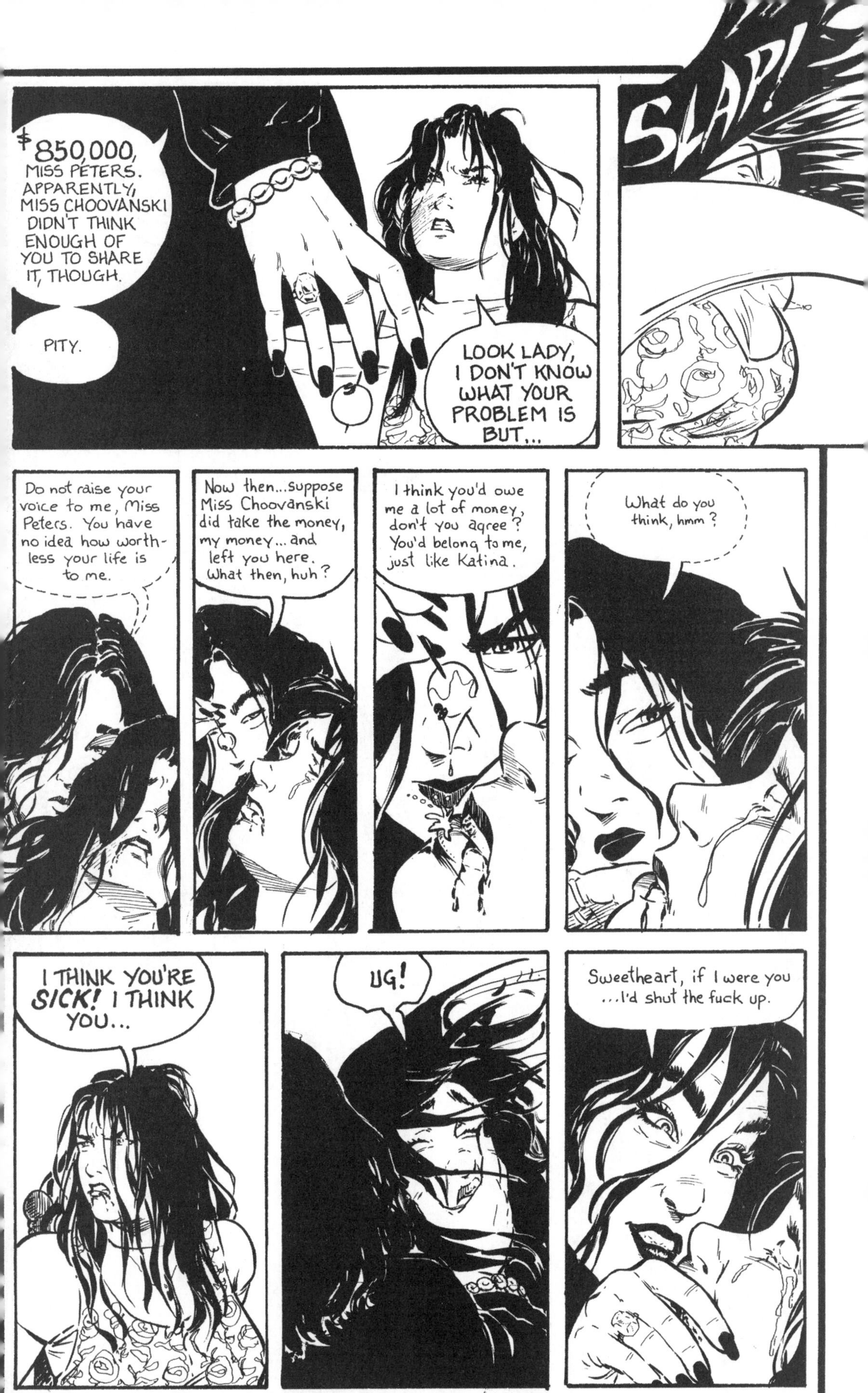
$850,000, MISS PETERS. APPARENTLY, MISS CHOOVANSKI DIDN'T THINK ENOUGH OF YOU TO SHARE IT, THOUGH.
PITY.
LOOK LADY, I DON'T KNOW WHAT YOUR PROBLEM IS BUT...
SLAP!
Do not raise your voice to me, Miss Peters. You have no idea how worthless your life is to me.
Now then...suppose Miss Choovanski did take the money, my money... and left you here. What then, huh?
I think you'd owe me a lot of money, don't you agree? You'd belong to me, just like Katina.
What do you think, hmm?
I THINK YOU'RE SICK! I THINK YOU...
UG!
Sweetheart, if I were you ...I'd shut the fuck up.

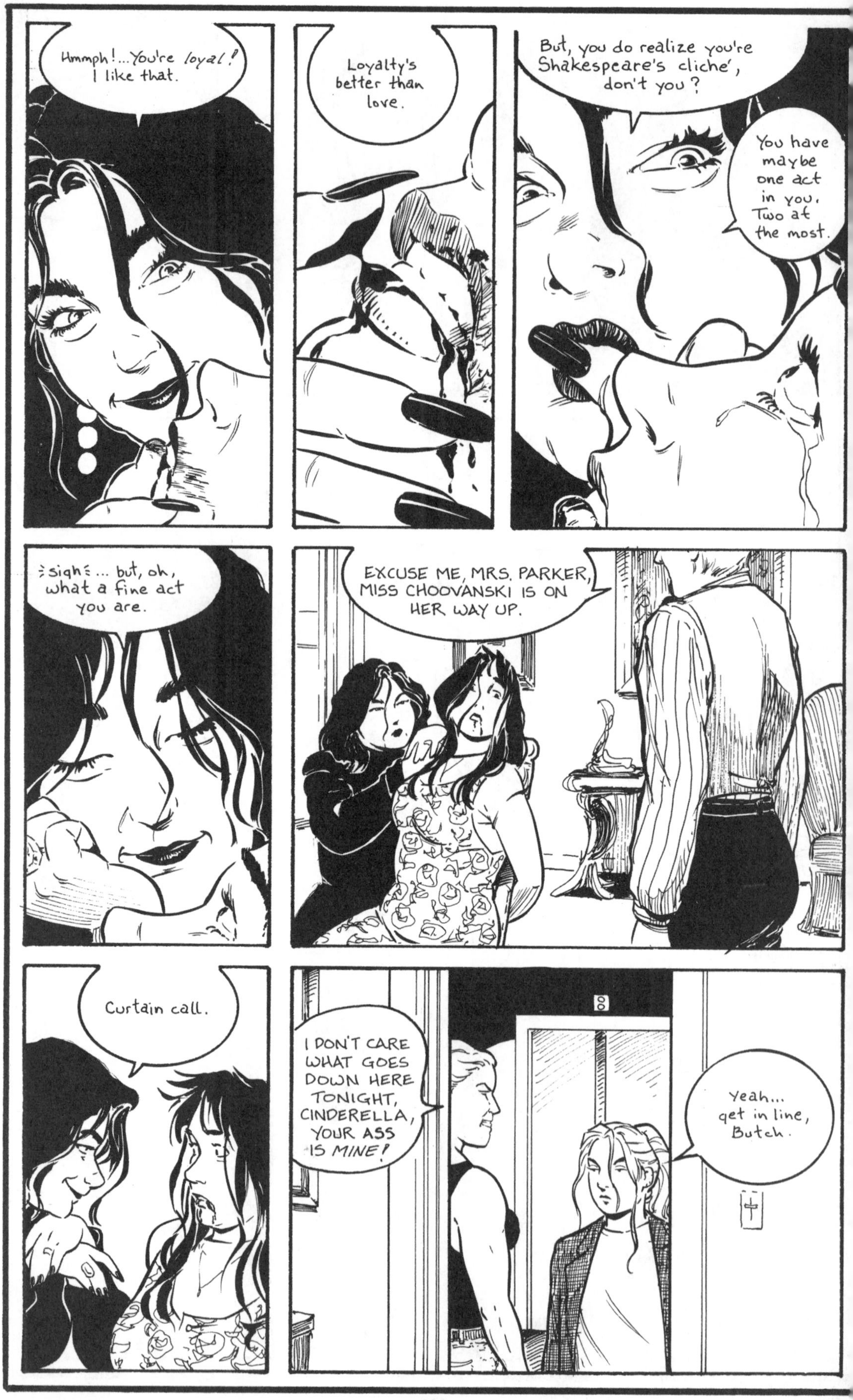
Hmmph!...You're *loyal*! I like that.
Loyalty's better than love.
But, you do realize you're Shakespeare's cliche', don't you?
You have maybe one act in you. Two at the most.
≷sigh≷... but, oh, what a fine act you are.
EXCUSE ME, MRS. PARKER, MISS CHOOVANSKI IS ON HER WAY UP.
Curtain call.
I DON'T CARE WHAT GOES DOWN HERE TONIGHT, CINDERELLA, YOUR ASS IS *MINE*!
Yeah... get in line, Butch.

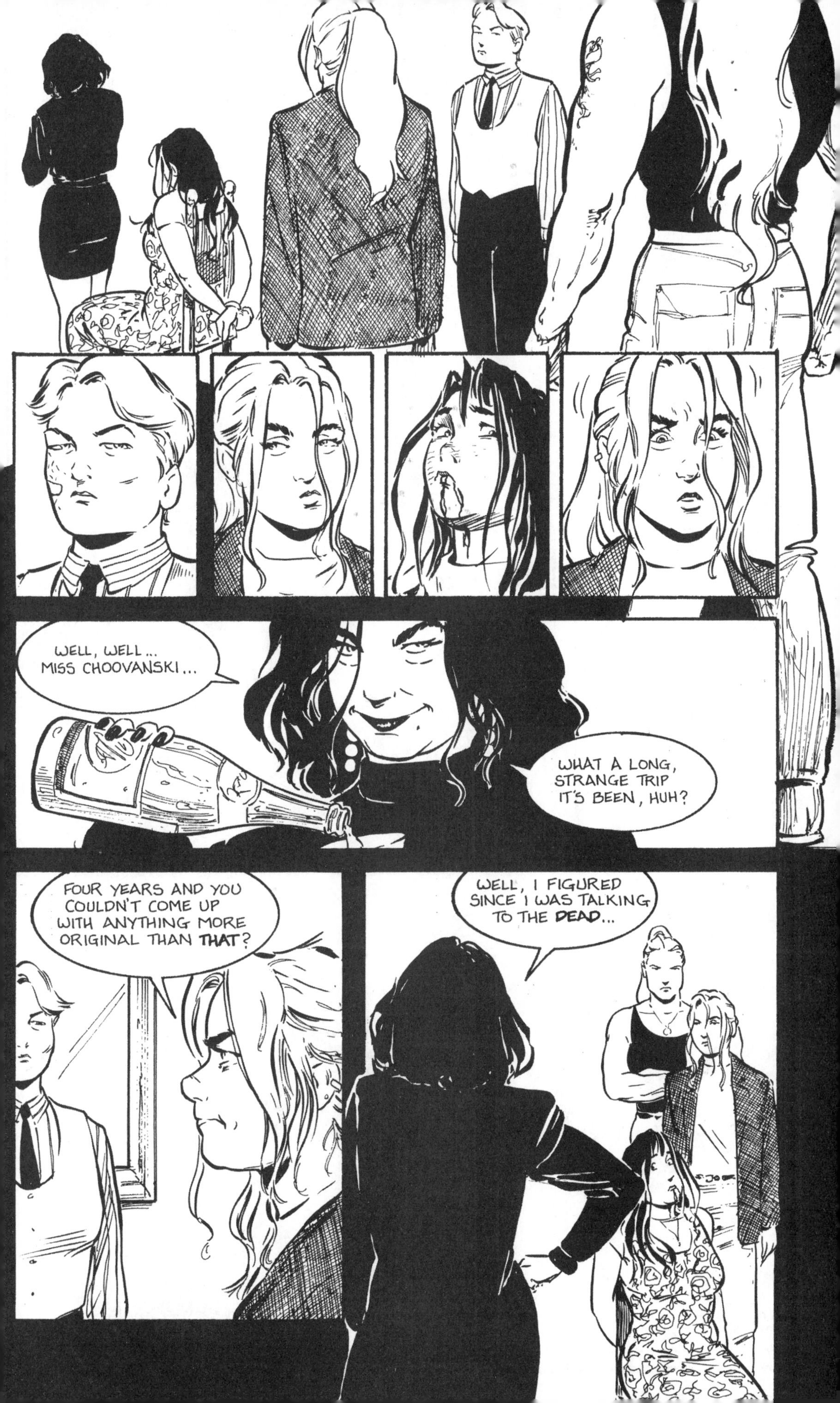
WELL, WELL...
MISS CHOOVANSKI...
WHAT A LONG, STRANGE TRIP IT'S BEEN, HUH?
FOUR YEARS AND YOU COULDN'T COME UP WITH ANYTHING MORE ORIGINAL THAN **THAT**?
WELL, I FIGURED SINCE I WAS TALKING TO THE **DEAD**...

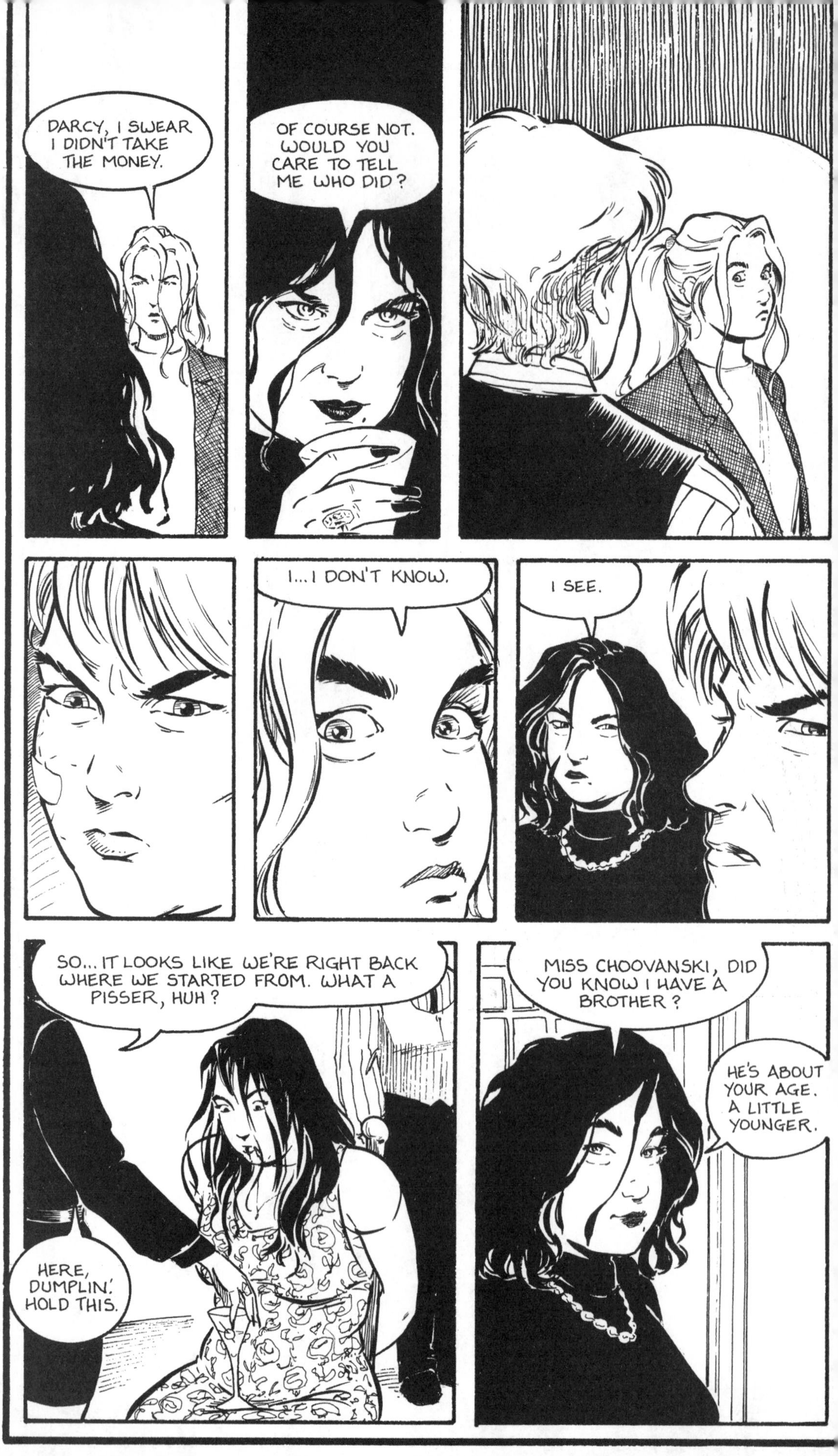
DARCY, I SWEAR I DIDN'T TAKE THE MONEY.
OF COURSE NOT. WOULD YOU CARE TO TELL ME WHO DID?
I... I DON'T KNOW.
I SEE.
SO... IT LOOKS LIKE WE'RE RIGHT BACK WHERE WE STARTED FROM. WHAT A PISSER, HUH?
HERE, DUMPLIN'. HOLD THIS.
MISS CHOOVANSKI, DID YOU KNOW I HAVE A BROTHER?
HE'S ABOUT YOUR AGE. A LITTLE YOUNGER.

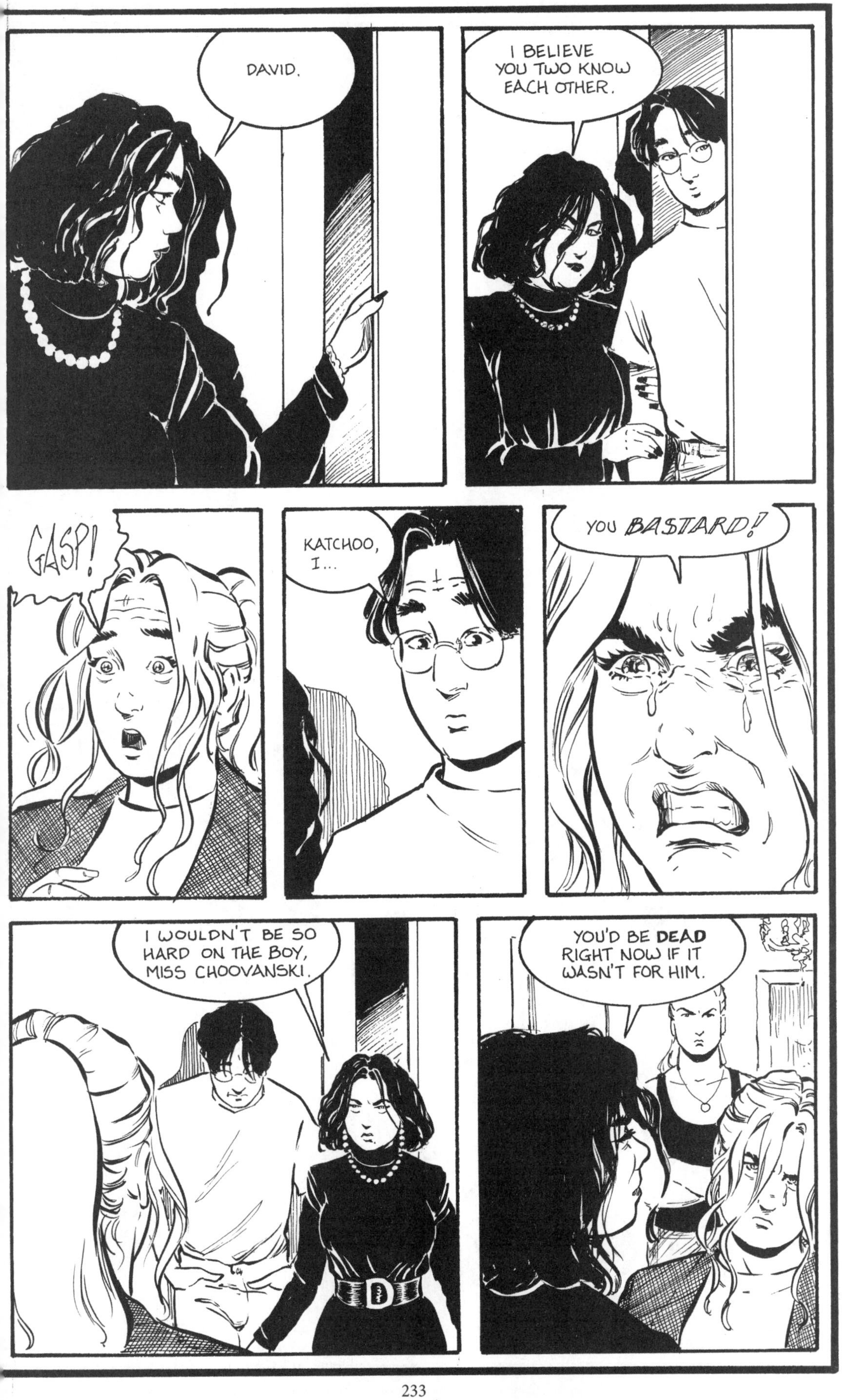
DAVID.
I BELIEVE YOU TWO KNOW EACH OTHER.
GASP!
KATCHOO, I...
YOU BASTARD!
I WOULDN'T BE SO HARD ON THE BOY, MISS CHOOVANSKI.
YOU'D BE DEAD RIGHT NOW IF IT WASN'T FOR HIM.

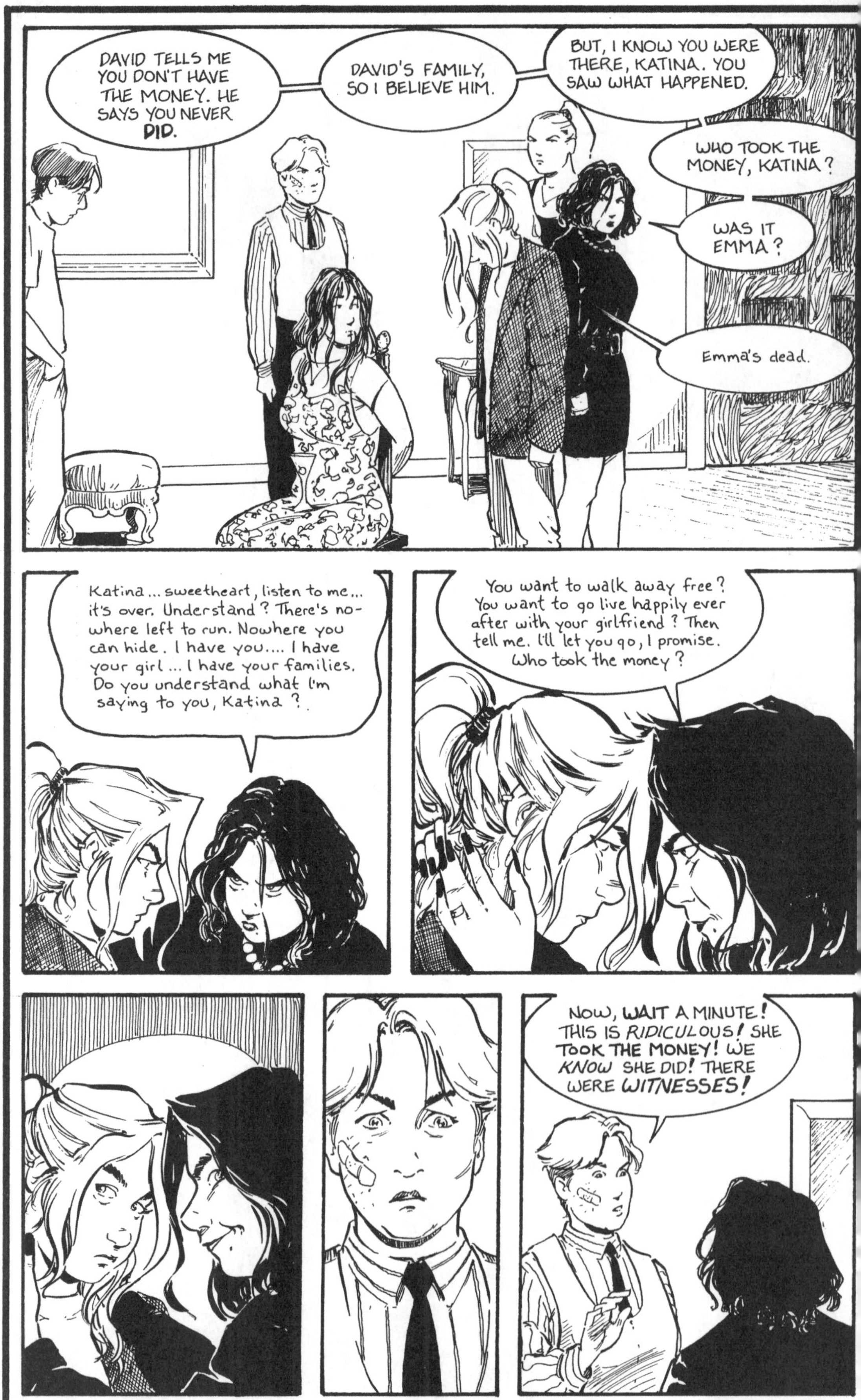
DAVID TELLS ME YOU DON'T HAVE THE MONEY. HE SAYS YOU NEVER DID.
DAVID'S FAMILY, SO I BELIEVE HIM.
BUT, I KNOW YOU WERE THERE, KATINA. YOU SAW WHAT HAPPENED.
WHO TOOK THE MONEY, KATINA?
WAS IT EMMA?
Emma's dead.
Katina ... sweetheart, listen to me... it's over. Understand? There's nowhere left to run. Nowhere you can hide. I have you.... I have your girl ... I have your families. Do you understand what I'm saying to you, Katina?.
You want to walk away free? You want to go live happily ever after with your girlfriend? Then tell me. I'll let you go, I promise. Who took the money?
NOW, WAIT A MINUTE! THIS IS RIDICULOUS! SHE TOOK THE MONEY! WE KNOW SHE DID! THERE WERE WITNESSES!

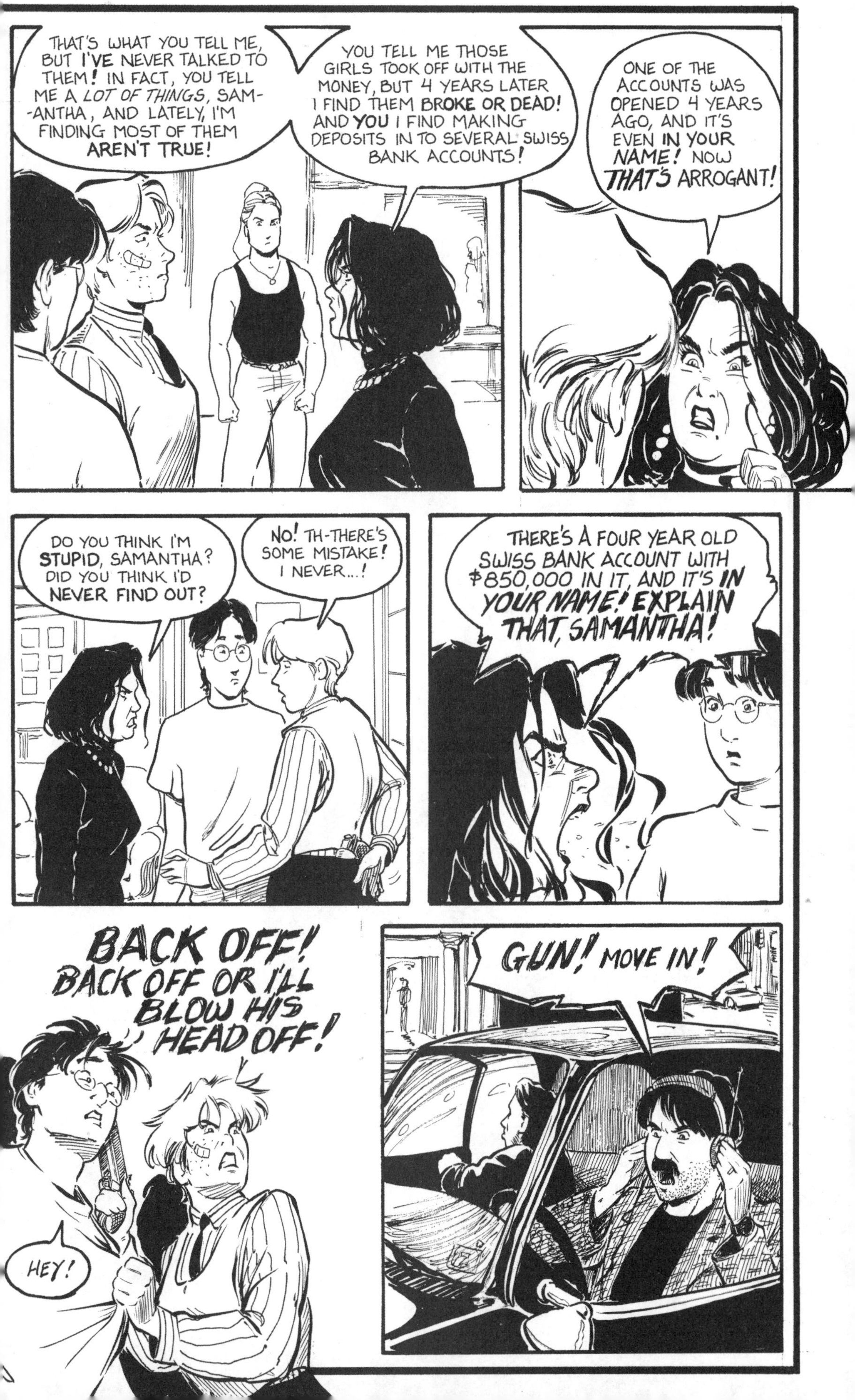
THAT'S WHAT YOU TELL ME, BUT I'VE NEVER TALKED TO THEM! IN FACT, YOU TELL ME A LOT OF THINGS, SAMANTHA, AND LATELY, I'M FINDING MOST OF THEM AREN'T TRUE!
YOU TELL ME THOSE GIRLS TOOK OFF WITH THE MONEY, BUT 4 YEARS LATER I FIND THEM BROKE OR DEAD! AND YOU I FIND MAKING DEPOSITS IN TO SEVERAL SWISS BANK ACCOUNTS!
ONE OF THE ACCOUNTS WAS OPENED 4 YEARS AGO, AND IT'S EVEN IN YOUR NAME! NOW THAT'S ARROGANT!
DO YOU THINK I'M STUPID, SAMANTHA? DID YOU THINK I'D NEVER FIND OUT?
NO! TH-THERE'S SOME MISTAKE! I NEVER...!
THERE'S A FOUR YEAR OLD SWISS BANK ACCOUNT WITH $850,000 IN IT, AND IT'S IN YOUR NAME! EXPLAIN THAT, SAMANTHA!
BACK OFF! BACK OFF OR I'LL BLOW HIS HEAD OFF!
HEY!
GUN! MOVE IN!

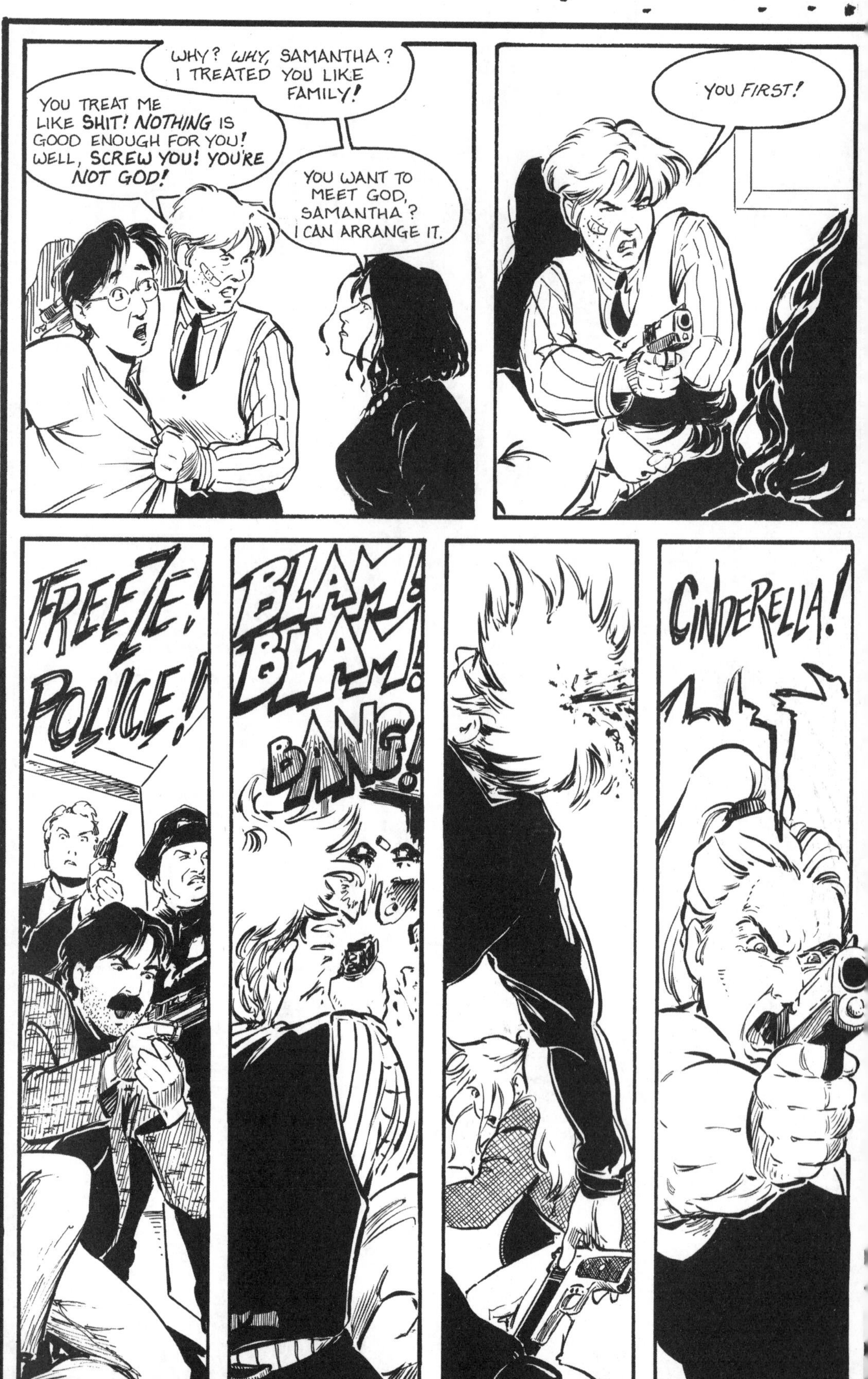
WHY? WHY, SAMANTHA? I TREATED YOU LIKE FAMILY!
YOU TREAT ME LIKE SHIT! NOTHING IS GOOD ENOUGH FOR YOU! WELL, SCREW YOU! YOU'RE NOT GOD!
YOU WANT TO MEET GOD, SAMANTHA? I CAN ARRANGE IT.
YOU FIRST!
FREEZE! POLICE!
BLAM! BLAM!
BANG!
CINDERELLA!

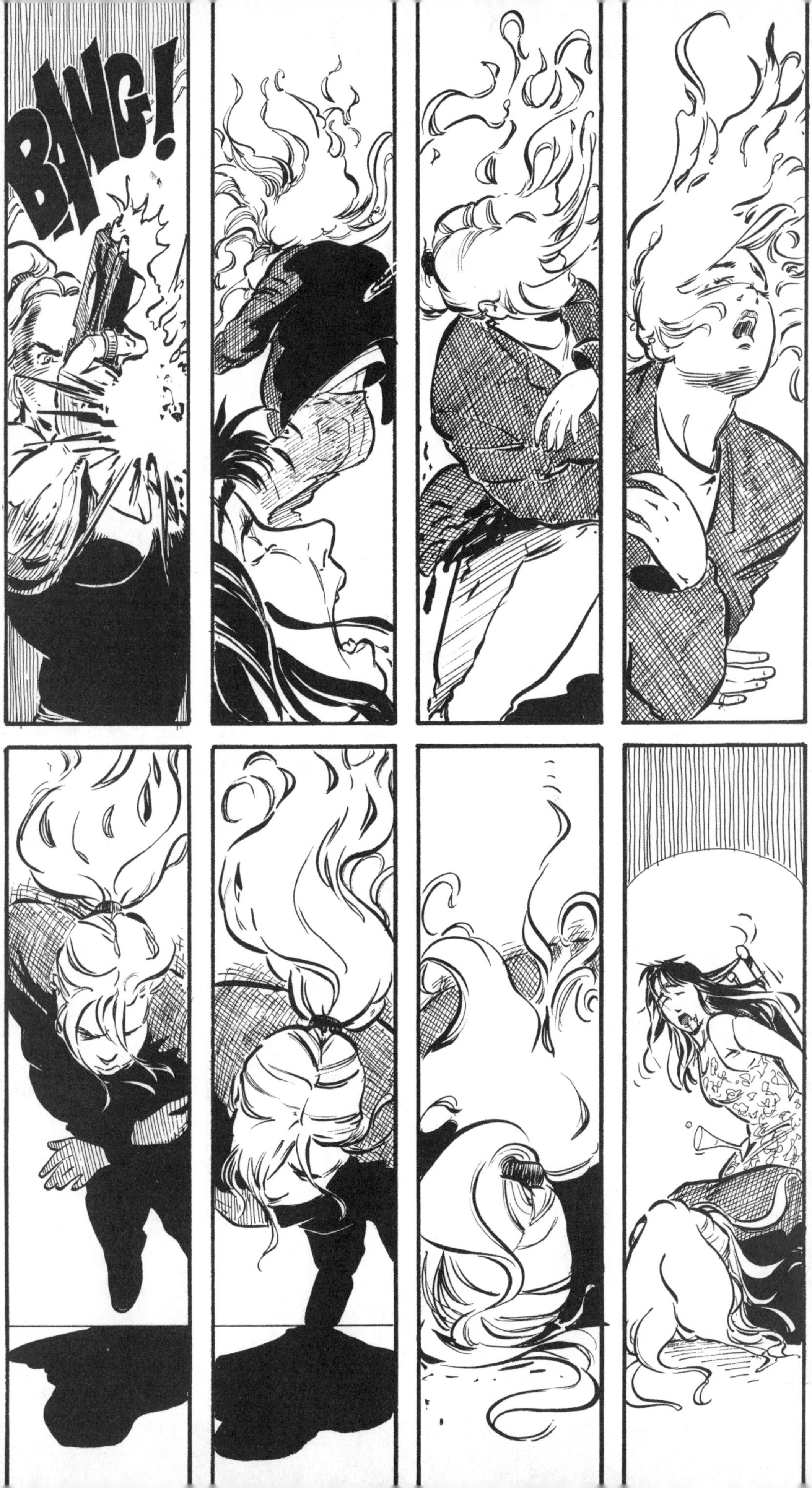
BANG!

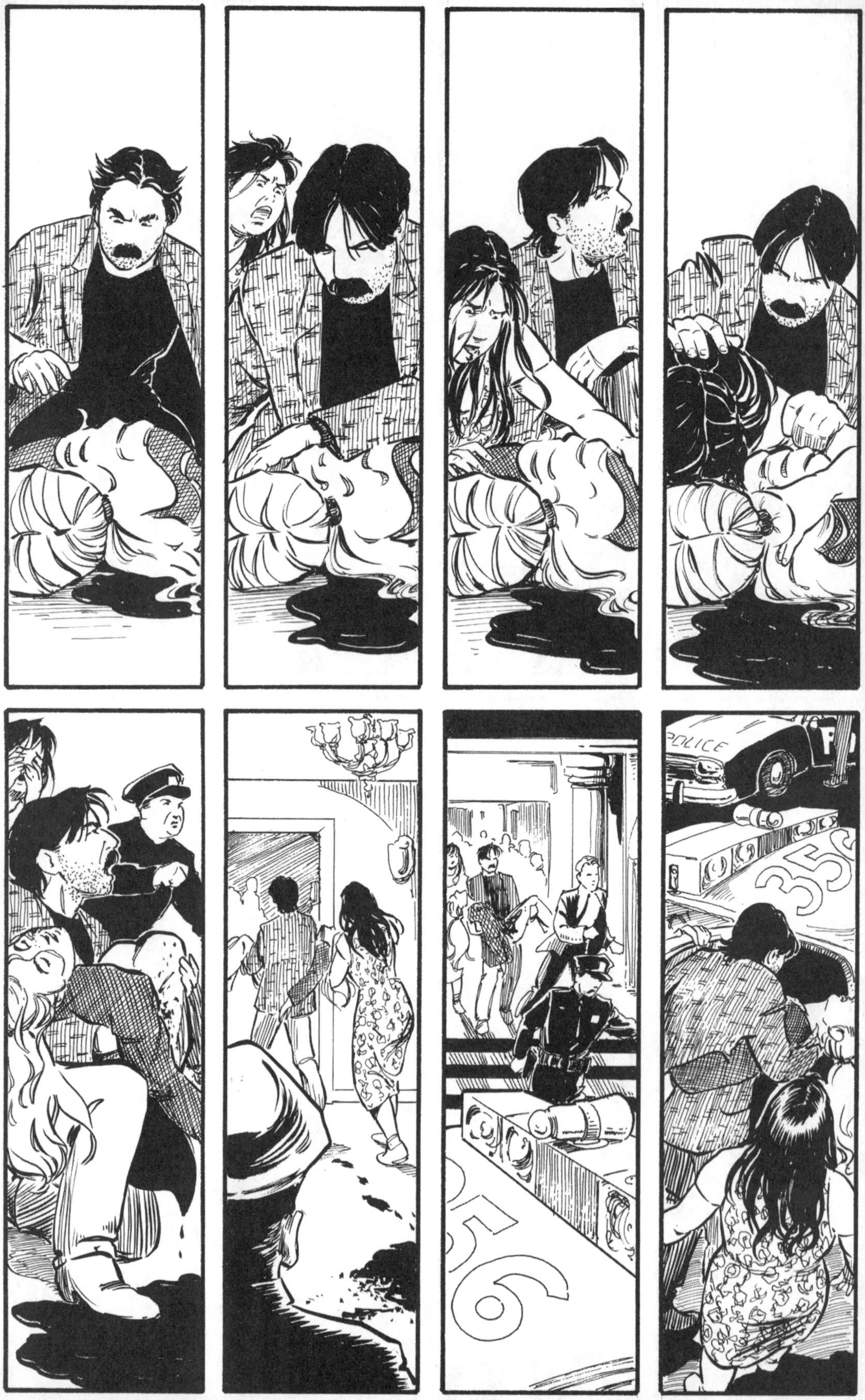
POLICE

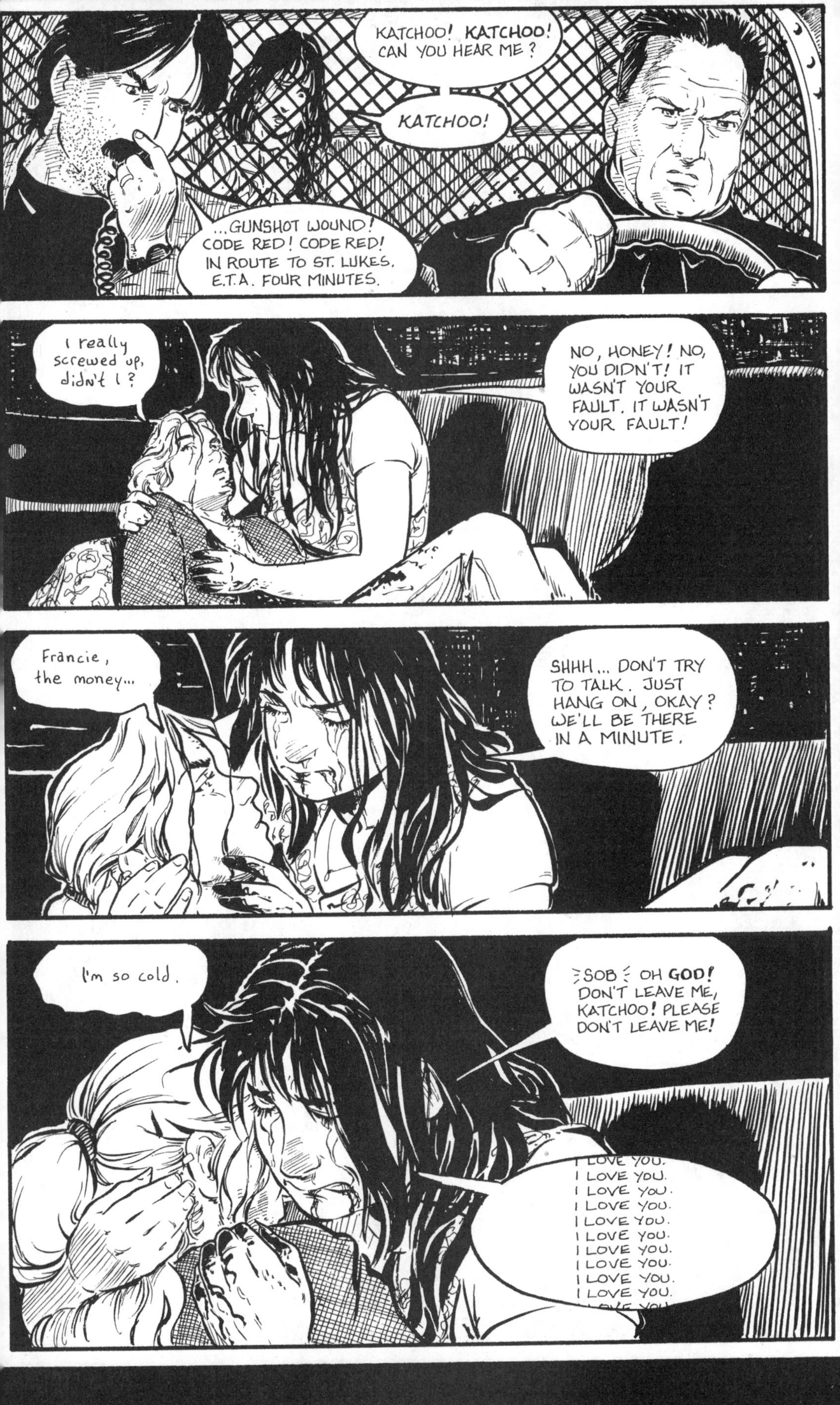
KATCHOO! KATCHOO! CAN YOU HEAR ME?
KATCHOO!
...GUNSHOT WOUND! CODE RED! CODE RED! IN ROUTE TO ST. LUKES. E.T.A. FOUR MINUTES.
I really screwed up, didn't I?
NO, HONEY! NO, YOU DIDN'T! IT WASN'T YOUR FAULT. IT WASN'T YOUR FAULT!
Francie, the money...
SHHH... DON'T TRY TO TALK. JUST HANG ON, OKAY? WE'LL BE THERE IN A MINUTE.
I'm so cold.
SOB OH GOD! DON'T LEAVE ME, KATCHOO! PLEASE DON'T LEAVE ME!
I LOVE YOU.
I LOVE YOU.
I LOVE YOU.
I LOVE YOU.
I LOVE YOU.
I LOVE YOU.
I LOVE YOU.
I LOVE YOU.
I LOVE YOU.
I LOVE YOU.

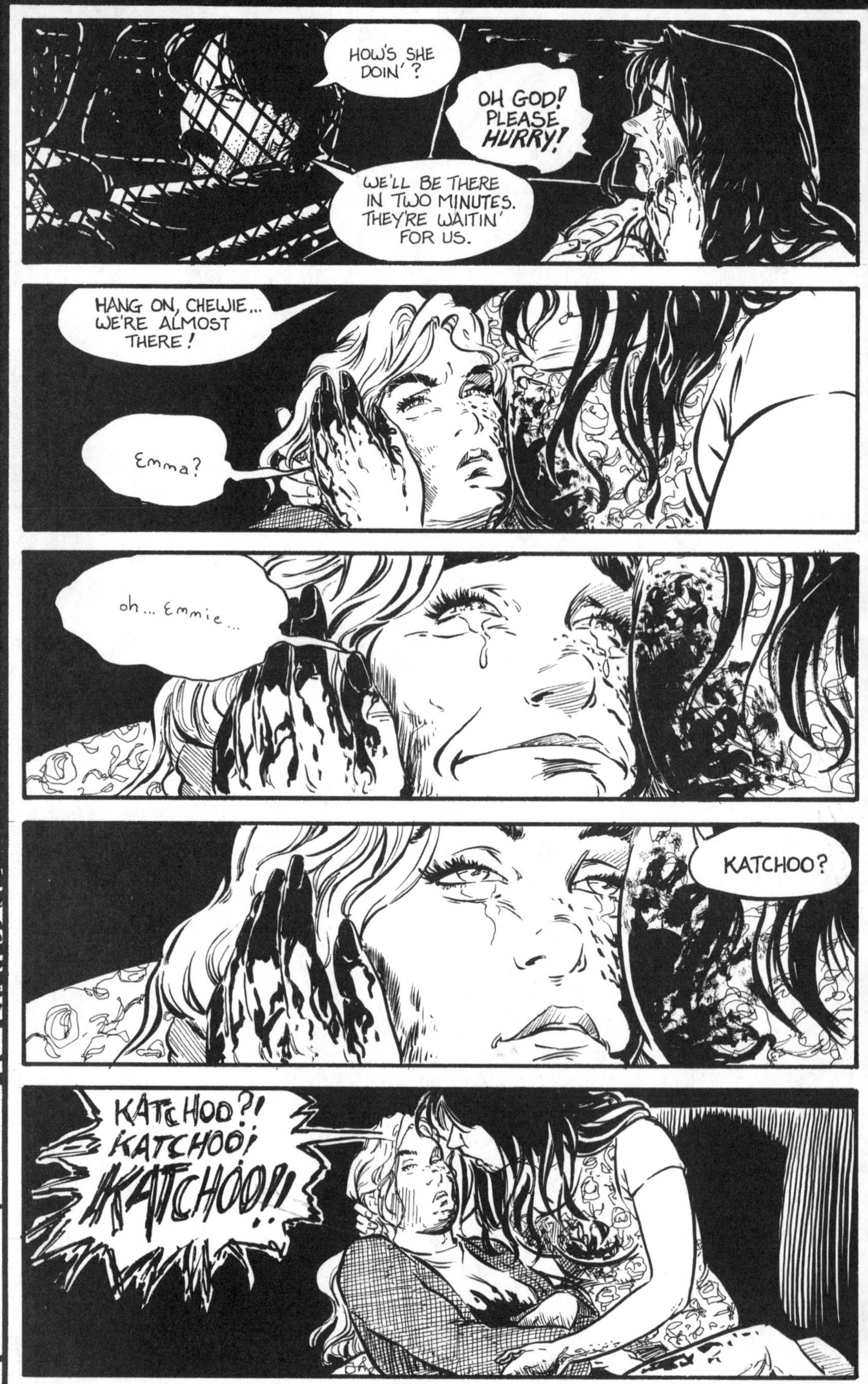
HOW'S SHE DOIN'?
OH GOD! PLEASE HURRY!
WE'LL BE THERE IN TWO MINUTES. THEY'RE WAITIN' FOR US.
HANG ON, CHEWIE... WE'RE ALMOST THERE!
Emma?
oh... Emmie...
KATCHOO?
KATCHOO?! KATCHOO! KATCHOO!!

Somewhere far away, the sky cries
out in thunder.
And there's nothing I can do.
So I wait. And I watch. And
I feel his breath against my face.
Cool and brave.
His salt licks my skin, his promise
brushes my hair.
His fury drives the wind to touch
my cheek,
And whisper something I can't hear.
I think he loves me. I think he
comes to see me.
I am young.
I will learn.

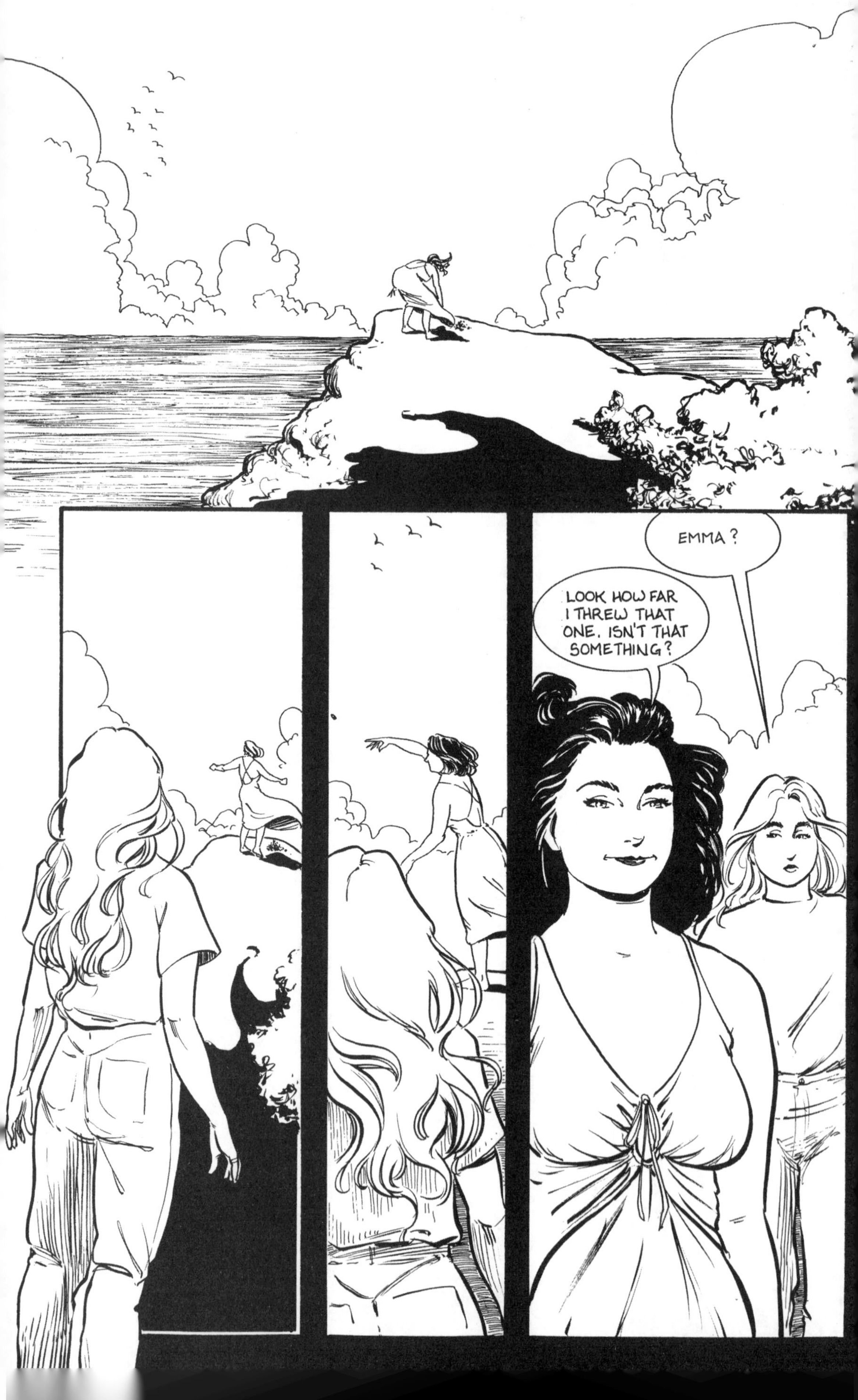
EMMA?
LOOK HOW FAR I THREW THAT ONE. ISN'T THAT SOMETHING?

WHERE ARE WE? HEAVEN?

YEAH. SORT OF. YOU CAN SEE IT FROM HERE.

LOOKS LIKE HANA— LIKE HAWAII.

I KNOW. IT'S BEAUTIFUL, ISN'T IT?

HERE, YOU THROW ONE.

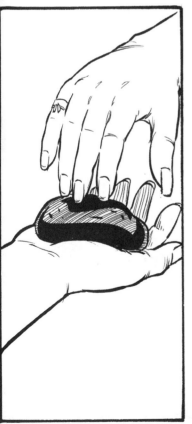

OH, EMMIE,... I MISS YOU SO MUCH.

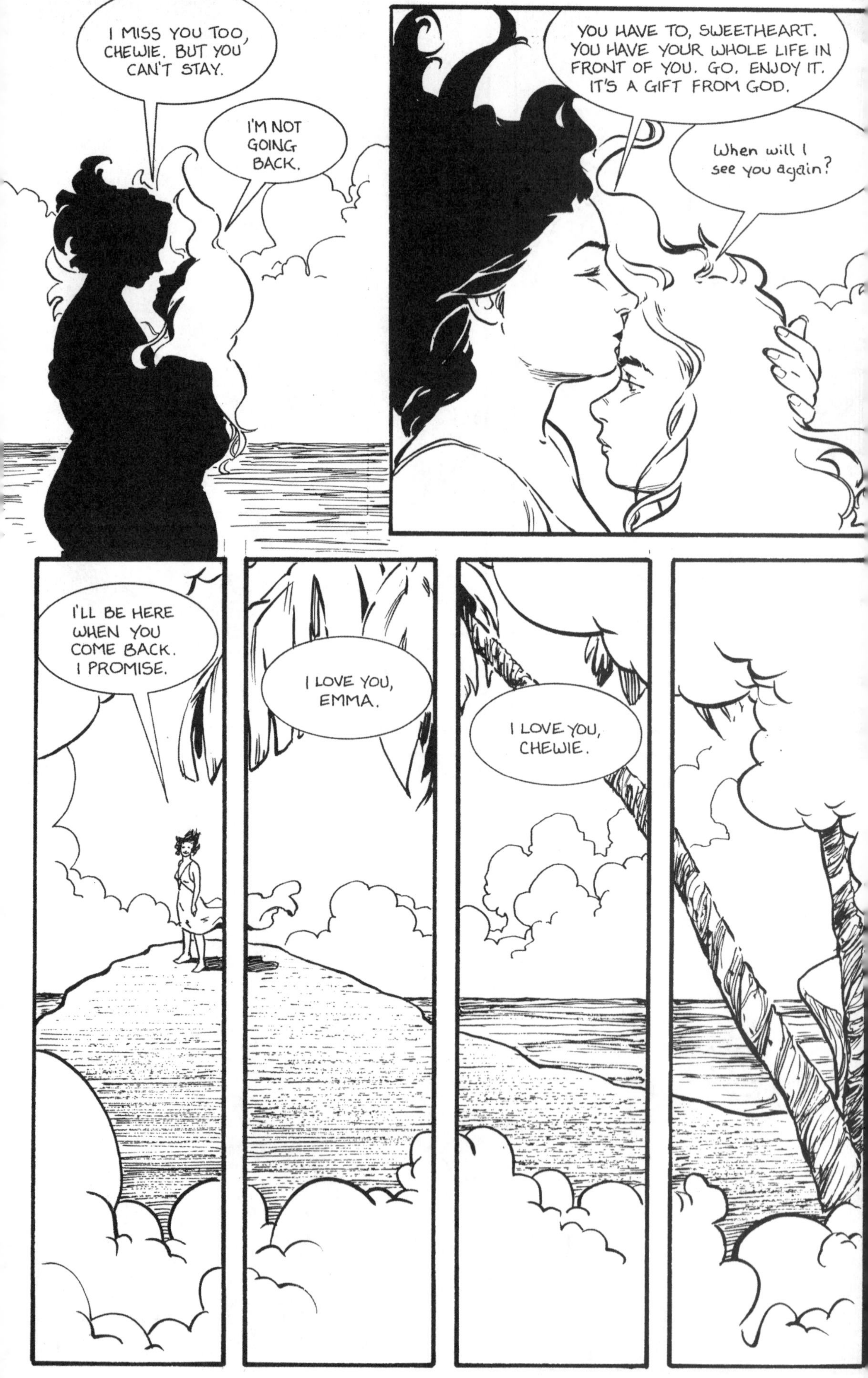
I MISS YOU TOO, CHEWIE. BUT YOU CAN'T STAY.
I'M NOT GOING BACK.
YOU HAVE TO, SWEETHEART. YOU HAVE YOUR WHOLE LIFE IN FRONT OF YOU. GO. ENJOY IT. IT'S A GIFT FROM GOD.
When will I see you again?
I'LL BE HERE WHEN YOU COME BACK. I PROMISE.
I LOVE YOU, EMMA.
I LOVE YOU, CHEWIE.

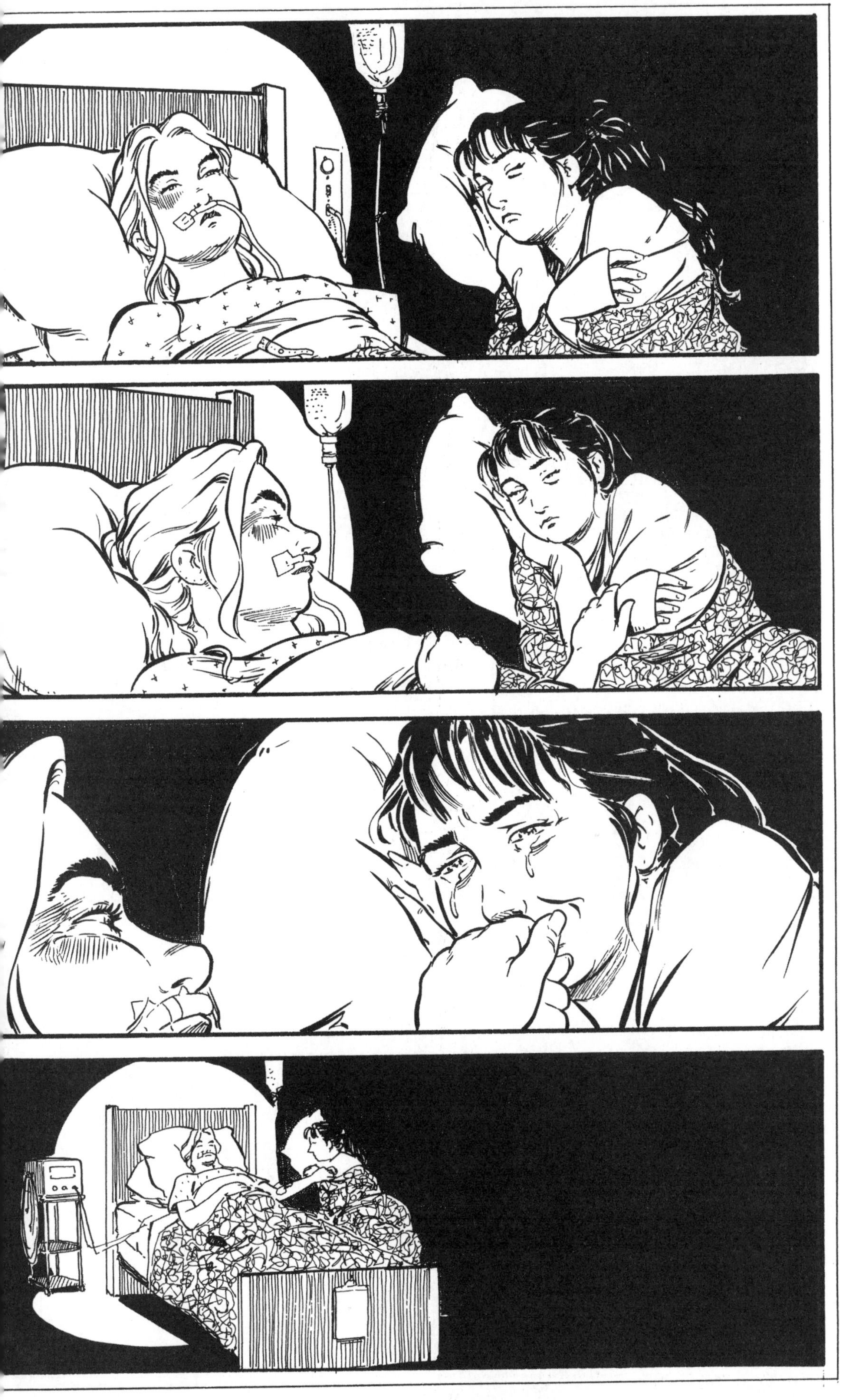

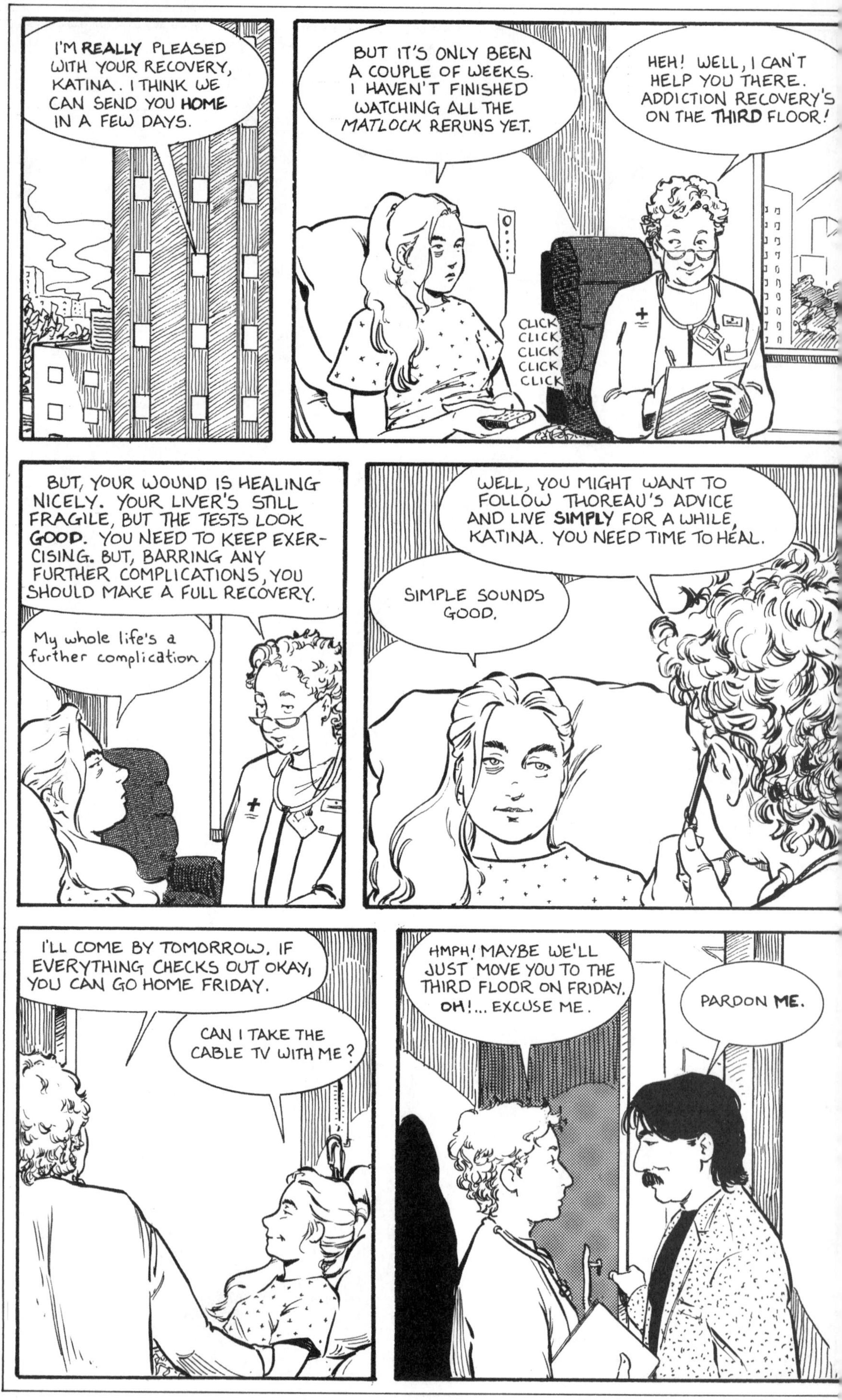
I'M REALLY PLEASED WITH YOUR RECOVERY, KATINA. I THINK WE CAN SEND YOU HOME IN A FEW DAYS.
BUT IT'S ONLY BEEN A COUPLE OF WEEKS. I HAVEN'T FINISHED WATCHING ALL THE MATLOCK RERUNS YET.
HEH! WELL, I CAN'T HELP YOU THERE. ADDICTION RECOVERY'S ON THE THIRD FLOOR!
CLICK CLICK CLICK CLICK CLICK
BUT, YOUR WOUND IS HEALING NICELY. YOUR LIVER'S STILL FRAGILE, BUT THE TESTS LOOK GOOD. YOU NEED TO KEEP EXERCISING. BUT, BARRING ANY FURTHER COMPLICATIONS, YOU SHOULD MAKE A FULL RECOVERY.
My whole life's a further complication.
WELL, YOU MIGHT WANT TO FOLLOW THOREAU'S ADVICE AND LIVE SIMPLY FOR A WHILE, KATINA. YOU NEED TIME TO HEAL.
SIMPLE SOUNDS GOOD.
I'LL COME BY TOMORROW. IF EVERYTHING CHECKS OUT OKAY, YOU CAN GO HOME FRIDAY.
CAN I TAKE THE CABLE TV WITH ME?
HMPH! MAYBE WE'LL JUST MOVE YOU TO THE THIRD FLOOR ON FRIDAY. OH!... EXCUSE ME.
PARDON ME.

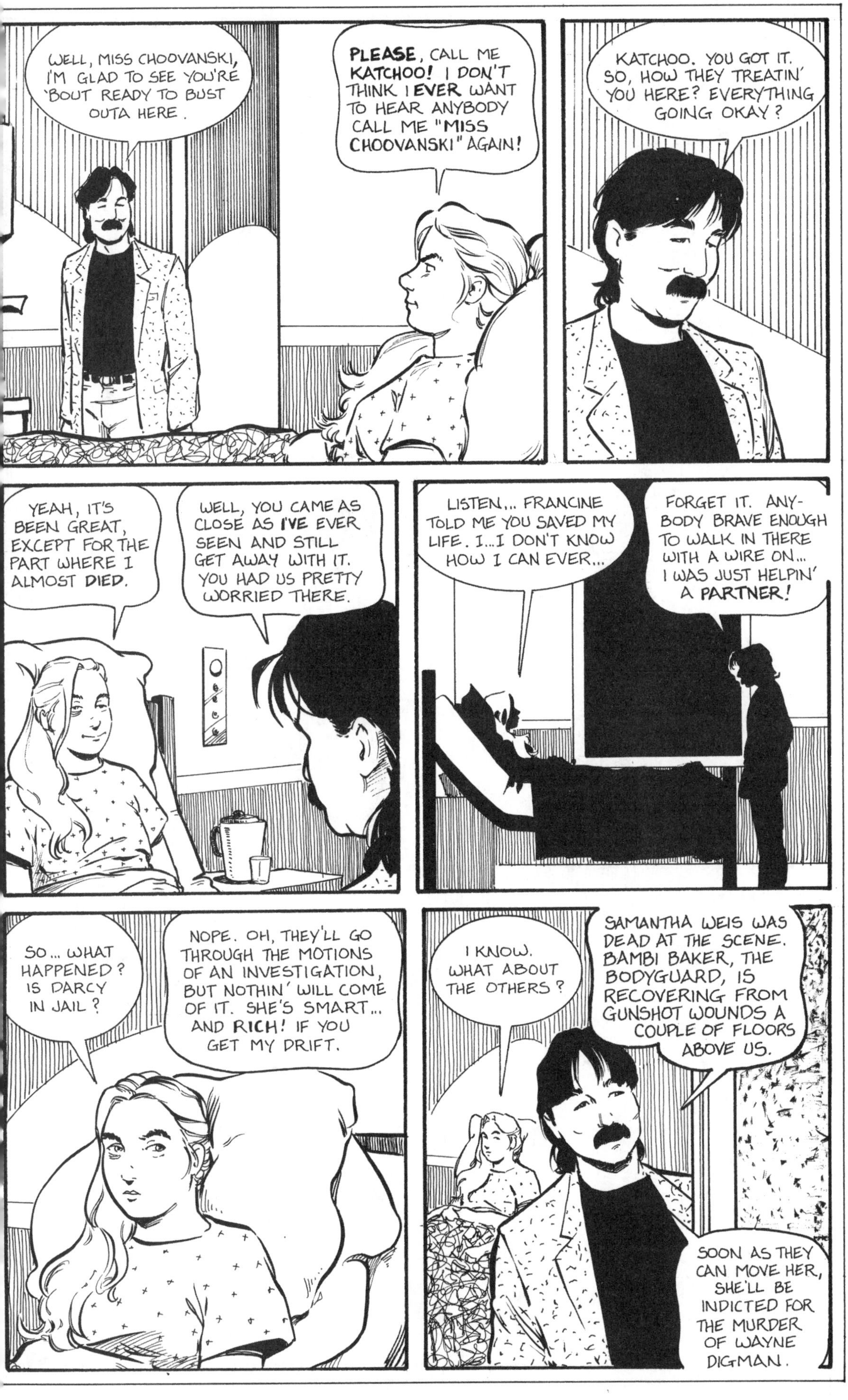

WELL, MISS CHOOVANSKI, I'M GLAD TO SEE YOU'RE 'BOUT READY TO BUST OUTA HERE.
PLEASE, CALL ME KATCHOO! I DON'T THINK I EVER WANT TO HEAR ANYBODY CALL ME "MISS CHOOVANSKI" AGAIN!
KATCHOO. YOU GOT IT. SO, HOW THEY TREATIN' YOU HERE? EVERYTHING GOING OKAY?
YEAH, IT'S BEEN GREAT, EXCEPT FOR THE PART WHERE I ALMOST DIED.
WELL, YOU CAME AS CLOSE AS I'VE EVER SEEN AND STILL GET AWAY WITH IT. YOU HAD US PRETTY WORRIED THERE.
LISTEN... FRANCINE TOLD ME YOU SAVED MY LIFE. I...I DON'T KNOW HOW I CAN EVER...
FORGET IT. ANYBODY BRAVE ENOUGH TO WALK IN THERE WITH A WIRE ON... I WAS JUST HELPIN' A PARTNER!
SO... WHAT HAPPENED? IS DARCY IN JAIL?
NOPE. OH, THEY'LL GO THROUGH THE MOTIONS OF AN INVESTIGATION, BUT NOTHIN' WILL COME OF IT. SHE'S SMART... AND RICH! IF YOU GET MY DRIFT.
I KNOW. WHAT ABOUT THE OTHERS?
SAMANTHA WEIS WAS DEAD AT THE SCENE. BAMBI BAKER, THE BODYGUARD, IS RECOVERING FROM GUNSHOT WOUNDS A COUPLE OF FLOORS ABOVE US.
SOON AS THEY CAN MOVE HER, SHE'LL BE INDICTED FOR THE MURDER OF WAYNE DIGMAN.

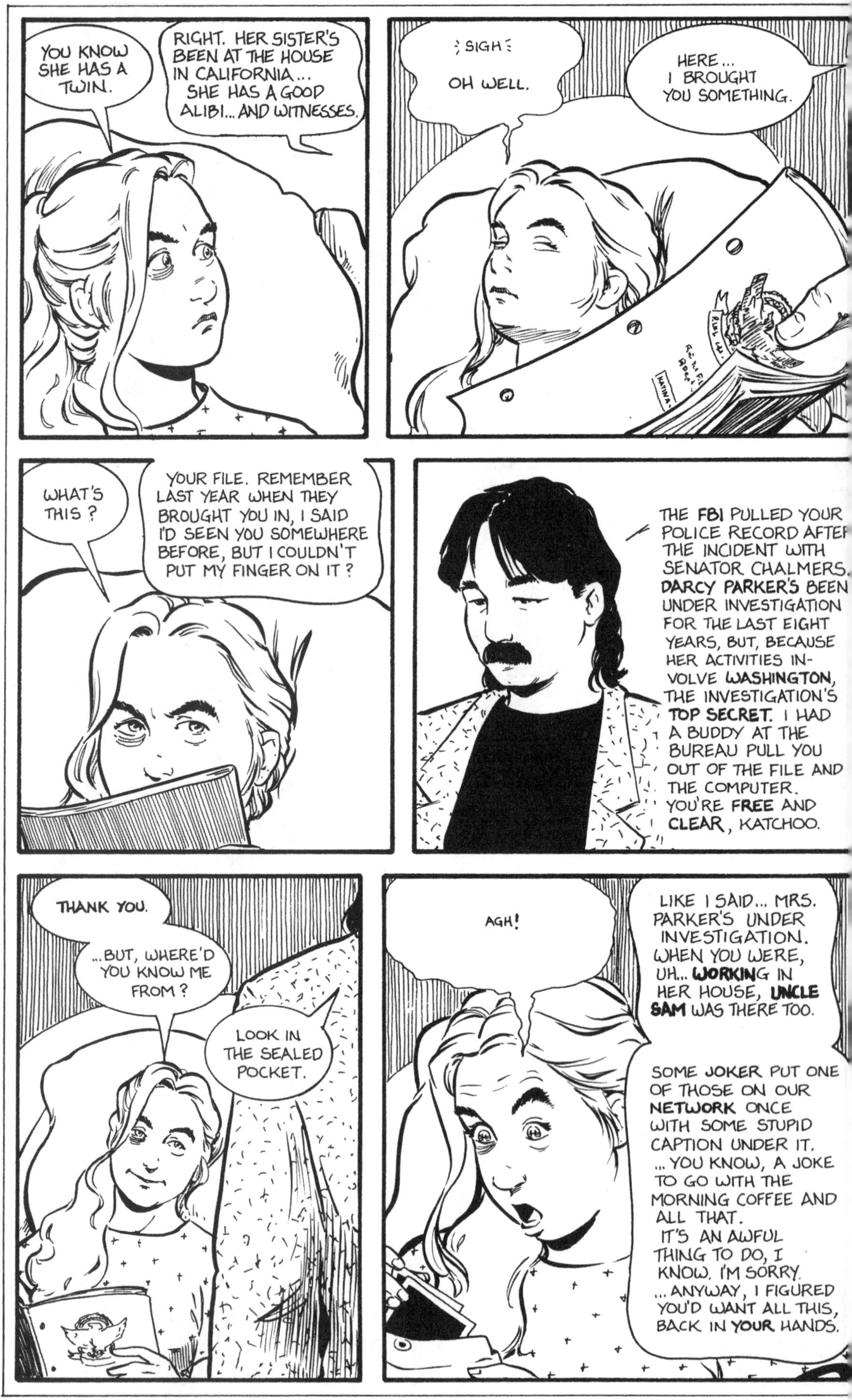

YOU KNOW SHE HAS A TWIN.
RIGHT. HER SISTER'S BEEN AT THE HOUSE IN CALIFORNIA... SHE HAS A GOOD ALIBI... AND WITNESSES.
SIGH
OH WELL.
HERE... I BROUGHT YOU SOMETHING.
WHAT'S THIS ?
YOUR FILE. REMEMBER LAST YEAR WHEN THEY BROUGHT YOU IN, I SAID I'D SEEN YOU SOMEWHERE BEFORE, BUT I COULDN'T PUT MY FINGER ON IT ?
THE FBI PULLED YOUR POLICE RECORD AFTER THE INCIDENT WITH SENATOR CHALMERS. DARCY PARKER'S BEEN UNDER INVESTIGATION FOR THE LAST EIGHT YEARS, BUT, BECAUSE HER ACTIVITIES INVOLVE WASHINGTON, THE INVESTIGATION'S TOP SECRET. I HAD A BUDDY AT THE BUREAU PULL YOU OUT OF THE FILE AND THE COMPUTER. YOU'RE FREE AND CLEAR, KATCHOO.
THANK YOU.
...BUT, WHERE'D YOU KNOW ME FROM ?
LOOK IN THE SEALED POCKET.
AGH!
LIKE I SAID... MRS. PARKER'S UNDER INVESTIGATION. WHEN YOU WERE, UH... WORKING IN HER HOUSE, UNCLE SAM WAS THERE TOO.
SOME JOKER PUT ONE OF THOSE ON OUR NETWORK ONCE WITH SOME STUPID CAPTION UNDER IT. ... YOU KNOW, A JOKE TO GO WITH THE MORNING COFFEE AND ALL THAT. IT'S AN AWFUL THING TO DO, I KNOW. I'M SORRY. ... ANYWAY, I FIGURED YOU'D WANT ALL THIS, BACK IN YOUR HANDS.

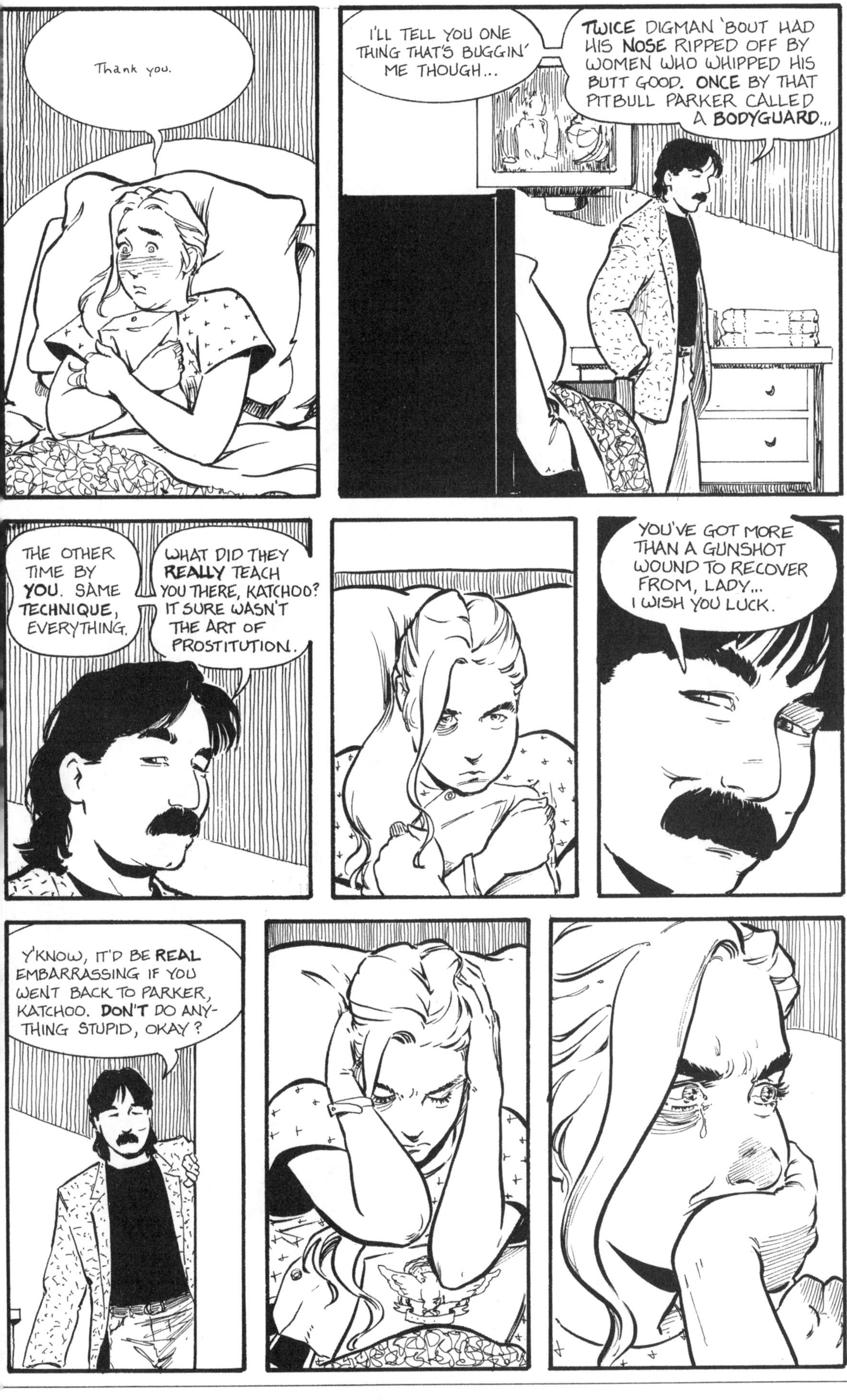

Thank you.
I'LL TELL YOU ONE THING THAT'S BUGGIN' ME THOUGH...
TWICE DIGMAN 'BOUT HAD HIS NOSE RIPPED OFF BY WOMEN WHO WHIPPED HIS BUTT GOOD. ONCE BY THAT PITBULL PARKER CALLED A BODYGUARD...
THE OTHER TIME BY YOU. SAME TECHNIQUE, EVERYTHING.
WHAT DID THEY REALLY TEACH YOU THERE, KATCHOO? IT SURE WASN'T THE ART OF PROSTITUTION.
YOU'VE GOT MORE THAN A GUNSHOT WOUND TO RECOVER FROM, LADY... I WISH YOU LUCK.
Y'KNOW, IT'D BE REAL EMBARRASSING IF YOU WENT BACK TO PARKER, KATCHOO. DON'T DO ANYTHING STUPID, OKAY?

Freddie Femurs nursed the imported beer from the bottle he kept propped to his mouth and watched the blonde waitress who never responded to his smile talk warmly with a table nearby.

"So, you're really gonna go through with it, huh?" said Chuck. It was the first thing that crossed his mind. The silence was awkward for him and he felt compelled to say something.

"Go through with what?" Freddie replied. He watched the blonde closely, searching for clues.

"The wedding. You and Casey. You're finally going to tie the knot, huh? You must be getting pretty excited."

Freddie looked at Chuck as if he'd just peed on himself. He was beginning to wonder why he continued to meet Chuck here every Friday afternoon for a beer. When they had worked together at McNeil and Lambart's it had been to Freddie's advantage to strike up a friendship with Chuck, who held the enviable position of personnel advisor to McNeil himself. Now that Freddie had left the firm to strike out on his own, Chuck was just a pain in the butt, but still of some use as an inside man. Freddie reminded himself of this as he forced a tight smile. "Oh....yeah. I suppose," he replied.

"Listen to you," Chuck laughed, "Mr. Cool. You're marrying Casey Jansen, man! You're going to Hawaii to marry the hottest aerobics instructor in town! All I've got to say is you better be in shape. Know what I mean?"

"It's not like you think. Casey's a great girl and all that, but...it's not like you think."

"What do you mean?"

Freddie finished off the rest of his beer and set the bottle by the edge of the table. The callous blonde waitress glided by and picked up the bottle on the run, disappearing into the crowd. The image of her blue jeaned bottom burned in Freddie's brain for several moments after she left.

Freddie turned to Chuck and leaned forward in confidence, "Can you keep a secret?" he whispered, " I mean, you have to swear to me this will go no further."

Chuck wiped his mouth with the back of his hand and leaned forward to tent the table in secrecy. "I'm here for you, buddy," he said.

"We were at her mother's last weekend and she shows me pictures of Casey when she was in high school. I didn't even recognize her! Turns out she's had two nose jobs! She's had her chin done, her lips puffed..."

"Puffed?" Chuck frowned.

"Puffed. I mean it's bad enough she's got these implants I'm not allowed to squeeze or lay on, now I'm wondering what's going to happen to her face if she gets too close to a microwave, you know?"

"Hey, I never thought of that," Chuck nodded solemnly.

Chuck wiped his mouth with the back of his hand and leaned forward to tent the table in secrecy, "I'm here for you, buddy."

"Then Casey gets all upset because her mother shows me these pictures and I have to lie to her and tell her it doesn't matter, but inside I'm thinking, "Geez, who the hell are you, really?"

Freddie glared his point home to Chuck for several moments, awaiting his reaction.

Chuck leaned back and shook his head, "Oh man."

The ice queen brought Freddie another beer, and for once he didn't acknowledge her. The thought crossed his mind she might notice this and it would bother her the rest of the night. That would be a good thing.

Chuck and Freddie slumped over their beers in wrinkled business suits and loosened ties, listening to the music and the din of the growing happy hour crowd. Freddie evaluated every woman in the bar on a desert island basis. Chuck pretended to contemplate his friends dilemma while watching ESPN on the television set reflected in the mirror behind him. When they broke to commercial, Chuck sniffed, sat up straight and ordered another beer. He smiled hopefully at his companion and attempted to turn the mood, "Aw, it'll work out, buddy. Casey's a sweet girl. You two look good together."

Freddie smirked as he stuffed a palm full of nuts into his mouth, "Yeah. We *look* good alright."

Chuck tried harder, "Better than when you were with Francine. She was too tall for you."

Freddie smiled for the first time. "Francine. Yeah." he said, " She was like, 5, 9... 5, 10 something... 6 feet in heels."

"Big girl."

"And getting bigger. Casey and I ran into her at the grocery store about a month ago, and man, she was fat! She's put on thirty pounds. Why do women let themselves go like that?" Freddie shook his head.

"Francine's pretty though."

"When she wants to be. She can be a real slob, too."

"Yeah, but that can be cool too, sometimes, you know?" Chuck interjected, "I mean, she wasn't real uptight about her appearance all the time, like some women."

"You mean like Casey," Freddie frowned.

"Oh no, no! I didn't mean..."

"And how come you know so much about Francine, huh?" Freddie scowled.

Chuck shifted uneasily in his seat, "Well, I wasn't going to say anything, but I guess I can tell you now that you're getting married. I mean, it's all in the past now, right?"

"What's in the past?"

"Francine. And me. We... we were together for awhile. You know, your basic summer romance type thing," Chuck laughed nervously.

Freddie evaluated every woman in the bar on a desert island basis.

"Even when we went out she would, like... grab me, at the most inappropriate times. It was like a game she played."

"What? When was this?" Freddie snapped bac[k]

"Before you knew her, I don't know, two... thr[ee] years ago."

"You never told me this."

"Well, I didn't want to piss you off, you know? Once you guys got together, I figured I'd just kee[p] my mouth shut."

"Mm hmm," Freddie murmured as he pulled a long, slow drink from his bottle. "What do you mean you were... 'together'?"

"I mean we were a couple, man. We practical[ly] lived together."

"Serious?"

"Depends on what you mean by serious. If you go by intensity, then yeah, it was serious. It was intense, man. Francine was intense. I thought she was going to kill me sometimes."

"What do you mean?" Freddie perked up, ready to hear another man's troubles with the woman who had eluded him.

"Oh, Francine's a sweet girl and all, you know, real laid back and kind of ditzy. But the sex... the sex was incredible! I mean, it's like she couldn't get enough, you know? After we broke up I realized she had some emotional problems, real insecure. But at the time... man, it was fun! We did it all the time, every night. Even when we went out she would, like... grab me, at the most inappropriate times. It was like a game she played. I'd be dying and she thought it was funny!"

"FRANCINE?!" Freddie exclaimed in disbelief.

"Yeah! One time I took her to Cancun for the weekend and she bought this little string bikini especially for the trip.... I thought I was going to have a stroke! I was a drooling idiot the whole tim[e] we were there. I took lots of pictures!" Chuck laughed. "I loved that bikini so much she gave it t[o] me on the plane ride home. I still have it. Man! Sh[e] was hot."

"Alright, I get the point! Francine was hot." Freddie groaned.

"She wasn't just hot, man, she was *hot to trot!*"

"I said I get the point, okay? Can we drop it?"

Chuck rocked his bottle slowly back and forth upon the table, smiling smugly, "Yep, she was ooooooone hot patootie!"

"Hey! I said SHUT UP!"

Chuck watched the vein on Freddie's forehead pulse and pound. "I'm sorry, you still care for her, don't you?" he said, regretting his confession. "I shouldn't be telling you this. Besides, you were with her too. You don't need to hear my version of what it's like to be with Francine. I'm sure it was the same for you."

Freddie's stomach turned sour. That was just the point, it hadn't been like that at all between him and Francine.

In the entire year they were together, she had never slept with him. She refused to.

Freddie winced as the memory of Francine overwhelmed him. Whether Freddie wanted to admit it or not, he missed her. He missed her slow, southern drawl and the way she used to look at him when they danced. He missed those big brown eyes, the squeezable breasts and pouting belly. He missed the soft, red lips that had never criticised him.

Nobody else felt like Francine. Nobody else smelled like her. She used to laugh and say it was the baby powder, but Freddie knew it was more than that. He didn't know the word for it, but there was something special about Francine. It radiated from her like body heat. It warmed her breath and flushed her cheeks and hung on every word she said. It swelled her breasts, it tilted her hips, it filled her thighs and moved her around him in slow motion. It sparkled in her eyes when he handed her an ice cream cone and chuckled deeply in the back of her throat when she laughed at his jokes.

God help him, it drove him crazy.

Freddie had wanted Francine more than he wanted anyone or anything in his life. She said she loved him too, but... nothing happened. He invested a year of his life trying to win her confidence, trying to reassure her. Trying to make her. The harder he tried the more she resisted. It became an obsession with him, a challenge to every fiber of his manhood.

Nothing.

Despite her protests and chaste demeanour, Francine drove him to despair seducing him with her desperate struggle to restrain herself, to quiet the sensuous woman within. A woman that screamed to Freddie like a third voice in the arguments and mumbled like a forgotten widow during their conversations. Like a siren on the rocks, the woman within Francine called to Freddie, and her unspoken message was clear, "You've never been with anybody like me."

Freddie knew it was the truth. It drove him insane with desire, and in the end, it drove him away.

She refused to sleep with him. She said every man left her once she gave herself to him. Freddie was different, she said. She loved him, she didn't want to lose him. So she hid her desires from him. He was denied.

This tormented Freddie. Francine was a riddle he could not solve. Any man could have her but the one she loved? Any man but him?

As time went on, Freddie found himself increasingly abusive with Francine, angrily attempting to get what he wanted by losing his special status.

Needless to say, it ended badly.

Her unspoken message was clear, "You've never been with anybody like me."

"She met you."

Frustrated with his dilemma, Freddie had begun an affair with Barbara, an administrative assistant in his office. Francine caught them making love in his office one rainy afternoon in November. She burst through the door wearing nothing but a coat and satin underwear.

She'd come to surrender.

The next day they met in the park. Freddie told Francine it was over between them, despite her pleas and promises that she would do anything to keep them together. Later those words haunted him; the lost opportunity intoxicating. If he'd kept his head, he could have taken her at her word and ended up with what he'd wanted all along. But at the time he wanted only to deny her a happy ending, to punish her for his year of frustration. If she'd wanted to break up with him, he would have begged her to stay. Since she wanted him back, he left her.

In retrospect, Freddie cursed himself for not taking advantage of the situation. He'd finally broken Francine's spirit. He could have had everything his way from that moment on. That would have been a good thing, wouldn't it?

A few months later, Freddie met Casey, the kind of girl he understood and was comfortable with. He thought marrying Casey would make him forget Francine. He was wrong. It only made him realize how much he missed her...

"If it makes you feel any better, it got real old," Chuck muttered.

...and this clod across the table wasn't helping matters one bit.

"She was kind of suffocating, you know? She was so insecure, so..." Chuck searched for the proper word, "...dependent. She needed a lot of love, the kind where you're together every minute of your lives. After awhile I saw that's what it was really about and it scared me."

Chuck's face fell and his eyes stayed fixed on a peanut he worried back and forth across his napkin. "But, to tell you the truth, Freddie, I think I did fall in love with her," he mumbled, "I mean, sure, she had problems, but who doesn't, you know? Maybe if I'd had the chance to tell her that..."

Freddie swallowed his anger and took several deep breaths to compose himself. Information was better than warfare.

"So," he smiled grimly, "what happened? If you loved her, why'd you break up? Why'd you dump her?"

Chuck looked up at Freddie with tears in his eyes, "I didn't. She left me."

"Why?"

"She met you."

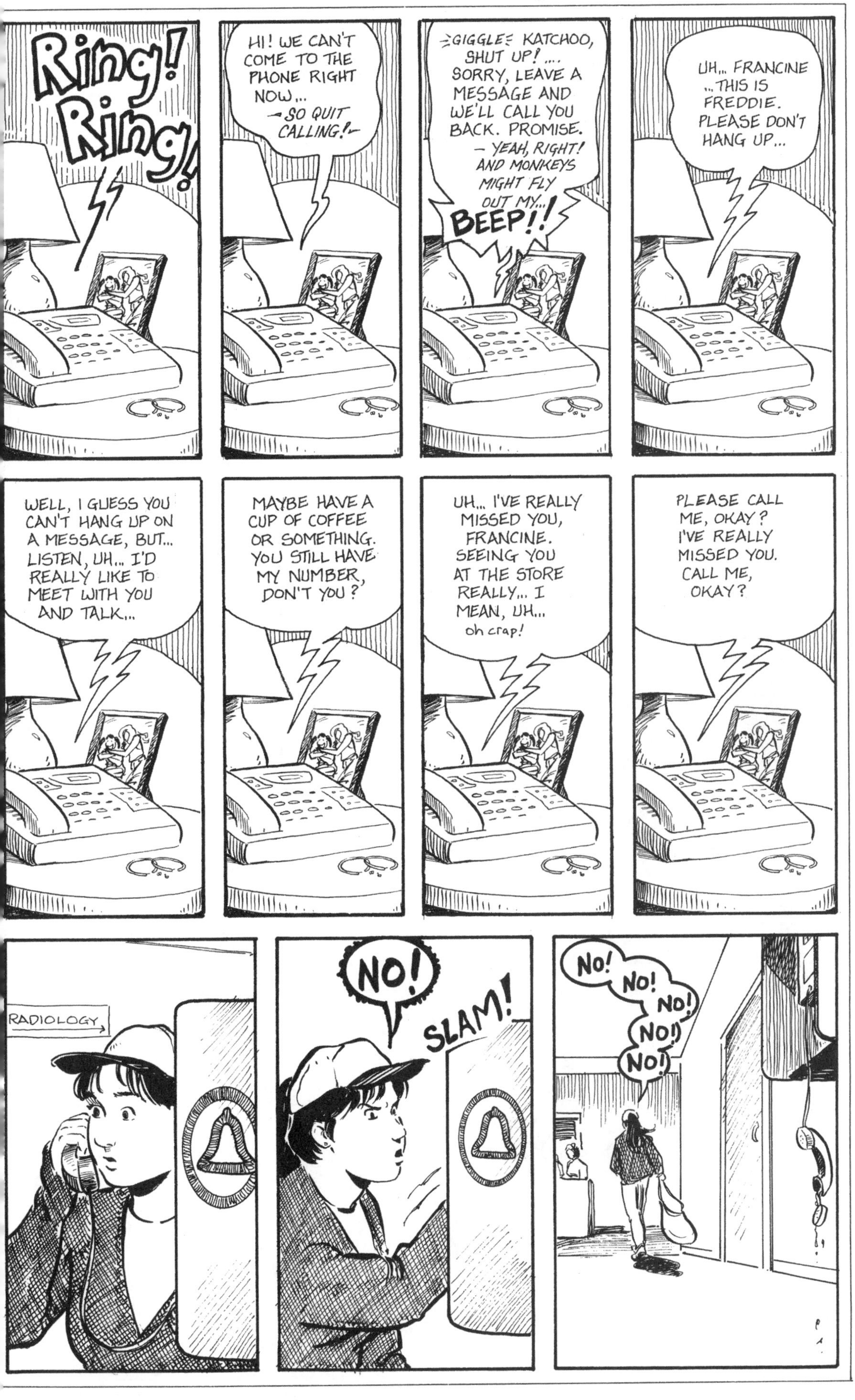
Ring! Ring!
HI! WE CAN'T COME TO THE PHONE RIGHT NOW... —SO QUIT CALLING!—
=GIGGLE= KATCHOO, SHUT UP!.... SORRY, LEAVE A MESSAGE AND WE'LL CALL YOU BACK. PROMISE. —YEAH, RIGHT! AND MONKEYS MIGHT FLY OUT MY...
BEEP!!
UH... FRANCINE ...THIS IS FREDDIE. PLEASE DON'T HANG UP...
WELL, I GUESS YOU CAN'T HANG UP ON A MESSAGE, BUT... LISTEN, UH... I'D REALLY LIKE TO MEET WITH YOU AND TALK...
MAYBE HAVE A CUP OF COFFEE OR SOMETHING. YOU STILL HAVE MY NUMBER, DON'T YOU?
UH... I'VE REALLY MISSED YOU, FRANCINE. SEEING YOU AT THE STORE REALLY... I MEAN, UH... oh crap!
PLEASE CALL ME, OKAY? I'VE REALLY MISSED YOU. CALL ME, OKAY?
RADIOLOGY
NO!
SLAM!
No! No! No! No! No!

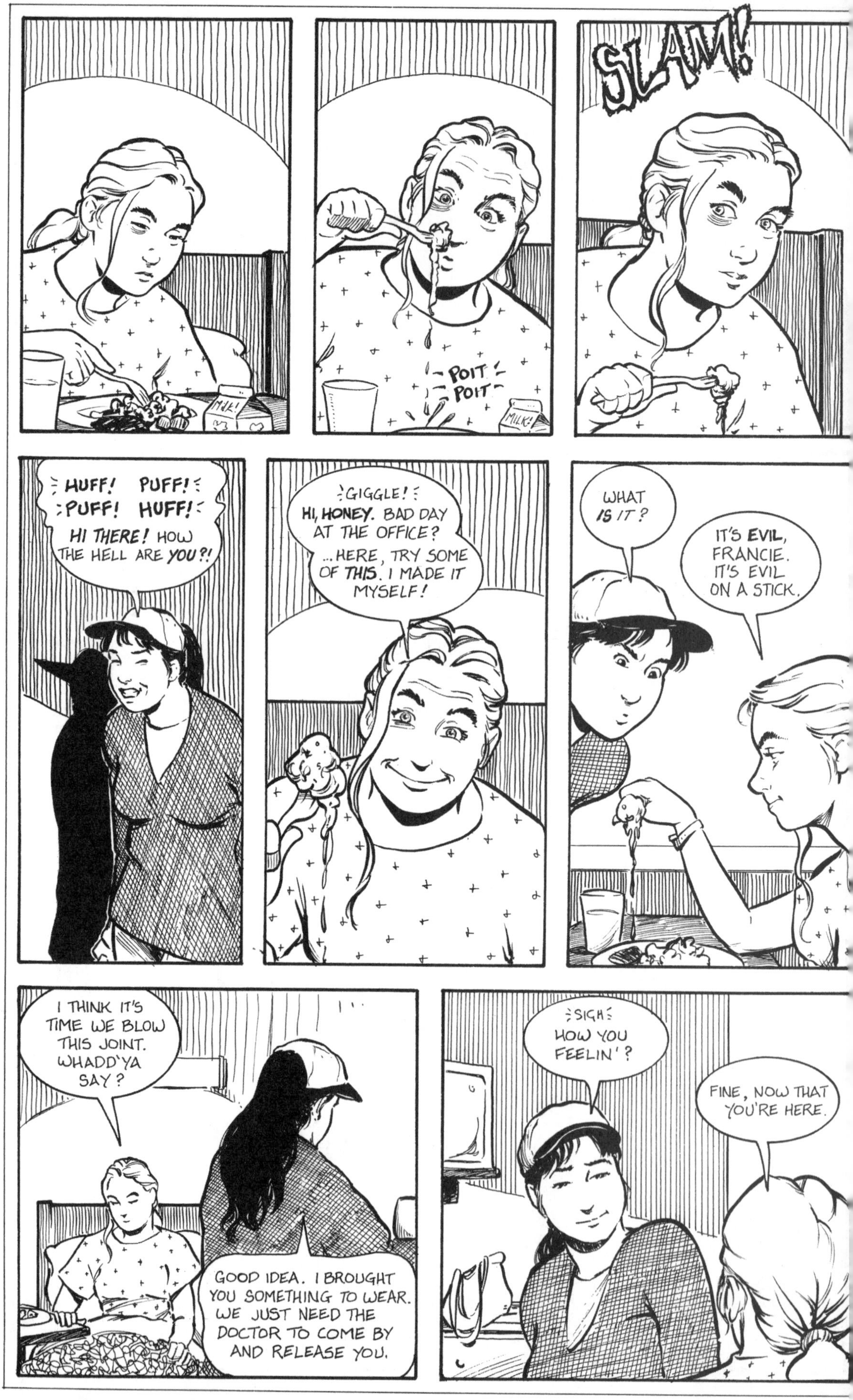
SLAM!
POIT POIT
HUFF! PUFF! PUFF! HUFF!
HI THERE! HOW THE HELL ARE YOU?!
GIGGLE!
HI, HONEY. BAD DAY AT THE OFFICE?
...HERE, TRY SOME OF THIS. I MADE IT MYSELF!
WHAT IS IT?
IT'S EVIL, FRANCIE. IT'S EVIL ON A STICK.
I THINK IT'S TIME WE BLOW THIS JOINT. WHADD'YA SAY?
GOOD IDEA. I BROUGHT YOU SOMETHING TO WEAR. WE JUST NEED THE DOCTOR TO COME BY AND RELEASE YOU.
SIGH
HOW YOU FEELIN'?
FINE, NOW THAT YOU'RE HERE.

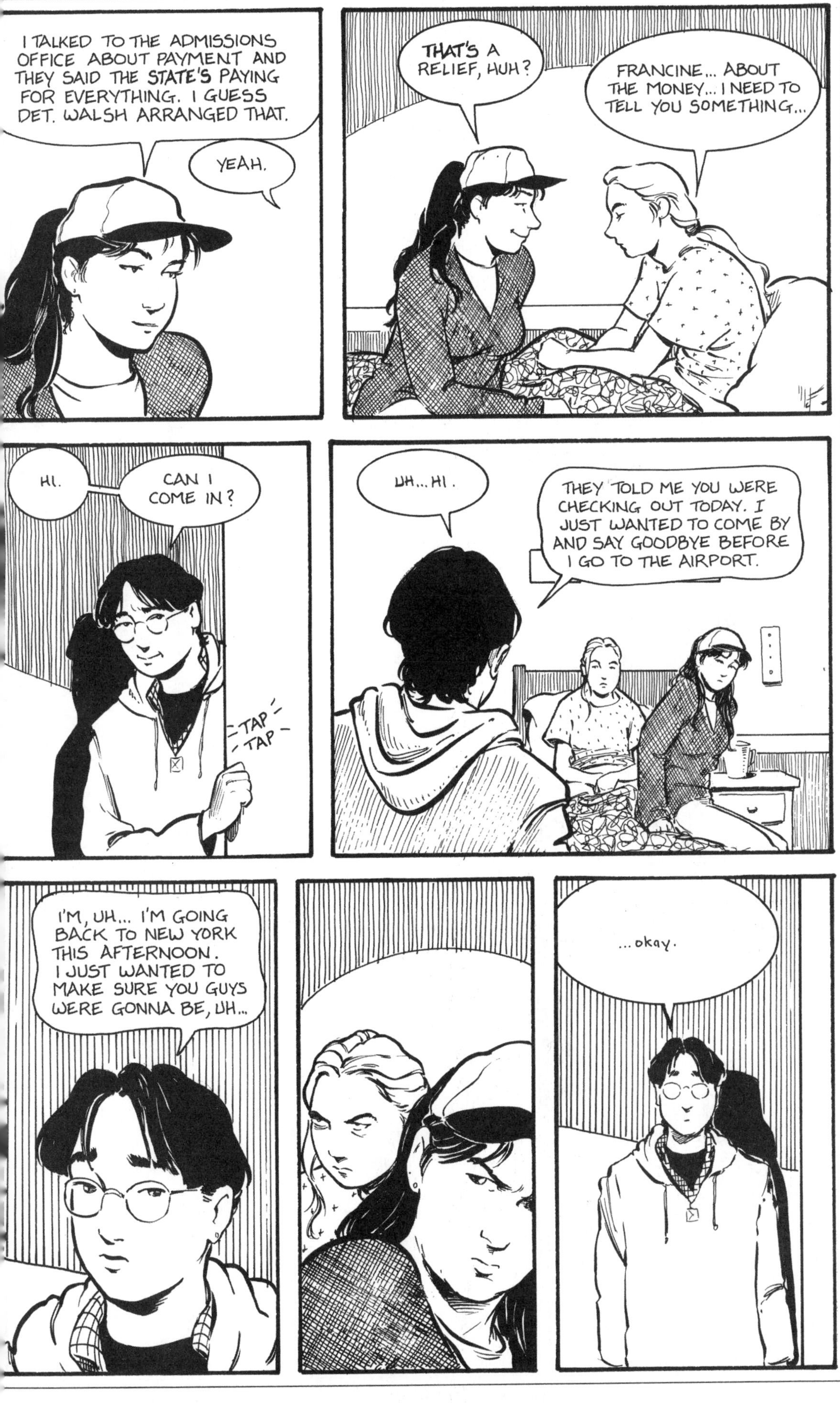
I TALKED TO THE ADMISSIONS OFFICE ABOUT PAYMENT AND THEY SAID THE STATE'S PAYING FOR EVERYTHING. I GUESS DET. WALSH ARRANGED THAT.
YEAH.
THAT'S A RELIEF, HUH?
FRANCINE... ABOUT THE MONEY... I NEED TO TELL YOU SOMETHING...
HI.
CAN I COME IN?
TAP TAP
UH... HI.
THEY TOLD ME YOU WERE CHECKING OUT TODAY. I JUST WANTED TO COME BY AND SAY GOODBYE BEFORE I GO TO THE AIRPORT.
I'M, UH... I'M GOING BACK TO NEW YORK THIS AFTERNOON. I JUST WANTED TO MAKE SURE YOU GUYS WERE GONNA BE, UH...
...okay.

HERE... I GOT YOU SOMETHING. SORT OF A GOOD-BYE PRESENT.

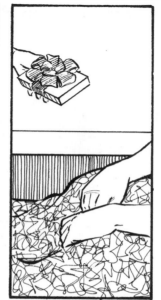

I'LL JUST LEAVE IT HERE.

I JUST WANTED TO SAY I'M SORRY... ABOUT THE WAY THINGS TURNED OUT. I DIDN'T MEAN TO HURT YOU GUYS, BUT I SEE NOW THAT I DID.

YOU TRUSTED ME, AND I KNOW HOW HARD THAT IS FOR YOU BOTH. I JUST COULDN'T BRING MYSELF TO TELL YOU WHO I WAS... AM. I WAS AFRAID YOU'D DO SOMETHING RASH AND END UP GETTING HURT.

HMPH... LIKE YOU WERE SAFE WITH ME.

LOOKS LIKE I REALLY MADE A MESS OF EVERY-THING. >SIGH< I JUST WANT TO SAY I'M SORRY.

TELL YOUR SISTER TO GIVE YOU A RAISE, YOU DID A GREAT JOB. YOU HAD ME FOOLED.

I DON'T WORK FOR DARCY. I'M JUST AN ART STUDENT AT NYU. I CAME HERE BECAUSE SHE ASKED ME TO, AS A FAVOR TO HER. WHEN SHE SHOWED ME YOUR PICTURE, I... >whew<

LOOK, I DON'T UNDER-STAND WHAT'S GOING ON BETWEEN YOU AND DARCY. AND I **DON'T CARE** WHO TOOK THE MONEY. SHE HAS MORE MONEY THAN SHE CAN SPEND ANYWAY.

ALL I KNOW IS I'VE LOST THE BEST FRIEND I EVER HAD.

...AND NO AMOUNT OF MONEY IS WORTH THAT.

; SIGH. ;

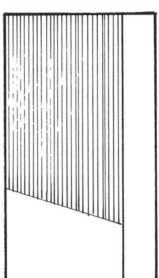

WHAT IS IT?

; SNIFF ;

THAT LOOKS LIKE THE BEACH HOUSE IN YOUR PICTURES OF HAWAII.

IT IS, THAT'S THE HOUSE I STAYED AT WITH EMMA.

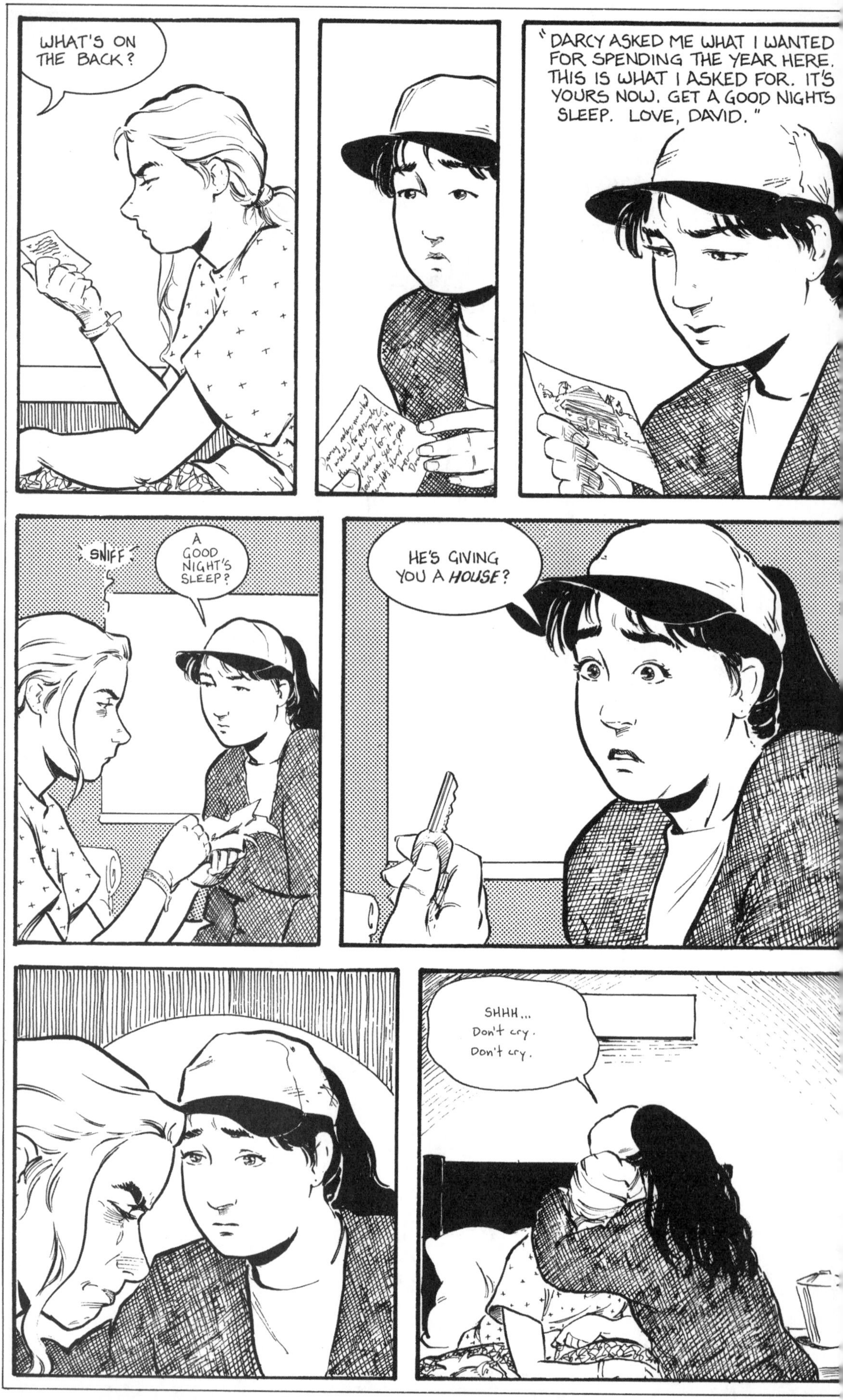
WHAT'S ON THE BACK?
"DARCY ASKED ME WHAT I WANTED FOR SPENDING THE YEAR HERE. THIS IS WHAT I ASKED FOR. IT'S YOURS NOW. GET A GOOD NIGHTS SLEEP. LOVE, DAVID."
SNIFF
A GOOD NIGHT'S SLEEP?
HE'S GIVING YOU A HOUSE?
SHHH... Don't cry. Don't cry.

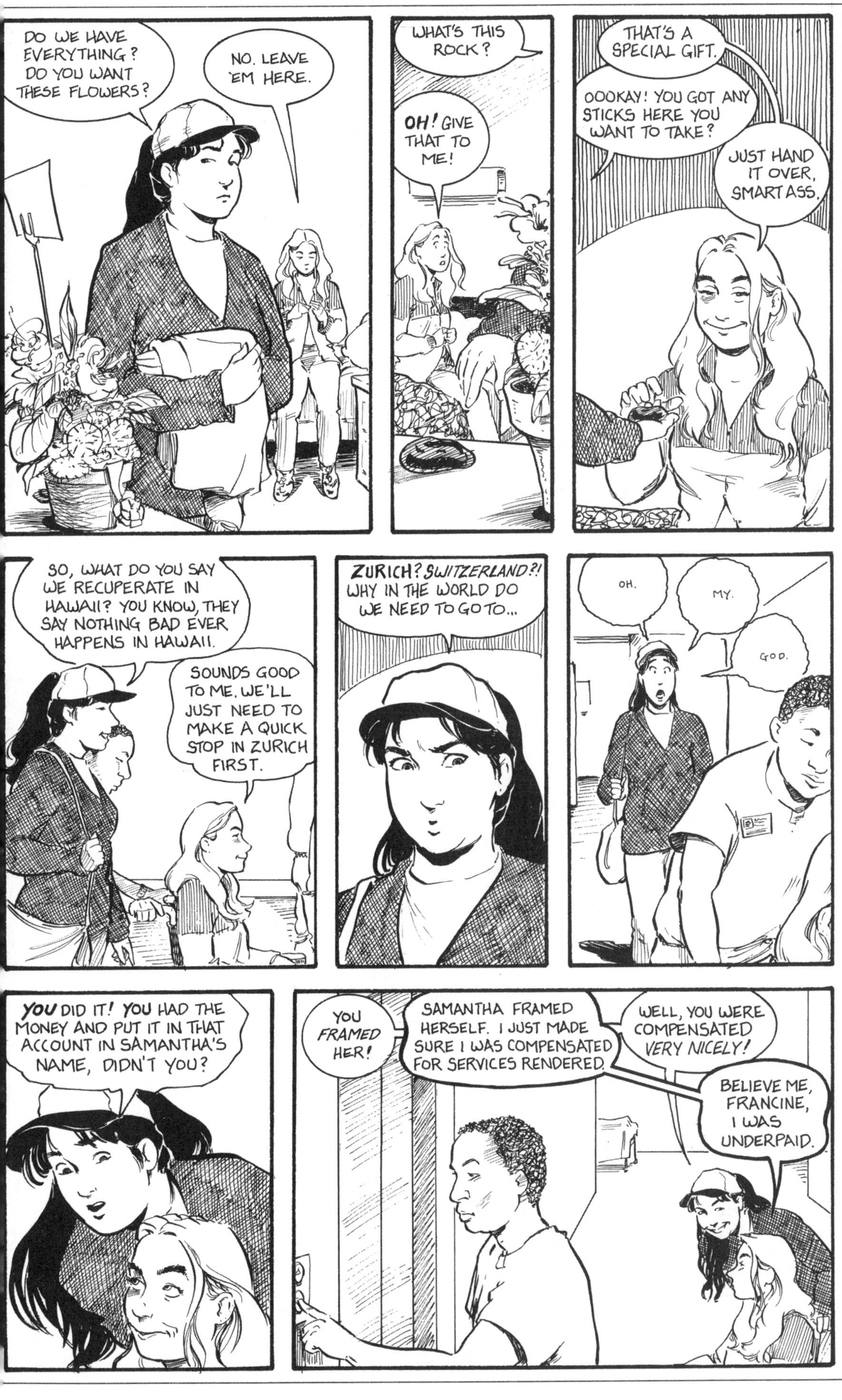
DO WE HAVE EVERYTHING? DO YOU WANT THESE FLOWERS?
NO. LEAVE 'EM HERE.
WHAT'S THIS ROCK?
OH! GIVE THAT TO ME!
THAT'S A SPECIAL GIFT.
OOOKAY! YOU GOT ANY STICKS HERE YOU WANT TO TAKE?
JUST HAND IT OVER, SMARTASS.
SO, WHAT DO YOU SAY WE RECUPERATE IN HAWAII? YOU KNOW, THEY SAY NOTHING BAD EVER HAPPENS IN HAWAII.
SOUNDS GOOD TO ME. WE'LL JUST NEED TO MAKE A QUICK STOP IN ZURICH FIRST.
ZURICH? SWITZERLAND?! WHY IN THE WORLD DO WE NEED TO GO TO...
OH.
MY.
GOD.
YOU DID IT! YOU HAD THE MONEY AND PUT IT IN THAT ACCOUNT IN SAMANTHA'S NAME, DIDN'T YOU?
YOU FRAMED HER!
SAMANTHA FRAMED HERSELF. I JUST MADE SURE I WAS COMPENSATED FOR SERVICES RENDERED.
WELL, YOU WERE COMPENSATED VERY NICELY!
BELIEVE ME, FRANCINE, I WAS UNDERPAID.

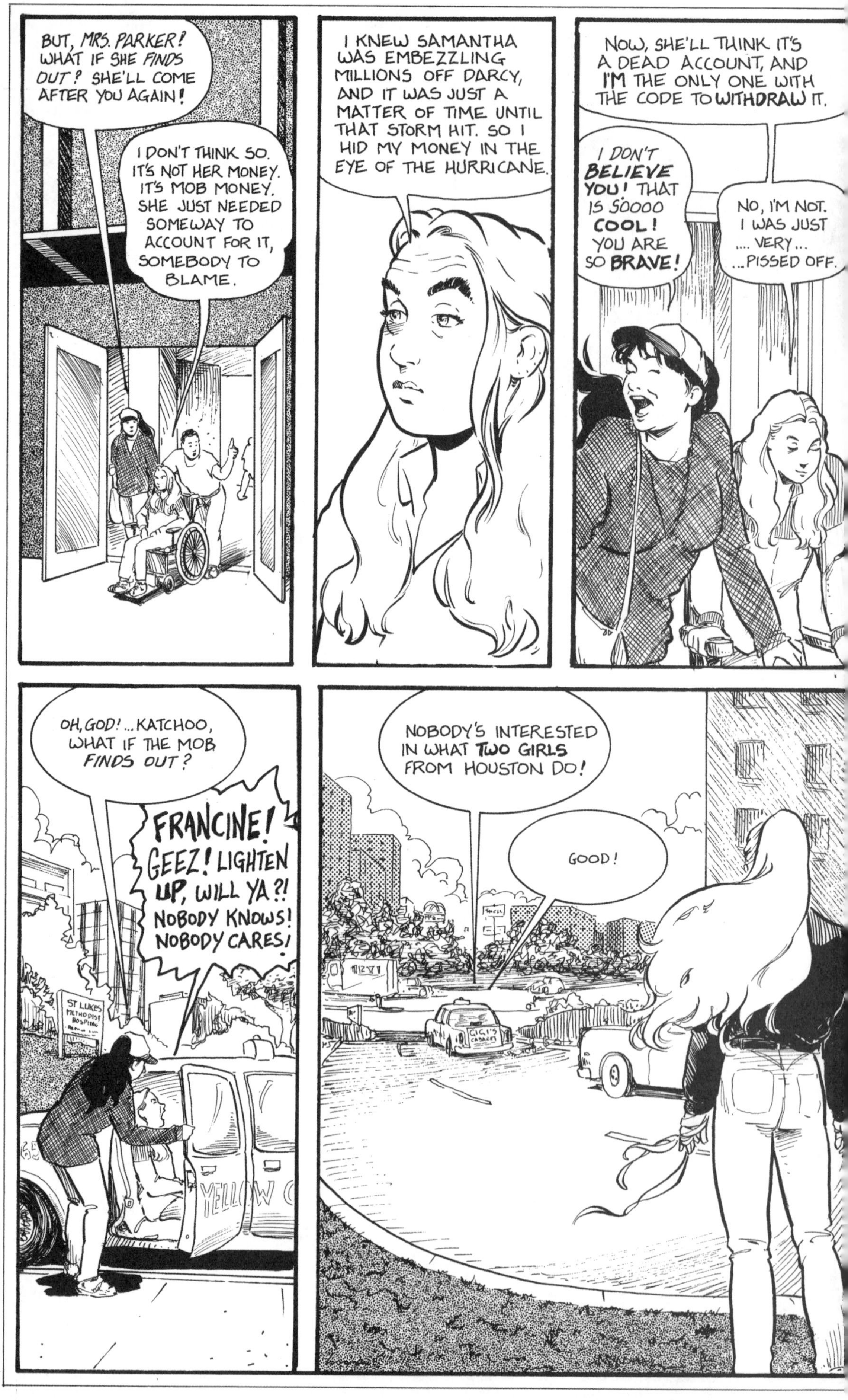

BUT, MRS. PARKER? WHAT IF SHE FINDS OUT? SHE'LL COME AFTER YOU AGAIN!
I DON'T THINK SO. IT'S NOT HER MONEY. IT'S MOB MONEY. SHE JUST NEEDED SOMEWAY TO ACCOUNT FOR IT, SOMEBODY TO BLAME.
I KNEW SAMANTHA WAS EMBEZZLING MILLIONS OFF DARCY, AND IT WAS JUST A MATTER OF TIME UNTIL THAT STORM HIT. SO I HID MY MONEY IN THE EYE OF THE HURRICANE.
NOW, SHE'LL THINK IT'S A DEAD ACCOUNT, AND I'M THE ONLY ONE WITH THE CODE TO WITHDRAW IT.
I DON'T BELIEVE YOU! THAT IS SOOOO COOL! YOU ARE SO BRAVE!
NO, I'M NOT. I WAS JUST .... VERY... ...PISSED OFF.
OH, GOD! ...KATCHOO, WHAT IF THE MOB FINDS OUT?
FRANCINE! GEEZ! LIGHTEN UP, WILL YA?! NOBODY KNOWS! NOBODY CARES!
ST LUKES METHODIST HOSPITAL
YELLOW C
NOBODY'S INTERESTED IN WHAT TWO GIRLS FROM HOUSTON DO!
GOOD!
GIGI'S CABARET

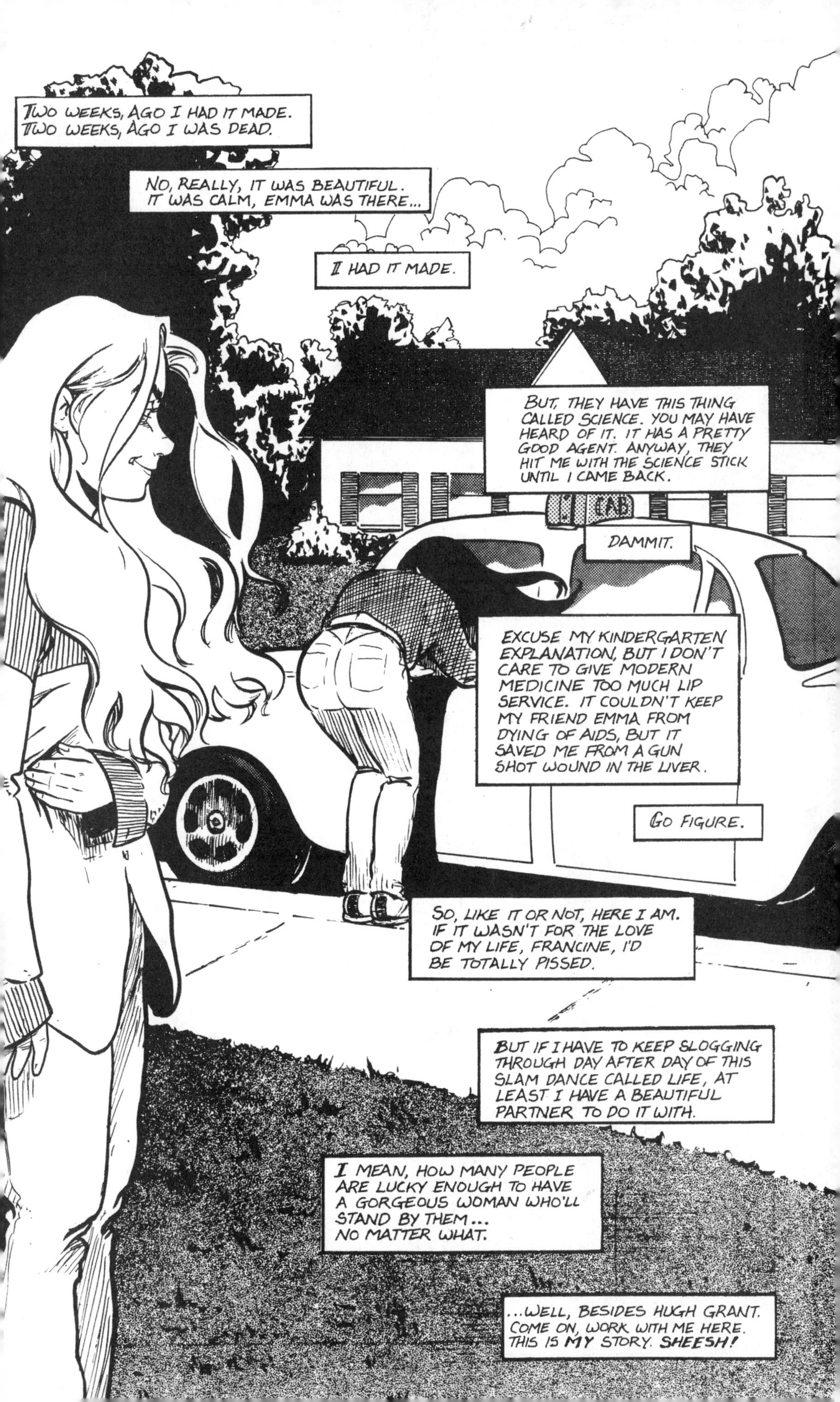

TWO WEEKS, AGO I HAD IT MADE.
TWO WEEKS, AGO I WAS DEAD.
NO, REALLY, IT WAS BEAUTIFUL. IT WAS CALM, EMMA WAS THERE...
I HAD IT MADE.
BUT, THEY HAVE THIS THING CALLED SCIENCE. YOU MAY HAVE HEARD OF IT. IT HAS A PRETTY GOOD AGENT. ANYWAY, THEY HIT ME WITH THE SCIENCE STICK UNTIL I CAME BACK.
CAB
DAMMIT.
EXCUSE MY KINDERGARTEN EXPLANATION, BUT I DON'T CARE TO GIVE MODERN MEDICINE TOO MUCH LIP SERVICE. IT COULDN'T KEEP MY FRIEND EMMA FROM DYING OF AIDS, BUT IT SAVED ME FROM A GUN SHOT WOUND IN THE LIVER.
GO FIGURE.
SO, LIKE IT OR NOT, HERE I AM. IF IT WASN'T FOR THE LOVE OF MY LIFE, FRANCINE, I'D BE TOTALLY PISSED.
BUT IF I HAVE TO KEEP SLOGGING THROUGH DAY AFTER DAY OF THIS SLAM DANCE CALLED LIFE, AT LEAST I HAVE A BEAUTIFUL PARTNER TO DO IT WITH.
I MEAN, HOW MANY PEOPLE ARE LUCKY ENOUGH TO HAVE A GORGEOUS WOMAN WHO'LL STAND BY THEM... NO MATTER WHAT.
...WELL, BESIDES HUGH GRANT. COME ON, WORK WITH ME HERE. THIS IS MY STORY. SHEESH!

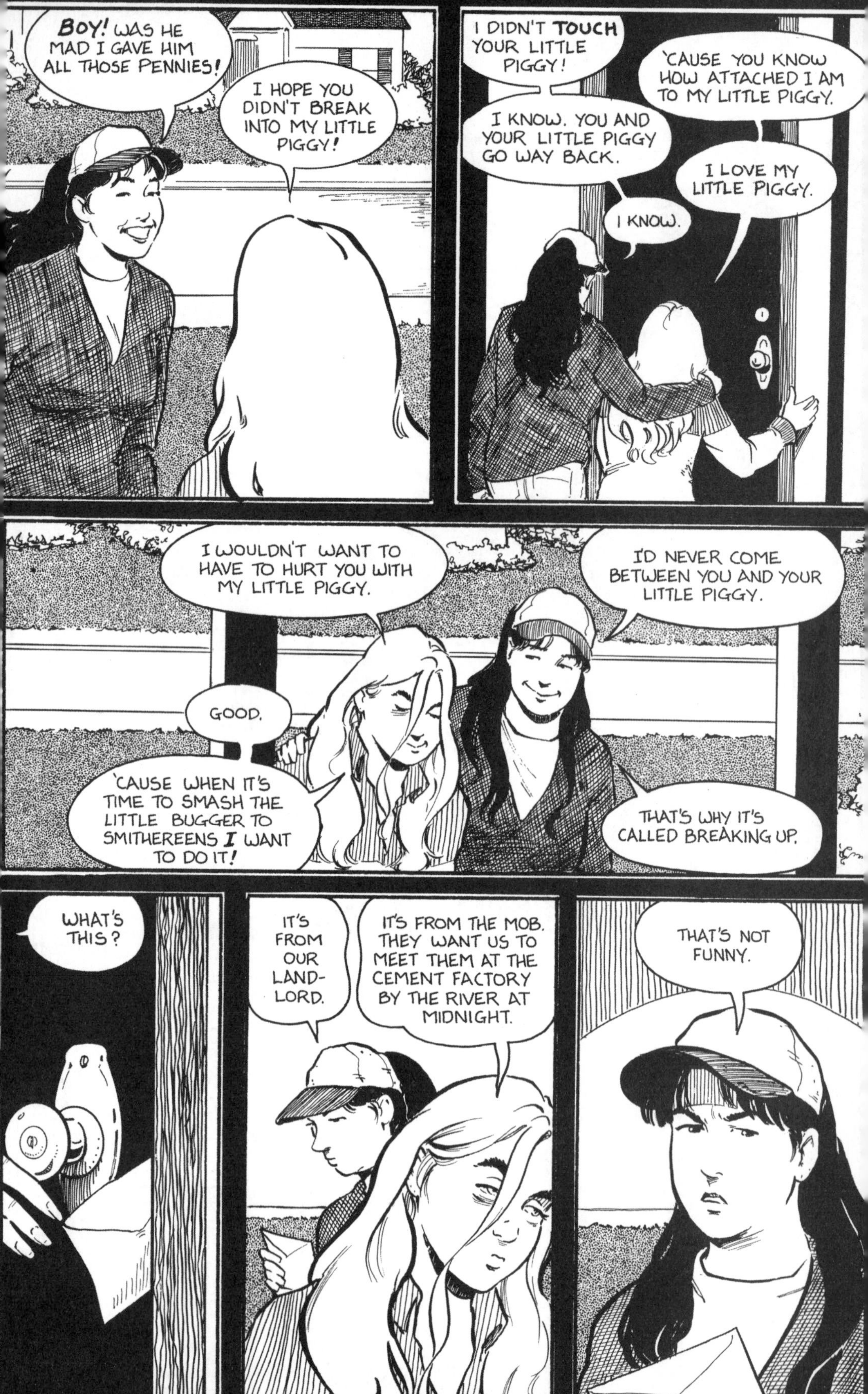

BOY! WAS HE MAD I GAVE HIM ALL THOSE PENNIES!
I HOPE YOU DIDN'T BREAK INTO MY LITTLE PIGGY!
I DIDN'T TOUCH YOUR LITTLE PIGGY!
'CAUSE YOU KNOW HOW ATTACHED I AM TO MY LITTLE PIGGY.
I KNOW. YOU AND YOUR LITTLE PIGGY GO WAY BACK.
I LOVE MY LITTLE PIGGY.
I KNOW.
I WOULDN'T WANT TO HAVE TO HURT YOU WITH MY LITTLE PIGGY.
I'D NEVER COME BETWEEN YOU AND YOUR LITTLE PIGGY.
GOOD.
'CAUSE WHEN IT'S TIME TO SMASH THE LITTLE BUGGER TO SMITHEREENS I WANT TO DO IT!
THAT'S WHY IT'S CALLED BREAKING UP.
WHAT'S THIS?
IT'S FROM OUR LAND-LORD.
IT'S FROM THE MOB. THEY WANT US TO MEET THEM AT THE CEMENT FACTORY BY THE RIVER AT MIDNIGHT.
THAT'S NOT FUNNY.

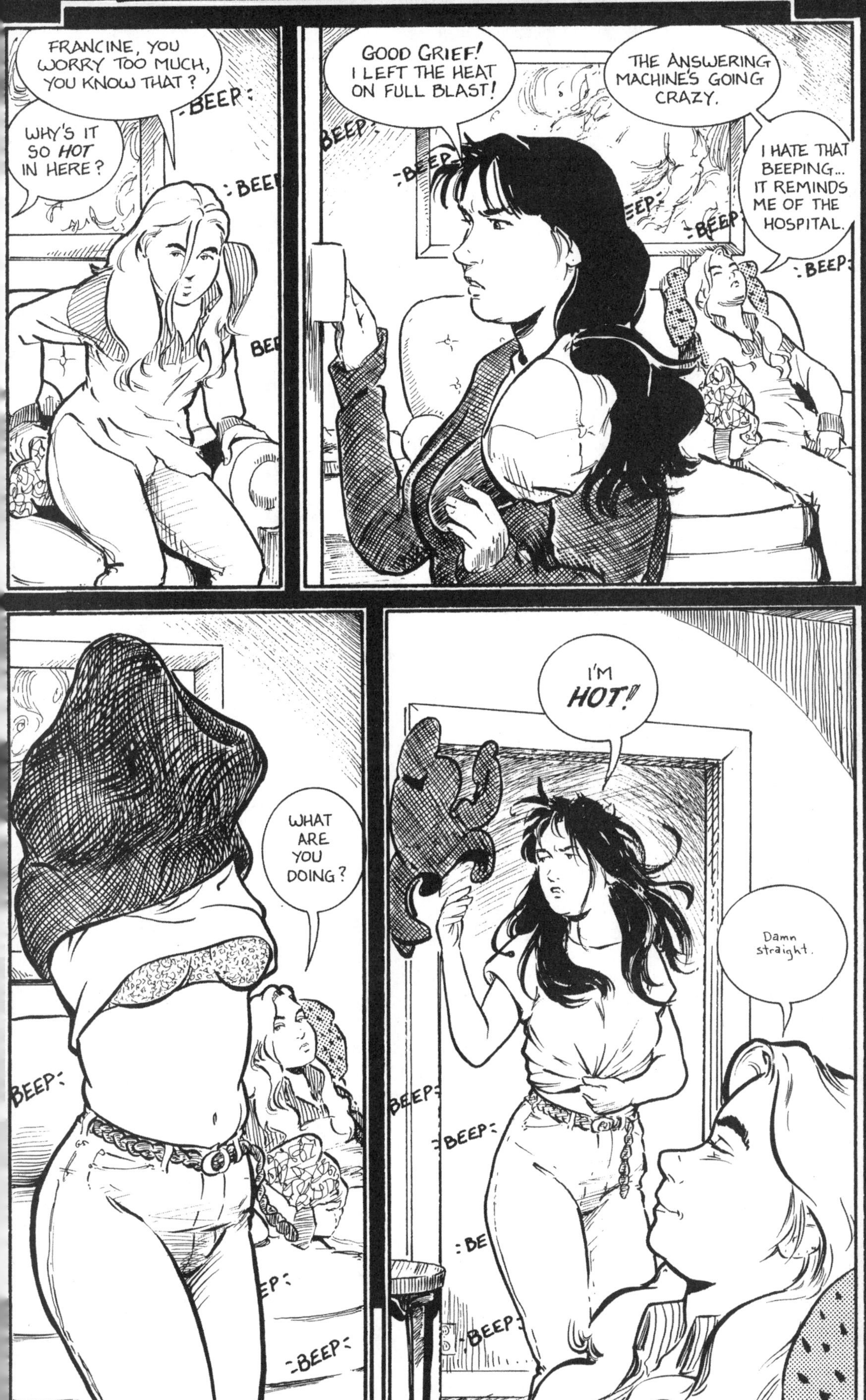

FRANCINE, YOU WORRY TOO MUCH, YOU KNOW THAT?
WHY'S IT SO HOT IN HERE?
-BEEP-
-BEEP
BEE
GOOD GRIEF! I LEFT THE HEAT ON FULL BLAST!
THE ANSWERING MACHINE'S GOING CRAZY.
I HATE THAT BEEPING... IT REMINDS ME OF THE HOSPITAL.
BEEP-
-BEEP-
-BEEP-
WHAT ARE YOU DOING?
BEEP-
-BEEP-
I'M HOT!
Damn straight.
BEEP-
-BEEP-
-BE
-BEEP-

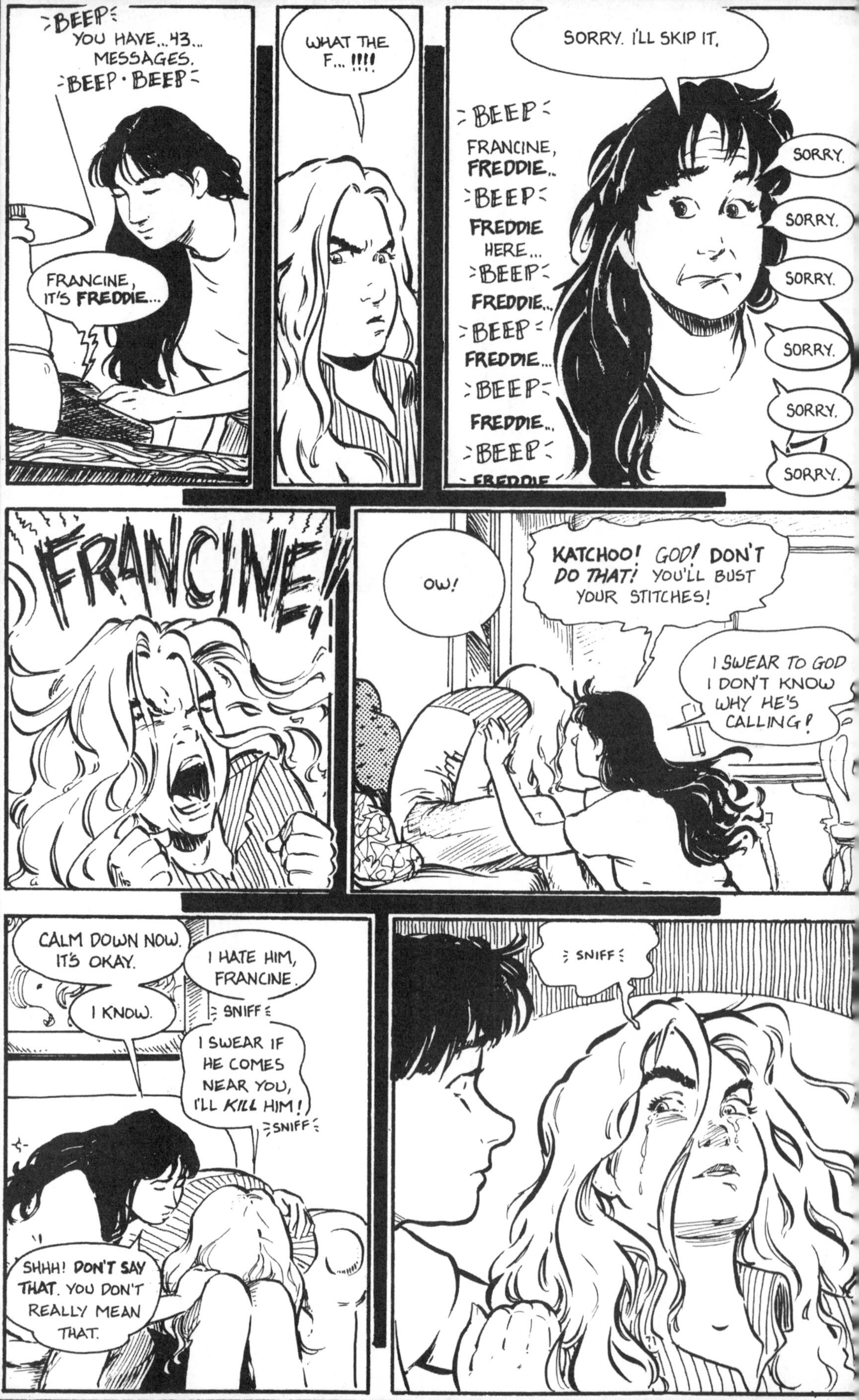

BEEP
YOU HAVE...43... MESSAGES.
BEEP · BEEP
FRANCINE, IT'S FREDDIE...
WHAT THE F... !!!!
SORRY. I'LL SKIP IT.
BEEP
FRANCINE, FREDDIE...
BEEP
FREDDIE HERE...
BEEP
FREDDIE...
BEEP
FREDDIE...
BEEP
FREDDIE...
BEEP
SORRY.
SORRY.
SORRY.
SORRY.
SORRY.
SORRY.
FRANCINE!!
OW!
KATCHOO! GOD! DON'T DO THAT! YOU'LL BUST YOUR STITCHES!
I SWEAR TO GOD I DON'T KNOW WHY HE'S CALLING!
CALM DOWN NOW. IT'S OKAY.
I HATE HIM, FRANCINE.
I KNOW.
SNIFF
I SWEAR IF HE COMES NEAR YOU, I'LL KILL HIM!
SNIFF
SHHH! DON'T SAY THAT. YOU DON'T REALLY MEAN THAT.
SNIFF

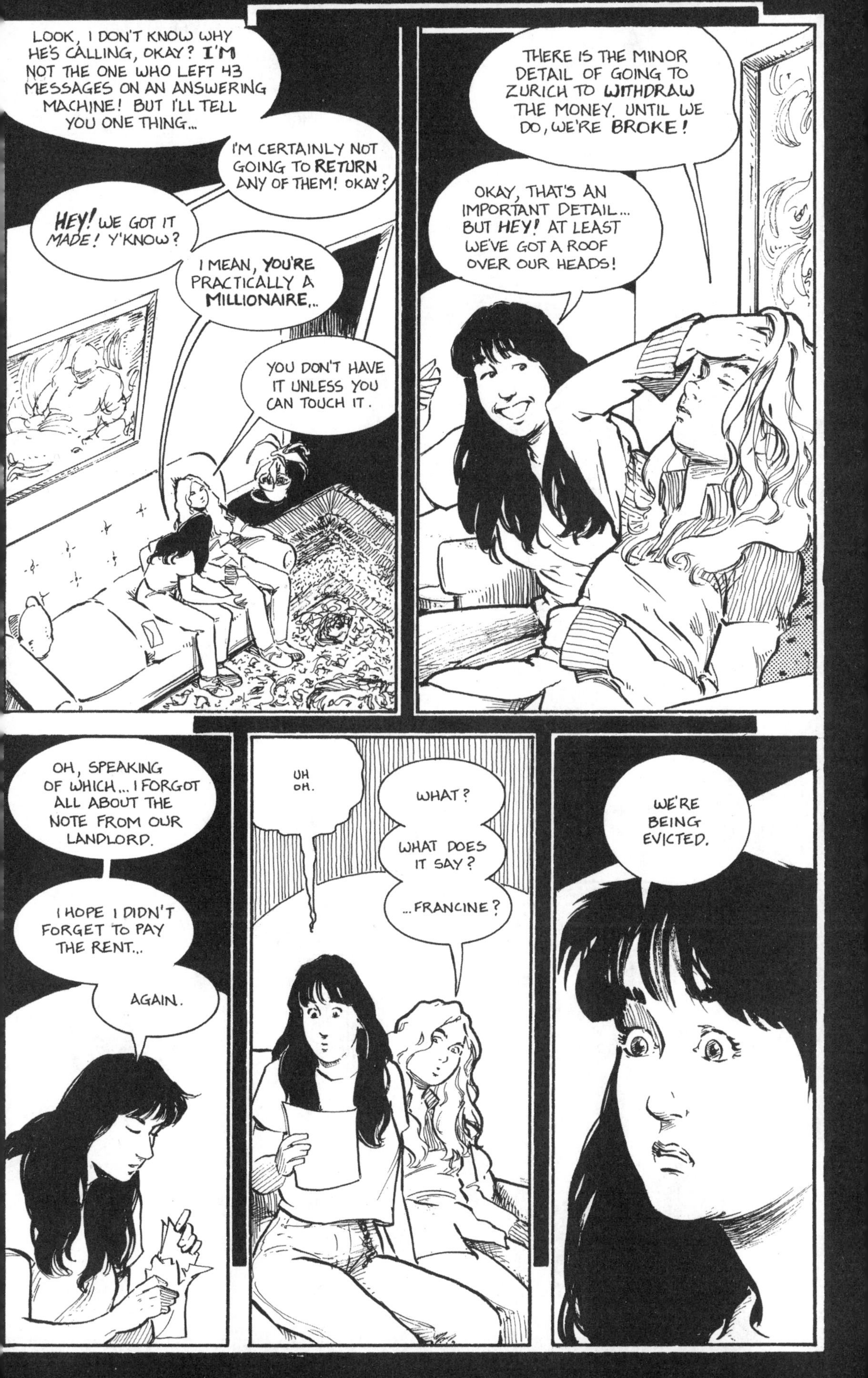
LOOK, I DON'T KNOW WHY HE'S CALLING, OKAY? I'M NOT THE ONE WHO LEFT 43 MESSAGES ON AN ANSWERING MACHINE! BUT I'LL TELL YOU ONE THING...
I'M CERTAINLY NOT GOING TO RETURN ANY OF THEM! OKAY?
HEY! WE GOT IT MADE! Y'KNOW?
I MEAN, YOU'RE PRACTICALLY A MILLIONAIRE...
YOU DON'T HAVE IT UNLESS YOU CAN TOUCH IT.
THERE IS THE MINOR DETAIL OF GOING TO ZURICH TO WITHDRAW THE MONEY. UNTIL WE DO, WE'RE BROKE!
OKAY, THAT'S AN IMPORTANT DETAIL... BUT HEY! AT LEAST WE'VE GOT A ROOF OVER OUR HEADS!
OH, SPEAKING OF WHICH... I FORGOT ALL ABOUT THE NOTE FROM OUR LANDLORD.
I HOPE I DIDN'T FORGET TO PAY THE RENT...
AGAIN.
UH OH.
WHAT?
WHAT DOES IT SAY?
...FRANCINE?
WE'RE BEING EVICTED.

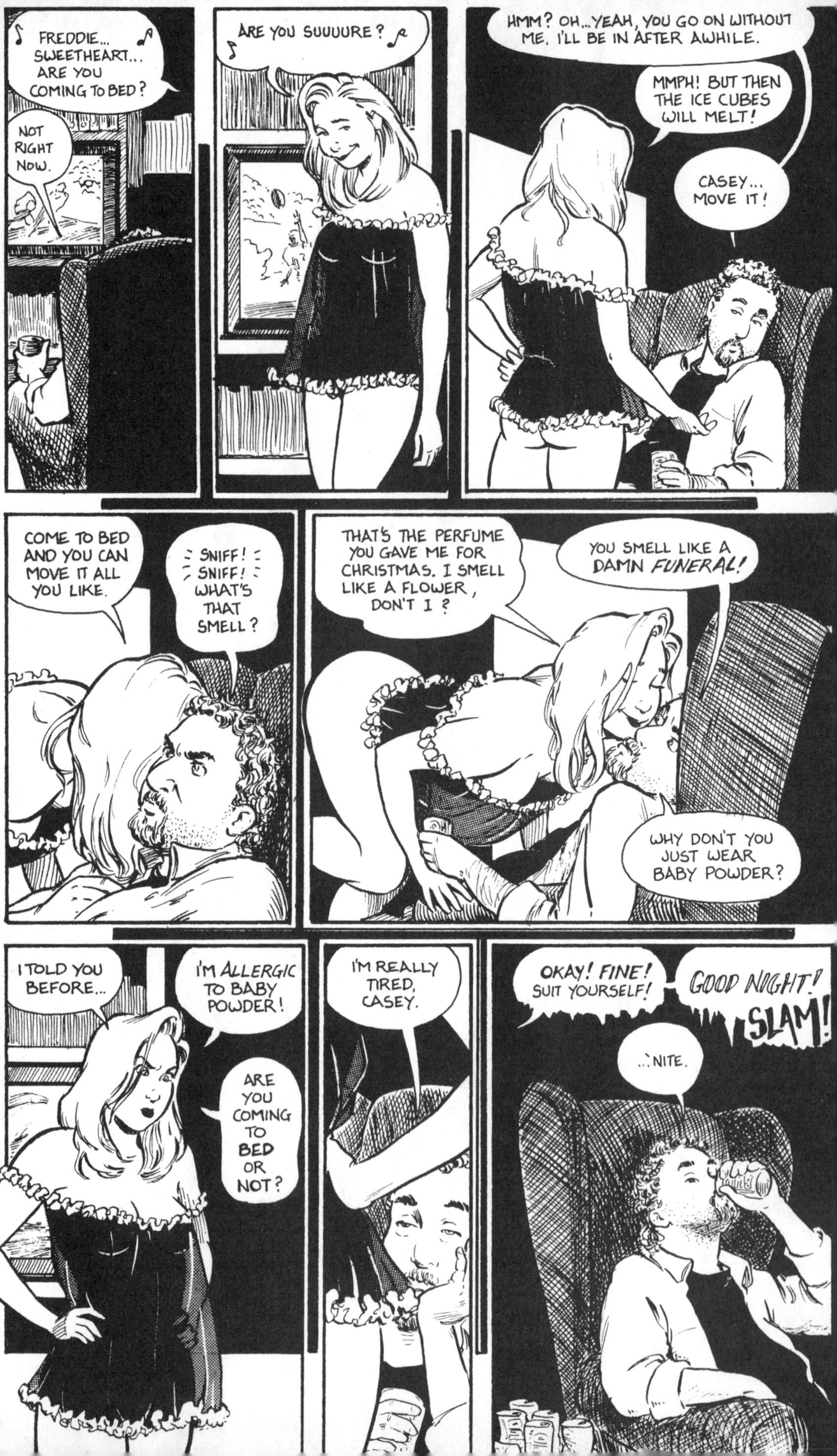
FREDDIE... SWEETHEART... ARE YOU COMING TO BED?
NOT RIGHT NOW.
ARE YOU SUUUURE?
HMM? OH...YEAH, YOU GO ON WITHOUT ME. I'LL BE IN AFTER AWHILE.
MMPH! BUT THEN THE ICE CUBES WILL MELT!
CASEY... MOVE IT!
COME TO BED AND YOU CAN MOVE IT ALL YOU LIKE.
SNIFF! SNIFF! WHAT'S THAT SMELL?
THAT'S THE PERFUME YOU GAVE ME FOR CHRISTMAS. I SMELL LIKE A FLOWER, DON'T I?
YOU SMELL LIKE A DAMN FUNERAL!
WHY DON'T YOU JUST WEAR BABY POWDER?
I TOLD YOU BEFORE...
I'M ALLERGIC TO BABY POWDER!
ARE YOU COMING TO BED OR NOT?
I'M REALLY TIRED, CASEY.
OKAY! FINE! SUIT YOURSELF!
GOOD NIGHT!
SLAM!
...'NITE.

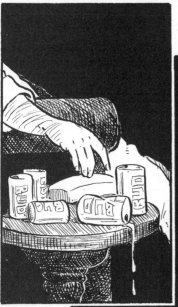

:RING RING: :CLICK: HI! WE CAN'T COME TO THE PHONE RIGHT NOW...
:SO QUIT CALLING!:

:GIGGLE: KATCHOO! SHUT UP!... SORRY, LEAVE A MESSAGE AND...

I HOPE YOU REALIZE I'M ABOUT TO START MY **PERIOD** AND *NOW* YOU WON'T GET ANY FOR A *WHOLE WEEK!*

GOOD.

SLAM!

...AND MONKEY'S MIGHT FLY OUT MY *BEEP!*

FRANCINE... IT'S FREDDIE. I KNOW YOU'RE THERE...

PLEASE TALK TO ME. I'M FALLING APART HERE, Y'KNOW WHAT I'M SAYIN'? PLEASE... JUST TALK TO ME, OKAY? THAT'S ALL. JUST... **TALK** TO ME.

FRANCINE? FRANCINE? PLEASE? ...

DANIEL O. SELZNICK PRESENTS
CLARK GABLE - VIVIAN LEIGH
C.O.P.
WEEK END SPECIAL
ITCHY & SCRATCHY THE MOVIE
MATA HARI
FELLINI ITALIAN
DOGS OF ITALY
PULP FICTION
HOW TO MURDER
SEX: THE MOVIE
PATRICIA N.
BED JELLY
WESTERN WAY
MUPPETS TAKE GERMANY
GARDENING
BATMAN
DYING: THE MARVEL
AUTO SURGERY
TOO MUCH COFFEE MAN
FERRARI
FRANCE IS
STING
HEIDI THE TOOL GIRL
BJORK DOWN
THE ALAMO
NINE WEEKS
TV
RADIO
LI'L ABNER
SHI MOVIE
FOOD
THE STING
HEY!
OH SHEESH! I'M SORR... FRANCINE!!

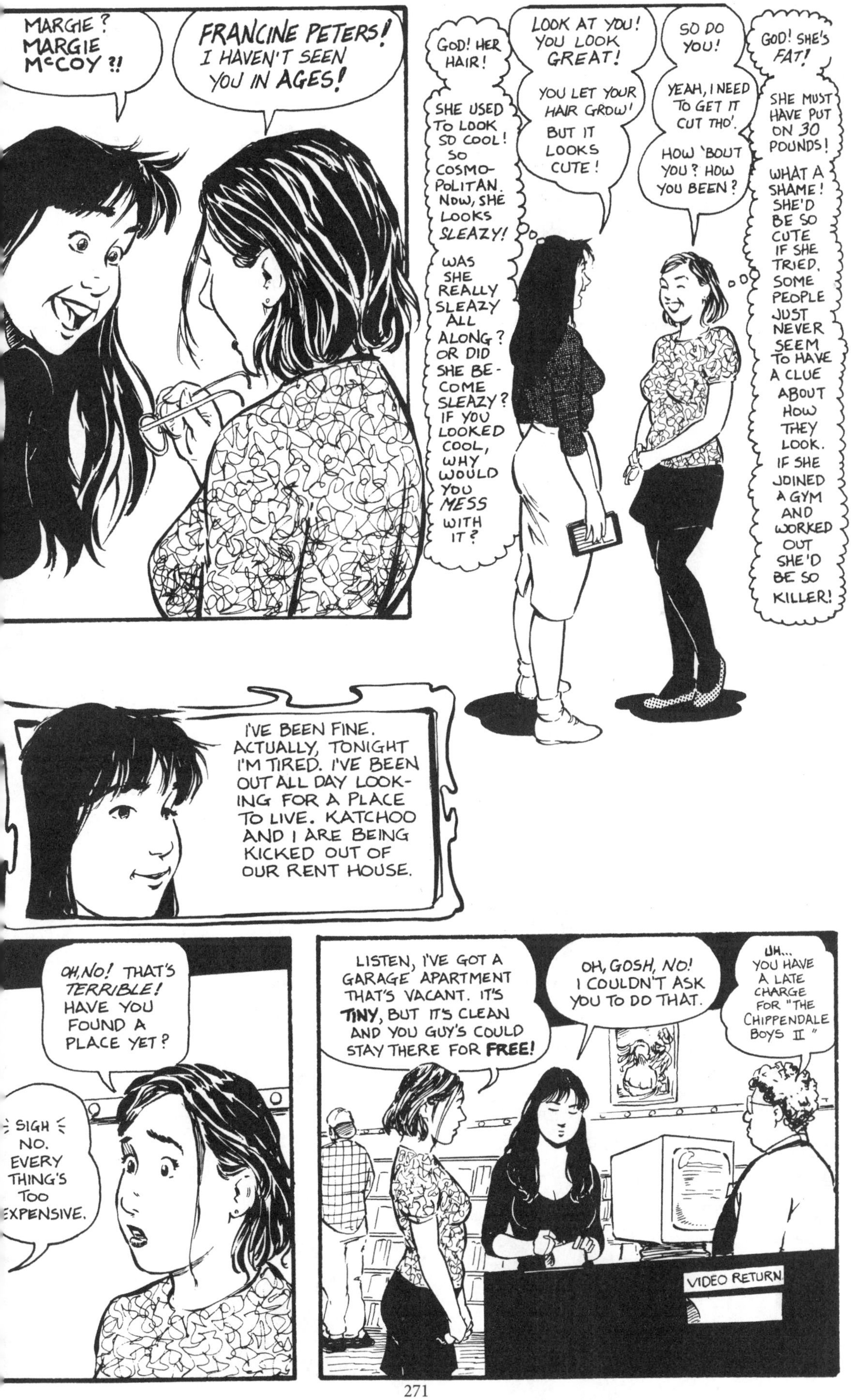

MARGIE? MARGIE McCOY?!
FRANCINE PETERS! I HAVEN'T SEEN YOU IN AGES!
GOD! HER HAIR!
SHE USED TO LOOK SO COOL! SO COSMO-POLITAN. NOW, SHE LOOKS SLEAZY!
WAS SHE REALLY SLEAZY ALL ALONG? OR DID SHE BE-COME SLEAZY? IF YOU LOOKED COOL, WHY WOULD YOU MESS WITH IT?
LOOK AT YOU! YOU LOOK GREAT!
YOU LET YOUR HAIR GROW! BUT IT LOOKS CUTE!
SO DO YOU!
YEAH, I NEED TO GET IT CUT THO'.
HOW 'BOUT YOU? HOW YOU BEEN?
GOD! SHE'S FAT!
SHE MUST HAVE PUT ON 30 POUNDS!
WHAT A SHAME! SHE'D BE SO CUTE IF SHE TRIED. SOME PEOPLE JUST NEVER SEEM TO HAVE A CLUE ABOUT HOW THEY LOOK. IF SHE JOINED A GYM AND WORKED OUT SHE'D BE SO KILLER!
I'VE BEEN FINE. ACTUALLY, TONIGHT I'M TIRED. I'VE BEEN OUT ALL DAY LOOK-ING FOR A PLACE TO LIVE. KATCHOO AND I ARE BEING KICKED OUT OF OUR RENT HOUSE.
OH, NO! THAT'S TERRIBLE! HAVE YOU FOUND A PLACE YET?
SIGH
NO. EVERY THING'S TOO EXPENSIVE.
LISTEN, I'VE GOT A GARAGE APARTMENT THAT'S VACANT. IT'S TINY, BUT IT'S CLEAN AND YOU GUY'S COULD STAY THERE FOR FREE!
OH, GOSH, NO! I COULDN'T ASK YOU TO DO THAT.
UH... YOU HAVE A LATE CHARGE FOR "THE CHIPPENDALE BOYS II"
VIDEO RETURN

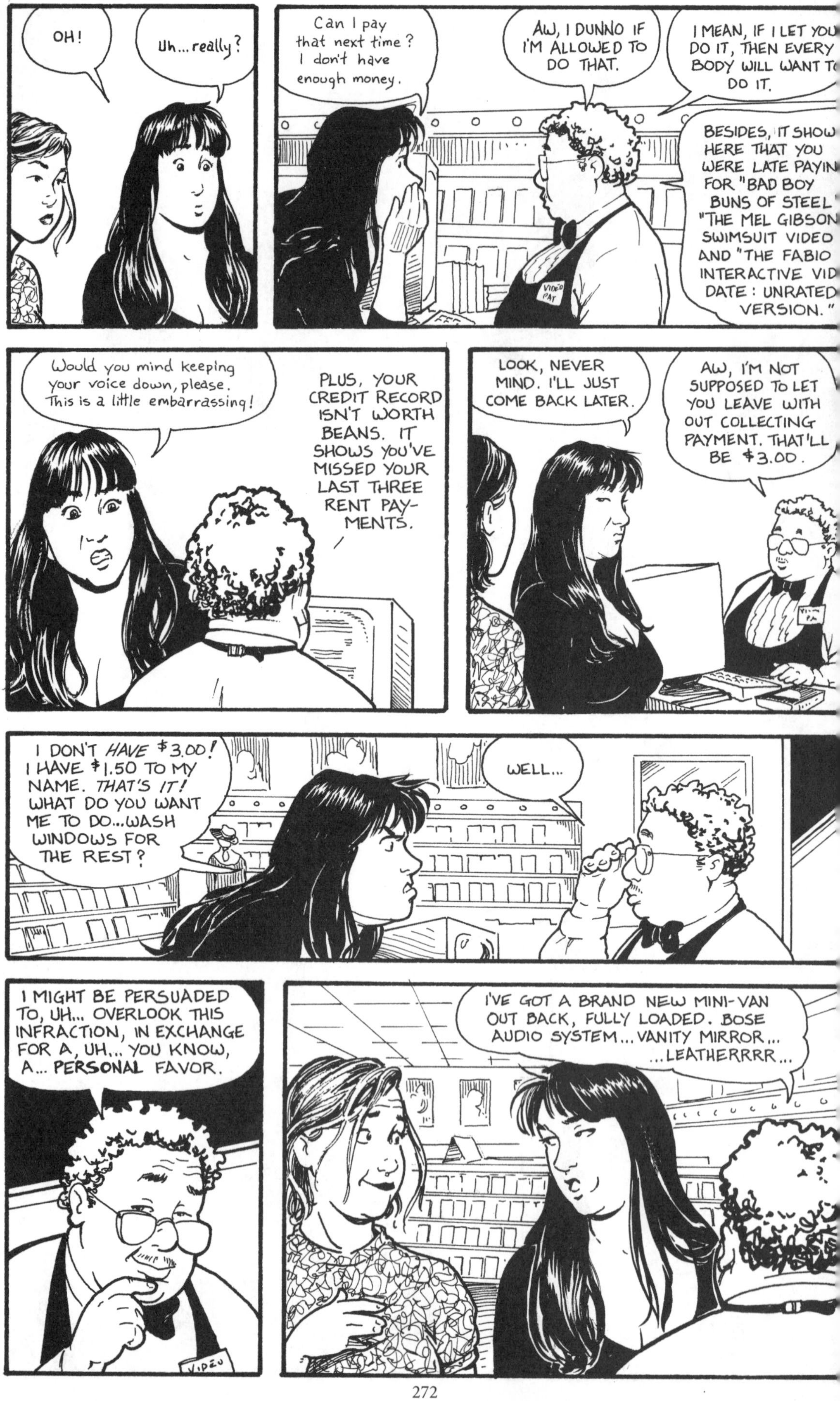
OH!
Uh...really?
Can I pay that next time? I don't have enough money.
AW, I DUNNO IF I'M ALLOWED TO DO THAT.
I MEAN, IF I LET YOU DO IT, THEN EVERY BODY WILL WANT TO DO IT.
BESIDES, IT SHOW HERE THAT YOU WERE LATE PAYIN FOR "BAD BOY BUNS OF STEEL" "THE MEL GIBSON SWIMSUIT VIDEO AND "THE FABIO INTERACTIVE VID DATE: UNRATED VERSION."
VIDEO PAT
Would you mind keeping your voice down, please. This is a little embarrassing!
PLUS, YOUR CREDIT RECORD ISN'T WORTH BEANS. IT SHOWS YOU'VE MISSED YOUR LAST THREE RENT PAYMENTS.
LOOK, NEVER MIND. I'LL JUST COME BACK LATER.
AW, I'M NOT SUPPOSED TO LET YOU LEAVE WITH OUT COLLECTING PAYMENT. THAT'LL BE $3.00.
I DON'T HAVE $3.00! I HAVE $1.50 TO MY NAME. THAT'S IT! WHAT DO YOU WANT ME TO DO...WASH WINDOWS FOR THE REST?
WELL...
I MIGHT BE PERSUADED TO, UH... OVERLOOK THIS INFRACTION, IN EXCHANGE FOR A, UH... YOU KNOW, A... PERSONAL FAVOR.
VIDEO
I'VE GOT A BRAND NEW MINI-VAN OUT BACK, FULLY LOADED. BOSE AUDIO SYSTEM... VANITY MIRROR... ...LEATHERRRR...

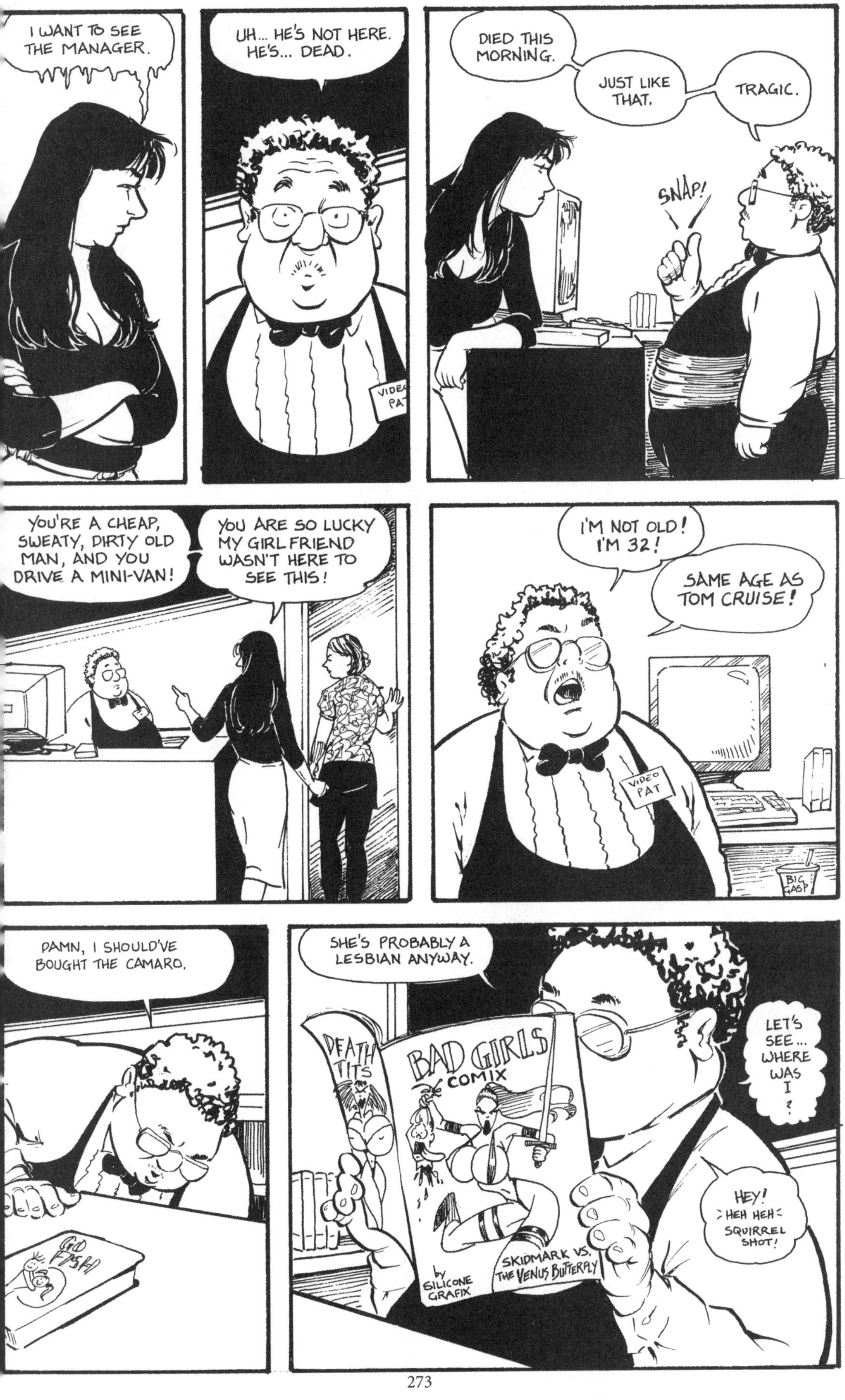
I WANT TO SEE THE MANAGER.
UH... HE'S NOT HERE. HE'S... DEAD.
DIED THIS MORNING.
JUST LIKE THAT.
TRAGIC.
SNAP!
VIDEO PAT
YOU'RE A CHEAP, SWEATY, DIRTY OLD MAN, AND YOU DRIVE A MINI-VAN!
YOU ARE SO LUCKY MY GIRLFRIEND WASN'T HERE TO SEE THIS!
I'M NOT OLD! I'M 32!
SAME AGE AS TOM CRUISE!
VIDEO PAT
BIG GASP
DAMN, I SHOULD'VE BOUGHT THE CAMARO.
GO FISH
SHE'S PROBABLY A LESBIAN ANYWAY.
DEATH TITS
BAD GIRLS COMIX
SKIDMARK VS. THE VENUS BUTTERFLY
by SILICONE GRAFIX
LET'S SEE... WHERE WAS I?
HEY! HEH HEH SQUIRREL SHOT!

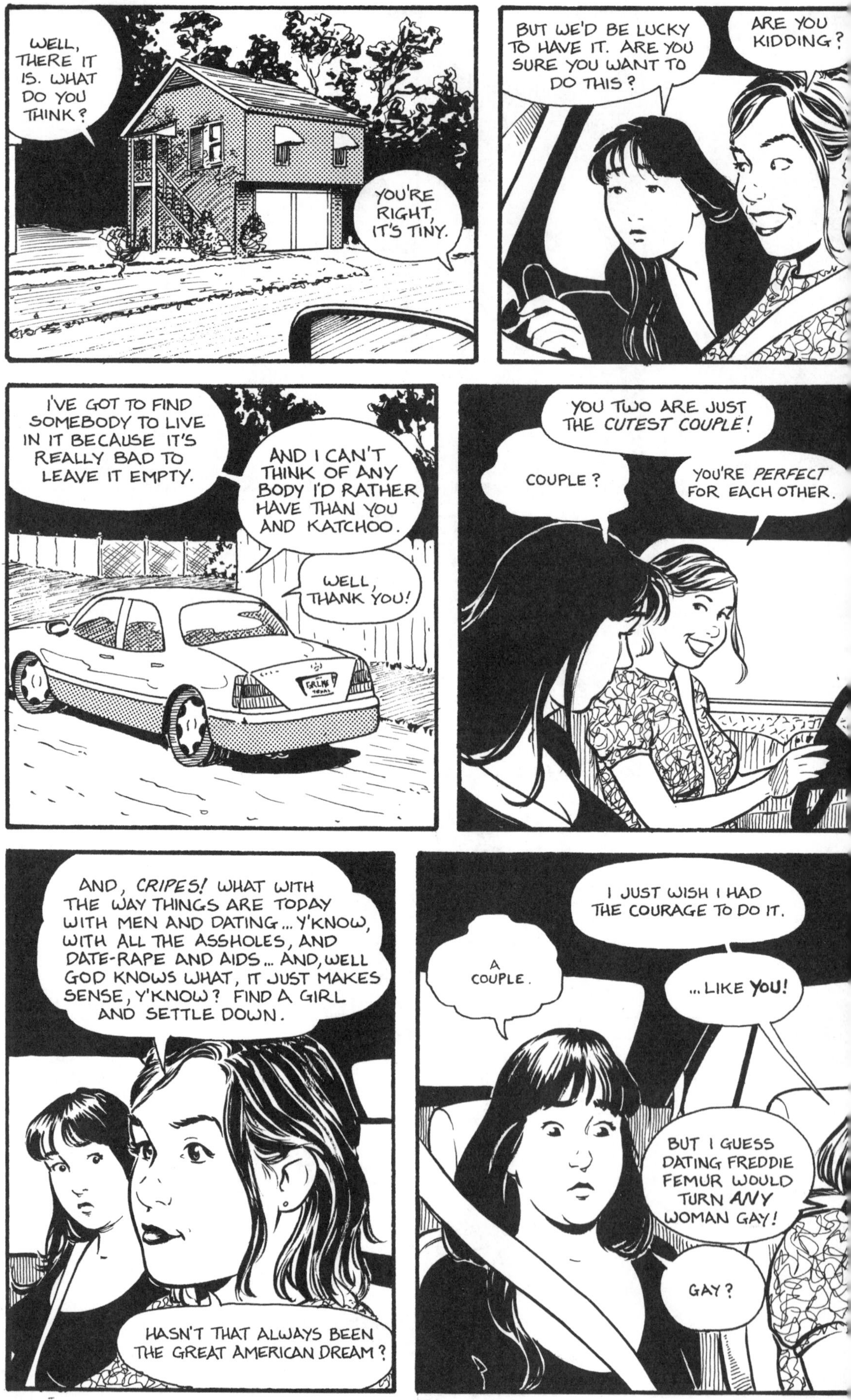
WELL, THERE IT IS. WHAT DO YOU THINK?
YOU'RE RIGHT, IT'S TINY.
BUT WE'D BE LUCKY TO HAVE IT. ARE YOU SURE YOU WANT TO DO THIS?
ARE YOU KIDDING?
I'VE GOT TO FIND SOMEBODY TO LIVE IN IT BECAUSE IT'S REALLY BAD TO LEAVE IT EMPTY.
AND I CAN'T THINK OF ANY BODY I'D RATHER HAVE THAN YOU AND KATCHOO.
WELL, THANK YOU!
YOU TWO ARE JUST THE *CUTEST COUPLE*!
COUPLE?
YOU'RE *PERFECT* FOR EACH OTHER.
AND, *CRIPES!* WHAT WITH THE WAY THINGS ARE TODAY WITH MEN AND DATING... Y'KNOW, WITH ALL THE ASSHOLES, AND DATE-RAPE AND AIDS... AND, WELL GOD KNOWS WHAT, IT JUST MAKES SENSE, Y'KNOW? FIND A GIRL AND SETTLE DOWN.
HASN'T THAT ALWAYS BEEN THE GREAT AMERICAN DREAM?
I JUST WISH I HAD THE COURAGE TO DO IT.
A COUPLE.
...LIKE **YOU**!
BUT I GUESS DATING FREDDIE FEMUR WOULD TURN *ANY* WOMAN GAY!
GAY?

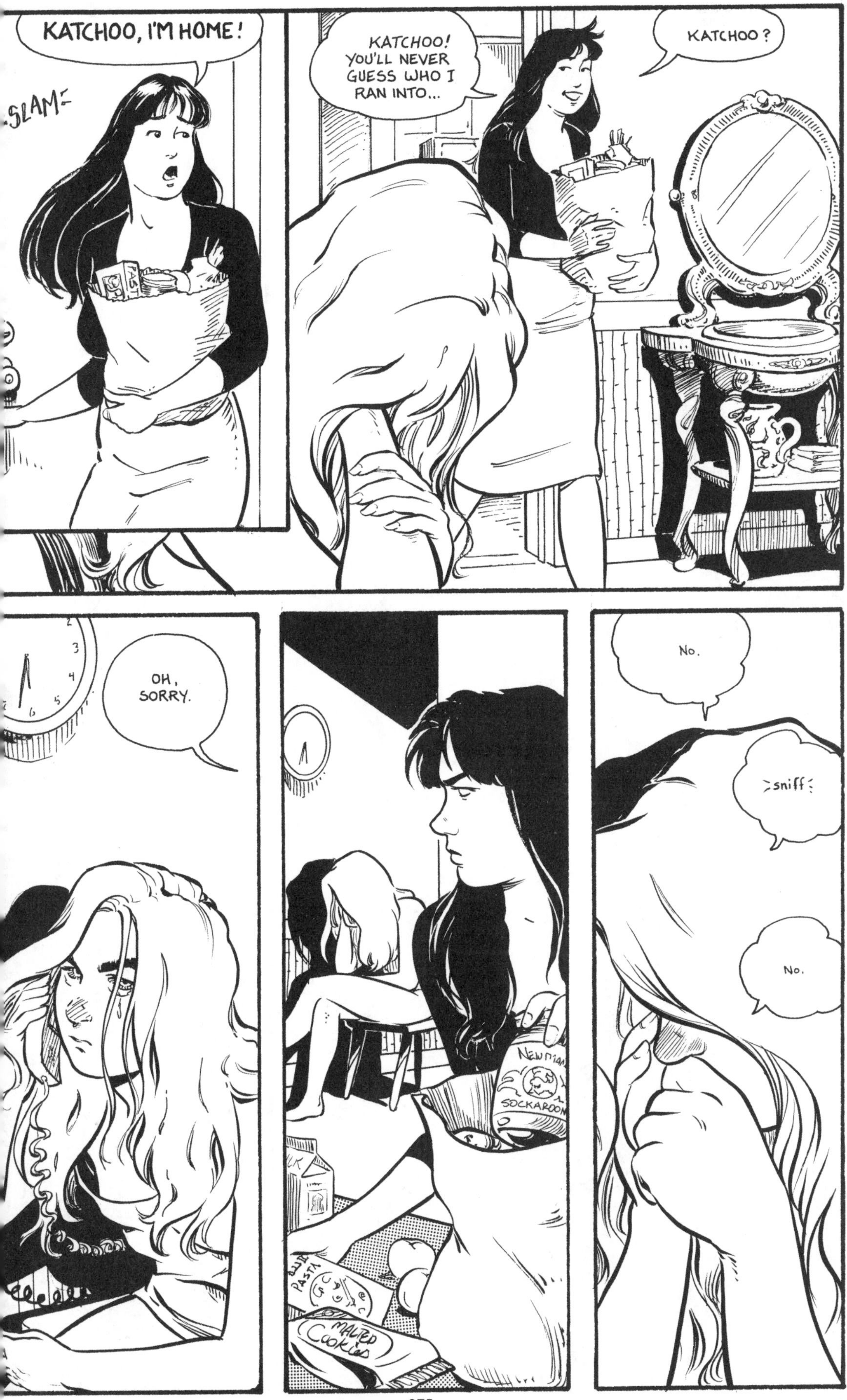
KATCHOO, I'M HOME!
SLAM
KATCHOO! YOU'LL NEVER GUESS WHO I RAN INTO...
KATCHOO?
OH, SORRY.
NEWMAN
SOCKAROONI
PASTA
MALTED Cookies
No.
sniff
No.

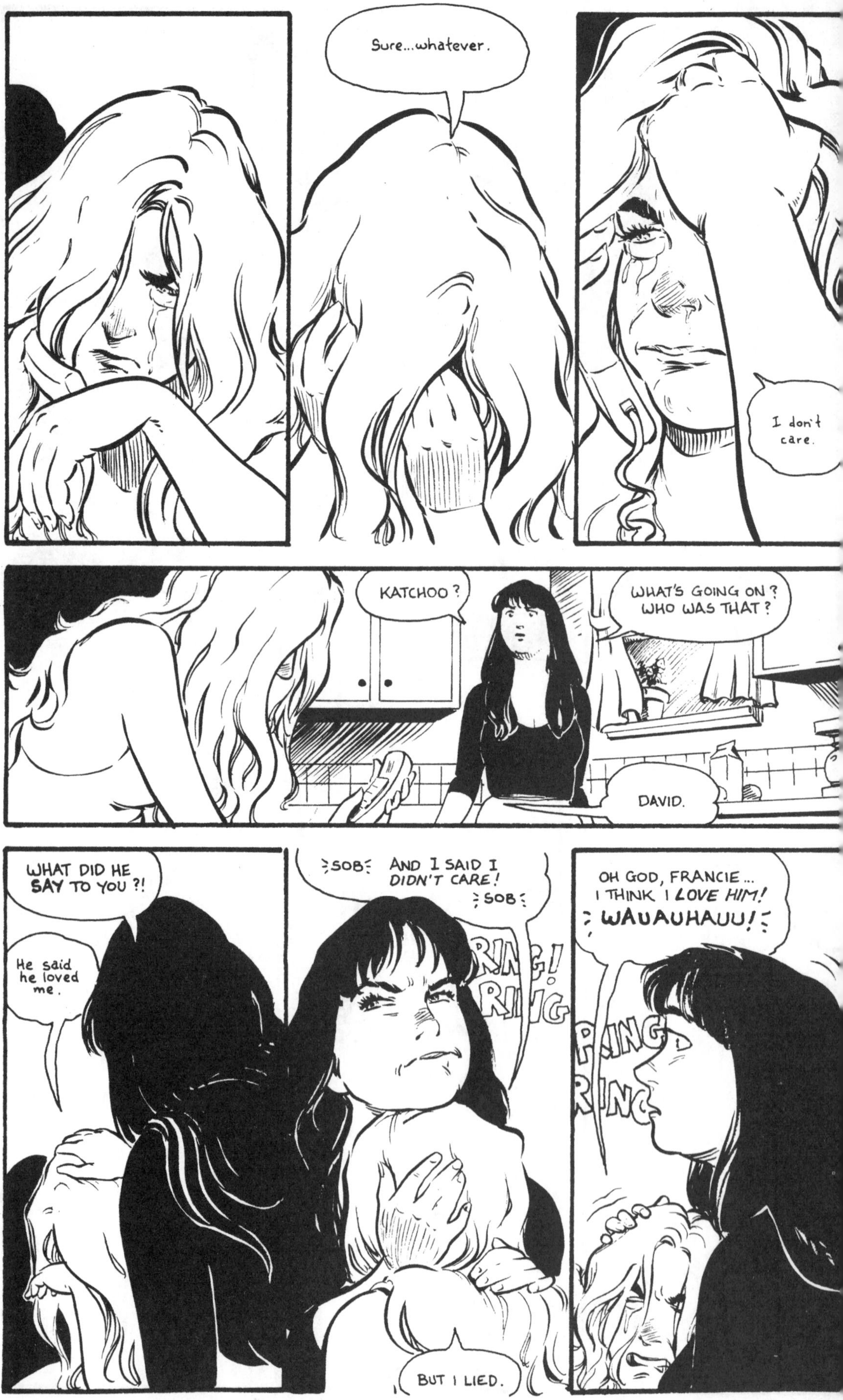

Sure...whatever.
I don't care.
KATCHOO?
WHAT'S GOING ON? WHO WAS THAT?
DAVID.
WHAT DID HE SAY TO YOU?!
He said he loved me.
SOB AND I SAID I DIDN'T CARE! SOB
BUT I LIED.
RING! RING
OH GOD, FRANCIE... I THINK I LOVE HIM! WAUAUHAUU!
RING RING

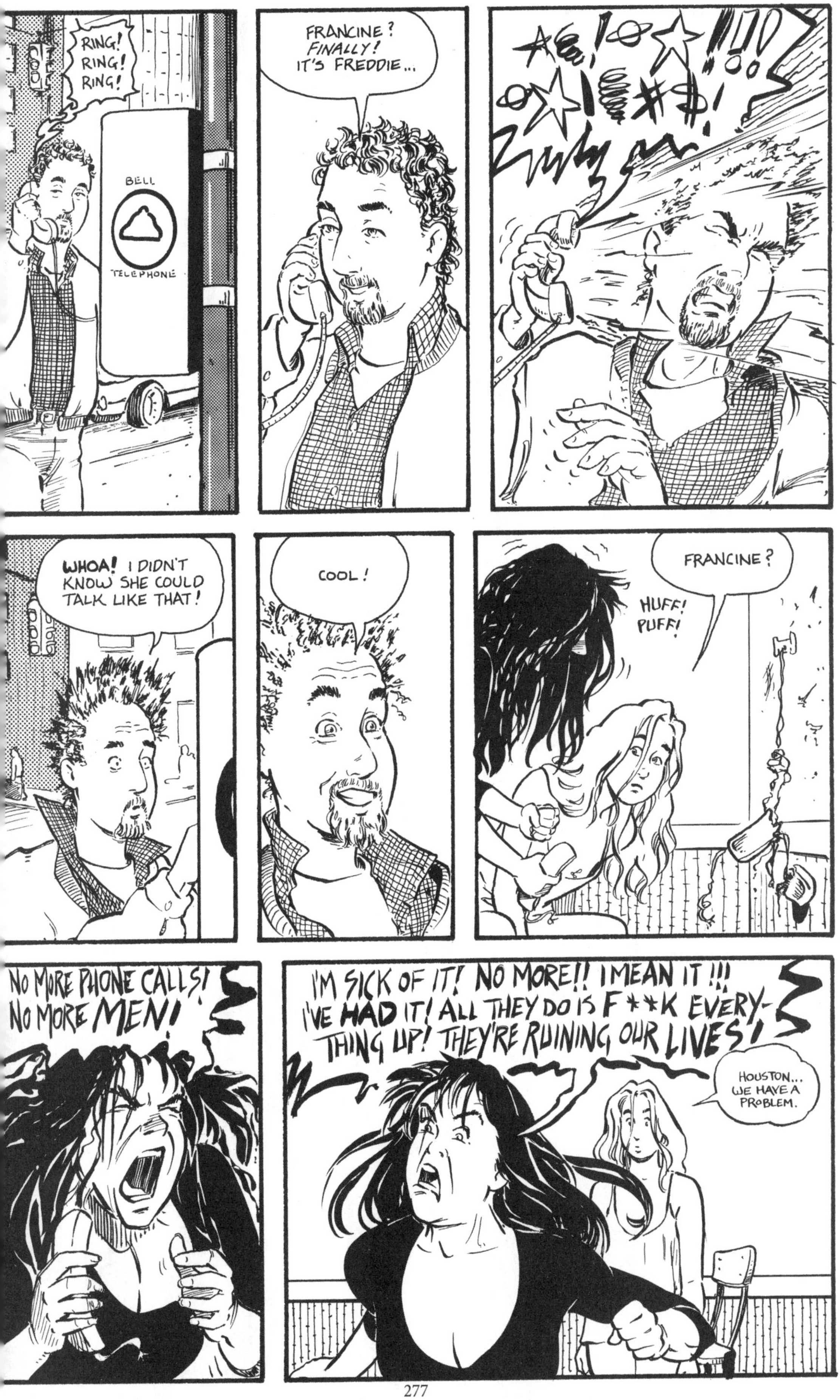
RING! RING! RING!
BELL
TELEPHONE
FRANCINE? FINALLY! IT'S FREDDIE...
WHOA! I DIDN'T KNOW SHE COULD TALK LIKE THAT!
COOL!
FRANCINE?
HUFF! PUFF!
NO MORE PHONE CALLS! NO MORE MEN!
I'M SICK OF IT! NO MORE!! I MEAN IT!!! I'VE HAD IT! ALL THEY DO IS F**K EVERY-THING UP! THEY'RE RUINING OUR LIVES!
HOUSTON... WE HAVE A PROBLEM.

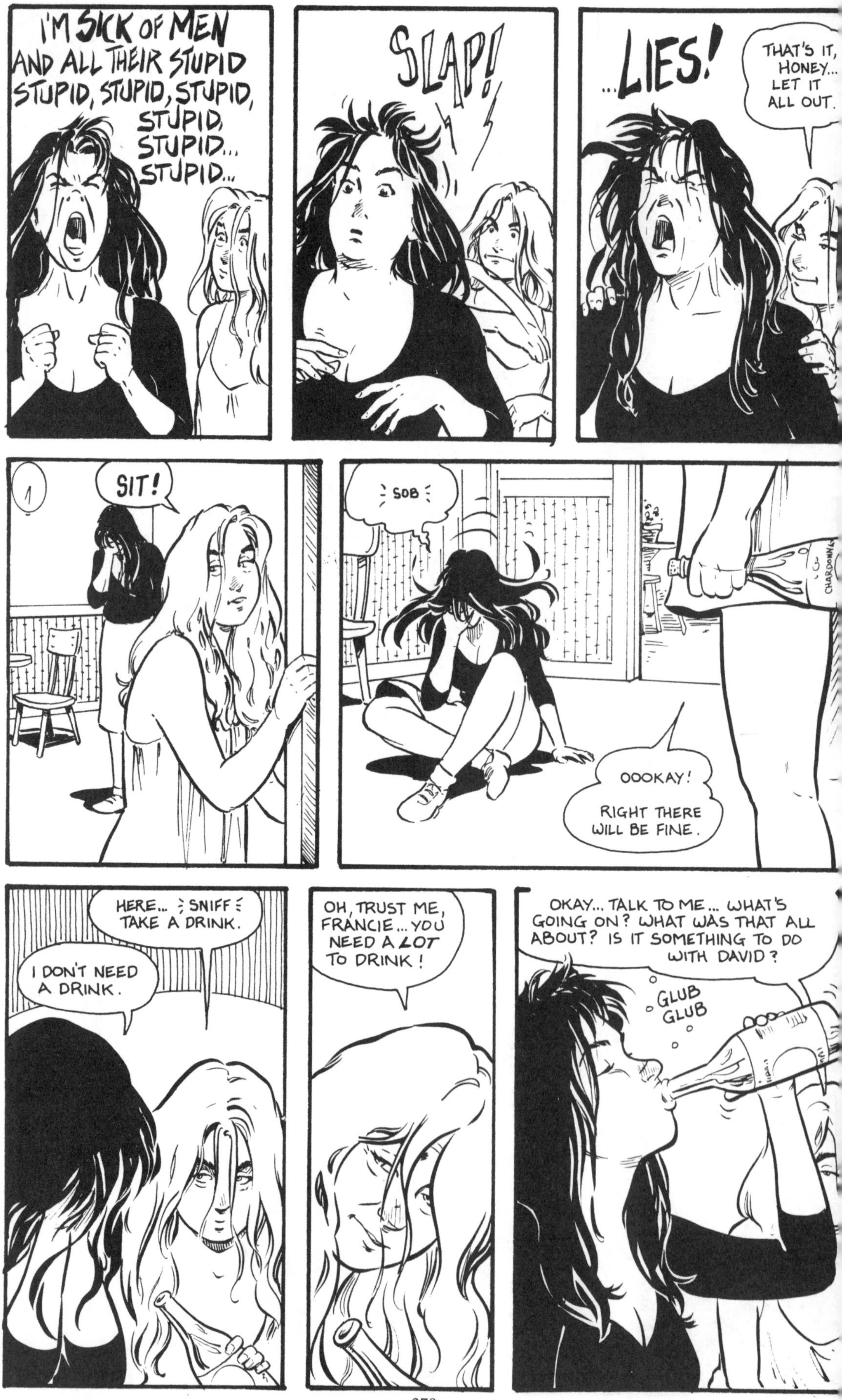
I'M SICK OF MEN AND ALL THEIR STUPID STUPID, STUPID, STUPID, STUPID, STUPID... STUPID...
SLAP!
...LIES!
THAT'S IT, HONEY... LET IT ALL OUT.
SIT!
SOB
OOOKAY!
RIGHT THERE WILL BE FINE.
CHARDONNAY
HERE... SNIFF TAKE A DRINK.
I DON'T NEED A DRINK.
OH, TRUST ME, FRANCIE... YOU NEED A LOT TO DRINK!
OKAY... TALK TO ME... WHAT'S GOING ON? WHAT WAS THAT ALL ABOUT? IS IT SOMETHING TO DO WITH DAVID?
GLUB GLUB

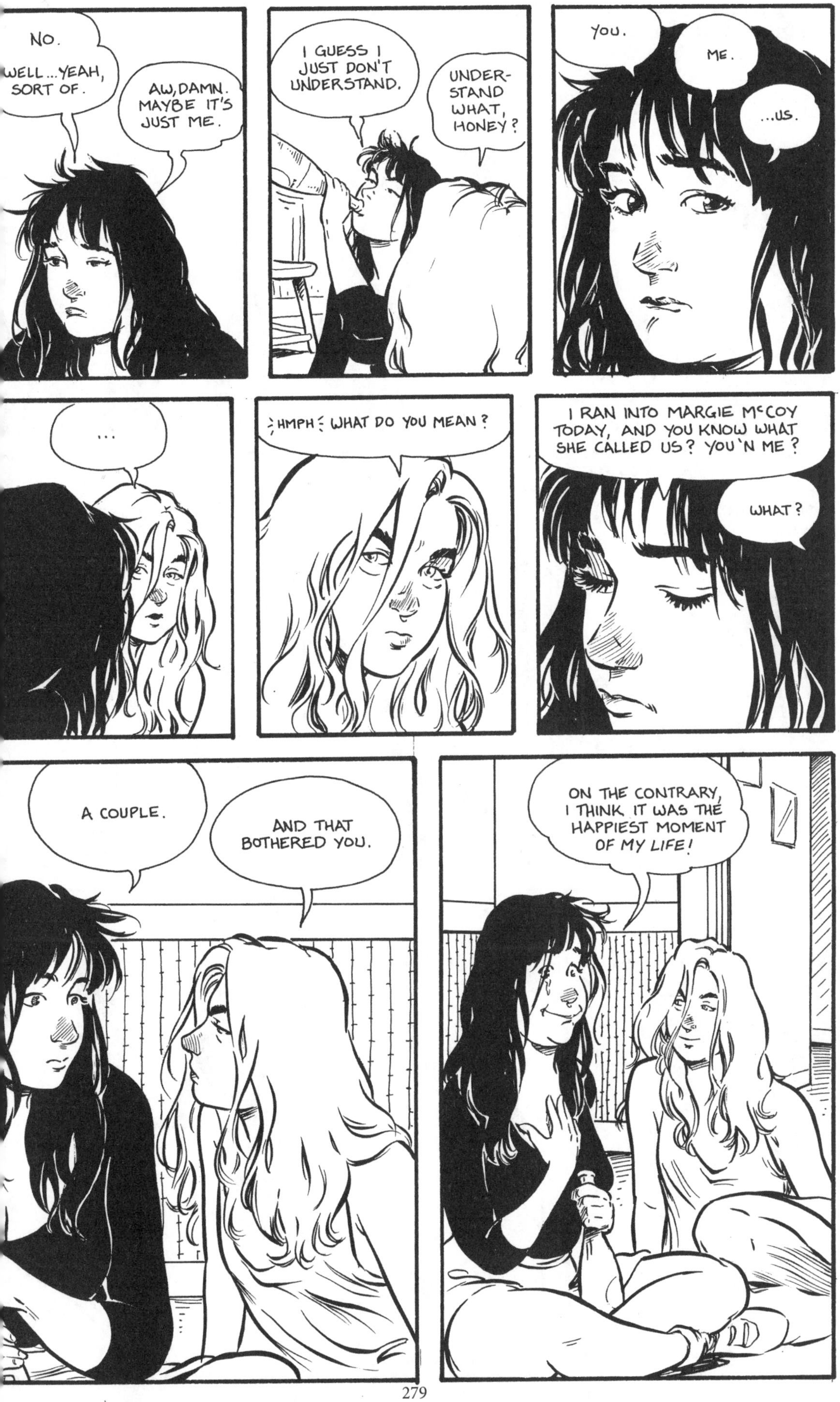
NO.
WELL...YEAH, SORT OF.
AW, DAMN. MAYBE IT'S JUST ME.
I GUESS I JUST DON'T UNDERSTAND.
UNDER-STAND WHAT, HONEY?
YOU.
ME.
...US.
...
HMPH WHAT DO YOU MEAN?
I RAN INTO MARGIE McCOY TODAY, AND YOU KNOW WHAT SHE CALLED US? YOU'N ME?
WHAT?
A COUPLE.
AND THAT BOTHERED YOU.
ON THE CONTRARY, I THINK IT WAS THE HAPPIEST MOMENT OF MY LIFE!

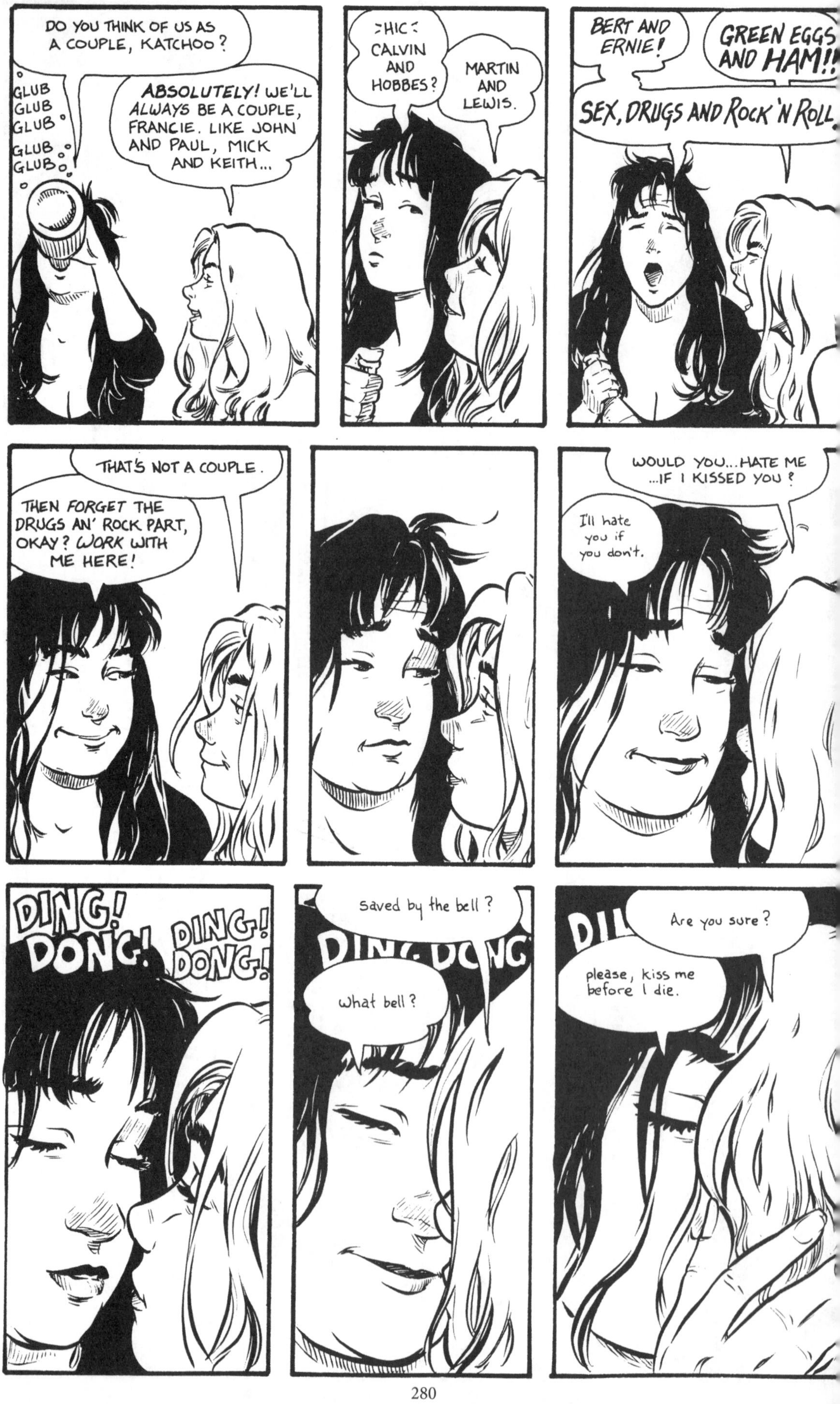

DO YOU THINK OF US AS A COUPLE, KATCHOO?
GLUB GLUB GLUB GLUB GLUB
ABSOLUTELY! WE'LL ALWAYS BE A COUPLE, FRANCIE. LIKE JOHN AND PAUL, MICK AND KEITH...
HIC CALVIN AND HOBBES?
MARTIN AND LEWIS.
BERT AND ERNIE!
GREEN EGGS AND HAM!!
SEX, DRUGS AND ROCK 'N ROLL
THAT'S NOT A COUPLE.
THEN FORGET THE DRUGS AN' ROCK PART, OKAY? WORK WITH ME HERE!
WOULD YOU...HATE ME ...IF I KISSED YOU?
I'll hate you if you don't.
DING! DONG! DING! DONG!
saved by the bell?
what bell?
Are you sure?
please, kiss me before I die.

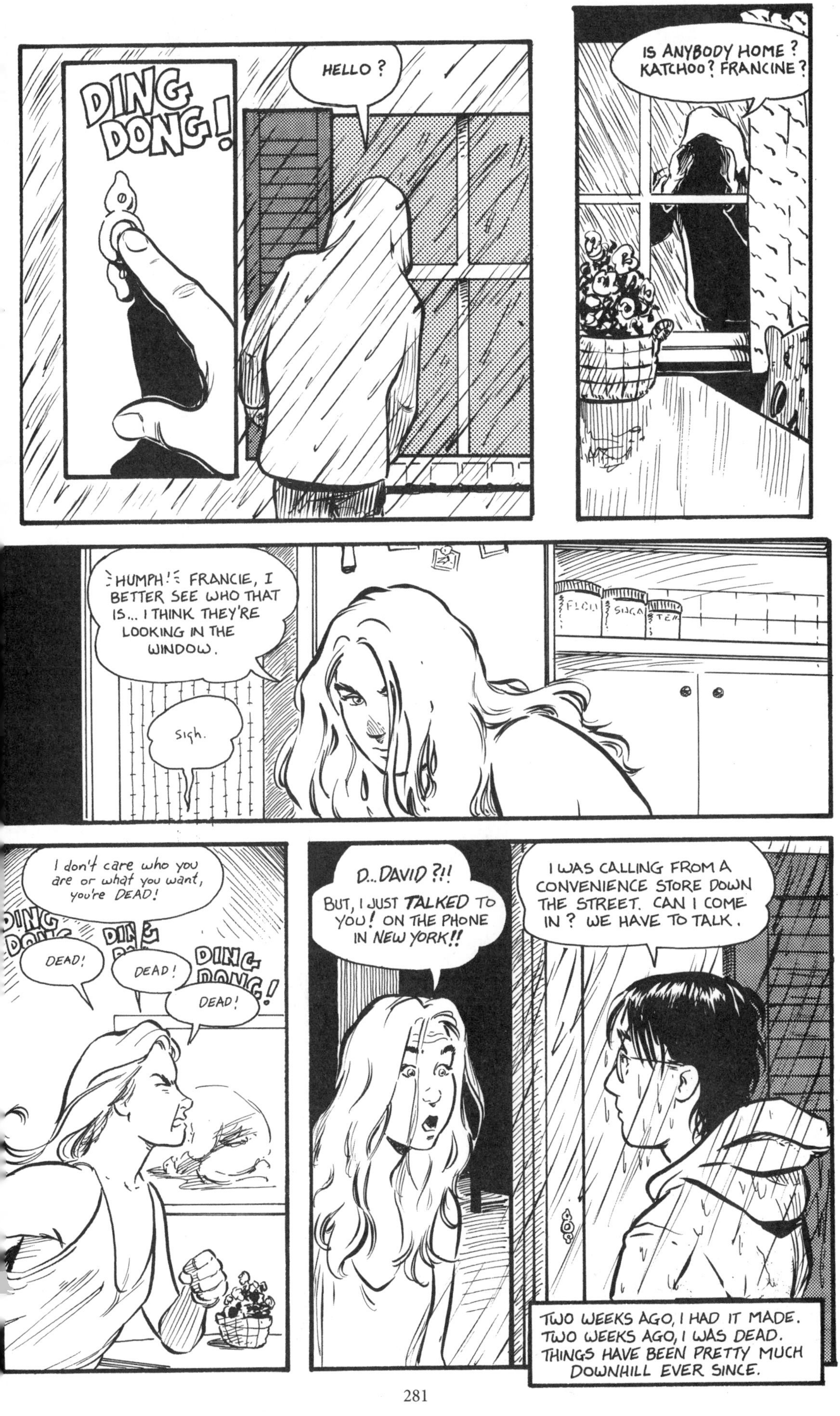
DING DONG!
HELLO?
IS ANYBODY HOME? KATCHOO? FRANCINE?
HUMPH! FRANCIE, I BETTER SEE WHO THAT IS... I THINK THEY'RE LOOKING IN THE WINDOW.
Sigh.
I don't care who you are or what you want, you're DEAD!
DING DONG
DEAD!
DEAD!
DING DONG!
DEAD!
D...DAVID?!!
BUT, I JUST TALKED TO YOU! ON THE PHONE IN NEW YORK!!
I WAS CALLING FROM A CONVENIENCE STORE DOWN THE STREET. CAN I COME IN? WE HAVE TO TALK.
TWO WEEKS AGO, I HAD IT MADE. TWO WEEKS AGO, I WAS DEAD. THINGS HAVE BEEN PRETTY MUCH DOWNHILL EVER SINCE.

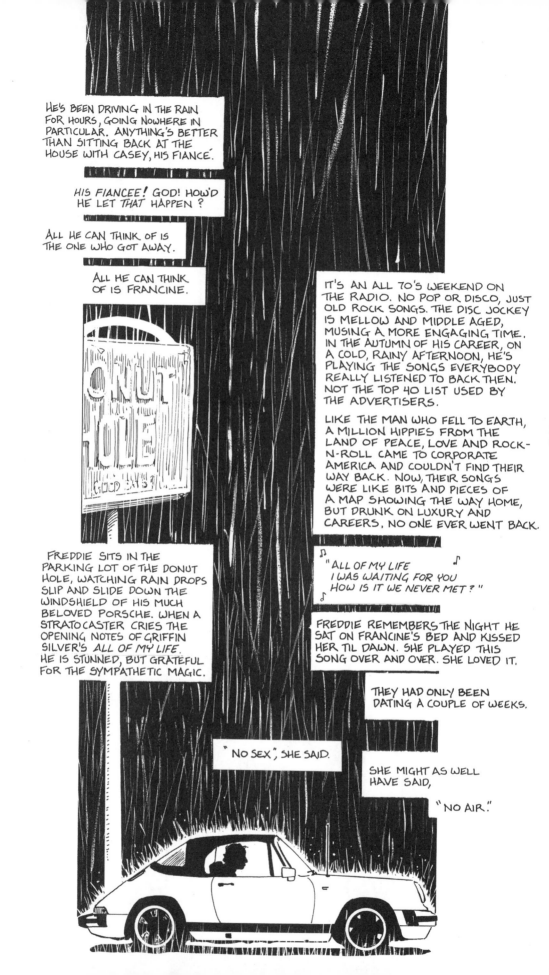

HE'S BEEN DRIVING IN THE RAIN FOR HOURS, GOING NOWHERE IN PARTICULAR. ANYTHING'S BETTER THAN SITTING BACK AT THE HOUSE WITH CASEY, HIS FIANCÉ.

HIS FIANCEE! GOD! HOW'D HE LET *THAT* HAPPEN?

ALL HE CAN THINK OF IS THE ONE WHO GOT AWAY.

ALL HE CAN THINK OF IS FRANCINE.

ONUT HOLE
GOOD EATS

IT'S AN ALL 70'S WEEKEND ON THE RADIO. NO POP OR DISCO, JUST OLD ROCK SONGS. THE DISC JOCKEY IS MELLOW AND MIDDLE AGED, MUSING A MORE ENGAGING TIME. IN THE AUTUMN OF HIS CAREER, ON A COLD, RAINY AFTERNOON, HE'S PLAYING THE SONGS EVERYBODY REALLY LISTENED TO BACK THEN. NOT THE TOP 40 LIST USED BY THE ADVERTISERS.

LIKE THE MAN WHO FELL TO EARTH, A MILLION HIPPIES FROM THE LAND OF PEACE, LOVE AND ROCK-N-ROLL CAME TO CORPORATE AMERICA AND COULDN'T FIND THEIR WAY BACK. NOW, THEIR SONGS WERE LIKE BITS AND PIECES OF A MAP SHOWING THE WAY HOME, BUT DRUNK ON LUXURY AND CAREERS, NO ONE EVER WENT BACK.

FREDDIE SITS IN THE PARKING LOT OF THE DONUT HOLE, WATCHING RAIN DROPS SLIP AND SLIDE DOWN THE WINDSHIELD OF HIS MUCH BELOVED PORSCHE. WHEN A STRATOCASTER CRIES THE OPENING NOTES OF GRIFFIN SILVER'S *ALL OF MY LIFE* HE IS STUNNED, BUT GRATEFUL FOR THE SYMPATHETIC MAGIC.

"ALL OF MY LIFE
I WAS WAITING FOR YOU
HOW IS IT WE NEVER MET?"

FREDDIE REMEMBERS THE NIGHT HE SAT ON FRANCINE'S BED AND KISSED HER TIL DAWN. SHE PLAYED THIS SONG OVER AND OVER. SHE LOVED IT.

THEY HAD ONLY BEEN DATING A COUPLE OF WEEKS.

"NO SEX", SHE SAID.

SHE MIGHT AS WELL HAVE SAID,

"NO AIR."

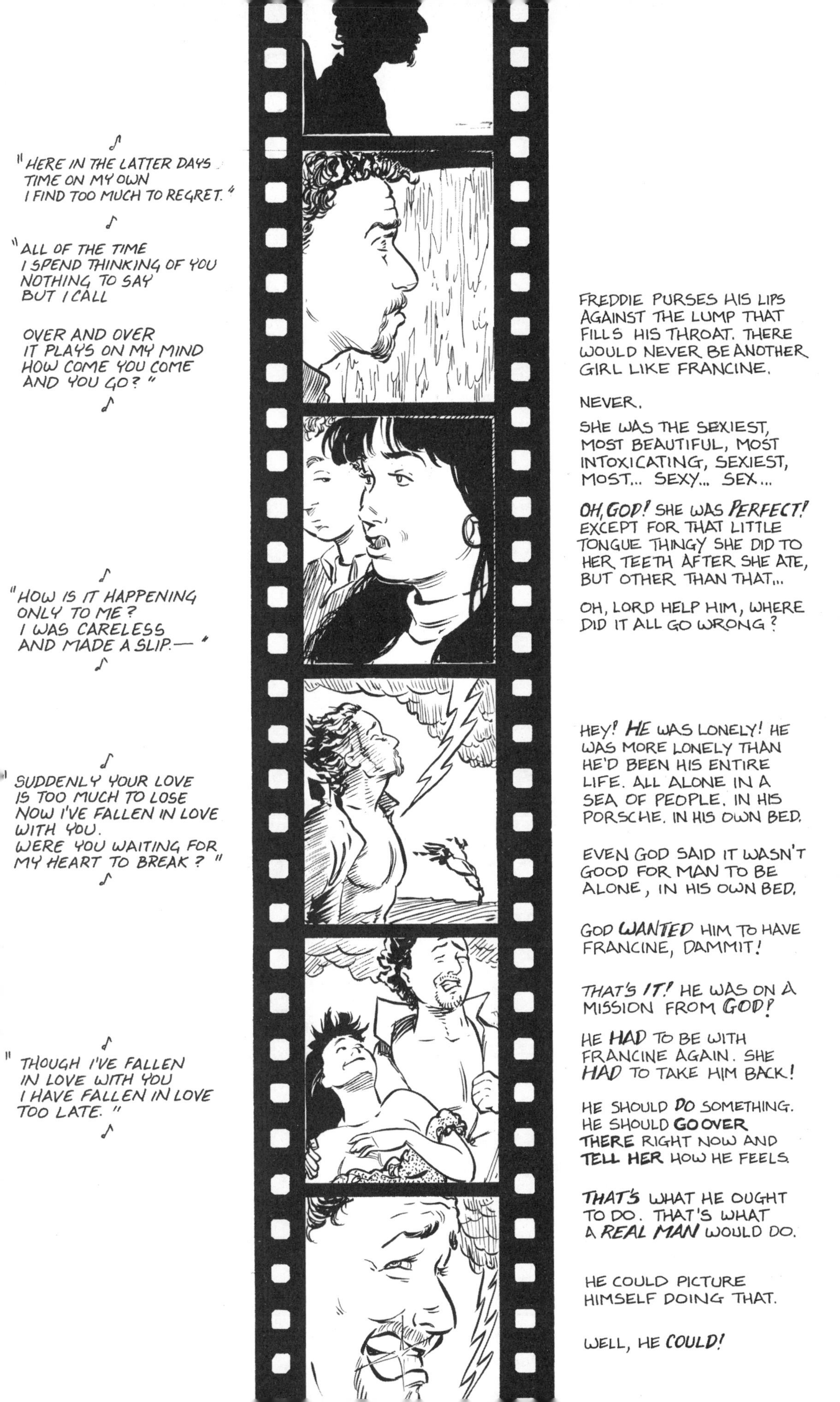

"HERE IN THE LATTER DAYS TIME ON MY OWN I FIND TOO MUCH TO REGRET."
"ALL OF THE TIME I SPEND THINKING OF YOU NOTHING TO SAY BUT I CALL
OVER AND OVER IT PLAYS ON MY MIND HOW COME YOU COME AND YOU GO?"
FREDDIE PURSES HIS LIPS AGAINST THE LUMP THAT FILLS HIS THROAT. THERE WOULD NEVER BE ANOTHER GIRL LIKE FRANCINE.
NEVER.
SHE WAS THE SEXIEST, MOST BEAUTIFUL, MOST INTOXICATING, SEXIEST, MOST... SEXY... SEX...
OH, GOD! SHE WAS PERFECT! EXCEPT FOR THAT LITTLE TONGUE THINGY SHE DID TO HER TEETH AFTER SHE ATE, BUT OTHER THAN THAT...
"HOW IS IT HAPPENING ONLY TO ME? I WAS CARELESS AND MADE A SLIP.—"
OH, LORD HELP HIM, WHERE DID IT ALL GO WRONG?
HEY! HE WAS LONELY! HE WAS MORE LONELY THAN HE'D BEEN HIS ENTIRE LIFE. ALL ALONE IN A SEA OF PEOPLE. IN HIS PORSCHE. IN HIS OWN BED.
"SUDDENLY YOUR LOVE IS TOO MUCH TO LOSE NOW I'VE FALLEN IN LOVE WITH YOU. WERE YOU WAITING FOR MY HEART TO BREAK?"
EVEN GOD SAID IT WASN'T GOOD FOR MAN TO BE ALONE, IN HIS OWN BED.
GOD WANTED HIM TO HAVE FRANCINE, DAMMIT!
THAT'S IT! HE WAS ON A MISSION FROM GOD!
HE HAD TO BE WITH FRANCINE AGAIN. SHE HAD TO TAKE HIM BACK!
"THOUGH I'VE FALLEN IN LOVE WITH YOU I HAVE FALLEN IN LOVE TOO LATE."
HE SHOULD DO SOMETHING. HE SHOULD GO OVER THERE RIGHT NOW AND TELL HER HOW HE FEELS.
THAT'S WHAT HE OUGHT TO DO. THAT'S WHAT A REAL MAN WOULD DO.
HE COULD PICTURE HIMSELF DOING THAT.
WELL, HE COULD!

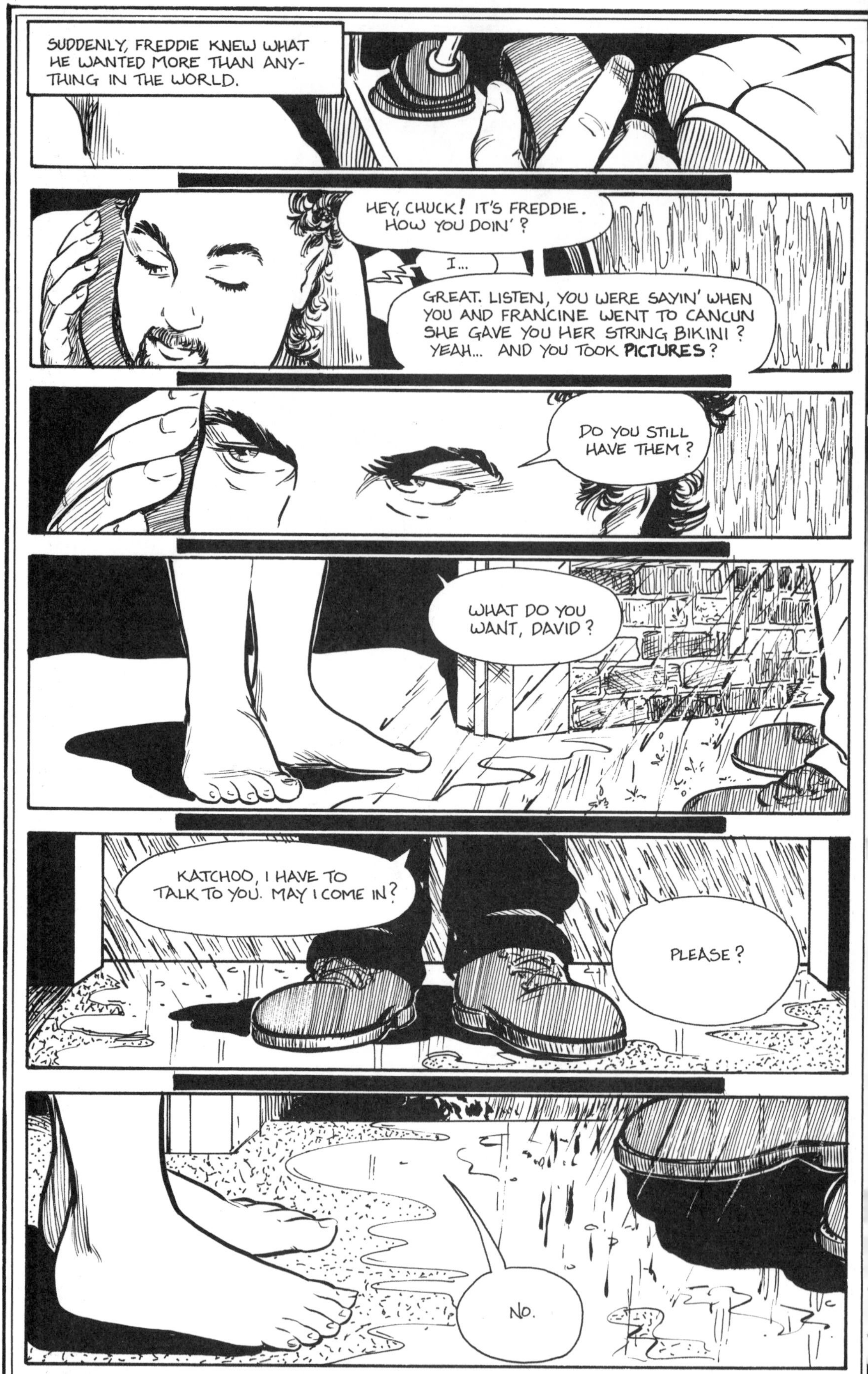
SUDDENLY, FREDDIE KNEW WHAT HE WANTED MORE THAN ANYTHING IN THE WORLD.
HEY, CHUCK! IT'S FREDDIE. HOW YOU DOIN'?
I...
GREAT. LISTEN, YOU WERE SAYIN' WHEN YOU AND FRANCINE WENT TO CANCUN SHE GAVE YOU HER STRING BIKINI? YEAH... AND YOU TOOK **PICTURES**?
DO YOU STILL HAVE THEM?
WHAT DO YOU WANT, DAVID?
KATCHOO, I HAVE TO TALK TO YOU. MAY I COME IN?
PLEASE?
NO.

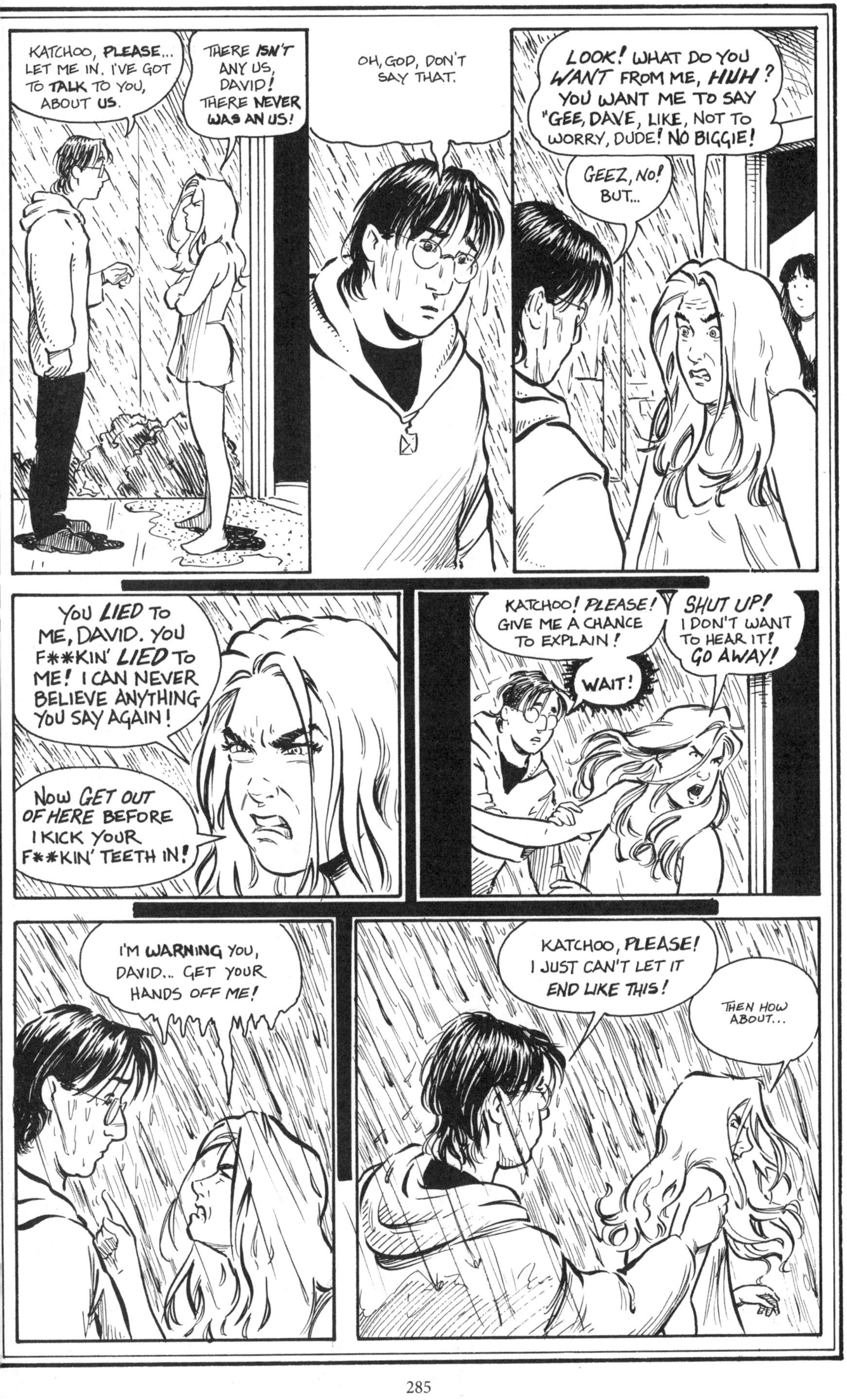
KATCHOO, PLEASE... LET ME IN. I'VE GOT TO TALK TO YOU, ABOUT US.
THERE ISN'T ANY US, DAVID! THERE NEVER WAS AN US!
OH, GOD, DON'T SAY THAT.
LOOK! WHAT DO YOU WANT FROM ME, HUH? YOU WANT ME TO SAY "GEE, DAVE, LIKE, NOT TO WORRY, DUDE! NO BIGGIE!
GEEZ, NO! BUT...
YOU LIED TO ME, DAVID. YOU F**KIN' LIED TO ME! I CAN NEVER BELIEVE ANYTHING YOU SAY AGAIN!
NOW GET OUT OF HERE BEFORE I KICK YOUR F**KIN' TEETH IN!
KATCHOO! PLEASE! GIVE ME A CHANCE TO EXPLAIN!
SHUT UP! I DON'T WANT TO HEAR IT! GO AWAY!
WAIT!
I'M WARNING YOU, DAVID... GET YOUR HANDS OFF ME!
KATCHOO, PLEASE! I JUST CAN'T LET IT END LIKE THIS!
THEN HOW ABOUT...

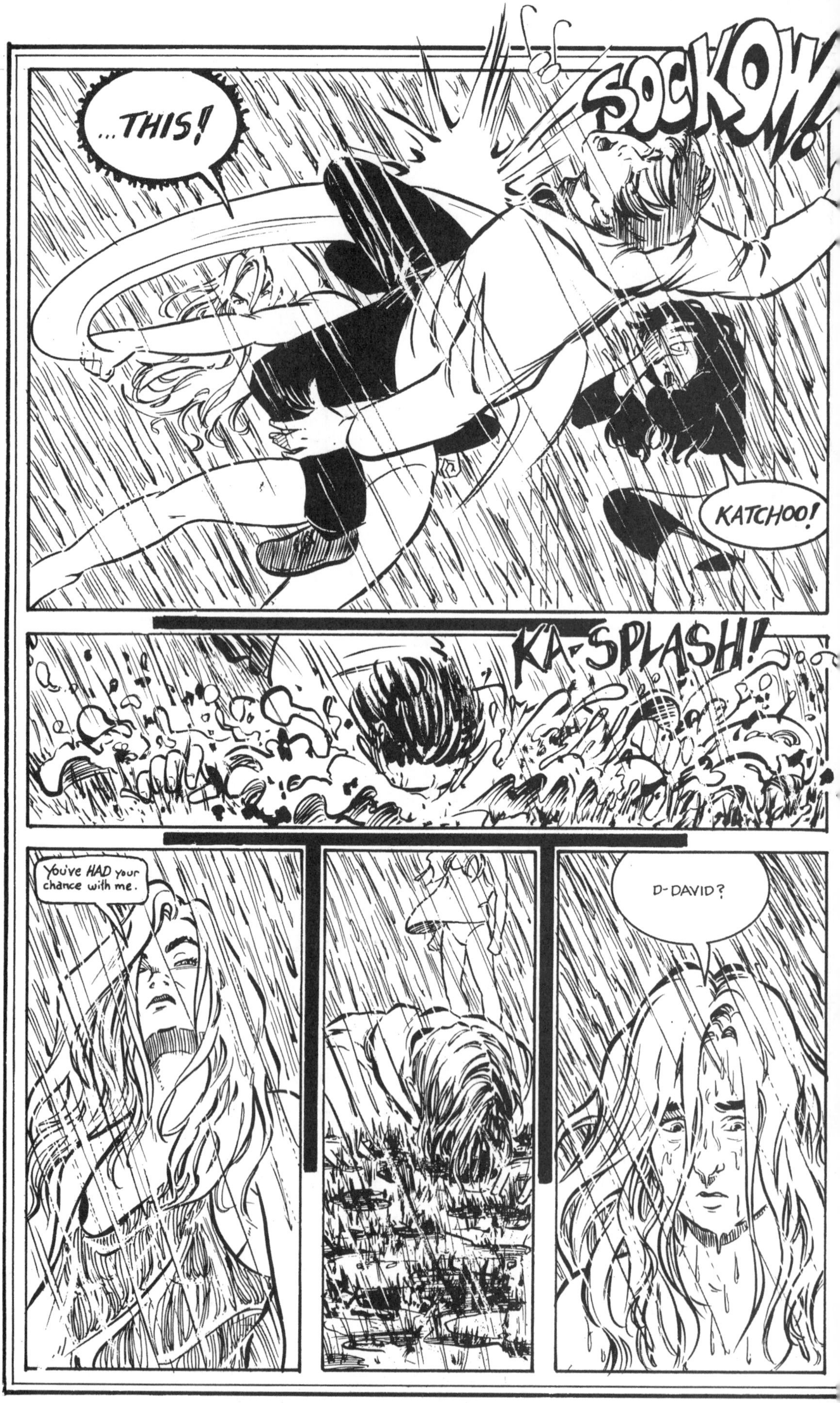
...THIS!
SOCKOW!
KATCHOO!
KA-SPLASH!
You've HAD your chance with me.
D-DAVID?

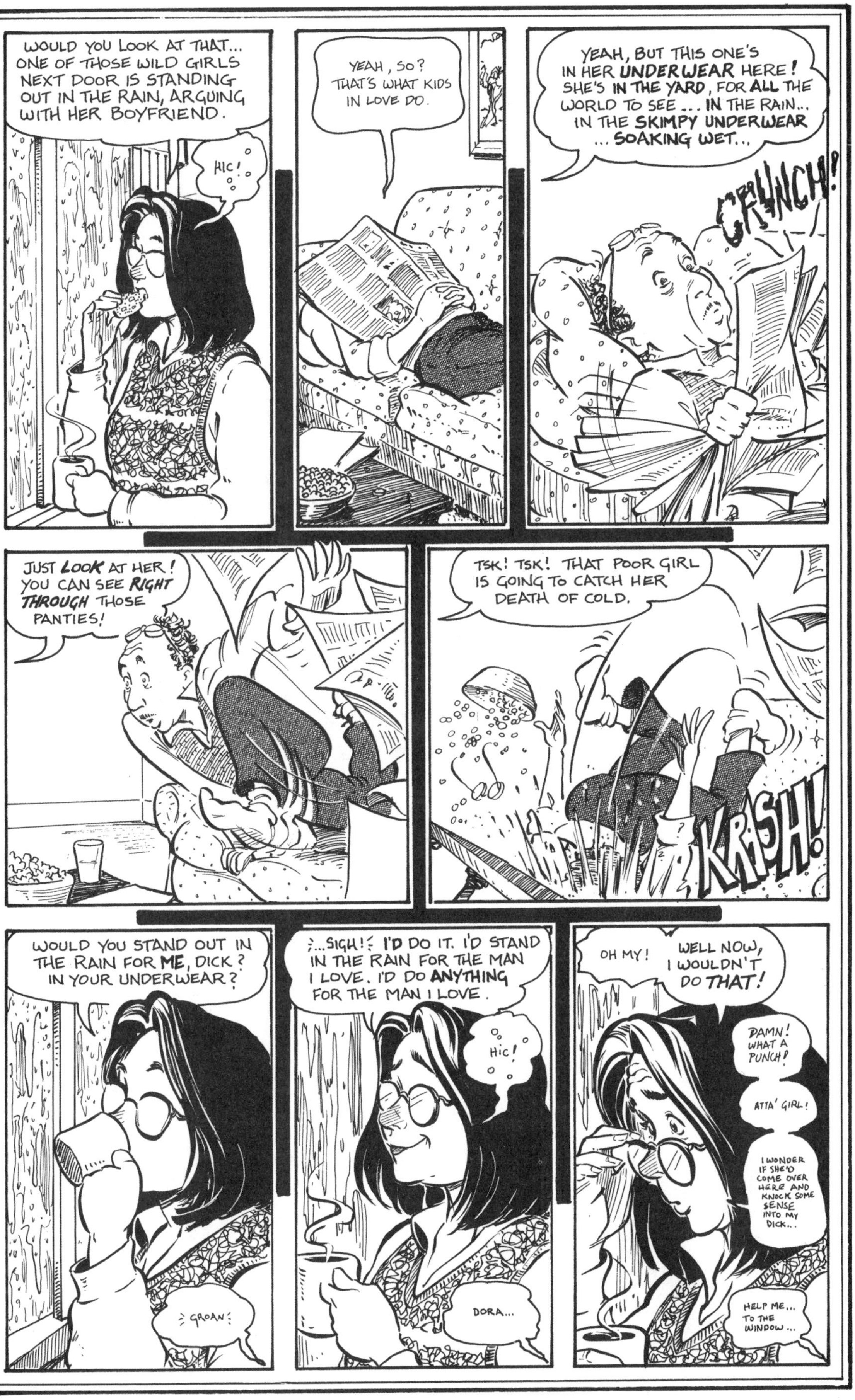
WOULD YOU LOOK AT THAT... ONE OF THOSE WILD GIRLS NEXT DOOR IS STANDING OUT IN THE RAIN, ARGUING WITH HER BOYFRIEND.
HIC!
YEAH, SO? THAT'S WHAT KIDS IN LOVE DO.
YEAH, BUT THIS ONE'S IN HER UNDERWEAR HERE! SHE'S IN THE YARD, FOR ALL THE WORLD TO SEE ... IN THE RAIN... IN THE SKIMPY UNDERWEAR ... SOAKING WET...
CRUNCH!
JUST LOOK AT HER! YOU CAN SEE RIGHT THROUGH THOSE PANTIES!
TSK! TSK! THAT POOR GIRL IS GOING TO CATCH HER DEATH OF COLD.
KRASH!
WOULD YOU STAND OUT IN THE RAIN FOR ME, DICK? IN YOUR UNDERWEAR?
GROAN
...SIGH! I'D DO IT. I'D STAND IN THE RAIN FOR THE MAN I LOVE. I'D DO ANYTHING FOR THE MAN I LOVE.
HIC!
DORA...
OH MY!
WELL NOW, I WOULDN'T DO THAT!
DAMN! WHAT A PUNCH!
ATTA' GIRL!
I WONDER IF SHE'D COME OVER HERE AND KNOCK SOME SENSE INTO MY DICK...
HELP ME... TO THE WINDOW...

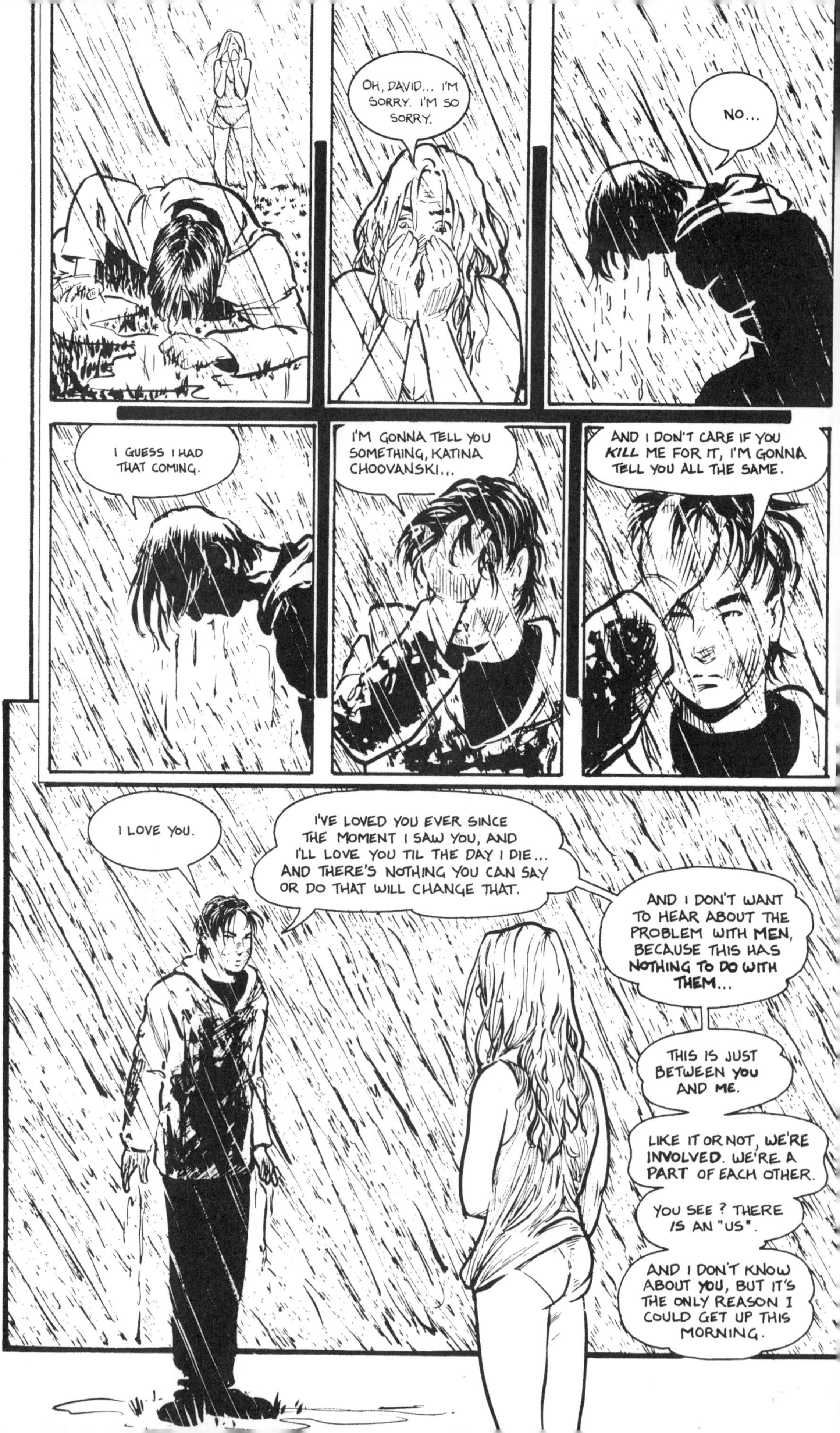
OH, DAVID... I'M SORRY. I'M SO SORRY.
NO...
I GUESS I HAD THAT COMING.
I'M GONNA TELL YOU SOMETHING, KATINA CHOOVANSKI...
AND I DON'T CARE IF YOU KILL ME FOR IT, I'M GONNA TELL YOU ALL THE SAME.
I LOVE YOU.
I'VE LOVED YOU EVER SINCE THE MOMENT I SAW YOU, AND I'LL LOVE YOU TIL THE DAY I DIE... AND THERE'S NOTHING YOU CAN SAY OR DO THAT WILL CHANGE THAT.
AND I DON'T WANT TO HEAR ABOUT THE PROBLEM WITH MEN, BECAUSE THIS HAS NOTHING TO DO WITH THEM...
THIS IS JUST BETWEEN YOU AND ME.
LIKE IT OR NOT, WE'RE INVOLVED. WE'RE A PART OF EACH OTHER.
YOU SEE? THERE IS AN "US".
AND I DON'T KNOW ABOUT YOU, BUT IT'S THE ONLY REASON I COULD GET UP THIS MORNING.

DAVID, I JUST CAN'T... I DON'T SEE US...

I LOVE YOU, KATCHOO.

LOOK DAVID, YOU DON'T UNDERSTAND WHAT I'VE BEEN THROUGH! THE THINGS I'VE SEEN MEN DO...

I LOVE YOU, KATCHOO. MORE THAN ANYTHING IN THE WORLD.

LISTEN TO ME YOU STUPID BOY!

YOU DON'T KNOW WHAT YOU'RE SAYING! YOU THINK I'M SOME PRINCESS OR SOMETHING BUT I'M NOT! CAN'T YOU GET IT THR OUR E...

IF YOU HA ANY IDEA TH THINGS THAT I'VE DONE, THE KIND OF PEOPLE I'VE BEEN WITH! THE PEOPLE I'V SLEPT WITH SER A RY N BE FR DE N TO UR SO WONG A SO WHY DON'T YOU JUST LEAVE ME TH F**K ALONE SO I CAN GET ON WITH M LIFE! GO FIND SOME AIRHEAD COED WHO'LL WORSHIP THE GROUND YOU WALK ON AND LET YOU GET HER PREGNANT

ALL I KNOW IS I LOVE YOU.

SHUT UP DAMMIT! SHUT UP!

SLAP!

I LOVE YOU, KATINA CHOOVANSKI... AND YOU'RE NEVER GONNA BEAT THAT OUT OF ME.

BUT IF THAT'S HOW YOU WANT TO SPEND OUR TIME TOGETHER, THEN I'LL ACCEPT THAT.

AT LEAST IT'LL BE YOUR FISTS THAT BEAT ME.

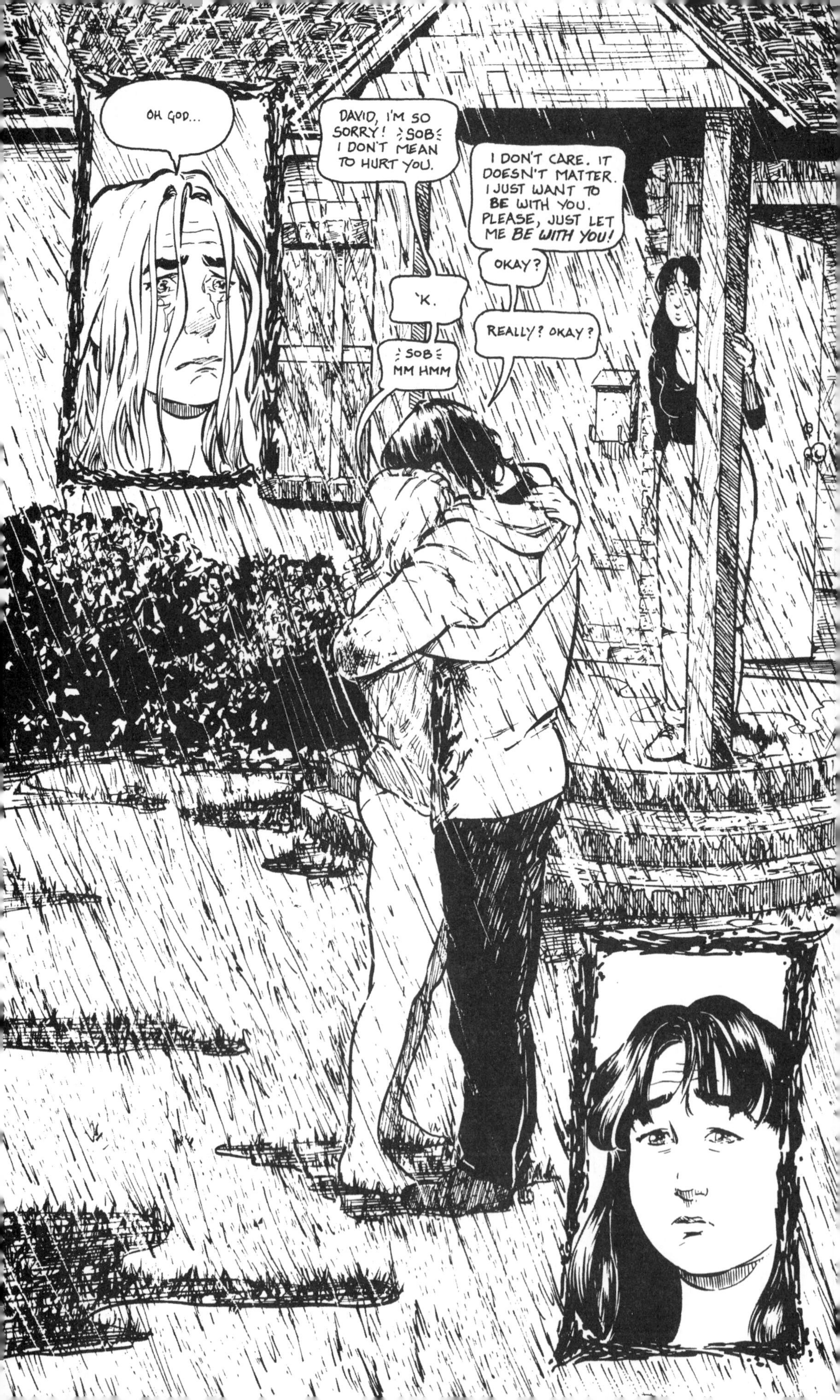

OH GOD...
DAVID, I'M SO SORRY! SOB I DON'T MEAN TO HURT YOU.
I DON'T CARE. IT DOESN'T MATTER. I JUST WANT TO BE WITH YOU. PLEASE, JUST LET ME BE WITH YOU!
OKAY?
`K.
REALLY? OKAY?
SOB MM HMM

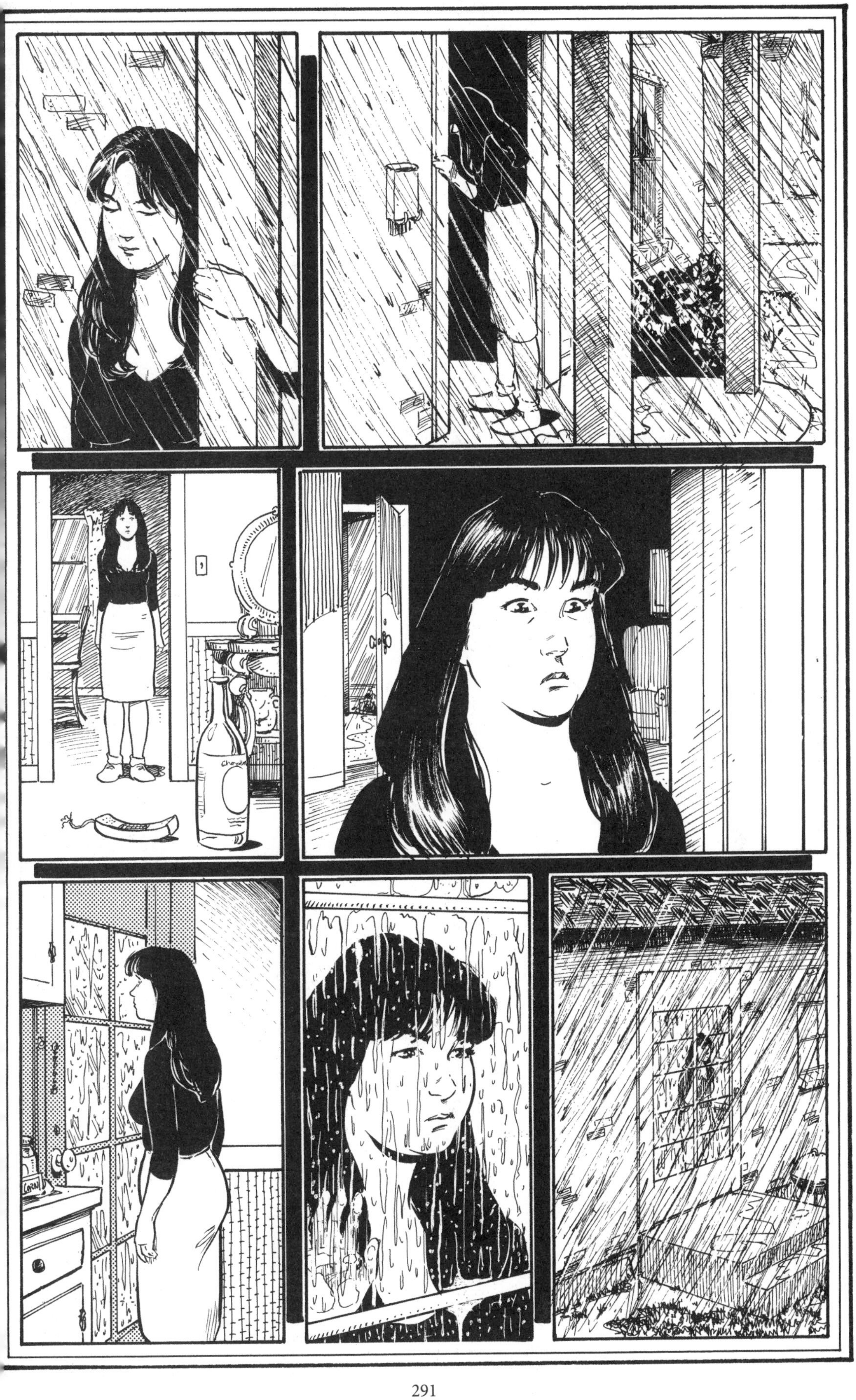

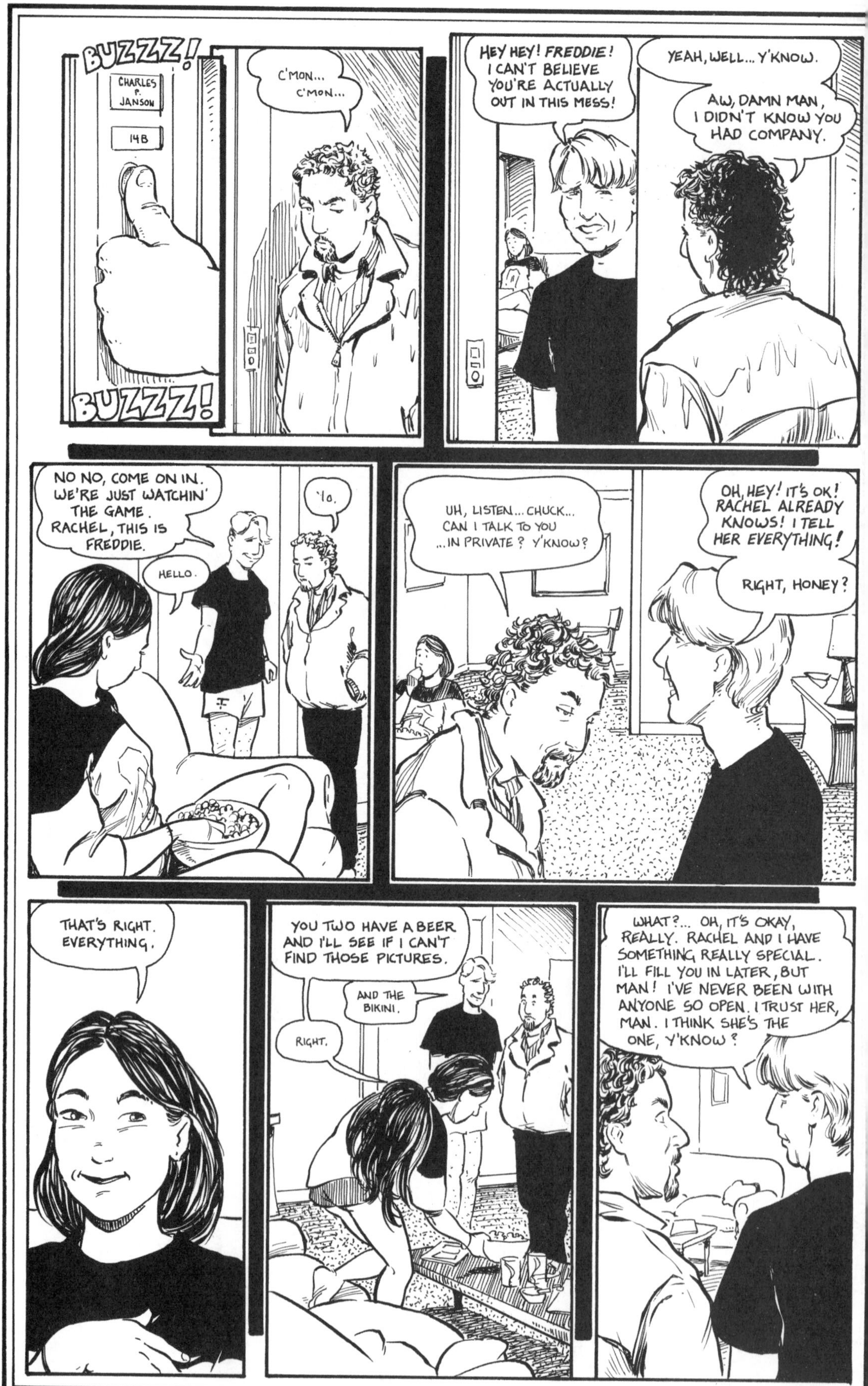
BUZZZ!
CHARLES P. JANSON
14B
BUZZZ!
C'MON... C'MON...
HEY HEY! FREDDIE! I CAN'T BELIEVE YOU'RE ACTUALLY OUT IN THIS MESS!
YEAH, WELL... Y'KNOW.
AW, DAMN MAN, I DIDN'T KNOW YOU HAD COMPANY.
NO NO, COME ON IN. WE'RE JUST WATCHIN' THE GAME. RACHEL, THIS IS FREDDIE.
'LO.
HELLO.
UH, LISTEN... CHUCK... CAN I TALK TO YOU ...IN PRIVATE? Y'KNOW?
OH, HEY! IT'S OK! RACHEL ALREADY KNOWS! I TELL HER EVERYTHING!
RIGHT, HONEY?
THAT'S RIGHT. EVERYTHING.
YOU TWO HAVE A BEER AND I'LL SEE IF I CAN'T FIND THOSE PICTURES.
AND THE BIKINI.
RIGHT.
WHAT?... OH, IT'S OKAY, REALLY. RACHEL AND I HAVE SOMETHING REALLY SPECIAL. I'LL FILL YOU IN LATER, BUT MAN! I'VE NEVER BEEN WITH ANYONE SO OPEN. I TRUST HER, MAN. I THINK SHE'S THE ONE, Y'KNOW?

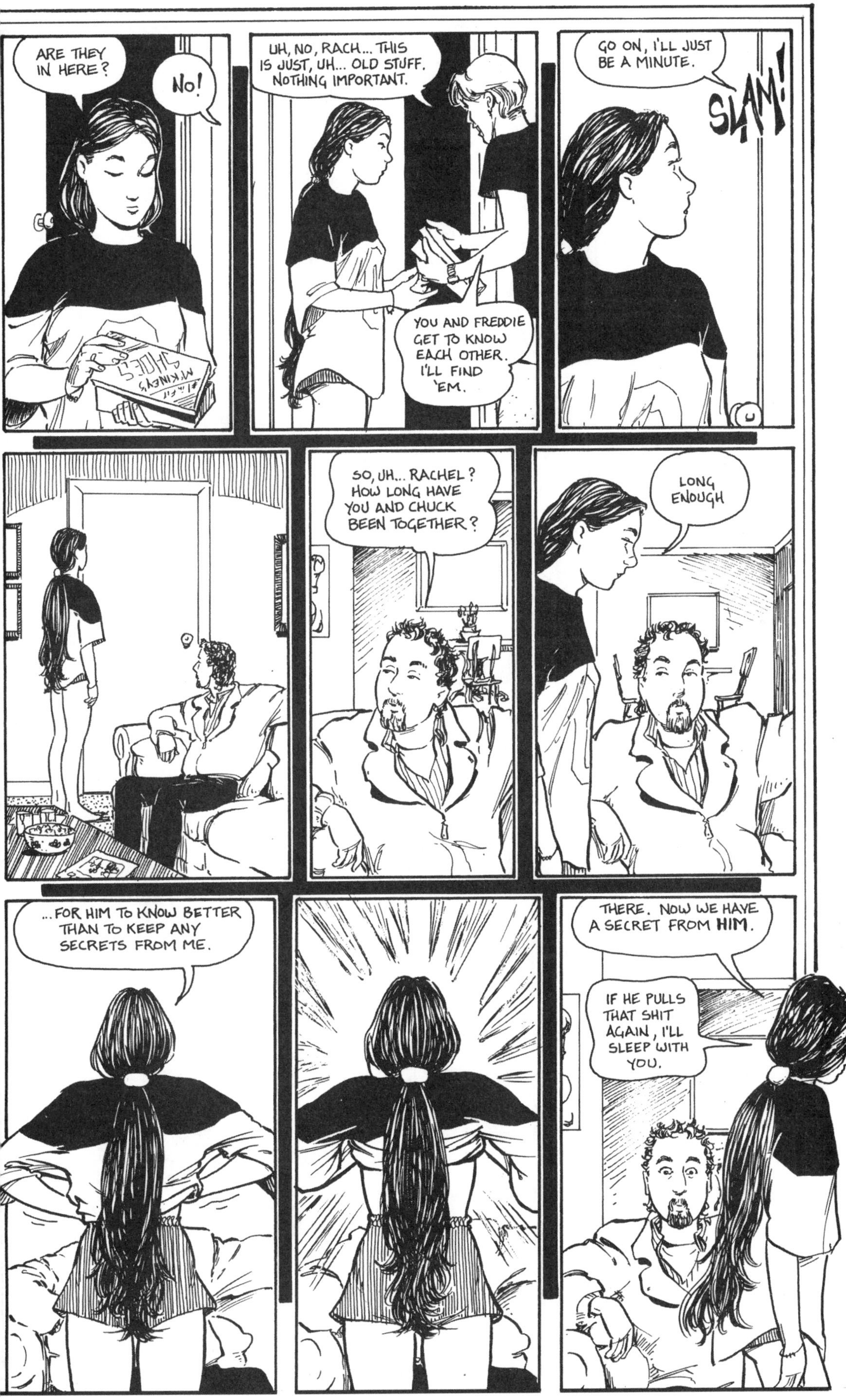
ARE THEY IN HERE?
No!
#1 FIT M'KINLEY'S SHOES
UH, NO, RACH... THIS IS JUST, UH... OLD STUFF. NOTHING IMPORTANT.
YOU AND FREDDIE GET TO KNOW EACH OTHER. I'LL FIND 'EM.
GO ON, I'LL JUST BE A MINUTE.
SLAM!
SO, UH... RACHEL? HOW LONG HAVE YOU AND CHUCK BEEN TOGETHER?
LONG ENOUGH
...FOR HIM TO KNOW BETTER THAN TO KEEP ANY SECRETS FROM ME.
THERE. NOW WE HAVE A SECRET FROM HIM.
IF HE PULLS THAT SHIT AGAIN, I'LL SLEEP WITH YOU.

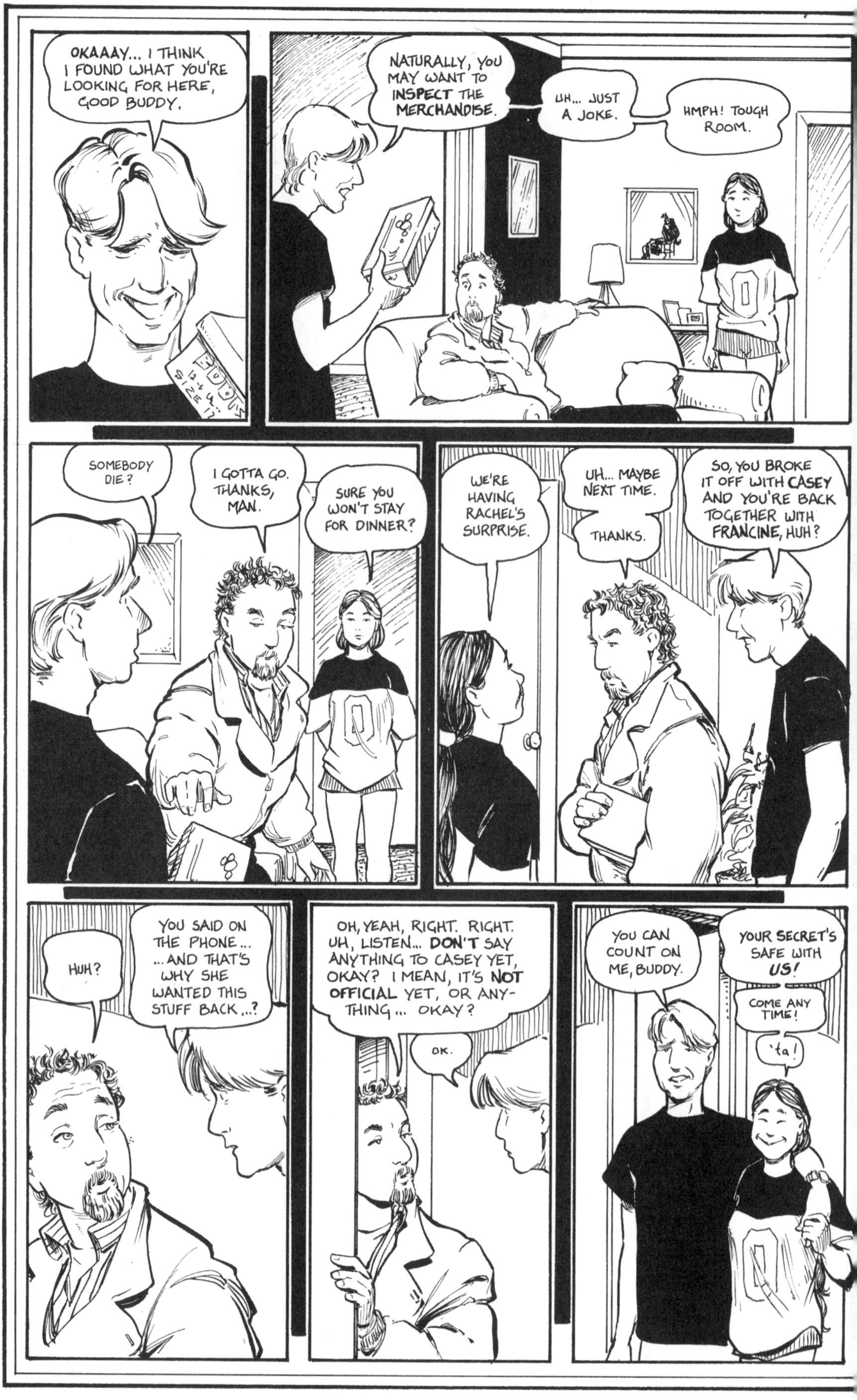
OKAAAY... I THINK I FOUND WHAT YOU'RE LOOKING FOR HERE, GOOD BUDDY.
NATURALLY, YOU MAY WANT TO INSPECT THE MERCHANDISE.
UH... JUST A JOKE.
HMPH! TOUGH ROOM.
SOMEBODY DIE?
I GOTTA GO. THANKS, MAN.
SURE YOU WON'T STAY FOR DINNER?
WE'RE HAVING RACHEL'S SURPRISE.
UH... MAYBE NEXT TIME.
THANKS.
SO, YOU BROKE IT OFF WITH CASEY AND YOU'RE BACK TOGETHER WITH FRANCINE, HUH?
HUH?
YOU SAID ON THE PHONE... ...AND THAT'S WHY SHE WANTED THIS STUFF BACK...?
OH, YEAH, RIGHT. RIGHT. UH, LISTEN... DON'T SAY ANYTHING TO CASEY YET, OKAY? I MEAN, IT'S NOT OFFICIAL YET, OR ANYTHING... OKAY?
OK.
YOU CAN COUNT ON ME, BUDDY.
YOUR SECRET'S SAFE WITH US!
COME ANY TIME!
'ta!

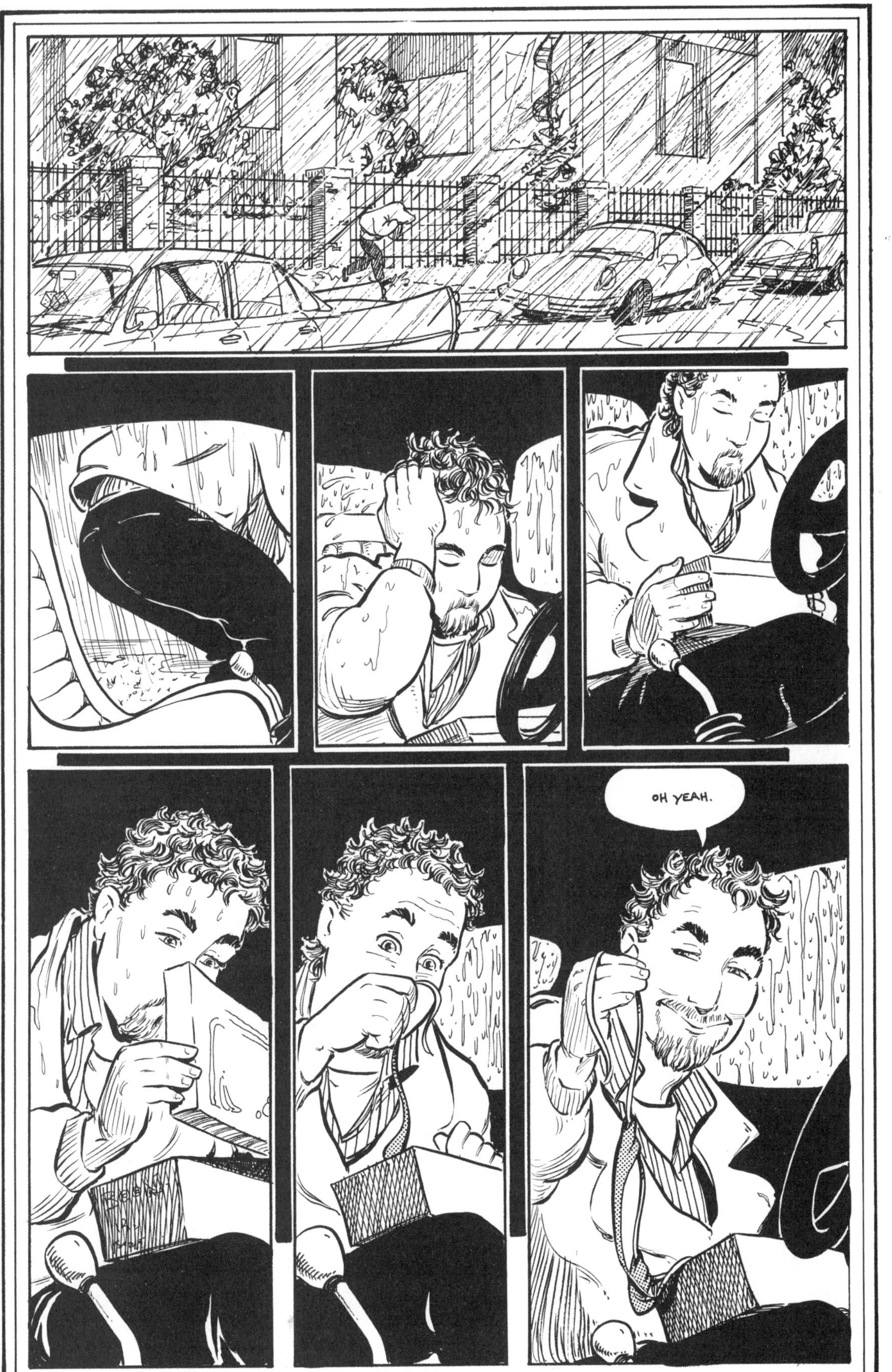
OH YEAH.

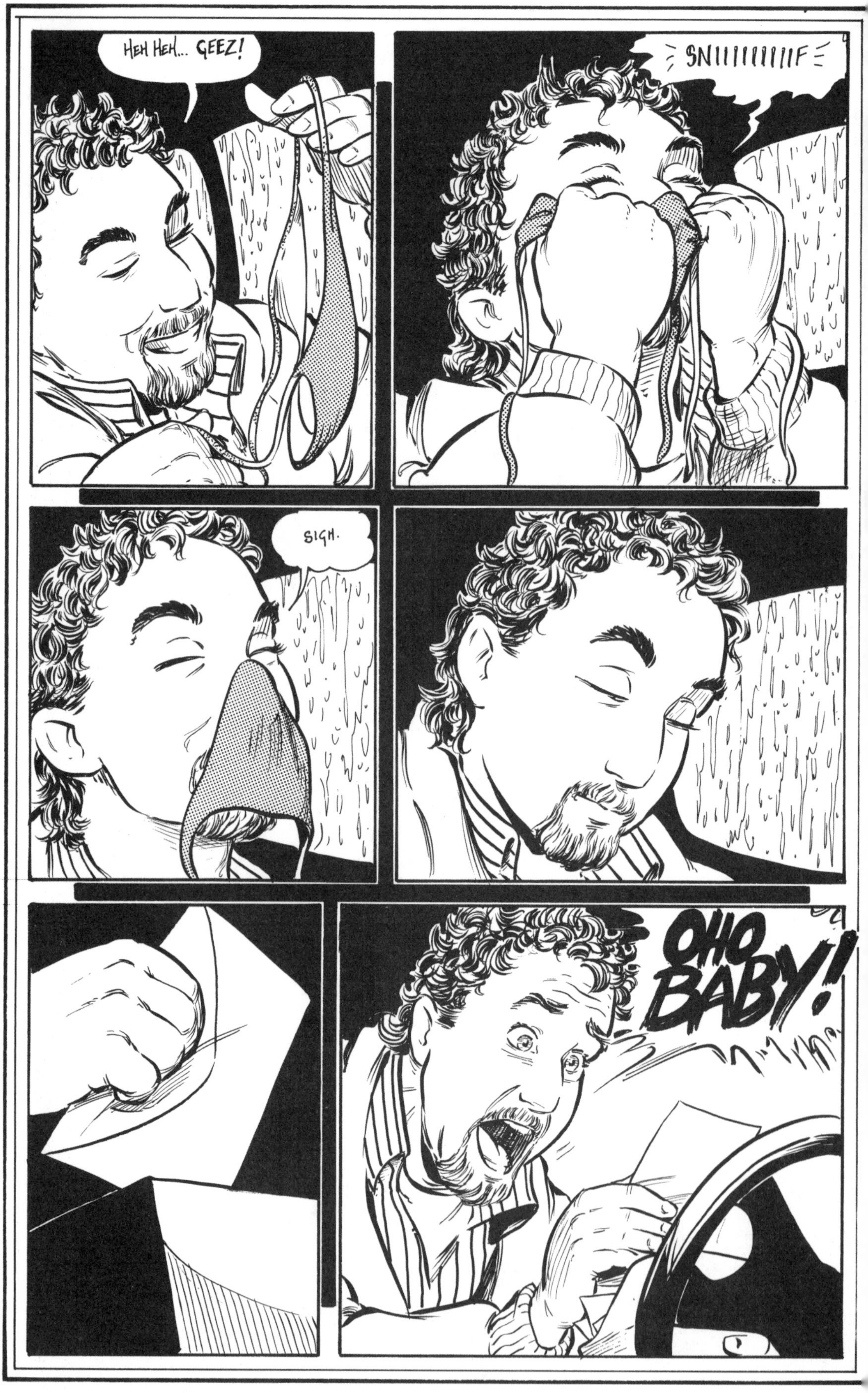
HEH HEH... GEEZ!
SNIIIIIIIIIF
SIGH.
OHO BABY!

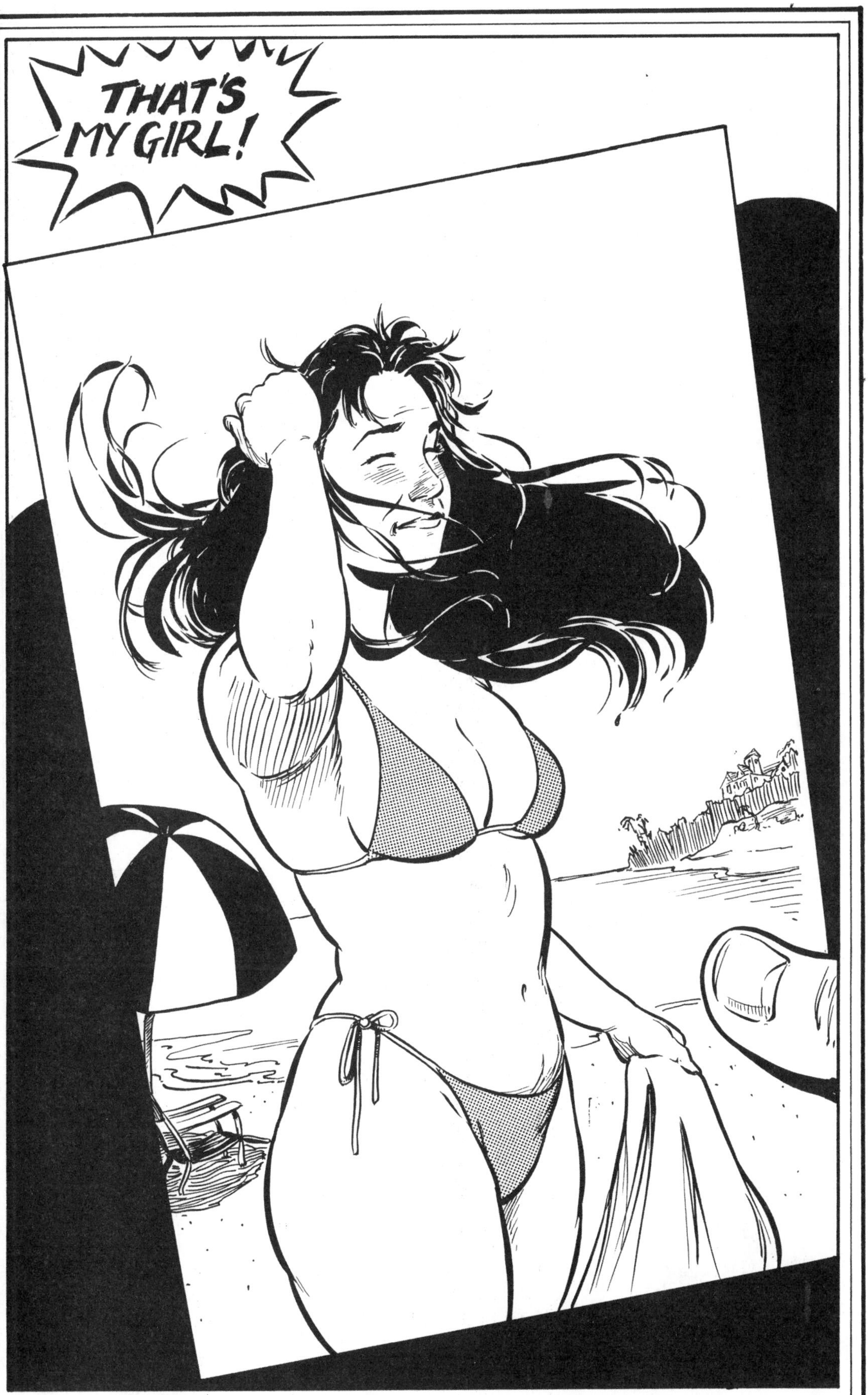
THAT'S MY GIRL!

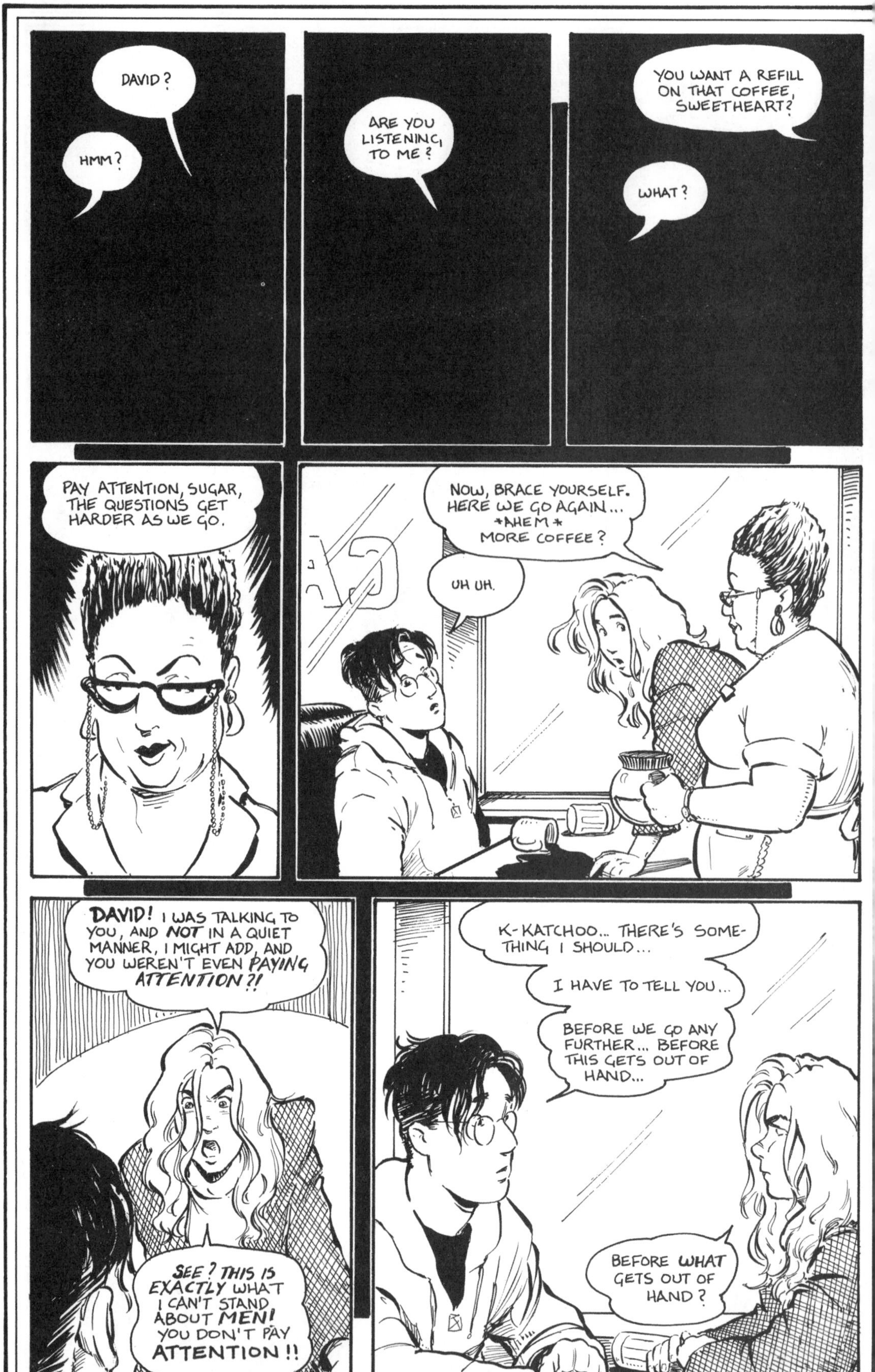
DAVID?
HMM?
ARE YOU LISTENING, TO ME?
YOU WANT A REFILL ON THAT COFFEE, SWEETHEART?
WHAT?
PAY ATTENTION, SUGAR, THE QUESTIONS GET HARDER AS WE GO.
NOW, BRACE YOURSELF. HERE WE GO AGAIN... *AHEM* MORE COFFEE?
UH UH.
DAVID! I WAS TALKING TO YOU, AND NOT IN A QUIET MANNER, I MIGHT ADD, AND YOU WEREN'T EVEN PAYING ATTENTION?!
SEE? THIS IS EXACTLY WHAT I CAN'T STAND ABOUT MEN! YOU DON'T PAY ATTENTION!!
K-KATCHOO... THERE'S SOMETHING I SHOULD...
I HAVE TO TELL YOU...
BEFORE WE GO ANY FURTHER... BEFORE THIS GETS OUT OF HAND...
BEFORE WHAT GETS OUT OF HAND?

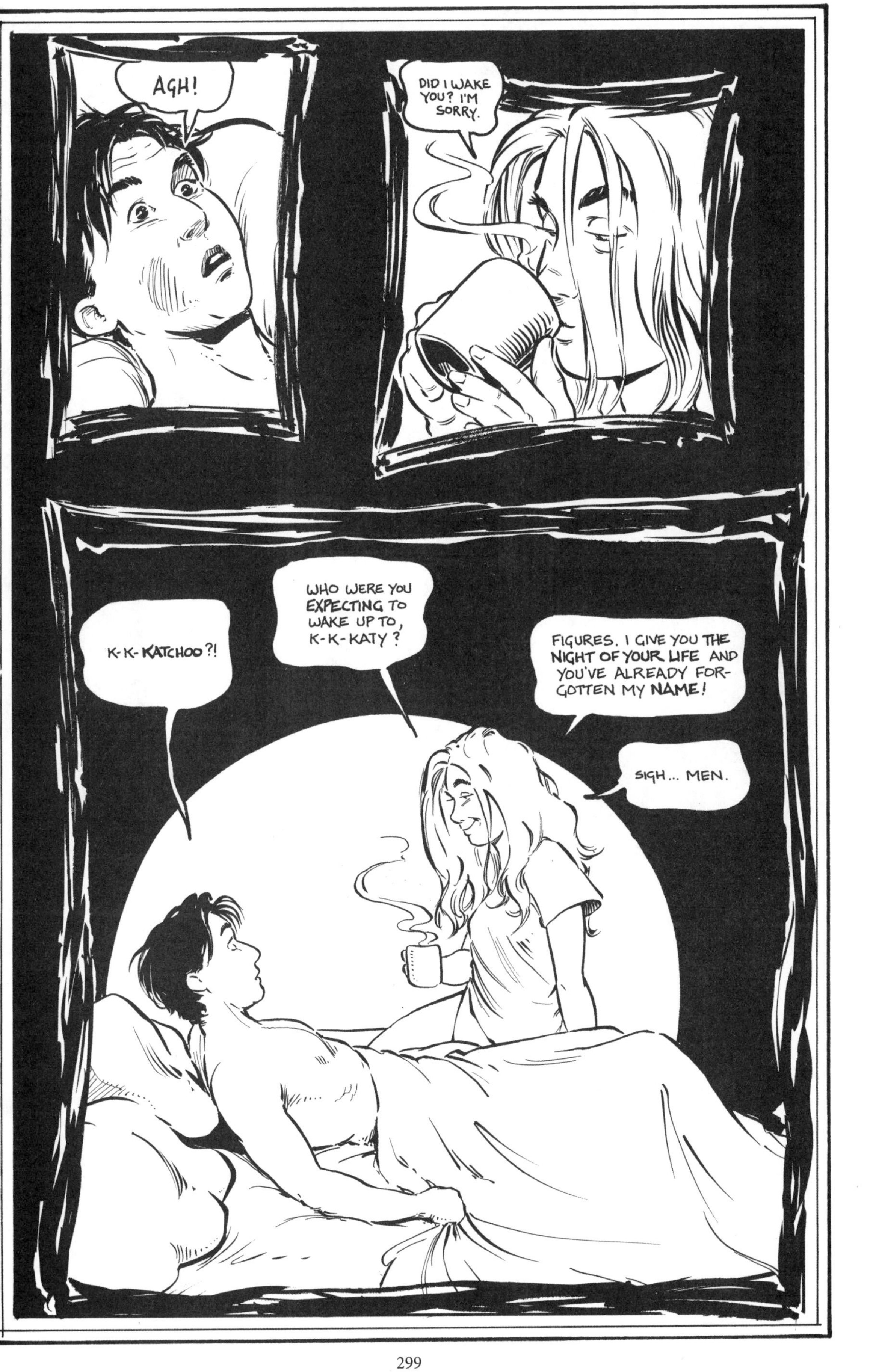
AGH!
DID I WAKE YOU? I'M SORRY.
K-K-KATCHOO?!
WHO WERE YOU EXPECTING TO WAKE UP TO, K-K-KATY?
FIGURES. I GIVE YOU THE NIGHT OF YOUR LIFE AND YOU'VE ALREADY FOR-GOTTEN MY NAME!
SIGH... MEN.

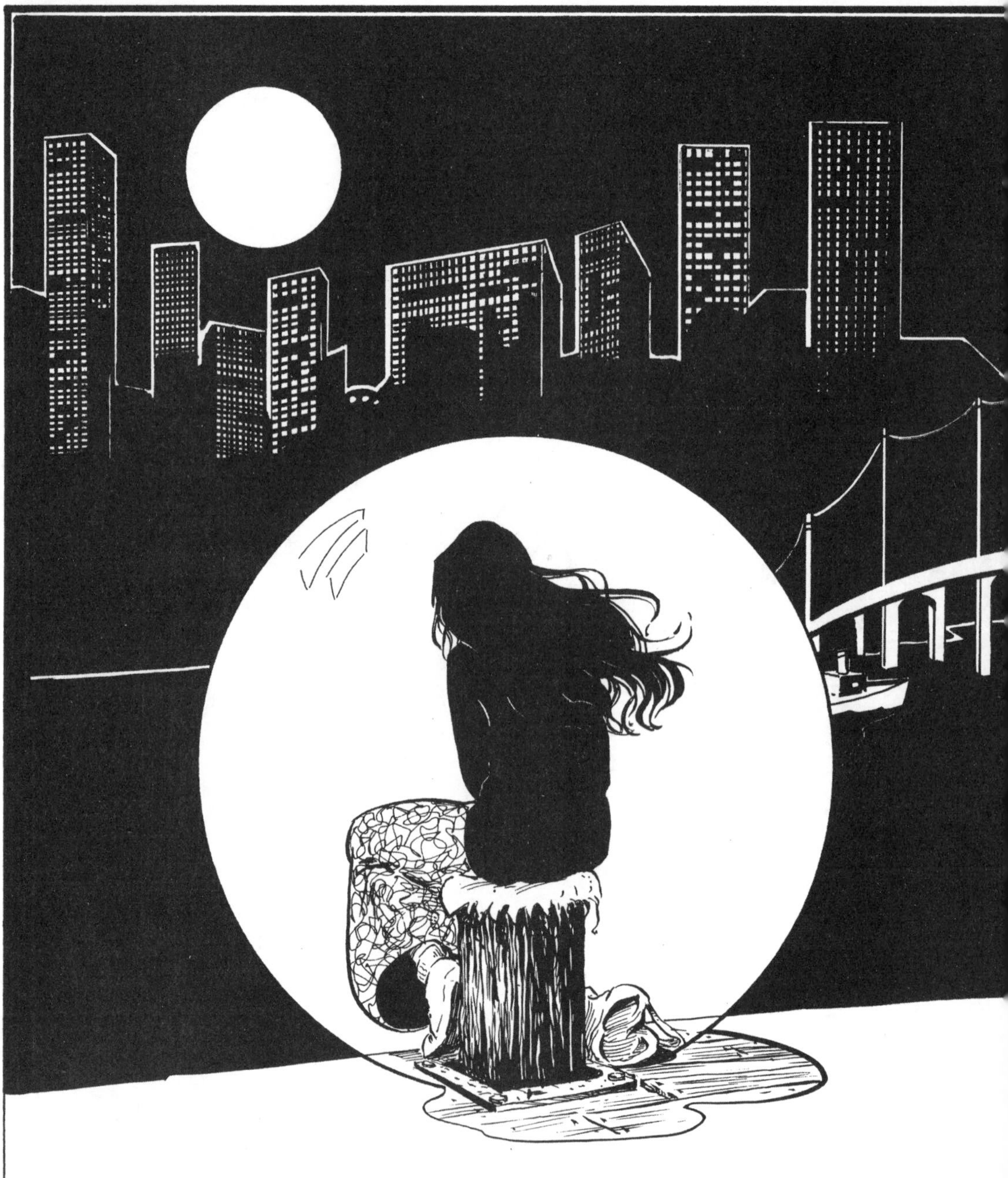

If you're leaving me
please don't tell me
You're still pleasing me
Do I fail you
I will wonder today
if tomorrow you'll stay
I can hear your voice turn cold

when you turn to me I know
I'm the one who won't let go
Are you blaming me
for holding on
when you let me know
it's my last chance
And I know it's gone

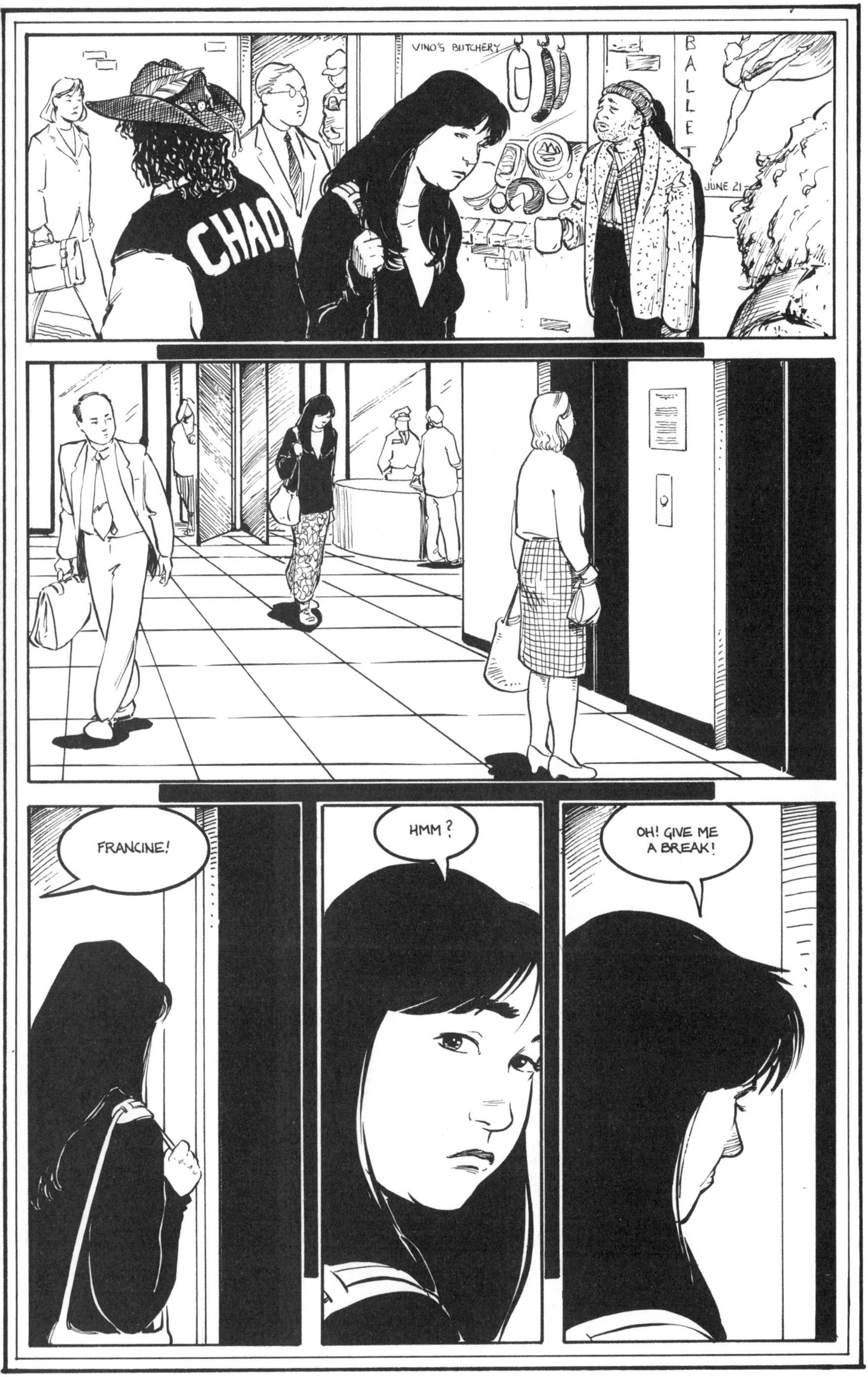

VINO'S BUTCHERY
BALLET
JUNE 21
CHAO
FRANCINE!
HMM ?
OH! GIVE ME A BREAK!

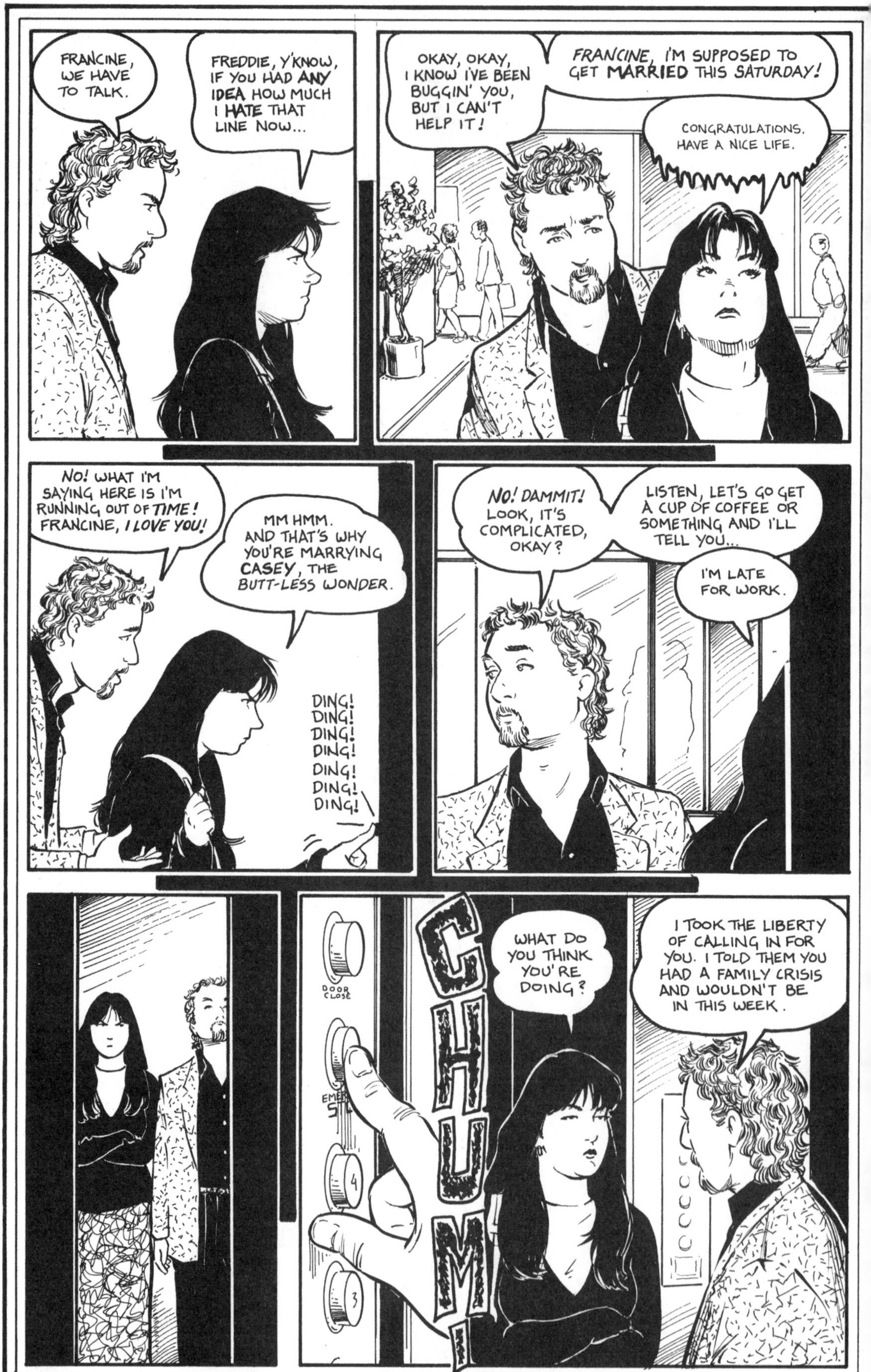
FRANCINE, WE HAVE TO TALK.
FREDDIE, Y'KNOW, IF YOU HAD ANY IDEA HOW MUCH I HATE THAT LINE NOW...
OKAY, OKAY, I KNOW I'VE BEEN BUGGIN' YOU, BUT I CAN'T HELP IT!
FRANCINE, I'M SUPPOSED TO GET MARRIED THIS SATURDAY!
CONGRATULATIONS. HAVE A NICE LIFE.
NO! WHAT I'M SAYING HERE IS I'M RUNNING OUT OF TIME! FRANCINE, I LOVE YOU!
MM HMM. AND THAT'S WHY YOU'RE MARRYING CASEY, THE BUTT-LESS WONDER.
DING! DING! DING! DING! DING! DING! DING!
NO! DAMMIT! LOOK, IT'S COMPLICATED, OKAY?
LISTEN, LET'S GO GET A CUP OF COFFEE OR SOMETHING AND I'LL TELL YOU...
I'M LATE FOR WORK.
DOOR CLOSE
CHUM!
WHAT DO YOU THINK YOU'RE DOING?
I TOOK THE LIBERTY OF CALLING IN FOR YOU. I TOLD THEM YOU HAD A FAMILY CRISIS AND WOULDN'T BE IN THIS WEEK.

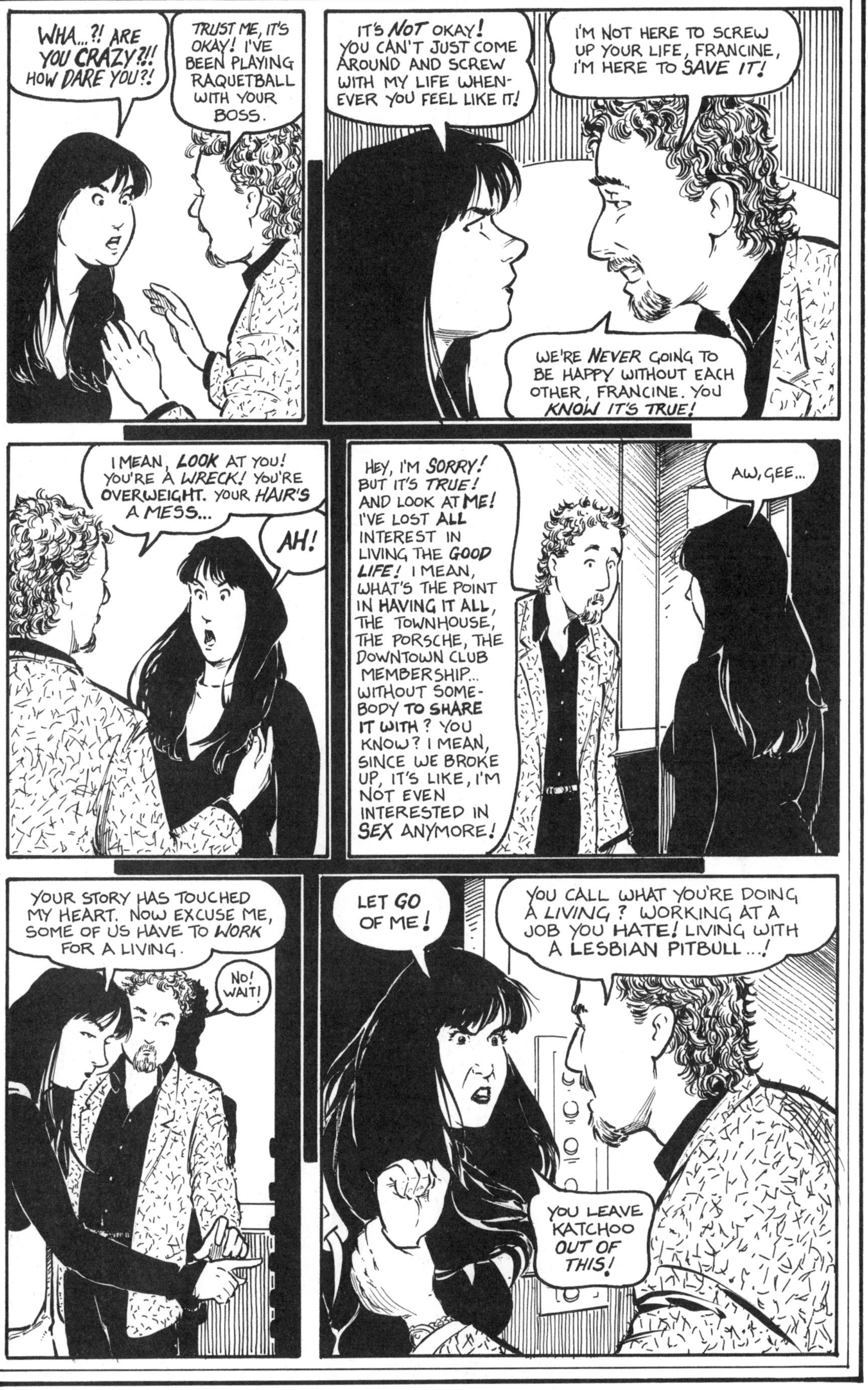
WHA...?! ARE YOU CRAZY?!! HOW DARE YOU?!
TRUST ME, IT'S OKAY! I'VE BEEN PLAYING RAQUETBALL WITH YOUR BOSS.
IT'S NOT OKAY! YOU CAN'T JUST COME AROUND AND SCREW WITH MY LIFE WHENEVER YOU FEEL LIKE IT!
I'M NOT HERE TO SCREW UP YOUR LIFE, FRANCINE, I'M HERE TO SAVE IT!
WE'RE NEVER GOING TO BE HAPPY WITHOUT EACH OTHER, FRANCINE. YOU KNOW IT'S TRUE!
I MEAN, LOOK AT YOU! YOU'RE A WRECK! YOU'RE OVERWEIGHT. YOUR HAIR'S A MESS...
AH!
HEY, I'M SORRY! BUT IT'S TRUE! AND LOOK AT ME! I'VE LOST ALL INTEREST IN LIVING THE GOOD LIFE! I MEAN, WHAT'S THE POINT IN HAVING IT ALL, THE TOWNHOUSE, THE PORSCHE, THE DOWNTOWN CLUB MEMBERSHIP... WITHOUT SOMEBODY TO SHARE IT WITH? YOU KNOW? I MEAN, SINCE WE BROKE UP, IT'S LIKE, I'M NOT EVEN INTERESTED IN SEX ANYMORE!
AW, GEE...
YOUR STORY HAS TOUCHED MY HEART. NOW EXCUSE ME, SOME OF US HAVE TO WORK FOR A LIVING.
NO! WAIT!
LET GO OF ME!
YOU CALL WHAT YOU'RE DOING A LIVING? WORKING AT A JOB YOU HATE! LIVING WITH A LESBIAN PITBULL...!
YOU LEAVE KATCHOO OUT OF THIS!

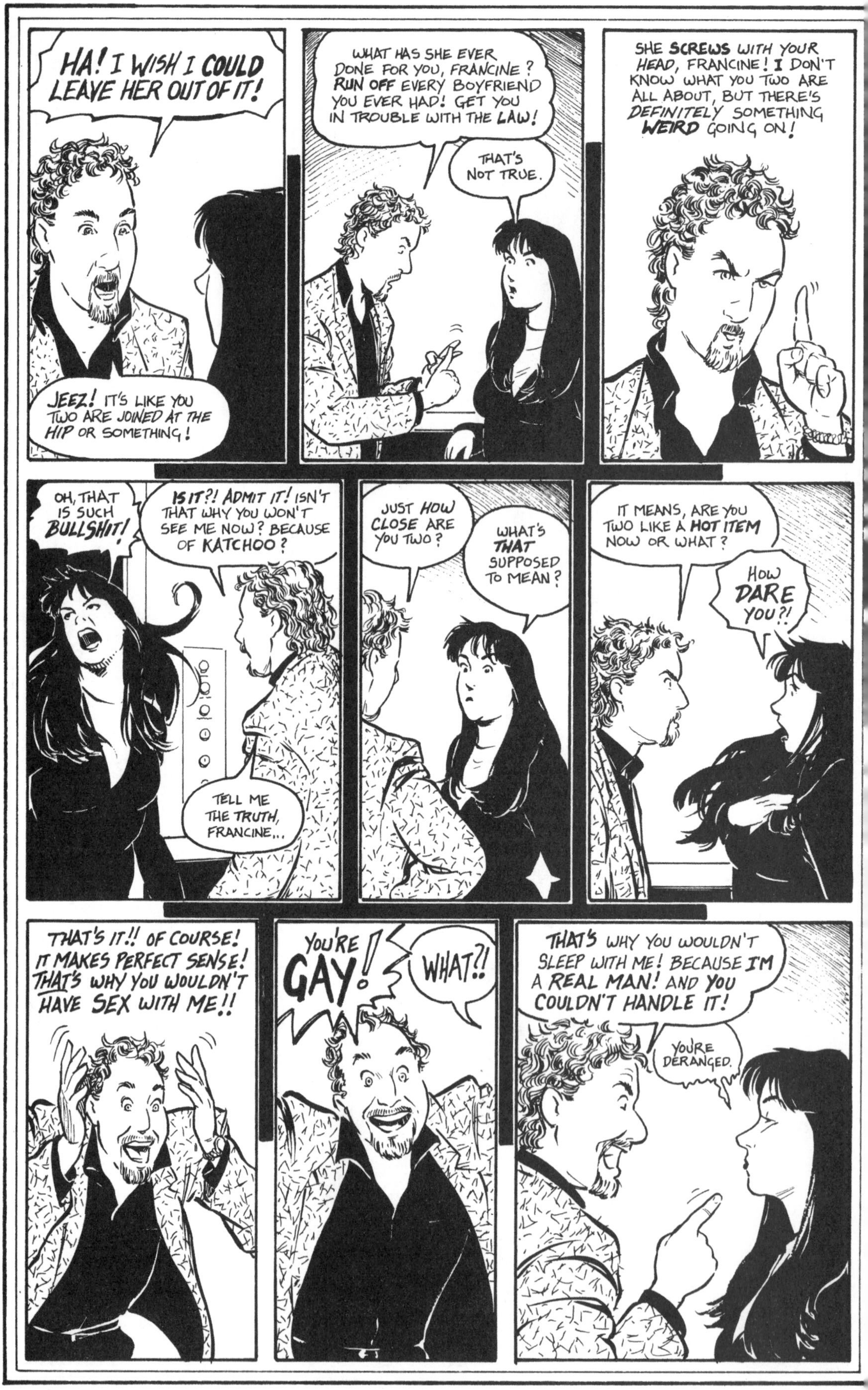
HA! I WISH I COULD LEAVE HER OUT OF IT!
JEEZ! IT'S LIKE YOU TWO ARE JOINED AT THE HIP OR SOMETHING!
WHAT HAS SHE EVER DONE FOR YOU, FRANCINE? RUN OFF EVERY BOYFRIEND YOU EVER HAD! GET YOU IN TROUBLE WITH THE LAW!
THAT'S NOT TRUE.
SHE SCREWS WITH YOUR HEAD, FRANCINE! I DON'T KNOW WHAT YOU TWO ARE ALL ABOUT, BUT THERE'S DEFINITELY SOMETHING WEIRD GOING ON!
OH, THAT IS SUCH BULLSHIT!
IS IT?! ADMIT IT! ISN'T THAT WHY YOU WON'T SEE ME NOW? BECAUSE OF KATCHOO?
TELL ME THE TRUTH, FRANCINE...
JUST HOW CLOSE ARE YOU TWO?
WHAT'S THAT SUPPOSED TO MEAN?
IT MEANS, ARE YOU TWO LIKE A HOT ITEM NOW OR WHAT?
HOW DARE YOU?!
THAT'S IT!! OF COURSE! IT MAKES PERFECT SENSE! THAT'S WHY YOU WOULDN'T HAVE SEX WITH ME!!
YOU'RE GAY!
WHAT?!
THAT'S WHY YOU WOULDN'T SLEEP WITH ME! BECAUSE I'M A REAL MAN! AND YOU COULDN'T HANDLE IT!
YOU'RE DERANGED.

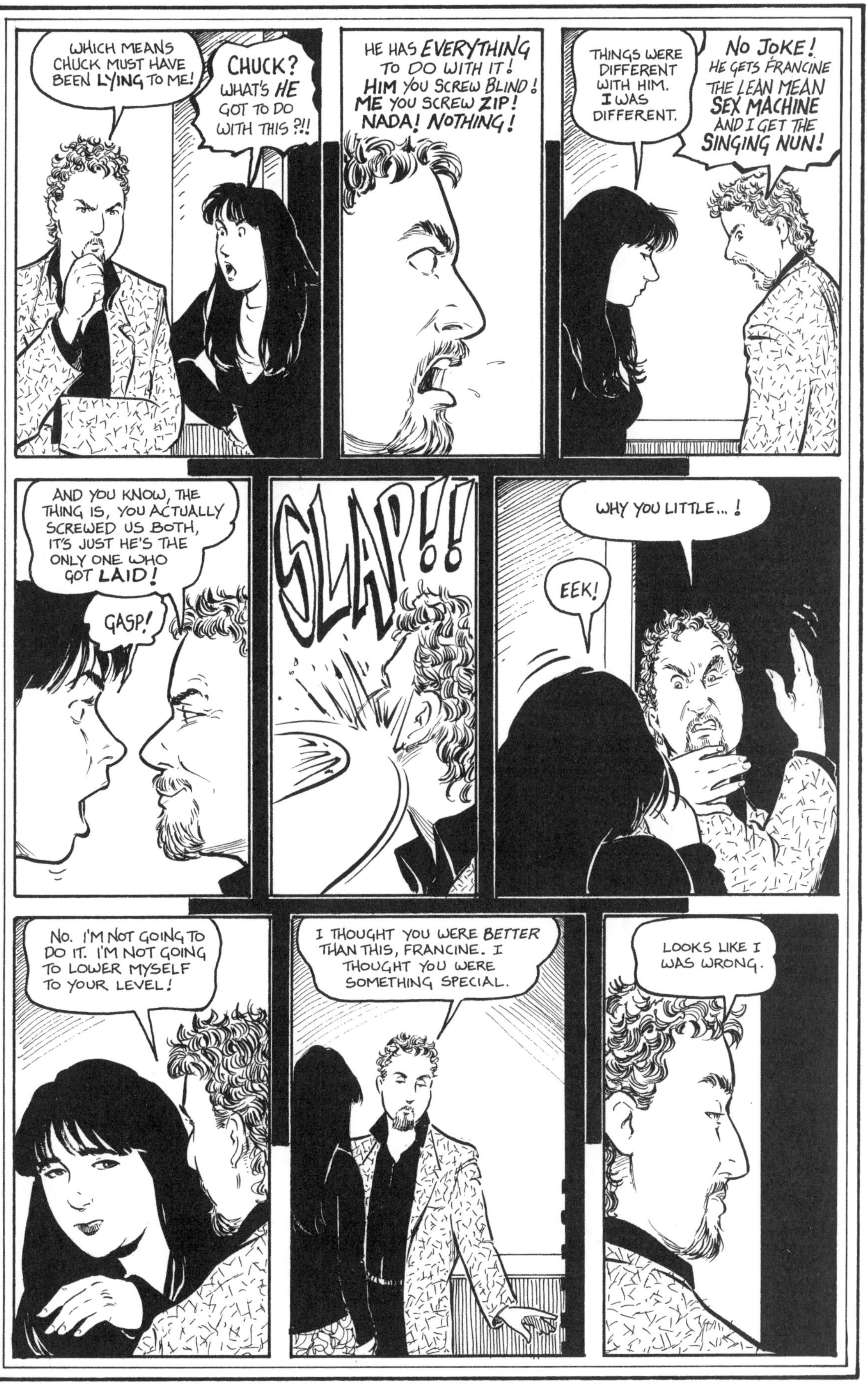
WHICH MEANS CHUCK MUST HAVE BEEN LYING TO ME!
CHUCK? WHAT'S HE GOT TO DO WITH THIS ?!!
HE HAS EVERYTHING TO DO WITH IT! HIM YOU SCREW BLIND! ME YOU SCREW ZIP! NADA! NOTHING!
THINGS WERE DIFFERENT WITH HIM. I WAS DIFFERENT.
NO JOKE! HE GETS FRANCINE THE LEAN MEAN SEX MACHINE AND I GET THE SINGING NUN!
AND YOU KNOW, THE THING IS, YOU ACTUALLY SCREWED US BOTH, IT'S JUST HE'S THE ONLY ONE WHO GOT LAID!
GASP!
SLAP!!
WHY YOU LITTLE... !
EEK!
NO. I'M NOT GOING TO DO IT. I'M NOT GOING TO LOWER MYSELF TO YOUR LEVEL!
I THOUGHT YOU WERE BETTER THAN THIS, FRANCINE. I THOUGHT YOU WERE SOMETHING SPECIAL.
LOOKS LIKE I WAS WRONG.

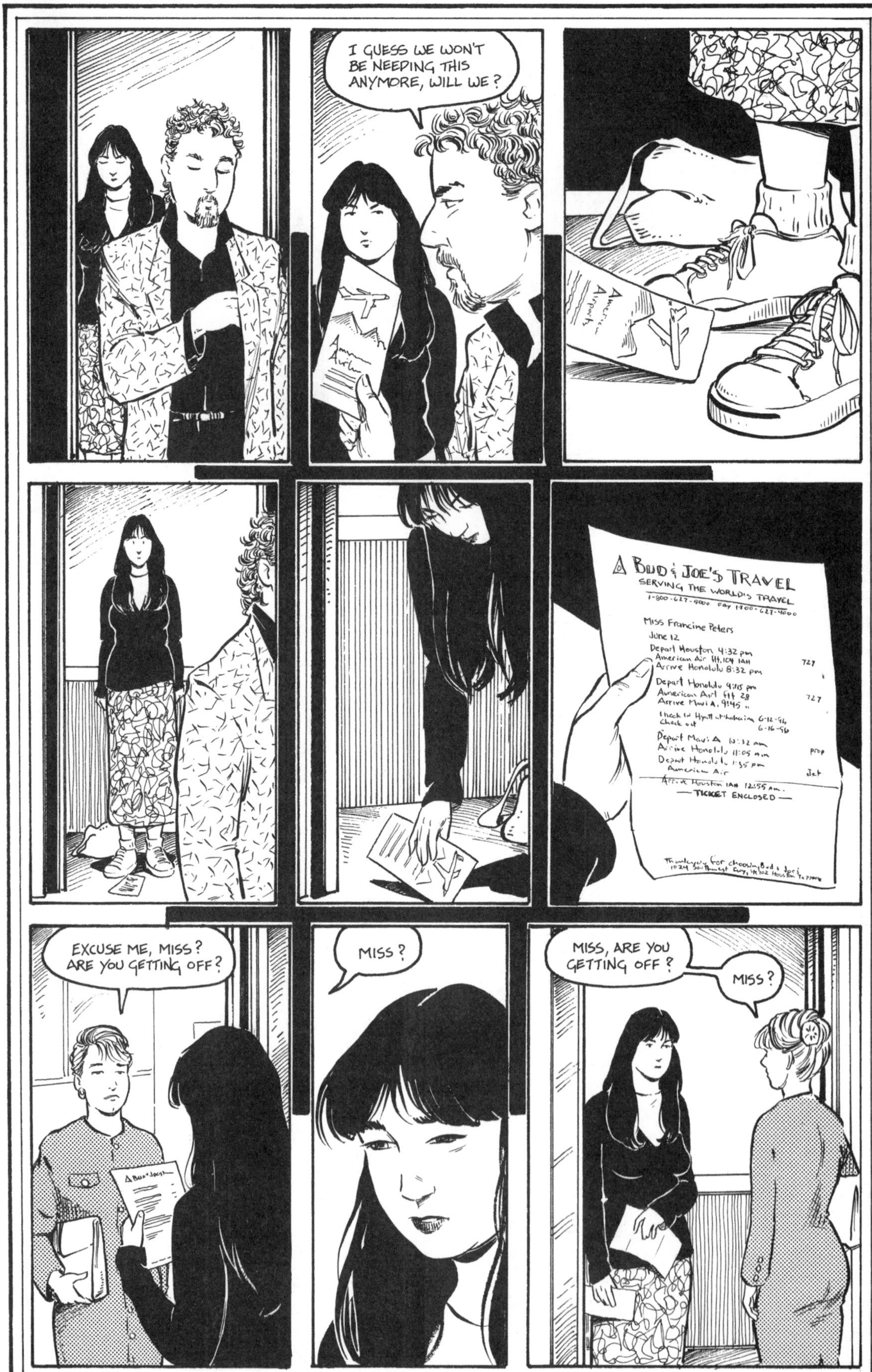
I GUESS WE WON'T BE NEEDING THIS ANYMORE, WILL WE?
BUD & JOE'S TRAVEL
SERVING THE WORLD'S TRAVEL
1-800-627-9000 FAX 1-800-627-4000
Miss Francine Peters
June 12
Depart Houston 4:32 pm
American Air flt. 104 IAH
727
Arrive Honolulu 8:32 pm
Depart Honolulu 9:15 pm
American Air flt 28
727
Arrive Maui A. 9:45
6-12-96
Check out
6-16-96
Depart Maui A 10:32 am
Arrive Honolulu 11:05 a.m
prop
Depart Honolulu 1:35 pm
American Air
Jet
Arrive Houston IAH 12:55 am.
—TICKET ENCLOSED—
EXCUSE ME, MISS? ARE YOU GETTING OFF?
MISS?
MISS, ARE YOU GETTING OFF?
MISS?

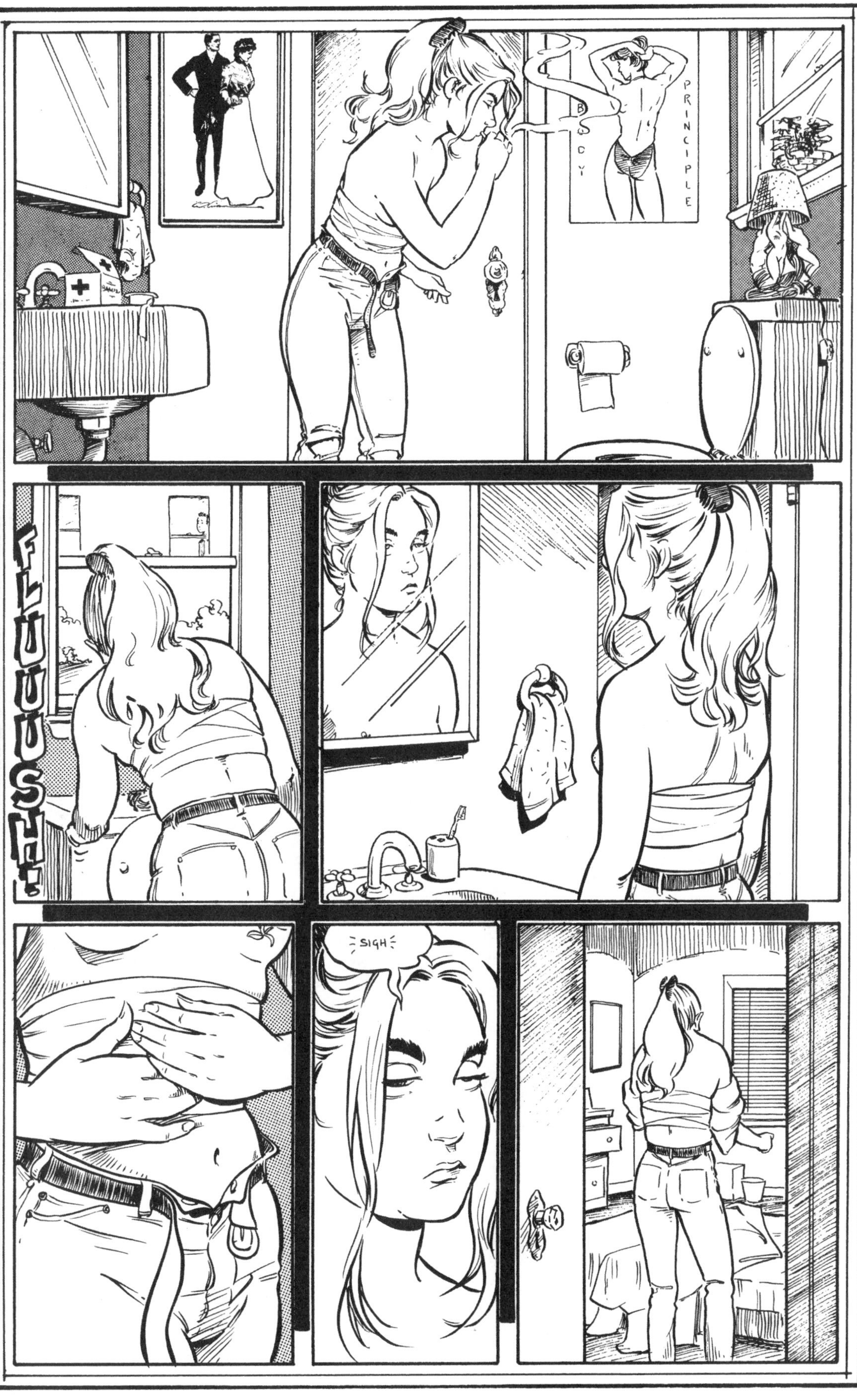

BODY PRINCIPLE
FLUUUUSH!
SIGH

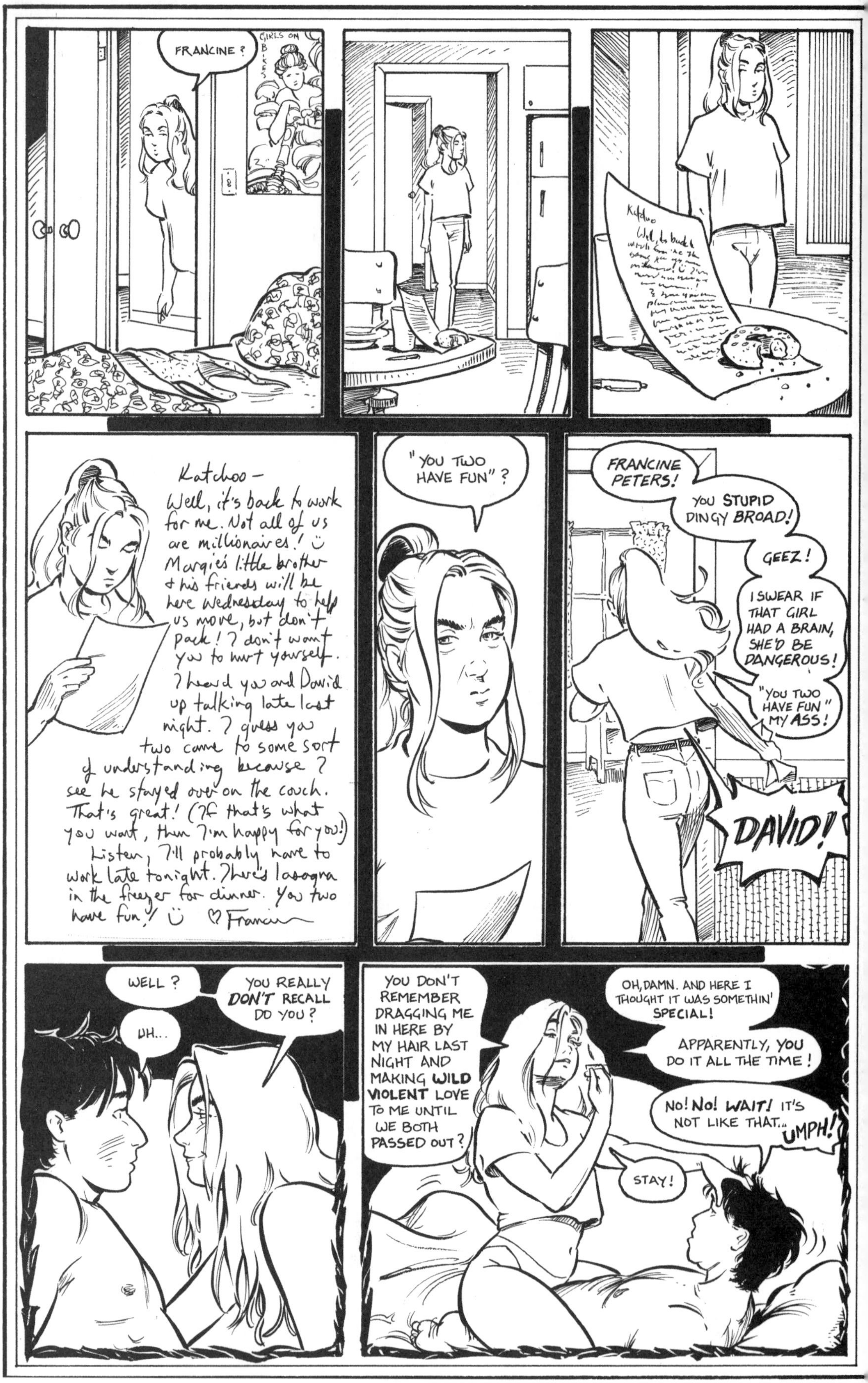
FRANCINE?
GIRLS ON BIKES
Katchoo—
Well, it's back to work for me. Not all of us are millionaires! ☺
Margie's little brother & his friends will be here Wednesday to help us move, but don't pack! I don't want you to hurt yourself.
I heard you and David up talking late last night. I guess you two came to some sort of understanding because I see he stayed over on the couch. That's great! (If that's what you want, then I'm happy for you!)
Listen, I'll probably have to work late tonight. There's lasagna in the freezer for dinner. You two have fun! ☺ ♡ Francine
"YOU TWO HAVE FUN"?
FRANCINE PETERS!
YOU STUPID DINGY BROAD!
GEEZ!
I SWEAR IF THAT GIRL HAD A BRAIN, SHE'D BE DANGEROUS!
"YOU TWO HAVE FUN" MY ASS!
DAVID!
WELL?
UH...
YOU REALLY DON'T RECALL DO YOU?
YOU DON'T REMEMBER DRAGGING ME IN HERE BY MY HAIR LAST NIGHT AND MAKING WILD VIOLENT LOVE TO ME UNTIL WE BOTH PASSED OUT?
OH, DAMN. AND HERE I THOUGHT IT WAS SOMETHIN' SPECIAL!
APPARENTLY, YOU DO IT ALL THE TIME!
NO! NO! WAIT! IT'S NOT LIKE THAT... UMPH!
STAY!

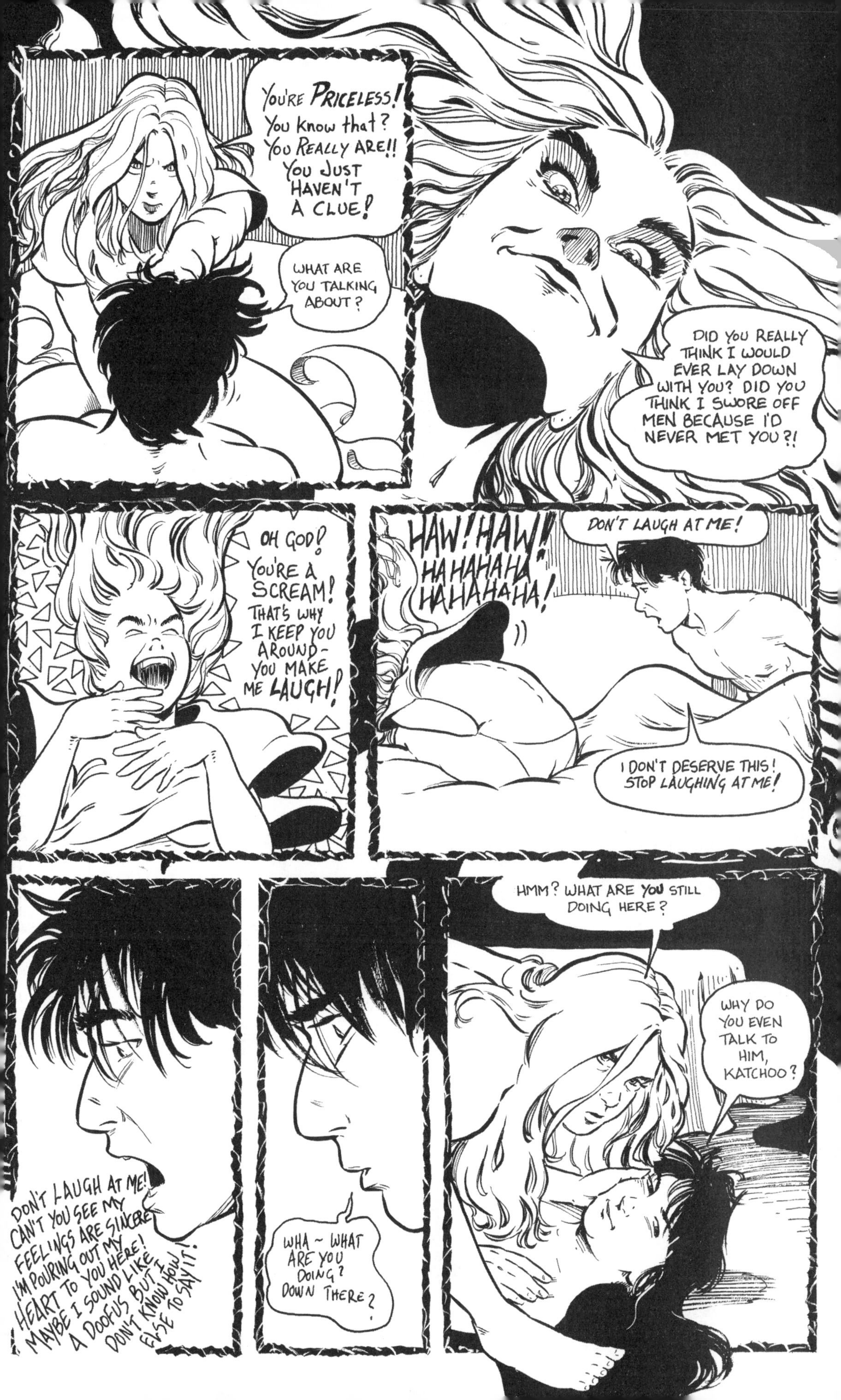
You're PRICELESS! You know that? You REALLY ARE!! You JUST HAVEN'T A CLUE!
WHAT ARE YOU TALKING ABOUT?
DID YOU REALLY THINK I WOULD EVER LAY DOWN WITH YOU? DID YOU THINK I SWORE OFF MEN BECAUSE I'D NEVER MET YOU?!
OH GOD! You're A SCREAM! THAT'S WHY I KEEP YOU AROUND - YOU MAKE ME LAUGH!
HAW! HAW! HAHAHAHA HAHAHAHA!
DON'T LAUGH AT ME!
I DON'T DESERVE THIS! STOP LAUGHING AT ME!
DON'T LAUGH AT ME! CAN'T YOU SEE MY FEELINGS ARE SINCERE! I'M POURING OUT MY HEART TO YOU HERE! MAYBE I SOUND LIKE A DOOFUS BUT I DON'T KNOW HOW ELSE TO SAY IT!
WHA ~ WHAT ARE YOU DOING? DOWN THERE?
HMM? WHAT ARE YOU STILL DOING HERE?
WHY DO YOU EVEN TALK TO HIM, KATCHOO?

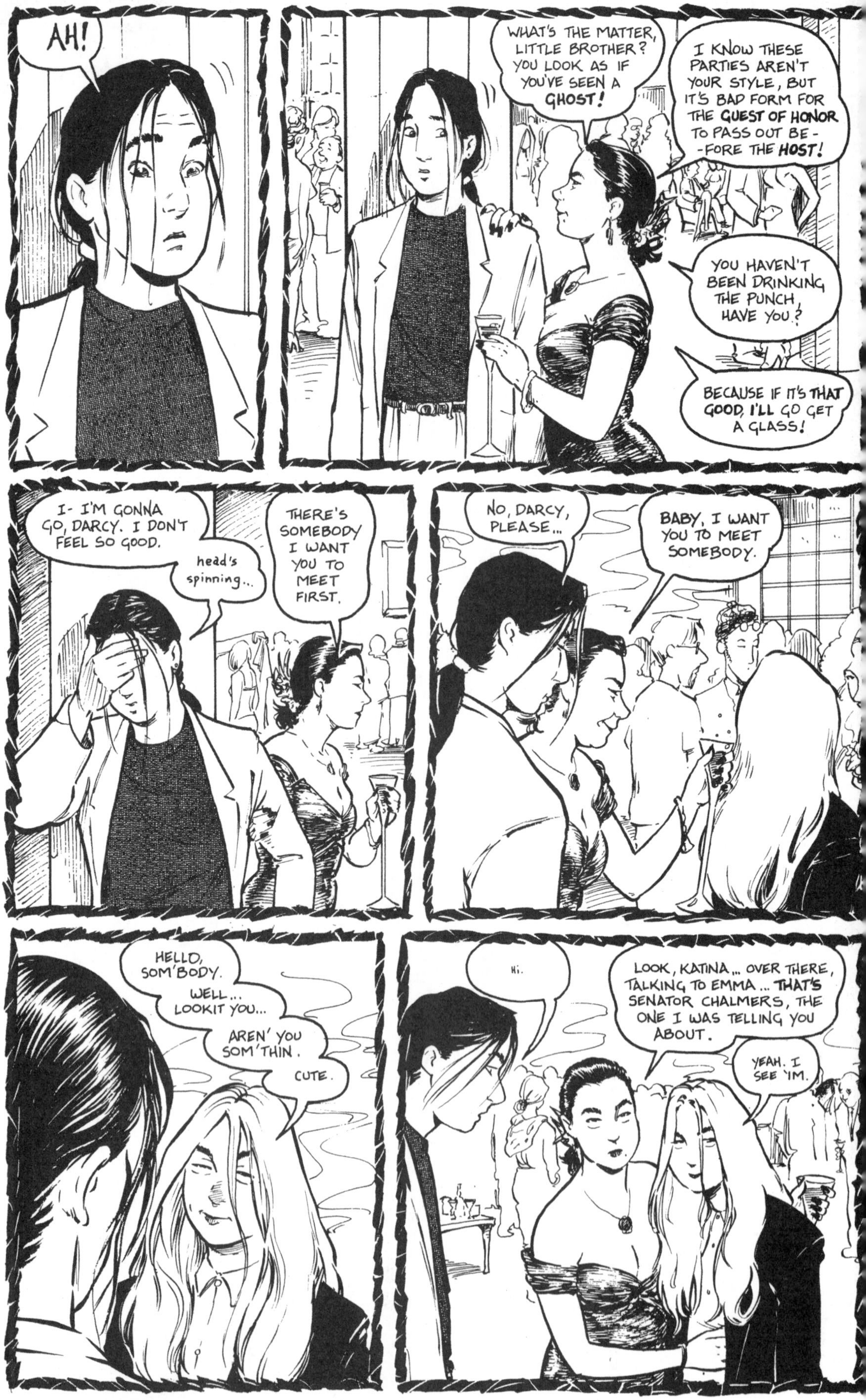
AH!
WHAT'S THE MATTER, LITTLE BROTHER? YOU LOOK AS IF YOU'VE SEEN A GHOST!
I KNOW THESE PARTIES AREN'T YOUR STYLE, BUT IT'S BAD FORM FOR THE GUEST OF HONOR TO PASS OUT BE- -FORE THE HOST!
YOU HAVEN'T BEEN DRINKING THE PUNCH, HAVE YOU?
BECAUSE IF IT'S THAT GOOD, I'LL GO GET A GLASS!
I- I'M GONNA GO, DARCY. I DON'T FEEL SO GOOD.
head's spinning...
THERE'S SOMEBODY I WANT YOU TO MEET FIRST.
NO, DARCY, PLEASE...
BABY, I WANT YOU TO MEET SOMEBODY.
HELLO, SOM'BODY.
WELL... LOOKIT YOU...
AREN' YOU SOM'THIN.
CUTE.
Hi.
LOOK, KATINA... OVER THERE, TALKING TO EMMA... THAT'S SENATOR CHALMERS, THE ONE I WAS TELLING YOU ABOUT.
YEAH. I SEE 'IM.

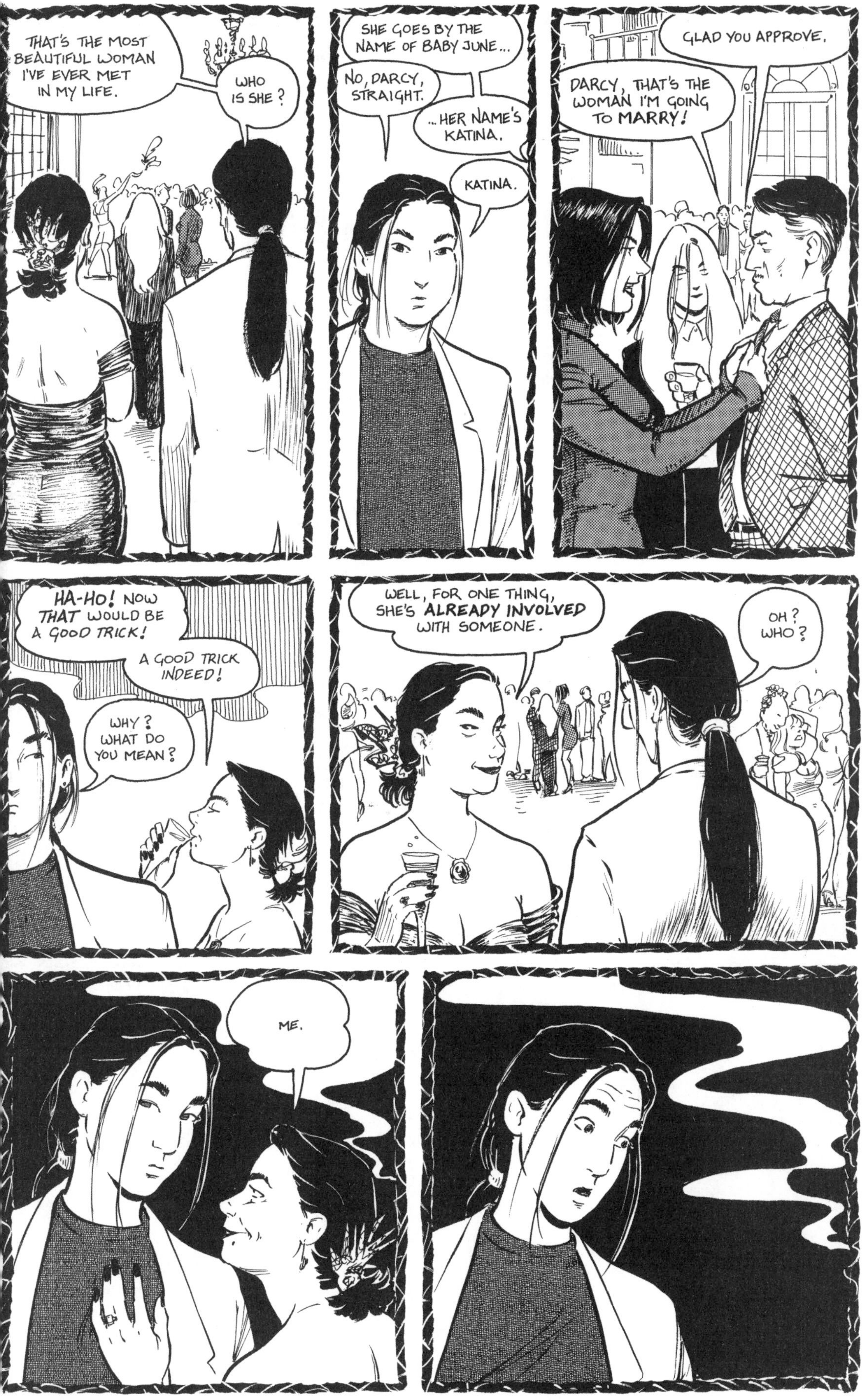
THAT'S THE MOST BEAUTIFUL WOMAN I'VE EVER MET IN MY LIFE.
WHO IS SHE?
SHE GOES BY THE NAME OF BABY JUNE...
NO, DARCY, STRAIGHT.
...HER NAME'S KATINA.
KATINA.
GLAD YOU APPROVE.
DARCY, THAT'S THE WOMAN I'M GOING TO MARRY!
HA-HO! NOW THAT WOULD BE A GOOD TRICK!
A GOOD TRICK INDEED!
WHY? WHAT DO YOU MEAN?
WELL, FOR ONE THING, SHE'S ALREADY INVOLVED WITH SOMEONE.
OH? WHO?
ME.

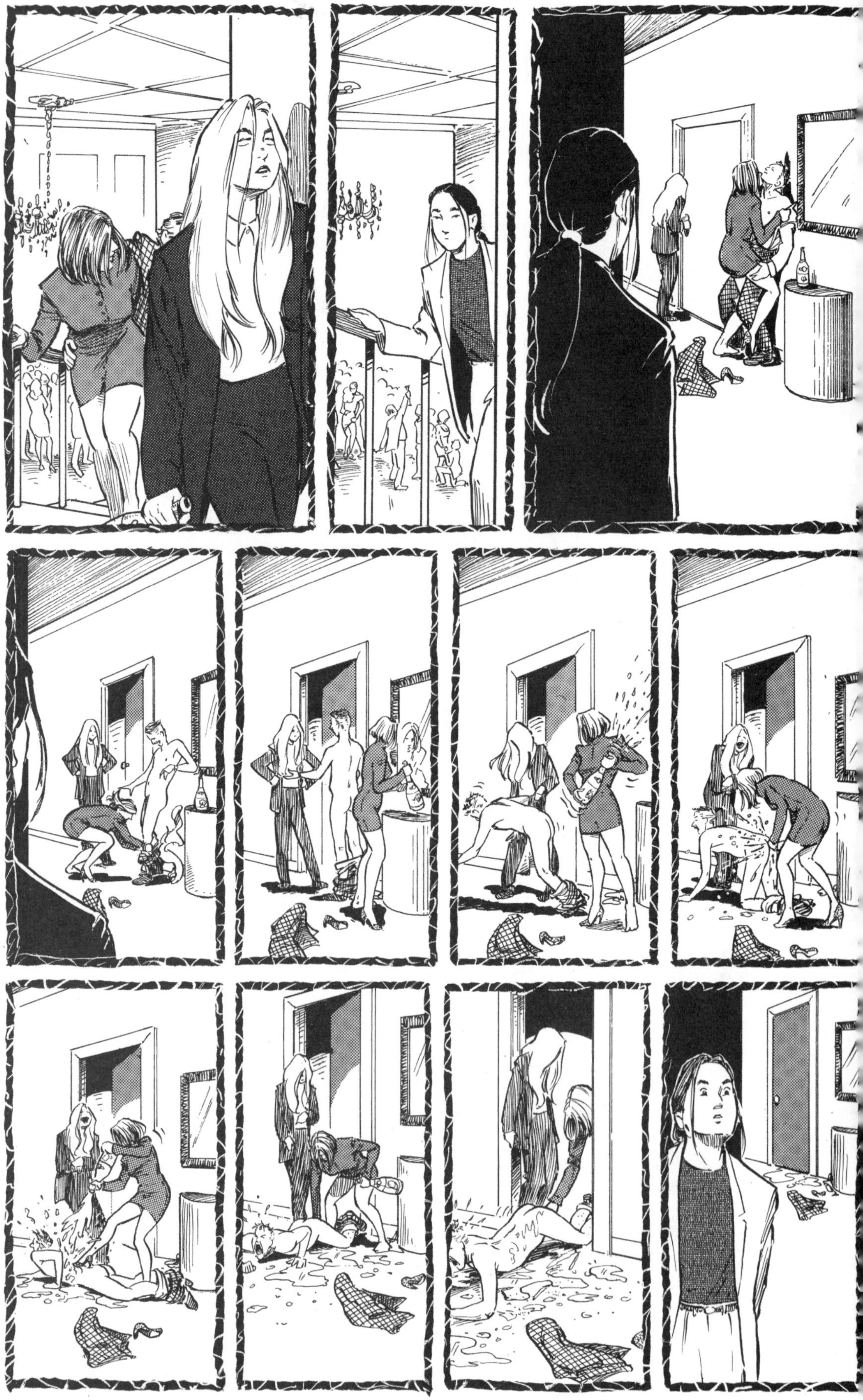

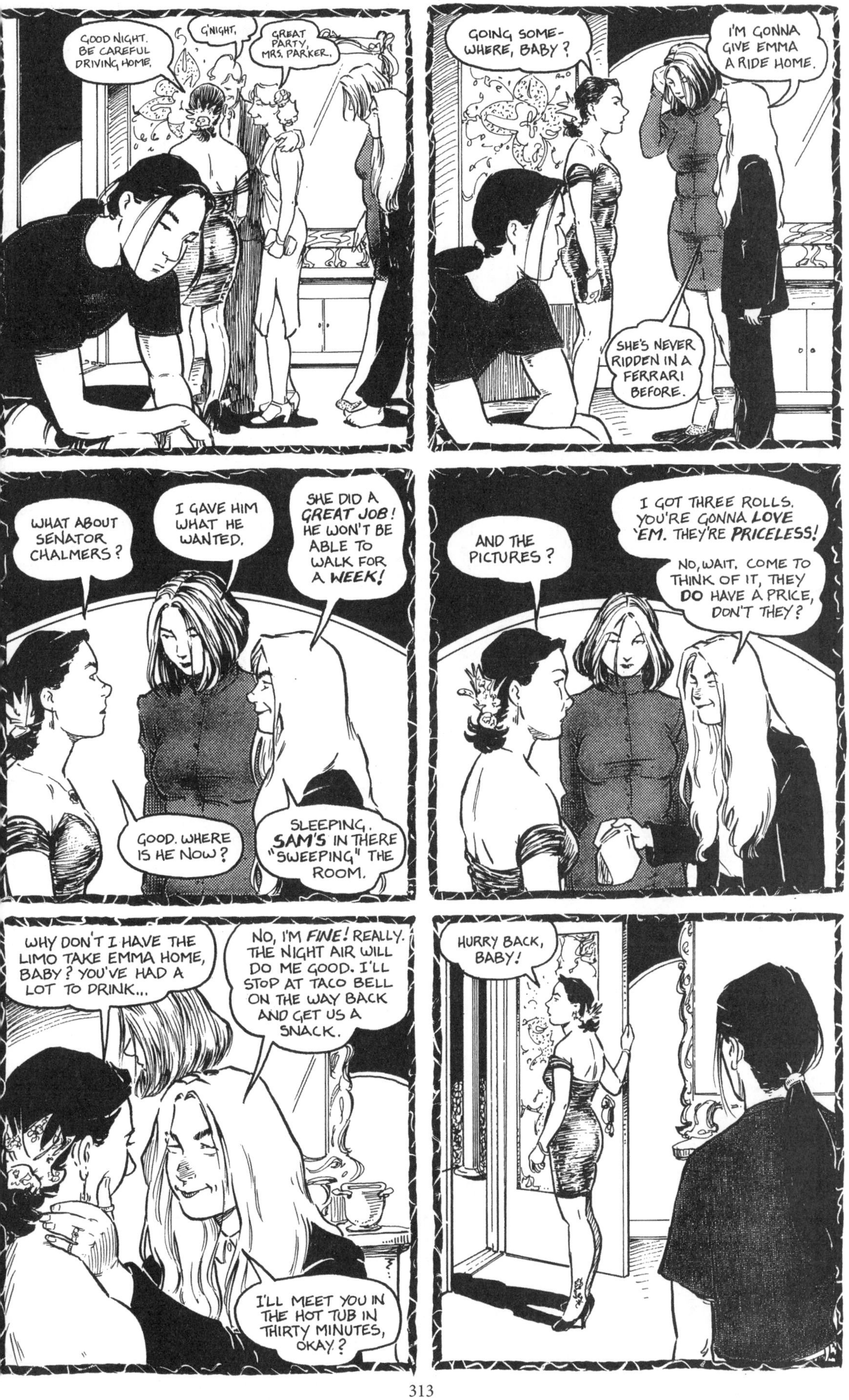
GOOD NIGHT. BE CAREFUL DRIVING HOME.
G'NIGHT.
GREAT PARTY, MRS. PARKER.
GOING SOME-WHERE, BABY?
I'M GONNA GIVE EMMA A RIDE HOME.
SHE'S NEVER RIDDEN IN A FERRARI BEFORE.
WHAT ABOUT SENATOR CHALMERS?
I GAVE HIM WHAT HE WANTED.
SHE DID A GREAT JOB! HE WON'T BE ABLE TO WALK FOR A WEEK!
GOOD. WHERE IS HE NOW?
SLEEPING. SAM'S IN THERE "SWEEPING" THE ROOM.
AND THE PICTURES?
I GOT THREE ROLLS. YOU'RE GONNA LOVE 'EM. THEY'RE PRICELESS!
NO, WAIT. COME TO THINK OF IT, THEY DO HAVE A PRICE, DON'T THEY?
WHY DON'T I HAVE THE LIMO TAKE EMMA HOME, BABY? YOU'VE HAD A LOT TO DRINK...
NO, I'M FINE! REALLY. THE NIGHT AIR WILL DO ME GOOD. I'LL STOP AT TACO BELL ON THE WAY BACK AND GET US A SNACK.
I'LL MEET YOU IN THE HOT TUB IN THIRTY MINUTES, OKAY?
HURRY BACK, BABY!

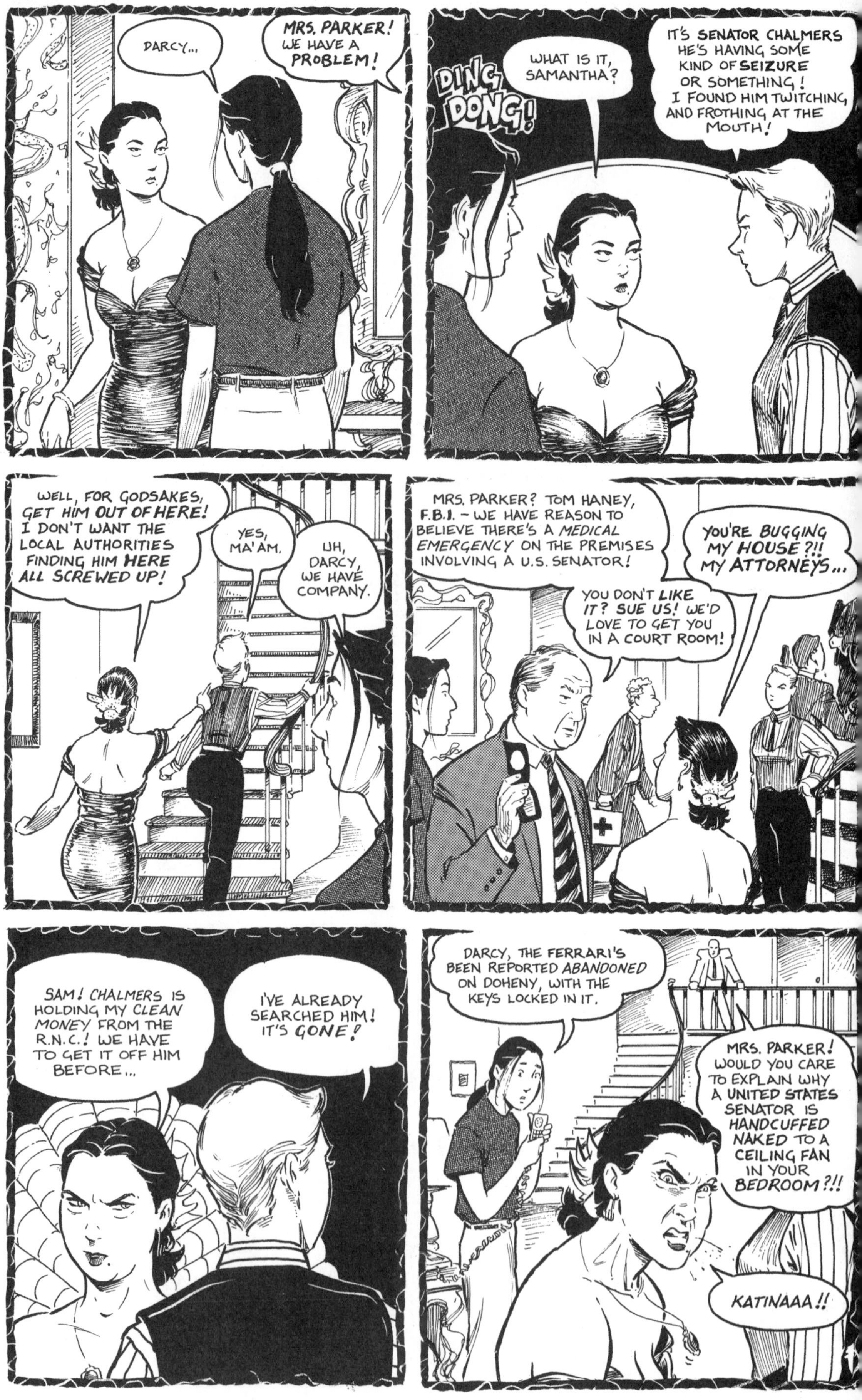
DARCY...
MRS. PARKER! WE HAVE A PROBLEM!
DING DONG!
WHAT IS IT, SAMANTHA?
IT'S SENATOR CHALMERS HE'S HAVING SOME KIND OF SEIZURE OR SOMETHING! I FOUND HIM TWITCHING AND FROTHING AT THE MOUTH!
WELL, FOR GODSAKES, GET HIM OUT OF HERE! I DON'T WANT THE LOCAL AUTHORITIES FINDING HIM HERE ALL SCREWED UP!
YES, MA'AM.
UH, DARCY, WE HAVE COMPANY.
MRS. PARKER? TOM HANEY, F.B.I. - WE HAVE REASON TO BELIEVE THERE'S A MEDICAL EMERGENCY ON THE PREMISES INVOLVING A U.S. SENATOR!
YOU'RE BUGGING MY HOUSE?!! MY ATTORNEYS...
YOU DON'T LIKE IT? SUE US! WE'D LOVE TO GET YOU IN A COURT ROOM!
SAM! CHALMERS IS HOLDING MY CLEAN MONEY FROM THE R.N.C.! WE HAVE TO GET IT OFF HIM BEFORE...
I'VE ALREADY SEARCHED HIM! IT'S GONE!
DARCY, THE FERRARI'S BEEN REPORTED ABANDONED ON DOHENY, WITH THE KEYS LOCKED IN IT.
MRS. PARKER! WOULD YOU CARE TO EXPLAIN WHY A UNITED STATES SENATOR IS HANDCUFFED NAKED TO A CEILING FAN IN YOUR BEDROOM?!!
KATINAAA!!

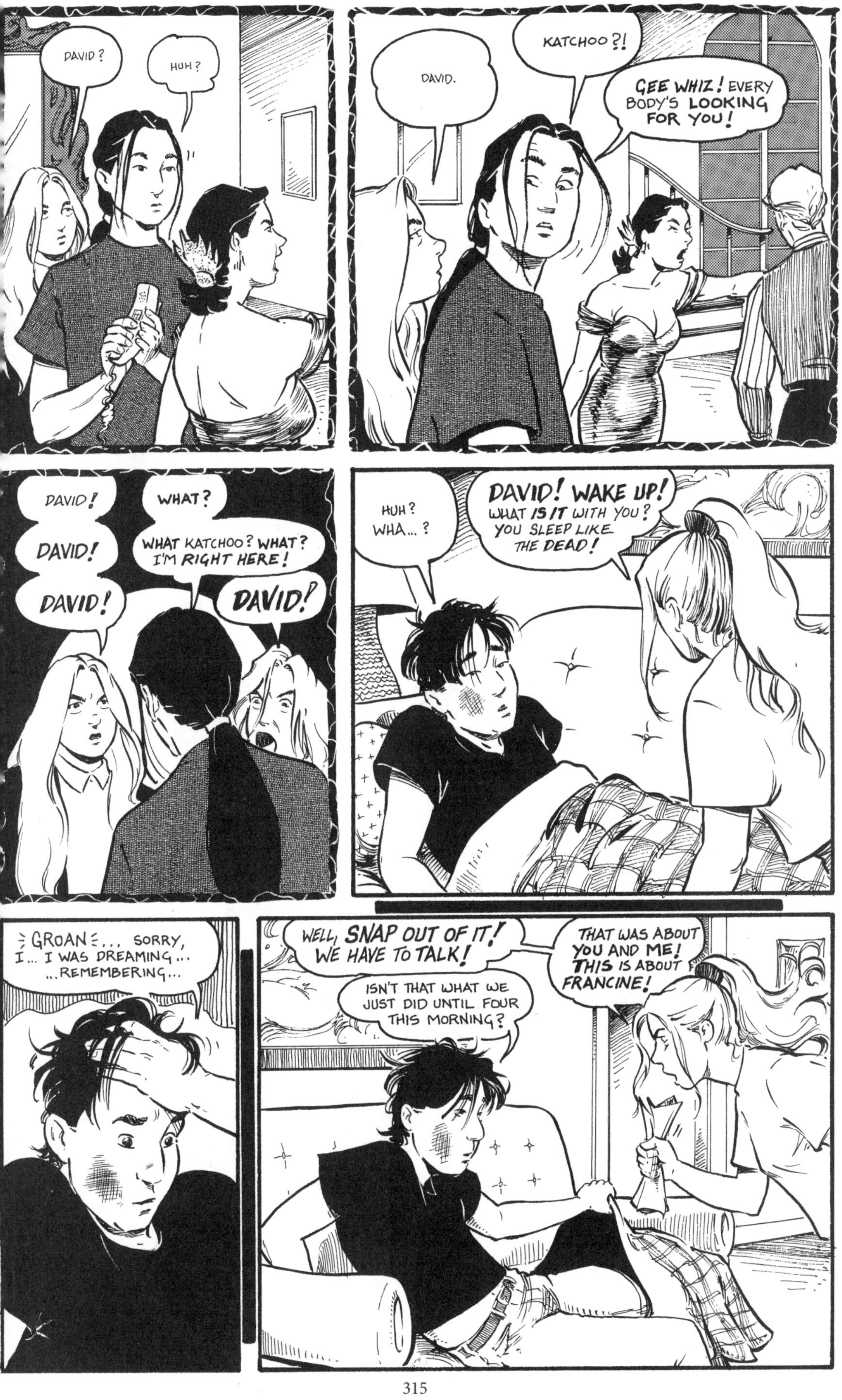
DAVID?
HUH?
DAVID.
KATCHOO?!
GEE WHIZ! EVERY BODY'S LOOKING FOR YOU!
DAVID!
DAVID!
DAVID!
WHAT?
WHAT KATCHOO? WHAT? I'M RIGHT HERE!
DAVID!
HUH? WHA...?
DAVID! WAKE UP! WHAT IS IT WITH YOU? YOU SLEEP LIKE THE DEAD!
GROAN... SORRY, I... I WAS DREAMING... ...REMEMBERING...
WELL, SNAP OUT OF IT! WE HAVE TO TALK!
ISN'T THAT WHAT WE JUST DID UNTIL FOUR THIS MORNING?
THAT WAS ABOUT YOU AND ME! THIS IS ABOUT FRANCINE!

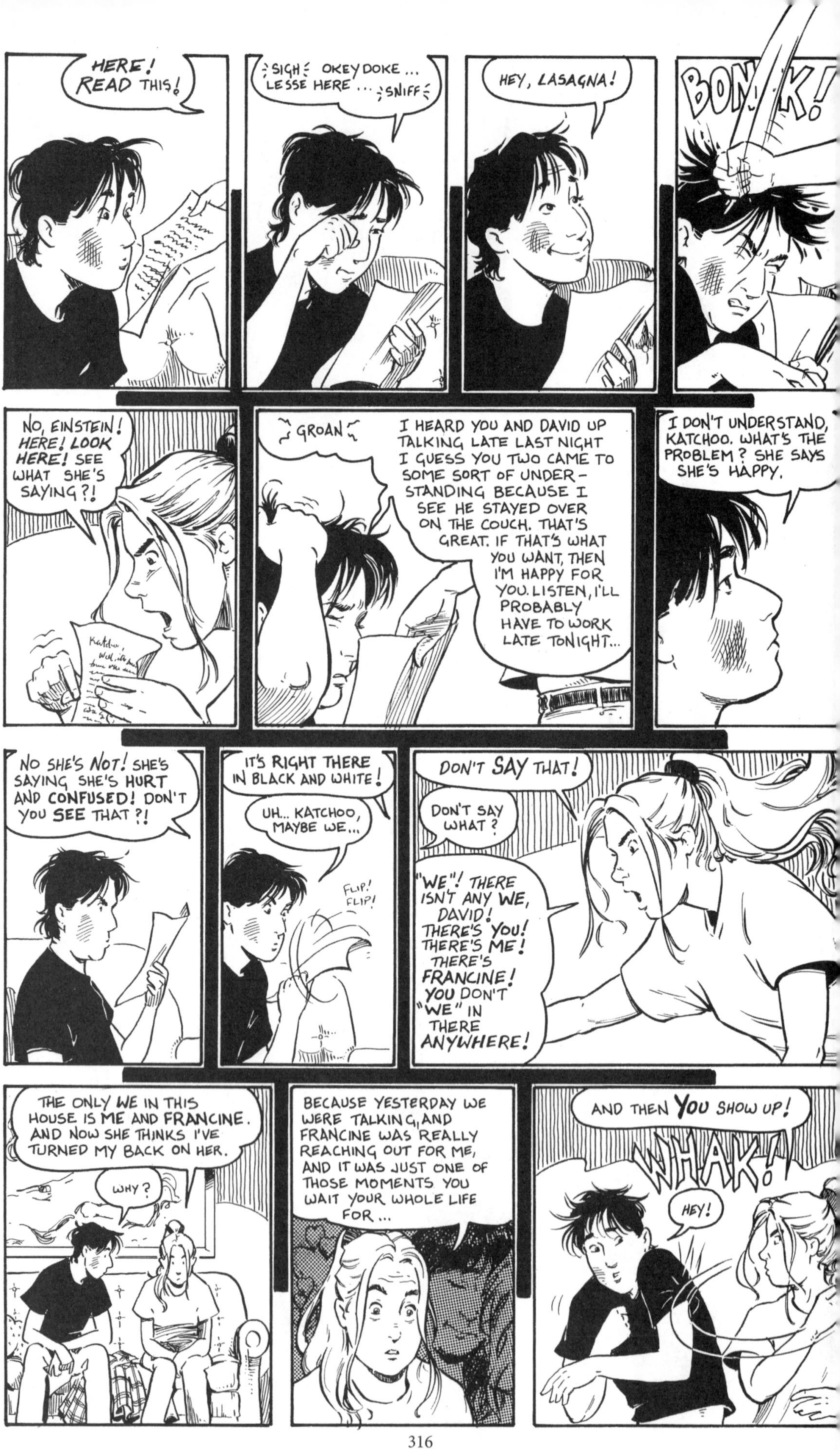
HERE! READ THIS!
SIGH OKEYDOKE... LESSE HERE... SNIFF
HEY, LASAGNA!
BONK!
NO, EINSTEIN! HERE! LOOK HERE! SEE WHAT SHE'S SAYING?!
GROAN
I HEARD YOU AND DAVID UP TALKING LATE LAST NIGHT I GUESS YOU TWO CAME TO SOME SORT OF UNDER-STANDING BECAUSE I SEE HE STAYED OVER ON THE COUCH. THAT'S GREAT. IF THAT'S WHAT YOU WANT, THEN I'M HAPPY FOR YOU. LISTEN, I'LL PROBABLY HAVE TO WORK LATE TONIGHT...
I DON'T UNDERSTAND, KATCHOO. WHAT'S THE PROBLEM? SHE SAYS SHE'S HAPPY.
NO SHE'S NOT! SHE'S SAYING SHE'S HURT AND CONFUSED! DON'T YOU SEE THAT?!
IT'S RIGHT THERE IN BLACK AND WHITE!
UH... KATCHOO, MAYBE WE...
FLIP! FLIP!
DON'T SAY THAT!
DON'T SAY WHAT?
"WE"! THERE ISN'T ANY WE, DAVID! THERE'S YOU! THERE'S ME! THERE'S FRANCINE! YOU DON'T "WE" IN THERE ANYWHERE!
THE ONLY WE IN THIS HOUSE IS ME AND FRANCINE. AND NOW SHE THINKS I'VE TURNED MY BACK ON HER.
WHY?
BECAUSE YESTERDAY WE WERE TALKING, AND FRANCINE WAS REALLY REACHING OUT FOR ME, AND IT WAS JUST ONE OF THOSE MOMENTS YOU WAIT YOUR WHOLE LIFE FOR...
AND THEN YOU SHOW UP!
WHAK!
HEY!

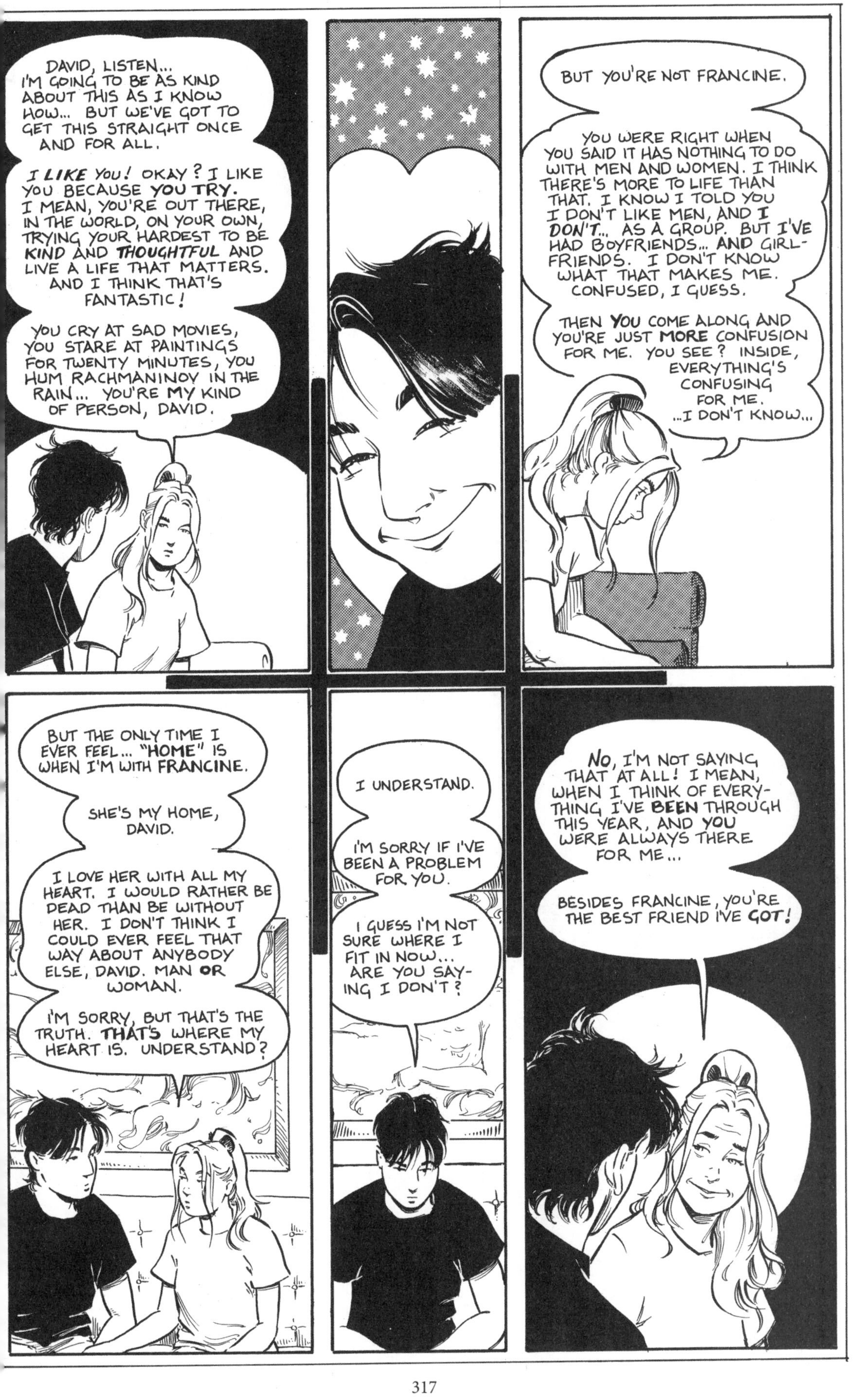
DAVID, LISTEN... I'M GOING TO BE AS KIND ABOUT THIS AS I KNOW HOW... BUT WE'VE GOT TO GET THIS STRAIGHT ONCE AND FOR ALL.
I LIKE YOU! OKAY? I LIKE YOU BECAUSE YOU TRY. I MEAN, YOU'RE OUT THERE, IN THE WORLD, ON YOUR OWN, TRYING YOUR HARDEST TO BE KIND AND THOUGHTFUL AND LIVE A LIFE THAT MATTERS. AND I THINK THAT'S FANTASTIC!
YOU CRY AT SAD MOVIES, YOU STARE AT PAINTINGS FOR TWENTY MINUTES, YOU HUM RACHMANINOV IN THE RAIN... YOU'RE MY KIND OF PERSON, DAVID.
BUT YOU'RE NOT FRANCINE.
YOU WERE RIGHT WHEN YOU SAID IT HAS NOTHING TO DO WITH MEN AND WOMEN. I THINK THERE'S MORE TO LIFE THAN THAT. I KNOW I TOLD YOU I DON'T LIKE MEN, AND I DON'T... AS A GROUP. BUT I'VE HAD BOYFRIENDS... AND GIRL-FRIENDS. I DON'T KNOW WHAT THAT MAKES ME. CONFUSED, I GUESS.
THEN YOU COME ALONG AND YOU'RE JUST MORE CONFUSION FOR ME. YOU SEE? INSIDE, EVERYTHING'S CONFUSING FOR ME. ...I DON'T KNOW...
BUT THE ONLY TIME I EVER FEEL... "HOME" IS WHEN I'M WITH FRANCINE.
SHE'S MY HOME, DAVID.
I LOVE HER WITH ALL MY HEART. I WOULD RATHER BE DEAD THAN BE WITHOUT HER. I DON'T THINK I COULD EVER FEEL THAT WAY ABOUT ANYBODY ELSE, DAVID. MAN OR WOMAN.
I'M SORRY, BUT THAT'S THE TRUTH. THAT'S WHERE MY HEART IS. UNDERSTAND?
I UNDERSTAND.
I'M SORRY IF I'VE BEEN A PROBLEM FOR YOU.
I GUESS I'M NOT SURE WHERE I FIT IN NOW... ARE YOU SAYING I DON'T?
NO, I'M NOT SAYING THAT AT ALL! I MEAN, WHEN I THINK OF EVERYTHING I'VE BEEN THROUGH THIS YEAR, AND YOU WERE ALWAYS THERE FOR ME...
BESIDES FRANCINE, YOU'RE THE BEST FRIEND I'VE GOT!

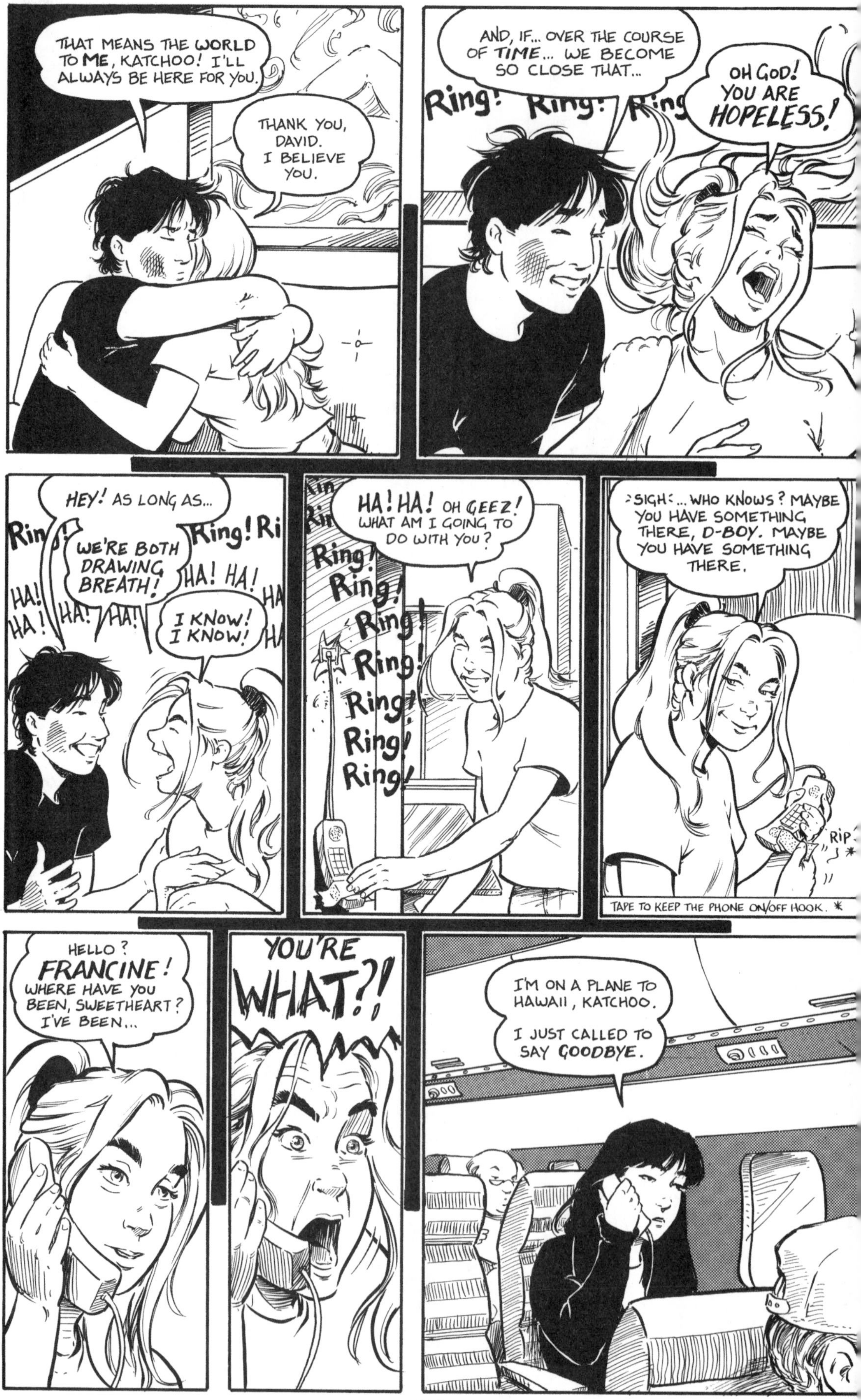
THAT MEANS THE WORLD TO ME, KATCHOO! I'LL ALWAYS BE HERE FOR YOU.
THANK YOU, DAVID. I BELIEVE YOU.
AND, IF... OVER THE COURSE OF TIME... WE BECOME SO CLOSE THAT...
Ring! Ring! Ring
OH GOD! YOU ARE HOPELESS!
HEY! AS LONG AS...
WE'RE BOTH DRAWING BREATH!
Ring! Ring! Ri
HA! HA! HA! HA! HA!
HA! HA! HA! HA!
I KNOW! I KNOW!
HA! HA! OH GEEZ! WHAT AM I GOING TO DO WITH YOU?
Ring! Ring! Ring! Ring! Ring! Ring! Ring! Ring!
SIGH... WHO KNOWS? MAYBE YOU HAVE SOMETHING THERE, D-BOY. MAYBE YOU HAVE SOMETHING THERE.
RIP
TAPE TO KEEP THE PHONE ON/OFF HOOK. *
HELLO? FRANCINE! WHERE HAVE YOU BEEN, SWEETHEART? I'VE BEEN...
YOU'RE WHAT?!
I'M ON A PLANE TO HAWAII, KATCHOO.
I JUST CALLED TO SAY GOODBYE.

All of my life
I was waiting for you
How is it we never met?
Here in the latter days
Time on my own
I find too much to regret.
All of the time I spend
Thinking of you
Nothing to say but I call.
Over and Over
It plays on my mind
How come you come and you go?
How is it happening only to me?
Now after all of the time we spent
I was careless and made a slip
Suddenly your love is
Too much to lose
Now I've fallen in love with you.
Were you waiting for
My heart to break?
Though I've fallen
In love with you
I have fallen in love
Too late.

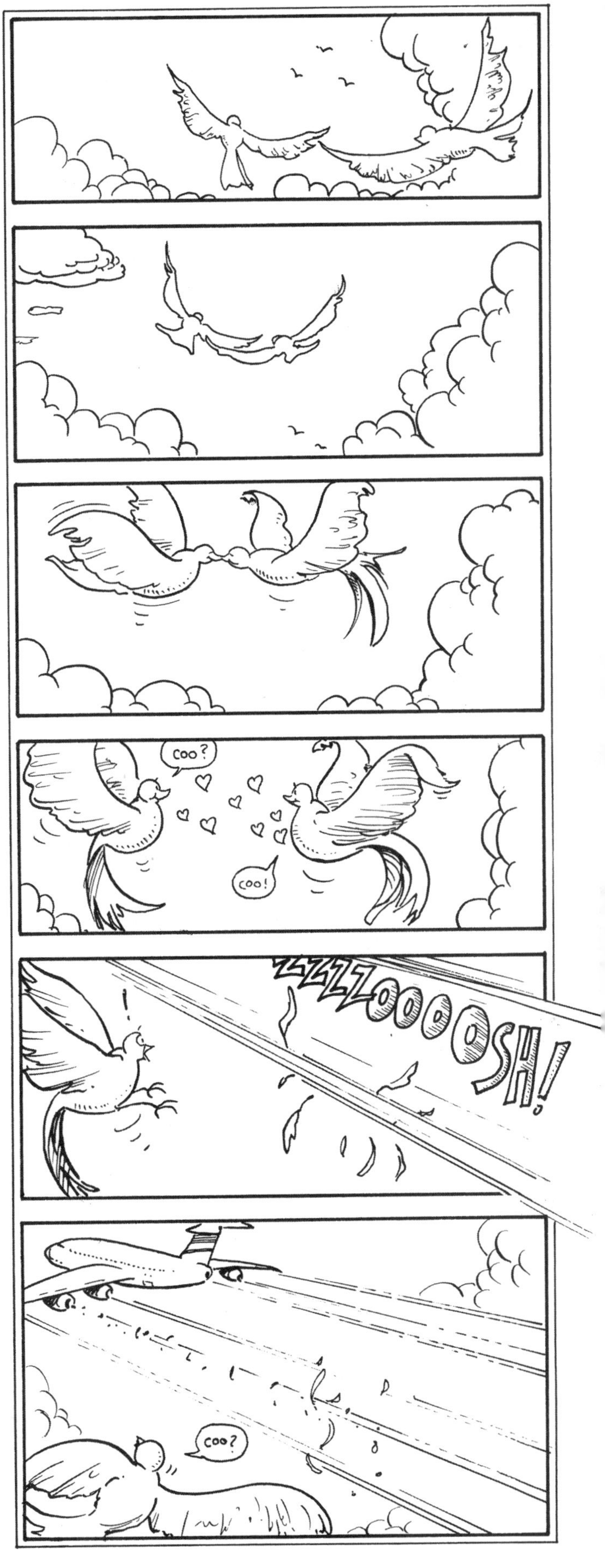

COO?
COO!
!
ZZZZOOOOOSH!
COO?

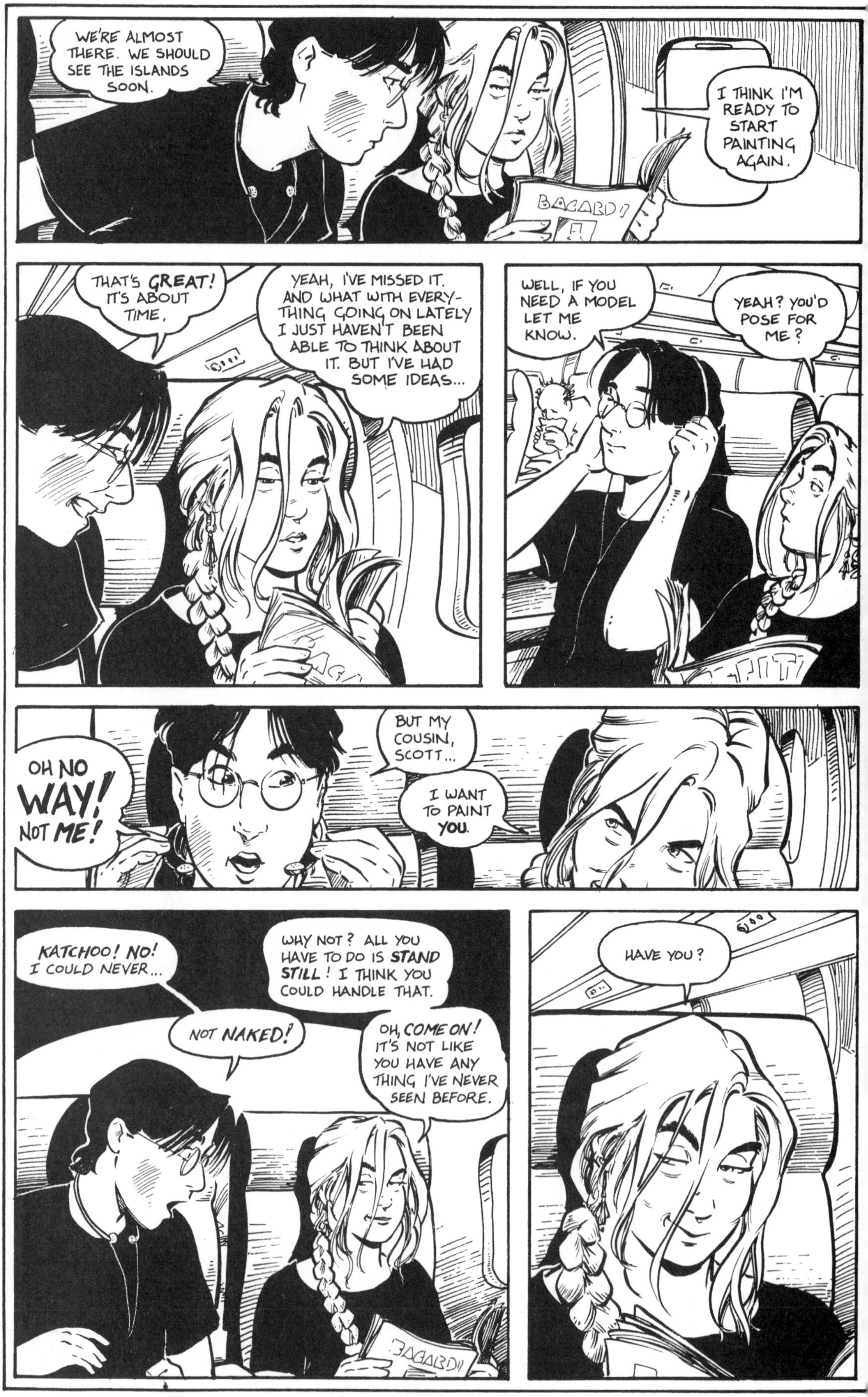

WE'RE ALMOST THERE. WE SHOULD SEE THE ISLANDS SOON.
I THINK I'M READY TO START PAINTING AGAIN.
BACARDI
THAT'S **GREAT!** IT'S ABOUT TIME.
YEAH, I'VE MISSED IT. AND WHAT WITH EVERY-THING GOING ON LATELY I JUST HAVEN'T BEEN ABLE TO THINK ABOUT IT. BUT I'VE HAD SOME IDEAS...
WELL, IF YOU NEED A MODEL LET ME KNOW.
YEAH? YOU'D POSE FOR ME?
OH NO **WAY!** NOT **ME!**
BUT MY COUSIN, SCOTT...
I WANT TO PAINT **YOU**.
KATCHOO! NO! I COULD NEVER...
WHY NOT? ALL YOU HAVE TO DO IS **STAND STILL**! I THINK YOU COULD HANDLE THAT.
NOT **NAKED!**
OH, **COME ON!** IT'S NOT LIKE YOU HAVE ANY THING I'VE NEVER SEEN BEFORE.
HAVE YOU?

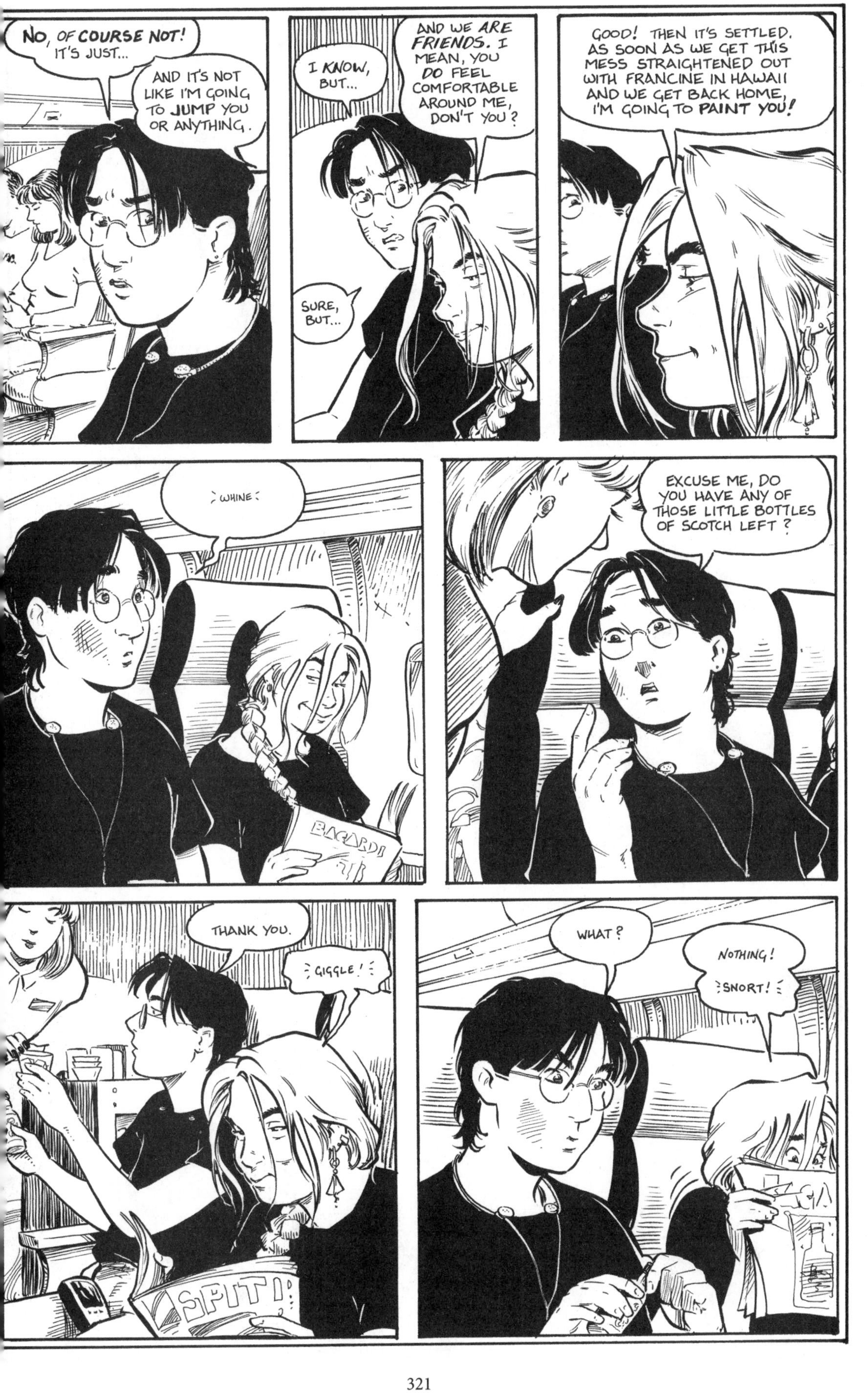
NO, OF COURSE NOT! IT'S JUST...
AND IT'S NOT LIKE I'M GOING TO JUMP YOU OR ANYTHING.
I KNOW, BUT...
AND WE ARE FRIENDS. I MEAN, YOU DO FEEL COMFORTABLE AROUND ME, DON'T YOU?
SURE, BUT...
GOOD! THEN IT'S SETTLED. AS SOON AS WE GET THIS MESS STRAIGHTENED OUT WITH FRANCINE IN HAWAII AND WE GET BACK HOME, I'M GOING TO PAINT YOU!
WHINE
BACARDI
EXCUSE ME, DO YOU HAVE ANY OF THOSE LITTLE BOTTLES OF SCOTCH LEFT?
THANK YOU.
GIGGLE!
SPIT!
WHAT?
NOTHING!
SNORT!

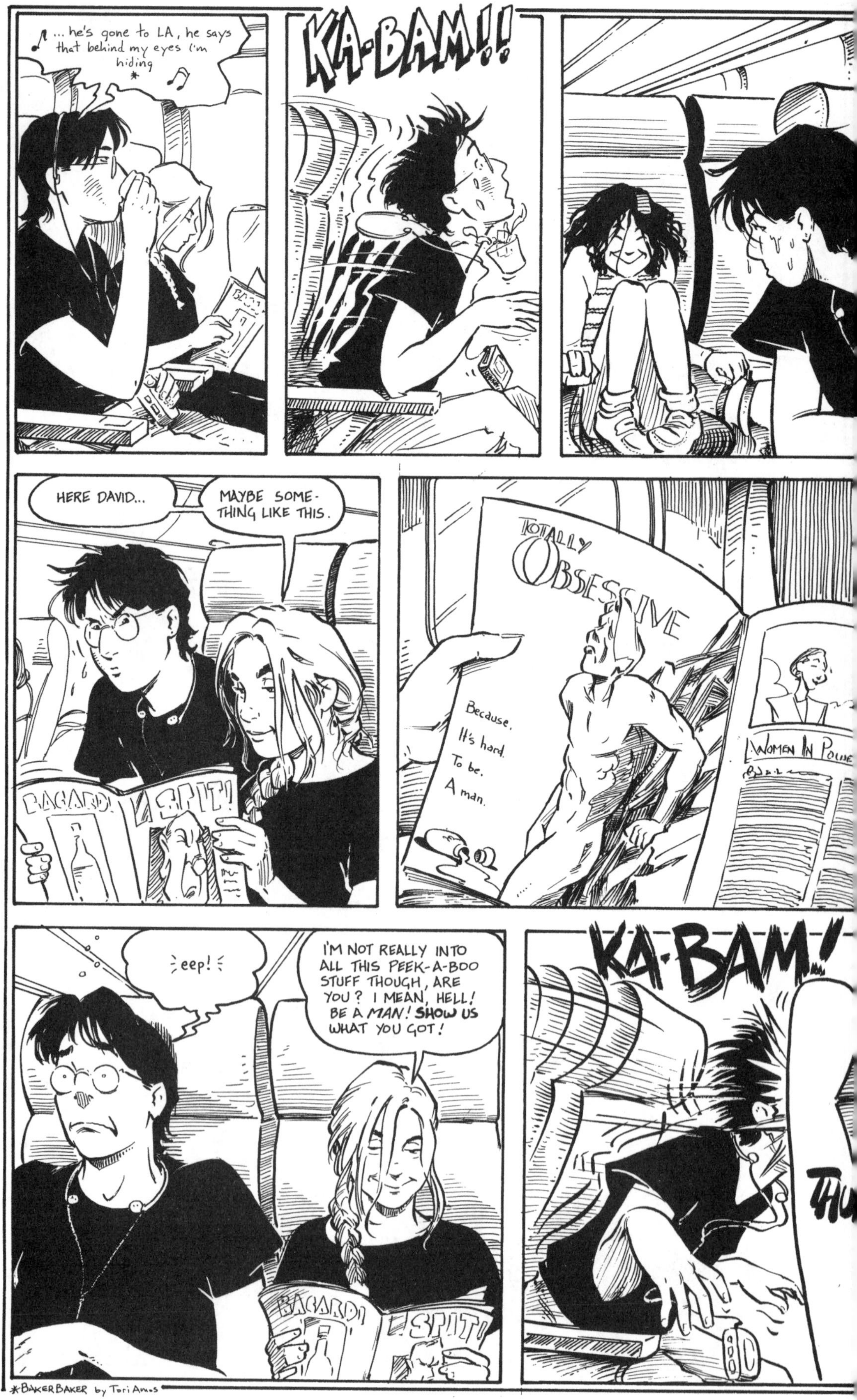

... he's gone to LA, he says that behind my eyes i'm hiding *
KA-BAM!!
HERE DAVID...
MAYBE SOME-THING LIKE THIS.
BACARDI
SPIT!
TOTALLY OBSSESSIVE
Because. It's hard. To be. A man.
eep!
I'M NOT REALLY INTO ALL THIS PEEK-A-BOO STUFF THOUGH, ARE YOU? I MEAN, HELL! BE A MAN! SHOW US WHAT YOU GOT!
BACARDI
SPIT!
KA-BAM!
*BAKER BAKER by Tori Amos

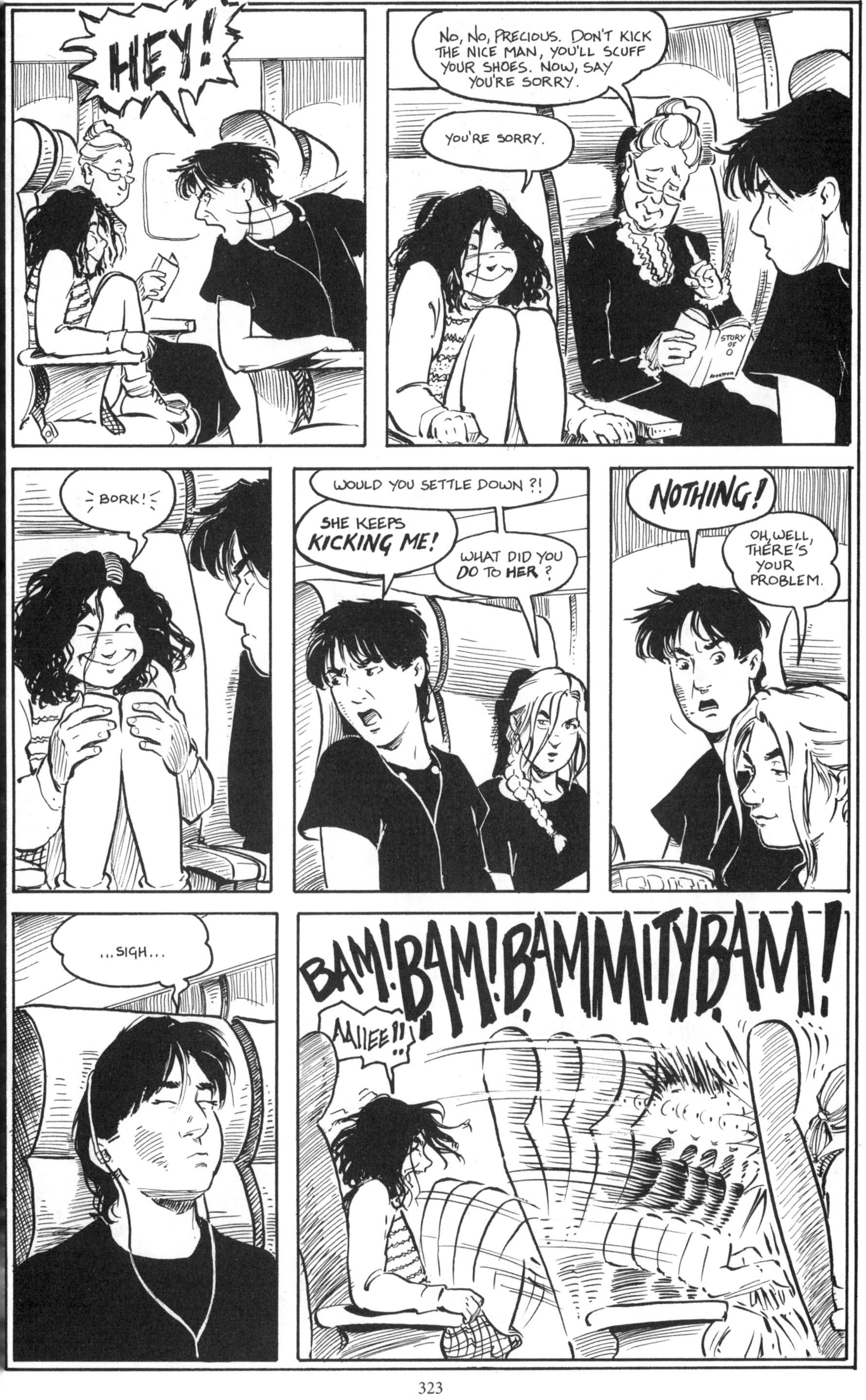
HEY!
NO, NO, PRECIOUS. DON'T KICK THE NICE MAN, YOU'LL SCUFF YOUR SHOES. NOW, SAY YOU'RE SORRY.
YOU'RE SORRY.
STORY OF O
BORK!
WOULD YOU SETTLE DOWN ?!
SHE KEEPS KICKING ME!
WHAT DID YOU DO TO HER ?
NOTHING!
OH, WELL, THERE'S YOUR PROBLEM.
...SIGH...
BAM! BAM! BAMMITYBAM!
AAIIEE!!

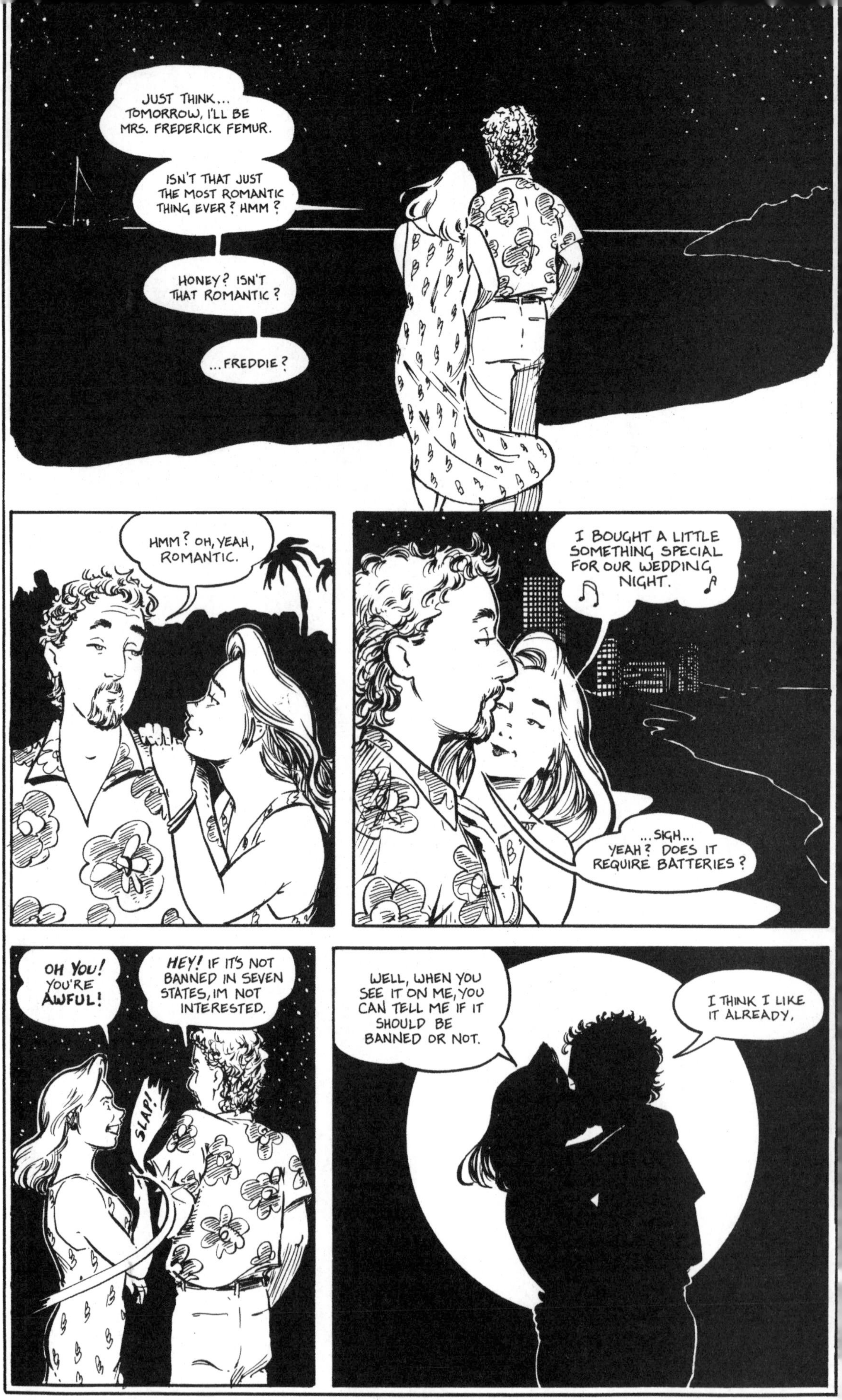
JUST THINK... TOMORROW, I'LL BE MRS. FREDERICK FEMUR.
ISN'T THAT JUST THE MOST ROMANTIC THING EVER? HMM?
HONEY? ISN'T THAT ROMANTIC?
...FREDDIE?
HMM? OH, YEAH, ROMANTIC.
I BOUGHT A LITTLE SOMETHING SPECIAL FOR OUR WEDDING NIGHT.
...SIGH... YEAH? DOES IT REQUIRE BATTERIES?
OH YOU! YOU'RE AWFUL!
HEY! IF IT'S NOT BANNED IN SEVEN STATES, IM NOT INTERESTED.
SLAP!
WELL, WHEN YOU SEE IT ON ME, YOU CAN TELL ME IF IT SHOULD BE BANNED OR NOT.
I THINK I LIKE IT ALREADY.

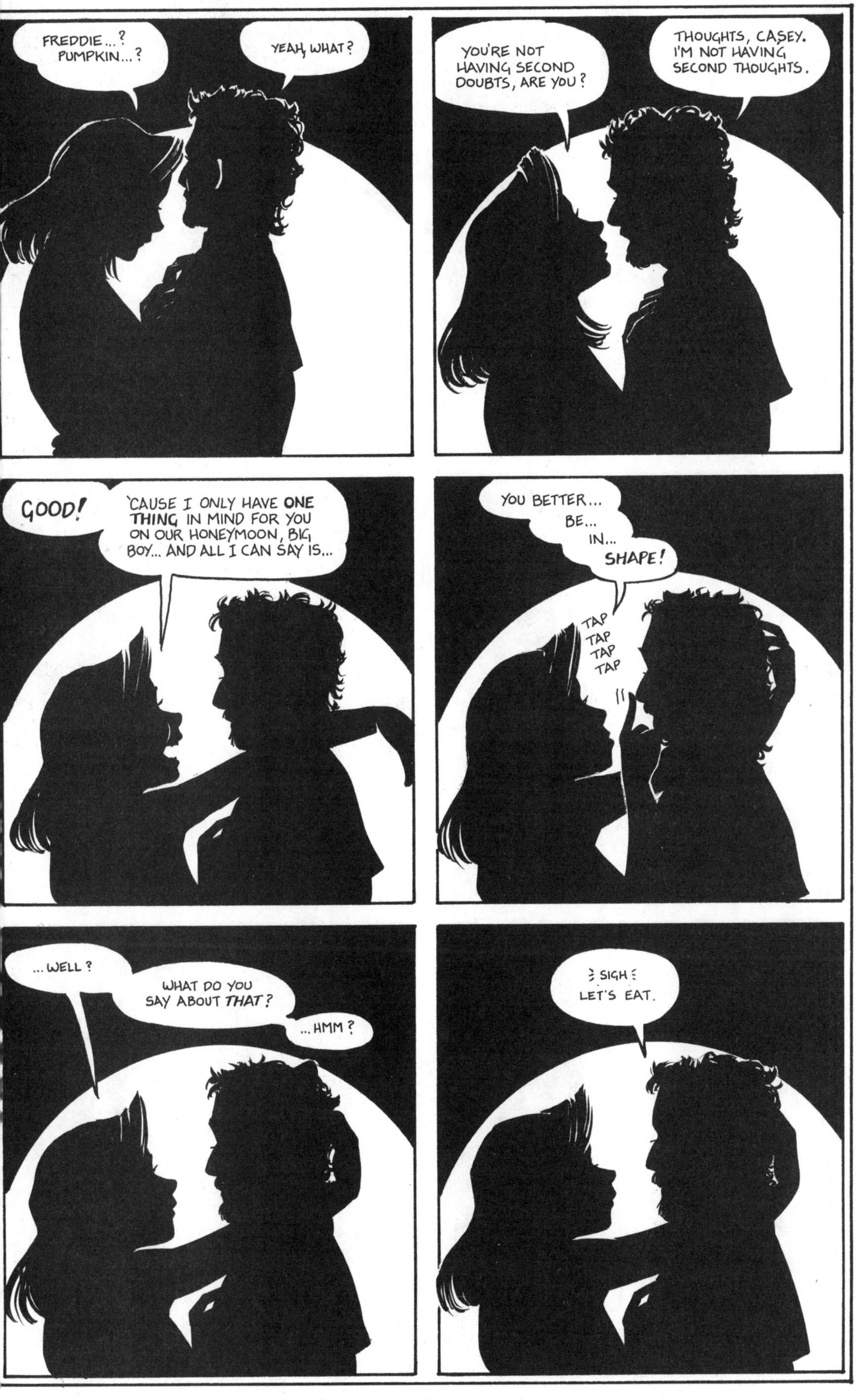
FREDDIE...? PUMPKIN...?
YEAH, WHAT?
YOU'RE NOT HAVING SECOND DOUBTS, ARE YOU?
THOUGHTS, CASEY. I'M NOT HAVING SECOND THOUGHTS.
GOOD!
'CAUSE I ONLY HAVE ONE THING IN MIND FOR YOU ON OUR HONEYMOON, BIG BOY... AND ALL I CAN SAY IS...
YOU BETTER... BE... IN... SHAPE!
TAP TAP TAP TAP
...WELL?
WHAT DO YOU SAY ABOUT THAT?
...HMM?
SIGH
LET'S EAT.

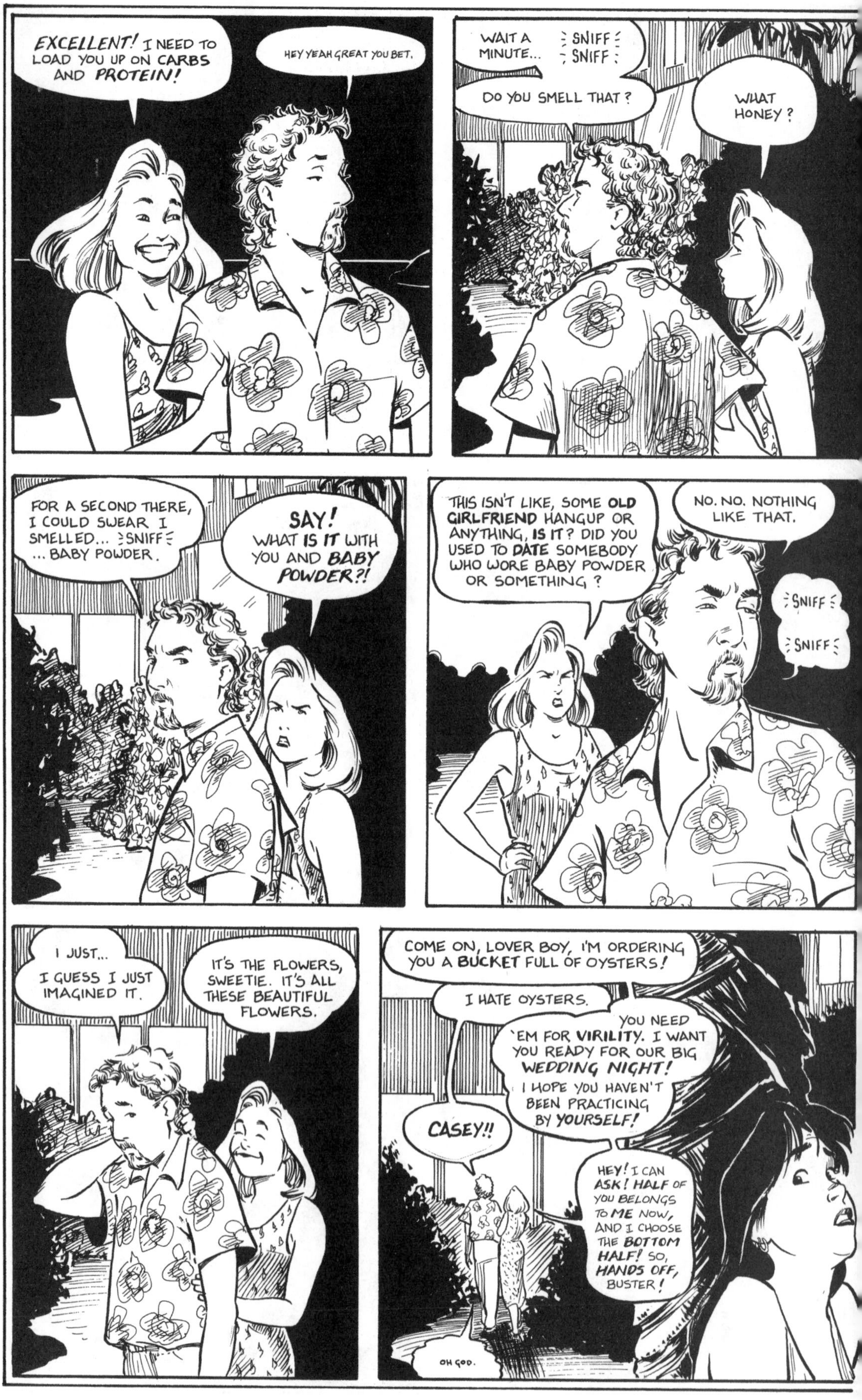
EXCELLENT! I NEED TO LOAD YOU UP ON CARBS AND PROTEIN!
HEY YEAH GREAT YOU BET.
WAIT A MINUTE... SNIFF SNIFF
DO YOU SMELL THAT?
WHAT HONEY?
FOR A SECOND THERE, I COULD SWEAR I SMELLED... SNIFF ... BABY POWDER.
SAY! WHAT IS IT WITH YOU AND BABY POWDER?!
THIS ISN'T LIKE, SOME OLD GIRLFRIEND HANGUP OR ANYTHING, IS IT? DID YOU USED TO DATE SOMEBODY WHO WORE BABY POWDER OR SOMETHING?
NO. NO. NOTHING LIKE THAT.
SNIFF
SNIFF
I JUST... I GUESS I JUST IMAGINED IT.
IT'S THE FLOWERS, SWEETIE. IT'S ALL THESE BEAUTIFUL FLOWERS.
COME ON, LOVER BOY, I'M ORDERING YOU A BUCKET FULL OF OYSTERS!
I HATE OYSTERS.
YOU NEED 'EM FOR VIRILITY. I WANT YOU READY FOR OUR BIG WEDDING NIGHT! I HOPE YOU HAVEN'T BEEN PRACTICING BY YOURSELF!
CASEY!!
HEY! I CAN ASK! HALF OF YOU BELONGS TO ME NOW, AND I CHOOSE THE BOTTOM HALF! SO, HANDS OFF, BUSTER!
OH GOD.

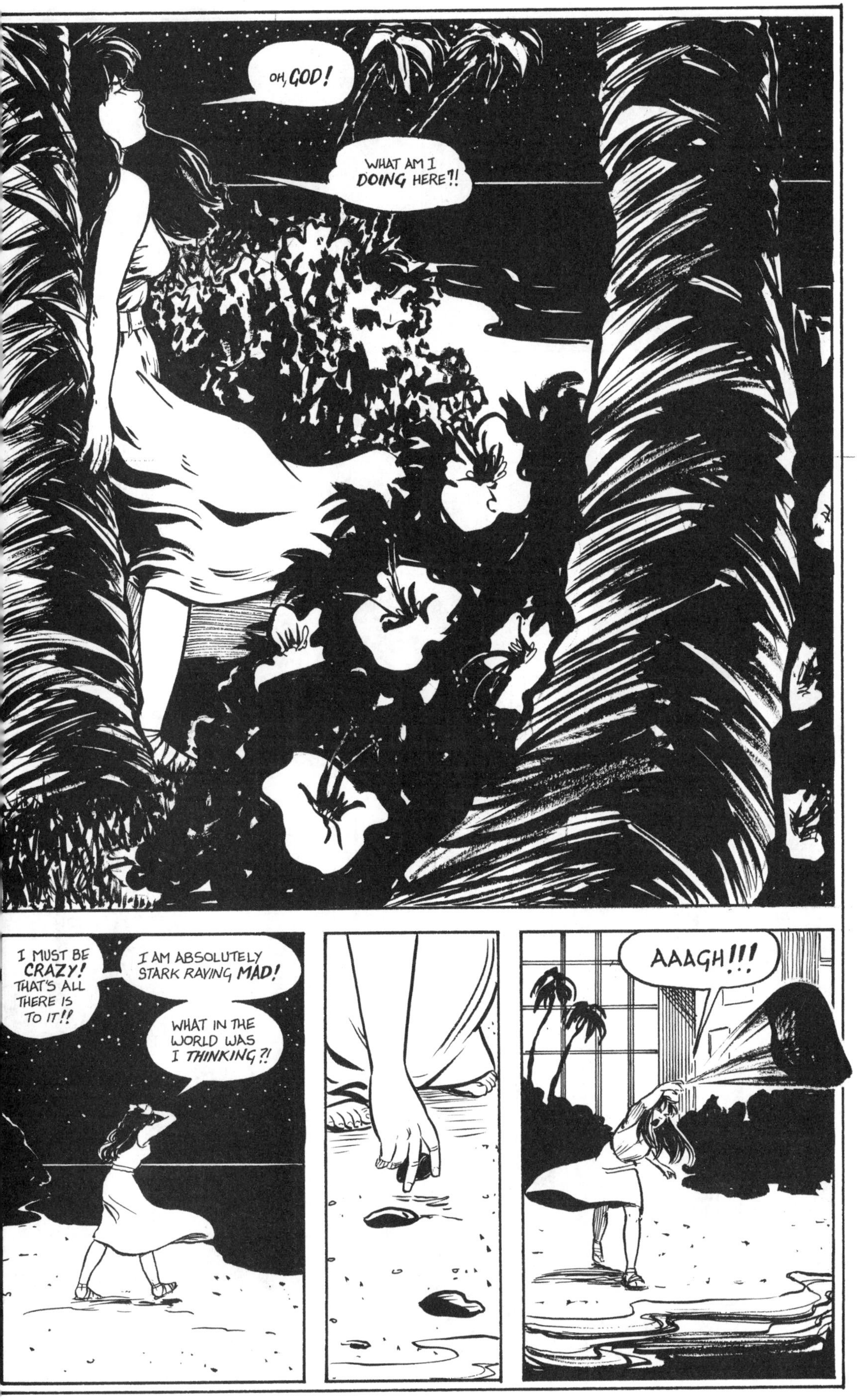

OH, GOD!
WHAT AM I DOING HERE?!
I MUST BE CRAZY! THAT'S ALL THERE IS TO IT!!
I AM ABSOLUTELY STARK RAVING MAD!
WHAT IN THE WORLD WAS I THINKING?!
AAAGH!!!

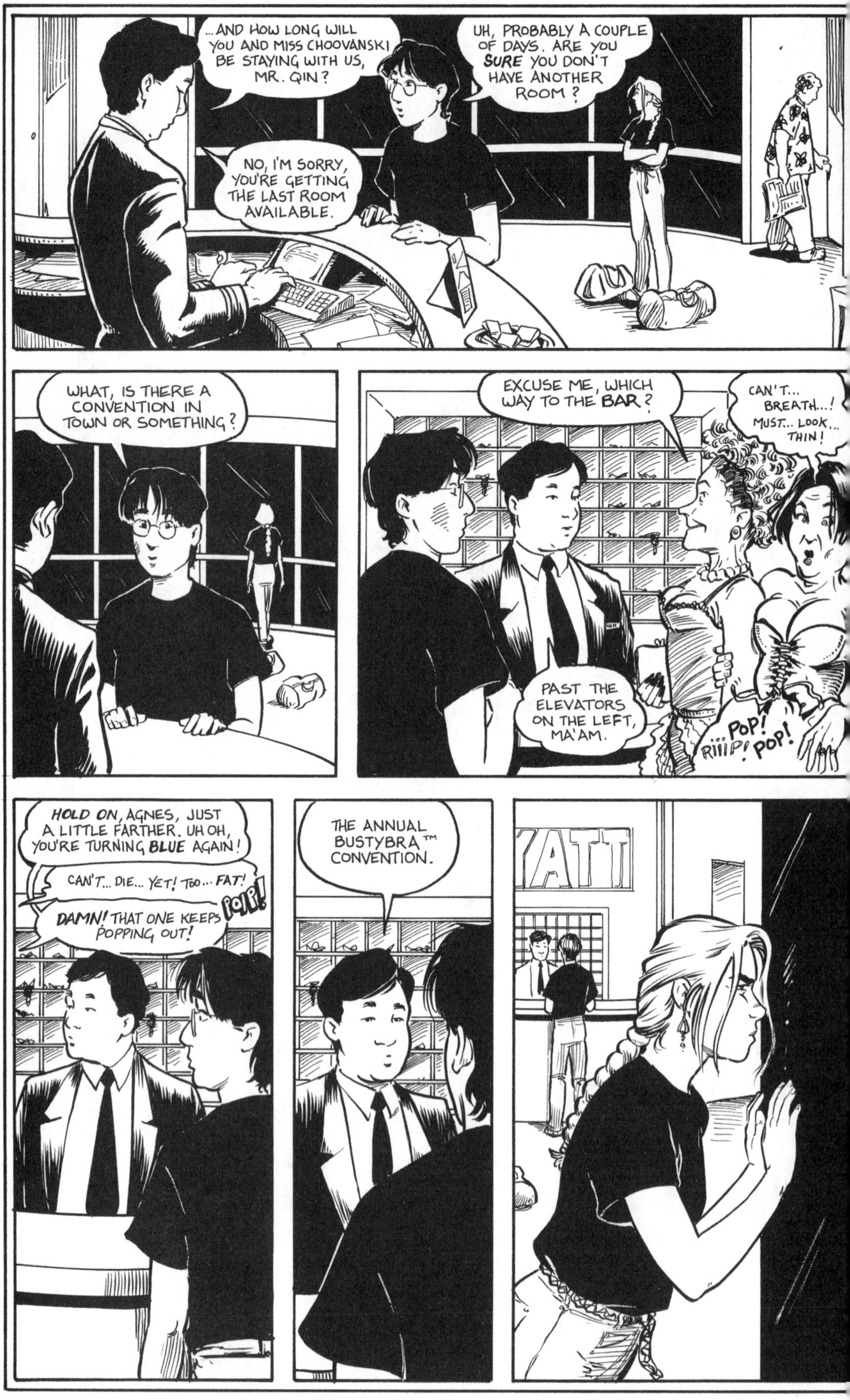
...AND HOW LONG WILL YOU AND MISS CHOOVANSKI BE STAYING WITH US, MR. QIN?
UH, PROBABLY A COUPLE OF DAYS. ARE YOU SURE YOU DON'T HAVE ANOTHER ROOM?
NO, I'M SORRY, YOU'RE GETTING THE LAST ROOM AVAILABLE.
WHAT, IS THERE A CONVENTION IN TOWN OR SOMETHING?
EXCUSE ME, WHICH WAY TO THE BAR?
CAN'T... BREATH...! MUST... LOOK... THIN!
PAST THE ELEVATORS ON THE LEFT, MA'AM.
RIIIP! POP! POP!
HOLD ON, AGNES, JUST A LITTLE FARTHER. UH OH, YOU'RE TURNING BLUE AGAIN!
CAN'T... DIE... YET! TOO... FAT!
DAMN! THAT ONE KEEPS POPPING OUT!
POP!
THE ANNUAL BUSTYBRA™ CONVENTION.
YATT

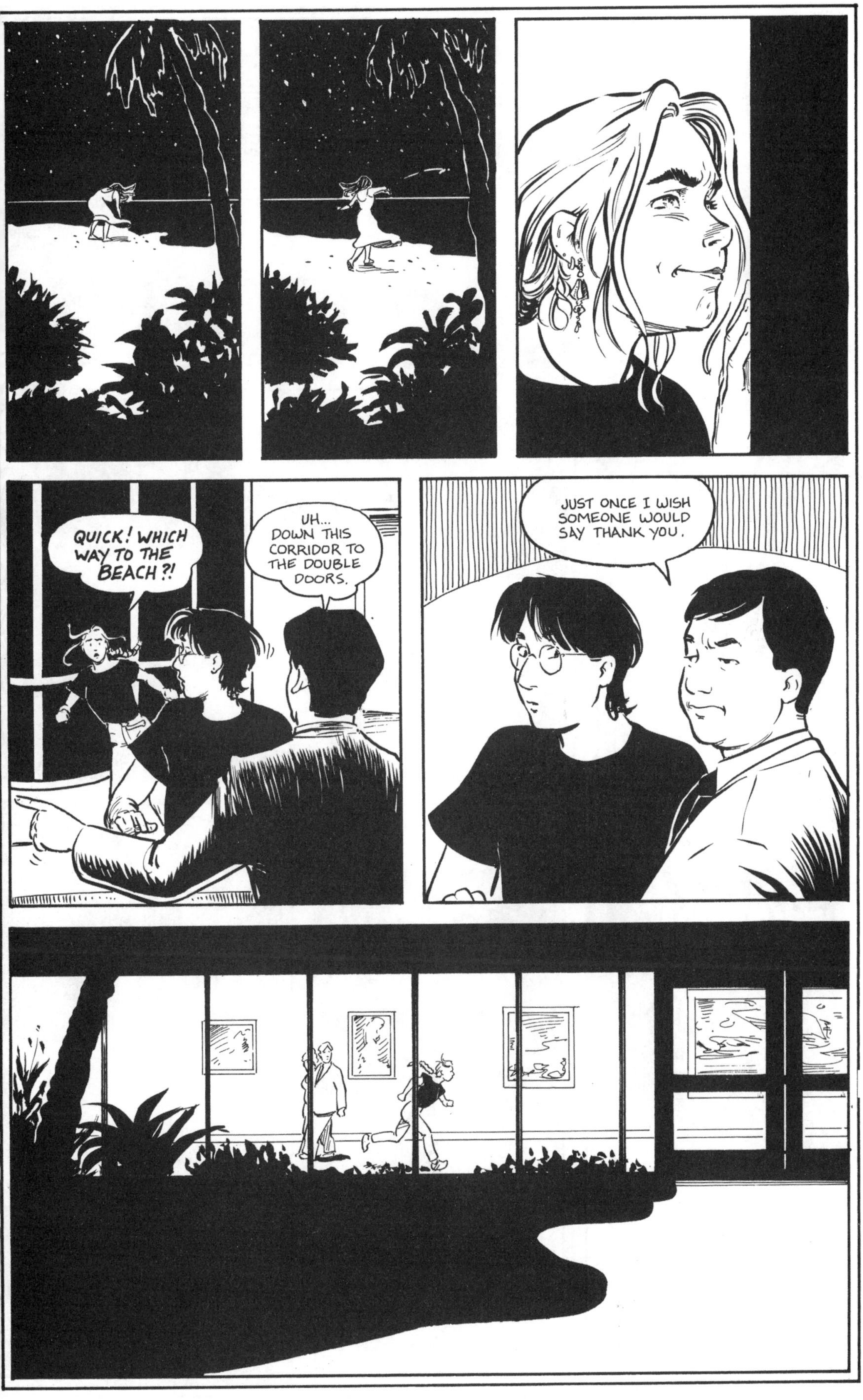
QUICK! WHICH WAY TO THE BEACH?!
UH... DOWN THIS CORRIDOR TO THE DOUBLE DOORS.
JUST ONCE I WISH SOMEONE WOULD SAY THANK YOU.

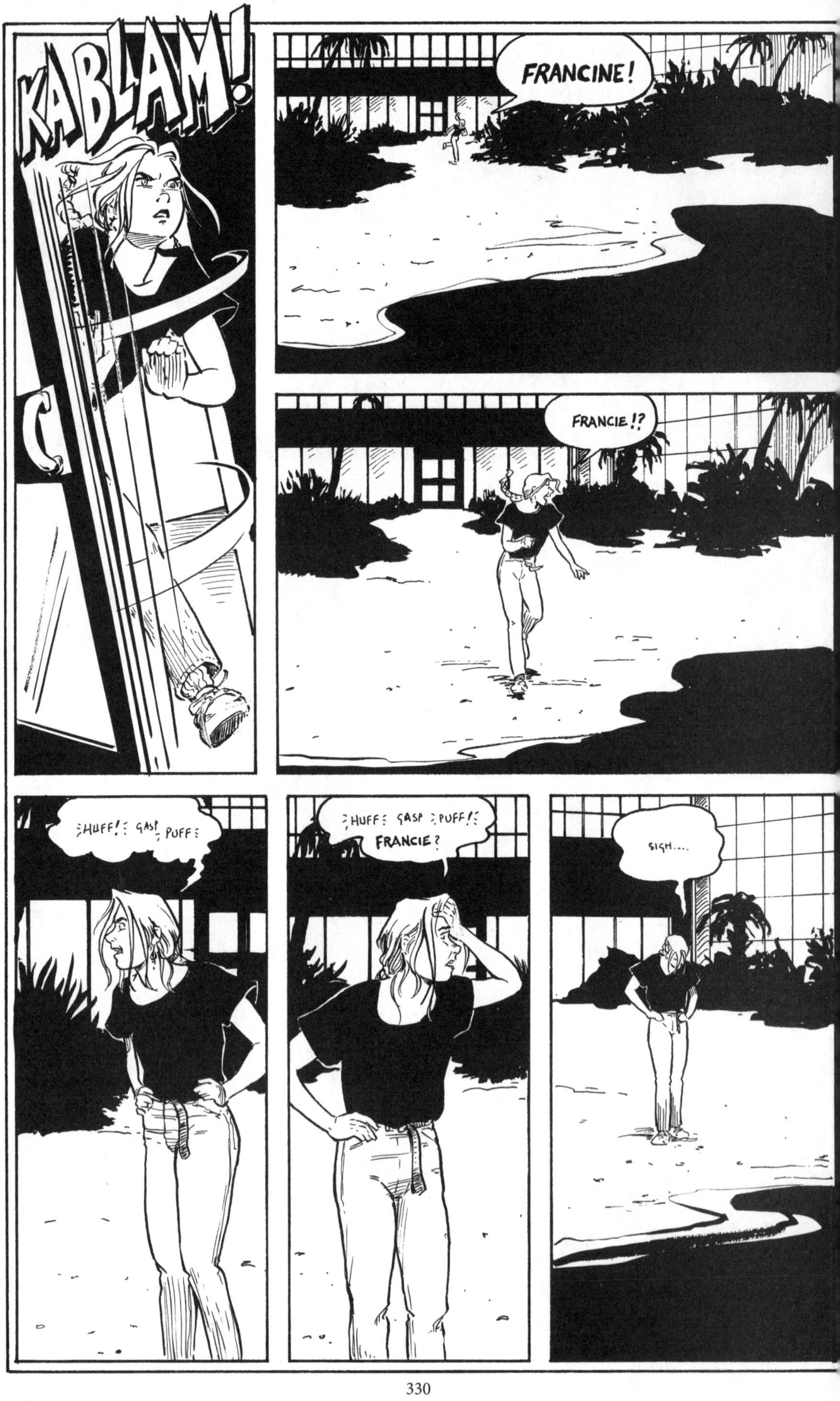
KABLAM!
FRANCINE!
FRANCIE!?
HUFF! GASP PUFF
HUFF GASP PUFF!
FRANCIE?
SIGH....

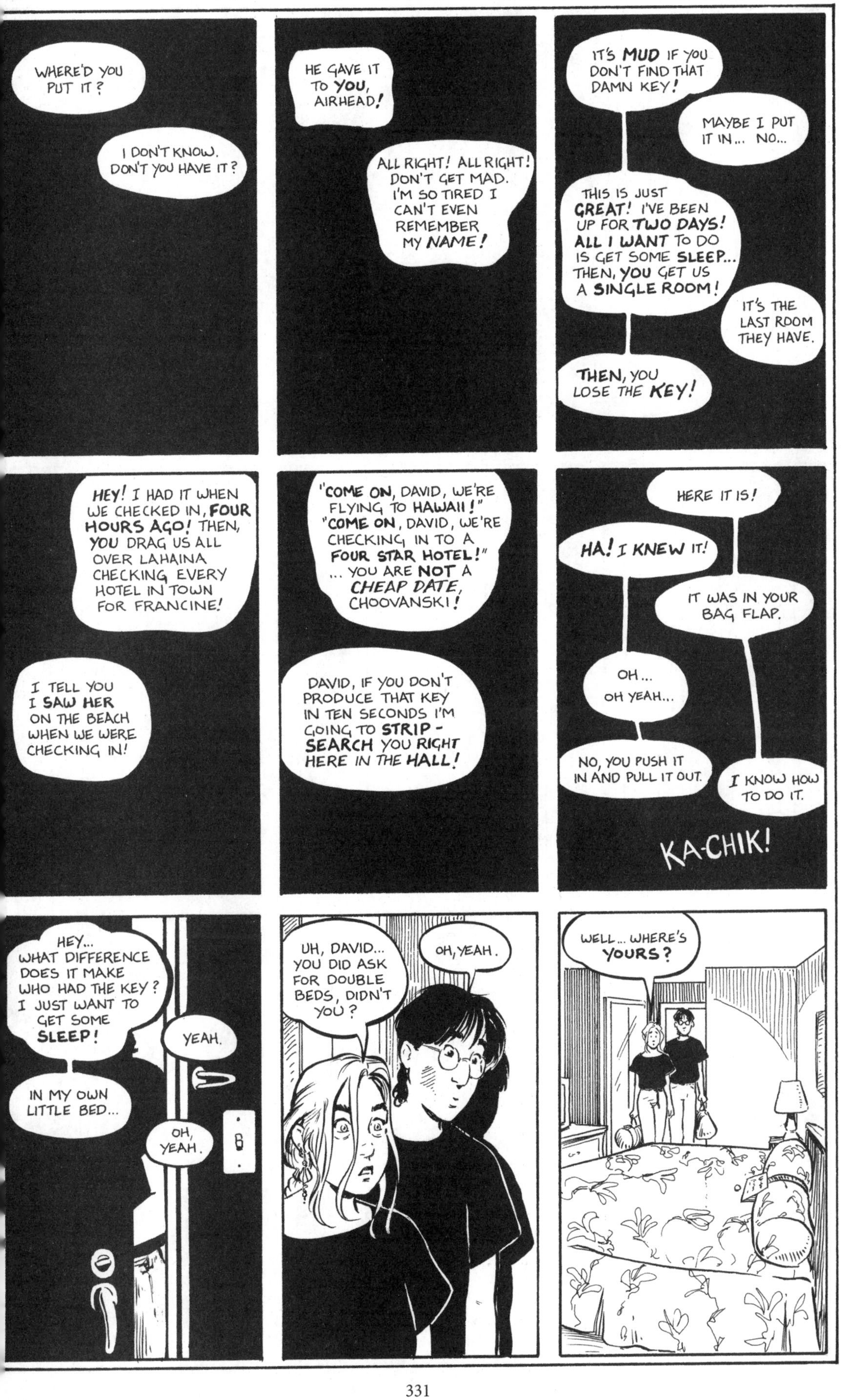
WHERE'D YOU PUT IT?
I DON'T KNOW. DON'T YOU HAVE IT?
HE GAVE IT TO YOU, AIRHEAD!
ALL RIGHT! ALL RIGHT! DON'T GET MAD. I'M SO TIRED I CAN'T EVEN REMEMBER MY NAME!
IT'S MUD IF YOU DON'T FIND THAT DAMN KEY!
MAYBE I PUT IT IN... NO...
THIS IS JUST GREAT! I'VE BEEN UP FOR TWO DAYS! ALL I WANT TO DO IS GET SOME SLEEP... THEN, YOU GET US A SINGLE ROOM!
IT'S THE LAST ROOM THEY HAVE.
THEN, YOU LOSE THE KEY!
HEY! I HAD IT WHEN WE CHECKED IN, FOUR HOURS AGO! THEN, YOU DRAG US ALL OVER LAHAINA CHECKING EVERY HOTEL IN TOWN FOR FRANCINE!
I TELL YOU I SAW HER ON THE BEACH WHEN WE WERE CHECKING IN!
"COME ON, DAVID, WE'RE FLYING TO HAWAII!" "COME ON, DAVID, WE'RE CHECKING IN TO A FOUR STAR HOTEL!" ... YOU ARE NOT A CHEAP DATE, CHOOVANSKI!
DAVID, IF YOU DON'T PRODUCE THAT KEY IN TEN SECONDS I'M GOING TO STRIP-SEARCH YOU RIGHT HERE IN THE HALL!
HERE IT IS!
HA! I KNEW IT!
IT WAS IN YOUR BAG FLAP.
OH... OH YEAH...
NO, YOU PUSH IT IN AND PULL IT OUT.
I KNOW HOW TO DO IT.
KA-CHIK!
HEY... WHAT DIFFERENCE DOES IT MAKE WHO HAD THE KEY? I JUST WANT TO GET SOME SLEEP!
YEAH.
IN MY OWN LITTLE BED...
OH, YEAH.
UH, DAVID... YOU DID ASK FOR DOUBLE BEDS, DIDN'T YOU?
OH, YEAH.
WELL... WHERE'S YOURS?

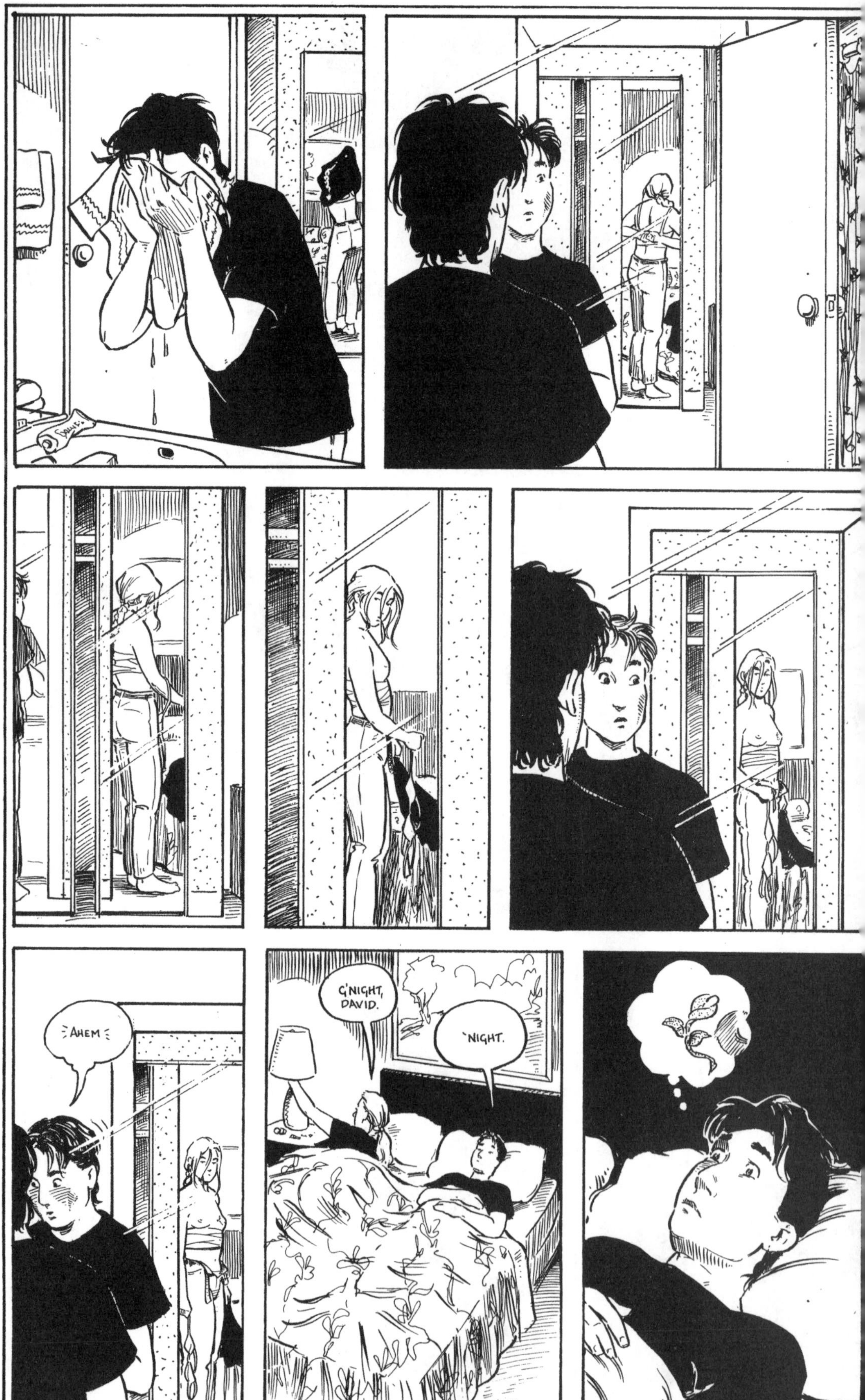
AHEM
G'NIGHT, DAVID.
`NIGHT.

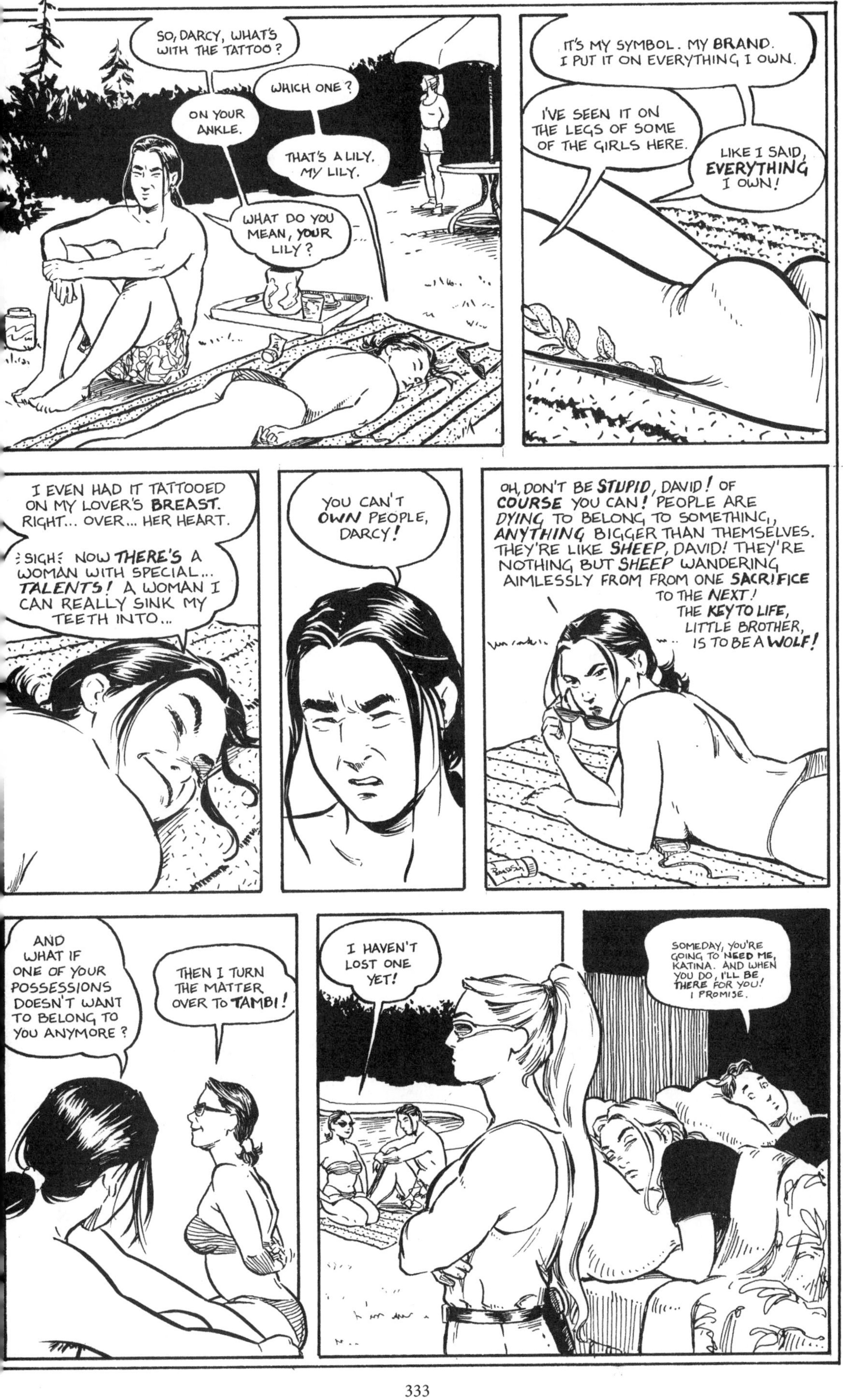

SO, DARCY, WHAT'S WITH THE TATTOO?
WHICH ONE?
ON YOUR ANKLE.
THAT'S A LILY. MY LILY.
WHAT DO YOU MEAN, YOUR LILY?
IT'S MY SYMBOL. MY BRAND. I PUT IT ON EVERYTHING I OWN.
I'VE SEEN IT ON THE LEGS OF SOME OF THE GIRLS HERE.
LIKE I SAID, EVERYTHING I OWN!
I EVEN HAD IT TATTOOED ON MY LOVER'S BREAST. RIGHT... OVER... HER HEART.
SIGH NOW THERE'S A WOMAN WITH SPECIAL... TALENTS! A WOMAN I CAN REALLY SINK MY TEETH INTO...
YOU CAN'T OWN PEOPLE, DARCY!
OH, DON'T BE STUPID, DAVID! OF COURSE YOU CAN! PEOPLE ARE DYING TO BELONG TO SOMETHING, ANYTHING BIGGER THAN THEMSELVES. THEY'RE LIKE SHEEP, DAVID! THEY'RE NOTHING BUT SHEEP WANDERING AIMLESSLY FROM FROM ONE SACRIFICE TO THE NEXT! THE KEY TO LIFE, LITTLE BROTHER, IS TO BE A WOLF!
AND WHAT IF ONE OF YOUR POSSESSIONS DOESN'T WANT TO BELONG TO YOU ANYMORE?
THEN I TURN THE MATTER OVER TO TAMBI!
I HAVEN'T LOST ONE YET!
SOMEDAY, YOU'RE GOING TO NEED ME, KATINA. AND WHEN YOU DO, I'LL BE THERE FOR YOU! I PROMISE.

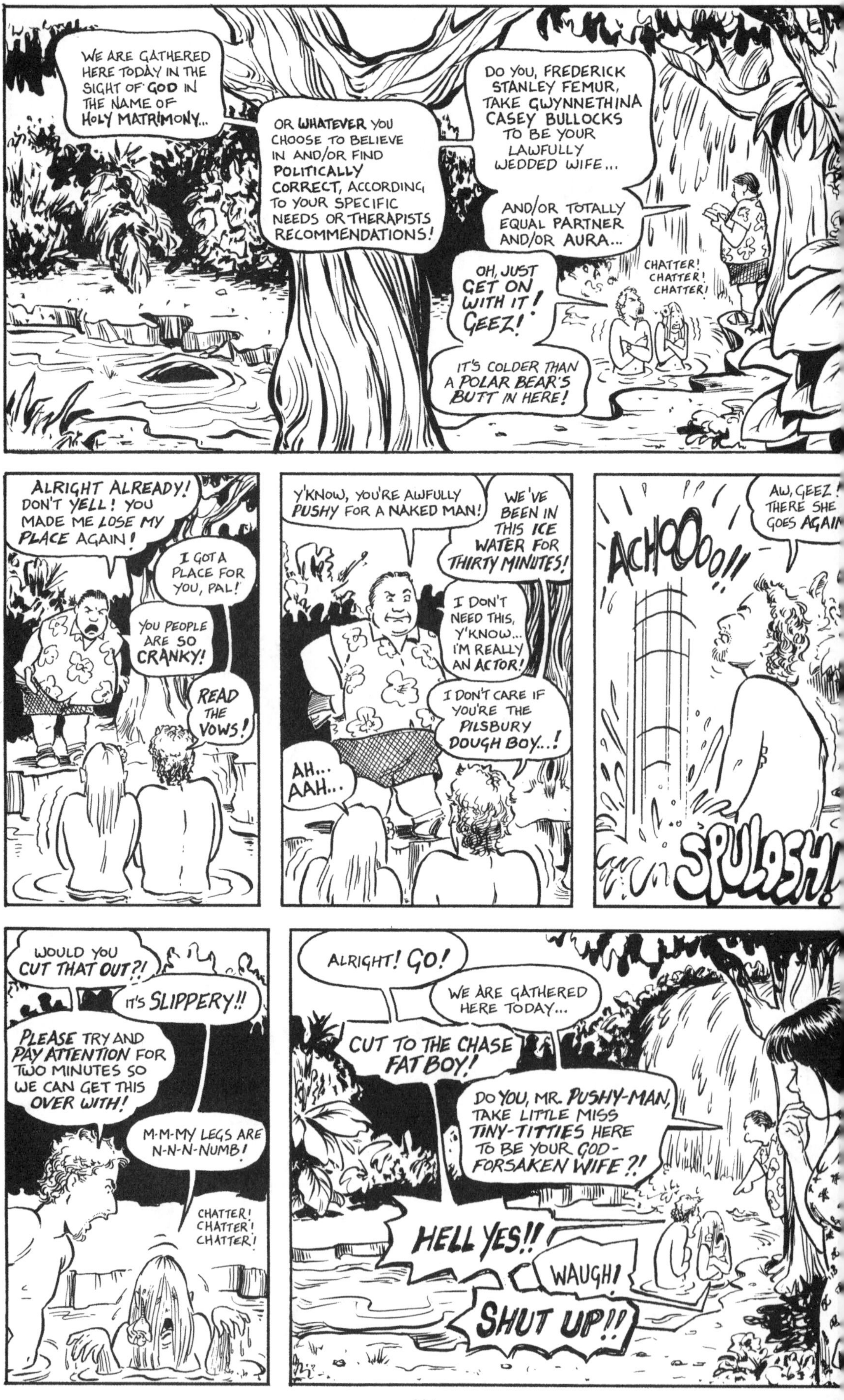

WE ARE GATHERED HERE TODAY IN THE SIGHT OF GOD IN THE NAME OF HOLY MATRIMONY...
OR WHATEVER YOU CHOOSE TO BELIEVE IN AND/OR FIND POLITICALLY CORRECT, ACCORDING TO YOUR SPECIFIC NEEDS OR THERAPISTS RECOMMENDATIONS!
DO YOU, FREDERICK STANLEY FEMUR, TAKE GWYNNETHINA CASEY BULLOCKS TO BE YOUR LAWFULLY WEDDED WIFE...
AND/OR TOTALLY EQUAL PARTNER AND/OR AURA...
OH, JUST GET ON WITH IT! GEEZ!
IT'S COLDER THAN A POLAR BEAR'S BUTT IN HERE!
CHATTER! CHATTER! CHATTER!
ALRIGHT ALREADY! DON'T YELL! YOU MADE ME LOSE MY PLACE AGAIN!
I GOT A PLACE FOR YOU, PAL!
YOU PEOPLE ARE SO CRANKY!
READ THE VOWS!
Y'KNOW, YOU'RE AWFULLY PUSHY FOR A NAKED MAN!
WE'VE BEEN IN THIS ICE WATER FOR THIRTY MINUTES!
I DON'T NEED THIS, Y'KNOW... I'M REALLY AN ACTOR!
I DON'T CARE IF YOU'RE THE PILSBURY DOUGH BOY...!
AH... AAH...
ACHOOOOO!!
AW, GEEZ! THERE SHE GOES AGAIN
SPULOSH!
WOULD YOU CUT THAT OUT?!
IT'S SLIPPERY!!
PLEASE TRY AND PAY ATTENTION FOR TWO MINUTES SO WE CAN GET THIS OVER WITH!
M-M-MY LEGS ARE N-N-N-NUMB!
CHATTER! CHATTER! CHATTER!
ALRIGHT! GO!
WE ARE GATHERED HERE TODAY...
CUT TO THE CHASE FAT BOY!
DO YOU, MR. PUSHY-MAN, TAKE LITTLE MISS TINY-TITTIES HERE TO BE YOUR GOD-FORSAKEN WIFE?!
HELL YES!!
WAUGH!
SHUT UP!!

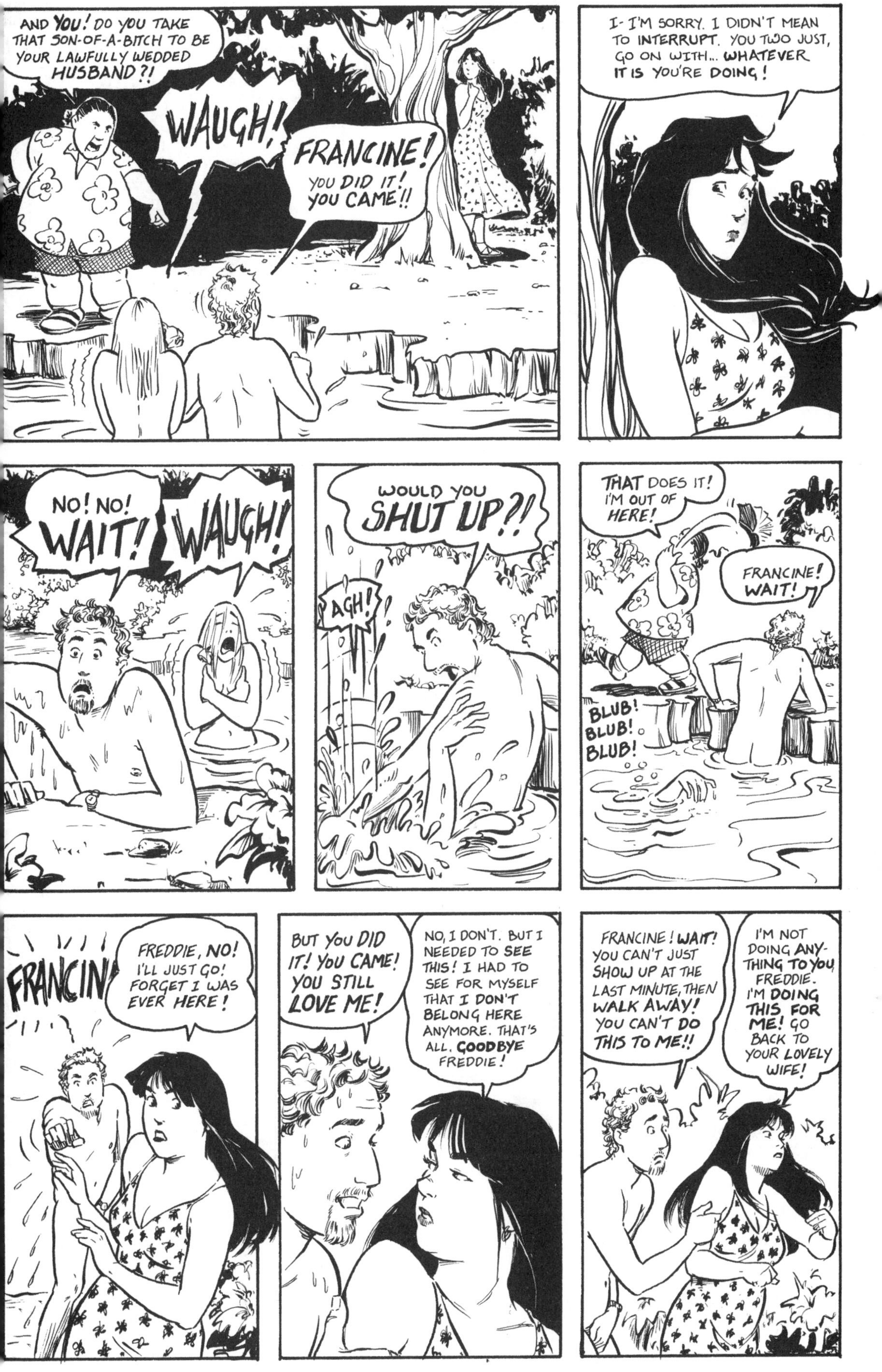
AND YOU! DO YOU TAKE THAT SON-OF-A-BITCH TO BE YOUR LAWFULLY WEDDED HUSBAND?!
WAUGH!
FRANCINE! YOU DID IT! YOU CAME!!
I- I'M SORRY. I DIDN'T MEAN TO INTERRUPT. YOU TWO JUST, GO ON WITH... WHATEVER IT IS YOU'RE DOING!
NO! NO! WAIT!
WAUGH!
WOULD YOU SHUT UP?!
AGH!
THAT DOES IT! I'M OUT OF HERE!
FRANCINE! WAIT!
BLUB! BLUB! BLUB!
FRANCIN
FREDDIE, NO! I'LL JUST GO! FORGET I WAS EVER HERE!
BUT YOU DID IT! YOU CAME! YOU STILL LOVE ME!
NO, I DON'T. BUT I NEEDED TO SEE THIS! I HAD TO SEE FOR MYSELF THAT I DON'T BELONG HERE ANYMORE. THAT'S ALL. GOODBYE FREDDIE!
FRANCINE! WAIT! YOU CAN'T JUST SHOW UP AT THE LAST MINUTE, THEN WALK AWAY! YOU CAN'T DO THIS TO ME!!
I'M NOT DOING ANY-THING TO YOU, FREDDIE. I'M DOING THIS FOR ME! GO BACK TO YOUR LOVELY WIFE!

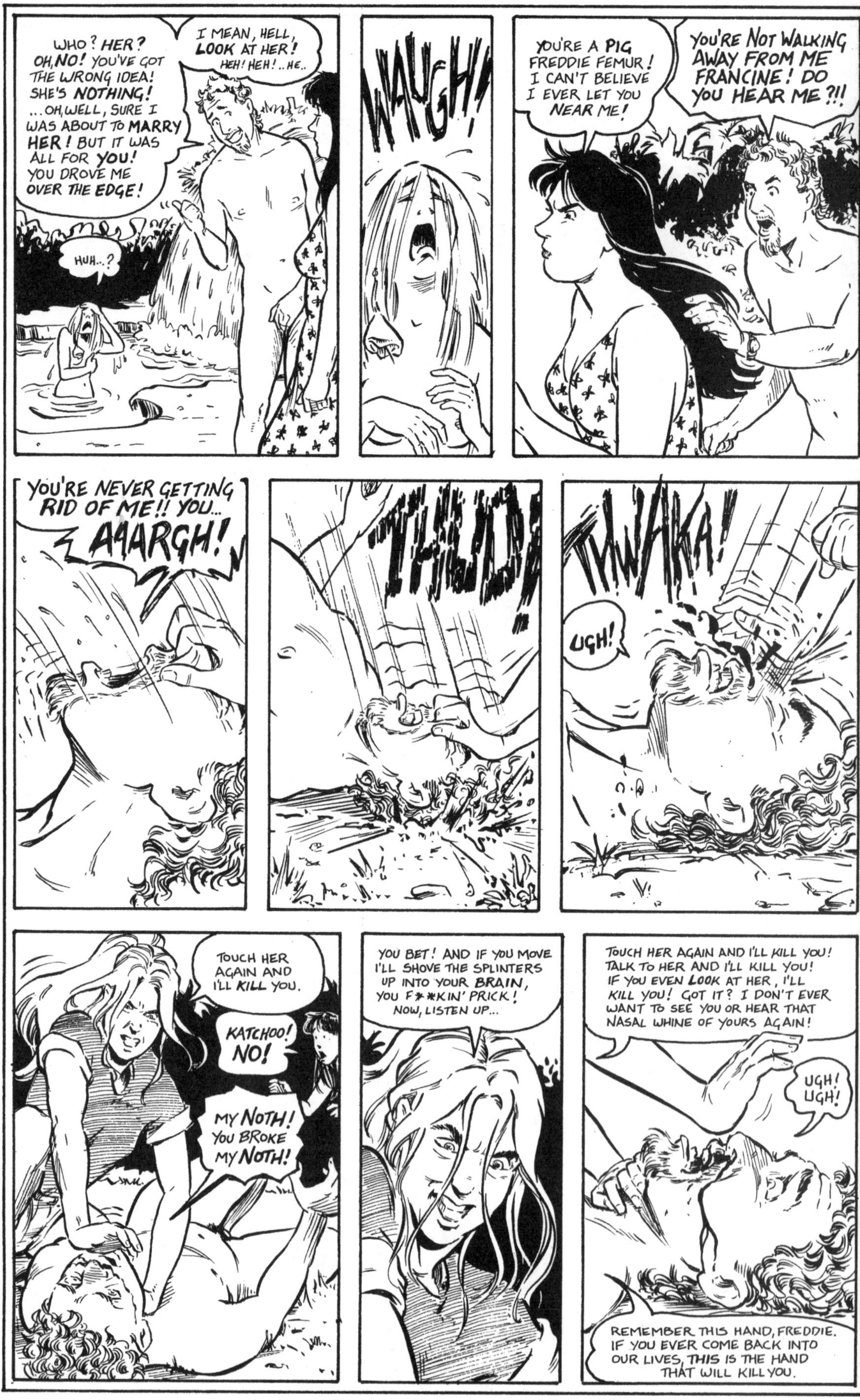
WHO? HER? OH, NO! YOU'VE GOT THE WRONG IDEA! SHE'S NOTHING! ...OH, WELL, SURE I WAS ABOUT TO MARRY HER! BUT IT WAS ALL FOR YOU! YOU DROVE ME OVER THE EDGE!
I MEAN, HELL, LOOK AT HER! HEH! HEH! ..HE..
HUH..?
WAUGH!!
YOU'RE A PIG FREDDIE FEMUR! I CAN'T BELIEVE I EVER LET YOU NEAR ME!
YOU'RE NOT WALKING AWAY FROM ME FRANCINE! DO YOU HEAR ME ?!!
YOU'RE NEVER GETTING RID OF ME!! YOU... AAARGH!
THUD!
TWAKA!
UGH!
TOUCH HER AGAIN AND I'LL KILL YOU.
KATCHOO! NO!
MY NOTH! YOU BROKE MY NOTH!
YOU BET! AND IF YOU MOVE I'LL SHOVE THE SPLINTERS UP INTO YOUR BRAIN, YOU F**KIN' PRICK! NOW, LISTEN UP...
TOUCH HER AGAIN AND I'LL KILL YOU! TALK TO HER AND I'LL KILL YOU! IF YOU EVEN LOOK AT HER, I'LL KILL YOU! GOT IT? I DON'T EVER WANT TO SEE YOU OR HEAR THAT NASAL WHINE OF YOURS AGAIN!
UGH! UGH!
REMEMBER THIS HAND, FREDDIE. IF YOU EVER COME BACK INTO OUR LIVES, THIS IS THE HAND THAT WILL KILL YOU.

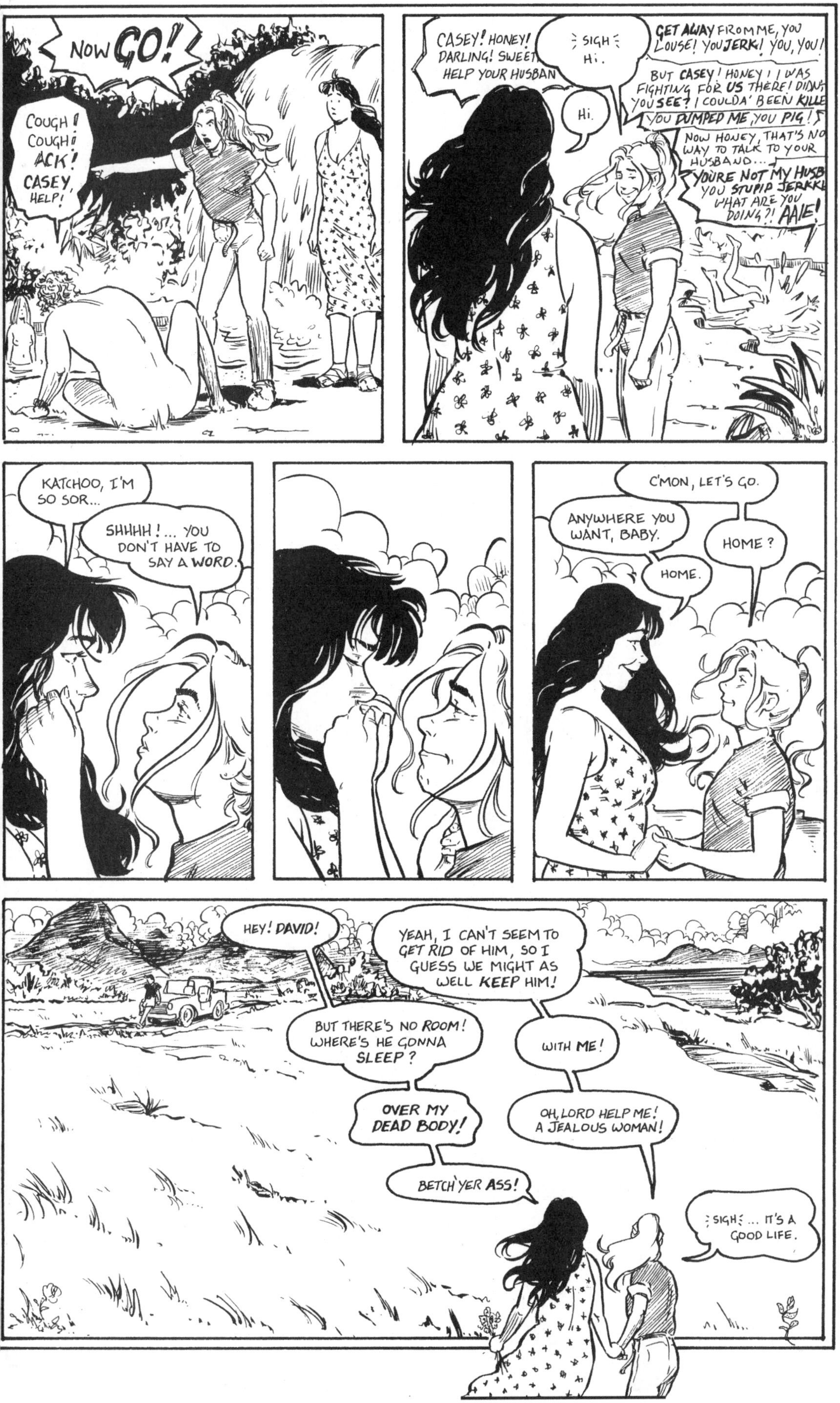

NOW GO!!
COUGH! COUGH! ACK! CASEY, HELP!
CASEY! HONEY! DARLING! SWEET HELP YOUR HUSBAN
SIGH Hi.
Hi.
GET AWAY FROM ME, YOU LOUSE! YOU JERK! YOU, YOU!
BUT CASEY! HONEY! I WAS FIGHTING FOR US THERE! DIDN'T YOU SEE? I COULDA' BEEN KILLE
YOU DUMPED ME, YOU PIG!
NOW HONEY, THAT'S NO WAY TO TALK TO YOUR HUSBAND...
YOU'RE NOT MY HUSB YOU STUPID JERKK! WHAT ARE YOU DOING?! AAIE!
KATCHOO, I'M SO SOR...
SHHHH!... YOU DON'T HAVE TO SAY A WORD.
C'MON, LET'S GO.
ANYWHERE YOU WANT, BABY.
HOME?
HOME.
HEY! DAVID!
YEAH, I CAN'T SEEM TO GET RID OF HIM, SO I GUESS WE MIGHT AS WELL KEEP HIM!
BUT THERE'S NO ROOM! WHERE'S HE GONNA SLEEP?
WITH ME!
OVER MY DEAD BODY!
OH, LORD HELP ME! A JEALOUS WOMAN!
BETCH'YER ASS!
SIGH ... IT'S A GOOD LIFE.

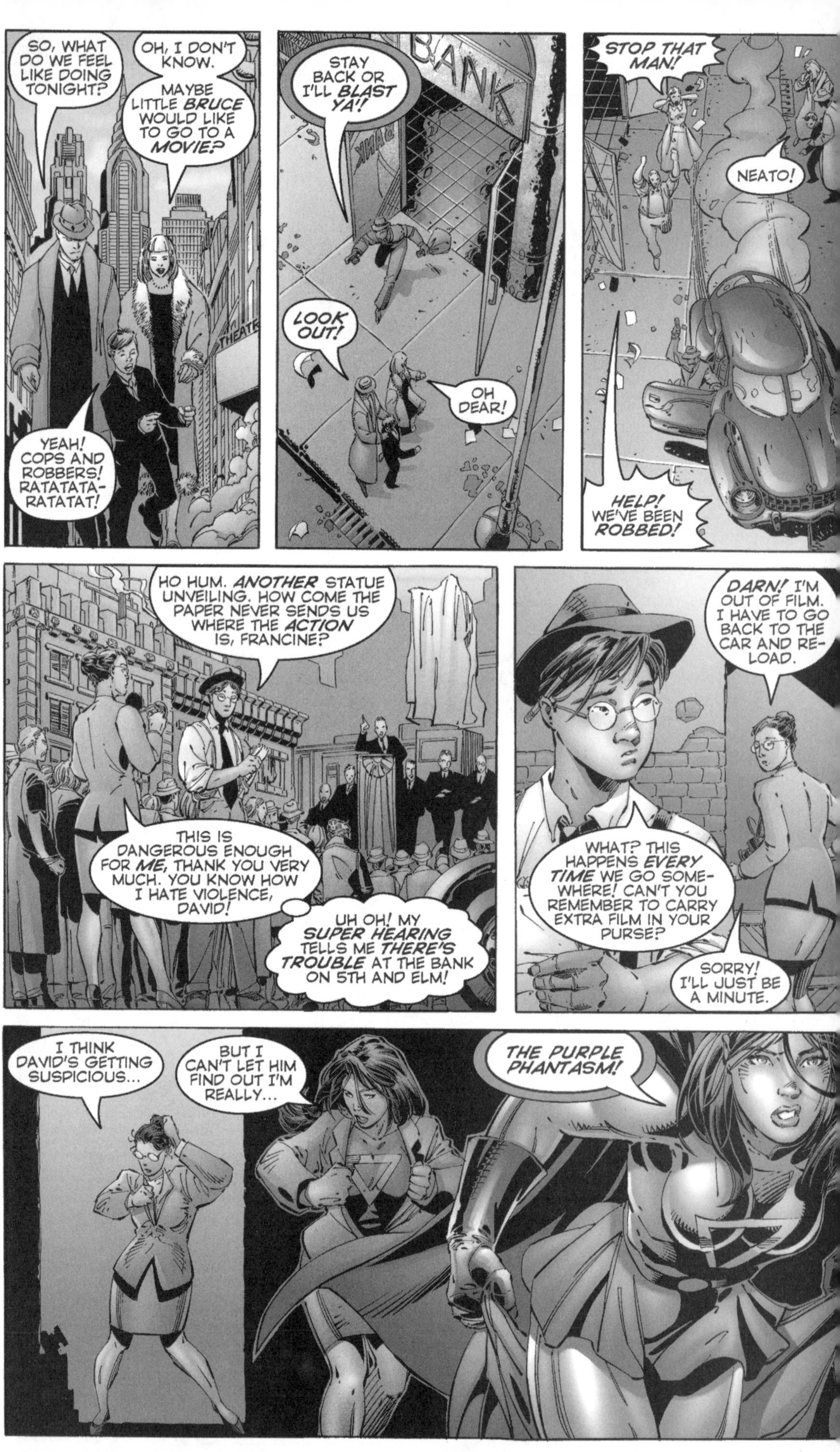

SO, WHAT DO WE FEEL LIKE DOING TONIGHT?
OH, I DON'T KNOW.
MAYBE LITTLE BRUCE WOULD LIKE TO GO TO A MOVIE?
YEAH! COPS AND ROBBERS! RATATATA-RATATAT!
THEATR
BANK
STAY BACK OR I'LL BLAST YA!!
LOOK OUT!
OH DEAR!
STOP THAT MAN!
NEATO!
HELP! WE'VE BEEN ROBBED!
HO HUM. ANOTHER STATUE UNVEILING. HOW COME THE PAPER NEVER SENDS US WHERE THE ACTION IS, FRANCINE?
THIS IS DANGEROUS ENOUGH FOR ME, THANK YOU VERY MUCH. YOU KNOW HOW I HATE VIOLENCE, DAVID!
UH OH! MY SUPER HEARING TELLS ME THERE'S TROUBLE AT THE BANK ON 5TH AND ELM!
DARN! I'M OUT OF FILM. I HAVE TO GO BACK TO THE CAR AND RE-LOAD.
WHAT? THIS HAPPENS EVERY TIME WE GO SOME-WHERE! CAN'T YOU REMEMBER TO CARRY EXTRA FILM IN YOUR PURSE?
SORRY! I'LL JUST BE A MINUTE.
I THINK DAVID'S GETTING SUSPICIOUS...
BUT I CAN'T LET HIM FIND OUT I'M REALLY...
THE PURPLE PHANTASM!

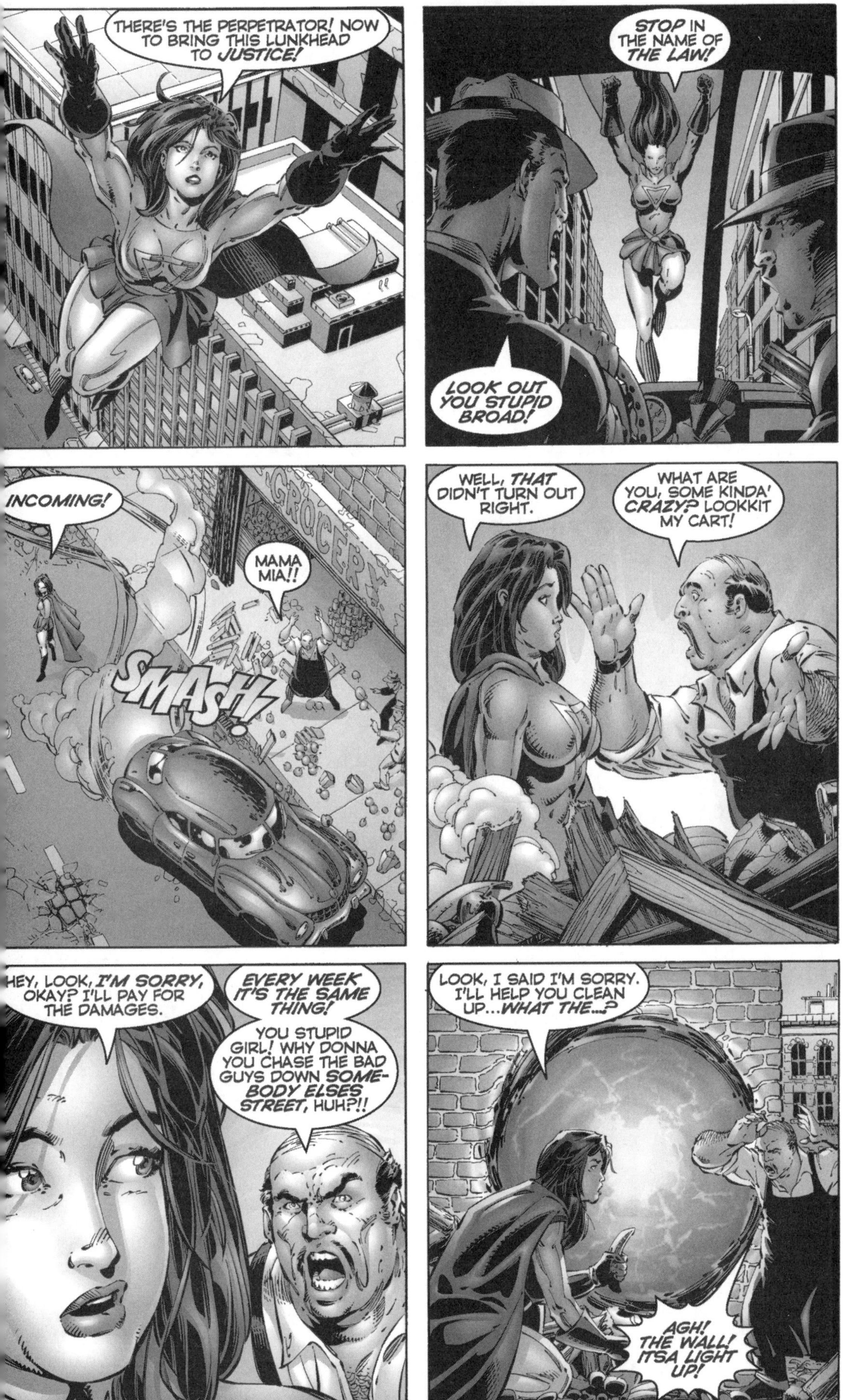
THERE'S THE PERPETRATOR! NOW TO BRING THIS LUNKHEAD TO JUSTICE!
STOP IN THE NAME OF THE LAW!
LOOK OUT YOU STUPID BROAD!
INCOMING!
MAMA MIA!!
SMASH!
WELL, THAT DIDN'T TURN OUT RIGHT.
WHAT ARE YOU, SOME KINDA' CRAZY? LOOKKIT MY CART!
HEY, LOOK, I'M SORRY, OKAY? I'LL PAY FOR THE DAMAGES.
EVERY WEEK IT'S THE SAME THING!
YOU STUPID GIRL! WHY DONNA YOU CHASE THE BAD GUYS DOWN SOMEBODY ELSES STREET, HUH?!!
LOOK, I SAID I'M SORRY. I'LL HELP YOU CLEAN UP...WHAT THE...?
AGH! THE WALL! ITSA LIGHT UP!

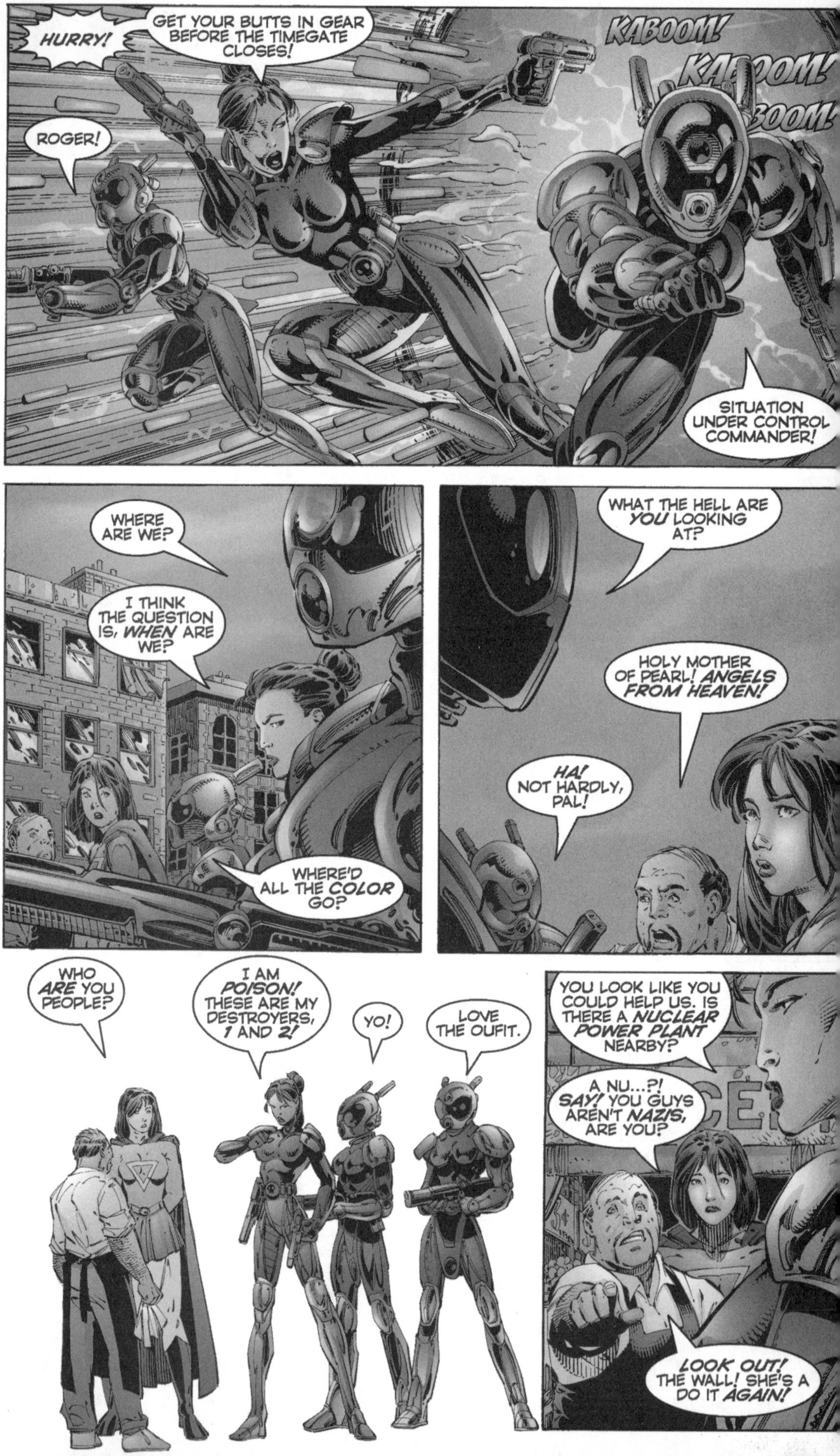
HURRY!
GET YOUR BUTTS IN GEAR BEFORE THE TIMEGATE CLOSES!
KABOOM!
ROGER!
SITUATION UNDER CONTROL COMMANDER!
WHERE ARE WE?
I THINK THE QUESTION IS, WHEN ARE WE?
WHERE'D ALL THE COLOR GO?
WHAT THE HELL ARE YOU LOOKING AT?
HOLY MOTHER OF PEARL! ANGELS FROM HEAVEN!
HA! NOT HARDLY, PAL!
WHO ARE YOU PEOPLE?
I AM POISON! THESE ARE MY DESTROYERS, 1 AND 2!
YO!
LOVE THE OUFIT.
YOU LOOK LIKE YOU COULD HELP US. IS THERE A NUCLEAR POWER PLANT NEARBY?
A NU...?! SAY! YOU GUYS AREN'T NAZIS, ARE YOU?
LOOK OUT! THE WALL! SHE'S A DO IT AGAIN!

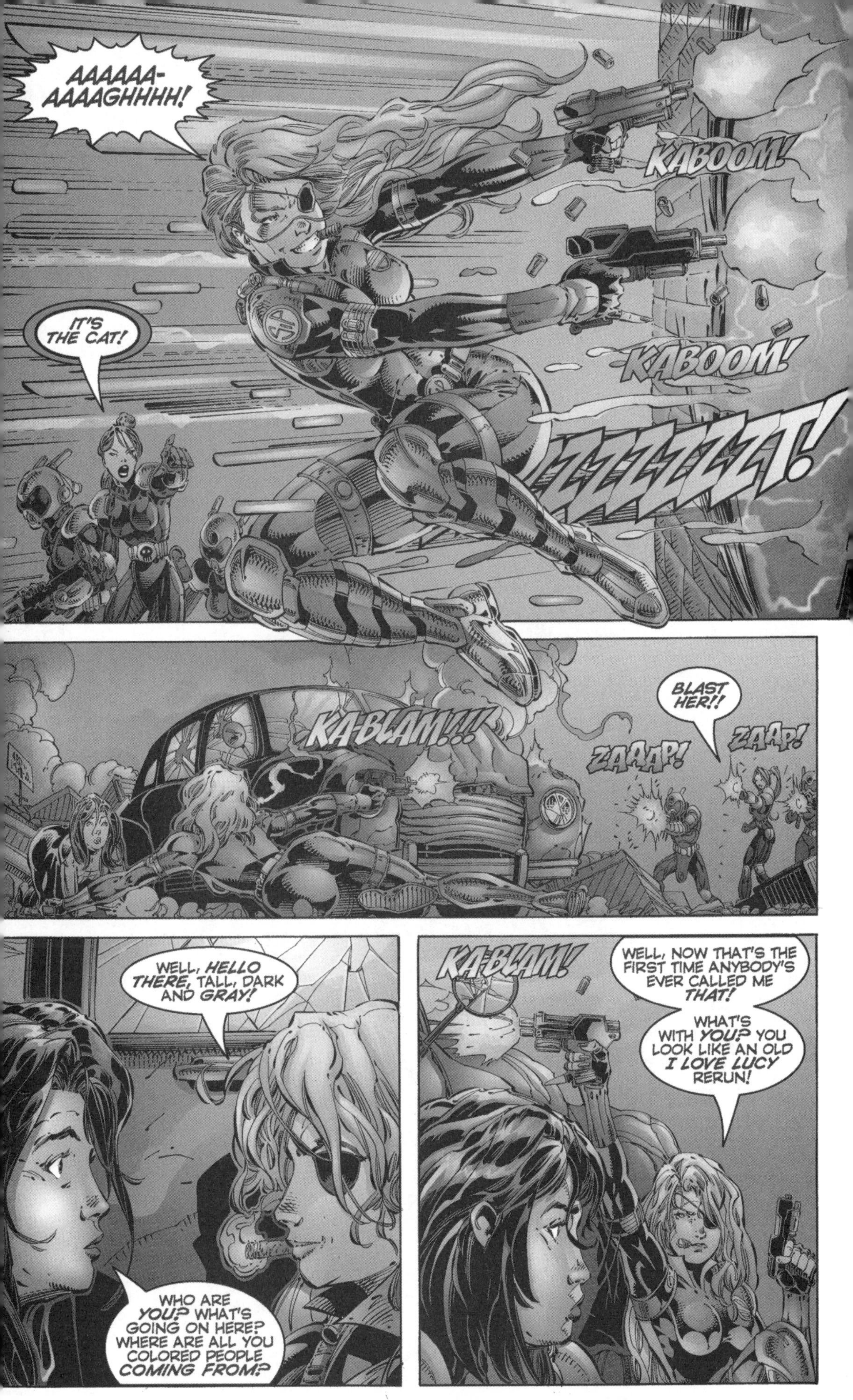
AAAAAA-
AAAAGHHHH!
KABOOM!
IT'S THE CAT!
KABOOM!
ZZZZZZZZT!
KA-BLAM!!!
ZAAAP!
BLAST HER!!
ZAAP!
WELL, HELLO THERE, TALL, DARK AND GRAY!
WHO ARE YOU? WHAT'S GOING ON HERE? WHERE ARE ALL YOU COLORED PEOPLE COMING FROM?
KA-BLAM!
WELL, NOW THAT'S THE FIRST TIME ANYBODY'S EVER CALLED ME THAT!
WHAT'S WITH YOU? YOU LOOK LIKE AN OLD I LOVE LUCY RERUN!

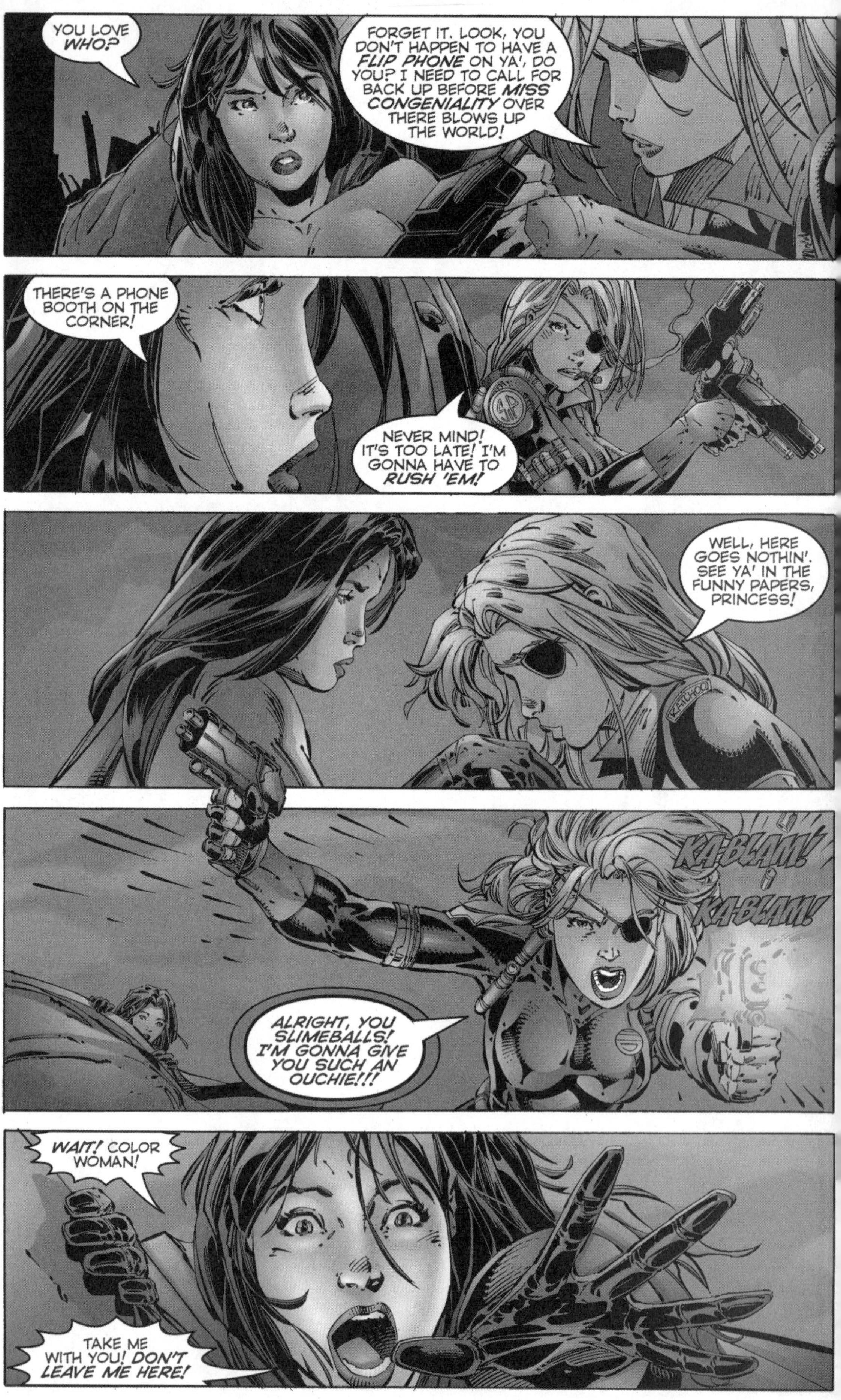
YOU LOVE *WHO?*
FORGET IT. LOOK, YOU DON'T HAPPEN TO HAVE A *FLIP PHONE* ON YA', DO YOU? I NEED TO CALL FOR BACK UP BEFORE *MISS CONGENIALITY* OVER THERE BLOWS UP THE WORLD!
THERE'S A PHONE BOOTH ON THE CORNER!
NEVER MIND! IT'S TOO LATE! I'M GONNA HAVE TO *RUSH 'EM!*
WELL, HERE GOES NOTHIN'. SEE YA' IN THE FUNNY PAPERS, PRINCESS!
KA-BLAM!
KA-BLAM!
ALRIGHT, YOU SLIMEBALLS! I'M GONNA GIVE YOU SUCH AN OUCHIE!!!
WAIT! COLOR WOMAN!
TAKE ME WITH YOU! *DON'T LEAVE ME HERE!*

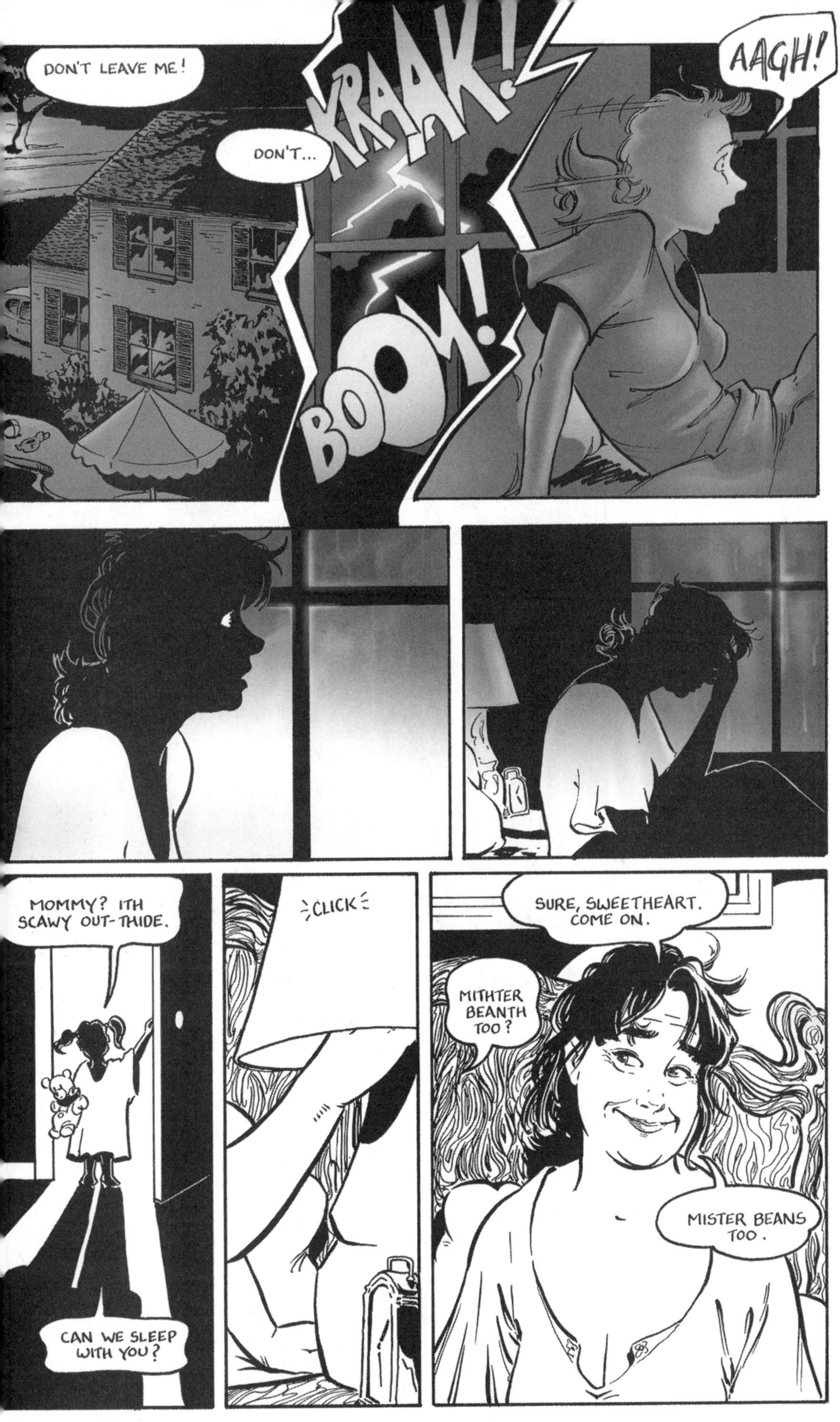
DON'T LEAVE ME!
DON'T...
KRAAK!
BOOM!
AAGH!
MOMMY? ITH SCAWY OUT-THIDE.
CAN WE SLEEP WITH YOU?
CLICK
SURE, SWEETHEART. COME ON.
MITHTER BEANTH TOO?
MISTER BEANS TOO.

WHERE'S DADDY?

I GUESS HE HAD TO WORK LATE, SWEETHEART.

HETH ALWATH WORKING LATE, MOMMY.

I KNOW, HONEY. I KNOW.

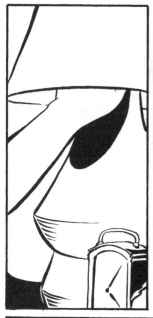

MOMMY?

SSSSH... GO TO SLEEP, SWEET-HEART. GO TO SLEEP.

THWEET DWEEMTH, MOMMY.

SWEET DREAMS, HONEY.

SO WHAT YOU'RE SAYING IS, YOU AND RAUL WERE MARRIED FOR TWO YEARS BEFORE YOU DISCOVERED YOU WERE *BOTH* TRANSSEXUALS?

THAT IS CORRECT, YES.

I WAS STUNNED.

344

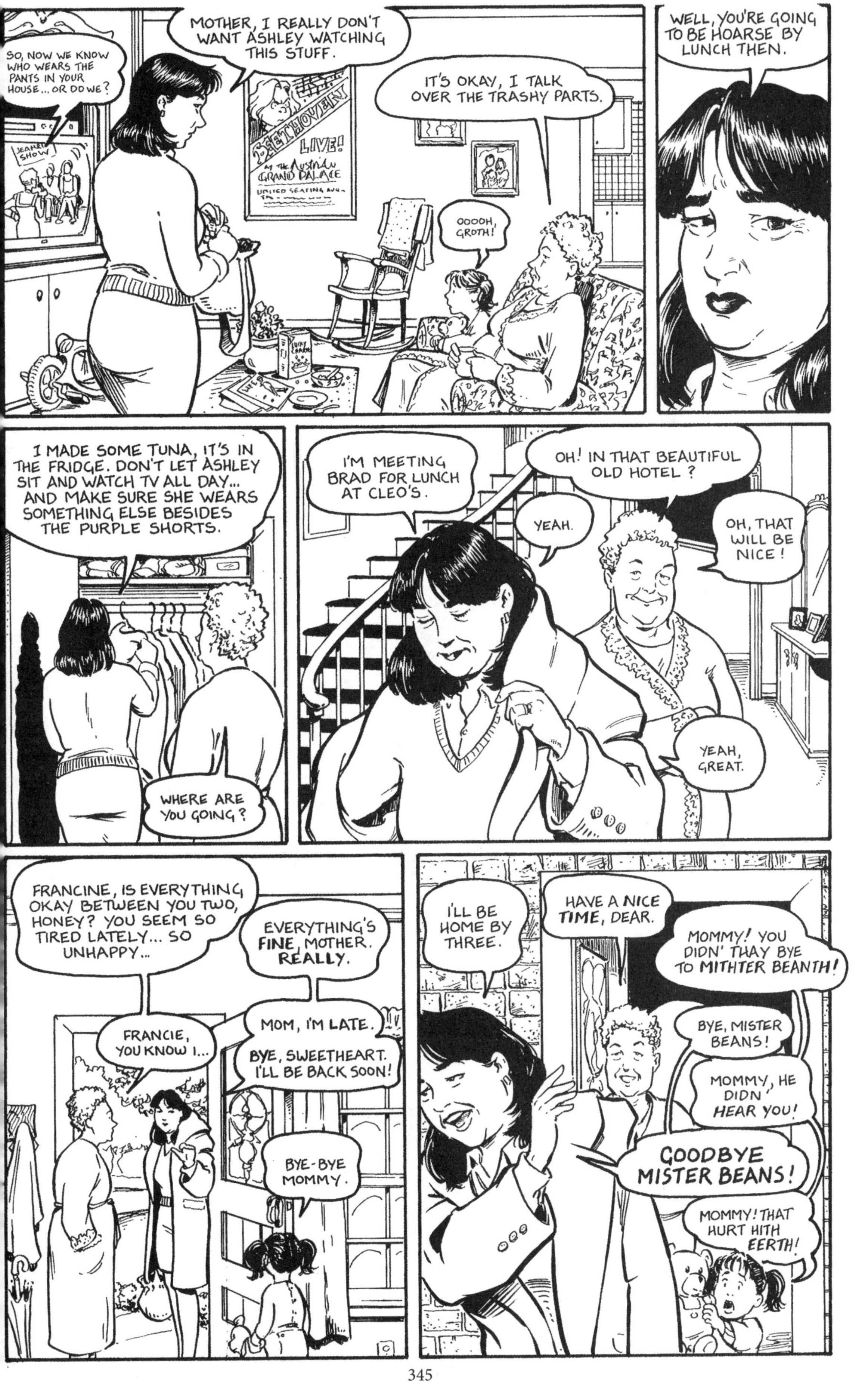
SO, NOW WE KNOW WHO WEARS THE PANTS IN YOUR HOUSE... OR DO WE?
JEANNE SHOW
MOTHER, I REALLY DON'T WANT ASHLEY WATCHING THIS STUFF.
BEETHOVEN LIVE! AT THE Austrian GRAND PALACE
IT'S OKAY, I TALK OVER THE TRASHY PARTS.
OOOOH, GROTH!
WELL, YOU'RE GOING TO BE HOARSE BY LUNCH THEN.
I MADE SOME TUNA, IT'S IN THE FRIDGE. DON'T LET ASHLEY SIT AND WATCH TV ALL DAY... AND MAKE SURE SHE WEARS SOMETHING ELSE BESIDES THE PURPLE SHORTS.
WHERE ARE YOU GOING?
I'M MEETING BRAD FOR LUNCH AT CLEO'S.
OH! IN THAT BEAUTIFUL OLD HOTEL?
YEAH.
OH, THAT WILL BE NICE!
YEAH, GREAT.
FRANCINE, IS EVERYTHING OKAY BETWEEN YOU TWO, HONEY? YOU SEEM SO TIRED LATELY... SO UNHAPPY...
EVERYTHING'S FINE, MOTHER. REALLY.
FRANCIE, YOU KNOW I...
MOM, I'M LATE.
BYE, SWEETHEART. I'LL BE BACK SOON!
BYE-BYE MOMMY.
I'LL BE HOME BY THREE.
HAVE A NICE TIME, DEAR.
MOMMY! YOU DIDN' THAY BYE TO MITHTER BEANTH!
BYE, MISTER BEANS!
MOMMY, HE DIDN' HEAR YOU!
GOODBYE MISTER BEANS!
MOMMY! THAT HURT HITH EERTH!

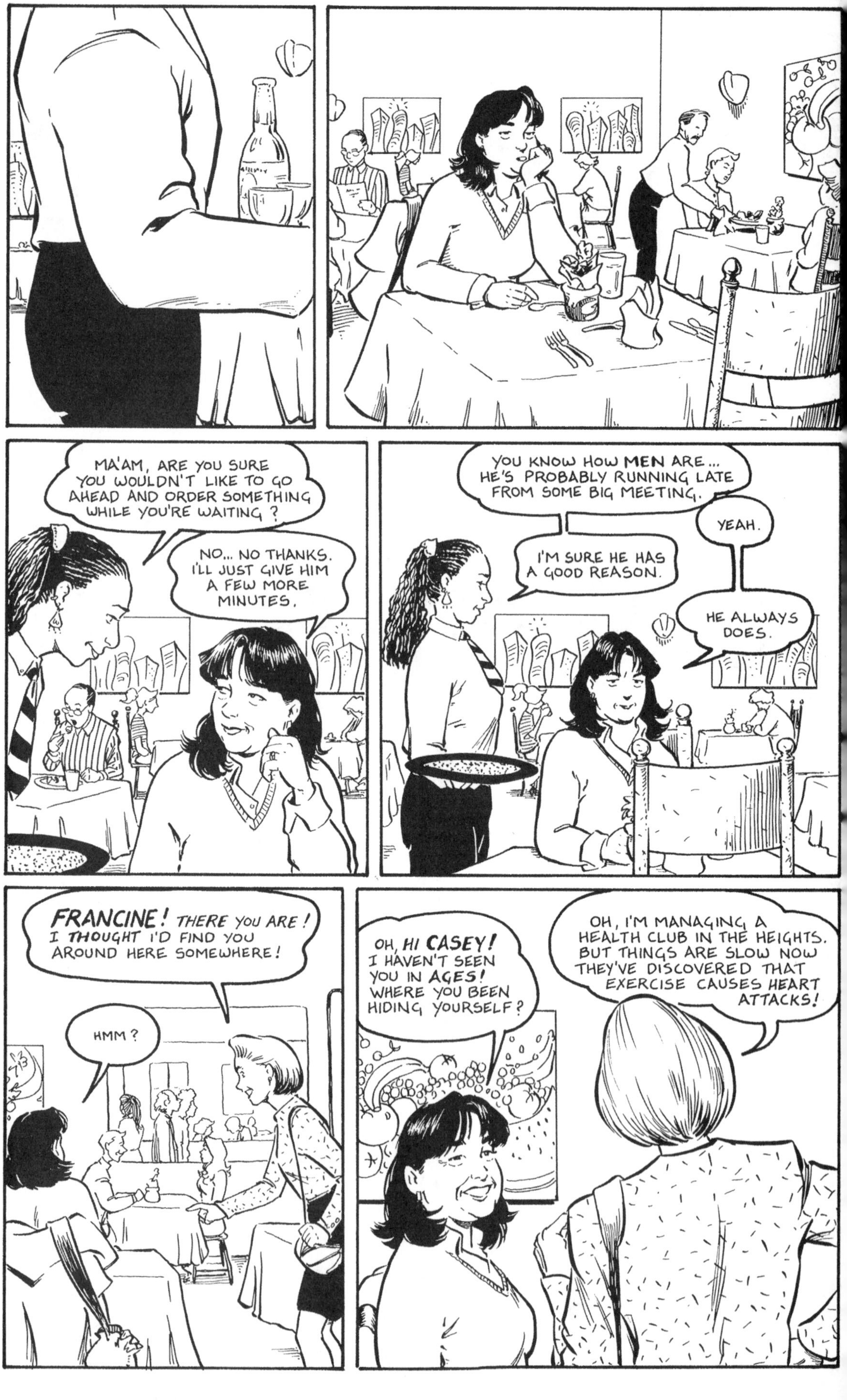
MA'AM, ARE YOU SURE YOU WOULDN'T LIKE TO GO AHEAD AND ORDER SOMETHING WHILE YOU'RE WAITING?
NO... NO THANKS. I'LL JUST GIVE HIM A FEW MORE MINUTES.
YOU KNOW HOW MEN ARE... HE'S PROBABLY RUNNING LATE FROM SOME BIG MEETING.
I'M SURE HE HAS A GOOD REASON.
YEAH.
HE ALWAYS DOES.
FRANCINE! THERE YOU ARE! I THOUGHT I'D FIND YOU AROUND HERE SOMEWHERE!
HMM?
OH, HI CASEY! I HAVEN'T SEEN YOU IN AGES! WHERE YOU BEEN HIDING YOURSELF?
OH, I'M MANAGING A HEALTH CLUB IN THE HEIGHTS. BUT THINGS ARE SLOW NOW THEY'VE DISCOVERED THAT EXERCISE CAUSES HEART ATTACKS!

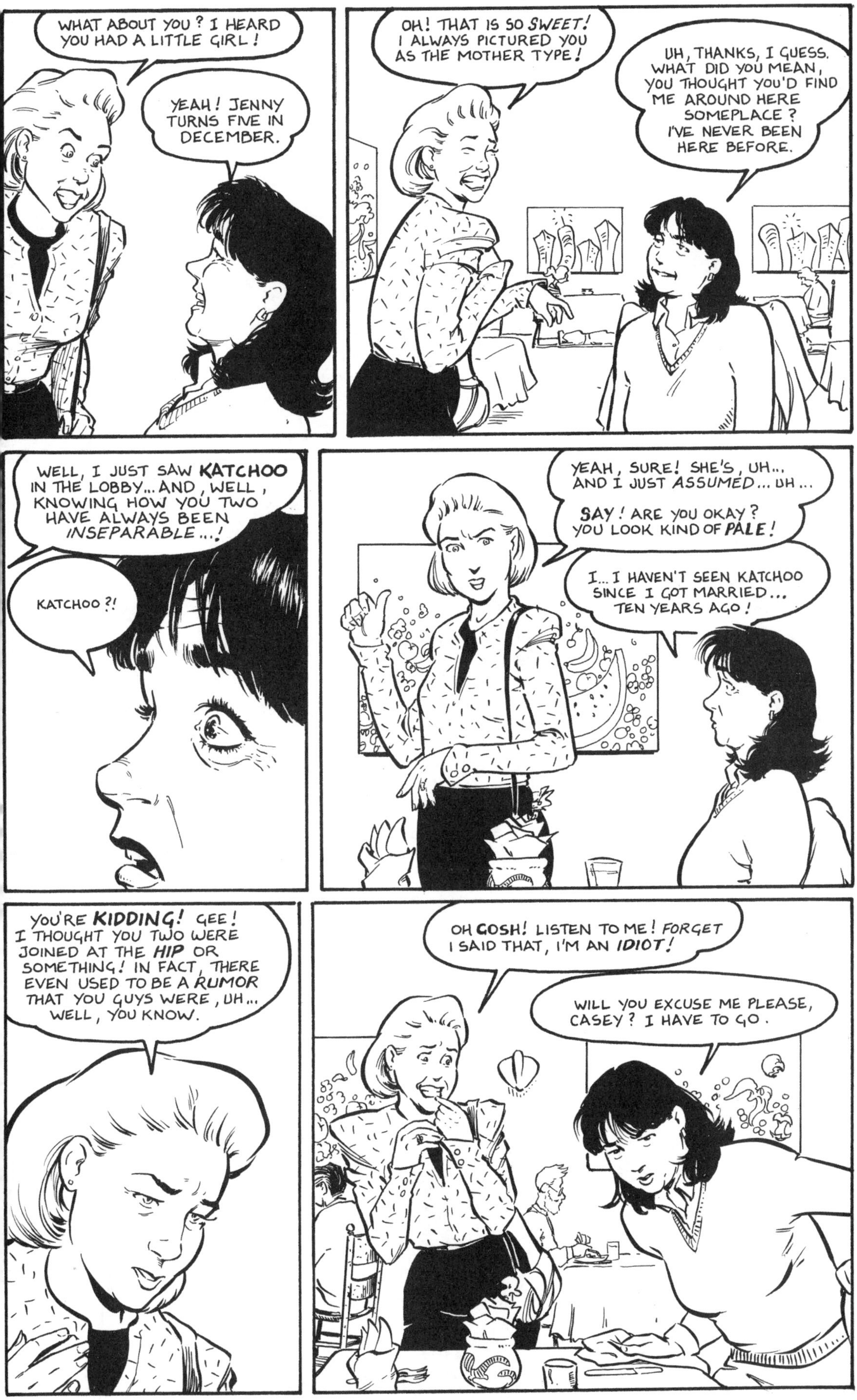
WHAT ABOUT YOU? I HEARD YOU HAD A LITTLE GIRL!
YEAH! JENNY TURNS FIVE IN DECEMBER.
OH! THAT IS SO *SWEET*! I ALWAYS PICTURED YOU AS THE MOTHER TYPE!
UH, THANKS, I GUESS. WHAT DID YOU MEAN, YOU THOUGHT YOU'D FIND ME AROUND HERE SOMEPLACE? I'VE NEVER BEEN HERE BEFORE.
WELL, I JUST SAW **KATCHOO** IN THE LOBBY... AND, WELL, KNOWING HOW YOU TWO HAVE ALWAYS BEEN *INSEPARABLE*...!
KATCHOO?!
YEAH, SURE! SHE'S, UH... AND I JUST *ASSUMED*... UH...
SAY! ARE YOU OKAY? YOU LOOK KIND OF **PALE**!
I... I HAVEN'T SEEN KATCHOO SINCE I GOT MARRIED... TEN YEARS AGO!
YOU'RE **KIDDING**! GEE! I THOUGHT YOU TWO WERE JOINED AT THE ***HIP*** OR SOMETHING! IN FACT, THERE EVEN USED TO BE A *RUMOR* THAT YOU GUYS WERE, UH... WELL, YOU KNOW.
OH **GOSH**! LISTEN TO ME! *FORGET* I SAID THAT, I'M AN ***IDIOT***!
WILL YOU EXCUSE ME PLEASE, CASEY? I HAVE TO GO.

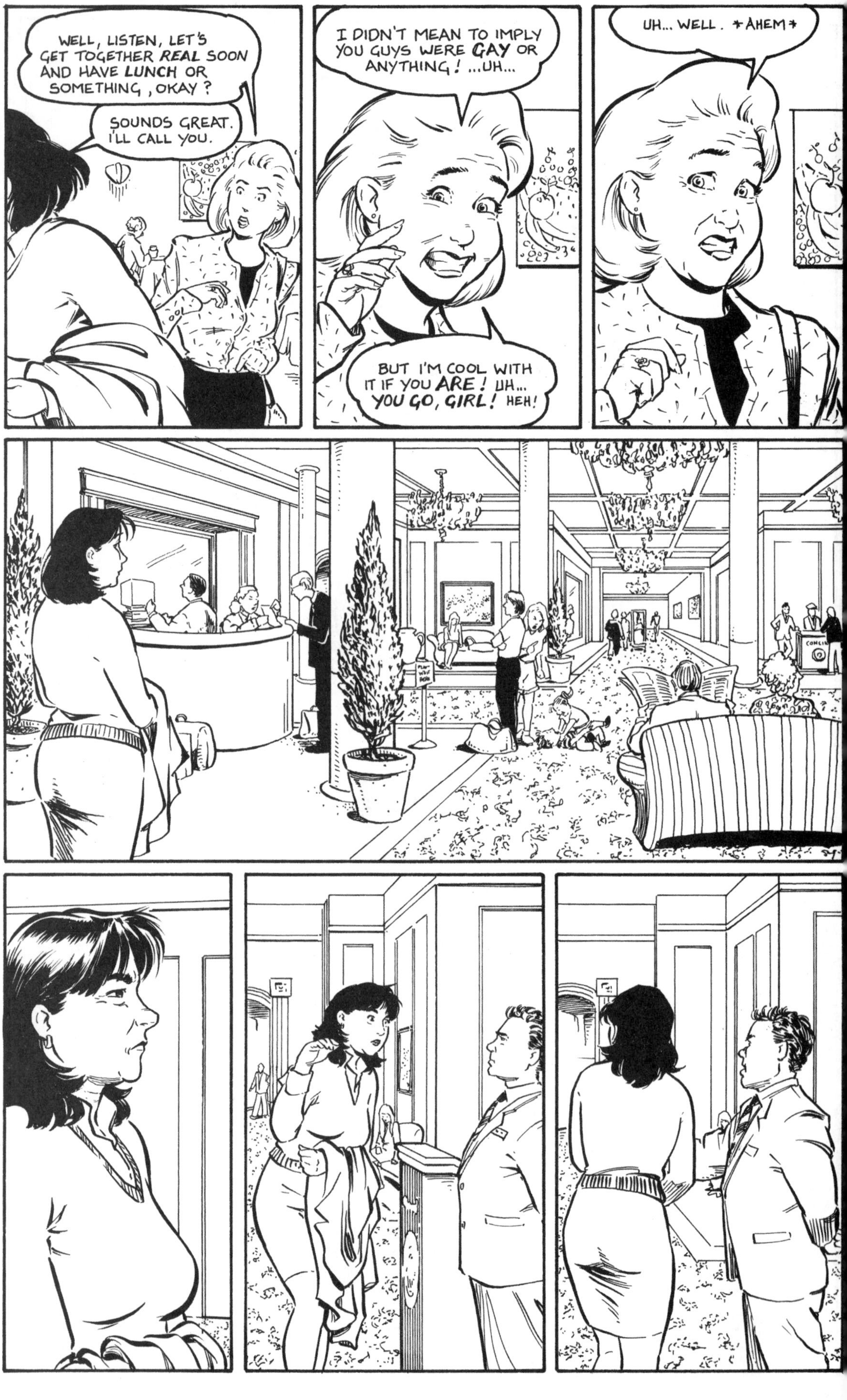
WELL, LISTEN, LET'S GET TOGETHER REAL SOON AND HAVE LUNCH OR SOMETHING, OKAY?
SOUNDS GREAT. I'LL CALL YOU.
I DIDN'T MEAN TO IMPLY YOU GUYS WERE GAY OR ANYTHING! ...UH...
BUT I'M COOL WITH IT IF YOU ARE! UH... YOU GO, GIRL! HEH!
UH... WELL. *AHEM*

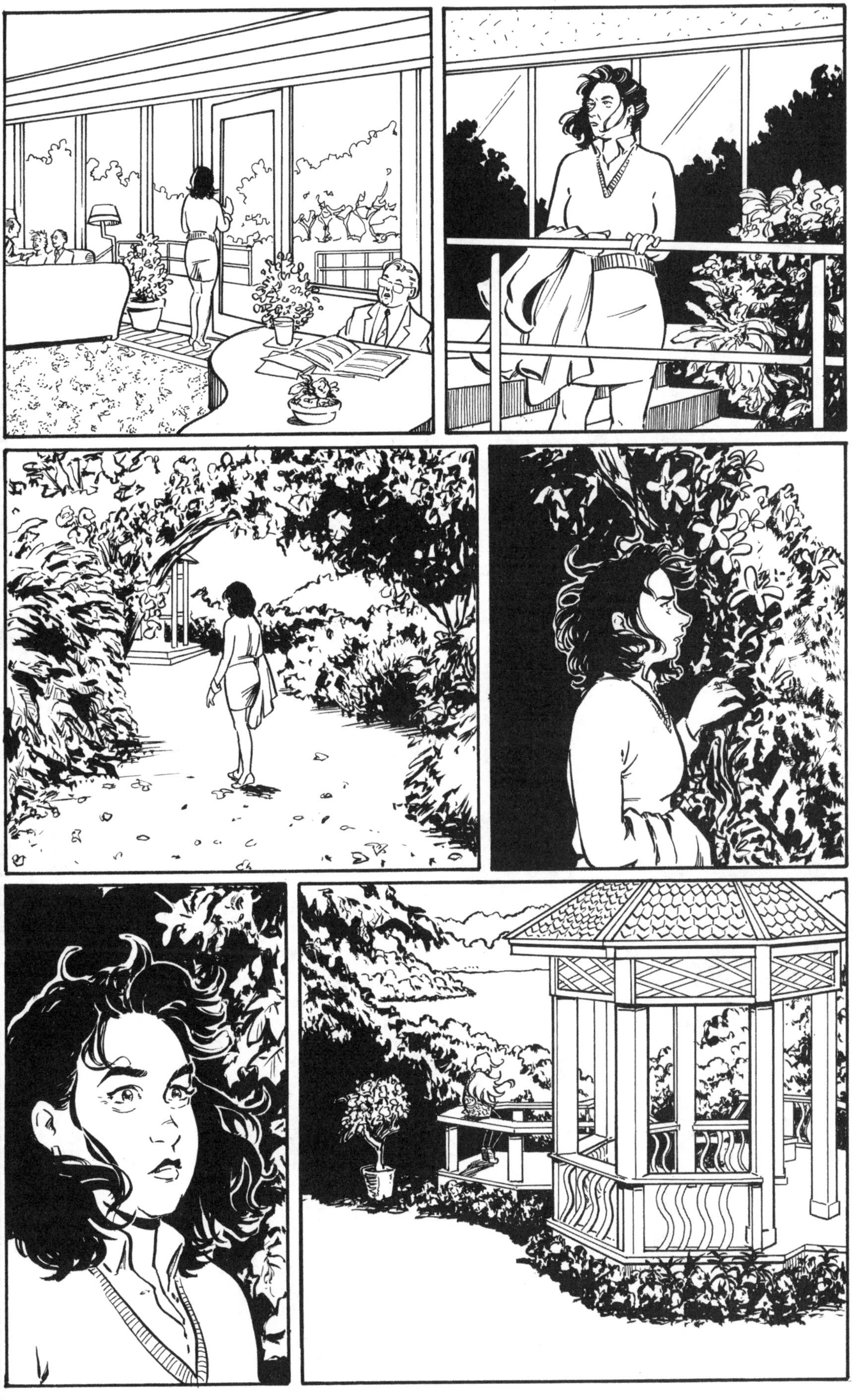

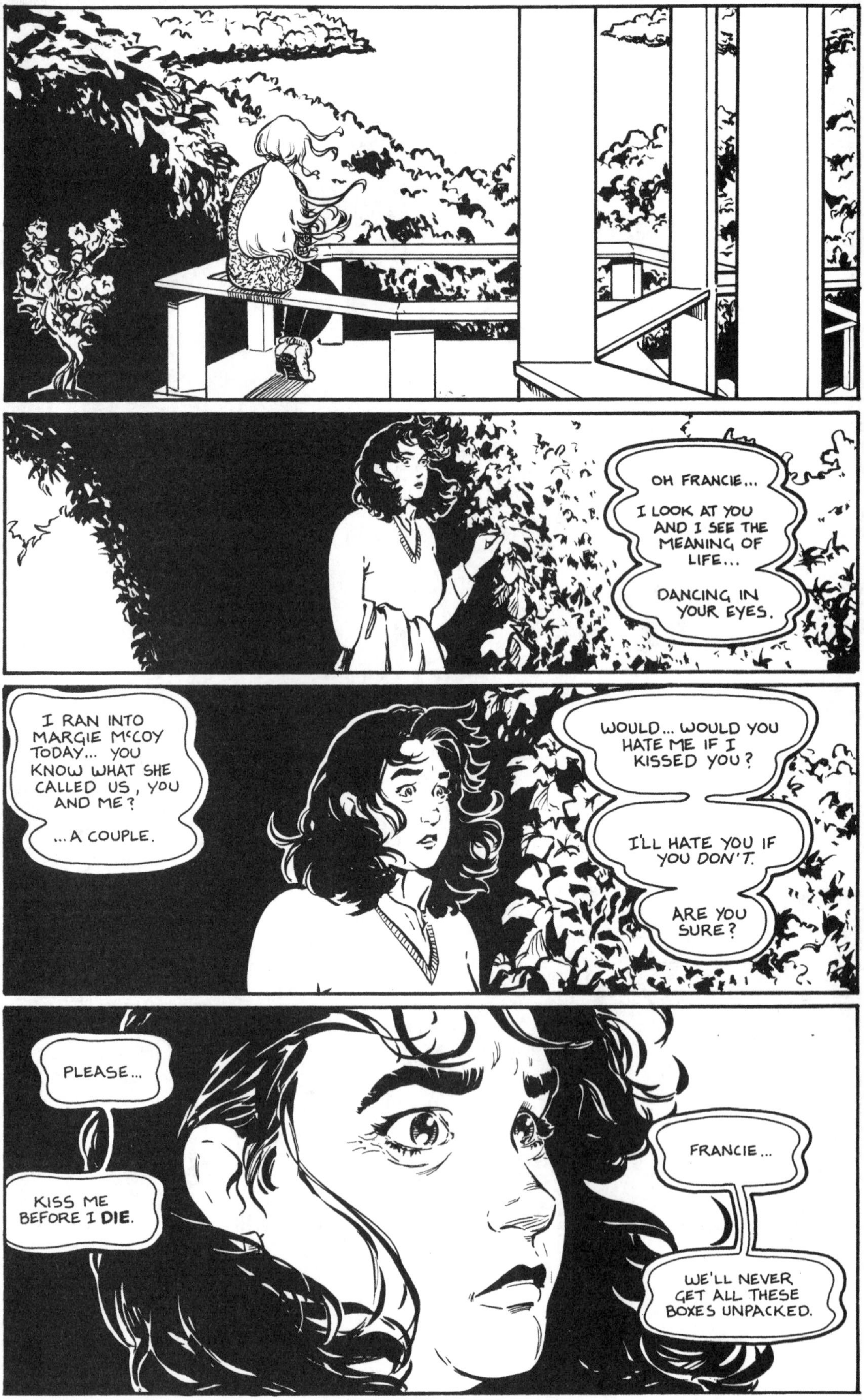
OH FRANCIE...
I LOOK AT YOU AND I SEE THE MEANING OF LIFE...
DANCING IN YOUR EYES.
I RAN INTO MARGIE McCOY TODAY... YOU KNOW WHAT SHE CALLED US, YOU AND ME?
...A COUPLE.
WOULD... WOULD YOU HATE ME IF I KISSED YOU?
I'LL HATE YOU IF YOU DON'T.
ARE YOU SURE?
PLEASE...
KISS ME BEFORE I DIE.
FRANCIE...
WE'LL NEVER GET ALL THESE BOXES UNPACKED.

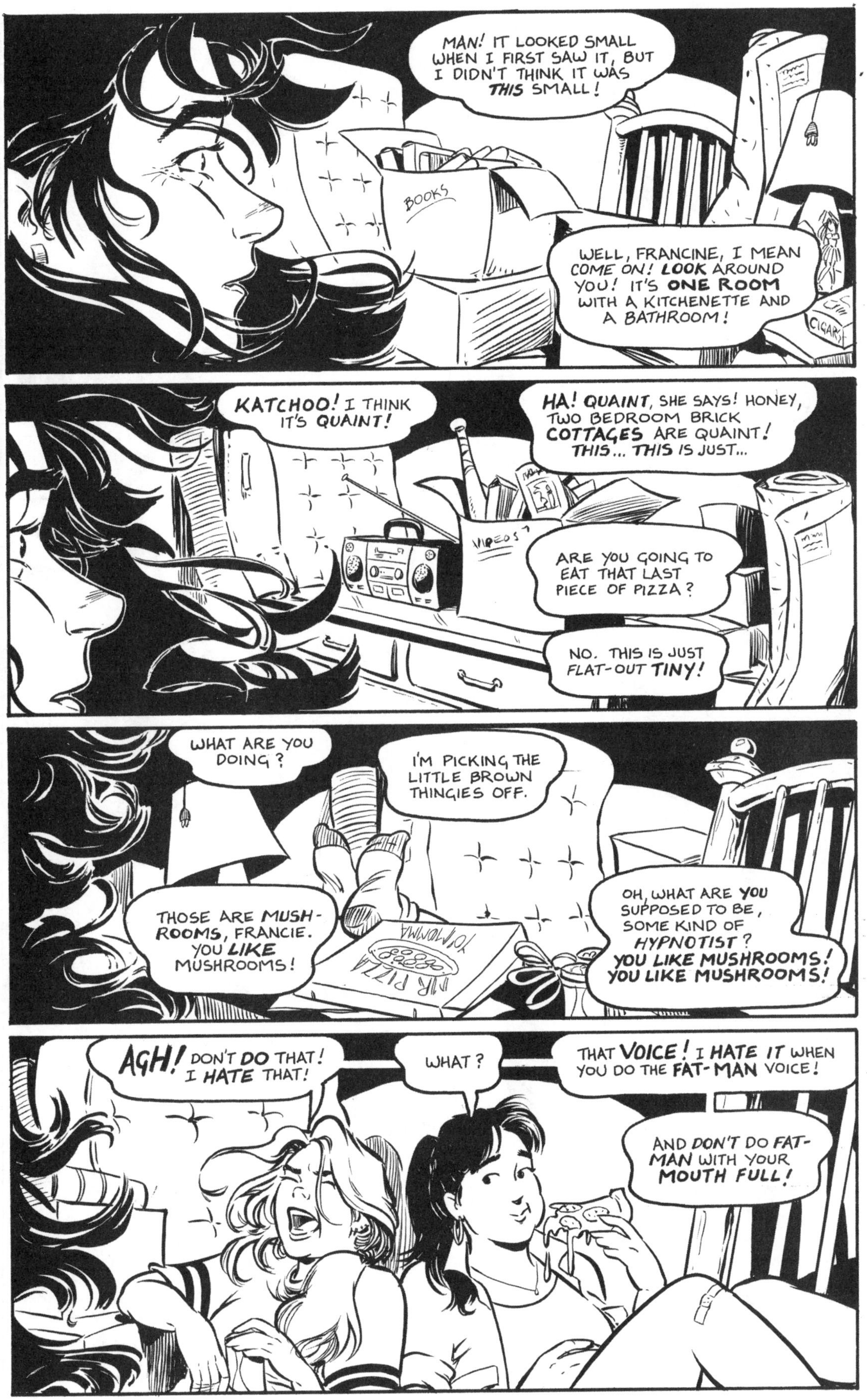
MAN! IT LOOKED SMALL WHEN I FIRST SAW IT, BUT I DIDN'T THINK IT WAS THIS SMALL!
BOOKS
WELL, FRANCINE, I MEAN COME ON! LOOK AROUND YOU! IT'S ONE ROOM WITH A KITCHENETTE AND A BATHROOM!
CIGARS
KATCHOO! I THINK IT'S QUAINT!
HA! QUAINT, SHE SAYS! HONEY, TWO BEDROOM BRICK COTTAGES ARE QUAINT! THIS... THIS IS JUST...
ARE YOU GOING TO EAT THAT LAST PIECE OF PIZZA?
NO. THIS IS JUST FLAT-OUT TINY!
WHAT ARE YOU DOING?
I'M PICKING THE LITTLE BROWN THINGIES OFF.
THOSE ARE MUSHROOMS, FRANCIE. YOU LIKE MUSHROOMS!
OH, WHAT ARE YOU SUPPOSED TO BE, SOME KIND OF HYPNOTIST? YOU LIKE MUSHROOMS! YOU LIKE MUSHROOMS!
AGH! DON'T DO THAT! I HATE THAT!
WHAT?
THAT VOICE! I HATE IT WHEN YOU DO THE FAT-MAN VOICE!
AND DON'T DO FAT-MAN WITH YOUR MOUTH FULL!

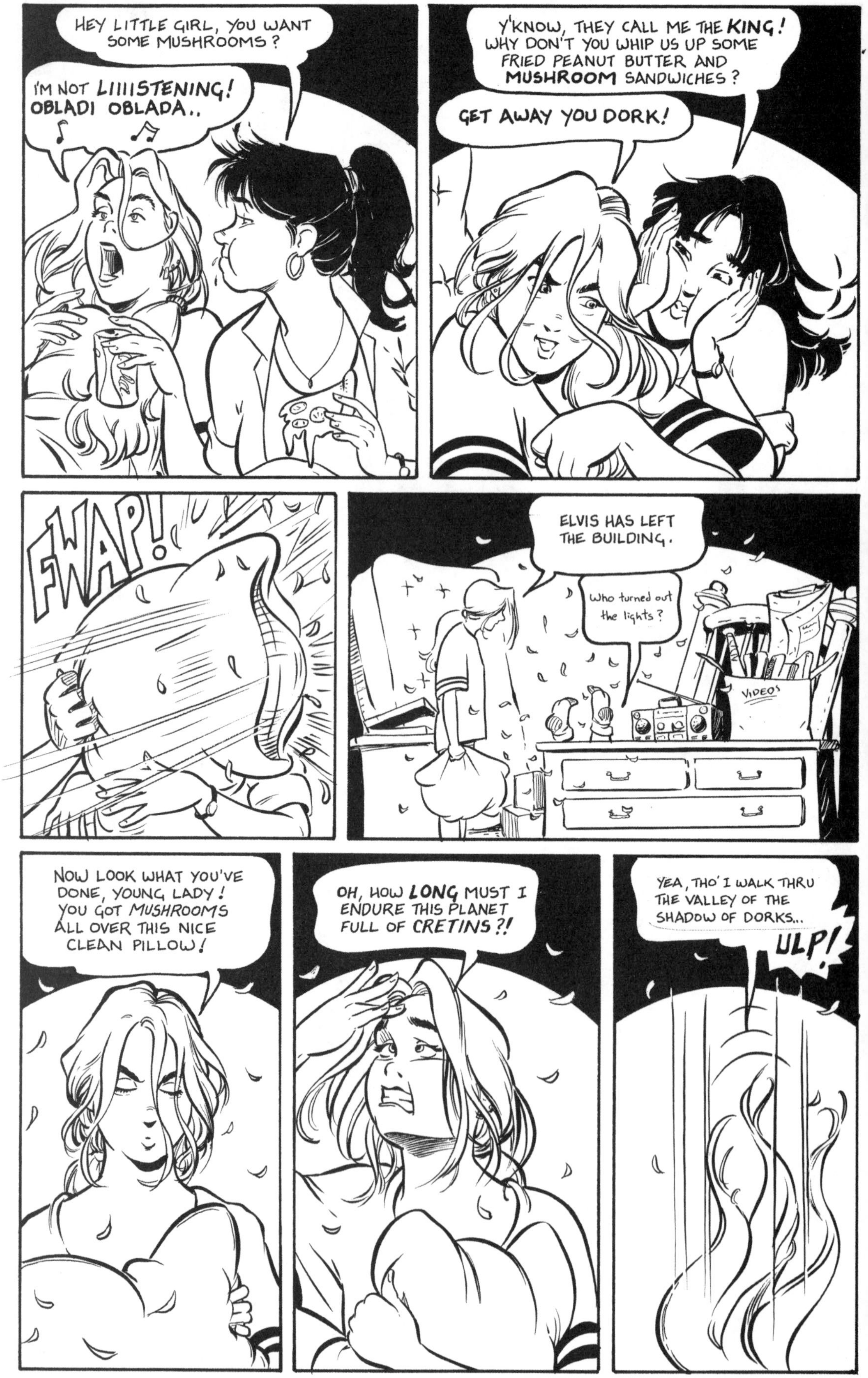

HEY LITTLE GIRL, YOU WANT SOME MUSHROOMS?
I'M NOT LIIIISTENING! OBLADI OBLADA..
Y'KNOW, THEY CALL ME THE KING! WHY DON'T YOU WHIP US UP SOME FRIED PEANUT BUTTER AND MUSHROOM SANDWICHES?
GET AWAY YOU DORK!
FWAP!
ELVIS HAS LEFT THE BUILDING.
Who turned out the lights?
VIDEOS
NOW LOOK WHAT YOU'VE DONE, YOUNG LADY! YOU GOT MUSHROOMS ALL OVER THIS NICE CLEAN PILLOW!
OH, HOW LONG MUST I ENDURE THIS PLANET FULL OF CRETINS?!
YEA, THO' I WALK THRU THE VALLEY OF THE SHADOW OF DORKS..
ULP!

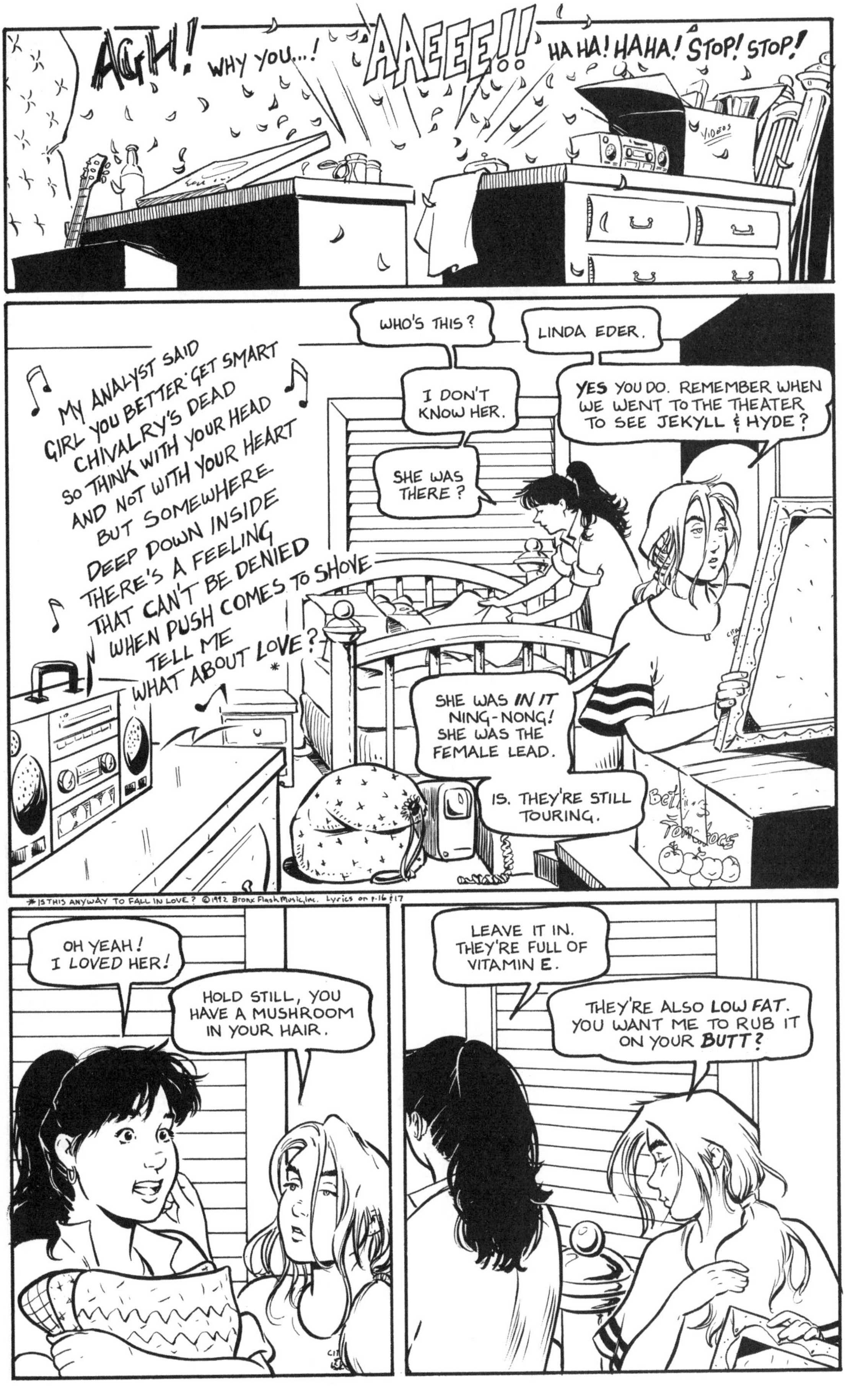
AGH!
WHY YOU...!
AAEEE!!
HA HA! HAHA! STOP! STOP!
VIDEOS
WHO'S THIS?
LINDA EDER.
MY ANALYST SAID GIRL YOU BETTER GET SMART CHIVALRY'S DEAD SO THINK WITH YOUR HEAD AND NOT WITH YOUR HEART BUT SOMEWHERE DEEP DOWN INSIDE THERE'S A FEELING THAT CAN'T BE DENIED WHEN PUSH COMES TO SHOVE TELL ME WHAT ABOUT LOVE?*
I DON'T KNOW HER.
YES YOU DO. REMEMBER WHEN WE WENT TO THE THEATER TO SEE JEKYLL & HYDE?
SHE WAS THERE?
SHE WAS IN IT NING-NONG! SHE WAS THE FEMALE LEAD.
IS. THEY'RE STILL TOURING.
*IS THIS ANYWAY TO FALL IN LOVE? ©1992 Bronx Flash Music, Inc. Lyrics on p.16 & 17
OH YEAH! I LOVED HER!
HOLD STILL, YOU HAVE A MUSHROOM IN YOUR HAIR.
LEAVE IT IN. THEY'RE FULL OF VITAMIN E.
THEY'RE ALSO LOW FAT. YOU WANT ME TO RUB IT ON YOUR BUTT?

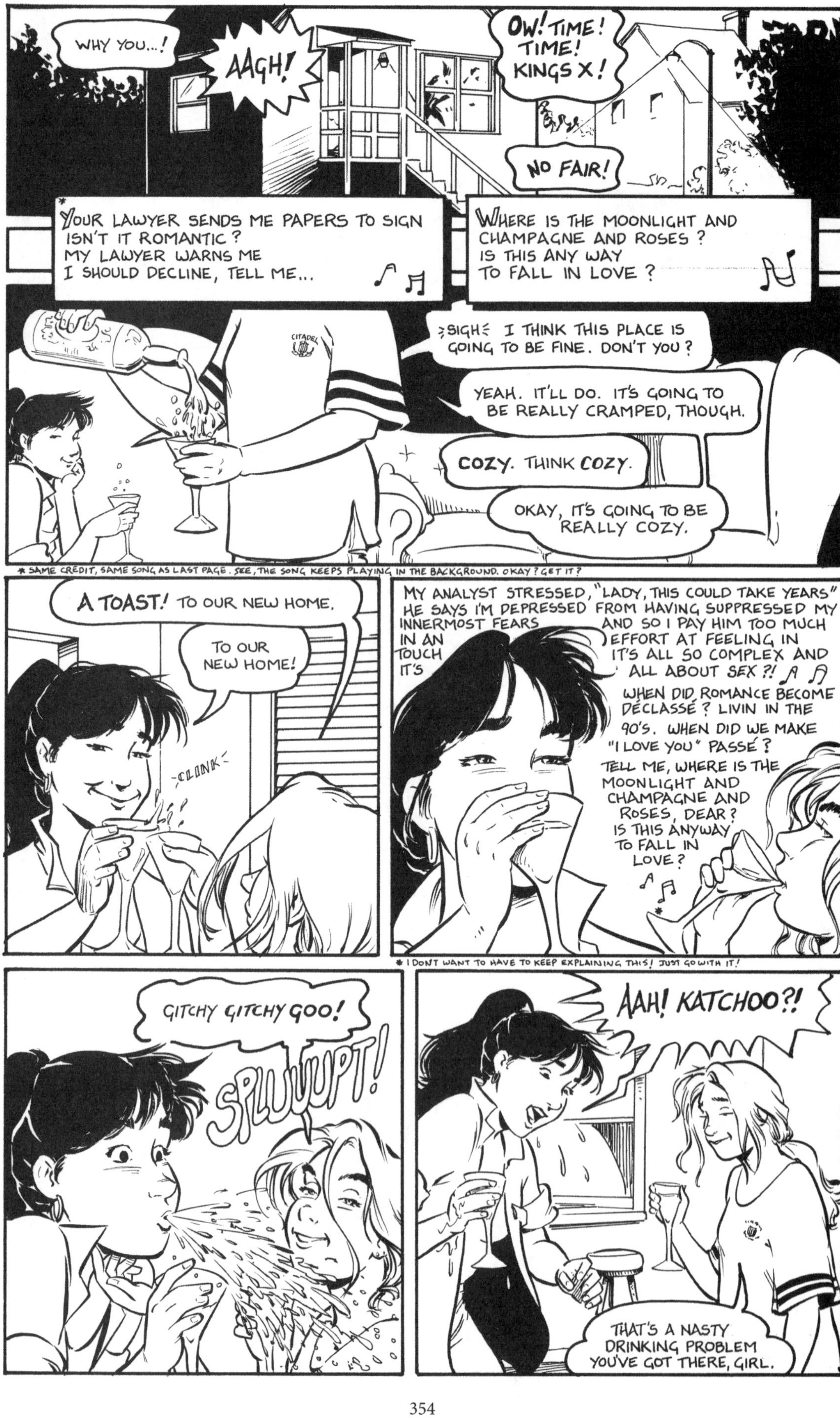

WHY YOU...!
AAGH!
OW! TIME! TIME! KINGS X!
NO FAIR!
*YOUR LAWYER SENDS ME PAPERS TO SIGN
ISN'T IT ROMANTIC?
MY LAWYER WARNS ME
I SHOULD DECLINE, TELL ME...
WHERE IS THE MOONLIGHT AND
CHAMPAGNE AND ROSES?
IS THIS ANY WAY
TO FALL IN LOVE?
CITADEL
SIGH I THINK THIS PLACE IS GOING TO BE FINE. DON'T YOU?
YEAH. IT'LL DO. IT'S GOING TO BE REALLY CRAMPED, THOUGH.
COZY. THINK COZY.
OKAY, IT'S GOING TO BE REALLY COZY.
* SAME CREDIT, SAME SONG AS LAST PAGE. SEE, THE SONG KEEPS PLAYING IN THE BACKGROUND. OKAY? GET IT?
A TOAST! TO OUR NEW HOME.
TO OUR NEW HOME!
CLINK
MY ANALYST STRESSED, "LADY, THIS COULD TAKE YEARS"
HE SAYS I'M DEPRESSED FROM HAVING SUPPRESSED MY
INNERMOST FEARS AND SO I PAY HIM TOO MUCH
IN AN EFFORT AT FEELING IN
TOUCH IT'S ALL SO COMPLEX AND
IT'S ALL ABOUT SEX?!
WHEN DID ROMANCE BECOME
DÉCLASSÉ? LIVIN IN THE
90'S. WHEN DID WE MAKE
"I LOVE YOU" PASSÉ?
TELL ME, WHERE IS THE
MOONLIGHT AND
CHAMPAGNE AND
ROSES, DEAR?
IS THIS ANYWAY
TO FALL IN
LOVE?
* I DON'T WANT TO HAVE TO KEEP EXPLAINING THIS! JUST GO WITH IT!
GITCHY GITCHY GOO!
SPLUUUPT!
AAH! KATCHOO?!
THAT'S A NASTY DRINKING PROBLEM YOU'VE GOT THERE, GIRL.

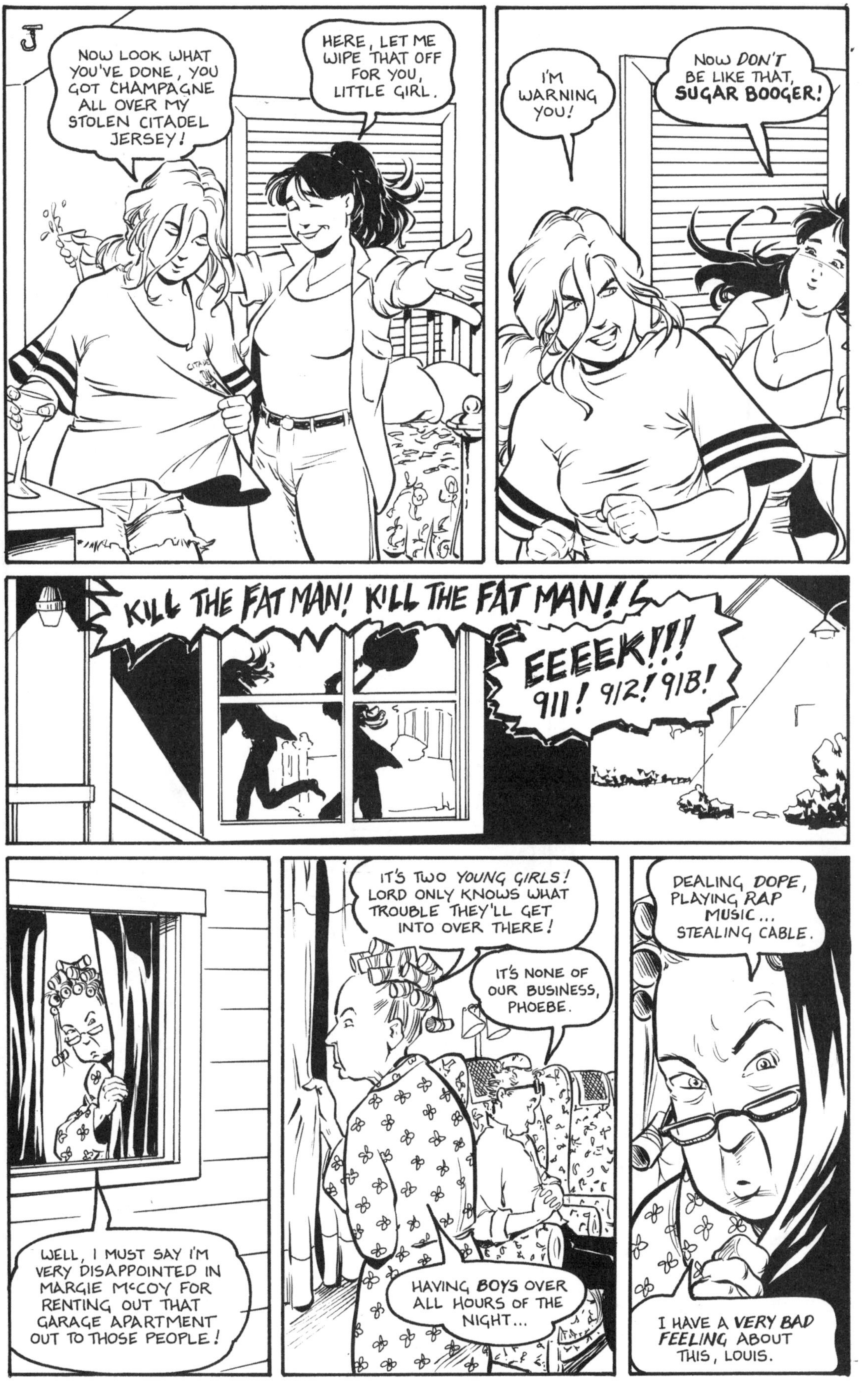

J
NOW LOOK WHAT YOU'VE DONE, YOU GOT CHAMPAGNE ALL OVER MY STOLEN CITADEL JERSEY!
HERE, LET ME WIPE THAT OFF FOR YOU, LITTLE GIRL.
CITADEL
I'M WARNING YOU!
NOW DON'T BE LIKE THAT, SUGAR BOOGER!
KILL THE FAT MAN! KILL THE FAT MAN!
EEEEK!!! 911! 912! 913!
WELL, I MUST SAY I'M VERY DISAPPOINTED IN MARGIE McCOY FOR RENTING OUT THAT GARAGE APARTMENT OUT TO THOSE PEOPLE!
IT'S TWO YOUNG GIRLS! LORD ONLY KNOWS WHAT TROUBLE THEY'LL GET INTO OVER THERE!
IT'S NONE OF OUR BUSINESS, PHOEBE.
HAVING BOYS OVER ALL HOURS OF THE NIGHT...
DEALING DOPE, PLAYING RAP MUSIC... STEALING CABLE.
I HAVE A VERY BAD FEELING ABOUT THIS, LOUIS.

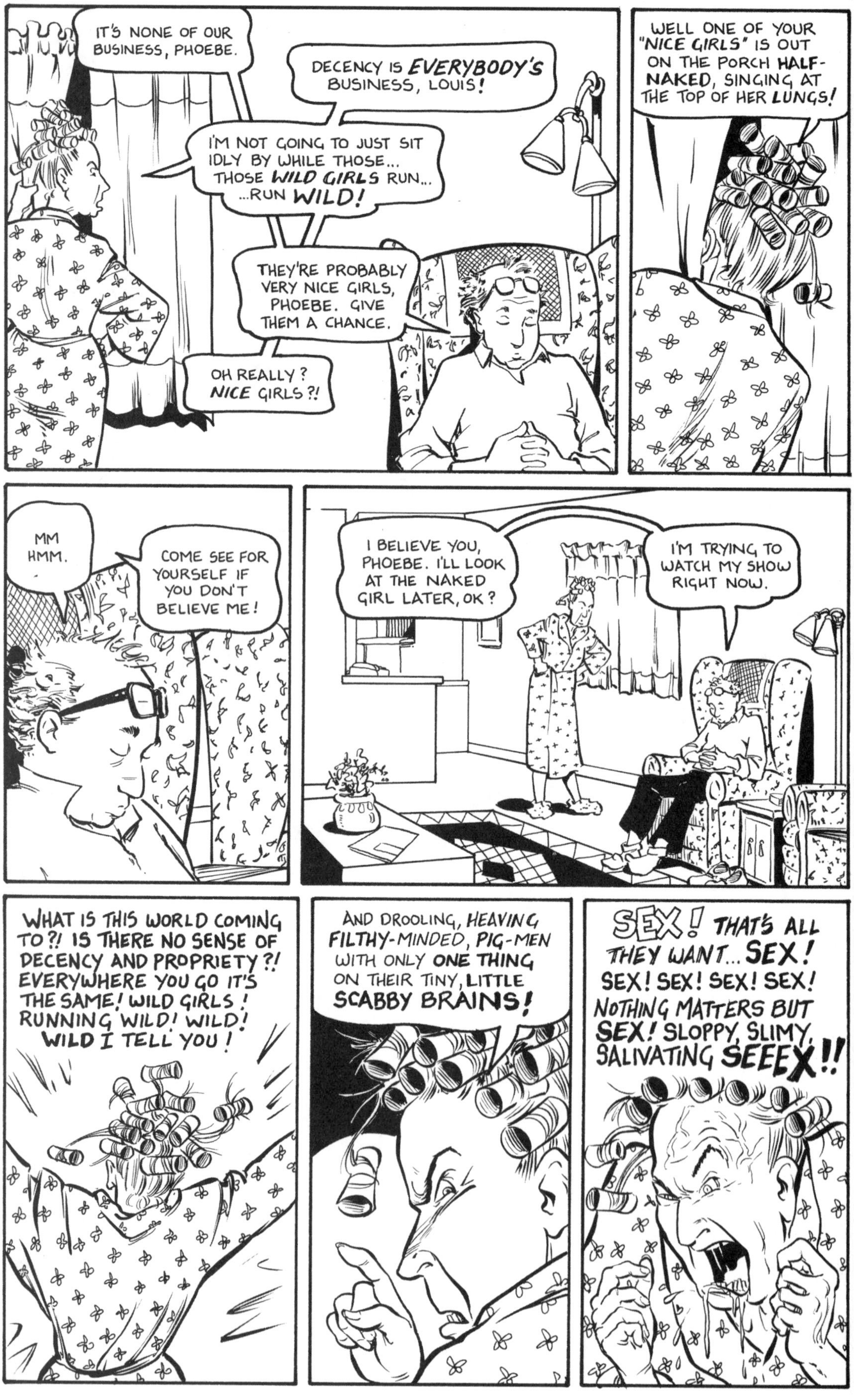
IT'S NONE OF OUR BUSINESS, PHOEBE.
DECENCY IS EVERYBODY'S BUSINESS, LOUIS!
I'M NOT GOING TO JUST SIT IDLY BY WHILE THOSE... THOSE WILD GIRLS RUN... ...RUN WILD!
THEY'RE PROBABLY VERY NICE GIRLS, PHOEBE. GIVE THEM A CHANCE.
OH REALLY? NICE GIRLS?!
WELL ONE OF YOUR "NICE GIRLS" IS OUT ON THE PORCH HALF-NAKED, SINGING AT THE TOP OF HER LUNGS!
MM HMM.
COME SEE FOR YOURSELF IF YOU DON'T BELIEVE ME!
I BELIEVE YOU, PHOEBE. I'LL LOOK AT THE NAKED GIRL LATER, OK?
I'M TRYING TO WATCH MY SHOW RIGHT NOW.
WHAT IS THIS WORLD COMING TO?! IS THERE NO SENSE OF DECENCY AND PROPRIETY?! EVERYWHERE YOU GO IT'S THE SAME! WILD GIRLS! RUNNING WILD! WILD! WILD I TELL YOU!
AND DROOLING, HEAVING FILTHY-MINDED, PIG-MEN WITH ONLY ONE THING ON THEIR TINY, LITTLE SCABBY BRAINS!
SEX! THAT'S ALL THEY WANT... SEX! SEX! SEX! SEX! SEX! NOTHING MATTERS BUT SEX! SLOPPY, SLIMY, SALIVATING SEEEX!!

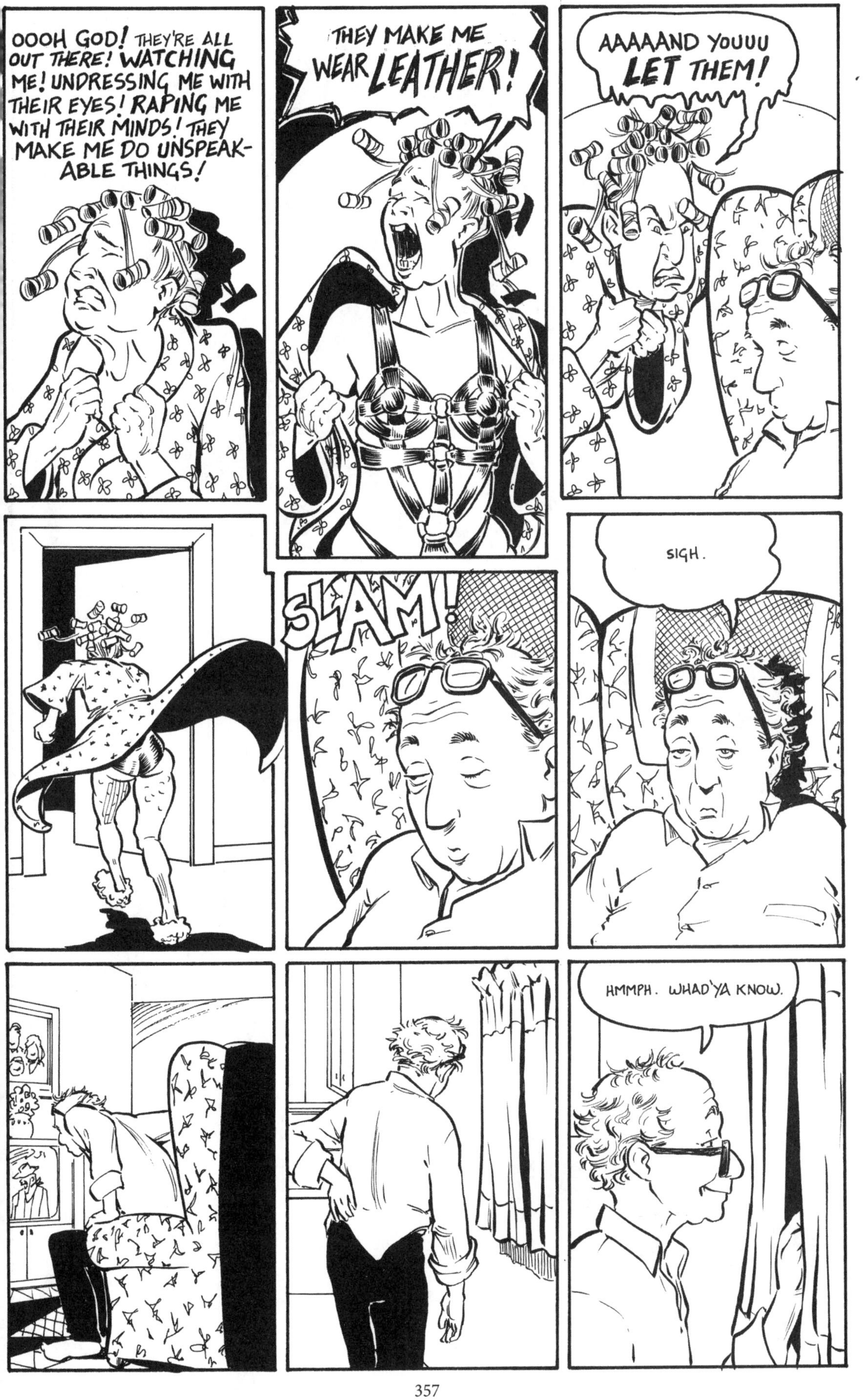
OOOH GOD! THEY'RE ALL OUT THERE! WATCHING ME! UNDRESSING ME WITH THEIR EYES! RAPING ME WITH THEIR MINDS! THEY MAKE ME DO UNSPEAKABLE THINGS!
THEY MAKE ME WEAR LEATHER!
AAAAAND YOUUU LET THEM!
SLAM!
SIGH.
HMMPH. WHAD'YA KNOW.

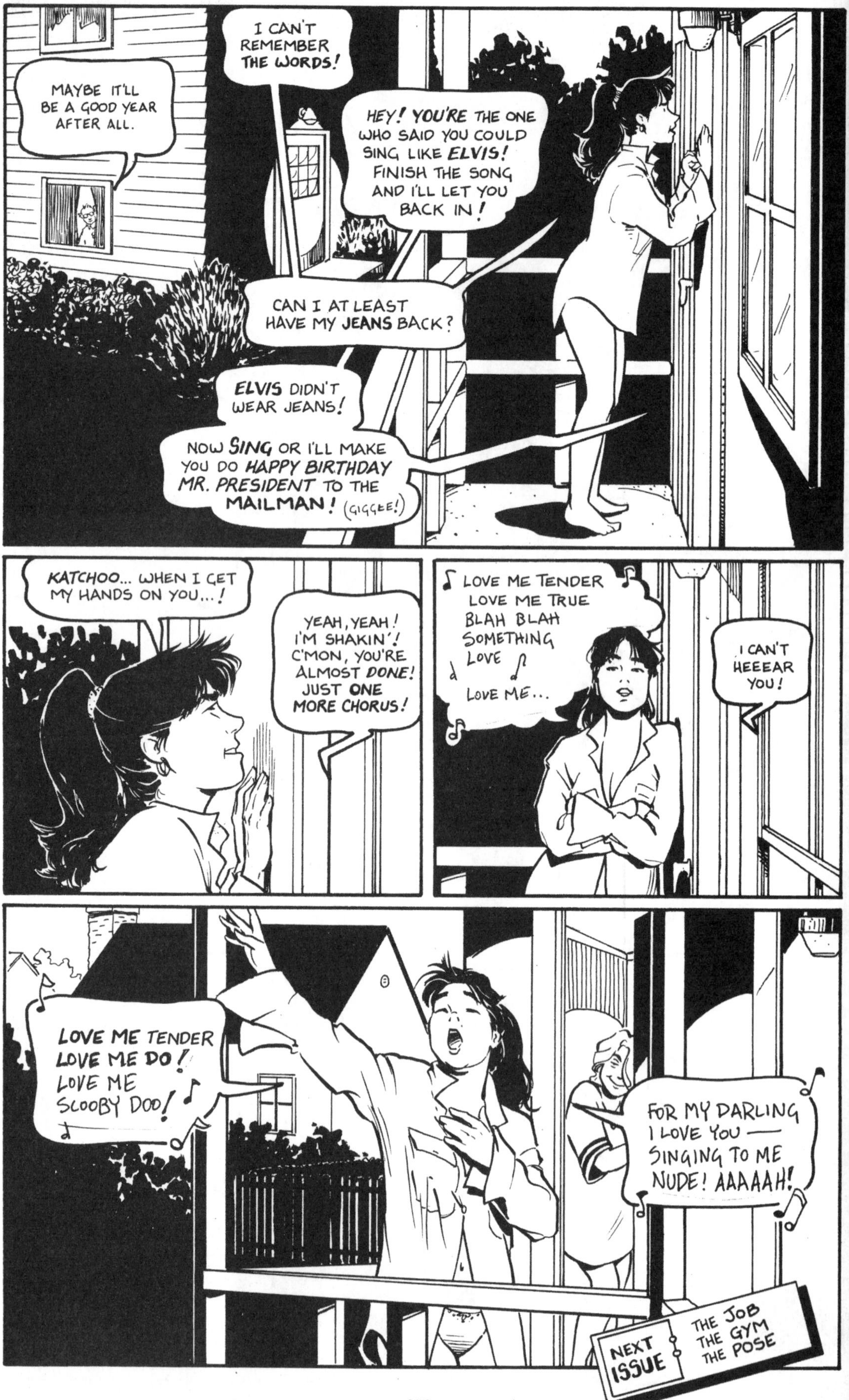
MAYBE IT'LL BE A GOOD YEAR AFTER ALL.
I CAN'T REMEMBER THE WORDS!
HEY! YOU'RE THE ONE WHO SAID YOU COULD SING LIKE ELVIS! FINISH THE SONG AND I'LL LET YOU BACK IN!
CAN I AT LEAST HAVE MY JEANS BACK?
ELVIS DIDN'T WEAR JEANS!
NOW SING OR I'LL MAKE YOU DO HAPPY BIRTHDAY MR. PRESIDENT TO THE MAILMAN! (GIGGLE!)
KATCHOO... WHEN I GET MY HANDS ON YOU...!
YEAH, YEAH! I'M SHAKIN'! C'MON, YOU'RE ALMOST DONE! JUST ONE MORE CHORUS!
LOVE ME TENDER LOVE ME TRUE BLAH BLAH SOMETHING LOVE LOVE ME...
I CAN'T HEEEAR YOU!
LOVE ME TENDER LOVE ME DO! LOVE ME SCOOBY DOO!
FOR MY DARLING I LOVE YOU — SINGING TO ME NUDE! AAAAAH!
NEXT ISSUE
THE JOB THE GYM THE POSE

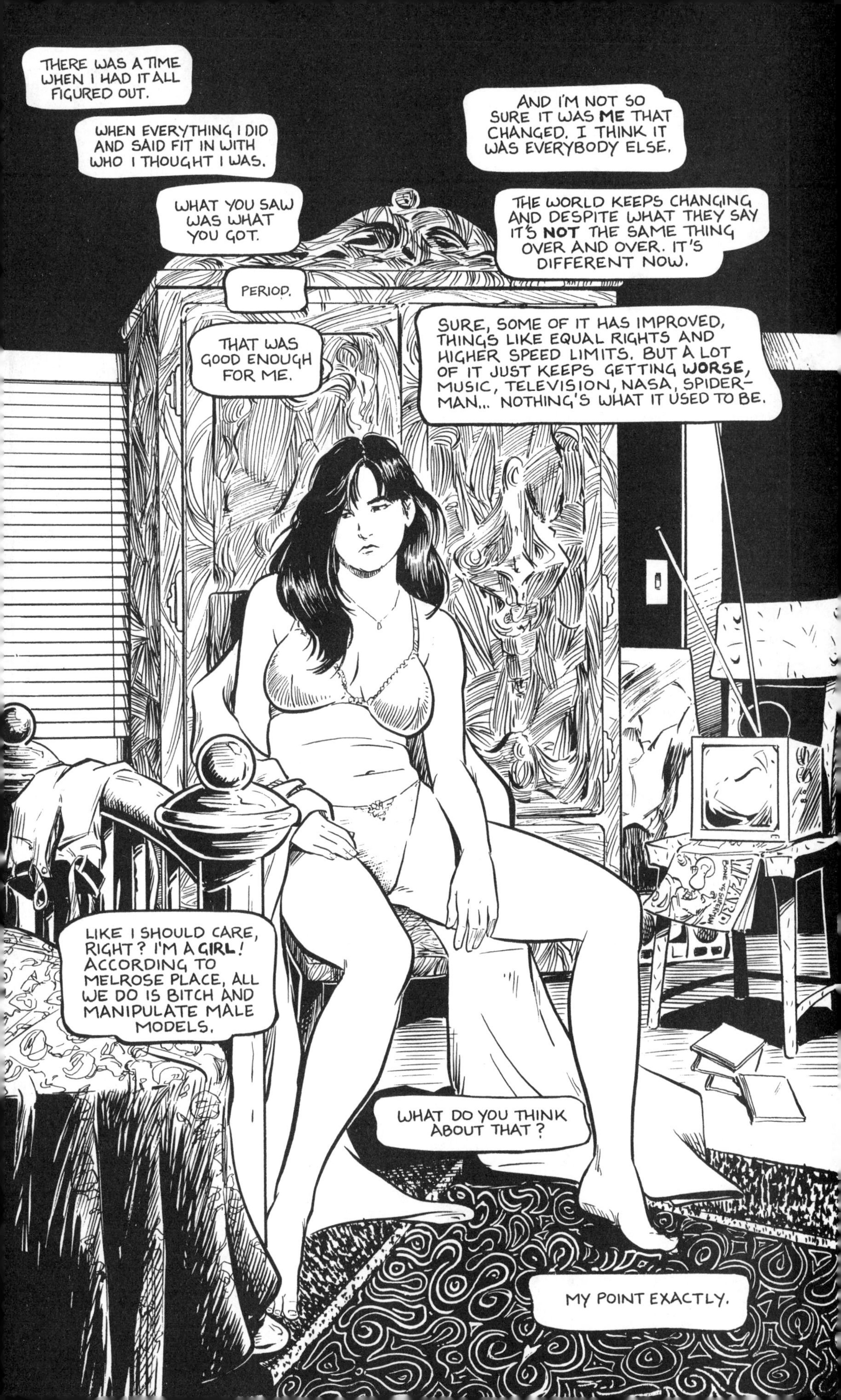

THERE WAS A TIME WHEN I HAD IT ALL FIGURED OUT.
WHEN EVERYTHING I DID AND SAID FIT IN WITH WHO I THOUGHT I WAS.
WHAT YOU SAW WAS WHAT YOU GOT.
PERIOD.
THAT WAS GOOD ENOUGH FOR ME.
AND I'M NOT SO SURE IT WAS **ME** THAT CHANGED. I THINK IT WAS EVERYBODY ELSE.
THE WORLD KEEPS CHANGING AND DESPITE WHAT THEY SAY IT'S **NOT** THE SAME THING OVER AND OVER. IT'S DIFFERENT NOW.
SURE, SOME OF IT HAS IMPROVED, THINGS LIKE EQUAL RIGHTS AND HIGHER SPEED LIMITS. BUT A LOT OF IT JUST KEEPS GETTING **WORSE**, MUSIC, TELEVISION, NASA, SPIDER-MAN... NOTHING'S WHAT IT USED TO BE.
LIKE I SHOULD CARE, RIGHT? I'M A **GIRL**! ACCORDING TO MELROSE PLACE, ALL WE DO IS BITCH AND MANIPULATE MALE MODELS.
WHAT DO YOU THINK ABOUT THAT?
MY POINT EXACTLY.

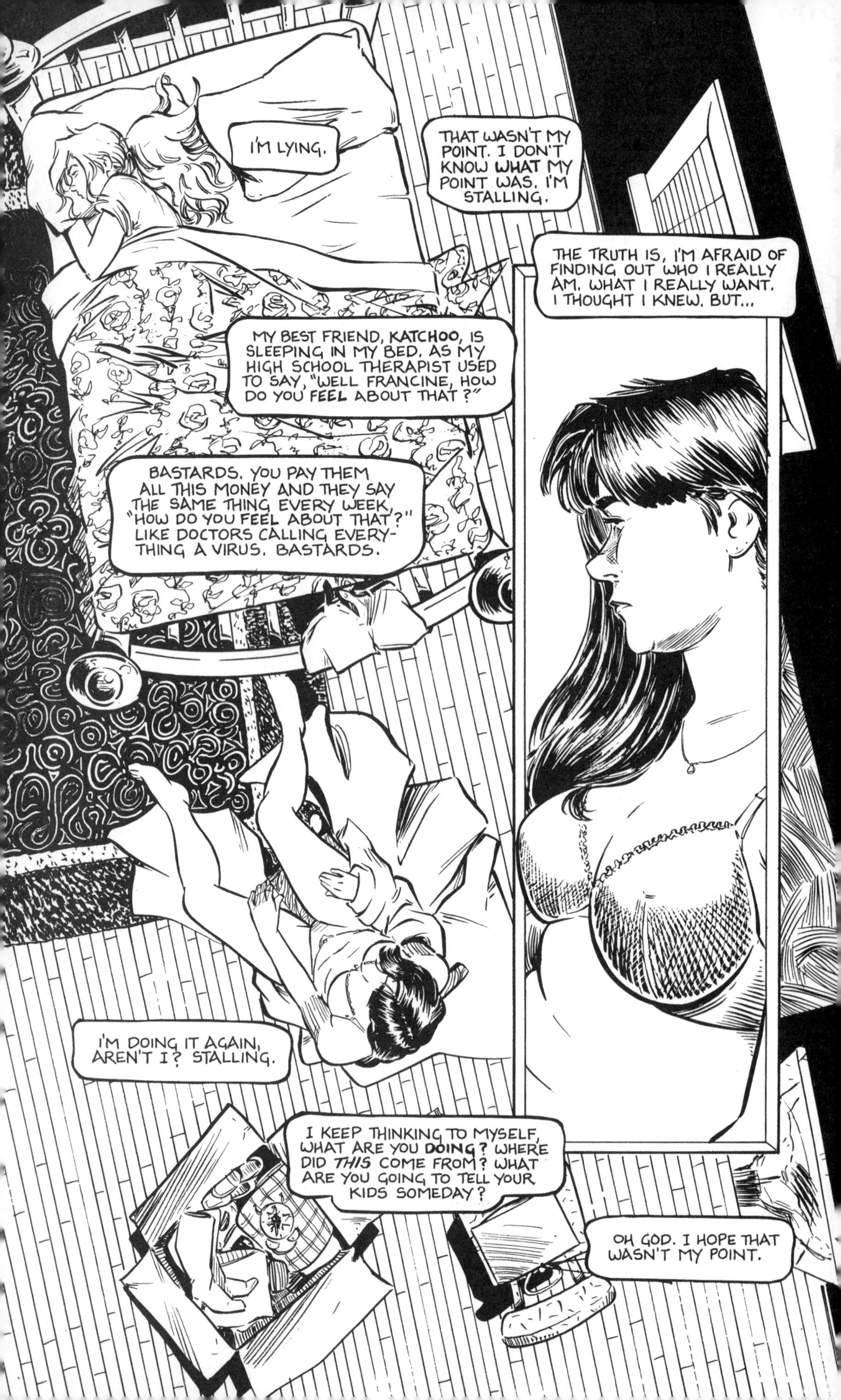
I'M LYING.
THAT WASN'T MY POINT. I DON'T KNOW **WHAT** MY POINT WAS. I'M STALLING.
THE TRUTH IS, I'M AFRAID OF FINDING OUT WHO I REALLY AM. WHAT I REALLY WANT. I THOUGHT I KNEW. BUT...
MY BEST FRIEND, **KATCHOO**, IS SLEEPING IN MY BED. AS MY HIGH SCHOOL THERAPIST USED TO SAY, "WELL FRANCINE, HOW DO YOU **FEEL** ABOUT THAT?"
BASTARDS. YOU PAY THEM ALL THIS MONEY AND THEY SAY THE SAME THING EVERY WEEK, "HOW DO YOU FEEL ABOUT THAT?" LIKE DOCTORS CALLING EVERY-THING A VIRUS. BASTARDS.
I'M DOING IT AGAIN, AREN'T I? STALLING.
I KEEP THINKING TO MYSELF, WHAT ARE YOU **DOING**? WHERE DID *THIS* COME FROM? WHAT ARE YOU GOING TO TELL YOUR KIDS SOMEDAY?
OH GOD. I HOPE THAT WASN'T MY POINT.

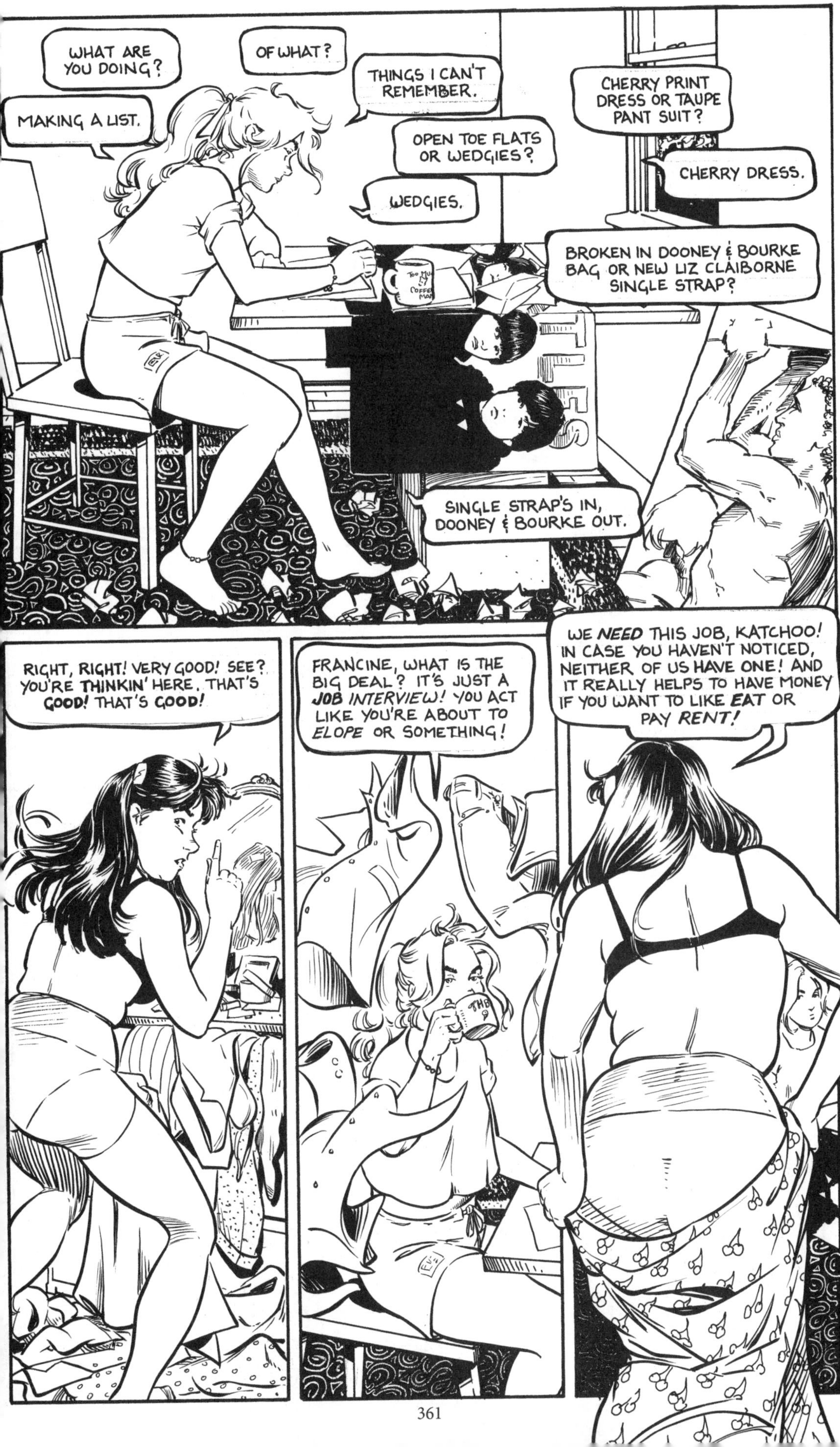
WHAT ARE YOU DOING?
MAKING A LIST.
OF WHAT?
THINGS I CAN'T REMEMBER.
OPEN TOE FLATS OR WEDGIES?
WEDGIES.
CHERRY PRINT DRESS OR TAUPE PANT SUIT?
CHERRY DRESS.
BROKEN IN DOONEY & BOURKE BAG OR NEW LIZ CLAIBORNE SINGLE STRAP?
SINGLE STRAP'S IN, DOONEY & BOURKE OUT.
RIGHT, RIGHT! VERY GOOD! SEE? YOU'RE THINKIN' HERE. THAT'S GOOD! THAT'S GOOD!
FRANCINE, WHAT IS THE BIG DEAL? IT'S JUST A JOB INTERVIEW! YOU ACT LIKE YOU'RE ABOUT TO ELOPE OR SOMETHING!
WE NEED THIS JOB, KATCHOO! IN CASE YOU HAVEN'T NOTICED, NEITHER OF US HAVE ONE! AND IT REALLY HELPS TO HAVE MONEY IF YOU WANT TO LIKE EAT OR PAY RENT!

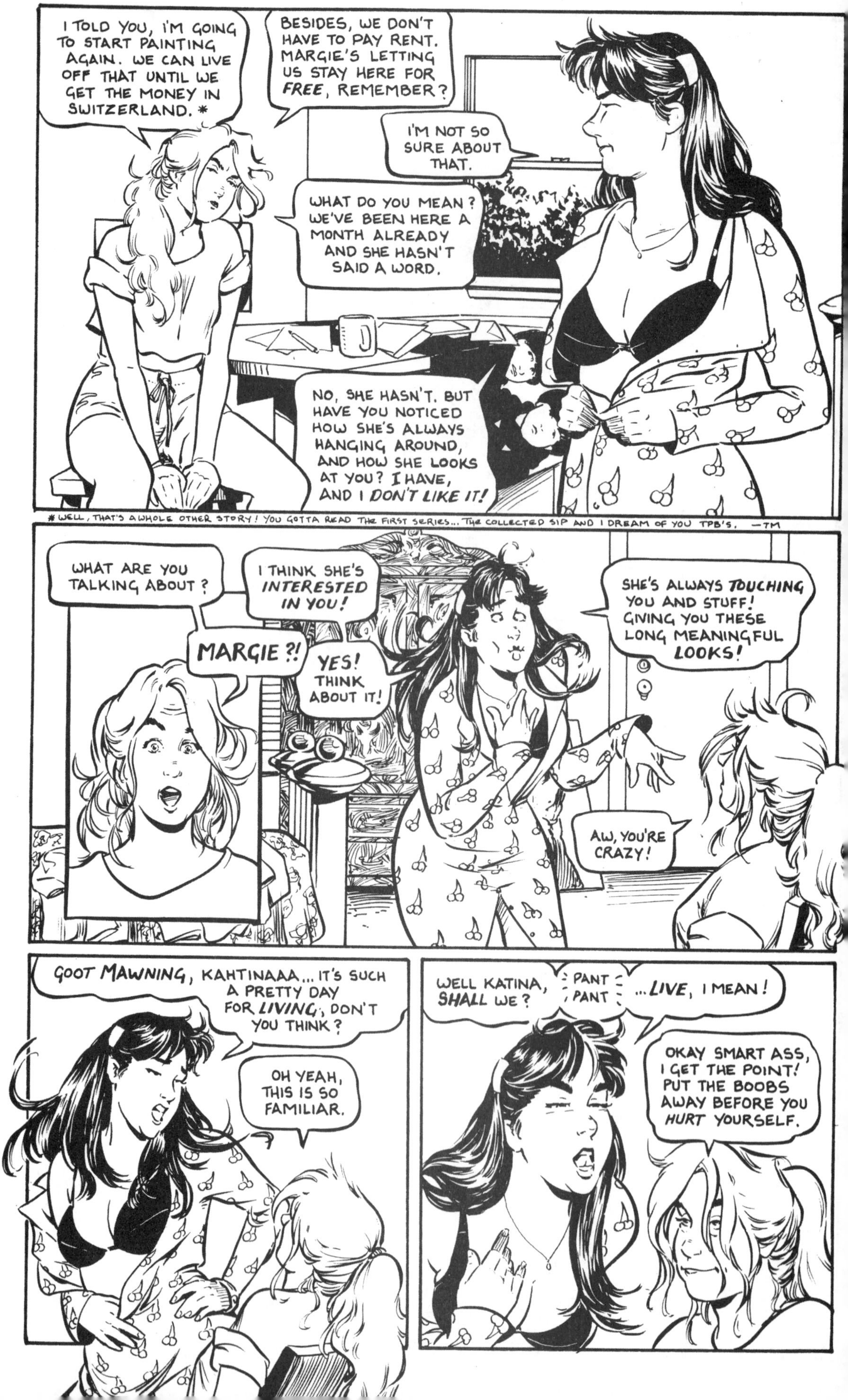
I TOLD YOU, I'M GOING TO START PAINTING AGAIN. WE CAN LIVE OFF THAT UNTIL WE GET THE MONEY IN SWITZERLAND. *
BESIDES, WE DON'T HAVE TO PAY RENT. MARGIE'S LETTING US STAY HERE FOR FREE, REMEMBER?
I'M NOT SO SURE ABOUT THAT.
WHAT DO YOU MEAN? WE'VE BEEN HERE A MONTH ALREADY AND SHE HASN'T SAID A WORD.
NO, SHE HASN'T. BUT HAVE YOU NOTICED HOW SHE'S ALWAYS HANGING AROUND, AND HOW SHE LOOKS AT YOU? I HAVE, AND I DON'T LIKE IT!
* WELL, THAT'S A WHOLE OTHER STORY! YOU GOTTA READ THE FIRST SERIES... THE COLLECTED SIP AND I DREAM OF YOU TPB'S. —TM
WHAT ARE YOU TALKING ABOUT?
I THINK SHE'S INTERESTED IN YOU!
MARGIE?!
YES! THINK ABOUT IT!
SHE'S ALWAYS TOUCHING YOU AND STUFF! GIVING YOU THESE LONG MEANINGFUL LOOKS!
AW, YOU'RE CRAZY!
GOOT MAWNING, KAHTINAAA... IT'S SUCH A PRETTY DAY FOR LIVING, DON'T YOU THINK?
OH YEAH, THIS IS SO FAMILIAR.
WELL KATINA, SHALL WE?
PANT PANT
...LIVE, I MEAN!
OKAY SMART ASS, I GET THE POINT! PUT THE BOOBS AWAY BEFORE YOU HURT YOURSELF.

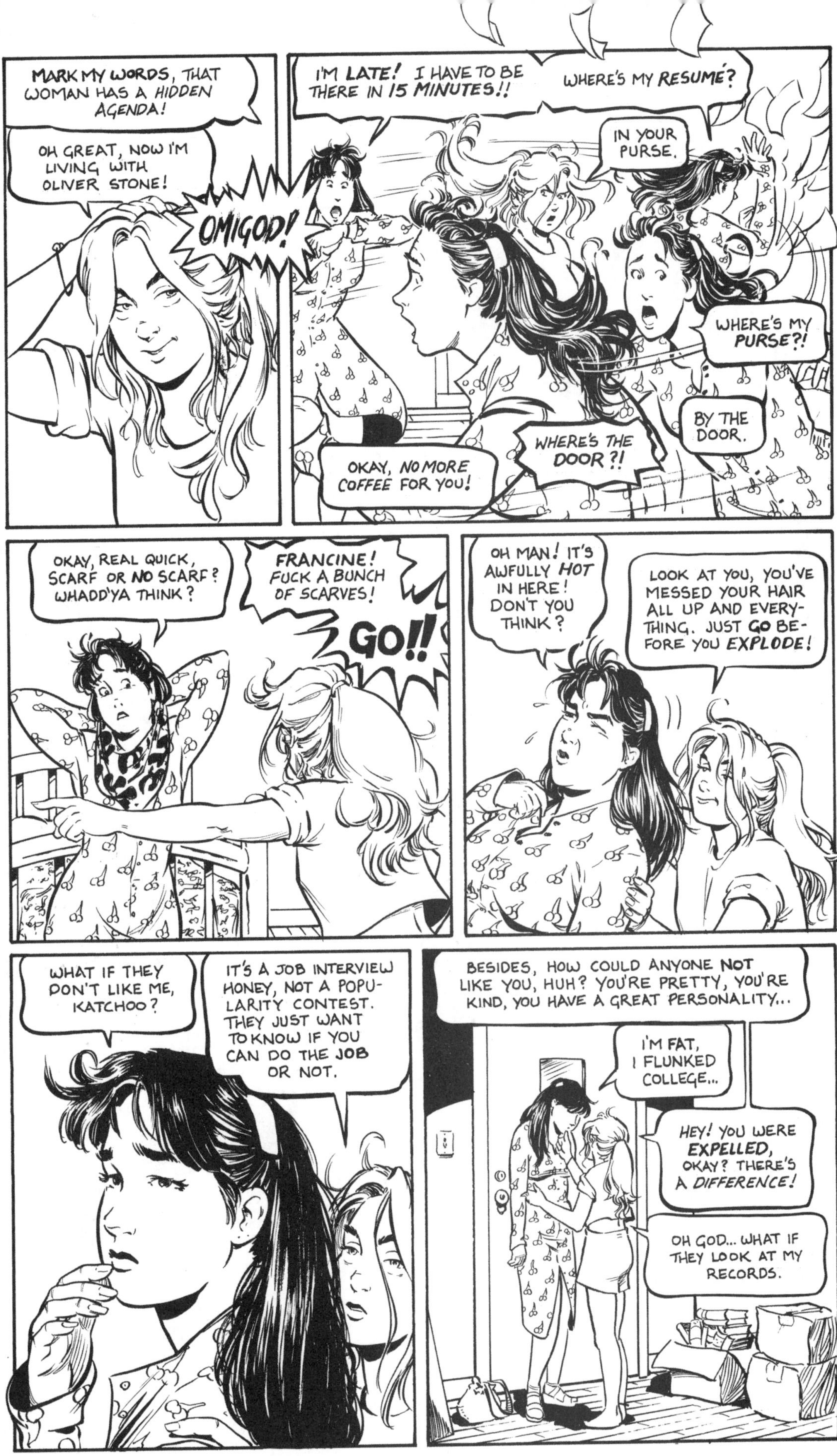
MARK MY WORDS, THAT WOMAN HAS A HIDDEN AGENDA!
OH GREAT, NOW I'M LIVING WITH OLIVER STONE!
OMIGOD!
I'M LATE! I HAVE TO BE THERE IN 15 MINUTES!!
WHERE'S MY RESUMÉ?
IN YOUR PURSE.
WHERE'S MY PURSE?!
BY THE DOOR.
WHERE'S THE DOOR?!
OKAY, NO MORE COFFEE FOR YOU!
OKAY, REAL QUICK, SCARF OR NO SCARF? WHADD'YA THINK?
FRANCINE! FUCK A BUNCH OF SCARVES!
GO!!
OH MAN! IT'S AWFULLY HOT IN HERE! DON'T YOU THINK?
LOOK AT YOU, YOU'VE MESSED YOUR HAIR ALL UP AND EVERY-THING. JUST GO BE-FORE YOU EXPLODE!
WHAT IF THEY DON'T LIKE ME, KATCHOO?
IT'S A JOB INTERVIEW HONEY, NOT A POPU-LARITY CONTEST. THEY JUST WANT TO KNOW IF YOU CAN DO THE JOB OR NOT.
BESIDES, HOW COULD ANYONE NOT LIKE YOU, HUH? YOU'RE PRETTY, YOU'RE KIND, YOU HAVE A GREAT PERSONALITY...
I'M FAT, I FLUNKED COLLEGE...
HEY! YOU WERE EXPELLED, OKAY? THERE'S A DIFFERENCE!
OH GOD... WHAT IF THEY LOOK AT MY RECORDS.

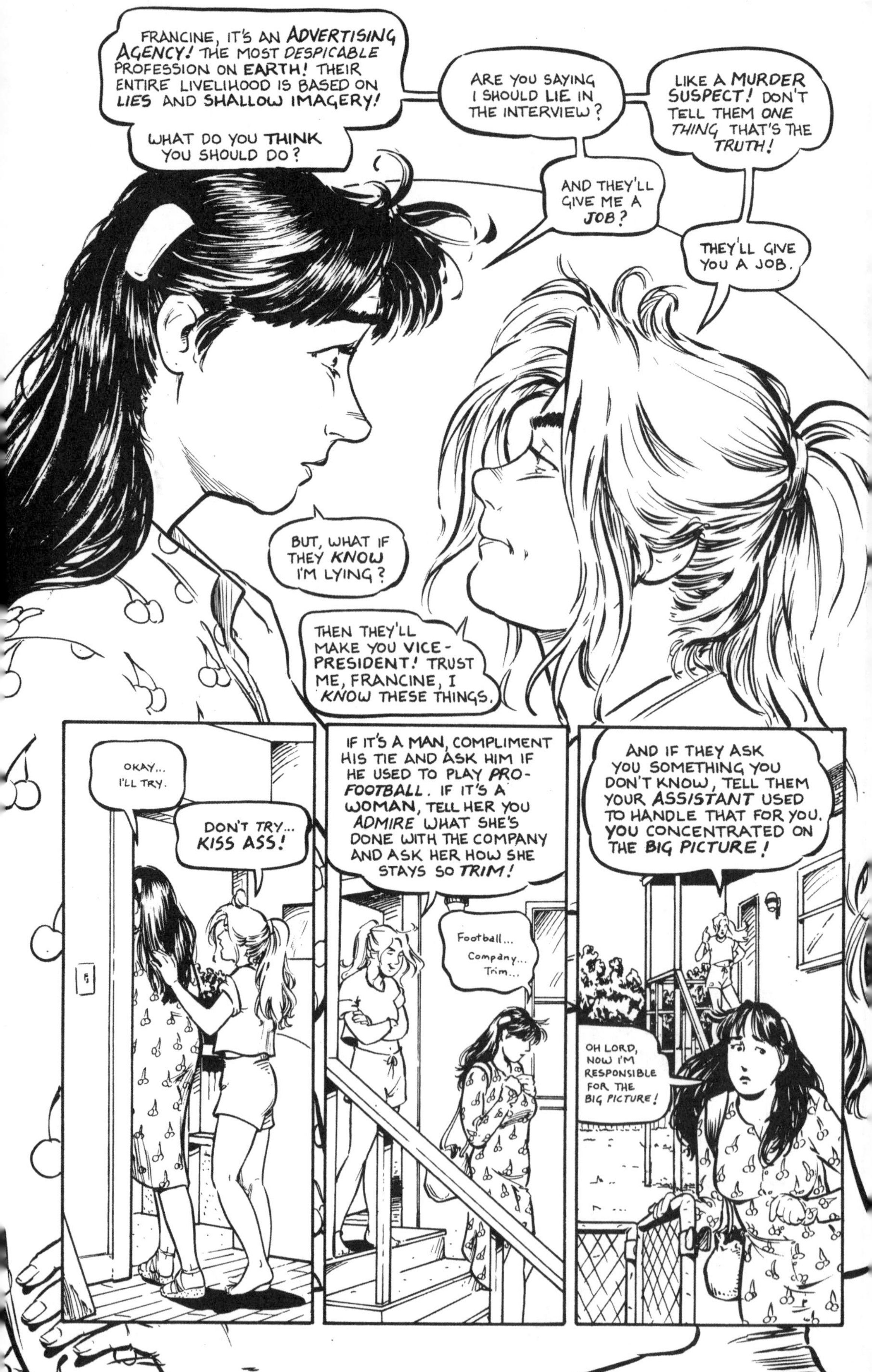
FRANCINE, IT'S AN ADVERTISING AGENCY! THE MOST DESPICABLE PROFESSION ON EARTH! THEIR ENTIRE LIVELIHOOD IS BASED ON LIES AND SHALLOW IMAGERY!
WHAT DO YOU THINK YOU SHOULD DO?
ARE YOU SAYING I SHOULD LIE IN THE INTERVIEW?
LIKE A MURDER SUSPECT! DON'T TELL THEM ONE THING THAT'S THE TRUTH!
AND THEY'LL GIVE ME A JOB?
THEY'LL GIVE YOU A JOB.
BUT, WHAT IF THEY KNOW I'M LYING?
THEN THEY'LL MAKE YOU VICE-PRESIDENT! TRUST ME, FRANCINE, I KNOW THESE THINGS.
OKAY... I'LL TRY.
DON'T TRY... KISS ASS!
IF IT'S A MAN, COMPLIMENT HIS TIE AND ASK HIM IF HE USED TO PLAY PRO-FOOTBALL. IF IT'S A WOMAN, TELL HER YOU ADMIRE WHAT SHE'S DONE WITH THE COMPANY AND ASK HER HOW SHE STAYS SO TRIM!
Football... Company... Trim...
AND IF THEY ASK YOU SOMETHING YOU DON'T KNOW, TELL THEM YOUR ASSISTANT USED TO HANDLE THAT FOR YOU. YOU CONCENTRATED ON THE BIG PICTURE!
OH LORD, NOW I'M RESPONSIBLE FOR THE BIG PICTURE!

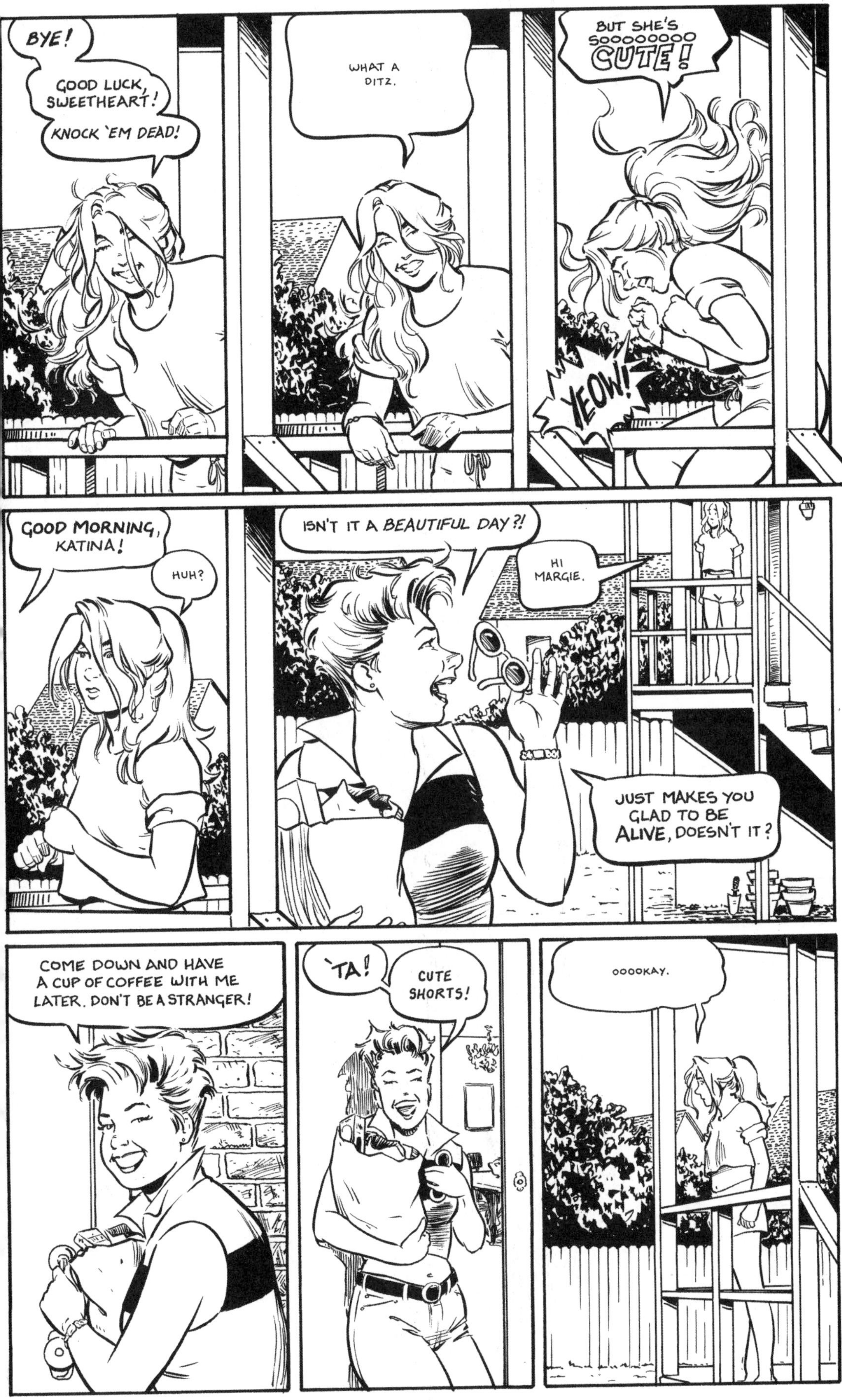
BYE!
GOOD LUCK, SWEETHEART!
KNOCK `EM DEAD!
WHAT A DITZ.
BUT SHE'S SOOOOOOOO CUTE!
YEOW!
GOOD MORNING, KATINA!
HUH?
ISN'T IT A BEAUTIFUL DAY?!
HI MARGIE.
JUST MAKES YOU GLAD TO BE ALIVE, DOESN'T IT?
COME DOWN AND HAVE A CUP OF COFFEE WITH ME LATER. DON'T BE A STRANGER!
`TA!
CUTE SHORTS!
OOOOKAY.

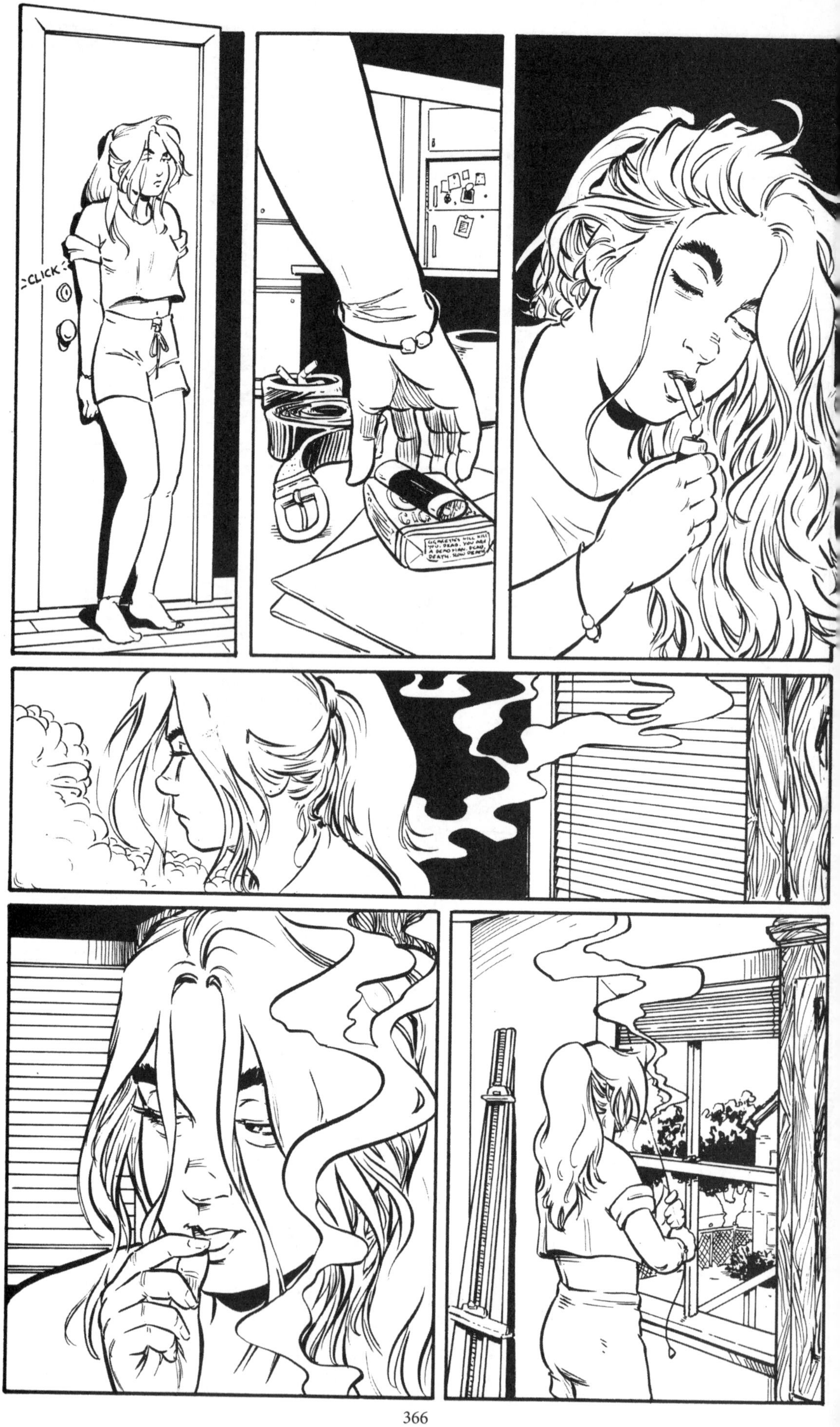
CLICK

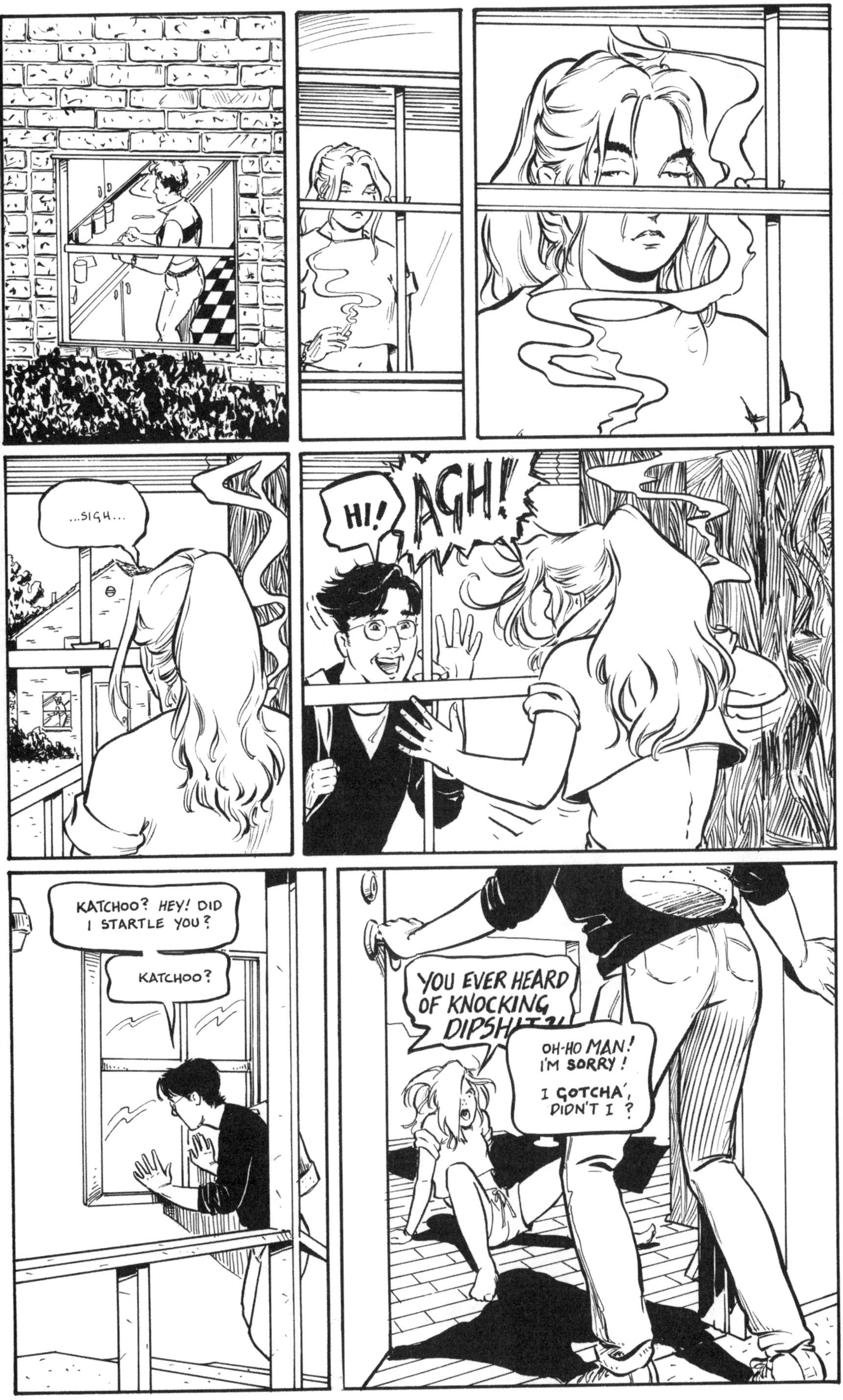
...SIGH...
HI!
AGH!
KATCHOO? HEY! DID I STARTLE YOU?
KATCHOO?
YOU EVER HEARD OF KNOCKING DIPSHIT?!
OH-HO MAN! I'M SORRY!
I GOTCHA', DIDN'T I?

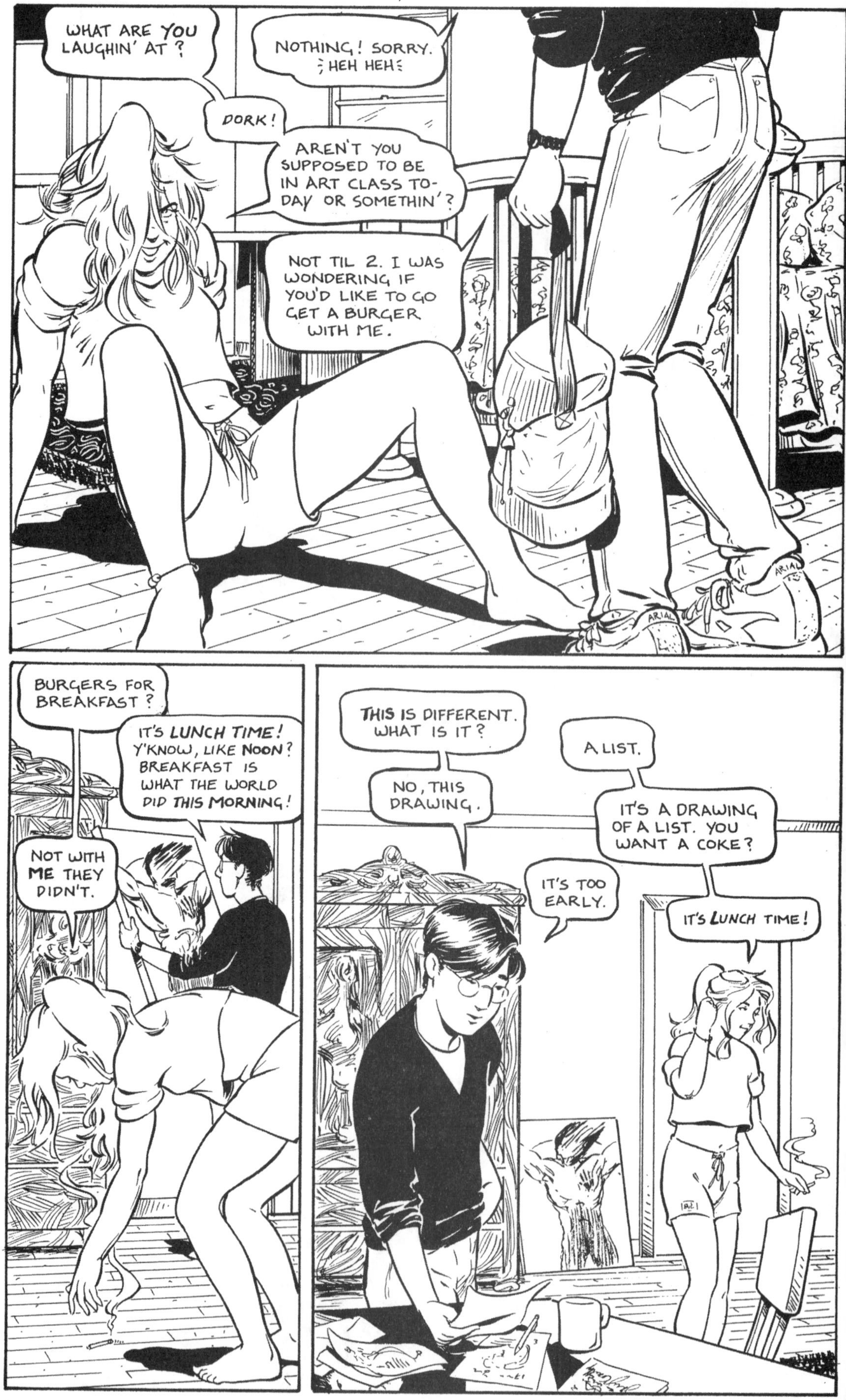
WHAT ARE YOU LAUGHIN' AT ?
NOTHING! SORRY. HEH HEH
DORK!
AREN'T YOU SUPPOSED TO BE IN ART CLASS TO-DAY OR SOMETHIN'?
NOT TIL 2. I WAS WONDERING IF YOU'D LIKE TO GO GET A BURGER WITH ME.
ARIAL
ARIAL
BURGERS FOR BREAKFAST ?
IT'S LUNCH TIME! Y'KNOW, LIKE NOON? BREAKFAST IS WHAT THE WORLD DID THIS MORNING!
NOT WITH ME THEY DIDN'T.
THIS IS DIFFERENT. WHAT IS IT ?
NO, THIS DRAWING.
A LIST.
IT'S A DRAWING OF A LIST. YOU WANT A COKE?
IT'S TOO EARLY.
IT'S LUNCH TIME!

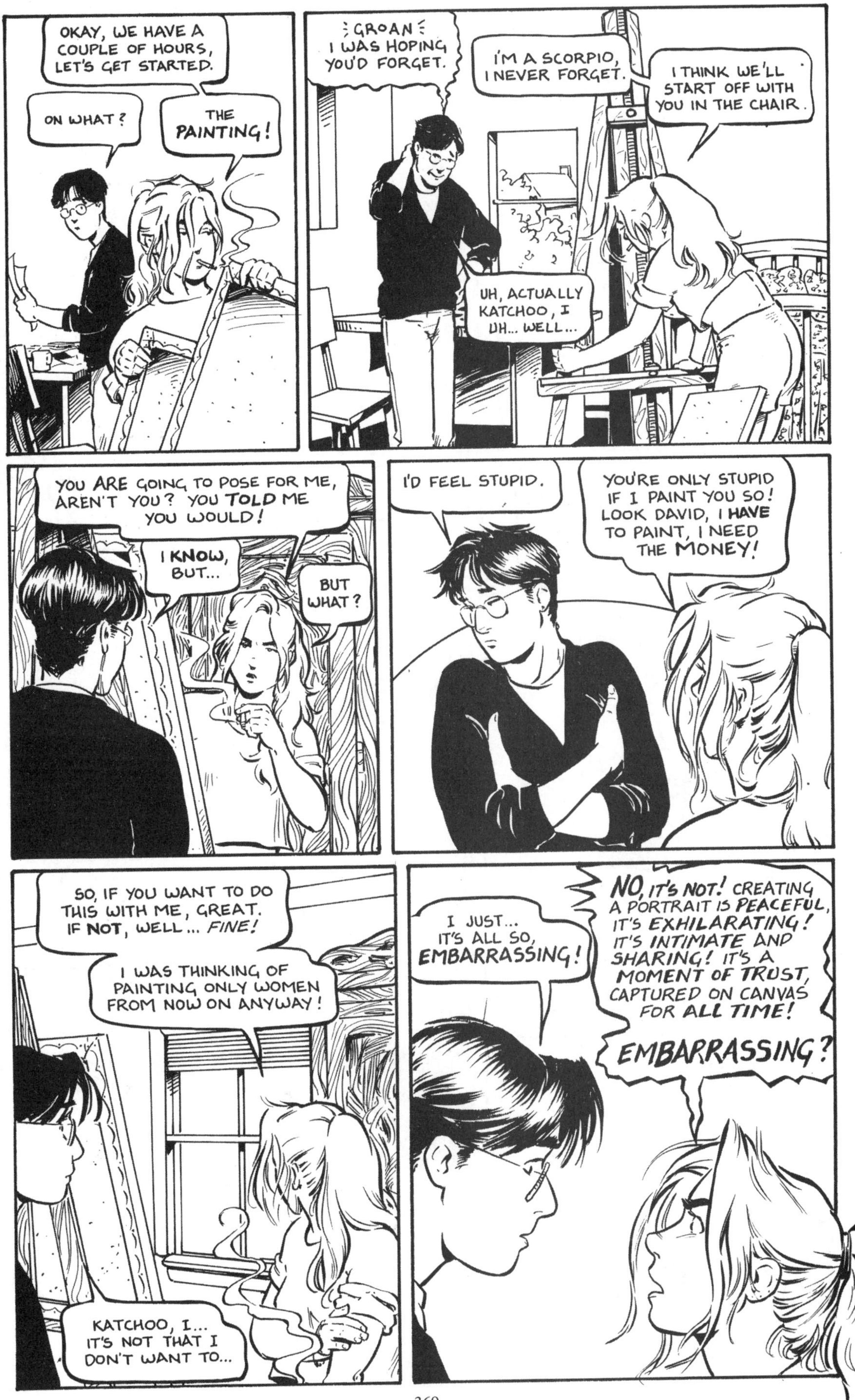
OKAY, WE HAVE A COUPLE OF HOURS, LET'S GET STARTED.
ON WHAT?
THE PAINTING!
GROAN I WAS HOPING YOU'D FORGET.
I'M A SCORPIO, I NEVER FORGET.
I THINK WE'LL START OFF WITH YOU IN THE CHAIR.
UH, ACTUALLY KATCHOO, I UH... WELL...
YOU ARE GOING TO POSE FOR ME, AREN'T YOU? YOU TOLD ME YOU WOULD!
I KNOW, BUT...
BUT WHAT?
I'D FEEL STUPID.
YOU'RE ONLY STUPID IF I PAINT YOU SO! LOOK DAVID, I HAVE TO PAINT, I NEED THE MONEY!
SO, IF YOU WANT TO DO THIS WITH ME, GREAT. IF NOT, WELL... FINE!
I WAS THINKING OF PAINTING ONLY WOMEN FROM NOW ON ANYWAY!
KATCHOO, I... IT'S NOT THAT I DON'T WANT TO...
I JUST... IT'S ALL SO, EMBARRASSING!
NO, IT'S NOT! CREATING A PORTRAIT IS PEACEFUL, IT'S EXHILARATING! IT'S INTIMATE AND SHARING! IT'S A MOMENT OF TRUST, CAPTURED ON CANVAS FOR ALL TIME!
EMBARRASSING?

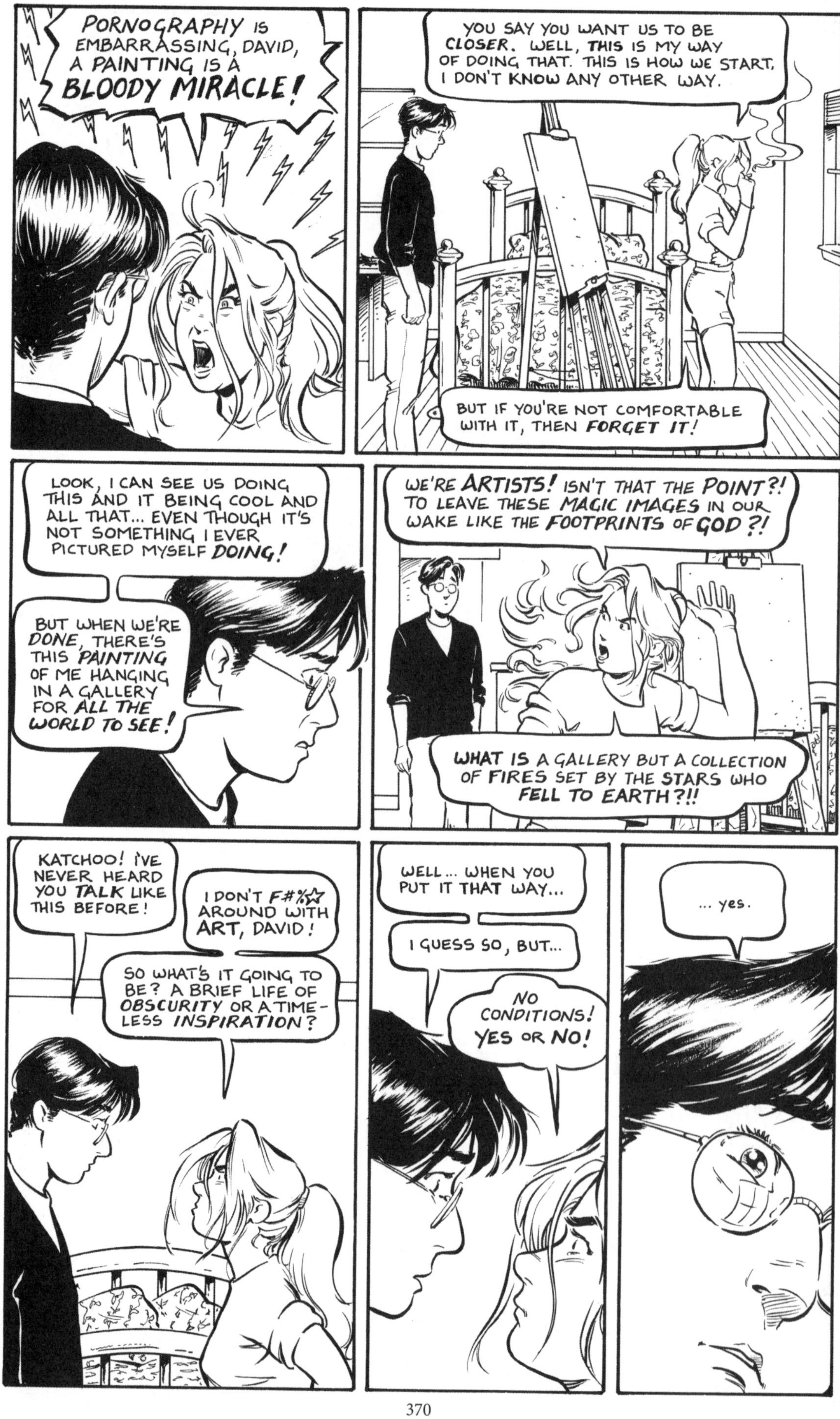
PORNOGRAPHY IS EMBARRASSING, DAVID, A PAINTING IS A BLOODY MIRACLE!
YOU SAY YOU WANT US TO BE CLOSER. WELL, THIS IS MY WAY OF DOING THAT. THIS IS HOW WE START. I DON'T KNOW ANY OTHER WAY.
BUT IF YOU'RE NOT COMFORTABLE WITH IT, THEN FORGET IT!
LOOK, I CAN SEE US DOING THIS AND IT BEING COOL AND ALL THAT... EVEN THOUGH IT'S NOT SOMETHING I EVER PICTURED MYSELF DOING!
BUT WHEN WE'RE DONE, THERE'S THIS PAINTING OF ME HANGING IN A GALLERY FOR ALL THE WORLD TO SEE!
WE'RE ARTISTS! ISN'T THAT THE POINT?! TO LEAVE THESE MAGIC IMAGES IN OUR WAKE LIKE THE FOOTPRINTS OF GOD?!
WHAT IS A GALLERY BUT A COLLECTION OF FIRES SET BY THE STARS WHO FELL TO EARTH?!!
KATCHOO! I'VE NEVER HEARD YOU TALK LIKE THIS BEFORE!
I DON'T F#%☆ AROUND WITH ART, DAVID!
SO WHAT'S IT GOING TO BE? A BRIEF LIFE OF OBSCURITY OR A TIMELESS INSPIRATION?
WELL... WHEN YOU PUT IT THAT WAY...
I GUESS SO, BUT...
NO CONDITIONS! YES OR NO!
... yes.

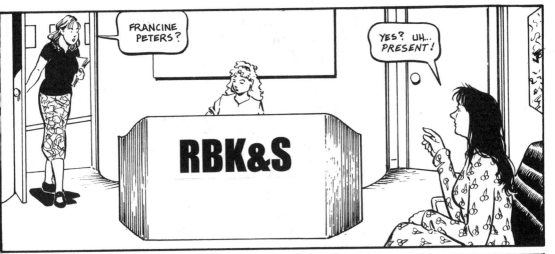

FRANCINE PETERS?

YES? UH... PRESENT!

RBK&S

I'M ALLISON WEBER, ASSOCIATE PRODUCER HERE AT RUTNER BOVIS KLEINENBAUMENSTEINENBERGER AND SMITH!

HI.

MS. FEINSTEIN ASKED ME TO SHOW YOU BACK TO THE CONFERENCE ROOM. WE'RE HAVING LUNCH BROUGHT IN.

THAT SOUNDS FUN!

HARDLY!

WE'VE BEEN UP FOR *TWO* DAYS STRAIGHT! TRYING TO COME UP WITH A NEW PITCH FOR THE *COMMAND PURPOSE* CONDOMS ACCOUNT.

SO, WHERE WERE YOU BEFORE THIS? HEY GAREB!

'MORNING ALLISON!

HOME.

HA! NO, I MEAN, WHERE WERE YOU *WORKING*?

OH! UH, I WAS AT SMITH SMITH SMITH AND, UH... SMITH!

FOUR SMITHS?!

ACTUALLY, I THINK THERE WAS ONLY *ONE* SMITH WITH *FOUR DESKS*! IT WASN'T A BIG AGENCY.

FOUR SMITHS!

IT WAS A VERY SMALL PLACE.

FOUR OF THEM.

TINY.

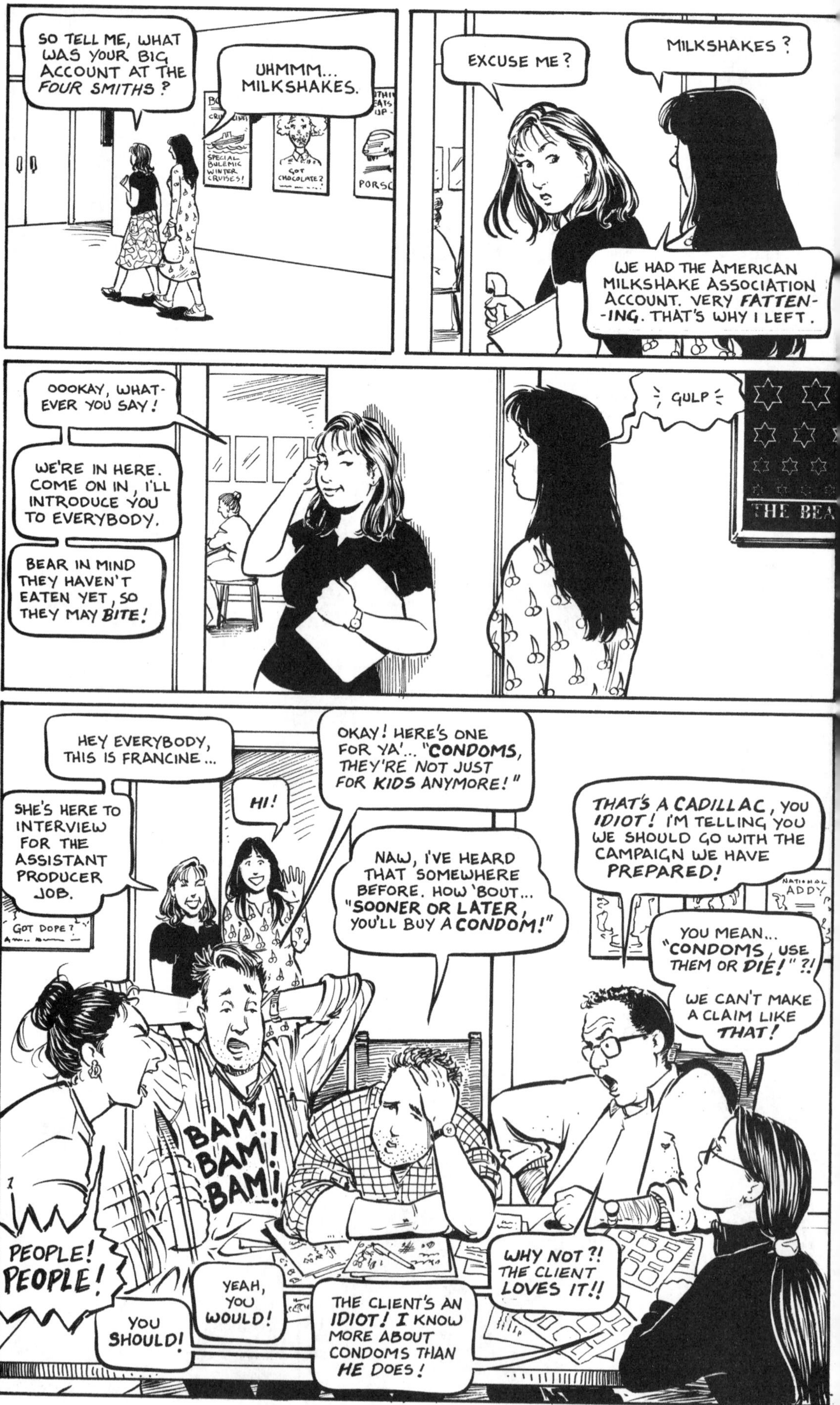

SO TELL ME, WHAT WAS YOUR BIG ACCOUNT AT THE FOUR SMITHS?
UHMMM... MILKSHAKES.
SPECIAL BULEMIC WINTER CRUISES!
GOT CHOCOLATE?
PORSC
EXCUSE ME?
MILKSHAKES?
WE HAD THE AMERICAN MILKSHAKE ASSOCIATION ACCOUNT. VERY FATTEN-ING. THAT'S WHY I LEFT.
OOOKAY, WHAT-EVER YOU SAY!
WE'RE IN HERE. COME ON IN, I'LL INTRODUCE YOU TO EVERYBODY.
BEAR IN MIND THEY HAVEN'T EATEN YET, SO THEY MAY BITE!
GULP
THE BEA
HEY EVERYBODY, THIS IS FRANCINE...
SHE'S HERE TO INTERVIEW FOR THE ASSISTANT PRODUCER JOB.
HI!
GOT DOPE?
OKAY! HERE'S ONE FOR YA'... "CONDOMS, THEY'RE NOT JUST FOR KIDS ANYMORE!"
NAW, I'VE HEARD THAT SOMEWHERE BEFORE. HOW 'BOUT... "SOONER OR LATER, YOU'LL BUY A CONDOM!"
THAT'S A CADILLAC, YOU IDIOT! I'M TELLING YOU WE SHOULD GO WITH THE CAMPAIGN WE HAVE PREPARED!
NATIONAL ADDY
YOU MEAN... "CONDOMS, USE THEM OR DIE!"?!
WE CAN'T MAKE A CLAIM LIKE THAT!
BAM! BAM! BAM!
PEOPLE! PEOPLE!
YOU SHOULD!
YEAH, YOU WOULD!
THE CLIENT'S AN IDIOT! I KNOW MORE ABOUT CONDOMS THAN HE DOES!
WHY NOT?! THE CLIENT LOVES IT!!

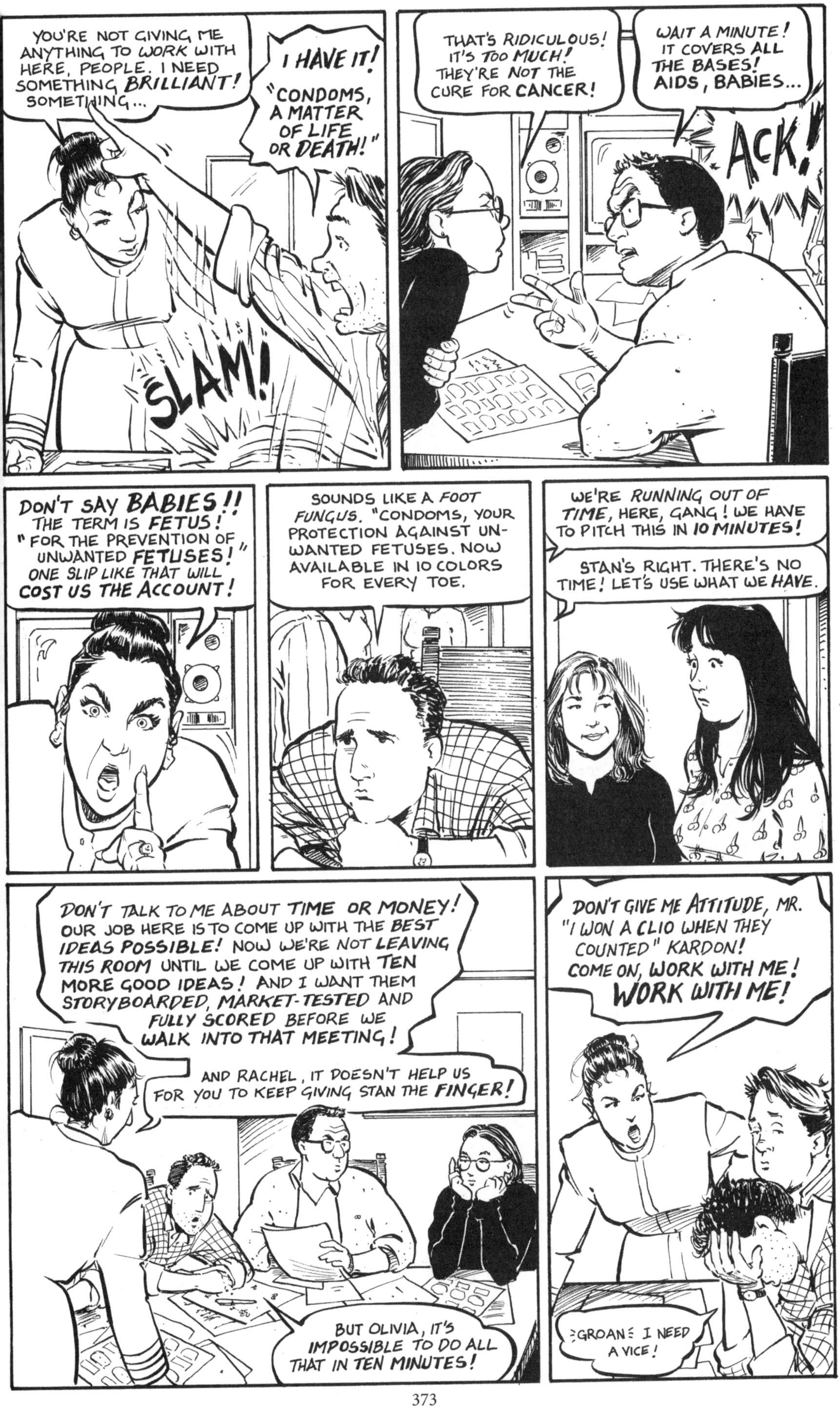
YOU'RE NOT GIVING ME ANYTHING TO WORK WITH HERE, PEOPLE. I NEED SOMETHING BRILLIANT! SOMETHING...
I HAVE IT! "CONDOMS, A MATTER OF LIFE OR DEATH!"
SLAM!
THAT'S RIDICULOUS! IT'S TOO MUCH! THEY'RE NOT THE CURE FOR CANCER!
WAIT A MINUTE! IT COVERS ALL THE BASES! AIDS, BABIES...
ACK!
DON'T SAY BABIES!! THE TERM IS FETUS! "FOR THE PREVENTION OF UNWANTED FETUSES!" ONE SLIP LIKE THAT WILL COST US THE ACCOUNT!
SOUNDS LIKE A FOOT FUNGUS. "CONDOMS, YOUR PROTECTION AGAINST UNWANTED FETUSES. NOW AVAILABLE IN 10 COLORS FOR EVERY TOE.
WE'RE RUNNING OUT OF TIME, HERE, GANG! WE HAVE TO PITCH THIS IN 10 MINUTES!
STAN'S RIGHT. THERE'S NO TIME! LET'S USE WHAT WE HAVE.
DON'T TALK TO ME ABOUT TIME OR MONEY! OUR JOB HERE IS TO COME UP WITH THE BEST IDEAS POSSIBLE! NOW WE'RE NOT LEAVING THIS ROOM UNTIL WE COME UP WITH TEN MORE GOOD IDEAS! AND I WANT THEM STORYBOARDED, MARKET-TESTED AND FULLY SCORED BEFORE WE WALK INTO THAT MEETING!
AND RACHEL, IT DOESN'T HELP US FOR YOU TO KEEP GIVING STAN THE FINGER!
BUT OLIVIA, IT'S IMPOSSIBLE TO DO ALL THAT IN TEN MINUTES!
DON'T GIVE ME ATTITUDE, MR. "I WON A CLIO WHEN THEY COUNTED" KARDON! COME ON, WORK WITH ME! WORK WITH ME!
GROAN I NEED A VICE!

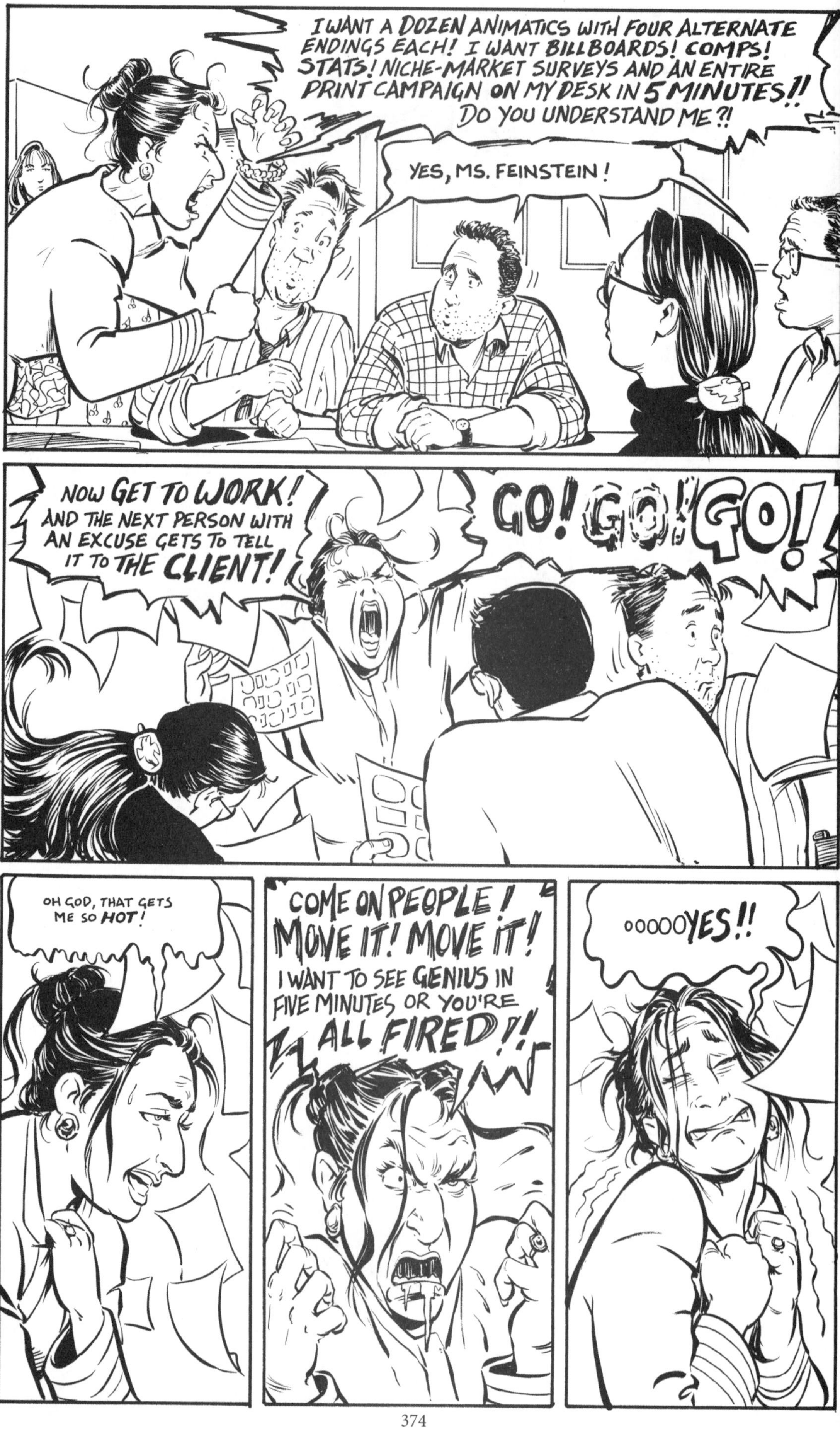
I WANT A DOZEN ANIMATICS WITH FOUR ALTERNATE ENDINGS EACH! I WANT BILLBOARDS! COMPS! STATS! NICHE-MARKET SURVEYS AND AN ENTIRE PRINT CAMPAIGN ON MY DESK IN 5 MINUTES!! DO YOU UNDERSTAND ME?!
YES, MS. FEINSTEIN!
NOW GET TO WORK! AND THE NEXT PERSON WITH AN EXCUSE GETS TO TELL IT TO THE CLIENT!
GO! GO! GO!
OH GOD, THAT GETS ME SO HOT!
COME ON PEOPLE! MOVE IT! MOVE IT! I WANT TO SEE GENIUS IN FIVE MINUTES OR YOU'RE ALL FIRED!!
OOOOOYES!!

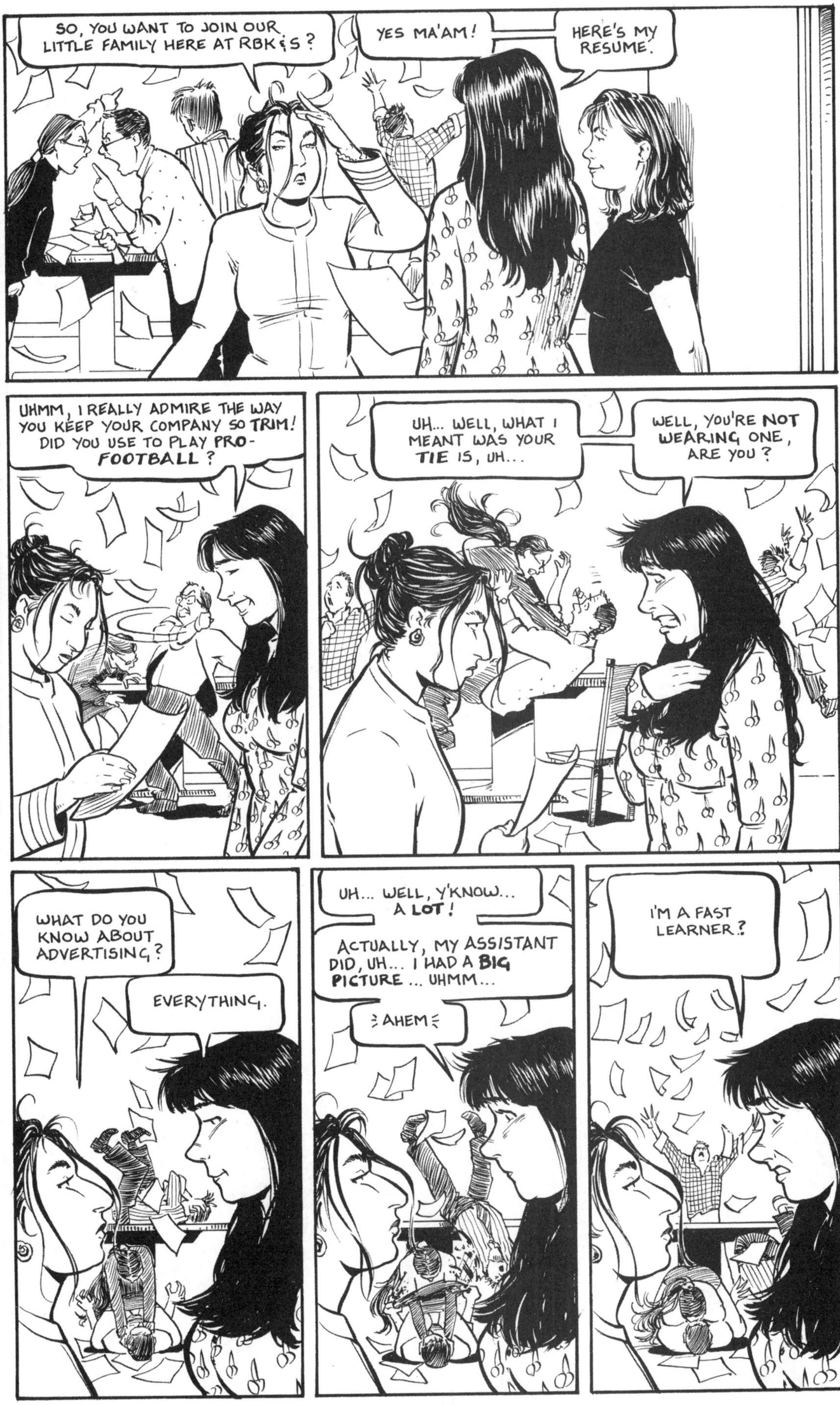
SO, YOU WANT TO JOIN OUR LITTLE FAMILY HERE AT RBK&S?
YES MA'AM!
HERE'S MY RESUME.
UHMM, I REALLY ADMIRE THE WAY YOU KEEP YOUR COMPANY SO TRIM! DID YOU USE TO PLAY PRO-FOOTBALL?
UH... WELL, WHAT I MEANT WAS YOUR TIE IS, UH...
WELL, YOU'RE NOT WEARING ONE, ARE YOU?
WHAT DO YOU KNOW ABOUT ADVERTISING?
EVERYTHING.
UH... WELL, Y'KNOW... A LOT!
ACTUALLY, MY ASSISTANT DID, UH... I HAD A BIG PICTURE ... UHMM...
AHEM
I'M A FAST LEARNER?

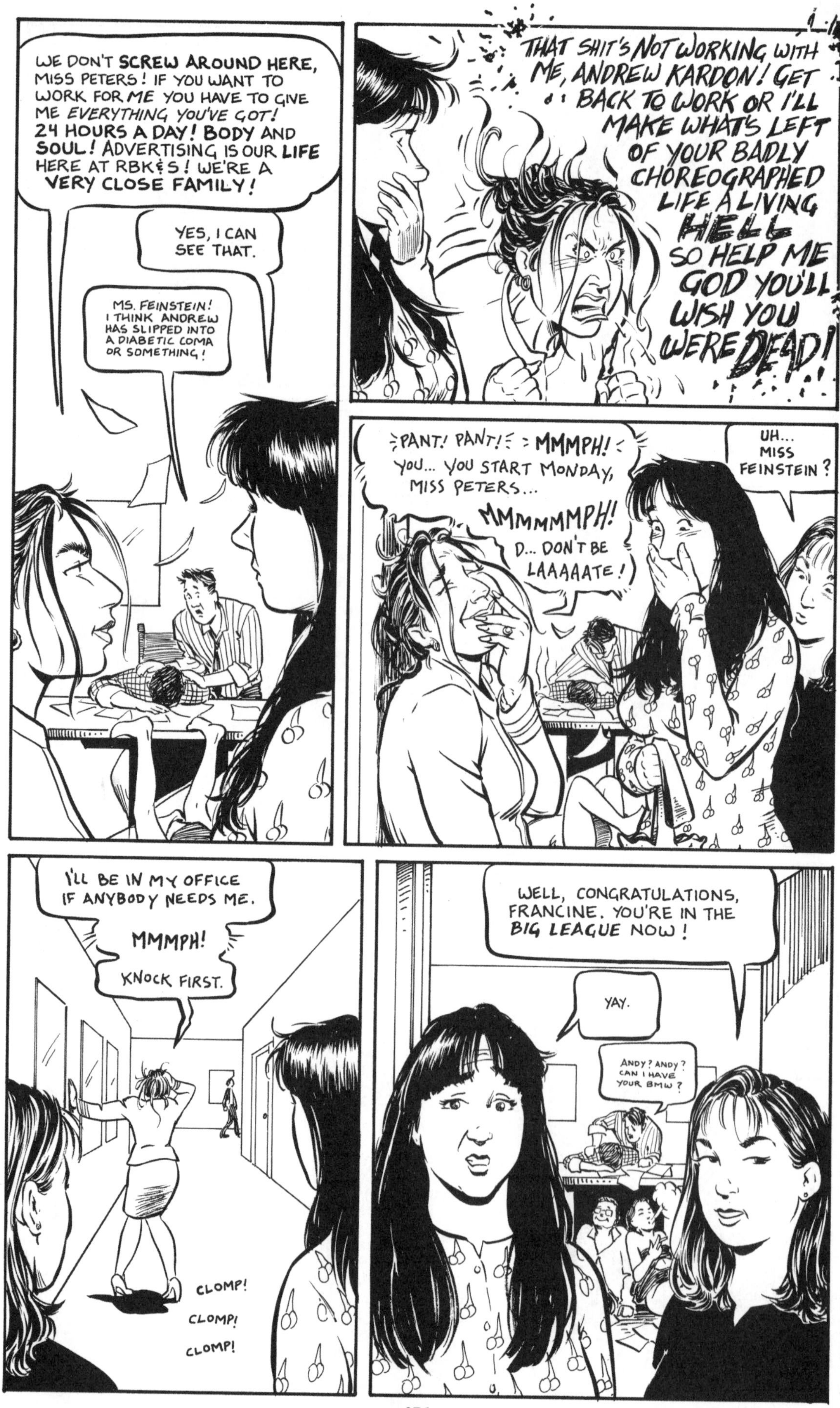
WE DON'T SCREW AROUND HERE, MISS PETERS! IF YOU WANT TO WORK FOR ME YOU HAVE TO GIVE ME EVERYTHING YOU'VE GOT! 24 HOURS A DAY! BODY AND SOUL! ADVERTISING IS OUR LIFE HERE AT RBK&S! WE'RE A VERY CLOSE FAMILY!
YES, I CAN SEE THAT.
MS. FEINSTEIN! I THINK ANDREW HAS SLIPPED INTO A DIABETIC COMA OR SOMETHING!
THAT SHIT'S NOT WORKING WITH ME, ANDREW KARDON! GET BACK TO WORK OR I'LL MAKE WHAT'S LEFT OF YOUR BADLY CHOREOGRAPHED LIFE A LIVING HELL SO HELP ME GOD YOU'LL WISH YOU WERE DEAD!
PANT! PANT! MMMPH! YOU... YOU START MONDAY, MISS PETERS...
MMMMMMPH! D... DON'T BE LAAAAATE!
UH... MISS FEINSTEIN?
I'LL BE IN MY OFFICE IF ANYBODY NEEDS ME.
MMMPH!
KNOCK FIRST.
CLOMP!
CLOMP!
CLOMP!
WELL, CONGRATULATIONS, FRANCINE. YOU'RE IN THE BIG LEAGUE NOW!
YAY.
ANDY? ANDY? CAN I HAVE YOUR BMW?

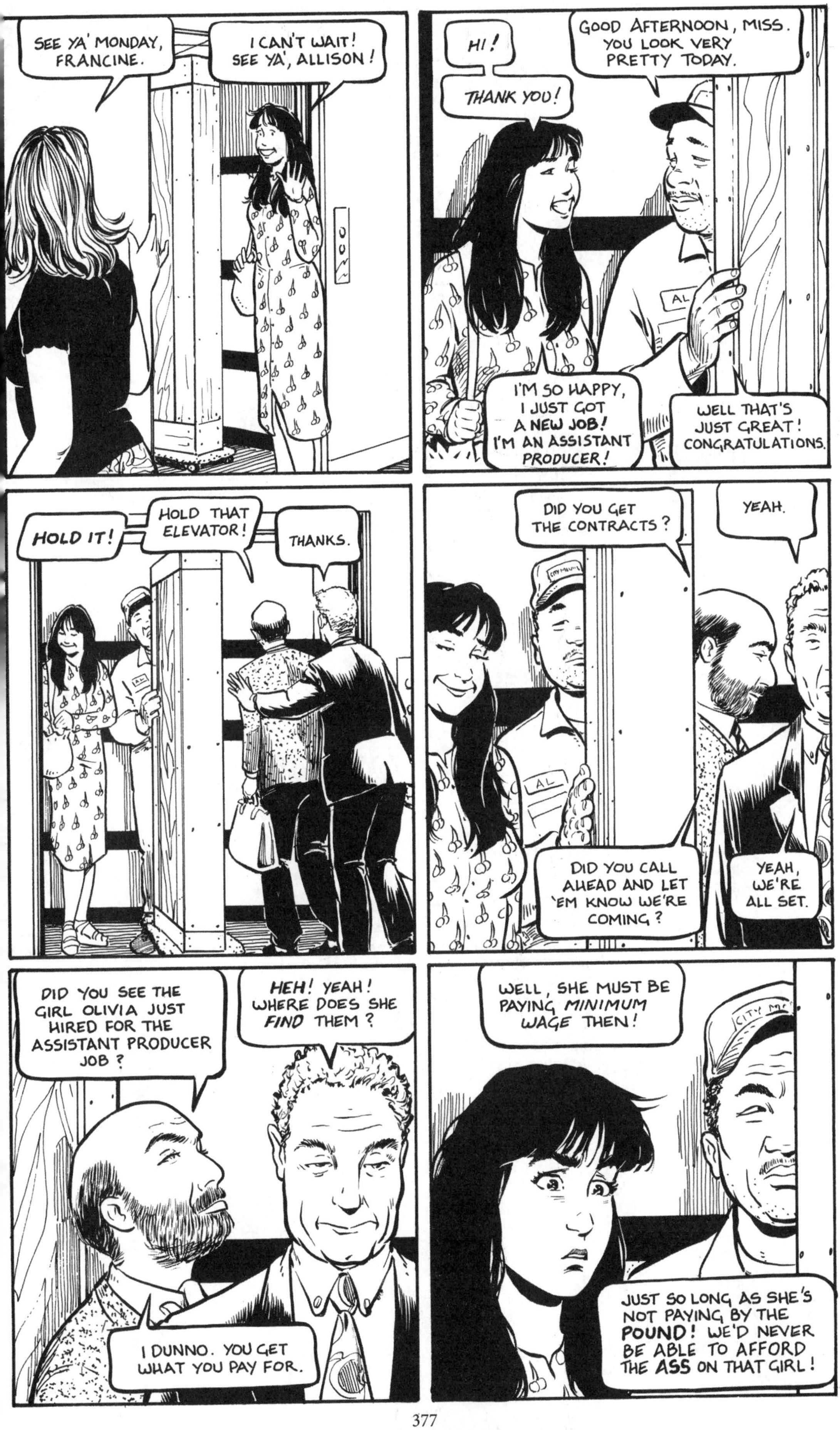
SEE YA' MONDAY, FRANCINE.
I CAN'T WAIT! SEE YA', ALLISON!
HI!
THANK YOU!
GOOD AFTERNOON, MISS. YOU LOOK VERY PRETTY TODAY.
I'M SO HAPPY, I JUST GOT A NEW JOB! I'M AN ASSISTANT PRODUCER!
WELL THAT'S JUST GREAT! CONGRATULATIONS.
HOLD IT!
HOLD THAT ELEVATOR!
THANKS.
DID YOU GET THE CONTRACTS?
YEAH.
DID YOU CALL AHEAD AND LET 'EM KNOW WE'RE COMING?
YEAH, WE'RE ALL SET.
DID YOU SEE THE GIRL OLIVIA JUST HIRED FOR THE ASSISTANT PRODUCER JOB?
HEH! YEAH! WHERE DOES SHE FIND THEM?
I DUNNO. YOU GET WHAT YOU PAY FOR.
WELL, SHE MUST BE PAYING MINIMUM WAGE THEN!
JUST SO LONG AS SHE'S NOT PAYING BY THE POUND! WE'D NEVER BE ABLE TO AFFORD THE ASS ON THAT GIRL!

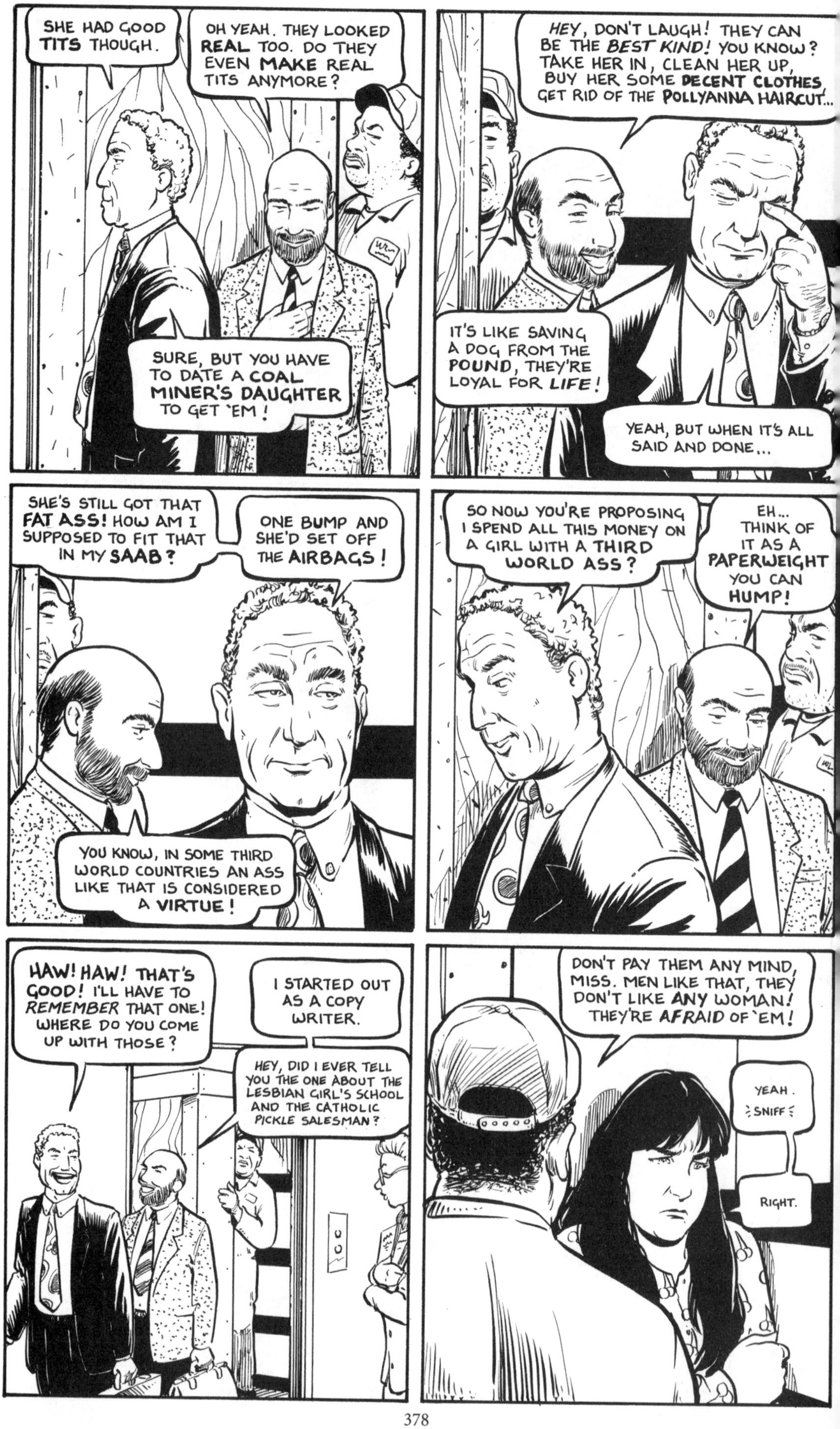
SHE HAD GOOD TITS THOUGH.
OH YEAH. THEY LOOKED REAL TOO. DO THEY EVEN MAKE REAL TITS ANYMORE?
SURE, BUT YOU HAVE TO DATE A COAL MINER'S DAUGHTER TO GET 'EM!
HEY, DON'T LAUGH! THEY CAN BE THE BEST KIND! YOU KNOW? TAKE HER IN, CLEAN HER UP, BUY HER SOME DECENT CLOTHES GET RID OF THE POLLYANNA HAIRCUT...
IT'S LIKE SAVING A DOG FROM THE POUND, THEY'RE LOYAL FOR LIFE!
YEAH, BUT WHEN IT'S ALL SAID AND DONE...
SHE'S STILL GOT THAT FAT ASS! HOW AM I SUPPOSED TO FIT THAT IN MY SAAB?
ONE BUMP AND SHE'D SET OFF THE AIRBAGS!
YOU KNOW, IN SOME THIRD WORLD COUNTRIES AN ASS LIKE THAT IS CONSIDERED A VIRTUE!
SO NOW YOU'RE PROPOSING I SPEND ALL THIS MONEY ON A GIRL WITH A THIRD WORLD ASS?
EH... THINK OF IT AS A PAPERWEIGHT YOU CAN HUMP!
HAW! HAW! THAT'S GOOD! I'LL HAVE TO REMEMBER THAT ONE! WHERE DO YOU COME UP WITH THOSE?
I STARTED OUT AS A COPY WRITER.
HEY, DID I EVER TELL YOU THE ONE ABOUT THE LESBIAN GIRL'S SCHOOL AND THE CATHOLIC PICKLE SALESMAN?
DON'T PAY THEM ANY MIND, MISS. MEN LIKE THAT, THEY DON'T LIKE ANY WOMAN! THEY'RE AFRAID OF 'EM!
YEAH.
SNIFF
RIGHT.

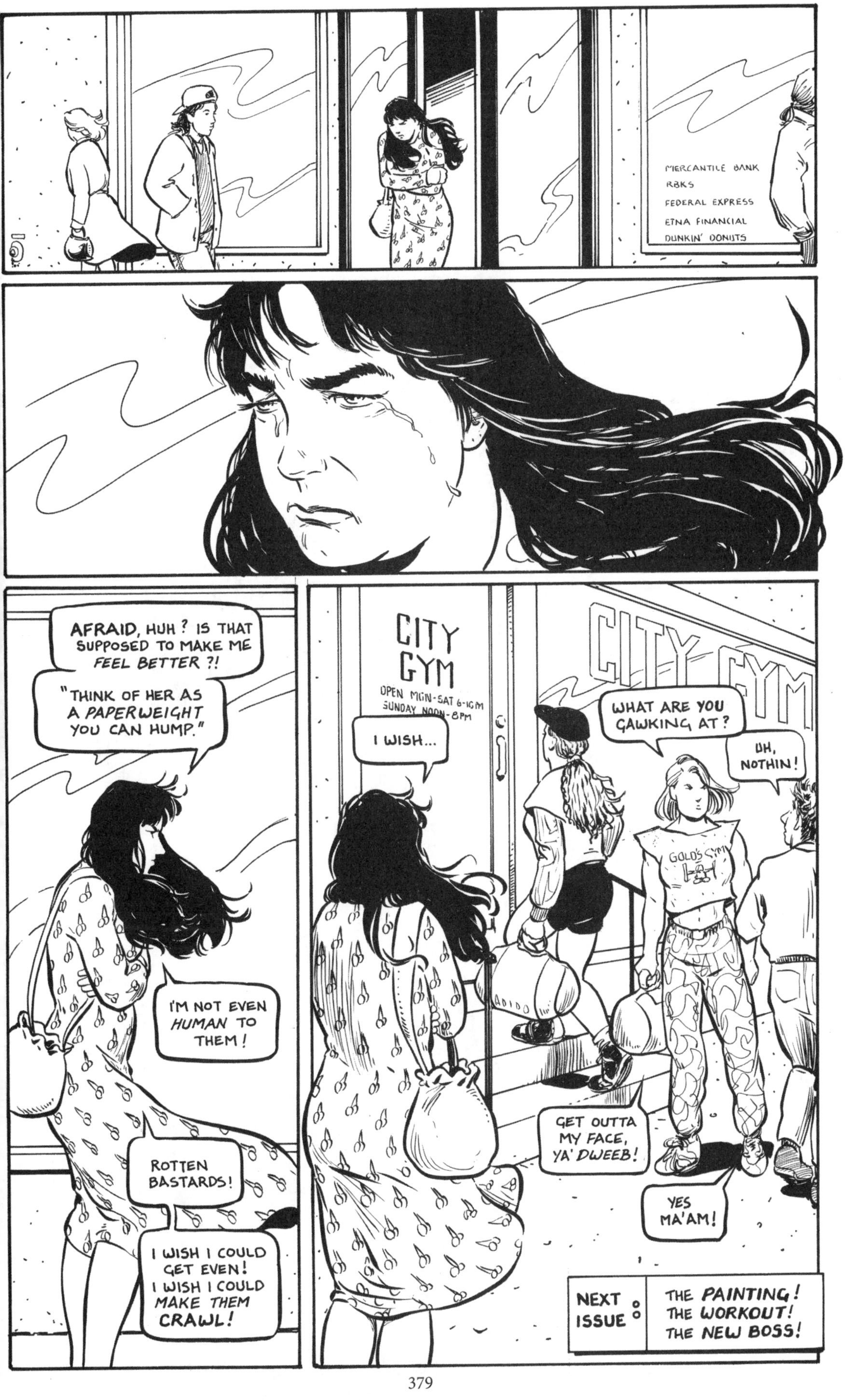
MERCANTILE BANK
RBKS
FEDERAL EXPRESS
ETNA FINANCIAL
DUNKIN' DONUTS
AFRAID, HUH? IS THAT SUPPOSED TO MAKE ME FEEL BETTER?!
"THINK OF HER AS A PAPERWEIGHT YOU CAN HUMP."
I'M NOT EVEN HUMAN TO THEM!
ROTTEN BASTARDS!
I WISH I COULD GET EVEN! I WISH I COULD MAKE THEM CRAWL!
CITY GYM
OPEN MON-SAT 6-10PM
SUNDAY NOON-8PM
CITY GYM
I WISH...
WHAT ARE YOU GAWKING AT?
UH, NOTHIN!
GOLD'S GYM
GET OUTTA MY FACE, YA' DWEEB!
YES MA'AM!
NEXT ISSUE:
THE PAINTING! THE WORKOUT! THE NEW BOSS!

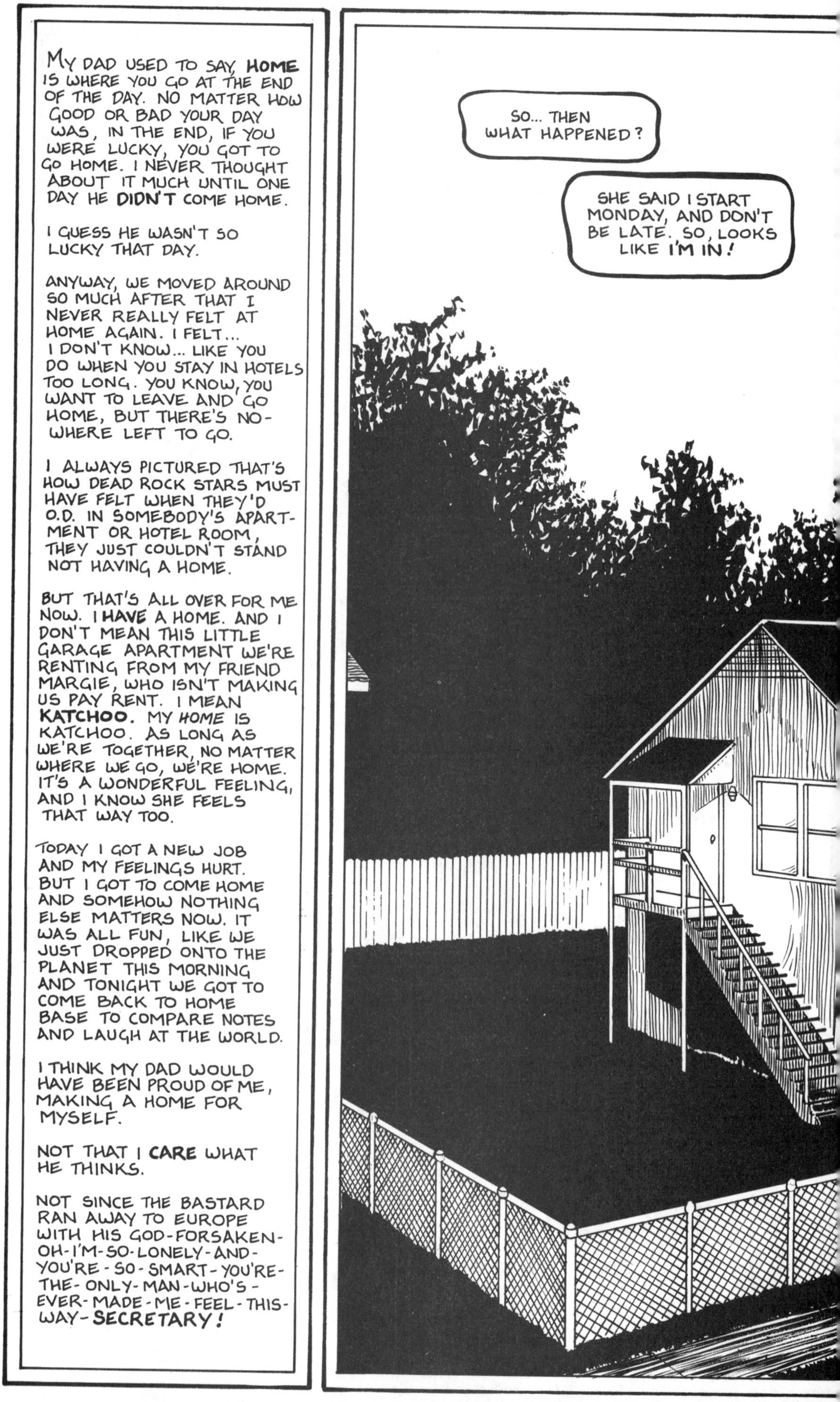
MY DAD USED TO SAY, HOME IS WHERE YOU GO AT THE END OF THE DAY. NO MATTER HOW GOOD OR BAD YOUR DAY WAS, IN THE END, IF YOU WERE LUCKY, YOU GOT TO GO HOME. I NEVER THOUGHT ABOUT IT MUCH UNTIL ONE DAY HE DIDN'T COME HOME.
I GUESS HE WASN'T SO LUCKY THAT DAY.
ANYWAY, WE MOVED AROUND SO MUCH AFTER THAT I NEVER REALLY FELT AT HOME AGAIN. I FELT... I DON'T KNOW... LIKE YOU DO WHEN YOU STAY IN HOTELS TOO LONG. YOU KNOW, YOU WANT TO LEAVE AND GO HOME, BUT THERE'S NO-WHERE LEFT TO GO.
I ALWAYS PICTURED THAT'S HOW DEAD ROCK STARS MUST HAVE FELT WHEN THEY'D O.D. IN SOMEBODY'S APART-MENT OR HOTEL ROOM, THEY JUST COULDN'T STAND NOT HAVING A HOME.
BUT THAT'S ALL OVER FOR ME NOW. I HAVE A HOME. AND I DON'T MEAN THIS LITTLE GARAGE APARTMENT WE'RE RENTING FROM MY FRIEND MARGIE, WHO ISN'T MAKING US PAY RENT. I MEAN KATCHOO. MY HOME IS KATCHOO. AS LONG AS WE'RE TOGETHER, NO MATTER WHERE WE GO, WE'RE HOME. IT'S A WONDERFUL FEELING, AND I KNOW SHE FEELS THAT WAY TOO.
TODAY I GOT A NEW JOB AND MY FEELINGS HURT. BUT I GOT TO COME HOME AND SOMEHOW NOTHING ELSE MATTERS NOW. IT WAS ALL FUN, LIKE WE JUST DROPPED ONTO THE PLANET THIS MORNING AND TONIGHT WE GOT TO COME BACK TO HOME BASE TO COMPARE NOTES AND LAUGH AT THE WORLD.
I THINK MY DAD WOULD HAVE BEEN PROUD OF ME, MAKING A HOME FOR MYSELF.
NOT THAT I CARE WHAT HE THINKS.
NOT SINCE THE BASTARD RAN AWAY TO EUROPE WITH HIS GOD-FORSAKEN-OH-I'M-SO-LONELY-AND-YOU'RE-SO-SMART-YOU'RE-THE-ONLY-MAN-WHO'S-EVER-MADE-ME-FEEL-THIS-WAY-SECRETARY!
SO... THEN WHAT HAPPENED?
SHE SAID I START MONDAY, AND DON'T BE LATE. SO, LOOKS LIKE I'M IN!

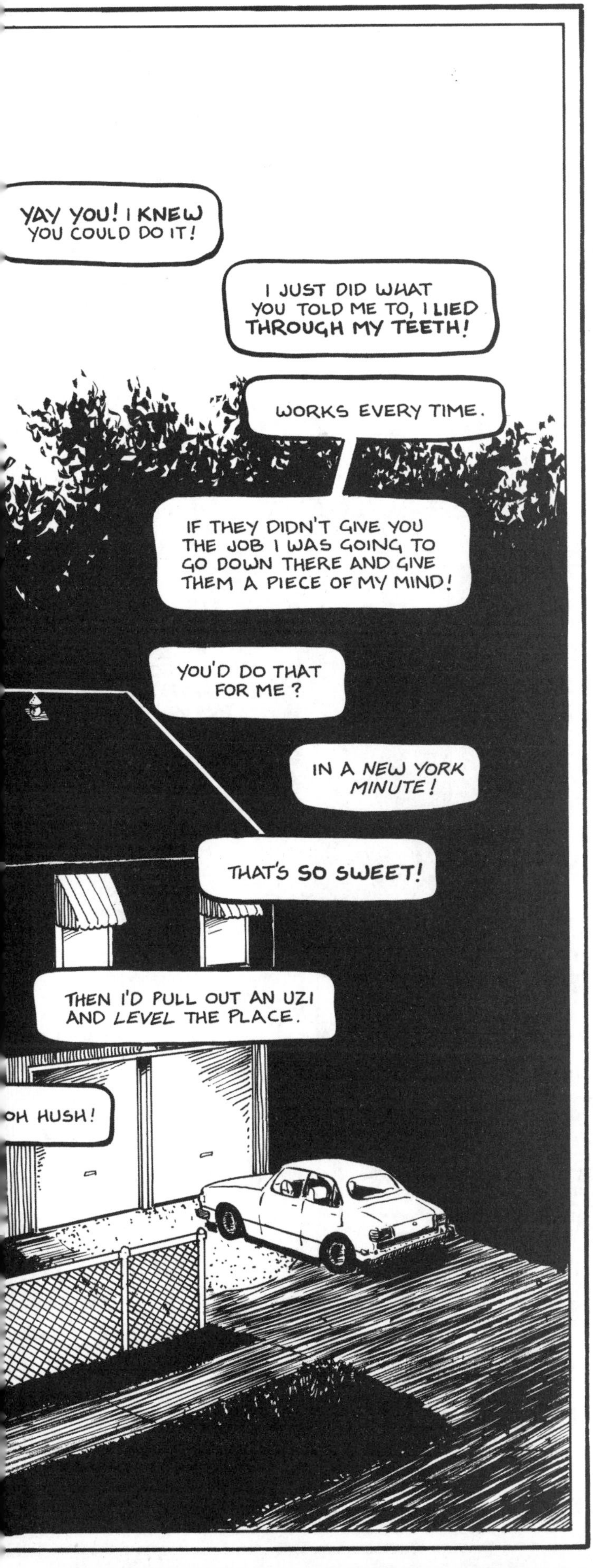
YAY YOU! I KNEW YOU COULD DO IT!
I JUST DID WHAT YOU TOLD ME TO, I LIED THROUGH MY TEETH!
WORKS EVERY TIME.
IF THEY DIDN'T GIVE YOU THE JOB I WAS GOING TO GO DOWN THERE AND GIVE THEM A PIECE OF MY MIND!
YOU'D DO THAT FOR ME?
IN A NEW YORK MINUTE!
THAT'S SO SWEET!
THEN I'D PULL OUT AN UZI AND LEVEL THE PLACE.
OH HUSH!

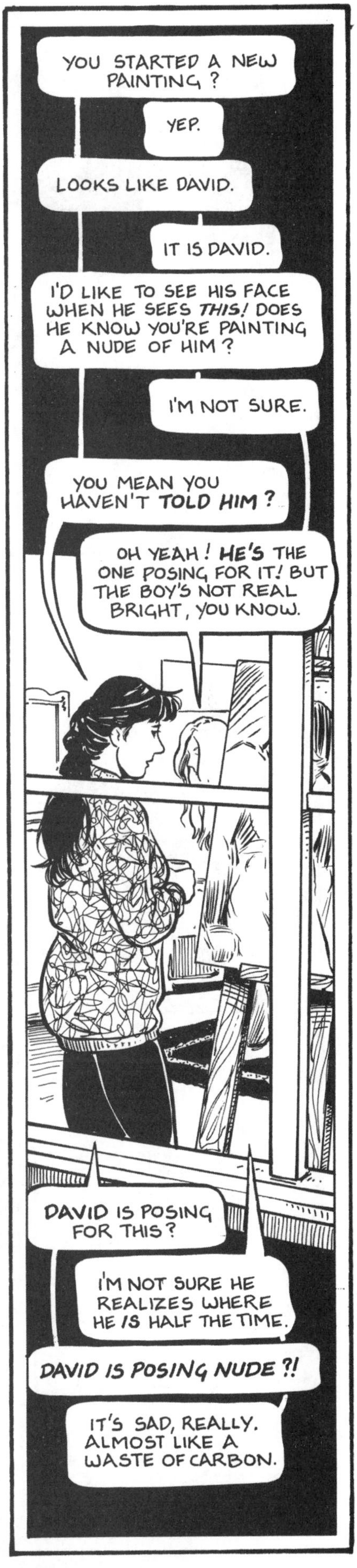
YOU STARTED A NEW PAINTING?
YEP.
LOOKS LIKE DAVID.
IT IS DAVID.
I'D LIKE TO SEE HIS FACE WHEN HE SEES THIS! DOES HE KNOW YOU'RE PAINTING A NUDE OF HIM?
I'M NOT SURE.
YOU MEAN YOU HAVEN'T TOLD HIM?
OH YEAH! HE'S THE ONE POSING FOR IT! BUT THE BOY'S NOT REAL BRIGHT, YOU KNOW.
DAVID IS POSING FOR THIS?
I'M NOT SURE HE REALIZES WHERE HE IS HALF THE TIME.
DAVID IS POSING NUDE?!
IT'S SAD, REALLY. ALMOST LIKE A WASTE OF CARBON.

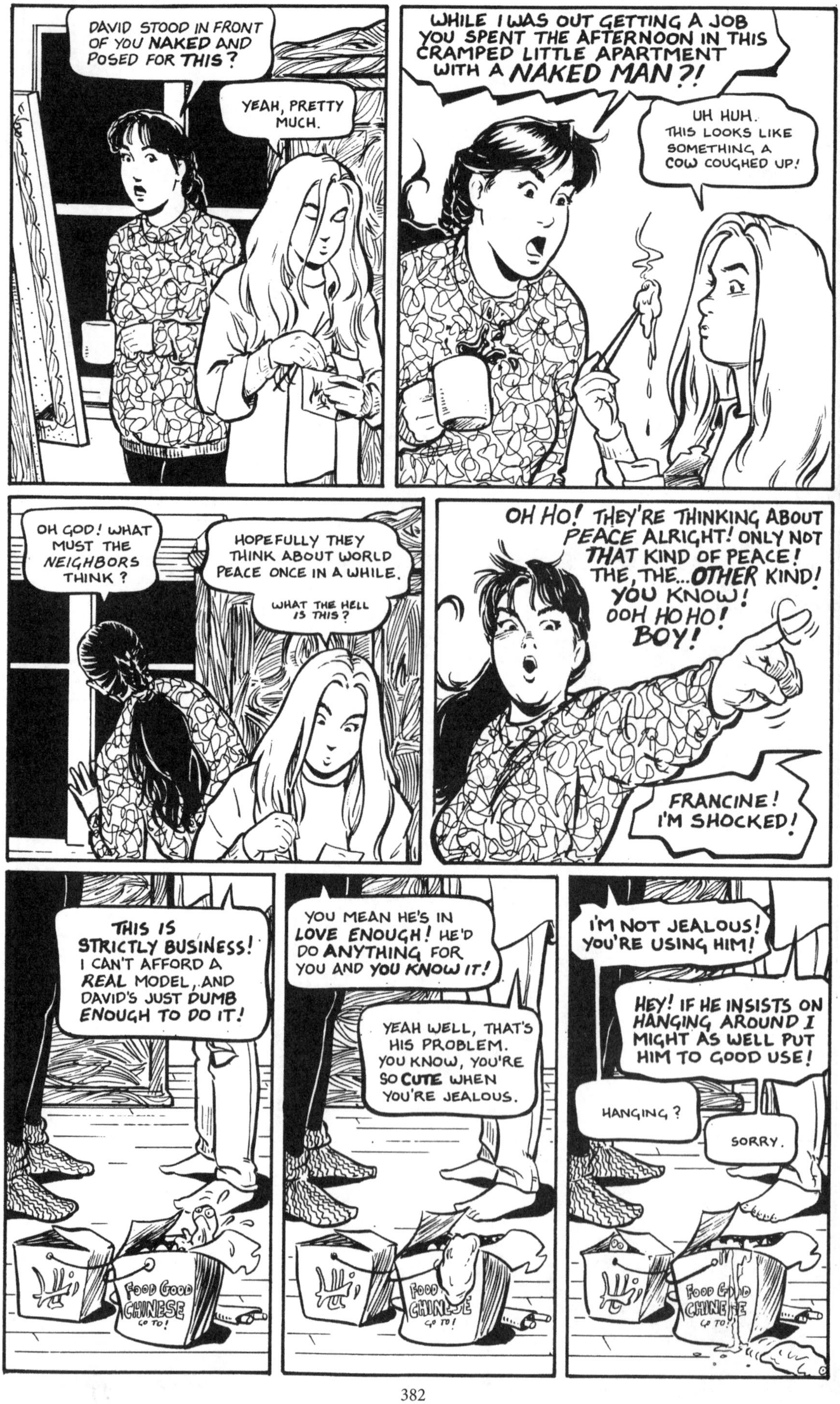
DAVID STOOD IN FRONT OF YOU NAKED AND POSED FOR THIS?
YEAH, PRETTY MUCH.
WHILE I WAS OUT GETTING A JOB YOU SPENT THE AFTERNOON IN THIS CRAMPED LITTLE APARTMENT WITH A NAKED MAN?!
UH HUH. THIS LOOKS LIKE SOMETHING A COW COUGHED UP!
OH GOD! WHAT MUST THE NEIGHBORS THINK?
HOPEFULLY THEY THINK ABOUT WORLD PEACE ONCE IN A WHILE.
WHAT THE HELL IS THIS?
OH HO! THEY'RE THINKING ABOUT PEACE ALRIGHT! ONLY NOT THAT KIND OF PEACE! THE, THE...OTHER KIND! YOU KNOW! OOH HO HO! BOY!
FRANCINE! I'M SHOCKED!
THIS IS STRICTLY BUSINESS! I CAN'T AFFORD A REAL MODEL, AND DAVID'S JUST DUMB ENOUGH TO DO IT!
FOOD GOOD CHINESE GO TO!
YOU MEAN HE'S IN LOVE ENOUGH! HE'D DO ANYTHING FOR YOU AND YOU KNOW IT!
YEAH WELL, THAT'S HIS PROBLEM. YOU KNOW, YOU'RE SO CUTE WHEN YOU'RE JEALOUS.
I'M NOT JEALOUS! YOU'RE USING HIM!
HEY! IF HE INSISTS ON HANGING AROUND I MIGHT AS WELL PUT HIM TO GOOD USE!
HANGING?
SORRY.

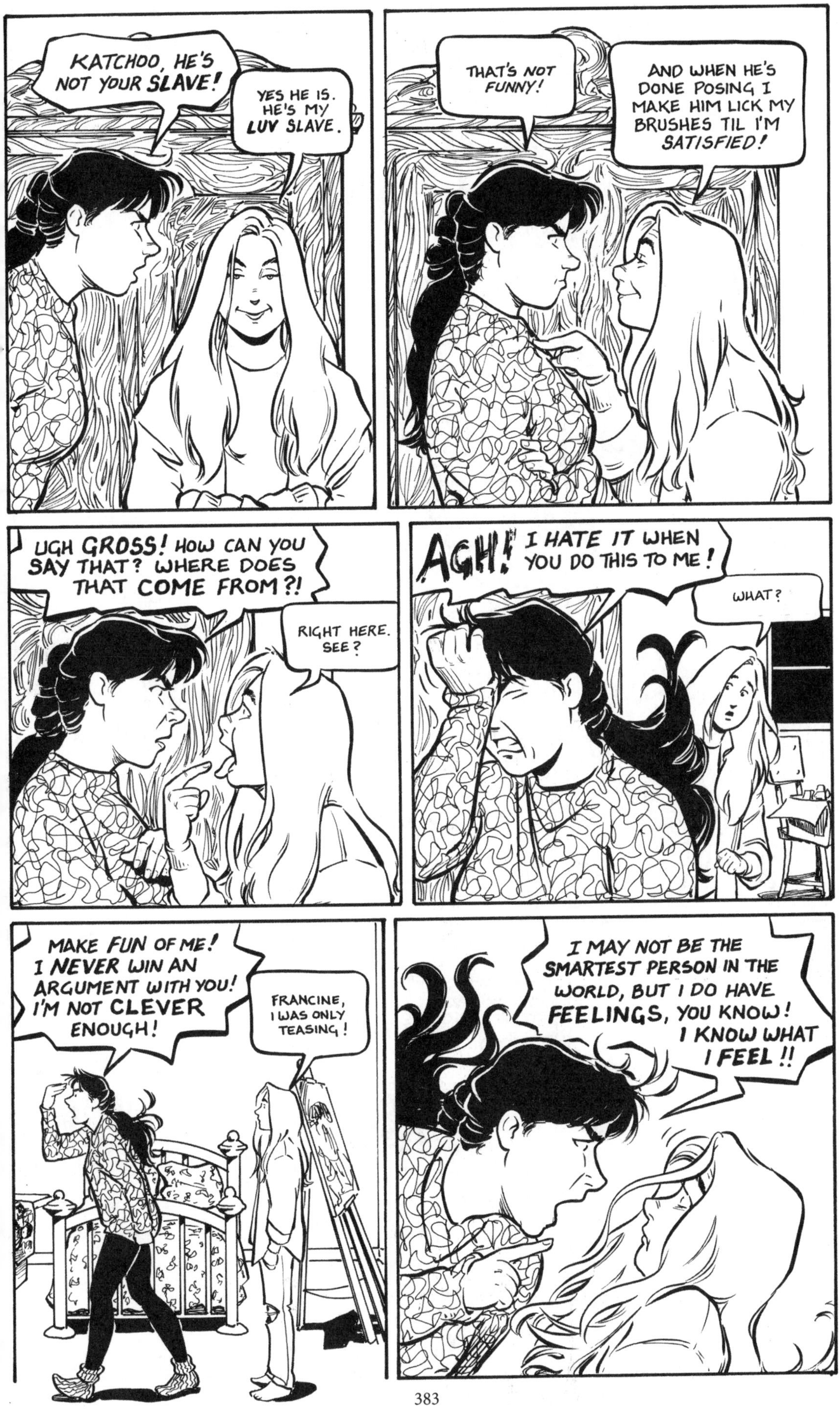
KATCHOO, HE'S NOT YOUR SLAVE!
YES HE IS. HE'S MY LUV SLAVE.
THAT'S NOT FUNNY!
AND WHEN HE'S DONE POSING I MAKE HIM LICK MY BRUSHES TIL I'M SATISFIED!
UGH GROSS! HOW CAN YOU SAY THAT? WHERE DOES THAT COME FROM?!
RIGHT HERE. SEE?
AGH! I HATE IT WHEN YOU DO THIS TO ME!
WHAT?
MAKE FUN OF ME! I NEVER WIN AN ARGUMENT WITH YOU! I'M NOT CLEVER ENOUGH!
FRANCINE, I WAS ONLY TEASING!
I MAY NOT BE THE SMARTEST PERSON IN THE WORLD, BUT I DO HAVE FEELINGS, YOU KNOW! I KNOW WHAT I FEEL!!

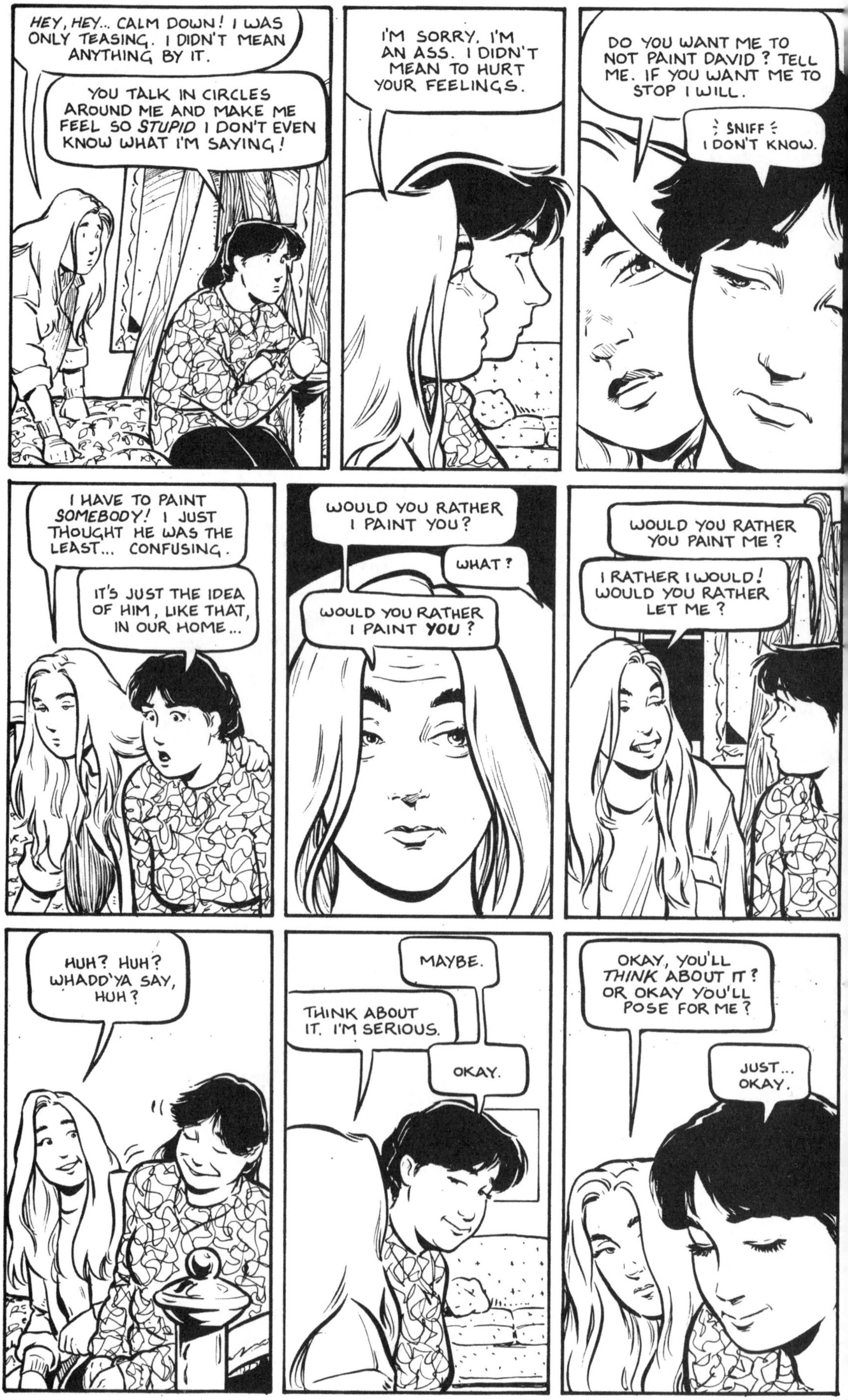
HEY, HEY... CALM DOWN! I WAS ONLY TEASING. I DIDN'T MEAN ANYTHING BY IT.
YOU TALK IN CIRCLES AROUND ME AND MAKE ME FEEL SO *STUPID* I DON'T EVEN KNOW WHAT I'M SAYING!
I'M SORRY, I'M AN ASS. I DIDN'T MEAN TO HURT YOUR FEELINGS.
DO YOU WANT ME TO NOT PAINT DAVID? TELL ME. IF YOU WANT ME TO STOP I WILL.
SNIFF I DON'T KNOW.
I HAVE TO PAINT *SOMEBODY*! I JUST THOUGHT HE WAS THE LEAST... CONFUSING.
IT'S JUST THE IDEA OF HIM, LIKE THAT, IN OUR HOME...
WOULD YOU RATHER I PAINT YOU?
WHAT?
WOULD YOU RATHER I PAINT **YOU**?
WOULD YOU RATHER YOU PAINT ME?
I RATHER I WOULD! WOULD YOU RATHER LET ME?
HUH? HUH? WHADD'YA SAY, HUH?
THINK ABOUT IT. I'M SERIOUS.
MAYBE.
OKAY.
OKAY, YOU'LL *THINK* ABOUT IT? OR OKAY YOU'LL POSE FOR ME?
JUST... OKAY.

WELL, WHEN YOU FIGURE OUT WHAT YOU WANT, LET ME KNOW, OKAY?

MMHMM.

OKAY.

OKAY.

MY LAST YEAR OF HIGH SCHOOL I WAS IN THE SENIOR PLAY AND MISSED MY CUE EVERY NIGHT. IT MADE EVERYBODY SO MAD. I ACTED LIKE I DIDN'T CARE, BUT I DID. I CARED MORE THAN ANYTHING IN THE WORLD. IT JUST ALL HAPPENED TOO FAST FOR ME, THAT'S ALL.

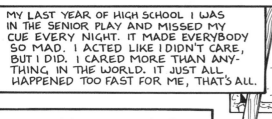

EVERYTHING HAPPENS *SO FAST*, IT'S HARD TO KEEP UP.

BUT, SOMETIMES I GO SLOW ON PURPOSE. WHEN IT'S *REALLY* IMPORTANT, I TAKE MY TIME.

AND YOU KNOW WHAT? THE REAL THINGS... THE THINGS THAT *LAST*... THEY *WAIT* FOR YOU.

SOMETIMES THAT'S THE ONLY WAY I CAN TELL IF SOMETHING'S *REAL* OR NOT. I GO *REAL SLOW*, AND IF IT STAYS WITH ME, I KNOW IT'S FOR REAL.

UNLIKE MY *BASTARD DAD*, WHO'S TRAMPING ALL OVER EUROPE WITH THE INFLATABLE DOLL *HE* CALLED A SECRETARY!

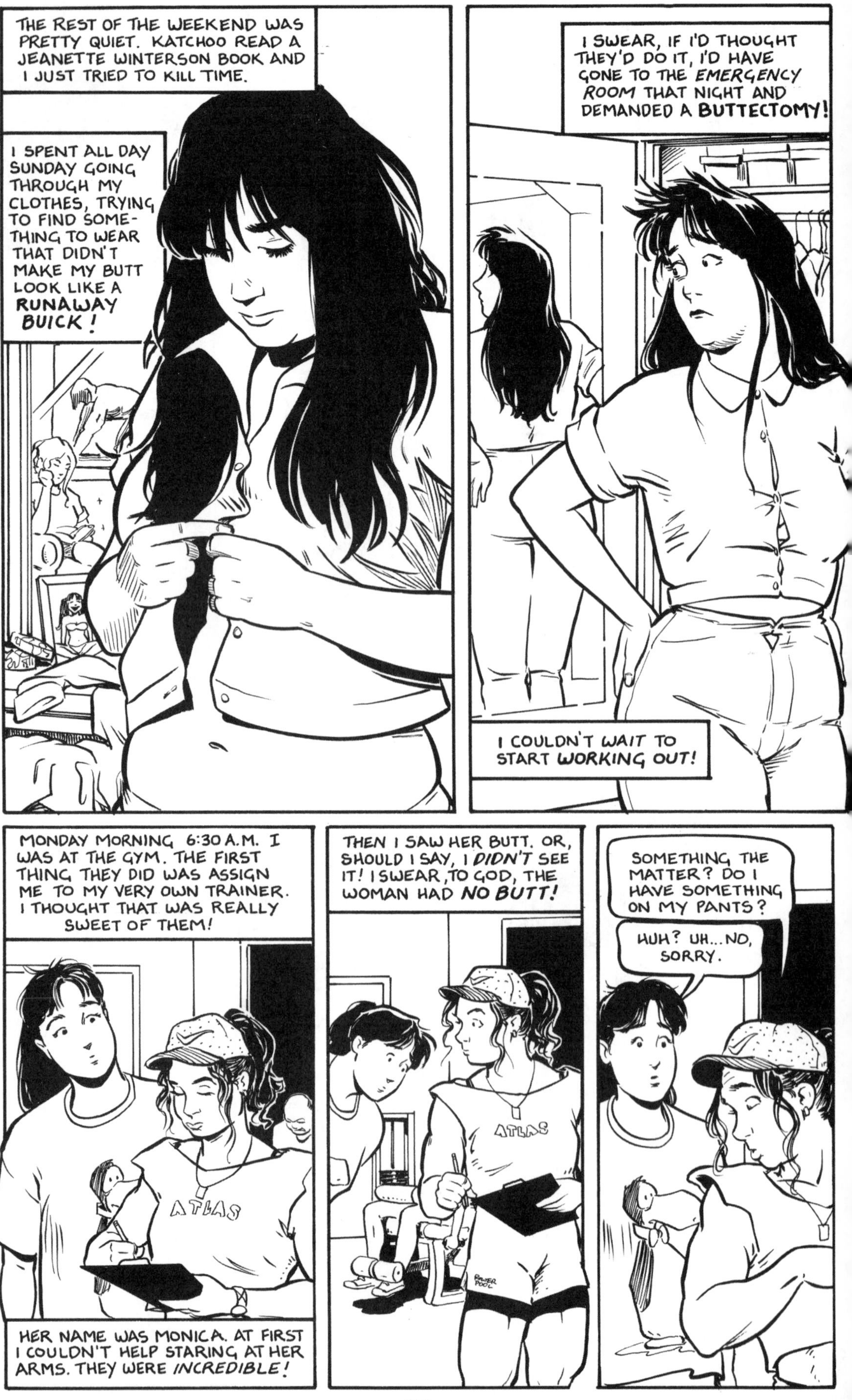

THE REST OF THE WEEKEND WAS PRETTY QUIET. KATCHOO READ A JEANETTE WINTERSON BOOK AND I JUST TRIED TO KILL TIME.
I SPENT ALL DAY SUNDAY GOING THROUGH MY CLOTHES, TRYING TO FIND SOMETHING TO WEAR THAT DIDN'T MAKE MY BUTT LOOK LIKE A **RUNAWAY BUICK!**
I SWEAR, IF I'D THOUGHT THEY'D DO IT, I'D HAVE GONE TO THE *EMERGENCY ROOM* THAT NIGHT AND DEMANDED A **BUTTECTOMY!**
I COULDN'T *WAIT* TO START **WORKING OUT!**
MONDAY MORNING 6:30 A.M. I WAS AT THE GYM. THE FIRST THING THEY DID WAS ASSIGN ME TO MY VERY OWN TRAINER. I THOUGHT THAT WAS REALLY SWEET OF THEM!
ATLAS
HER NAME WAS MONICA. AT FIRST I COULDN'T HELP STARING AT HER ARMS. THEY WERE *INCREDIBLE!*
THEN I SAW HER BUTT. OR, SHOULD I SAY, I *DIDN'T* SEE IT! I SWEAR, TO GOD, THE WOMAN HAD **NO BUTT!**
ATLAS
POWER POOL
SOMETHING THE MATTER? DO I HAVE SOMETHING ON MY PANTS?
HUH? UH... NO, SORRY.

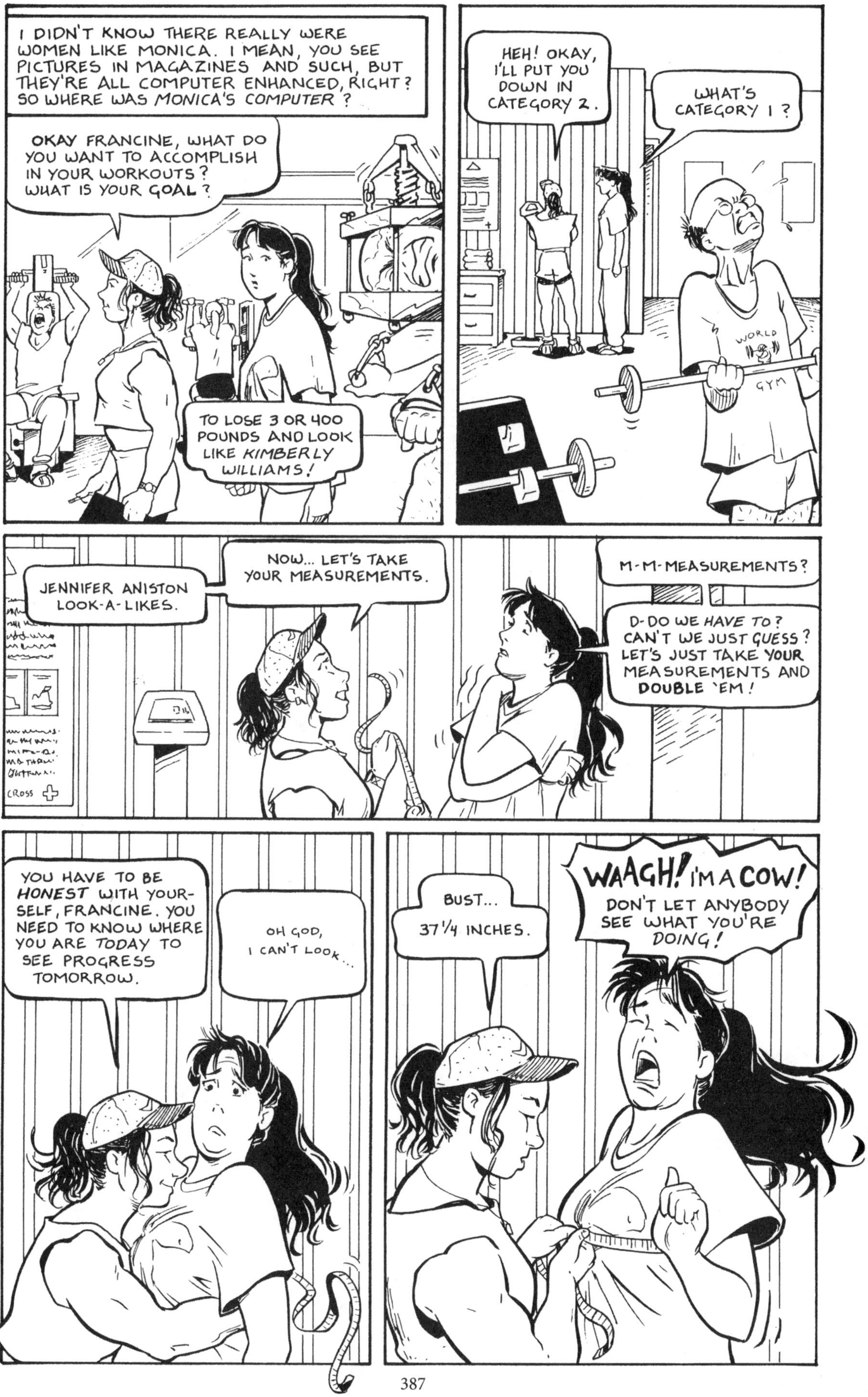

I DIDN'T KNOW THERE REALLY WERE WOMEN LIKE MONICA. I MEAN, YOU SEE PICTURES IN MAGAZINES AND SUCH, BUT THEY'RE ALL COMPUTER ENHANCED, RIGHT? SO WHERE WAS *MONICA'S COMPUTER*?
OKAY FRANCINE, WHAT DO YOU WANT TO ACCOMPLISH IN YOUR WORKOUTS? WHAT IS YOUR **GOAL**?
TO LOSE 3 OR 400 POUNDS AND LOOK LIKE *KIMBERLY WILLIAMS*!
HEH! OKAY, I'LL PUT YOU DOWN IN CATEGORY 2.
WHAT'S CATEGORY 1?
WORLD GYM
JENNIFER ANISTON LOOK-A-LIKES.
NOW... LET'S TAKE YOUR MEASUREMENTS.
CROSS
M-M-MEASUREMENTS?
D-DO WE *HAVE TO*? CAN'T WE JUST *GUESS*? LET'S JUST TAKE **YOUR** MEASUREMENTS AND **DOUBLE** 'EM!
YOU HAVE TO BE ***HONEST*** WITH YOURSELF, FRANCINE. YOU NEED TO KNOW WHERE YOU ARE *TODAY* TO SEE PROGRESS TOMORROW.
OH GOD, I CAN'T LOOK...
BUST... 37¼ INCHES.
WAAGH! I'M A **COW!** DON'T LET ANYBODY SEE WHAT YOU'RE *DOING*!

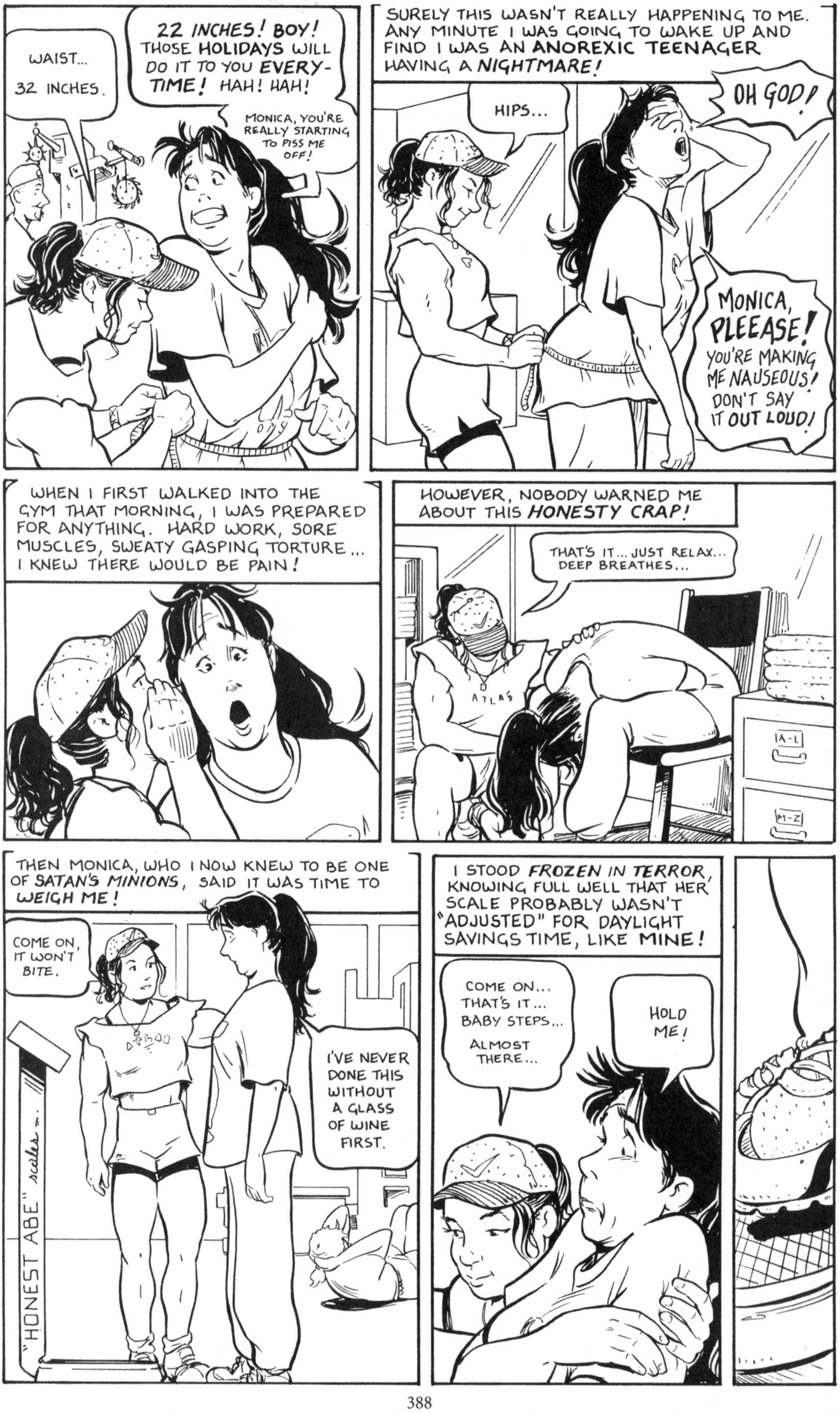
WAIST... 32 INCHES.
22 INCHES! BOY! THOSE HOLIDAYS WILL DO IT TO YOU EVERY-TIME! HAH! HAH!
MONICA, YOU'RE REALLY STARTING TO PISS ME OFF!
SURELY THIS WASN'T REALLY HAPPENING TO ME. ANY MINUTE I WAS GOING TO WAKE UP AND FIND I WAS AN ANOREXIC TEENAGER HAVING A NIGHTMARE!
HIPS...
OH GOD!
MONICA, PLEEASE! YOU'RE MAKING ME NAUSEOUS! DON'T SAY IT OUT LOUD!
WHEN I FIRST WALKED INTO THE GYM THAT MORNING, I WAS PREPARED FOR ANYTHING. HARD WORK, SORE MUSCLES, SWEATY GASPING TORTURE... I KNEW THERE WOULD BE PAIN!
HOWEVER, NOBODY WARNED ME ABOUT THIS HONESTY CRAP!
THAT'S IT... JUST RELAX... DEEP BREATHES...
ATLAS
A-L
M-Z
THEN MONICA, WHO I NOW KNEW TO BE ONE OF SATAN'S MINIONS, SAID IT WAS TIME TO WEIGH ME!
COME ON, IT WON'T BITE.
I'VE NEVER DONE THIS WITHOUT A GLASS OF WINE FIRST.
"HONEST ABE" scales
I STOOD FROZEN IN TERROR, KNOWING FULL WELL THAT HER SCALE PROBABLY WASN'T "ADJUSTED" FOR DAYLIGHT SAVINGS TIME, LIKE MINE!
COME ON... THAT'S IT... BABY STEPS... ALMOST THERE...
HOLD ME!

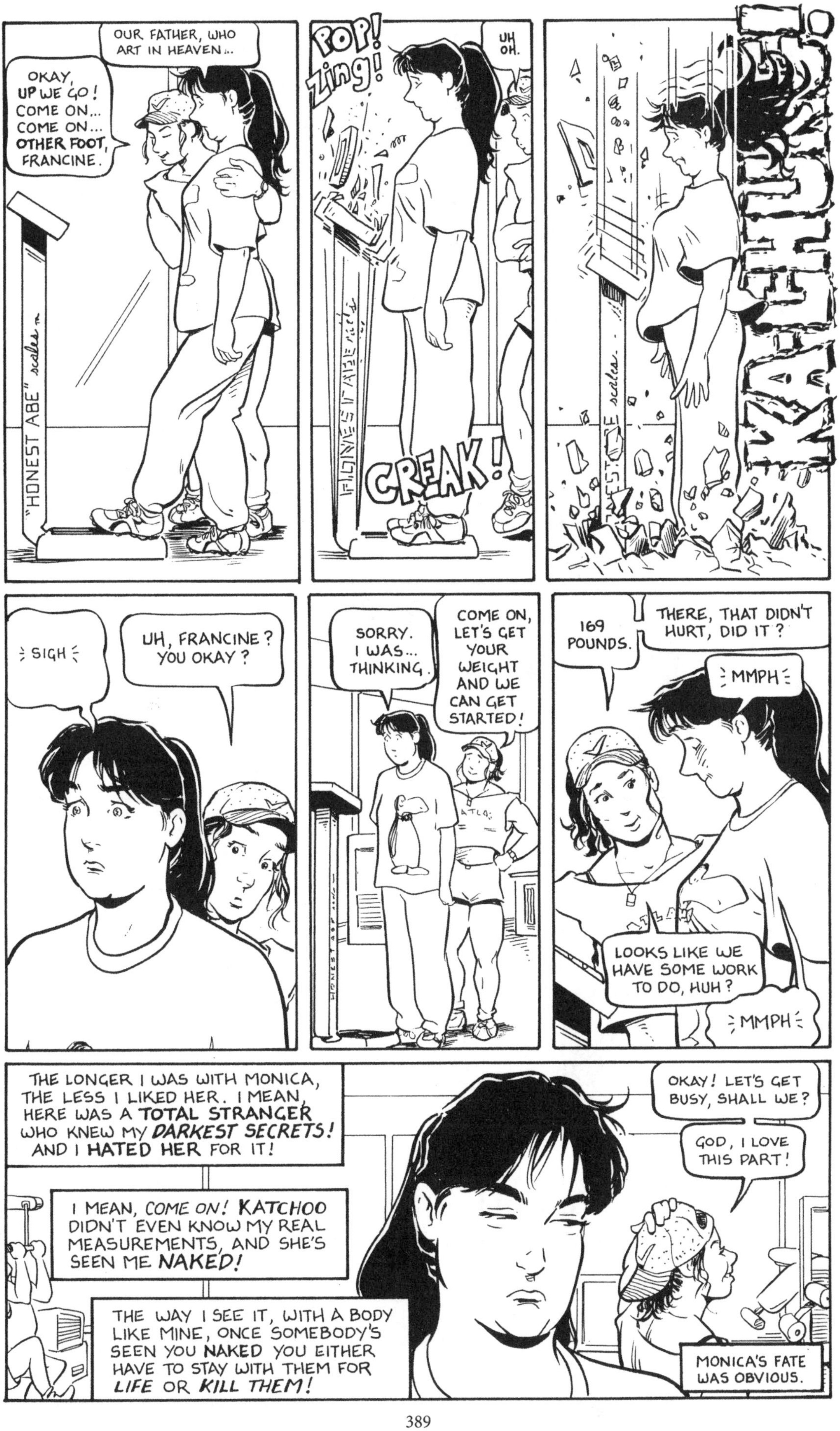
OUR FATHER, WHO ART IN HEAVEN...
OKAY, UP WE GO! COME ON... COME ON... OTHER FOOT, FRANCINE.
"HONEST ABE" scales
POP! zing!
UH OH.
CREAK!
KA-CHUNK!
SIGH
UH, FRANCINE? YOU OKAY?
SORRY. I WAS... THINKING.
COME ON, LET'S GET YOUR WEIGHT AND WE CAN GET STARTED!
169 POUNDS.
THERE, THAT DIDN'T HURT, DID IT?
MMPH
LOOKS LIKE WE HAVE SOME WORK TO DO, HUH?
MMPH
THE LONGER I WAS WITH MONICA, THE LESS I LIKED HER. I MEAN, HERE WAS A TOTAL STRANGER WHO KNEW MY DARKEST SECRETS! AND I HATED HER FOR IT!
I MEAN, COME ON! KATCHOO DIDN'T EVEN KNOW MY REAL MEASUREMENTS, AND SHE'S SEEN ME NAKED!
THE WAY I SEE IT, WITH A BODY LIKE MINE, ONCE SOMEBODY'S SEEN YOU NAKED YOU EITHER HAVE TO STAY WITH THEM FOR LIFE OR KILL THEM!
OKAY! LET'S GET BUSY, SHALL WE?
GOD, I LOVE THIS PART!
MONICA'S FATE WAS OBVIOUS.

BEING THE SWEET-NATURED GIRL THAT I AM, I RESOLVED TO LET MONICA LIVE LONG ENOUGH TO GET ME IN SHAPE. BUT AFTER THAT, IT WAS *CURTAINS!*

AT FIRST I PICTURED SOMETHING SUBTLE. SOMETHING SO **CLEVER** IN IT'S CONCEPT AND EXECUTION THAT NO OVERWEIGHT JURY WOULD *EVER CONVICT ME*, BUT INSTEAD WOULD PRAISE ME FOR MY *INGENUITY!*

BUT THEN, I'D NEED A *CALIFORNIA* JURY FOR THAT, WOULDN'T I?

HOWEVER, ALL MY MERCIFUL GOODWILL WENT OUT THE WINDOW ONCE MONICA BEGAN TORTURING ME WITH HER ARRAY OF *MANIACAL MACHINES!*

MONICA, PHONE.

HERE FRANCINE, TUG ON THIS TIL I GET BACK.

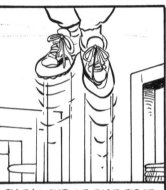

BY THE END OF THAT FIRST WORKOUT I DECIDED TO KILL MONICA WITH THE NEAREST BLUNT, HEAVY OBJECT AROUND...

MY BUTT!

THAT'S IT... I'D *SIT ON HER!* I'D SIT ON HER TIL SHE SCREAMED FOR MERCY AND POUNDED THE CARPET IN *RECIPROCAL PAIN!*

FIRST DAY?

HUH? OH...YEAH.

ME TOO.

INVIGORATING, ISN'T IT?

"LET ME LIVE!" SHE'D HOWL. *"DIE! YOU BUTTLESS FREAK!"* I'D SMILE, KNOWING MY MEASUREMENTS WERE SAFE ONCE MORE FROM THE *TYRANNY OF FITNESS!*

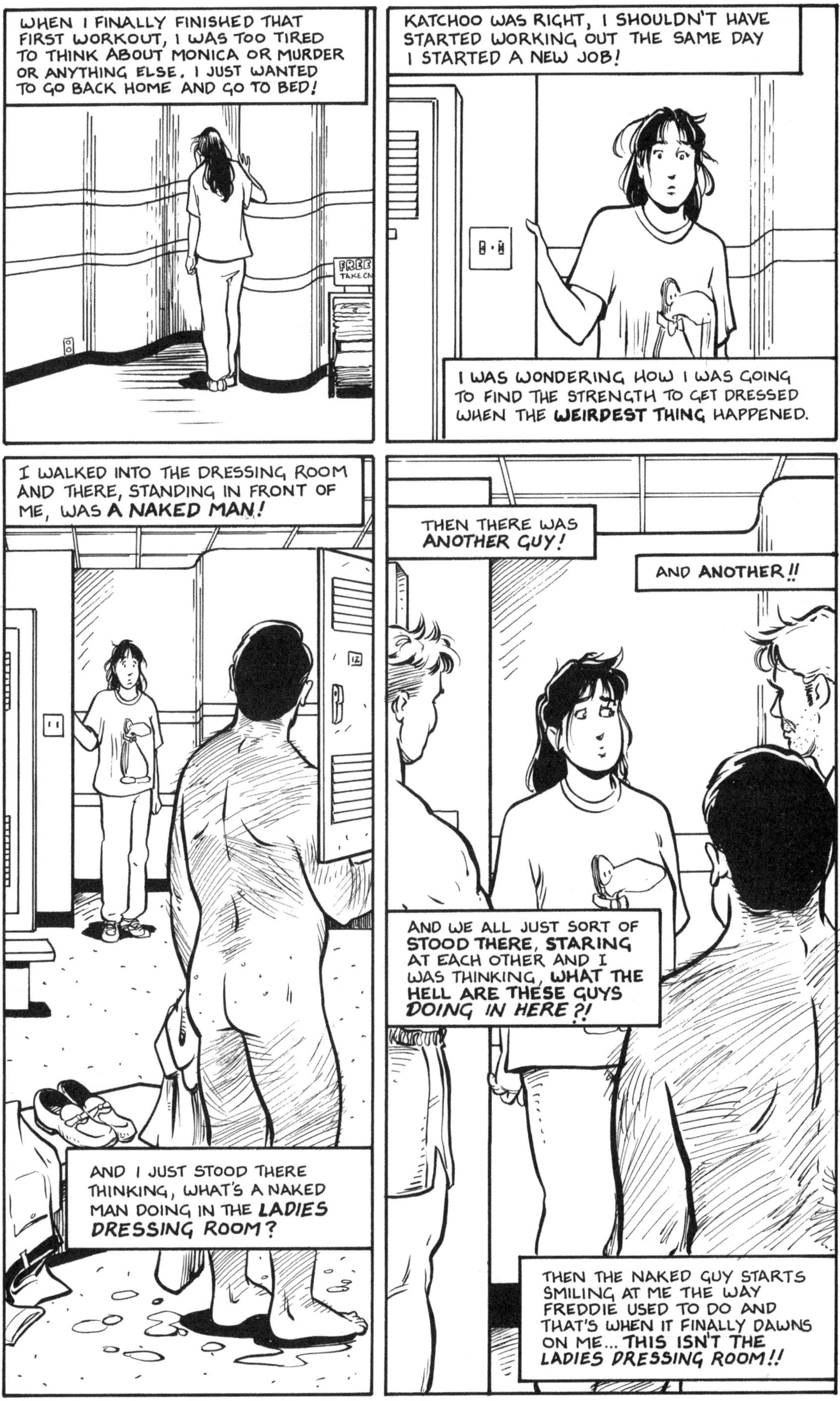

WHEN I FINALLY FINISHED THAT FIRST WORKOUT, I WAS TOO TIRED TO THINK ABOUT MONICA OR MURDER OR ANYTHING ELSE. I JUST WANTED TO GO BACK HOME AND GO TO BED!
FREE TAKE ONE
KATCHOO WAS RIGHT, I SHOULDN'T HAVE STARTED WORKING OUT THE SAME DAY I STARTED A NEW JOB!
I WAS WONDERING HOW I WAS GOING TO FIND THE STRENGTH TO GET DRESSED WHEN THE **WEIRDEST THING** HAPPENED.
I WALKED INTO THE DRESSING ROOM AND THERE, STANDING IN FRONT OF ME, WAS **A NAKED MAN!**
12
AND I JUST STOOD THERE THINKING, WHAT'S A NAKED MAN DOING IN THE ***LADIES DRESSING ROOM?***
THEN THERE WAS **ANOTHER GUY!**
AND **ANOTHER!!**
AND WE ALL JUST SORT OF **STOOD THERE, STARING** AT EACH OTHER AND I WAS THINKING, **WHAT THE HELL ARE THESE GUYS *DOING IN HERE?!***
THEN THE NAKED GUY STARTS SMILING AT ME THE WAY FREDDIE USED TO DO AND THAT'S WHEN IT FINALLY DAWNS ON ME... **THIS ISN'T THE *LADIES DRESSING ROOM!!***

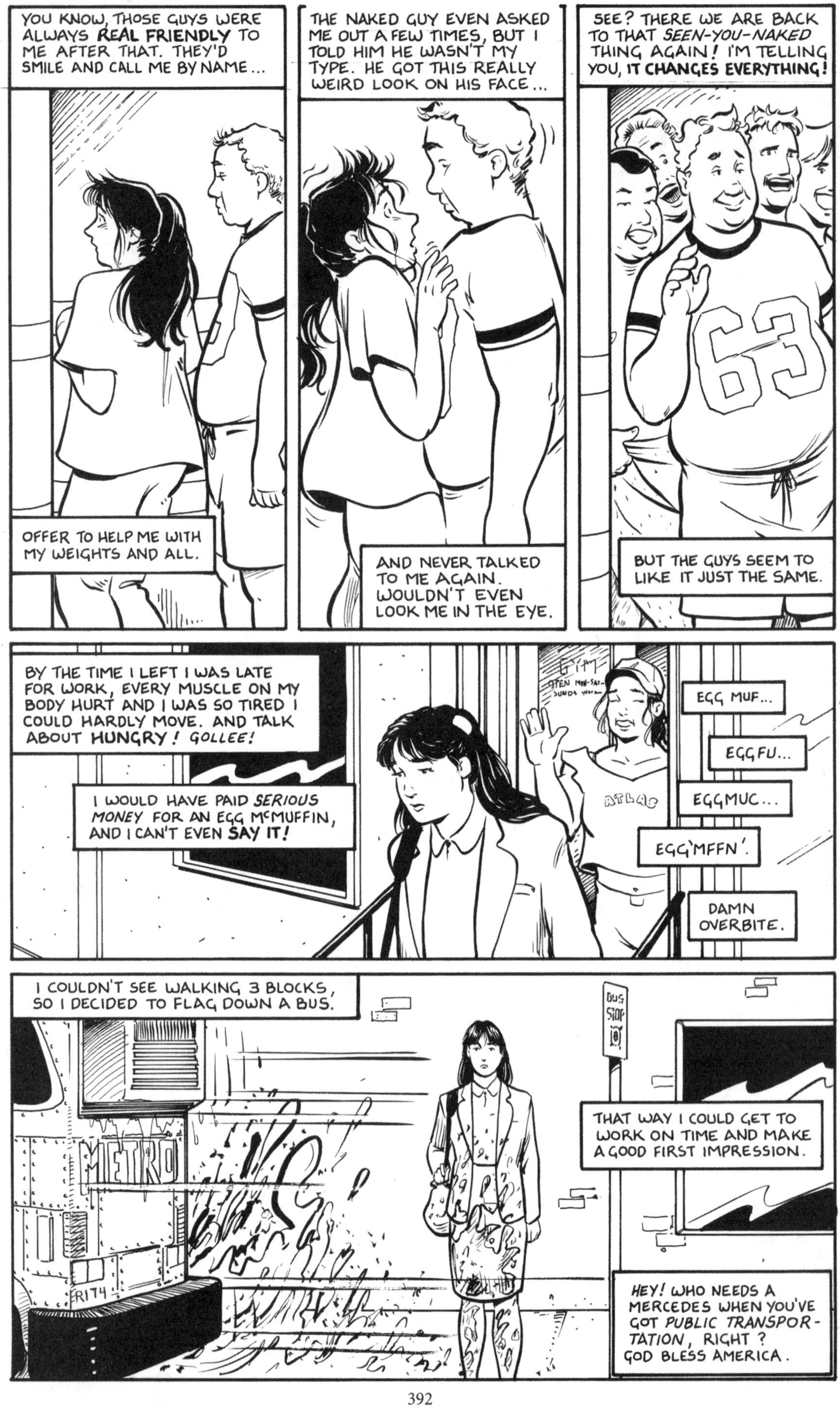
YOU KNOW, THOSE GUYS WERE ALWAYS **REAL FRIENDLY** TO ME AFTER THAT. THEY'D SMILE AND CALL ME BY NAME...
OFFER TO HELP ME WITH MY WEIGHTS AND ALL.
THE NAKED GUY EVEN ASKED ME OUT A FEW TIMES, BUT I TOLD HIM HE WASN'T MY TYPE. HE GOT THIS REALLY WEIRD LOOK ON HIS FACE...
AND NEVER TALKED TO ME AGAIN. WOULDN'T EVEN LOOK ME IN THE EYE.
SEE? THERE WE ARE BACK TO THAT *SEEN-YOU-NAKED* THING AGAIN! I'M TELLING YOU, **IT CHANGES EVERYTHING!**
63
BUT THE GUYS SEEM TO LIKE IT JUST THE SAME.
BY THE TIME I LEFT I WAS LATE FOR WORK, EVERY MUSCLE ON MY BODY HURT AND I WAS SO TIRED I COULD HARDLY MOVE. AND TALK ABOUT **HUNGRY**! *GOLLEE!*
I WOULD HAVE PAID *SERIOUS MONEY* FOR AN EGG McMUFFIN, AND I CAN'T EVEN **SAY IT**!
GYM
ATLAS
EGG MUF...
EGGFU...
EGGMUC...
EGG'MFFN'.
DAMN OVERBITE.
I COULDN'T SEE WALKING 3 BLOCKS, SO I DECIDED TO FLAG DOWN A BUS.
BUS STOP
METRO
R174
THAT WAY I COULD GET TO WORK ON TIME AND MAKE A GOOD FIRST IMPRESSION.
HEY! WHO NEEDS A MERCEDES WHEN YOU'VE GOT *PUBLIC TRANSPORTATION*, RIGHT? GOD BLESS AMERICA.

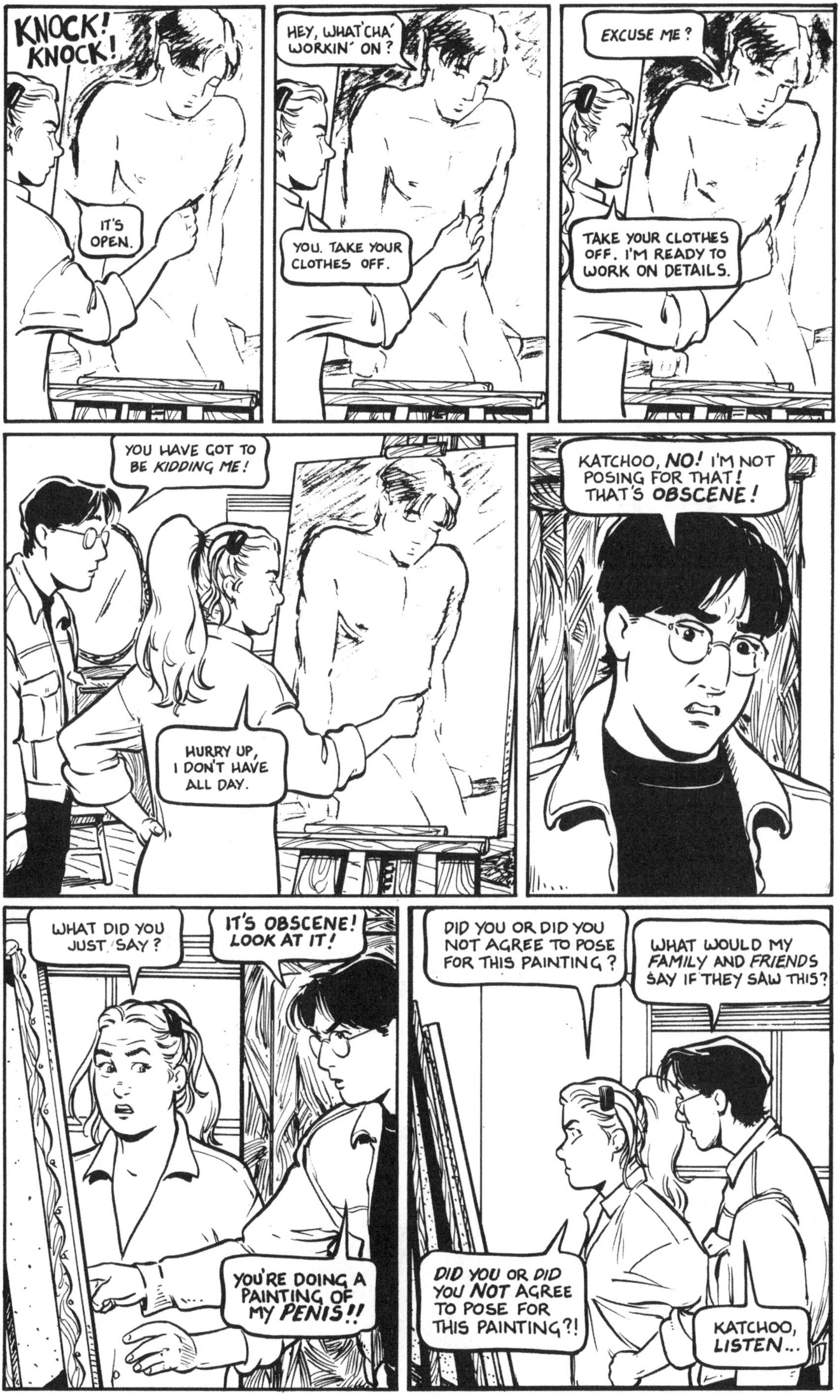
KNOCK! KNOCK!
IT'S OPEN.
HEY, WHAT'CHA' WORKIN' ON?
YOU. TAKE YOUR CLOTHES OFF.
EXCUSE ME?
TAKE YOUR CLOTHES OFF. I'M READY TO WORK ON DETAILS.
YOU HAVE GOT TO BE KIDDING ME!
HURRY UP, I DON'T HAVE ALL DAY.
KATCHOO, NO! I'M NOT POSING FOR THAT! THAT'S OBSCENE!
WHAT DID YOU JUST SAY?
IT'S OBSCENE! LOOK AT IT!
YOU'RE DOING A PAINTING OF MY PENIS!!
DID YOU OR DID YOU NOT AGREE TO POSE FOR THIS PAINTING?
WHAT WOULD MY FAMILY AND FRIENDS SAY IF THEY SAW THIS?
DID YOU OR DID YOU NOT AGREE TO POSE FOR THIS PAINTING?!
KATCHOO, LISTEN...

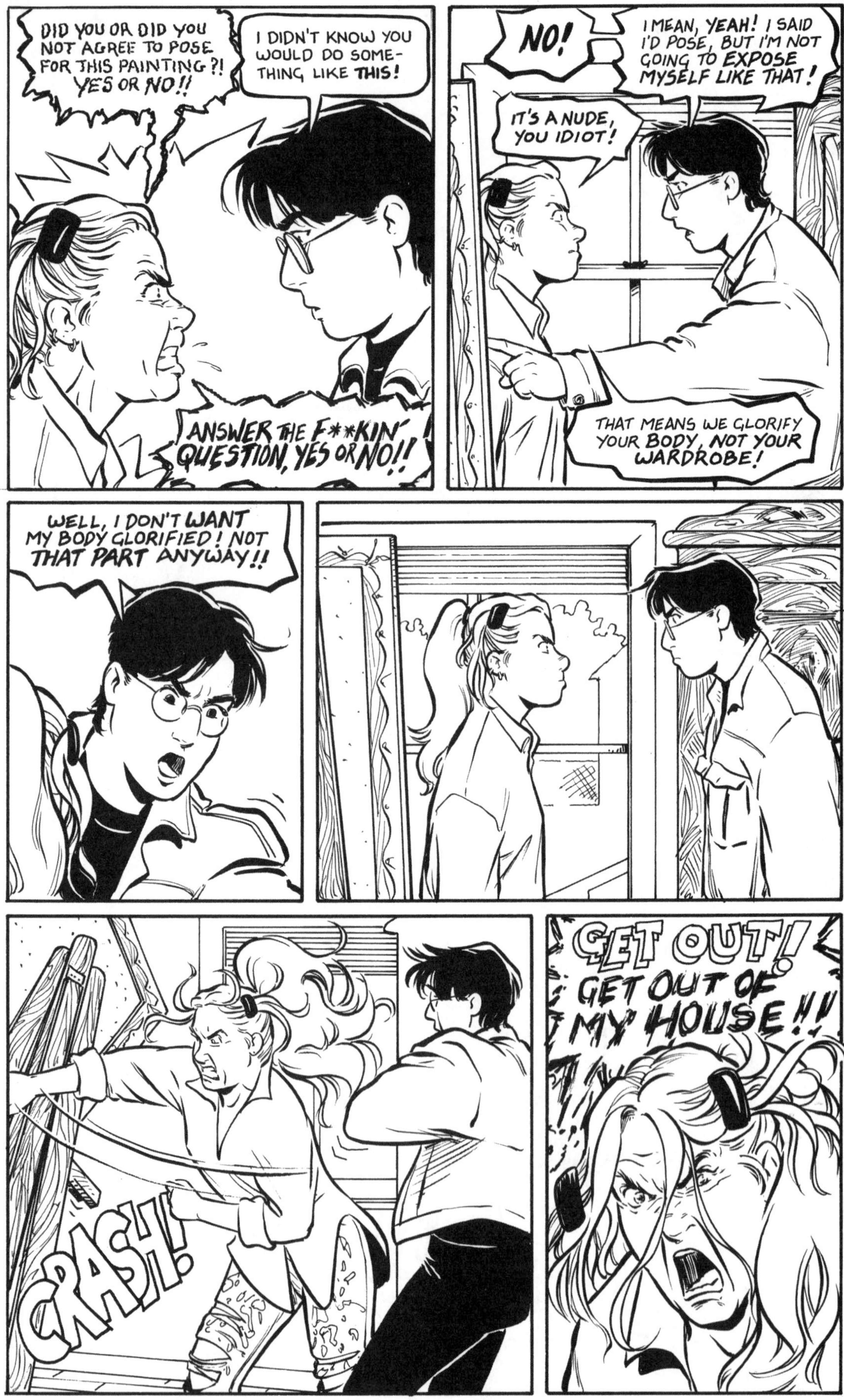
DID YOU OR DID YOU NOT AGREE TO POSE FOR THIS PAINTING ?! YES OR NO!!
I DIDN'T KNOW YOU WOULD DO SOME-THING LIKE THIS!
ANSWER THE F**KIN' QUESTION, YES OR NO!!
NO!
I MEAN, YEAH! I SAID I'D POSE, BUT I'M NOT GOING TO EXPOSE MYSELF LIKE THAT!
IT'S A NUDE, YOU IDIOT!
THAT MEANS WE GLORIFY YOUR BODY, NOT YOUR WARDROBE!
WELL, I DON'T WANT MY BODY GLORIFIED! NOT THAT PART ANYWAY!!
CRASH!
GET OUT!
GET OUT OF MY HOUSE!!

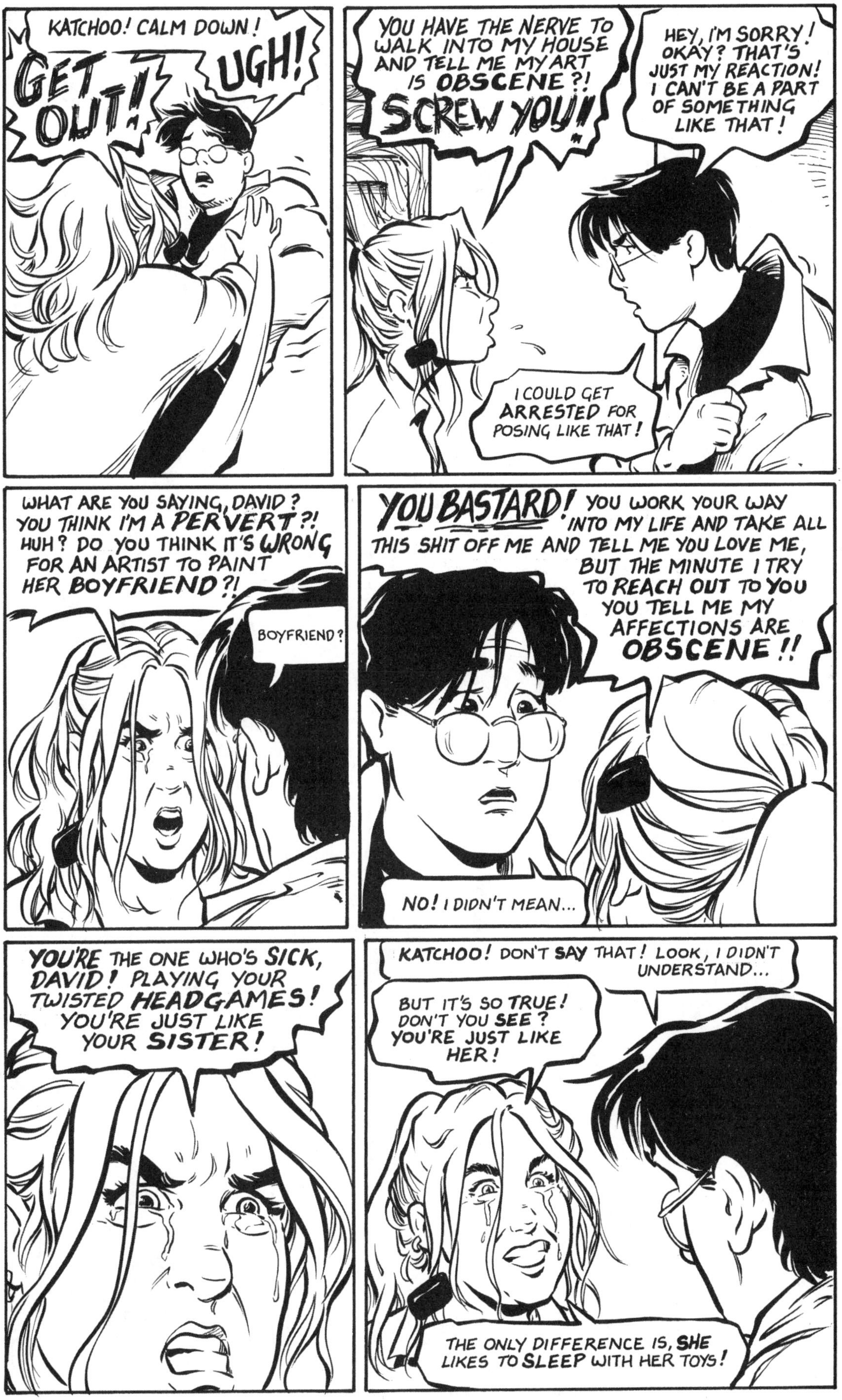
KATCHOO! CALM DOWN!
GET OUT!!
UGH!
YOU HAVE THE NERVE TO WALK INTO MY HOUSE AND TELL ME MY ART IS OBSCENE?!
SCREW YOU!!
HEY, I'M SORRY! OKAY? THAT'S JUST MY REACTION! I CAN'T BE A PART OF SOMETHING LIKE THAT!
I COULD GET ARRESTED FOR POSING LIKE THAT!
WHAT ARE YOU SAYING, DAVID? YOU THINK I'M A PERVERT?! HUH? DO YOU THINK IT'S WRONG FOR AN ARTIST TO PAINT HER BOYFRIEND?!
BOYFRIEND?
YOU BASTARD! YOU WORK YOUR WAY INTO MY LIFE AND TAKE ALL THIS SHIT OFF ME AND TELL ME YOU LOVE ME, BUT THE MINUTE I TRY TO REACH OUT TO YOU YOU TELL ME MY AFFECTIONS ARE OBSCENE!!
NO! I DIDN'T MEAN...
YOU'RE THE ONE WHO'S SICK, DAVID! PLAYING YOUR TWISTED HEADGAMES! YOU'RE JUST LIKE YOUR SISTER!
KATCHOO! DON'T SAY THAT! LOOK, I DIDN'T UNDERSTAND...
BUT IT'S SO TRUE! DON'T YOU SEE? YOU'RE JUST LIKE HER!
THE ONLY DIFFERENCE IS, SHE LIKES TO SLEEP WITH HER TOYS!

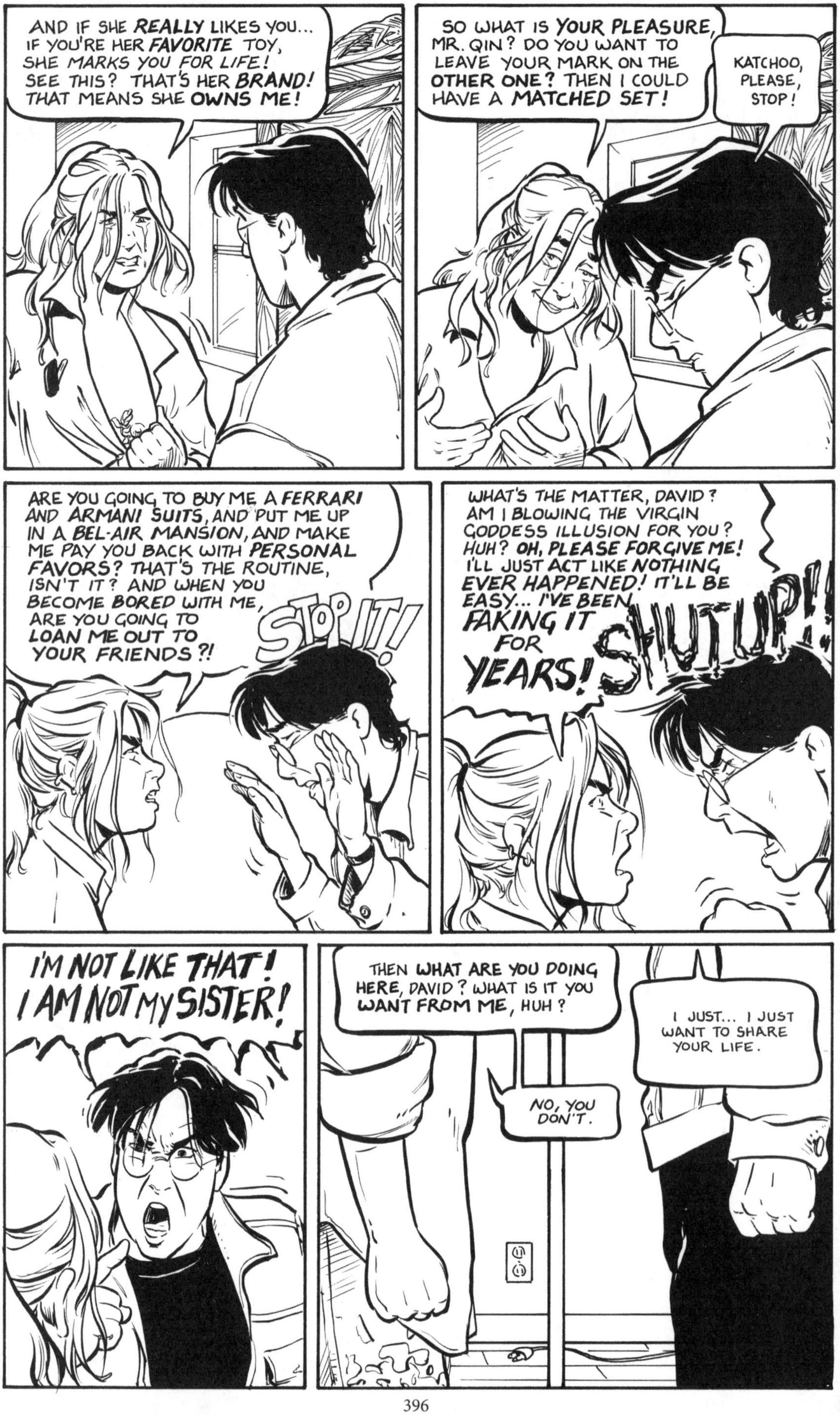
AND IF SHE REALLY LIKES YOU... IF YOU'RE HER FAVORITE TOY, SHE MARKS YOU FOR LIFE! SEE THIS? THAT'S HER BRAND! THAT MEANS SHE OWNS ME!
SO WHAT IS YOUR PLEASURE, MR. QIN? DO YOU WANT TO LEAVE YOUR MARK ON THE OTHER ONE? THEN I COULD HAVE A MATCHED SET!
KATCHOO, PLEASE, STOP!
ARE YOU GOING TO BUY ME A FERRARI AND ARMANI SUITS, AND PUT ME UP IN A BEL-AIR MANSION, AND MAKE ME PAY YOU BACK WITH PERSONAL FAVORS? THAT'S THE ROUTINE, ISN'T IT? AND WHEN YOU BECOME BORED WITH ME, ARE YOU GOING TO LOAN ME OUT TO YOUR FRIENDS?!
STOP IT!
WHAT'S THE MATTER, DAVID? AM I BLOWING THE VIRGIN GODDESS ILLUSION FOR YOU? HUH? OH, PLEASE FORGIVE ME! I'LL JUST ACT LIKE NOTHING EVER HAPPENED! IT'LL BE EASY... I'VE BEEN FAKING IT FOR YEARS!
SHUTUP!!
I'M NOT LIKE THAT! I AM NOT MY SISTER!
THEN WHAT ARE YOU DOING HERE, DAVID? WHAT IS IT YOU WANT FROM ME, HUH?
I JUST... I JUST WANT TO SHARE YOUR LIFE.
NO, YOU DON'T.

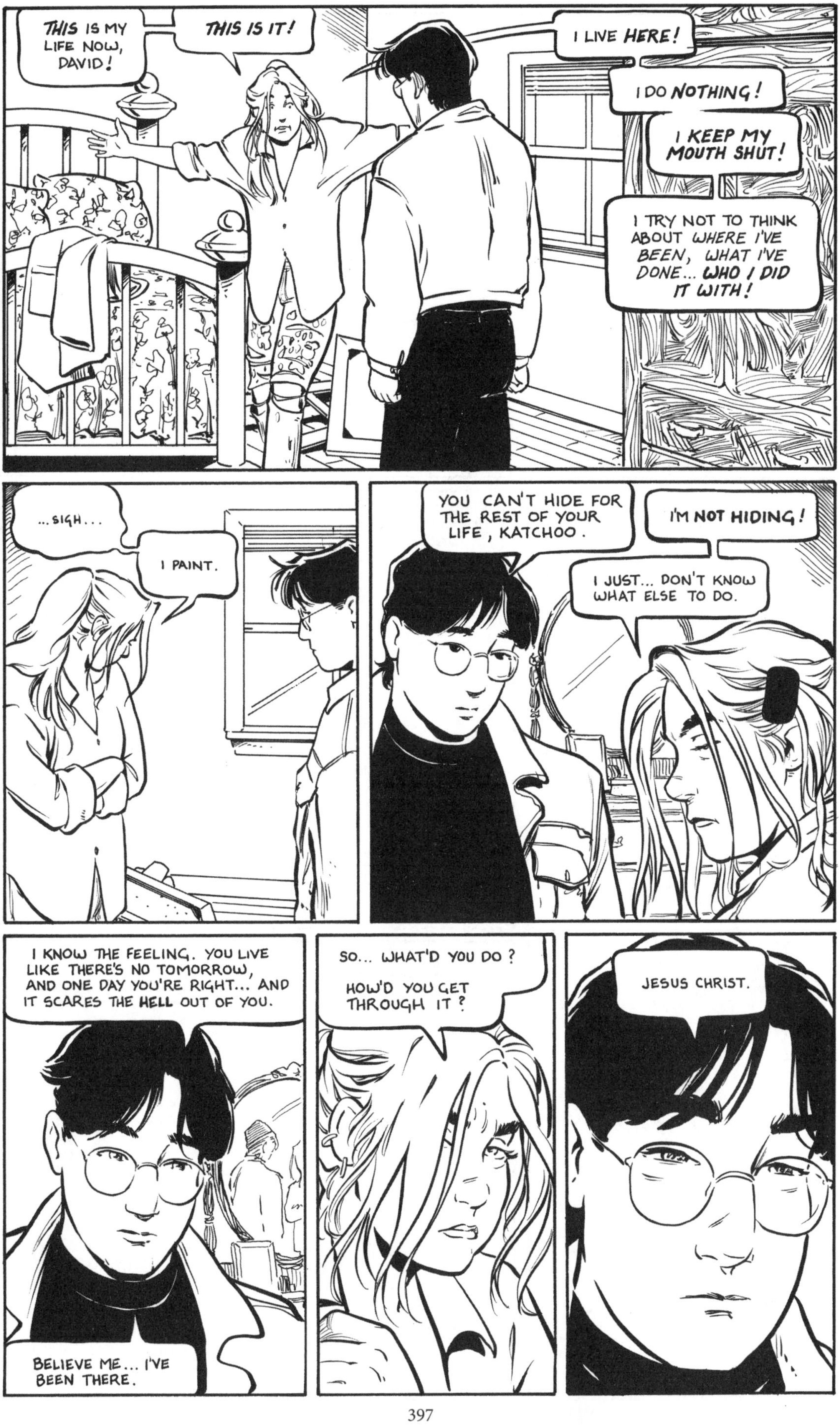
THIS IS MY LIFE NOW, DAVID!
THIS IS IT!
I LIVE HERE!
I DO NOTHING!
I KEEP MY MOUTH SHUT!
I TRY NOT TO THINK ABOUT WHERE I'VE BEEN, WHAT I'VE DONE... WHO I DID IT WITH!
...SIGH...
I PAINT.
YOU CAN'T HIDE FOR THE REST OF YOUR LIFE, KATCHOO.
I'M NOT HIDING!
I JUST... DON'T KNOW WHAT ELSE TO DO.
I KNOW THE FEELING. YOU LIVE LIKE THERE'S NO TOMORROW, AND ONE DAY YOU'RE RIGHT... AND IT SCARES THE HELL OUT OF YOU.
BELIEVE ME... I'VE BEEN THERE.
SO... WHAT'D YOU DO?
HOW'D YOU GET THROUGH IT?
JESUS CHRIST.

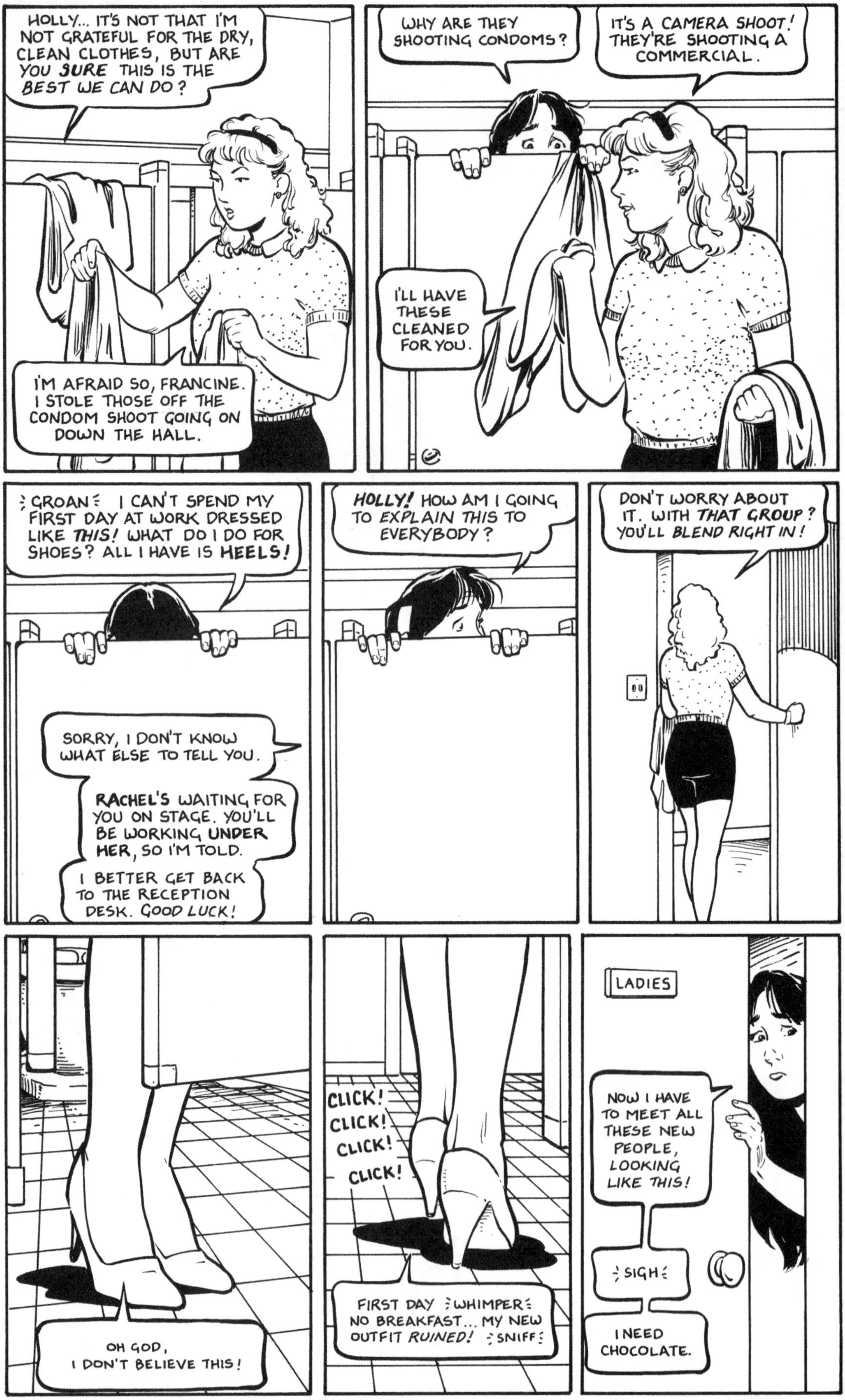
HOLLY... IT'S NOT THAT I'M NOT GRATEFUL FOR THE DRY, CLEAN CLOTHES, BUT ARE YOU SURE THIS IS THE BEST WE CAN DO?
I'M AFRAID SO, FRANCINE. I STOLE THOSE OFF THE CONDOM SHOOT GOING ON DOWN THE HALL.
WHY ARE THEY SHOOTING CONDOMS?
IT'S A CAMERA SHOOT! THEY'RE SHOOTING A COMMERCIAL.
I'LL HAVE THESE CLEANED FOR YOU.
GROAN I CAN'T SPEND MY FIRST DAY AT WORK DRESSED LIKE THIS! WHAT DO I DO FOR SHOES? ALL I HAVE IS HEELS!
SORRY, I DON'T KNOW WHAT ELSE TO TELL YOU.
RACHEL'S WAITING FOR YOU ON STAGE. YOU'LL BE WORKING UNDER HER, SO I'M TOLD.
I BETTER GET BACK TO THE RECEPTION DESK. GOOD LUCK!
HOLLY! HOW AM I GOING TO EXPLAIN THIS TO EVERYBODY?
DON'T WORRY ABOUT IT. WITH THAT GROUP? YOU'LL BLEND RIGHT IN!
OH GOD, I DON'T BELIEVE THIS!
CLICK! CLICK! CLICK! CLICK!
FIRST DAY WHIMPER NO BREAKFAST... MY NEW OUTFIT RUINED! SNIFF
LADIES
NOW I HAVE TO MEET ALL THESE NEW PEOPLE, LOOKING LIKE THIS!
SIGH
I NEED CHOCOLATE.

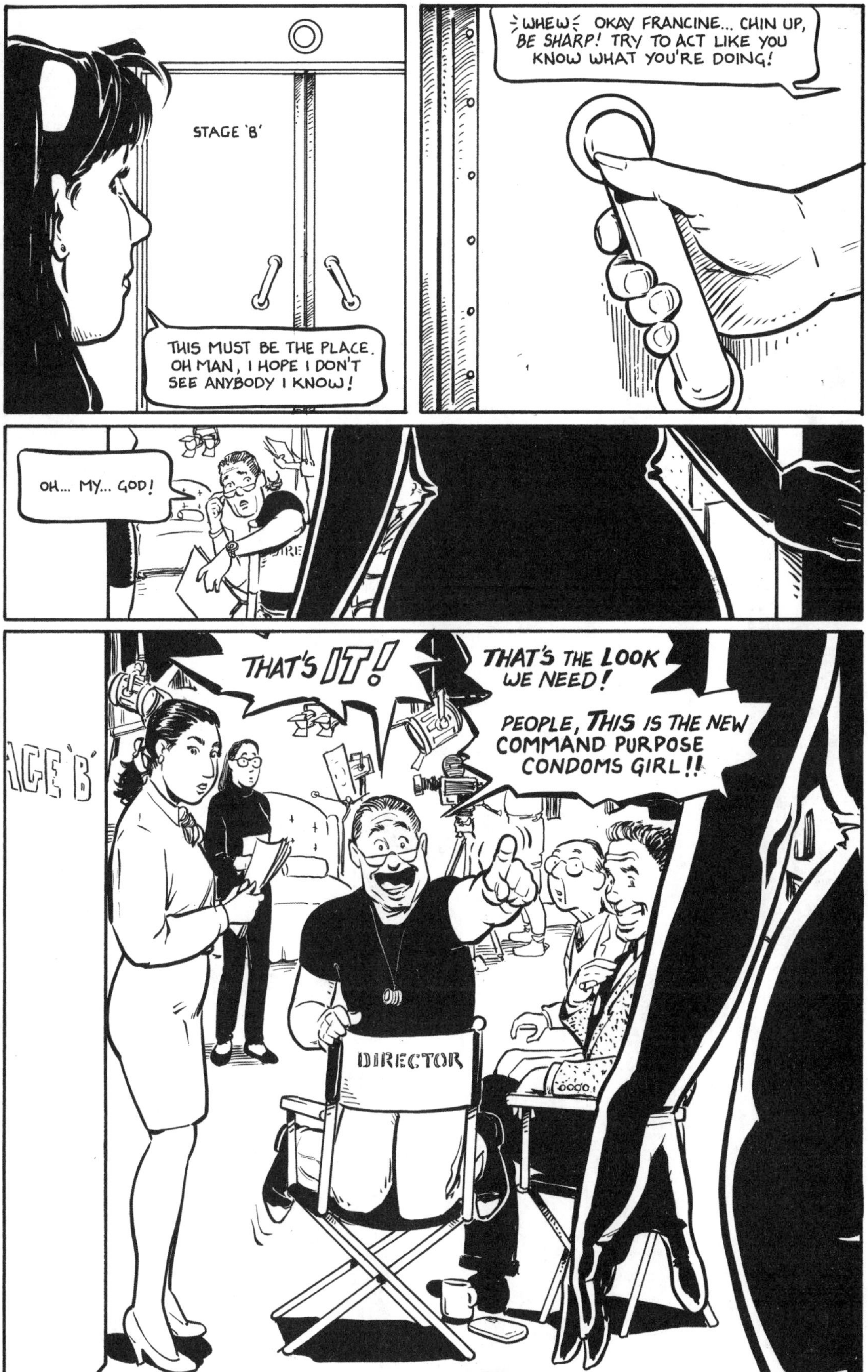
STAGE 'B'
THIS MUST BE THE PLACE. OH MAN, I HOPE I DON'T SEE ANYBODY I KNOW!
WHEW OKAY FRANCINE... CHIN UP, BE SHARP! TRY TO ACT LIKE YOU KNOW WHAT YOU'RE DOING!
OH... MY... GOD!
THAT'S IT!
THAT'S THE LOOK WE NEED!
PEOPLE, THIS IS THE NEW COMMAND PURPOSE CONDOMS GIRL!!
DIRECTOR
TO BE CONTINUED!

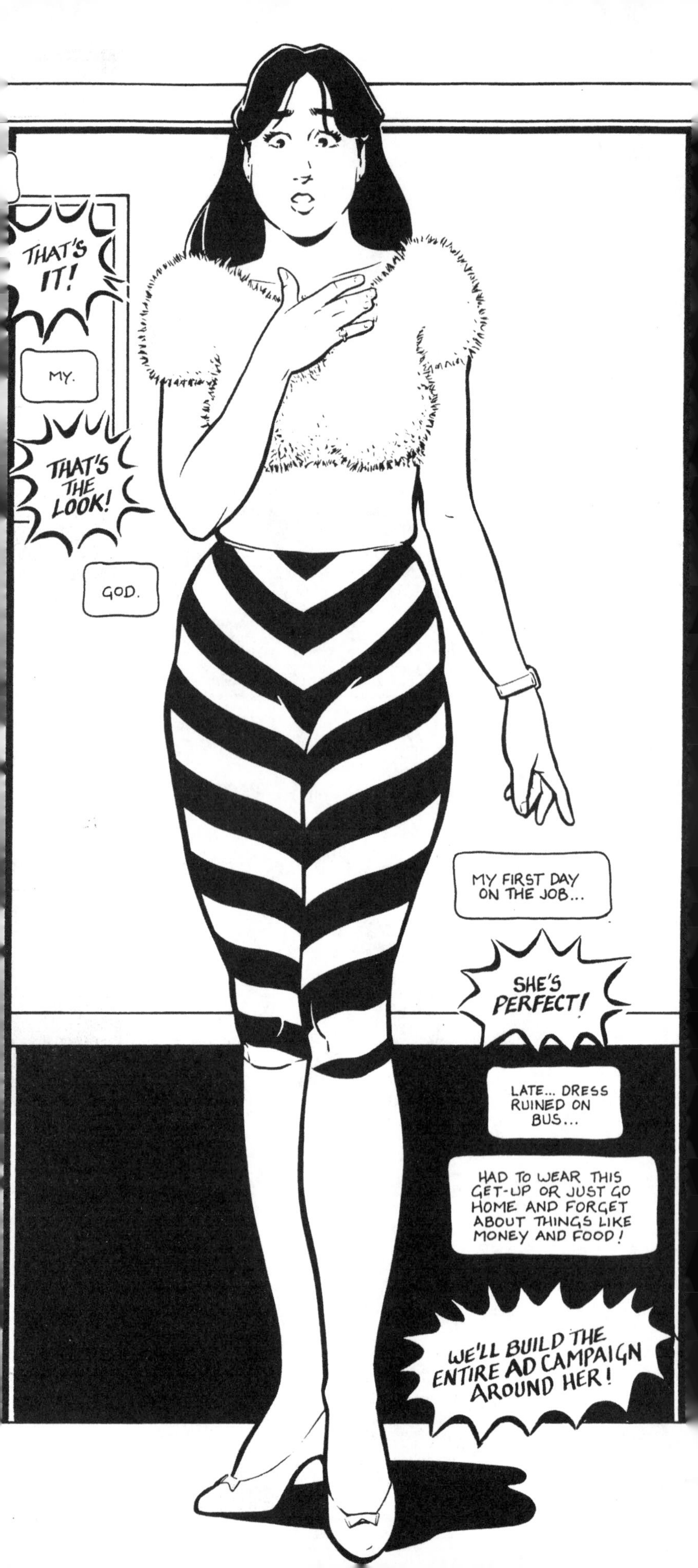
THAT'S IT!
MY.
THAT'S THE LOOK!
GOD.
MY FIRST DAY ON THE JOB...
SHE'S PERFECT!
LATE... DRESS RUINED ON BUS...
HAD TO WEAR THIS GET-UP OR JUST GO HOME AND FORGET ABOUT THINGS LIKE MONEY AND FOOD!
WE'LL BUILD THE ENTIRE AD CAMPAIGN AROUND HER!

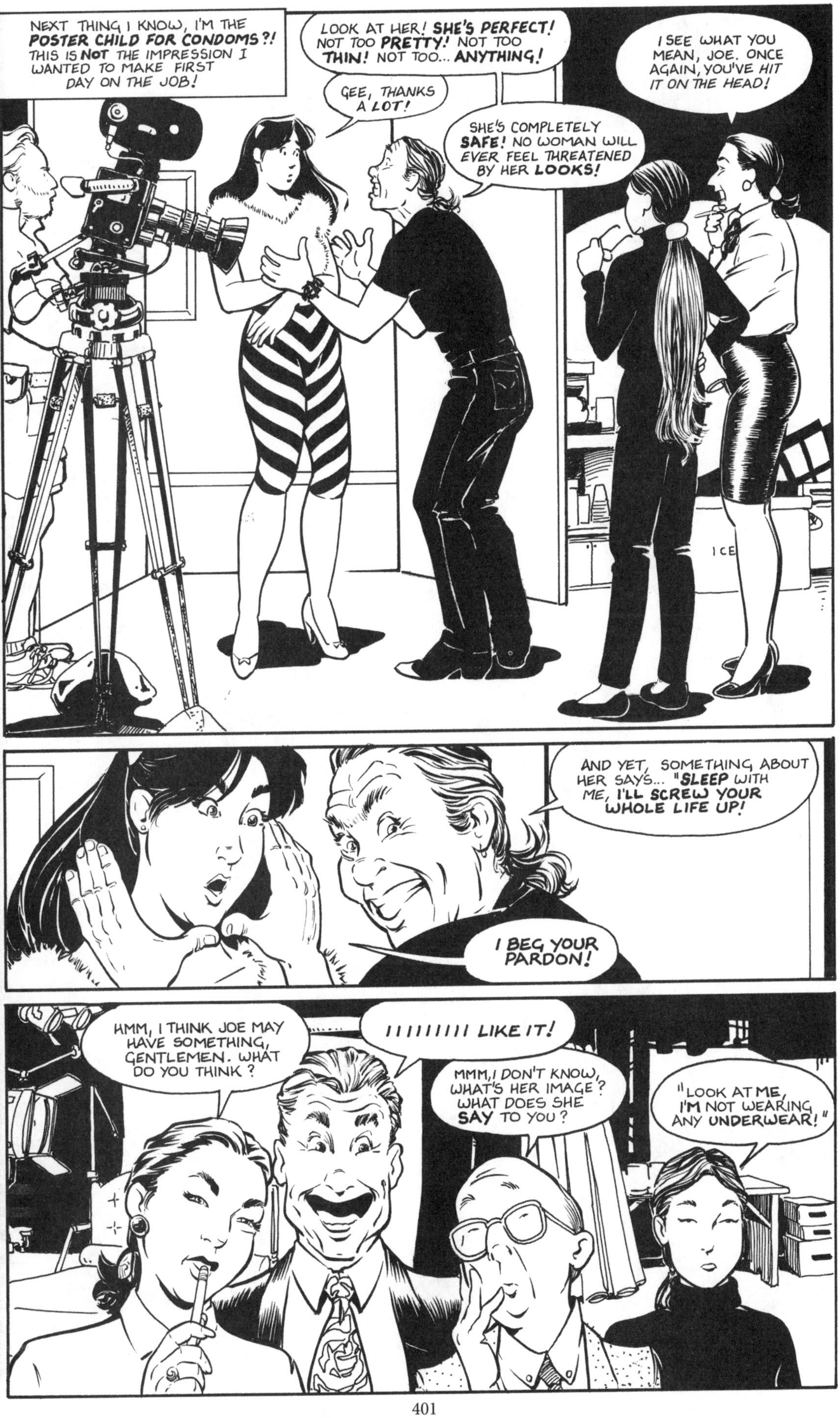
NEXT THING I KNOW, I'M THE POSTER CHILD FOR CONDOMS?! THIS IS NOT THE IMPRESSION I WANTED TO MAKE FIRST DAY ON THE JOB!
LOOK AT HER! SHE'S PERFECT! NOT TOO PRETTY! NOT TOO THIN! NOT TOO... ANYTHING!
GEE, THANKS A LOT!
I SEE WHAT YOU MEAN, JOE. ONCE AGAIN, YOU'VE HIT IT ON THE HEAD!
SHE'S COMPLETELY SAFE! NO WOMAN WILL EVER FEEL THREATENED BY HER LOOKS!
ICE
AND YET, SOMETHING ABOUT HER SAYS... "SLEEP WITH ME, I'LL SCREW YOUR WHOLE LIFE UP!
I BEG YOUR PARDON!
HMM, I THINK JOE MAY HAVE SOMETHING, GENTLEMEN. WHAT DO YOU THINK?
IIIIIIIII LIKE IT!
MMM, I DON'T KNOW, WHAT'S HER IMAGE? WHAT DOES SHE SAY TO YOU?
"LOOK AT ME, I'M NOT WEARING ANY UNDERWEAR!"

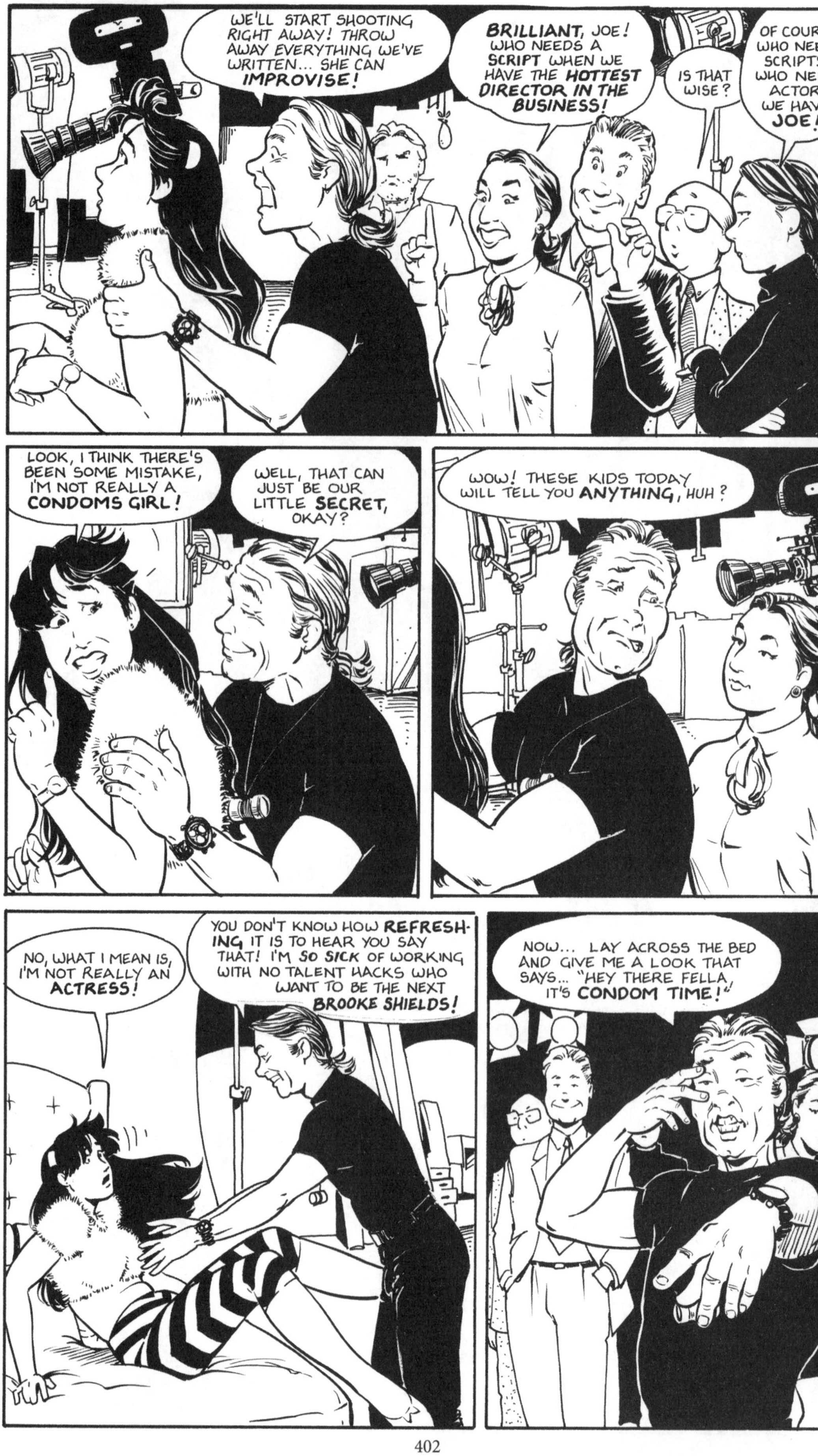
WE'LL START SHOOTING RIGHT AWAY! THROW AWAY EVERYTHING WE'VE WRITTEN... SHE CAN IMPROVISE!
BRILLIANT, JOE! WHO NEEDS A SCRIPT WHEN WE HAVE THE HOTTEST DIRECTOR IN THE BUSINESS!
IS THAT WISE?
OF COURSE! WHO NEEDS SCRIPTS? WHO NEEDS ACTORS? WE HAVE JOE!
LOOK, I THINK THERE'S BEEN SOME MISTAKE, I'M NOT REALLY A CONDOMS GIRL!
WELL, THAT CAN JUST BE OUR LITTLE SECRET, OKAY?
WOW! THESE KIDS TODAY WILL TELL YOU ANYTHING, HUH?
NO, WHAT I MEAN IS, I'M NOT REALLY AN ACTRESS!
YOU DON'T KNOW HOW REFRESHING IT IS TO HEAR YOU SAY THAT! I'M SO SICK OF WORKING WITH NO TALENT HACKS WHO WANT TO BE THE NEXT BROOKE SHIELDS!
NOW... LAY ACROSS THE BED AND GIVE ME A LOOK THAT SAYS... "HEY THERE FELLA, IT'S CONDOM TIME!"

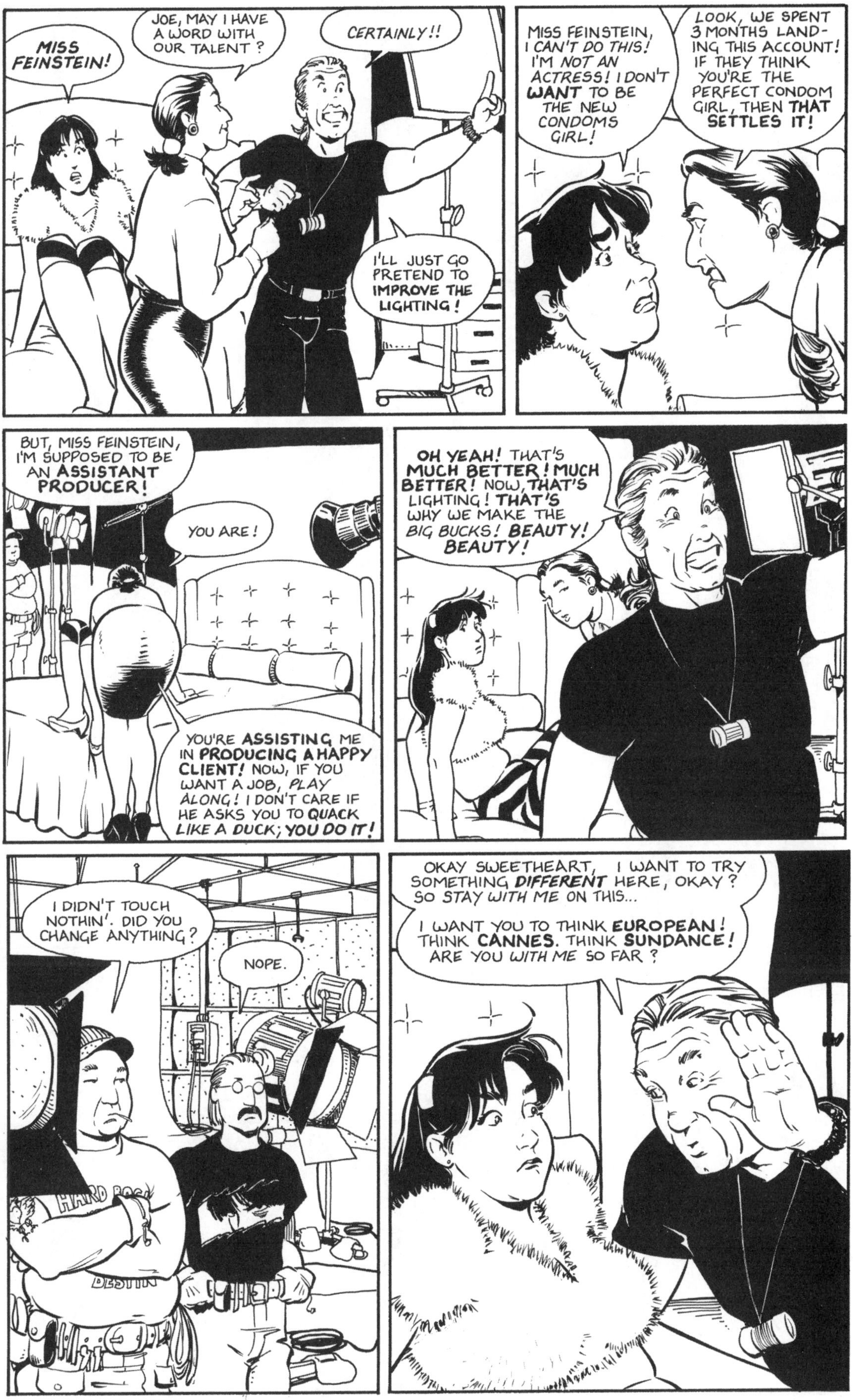
MISS FEINSTEIN!
JOE, MAY I HAVE A WORD WITH OUR TALENT ?
CERTAINLY!!
I'LL JUST GO PRETEND TO IMPROVE THE LIGHTING!
MISS FEINSTEIN, I CAN'T DO THIS! I'M NOT AN ACTRESS! I DON'T WANT TO BE THE NEW CONDOMS GIRL!
LOOK, WE SPENT 3 MONTHS LANDING THIS ACCOUNT! IF THEY THINK YOU'RE THE PERFECT CONDOM GIRL, THEN THAT SETTLES IT!
BUT, MISS FEINSTEIN, I'M SUPPOSED TO BE AN ASSISTANT PRODUCER!
YOU ARE!
YOU'RE ASSISTING ME IN PRODUCING A HAPPY CLIENT! NOW, IF YOU WANT A JOB, PLAY ALONG! I DON'T CARE IF HE ASKS YOU TO QUACK LIKE A DUCK; YOU DO IT!
OH YEAH! THAT'S MUCH BETTER! MUCH BETTER! NOW, THAT'S LIGHTING! THAT'S WHY WE MAKE THE BIG BUCKS! BEAUTY! BEAUTY!
I DIDN'T TOUCH NOTHIN'. DID YOU CHANGE ANYTHING?
NOPE.
OKAY SWEETHEART, I WANT TO TRY SOMETHING DIFFERENT HERE, OKAY? SO STAY WITH ME ON THIS...
I WANT YOU TO THINK EUROPEAN! THINK CANNES. THINK SUNDANCE! ARE YOU WITH ME SO FAR?

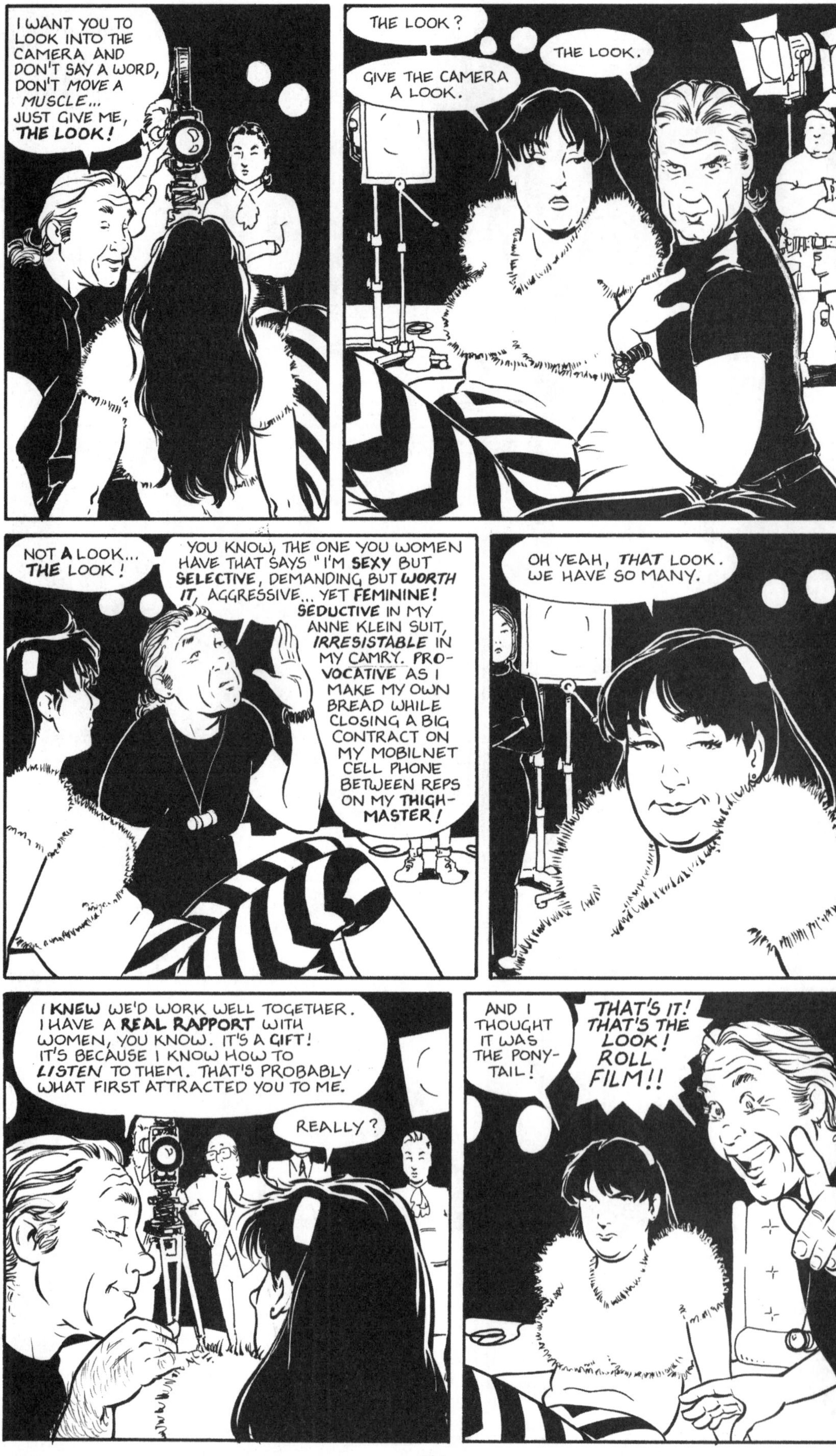

I WANT YOU TO LOOK INTO THE CAMERA AND DON'T SAY A WORD, DON'T MOVE A MUSCLE... JUST GIVE ME, THE LOOK!
THE LOOK?
GIVE THE CAMERA A LOOK.
THE LOOK.
NOT A LOOK... THE LOOK!
YOU KNOW, THE ONE YOU WOMEN HAVE THAT SAYS "I'M SEXY BUT SELECTIVE, DEMANDING BUT WORTH IT, AGGRESSIVE... YET FEMININE! SEDUCTIVE IN MY ANNE KLEIN SUIT, IRRESISTABLE IN MY CAMRY. PROVOCATIVE AS I MAKE MY OWN BREAD WHILE CLOSING A BIG CONTRACT ON MY MOBILNET CELL PHONE BETWEEN REPS ON MY THIGH-MASTER!
OH YEAH, THAT LOOK. WE HAVE SO MANY.
I KNEW WE'D WORK WELL TOGETHER. I HAVE A REAL RAPPORT WITH WOMEN, YOU KNOW. IT'S A GIFT! IT'S BECAUSE I KNOW HOW TO LISTEN TO THEM. THAT'S PROBABLY WHAT FIRST ATTRACTED YOU TO ME.
REALLY?
AND I THOUGHT IT WAS THE PONY-TAIL!
THAT'S IT! THAT'S THE LOOK! ROLL FILM!!

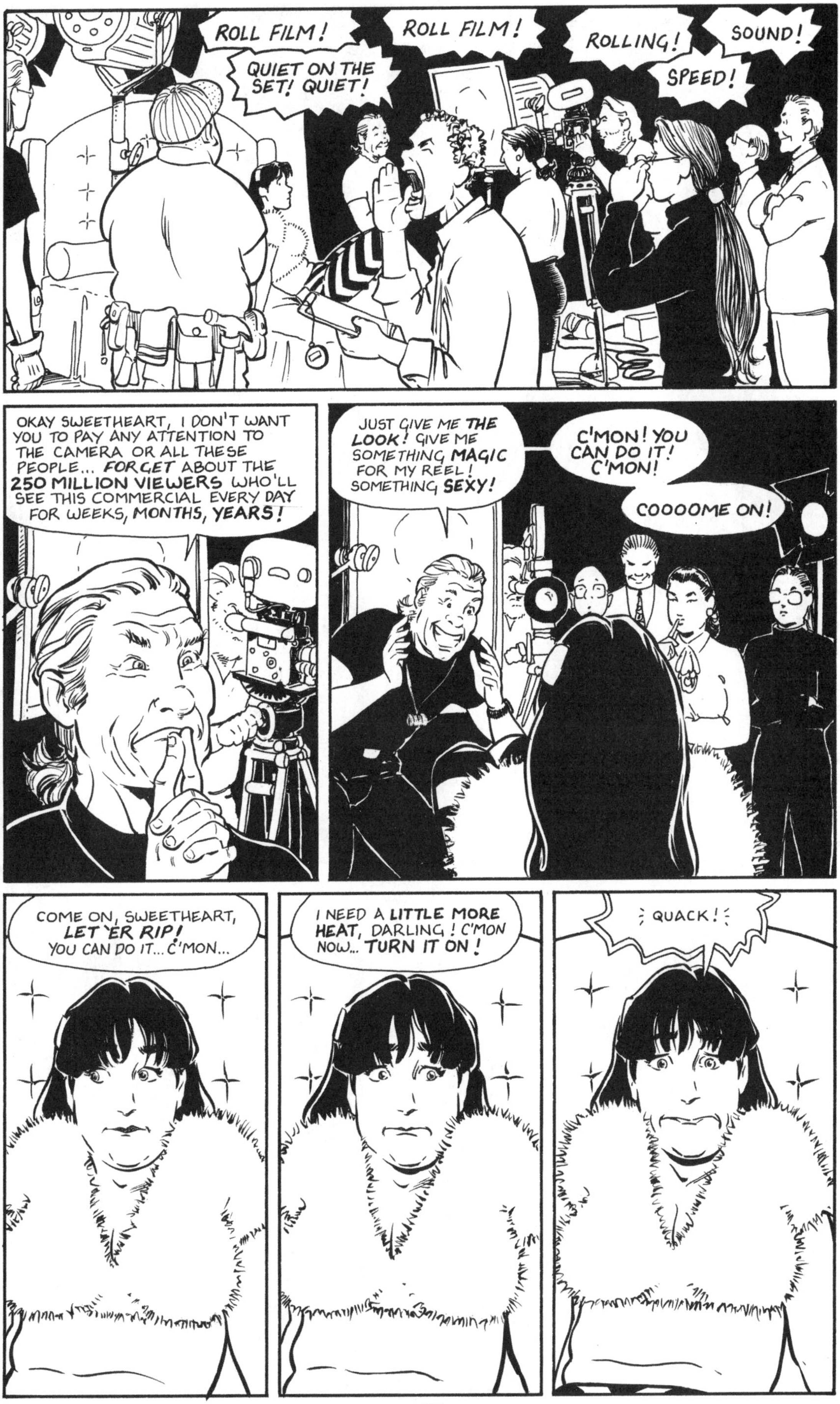

ROLL FILM!
QUIET ON THE SET! QUIET!
ROLL FILM!
ROLLING!
SOUND!
SPEED!
OKAY SWEETHEART, I DON'T WANT YOU TO PAY ANY ATTENTION TO THE CAMERA OR ALL THESE PEOPLE... FORGET ABOUT THE 250 MILLION VIEWERS WHO'LL SEE THIS COMMERCIAL EVERY DAY FOR WEEKS, MONTHS, YEARS!
JUST GIVE ME THE LOOK! GIVE ME SOMETHING MAGIC FOR MY REEL! SOMETHING SEXY!
C'MON! YOU CAN DO IT! C'MON!
COOOOME ON!
COME ON, SWEETHEART, LET 'ER RIP! YOU CAN DO IT... C'MON...
I NEED A LITTLE MORE HEAT, DARLING! C'MON NOW... TURN IT ON!
QUACK!

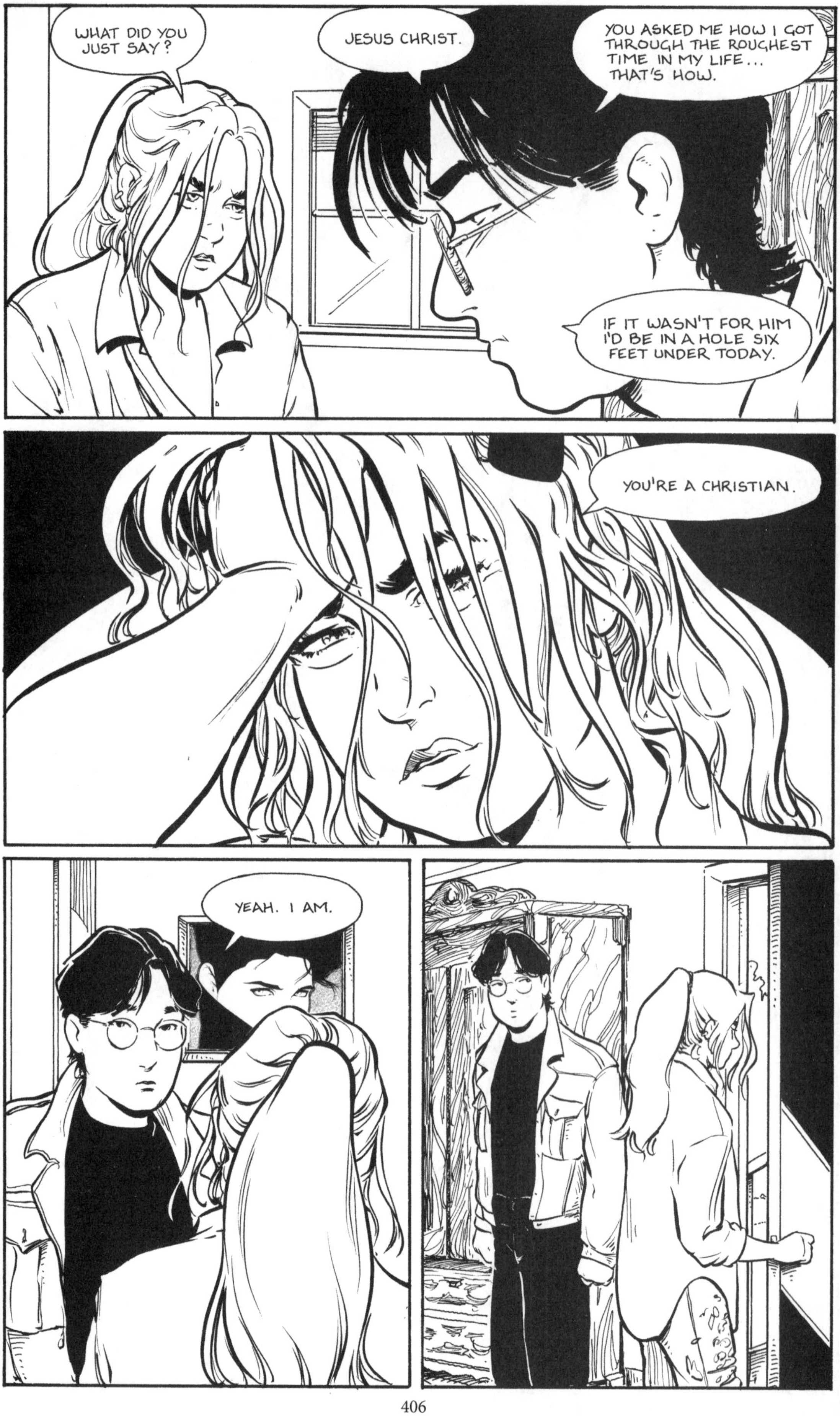
WHAT DID YOU JUST SAY?
JESUS CHRIST.
YOU ASKED ME HOW I GOT THROUGH THE ROUGHEST TIME IN MY LIFE... THAT'S HOW.
IF IT WASN'T FOR HIM I'D BE IN A HOLE SIX FEET UNDER TODAY.
YOU'RE A CHRISTIAN.
YEAH. I AM.

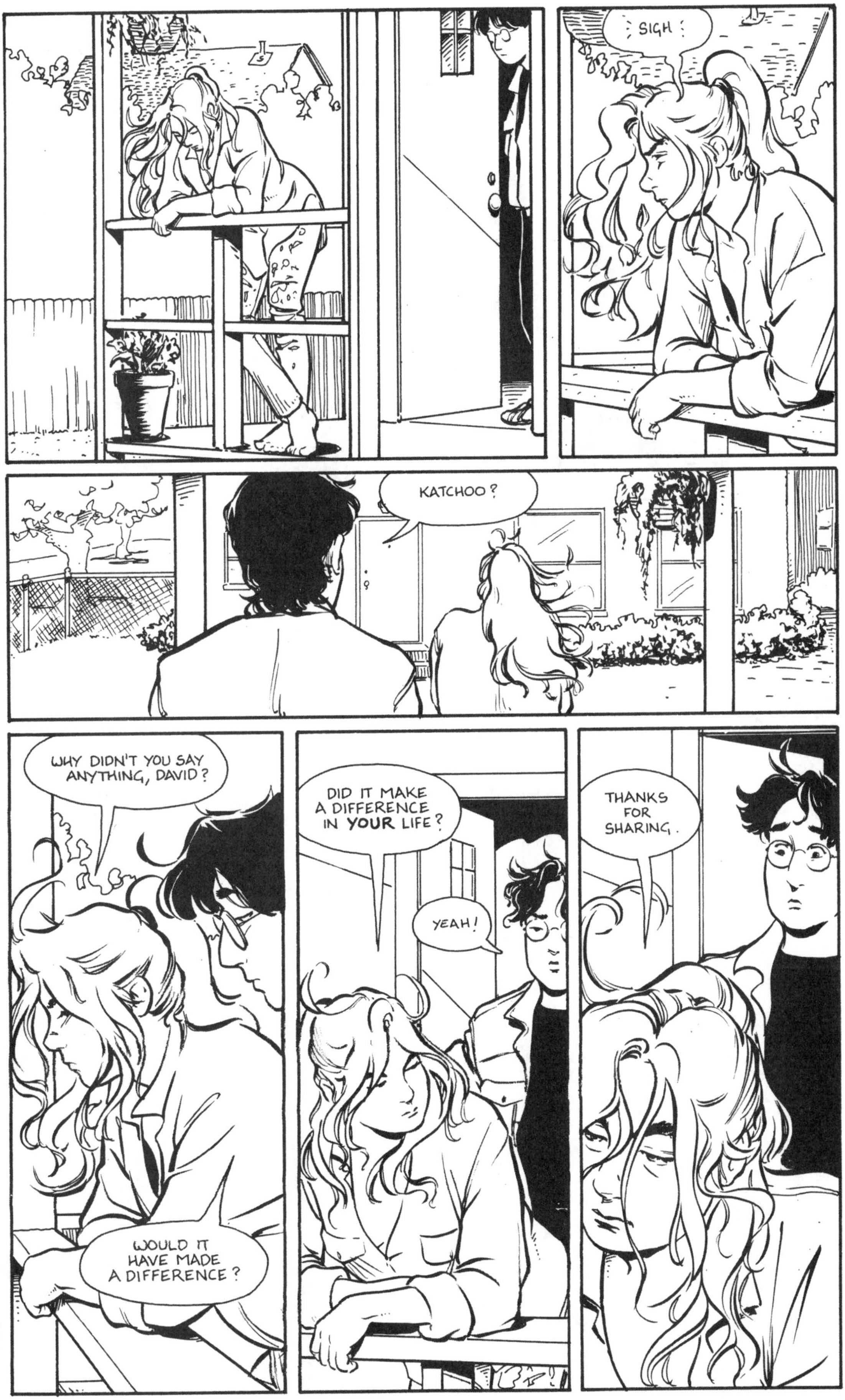
SIGH
KATCHOO?
WHY DIDN'T YOU SAY ANYTHING, DAVID?
WOULD IT HAVE MADE A DIFFERENCE?
DID IT MAKE A DIFFERENCE IN YOUR LIFE?
YEAH!
THANKS FOR SHARING.

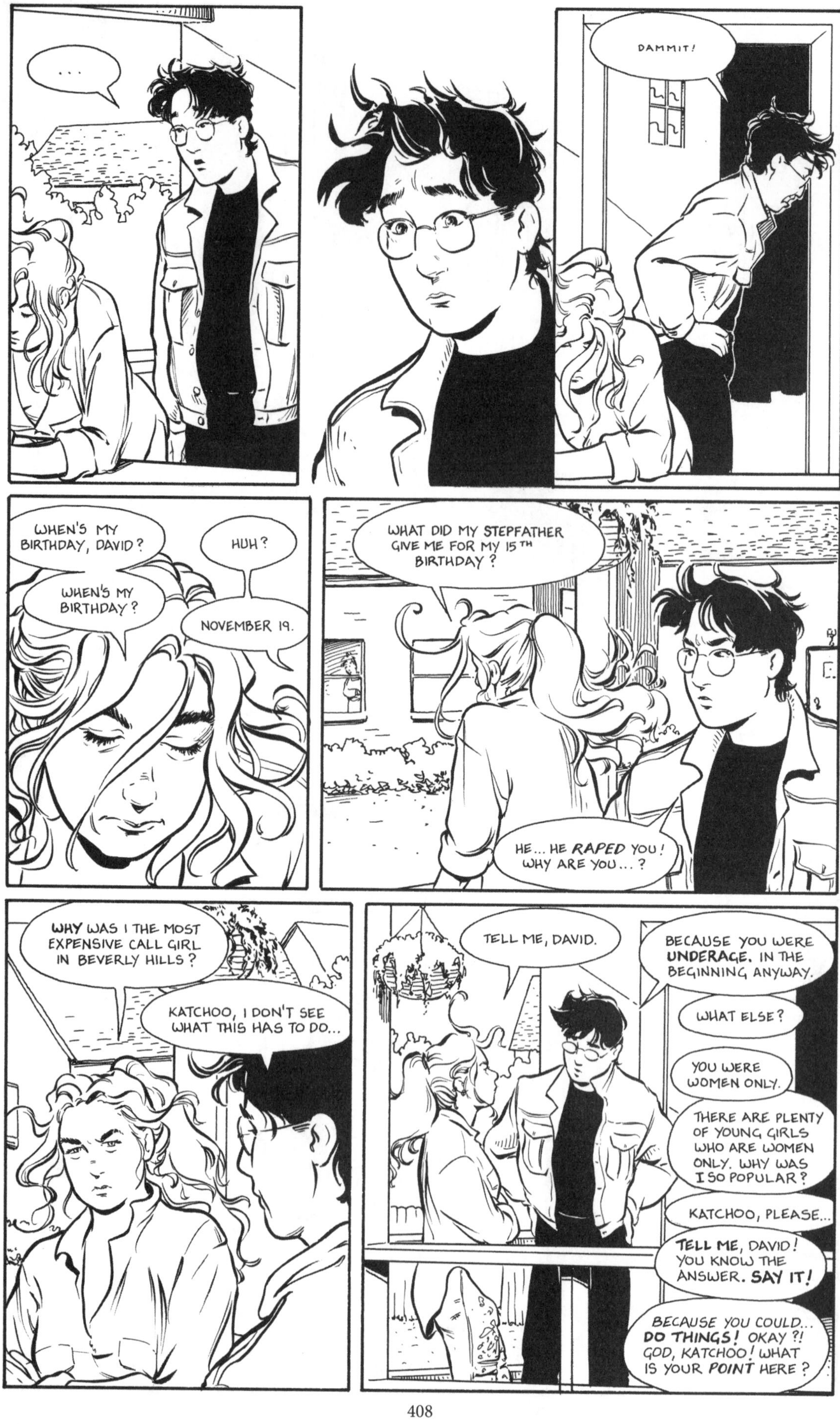
...
DAMMIT!
WHEN'S MY BIRTHDAY, DAVID?
HUH?
WHEN'S MY BIRTHDAY?
NOVEMBER 19.
WHAT DID MY STEPFATHER GIVE ME FOR MY 15TH BIRTHDAY?
HE... HE RAPED YOU! WHY ARE YOU...?
WHY WAS I THE MOST EXPENSIVE CALL GIRL IN BEVERLY HILLS?
KATCHOO, I DON'T SEE WHAT THIS HAS TO DO...
TELL ME, DAVID.
BECAUSE YOU WERE UNDERAGE. IN THE BEGINNING ANYWAY.
WHAT ELSE?
YOU WERE WOMEN ONLY.
THERE ARE PLENTY OF YOUNG GIRLS WHO ARE WOMEN ONLY. WHY WAS I SO POPULAR?
KATCHOO, PLEASE...
TELL ME, DAVID! YOU KNOW THE ANSWER. SAY IT!
BECAUSE YOU COULD... DO THINGS! OKAY?! GOD, KATCHOO! WHAT IS YOUR POINT HERE?

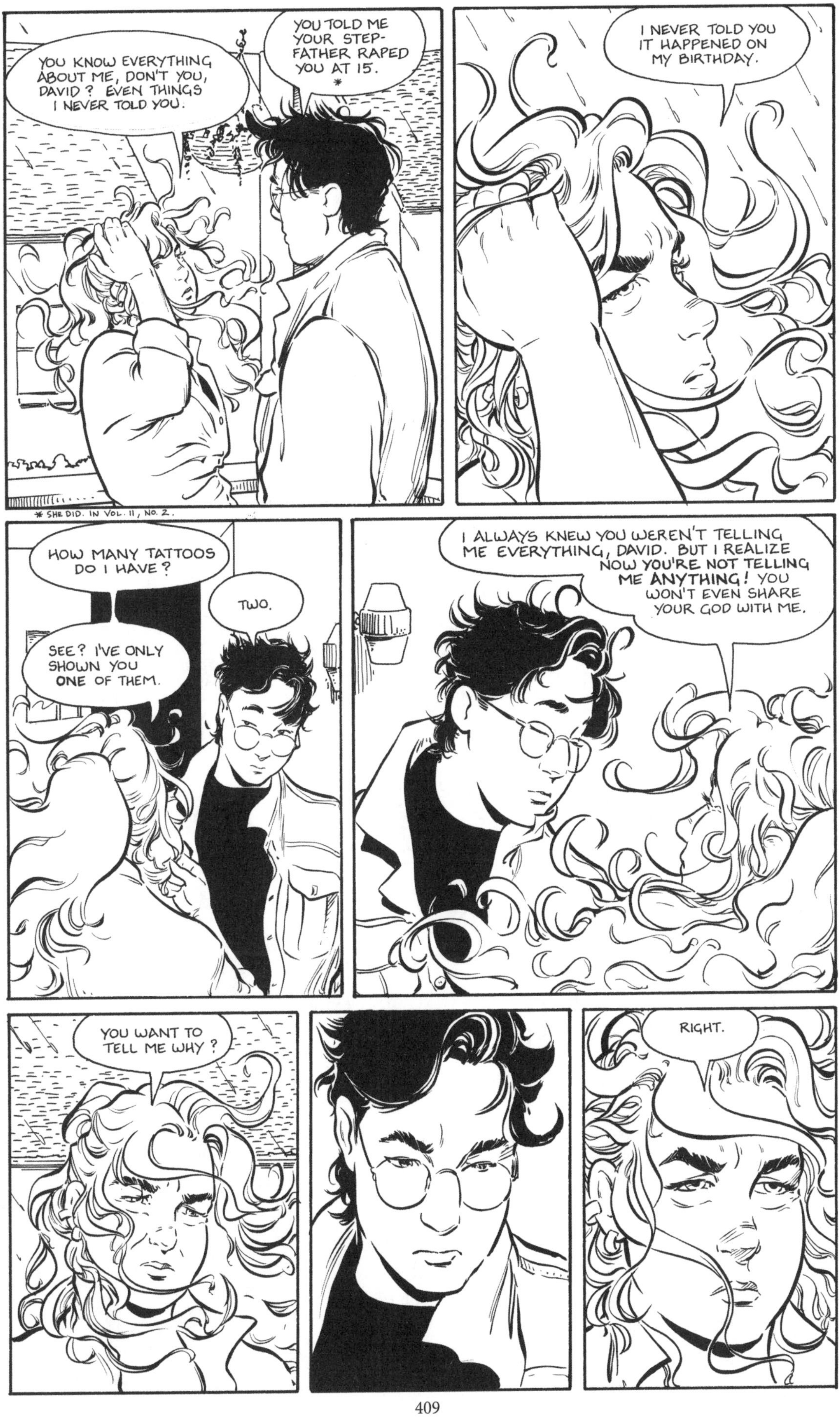
YOU KNOW EVERYTHING ABOUT ME, DON'T YOU, DAVID? EVEN THINGS I NEVER TOLD YOU.
YOU TOLD ME YOUR STEP-FATHER RAPED YOU AT 15. *
I NEVER TOLD YOU IT HAPPENED ON MY BIRTHDAY.
* SHE DID. IN VOL. II, NO. 2.
HOW MANY TATTOOS DO I HAVE?
TWO.
SEE? I'VE ONLY SHOWN YOU ONE OF THEM.
I ALWAYS KNEW YOU WEREN'T TELLING ME EVERYTHING, DAVID. BUT I REALIZE NOW YOU'RE NOT TELLING ME ANYTHING! YOU WON'T EVEN SHARE YOUR GOD WITH ME.
YOU WANT TO TELL ME WHY?
RIGHT.

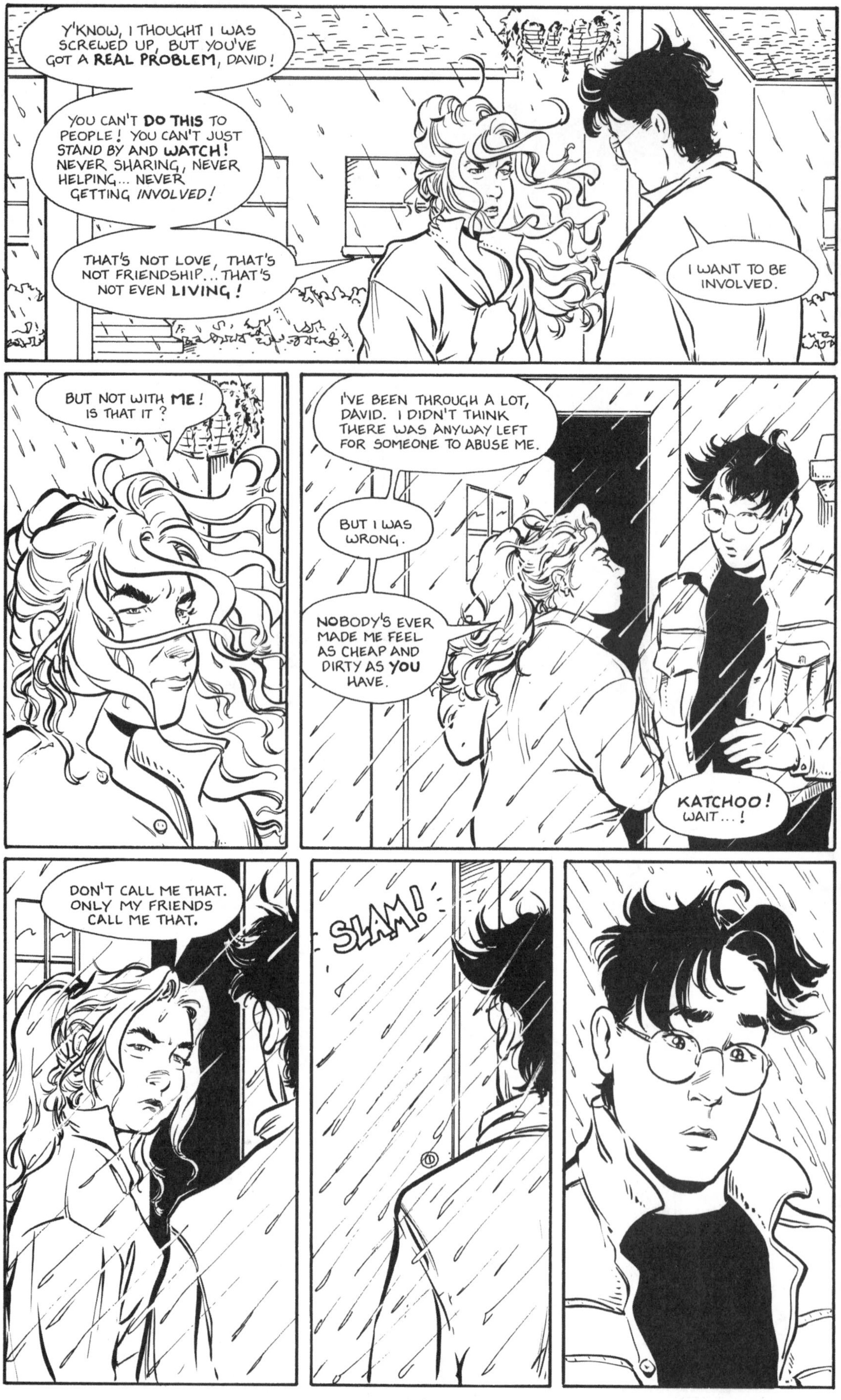
Y'KNOW, I THOUGHT I WAS SCREWED UP, BUT YOU'VE GOT A REAL PROBLEM, DAVID!
YOU CAN'T DO THIS TO PEOPLE! YOU CAN'T JUST STAND BY AND WATCH! NEVER SHARING, NEVER HELPING... NEVER GETTING INVOLVED!
THAT'S NOT LOVE, THAT'S NOT FRIENDSHIP... THAT'S NOT EVEN LIVING!
I WANT TO BE INVOLVED.
BUT NOT WITH ME! IS THAT IT?
I'VE BEEN THROUGH A LOT, DAVID. I DIDN'T THINK THERE WAS ANYWAY LEFT FOR SOMEONE TO ABUSE ME.
BUT I WAS WRONG.
NOBODY'S EVER MADE ME FEEL AS CHEAP AND DIRTY AS YOU HAVE.
KATCHOO! WAIT...!
DON'T CALL ME THAT. ONLY MY FRIENDS CALL ME THAT.
SLAM!

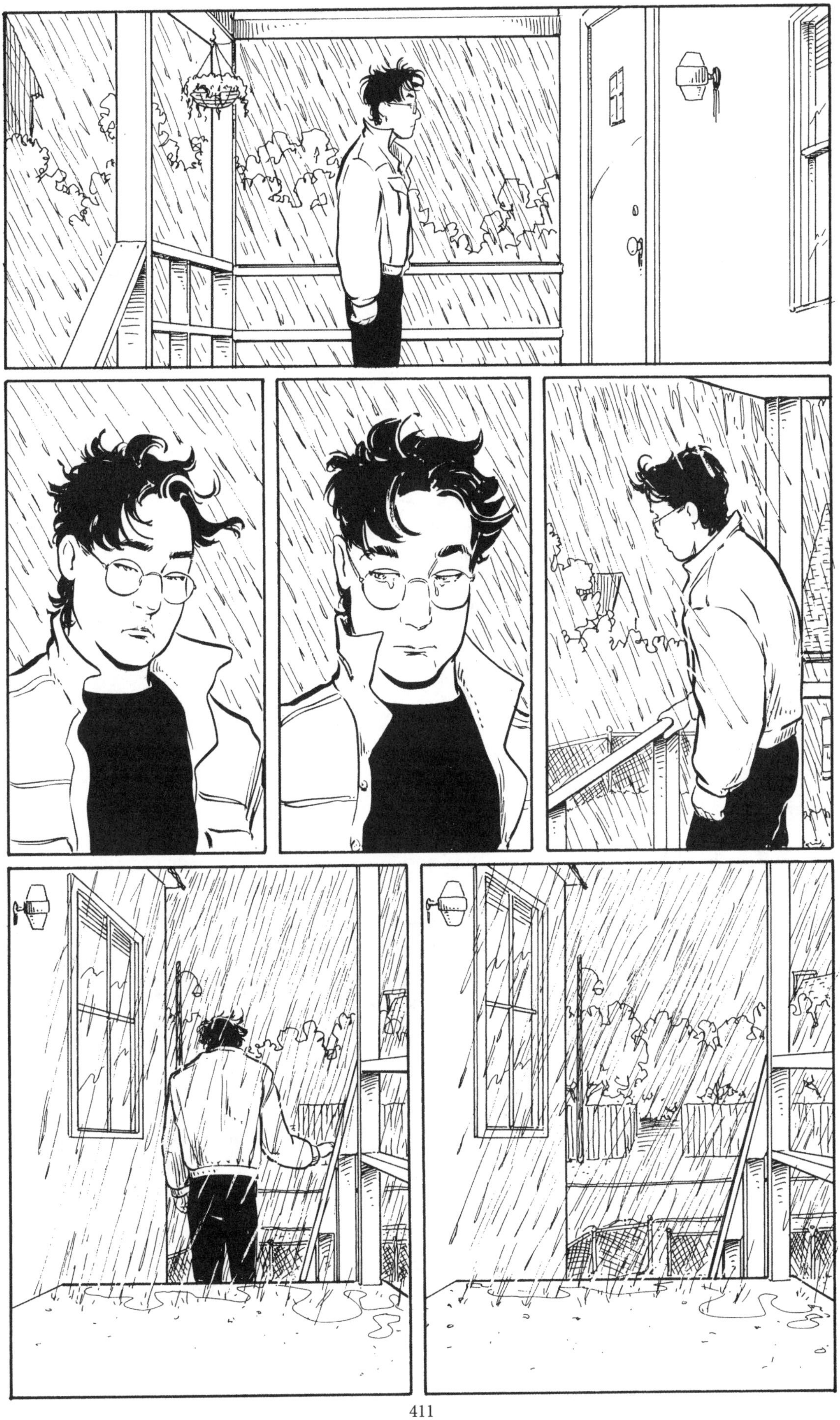

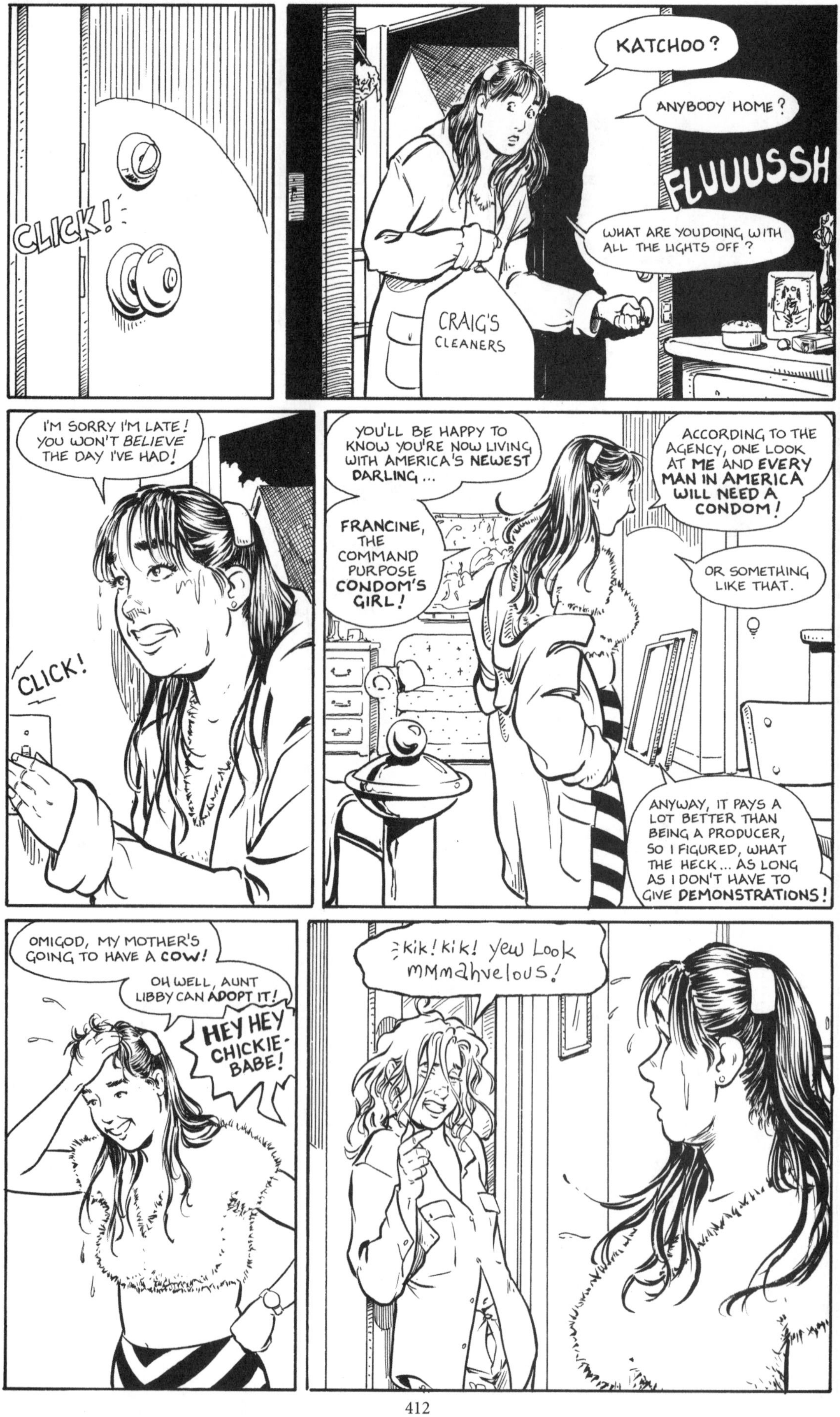

CLICK!
KATCHOO?
ANYBODY HOME?
FLUUUSSH
WHAT ARE YOU DOING WITH ALL THE LIGHTS OFF?
CRAIG'S CLEANERS
I'M SORRY I'M LATE! YOU WON'T BELIEVE THE DAY I'VE HAD!
CLICK!
YOU'LL BE HAPPY TO KNOW YOU'RE NOW LIVING WITH AMERICA'S NEWEST DARLING...
FRANCINE, THE COMMAND PURPOSE CONDOM'S GIRL!
ACCORDING TO THE AGENCY, ONE LOOK AT ME AND EVERY MAN IN AMERICA WILL NEED A CONDOM!
OR SOMETHING LIKE THAT.
ANYWAY, IT PAYS A LOT BETTER THAN BEING A PRODUCER, SO I FIGURED, WHAT THE HECK... AS LONG AS I DON'T HAVE TO GIVE DEMONSTRATIONS!
OMIGOD, MY MOTHER'S GOING TO HAVE A COW!
OH WELL, AUNT LIBBY CAN ADOPT IT!
HEY HEY CHICKIE-BABE!
kik! kik! yew Look mmmahvelous!

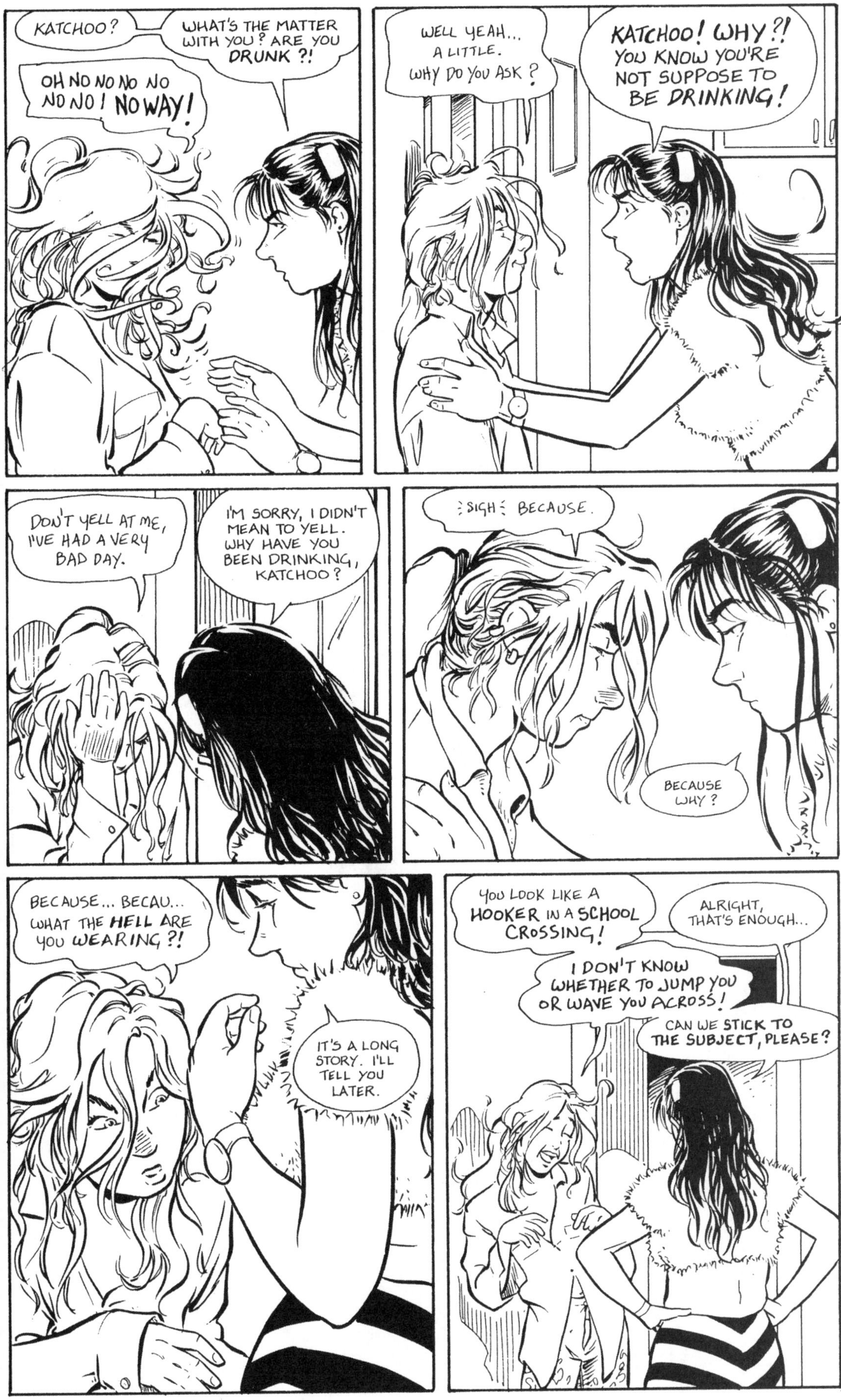

KATCHOO?
WHAT'S THE MATTER WITH YOU? ARE YOU DRUNK?!
OH NO NO NO NO NO NO! NO WAY!
WELL YEAH... A LITTLE. WHY DO YOU ASK?
KATCHOO! WHY?! YOU KNOW YOU'RE NOT SUPPOSE TO BE DRINKING!
DON'T YELL AT ME, I'VE HAD A VERY BAD DAY.
I'M SORRY, I DIDN'T MEAN TO YELL. WHY HAVE YOU BEEN DRINKING, KATCHOO?
:SIGH: BECAUSE.
BECAUSE WHY?
BECAUSE... BECAU... WHAT THE HELL ARE YOU WEARING?!
IT'S A LONG STORY. I'LL TELL YOU LATER.
YOU LOOK LIKE A HOOKER IN A SCHOOL CROSSING!
ALRIGHT, THAT'S ENOUGH...
I DON'T KNOW WHETHER TO JUMP YOU OR WAVE YOU ACROSS!
CAN WE STICK TO THE SUBJECT, PLEASE?

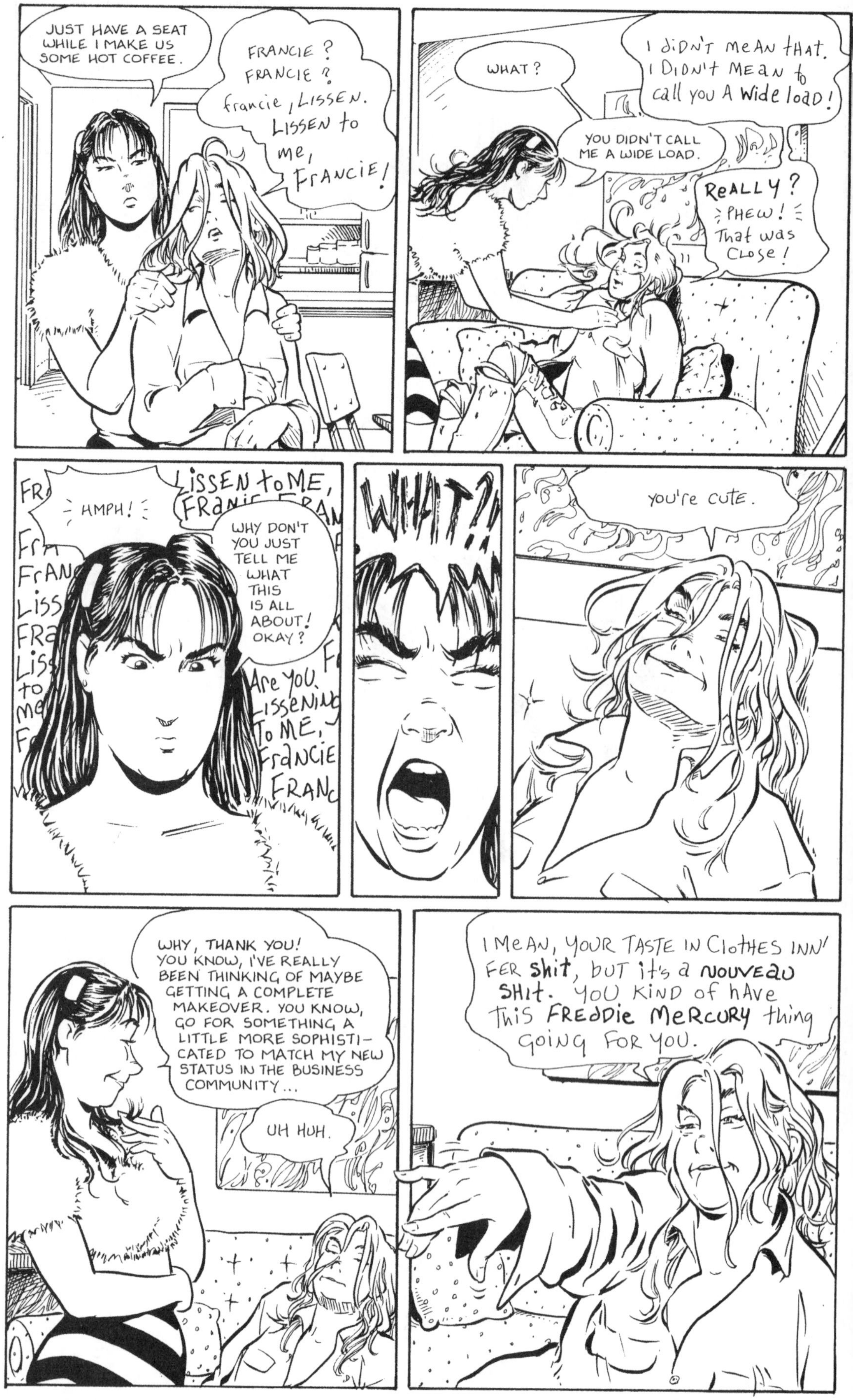
JUST HAVE A SEAT WHILE I MAKE US SOME HOT COFFEE.
FRANCIE? FRANCIE? francie, LISSEN. LISSEN to me, FRANCIE!
WHAT?
I DIDN'T MEAN THAT. I DIDN'T MEAN to call you A Wide load!
YOU DIDN'T CALL ME A WIDE LOAD.
REALLY? PHEW! That was Close!
HMPH!
WHY DON'T YOU JUST TELL ME WHAT THIS IS ALL ABOUT! OKAY?
WHAT?!
you're cute.
WHY, THANK YOU! YOU KNOW, I'VE REALLY BEEN THINKING OF MAYBE GETTING A COMPLETE MAKEOVER. YOU KNOW, GO FOR SOMETHING A LITTLE MORE SOPHISTI-CATED TO MATCH MY NEW STATUS IN THE BUSINESS COMMUNITY...
UH HUH.
I MEAN, YOUR TASTE IN CLOTHES INN' FER SHIT, BUT IT'S A NOUVEAU SHIT. YOU KIND OF HAVE THIS FREDDIE MERCURY thing GOING FOR YOU.

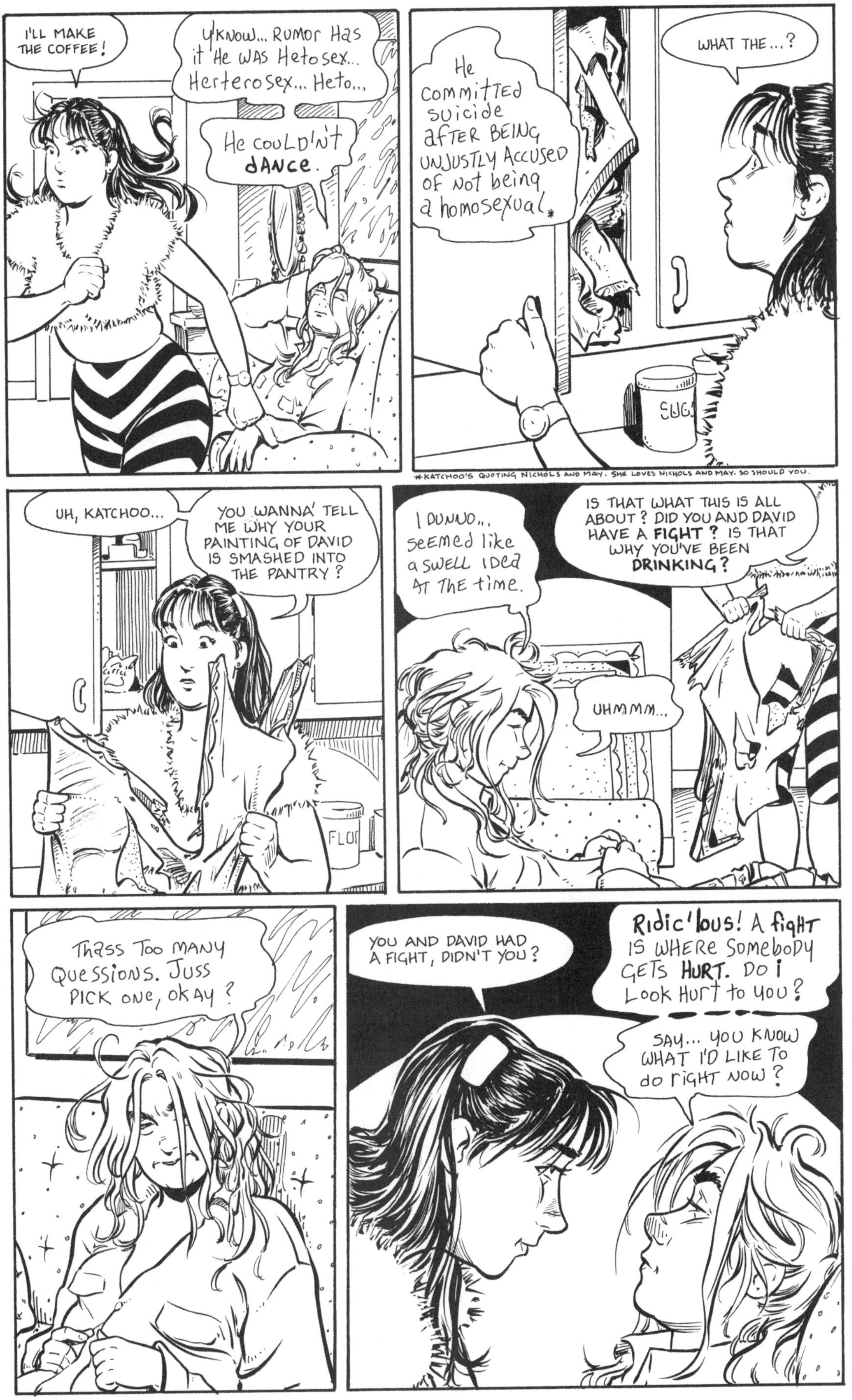

I'LL MAKE THE COFFEE!
Y'KNOW... RUMOR HAS IT HE WAS HETOSEX... HERTEROSEX... HETO...
HE COULDN'T DANCE.
HE COMMITTED SUICIDE AFTER BEING UNJUSTLY ACCUSED OF NOT BEING A HOMOSEXUAL.*
WHAT THE...?
SUG
*KATCHOO'S QUOTING NICHOLS AND MAY. SHE LOVES NICHOLS AND MAY. SO SHOULD YOU.
UH, KATCHOO...
YOU WANNA' TELL ME WHY YOUR PAINTING OF DAVID IS SMASHED INTO THE PANTRY?
FLOU
I DUNNO... SEEMED LIKE A SWELL IDEA AT THE TIME.
IS THAT WHAT THIS IS ALL ABOUT? DID YOU AND DAVID HAVE A FIGHT? IS THAT WHY YOU'VE BEEN DRINKING?
UHMMM...
THASS TOO MANY QUESSIONS. JUSS PICK ONE, OKAY?
YOU AND DAVID HAD A FIGHT, DIDN'T YOU?
RIDIC'LOUS! A FIGHT IS WHERE SOMEBODY GETS HURT. DO I LOOK HURT TO YOU?
SAY... YOU KNOW WHAT I'D LIKE TO DO RIGHT NOW?

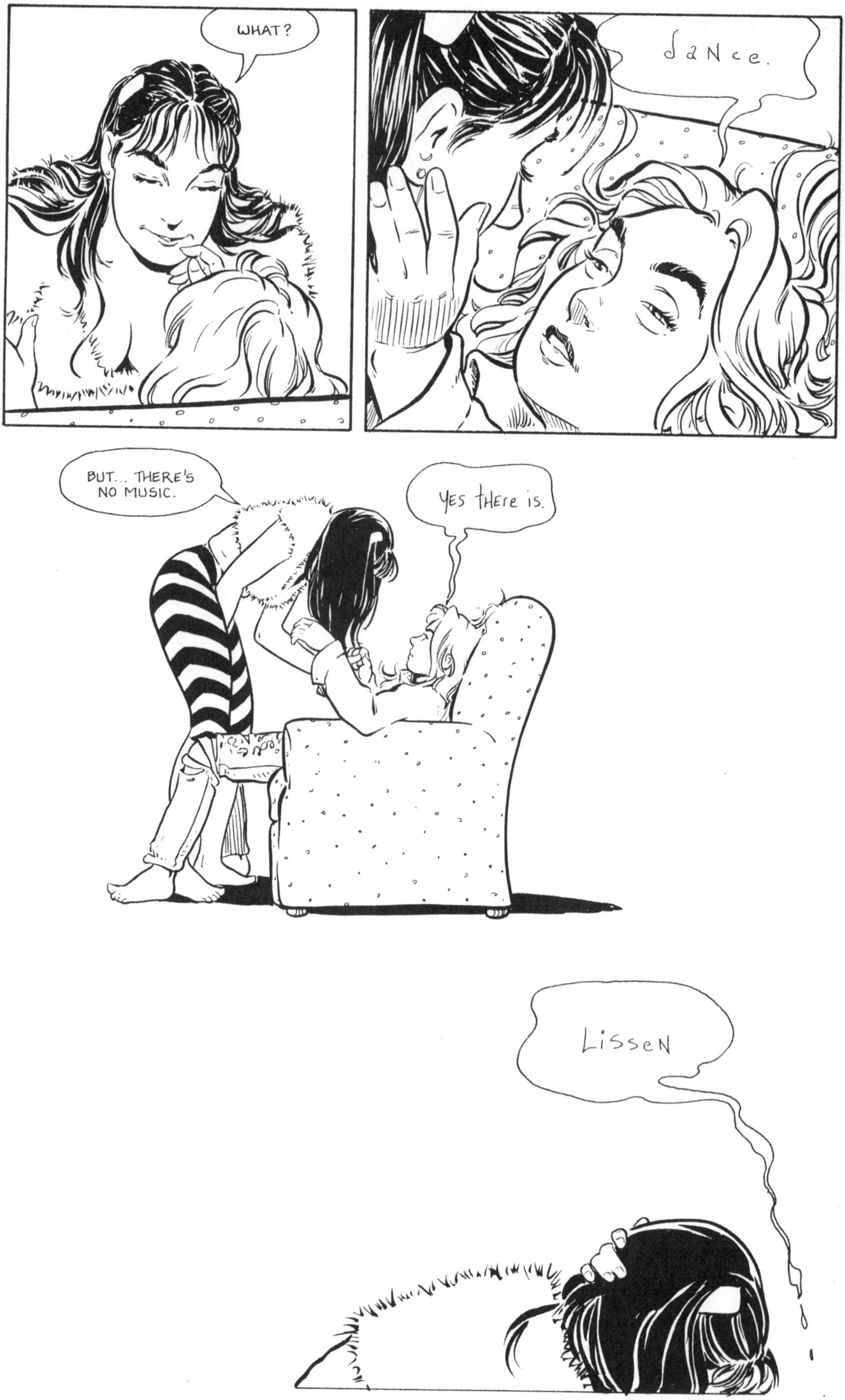
WHAT?
dance.
BUT... THERE'S NO MUSIC.
yes there is.
Lissen

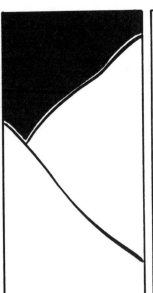

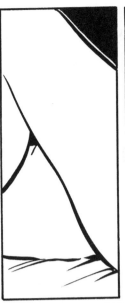

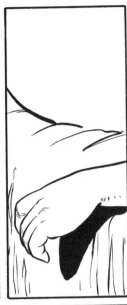

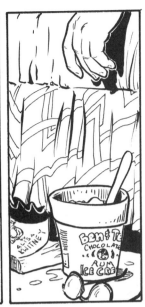

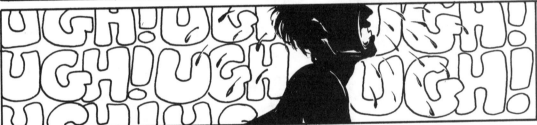

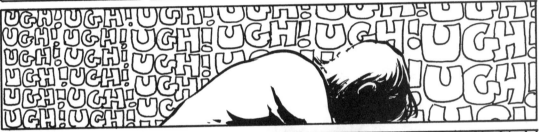

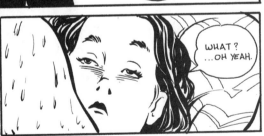

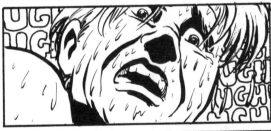

UGH! UGH! UGH! UGH! UGH!
UGH! UGH! UGH!
WHAT? ...OH YEAH.
COME ON BABY, COME ON. OH GOD, THAT FEELS SO GOOD. OH YES, LIKE THAT. THAT'S IT. OH GOD, YOU'RE AN ANIMAL. DO IT. YES. YES. YES.
OH YES, I'M CO... YAWN!
OH GOD THAT WAS INCREDIBLE. IT'S NEVER FELT LIKE THAT BEFORE. I WON'T BE ABLE TO WALK FOR A WEEK.
PANT! PANT! PANT

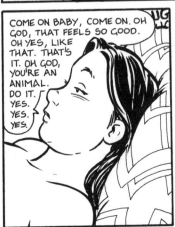

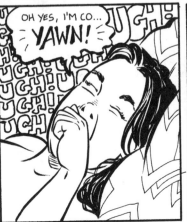

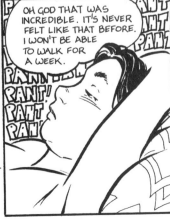

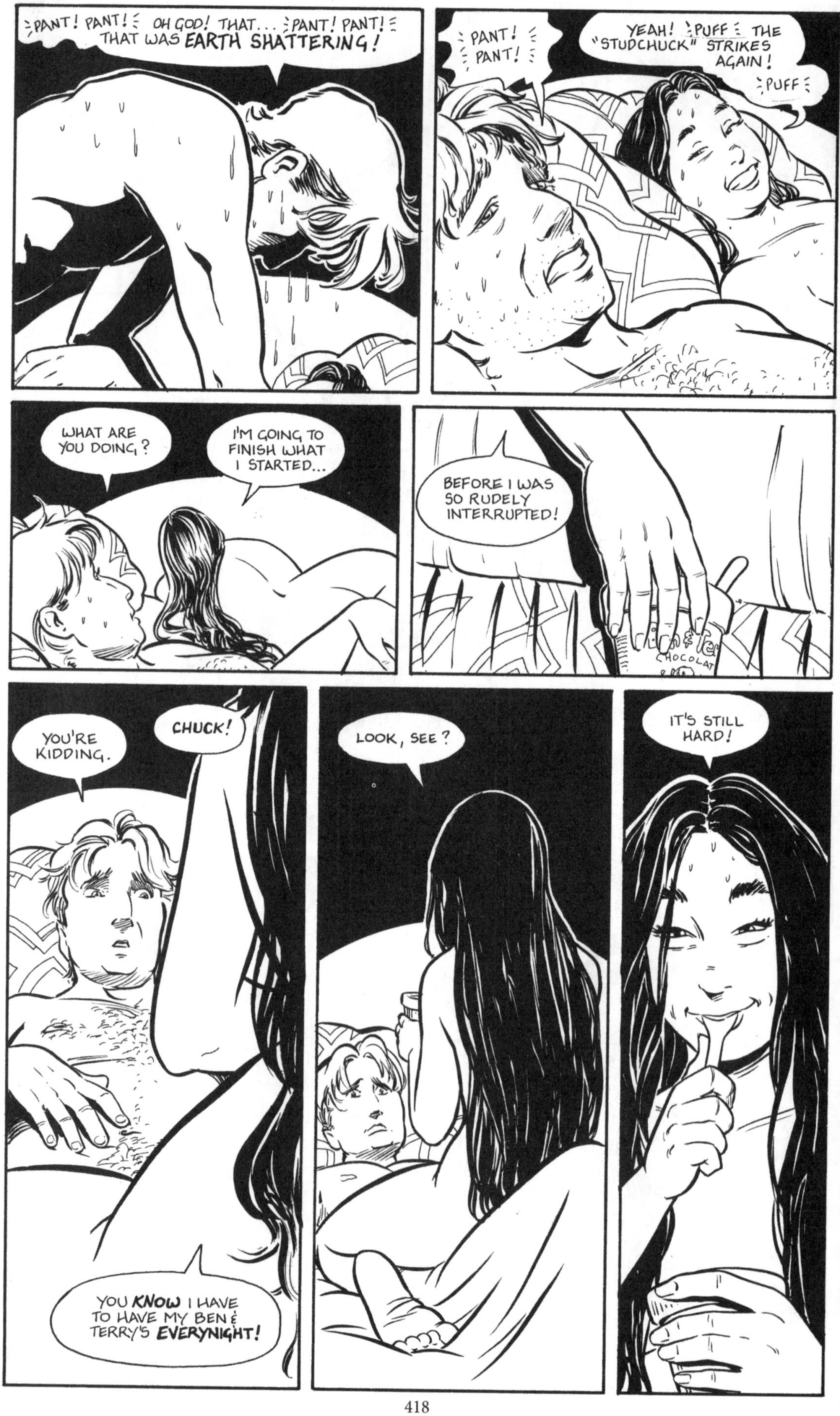
PANT! PANT! OH GOD! THAT... PANT! PANT! THAT WAS EARTH SHATTERING!
PANT! PANT!
YEAH! PUFF THE "STUDCHUCK" STRIKES AGAIN! PUFF
WHAT ARE YOU DOING?
I'M GOING TO FINISH WHAT I STARTED...
BEFORE I WAS SO RUDELY INTERRUPTED!
YOU'RE KIDDING.
CHUCK!
YOU KNOW I HAVE TO HAVE MY BEN & TERRY'S EVERYNIGHT!
LOOK, SEE?
IT'S STILL HARD!

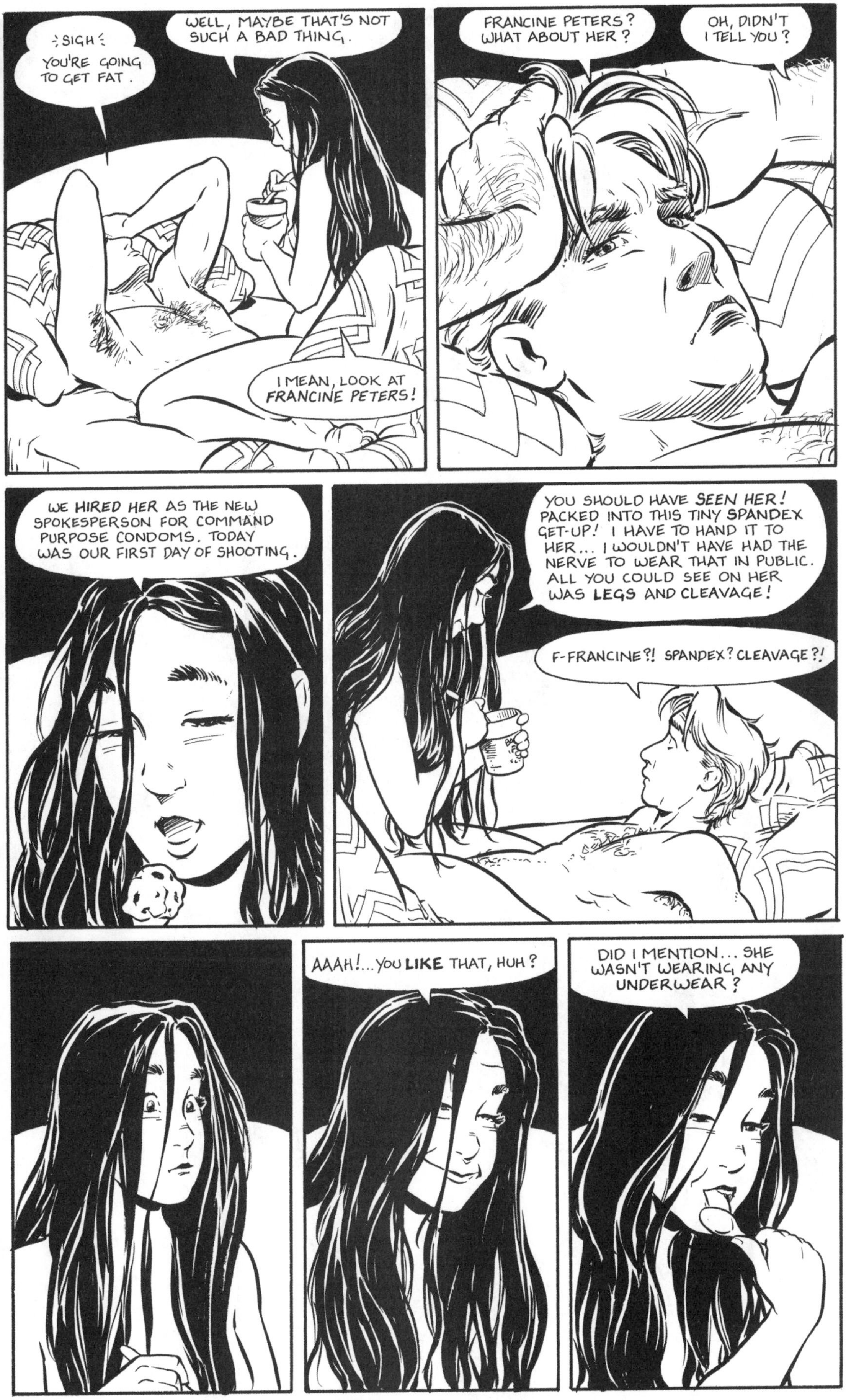
⁝SIGH⁝ YOU'RE GOING TO GET FAT.
WELL, MAYBE THAT'S NOT SUCH A BAD THING.
I MEAN, LOOK AT FRANCINE PETERS!
FRANCINE PETERS? WHAT ABOUT HER?
OH, DIDN'T I TELL YOU?
WE HIRED HER AS THE NEW SPOKESPERSON FOR COMMAND PURPOSE CONDOMS. TODAY WAS OUR FIRST DAY OF SHOOTING.
YOU SHOULD HAVE SEEN HER! PACKED INTO THIS TINY SPANDEX GET-UP! I HAVE TO HAND IT TO HER... I WOULDN'T HAVE HAD THE NERVE TO WEAR THAT IN PUBLIC. ALL YOU COULD SEE ON HER WAS LEGS AND CLEAVAGE!
F-FRANCINE?! SPANDEX? CLEAVAGE?!
AAAH!...YOU LIKE THAT, HUH?
DID I MENTION... SHE WASN'T WEARING ANY UNDERWEAR?

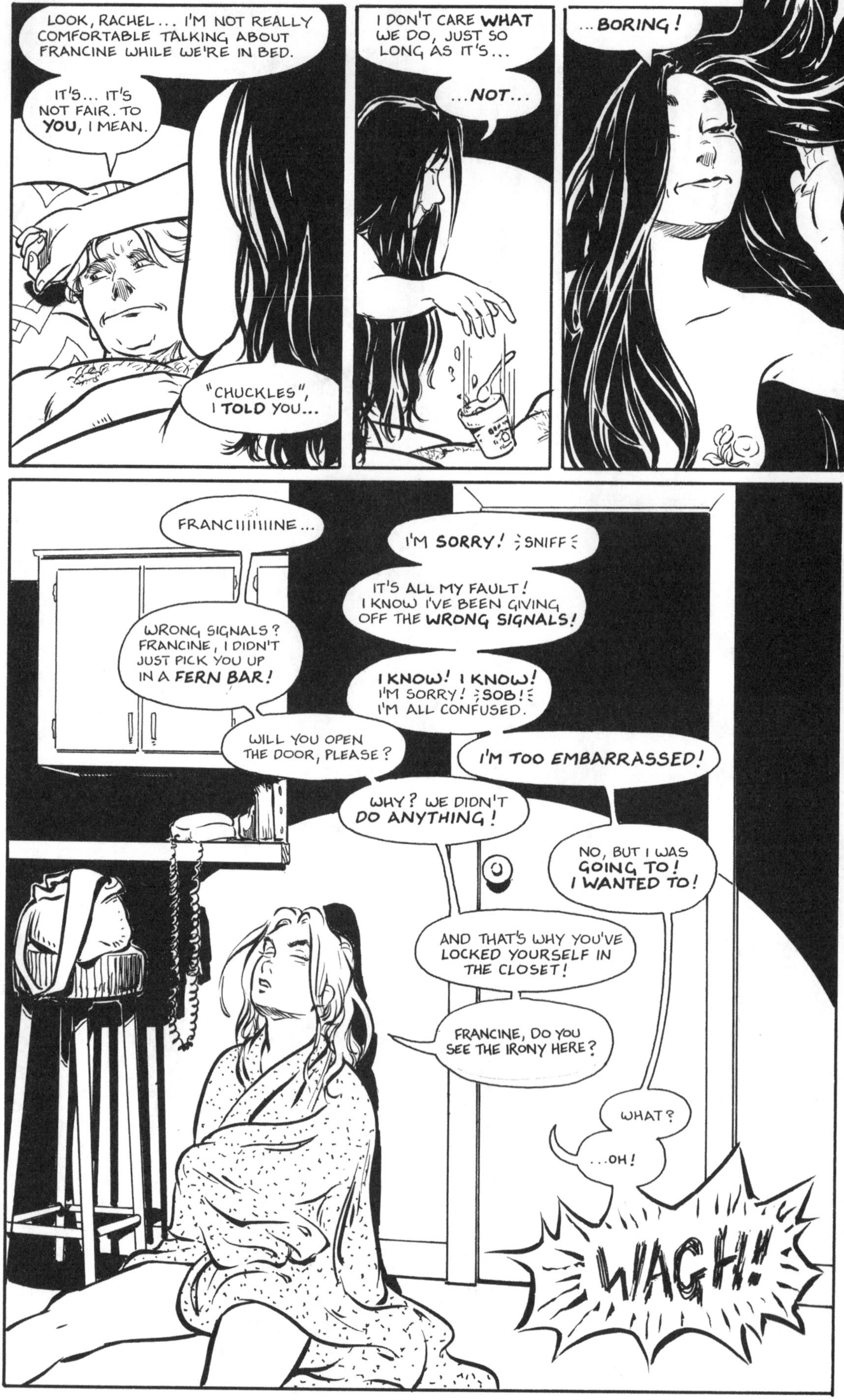

LOOK, RACHEL... I'M NOT REALLY COMFORTABLE TALKING ABOUT FRANCINE WHILE WE'RE IN BED.
IT'S... IT'S NOT FAIR. TO YOU, I MEAN.
"CHUCKLES", I TOLD YOU...
I DON'T CARE WHAT WE DO, JUST SO LONG AS IT'S...
...NOT...
...BORING!
FRANCIIIIIIINE...
I'M SORRY! ;SNIFF;
IT'S ALL MY FAULT! I KNOW I'VE BEEN GIVING OFF THE WRONG SIGNALS!
WRONG SIGNALS? FRANCINE, I DIDN'T JUST PICK YOU UP IN A FERN BAR!
I KNOW! I KNOW! I'M SORRY! ;SOB! I'M ALL CONFUSED.
WILL YOU OPEN THE DOOR, PLEASE?
I'M TOO EMBARRASSED!
WHY? WE DIDN'T DO ANYTHING!
NO, BUT I WAS GOING TO! I WANTED TO!
AND THAT'S WHY YOU'VE LOCKED YOURSELF IN THE CLOSET!
FRANCINE, DO YOU SEE THE IRONY HERE?
WHAT?
...OH!
WAGH!!

WHAT'S THE MOST **EMBARRASS-ING** THING THAT'S EVER HAPPENED TO YOU?

DID YOU SPEND YOUR FIRST DATE WITH FOOD ON YOUR TEETH?

DID YOU GET CAUGHT SHOP-LIFTING IN THE MALL WHEN YOU WERE 15?

DID YOUR ROBE COME OFF DURING THE SENIOR PLAY?

MAYBE YOU CALLED YOUR FIRST BOSS BILL FOR A WEEK BEFORE SOMEBODY TOLD YOU IT WAS BOB.

OR MAYBE YOU ALMOST HAD **SEX** WITH YOUR BEST FRIEND BUT COULDN'T GO THROUGH WITH IT AND LOCKED YOUR-SELF IN THE CLOSET BE-CAUSE YOU WERE **SO EM-BARRASSED** AND YOU WOULDN'T COME OUT AND YOUR BEST FRIEND SAT OUTSIDE THE DOOR HALF THE NIGHT UNTIL SHE FELL ASLEEP AND YOU SPENT THE REST OF THE NIGHT ON THE COUCH AND TRIED TO **SNEAK OUT** TO WORK THE NEXT MORNING WITHOUT WAKING HER UP AND SHE CAUGHT YOU DOING IT AND TOOK A **POLOROID** OF YOU DOING IT TO SHOW YOU HOW **STUPID** YOU LOOKED DOING IT.

K-FLASH!

OKAY, SO MAYBE YOUR ROBE *DIDN'T* COME OFF DURING THE SENIOR PLAY. IT DOESN'T MATTER...

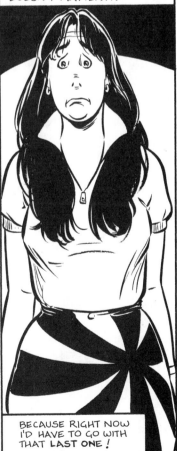

BECAUSE RIGHT NOW I'D HAVE TO GO WITH THAT **LAST ONE!**

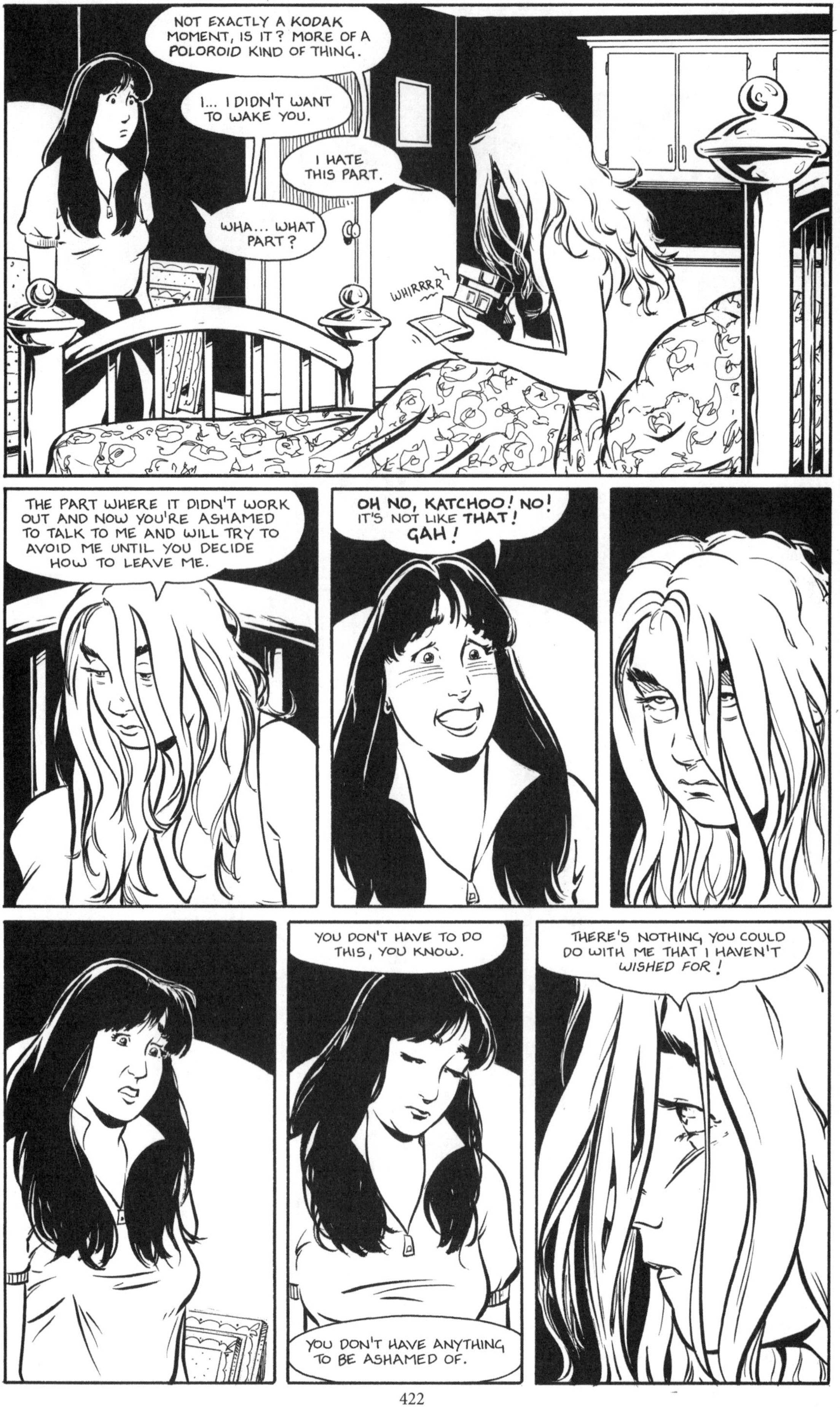

NOT EXACTLY A KODAK MOMENT, IS IT? MORE OF A POLOROID KIND OF THING.
I... I DIDN'T WANT TO WAKE YOU.
I HATE THIS PART.
WHA... WHAT PART?
WHIRRRR
THE PART WHERE IT DIDN'T WORK OUT AND NOW YOU'RE ASHAMED TO TALK TO ME AND WILL TRY TO AVOID ME UNTIL YOU DECIDE HOW TO LEAVE ME.
OH NO, KATCHOO! NO! IT'S NOT LIKE THAT! GAH!
YOU DON'T HAVE TO DO THIS, YOU KNOW.
YOU DON'T HAVE ANYTHING TO BE ASHAMED OF.
THERE'S NOTHING YOU COULD DO WITH ME THAT I HAVEN'T WISHED FOR!

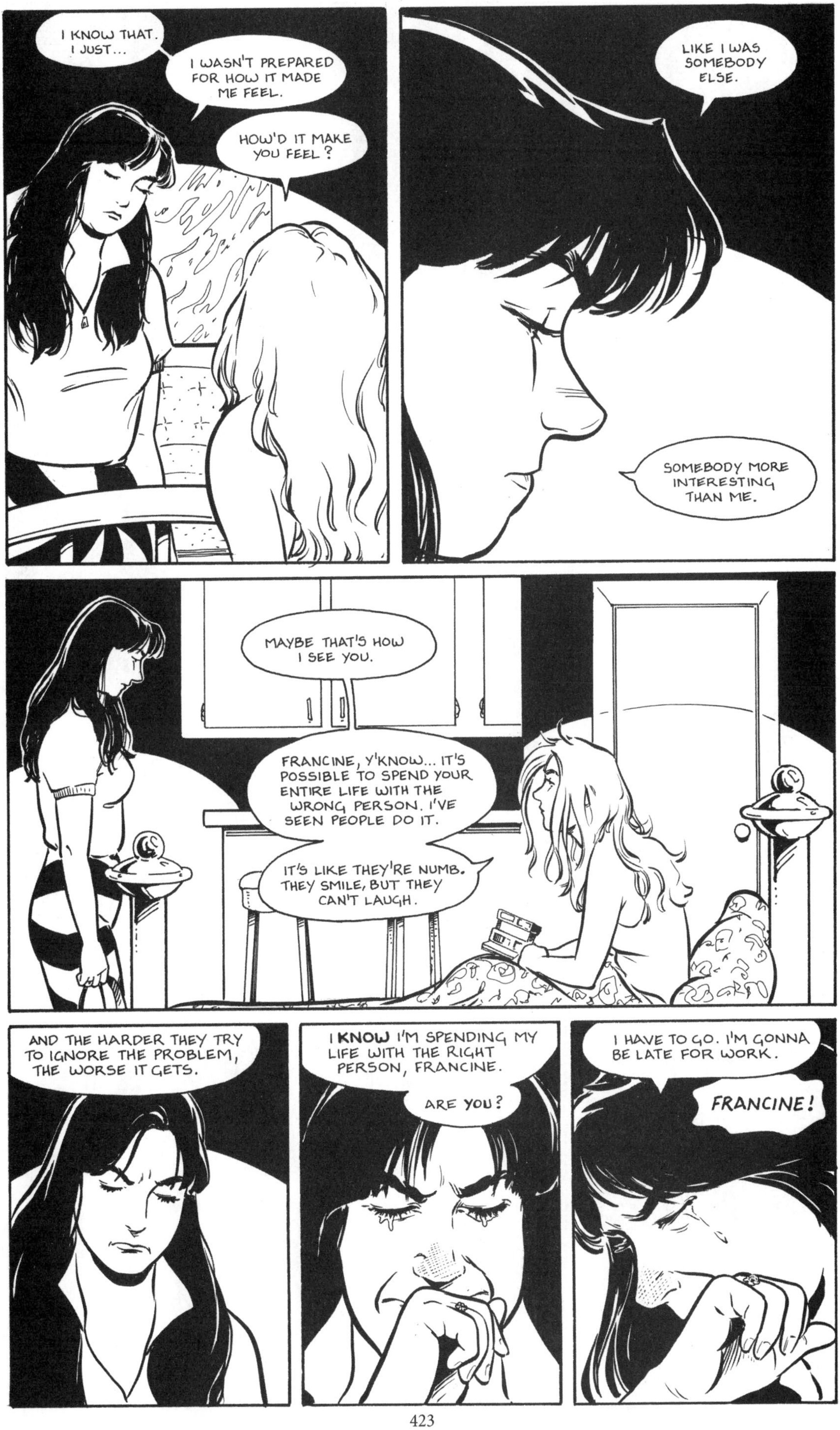
I KNOW THAT. I JUST...
I WASN'T PREPARED FOR HOW IT MADE ME FEEL.
HOW'D IT MAKE YOU FEEL?
LIKE I WAS SOMEBODY ELSE.
SOMEBODY MORE INTERESTING THAN ME.
MAYBE THAT'S HOW I SEE YOU.
FRANCINE, Y'KNOW... IT'S POSSIBLE TO SPEND YOUR ENTIRE LIFE WITH THE WRONG PERSON. I'VE SEEN PEOPLE DO IT.
IT'S LIKE THEY'RE NUMB. THEY SMILE, BUT THEY CAN'T LAUGH.
AND THE HARDER THEY TRY TO IGNORE THE PROBLEM, THE WORSE IT GETS.
I KNOW I'M SPENDING MY LIFE WITH THE RIGHT PERSON, FRANCINE.
ARE YOU?
I HAVE TO GO. I'M GONNA BE LATE FOR WORK.
FRANCINE!

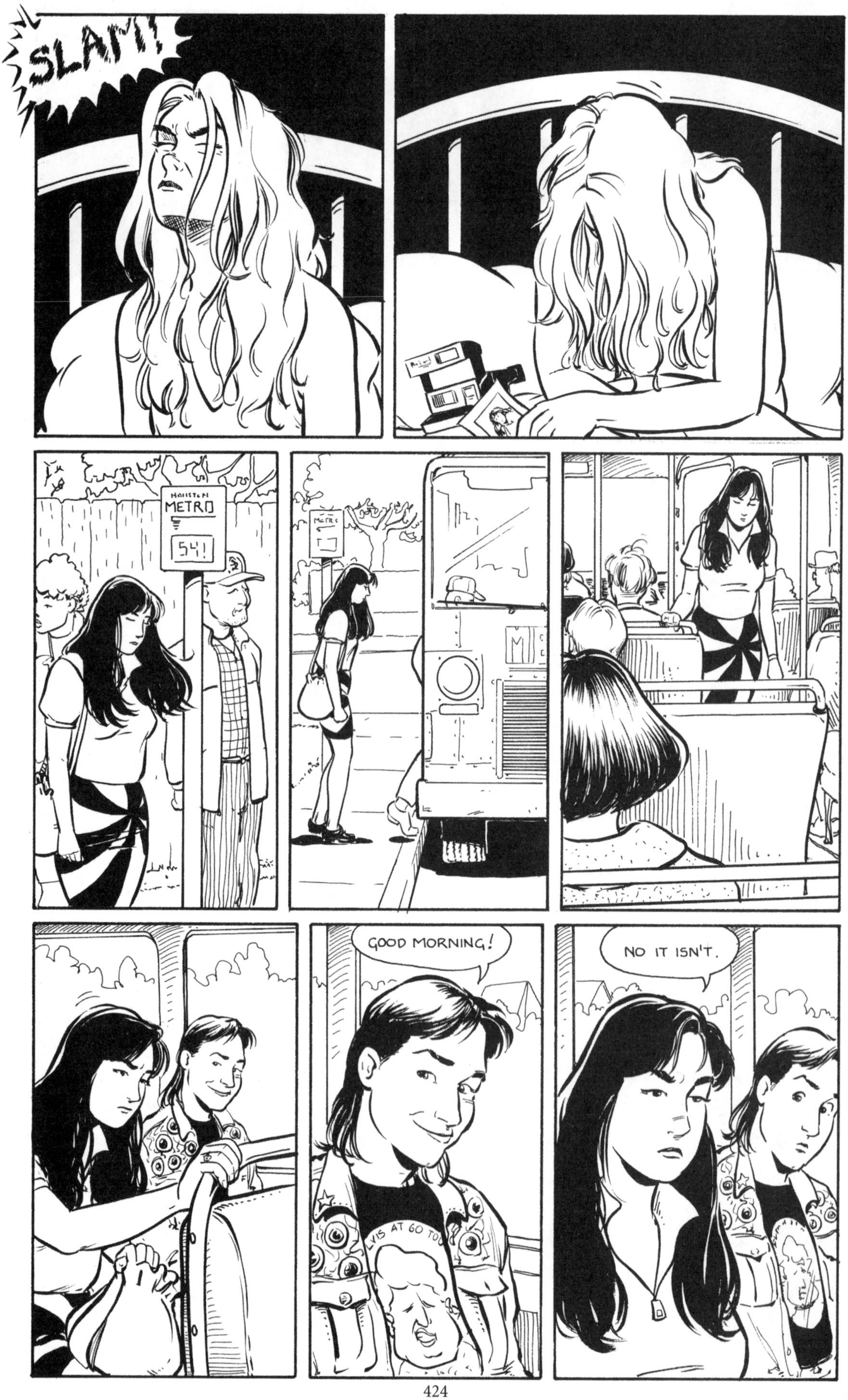
SLAM!
HOUSTON
METRO
54!
GOOD MORNING!
NO IT ISN'T.

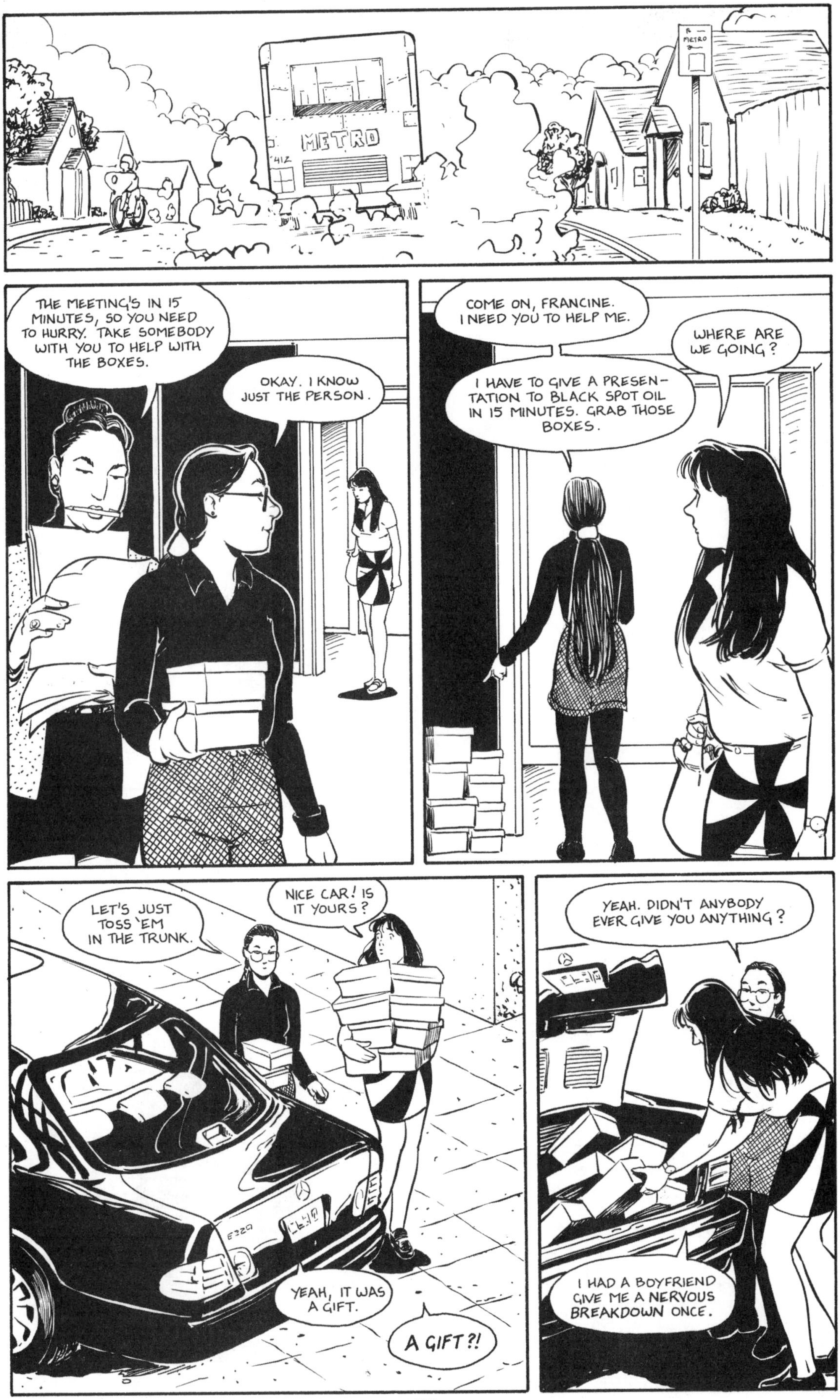
METRO
412
METRO
THE MEETING'S IN 15 MINUTES, SO YOU NEED TO HURRY. TAKE SOMEBODY WITH YOU TO HELP WITH THE BOXES.
OKAY. I KNOW JUST THE PERSON.
COME ON, FRANCINE. I NEED YOU TO HELP ME.
I HAVE TO GIVE A PRESENTATION TO BLACK SPOT OIL IN 15 MINUTES. GRAB THOSE BOXES.
WHERE ARE WE GOING?
LET'S JUST TOSS 'EM IN THE TRUNK.
NICE CAR! IS IT YOURS?
YEAH, IT WAS A GIFT.
A GIFT?!
YEAH. DIDN'T ANYBODY EVER GIVE YOU ANYTHING?
I HAD A BOYFRIEND GIVE ME A NERVOUS BREAKDOWN ONCE.

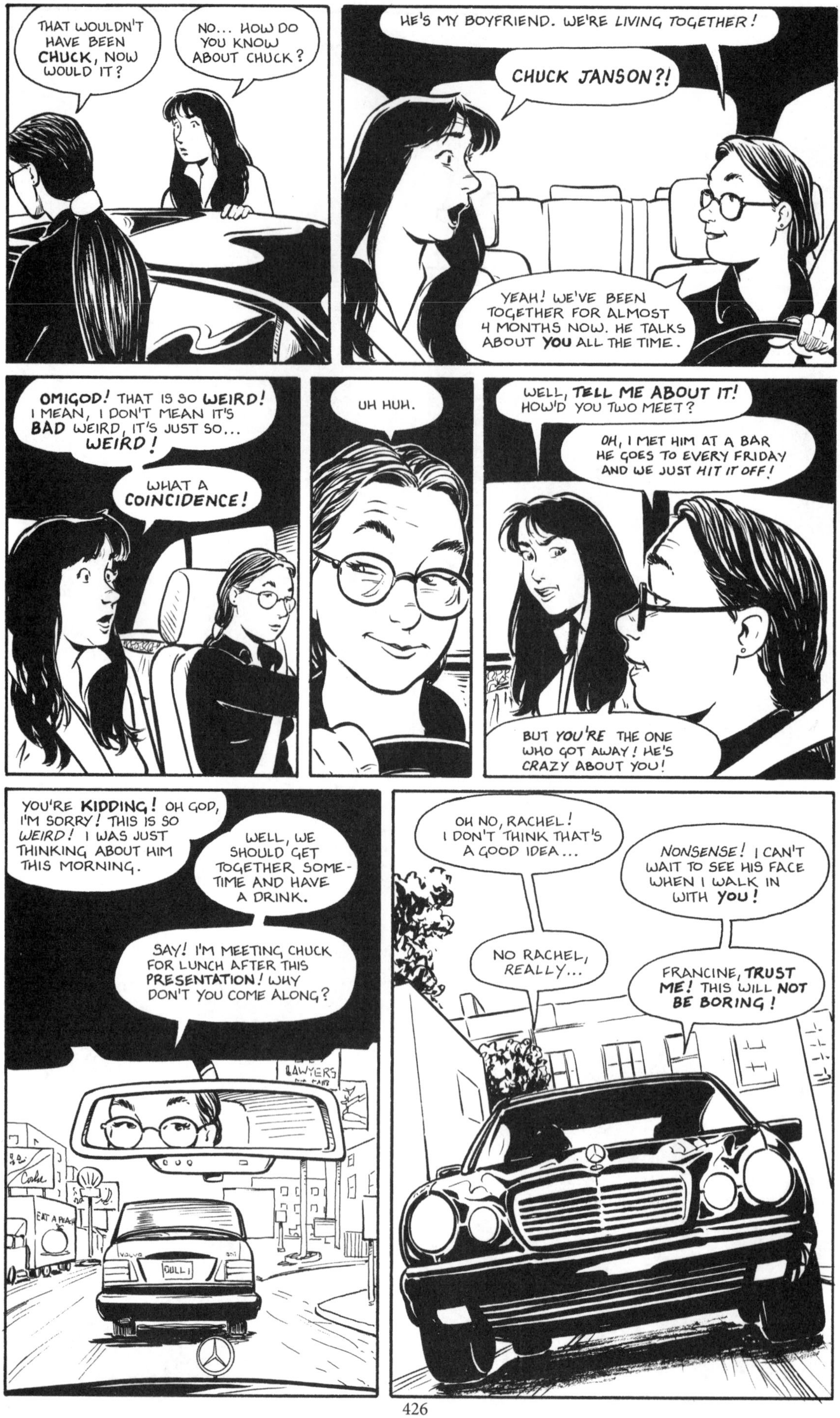
THAT WOULDN'T HAVE BEEN **CHUCK**, NOW WOULD IT?
NO... HOW DO YOU KNOW ABOUT CHUCK?
HE'S MY BOYFRIEND. WE'RE *LIVING TOGETHER!*
CHUCK JANSON?!
YEAH! WE'VE BEEN TOGETHER FOR ALMOST 4 MONTHS NOW. HE TALKS ABOUT **YOU** ALL THE TIME.
OMIGOD! THAT IS SO **WEIRD!** I MEAN, I DON'T MEAN IT'S **BAD** WEIRD, IT'S JUST SO... **WEIRD!**
WHAT A **COINCIDENCE!**
UH HUH.
WELL, **TELL ME ABOUT IT!** HOW'D YOU TWO MEET?
OH, I MET HIM AT A BAR HE GOES TO EVERY FRIDAY AND WE JUST *HIT IT OFF!*
BUT *YOU'RE* THE ONE WHO GOT AWAY! HE'S *CRAZY* ABOUT YOU!
YOU'RE **KIDDING!** OH GOD, I'M SORRY! THIS IS SO *WEIRD!* I WAS JUST THINKING ABOUT HIM THIS MORNING.
WELL, WE SHOULD GET TOGETHER SOMETIME AND HAVE A DRINK.
SAY! I'M MEETING CHUCK FOR LUNCH AFTER THIS **PRESENTATION!** WHY DON'T YOU COME ALONG?
LAWYERS
EAT A PEACH
OH NO, RACHEL! I DON'T THINK THAT'S A GOOD IDEA...
NONSENSE! I CAN'T WAIT TO SEE HIS FACE WHEN I WALK IN WITH **YOU!**
NO RACHEL, *REALLY...*
FRANCINE, **TRUST ME!** THIS WILL **NOT BE BORING!**

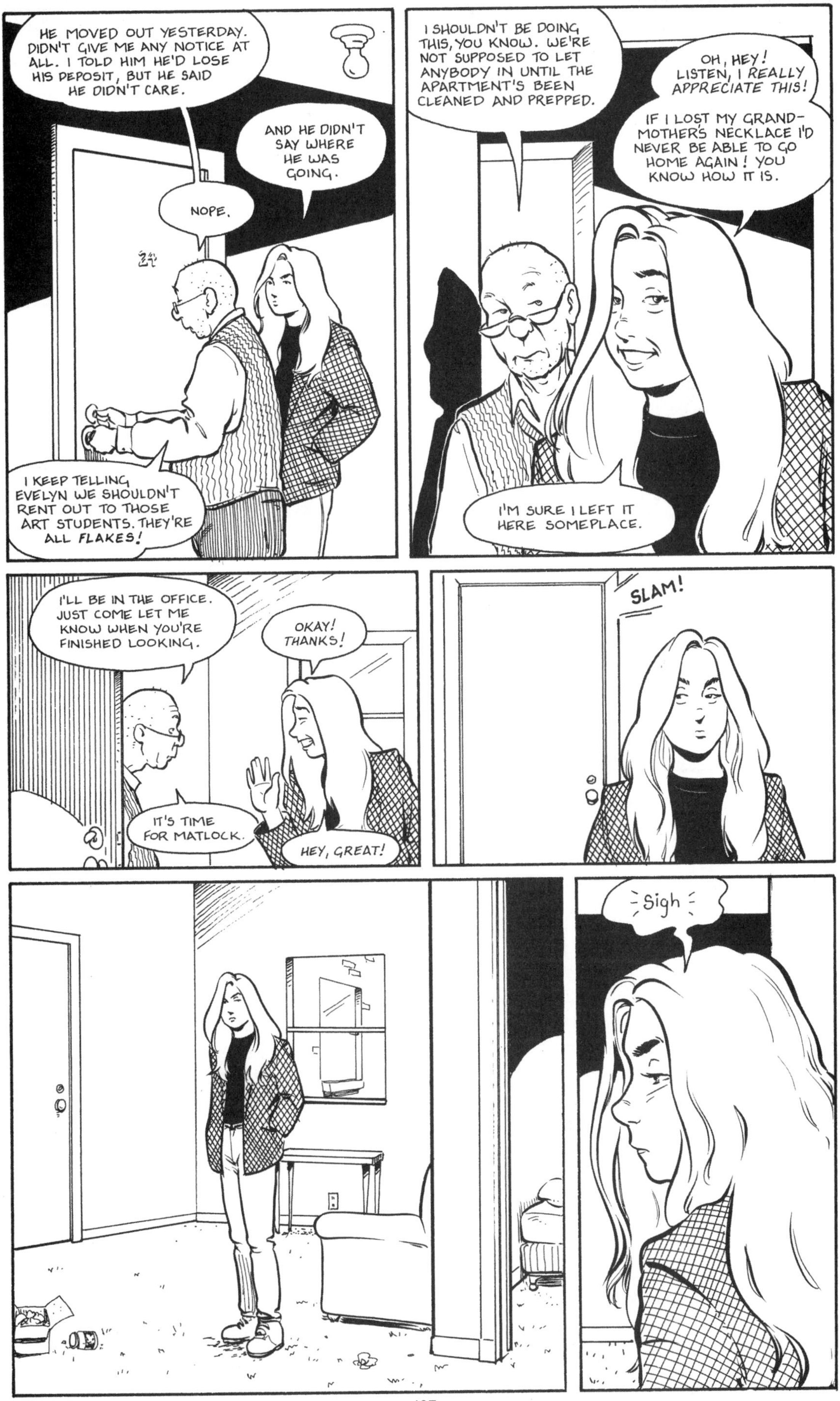
HE MOVED OUT YESTERDAY. DIDN'T GIVE ME ANY NOTICE AT ALL. I TOLD HIM HE'D LOSE HIS DEPOSIT, BUT HE SAID HE DIDN'T CARE.
AND HE DIDN'T SAY WHERE HE WAS GOING.
NOPE.
I KEEP TELLING EVELYN WE SHOULDN'T RENT OUT TO THOSE ART STUDENTS. THEY'RE ALL FLAKES!
I SHOULDN'T BE DOING THIS, YOU KNOW. WE'RE NOT SUPPOSED TO LET ANYBODY IN UNTIL THE APARTMENT'S BEEN CLEANED AND PREPPED.
OH, HEY! LISTEN, I REALLY APPRECIATE THIS!
IF I LOST MY GRAND-MOTHER'S NECKLACE I'D NEVER BE ABLE TO GO HOME AGAIN! YOU KNOW HOW IT IS.
I'M SURE I LEFT IT HERE SOMEPLACE.
I'LL BE IN THE OFFICE. JUST COME LET ME KNOW WHEN YOU'RE FINISHED LOOKING.
OKAY! THANKS!
IT'S TIME FOR MATLOCK.
HEY, GREAT!
SLAM!
Sigh

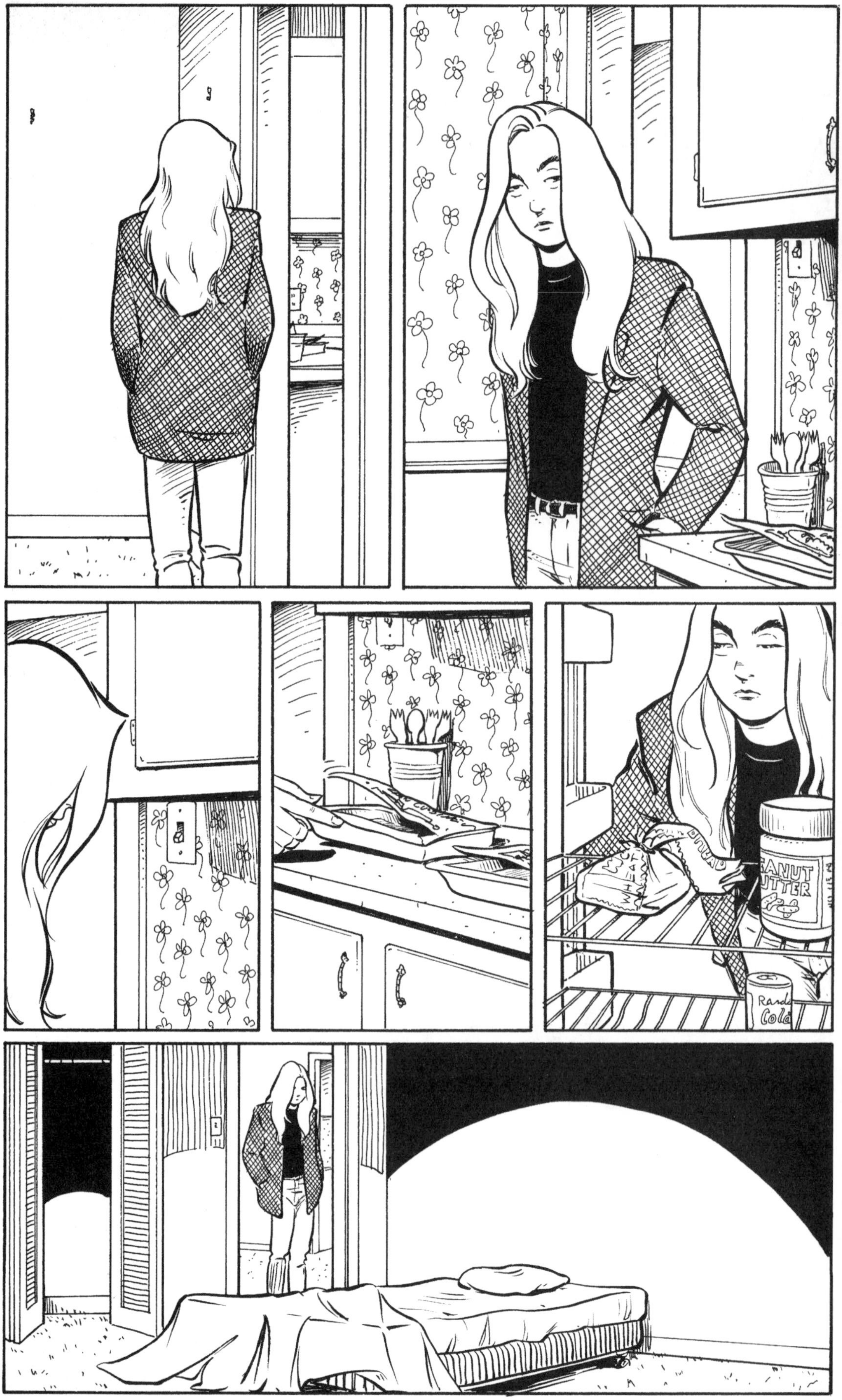
EANUT
UTTER
Cola

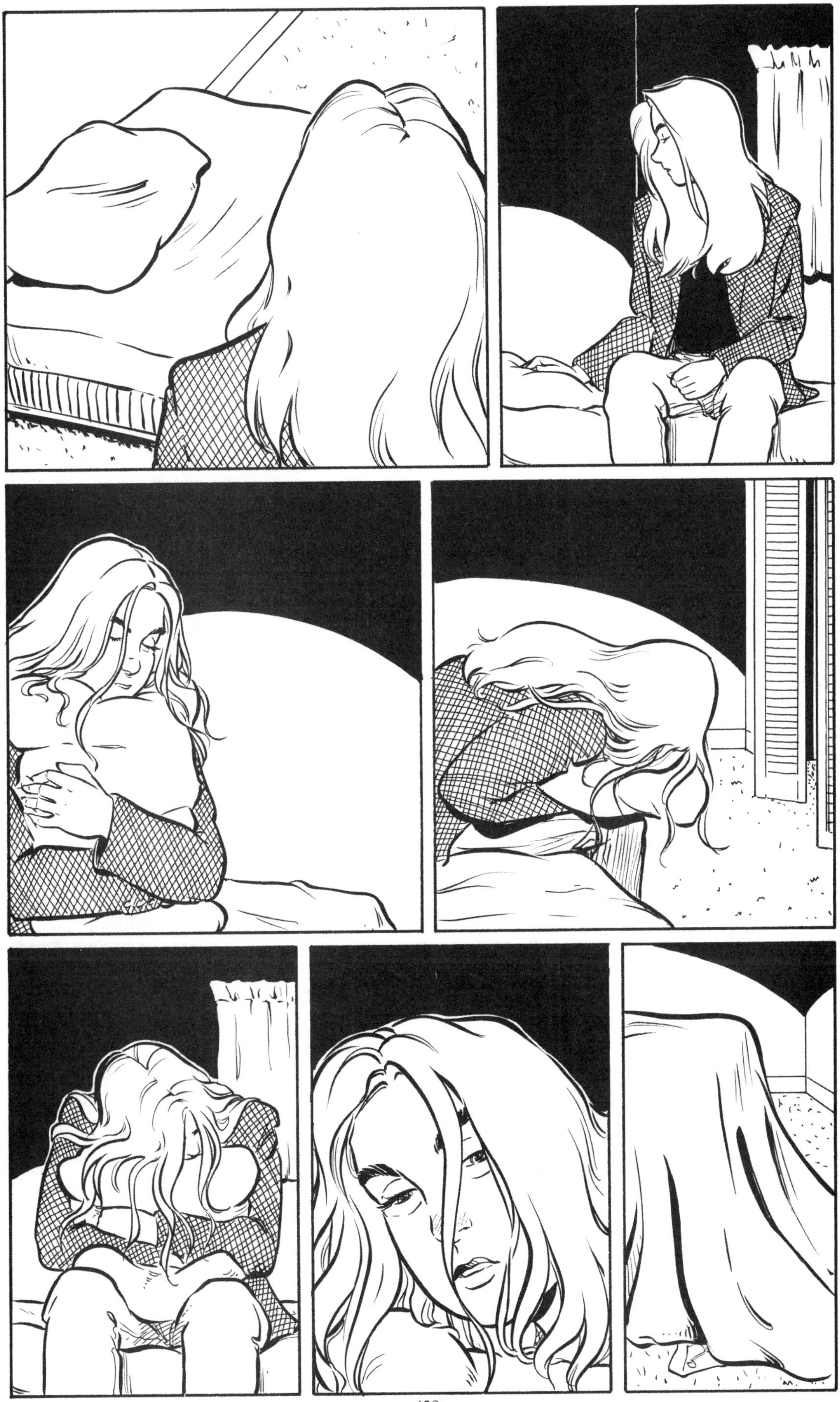

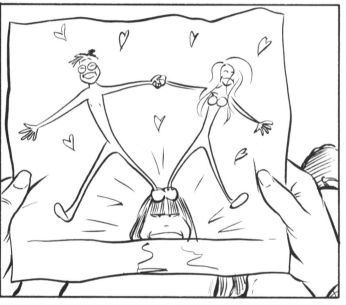

giggle

HA! HA! HA! HA! HA!

430

AS YOU CAN SEE, RUTNER BOVIS' PLAN WILL GIVE BLACK SPOT OIL ALMOST **60% RECOGNITION** WITHIN A 12 MONTH PERIOD, UP FROM YOUR CURRENT **3%!** AND WE CAN ACCOMPLISH THIS **WITHIN** YOUR REQUIRED BUDGET!

☐ = RBKS PLAN
☐ = PRESENT

60% BSO — 3% THE COMPETITION

BLACK SPOT OIL Co 1997 MARKET GROWTH CONSUMER SHARE

RATHER IMPRESSIVE, WOULDN'T YOU SAY?

YES. WELL...

* AHEM *

PERHAPS I SHOULD TRY PUTTING IT ANOTHER WAY.

FRANCINE, WILL YOU GIVE ME A HAND HERE PLEASE? YES, **YOU.** COME ON.

IF YOU'LL JUST HOLD THIS FOR ME. HERE, BRACE IT AGAINST YOU LIKE THIS...

BSO w/ RBKS

COMPETITION

NOW THEN, GENTLEMEN... IF YOU'LL LOOK **CLOSELY** AT THIS CHART... YOU CAN...

BSO w/ RBKS

COMPETITION

...**CLEARLY** SEE THE **GROWTH**...

...AS WE **EXPAND** THROUGH THE **COMING YEAR**...

...UNTIL WE **BUST** RIGHT THROUGH EVERY RESTRAINT THE MARKET HAS...

...**STRIPPING** THE COMPETITION **BARE**!

MAKING **BLACK SPOT OIL** THE *NUMBER ONE* **BULL** IN AMERICA'S **BEAR** MARKET, THE CONSUMER'S CHOICE FOR ALL HER **SLIPPERY NEEDS**! THAT IS, **IF** YOU DECIDE TO GO WITH *RUTNER BOVIS*!

ALL WE ASK IS YOU GIVE US A CHANCE TO **SHOW YOU WHAT WE'VE GOT**!

BRAVO! BRAVO! CLAP! CLA CLAP! CLA YES!

CLAP! CLAP! CLAP! CL CLAP! CL CLAP

ACCOUNT, HELL! GIVE HER THE WHOLE DAMN COMPANY!

CLAP! CLAP! CLAP!

JUST SAY THE WORD AND I'LL BUY YOU A CORVETTE AND A NICE LITTLE CONDO BY THE PARK!

CLAP! CLAP! CLAP!

WHAT THE HELL DO YOU THINK YOU'RE DOING?!

WINNING THE ACCOUNT.

I'VE NEVER BEEN SO EMBARRASSED IN MY ENTIRE LIFE!

THEN YOU NEED TO GET OUT MORE OFTEN.

BLACK SPO PLAZ

LOOK, I JUST SHOWED YOU THE ANSWER TO LIFE, THE UNIVERSE AND EVERYTHING! NOW WHAT YOU DO WITH THAT POWER IS UP TO YOU, BUT I SUGGEST WE BREAK FOR LUNCH FIRST!

C'MON, "BUBBLES"!

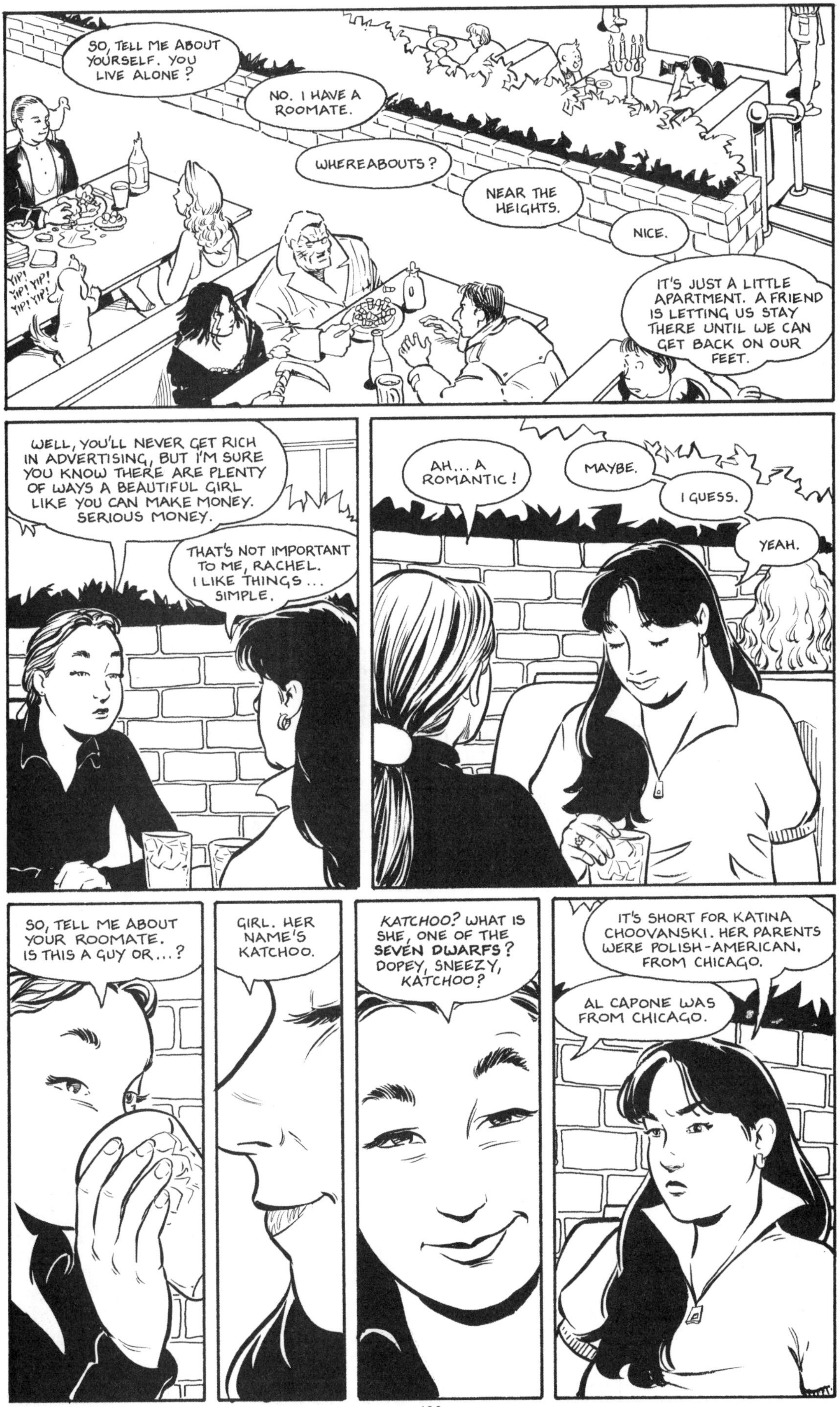
SO, TELL ME ABOUT YOURSELF. YOU LIVE ALONE?
NO. I HAVE A ROOMATE.
WHEREABOUTS?
NEAR THE HEIGHTS.
NICE.
IT'S JUST A LITTLE APARTMENT. A FRIEND IS LETTING US STAY THERE UNTIL WE CAN GET BACK ON OUR FEET.
YIP! YIP! YIP! YIP! YIP! YIP!
WELL, YOU'LL NEVER GET RICH IN ADVERTISING, BUT I'M SURE YOU KNOW THERE ARE PLENTY OF WAYS A BEAUTIFUL GIRL LIKE YOU CAN MAKE MONEY. SERIOUS MONEY.
THAT'S NOT IMPORTANT TO ME, RACHEL. I LIKE THINGS... SIMPLE.
AH... A ROMANTIC!
MAYBE.
I GUESS.
YEAH.
SO, TELL ME ABOUT YOUR ROOMATE. IS THIS A GUY OR...?
GIRL. HER NAME'S KATCHOO.
KATCHOO? WHAT IS SHE, ONE OF THE SEVEN DWARFS? DOPEY, SNEEZY, KATCHOO?
IT'S SHORT FOR KATINA CHOOVANSKI. HER PARENTS WERE POLISH-AMERICAN, FROM CHICAGO.
AL CAPONE WAS FROM CHICAGO.

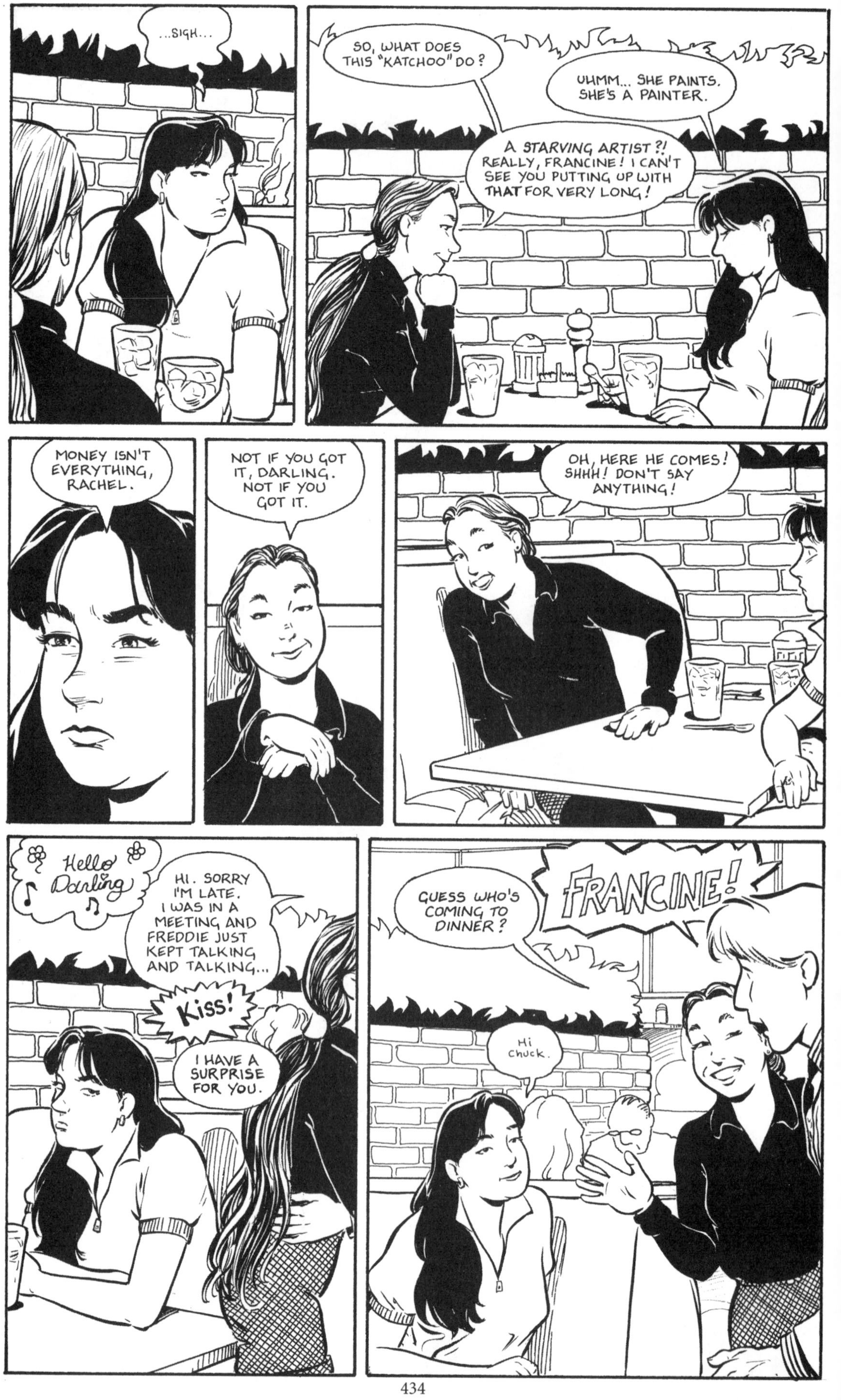
...SIGH...
SO, WHAT DOES THIS "KATCHOO" DO?
UHMM... SHE PAINTS. SHE'S A PAINTER.
A STARVING ARTIST?! REALLY, FRANCINE! I CAN'T SEE YOU PUTTING UP WITH THAT FOR VERY LONG!
MONEY ISN'T EVERYTHING, RACHEL.
NOT IF YOU GOT IT, DARLING. NOT IF YOU GOT IT.
OH, HERE HE COMES! SHHH! DON'T SAY ANYTHING!
Hello Darling
HI. SORRY I'M LATE. I WAS IN A MEETING AND FREDDIE JUST KEPT TALKING AND TALKING...
KISS!
I HAVE A SURPRISE FOR YOU.
GUESS WHO'S COMING TO DINNER?
FRANCINE!
Hi Chuck.

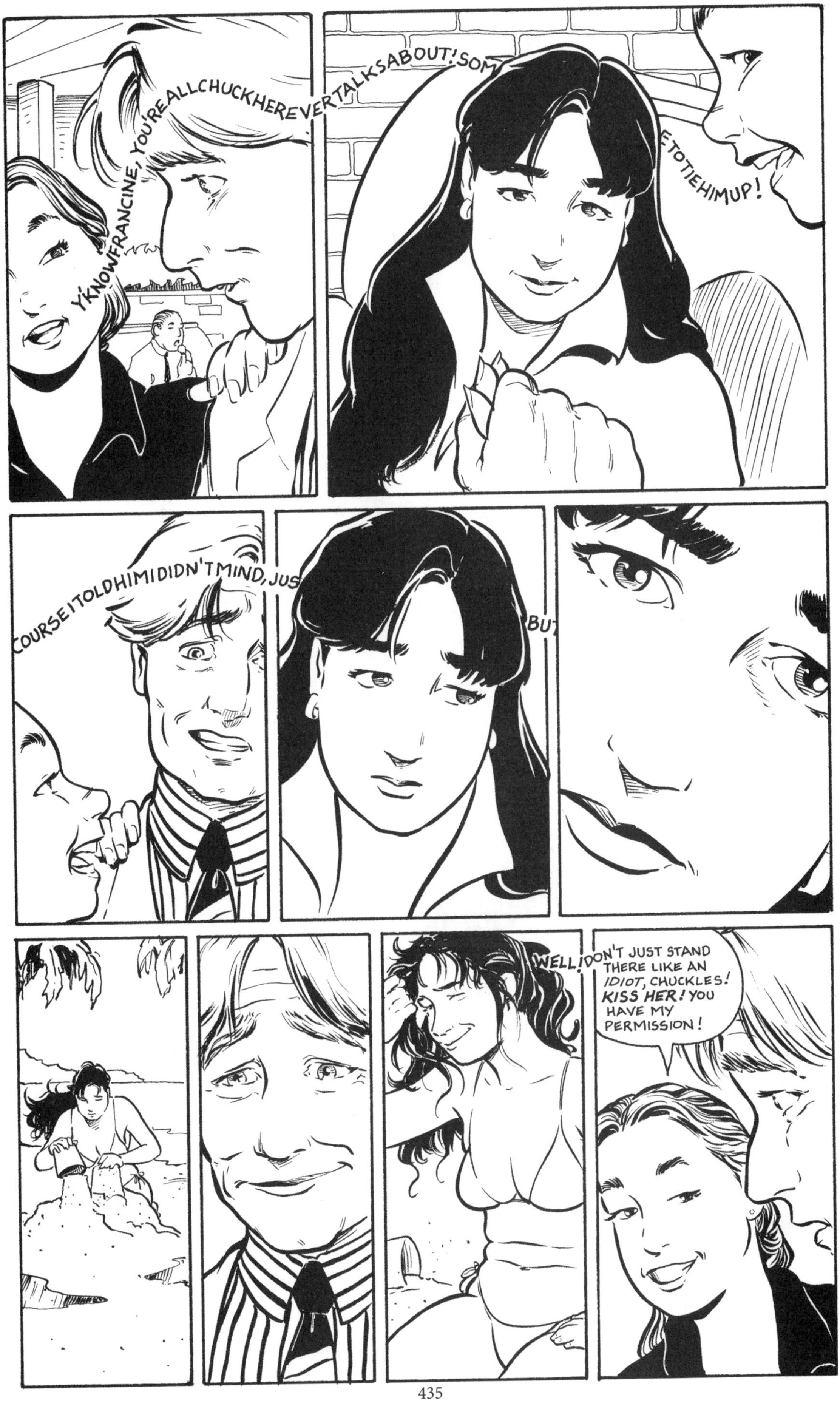
Y'KNOWFRANCINE, YOU'REALLCHUCKHEREVERTALKSABOUT!SOM
ETOTIEHIMUP!
COURSEITOLDHIMIDIDN'TMIND,JUS
BU
WELL!
DON'T JUST STAND THERE LIKE AN IDIOT, CHUCKLES! KISS HER! YOU HAVE MY PERMISSION!

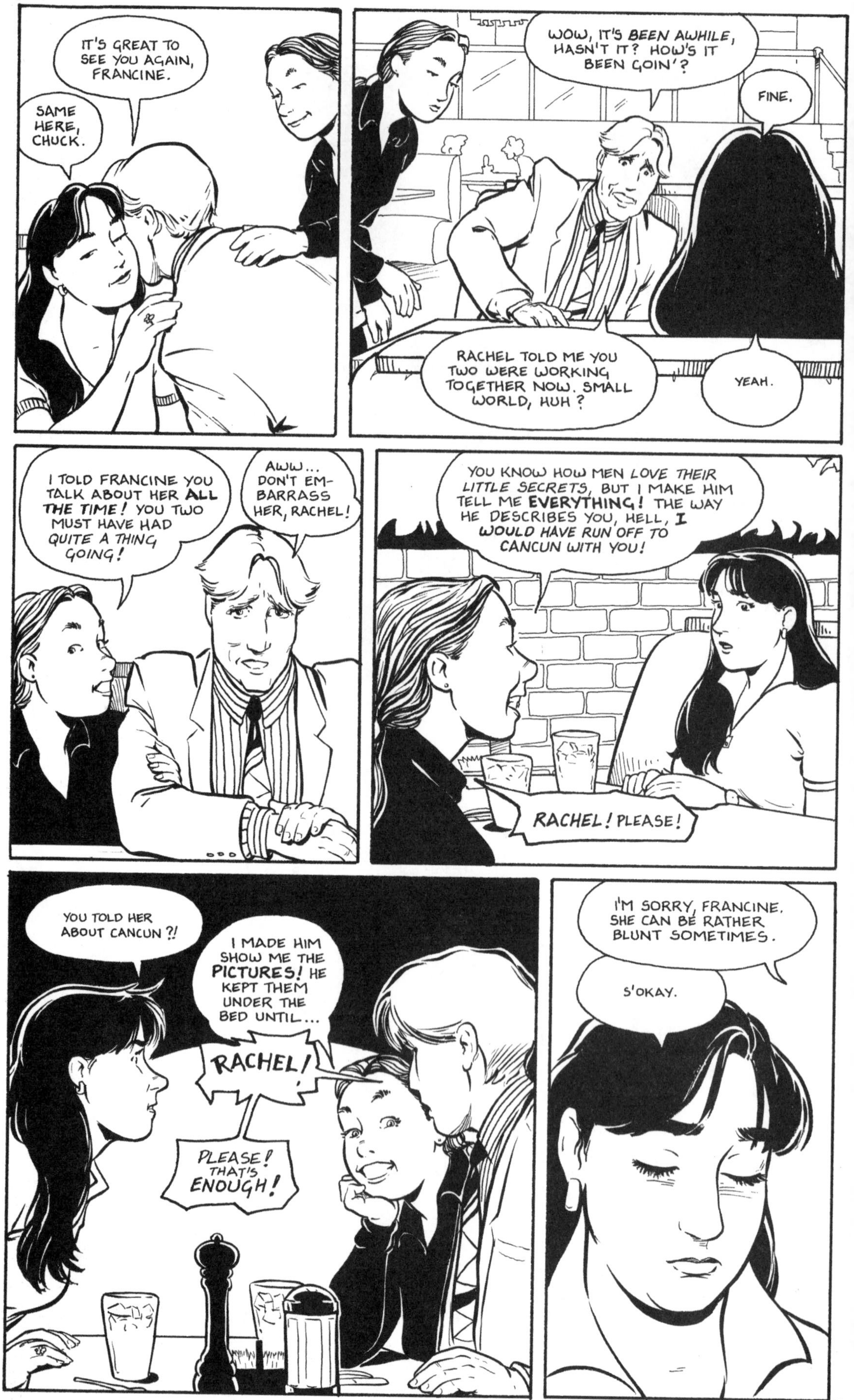
IT'S GREAT TO SEE YOU AGAIN, FRANCINE.
SAME HERE, CHUCK.
WOW, IT'S BEEN AWHILE, HASN'T IT? HOW'S IT BEEN GOIN'?
FINE.
RACHEL TOLD ME YOU TWO WERE WORKING TOGETHER NOW. SMALL WORLD, HUH?
YEAH.
I TOLD FRANCINE YOU TALK ABOUT HER ALL THE TIME! YOU TWO MUST HAVE HAD QUITE A THING GOING!
AWW... DON'T EM-BARRASS HER, RACHEL!
YOU KNOW HOW MEN LOVE THEIR LITTLE SECRETS, BUT I MAKE HIM TELL ME EVERYTHING! THE WAY HE DESCRIBES YOU, HELL, I WOULD HAVE RUN OFF TO CANCUN WITH YOU!
RACHEL! PLEASE!
YOU TOLD HER ABOUT CANCUN ?!
I MADE HIM SHOW ME THE PICTURES! HE KEPT THEM UNDER THE BED UNTIL...
RACHEL!
PLEASE! THAT'S ENOUGH!
I'M SORRY, FRANCINE. SHE CAN BE RATHER BLUNT SOMETIMES.
S'OKAY.

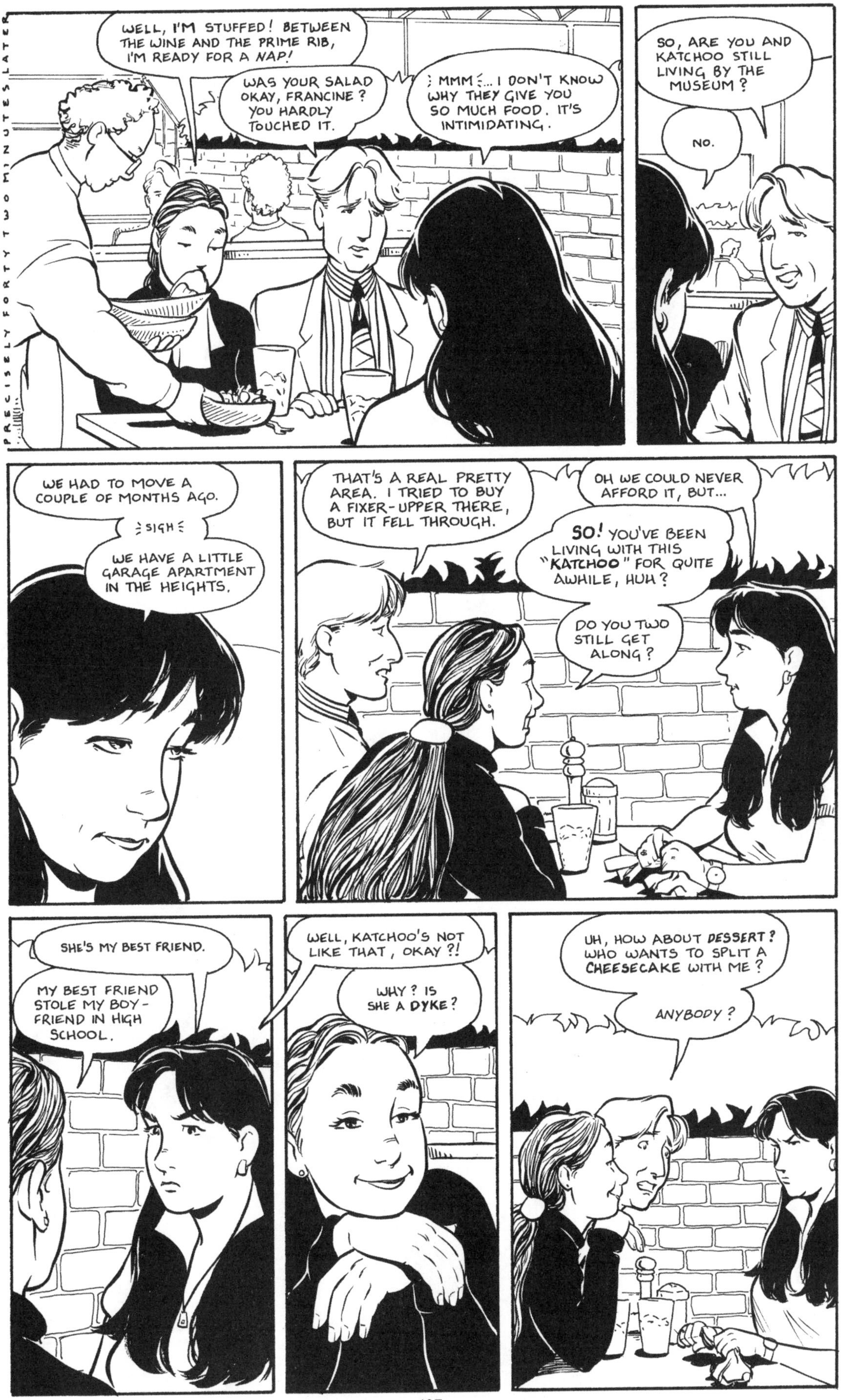
PRECISELY FORTY TWO MINUTES LATER
WELL, I'M STUFFED! BETWEEN THE WINE AND THE PRIME RIB, I'M READY FOR A NAP!
WAS YOUR SALAD OKAY, FRANCINE? YOU HARDLY TOUCHED IT.
MMM... I DON'T KNOW WHY THEY GIVE YOU SO MUCH FOOD. IT'S INTIMIDATING.
SO, ARE YOU AND KATCHOO STILL LIVING BY THE MUSEUM?
NO.
WE HAD TO MOVE A COUPLE OF MONTHS AGO.
SIGH
WE HAVE A LITTLE GARAGE APARTMENT IN THE HEIGHTS.
THAT'S A REAL PRETTY AREA. I TRIED TO BUY A FIXER-UPPER THERE, BUT IT FELL THROUGH.
OH WE COULD NEVER AFFORD IT, BUT...
SO! YOU'VE BEEN LIVING WITH THIS "KATCHOO" FOR QUITE AWHILE, HUH?
DO YOU TWO STILL GET ALONG?
SHE'S MY BEST FRIEND.
MY BEST FRIEND STOLE MY BOY-FRIEND IN HIGH SCHOOL.
WELL, KATCHOO'S NOT LIKE THAT, OKAY?!
WHY? IS SHE A DYKE?
UH, HOW ABOUT DESSERT? WHO WANTS TO SPLIT A CHEESECAKE WITH ME?
ANYBODY?

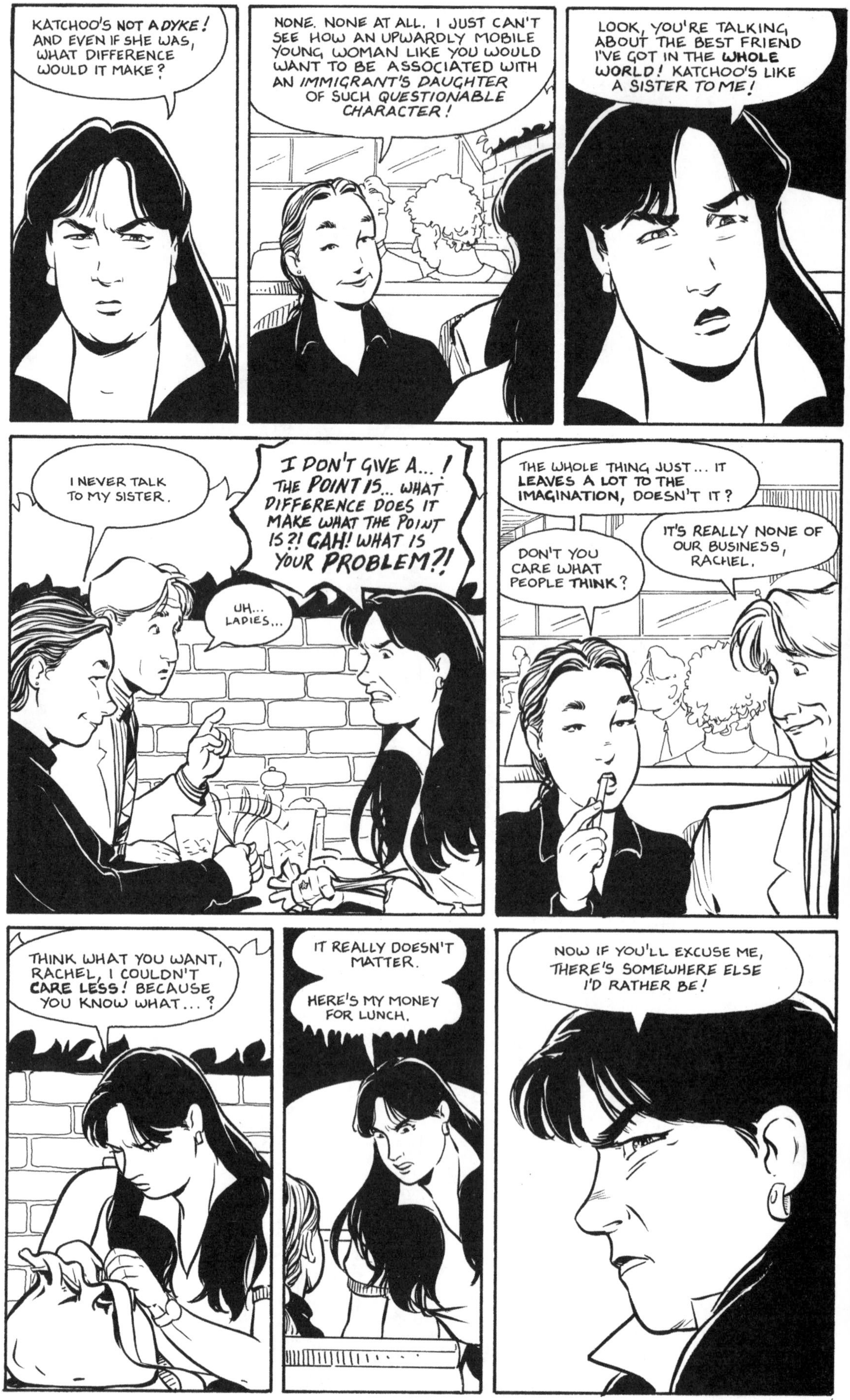
KATCHOO'S NOT A DYKE! AND EVEN IF SHE WAS, WHAT DIFFERENCE WOULD IT MAKE?
NONE. NONE AT ALL. I JUST CAN'T SEE HOW AN UPWARDLY MOBILE YOUNG WOMAN LIKE YOU WOULD WANT TO BE ASSOCIATED WITH AN IMMIGRANT'S DAUGHTER OF SUCH QUESTIONABLE CHARACTER!
LOOK, YOU'RE TALKING ABOUT THE BEST FRIEND I'VE GOT IN THE WHOLE WORLD! KATCHOO'S LIKE A SISTER TO ME!
I NEVER TALK TO MY SISTER.
I DON'T GIVE A...! THE POINT IS... WHAT DIFFERENCE DOES IT MAKE WHAT THE POINT IS?! GAH! WHAT IS YOUR PROBLEM?!
UH... LADIES...
THE WHOLE THING JUST... IT LEAVES A LOT TO THE IMAGINATION, DOESN'T IT?
DON'T YOU CARE WHAT PEOPLE THINK?
IT'S REALLY NONE OF OUR BUSINESS, RACHEL.
THINK WHAT YOU WANT, RACHEL, I COULDN'T CARE LESS! BECAUSE YOU KNOW WHAT...?
IT REALLY DOESN'T MATTER.
HERE'S MY MONEY FOR LUNCH.
NOW IF YOU'LL EXCUSE ME, THERE'S SOMEWHERE ELSE I'D RATHER BE!

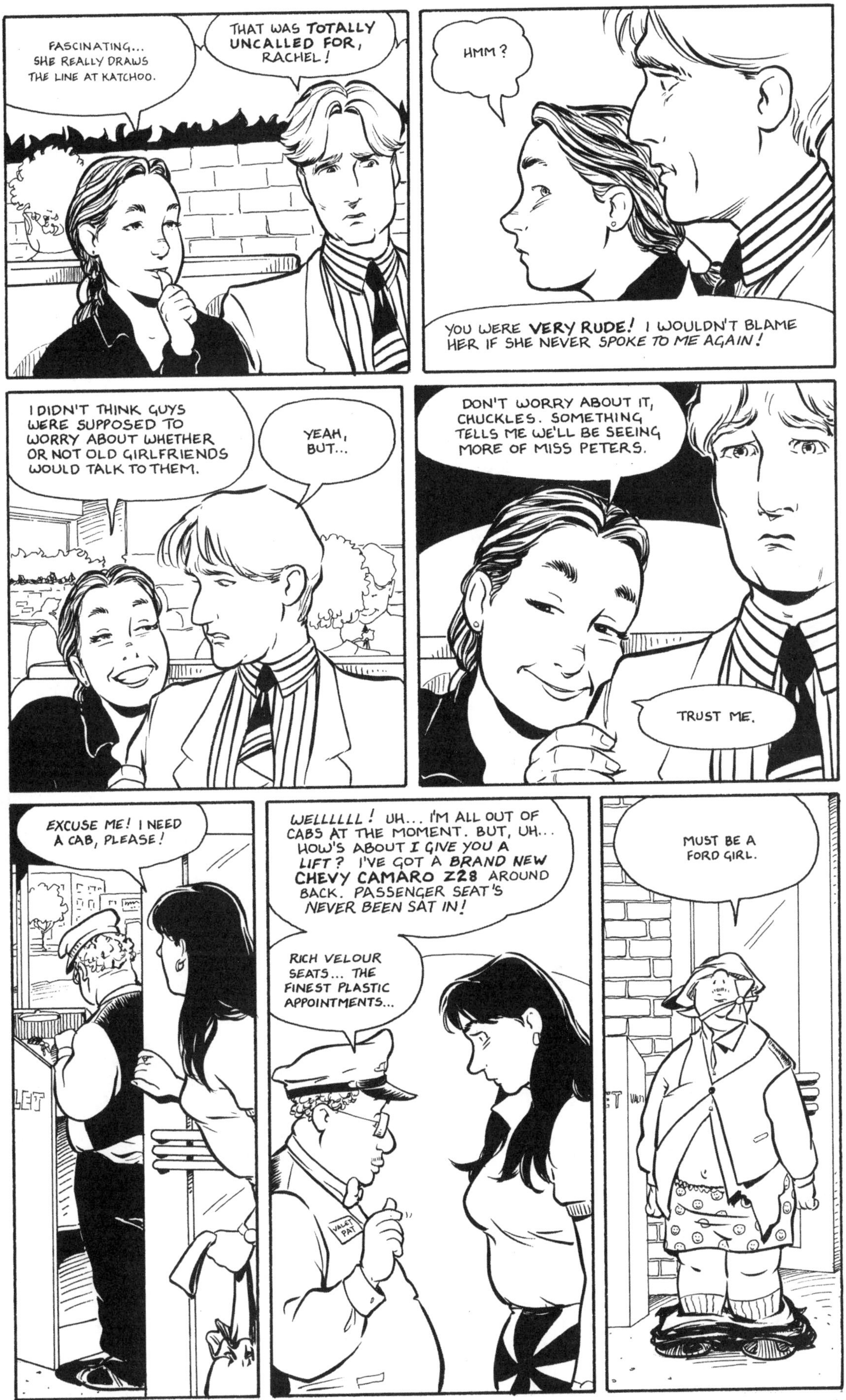
FASCINATING... SHE REALLY DRAWS THE LINE AT KATCHOO.
THAT WAS TOTALLY UNCALLED FOR, RACHEL!
HMM?
YOU WERE VERY RUDE! I WOULDN'T BLAME HER IF SHE NEVER SPOKE TO ME AGAIN!
I DIDN'T THINK GUYS WERE SUPPOSED TO WORRY ABOUT WHETHER OR NOT OLD GIRLFRIENDS WOULD TALK TO THEM.
YEAH, BUT...
DON'T WORRY ABOUT IT, CHUCKLES. SOMETHING TELLS ME WE'LL BE SEEING MORE OF MISS PETERS.
TRUST ME.
EXCUSE ME! I NEED A CAB, PLEASE!
WELLLLLL! UH... I'M ALL OUT OF CABS AT THE MOMENT. BUT, UH... HOW'S ABOUT I GIVE YOU A LIFT? I'VE GOT A BRAND NEW CHEVY CAMARO Z28 AROUND BACK. PASSENGER SEAT'S NEVER BEEN SAT IN!
RICH VELOUR SEATS... THE FINEST PLASTIC APPOINTMENTS...
VALET PAT
MUST BE A FORD GIRL.

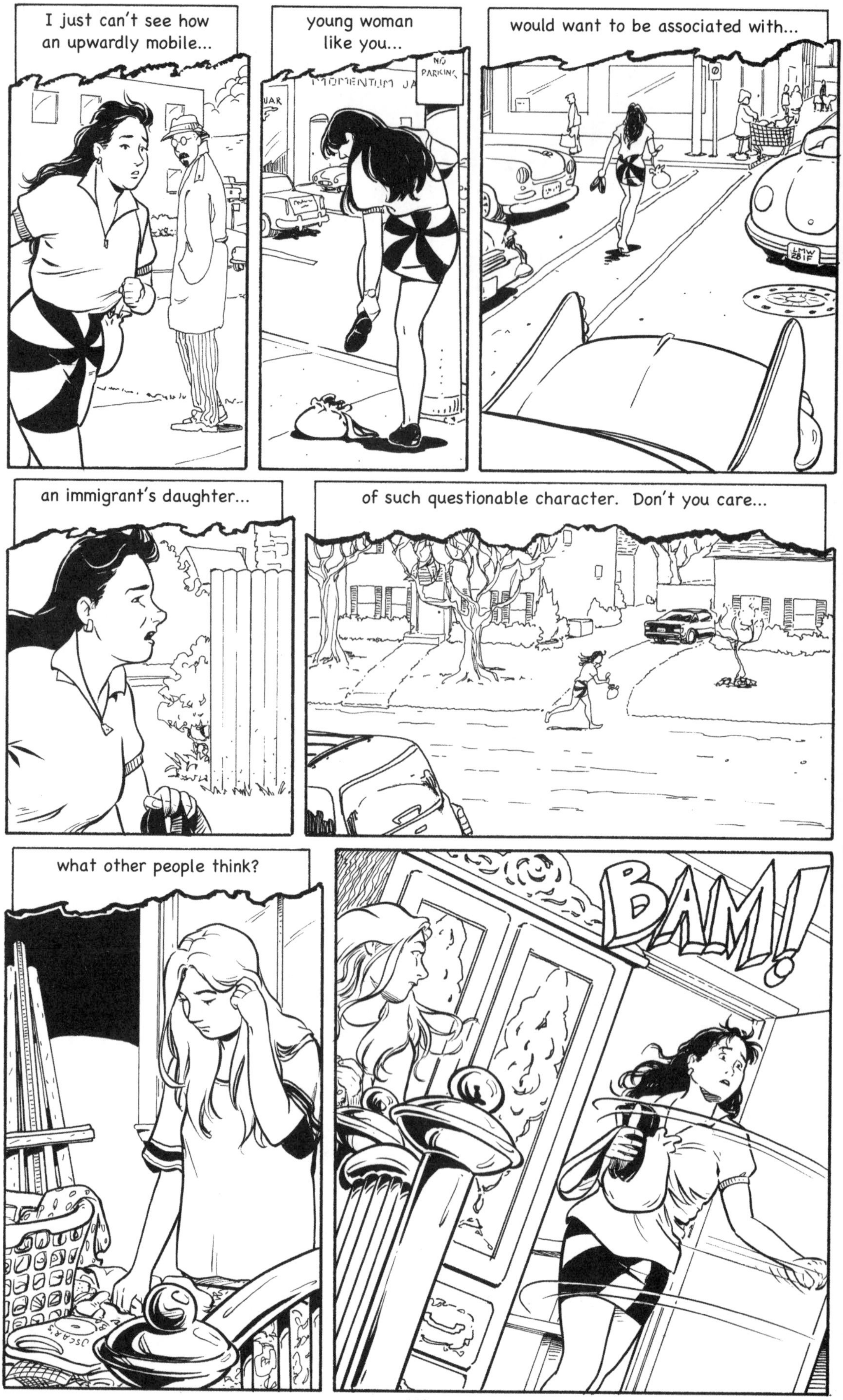
I just can't see how an upwardly mobile...
young woman like you...
NO PARKING
would want to be associated with...
an immigrant's daughter...
of such questionable character. Don't you care...
what other people think?
BAM!

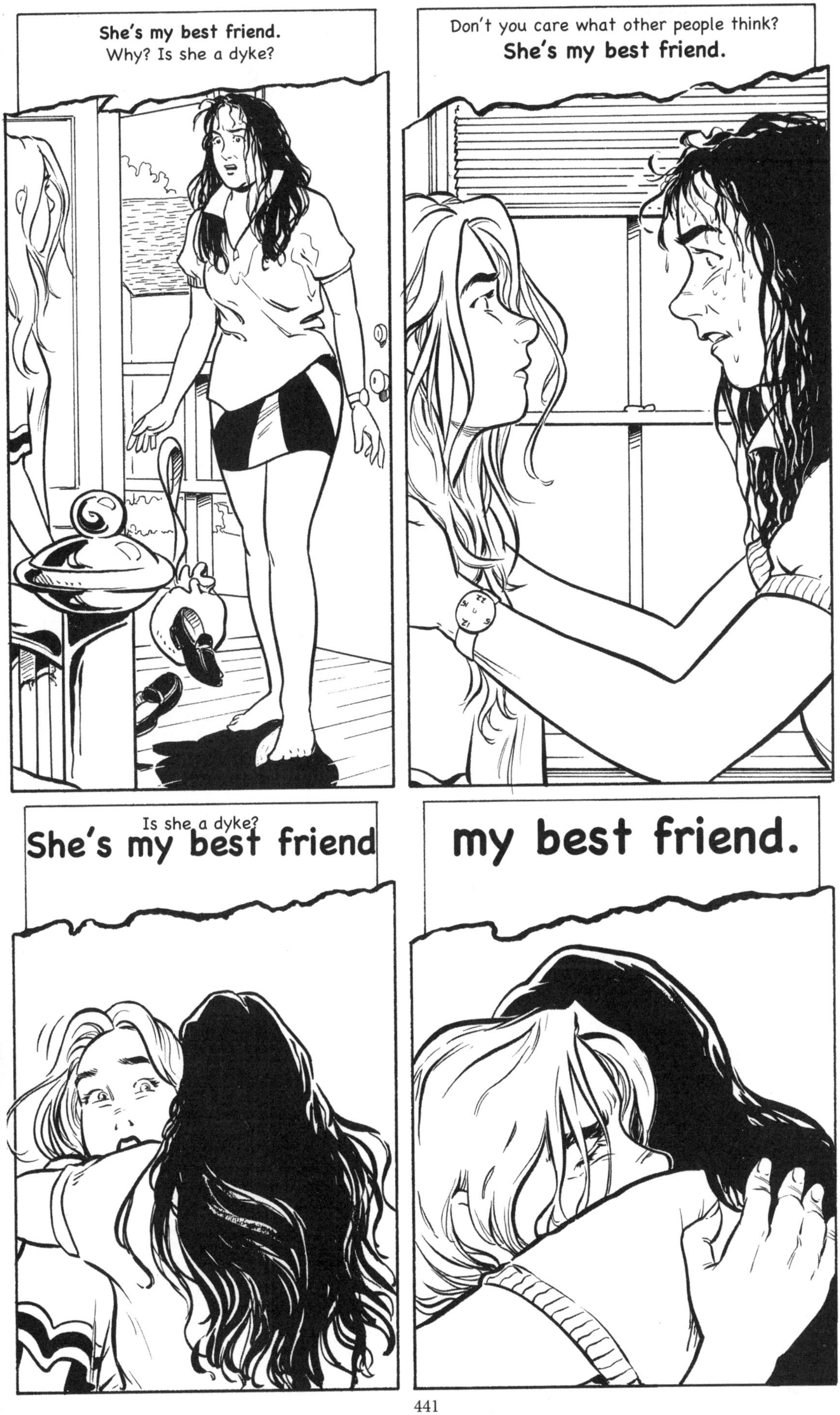
She's my best friend.
Why? Is she a dyke?
Don't you care what other people think?
She's my best friend.
Is she a dyke?
She's my best friend
my best friend.

A DISTANT SCREAM

SOMEDAYS I THINK
I'M GOING TO GIVE IT ALL AWAY
FIND A JOB THAT PAYS
SOME LETTERS BEHIND MY NAME.

SOMEDAYS I'LL BE
STANDING AT A MIRROR LOOKING IN
YOUR FACE STARTS FADING IN
THE FEELING COMES AGAIN.

I GUESS I'LL ALWAYS BE
THE LOSING SIDE OF YOU.
YOUR MISMATCHED OTHER SHOE
YOUR AFTER MIDNIGHT BLUES.

LOVE IS A MYSTERY TO ME.
A LOSER'S DREAM.

THESE DAYS ARE SPENT
IN HOT DESIRE TO BE THE WAY I WAS.
TO RIDE THE MAGIC BUS
TO TRY AND STAY IN TOUCH.

AFRAID MY FACE
IS JUST A MEMORY TO THOSE I KNEW.
AN INFLUENTIAL CLUE
TO WHAT THEY HAVE TO LOSE.

I GUESS I'LL ALWAYS BE
THE LOSING SIDE OF YOU.
YOUR MISMATCHED OTHER SHOE
YOUR AFTER MIDNIGHT BLUES.

LOVE IS A MYSTERY.
TO ME, A DISTANT SCREAM.

Words and Music by Griffin Silver
Copyright 1997 Dancers In The Valley Music, Inc.

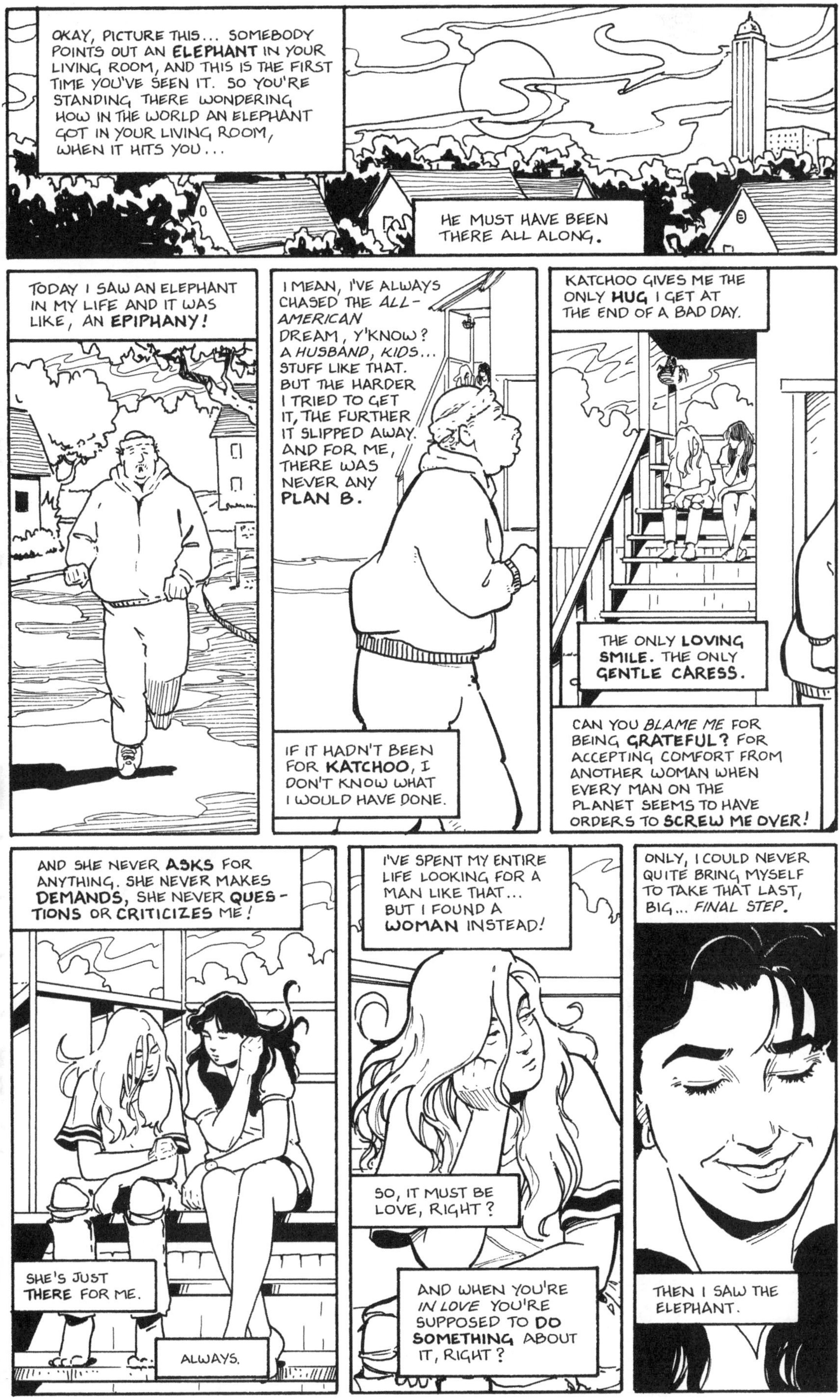
OKAY, PICTURE THIS... SOMEBODY POINTS OUT AN ELEPHANT IN YOUR LIVING ROOM, AND THIS IS THE FIRST TIME YOU'VE SEEN IT. SO YOU'RE STANDING THERE WONDERING HOW IN THE WORLD AN ELEPHANT GOT IN YOUR LIVING ROOM, WHEN IT HITS YOU...
HE MUST HAVE BEEN THERE ALL ALONG.
TODAY I SAW AN ELEPHANT IN MY LIFE AND IT WAS LIKE, AN EPIPHANY!
I MEAN, I'VE ALWAYS CHASED THE ALL-AMERICAN DREAM, Y'KNOW? A HUSBAND, KIDS... STUFF LIKE THAT. BUT THE HARDER I TRIED TO GET IT, THE FURTHER IT SLIPPED AWAY. AND FOR ME, THERE WAS NEVER ANY PLAN B.
IF IT HADN'T BEEN FOR KATCHOO, I DON'T KNOW WHAT I WOULD HAVE DONE.
KATCHOO GIVES ME THE ONLY HUG I GET AT THE END OF A BAD DAY.
THE ONLY LOVING SMILE. THE ONLY GENTLE CARESS.
CAN YOU BLAME ME FOR BEING GRATEFUL? FOR ACCEPTING COMFORT FROM ANOTHER WOMAN WHEN EVERY MAN ON THE PLANET SEEMS TO HAVE ORDERS TO SCREW ME OVER!
AND SHE NEVER ASKS FOR ANYTHING. SHE NEVER MAKES DEMANDS, SHE NEVER QUES-TIONS OR CRITICIZES ME!
SHE'S JUST THERE FOR ME.
ALWAYS.
I'VE SPENT MY ENTIRE LIFE LOOKING FOR A MAN LIKE THAT... BUT I FOUND A WOMAN INSTEAD!
SO, IT MUST BE LOVE, RIGHT?
AND WHEN YOU'RE IN LOVE YOU'RE SUPPOSED TO DO SOMETHING ABOUT IT, RIGHT?
ONLY, I COULD NEVER QUITE BRING MYSELF TO TAKE THAT LAST, BIG... FINAL STEP.
THEN I SAW THE ELEPHANT.

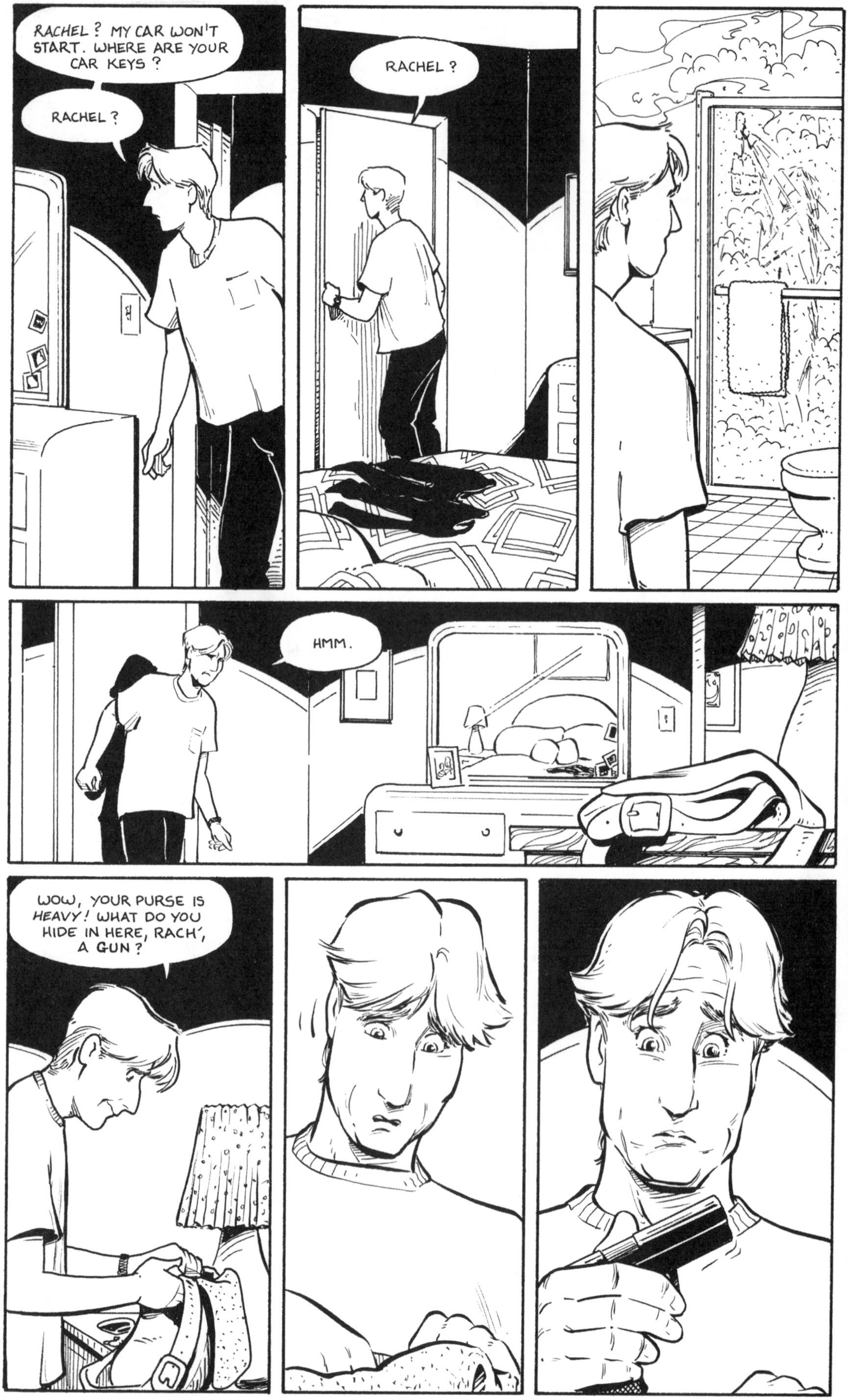
RACHEL ? MY CAR WON'T START. WHERE ARE YOUR CAR KEYS ?
RACHEL ?
RACHEL ?
HMM.
WOW, YOUR PURSE IS HEAVY! WHAT DO YOU HIDE IN HERE, RACH', A GUN ?

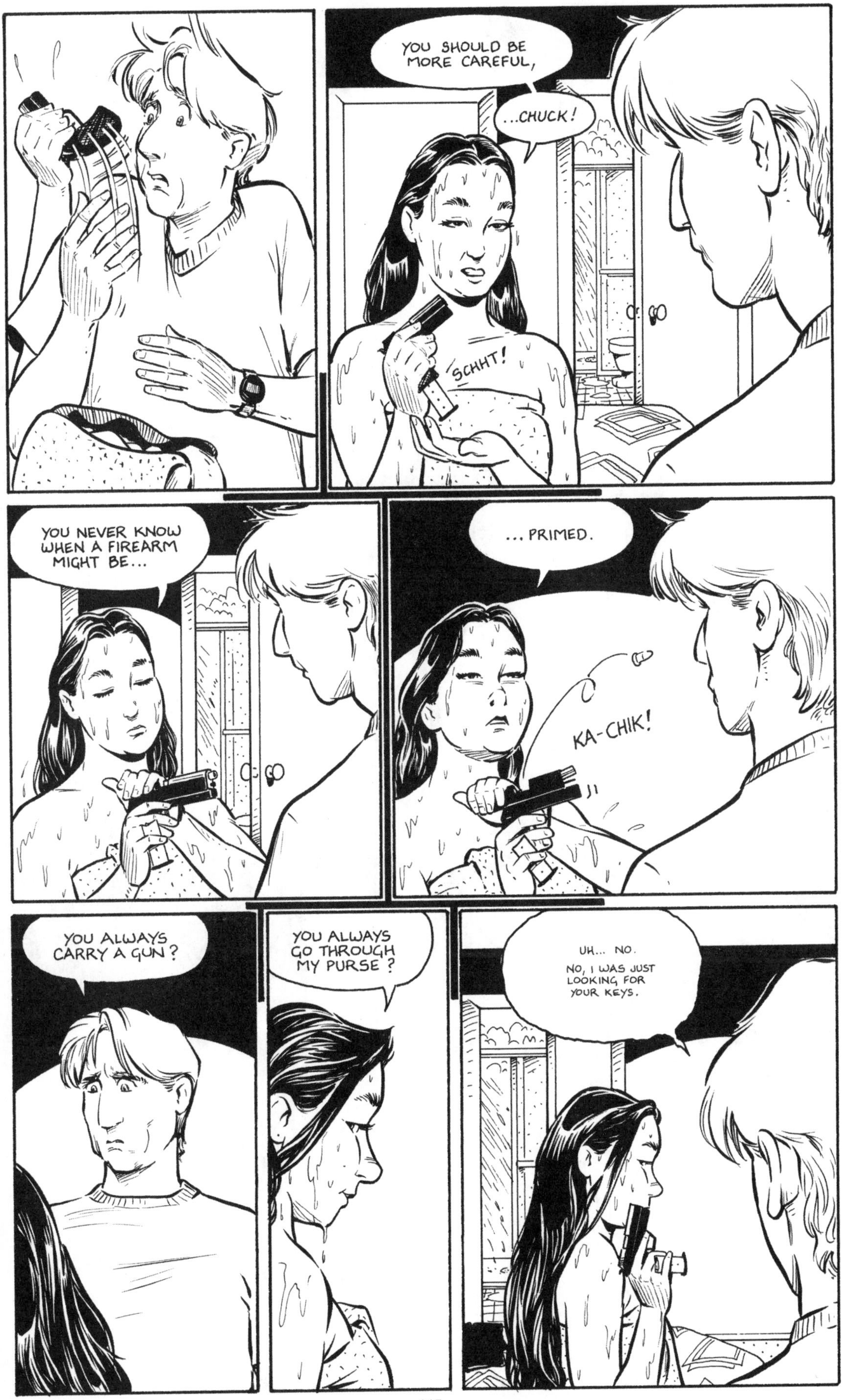
YOU SHOULD BE MORE CAREFUL,
...CHUCK!
SCHHT!
YOU NEVER KNOW WHEN A FIREARM MIGHT BE...
...PRIMED.
KA-CHIK!
YOU ALWAYS CARRY A GUN?
YOU ALWAYS GO THROUGH MY PURSE?
UH... NO.
NO, I WAS JUST LOOKING FOR YOUR KEYS.

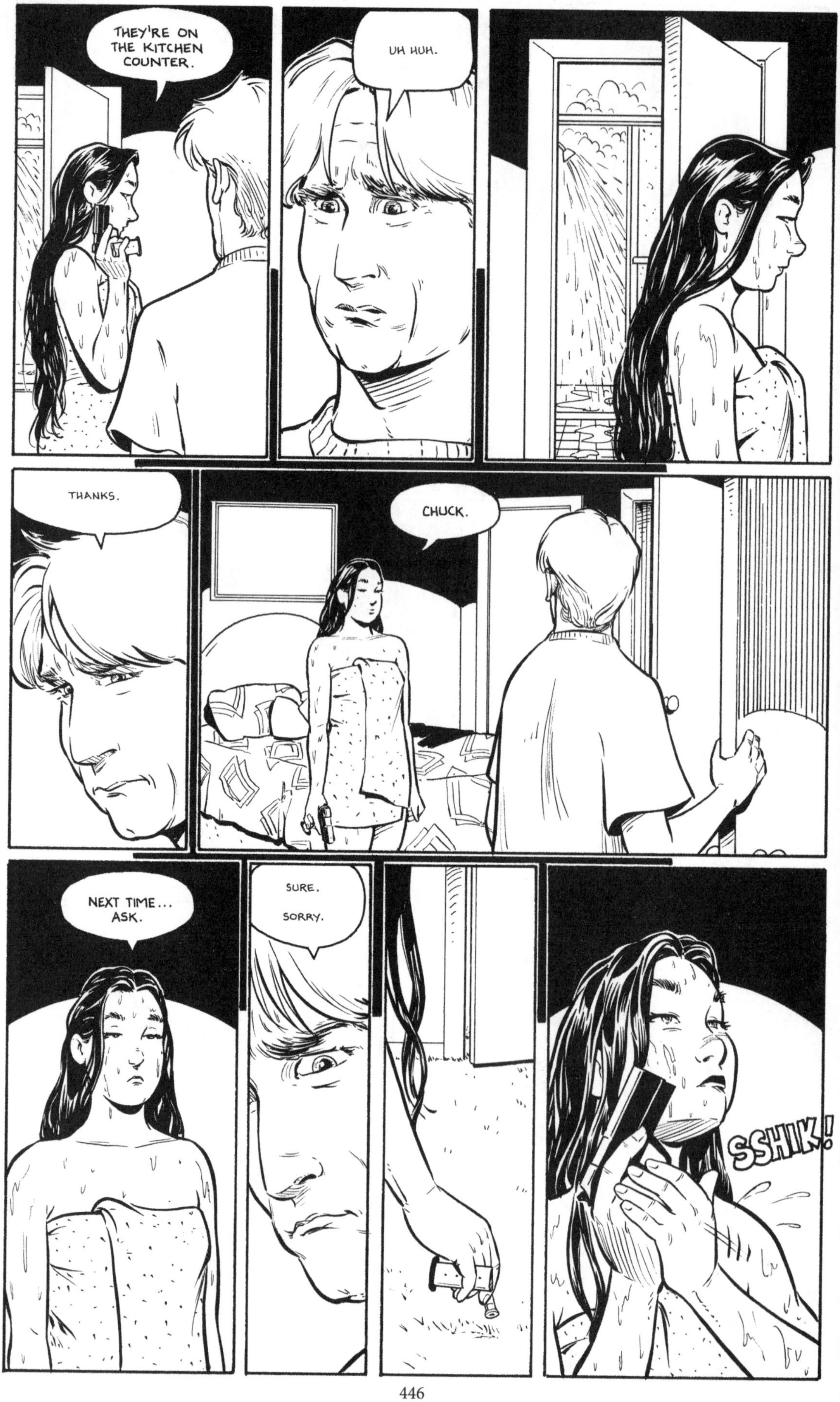
THEY'RE ON THE KITCHEN COUNTER.
UH HUH.
THANKS.
CHUCK.
NEXT TIME... ASK.
SURE.
SORRY.
SSHIK!

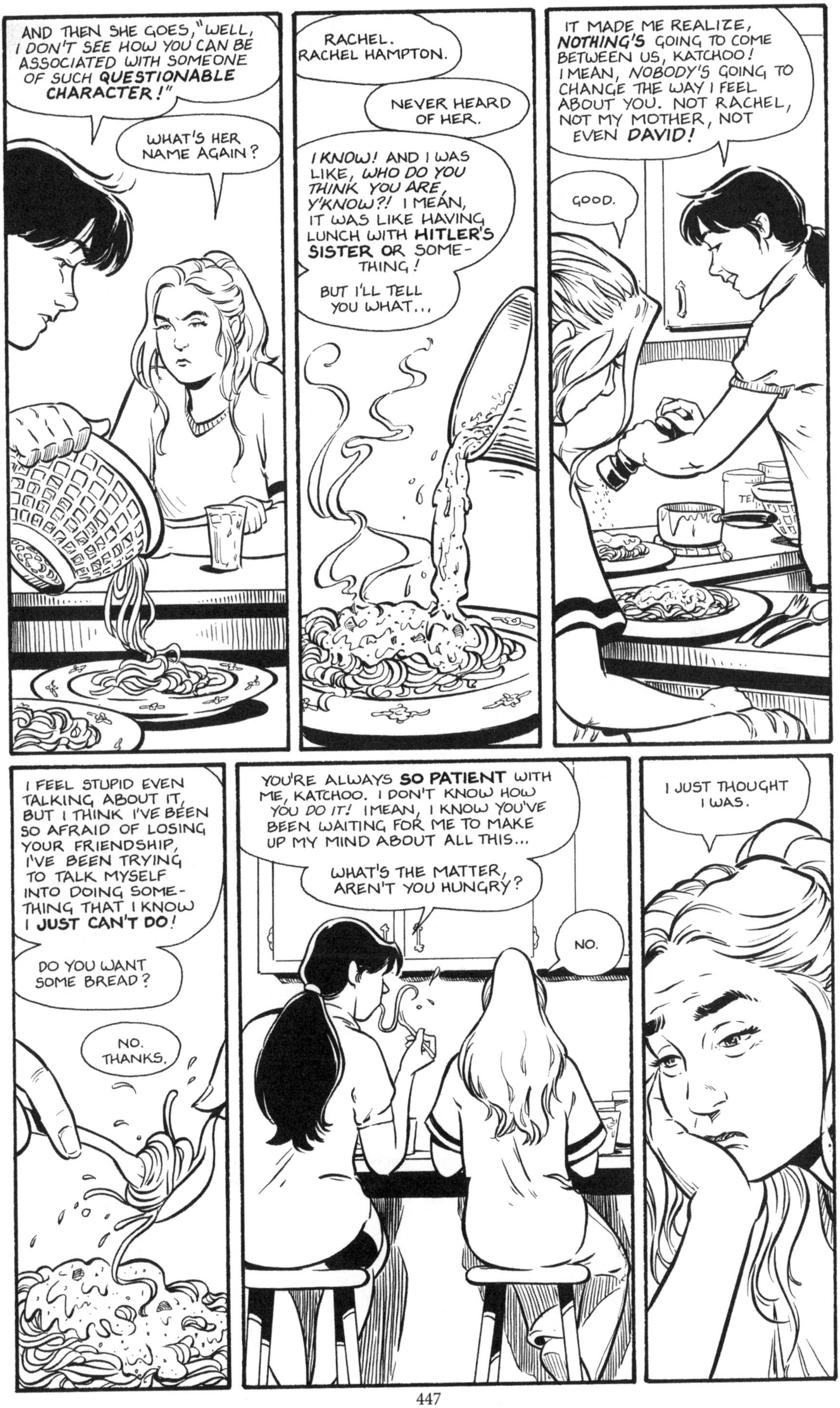
AND THEN SHE GOES, "WELL, I DON'T SEE HOW YOU CAN BE ASSOCIATED WITH SOMEONE OF SUCH QUESTIONABLE CHARACTER!"
WHAT'S HER NAME AGAIN?
RACHEL. RACHEL HAMPTON.
NEVER HEARD OF HER.
I KNOW! AND I WAS LIKE, WHO DO YOU THINK YOU ARE, Y'KNOW?! I MEAN, IT WAS LIKE HAVING LUNCH WITH HITLER'S SISTER OR SOMETHING!
BUT I'LL TELL YOU WHAT...
IT MADE ME REALIZE, NOTHING'S GOING TO COME BETWEEN US, KATCHOO! I MEAN, NOBODY'S GOING TO CHANGE THE WAY I FEEL ABOUT YOU. NOT RACHEL, NOT MY MOTHER, NOT EVEN DAVID!
GOOD.
I FEEL STUPID EVEN TALKING ABOUT IT, BUT I THINK I'VE BEEN SO AFRAID OF LOSING YOUR FRIENDSHIP, I'VE BEEN TRYING TO TALK MYSELF INTO DOING SOMETHING THAT I KNOW I JUST CAN'T DO!
DO YOU WANT SOME BREAD?
NO. THANKS.
YOU'RE ALWAYS SO PATIENT WITH ME, KATCHOO. I DON'T KNOW HOW YOU DO IT! I MEAN, I KNOW YOU'VE BEEN WAITING FOR ME TO MAKE UP MY MIND ABOUT ALL THIS...
WHAT'S THE MATTER, AREN'T YOU HUNGRY?
NO.
I JUST THOUGHT I WAS.

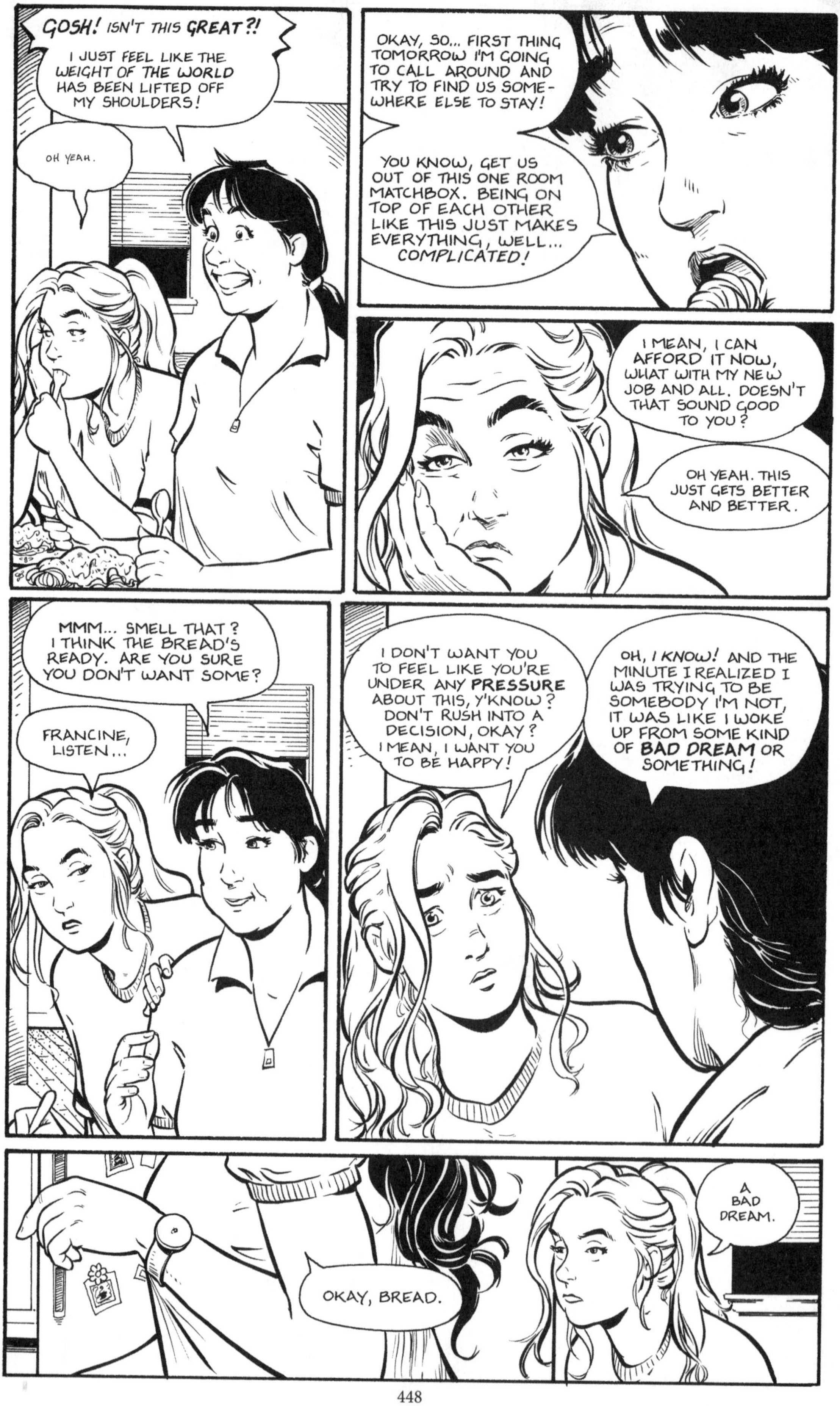
GOSH! ISN'T THIS GREAT?!
I JUST FEEL LIKE THE WEIGHT OF THE WORLD HAS BEEN LIFTED OFF MY SHOULDERS!
OH YEAH.
OKAY, SO... FIRST THING TOMORROW I'M GOING TO CALL AROUND AND TRY TO FIND US SOME-WHERE ELSE TO STAY!
YOU KNOW, GET US OUT OF THIS ONE ROOM MATCHBOX. BEING ON TOP OF EACH OTHER LIKE THIS JUST MAKES EVERYTHING, WELL... COMPLICATED!
I MEAN, I CAN AFFORD IT NOW, WHAT WITH MY NEW JOB AND ALL. DOESN'T THAT SOUND GOOD TO YOU?
OH YEAH. THIS JUST GETS BETTER AND BETTER.
MMM... SMELL THAT? I THINK THE BREAD'S READY. ARE YOU SURE YOU DON'T WANT SOME?
FRANCINE, LISTEN...
I DON'T WANT YOU TO FEEL LIKE YOU'RE UNDER ANY PRESSURE ABOUT THIS, Y'KNOW? DON'T RUSH INTO A DECISION, OKAY? I MEAN, I WANT YOU TO BE HAPPY!
OH, I KNOW! AND THE MINUTE I REALIZED I WAS TRYING TO BE SOMEBODY I'M NOT, IT WAS LIKE I WOKE UP FROM SOME KIND OF BAD DREAM OR SOMETHING!
OKAY, BREAD.
A BAD DREAM.

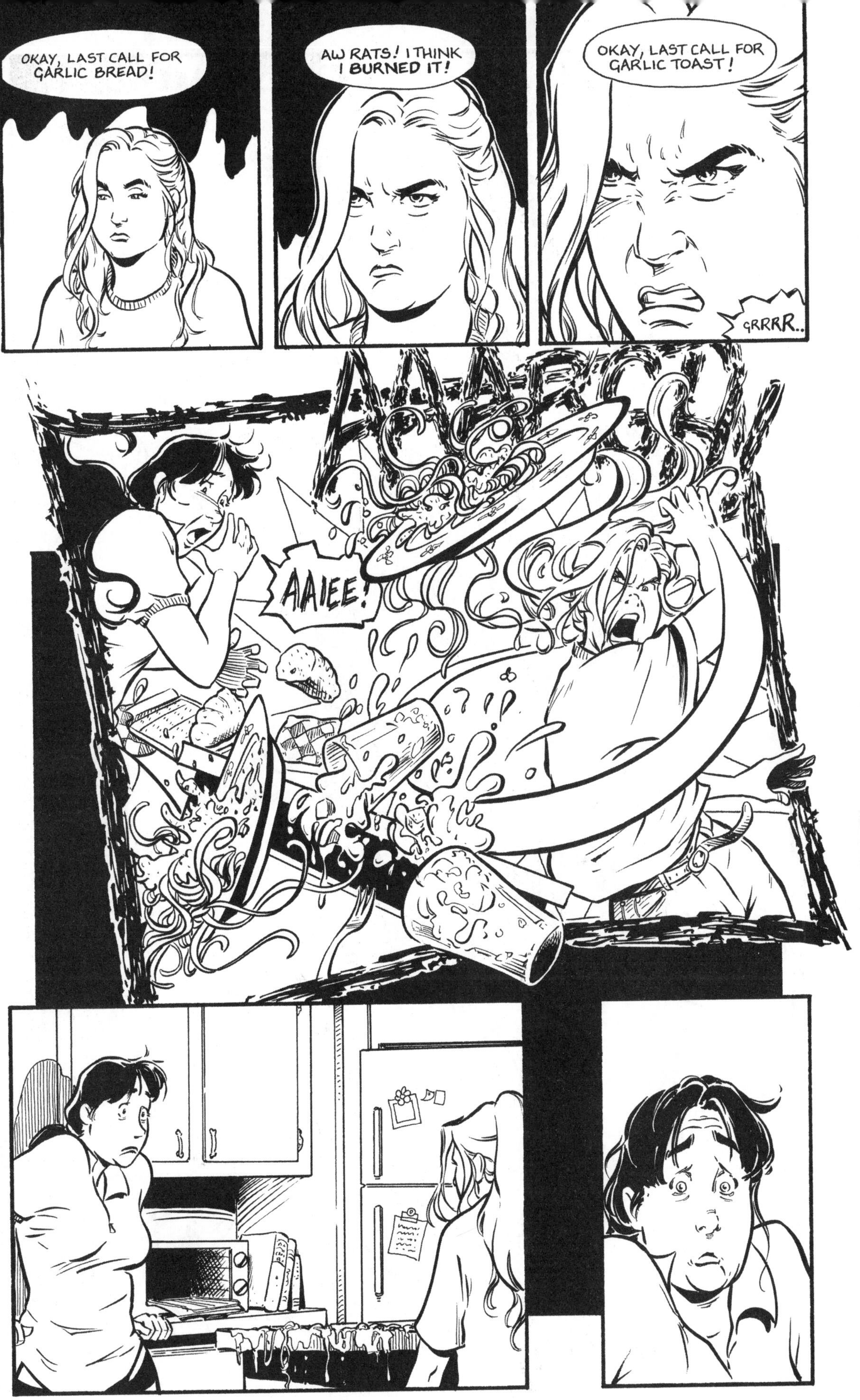
OKAY, LAST CALL FOR GARLIC BREAD!
AW RATS! I THINK I BURNED IT!
OKAY, LAST CALL FOR GARLIC TOAST!
GRRRR..
AAIEE!

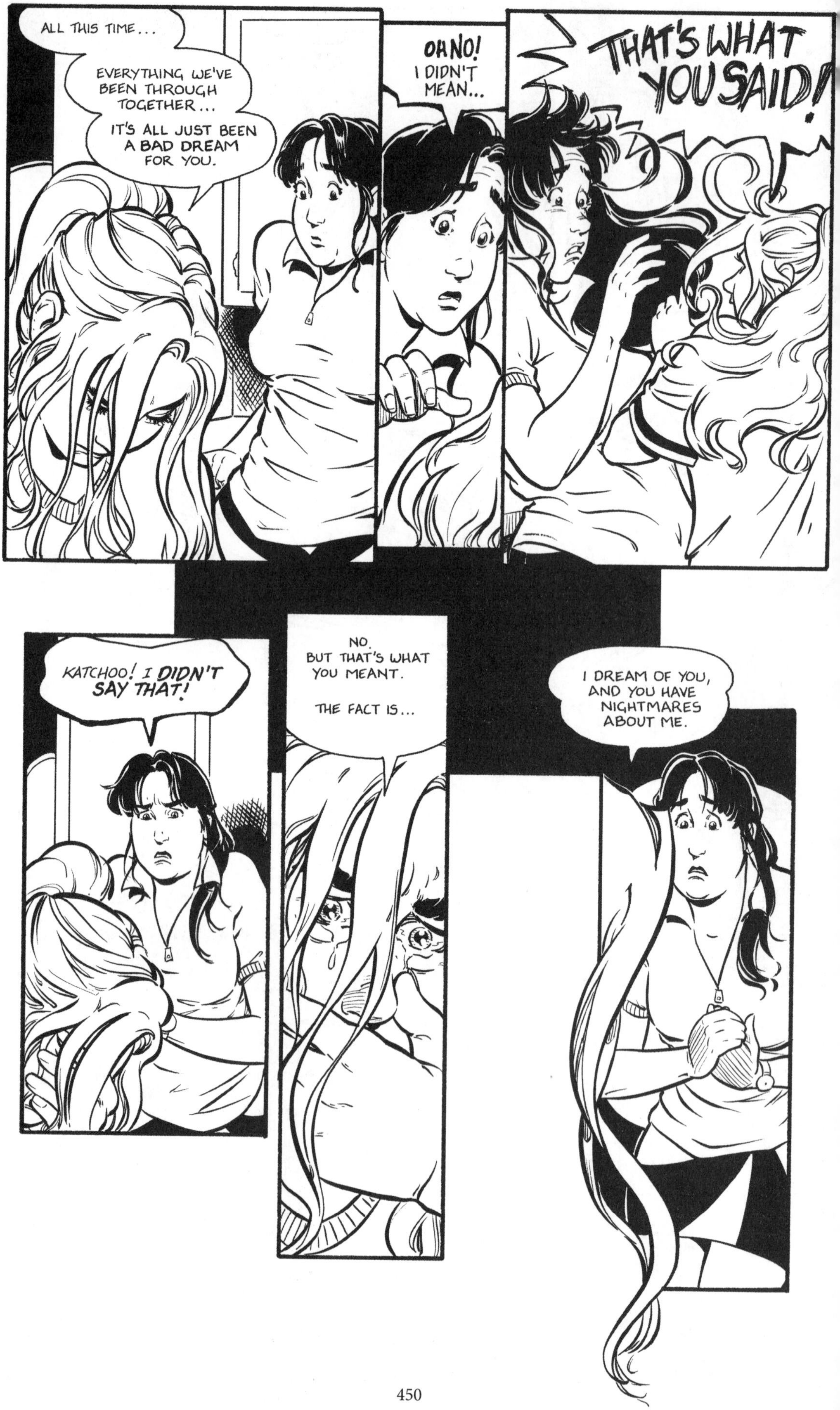

ALL THIS TIME...
EVERYTHING WE'VE BEEN THROUGH TOGETHER...
IT'S ALL JUST BEEN A BAD DREAM FOR YOU.
OH NO! I DIDN'T MEAN...
THAT'S WHAT YOU SAID!
KATCHOO! I DIDN'T SAY THAT!
NO. BUT THAT'S WHAT YOU MEANT.
THE FACT IS...
I DREAM OF YOU, AND YOU HAVE NIGHTMARES ABOUT ME.

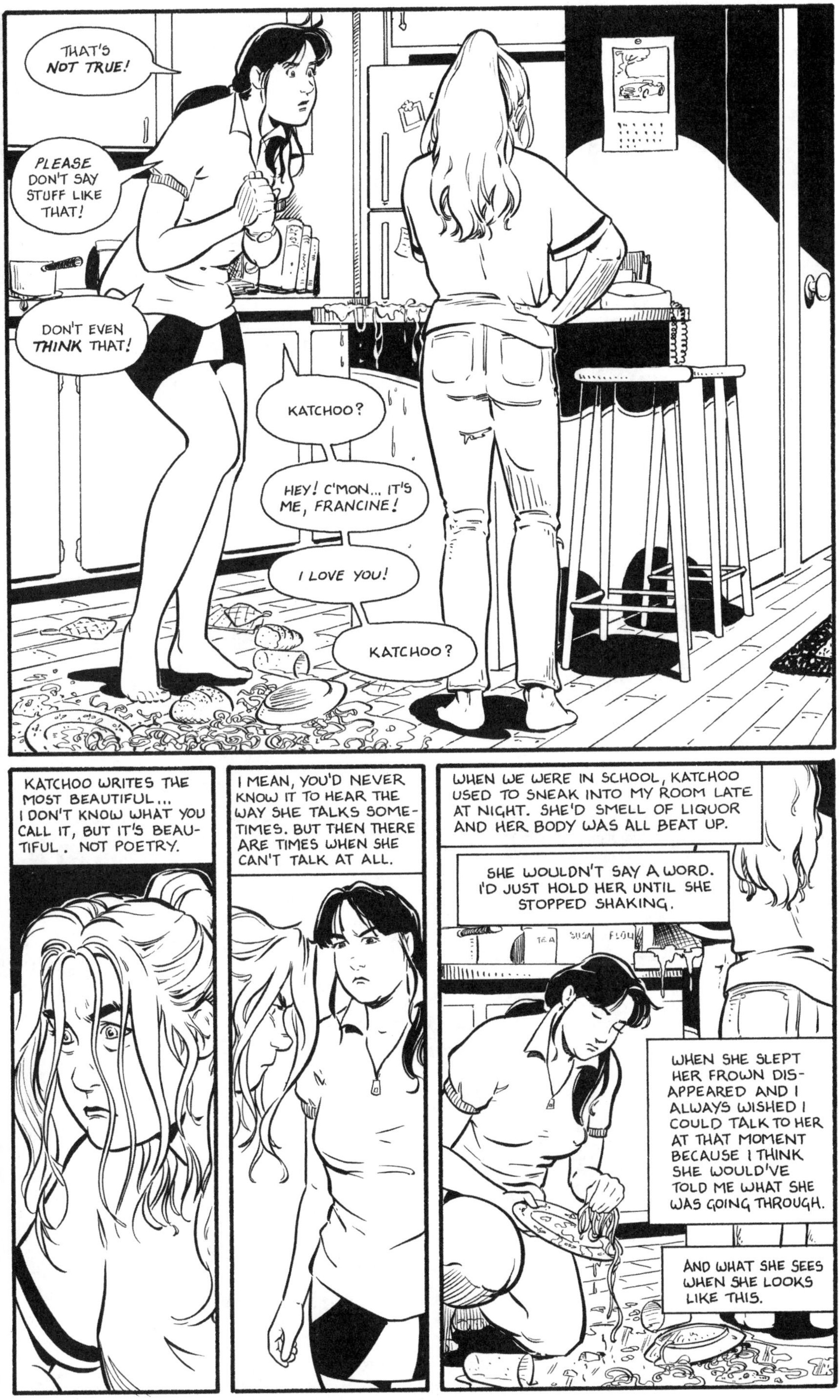
THAT'S NOT TRUE!
PLEASE DON'T SAY STUFF LIKE THAT!
DON'T EVEN THINK THAT!
KATCHOO?
HEY! C'MON... IT'S ME, FRANCINE!
I LOVE YOU!
KATCHOO?
KATCHOO WRITES THE MOST BEAUTIFUL... I DON'T KNOW WHAT YOU CALL IT, BUT IT'S BEAUTIFUL. NOT POETRY.
I MEAN, YOU'D NEVER KNOW IT TO HEAR THE WAY SHE TALKS SOMETIMES. BUT THEN THERE ARE TIMES WHEN SHE CAN'T TALK AT ALL.
WHEN WE WERE IN SCHOOL, KATCHOO USED TO SNEAK INTO MY ROOM LATE AT NIGHT. SHE'D SMELL OF LIQUOR AND HER BODY WAS ALL BEAT UP.
SHE WOULDN'T SAY A WORD. I'D JUST HOLD HER UNTIL SHE STOPPED SHAKING.
TEA
SUGA
FLOU
WHEN SHE SLEPT HER FROWN DISAPPEARED AND I ALWAYS WISHED I COULD TALK TO HER AT THAT MOMENT BECAUSE I THINK SHE WOULD'VE TOLD ME WHAT SHE WAS GOING THROUGH.
AND WHAT SHE SEES WHEN SHE LOOKS LIKE THIS.

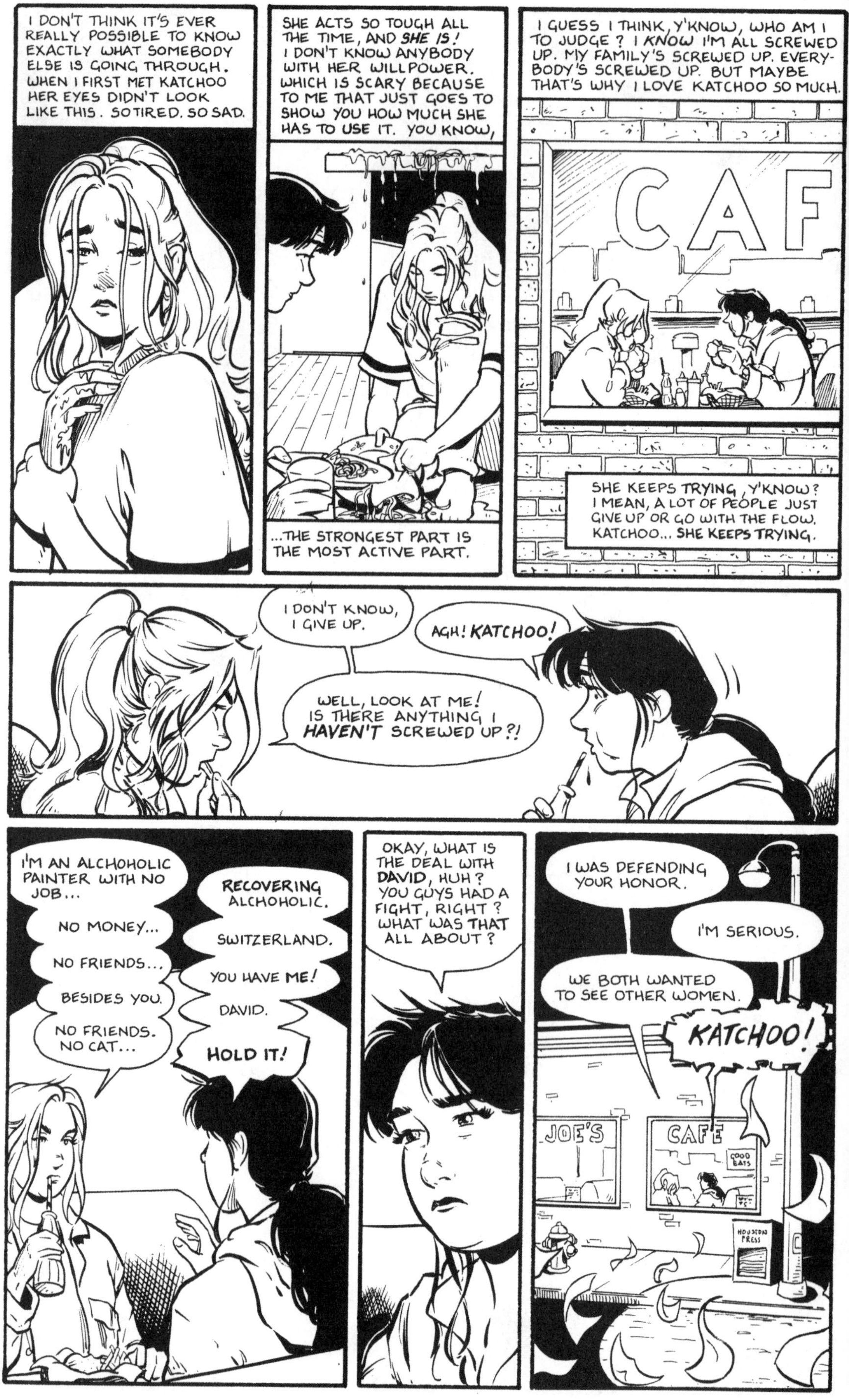
I DON'T THINK IT'S EVER REALLY POSSIBLE TO KNOW EXACTLY WHAT SOMEBODY ELSE IS GOING THROUGH. WHEN I FIRST MET KATCHOO HER EYES DIDN'T LOOK LIKE THIS. SO TIRED. SO SAD.
SHE ACTS SO TOUGH ALL THE TIME, AND SHE IS! I DON'T KNOW ANYBODY WITH HER WILLPOWER. WHICH IS SCARY BECAUSE TO ME THAT JUST GOES TO SHOW YOU HOW MUCH SHE HAS TO USE IT. YOU KNOW,
...THE STRONGEST PART IS THE MOST ACTIVE PART.
I GUESS I THINK, Y'KNOW, WHO AM I TO JUDGE? I KNOW I'M ALL SCREWED UP. MY FAMILY'S SCREWED UP. EVERYBODY'S SCREWED UP. BUT MAYBE THAT'S WHY I LOVE KATCHOO SO MUCH.
CAF
SHE KEEPS TRYING, Y'KNOW? I MEAN, A LOT OF PEOPLE JUST GIVE UP OR GO WITH THE FLOW. KATCHOO... SHE KEEPS TRYING.
I DON'T KNOW, I GIVE UP.
AGH! KATCHOO!
WELL, LOOK AT ME! IS THERE ANYTHING I HAVEN'T SCREWED UP?!
I'M AN ALCHOHOLIC PAINTER WITH NO JOB...
NO MONEY...
NO FRIENDS...
BESIDES YOU.
NO FRIENDS. NO CAT...
RECOVERING ALCHOHOLIC.
SWITZERLAND.
YOU HAVE ME!
DAVID.
HOLD IT!
OKAY, WHAT IS THE DEAL WITH DAVID, HUH? YOU GUYS HAD A FIGHT, RIGHT? WHAT WAS THAT ALL ABOUT?
I WAS DEFENDING YOUR HONOR.
I'M SERIOUS.
WE BOTH WANTED TO SEE OTHER WOMEN.
KATCHOO!
JOE'S
CAFE
GOOD EATS
HOUSTON PRESS

KATCHOO Alright, alright. I kicked him out.

FRANCINE Kicked him out?

KATCHOO Broke it off, something, whatever.

FRANCINE Why?

KATCHOO Because I realized we were never really friends to begin with, that's why. Besides, the last thing I need is for some guy to come along and try to worm his way into my life. I told him that the day I met him, but he just kept coming around, reading that asinine poetry of his.

FRANCINE Oh God forbid some nice guy wants to be with you.

KATCHOO That's not what I meant. Did you know he's a Christian?

FRANCINE No.

KATCHOO I didn't either until yesterday.

FRANCINE Makes sense though, doesn't it? When you think about it.

KATCHOO What do you mean?

FRANCINE I mean the way he acts, y'know. He's so... decent.

KATCHOO Don't you think that's the kind of thing friends should tell each other?

FRANCINE He told you.

KATCHOO Finally! A whole year later!

FRANCINE You don't like Christians? My family's Methodist. Well, except for Uncle Maury, but that's a long story.

KATCHOO I don't care! The point is he didn't think enough of me to tell me!

FRANCINE Oh.

KATCHOO Besides, he was really starting to creep me out. He knew all these weird little things about me. Private things. But I didn't know anything about him. He never told me anything.

FRANCINE Well maybe he was just more interested in you than him. I wish I could find a guy like that.

KATCHOO You don't understand.

FRANCINE Katchoo, I'm sorry but so far you've just described a guy half the women in America are looking for.

KATCHOO Well, they can have him.

(Silence as Francine studies Katchoo)
FRANCINE I'll take him.

KATCHOO Huh?

FRANCINE Hey, if you don't want him, I'll take him. He's better than anything I've been able to come up with. Of course, that's not saying much.

KATCHOO Get real.

FRANCINE No, I'm serious. I think he's cute. Of course, I'd have to make some changes. Get him out of that 60's John Lennon look, more into an Eddie Bauer thing.

KATCHOO What?!

FRANCINE Oh, you know, just clean his act up a little bit. And he'll tell me everything by God or I'll make his life a living hell! I don't care how hard it is for him to talk about it.

KATCHOO Talk about what?!

FRANCINE Oh, you know, obviously he had a traumatic childhood. He has all the signs. I wouldn't be surprised if he was an abused child. But hey, you already know that, don't you? I mean, you were the one he was trying to open up to all this time, for cryin' out loud.

(Katchoo turns pale)

FRANCINE You know how deep some things are, and it's just impossible to get them out? It all gets jumbled up inside. Love, hate, nightmares... dreams. Then you meet somebody you think will understand, but you don't know what to say. Then you're afraid to say anything.

(Katchoo begins to cry.)
KATCHOO Oh god.

FRANCINE I thought you saw that.

(Katchoo, hand over eyes, shakes her head.)

FRANCINE I don't know. Maybe I'm wrong. But that's what it looks like to me.

(Katchoo wipes her eyes angrily.)

FRANCINE (softly) I think you probably have more in common with David than you think.

KATCHOO (with shaking voice) I have to find him.

FRANCINE Just call him. I doubt if he's out on a date.

KATCHOO No, he's gone. Moved out. Disappeared. I've been looking everywhere for him.

FRANCINE Oh Katchoo.

KATCHOO I only know one more place to look.

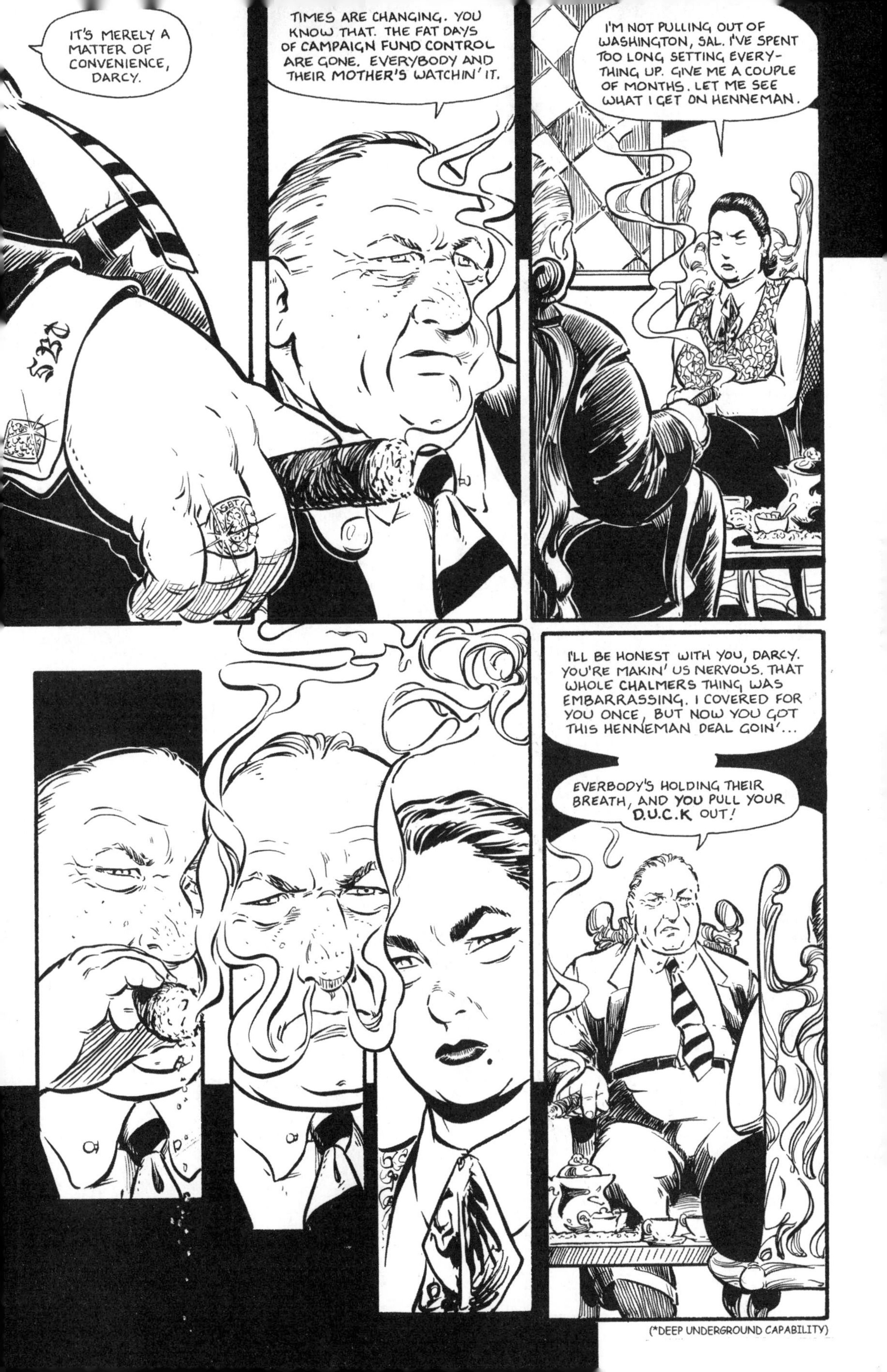
IT'S MERELY A MATTER OF CONVENIENCE, DARCY.
TIMES ARE CHANGING. YOU KNOW THAT. THE FAT DAYS OF CAMPAIGN FUND CONTROL ARE GONE. EVERYBODY AND THEIR MOTHER'S WATCHIN' IT.
I'M NOT PULLING OUT OF WASHINGTON, SAL. I'VE SPENT TOO LONG SETTING EVERY-THING UP. GIVE ME A COUPLE OF MONTHS. LET ME SEE WHAT I GET ON HENNEMAN.
I'LL BE HONEST WITH YOU, DARCY. YOU'RE MAKIN' US NERVOUS. THAT WHOLE CHALMERS THING WAS EMBARRASSING. I COVERED FOR YOU ONCE, BUT NOW YOU GOT THIS HENNEMAN DEAL GOIN'...
EVERBODY'S HOLDING THEIR BREATH, AND YOU PULL YOUR D.U.C.K OUT!
(*DEEP UNDERGROUND CAPABILITY)

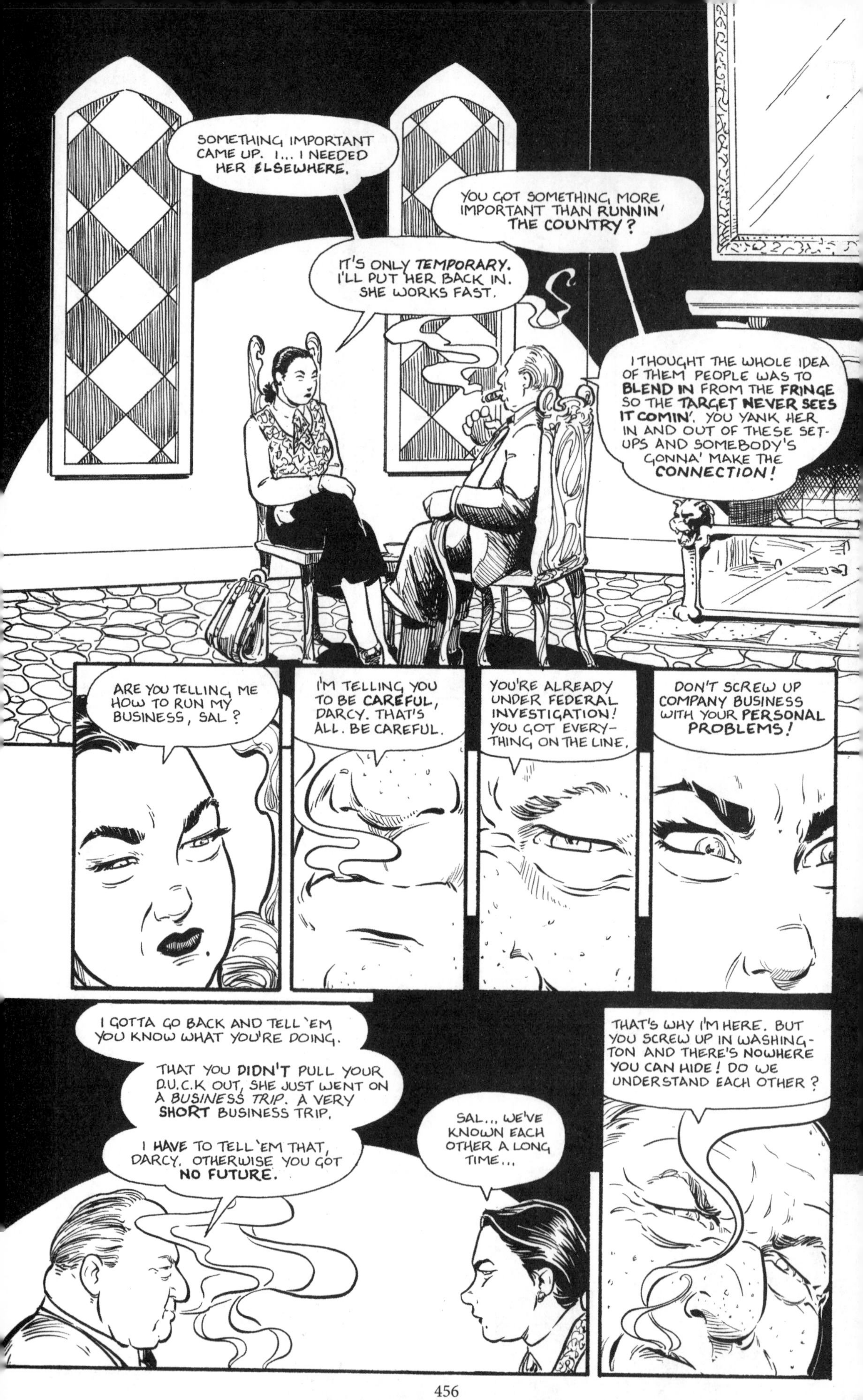
SOMETHING IMPORTANT CAME UP. I... I NEEDED HER ELSEWHERE.
YOU GOT SOMETHING MORE IMPORTANT THAN RUNNIN' THE COUNTRY?
IT'S ONLY TEMPORARY. I'LL PUT HER BACK IN. SHE WORKS FAST.
I THOUGHT THE WHOLE IDEA OF THEM PEOPLE WAS TO BLEND IN FROM THE FRINGE SO THE TARGET NEVER SEES IT COMIN'. YOU YANK HER IN AND OUT OF THESE SET-UPS AND SOMEBODY'S GONNA' MAKE THE CONNECTION!
ARE YOU TELLING ME HOW TO RUN MY BUSINESS, SAL?
I'M TELLING YOU TO BE CAREFUL, DARCY. THAT'S ALL. BE CAREFUL.
YOU'RE ALREADY UNDER FEDERAL INVESTIGATION! YOU GOT EVERY-THING ON THE LINE.
DON'T SCREW UP COMPANY BUSINESS WITH YOUR PERSONAL PROBLEMS!
I GOTTA GO BACK AND TELL 'EM YOU KNOW WHAT YOU'RE DOING.
THAT YOU DIDN'T PULL YOUR D.U.C.K OUT, SHE JUST WENT ON A BUSINESS TRIP. A VERY SHORT BUSINESS TRIP.
I HAVE TO TELL 'EM THAT, DARCY. OTHERWISE YOU GOT NO FUTURE.
SAL... WE'VE KNOWN EACH OTHER A LONG TIME...
THAT'S WHY I'M HERE. BUT YOU SCREW UP IN WASHING-TON AND THERE'S NOWHERE YOU CAN HIDE! DO WE UNDERSTAND EACH OTHER?

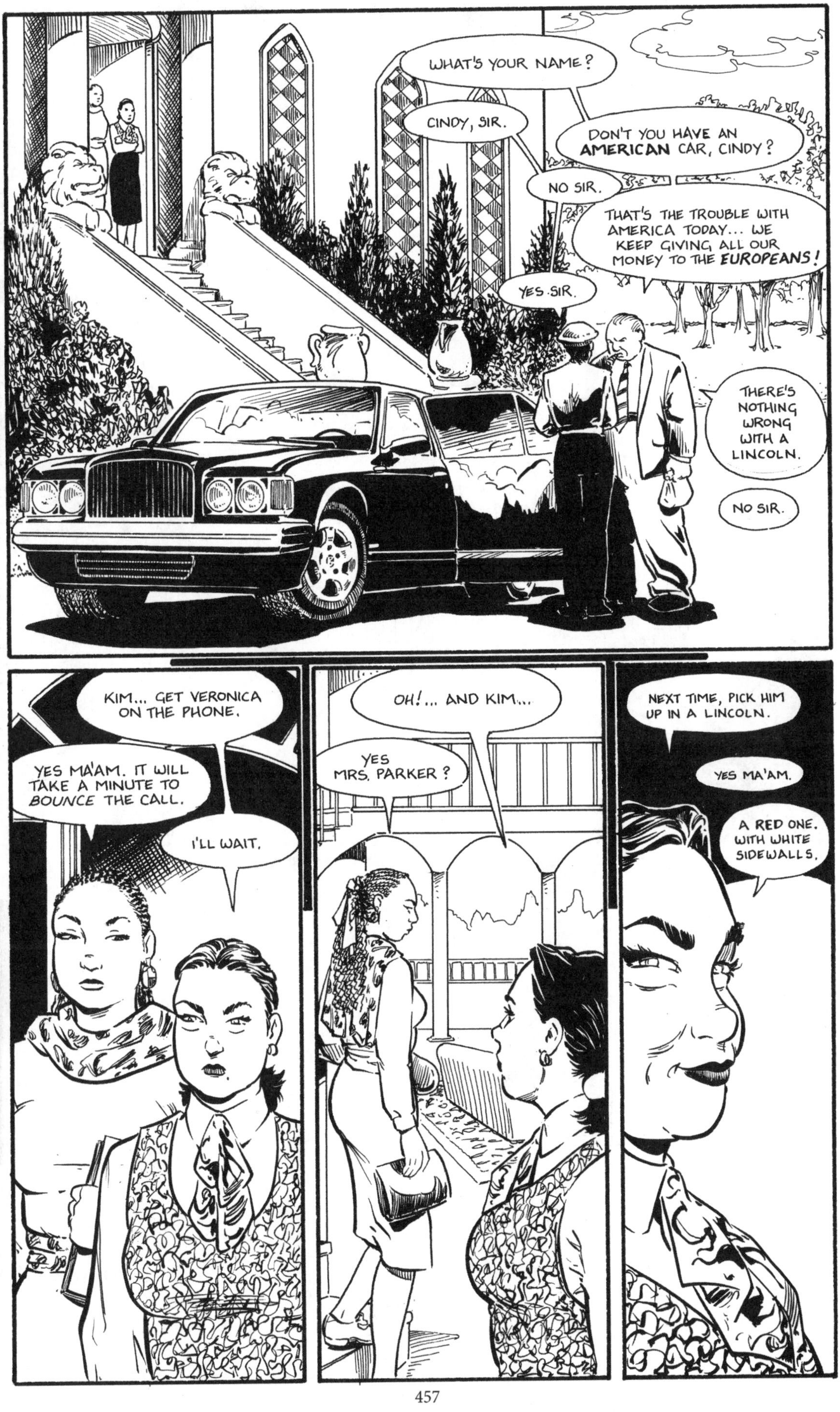
WHAT'S YOUR NAME?
CINDY, SIR.
DON'T YOU HAVE AN AMERICAN CAR, CINDY?
NO SIR.
THAT'S THE TROUBLE WITH AMERICA TODAY... WE KEEP GIVING ALL OUR MONEY TO THE EUROPEANS!
YES SIR.
THERE'S NOTHING WRONG WITH A LINCOLN.
NO SIR.
KIM... GET VERONICA ON THE PHONE.
YES MA'AM. IT WILL TAKE A MINUTE TO BOUNCE THE CALL.
I'LL WAIT.
OH!... AND KIM...
YES MRS. PARKER?
NEXT TIME, PICK HIM UP IN A LINCOLN.
YES MA'AM.
A RED ONE. WITH WHITE SIDEWALLS.

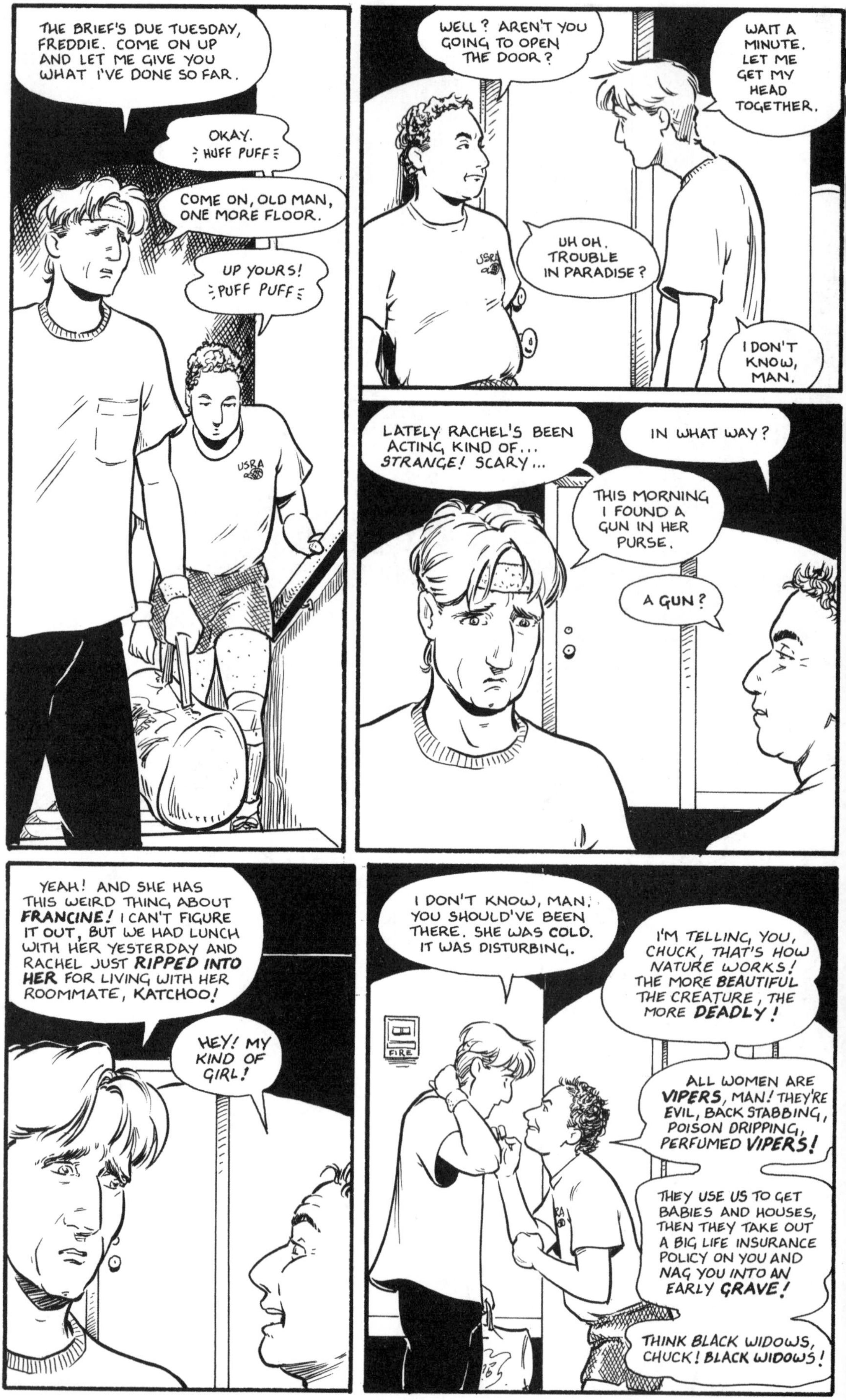
THE BRIEF'S DUE TUESDAY, FREDDIE. COME ON UP AND LET ME GIVE YOU WHAT I'VE DONE SO FAR.
OKAY. HUFF PUFF
COME ON, OLD MAN, ONE MORE FLOOR.
UP YOURS! PUFF PUFF
USRA
WELL? AREN'T YOU GOING TO OPEN THE DOOR?
WAIT A MINUTE. LET ME GET MY HEAD TOGETHER.
UH OH. TROUBLE IN PARADISE?
I DON'T KNOW, MAN.
LATELY RACHEL'S BEEN ACTING KIND OF... STRANGE! SCARY...
IN WHAT WAY?
THIS MORNING I FOUND A GUN IN HER PURSE.
A GUN?
YEAH! AND SHE HAS THIS WEIRD THING ABOUT FRANCINE! I CAN'T FIGURE IT OUT, BUT WE HAD LUNCH WITH HER YESTERDAY AND RACHEL JUST RIPPED INTO HER FOR LIVING WITH HER ROOMMATE, KATCHOO!
HEY! MY KIND OF GIRL!
I DON'T KNOW, MAN. YOU SHOULD'VE BEEN THERE. SHE WAS COLD. IT WAS DISTURBING.
I'M TELLING YOU, CHUCK, THAT'S HOW NATURE WORKS! THE MORE BEAUTIFUL THE CREATURE, THE MORE DEADLY!
FIRE
ALL WOMEN ARE VIPERS, MAN! THEY'RE EVIL, BACK STABBING, POISON DRIPPING, PERFUMED VIPERS!
THEY USE US TO GET BABIES AND HOUSES, THEN THEY TAKE OUT A BIG LIFE INSURANCE POLICY ON YOU AND NAG YOU INTO AN EARLY GRAVE!
THINK BLACK WIDOWS, CHUCK! BLACK WIDOWS!

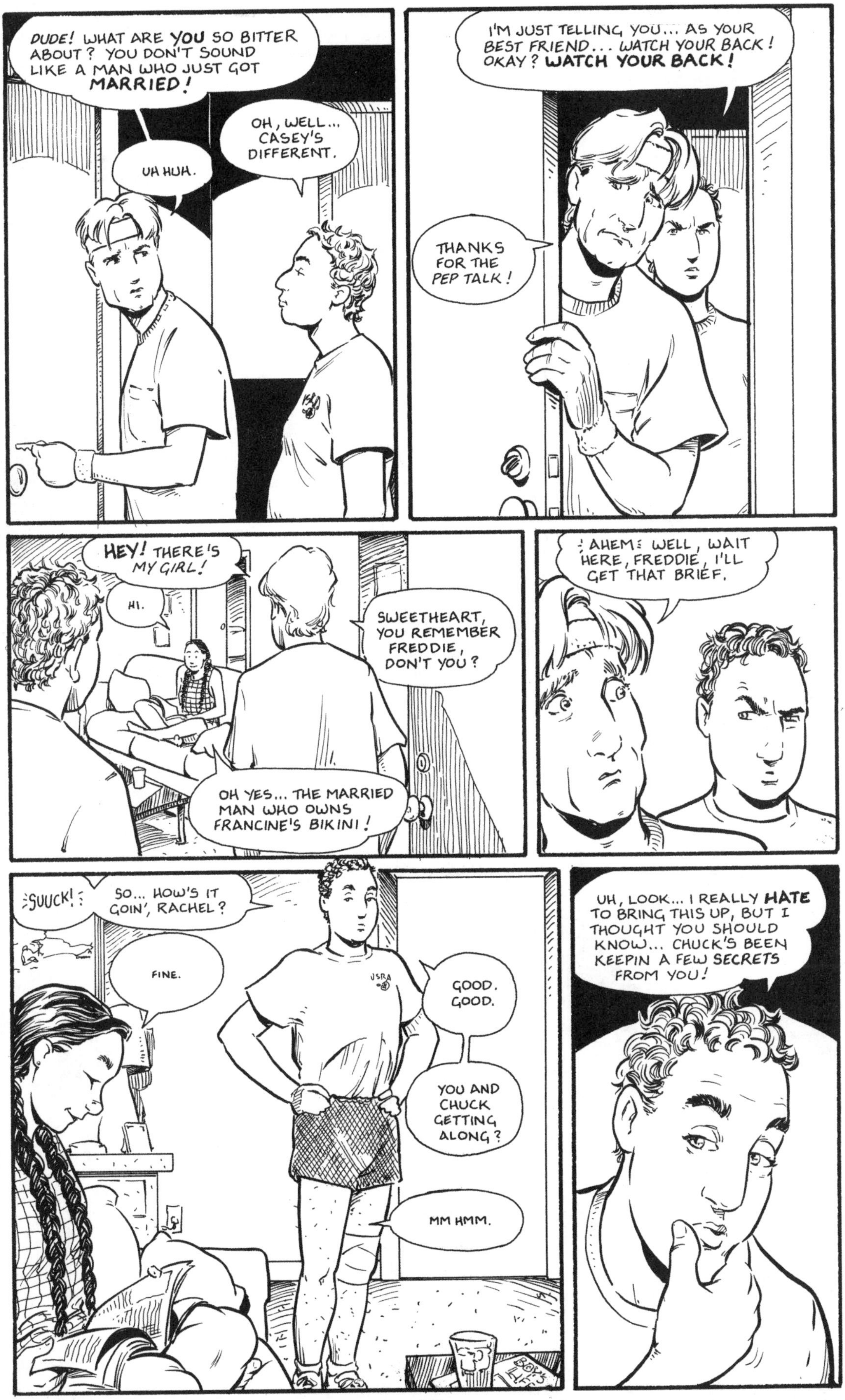
DUDE! WHAT ARE YOU SO BITTER ABOUT? YOU DON'T SOUND LIKE A MAN WHO JUST GOT MARRIED!
UH HUH.
OH, WELL... CASEY'S DIFFERENT.
I'M JUST TELLING YOU... AS YOUR BEST FRIEND... WATCH YOUR BACK! OKAY? WATCH YOUR BACK!
THANKS FOR THE PEP TALK!
HEY! THERE'S MY GIRL!
HI.
SWEETHEART, YOU REMEMBER FREDDIE, DON'T YOU?
OH YES... THE MARRIED MAN WHO OWNS FRANCINE'S BIKINI!
AHEM WELL, WAIT HERE, FREDDIE, I'LL GET THAT BRIEF.
SUUCK!
SO... HOW'S IT GOIN', RACHEL?
FINE.
GOOD. GOOD.
YOU AND CHUCK GETTING ALONG?
MM HMM.
UH, LOOK... I REALLY HATE TO BRING THIS UP, BUT I THOUGHT YOU SHOULD KNOW... CHUCK'S BEEN KEEPIN A FEW SECRETS FROM YOU!

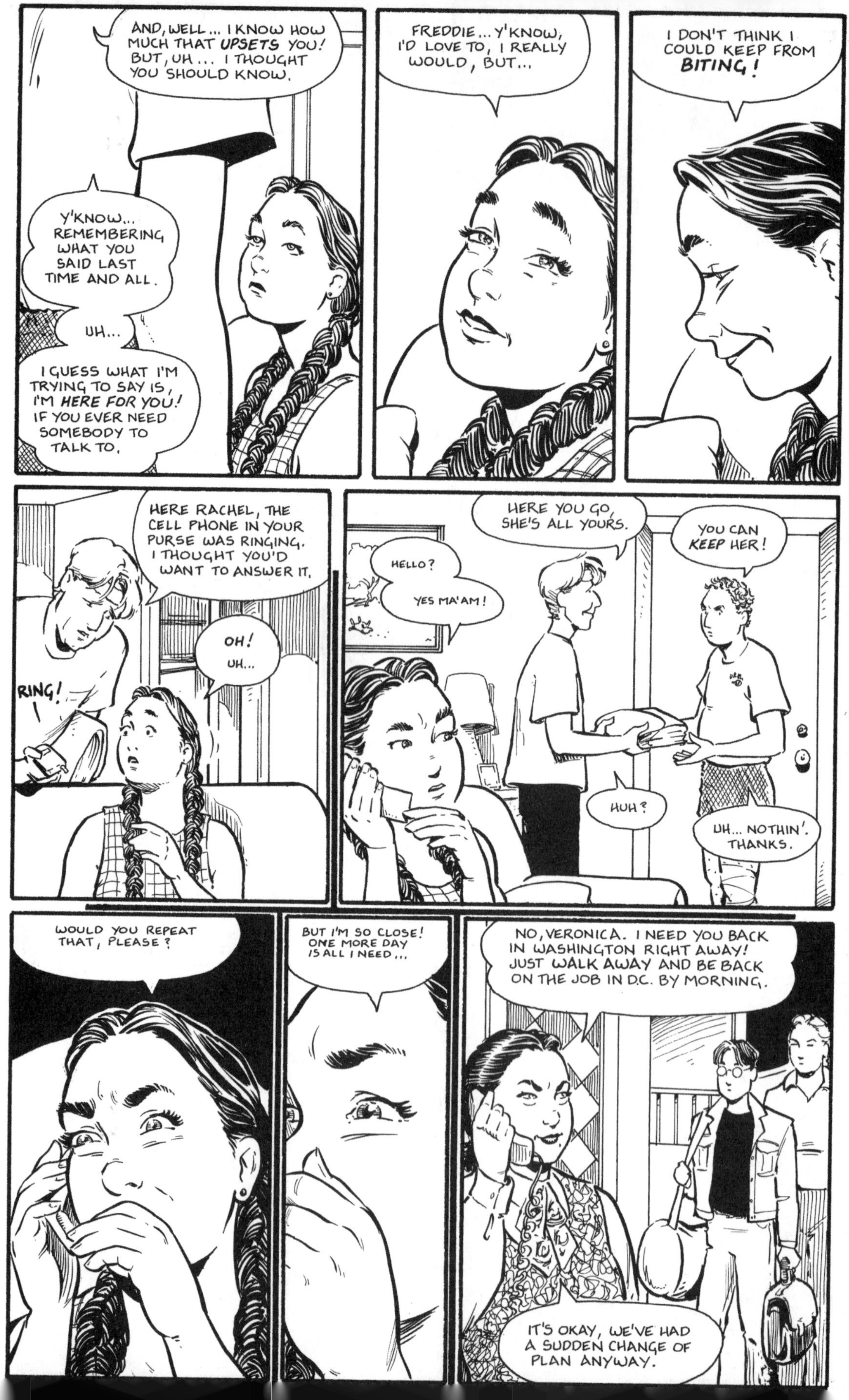
AND, WELL... I KNOW HOW MUCH THAT UPSETS YOU! BUT, UH... I THOUGHT YOU SHOULD KNOW.
Y'KNOW... REMEMBERING WHAT YOU SAID LAST TIME AND ALL.
UH...
I GUESS WHAT I'M TRYING TO SAY IS, I'M HERE FOR YOU! IF YOU EVER NEED SOMEBODY TO TALK TO.
FREDDIE... Y'KNOW, I'D LOVE TO, I REALLY WOULD, BUT...
I DON'T THINK I COULD KEEP FROM BITING!
HERE RACHEL, THE CELL PHONE IN YOUR PURSE WAS RINGING. I THOUGHT YOU'D WANT TO ANSWER IT.
RING!
OH! UH...
HERE YOU GO, SHE'S ALL YOURS.
YOU CAN KEEP HER!
HELLO?
YES MA'AM!
HUH?
UH... NOTHIN'. THANKS.
WOULD YOU REPEAT THAT, PLEASE?
BUT I'M SO CLOSE! ONE MORE DAY IS ALL I NEED...
NO, VERONICA. I NEED YOU BACK IN WASHINGTON RIGHT AWAY! JUST WALK AWAY AND BE BACK ON THE JOB IN D.C. BY MORNING.
IT'S OKAY, WE'VE HAD A SUDDEN CHANGE OF PLAN ANYWAY.

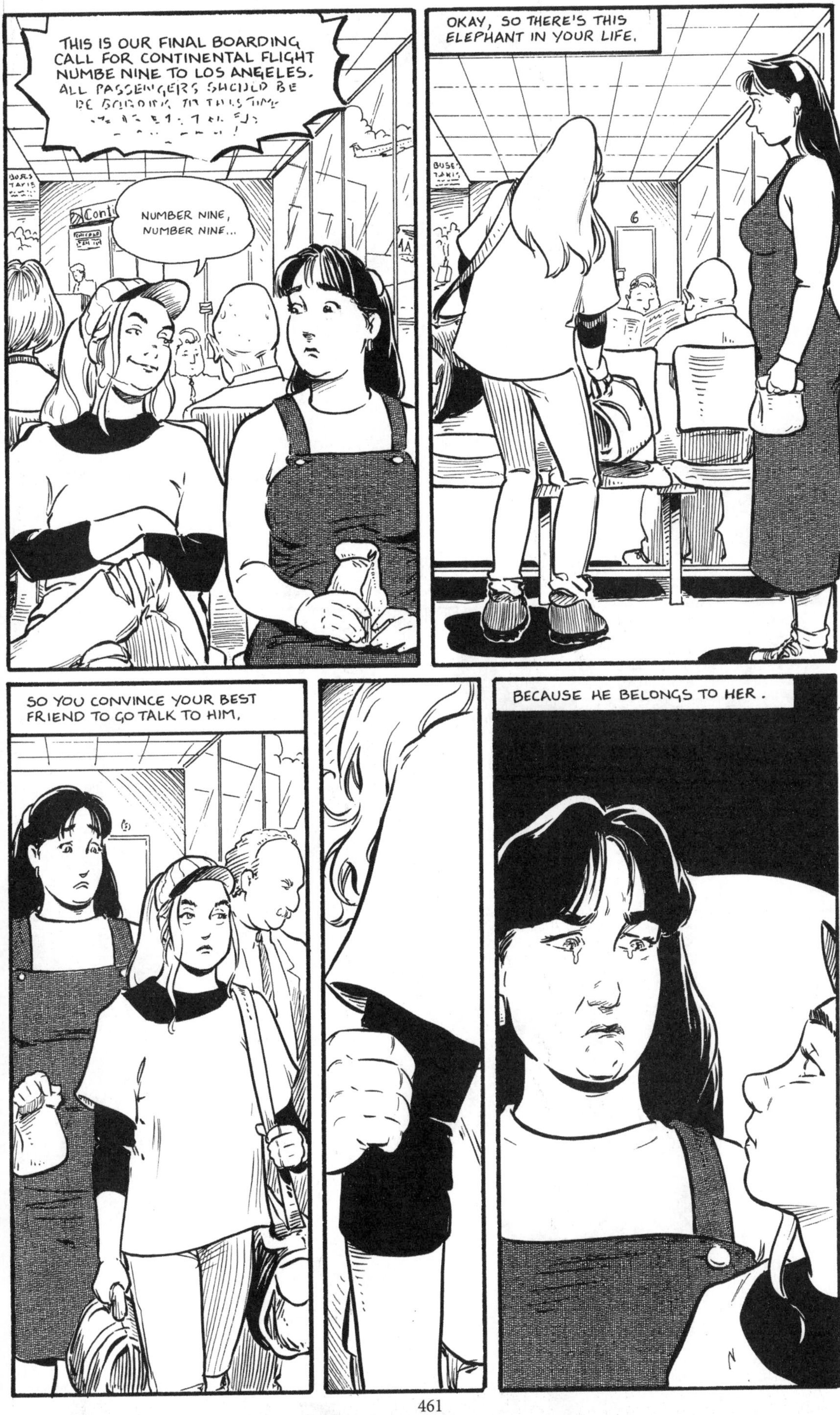
THIS IS OUR FINAL BOARDING CALL FOR CONTINENTAL FLIGHT NUMBE NINE TO LOS ANGELES.
ALL PASSENGERS SHOULD BE
NUMBER NINE, NUMBER NINE...
OKAY, SO THERE'S THIS ELEPHANT IN YOUR LIFE.
SO YOU CONVINCE YOUR BEST FRIEND TO GO TALK TO HIM,
BECAUSE HE BELONGS TO HER.

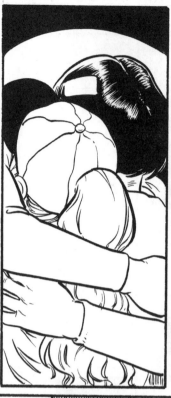

AND EVEN THOUGH YOU DON'T ALWAYS SEE HIM, YOU KNOW HE'S ALWAYS *THERE!* REMINDING HER OF THE PAST, THROWING SHADOWS IN YOUR WAY.

SO SHE WALKS AWAY AND THEY CLOSE THE DOOR AND IT'S ALL YOU CAN DO TO KEEP FROM RUNNING UP AND BEATING IT BACK OPEN WITH YOUR FISTS.

BECAUSE YOU KNOW THE ELEPHANT IS DEAD.

BUT SHE HAS TO SEE FOR HERSELF, BECAUSE AS LONG AS YOU'VE KNOWN HER, YOUR BEST FRIEND HAS BEEN A LITTLE GIRL WALKING THROUGH A GRAVEYARD.

NO ENTRY
ONCE DOOR IS CLOSED!

AND NOW ALL YOU CAN DO IS WAIT FOR HER TO COME OUT ON THE OTHER SIDE.

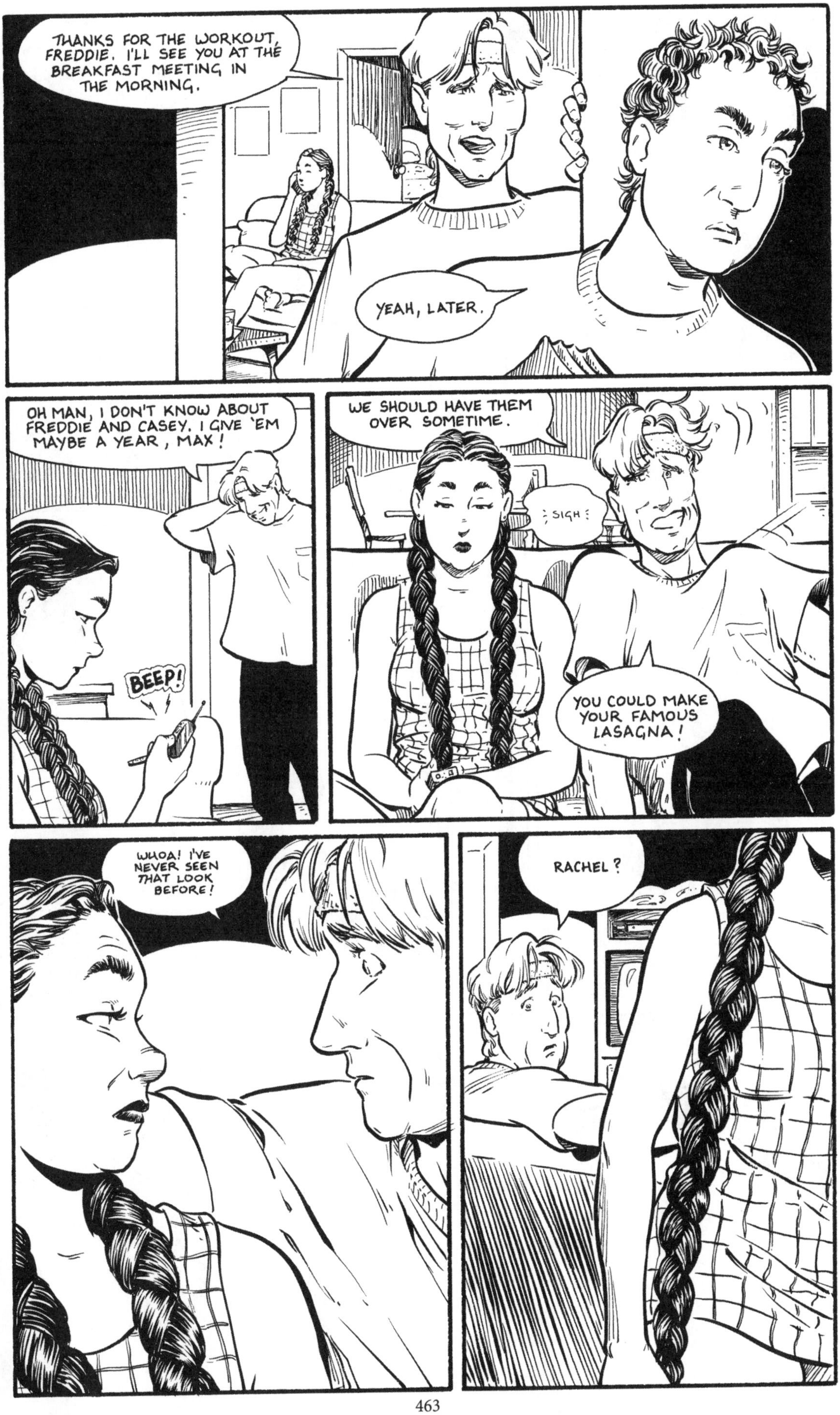
THANKS FOR THE WORKOUT, FREDDIE. I'LL SEE YOU AT THE BREAKFAST MEETING IN THE MORNING.
YEAH, LATER.
OH MAN, I DON'T KNOW ABOUT FREDDIE AND CASEY. I GIVE 'EM MAYBE A YEAR, MAX!
BEEP!
WE SHOULD HAVE THEM OVER SOMETIME.
SIGH
YOU COULD MAKE YOUR FAMOUS LASAGNA!
WHOA! I'VE NEVER SEEN THAT LOOK BEFORE!
RACHEL?

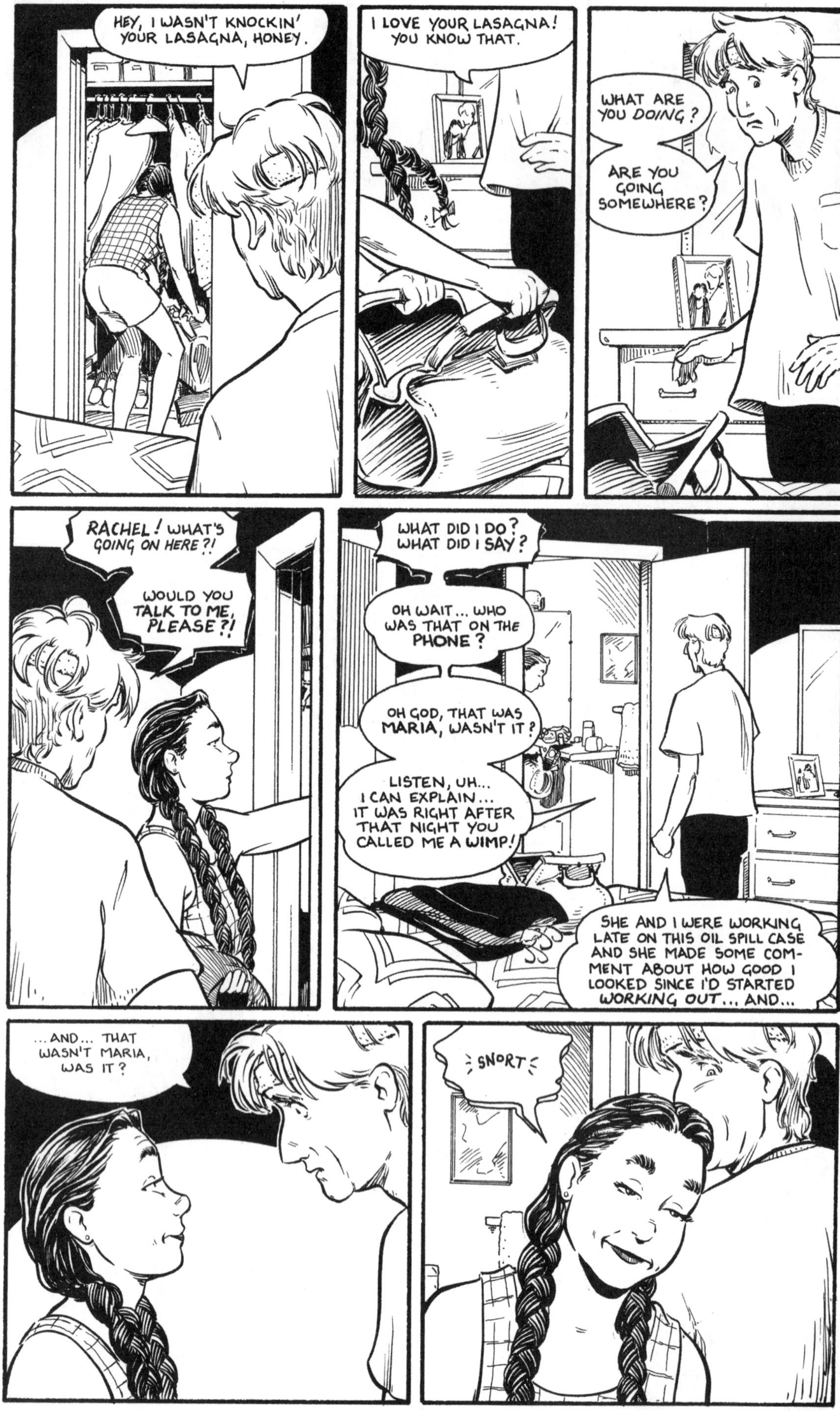
HEY, I WASN'T KNOCKIN' YOUR LASAGNA, HONEY.
I LOVE YOUR LASAGNA! YOU KNOW THAT.
WHAT ARE YOU DOING?
ARE YOU GOING SOMEWHERE?
RACHEL! WHAT'S GOING ON HERE?!
WOULD YOU TALK TO ME, PLEASE?!
WHAT DID I DO? WHAT DID I SAY?
OH WAIT... WHO WAS THAT ON THE PHONE?
OH GOD, THAT WAS MARIA, WASN'T IT?
LISTEN, UH... I CAN EXPLAIN... IT WAS RIGHT AFTER THAT NIGHT YOU CALLED ME A WIMP!
SHE AND I WERE WORKING LATE ON THIS OIL SPILL CASE AND SHE MADE SOME COMMENT ABOUT HOW GOOD I LOOKED SINCE I'D STARTED WORKING OUT... AND...
...AND... THAT WASN'T MARIA, WAS IT?
SNORT

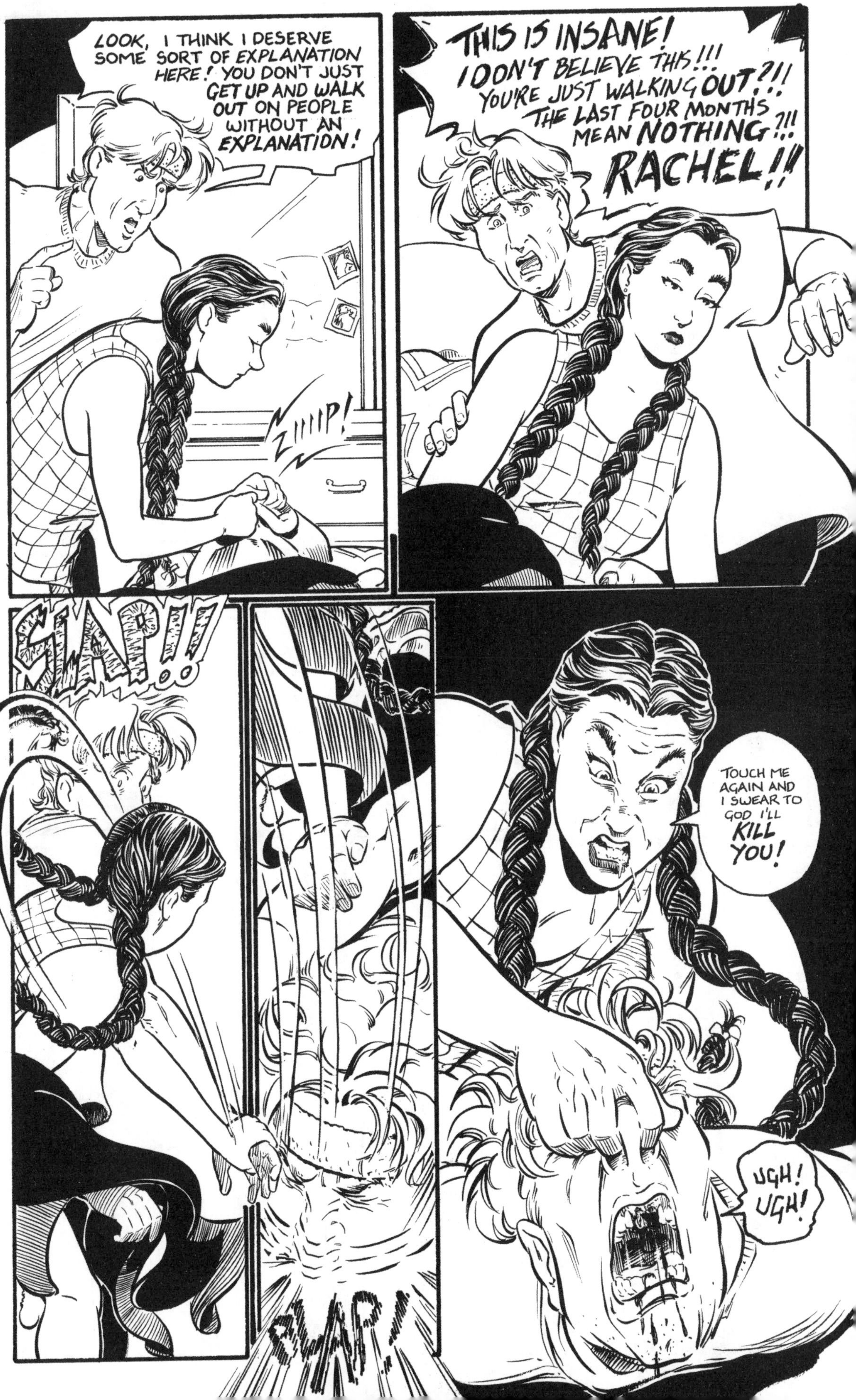
LOOK, I THINK I DESERVE SOME SORT OF EXPLANATION HERE! YOU DON'T JUST GET UP AND WALK OUT ON PEOPLE WITHOUT AN EXPLANATION!
ZIIIIP!
THIS IS INSANE! I DON'T BELIEVE THIS!!! YOU'RE JUST WALKING OUT?!! THE LAST FOUR MONTHS MEAN NOTHING?!! RACHEL!!
SLAP!!
SNAP!
TOUCH ME AGAIN AND I SWEAR TO GOD I'LL KILL YOU!
UGH! UGH!

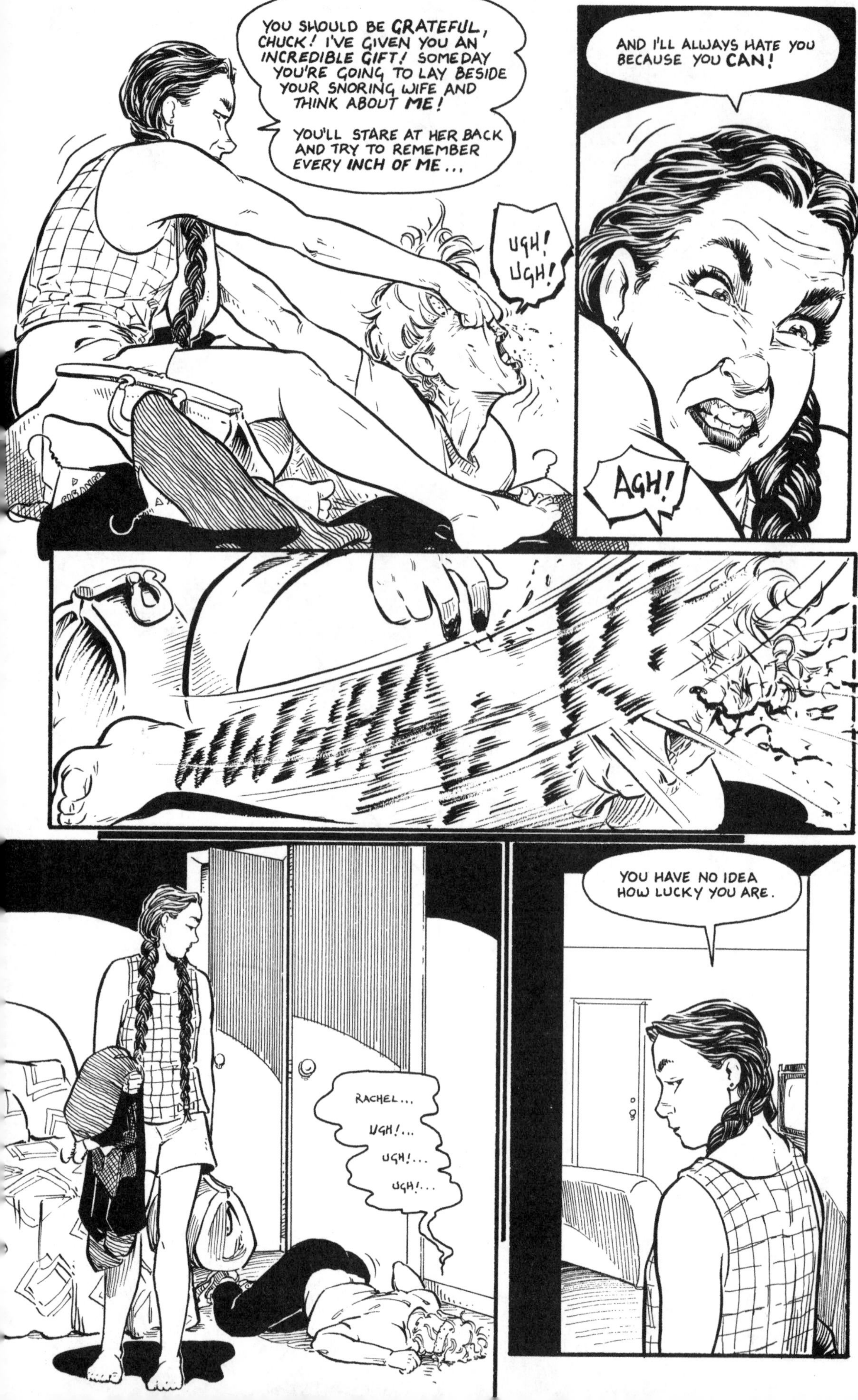
YOU SHOULD BE GRATEFUL, CHUCK! I'VE GIVEN YOU AN INCREDIBLE GIFT! SOMEDAY YOU'RE GOING TO LAY BESIDE YOUR SNORING WIFE AND THINK ABOUT ME!
YOU'LL STARE AT HER BACK AND TRY TO REMEMBER EVERY INCH OF ME...
UGH! UGH!
AND I'LL ALWAYS HATE YOU BECAUSE YOU CAN!
AGH!
RACHEL... UGH!... UGH!... UGH!...
YOU HAVE NO IDEA HOW LUCKY YOU ARE.

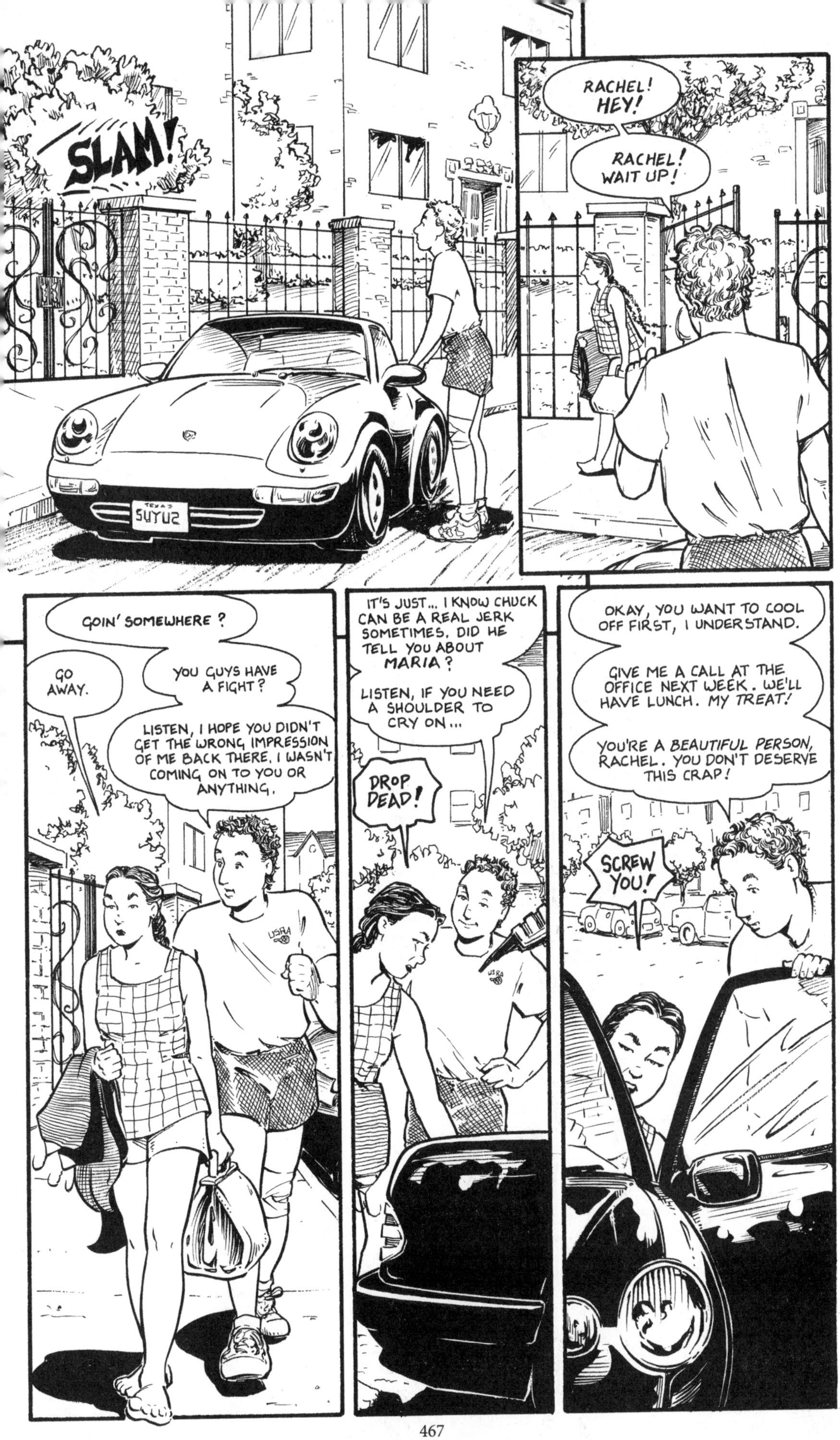

SLAM!
RACHEL! HEY!
RACHEL! WAIT UP!
GOIN' SOMEWHERE ?
GO AWAY.
YOU GUYS HAVE A FIGHT ?
LISTEN, I HOPE YOU DIDN'T GET THE WRONG IMPRESSION OF ME BACK THERE. I WASN'T COMING ON TO YOU OR ANYTHING.
IT'S JUST... I KNOW CHUCK CAN BE A REAL JERK SOMETIMES. DID HE TELL YOU ABOUT MARIA ?
LISTEN, IF YOU NEED A SHOULDER TO CRY ON...
DROP DEAD!
OKAY, YOU WANT TO COOL OFF FIRST, I UNDERSTAND.
GIVE ME A CALL AT THE OFFICE NEXT WEEK. WE'LL HAVE LUNCH. MY TREAT!
YOU'RE A BEAUTIFUL PERSON, RACHEL. YOU DON'T DESERVE THIS CRAP!
SCREW YOU!

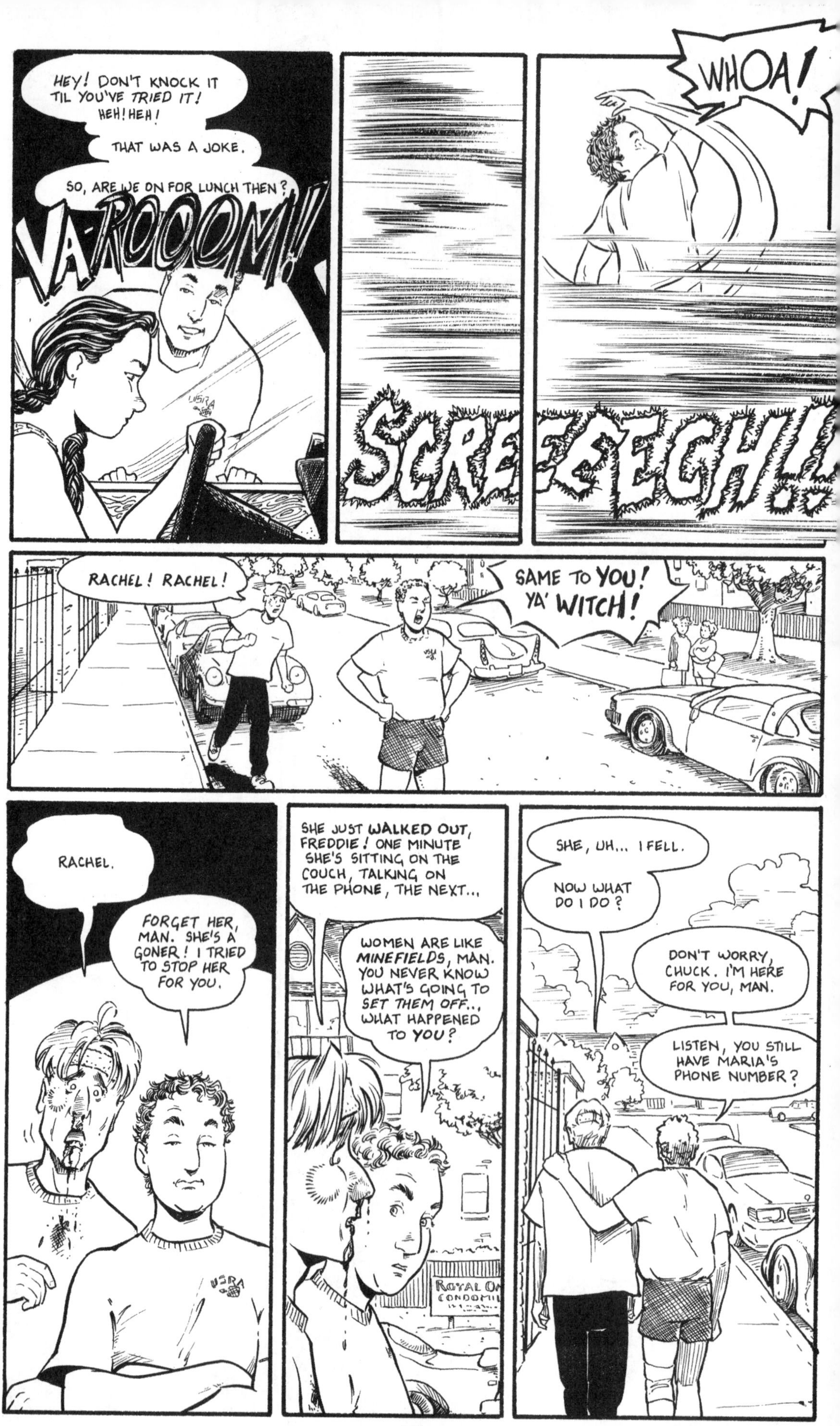

HEY! DON'T KNOCK IT TIL YOU'VE TRIED IT! HEH! HEH!
THAT WAS A JOKE.
SO, ARE WE ON FOR LUNCH THEN?
VA-ROOOM!!
WHOA!
SCREEECH!!
RACHEL! RACHEL!
SAME TO YOU! YA' WITCH!
RACHEL.
FORGET HER, MAN. SHE'S A GONER! I TRIED TO STOP HER FOR YOU.
SHE JUST WALKED OUT, FREDDIE! ONE MINUTE SHE'S SITTING ON THE COUCH, TALKING ON THE PHONE, THE NEXT...
WOMEN ARE LIKE MINEFIELDS, MAN. YOU NEVER KNOW WHAT'S GOING TO SET THEM OFF.., WHAT HAPPENED TO YOU?
SHE, UH... I FELL.
NOW WHAT DO I DO?
DON'T WORRY, CHUCK. I'M HERE FOR YOU, MAN.
LISTEN, YOU STILL HAVE MARIA'S PHONE NUMBER?

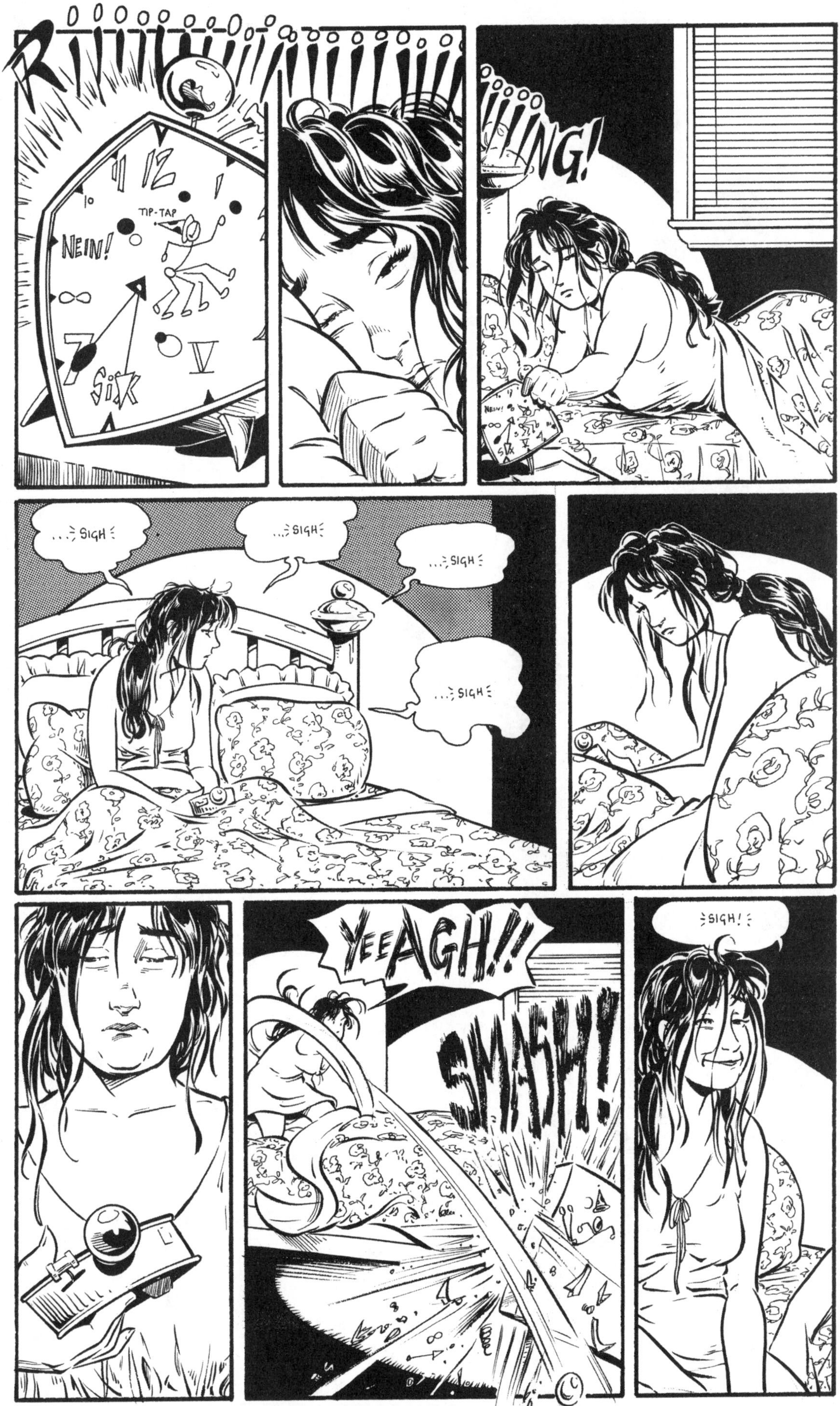
RIIIIIIIIIIIIIIIIIIIIIIIING!
TIP-TAP
NEIN!
SIX
V
...SIGH
...SIGH
...SIGH
...SIGH
YEEAGH!!
SMASH!
SIGH!

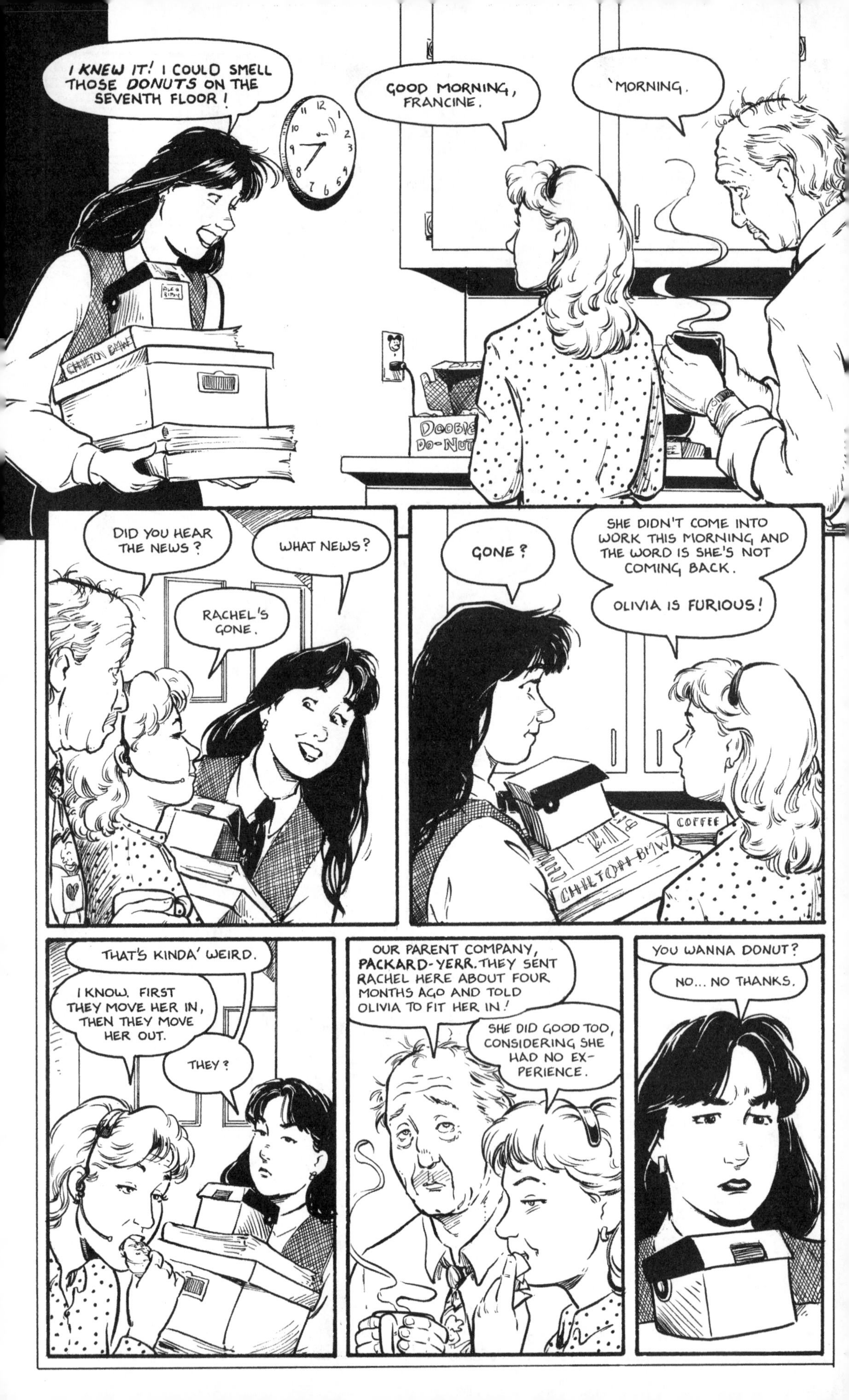
I KNEW IT! I COULD SMELL THOSE DONUTS ON THE SEVENTH FLOOR!
GOOD MORNING, FRANCINE.
`MORNING.
DOOBIE DO-NUT
CHILTON BMW
DID YOU HEAR THE NEWS?
WHAT NEWS?
RACHEL'S GONE.
GONE?
SHE DIDN'T COME INTO WORK THIS MORNING AND THE WORD IS SHE'S NOT COMING BACK.
OLIVIA IS FURIOUS!
COFFEE
CHILTON BMW
THAT'S KINDA' WEIRD.
I KNOW. FIRST THEY MOVE HER IN, THEN THEY MOVE HER OUT.
THEY?
OUR PARENT COMPANY, PACKARD-YERR. THEY SENT RACHEL HERE ABOUT FOUR MONTHS AGO AND TOLD OLIVIA TO FIT HER IN!
SHE DID GOOD TOO, CONSIDERING SHE HAD NO EX-PERIENCE.
YOU WANNA DONUT?
NO... NO THANKS.

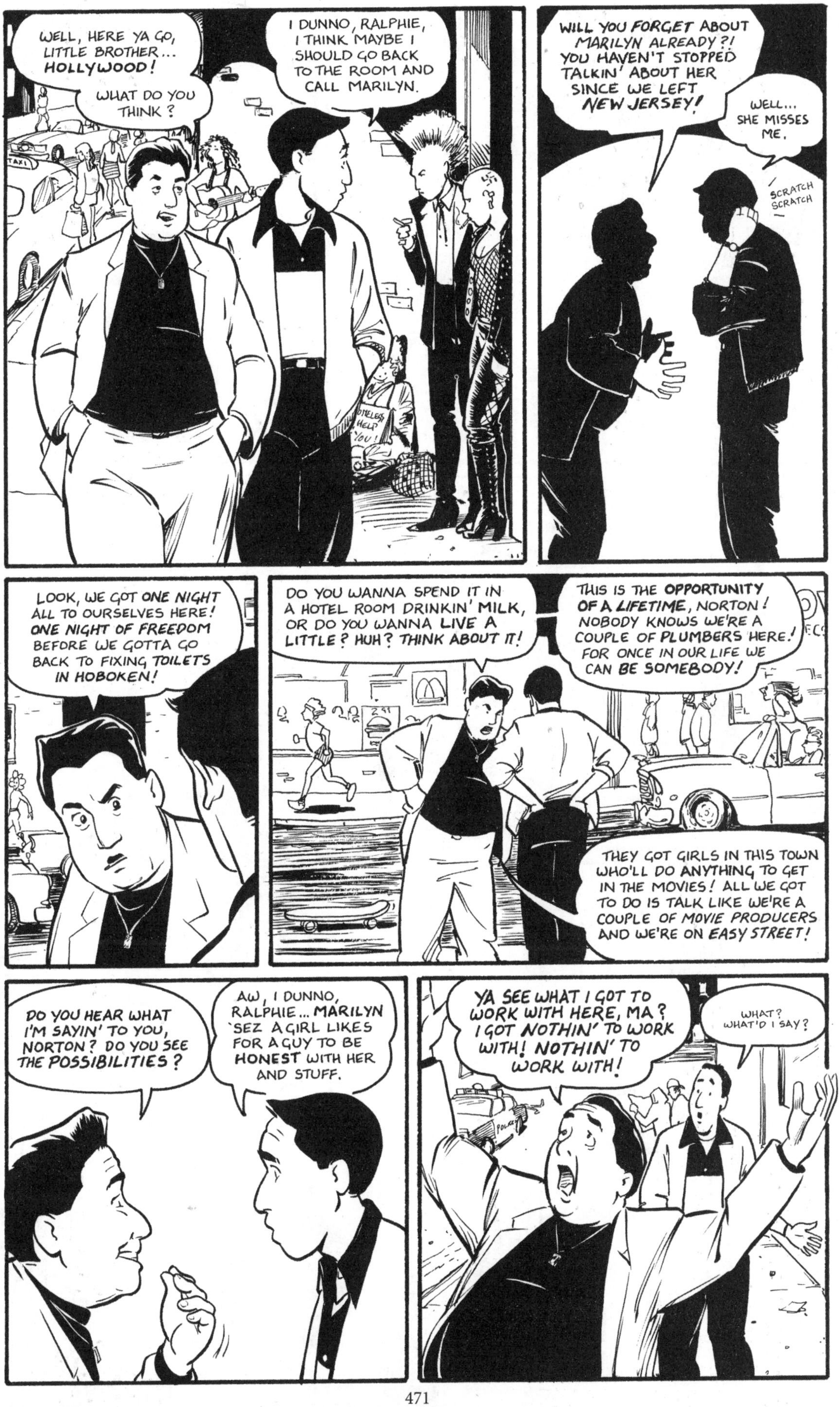
WELL, HERE YA GO, LITTLE BROTHER... HOLLYWOOD!
WHAT DO YOU THINK?
I DUNNO, RALPHIE, I THINK MAYBE I SHOULD GO BACK TO THE ROOM AND CALL MARILYN.
WILL YOU FORGET ABOUT MARILYN ALREADY?! YOU HAVEN'T STOPPED TALKIN' ABOUT HER SINCE WE LEFT NEW JERSEY!
WELL... SHE MISSES ME.
SCRATCH SCRATCH
LOOK, WE GOT ONE NIGHT ALL TO OURSELVES HERE! ONE NIGHT OF FREEDOM BEFORE WE GOTTA GO BACK TO FIXING TOILETS IN HOBOKEN!
DO YOU WANNA SPEND IT IN A HOTEL ROOM DRINKIN' MILK, OR DO YOU WANNA LIVE A LITTLE? HUH? THINK ABOUT IT!
THIS IS THE OPPORTUNITY OF A LIFETIME, NORTON! NOBODY KNOWS WE'RE A COUPLE OF PLUMBERS HERE! FOR ONCE IN OUR LIFE WE CAN BE SOMEBODY!
THEY GOT GIRLS IN THIS TOWN WHO'LL DO ANYTHING TO GET IN THE MOVIES! ALL WE GOT TO DO IS TALK LIKE WE'RE A COUPLE OF MOVIE PRODUCERS AND WE'RE ON EASY STREET!
DO YOU HEAR WHAT I'M SAYIN' TO YOU, NORTON? DO YOU SEE THE POSSIBILITIES?
AW, I DUNNO, RALPHIE... MARILYN SEZ A GUY LIKES FOR A GUY TO BE HONEST WITH HER AND STUFF.
YA SEE WHAT I GOT TO WORK WITH HERE, MA? I GOT NOTHIN' TO WORK WITH! NOTHIN' TO WORK WITH!
WHAT? WHAT'D I SAY?

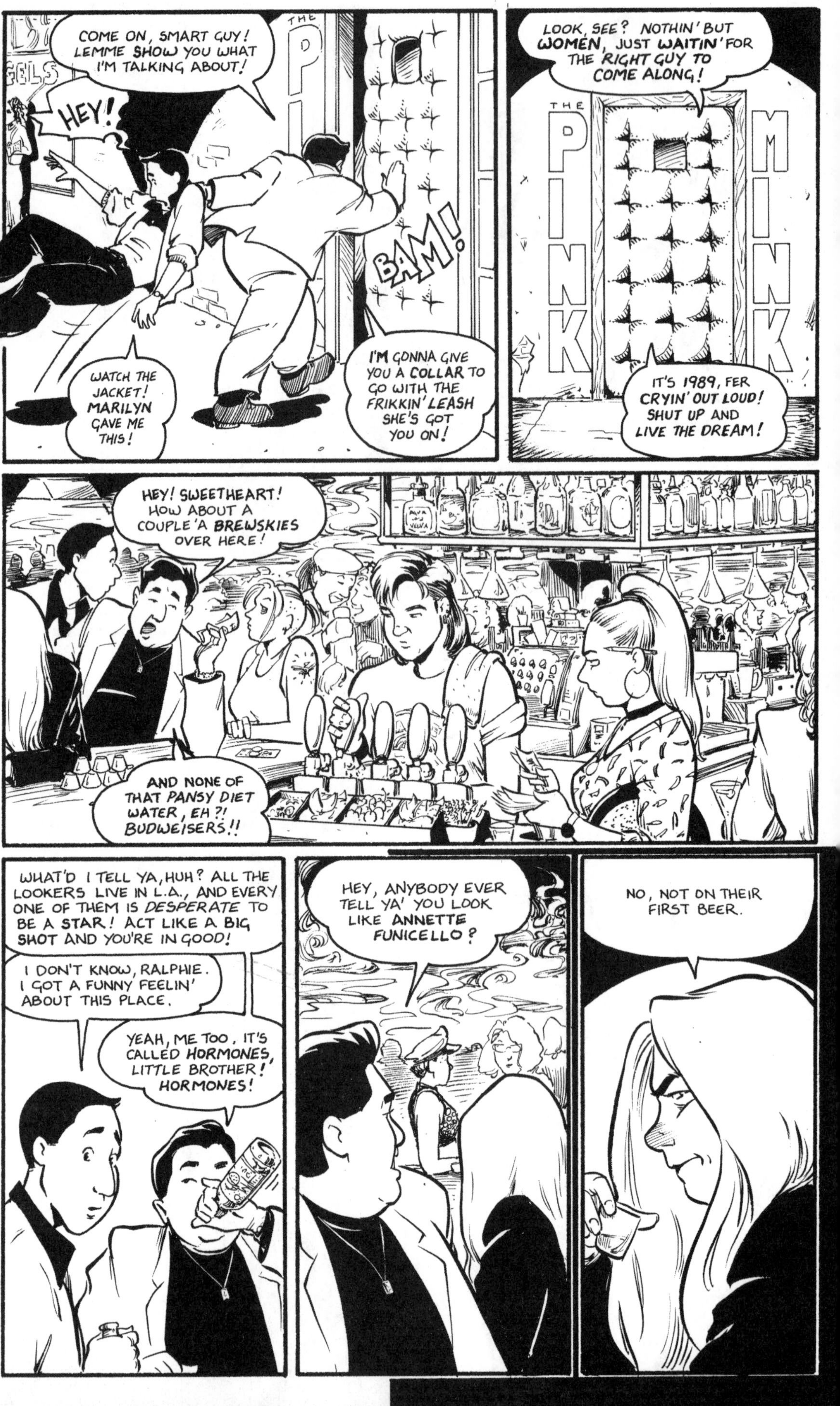
COME ON, SMART GUY! LEMME SHOW YOU WHAT I'M TALKING ABOUT!
HEY!
BAM!
WATCH THE JACKET! MARILYN GAVE ME THIS!
I'M GONNA GIVE YOU A COLLAR TO GO WITH THE FRIKKIN' LEASH SHE'S GOT YOU ON!
LOOK, SEE? NOTHIN' BUT WOMEN, JUST WAITIN' FOR THE RIGHT GUY TO COME ALONG!
THE PINK MINK
IT'S 1989, FER CRYIN' OUT LOUD! SHUT UP AND LIVE THE DREAM!
HEY! SWEETHEART! HOW ABOUT A COUPLE 'A BREWSKIES OVER HERE!
AND NONE OF THAT PANSY DIET WATER, EH?! BUDWEISERS!!
WHAT'D I TELL YA, HUH? ALL THE LOOKERS LIVE IN L.A., AND EVERY ONE OF THEM IS DESPERATE TO BE A STAR! ACT LIKE A BIG SHOT AND YOU'RE IN GOOD!
I DON'T KNOW, RALPHIE. I GOT A FUNNY FEELIN' ABOUT THIS PLACE.
YEAH, ME TOO, IT'S CALLED HORMONES, LITTLE BROTHER! HORMONES!
HEY, ANYBODY EVER TELL YA' YOU LOOK LIKE ANNETTE FUNICELLO?
NO, NOT ON THEIR FIRST BEER.

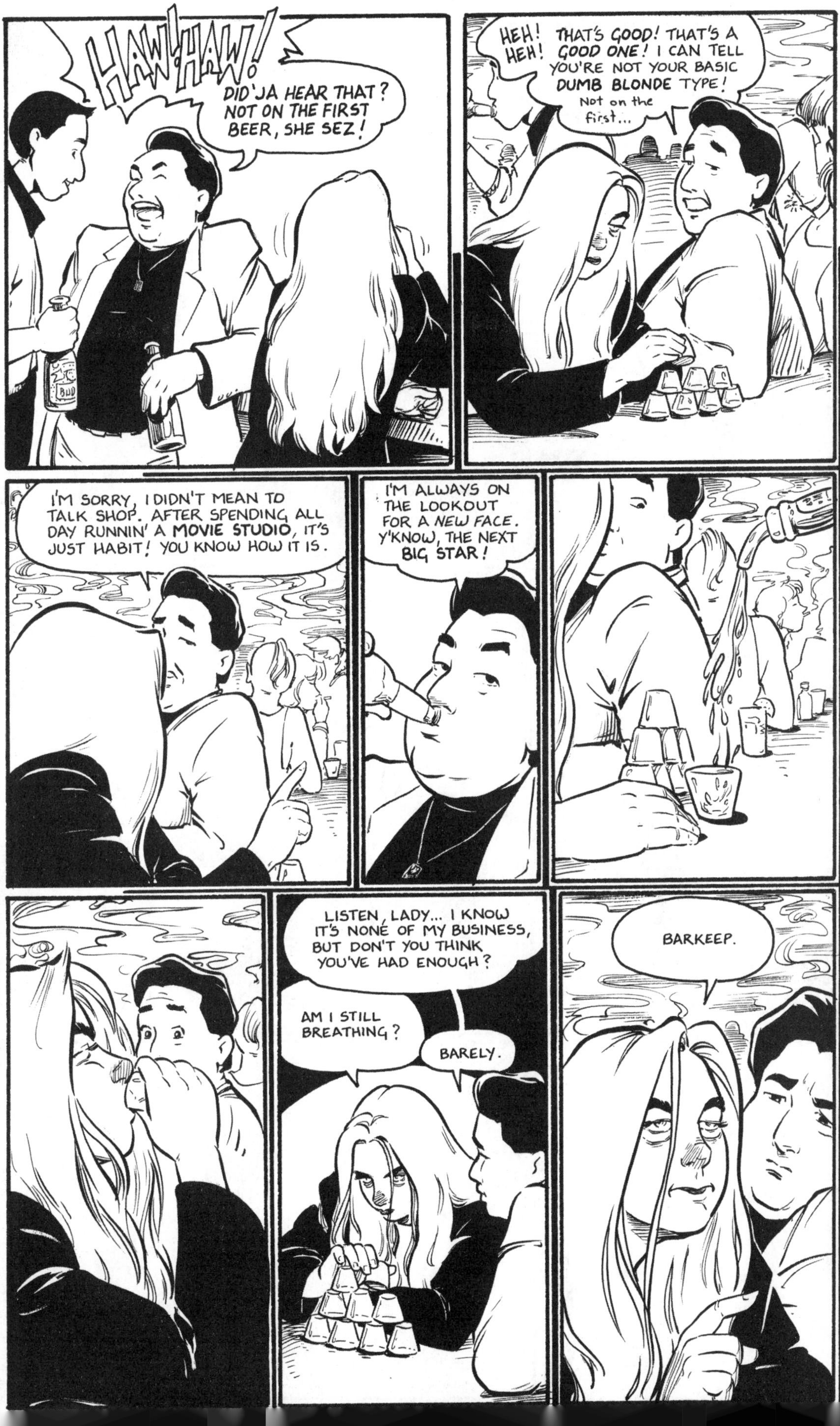
HAW! HAW!
DID'JA HEAR THAT? NOT ON THE FIRST BEER, SHE SEZ!
HEH! HEH!
THAT'S GOOD! THAT'S A GOOD ONE! I CAN TELL YOU'RE NOT YOUR BASIC DUMB BLONDE TYPE!
Not on the first...
I'M SORRY, I DIDN'T MEAN TO TALK SHOP. AFTER SPENDING ALL DAY RUNNIN' A MOVIE STUDIO, IT'S JUST HABIT! YOU KNOW HOW IT IS.
I'M ALWAYS ON THE LOOKOUT FOR A NEW FACE. Y'KNOW, THE NEXT BIG STAR!
LISTEN, LADY... I KNOW IT'S NONE OF MY BUSINESS, BUT DON'T YOU THINK YOU'VE HAD ENOUGH?
AM I STILL BREATHING?
BARELY.
BARKEEP.

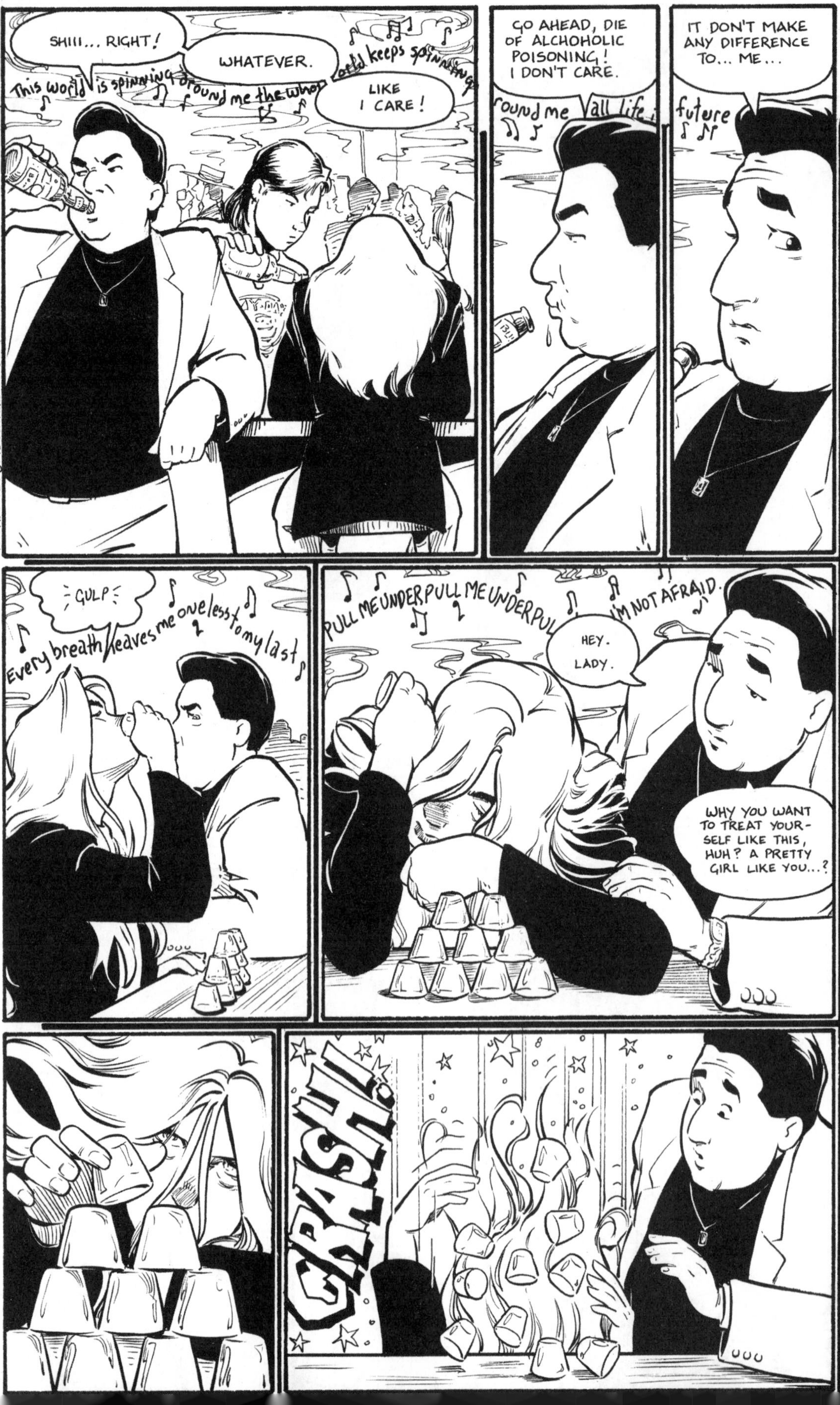
SHIII... RIGHT!
WHATEVER.
This world is spinning around me the whole world keeps spinning
LIKE I CARE!
GO AHEAD, DIE OF ALCHOHOLIC POISONING! I DON'T CARE.
round me all life i
IT DON'T MAKE ANY DIFFERENCE TO... ME...
future
GULP
Every breath leaves me one less to my last
PULL ME UNDER PULL ME UNDER PUL I'M NOT AFRAID.
HEY. LADY.
WHY YOU WANT TO TREAT YOURSELF LIKE THIS, HUH? A PRETTY GIRL LIKE YOU...?
CRASH!

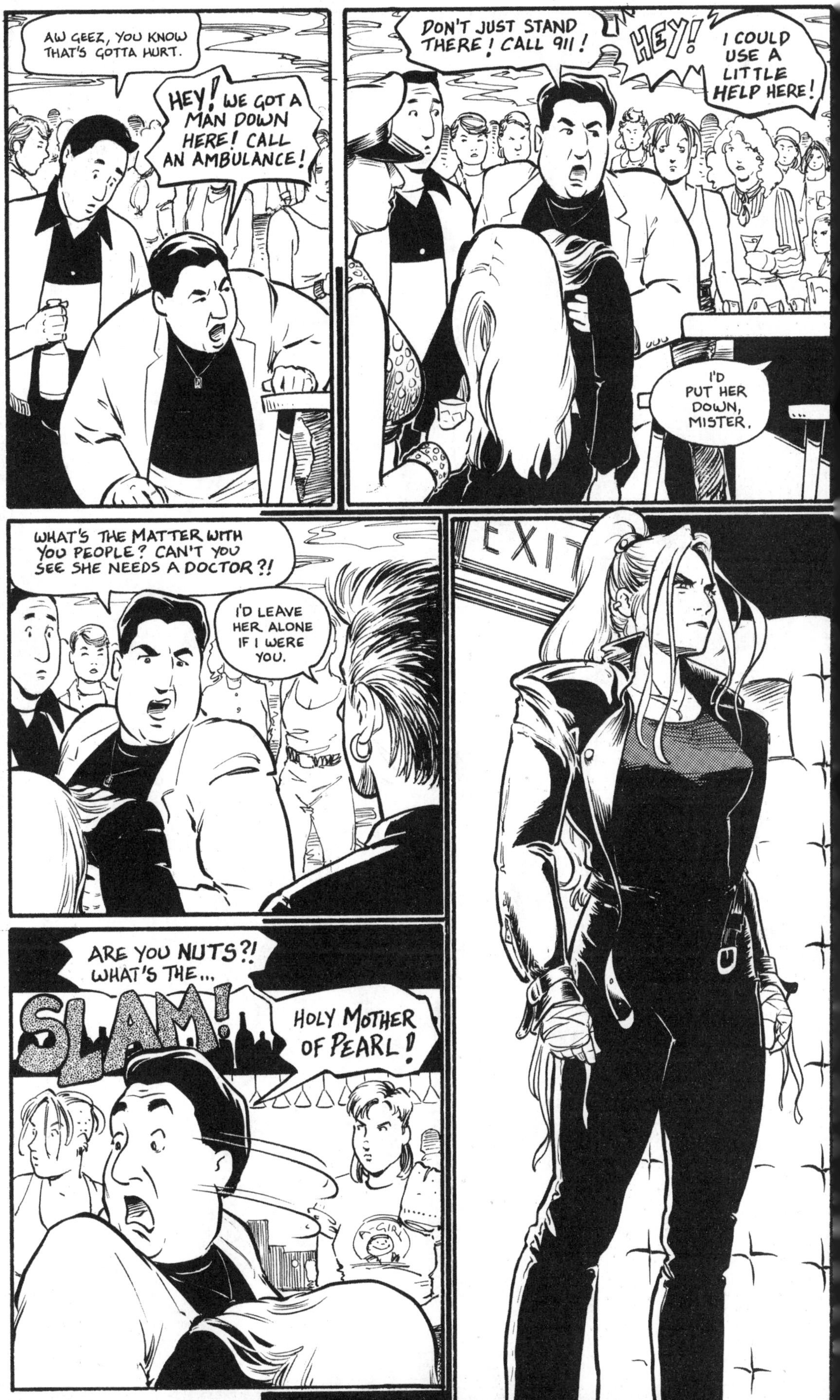
AW GEEZ, YOU KNOW THAT'S GOTTA HURT.
HEY! WE GOT A MAN DOWN HERE! CALL AN AMBULANCE!
DON'T JUST STAND THERE! CALL 911!
HEY!
I COULD USE A LITTLE HELP HERE!
I'D PUT HER DOWN, MISTER.
WHAT'S THE MATTER WITH YOU PEOPLE? CAN'T YOU SEE SHE NEEDS A DOCTOR?!
I'D LEAVE HER ALONE IF I WERE YOU.
EXIT
ARE YOU NUTS?! WHAT'S THE...
SLAM!
HOLY MOTHER OF PEARL!

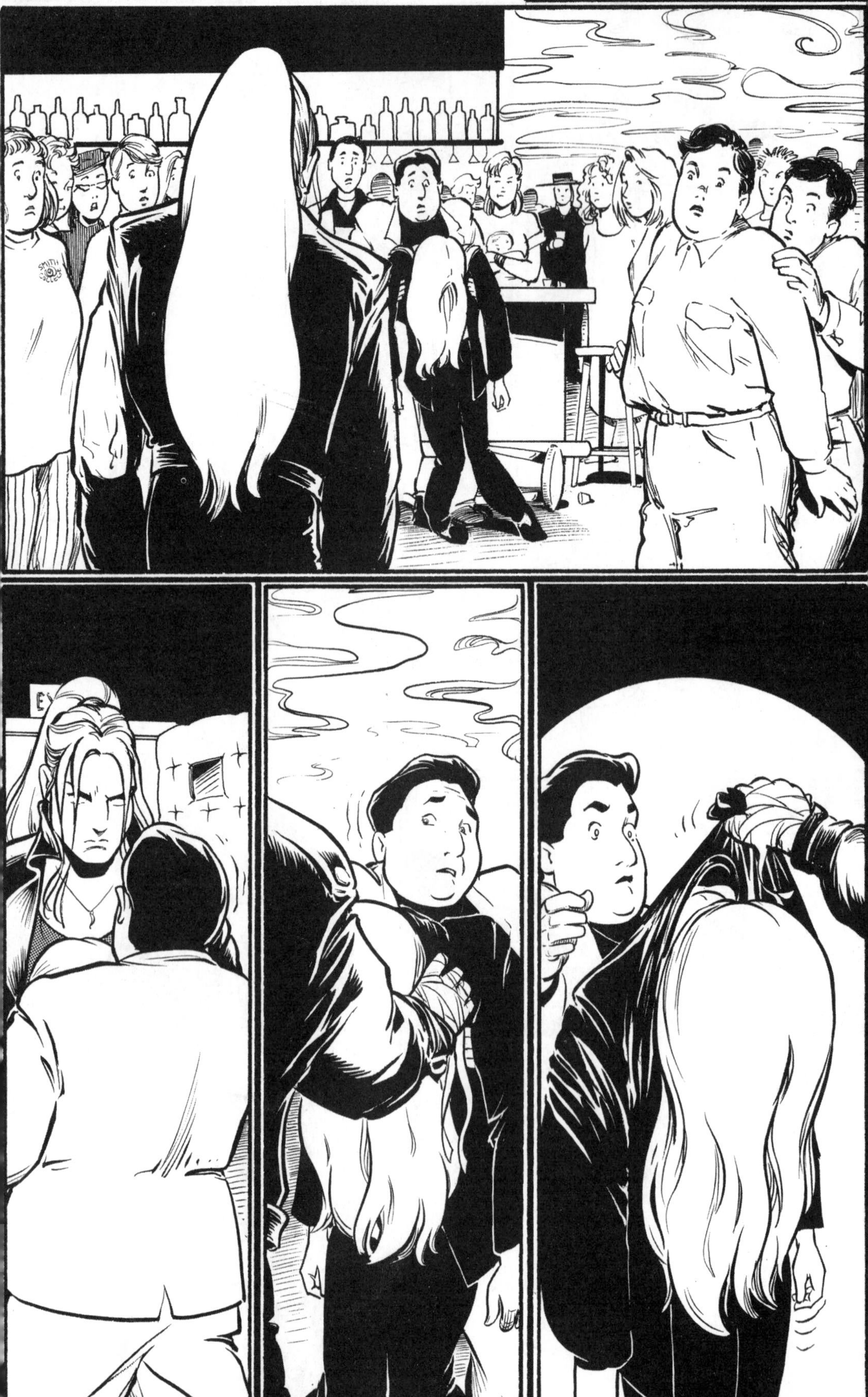

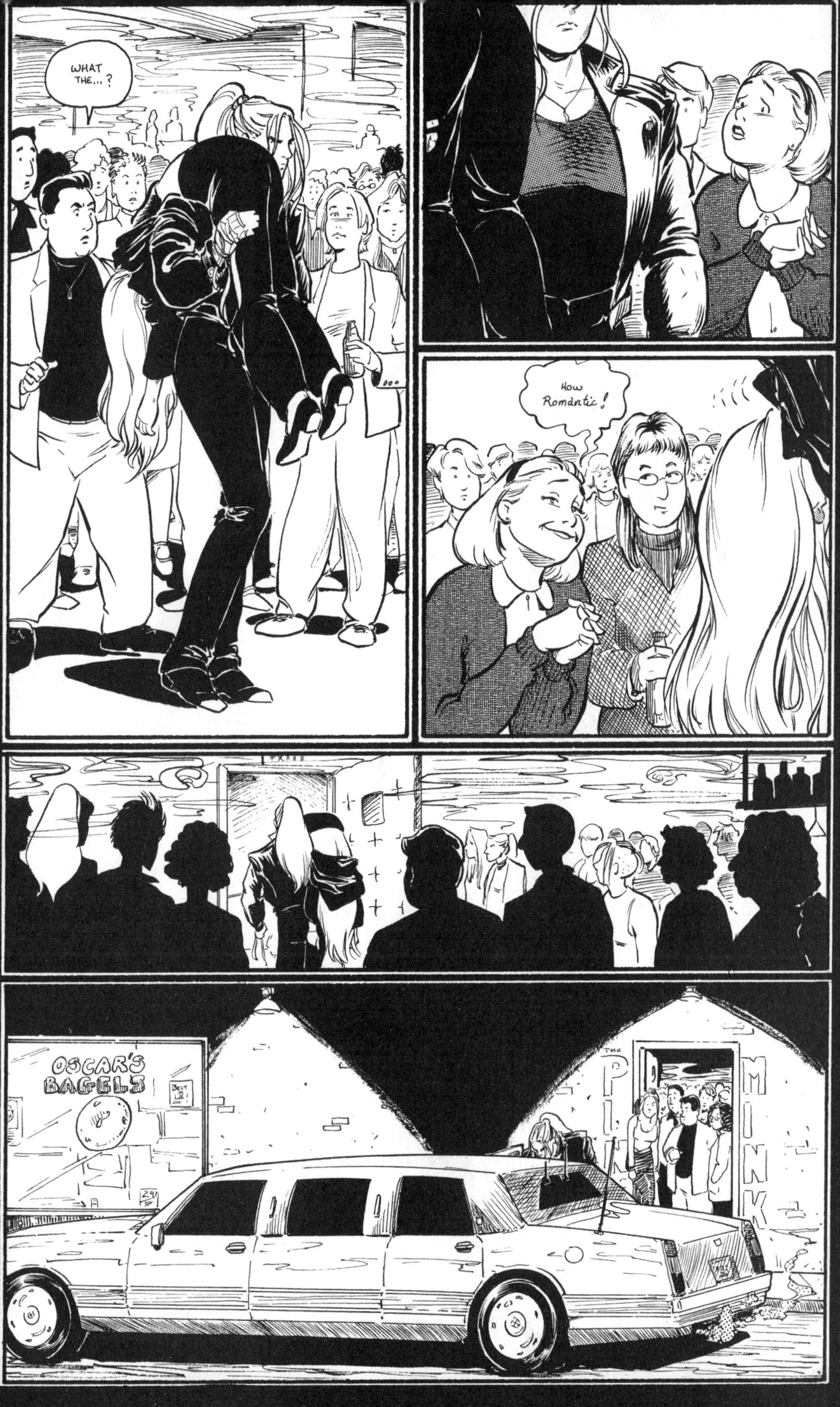
WHAT THE...?
How Romantic!
OSCAR'S BAGELS
THE PINK MINK

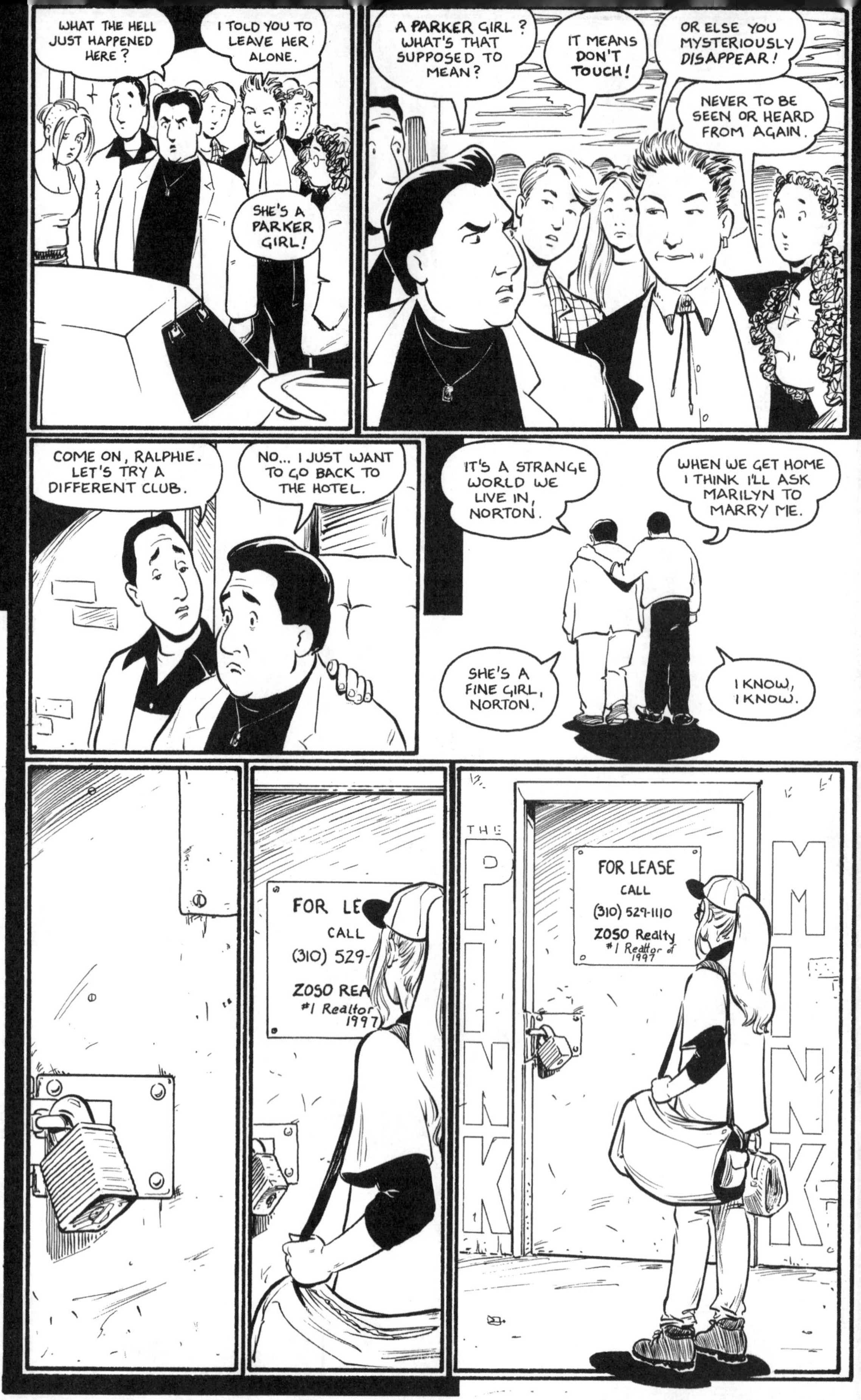
WHAT THE HELL JUST HAPPENED HERE?
I TOLD YOU TO LEAVE HER ALONE.
SHE'S A PARKER GIRL!
A PARKER GIRL? WHAT'S THAT SUPPOSED TO MEAN?
IT MEANS DON'T TOUCH!
OR ELSE YOU MYSTERIOUSLY DISAPPEAR!
NEVER TO BE SEEN OR HEARD FROM AGAIN.
COME ON, RALPHIE. LET'S TRY A DIFFERENT CLUB.
NO... I JUST WANT TO GO BACK TO THE HOTEL.
IT'S A STRANGE WORLD WE LIVE IN, NORTON.
WHEN WE GET HOME I THINK I'LL ASK MARILYN TO MARRY ME.
SHE'S A FINE GIRL, NORTON.
I KNOW, I KNOW.
FOR LEASE
CALL
(310) 529-1110
ZOSO Realty
#1 Realtor of 1997
THE PINK MINK

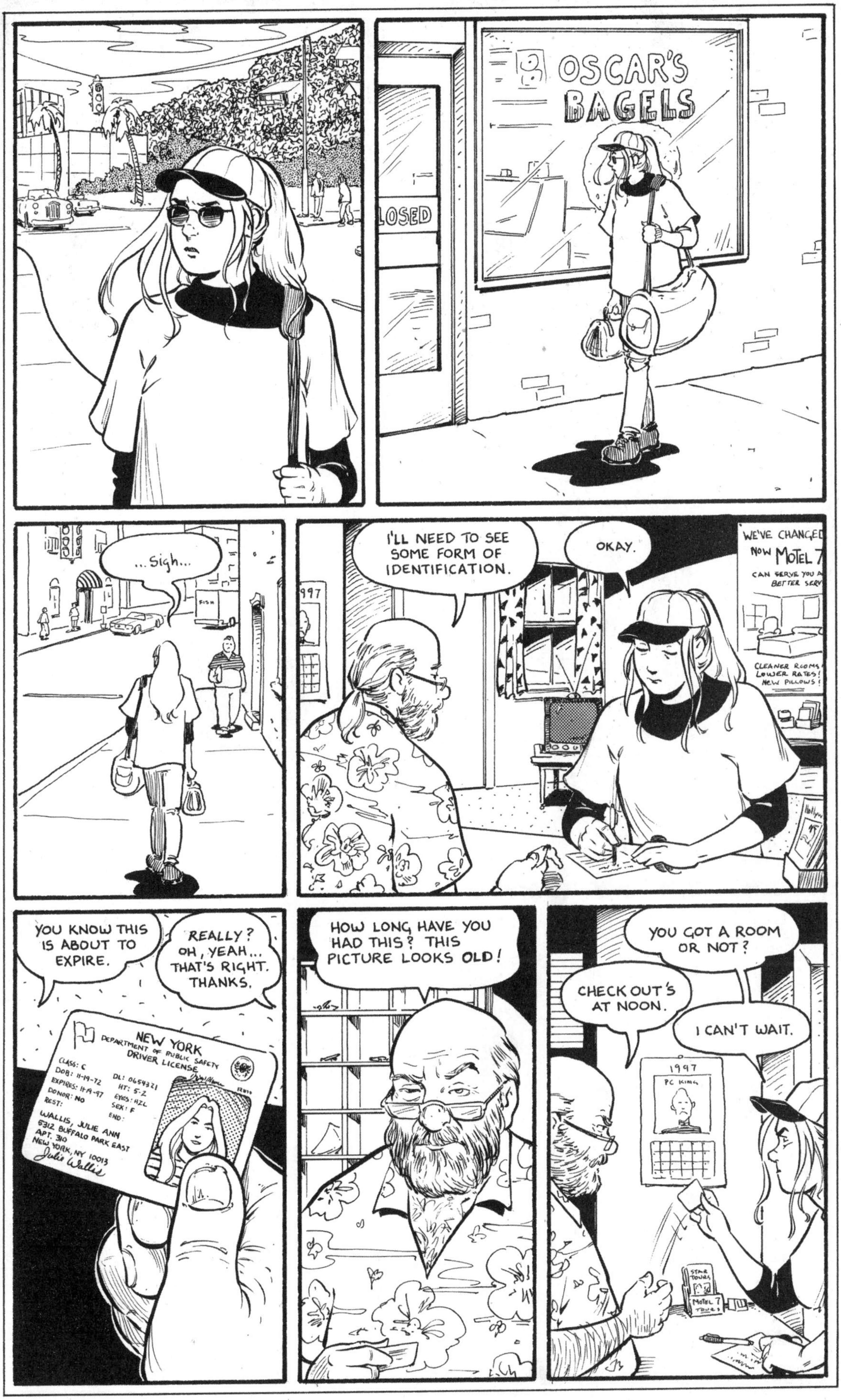
OSCAR'S
BAGELS
LOSED
...Sigh...
FISH
I'LL NEED TO SEE SOME FORM OF IDENTIFICATION.
OKAY.
WE'VE CHANGED
NOW MOTEL 7
CAN SERVE YOU A
BETTER SERV
CLEANER ROOMS! LOWER RATES! NEW PILLOWS!
1997
YOU KNOW THIS IS ABOUT TO EXPIRE.
REALLY? OH, YEAH... THAT'S RIGHT. THANKS.
NEW YORK
DEPARTMENT OF PUBLIC SAFETY
DRIVER LICENSE
CLASS: C
DOB: 11-19-72
EXPIRES: 11-19-97
DONOR: NO
REST:
DL: 0654321
HT: 5-2
EYES: HZL
SEX: F
END:
WALLIS, JULIE ANN
6312 BUFFALO PARK EAST
APT. 310
NEW YORK, NY 10013
Julie Wallis
HOW LONG HAVE YOU HAD THIS? THIS PICTURE LOOKS OLD!
YOU GOT A ROOM OR NOT?
CHECK OUT'S AT NOON.
I CAN'T WAIT.
1997
PC KING
STAR TOURS
MOTEL 7 TOURS

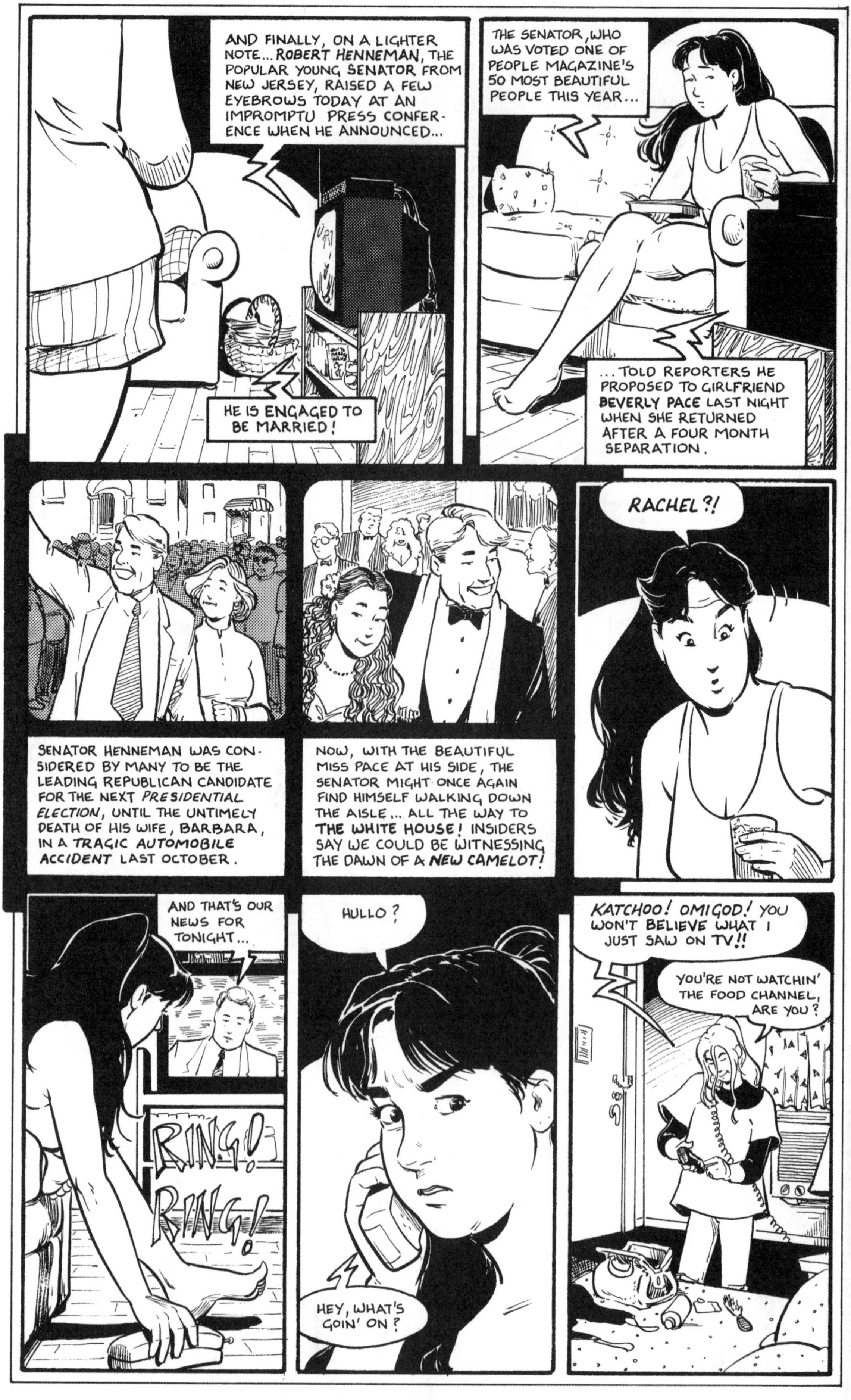
AND FINALLY, ON A LIGHTER NOTE... ROBERT HENNEMAN, THE POPULAR YOUNG SENATOR FROM NEW JERSEY, RAISED A FEW EYEBROWS TODAY AT AN IMPROMPTU PRESS CONFERENCE WHEN HE ANNOUNCED...
HE IS ENGAGED TO BE MARRIED!
THE SENATOR, WHO WAS VOTED ONE OF PEOPLE MAGAZINE'S 50 MOST BEAUTIFUL PEOPLE THIS YEAR...
...TOLD REPORTERS HE PROPOSED TO GIRLFRIEND BEVERLY PACE LAST NIGHT WHEN SHE RETURNED AFTER A FOUR MONTH SEPARATION.
SENATOR HENNEMAN WAS CONSIDERED BY MANY TO BE THE LEADING REPUBLICAN CANDIDATE FOR THE NEXT PRESIDENTIAL ELECTION, UNTIL THE UNTIMELY DEATH OF HIS WIFE, BARBARA, IN A TRAGIC AUTOMOBILE ACCIDENT LAST OCTOBER.
NOW, WITH THE BEAUTIFUL MISS PACE AT HIS SIDE, THE SENATOR MIGHT ONCE AGAIN FIND HIMSELF WALKING DOWN THE AISLE... ALL THE WAY TO THE WHITE HOUSE! INSIDERS SAY WE COULD BE WITNESSING THE DAWN OF A NEW CAMELOT!
RACHEL?!
AND THAT'S OUR NEWS FOR TONIGHT...
RING! RING!
HULLO?
HEY, WHAT'S GOIN' ON?
KATCHOO! OMIGOD! YOU WON'T BELIEVE WHAT I JUST SAW ON TV!!
YOU'RE NOT WATCHIN' THE FOOD CHANNEL, ARE YOU?

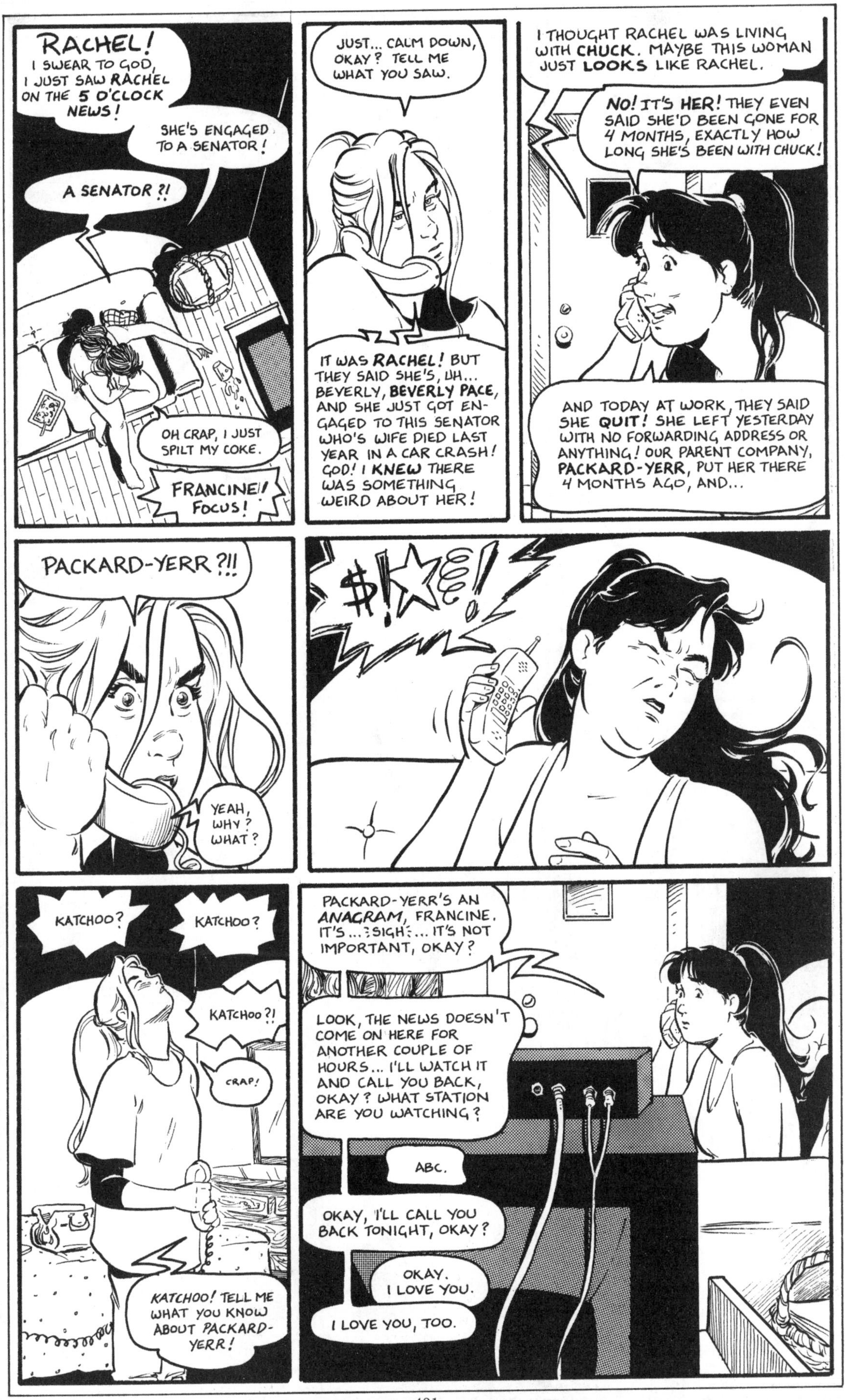

RACHEL! I SWEAR TO GOD, I JUST SAW RACHEL ON THE 5 O'CLOCK NEWS!
SHE'S ENGAGED TO A SENATOR!
A SENATOR?!
OH CRAP, I JUST SPILT MY COKE.
FRANCINE! FOCUS!
JUST... CALM DOWN, OKAY? TELL ME WHAT YOU SAW.
IT WAS RACHEL! BUT THEY SAID SHE'S, UH... BEVERLY, BEVERLY PACE, AND SHE JUST GOT ENGAGED TO THIS SENATOR WHO'S WIFE DIED LAST YEAR IN A CAR CRASH! GOD! I KNEW THERE WAS SOMETHING WEIRD ABOUT HER!
I THOUGHT RACHEL WAS LIVING WITH CHUCK. MAYBE THIS WOMAN JUST LOOKS LIKE RACHEL.
NO! IT'S HER! THEY EVEN SAID SHE'D BEEN GONE FOR 4 MONTHS, EXACTLY HOW LONG SHE'S BEEN WITH CHUCK!
AND TODAY AT WORK, THEY SAID SHE QUIT! SHE LEFT YESTERDAY WITH NO FORWARDING ADDRESS OR ANYTHING! OUR PARENT COMPANY, PACKARD-YERR, PUT HER THERE 4 MONTHS AGO, AND...
PACKARD-YERR?!!
YEAH, WHY? WHAT?
KATCHOO?
KATCHOO?
KATCHOO?!
CRAP!
KATCHOO! TELL ME WHAT YOU KNOW ABOUT PACKARD-YERR!
PACKARD-YERR'S AN ANAGRAM, FRANCINE. IT'S... SIGH... IT'S NOT IMPORTANT, OKAY?
LOOK, THE NEWS DOESN'T COME ON HERE FOR ANOTHER COUPLE OF HOURS... I'LL WATCH IT AND CALL YOU BACK, OKAY? WHAT STATION ARE YOU WATCHING?
ABC.
OKAY, I'LL CALL YOU BACK TONIGHT, OKAY?
OKAY. I LOVE YOU.
I LOVE YOU, TOO.

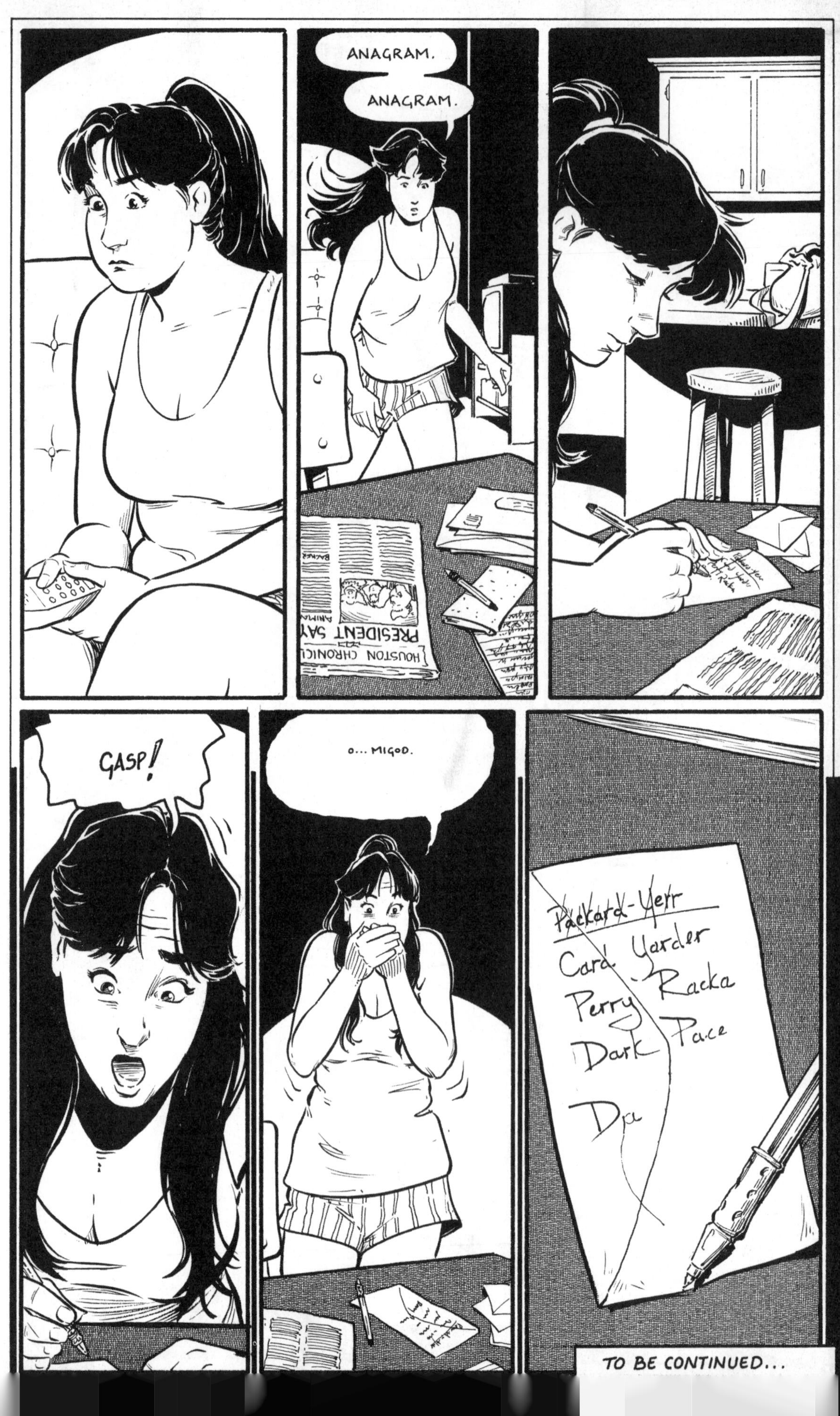
ANAGRAM.
ANAGRAM.
HOUSTON CHRONICLE
PRESIDENT SAYS
GASP!
O... MIGOD.
Packard-Yerr
Card Yarder
Perry Racka
Dark Pace
Da
TO BE CONTINUED...

Other Books by Terry Moore

Echo
Rachel Rising
Motor Girl
SiP Kids
Paradise TOO!
Ever
Strangers In Paradise XXV
Five Years
Serial
Parker Girls